THE SPORT AMERICANA®

TEAM

CHECKLIST

NO. 5

By
JEFF FRITSCH
AND
DENNIS W. ECKES

ISBN 0-937424-47-1

SPORT AMERICANA BASEBALL
TEAM CHECKLIST
TABLE OF CONTENTS

OLD TIMERS and GROUP PHOTOS

GREAT FOR AUTOGRAPHS

1 to 9 ar $ 3.00 each plus postage & handling
10 to 24 at $ 2.50 each plus postage & handling
25 or more at $ 2.25 each plus postage & handling

NEW LARGER EXPANDED LIST

OLD TIMERS
- ☐ Aaron, Hank*
- ☐ Agee, Tommy
- ☐ Allen, Dick
- ☐ Alston, Walter*
- ☐ Aparico, Luis*
- ☐ Appling, Luke*
- ☐ Ashburn, Richie
- ☐ Banks, Ernie*
- ☐ Bauer, Hank
- ☐ Bell, Cool Papa
- ☐ Bench, Johnny*
- ☐ Berra, Yogi*
- ☐ Blue, Vida
- ☐ Bonds, Bobby
- ☐ Boudreau, Lou*
- ☐ Brock, Lou*
- ☐ Buhl, Bob
- ☐ Bunning, Jim
- ☐ Burdette, Lew
- ☐ Campanella, Roy*
- ☐ Carew, Rod
- ☐ Carlton, Steve
- ☐ Cepeda, Orlando
- ☐ Charboneau, Joe
- ☐ Crandell, Del
- ☐ Cueller, Mike
- ☐ Dandridge, Ray*
- ☐ Dark, Alvin
- ☐ Davis, Tommy
- ☐ DiMaggio, Joe*
- ☐ Doby, Larry
- ☐ Doerr, Bobby*
- ☐ Dropo, Walt
- ☐ Drysdale, Don*
- ☐ Erskine, Carl
- ☐ Face, Elroy
- ☐ Ferrell, Rick*
- ☐ Fingers, Rollie
- ☐ Flanagan, Mike
- ☐ Friend, Bob
- ☐ Garvey, Steve
- ☐ Gehrig, Lou*
- ☐ Gibson, Bob*
- ☐ Gomez, Lefty*
- ☐ Grant, Mud Cat
- ☐ Groat, Dick
- ☐ Guidry, Ron
- ☐ Howard, Ellie
- ☐ Hubbell, Carl*
- ☐ Hunter, Catfish*
- ☐ Irvin, Monte*
- ☐ Jackson, Reggie
- ☐ Jenkins, Ferguson
- ☐ Kaline, Al*
- ☐ Kell, George*
- ☐ Killebrew, Harmon*
- ☐ Kiner, Ralph*
- ☐ Kluzewski, Ted
- ☐ Koosman, Jerry
- ☐ Koufax, Sandy*
- ☐ Kranepool, Ed
- ☐ Kubek, Tony
- ☐ Labine, Clem
- ☐ Law, Vernon
- ☐ Lemon, Bob

OLD TIMERS
- ☐ Lolich, Mickey
- ☐ Lopat, Eddie
- ☐ Lopez, Al*
- ☐ Lyle, Sparky
- ☐ Mantle, Mickey*
- ☐ Marichal, Juan*
- ☐ Marion, Marty
- ☐ Maris, Roger
- ☐ Martin, Billy
- ☐ Mathews, Eddie*
- ☐ Mays, Willie*
- ☐ McCovey, Willie*
- ☐ McDougald, Gil
- ☐ McGraw, Tug
- ☐ McLain, Denny
- ☐ McNally, Dave
- ☐ Mize, Johnny*
- ☐ Morgan, Joe
- ☐ Mueller, Don
- ☐ Munson, Thurman
- ☐ Musial, Stan*
- ☐ Newcomb, Don
- ☐ Newhouser, Hal
- ☐ Oliva, Tony
- ☐ Palmer, Jim
- ☐ Perez, Tony
- ☐ Perry, Gaylord
- ☐ Perry, Jim
- ☐ Pierce, Billy
- ☐ Piniella, Lou
- ☐ Pinson, Vada
- ☐ Podres, Johnny
- ☐ Powell, Boog
- ☐ Reese, Pee Wee*
- ☐ Rizzuto, Phil
- ☐ Roberts, Robin*
- ☐ Robinson, Brooks*
- ☐ Robinson, Jackie*
- ☐ Robinson, Frank*
- ☐ Rosen, Al
- ☐ Ruth, Babe Player*
- ☐ Ruth, Babe Retired*
- ☐ Santo, Ron
- ☐ Sauer, Hank
- ☐ Mike Schmidt
- ☐ Schoendienst, Red*
- ☐ Score, Herb
- ☐ Seaver, Tom
- ☐ Sewell, Joe*
- ☐ Shantz, Bobby
- ☐ Sievers, Roy
- ☐ Slaughter, Enos*
- ☐ Snider, Duke*
- ☐ Spahn, Warren*
- ☐ Stargell, Willie*
- ☐ Stottlemyre, Mel
- ☐ Sutter, Bruce
- ☐ Tresh, Tommy
- ☐ Virdon, Bill
- ☐ Walker, Harry
- ☐ Wilhelm, Hoyt*
- ☐ Williams, Billy*
- ☐ Williams, Ted*
- ☐ Wills, Maury
- ☐ Wynn, Early*
- ☐ Yastrzemski, Carl*

GROUPS
- ☐ 1950 Phillies Team
- ☐ 1952 Giants Line Up
- ☐ 1955 Dodgers
- ☐ 1956 Dodgers
- ☐ 1961 Yankees Line Up
- ☐ 1962 Yankees Team
- ☐ 1963 Dodgers L.A.
- ☐ 1964 Cardinals Infield
- ☐ 1964 Yankees Team
- ☐ 1969 Mets Team
- ☐ 1973 Mets Team
- ☐ 1989 Mets Team
- ☐ Aaron & Mays
- ☐ Bench & Lasorda
- ☐ Bench & Perez
- ☐ Bench & Yastrzemski
- ☐ Brett & Bo Jackson
- ☐ Brett & Boggs
- ☐ Brett & Cal Ripken
- ☐ Brooks Robinson & Clete Boyer
- ☐ B. Robinson & Kaline
- ☐ Cal, Cal Sr. & Billy Ripken
- ☐ DiMaggio & Feller
- ☐ Downing, Stottlemyre, Peterson & Ford
- ☐ Gehrig, Foxx & Ruth
- ☐ Gehrig, Gehringer, Greenberg & Ruth
- ☐ Joe & Dom DiMaggio
- ☐ K. Hernandez & Will Clark
- ☐ Mantle, DiMaggio, & Williams
- ☐ Mantle, Houk, Pepitone, B. Robinson & Tresh

GROUPS
- ☐ Mantle, Maris, Keane & Tresh
- ☐ Mantle, Maris & Berra
- ☐ Mantle, Mays & Killebrew
- ☐ Mantle & Maris
- ☐ Mantle & Mays
- ☐ Mattingly, Brett & Boggs
- ☐ Mattingly & Boggs
- ☐ Mattingly & Brett
- ☐ Mattingly & Hernandez
- ☐ Mattingly & Joyner
- ☐ Mattingly & Rose
- ☐ Mattingly & Strawberry
- ☐ Mattingly & Winfield
- ☐ McGwire, Canseco & Weiss
- ☐ McGwire & Joyner
- ☐ Phil & Joe Niekro
- ☐ Preacher Roe & Johnny Podres
- ☐ Roberto, Sandy & Sandy Jr. Alomar
- ☐ Roberto & Sandy Jr. Alomar
- ☐ Rose, Morgan, Bench & Perez
- ☐ Rose & Hernandez
- ☐ Rose & McGee
- ☐ Rose & Puckett
- ☐ Rose & Ryan
- ☐ Seaver, Cardwell, & Al Jackson
- ☐ Seaver & Stottlemyre
- ☐ Strawberry & Davis
- ☐ Strawberry & Dykstra
- ☐ Strawberry & McGee
- ☐ Winfield & Reggie Jackson
- ☐ Will Clark & Mitchell

SEND ONLY $ 1.00 for DEN'S BIG CATALOGUE CATALOGUE sent FREE with each ORDER

*Hall of Fame

NOTE: Most photos are in full color. Some of the older players are in a sepia color as no color negatives are available.

HOW TO USE THE TEAM CHECKLIST

While the text of this book is straight forward and easy to follow, several conventions and clarifying abbreviations are used in the text to attain consistency. These abbreviations and conventions are explained below.

ABBREVIATIONS

(B)   BACK ONLY—appears when the team name of a player is different on the back from that on the front.

(C)   COACH—appears when the card is of a coach of that particular team.

(F))   FRONT ONLY—appears when the team name of a player is different on the front from that on the back.

(FS)   FUTURE STAR—more than one player per card listed as Future Stars.

(HC)   HEAD COACH—appears only on the Topps cards of Bob Kennedy of 1964 and 1965 when he is listed as Head Coach of the Cubs, and on the 1985 Topps and 1988 Topps traded cards of the Olympic coaches.

(M)   MANAGER—appears when the card is a manager of that particular team.

(P)   PROSPECT—more than one player per card; listed as Prospect in 1979 Topps and Major League Prospect in 1985-1990 Fleer.

(R)   ROOKIE—more than one player per card listed as Rookie Stars.

CONVENTIONS

For Bowman, Goudey and Play Ball issues, the team on the front of the card is determined by the uniform worn. The team on the back of the card is determined by the team name actually printed on the back. For all Topps, Fleer, and Donruss issues (except the 1951 Topps Red and Blue Backs which have no writing on the back), the team name is determined by the team name printed on the front and back respectively. When a difference in the team name printed on the front and back exists; e.g., 1979 Topps Bump Wills exist with both the Rangers (correct) and Blue Jays (error) printed on the front, and the 1969 Topps Donn Clendenon exists with both Houston (correct) and Expos (error) printed on the front; the correct version only is used in the text.

Individuals sharing the same name are noted by the inclusion of middle initials or names. This situation occurs only when the Major League careers of the players sharing the same name overlap. Such is the case of Hal R. Smith and Hal W. Smith. Contrastly, Ron Jackson whose card appears in the late 1950's and early 1960's is not distinguished from the Ron Jackson whose card appears in the late 1970's. Kindly refer to the Encyclopedia of Baseball, Baseball Register, etc., for correct identifications. In the case of Bob Sadowski, pitcher, certain publications list him as having the middle initial "F". Through research, this information has been found to be in error; in fact, he has neither a middle initial nor a middle name. To differentiate him from Bob Sadowski, infielder, he is listed herein as merely "Bob Sadowski," while the infielder is listed as "Bob Frank Sadowski". Frank Baker whose card appears in 1970 and 1971 has no middle name or initial; he is listed as Frank Baker. Frank Baker whose card appears in 1971, 1972, and 1974 is referred to as Frank W. Baker. There are several cards in many of the sets that have been omitted from the checklists within because the players are not committed to any current team; e.g., old timers from the 1940 Play Ball set, 1976 Topps All-Time Greats, 1933 Goudey Lajoie, etc. Likewise, special cards have been omitted, e.g., All-Star Cards, multiplayer cards, league leader cards, Donruss Diamond Kings, boyhood picture cards, etc. All sets are in color unless noted as being in black and white.

Several of the card sets included in this book contain special instructions to the sets because of indiginous peculiarities of the sets themselves. The 1934-36 Diamond Stars and the Sportflics are preceded by clarifying narratives. Please read these narratives before attempting to use the team checklist for these sets.

1948 BOWMAN (48)
2 1/16" X 2 1/2"
BLACK & WHITE

BOSTON BRAVES

- ☐ 1. BOB ELLIOTT
- ☐ 12. JOHNNY SAIN
- ☐ 18. WARREN SPAHN

BOSTON RED SOX

NO CARDS ISSUED

BROOKLYN DODGERS

- ☐ 7. PETE REISER
- ☐ 41. REX BARNEY
- ☐ 43. BRUCE EDWARDS

CHICAGO CUBS

NO CARDS ISSUED

CHICAGO WHITE SOX

NO CARDS ISSUED

CINCINATTI REDS

- ☐ 2. EWELL BLACKWELL
- ☐ 39. AUGIE GALAN
- ☐ 44. JOHNNY WYROSTEK
- ☐ 45. HANK SAUER
- ☐ 46. HERMAN WEHMEIER

CLEVELAND INDIANS

- ☐ 5. BOB FELLER

DETROIT TIGERS

NO CARDS ISSUED

NEW YORK GIANTS

- ☐ 4. JOHNNY MIZE
- ☐ 9. WALKER COOPER
- ☐ 13. WILLARD MARSHALL
- ☐ 16. JACK LOHRKE
- ☐ 20. BUDDY KERR
- ☐ 23. LARRY JANSEN
- ☐ 27. SID GORDON
- ☐ 30. WHITEY LOCKMAN
- ☐ 32. BILL RIGNEY
- ☐ 34. SHELDON JONES
- ☐ 37. CLINT HARTUNG
- ☐ 42. RAY POAT
- ☐ 47. BOBBY THOMSON
- ☐ 48. DAVE KOSLO

NEW YORK YANKEES

- ☐ 6. YOGI BERRA
- ☐ 8. PHIL RIZZUTO
- ☐ 11. JOHNNY LINDELL
- ☐ 14. ALLIE REYNOLDS
- ☐ 19. TOMMY HENRICH
- ☐ 22. BILL BEVENS
- ☐ 26. FRANK SHEA
- ☐ 29. JOE PAGE
- ☐ 33. BILLY JOHNSON
- ☐ 35. GEORGE STIRNWEISS

PHILADELPHIA ATHLETICS

- ☐ 10. BUDDY ROSAR
- ☐ 15. EDDIE JOOST
- ☐ 21. FERRIS FAIN
- ☐ 25. BARNEY MCCOSKEY
- ☐ 31. BILL MCCAHAN

PHILADELPHIA PHILLIES

- ☐ 24. DUTCH LEONARD
- ☐ 28. EMIL VERBAN

PITTSBURGH PIRATES

- ☐ 3. RALPH KINER

ST. LOUIS BROWNS

NO CARDS ISSUED

ST. LOUIS CARDINALS

- ☐ 17. ENOS SLAUGHTER
- ☐ 36. STAN MUSIAL
- ☐ 38. RED SCHOENDIENST
- ☐ 40. MARTY MARION

WASHINGTON SENATORS

NO CARDS ISSUED

1949 BOWMAN (240)
2 1/16" X 2 1/2"

BOSTON BRAVES

- ☐ 1. VERN BICKFORD
- ☐ 17. EARL TORGESON
- ☐ 33. WARREN SPAHN
- ☐ 47. JOHNNY SAIN
- ☐ 58. BOB ELLIOTT
- ☐ 67. ALVIN DARK
- ☐ 72. TOMMY HOLMES
- ☐ 88. BILL SALKELD
- ☐ 104. ED STANKY

- ☐ 153. PHIL MASI
- ☐ 169. JEFF HEATH
- ☐ 185. PETE REISER
- ☐ 201. SIBBY SISTI
- ☐ 213. CHARLES BARRETT
- ☐ 235. JIM RUSSELL
- ☐ 239. FRANK MCCORMICK

BOSTON RED SOX

- ☐ 7. JOE DOBSON
- ☐ 23. BOBBY DOERR
- ☐ 39. BILL GOODMAN
- ☐ 53. JACK KRAMER
- ☐ 64. DOM DIMAGGIO
- ☐ 71. VERN STEPHENS
- ☐ 86. JOHNNY PESKY
- ☐ 102. STAN SPENCE
- ☐ 118. SAM MELE
- ☐ 151. MICKEY HARRIS
- ☐ 167. BORIS MARTIN
- ☐ 183. LOU STRINGER
- ☐ 199. TEX HUGHSON
- ☐ 211. DAVE FERRISS
- ☐ 231. EARL JOHNSON

BROOKLYN DODGERS

- ☐ 20. GENE HERMANSKI
- ☐ 36. PEE WEE REESE
- ☐ 50. JACKIE ROBINSON
- ☐ 61. REX BARNEY
- ☐ 70. CARL FURILLO
- ☐ 73. BILLY COX
- ☐ 84. ROY CAMPANELLA
- ☐ 100. GIL HODGES
- ☐ 116. JOE HATTEN
- ☐ 146. MIKE MCCORMICK
- ☐ 162. PREACHER ROE
- ☐ 178. TOMMY BROWN
- ☐ 179. HUGH CASEY(F)
- ☐ 194. RALPH BRANCA
- ☐ 206. BRUCE EDWARDS
- ☐ 226. DUKE SNIDER

CHICAGO CUBS

- ☐ 6. PHIL CAVARRETTA
- ☐ 22. PEANUTS LOWREY
- ☐ 38. EMIL VERBAN
- ☐ 52. JOHNNY SCHMITZ
- ☐ 63. ANDY PAFKO
- ☐ 76. BILL NICHOLSON(F)
- ☐ 83. BOB SCHEFFING
- ☐ 99. FRANK GUSTINE(B)
- ☐ 115. DUTCH LEONARD(B)
- ☐ 130. HARRY WALKER(B)
- ☐ 134. HANK BOROWY(F)
- ☐ 142. EDDIE WAITKUS(F)
- ☐ 152. CLARENCE MADDERN
- ☐ 168. DOYLE LADE
- ☐ 184. BOB CHIPMAN
- ☐ 200. JESS DOBERNIC
- ☐ 212. RALPH HAMNER

CHICAGO WHITE SOX

- ☐ 12. CASS MICHAELS
- ☐ 28. DON KOLLOWAY
- ☐ 44. DAVE PHILLEY
- ☐ 87. RANDY GUMPERT(B)
- ☐ 96. TAFT WRIGHT(F)
- ☐ 103. JOE TIPTON(B)
- ☐ 119. FLOYD BAKER
- ☐ 133. AARON ROBINSON(F)
- ☐ 141. TONY LUPIEN(F)
- ☐ 159. GLEN MOULDER

☐ 175. LUKE APPLING
☐ 191. JOE HAYNES
☐ 217. MARINO PIERETTI

CINCINNATI REDS

☐ 5. HANK SAUER
☐ 21. FRANK BAUMHOLTZ
☐ 37. JOHN WYROSTEK
☐ 51. HERMAN WEHMEIER
☐ 62. GRADY HATTON
☐ 81. VIRGIL STALLCUP
☐ 97. DANNY LITWHILER
☐ 113. RAY LAMANNO
☐ 128. JOHNNY VANDER MEER
☐ 160. JIM BLACKBURN
☐ 176. KEN RAFFENSBERGER
☐ 192. HARRY GUMBERT

KEN KELTNER

CLEVELAND INDIANS

☐ 11. LOU BOUDREAU(M)
☐ 27. BOB FELLER
☐ 43. DALE MITCHELL
☐ 57. GENE BEARDEN
☐ 78. SAM ZOLDAK
☐ 94. MICKEY VERNON(B)
☐ 103. JOE TIPTON(F)
☐ 110. EARLY WYNN(B)
☐ 125. KEN KELTNER
☐ 136. HANK EDWARDS
☐ 150. ALLIE CLARK
☐ 166. MIKE TRESH
☐ 182. HAL PECK
☐ 198. STEVE GROMEK
☐ 210. JOE GORDON
☐ 224. SATCHELL PAIGE
☐ 233. LARRY DOBY
☐ 238. BOB LEMON

DETROIT TIGERS

☐ 10. TED GRAY
☐ 26. GEORGE KELL
☐ 42. HOOT EVERS
☐ 56. PAT MULLIN
☐ 75. EDDIE MAYO
☐ 91. DICK WAKEFIELD
☐ 107. EDDIE LAKE
☐ 122. GEORGE VICO
☐ 133. AARON ROBINSON(B)
☐ 141. TONY LUPIEN(B)
☐ 148. BOB SWIFT
☐ 164. VIC WERTZ
☐ 180. CONNIE BERRY
☐ 196. FRED HUTCHINSON
☐ 208. DIZZY TROUT
☐ 219. VIRGIL TRUCKS

NEW YORK GIANTS

☐ 2. WHITEY LOCKMAN
☐ 18. BOBBY THOMSON
☐ 34. DAVE KOSLO
☐ 48. WILLARD MARSHALL
☐ 59. JACK LOHRKE
☐ 68. SHELDON JONES
☐ 85. JOHNNY MIZE
☐ 101. SID GORDON
☐ 117. WALKER COOPER
☐ 154. CLINT HARTUNG
☐ 170. BILL RIGNEY
☐ 186. BUDDY KERR
☐ 202. LARRY JANSEN
☐ 220. JOHNNY MCCARTHY
☐ 221. BOB MUNCRIEF(F)

☐ 223. BOB HOFMAN
☐ 230. AUGIE GALAN
☐ 237. MONTE KENNEDY

NEW YORK YANKEES

☐ 3. BOB PORTERFIELD
☐ 19. BOBBY BROWN
☐ 35. VIC RASCHI
☐ 49. FRANK SHEA
☐ 60. YOGI BERRA
☐ 69. TOMMY HENRICH
☐ 82. JOE PAGE
☐ 87. RANDY GUMPERT(F)
☐ 98. PHIL RIZZUTO
☐ 114. ALLIE REYNOLDS
☐ 129. BILL JOHNSON
☐ 149. ROY PARTEE
☐ 165. GEORGE STIRNWEISS
☐ 181. GUS NIARHOS
☐ 197. JOHNNY LINDELL
☐ 209. CHARLIE KELLER
☐ 218. DICK KRYHOSKI
☐ 225. GERRY COLEMAN
☐ 229. ED LOPAT
☐ 232. GEORGE MCQUINN
☐ 236. FRED SANFORD
☐ 240. NORMAN YOUNG

PHILDELPHIA ATHLETICS

☐ 9. FERRIS FAIN
☐ 25. CARL SHEIB
☐ 41. LOU BRISSIE
☐ 55. EDDIE JOOST
☐ 66. ELMER VALO
☐ 80. BILL MCCAHAN
☐ 96. TAFT WRIGHT(B)
☐ 112. SAM CHAPMAN
☐ 127. HENRY MAJESKI
☐ 138. BUDDY ROSAR
☐ 155. MIKE GUERRA
☐ 171. DICK FOWLER
☐ 187. PHIL MARCHILDON
☐ 203. BARNEY MCCOSKY
☐ 222. ALEX KELLNER

PHILADELPHIA PHILLIES

☐ 14. CURT SIMMONS
☐ 30. ANDY SEMINICK
☐ 46. ROBIN ROBERTS
☐ 76. BILL NICHOLSON(B)
☐ 92. WILLIE JONES
☐ 108. KEN HEINTZELMAN
☐ 115. DUTCH LEONARD(F)
☐ 123. JOHNNY BLATNIK
☐ 130. HARRY WALKER(F)
☐ 134. HANK BOROWY(B)
☐ 142. EDDIE WAITKUS(B)
☐ 145. BLIX DONNELLY
☐ 161. JOCKO THOMPSON
☐ 177. STAN LOPATA
☐ 193. KEN TRINKLE
☐ 205. DICK SISLER
☐ 214. RICHIE ASHBURN
☐ 216. SCHOOLBOY ROWE
☐ 228. JACKIE MAYO

PITTSBURGH PIRATES

☐ 8. MURRY DICKSON
☐ 13. BOB CHESNES
☐ 29. RALPH KINER
☐ 45. WALLY WESTLAKE
☐ 77. ERNIE BONHAM
☐ 93. ED STEVENS
☐ 99. FRANK GUSTINE(F)
☐ 109. ED FITZGERALD
☐ 124. DANNY MURTAUGH
☐ 135. STAN ROJEK
☐ 147. BERT SINGLETON
☐ 163. CLYDE MCCULLOUGH
☐ 179. HUGH CASEY(B)
☐ 195. EDDIE BOCKMAN
☐ 207. JOHNNY HOPP
☐ 215. KIRBY HIGBE
☐ 221. BOB MUNCRIEF(B)
☐ 227. FRITZ OSTERMUELLER
☐ 234. RIP SEWELL

ST. LOUIS BROWNS

☐ 4. JERRY PRIDDY
☐ 15. NED GARVER
☐ 31. DICK KOKOS
☐ 89. MIZELL PLATT
☐ 105. BILL KENNEDY
☐ 120. CLIFF FANNIN
☐ 131. PAUL LEHNER
☐ 139. HANK ARFT
☐ 143. BOB DILLINGER
☐ 156. AL ZARILLA
☐ 172. EDDIE PELLAGRINI
☐ 188. KARL DREWS
☐ 204. BOB SAVAGE

ST. LOUIS CARDINALS

☐ 24. STAN MUSIAL
☐ 40. RED MUNGER
☐ 54. MARTY MARION
☐ 65. ENOS SLAUGHTER
☐ 79. RON NORTHEY
☐ 95. HOWIE POLLET
☐ 111. RED SCHOENDIENST
☐ 126. AL BRAZLE
☐ 137. TED WILKS
☐ 158. HARRY BRECHEEN
☐ 174. TERRY MOORE(C)
☐ 190. JIM HEARN

WASHINGTON SENATORS

☐ 16. AL KOZAR
☐ 32. EDDIE YOST
☐ 74. TOM MCBRIDE
☐ 90. GIL COAN
☐ 94. MICKEY VERNON(F)
☐ 106. JAKE EARLY
☐ 110. EARLY WYNN(F)
☐ 121. MARK CHRISTMAN
☐ 132. AL EVANS
☐ 140. RAY SCARBOROUGH
☐ 144. MICKEY HAEFNER
☐ 157. WALT MASTERSON
☐ 173. EDDIE STEWART
☐ 189. EARL WOOTEN

1950 BOWMAN (252)
2 1/16" X 2 1/2"

BOSTON BRAVES

☐ 19. WARREN SPAHN
☐ 20. BOB ELLIOTT
☐ 55. BUDDY KERR
☐ 56. DEL CRANDALL
☐ 57. VERN BICKFORD
☐ 73. WILLARD MARSHALL
☐ 74. JOHNNY ANTONELLI
☐ 109. SID GORDON
☐ 110. TOMMY HOLMES
☐ 111. WALKER COOPER
☐ 163. EARL TORGESON
☐ 164. SIBBY SISTI
☐ 192. BOB CHIPMAN
☐ 193. PETE REISER
☐ 248. SAM JETHROE

BOSTON RED SOX

- ☐ 1. MEL PARNELL
- ☐ 2. VERN STEPHENS
- ☐ 3. DOM DIMAGGIO
- ☐ 43. BOBBY DOERR
- ☐ 44. JOE DOBSON
- ☐ 45. AL ZARILLA
- ☐ 97. MICKEY MCDERMOTT
- ☐ 98. TED WILLIAMS
- ☐ 99. BILLY GOODMAN
- ☐ 136. WARREN ROSAR
- ☐ 137. JOHNNY PESKY
- ☐ 152. ELLIS KINDER
- ☐ 153. WALT MASTERSON
- ☐ 186. KEN KELTNER
- ☐ 187. LOU STRINGER
- ☐ 188. EARL JOHNSON
- ☐ 245. AL PAPAI
- ☐ 246. WALT DROPO

BROOKLYN DODGERS

- ☐ 21. PEE WEE REESE
- ☐ 22. JACKIE ROBINSON
- ☐ 23. DON NEWCOMBE
- ☐ 58. CARL FURILLO
- ☐ 59. RALPH BRANCA
- ☐ 75. ROY CAMPANELLA
- ☐ 76. REX BARNEY
- ☐ 77. DUKE SNIDER
- ☐ 112. GIL HODGES
- ☐ 113. GENE HERMANSKI
- ☐ 165. BRUCE EDWARDS
- ☐ 166. JOE HATTEN
- ☐ 167. PREACHER ROE
- ☐ 194. BILLY COX
- ☐ 222. BOBBY MORGAN
- ☐ 223. JIMMY RUSSELL
- ☐ 224. JACK BANTA

CHICAGO CUBS

- ☐ 24. JOHNNY SCHMITZ
- ☐ 25. HANK SAUER
- ☐ 60. ANDY PAFKO
- ☐ 61. BOB RUSH
- ☐ 78. MICKEY OWEN
- ☐ 79. JOHNNY VANDER MEER
- ☐ 114. WAYNE TERWILLIGER
- ☐ 115. ROY SMALLEY
- ☐ 169. HANK EDWARDS
- ☐ 170. EMIL LEONARD
- ☐ 195. PHIL CAVARRETTA
- ☐ 196. DOYLE LADE
- ☐ 229. FRANK FRISCH(M)
- ☐ 230. BILL SERENA
- ☐ 231. PRESTON WARD

CHICAGO WHITE SOX

- ☐ 4. GUS ZERNIAL
- ☐ 5. BOB KUZAVA
- ☐ 37. LUKE APPLING
- ☐ 38. BILL WIGHT
- ☐ 91. CASS MICHAELS
- ☐ 92. HANK MAJESKI
- ☐ 127. DAVE PHILLEY
- ☐ 128. PHIL MASI
- ☐ 146. FLOYD BAKER
- ☐ 183. MICKEY HAEFNER
- ☐ 184. RANDY GUMPERT
- ☐ 185. HOWIE JUDSON
- ☐ 236. BOB CAIN
- ☐ 237. BILL SALKELD

CINCINNATI REDS

- ☐ 26. GRADY HATTON
- ☐ 27. HERMAN WEHMEIER
- ☐ 62. TED KLUSZEWSKI
- ☐ 63. EWELL BLACKWELL
- ☐ 80. HOWARD FOX
- ☐ 81. RON NORTHEY
- ☐ 116. VIRGIL STALLCUP
- ☐ 168. BOB SCHEFFING
- ☐ 172. PEANUTS LOWREY
- ☐ 173. LLOYD MERRIMAN
- ☐ 197. JOHNNY WYROSTEK
- ☐ 198. DANNY LITWHILER

CLEVELAND INDIANS

- ☐ 6. BOB FELLER
- ☐ 7. JIM HEGAN
- ☐ 39. LARRY DOBY
- ☐ 40. BOB LEMON
- ☐ 93. GENE BEARDEN
- ☐ 94. LOU BOUDREAU(M)
- ☐ 129. JOE GORDON
- ☐ 130. DALE MITCHELL
- ☐ 131. STEVE GROMEK
- ☐ 132. MICKEY VERNON
- ☐ 147. MIKE GARCIA
- ☐ 148. EARLY WYNN
- ☐ 181. MARINO PIERETTI
- ☐ 182. SAM ZOLDAK
- ☐ 232. AL ROSEN
- ☐ 233. ALLIE CLARK

DETROIT TIGERS

- ☐ 8. GEORGE KELL
- ☐ 9. VIC WERTZ
- ☐ 41. HOOT EVERS
- ☐ 42. ART HOUTTEMAN
- ☐ 95. AARON ROBINSON
- ☐ 96. VIRGIL TRUCKS
- ☐ 133. DON KOLLOWAY
- ☐ 134. DIZZY TROUT
- ☐ 135. PAT MULLIN
- ☐ 149. BOB SWIFT
- ☐ 150. GEORGE VICO
- ☐ 151. FRED HUTCHINSON
- ☐ 210. TED GRAY
- ☐ 211. CHARLIE KELLER
- ☐ 212. GERRY PRIDDY
- ☐ 240. EDDIE LAKE
- ☐ 241. NEIL BERRY
- ☐ 242. DICK KRYHOSKI
- ☐ 243. JOHNNY GROTH

NEW YORK GIANTS

- ☐ 28. BOBBY THOMSON
- ☐ 29. ED STANKY
- ☐ 64. AL DARK
- ☐ 65. DAVE KOSLO
- ☐ 66. LARRY JANSEN
- ☐ 82. WHITEY LOCKMAN
- ☐ 83. SHELDON JONES
- ☐ 117. BILL RIGNEY
- ☐ 118. CLINT HARTUNG
- ☐ 174. HANK THOMPSON
- ☐ 175. MONTE KENNEDY
- ☐ 199. JACK KRAMER
- ☐ 200. KIRBY HIGBE
- ☐ 220. LEO DUROCHER(M)
- ☐ 221. DON MUELLER
- ☐ 235. TOOKIE GILBERT

NEW YORK YANKEES

- ☐ 10. TOMMY HENRICH
- ☐ 11. PHIL RIZZUTO
- ☐ 12. JOE PAGE
- ☐ 46. YOGI BERRA
- ☐ 47. JERRY COLEMAN
- ☐ 100. VIC RASCHI
- ☐ 101. BOBBY BROWN
- ☐ 102. BILLY JOHNSON
- ☐ 138. ALLIE REYNOLDS
- ☐ 139. JOHNNY MIZE
- ☐ 154. GUS NIARHOS
- ☐ 155. FRANK SHEA
- ☐ 156. FRED SANFORD
- ☐ 215. ED LOPAT
- ☐ 216. BOB PORTERFIELD
- ☐ 217. CASEY STENGEL(M)
- ☐ 218. CLIFF MAPES
- ☐ 219. HANK BAUER

PHILADELPHIA ATHLETICS

- ☐ 13. FERRIS FAIN
- ☐ 14. ALEX KELLNER
- ☐ 48. LOU BRISSIE
- ☐ 49. ELMER VALO
- ☐ 103. EDDIE JOOST
- ☐ 104. SAM CHAPMAN
- ☐ 105. BOB DILLINGER
- ☐ 140. PETE SUDER
- ☐ 141. JOE COLEMAN
- ☐ 157. MIKE GUERRA
- ☐ 158. PAUL LEHNER
- ☐ 159. JOE TIPTON
- ☐ 213. CARL SCHEIB
- ☐ 214. DICK FOWLER
- ☐ 234. BOBBY SHANTZ

PHILADELPHIA PHILLIES

- ☐ 30. EDDIE WAITKUS
- ☐ 31. DEL ENNIS
- ☐ 32. ROBIN ROBERTS
- ☐ 67. WILLIE JONES
- ☐ 68. CURT SIMMONS
- ☐ 84. RICHIE ASHBURN
- ☐ 85. KEN HEINTZELMAN
- ☐ 119. DICK SISLER
- ☐ 120. JOHN THOMPSON
- ☐ 121. ANDY SEMINICK
- ☐ 176. BLIX DONNELLY
- ☐ 177. HANK BOROWY
- ☐ 204. GRANNY HAMNER
- ☐ 205. MIKE GOLIAT
- ☐ 206. STAN LOPATA
- ☐ 225. EDDIE SAWYER(M)
- ☐ 226. JIM KONSTANTY
- ☐ 227. BOB J. MILLER
- ☐ 228. BILL NICHOLSON

PITTSBURGH PIRATES

- ☐ 33. RALPH KINER
- ☐ 34. MURRY DICKSON
- ☐ 69. WALLY WESTLAKE
- ☐ 70. BOB CHESNES
- ☐ 86. STAN ROJEK
- ☐ 87. BILL WERLE
- ☐ 122. JOHNNY HOPP
- ☐ 123. DINO RESTELLI
- ☐ 124. CLYDE MCCULLOUGH
- ☐ 171. HARRY GUMBERT
- ☐ 178. ED FITZGERALD
- ☐ 201. PETE CASTIGLIONE
- ☐ 202. CLIFF CHAMBERS
- ☐ 203. DANNY MURTAUGH
- ☐ 244. DALE COOGAN

ST. LOUIS BROWNS

- ☐ 16. ROY SIEVERS
- ☐ 50. DICK KOKOS
- ☐ 51. NED GARVER
- ☐ 106. CLIFF FANNIN
- ☐ 142. SHERMAN LOLLAR
- ☐ 145. JACK GRAHAM
- ☐ 189. OWEN FRIEND
- ☐ 190. KEN WOOD
- ☐ 191. DICK STARR
- ☐ 249. GEORGE STIRNWEISS
- ☐ 250. RAY COLEMAN
- ☐ 251. LES MOSS
- ☐ 252. BILLY DEMARS

ST. LOUIS CARDINALS

- ☐ 35. ENOS SLAUGHTER
- ☐ 36. EDDIE KAZAK
- ☐ 71. RED SCHOENDIENST
- ☐ 72. HOWIE POLLET
- ☐ 88. MARTY MARION
- ☐ 89. RED MUNGER
- ☐ 90. HARRY BRECHEEN
- ☐ 125. DEL RICE

□ 126. AL BRAZLE
□ 179. CHUCK DIERING
□ 180. HARRY WALKER
□ 207. MAX LANIER
□ 208. JIM HEARN
□ 209. JOHNNY LINDELL
□ 238. NIPPY JONES
□ 239. BILL HOWERTON

WASHINGTON SENATORS

□ 15. AL KOZAR
□ 17. SID HUDSON
□ 18. EDDIE ROBINSON
□ 52. SAM MELE
□ 53. CLYDE VOLLMER
□ 54. GIL COAN
□ 107. SAM DENTE
□ 108. RAY SCARBOROUGH
□ 143. EDDIE STEWART
□ 144. AL EVANS
□ 160. MICKEY HARRIS
□ 161. SHERRY ROBERTSON
□ 162. EDDIE YOST
□ 247. IRV NOREN

1951 BOWMAN (324)
2 1/16" X 3 1/8"

VIRGIL "FIRE" TRUCKS

BOSTON BRAVES

□ 19. SID GORDON
□ 20. DEL CRANDALL
□ 42. VERN BICKFORD
□ 66. BOB ELLIOTT
□ 98. WILLARD MARSHALL
□ 99. EARL TORGESON
□ 134. WARREN SPAHN
□ 135. WALKER COOPER
□ 170. SIBBY SISTI
□ 171. BUDDY KERR
□ 207. BILLY SOUTHWORTH(M)
□ 208. BLIX DONNELLY
□ 242. SAM JETHROE
□ 243. JOHNNY ANTONELLI
□ 277. ROY HARTSFIELD
□ 278. NORMAN ROY
□ 312. GENE MAUCH
□ 313. RAY MUELLER
□ 314. JOHNNY SAIN

BOSTON RED SOX

□ 15. JOHNNY PESKY
□ 16. MICKEY MCDERMOTT
□ 38. AL EVANS
□ 39. RAY SCARBOROUGH
□ 62. LOU BOUDREAU
□ 91. CLYDE VOLLMER
□ 92. VERN STEPHENS
□ 128. ELLIS KINDER
□ 129. MATT BATTS
□ 164. BILL WIGHT
□ 165. TED WILLIAMS
□ 201. STEVE O'NEIL(M)
□ 202. MIKE GUERRA(F)
□ 210. LES MOSS(B)
□ 236. WARREN ROSAR
□ 237. BILLY GOODMAN
□ 270. WILLARD NIXON
□ 271. TOMMY WRIGHT
□ 306. JIM PIERSALL
□ 307. WALT MASTERSON

BROOKLYN DODGERS

□ 6. DON NEWCOMBE
□ 7. GIL HODGES
□ 31. ROY CAMPANELLA
□ 32. DUKE SNIDER
□ 55. GENE HERMANSKI
□ 56. RALPH BRANCA
□ 80. PEE WEE REESE
□ 81. CARL FURILLO
□ 116. BRUCE EDWARDS
□ 117. EDDIE MIKSIS
□ 118. PREACHER ROE
□ 152. CAL ABRAMS
□ 153. REX BARNEY
□ 189. ERV PALICA
□ 190. JOE HATTEN
□ 224. BILLY COX
□ 225. DAN BANKHEAD
□ 259. CHARLIE DRESSEN(M)
□ 260. CARL ERSKINE
□ 299. CLYDE KING

CHICAGO CUBS

□ 22. HANK SAUER
□ 44. ROY SMALLEY
□ 69. JOHNNY SCHMITZ
□ 70. RON NORTHEY
□ 102. DUTCH LEONARD
□ 103. ANDY PAFKO
□ 138. PHIL CAVARRETTA
□ 139. DOYLE LADE
□ 174. MICKEY OWEN
□ 175. WAYNE TERWILLIGER
□ 211. HAL JEFFCOAT
□ 212. BOB RUSH
□ 246. BILL SERENA
□ 247. BOB RAMAZZOTTI
□ 248. JOHNNY KLIPPSTEIN
□ 282. FRANK FRISCH(M)
□ 283. WALT DUBIEL
□ 317. SMOKY BURGESS
□ 318. WARREN HACKER

CHICAGO WHITE SOX

□ 12. HANK MAJESKI
□ 35. AL ZARILLA
□ 36. JOE DOBSON
□ 59. RANDY GUMPERT
□ 60. CHICO CARRASQUEL
□ 87. FLOYD BAKER
□ 88. EDDIE ROBINSON
□ 123. HOWIE JUDSON
□ 124. GUS NIARHOS
□ 159. EDDIE STEWART
□ 160. PHIL MASI
□ 195. PAUL RICHARDS(M)
□ 196. BILLY PIERCE
□ 197. BOB CAIN(F)
□ 231. LUIS ALOMA
□ 232. NELSON FOX
□ 266. HARRY DORISH
□ 267. KEN HOLCOMBE
□ 302. JIM BUSBY
□ 303. MARV ROTBLATT

CINCINNATI REDS

□ 24. EWELL BLACKWELL
□ 47. GRADY HATTON
□ 48. KEN RAFFENSBERGER
□ 72. LLOYD MERRIMAN
□ 107. JOHNNY WYROSTEK
□ 108. VIRGIL STALLCUP
□ 143. TED KLUSZEWSKI
□ 144. HERMAN WEHMEIER
□ 179. DANNY LITWHILER
□ 180. HOWIE FOX
□ 215. KEN PETERSON
□ 216. CONNIE RYAN
□ 251. WILLARD RAMSDELL
□ 252. DIXIE HOWELL
□ 286. BOB USHER
□ 287. JIM BLACKBURN
□ 288. BOBBY ADAMS
□ 322. LUKE SEWELL(M)
□ 323. JOE ADCOCK
□ 324. JOHNNY PRAMESA

CLEVELAND INDIANS

□ 5. DALE MITCHELL
□ 21. GEORGE STIRNWEISS(B)
□ 29. ALLIE CLARK
□ 30. BOB FELLER
□ 53. BOB LEMON
□ 54. RAY BOONE
□ 78. EARLY WYNN
□ 79. JIM HEGAN
□ 114. SAM ZOLDAK(F)
□ 115. STEVE GROMEK
□ 150. MIKE GARCIA
□ 151. LARRY DOBY
□ 155. LOU BRISSIE(B)
□ 187. AL ROSEN
□ 188. BOBBY AVILA
□ 222. THURMAN TUCKER
□ 223. JOHNNY VANDER MEER
□ 257. BIRDIE TEBBETTS
□ 258. LUKE EASTER
□ 295. AL LOPEZ(M)
□ 296. BOB KENNEDY

RAY BOONE

DETROIT TIGERS

□ 23. HOOT EVERS
□ 45. ART HOUTTEMAN
□ 46. GEORGE KELL
□ 71. JERRY PRIDDY
□ 104. VIRGIL TRUCKS
□ 105. DON KOLLOWAY
□ 106. PAT MULLIN
□ 140. EDDIE LAKE
□ 141. FRED HUTCHINSON
□ 142. AARON ROBINSON
□ 176. VIC WERTZ
□ 177. CHARLIE KELLER
□ 178. TED GRAY
□ 197. BOB CAIN(B)
□ 213. NEIL BERRY
□ 214. BOB SWIFT
□ 249. JOHNNY GROTH
□ 250. HANK BOROWY
□ 284. GENE BEARDEN
□ 285. JOHNNY LIPON
□ 319. RED ROLFE(M)
□ 320. HAL WHITE
□ 321. EARL JOHNSON

1951 Bowman

NEW YORK GIANTS

- 13. ED STANKY
- 14. AL DARK
- 37. WHITEY LOCKMAN
- 61. JIM HEARN
- 89. HENRY THOMPSON
- 90. DAVE KOSLO
- 125. BILL RIGNEY
- 126. BOBBY THOMSON
- 127. SAL MAGLIE
- 161. WES WESTRUM
- 162. LARRY JANSEN
- 163. MONTE KENNEDY
- 198. MONTE IRVIN
- 199. SHELDON JONES
- 200. JACK KRAMER(F)
- 233. LEO DUROCHER(M)
- 234. CLINT HARTUNG
- 235. JACK LOHRKE
- 268. DON MUELLER
- 269. RAY NOBLE
- 304. ALLEN GETTEL
- 305. WILLIE MAYS

NEW YORK YANKEES

- 1. WHITEY FORD
- 2. YOGI BERRA
- 25. VIC RASCHI
- 26. PHIL RIZZUTO
- 49. JERRY COLEMAN
- 50. JOHNNY MIZE
- 73. TOMMY BYRNE
- 74. BILLY JOHNSON
- 109. ALLIE REYNOLDS
- 110. BOBBY BROWN
- 145. FRED SANFORD
- 146. JOHNNY HOPP
- 181. CASEY STENGEL(M)
- 182. TOM FERRICK
- 183. HANK BAUER
- 200. JACK KRAMER(B)
- 217. JOE PAGE
- 218. ED LOPAT
- 219. GENE WOODLING
- 253. MICKEY MANTLE
- 254. JACKIE JENSEN
- 280. FRANK OVERMIRE(B)
- 289. CLIFF MAPES
- 290. BILL DICKEY(C)
- 291. TOMMY HENRICH(C)

PHILADELPHIA ATHLETICS

- 8. PAUL LEHNER
- 9. SAM CHAPMAN
- 33. BOB HOOPER
- 57. ALEX KELLNER
- 82. JOE TIPTON
- 83. CARL SCHEIB
- 84. BARNEY MCCOSKY
- 114. SAM ZOLDAK(B)
- 119. EDDIE JOOST
- 120. JOE COLEMAN
- 154. PETE SUDER
- 155. LOU BRISSIE(F)
- 191. BILLY HITCHCOCK
- 192. HANK WYSE(F)
- 226. JIMMY DYKES(M)
- 227. BOBBY SHANTZ
- 261. WALLY MOSES
- 262. GUS ZERNIAL
- 297. DAVE PHILLEY
- 298. JOE ASTROTH

PHILADELPHIA PHILLIES

- 3. ROBIN ROBERTS
- 4. DEL ENNIS
- 27. JIM KONSTANTY
- 28. EDDIE WAITKUS
- 51. ANDY SEMINICK
- 52. DICK SISLER
- 75. RUSS MEYER
- 76. STAN LOPATA
- 77. MIKE GOLIAT
- 111. CURT SIMMONS
- 112. WILLIE JONES
- 113. BILL NICHOLSON
- 147. KEN HEINTZELMAN
- 148. GRANNY HAMNER
- 149. BUBBA CHURCH

- 184. EDDIE SAWYER(M)
- 185. JIMMY BLOODWORTH
- 186. RICHIE ASHBURN
- 220. BOB J. MILLER
- 221. DICK WHITMAN
- 255. MILO CANDINI
- 256. KEN SILVESTRI
- 292. EDDIE PELLAGRINI
- 293. KEN JOHNSON
- 294. JOCKO THOMPSON

PITTSBURGH PIRATES

- 17. PETE CASTIGLIONE
- 40. GUS BELL
- 63. BOB DILLINGER
- 64. BILL WERLE
- 93. DANNY O'CONNELL
- 94. CLYDE MCCULLOUGH
- 130. TOM SAFFELL
- 131. CLIFF CHAMBERS
- 166. STAN ROJEK(F)
- 167. MURRY DICKSON
- 203. VERNON LAW
- 204. VIC LOMBARDI
- 229. BILL HOWERTON(B)
- 238. PETE REISER
- 239. BILL MACDONALD
- 263. HOWIE POLLET(B)
- 272. BILLY MEYER(M)
- 273. DANNY MURTAUGH
- 274. GEORGE METKOVICH
- 308. TED BEARD
- 309. MEL QUEEN
- 310. ERV DUSAK

ST. LOUIS BROWNS

- 21. GEORGE STIRNWEISS(F)
- 43. BILLY DEMARS
- 67. ROY SIEVERS
- 68. DICK KOKOS
- 100. SHERM LOLLAR
- 101. OWEN FRIEND
- 136. RAY COLEMAN
- 137. DICK STARR
- 172. NED GARVER
- 173. HANK ARFT
- 209. KEN WOOD
- 210. LES MOSS(F)
- 244. CLIFF FANNIN
- 245. JOHN BERARDINO
- 279. JIM DELSING
- 280. FRANK OVERMIRE(F)
- 281. AL WIDMAR
- 315. ZACK TAYLOR(M)
- 316. DUANE PILLETTE

ST. LOUIS CARDINALS

- 10. RED SCHOENDIENST
- 11. RED MUNGER
- 34. MARTY MARION(M)
- 58. ENOS SLAUGHTER
- 85. EDDIE KAZAK
- 86. HARRY BRECHEEN
- 121. GERRY STALEY
- 122. JOE GARAGIOLA
- 156. DEL RICE
- 157. AL BRAZLE
- 158. CHUCK DIERING
- 166. STAN ROJEK(B)
- 193. TED WILKS
- 194. HARRY LOWREY
- 228. CLOYD BOYER
- 229. BILL HOWERTON(F)
- 230. MAX LANIER
- 263. HOWIE POLLET(F)
- 264. DON RICHMOND
- 265. STEVE BILKO
- 300. HAL RICE
- 301. TOMMY GLAVIANO

WASHINGTON SENATORS

- 18. GIL COAN
- 41. EDDIE YOST
- 65. MICKEY VERNON
- 95. SHERRY ROBERTSON
- 96. SANDY CONSUEGRA
- 97. BOB KUZAVA
- 132. CASS MICHAELS
- 133. SAM DENTE
- 168. SAM MELE
- 169. SID HUDSON
- 192. HANK WYSE(B)
- 202. MIKE GUERRA(B)
- 205. MICKEY GRASSO
- 206. CONRADO MARRERO
- 240. JOE HAYNES
- 241. IRV NOREN
- 275. BUCKY HARRIS(M)
- 276. FRANK QUINN
- 311. MICKEY HARRIS

1952 BOWMAN (252)
2 1/16" X 3 1/8"

BOSTON BRAVES

- 12. MAX SURKONT
- 28. ROY HARTSFIELD
- 48. VERN BICKFORD
- 60. SID GORDON
- 72. EARL TORGESON
- 84. SAM JETHROE
- 97. WILLARD MARSHALL
- 100. SIBBY SISTI
- 120. CHET NICHOLS
- 132. DAVE COLE
- 156. WARREN SPAHN
- 172. EBBA ST. CLAIRE
- 192. JOHN CUSICK
- 208. WALKER COOPER
- 215. SHELDON JONES
- 228. BOB CHIPMAN
- 244. LEW BURDETTE

BOSTON RED SOX

- 9. VERN STEPHENS
- 25. MICKEY MCDERMOTT
- 45. JOHNNY PESKY
- 57. CLYDE VOLLMER

5

1952 Bowman

☐ 81. BILLY GOODMAN
☐ 106. RANDY GUMPERT
☐ 117. BILL WIGHT
☐ 129. GUS NIARHOS
☐ 140. RAY SCARBOROUGH
☐ 153. FRED HATFIELD
☐ 169. WALT DROPO
☐ 189. JIM PIERSALL
☐ 205. WALT MASTERSON
☐ 225. DEL WILBER
☐ 241. MEL PARNESS
☐ 250. IVAN DELOCK

BROOKLYN DODGERS

☐ 8. PEE WEE REESE
☐ 24. CARL FURILLO
☐ 44. ROY CAMPANELLA
☐ 56. CLYDE KING
☐ 70. CARL ERSKINE
☐ 80. GIL HODGES
☐ 86. CAL ABRAMS
☐ 96. RALPH BRANCA
☐ 116. DUKE SNIDER
☐ 128. DON NEWCOMBE
☐ 152. BILLY COX
☐ 168. PREACHER ROE
☐ 188. CHARLIE DRESSEN(M)
☐ 204. ANDY PAFKO
☐ 224. JOHNNY SCHMITZ
☐ 240. BILLY LOES

CHICAGO CUBS

☐ 16. TURK LOWN
☐ 22. WILLARD RAMSDELL
☐ 32. EDDIE MIKSIS
☐ 64. ROY SMALLEY
☐ 88. BRUCE EDWARDS
☐ 104. HAL JEFFCOAT
☐ 126. PHIL CAVARRETTA(M)
☐ 136. GENE HERMANSKI
☐ 144. JOE HATTEN
☐ 159. DUTCH LEONARD
☐ 175. RANSOM JACKSON
☐ 195. FRANK BAUMHOLTZ
☐ 211. PAUL MINNER
☐ 231. DEE FONDY
☐ 236. TOMMY BROWN(B)
☐ 247. JOHN PRAMESA

CHICAGO WHITE SOX

☐ 5. MINNIE MINOSO
☐ 21. NELSON FOX
☐ 41. CHICO CARRASQUEL
☐ 54. BILLY PIERCE
☐ 68. JIM BUSBY
☐ 77. EDDIE ROBINSON
☐ 93. PAUL RICHARDS(M)
☐ 113. AL ZARILLA
☐ 149. HOWIE JUDSON
☐ 165. SAUL ROGOVIN
☐ 185. EDDIE STEWART
☐ 201. RAY COLEMAN
☐ 221. LOU KRETLOW
☐ 237. SHERMAN LOLLAR

CINCINNATI REDS

☐ 6. VIRGIL STALLCUP
☐ 42. JOHNNY WYROSTEK
☐ 55. KEN RAFFENSBERGER
☐ 69. JOE ADCOCK
☐ 78. LLOYD MERRIMAN
☐ 94. LUKE SEWELL(M)
☐ 114. FRANK HILLER
☐ 127. DICK SISLER
☐ 141. HANK EDWARDS
☐ 150. HERMAN WEHMEIER
☐ 166. BOBBY ADAMS
☐ 186. FRANK SMITH
☐ 202. HARRY PERKOWSKI
☐ 222. DIXIE HOWELL
☐ 238. ROY MCMILLAN

CLEVELAND INDIANS

☐ 7. MIKE GARCIA
☐ 23. BOB LEMON
☐ 43. BOB FELLER

☐ 79. LOU BRISSIE
☐ 95. LUKE EASTER
☐ 115. LARRY DOBY
☐ 124. BIRDIE TEBBETTS
☐ 142. EARLY WYNN
☐ 151. AL ROSEN
☐ 167. BOB AVILA
☐ 187. JIM HEGAN
☐ 203. STEVE GROMEK
☐ 214. RAY BOONE
☐ 223. HARRY SIMPSON
☐ 239. DALE MITCHELL

DETROIT TIGERS

☐ 3. FRED HUTCHINSON
☐ 13. CLIFF MAPES
☐ 39. VIC WERTZ
☐ 67. JOHNNY GROTH
☐ 75. GEORGE KELL
☐ 91. DON KOLLOWAY
☐ 111. HOOT EVERS
☐ 131. BOB SWIFT
☐ 139. JERRY PRIDDY
☐ 147. MARLIN STUART
☐ 163. JOHNNY LIPON
☐ 183. PAT MULLIN
☐ 199. TED GRAY
☐ 209. DICK LITTLEFIELD
☐ 216. MATT BATTS
☐ 219. NEIL BERRY
☐ 235. STEVE SOUCHOCK

NEW YORK GIANTS

☐ 2. BOBBY THOMSON
☐ 18. DON MUELLER
☐ 34. AL DARK
☐ 38. WHITEY LOCKMAN
☐ 49. JIM HEARN
☐ 66. SAL MAGLIE
☐ 74. WES WESTRUM
☐ 90. LARRY JANSEN
☐ 110. MAX LANIER
☐ 121. AL CORWIN
☐ 146. LEO DUROCHER(M)
☐ 162. MONTE IRWIN
☐ 178. DAVE WILLIAMS
☐ 182. DAVE KOSLO
☐ 198. CHUCK DIERING
☐ 213. MONTE KENNEDY
☐ 218. WILLIE MAYS
☐ 234. FRED FITZSIMMONS(C)
☐ 249. HANK THOMPSON

NEW YORK YANKEES

☐ 1. YOGI BERRA
☐ 17. ED LOPAT
☐ 33. GIL MCDOUGALD
☐ 37. VIC RASCHI
☐ 52. PHIL RIZZUTO
☐ 65. HANK BAUER
☐ 73. JERRY COLEMAN
☐ 101. MICKEY MANTLE
☐ 105. BOBBY BROWN
☐ 109. TOM MORGAN
☐ 145. JOHNNY MIZE
☐ 161. JACKIE JENSEN(F)
☐ 177. GENE WOODLING
☐ 181. JOE COLLINS
☐ 197. CHARLIE SILVERA
☐ 217. CASEY STENGEL(M)
☐ 233. BOB KUZAVA
☐ 252. FRANK CROSETTI(C)

PHILADELPHIA ATHLETICS

☐ 10. BOB HOOPER
☐ 26. EDDIE JOOST
☐ 46. CARL SCHEIB
☐ 58. HANK MAJESKI
☐ 82. GUS ZERNIAL
☐ 89. BILLY HITCHCOCK
☐ 98. JIMMY DYKES(M)
☐ 118. RAY MURRAY
☐ 130. ALLIE CLARK
☐ 154. FERRIS FAIN
☐ 170. JOE ASTROTH
☐ 179. PETE SUDER
☐ 190. DICK FOWLER
☐ 206. ELMER VALO
☐ 226. ALEX KELLNER
☐ 242. EVERETT KELL

PHILADELPHIA PHILLIES

☐ 4. ROBIN ROBERTS
☐ 20. WILLIE JONES
☐ 35. GRANNY HAMNER
☐ 40. BUBBA CHURCH
☐ 53. RICHIE ASHBURN
☐ 76. DEL ENNIS
☐ 92. EDDIE WAITKUS
☐ 112. SMOKEY BURGESS
☐ 125. HOWIE FOX
☐ 148. KEN HEINTZELMAN
☐ 164. CONNIE RYAN
☐ 184. CURT SIMMONS
☐ 200. KEN SILVESTRI
☐ 220. RUSS MEYER
☐ 236. TOMMY BROWN(F)
☐ 251. JACK LOHRKE

PITTSBURGH PIRATES

☐ 11. RALPH KINER
☐ 27. JOE GARAGIOLA
☐ 47. PETE CASTIGLIONE
☐ 59. MURRAY DICKSON
☐ 71. VERNON LAW
☐ 83. HOWIE POLLET
☐ 99. CLYDE MCCULLOUGH
☐ 108. GEORGE METKOVICH
☐ 119. BILL HOWERTON
☐ 138. TED WILKS
☐ 155. BILL MEYER(M)
☐ 171. MEL QUEEN
☐ 180. ED FITZ GERALD
☐ 191. BOB FRIEND
☐ 207. GEORGE STRICKLAND
☐ 227. CLYDE SUKEFORTH(C)
☐ 243. RED MUNGER

1952 Bowman

ST. LOUIS BROWNS

- ☐ 19. BOB CAIN
- ☐ 29. NED GARVER
- ☐ 61. TOMMY BYRNE
- ☐ 85. MARTY MARION(C)
- ☐ 133. DICK KRYHOSKI
- ☐ 137. STAN ROJEK
- ☐ 157. JIM DELSING
- ☐ 173. GENE BEARDEN
- ☐ 193. BOBBY YOUNG
- ☐ 229. HANK ARFT
- ☐ 245. GEORGE SCHMEES

ST. LOUIS CARDINALS

- ☐ 14. CLIFF CHAMBERS
- ☐ 30. RED SCHOENDIENST
- ☐ 50. GERRY STALEY
- ☐ 62. JOE PRESKO
- ☐ 102. PEANUTS LOWREY
- ☐ 107. DEL RICE
- ☐ 122. BILLY JOHNSON
- ☐ 134. AL BRAZLE
- ☐ 160. EDDIE STANKY(M)
- ☐ 176. HARRY BRECHEEN
- ☐ 196. STAN MUSIAL
- ☐ 212. SOLLY HEMUS
- ☐ 232. ENOS SLAUGHTER
- ☐ 248. BILL WERLE

WASHINGTON SENATORS

- ☐ 15. SAM MELE
- ☐ 31. EDDIE YOST
- ☐ 36. CASS MICHAELS
- ☐ 51. GIL COAN
- ☐ 63. IRV NOREN
- ☐ 87. MICKEY VERNON
- ☐ 103. JOE HAYNES
- ☐ 123. SID HUDSON
- ☐ 135. MICKEY HARRIS
- ☐ 143. SANDY CONSUEGRA
- ☐ 158. BUCKY HARRIS(M)
- ☐ 161. JACKIE JENSEN(B)
- ☐ 174. MICKEY GRASSO
- ☐ 194. BOB PORTERFIELD
- ☐ 210. ARCHIE WILSON
- ☐ 230. FRANK SHEA
- ☐ 246. JERRY SNYDER

1953 BOWMAN (160)
2 1/2" X 3 3/4"
COLOR

BOSTON RED SOX

- ☐ 25. HOOT EVERS
- ☐ 35. MICKEY MCDERMOTT
- ☐ 41. SAMMY WHITE
- ☐ 57. LOU BOUDREAU(M)
- ☐ 61. GEORGE KELL
- ☐ 66. MEL PARNELL
- ☐ 123. JOHNNY LIPON
- ☐ 148. BILLY GOODMAN

BROOKLYN DODGERS

- ☐ 12. CARL ERSKINE
- ☐ 14. BILLY LOES
- ☐ 33. PEE WEE REESE
- ☐ 46. ROY CAMPANELLA
- ☐ 78. CARL FURILLO
- ☐ 92. GIL HODGES
- ☐ 117. DUKE SNIDER
- ☐ 124. CHARLIE DRESSEN(M)
- ☐ 129. RUSS MEYER
- ☐ 135. BOBBY MORGAN
- ☐ 145. GEORGE SHUBA

CHICAGO CUBS

- ☐ 7. HARRY CHITI
- ☐ 30. PHIL CAVARRETTA(M)
- ☐ 42. TOMMY BROWN
- ☐ 48. HANK SAUER
- ☐ 71. PAUL MINNER
- ☐ 94. BOB ADDIS
- ☐ 110. BOB RUSH
- ☐ 112. TOBY ATWELL
- ☐ 122. BILL SERENA
- ☐ 144. WARREN HACKER
- ☐ 154. TURK LOWN

CHICAGO WHITE SOX

- ☐ 18. NELSON FOX
- ☐ 36. MINNIE MINOSO
- ☐ 39. PAUL RICHARDS(M)
- ☐ 50. LOU KRETLOW
- ☐ 54. CHICO CARRASQUEL
- ☐ 73. BILLY PIERCE
- ☐ 75. SAUL ROGOVIN
- ☐ 88. JOE DOBSON
- ☐ 98. HECTOR RODRIQUEZ
- ☐ 137. SAM DENTE
- ☐ 157. SHERMAN LOLLAR

CINCINNATI REDS

- ☐ 23. HERMAN WEHMEIER
- ☐ 26. ROY MCMILLAN
- ☐ 58. WILLARD MARSHALL
- ☐ 62. TED KLUSZEWSKI
- ☐ 87. HARRY PERKOWSKI
- ☐ 90. JOE NUXHALL

- ☐ 106. KEN RAFFENSBERGER
- ☐ 108. BOBBY ADAMS
- ☐ 138. BUBBA CHURCH

CLEVELAND INDIANS

- ☐ 8. AL ROSEN
- ☐ 29. BOBBY AVILA
- ☐ 40. LARRY DOBY
- ☐ 43. MIKE GARCIA
- ☐ 79. RAY BOONE
- ☐ 86. HARRY SIMPSON
- ☐ 102. JIM HEGAN
- ☐ 104. LUKE EASTER
- ☐ 114. BOB FELLER
- ☐ 119. DALE MITCHELL
- ☐ 143. AL LOPEZ(M)
- ☐ 146. EARLY WYNN

DETROIT TIGERS

- ☐ 4. ART HOUTTEMAN
- ☐ 6. JOE GINSBERG
- ☐ 45. WALT DROPO
- ☐ 47. NED GARVER
- ☐ 72. TED GRAY
- ☐ 91. STEVE SOUCHOCK
- ☐ 100. BILL WIGHT
- ☐ 125. FRED HATFIELD
- ☐ 132. FRED HUTCHINSON(M)
- ☐ 134. JOHNNY PESKY

MIKWAUKEE BRAVES

- ☐ 3. SAM JETHROE*
- ☐ 5. SID GORDON*
- ☐ 37. JIM WILSON*
- ☐ 69. CHARLIE GRIMM(M)
- ☐ 83. JACK DANIELS
- ☐ 97. EDDIE MATHEWS
- ☐ 99. WARREN SPAHN
- ☐ 151. JOE ADCOCK
- ☐ 156. MAX SURKONT

NEW YORK GIANTS

- ☐ 1. DAVEY WILLIAMS
- ☐ 19. AL DARK
- ☐ 51. MONTE IRVIN
- ☐ 55. LEO DUROCHER(M)
- ☐ 74. DON MUELLER
- ☐ 76. JIM HEARN
- ☐ 96. SAL MAGLIE
- ☐ 126. AL CORWIN
- ☐ 128. WHITEY LOCKMAN
- ☐ 149. AL CORWIN

NEW YORK YANKEES

- ☐ 9. PHIL RIZZUTO
- ☐ 27. VIC RASCHI
- ☐ 59. MICKEY MANTLE
- ☐ 63. GIL MCDOUGALD
- ☐ 68. ALLIE REYNOLDS
- ☐ 84. HANK BAUER
- ☐ 118. BILLY MARTIN
- ☐ 121. YOGI BERRA
- ☐ 136. JIM BRIDEWESER
- ☐ 153. WHITEY FORD

PHILADELPHIA ATHLETICS

- ☐ 11. BOBBY SHANTZ
- ☐ 13. GUS ZERNIAL
- ☐ 31. JIMMY DYKES(M)
- ☐ 38. HARRY BYRD
- ☐ 82. JOE ASTROTH
- ☐ 95. WALLY MOSES(C)
- ☐ 105. EDDIE JOOST
- ☐ 107. ALEX KELLNER
- ☐ 130. CASS MICHAELS
- ☐ 150. CARL SCHEIB
- ☐ 155. ALLIE CLARK

PHILADELPHIA PHILLIES

- ☐ 10. RICHIE ASHBURN
- ☐ 28. SMOKY BURGESS
- ☐ 60. GRANNY HAMNER
- ☐ 64. CURT SIMMONS
- ☐ 65. ROBIN ROBERTS

7

* Nos. 3, 5, 37 appear with Boston Braves on the back of the card.

☐ 67. MEL CLARK
☐ 103. DEL ENNIS
☐ 113. KARL DREWS
☐ 131. CONNIE RYAN
☐ 133. WILLIE JONES
☐ 158. HOWARD FOX

PITTSBURGH PIRATES

☐ 16. BOB FRIEND
☐ 21. JOE GARAGIOLA
☐ 80. RALPH KINER
☐ 147. CLEM KOSHOREK
☐ 160. CAL ABRAMS

ST. LOUIS BROWNS

☐ 2. VIC WERTZ
☐ 20. DON LENHARDT
☐ 52. MARTY MARION(M)
☐ 56. BOB CAIN
☐ 70. CLINT COURTNEY
☐ 111. JIM DYCK
☐ 120. MARLIN STUART
☐ 127. DICK KRYHOSKI

ST. LOUIS CARDINALS

☐ 17. GERRY STALEY
☐ 32. STAN MUSIAL
☐ 49. EDDIE STANKY(M)
☐ 53. DEL RICE
☐ 81. ENOS SLAUGHTER
☐ 85. SOLLY HEMUS
☐ 101. RED SCHOENDIENST
☐ 115. CLOYD BOYER
☐ 140. AL BRAZLE
☐ 142. LARRY MIGGINS

WASHINGTON SENATORS

☐ 15. JIM BUSBY
☐ 22. BOB PORTERFIELD
☐ 24. JACKIE JENSEN
☐ 34. GIL COAN
☐ 77. MICKEY GRASSO

☐ 89. SANDY CONSUEGRA
☐ 109. KEN WOOD
☐ 116. EDDIE YOST
☐ 139. PETE RUNNELS
☐ 141. FRANK SHEA
☐ 152. CLYDE VOLLMER
☐ 159. MICKEY VERNON

1953 BOWMAN (64)
2 1/2″ X 3 3/4″
BLACK & WHITE

BOSTON RED SOX

☐ 2. WILLARD NIXON
☐ 11. DICK GERNERT
☐ 24. DEL WILBER
☐ 29. SID HUDSON
☐ 36. JIM PIERSALL
☐ 49. FLOYD BAKER

BROOKLYN DODGERS

☐ 26. PREACHER ROE
☐ 52. RALPH BRANCA
☐ 60. BILLY COX

CHICAGO CUBS

☐ 5. DEE FONDY
☐ 12. RANDY JACKSON
☐ 37. HAL JEFFCOAT
☐ 41. BOB RAMAZZOTTI
☐ 50. DUTCH LEONARD
☐ 56. ROY SMALLEY

CHICAGO WHITE SOX

NO CARDS ISSUED

CINCINATTI REDS

☐ 1. GUS BELL
☐ 7. ANDY SEMINICK
☐ 21. BUD PODBIELAN
☐ 32. ROCKY BRIDGES
☐ 42. HOWIE JUDSON

CLEVELAND INDIANS

☐ 13. JOE TIPTON
☐ 27. BOB LEMON
☐ 63. STEVE GROMEK

DETROIT TIGERS

☐ 4. PAT MULLIN
☐ 18. BILLY HOEFT
☐ 22. MATT BATTS
☐ 44. JIM DELSING

MILWAUKEE BRAVES

☐ 30. WALKER COOPER
☐ 34. EBBA ST. CLAIR
☐ 38. DAVE COLE
☐ 51. LOU BURDETTE
☐ 57. ANDY PAFKO

NEW YORK GIANTS

☐ 3. BILL RIGNEY
☐ 28. HOYT WILHELM
☐ 40. LARRY JANSEN

NEW YORK YANKEES

☐ 15. JOHNNY MIZE
☐ 25. JOHN SAIN
☐ 31. GENE WOODLING
☐ 33. BOB KUZAVA
☐ 39. CASEY STENGEL(M)
☐ 45. IRV NOREN
☐ 54. BILL MILLER
☐ 61. TOM GORMAN

PHILADELPHIA ATHLETICS

☐ 6. RAY MURRAY
☐ 8. PETE SUDER
☐ 20. EDDIE ROBINSON
☐ 43. HAL BEVAN
☐ 53. MORRIS MARTIN
☐ 62. KEITH THOMAS

PHILADELPHIA PHILLIES

☐ 14. BILL NICHOLSON
☐ 35. JOHNNY WYROSTEK
☐ 47. JACK LOHRKE
☐ 48. STEVE RIDZIK
☐ 58. JIM KONSTANTY
☐ 64. ANDY HANSEN

PITTSBURGH PIRATES

☐ 19. PAUL LA PALME

1953 Bowman B & W

ST. LOUIS BROWNS

- ☐ 17. VIRGIL TRUCKS
- ☐ 59. DUANE PILLETTE

ST. LOUIS CARDINALS

- ☐ 10. DICK SISLER
- ☐ 16. STU MILLER
- ☐ 23. WILMER MIZELL

WASHINGTON SENATORS

- ☐ 9. WALT MASTERSON
- ☐ 46. BUCKY HARRIS(M)
- ☐ 55. DON JOHNSON

1954 BOWMAN (224)
2 1/2″ X 3 3/4″

BALTIMORE ORIOLES

- ☐ 5. BILL HUNTER
- ☐ 21. VIC WERTZ
- ☐ 37. DICK KOKOS
- ☐ 53. DON LENHARDT
- ☐ 69. CLINT COURTNEY
- ☐ 85. JIM DYCK
- ☐ 101. DON LARSEN
- ☐ 117. DICK KRYHOSKI
- ☐ 133. DUANE PILLETTE
- ☐ 149. BOB YOUNG
- ☐ 165. JOHNNY GROTH
- ☐ 181. LES MOSS
- ☐ 197. LOU KRETLOW
- ☐ 213. DICK LITTLEFIELD

BOSTON RED SOX

- ☐ 2. JACKIE JENSEN
- ☐ 18. HOOT EVERS
- ☐ 34. SAMMY WHITE
- ☐ 50. GEORGE KELL
- ☐ 66. TED WILLIAMS
- ☐ 66. JIM PIERSALL
- ☐ 82. BILLY GOODMAN
- ☐ 98. ELLIS KINDER
- ☐ 114. WILLARD NIXON
- ☐ 130. MILT BOLLING
- ☐ 146. DICK GERNERT
- ☐ 162. TED LEPCIO
- ☐ 178. DEL WILBER
- ☐ 194. SID HUDSON
- ☐ 210. JIM PIERSALL

BROOKLYN DODGERS

- ☐ 10. CARL ERSKINE
- ☐ 26. BILLY COX
- ☐ 42. BILLY LOES
- ☐ 58. PEE WEE REESE
- ☐ 74. JIM GILLIAM
- ☐ 90. ROY CAMPANELLA
- ☐ 106. CLEM LABINE
- ☐ 122. CARL FURILLO
- ☐ 138. GIL HODGES
- ☐ 154. DON NEWCOMBE
- ☐ 170. DUKE SNIDER
- ☐ 186. RUSS MEYER
- ☐ 202. GEORGE SHUBA
- ☐ 218. PREACHER ROE

CHICAGO CUBS

- ☐ 13. PAUL MINNER
- ☐ 29. JOHNNY KLIPPSTEIN
- ☐ 45. RALPH KINER
- ☐ 61. EDDIE MIKSIS
- ☐ 77. BOB RUSH
- ☐ 93. BILL SERENA
- ☐ 109. ROY SMALLEY
- ☐ 125. WARREN HACKER
- ☐ 141. JOE GARAGIOLA
- ☐ 157. TURK LOWN
- ☐ 173. DEE FONDY
- ☐ 189. RANDY JACKSON
- ☐ 205. HAL JEFFCOAT
- ☐ 221. FRANK BAUMHOLTZ

CHICAGO WHITE SOX

- ☐ 6. NELSON FOX
- ☐ 22. SAM MELE
- ☐ 38. MINNIE MINOSO
- ☐ 54. CHICO CARRASQUEL
- ☐ 70. WILLARD MARSHALL(B)
- ☐ 86. HARRY DORISH
- ☐ 102. BILLY PIERCE
- ☐ 118. BOB BOYD
- ☐ 134. LUIS ALOMA
- ☐ 150. CASS MICHAELS
- ☐ 166. SANDY CONSUEGRA
- ☐ 182. SHERMAN LOLLAR
- ☐ 198. VIRGIL TRUCKS
- ☐ 214. FERRIS FAIN

CINCINNATI REDS

- ☐ 12. ROY MCMILLAN
- ☐ 28. JIM GREENGRASS
- ☐ 44. HARRY PERKOWSKI
- ☐ 60. FRED BACZEWSKI
- ☐ 70. WILLARD MARSHALL(F)
- ☐ 76. JOE NUXHALL
- ☐ 92. KEN RAFFENSBERGER
- ☐ 108. BOBBY ADAMS
- ☐ 124. GUS BELL
- ☐ 140. SAUL ROGOVIN
- ☐ 156. ROCKY BRIDGES
- ☐ 172. ANDY SEMINICK
- ☐ 188. FRANK SMITH
- ☐ 204. JACKIE COLLUM
- ☐ 220. HOBIE LANDRITH

CLEVELAND INDIANS

- ☐ 4. BOB HOOPER
- ☐ 20. ART HOUTTEMAN
- ☐ 36. GEORGE STRICKLAND
- ☐ 52. JOE GINSBERG
- ☐ 68. BOBBY AVILA
- ☐ 84. LARRY DOBY
- ☐ 100. MIKE GARCIA
- ☐ 116. LUKE EASTER
- ☐ 132. BOB FELLER
- ☐ 148. DALE MITCHELL
- ☐ 164. EARLY WYNN
- ☐ 184. MICKEY GRASSO
- ☐ 196. BOB LEMON
- ☐ 212. OWEN FRIEND

DETROIT TIGERS

- ☐ 7. WALT DROPO
- ☐ 23. HARVEY KUENN
- ☐ 39. NED GARVER
- ☐ 55. JIM DELSING
- ☐ 71. TED GRAY
- ☐ 87. DON LUND
- ☐ 103. STEVE SOUCHOCK
- ☐ 119. FRED HATFIELD
- ☐ 135. JOHNNY PESKY
- ☐ 151. PAT MULLIN
- ☐ 167. BILLY HOEFT
- ☐ 183. MATT BATTS
- ☐ 199. STEVE GROMEK
- ☐ 215. JOHNNY BUCHA

MILWAUKEE BRAVES

- ☐ 16. JIM WILSON
- ☐ 32. DEL CRANDALL
- ☐ 48. JACK DITTMER
- ☐ 64. EDDIE MATHEWS
- ☐ 80. JOHNNY LOGAN
- ☐ 96. JOE ADCOCK
- ☐ 112. ANDY PAFKO
- ☐ 144. ERNIE JOHNSON
- ☐ 160. DANNY O'CONNELL
- ☐ 176. VERN BICKFORD
- ☐ 192. LEW BURDETTE
- ☐ 201. BOBBY THOMSON
- ☐ 224. BILL BRUTON

NEW YORK GIANTS

- ☐ 9. DAVE WILLIAMS
- ☐ 25. WES WESTRUM
- ☐ 41. AL DARK
- ☐ 57. HOYT WILHELM
- ☐ 73. DON MUELLER
- ☐ 89. WILLIE MAYS
- ☐ 105. SAL MAGLIE
- ☐ 121. RAY KATT
- ☐ 128. EBBA ST. CLAIRE
- ☐ 137. AL CORWIN
- ☐ 153. WHITEY LOCKMAN
- ☐ 169. LARRY JANSEN
- ☐ 185. DARYL SPENCER
- ☐ 208. JOHNNY ANTONELLI
- ☐ 217. HANK THOMPSON

NEW YORK YANKEES

- ☐ 1. PHIL RIZZUTO
- ☐ 17. TOM GORMAN
- ☐ 33. VIC RASCHI
- ☐ 49. HARRY BYRD
- ☐ 65. MICKEY MANTLE
- ☐ 81. JERRY COLEMAN
- ☐ 97. GIL MCDOUGALD
- ☐ 113. ALLIE REYNOLDS
- ☐ 129. HANK BAUER
- ☐ 145. BILLY MARTIN
- ☐ 161. YOGI BERRA
- ☐ 177. WHITEY FORD
- ☐ 193. EDDIE ROBINSON
- ☐ 209. GENE WOODLING

PHILADELPHIA ATHLETICS

- ☐ 3. MARION FRICANO
- ☐ 19. BOBBY SHANTZ
- ☐ 35. EDDIE JOOST
- ☐ 51. ALEX KELLNER
- ☐ 67. CARL SCHEIB
- ☐ 83. RAY MURRAY
- ☐ 99. PETE SUDER
- ☐ 115. DON BOLLWEG
- ☐ 131. JOE ASTROTH
- ☐ 147. JOE DEMAESTRI
- ☐ 163. DAVE PHILLEY
- ☐ 179. MORRIS MARTIN
- ☐ 195. BOB CAIN
- ☐ 211. AL ROBERTSON

PHILADELPHIA PHILLIES

- ☐ 15. RICHIE ASHBURN
- ☐ 31. SMOKEY BURGESS
- ☐ 47. GRANNY HAMNER
- ☐ 63. EARL TORGESON
- ☐ 79. CURT SIMMONS
- ☐ 95. ROBIN ROBERTS
- ☐ 111. MURRY DICKSON
- ☐ 127. DEL ENNIS
- ☐ 143. WILLIE JONES
- ☐ 159. JOHNNY LINDELL
- ☐ 175. MEL CLARK
- ☐ 191. KARL DREWS
- ☐ 207. STAN LOPATA
- ☐ 223. STEVE RIDZIK

PITTSBURGH PIRATES

- ☐ 11. SID GORDON
- ☐ 27. DICK COLE
- ☐ 43. BOB FRIEND
- ☐ 59. BOB SCHULTZ
- ☐ 75. MAX SURKONT
- ☐ 91. CAL ABRAMS
- ☐ 107. PAUL LA PALME
- ☐ 123. TOBY ATWELL
- ☐ 139. PRESTON WARD
- ☐ 155. FRANK THOMAS
- ☐ 171. CARLOS BERNIER
- ☐ 187. VERN LAW
- ☐ 203. VIC JANOWICZ
- ☐ 219. HAL RICE

ST. LOUIS CARDINALS

- ☐ 14. GERRY STALEY
- ☐ 30. DEL RICE
- ☐ 46. RIP REPULSKI
- ☐ 62. ENOS SLAUGHTER
- ☐ 78. SAL YVARS
- ☐ 94. SOLLY HEMUS
- ☐ 110. RED SCHOENDIENST
- ☐ 126. CLIFF CHAMBERS
- ☐ 142. AL BRAZLE
- ☐ 158. STU MILLER
- ☐ 174. PETE CASTIGLIONE
- ☐ 190. JOE PRESKO
- ☐ 206. STEVE BILKO
- ☐ 222. MEMO LUNA

WASHINGTON SENATORS

- ☐ 8. JIM BUSBY
- ☐ 24. BOB PORTERFIELD
- ☐ 40. GIL COAN
- ☐ 56. MICKEY MCDERMOTT
- ☐ 72. EDDIE YOST
- ☐ 88. TOM UMPHLETT
- ☐ 104. FRANK SHEA
- ☐ 120. MEL HODERLEIN
- ☐ 136. CLYDE VOLLMER
- ☐ 152. MICKEY VERNON
- ☐ 168. ED FITZ GERALD
- ☐ 180. JOE TIPTON
- ☐ 200. CONNIE MARRERO
- ☐ 216. JERRY SNYDER

1955 BOWMAN (320)
2 1/2" X 3 3/4"

BALTIMORE ORIOLES

- ☐ 3. JOE COLEMAN
- ☐ 4. EDDIE WAITKUS
- ☐ 55. CAL ABRAMS
- ☐ 56. BILLY COX
- ☐ 77. JIM MCDONALD
- ☐ 78. GIL COAN
- ☐ 79. WILLIE MIRANDA
- ☐ 101. DON JOHNSON
- ☐ 108. LOU KRETLOW
- ☐ 109. VERN STEPHENS
- ☐ 159. HARRY BYRD
- ☐ 161. MATT BATTS
- ☐ 162. CHARLIE MAXWELL
- ☐ 215. BOB KUZAVA
- ☐ 216. PREACHER ROE
- ☐ 225. PAUL RICHARDS(M)
- ☐ 241. JOHN PESKY
- ☐ 244. DUANE PILLETTE
- ☐ 245. BILL MILLER

BOSTON RED SOX

- ☐ 15. FRANK SULLIVAN
- ☐ 16. JIM PIERSALL
- ☐ 47. SAMMY WHITE
- ☐ 48. MILT BOLLING
- ☐ 126. BILLY GOODMAN
- ☐ 147. SAM MELE
- ☐ 150. BILL KLAUS
- ☐ 177. WILLARD NIXON
- ☐ 178. TOM BREWER
- ☐ 221. HECTOR BROWN
- ☐ 222. RUSS KEMMERER
- ☐ 256. OWEN FRIEND
- ☐ 264. BILL R. HENRY
- ☐ 276. IVAN DELOCK
- ☐ 290. HERSHELL FREEMAN
- ☐ 302. FRANK MALZONE
- ☐ 318. SID HUDSON
- ☐ 319. AL SCHROLL
- ☐ 320. GEORGE SUSCE

BROOKLYN DODGERS

- ☐ 21. DON HOAK
- ☐ 22. ROY CAMPANELLA
- ☐ 37. PEE WEE REESE
- ☐ 39. BOB DARNELL
- ☐ 65. DON ZIMMER
- ☐ 66. GEORGE SHUBA
- ☐ 97. JOHNNY PODRES
- ☐ 98. JIM GILLIAM
- ☐ 143. DON NEWCOMBE
- ☐ 156. JIM HUGHES
- ☐ 158. GIL HODGES
- ☐ 169. CARL FURILLO
- ☐ 170. CARL ERSKINE
- ☐ 195. ERV PALICA
- ☐ 196. RUSS MEYER
- ☐ 240. BILLY LOES
- ☐ 261. WALT MORYN
- ☐ 270. CHICO FERNANDEZ
- ☐ 278. CHARLIE NEAL
- ☐ 310. KEN LEHMAN

CHICAGO CUBS

- ☐ 7. GENE BAKER
- ☐ 8. WARREN HACKER
- ☐ 52. HAL RICE
- ☐ 87. RANDY JACKSON
- ☐ 88. STEVE BILKO
- ☐ 137. BOB TALBOT
- ☐ 181. EDDIE MIKSIS
- ☐ 182. BOB RUSH
- ☐ 223. HAL JEFFCOAT
- ☐ 224. DEE FONDY
- ☐ 227. FRANK BAUMHOLTZ
- ☐ 229. JIM BROSNAN
- ☐ 242. ERNIE BANKS
- ☐ 247. DUTCH LEONARD(C)
- ☐ 273. BUBBA CHURCH
- ☐ 280. CLYDE MCCULLOUGH
- ☐ 304. HARRY CHITI

CHICAGO WHITE SOX

- ☐ 25. MINNIE MINOSO
- ☐ 26. VIRGIL TRUCKS
- ☐ 33. NELSON FOX
- ☐ 34. CLINT COURTNEY
- ☐ 85. CASS MICHAELS
- ☐ 86. TED GRAY
- ☐ 116. SANDY CONSUEGRA
- ☐ 117. JOHNNY GROTH
- ☐ 131. WILLARD MARSHALL
- ☐ 135. LLOYD MERRIMAN
- ☐ 145. BOB NIEMAN
- ☐ 148. BOB CHAKALES
- ☐ 151. JIM BRIDEWESER
- ☐ 173. CHICO CARRASQUEL
- ☐ 174. SHERMAN LOLLAR
- ☐ 213. GEORGE KELL
- ☐ 214. BILLY PIERCE
- ☐ 230. AL BRAZLE
- ☐ 233. BILL SERENA
- ☐ 248. HARRY DORISH
- ☐ 251. STAN JOK
- ☐ 266. MIKE FORNIELES
- ☐ 282. PHIL CAVARRETTA
- ☐ 285. WALT DROPO

CINCINNATI REDS

- ☐ 31. JOHNNY TEMPLE
- ☐ 32. WALLY POST
- ☐ 49. JIM GREENGRASS
- ☐ 50. HOBIE LANDRITH
- ☐ 51. ELVIN TAPPE
- ☐ 93. ANDY SEMINICK
- ☐ 118. BOBBY ADAMS
- ☐ 136. ROCKY BRIDGES
- ☐ 152. JOHNNY KLIPPSTEIN
- ☐ 155. GERRY STALEY
- ☐ 189. JACK COLLUM
- ☐ 190. FRED BACZEWSKI
- ☐ 193. HOWIE JUDSON
- ☐ 194. JOE NUXHALL
- ☐ 232. BIRDIE TEBBETTS(M)
- ☐ 234. DICK BARTELL(C)
- ☐ 243. GUS BELL

CLEVELAND INDIANS

- ☐ 19. BOBBY AVILA
- ☐ 20. AL SMITH
- ☐ 38. EARLY WYNN
- ☐ 40. VIC WERTZ
- ☐ 96. RAY NARLESKI
- ☐ 127. HANK MAJESKI

1955 Bowman

☐ 128. MIKE GARCIA
☐ 129. HAL NARAGON
☐ 134. BOB FELLER
☐ 142. RUDY REGALADO
☐ 144. ART HOUTTEMAN
☐ 191. BOB LEMON
☐ 192. GEORGE STRICKLAND
☐ 197. RALPH KINER
☐ 198. DAVE POPE
☐ 259. DON MOSSI
☐ 263. EDDIE JOOST
☐ 271. BOB HOOPER
☐ 308. AL LOPEZ(M)
☐ 312. BILL WIGHT
☐ 314. DALE MITCHELL

DETROIT TIGERS

☐ 23. AL KALINE
☐ 24. AL ABER
☐ 35. BILL TUTTLE
☐ 36. WAYNE BELARDI
☐ 91. DICK MARLOWE
☐ 92. GEORGE ZUVERINK
☐ 121. RUFUS CRAWFORD
☐ 132. HARVEY KUENN
☐ 133. CHARLES KING
☐ 154. FRANK LARY
☐ 187. FRED HATFIELD
☐ 188. NED GARVER
☐ 203. STEVE GROMEK
☐ 204. FRANK BOLLING
☐ 228. BUBBA PHILLIPS
☐ 254. BENNETT FLOWERS
☐ 274. JIM DELSING

KANSAS CITY ATHLETICS

☐ 5. JIM ROBERTSON
☐ 6. PETE SUDER
☐ 53. ALEX KELLNER
☐ 54. DON BOLLWEG
☐ 80. LOU LIMMER
☐ 89. LOU BOUDREAU(M)
☐ 90. ART DITMAR
☐ 119. JOE ASTROTH
☐ 120. ED BURTSCHY
☐ 140. BOBBY SHANTZ
☐ 149. CLOYD BOYER
☐ 175. BILLY SHANTZ
☐ 176. JOE DEMAESTRI
☐ 211. SONNY DIXON
☐ 316. MARION FRICANO

MILWAUKEE BRAVES

☐ 11. BILLY BRUTON
☐ 12. ANDY PAFKO
☐ 43. BOB BUHL
☐ 44. DANNY O'CONNELL
☐ 70. LOU BURDETTE
☐ 71. DAVE JOLLY
☐ 72. CHET NICHOLS
☐ 102. BOBBY THOMSON
☐ 103. EDDIE MATHEWS
☐ 157. ERNIE JOHNSON
☐ 179. HANK AARON
☐ 180. JOHNNY LOGAN
☐ 212. JACK DITTMER
☐ 217. DEL CRANDALL
☐ 218. JOE ADCOCK
☐ 252. ROY SMALLEY
☐ 253. JIM WILSON
☐ 298. CHARLIE GRIMM(M)

NEW YORK GIANTS

☐ 1. HOYT WILHELM
☐ 2. AL DARK
☐ 94. HANK THOMPSON
☐ 95. SAL MAGLIE
☐ 122. AL CORWIN
☐ 123. MARV GRISSOM
☐ 124. JOHNNY ANTONELLI
☐ 125. PAUL GIEL
☐ 138. DAVEY WILLIAMS
☐ 141. WES WESTRUM
☐ 146. DON LIDDLE
☐ 183. RAY KATT
☐ 184. WILLIE MAYS
☐ 219. WHITEY LOCKMAN
☐ 220. JIM HEARN
☐ 249. BILLY GARDNER
☐ 269. JOE AMALFITANO

NEW YORK YANKEES

☐ 9. GIL MCDOUGALD
☐ 10. PHIL RIZZUTO
☐ 59. WHITEY FORD
☐ 60. ENOS SLAUGHTER
☐ 63. IRV NOREN
☐ 67. DON LARSEN
☐ 68. ELSTON HOWARD
☐ 69. BILL HUNTER
☐ 99. JERRY COLEMAN
☐ 100. TOM MORGAN
☐ 153. EDDIE ROBINSON
☐ 160. BILL SKOWRON
☐ 167. BOB GRIM
☐ 168. YOGI BERRA
☐ 201. ALLIE REYNOLDS
☐ 202. MICKEY MANTLE
☐ 231. JIM KONSTANTY
☐ 246. HANK BAUER
☐ 300. TOMMY BYRNE
☐ 306. BOB CERV

PHILADELPHIA PHILLIES

☐ 17. DEL ENNIS
☐ 18. STAN LOPATA
☐ 41. MEL CLARK
☐ 42. BOB GREENWOOD
☐ 64. CURT SIMMONS
☐ 81. BOB MORGAN
☐ 110. BOB J. MILLER
☐ 111. STEVE RIDZIK
☐ 112. GRANNY HAMNER
☐ 130. RICHIE ASHBURN
☐ 171. ROBIN ROBERTS
☐ 172. WILLIE JONES
☐ 209. SMOKY BURGESS
☐ 210. EARL TORGESON
☐ 236. MURRAY DICKSON
☐ 237. JOHNNY WYROSTEK
☐ 287. RON MROZINSKI
☐ 292. MARV BLAYLOCK
☐ 294. WALLY MOSES(C)

PITTSBURGH PIRATES

☐ 27. PRESTON WARD
☐ 28. DICK COLE
☐ 57. BOB FRIEND
☐ 58. FRANK THOMAS
☐ 82. LEE WALLS
☐ 83. MAX SURKONT
☐ 84. GEORGE FREESE
☐ 113. BOB HALL
☐ 114. VIC JANOWICZ
☐ 115. ROGER BOWMAN
☐ 163. SID GORDON
☐ 164. TOBY ATWELL
☐ 199. VERNON LAW
☐ 200. DICK LITTLEFIELD
☐ 288. DICK SMITH

ST. LOUIS CARDINALS

☐ 29. RED SCHOENDIENST
☐ 30. BILL SARNI
☐ 61. PAUL LAPALME
☐ 62. ROYCE LINT
☐ 75. BROOKS LAWRENCE

☐ 76. TOM POHOLSKY
☐ 106. DEL RICE
☐ 107. SOLLY HEMUS
☐ 185. VIC RASCHI
☐ 186. ALEX GRAMMAS
☐ 205. RIP REPULSKI
☐ 206. RALPH BEARD
☐ 238. EDDIE STANKY(M)
☐ 257. TOM ALSTON
☐ 296. BILL VIRDON

WASHINGTON SENATORS

☐ 13. CLYDE VOLLMER
☐ 14. GUS KERIAZAKOS
☐ 45. TOM UMPHLETT
☐ 46. MICKEY VERNON
☐ 73. EDDIE YOST
☐ 74. JERRY SNYDER
☐ 104. BOB PORTERFIELD
☐ 105. JOHNNY SCHMITZ
☐ 165. MICKEY MCDERMOTT
☐ 166. JIM BUSBY
☐ 207. FRANK SHEA
☐ 208. ED FITZ GERALD
☐ 255. PETE RUNNELS
☐ 262. JIM LEMON
☐ 268. ROY HAWES

1989 BOWMAN (484)
2 1/2" X 3 3/4"

ATLANTA BRAVES

☐ 262. ZANE SMITH
☐ 263. CHARLIE PULEO
☐ 264. DEREK LILLIQUIST
☐ 265. PAUL ASSENMACHER
☐ 266. JOHN SMOLTZ
☐ 267. TOM GLAVINE
☐ 268. STEVE AVERY
☐ 269. PETE SMITH
☐ 270. JODY DAVIS
☐ 271. BRUCE BENEDICT
☐ 272. ANDRES THOMAS
☐ 273. GERALD PERRY
☐ 274. RON GANT
☐ 275. DARRELL EVANS
☐ 276. DALE MURPHY
☐ 277. DION JAMES
☐ 278. LONNIE SMITH
☐ 279. GERONIMO BERROA

BALTIMORE ORIOLES

☐ 1. OSWALD PERAZA
☐ 2. BRIAN HOLTON
☐ 3. JOSE BAUTISTA
☐ 4. PETE HARNISCH
☐ 5. DAVE SCHMIDT
☐ 6. GREGG OLSON
☐ 7. JEFF BALLARD
☐ 8. BOB MELVIN
☐ 9. CAL RIPKEN
☐ 10. RANDY MILLIGAN
☐ 11. JUAN BELL
☐ 12. BILLY RIPKEN
☐ 13. JIM TRABER

11

☐ 14. PETE STANICEK
☐ 15. STEVE FINLEY
☐ 16. LARRY SHEETS
☐ 17. PHIL BRADLEY
☐ 18. BRADY ANDERSON
☐ 260. CAL RIPKEN, SR. (C)

BOSTON RED SOX

☐ 19. LEE SMITH
☐ 20. TOM FISCHER
☐ 21. MIKE BODDICKER
☐ 22. ROB MURPHY
☐ 23. WES GARDNER
☐ 24. JOHN DOPSON
☐ 25. BOB STANLEY
☐ 26. ROGER CLEMENS
☐ 27. RICH GEDMAN
☐ 28. MARTY BARRETT
☐ 29. LUIS RIVERS
☐ 30. JODY REED
☐ 31. NICK ESASKY
☐ 32. WADE BOGGS
☐ 33. JIM RICE
☐ 34. MIKE GREENWELL
☐ 35. DWIGHT EVANS
☐ 36. ELLIS BURKS

CALIFORNIA ANGELS

☐ 37. CHUCK FINLEY
☐ 38. KIRK MCCASKILL
☐ 39. JIM ABBOTT
☐ 40. BRYAN HARVEY
☐ 41. BERT BLYLEVEN
☐ 42. MIKE WITT
☐ 43. BOB MCCLURE
☐ 44. BILL SCHROEDER
☐ 45. LANCE PARRISH
☐ 46. DICK SCHOFIELD
☐ 47. WALLY JOYNER
☐ 48. JACK HOWELL
☐ 49. JOHNNY RAY
☐ 50. CHILI DAVIS
☐ 51. TONY ARMAS
☐ 52. CLAUDELL WASHINGTON
☐ 53. BRIAN DOWNING
☐ 54. DEVON WHITE

CHICAGO CUBS

☐ 280. STEVE WILSON
☐ 281. RICK SUTCLIFFE
☐ 282. KEVIN COFFMAN
☐ 283. MITCH WILLIAMS
☐ 284. GREG MADDUX
☐ 285. PAUL KILGUS
☐ 286. MIKE HARKEY
☐ 287. LLOYD MCCLENDON
☐ 288. DAMON BERRYHILL
☐ 289. TY GRIFFIN
☐ 290. RYNE SANDBERG
☐ 291. MARK GRACE
☐ 292. CURT WILKERSON
☐ 293. VANCE LAW
☐ 294. SHAWON DUNSTON
☐ 295. JEROME WALTON
☐ 296. MITCH WEBSTER
☐ 297. DWIGHT SMITH
☐ 298. ANDRE DAWSON

CHICAGO WHITE SOX

☐ 55. BOBBY THIGPEN
☐ 56. BILL LONG
☐ 57. JERRY REUSS
☐ 58. SHAWN HILLEGAS
☐ 59. MELIDO PEREZ
☐ 60. JEFF BITTIGER
☐ 61. JACK MCDOWELL
☐ 62. CARLTON FISK
☐ 63. STEVE LYONS
☐ 64. OZZIE GUILLEN
☐ 65. ROBIN VENTURA
☐ 66. FRED MANRIQUE
☐ 67. DAN PASQUA
☐ 68. IVAN CALDERON
☐ 69. RON KITTLE
☐ 70. DARYL BOSTON
☐ 71. DAVE GALLAGHER
☐ 72. HAROLD BAINES

CINCINNATI REDS

☐ 259. KEN GRIFFEY
☐ 299. JEFF SELLERS
☐ 300. JOSE RIJO
☐ 301. JOHN FRANCO
☐ 302. RICK MAHLER
☐ 303. RON ROBINSON
☐ 304. DANNY JACKSON
☐ 305. ROB DIBBLE
☐ 306. TOM BROWNING
☐ 307. BO DIAZ
☐ 308. MANNY TRILLO
☐ 309. CHRIS SABO
☐ 310. RON OESTER
☐ 311. BARRY LARKIN
☐ 312. TODD BENZINGER
☐ 313. PAUL O'NEILL
☐ 314. KAL DANIELS
☐ 315. JOEL YOUNGBLOOD
☐ 316. ERIC DAVIS

CLEVELAND INDIANS

☐ 73. CHARLES NAGY
☐ 74. JOHN FARRELL
☐ 75. KEVIN WICKANDER
☐ 76. GREG SWINDELL
☐ 77. MIKE WALKER
☐ 78. DOUG JONES
☐ 79. RICH YETT
☐ 80. TOM CANDIOTTI
☐ 81. JESSE OROSCO
☐ 82. BUD BLACK
☐ 83. ANDY ALLANSON
☐ 84. PETE O'BRIEN
☐ 85. JERRY BROWNE
☐ 86. BROOK JACOBY
☐ 87. MARK LEWIS
☐ 88. LUIS AGUAYO
☐ 89. CORY SNYDER
☐ 90. ODDIBE MCDOWELL
☐ 91. JOE CARTER

DETROIT TIGERS

☐ 92. FRANK TANANA
☐ 93. JACK MORRIS
☐ 94. DOYLE ALEXANDER
☐ 95. STEVE SEARCY
☐ 96. RANDY BOCKUS
☐ 97. JEFF ROBINSON
☐ 98. MIKE HENNEMAN
☐ 99. PAUL GIBSON
☐ 100. FRANK WILLIAMS
☐ 101. MATT NOKES
☐ 102. RICCO BROGNA
☐ 103. LOU WHITAKER
☐ 104. AL PEDRIQUE
☐ 105. ALAN TRAMMELL
☐ 106. CHRIS BROWN
☐ 107. PAT SHERIDAN
☐ 108. CHET LEMON
☐ 109. KEITH MORELAND

HOUSTON ASTROS

☐ 317. DAVE SMITH
☐ 318. MARK PORTUGAL
☐ 319. BRIAN MEYER

☐ 320. JIM DESHAIES
☐ 321. JUAN AGOSTO
☐ 322. MIKE SCOTT
☐ 323. RICK RHODEN
☐ 324. JIM CLANCY
☐ 325. LARRY ANDERSEN
☐ 326. ALEX TREVINO
☐ 327. ALAN ASHBY
☐ 328. CRAIG REYNOLDS
☐ 329. BILL DORAN
☐ 330. RAFAEL RAMIREZ
☐ 331. GLENN DAVIS
☐ 332. WILLIE ANSLEY
☐ 333. GERALD YOUNG
☐ 334. CAMERON DREW

KANSAS CITY ROYALS

☐ 110. MEL STOTTLEMYRE, JR.
☐ 111. BRET SABERHAGEN
☐ 112. FLOYD BANNISTER
☐ 113. JEFF MONTGOMERY
☐ 114. STEVE FARR
☐ 115. TOM GORDON
☐ 116. CHARLIE LEIBRANDT
☐ 117. MARK GUBICZA
☐ 118. MIKE MACFARLANE
☐ 119. BOB BOONE
☐ 120. KURT STILLWELL
☐ 121. GEORGE BRETT
☐ 122. FRANK WHITE
☐ 123. KEVIN SEITZER
☐ 124. WILLIE WILSON
☐ 125. PAT TABLER
☐ 126. BO JACKSON
☐ 127. HUGH WALKER
☐ 128. DANNY TARTABULL

LOS ANGELES DODGERS

☐ 335. JAY HOWELL
☐ 336. TIM BELCHER
☐ 337. FERNANDO VALENZUELA
☐ 338. RICKY HORTON
☐ 339. TIM LEARY
☐ 340. BILL BENE
☐ 341. OREL HERSHISER
☐ 342. MIKE SCIOSCIA
☐ 343. RICK DEMPSEY
☐ 344. WILLIE RANDOLPH
☐ 345. ALFREDO GRIFFIN
☐ 346. EDDIE MURRAY
☐ 347. MICKEY HATCHER
☐ 348. MIKE SHARPERSON
☐ 349. JOHN SHELBY
☐ 350. MIKE MARSHALL
☐ 351. KIRK GIBSON
☐ 352. MIKE DAVIS

MILWAUKEE BREWERS

☐ 129. TEDDY HIGUERA
☐ 130. DON AUGUST
☐ 131. JUAN NIEVES
☐ 132. MIKE BIRKBECK
☐ 133. DAN PLESAC
☐ 134. CHRIS BOSIO
☐ 135. BILL WEGMAN
☐ 136. CHUCK CRIM
☐ 137. B. J. SURHOFF
☐ 138. JOEY MEYER
☐ 139. DALE SVEUM
☐ 140. PAUL MOLITOR
☐ 141. JIM GANTNER
☐ 142. GARY SHEFFIELD
☐ 143. GREG BROCK
☐ 144. ROBIN YOUNT
☐ 145. GLENN BRAGGS
☐ 146. ROB DEER

MINNESOTA TWINS

☐ 147. FRED TOLIVER
☐ 148. JEFF REARDON
☐ 149. ALLAN ANDERSON
☐ 150. FRANK VIOLA
☐ 151. SHANE RAWLEY
☐ 152. JUAN BERENGUER
☐ 153. JOHNNY ARD
☐ 154. TIM LAUDNER
☐ 155. BRIAN HARPER
☐ 156. AL NEWMAN

☐ 157. KENT HRBEK
☐ 158. GARY GAETTI
☐ 159. WALLY BACKMAN
☐ 160. GENE LARKIN
☐ 161. GREG GAGNE
☐ 162. KIRBY PUCKETT
☐ 163. DANNY GLADDEN
☐ 164. RANDY BUSH

MONTREAL EXPOS

☐ 353. BRYN SMITH
☐ 354. PASCUAL PEREZ
☐ 355. KEVIN GROSS
☐ 356. ANDY MCGAFFIGAN
☐ 357. BRIAN HOLMAN
☐ 358. DAVE WAINHOUSE
☐ 359. DENNY MARTINEZ
☐ 360. TIM BURKE
☐ 361. NELSON SANTOVENIA
☐ 362. TIM WALLACH
☐ 363. SPIKE OWEN
☐ 364. REX HUDLER
☐ 365. ANDRES GALARRAGA
☐ 366. OTIS NIXON
☐ 367. HUBIE BROOKS
☐ 368. MIKE ALDRETE
☐ 369. TIM RAINES
☐ 370. DAVE MARTINEZ

NEW YORK METS

☐ 261. MEL STOTTLEMYRE (C)
☐ 371. BOB OJEDA
☐ 372. RON DARLING
☐ 373. WALLY WHITEHURST
☐ 374. RANDY MYERS
☐ 375. DAVID CONE
☐ 376. DWIGHT GOODEN
☐ 377. SID FERNANDEZ
☐ 378. DAVE PROCTOR
☐ 379. GARY CARTER
☐ 380. KEITH MILLER
☐ 381. GREGG JEFFERIES
☐ 382. TIM TEUFEL
☐ 383. KEVIN ELSTER
☐ 384. DAVE MAGADAN
☐ 385. KEITH HERNANDEZ
☐ 386. MOOKIE WILSON
☐ 387. DARRYL STRAWBERRY
☐ 388. KEVIN MCREYNOLDS
☐ 389. MARK CARREON

NEW YORK YANKEES

☐ 165. DAVE LAPOINT
☐ 166. ANDY HAWKINS
☐ 167. DAVE REGHETTI
☐ 168. LANCE MCCULLERS
☐ 169. JIMMY JONES
☐ 170. AL LEITER
☐ 171. JOHN CANDELARIA
☐ 172. DON SLAUGHT
☐ 173. JAMIE QUIRK
☐ 174. RAFAEL SANTANA
☐ 175. MIKE PAGLIARULO
☐ 176. DON MATTINGLY
☐ 177. KEN PHELPS
☐ 178. STEVE SAX
☐ 179. DAVE WINFIELD
☐ 180. STAN JEFFERSON
☐ 181. RICKEY HENDERSON
☐ 182. BOB BROWER
☐ 183. ROBERTO KELLY

OAKLAND A'S

☐ 184. CURT YOUNG
☐ 185. GENE NELSON
☐ 186. BOB WELCH
☐ 187. RICK HONEYCUTT
☐ 188. DAVE STEWART
☐ 189. MIKE MOORE
☐ 190. DENNIS ECKERSLEY
☐ 191. ERIC PLUNK
☐ 192. STORM DAVIS
☐ 193. TERRY STEINBACH
☐ 194. RON HASSEY
☐ 195. STAN ROYER
☐ 196. WALT WEISS
☐ 197. MARK MCGWIRE

☐ 198. CARNEY LANSFORD
☐ 199. GLENN HUBBARD
☐ 200. DAVE HENDERSON
☐ 201. JOSE CANSECO
☐ 202. DAVE PARKER

PHILADELPHIA PHILLIES

☐ 390. JEFF PARRETT
☐ 391. MIKE MADDUX
☐ 392. DON CARMAN
☐ 393. BRUCE RUFFIN
☐ 394. KEN HOWELL
☐ 395. STEVE BEDROSIAN
☐ 396. FLOYD YOUMANS
☐ 397. LARRY MCWILLIAMS
☐ 398. PAT COMBS
☐ 399. STEVE LAKE
☐ 400. DICKIE THON
☐ 401. RICKY JORDAN
☐ 402. MIKE SCHMIDT
☐ 403. TOM HERR
☐ 404. CHRIS JAMES
☐ 405. JUAN SAMUEL
☐ 406. VON HAYES
☐ 407. RON JONES
☐ 408. CURT FORD

PITTSBURGH PIRATES

☐ 409. BOB WALK
☐ 410. JEFF ROBINSON
☐ 411. JIM GOTT
☐ 412. SCOTT MEDVIN
☐ 413. JOHN SMILEY
☐ 414. BOB KIPPER
☐ 415. BRIAN FISHER
☐ 416. DOUG DRABEK
☐ 417. MIKE LAVALLIERE
☐ 418. KEN OBERKFELL
☐ 419. SID BREAM
☐ 420. AUSTIN MANAHAN
☐ 421. JOSE LIND
☐ 422. BOBBY BONILLA
☐ 423. GLENN WILSON
☐ 424. ANDY VAN SLYKE
☐ 425. GARY REDUS
☐ 426. BARRY BONDS

ST. LOUIS CARDINALS

☐ 427. DON HEINKEL
☐ 428. KEN DAYLEY
☐ 429. TODD WORRELL
☐ 430. BRAD DUVALL
☐ 431. JOSE DELEON
☐ 432. JOE MAGRANE
☐ 433. JOHN ERICKS
☐ 434. FRANK DIPINO
☐ 435. TONY PENA
☐ 436. OZZIE SMITH
☐ 437. TERRY PENDLETON
☐ 438. JOSE OQUENDO
☐ 439. TIM JONES
☐ 440. PEDRO GUERRERO
☐ 441. MILT THOMPSON
☐ 442. WILLIE MCGEE
☐ 443. VINCE COLEMAN
☐ 444. TOM BRUNANSKY

SAN DIEGO PADRES

☐ 258. SANDY ALOMAR (C)
☐ 445. WALT TERRELL
☐ 446. ERIC SHOW
☐ 447. MARK DAVIS
☐ 448. ANDY BENES
☐ 449. EDDIE WHITSON
☐ 450. DENNIS RASMUSSEN
☐ 451. BRUCE HURST
☐ 452. PAT CLEMENTS
☐ 453. BENNY SANTIAGO
☐ 454. SANDY ALOMAR, JR.
☐ 455. GARRY TEMPLETON
☐ 456. JACK CLARK
☐ 457. TIM FLANNERY
☐ 458. ROBERTO ALOMAR
☐ 459. CARMELO MARTINEZ
☐ 460. JOHN KRUK
☐ 461. TONY GWYNN
☐ 462. JERALD CLARK

SAN FRANCISCO GIANTS

☐ 463. DON ROBINSON
☐ 464. CRAIG LEFFERTS
☐ 465. KELLY DOWNS
☐ 466. RICK REUSCHEL
☐ 467. SCOTT GARRELTS
☐ 468. WIL TEJADA
☐ 469. KIRT MANWARING
☐ 470. TERRY KENNEDY
☐ 471. JOSE URIBE
☐ 472. ROYCE CLAYTON
☐ 473. ROBBY THOMPSON
☐ 474. KEVIN MITCHELL
☐ 475. ERNIE RILES
☐ 476. WILL CLARK
☐ 477. DONELL NIXON
☐ 478. CANDY MALDONADO
☐ 479. TRACY JONES
☐ 480. BRETT BULTER

SEATTLE MARINERS

☐ 203. SCOTT BANKHEAD
☐ 204. TOM NIEDENFUER
☐ 205. MARK LANGSTON
☐ 206. ERIK HANSON
☐ 207. MIKE JACKSON
☐ 208. DAVE VALLE
☐ 209. SCOTT BRADLEY
☐ 210. HAROLD REYNOLDS
☐ 211. TINO MARTINEZ
☐ 212. RICH RENTERIA
☐ 213. REY QUINONES
☐ 214. JIM PRESLEY
☐ 215. ALVIN DAVIS
☐ 216. EDGAR MARTINEZ
☐ 217. DARNELL COLES
☐ 218. JEFFREY LEONARD
☐ 219. JAY BUHNER
☐ 220. KEN GRIFFEY, JR.

TEXAS RANGERS

☐ 221. DREW HALL
☐ 222. BOBBY WITT
☐ 223. JAMIE MOYER
☐ 224. CHARLIE HOUGH
☐ 225. NOLAN RYAN
☐ 226. JEFF RUSSELL
☐ 227. JIM SUNDBERG
☐ 228. JULIO FRANCO
☐ 229. BUDDY BELL
☐ 230. SCOTT FLETCHER
☐ 231. JEFF KUNKEL
☐ 232. STEVE BUECHELE
☐ 233. MONTY FARISS
☐ 234. RICK LEACH
☐ 235. RUBEN SIERRA
☐ 236. CECIL ESPY
☐ 237. RAFAEL PALMEIRO
☐ 238. PETE INCAVIGLIA

TORONTO BLUE JAYS

☐ 239. DAVE STIEB
☐ 240. JEFF MUSSELMAN
☐ 241. MIKE FLANAGAN

☐ 242. TODD STOTTLEMYRE
☐ 243. JIMMY KEY
☐ 244. TONY CASTILLO
☐ 245. ALEX SANCHEZ
☐ 246. TOM HENKE
☐ 247. JOHN CERUTTI
☐ 248. ERNIE WHITT
☐ 249. BOB BRENLY
☐ 250. RANCE MULLINIKS
☐ 251. KELLY GRUBER
☐ 252. ED SPRAGUE
☐ 253. FRED MCGRIFF
☐ 254. TONY FERNANDEZ
☐ 255. TOM LAWLESS
☐ 256. GEORGE BELL
☐ 257. JESSE BARFIELD

Jeremy Fritsch

Jeremy & Jaycie Fritsch

Jaycie Fritsch

Jeff & Larry Fritsch

1934–36 DIAMOND STARS (108)
2 3/8" X 2 7/8"

The National Chicle Diamond Stars baseball cards were released over a period of three years. Some of the players changed teams during that period of time; consequently, some of the cards in the lists below appear with more than one team.

BOSTON BRAVES

- ☐ 3. WALTER (RABBIT) MARANVILLE
- ☐ 20. FRANCIS (FRANK) HOGAN
- ☐ 25. WALTER (WALLY) BERGER
- ☐ 37. BILL URBANSKI
- ☐ 49. BAXTER (BUCK) JORDAN
- ☐ 62. FRED FRANKHOUSE
- ☐ 82. JOHNNY BABICH
- ☐ 108. WALTER BERGER

BOSTON RED SOX

- ☐ 1. LEFTY GROVE
- ☐ 6. MAX BISHOP
- ☐ 30. HENRY (HEINIE) MANUSH
- ☐ 48. RICK FERRELL
- ☐ 61. BILLY WERBER
- ☐ 73. FRED (FRITZ) OSTERMUELLER
- ☐ 94. WES FERRELL

BROOKLYN DODGERS

- ☐ 19. VAN MUNGO
- ☐ 28. AL LOPEZ
- ☐ 55. TONY CUCCINELLO
- ☐ 68. SAM LESLIE
- ☐ 82. JOHNNY BABICH
- ☐ 89. JOE STRIPP
- ☐ 97. AL LOPEZ
- ☐ 102. VAN MUNGO

CHICAGO CUBS

- ☐ 31. HAZEN (KIKI) CUYLER
- ☐ 34. STANLEY HACK
- ☐ 52. GEORGE STAINBACK
- ☐ 107. STANLEY HACK

CHICAGO WHITE SOX

- ☐ 2. AL SIMMONS
- ☐ 7. LEW FONSECA
- ☐ 42. JIMMY DYKES
- ☐ 43. TED LYONS
- ☐ 51. JOHN WHITEHEAD
- ☐ 65. HENRY (ZEKE) BONURA
- ☐ 72. ANTHONY (TONY) PIET
- ☐ 95. LUKE APPLING

CINCINNATI REDS

- ☐ 18. CHARLES (CHICK) HAFEY
- ☐ 24. EARL (SPARKY) ADAMS
- ☐ 31. KIKI CUYLER
- ☐ 36. ERNEST (ERNIE) LOMBARDI
- ☐ 46. CHARLES (RED) LUCAS
- ☐ 59. JIMMY BOTTOMLEY
- ☐ 84. SAM BYRD
- ☐ 96. LEW RIGGS
- ☐ 105. ERNEST (ERNIE) LOMBARDI
- ☐ 106. CHARLES (RED) LUCAS

CLEVELAND INDIANS

- ☐ 2. JOE VOSMIK
- ☐ 13. GEORGE BLAEHOLDER
- ☐ 32. EDGAR (SAM) RICE
- ☐ 35. EARL AVERILL
- ☐ 58. GLENN MYATT
- ☐ 70. HAROLD (HAL) TROSKY
- ☐ 79. WILLIS HUDLIN
- ☐ 87. STEVE O'NEIL
- ☐ 100. EARL AVERILL

DETROIT TIGERS

- ☐ 2. AL SIMMONS
- ☐ 5. TOM BRIDGES
- ☐ 9. GORDON (MICKEY) COCHRANE
- ☐ 33. LYNWOOD (SCHOOLBOY) ROWE
- ☐ 45. JOYNER (JO-JO) WHITE
- ☐ 54. HANK GREENBERG
- ☐ 67. MARVIN OWEN
- ☐ 76. BILL ROGELL
- ☐ 77. CHARLEY GEHRINGER
- ☐ 90. RAY HAYWORTH
- ☐ 93. ALVIN CROWDER
- ☐ 98. LYNWOOD (SCHOOLBOY) ROWE

NEW YORK GIANTS

- ☐ 14. BILL TERRY
- ☐ 15. DICK BARTELL
- ☐ 21. JOHNNY VERGES
- ☐ 39. CARL HUBBELL
- ☐ 50. MEL OTT
- ☐ 63. TRAVIS JACKSON
- ☐ 101. DICK BARTELL

NEW YORK YANKEES

- ☐ 11. BILL DICKEY
- ☐ 12. FRED (DIXIE) WALKER
- ☐ 29. ROBERT (RED) ROLFE
- ☐ 38. WILLIAM (BEN) CHAPMAN
- ☐ 60. CHARLES (RED) RUFFING
- ☐ 74. ANTHONY (TONY) LAZZERI
- ☐ 86. FRANK CROSETTI
- ☐ 88. GEORGE SELKIRK
- ☐ 103. BILL DICKEY
- ☐ 104. ROBERT (RED) ROLFE

PHILADELPHIA ATHLETICS

- ☐ 10. ROY MAHAFFEY
- ☐ 64. JIMMIE("Y") FOXX

PHILADELPHIA PHILLIES

- ☐ 15. DICK BARTELL
- ☐ 21. JOHNNY VERGES
- ☐ 22. JIMMIE WILSON
- ☐ 40. JOHN (BLONDY) RYAN
- ☐ 41. HARVEY HENDRICK
- ☐ 80. LOU CHIOZZA
- ☐ 92. ETHAN ALLEN

PITTSBURGH PIRATES

- ☐ 16. LLOYD WANER
- ☐ 27. HAROLD (PIE) TRAYNOR
- ☐ 56. AUGUST (GUS) SUHR
- ☐ 57. DARRELL (CY) BLANTON
- ☐ 69. EARL GRACE
- ☐ 83. PAUL WANER
- ☐ 99. HAROLD (PIE) TRAYNOR

ST. LOUIS BROWNS

- ☐ 10. ROY MAHAFFEY
- ☐ 13. GEORGE BLAEHOLDER
- ☐ 44. ROGERS HORNSBY
- ☐ 53. OSCAR MELILLO
- ☐ 75. IRVING (JACK) BURNS
- ☐ 85. JULIUS SOLTERS

ST. LOUIS CARDINALS

- ☐ 17. FRANK FRISCH
- ☐ 23. BILL HALLAHAN
- ☐ 26. JOHN (PEPPER) MARTIN
- ☐ 66. JOSEPH (DUCKY) MEDWICK
- ☐ 81. BILL DELANCEY

WASHINGTON SENATORS

- ☐ 4. CHARLES (BUDDY) MEYER
- ☐ 30. HENRY (HEINIE) MANUSH
- ☐ 47. CLIFF BOLTON
- ☐ 71. OSWALD (OSSIE) BLUEGE
- ☐ 78. JOE KUHEL
- ☐ 91. BUCKY HARRIS

1981 DONRUSS (605)
2 1/2" X 3 1/2"

PETE ROSE FIRST BASE

ATLANTA BRAVES

- [ ] 66. JEFF BURROUGHS
- [ ] 77. GENE GARBER
- [ ] 88. LUIS GOMEZ
- [ ] 99. BOB HORNER
- [ ] 186. BRIAN ASSELSTINE
- [ ] 197. RICK CAMP
- [ ] 208. BRUCE BENEDICT
- [ ] 219. CHRIS CHAMBLISS
- [ ] 306. GARY MATTHEWS
- [ ] 317. RICK MATULA
- [ ] 328. PHIL NIEKRO
- [ ] 339. JERRY ROYSTER
- [ ] 426. BOBBY COX(M)
- [ ] 437. DALE MURPHY
- [ ] 448. DOYLE ALEXANDER
- [ ] 459. GLENN HUBBARD
- [ ] 523. PRESTON HANNA
- [ ] 550. AL HRABOSKY
- [ ] 584. LARRY BRADFORD
- [ ] 597. TOMMY BOGGS

BALTIMORE ORIOLES

- [ ] 112. EDDIE MURRAY
- [ ] 113. RICK DEMPSEY
- [ ] 114. SCOTT MCGREGOR
- [ ] 115. KEN SINGLETON
- [ ] 116. GARY ROENICKE
- [ ] 232. RICH DAUER
- [ ] 233. DAN GRAHAM
- [ ] 234. MIKE FLANAGAN
- [ ] 235. JOHN LOWENSTEIN
- [ ] 236. BENNY AYALA
- [ ] 352. DOUG DECINCES
- [ ] 353. JIM PALMER
- [ ] 354. TIPPY MARTINEZ
- [ ] 355. AL BUMBRY
- [ ] 356. EARL WEAVER(M)
- [ ] 472. MARK BELANGER
- [ ] 473. JIM PALMER
- [ ] 474. SAMMY STEWART
- [ ] 475. TIM STODDARD
- [ ] 476. STEVE STONE
- [ ] 499. LENN SAKATA
- [ ] 507. TERRY CROWLEY
- [ ] 514. KIKO GARCIA
- [ ] 533. DENNIS MARTINEZ
- [ ] 552. DAVE FORD
- [ ] 600. H. PAT KELLY

BOSTON RED SOX

- [ ] 94. CARL YASTRZEMSKI
- [ ] 95. GLENN HOFFMAN
- [ ] 96. DENNIS ECKERSLEY
- [ ] 97. TOM BURGMEIER
- [ ] 98. WIN REMMERSWAAL
- [ ] 214. CARL YASTRZEMSKI
- [ ] 215. JERRY REMY
- [ ] 216. MIKE TORREZ
- [ ] 217. SKIP LOCKWOOD
- [ ] 218. FRED LYNN

- [ ] 334. TONY PEREZ
- [ ] 335. CARLTON FISK
- [ ] 336. DICK DRAGO
- [ ] 337. STEVE RENKO
- [ ] 338. JIM RICE
- [ ] 454. RICK BURLESON
- [ ] 455. GARY ALLENSON
- [ ] 456. BOB STANLEY
- [ ] 457. JOHN TUDOR
- [ ] 458. DWIGHT EVANS
- [ ] 512. DAVE RADER
- [ ] 544. DAVE STAPLETON
- [ ] 577. JIM DWYER

CALIFORNIA ANGELS

- [ ] 49. ROD CAREW
- [ ] 50. BERT CAMPANERIS
- [ ] 51. TOM DONOHUE
- [ ] 52. DAVE FROST
- [ ] 53. ED HALICKI
- [ ] 54. DAN FORD
- [ ] 169. ROD CAREW
- [ ] 170. FRED PATEK
- [ ] 171. FRANK TANANA
- [ ] 172. ALFREDO MARTINEZ
- [ ] 173. CHRIS KNAPP
- [ ] 174. JOE RUDI
- [ ] 289. BOBBY GRICH
- [ ] 290. DICKIE THON
- [ ] 291. MARK CLEAR
- [ ] 292. DAVE LEMANCZYK
- [ ] 293. JASON THOMPSON
- [ ] 294. RICK MILLER
- [ ] 409. CARNEY LANSFORD
- [ ] 410. BRIAN DOWNING
- [ ] 411. DON AASE
- [ ] 412. JIM BARR
- [ ] 413. DON BAYLOR
- [ ] 414. JIM FREGOSI(M)
- [ ] 532. GEOFF ZAHN
- [ ] 542. BUTCH HOBSON
- [ ] 572. BOBBY CLARK
- [ ] 581. ANDY HASSLER

CHICAGO CUBS

- [ ] 482. BILL BUCKNER
- [ ] 483. IVAN DEJESUS
- [ ] 485. LENNY RANDLE
- [ ] 501. STEVE DILLAR
- [ ] 513. MICK KELLEHER
- [ ] 515. LARRY BIITTNER
- [ ] 519. SCOT THOMPSON
- [ ] 520. JIM TRACY
- [ ] 521. CARLOS LEZCANO
- [ ] 522. JOE AMALFITANO(M)
- [ ] 535. STEVE MACKO
- [ ] 551. DICK TIDROW
- [ ] 553. DAVE KINGMAN
- [ ] 558. BARRY FOOTE
- [ ] 559. TIM BLACKWELL
- [ ] 561. RICK REUSCHEL
- [ ] 562. LYNN MCGLOTHEN
- [ ] 573. DENNIS LAMP
- [ ] 586. BILL CAUDILL
- [ ] 587. DOUG CAPILLA
- [ ] 588. GEORGE RILEY
- [ ] 589. WILLIE HERNANDEZ

CHICAGO WHITE SOX

- [ ] 38. LAMAR JOHNSON
- [ ] 39. KEVIN BELL
- [ ] 40. ED FARMER
- [ ] 41. ROSS BAUMGARTEN
- [ ] 42. LEO SUTHERLAND
- [ ] 158. JIM MORRISON
- [ ] 159. GLENN BORGMANN
- [ ] 160. LAMARR HOYT
- [ ] 161. RICH WORTHAM
- [ ] 162. THAD BOSLEY
- [ ] 278. GREG PRYOR
- [ ] 279. BRITT BURNS
- [ ] 280. RICH DOTSON
- [ ] 281. CHET LEMON
- [ ] 282. RUSTY KUNTZ
- [ ] 398. MIKE SQUIRES
- [ ] 399. MARVIS FOLEY
- [ ] 400. STEVE TROUT

- [ ] 401. WAYNE NORDHAGEN
- [ ] 402. TONY LARUSSA(M)
- [ ] 503. JIM ESSIAN
- [ ] 576. RON LEFLORE
- [ ] 596. MIKE PROLY

CINCINNATI REDS

- [ ] 61. RAY KNIGHT
- [ ] 62. JOHNNY BENCH
- [ ] 63. MARIO SOTO
- [ ] 64. DOUG BAIR
- [ ] 65. GEORGE FOSTER
- [ ] 181. DAVE CONCEPCION
- [ ] 182. JOHNNY BENCH
- [ ] 183. MIKE LACOSS
- [ ] 184. KEN GRIFFEY
- [ ] 185. DAVE COLLINS
- [ ] 301. DAN DRIESSEN
- [ ] 302. JOE NOLAN
- [ ] 303. PAUL HOUSEHOLDER
- [ ] 304. HARRY SPILMAN
- [ ] 305. CESAR GERONIMO
- [ ] 421. CHARLIE LEIBRANDT
- [ ] 422. TOM SEAVER
- [ ] 423. RON OESTER
- [ ] 424. JUNIOR KENNEDY
- [ ] 425. TOM SEAVER
- [ ] 554. MIKE VAIL

CLEVELAND INDIANS

- [ ] 78. MIKE HARGROVE
- [ ] 79. DAVE ROSELLO
- [ ] 80. RON HASSEY
- [ ] 81. SID MONGE
- [ ] 82. JOE CHARBONEAU
- [ ] 198. ANDRE THORNTON
- [ ] 199. TOM VERYZER
- [ ] 200. GARY ALEXANDER
- [ ] 201. RICK WAITS
- [ ] 202. RICK MANNING
- [ ] 318. TOBY HARRAH
- [ ] 319. DUANE KUIPER
- [ ] 320. LEN BARKER
- [ ] 321. VICTOR CRUZ
- [ ] 322. DELL ALSTON
- [ ] 438. JERRY DYBZINSKI
- [ ] 439. JORGE ORTA
- [ ] 440. WAYNE GARLAND
- [ ] 441. MIGUEL DILONE
- [ ] 442. DAVE GARCIA(M)
- [ ] 517. BO DIAZ

DETROIT TIGERS

- [ ] 5. ALAN TRAMMELL
- [ ] 6. TOM BROOKENS
- [ ] 7. DUFFY DYER
- [ ] 8. MARK FIDRYCH
- [ ] 9. DAVE ROZEMA
- [ ] 10. RICKY PETERS
- [ ] 125. RICHIE HEBNER
- [ ] 126. MARK WAGNER
- [ ] 127. JACK MORRIS
- [ ] 128. DAN PETRY
- [ ] 129. BRUCE ROBBINS
- [ ] 130. CHAMP SUMMERS
- [ ] 245. JOHN WOCKENFUSS
- [ ] 246. STAN PAPI
- [ ] 247. MILT WILCOX
- [ ] 248. DAN SCHATZEDER
- [ ] 249. STEVE KEMP
- [ ] 250. JIM LENTINE
- [ ] 365. LOU WHITAKER
- [ ] 366. LANCE PARRISH
- [ ] 367. TIM CORCORAN
- [ ] 368. PAT UNDERWOOD
- [ ] 369. AL COWENS
- [ ] 370. SPARKY ANDERSON(M)

HOUSTON ASTROS

- [ ] 18. JOE MORGAN
- [ ] 19. RAFAEL LANDESTOY
- [ ] 20. BRUCE BOCHY
- [ ] 21. JOE SAMBITO
- [ ] 23. DAVE SMITH
- [ ] 24. TERRY PUHL
- [ ] 138. ENOS CABELL

☐ 139. DAVE BERGMAN
☐ 140. J.R. RICHARD
☐ 141. KEN FORSCH
☐ 143. FRANK LACORTE
☐ 144. DENNIS WALLING
☐ 258. ART HOWE
☐ 259. ALAN ASHBY
☐ 260. NOLAN RYAN
☐ 261. VERN RUHLE
☐ 263. CESAR CEDENO
☐ 264. JEFF LEONARD
☐ 378. CRAIG REYNOLDS
☐ 379. LUIS PUJOLS
☐ 380. JOE NIEKRO
☐ 381. JOAQUIN ANDUJAR
☐ 383. JOSE CRUZ
☐ 384. BILL VIRDON(M)
☐ 490. DAVE W. ROBERTS

KANSAS CITY ROYALS

☐ 100. GEORGE BRETT
☐ 101. DAVE CHALK
☐ 102. DENNIS LEONARD
☐ 103. RENIE MARTIN
☐ 104. AMOS OTIS
☐ 220. WILLIE AIKENS
☐ 221. JOHN WATHAN
☐ 222. DAN QUISENBERRY
☐ 223. WILLIE WILSON
☐ 224. CLINT HURDLE
☐ 340. FRANK WHITE
☐ 341. JAMIE QUIRK
☐ 342. PAUL SPLITTORFF
☐ 343. MARTY PATTIN
☐ 344. PETE LACOCK
☐ 460. U.L. WASHINGTON
☐ 461. LARRY GURA
☐ 462. RICH GALE
☐ 463. HAL MCRAE
☐ 464. JIM FREY(M)
☐ 504. RANCE MULLINIKS

TOMMY LaSORDA MANAGER

LOS ANGELES DODGERS

☐ 56. STEVE GARVEY
☐ 57. BILL RUSSELL
☐ 58. DON SUTTON
☐ 59. REGGIE SMITH
☐ 60. RICK MONDAY
☐ 176. STEVE GARVEY
☐ 177. JOE FERGUSON
☐ 178. BOB WELCH
☐ 179. DUSTY BAKER
☐ 180. RUDY LAW
☐ 296. RON CEY
☐ 297. STEVE YEAGER
☐ 298. BOBBY CASTILLO
☐ 299. MANNY MOTA
☐ 300. JAY JOHNSTONE
☐ 416. DAVE LOPES
☐ 417. JERRY REUSS
☐ 418. RICK SUTCLIFFE
☐ 419. DERREL THOMAS
☐ 420. TOM LASORDA(M)
☐ 511. STEVE HOWE
☐ 526. MICKEY HATCHER
☐ 534. GARY THOMASSON
☐ 541. BURT HOOTON
☐ 557. DON STANHOUSE

MILWAUKEE BREWERS

☐ 83. CECIL COOPER
☐ 84. SAL BANDO
☐ 85. MOOSE HAAS
☐ 86. MIKE CALDWELL
☐ 87. LARRY HISLE
☐ 203. PAUL MOLITOR
☐ 204. JIM GANTNER
☐ 205. PAUL MITCHELL
☐ 206. REGGIE CLEVELAND
☐ 207. SIXTO LEZCANO
☐ 323. ROBIN YOUNT
☐ 324. CHARLIE MOORE
☐ 325. LARY SORENSEN
☐ 326. GORMAN THOMAS
☐ 327. BOB RODGERS(M)
☐ 443. DON MONEY
☐ 444. BUCK MARTINEZ
☐ 445. JERRY AUGUSTINE
☐ 446. BEN OGLIVIE
☐ 447. JIM SLATON
☐ 508. BILL TRAVERS
☐ 510. BOB MCCLURE
☐ 528. DICK DAVIS
☐ 578. BILL CASTRO

MINNESOTA TWINS

☐ 487. ROY SMALLEY
☐ 488. JOHN CASTINO
☐ 489. RON JACKSON
☐ 492. MIKE CUBBAGE
☐ 493. ROB WILFONG
☐ 494. DANNY GOODWIN
☐ 495. JOSE MORALES
☐ 527. JOHN GORYL(M)
☐ 529. BUTCH WYNEGAR
☐ 530. SAL BUTERA
☐ 531. JERRY KOOSMAN
☐ 546. DOUG CORBETT
☐ 547. DARRELL JACKSON
☐ 548. PETE REDFERN
☐ 549. ROGER ERICKSON
☐ 564. JOHN VERHOEVEN
☐ 565. KEN LANDREAUX
☐ 566. GLENN ADAMS
☐ 567. HOSKEN POWELL
☐ 592. RICK SOFIELD
☐ 593. BOMBO RIVERA
☐ 594. GARY WARD

MONTREAL EXPOS

☐ 89. LARRY PARRISH
☐ 90. GARY CARTER
☐ 91. BILL GULLICKSON
☐ 92. FRED NORMAN
☐ 93. TOMMY HUTTON
☐ 209. RODNEY SCOTT
☐ 210. JOHN TAMARGO
☐ 211. BILL LEE
☐ 212. ANDRE DAWSON
☐ 213. ROWLAND OFFICE
☐ 329. CHRIS SPEIER
☐ 330. STEVE ROGERS
☐ 331. WOODIE FRYMAN
☐ 332. WARREN CROMARTIE
☐ 333. JERRY WHITE
☐ 449. TONY BERNAZARD
☐ 450. SCOTT SANDERSON
☐ 451. DAVE PALMER
☐ 452. STAN BAHNSEN
☐ 453. DICK WILLIAMS(M)
☐ 538. TIM RAINES
☐ 540. KEN MACHA
☐ 545. BOB PATE
☐ 599. ELIAS SOSA

NEW YORK METS

☐ 34. LEE MAZZILLI
☐ 35. JOHN STEARNS
☐ 36. ROY JACKSON
☐ 37. MIKE SCOTT
☐ 154. FRANK TAVERAS
☐ 155. CRAIG SWAN
☐ 156. JEFF REARDON
☐ 157. STEVE HENDERSON
☐ 274. MIKE JORGENSEN
☐ 275. PAT ZACHRY

☐ 276. NEIL ALLEN
☐ 277. JOEL YOUNGBLOOD
☐ 394. DOUG FLYNN
☐ 395. PETE FALCONE
☐ 396. TOM HAUSMAN
☐ 397. ELLIOTT MADDOX
☐ 506. JOE TORRE(M)
☐ 524. RAY BURRIS
☐ 575. MOOKIE WILSON

NEW YORK YANKEES

☐ 105. GRAIG NETTLES
☐ 106. ERIC SODERHOLM
☐ 107. TOMMY JOHN
☐ 108. TOM UNDERWOOD
☐ 109. LOU PINIELLA
☐ 111. BOBBY MURCER
☐ 225. BOB WATSON
☐ 226. JIM SPENCER
☐ 227. RON GUIDRY
☐ 228. REGGIE JACKSON
☐ 229. OSCAR GAMBLE
☐ 231. LUIS TIANT
☐ 345. WILLIE RANDOLPH
☐ 346. RICK CERONE
☐ 347. RICH GOSSAGE
☐ 348. REGGIE JACKSON
☐ 349. RUPPERT JONES
☐ 351. YOGI BERRA(C)
☐ 465. BUCKY DENT
☐ 466. DENNIS WERTH
☐ 467. RON DAVIS
☐ 468. REGGIE JACKSON
☐ 469. BOBBY BROWN
☐ 471. GAYLORD PERRY
☐ 486. LARRY MILBOURNE
☐ 500. GENE MICHAEL(M)
☐ 571. JOE LEFEBVRE

OAKLAND A'S

☐ 110. MICKEY KLUTTS
☐ 117. DAVE REVERING
☐ 118. MIKE NORRIS
☐ 119. RICKEY HENDERSON
☐ 120. MIKE HEATH
☐ 230. JEFF COX
☐ 237. WAYNE GROSS
☐ 238. RICK LANGFORD
☐ 239. TONY ARMAS
☐ 240. BOB LACEY
☐ 350. DAVE MCKAY
☐ 357. ROB PICCIOLO
☐ 358. MATT KEOUGH
☐ 359. DWAYNE MURPHY
☐ 360. BRIAN KINGMAN
☐ 470. MIKE DAVIS
☐ 477. JEFF NEWMAN
☐ 478. STEVE MCCATTY
☐ 479. BILLY MARTIN(M)
☐ 480. MITCHELL PAGE
☐ 484. CLIFF JOHNSON
☐ 497. MIKE EDWARDS
☐ 585. FRED STANLEY

PHILADELPHIA PHILLIES

☐ 11. MIKE SCHMIDT
☐ 22. MANNY TRILLO
☐ 33. STEVE CARLTON
☐ 44. RON REED
☐ 55. GARRY MADDOX
☐ 131. PETE ROSE
☐ 142. LARRY BOWA
☐ 153. DICK RUTHVEN
☐ 164. DEL UNSER
☐ 175. GREG LUZINSKI
☐ 251. PETE ROSE
☐ 262. BOB BOONE
☐ 273. TUG MCGRAW
☐ 284. SPARKY LYLE
☐ 295. LONNIE SMITH
☐ 371. PETE ROSE
☐ 382. KEITH MORELAND
☐ 393. BOB WALK
☐ 404. BAKE MCBRIDE
☐ 415. DALLAS GREEN(M)
☐ 568. DICK NOLES
☐ 574. RANDY LERCH
☐ 598. GREG GROSS

1981 Donruss

PITTSBURGH PIRATES

- [ ] 12. WILLIE STARGELL
- [ ] 13. TIM FOLI
- [ ] 14. MANNY SANGUILLEN
- [ ] 15. GRANT JACKSON
- [ ] 16. EDDIE SOLOMON
- [ ] 17. OMAR MORENO
- [ ] 132. WILLIE STARGELL
- [ ] 133. ED OTT
- [ ] 134. JIM BIBBY
- [ ] 135. BERT BLYLEVEN
- [ ] 136. DAVE PARKER
- [ ] 137. BILL ROBINSON
- [ ] 252. BILL MADLOCK
- [ ] 253. DALE BERRA
- [ ] 254. KENT TEKULVE
- [ ] 255. ENRIQUE ROMO
- [ ] 256. MIKE EASLER
- [ ] 257. CHUCK TANNER(M)
- [ ] 372. PHIL GARNER
- [ ] 373. STEVE NICOSIA
- [ ] 374. JOHN CANDELARIA
- [ ] 375. DON ROBINSON
- [ ] 376. LEE LACY
- [ ] 377. JOHN MILNER
- [ ] 563. BOB OWCHINKO

ST. LOUIS CARDINALS

- [ ] 67. KEITH HERNANDEZ
- [ ] 68. TOM HERR
- [ ] 69. BOB FORSCH
- [ ] 70. JOHN FULGHAM
- [ ] 71. BOBBY BONDS
- [ ] 187. GARRY TEMPLETON
- [ ] 188. MIKE PHILLIPS
- [ ] 189. PETE VUCKOVICH
- [ ] 190. JOHN URREA
- [ ] 191. TONY SCOTT
- [ ] 307. KEN REITZ
- [ ] 308. TED SIMMONS
- [ ] 309. JOHN LITTLEFIELD
- [ ] 310. GEORGE FRAZIER
- [ ] 311. DANE IORG
- [ ] 427. LEON DURHAM
- [ ] 428. TERRY KENNEDY
- [ ] 429. SILVIO MARTINEZ
- [ ] 430. GEORGE HENDRICK
- [ ] 431. RED SCHOENDIENST(C)
- [ ] 505. DARRELL PORTER
- [ ] 536. JIM KAAT
- [ ] 539. KEITH SMITH
- [ ] 560. BRUCE SUTTER
- [ ] 580. MARK LITTELL
- [ ] 583. KEN OBERKFELL

SAN DIEGO PADRES

- [ ] 1. OZZIE SMITH
- [ ] 2. ROLLIE FINGERS
- [ ] 3. RICK WISE
- [ ] 4. GENE RICHARDS
- [ ] 121. DAVE CASH
- [ ] 122. RANDY JONES
- [ ] 123. ERIC RASMUSSEN
- [ ] 124. JERRY MUMPHREY
- [ ] 241. GENE TENACE
- [ ] 242. BOB SHIRLEY
- [ ] 243. GARY LUCAS
- [ ] 244. JERRY TURNER
- [ ] 361. BILL FAHEY
- [ ] 362. STEVE MURA
- [ ] 363. DENNIS KINNEY
- [ ] 364. DAVE WINFIELD
- [ ] 525. BRODERICK PERKINS
- [ ] 595. DAVE EDWARDS

SAN FRANCISCO GIANTS

- [ ] 72. RENNIE STENNETT
- [ ] 73. JOE STRAIN
- [ ] 74. ED WHITSON
- [ ] 75. TOM GRIFFIN
- [ ] 76. BILL NORTH
- [ ] 192. DARRELL EVANS
- [ ] 193. MILT MAY
- [ ] 194. BOB KNEPPER
- [ ] 195. RANDY MOFFITT
- [ ] 196. LARRY HERNDON

- [ ] 312. MIKE IVIE
- [ ] 313. DENNIS LITTLEJOHN
- [ ] 314. GARY LAVELLE
- [ ] 315. JACK CLARK
- [ ] 316. JIM WOHLFORD
- [ ] 432. JOHN LEMASTER
- [ ] 433. VIDA BLUE
- [ ] 434. JOHN MONTEFUSCO
- [ ] 435. TERRY WHITFIELD
- [ ] 436. DAVE BRISTOL(M)
- [ ] 498. MIKE SADEK
- [ ] 555. JERRY MARTIN
- [ ] 556. JESUS FIGUEROA
- [ ] 579. GREG MINTON

SEATTLE MARINERS

- [ ] 43. DAN MEYER
- [ ] 45. MARIO MENDOZA
- [ ] 46. RICK HONEYCUTT
- [ ] 47. GLENN ABBOTT
- [ ] 48. LEON ROBERTS
- [ ] 163. JULIO CRUZ
- [ ] 165. JIM ANDERSON
- [ ] 166. JIM BEATTIE
- [ ] 167. SHANE RAWLEY
- [ ] 168. JOE SIMPSON
- [ ] 283. TED COX
- [ ] 285. LARRY COX
- [ ] 286. FLOYD BANNISTER
- [ ] 287. BYRON MCLAUGHLIN
- [ ] 288. RODNEY CRAIG
- [ ] 403. BRUCE BOCHTE
- [ ] 405. JERRY NARRON
- [ ] 406. ROB DRESSLER
- [ ] 407. DAVE HEAVERLO
- [ ] 408. TOM PACIOREK
- [ ] 501. DAVE A. ROBERTS
- [ ] 516. WILLIE NORWOOD
- [ ] 518. JUAN BENIQUEZ
- [ ] 543. BILL STEIN

TEXAS RANGERS

- [ ] 25. BUMP WILLS
- [ ] 26. JOHN ELLIS
- [ ] 27. JIM KERN
- [ ] 28. RICHIE ZISK
- [ ] 145. BUDDY BELL
- [ ] 146. FERGUSON JENKINS
- [ ] 147. DANNY DARWIN
- [ ] 148. JOHN GRUBB
- [ ] 265. PAT PUTNAM
- [ ] 266. JON MATLACK
- [ ] 267. DAVE RAJSICH
- [ ] 268. BILLY SAMPLE
- [ ] 385. JIM SUNDBERG
- [ ] 386. DOC MEDICH
- [ ] 387. AL OLIVER
- [ ] 388. JIM NORRIS
- [ ] 496. MICKEY RIVERS
- [ ] 509. NELSON NORMAN

Blue Jays

ALFREDO GRIFFIN SHORTSTOP

TORONTO BLUE JAYS

- [ ] 29. JOHN MAYBERRY
- [ ] 30. BOB DAVIS
- [ ] 31. JACKSON TODD
- [ ] 32. AL WOODS

- [ ] 149. ALFREDO GRIFFIN
- [ ] 150. JERRY GARVIN
- [ ] 151. PAUL MIRABELLA
- [ ] 152. RICK BOSETTI
- [ ] 269. DAMASO GARCIA
- [ ] 270. TOM BUSKEY
- [ ] 271. JOEY MCLAUGHLIN
- [ ] 272. BARRY BONNELL
- [ ] 389. BOB BAILOR
- [ ] 390. ERNIE WHITT
- [ ] 391. OTTO VELEZ
- [ ] 392. ROY HOWELL
- [ ] 569. DANNY AINGE
- [ ] 570. BOBBY MATTICK(M)
- [ ] 582. DAVE STIEB

1982 DONRUSS (660)
2 1/2" X 3 1/2"

ATLANTA BRAVES

- [ ] 47. CHRIS CHAMBLISS
- [ ] 58. CLAUDELL WASHINGTON
- [ ] 97. AL HRABOSKY
- [ ] 123. GENE GARBER
- [ ] 149. MATT SINATRO
- [ ] 173. BOB HORNER
- [ ] 184. BRIAN ASSELSTINE
- [ ] 223. RICK CAMP
- [ ] 249. TOMMY BOGGS
- [ ] 275. BRETT BUTLER
- [ ] 299. DALE MURPHY
- [ ] 310. RUFINO LINARES
- [ ] 349. MICKEY MAHLER
- [ ] 375. BRUCE BENEDICT
- [ ] 401. STEVE BEDROSIAN
- [ ] 425. EDDIE MILLER
- [ ] 436. GLENN HUBBARD
- [ ] 475. PHIL NIEKRO
- [ ] 501. KEN DAYLEY
- [ ] 527. LARRY MCWILLIAMS
- [ ] 543. GAYLORD PERRY
- [ ] 546. RAFAEL RAMIREZ
- [ ] 553. LARRY BRADFORD
- [ ] 555. JERRY ROYSTER

BALTIMORE ORIOLES

- [ ] 27. EARL WEAVER(M)
- [ ] 77. RICK DEMPSEY
- [ ] 79. DENNIS MARTINEZ
- [ ] 105. KEN SINGLETON
- [ ] 131. TIM STODDARD
- [ ] 153. AL BUMBRY
- [ ] 203. JOSE MORALES
- [ ] 205. TIPPY MARTINEZ
- [ ] 231. JIM PALMER
- [ ] 257. RICH DAUER
- [ ] 279. DOUG DECINCES
- [ ] 329. MIKE FLANAGAN
- [ ] 331. SCOTT MCGREGOR
- [ ] 357. STEVE STONE
- [ ] 383. TERRY CROWLEY
- [ ] 405. CAL RIPKEN
- [ ] 455. DAN GRAHAM
- [ ] 457. SAMMY STEWART
- [ ] 483. EDDIE MURRAY

□ 509. GARY ROENICKE
□ 579. CAL RIPKEN, SR.(C)
□ 581. BENNY AYALA
□ 597. DAVE FORD
□ 599. JOHN LOWENSTEIN
□ 610. BOB BONNER
□ 611. JIM DWYER
□ 644. LENN SAKATA

BOSTON RED SOX

□ 30. DENNIS ECKERSLEY
□ 74. CARL YASTRZEMSKI
□ 82. CARNEY LANSFORD
□ 109. DWIGHT EVANS
□ 134. BOB STANLEY
□ 156. JERRY REMY
□ 200. JIM RICE
□ 208. DAVE STAPLETON
□ 235. MIKE TORREZ
□ 260. JOHN TUDOR
□ 282. RALPH HOUK(M)
□ 326. FRANK TANANA
□ 334. RICK MILLER
□ 361. TOM BURGMEIER
□ 386. GARY ALLENSON
□ 408. TONY PEREZ
□ 452. MARK CLEAR
□ 460. GLENN HOFFMAN
□ 487. BILL CAMPBELL
□ 512. RICH GEDMAN
□ 540. BOB OJEDA
□ 560. JULIO VALDEZ
□ 564. STEVE CRAWFORD
□ 586. JOE RUDI
□ 608. GARRY HANCOCK
□ 632. REID NICHOLS

CALIFORNIA ANGELS

□ 38. STEVE RENKO
□ 66. BRUCE KISON
□ 90. BOBBY GRICH
□ 115. BRIAN DOWNING
□ 141. GENE MAUCH(M)
□ 164. GEOFF ZAHN
□ 192. ED OTT
□ 216. ROD CAREW
□ 241. FRED PATEK
□ 267. DON AASE
□ 290. DAVE FROST
□ 318. BOB CLARK
□ 342. RICK BURLESON
□ 367. FRED LYNN
□ 393. KEN FORSCH
□ 416. MIKE WITT
□ 444. JOHN HARRIS
□ 468. DAN FORD
□ 493. DON BAYLOR
□ 519. ANDY HASSLER
□ 577. BUTCH HOBSON
□ 587. JUAN BENIQUEZ
□ 593. BERT CAMPANERIS

CHICAGO CUBS

□ 48. IVAN DEJESUS
□ 57. HECTOR CRUZ
□ 99. TIM BLACKWELL
□ 126. RANDY MARTZ
□ 151. LEON DURHAM
□ 174. STEVE DILLARD
□ 183. STEVE HENDERSON
□ 225. JODY DAVIS
□ 252. LEE SMITH
□ 277. KEN REITZ
□ 300. MIKE LUM
□ 309. JERRY MORALES
□ 351. MIKE KRUKOW
□ 378. KEN KRAVEC
□ 403. BILL BUCKNER
□ 426. BILL CAUDILL
□ 435. MIKE TYSON
□ 477. DICK TIDROW
□ 504. DOUG BIRD
□ 529. PAT TABLER
□ 533. MIKE GRIFFIN
□ 554. SCOTT FLETCHER
□ 633. DAVE GEISEL

CHICAGO WHITE SOX

□ 39. MIKE SQUIRES
□ 67. WAYNE NORDHAGEN
□ 104. ROSS BAUMGARTEN
□ 117. LAMARR HOYT
□ 143. TONY BERNAZARD
□ 165. RON LEFLORE
□ 193. GREG LUZINSKI
□ 230. BRITT BURNS
□ 243. STEVE TROUT
□ 269. LAMAR JOHNSON
□ 291. CHET LEMON
□ 319. TONY LARUSSA(M)
□ 356. RICHARD DOTSON
□ 369. JIM ESSIAN
□ 395. JIM MORRISON
□ 417. BOB MOLINARO
□ 445. VADA PINSON(C)
□ 482. ED FARMER
□ 495. CARLTON FISK
□ 521. GREG PRYOR
□ 568. HAROLD BAINES
□ 603. JERRY KOOSMAN
□ 609. JERRY TURNER
□ 619. DENNIS LAMP
□ 631. KEVIN HICKEY
□ 637. BILL ALMON

CINCINNATI REDS

□ 43. LARRY BIITTNER
□ 62. JOE NOLAN
□ 103. MARIO SOTO
□ 122. FRANK PASTORE
□ 148. TOM SEAVER
□ 169. DAVE COLLINS
□ 188. JUNIOR KENNEDY
□ 229. TOM HUME
□ 248. DAN DRIESSEN
□ 274. GEORGE FOSTER
□ 295. SAM MEJIAS
□ 314. PAUL HOUSEHOLDER
□ 355. PAUL MOSKAU
□ 374. RAY KNIGHT
□ 400. JOHNNY BENCH
□ 421. DAVE CONCEPCION
□ 440. MIKE LACOSS
□ 481. JOE PRICE
□ 500. RON OESTER
□ 526. JOHN MCNAMARA(M)
□ 538. MIKE O'BERRY
□ 634. KEN GRIFFEY

CLEVELAND INDIANS

□ 33. RICK WAITS
□ 72. TOBY HARRAH
□ 85. RICK MANNING
□ 111. BERT BLYLEVEN
□ 137. LEN BARKER
□ 159. ALAN BANNISTER
□ 198. DUANE KUIPER
□ 211. JORGE ORTA
□ 237. VON HAYES
□ 263. BO DIAZ
□ 285. MIKE STANTON
□ 324. ANDRE THORNTON
□ 337. DAVE GARCIA(M)
□ 363. JOE CHARBONEAU
□ 389. MIKE HARGROVE
□ 411. DAN SPILLNER
□ 450. TOM VERYZER
□ 463. RON HASSEY
□ 489. WAYNE GARLAND
□ 515. MIGUEL DILONE
□ 551. CHRIS BANDO
□ 572. JOHN DENNY
□ 617. DAVE ROSELLO
□ 620. SID MONGE
□ 647. JERRY DYBZINSKI

DETROIT TIGERS

□ 29. SPARKY ANDERSON(M)
□ 76. ALAN TRAMMELL
□ 81. CHAMP SUMMERS
□ 107. JACK MORRIS
□ 133. DAN PETRY
□ 155. RICK PETERS
□ 202. TOM BROOKENS

□ 207. AL COWENS
□ 233. MILT WILCOX
□ 259. DAVE ROZEMA
□ 281. LANCE PARRISH
□ 328. RICHIE HEBNER
□ 333. STAN PAPI
□ 359. AURELIO LOPEZ
□ 385. DAN SCHATZEDER
□ 407. KIRK GIBSON
□ 454. LOU WHITAKER
□ 459. JOHN WOCKENFUSS
□ 485. KEVIN SAUCIER
□ 511. DAVE TOBIK
□ 542. LYNN JONES
□ 583. RICK LEACH
□ 594. STEVE KEMP
□ 601. MICK KELLEHER
□ 602. RON JACKSON

HOUSTON ASTROS

□ 41. BOB KNEPPER
□ 65. JOE SAMBITO
□ 92. ART HOWE
□ 118. CESAR CEDENO
□ 144. BILL VIRDON(M)
□ 167. JOE NIEKRO
□ 191. DAVE SMITH
□ 218. JOE PITTMAN
□ 244. JOSE CRUZ
□ 270. FRANK LACORTE
□ 293. VERN RUHLE
□ 317. ALAN ASHBY
□ 344. CRAIG REYNOLDS
□ 370. TERRY PUHL
□ 396. MIKE IVIE
□ 419. NOLAN RYAN
□ 443. DON SUTTON
□ 470. KIKO GARCIA
□ 496. DENNY WALLING
□ 522. TONY SCOTT
□ 544. PHIL GARNER
□ 576. LUIS PUJOLS
□ 625. DAVE W. ROBERTS

KANSAS CITY ROYALS

□ 34. GEORGE BRETT
□ 70. AMOS OTIS
□ 86. JOHN WATHAN
□ 112. DAN QUISENBERRY
□ 138. RICH GALE
□ 160. U.L. WASHINGTON
□ 196. HAL MCRAE
□ 212. JAMIE QUIRK
□ 238. RENIE MARTIN
□ 264. DENNIS LEONARD
□ 286. FRANK WHITE
□ 322. CESAR GERONIMO
□ 338. LARRY GURA
□ 364. KEN BRETT
□ 390. DARRYL MOTLEY
□ 412. WILLIE AIKENS
□ 448. WILLIE WILSON
□ 464. PAUL SPLITTORFF
□ 490. JIM L. WRIGHT
□ 516. CLINT HURDLE
□ 570. LEE MAY
□ 590. DAVE CHALK
□ 630. RANCE MULLINIKS

LOS ANGELES DODGERS

□ 32. BURT HOOTON
□ 75. BOB WELCH
□ 84. STEVE GARVEY
□ 110. TOM LASORDA(M)
□ 136. PEDRO GUERRERO
□ 158. STEVE HOWE
□ 201. STEVE YEAGER
□ 210. RON CEY
□ 236. BOBBY CASTILLO
□ 262. JAY JOHNSTONE
□ 284. JERRY REUSS
□ 327. DAVEY LOPES
□ 336. DUSTY BAKER
□ 362. TERRY FORSTER
□ 388. KEN LANDREAUX
□ 410. DAVE STEWART
□ 453. BILL RUSSELL

- ☐ 462. FERNANDO VALENZUELA
- ☐ 488. REGGIE SMITH
- ☐ 514. RICK MONDAY
- ☐ 537. DERREL THOMAS
- ☐ 562. MIKE MARSHALL
- ☐ 598. MIKE SCIOSCIA
- ☐ 604. DAVE GOLTZ
- ☐ 624. STEVE SAX

MILWAUKEE BREWERS

- ☐ 28. ROLLIE FINGERS
- ☐ 78. PAUL MOLITOR
- ☐ 80. JIM SLATON
- ☐ 106. TED SIMMONS
- ☐ 132. GORMAN THOMAS
- ☐ 154. MARK BROUHARD
- ☐ 204. ROY HOWELL
- ☐ 206. MOOSE HAAS
- ☐ 232. BOB RODGERS(M)
- ☐ 258. CECIL COOPER
- ☐ 280. CHARLIE MOORE
- ☐ 330. MIKE CALDWELL
- ☐ 332. JERRY AUGUSTINE
- ☐ 358. LARRY HISLE
- ☐ 384. DON MONEY
- ☐ 406. JIM GANTNER
- ☐ 456. REGGIE CLEVELAND
- ☐ 458. PETE VUCKOVICH
- ☐ 484. BEN OGLIVIE
- ☐ 510. ROBIN YOUNT
- ☐ 536. EDDIE ROMERO
- ☐ 578. HARVEY KUENN(C)
- ☐ 592. SAL BANDO
- ☐ 595. RANDY LERCH
- ☐ 618. RICKEY KEETON
- ☐ 623. JAMIE EASTERLY

MINNESOTA TWINS

- ☐ 51. PETE REDFERN
- ☐ 53. DOUG CORBETT
- ☐ 102. DAVE ENGLE
- ☐ 130. ROB WILFONG
- ☐ 177. FERNANDO ARROYO
- ☐ 179. DARRELL JACKSON
- ☐ 228. HOSKEN POWELL
- ☐ 256. JOHN CASTINO
- ☐ 303. ROGER ERICKSON
- ☐ 305. DANNY GOODWIN
- ☐ 354. PETE MACKANIN
- ☐ 382. BRAD HAVENS
- ☐ 429. AL WILLIAMS
- ☐ 431. GLENN ADAMS
- ☐ 480. MICKEY HATCHER
- ☐ 508. BUTCH WYNEGAR
- ☐ 532. SAL BUTERA
- ☐ 539. JACK O'CONNOR
- ☐ 549. TIM LAUDNER
- ☐ 557. KENT HRBEK
- ☐ 566. JOHNNY PODRES(C)
- ☐ 571. GARY WARD
- ☐ 573. ROY SMALLEY
- ☐ 591. BILLY GARDNER(M)

MONTREAL EXPOS

- ☐ 36. STEVE ROGERS
- ☐ 68. WOODIE FRYMAN
- ☐ 88. ANDRE DAWSON
- ☐ 114. GARY CARTER
- ☐ 140. TIM WALLACH
- ☐ 162. BILL GULLICKSON
- ☐ 194. BILL LEE
- ☐ 214. TIM RAINES
- ☐ 240. RODNEY SCOTT
- ☐ 266. JOHN MILNER
- ☐ 288. SCOTT SANDERSON
- ☐ 320. CHARLIE LEA
- ☐ 340. WARREN CROMARTIE
- ☐ 366. CHRIS SPEIER
- ☐ 392. STAN BAHNSEN
- ☐ 414. RAY BURRIS
- ☐ 446. ELIAS SOSA
- ☐ 466. LARRY PARRISH
- ☐ 492. JIM FANNING(M)
- ☐ 518. GRANT JACKSON
- ☐ 547. JEFF REARDON
- ☐ 621. JERRY WHITE
- ☐ 627. TERRY FRANCONA
- ☐ 650. FELIPE ALOU(C)

NEW YORK METS

- ☐ 49. LEE MAZZILLI
- ☐ 56. RUSTY STAUB
- ☐ 98. FRANK TAVERAS
- ☐ 128. MIKE SCOTT
- ☐ 175. MOOKIE WILSON
- ☐ 182. DAVE KINGMAN
- ☐ 224. MIKE JORGENSEN
- ☐ 254. PAT ZACHRY
- ☐ 301. TOM HAUSMAN
- ☐ 308. BOB BAILOR
- ☐ 350. ALEX TREVINO
- ☐ 380. PETE FALCONE
- ☐ 427. DOUG FLYNN
- ☐ 434. JOHN STEARNS
- ☐ 476. HUBIE BROOKS
- ☐ 506. NEIL ALLEN
- ☐ 589. CRAIG SWAN
- ☐ 605. ELLIS VALENTINE
- ☐ 613. JOEL YOUNGBLOOD
- ☐ 641. ED LYNCH
- ☐ 646. JESSE OROSCO
- ☐ 649. RON GARDENHIRE

NEW YORK YANKEES

- ☐ 31. DAVE WINFIELD
- ☐ 73. DAVE RIGHETTI
- ☐ 83. BARRY FOOTE
- ☐ 108. BOB WATSON
- ☐ 135. LOU PINIELLA
- ☐ 157. RICK REUSCHEL
- ☐ 199. RICK CERONE
- ☐ 209. BUCKY DENT
- ☐ 234. DAVE REVERING
- ☐ 261. JERRY MUMPHREY
- ☐ 283. RICH GOSSAGE
- ☐ 325. RUDY MAY
- ☐ 335. GRAIG NETTLES
- ☐ 360. OSCAR GAMBLE
- ☐ 387. YOGI BERRA(C)
- ☐ 409. TOMMY JOHN
- ☐ 451. RON DAVIS
- ☐ 461. WILLIE RANDOLPH
- ☐ 486. BOBBY MURCER
- ☐ 513. GENE NELSON
- ☐ 535. REGGIE JACKSON
- ☐ 548. RON GUIDRY
- ☐ 552. BOBBY BROWN
- ☐ 569. DAVE LAROCHE
- ☐ 584. GEORGE FRAZIER
- ☐ 614. LARRY MILBOURNE
- ☐ 635. BOB LEMON(M)

TONY ARMAS of

OAKLAND A'S

- ☐ 35. STEVE MCCATTY
- ☐ 71. MATT KEOUGH
- ☐ 87. BRIAN KINGMAN
- ☐ 113. RICKEY HENDERSON
- ☐ 139. WAYNE GROSS
- ☐ 161. RICK LANGFORD
- ☐ 197. MIKE NORRIS
- ☐ 213. JEFF JONES
- ☐ 239. DWAYNE MURPHY
- ☐ 265. JIM SPENCER
- ☐ 287. BOB OWCHINKO
- ☐ 323. TOM UNDERWOOD
- ☐ 339. CLIFF JOHNSON

- ☐ 365. TONY ARMAS
- ☐ 391. DAVE MCKAY
- ☐ 413. MIKE HEATH
- ☐ 449. FRED STANLEY
- ☐ 465. ROB PICCIOLO
- ☐ 491. BILLY MARTIN(M)
- ☐ 517. JEFF NEWMAN
- ☐ 534. KELVIN MOORE
- ☐ 556. SHOOTY BABITT
- ☐ 616. KEITH DRUMRIGHT
- ☐ 626. RICK BOSETTI

PHILADELPHIA PHILLIES

- ☐ 42. STEVE CARLTON
- ☐ 63. LARRY BOWA
- ☐ 93. MARTY BYSTROM
- ☐ 119. KEITH MORELAND
- ☐ 147. DICK DAVIS
- ☐ 168. PETE ROSE
- ☐ 189. SPARKY LYLE
- ☐ 219. LARRY CHRISTENSON
- ☐ 245. MANNY TRILLO
- ☐ 273. DEL UNSER
- ☐ 294. MIKE SCHMIDT
- ☐ 315. GARRY MADDOX
- ☐ 345. MIKE PROLY
- ☐ 371. GREG GROSS
- ☐ 399. RON REED
- ☐ 420. TUG MCGRAW
- ☐ 441. GARY MATTHEWS
- ☐ 471. BOB BOONE
- ☐ 497. BAKE MCBRIDE
- ☐ 525. DICK RUTHVEN
- ☐ 606. LONNIE SMITH
- ☐ 622. LUIS AGUAYO

PITTSBURGH PIRATES

- ☐ 45. STEVE NICOSIA
- ☐ 59. ENRIQUE ROMO
- ☐ 95. DAVE PARKER
- ☐ 124. TONY PENA
- ☐ 150. CHUCK TANNER(M)
- ☐ 171. JIM BIBBY
- ☐ 185. ROD SCURRY
- ☐ 221. MIKE EASLER
- ☐ 250. DALE BERRA
- ☐ 276. LEE LACY
- ☐ 297. JOHN CANDELARIA
- ☐ 311. KENT TEKULVE
- ☐ 347. OMAR MORENO
- ☐ 376. TIM FOLI
- ☐ 402. BILL ROBINSON
- ☐ 423. RICK RHODEN
- ☐ 437. EDDIE SOLOMON
- ☐ 473. RANDY NIEMANN
- ☐ 502. JASON THOMPSON
- ☐ 528. JOHNNY RAY
- ☐ 582. VANCE LAW
- ☐ 639. WILLIE STARGELL
- ☐ 651. HARVEY HADDIX(C)
- ☐ 653. BILL MADLOCK

ST. LOUIS CARDINALS

- ☐ 40. GEORGE HENDRICK
- ☐ 64. SIXTO LEZCANO
- ☐ 91. BOB FORSCH
- ☐ 120. BOB SHIRLEY
- ☐ 152. GENE TENACE
- ☐ 166. DANE IORG
- ☐ 190. WHITEY HERZOG(M)
- ☐ 217. JIM KAAT
- ☐ 246. LARY SORENSEN
- ☐ 278. KEITH HERNANDEZ
- ☐ 292. TITO LANDRUM
- ☐ 316. MIKE RAMSEY
- ☐ 343. JOHN MARTIN
- ☐ 372. BRUCE SUTTER
- ☐ 404. KEN OBERKFELL
- ☐ 418. STEVE BRAUN
- ☐ 442. MARK LITTELL
- ☐ 469. SILVIO MARTINEZ
- ☐ 498. DARRELL PORTER
- ☐ 530. TOM HERR
- ☐ 545. GARRY TEMPLETON
- ☐ 588. LUIS DELEON
- ☐ 607. JOAQUIN ANDUJAR
- ☐ 615. GENE ROOF

1982 Donruss

☐ 636. ORLANDO SANCHEZ
☐ 640. BOB SYKES
☐ 645. JULIO GONZALEZ

SAN DIEGO PADRES

☐ 44. CHRIS WELSH
☐ 61. TIM FLANNERY
☐ 94. OZZIE SMITH
☐ 121. TERRY KENNEDY
☐ 145. JOHN LITTLEFIELD
☐ 170. RICK WISE
☐ 187. DANNY BOONE
☐ 220. JUAN BONILLA
☐ 247. DAVE EDWARDS
☐ 271. BARRY EVANS
☐ 296. GARY LUCAS
☐ 313. JOHN URREA
☐ 346. RUPPERT JONES
☐ 373. JOE LEFEBVRE
☐ 397. BRODERICK PERKINS
☐ 422. JUAN EICHELBERGER
☐ 439. RANDY BASS
☐ 472. LUIS SALAZAR
☐ 499. GENE RICHARDS
☐ 523. STEVE MURA

SAN FRANCISCO GIANTS

☐ 46. JACK CLARK
☐ 60. GARY LAVELLE
☐ 96. DOYLE ALEXANDER
☐ 125. ALLEN RIPLEY
☐ 146. DAVE BERGMAN
☐ 172. LARRY HERNDON
☐ 186. FRED BREINING
☐ 222. VIDA BLUE
☐ 251. EDDIE WHITSON
☐ 272. ENOS CABELL
☐ 298. JERRY MARTIN
☐ 312. JOE MORGAN
☐ 348. GREG MINTON
☐ 377. AL HOLLAND
☐ 398. DARRELL EVANS
☐ 424. FRANK ROBINSON(M)
☐ 438. JEFF LEONARD
☐ 474. TOM GRIFFIN
☐ 503. MILT MAY
☐ 524. JOHNNIE LEMASTER
☐ 563. RENNIE STENNETT
☐ 574. BOB BRENLY

SEATTLE MARINERS

☐ 50. JULIO CRUZ
☐ 55. JOE SIMPSON
☐ 100. FLOYD BANNISTER
☐ 127. RICHIE ZISK
☐ 176. DAN MEYER
☐ 181. JIM ANDERSON
☐ 226. MIKE PARROTT
☐ 253. TOM PACIOREK
☐ 302. GLENN ABBOTT
☐ 307. LENNY RANDLE
☐ 352. SHANE RAWLEY
☐ 379. JEFF BURROUGHS
☐ 428. LARRY ANDERSEN
☐ 433. JERRY NARRON
☐ 478. JIM BEATTIE
☐ 505. BRUCE BOCHTE
☐ 567. PAUL SERNA
☐ 596. BRYAN CLARK
☐ 600. RENE LACHEMANN(M)
☐ 612. TERRY BULLING
☐ 648. TOMMY DAVIS(C)

TEXAS RANGERS

☐ 37. BILL STEIN
☐ 69. BILLY SAMPLE
☐ 89. JIM KERN
☐ 116. AL OLIVER
☐ 142. GEORGE MEDICH
☐ 163. MARK WAGNER
☐ 195. DON ZIMMER(M)
☐ 215. JON MATLACK
☐ 242. MICKEY RIVERS
☐ 268. JIM SUNDBERG
☐ 289. BUMP WILLS
☐ 321. DANNY DARWIN

☐ 341. STEVE COMER
☐ 368. BUDDY BELL
☐ 394. MARIO MENDOZA
☐ 415. LEON ROBERTS
☐ 447. CHARLIE HOUGH
☐ 467. JOHN GRUBB
☐ 494. RICK HONEYCUTT
☐ 520. PAT PUTNAM
☐ 550. JOHN HENRY JOHNSON
☐ 565. BOB BABCOCK
☐ 642. JOHN ELLIS
☐ 643. FERGIE JENKINS

TORONTO BLUE JAYS

☐ 52. DAVE STIEB
☐ 54. JORGE BELL
☐ 101. ALFREDO GRIFFIN
☐ 129. LLOYD MOSEBY
☐ 178. JACKSON TODD
☐ 180. AL WOODS
☐ 227. JIM CLANCY
☐ 255. LUIS LEAL
☐ 304. OTTO VELEZ
☐ 306. JOHN MAYBERRY
☐ 353. GARTH IORG
☐ 381. ERNIE WHITT
☐ 430. JERRY GARVIN
☐ 432. BARRY BONNELL
☐ 479. DAMASO GARCIA
☐ 507. JOEY MCLAUGHLIN
☐ 541. ROY LEE JACKSON
☐ 559. MARK BOMBACK
☐ 561. BUCK MARTINEZ
☐ 580. JUAN BERENGUER
☐ 629. PAUL MIRABELLA
☐ 638. DANNY AINGE
☐ 652. WILLIE UPSHAW

1983 DONRUSS (660)
2 1/2" X 3 1/2"

ATLANTA BRAVES

☐ 47. DALE MURPHY
☐ 58. BOB HORNER
☐ 97. PHIL NIEKRO
☐ 123. CHRIS CHAMBLISS

☐ 149. RICK CAMP
☐ 173. STEVE BEDROSIAN
☐ 184. GLENN HUBBARD
☐ 223. GENE GARBER
☐ 249. CLAUDELL WASHINGTON
☐ 275. RUFINO LINARES
☐ 299. BRUCE BENEDICT
☐ 310. RAFAEL RAMIREZ
☐ 349. TOMMY BOGGS
☐ 375. KEN DAYLEY
☐ 401. BOB WALK
☐ 425. JERRY ROYSTER
☐ 436. BIFF POCOROBA
☐ 475. AL HRABOSKY
☐ 501. LARRY WHISENTON
☐ 527. RICK MAHLER
☐ 551. BOB WATSON
☐ 557. PASCUAL PEREZ
☐ 562. CARLOS DIAZ
☐ 607. TERRY HARPER
☐ 622. MATT SINATRO
☐ 628. JOE TORRE(M)
☐ 636. BRETT BUTLER

BALTIMORE ORIOLES

☐ 27. GARY ROENICKE
☐ 77. JIM PALMER
☐ 79. JOE NOLAN
☐ 105. MIKE FLANAGAN
☐ 131. GLENN GULLIVER
☐ 153. JOHN LOWENSTEIN
☐ 203. SAMMY STEWART
☐ 205. LENN SAKATA
☐ 231. DENNIS MARTINEZ
☐ 257. KEN SINGLETON
☐ 279. CAL RIPKEN
☐ 329. RICK DEMPSEY
☐ 331. BENNY AYALA
☐ 357. TIPPY MARTINEZ
☐ 383. AL BUMBRY
☐ 405. EDDIE MURRAY
☐ 455. RICH DAUER
☐ 457. TERRY CROWLEY
☐ 483. SCOTT MCGREGOR
☐ 509. DAN FORD
☐ 581. TIM STODDARD
☐ 583. JIM DWYER
☐ 619. STORM DAVIS

BOSTON RED SOX

☐ 30. GARY ALLENSON
☐ 74. JERRY REMY
☐ 82. RICK MILLER
☐ 109. LUIS APONTE
☐ 134. BRUCE HURST
☐ 156. RICH GEDMAN
☐ 200. DAVE STAPLETON
☐ 208. JIM RICE
☐ 235. TOM BURGMEIER
☐ 260. BOB OJEDA
☐ 282. GLENN HOFFMAN
☐ 326. CARL YASTRZEMSKI
☐ 334. CHUCK RAINEY
☐ 361. MARK CLEAR
☐ 386. BOB STANLEY
☐ 408. CARNEY LANSFORD
☐ 452. DWIGHT EVANS

☐ 460. REID NICHOLS
☐ 487. DENNIS ECKERSLEY
☐ 512. MIKE TORREZ
☐ 534. ROGER LAFRANCOIS
☐ 563. JOHN TUDOR
☐ 578. TONY PEREZ
☐ 586. WADE BOGGS

CALIFORNIA ANGELS

☐ 38. DON AASE
☐ 66. GEOFF ZAHN
☐ 90. ROD CAREW
☐ 115. REGGIE JACKSON
☐ 141. DARYL SCONIERS
☐ 164. KEN FORSCH
☐ 192. BOB BOONE
☐ 216. DOUG DECINCES
☐ 241. FRED LYNN
☐ 267. BRUCE KISON
☐ 290. ANDY HASSLER
☐ 318. RICK BURLESON
☐ 342. TIM FOLI
☐ 367. BRIAN DOWNING
☐ 393. STEVE RENKO
☐ 416. MIKE WITT
☐ 444. BOBBY CLARK
☐ 468. BOBBY GRICH
☐ 493. DON BAYLOR
☐ 519. LUIS SANCHEZ
☐ 542. LUIS TIANT
☐ 570. TOMMY JOHN
☐ 604. JOE FERGUSON
☐ 612. ROB WILFONG
☐ 639. RON JACKSON
☐ 640. JUAN BENIQUEZ

CHICAGO CUBS

☐ 48. DOUG BIRD
☐ 57. ALLEN RIPLEY
☐ 99. BILL BUCKNER
☐ 126. MEL HALL
☐ 151. RANDY MARTZ
☐ 174. WILLIE HERNANDEZ
☐ 183. JODY DAVIS
☐ 225. MIKE PROLY
☐ 252. STEVE HENDERSON
☐ 277. RYNE SANDBERG
☐ 300. FERGIE JENKINS
☐ 309. KEITH MORELAND
☐ 351. BUMP WILLS
☐ 378. SCOT THOMPSON
☐ 403. LEE SMITH
☐ 426. DICKIE NOLES
☐ 435. LARRY BOWA
☐ 477. LEON DURHAM
☐ 504. BILL CAMPBELL
☐ 529. JUNIOR KENNEDY
☐ 552. PAT TABLER
☐ 561. JAY JOHNSTONE
☐ 596. BOBBY MOLINARO
☐ 614. LEE ELIA(M)
☐ 631. GARY WOODS

CHICAGO WHITE SOX

☐ 39. JERRY KOOSMAN
☐ 67. SALOME BAROJAS
☐ 104. CARLTON FISK
☐ 117. VANCE LAW
☐ 143. HAROLD BAINES
☐ 165. DENNIS LAMP
☐ 193. BRITT BURNS
☐ 230. MARC HILL
☐ 243. TOM PACIOREK
☐ 269. STEVE KEMP
☐ 291. ERNESTO ESCARREGA
☐ 319. RICHARD DOTSON
☐ 356. BILL ALMON
☐ 369. AURELIO RODRIGUEZ
☐ 395. GREG LUZINSKI
☐ 417. STEVE TROUT
☐ 445. KEVIN HICKEY
☐ 482. TONY BERNAZARD
☐ 495. MIKE SQUIRES
☐ 521. RUDY LAW
☐ 543. RON LEFLORE
☐ 571. TONY LARUSSA(M)
☐ 616. JERRY HAIRSTON
☐ 632. LAMARR HOYT
☐ 652. MARVIS FOLEY

CINCINNATI REDS

☐ 43. CESAR CEDENO
☐ 62. FRANK PASTORE
☐ 103. BRUCE BERENYI
☐ 122. TOM SEAVER
☐ 148. DAVE CONCEPCION
☐ 169. EDDIE MILNER
☐ 188. DAVE VANGORDER
☐ 229. TOM HUME
☐ 248. MARIO SOTO
☐ 274. DAN DRIESSEN
☐ 295. GREG HARRIS
☐ 314. WAYNE KRENCHICKI
☐ 355. JIM KERN
☐ 374. ALEX TREVINO
☐ 400. TOM LAWLESS
☐ 421. CHARLIE LIEBRANDT
☐ 440. LARRY BIITTNER
☐ 481. JOE PRICE
☐ 500. JOHNNY BENCH
☐ 526. RON OESTER
☐ 547. BRAD LESLEY
☐ 566. PAUL HOUSEHOLDER
☐ 597. MIKE VAIL
☐ 624. DUANE WALKER

CLEVELAND INDIANS

☐ 33. CHRIS BANDO
☐ 72. RICK SUTCLIFFE
☐ 85. MIGUEL DILONE
☐ 111. LEN BARKER
☐ 137. DAN SPILLNER
☐ 159. RON HASSEY
☐ 198. RICK MANNING
☐ 211. ANDRE THORNTON
☐ 237. JOHN DENNY
☐ 263. RICK WAITS
☐ 285. ALAN BANNISTER
☐ 324. VON HAYES
☐ 337. TOBY HARRAH
☐ 363. LARY SORENSEN
☐ 389. ED WHITSON
☐ 411. LARRY MILBOURNE
☐ 450. MIKE HARGROVE
☐ 463. JACK PERCONTE
☐ 489. MIKE FISCHLIN
☐ 515. RODNEY CRAIG
☐ 537. ED GLYNN
☐ 576. JERRY DYBZINSKI
☐ 589. BERT BLYLEVEN

DETROIT TIGERS

☐ 29. PAT UNDERWOOD
☐ 76. JOHN WOCKENFUSS
☐ 81. RICK LEACH
☐ 107. JACK MORRIS
☐ 133. DAVE ROZEMA
☐ 155. MILT WILCOX
☐ 202. ENOS CABELL
☐ 207. ALAN TRAMMELL
☐ 233. LARRY PASHNICK
☐ 259. ELIAS SOSA
☐ 281. BILL FAHEY
☐ 328. HOWARD JOHNSON
☐ 333. LOU WHITAKER
☐ 359. DAN PETRY
☐ 385. DAVE TOBIK
☐ 407. LANCE PARRISH
☐ 454. TOM BROOKENS
☐ 459. KIRK GIBSON
☐ 485. MIKE IVIE
☐ 511. CHET LEMON
☐ 533. SPARKY ANDERSON(M)
☐ 580. GLEN WILSON
☐ 585. LARRY HERNDON
☐ 600. JERRY UJDUR
☐ 641. DAVE RUCKER

HOUSTON ASTROS

☐ 41. JOSE CRUZ
☐ 65. HARRY SPILMAN
☐ 92. BOB KNEPPER
☐ 118. NOLAN RYAN
☐ 144. ALAN ASHBY
☐ 167. TERRY PUHL
☐ 191. DICKIE THON
☐ 218. FRANK LACORTE

☐ 244. JOE SAMBITO
☐ 270. PHIL GARNER
☐ 293. TONY SCOTT
☐ 317. CRAIG REYNOLDS
☐ 344. MIKE LACOSS
☐ 370. DAVE SMITH
☐ 396. ART HOWE
☐ 419. DENNY WALLING
☐ 443. DANNY HEEP
☐ 470. JOE NIEKRO
☐ 496. BERT ROBERGE
☐ 522. RAY KNIGHT
☐ 545. RANDY MOFFITT
☐ 569. KIKO GARCIA
☐ 620. ALAN KNICELY
☐ 627. VERN RUHLE
☐ 642. LUIS PUJOLS

KANSAS CITY ROYALS

☐ 34. VIDA BLUE
☐ 70. DAN QUISENBERRY
☐ 86. JOHN WATHAN
☐ 112. WILLIE WILSON
☐ 138. JERRY MARTIN
☐ 160. LARRY GURA
☐ 196. DON SLAUGHT
☐ 212. WILLIE AIKENS
☐ 238. HAL MCRAE
☐ 264. GREG PRYOR
☐ 286. PAUL SPLITTORFF
☐ 322. BUD BLACK
☐ 338. GEORGE BRETT
☐ 364. AMOS OTIS
☐ 390. DON HOOD
☐ 412. DENNIS LEONARD
☐ 448. CESAR GERONIMO
☐ 464. FRANK WHITE
☐ 490. U.L. WASHINGTON
☐ 516. ONIX CONCEPCION
☐ 538. LEE MAY
☐ 574. KEITH CREEL
☐ 590. DICK HOWSER(M)

LOS ANGELES DODGERS

☐ 32. BURT HOOTON
☐ 75. MIKE SCIOSCIA
☐ 84. RON CEY
☐ 110. PEDRO GUERRERO
☐ 136. TOM LASORDA(M)
☐ 158. JERRY REUSS
☐ 201. STEVE YEAGER
☐ 210. BILL RUSSELL
☐ 236. KEN LANDREAUX
☐ 262. CANDY MALDONADO
☐ 284. FERNANDO VALENZUELA
☐ 327. RON ROENICKE
☐ 336. STEVE SAX
☐ 362. MIKE MARSHALL
☐ 388. JORGE ORTA
☐ 410. BOB WELCH
☐ 453. TERRY FORSTER
☐ 462. DUSTY BAKER
☐ 488. STEVE GARVEY
☐ 514. MARK BELANGER
☐ 536. TOM NIEDENFUER
☐ 579. GREG BROCK
☐ 588. DAVE STEWART
☐ 630. STEVE HOWE
☐ 643. RICK MONDAY

MILWAUKEE BREWERS

☐ 28. DWIGHT BERNARD
☐ 78. ROLLIE FINGERS
☐ 80. PETE VUCKOVICH
☐ 106. CECIL COOPER
☐ 132. DON MONEY
☐ 154. MIKE CALDWELL
☐ 204. MOOSE HAAS
☐ 206. CHARLIE MOORE
☐ 232. JIM GANTNER
☐ 258. ROBIN YOUNT
☐ 280. JAMIE EASTERLY
☐ 330. JIM SLATON
☐ 332. TED SIMMONS
☐ 358. ROY HOWELL
☐ 384. BEN OGLIVIE
☐ 406. MARSHALL EDWARDS
☐ 456. ROB PICCIOLO

☐ 458. NED YOST
☐ 484. PAUL MOLITOR
☐ 510. GORMAN THOMAS
☐ 531. DON SUTTON
☐ 532. MARK BROUHARD
☐ 582. BOB MCCLURE
☐ 584. ED ROMERO
☐ 608. HARVEY KUENN(M)

MINNESOTA TWINS

☐ 51. JACK O'CONNOR
☐ 53. GARY GAETTI
☐ 102. BOBBY CASTILLO
☐ 130. JOHN PACELLA
☐ 177. TIM LAUDNER
☐ 179. KENT HRBEK
☐ 228. RON DAVIS
☐ 256. PETE REDFERN
☐ 303. JOHN CASTINO
☐ 305. RANDY JOHNSON
☐ 354. TERRY FELTON
☐ 382. FRANK VIOLA
☐ 429. GARY WARD
☐ 431. RON WASHINGTON
☐ 480. BRAD HAVENS
☐ 508. AL WILLIAMS
☐ 555. TOM BRUNANSKY
☐ 615. MICKEY HATCHER
☐ 646. DAVE ENGLE
☐ 650. JESUS VEGA

MONTREAL EXPOS

☐ 36. RAY BURRIS
☐ 68. DAVID PALMER
☐ 88. BYRN SMITH
☐ 114. MIKE GATES
☐ 140. AL OLIVER
☐ 162. WOODIE FRYMAN
☐ 194. JEFF REARDON
☐ 214. TIM BLACKWELL
☐ 240. DOUG FLYNN
☐ 266. CHRIS SPEIER
☐ 288. BILL GULLICKSON
☐ 320. STEVE ROGERS
☐ 340. GARY CARTER
☐ 366. BRAD MILLS
☐ 392. TIM WALLACH
☐ 414. CHARLIE LEA
☐ 446. SCOTT SANDERSON
☐ 466. WARREN CROMARTIE
☐ 492. ROY JOHNSON
☐ 518. ANDRE DAWSON
☐ 540. TIM RAINES
☐ 572. JOEL YOUNGBLOOD
☐ 592. TERRY FRANCONA
☐ 602. JERRY WHITE

JOHN STEARNS

NEW YORK METS

☐ 49. HUBIE BROOKS
☐ 56. MOOKIE WILSON
☐ 98. NEIL ALLEN
☐ 128. CHARLIE PULEO
☐ 175. RON GARDENHIRE
☐ 182. PETE FALCONE
☐ 224. SCOTT HOLMAN
☐ 254. CRAIG SWAN

☐ 301. DAVE KINGMAN
☐ 308. ED LYNCH
☐ 350. RUSTY STAUB
☐ 380. JOHN STEARNS
☐ 427. GEORGE FOSTER
☐ 434. JESSE OROSCO
☐ 476. RON HODGES
☐ 506. BOB BAILOR
☐ 553. BRENT GAFF
☐ 560. PAT ZACHRY
☐ 599. GARY RAJSICH
☐ 618. WALLY BACKMAN
☐ 634. TERRY LEACH

NEW YORK YANKEES

☐ 31. RON GUIDRY
☐ 73. STEVE BALBONI
☐ 83. GRAIG NETTLES
☐ 108. MIKE MORGAN
☐ 135. RUDY MAY
☐ 157. RICH GOSSAGE
☐ 199. DAVE RIGHETTI
☐ 209. ROY SMALLEY
☐ 234. DAVE COLLINS
☐ 261. BOBBY MURCER
☐ 283. WILLIE RANDOLPH
☐ 325. BUTCH WYNEGAR
☐ 335. LOU PINIELLA
☐ 360. JERRY MUMPHREY
☐ 387. ANDRE ROBERTSON
☐ 409. DAVE WINFIELD
☐ 451. DOYLE ALEXANDER
☐ 461. OSCAR GAMBLE
☐ 486. KEN GRIFFEY
☐ 513. SHANE RAWLEY
☐ 535. GEORGE FRAZIER
☐ 577. RICK CERONE
☐ 587. JAY HOWELL
☐ 638. LEE MAZZILLI

OAKLAND A'S

☐ 35. RICKEY HENDERSON
☐ 71. TONY ARMAS
☐ 87. KELVIN MOORE
☐ 113. DAVE BEARD
☐ 139. MIKE NORRIS
☐ 161. DWAYNE MURPHY
☐ 197. FRED STANLEY
☐ 213. DAVE MCKAY
☐ 239. MATT KEOUGH
☐ 265. BOB OWCHINKO
☐ 287. JOE RUDI
☐ 323. JEFF BURROUGHS
☐ 339. DAVEY LOPES
☐ 365. RICK LANGFORD
☐ 391. TOM UNDERWOOD
☐ 413. DAN MEYER
☐ 449. JIMMY SEXTON
☐ 465. MICKEY KLUTTS
☐ 491. STEVE MCCATTY
☐ 517. MIKE HEATH
☐ 539. BOB KEARNEY
☐ 575. BILLY MARTIN(M)
☐ 591. WAYNE GROSS
☐ 601. CLIFF JOHNSON
☐ 635. JEFF NEWMAN
☐ 651. JEFF JONES

PHILADELPHIA PHILLIES

☐ 42. PETE ROSE
☐ 63. GARRY MADDOX
☐ 93. MARTY BYSTROM
☐ 119. MIKE KRUKOW
☐ 147. BO DIAZ
☐ 168. MIKE SCHMIDT
☐ 189. BOB DERNIER
☐ 219. STEVE CARLTON
☐ 245. SID MONGE
☐ 273. DAVE W. ROBERTS
☐ 294. MANNY TRILLO
☐ 315. GEORGE VUKOVICH
☐ 345. LARRY CHRISTENSON
☐ 371. TUG MCGRAW
☐ 399. IVAN DEJESUS
☐ 420. GARY MATTHEWS
☐ 441. GREG GROSS
☐ 471. ED FARMER

☐ 497. DICK RUTHVEN
☐ 525. JULIO FRANCO
☐ 546. LUIS AGUAYO
☐ 567. RON REED
☐ 606. OZZIE VIRGIL
☐ 626. PAT CORRALES(M)

PITTSBURGH PIRATES

☐ 45. LARRY MCWILLIAMS
☐ 59. TONY PENA
☐ 95. JASON THOMPSON
☐ 124. CHUCK TANNER(M)
☐ 150. JIM MORRISON
☐ 171. DON ROBINSON
☐ 185. DALE BERRA
☐ 221. MIKE EASLER
☐ 250. RICK RHODEN
☐ 276. LEE LACY
☐ 297. KENT TEKULVE
☐ 311. BILL MADLOCK
☐ 347. OMAR MORENO
☐ 376. ROD SCURRY
☐ 402. JIMMY SMITH
☐ 423. MATT GUANTE
☐ 437. JOHNNY RAY
☐ 473. DAVE PARKER
☐ 502. MANNY SARMIENTO
☐ 528. STEVE NICOSIA
☐ 549. JOHN CANDELARIA
☐ 610. WILLIE STARGELL
☐ 647. DICK DAVIS

ST. LOUIS CARDINALS

☐ 40. BRUCE SUTTER
☐ 64. BOB FORSCH
☐ 91. LONNIE SMITH
☐ 120. OZZIE SMITH
☐ 152. KEITH HERNANDEZ
☐ 166. DAVID GREEN
☐ 190. WILLIE MCGEE
☐ 217. TOM HERR
☐ 246. KEN OBERKFELL
☐ 278. DARRELL PORTER
☐ 292. STEVE MURA
☐ 316. JOAQUIN ANDUJAR
☐ 343. JIM KAAT
☐ 372. DOUG BAIR
☐ 404. GEORGE HENDRICK
☐ 418. GLENN BRUMMER
☐ 442. GENE TENACE
☐ 469. DANE IORG
☐ 498. TITO LANDRUM
☐ 530. WHITEY HERZOG(M)
☐ 544. DAVE LAPOINT
☐ 568. MIKE RAMSEY
☐ 617. JOHN MARTIN
☐ 621. JOHN STUPER

SAN DIEGO PADRES

☐ 44. FLOYD CHIFFER
☐ 61. TIM LOLLAR
☐ 94. CHRIS WELSH
☐ 121. BRODERICK PERKINS
☐ 145. GARRY TEMPLETON
☐ 170. JOHN CURTIS
☐ 187. GARY LUCAS
☐ 220. TERRY KENNEDY
☐ 247. JOE PITTMAN
☐ 271. GENE RICHARDS
☐ 296. LUIS DELEON
☐ 313. JOHN MONTEFUSCO
☐ 346. JUAN BONILLA
☐ 373. RUPPERT JONES
☐ 397. ALAN WIGGINS
☐ 422. JUAN EICHELBERGER
☐ 439. ERIC SHOW
☐ 472. TIM FLANNERY
☐ 499. SIXTO LEZCANO
☐ 523. JOE LEFEBVRE
☐ 548. LUIS SALAZAR
☐ 565. DAVE EDWARDS
☐ 598. TONY GWYNN
☐ 625. DICK WILLIAMS(M)
☐ 633. STEVE SWISHER

SAN FRANCISCO GIANTS

- ☐ 46. ALAN FOWLKES
- ☐ 60. GARY LAVELLE
- ☐ 96. TOM O'MALLEY
- ☐ 125. JOHNNIE LEMASTER
- ☐ 146. AL HOLLAND
- ☐ 172. RICH GALE
- ☐ 186. GREG MINTON
- ☐ 222. JACK CLARK
- ☐ 251. DARRELL EVANS
- ☐ 272. RENIE MARTIN
- ☐ 298. ATLEE HAMMAKER
- ☐ 312. MILT MAY
- ☐ 348. CHARLES DAVIS
- ☐ 377. BOB BRENLY
- ☐ 398. JIM BARR
- ☐ 424. BILL LASKEY
- ☐ 438. JOE MORGAN
- ☐ 474. JEFF LEONARD
- ☐ 503. FRED BREINING
- ☐ 524. JIM WOHLFORD
- ☐ 550. DAVE BERGMAN
- ☐ 564. FRANK ROBINSON(M)
- ☐ 605. GUY SULARZ
- ☐ 611. REGGIE SMITH

SEATTLE MARINERS

- ☐ 50. FLOYD BANNISTER
- ☐ 55. GENE NELSON
- ☐ 100. ED VANDEBERG
- ☐ 127. BRUCE BOCHTE
- ☐ 176. JIM BEATTIE
- ☐ 181. LARRY ANDERSEN
- ☐ 226. TERRY BULLING
- ☐ 253. MANNY CASTILLO
- ☐ 302. BILL CAUDILL
- ☐ 307. GAYLORD PERRY
- ☐ 352. RICK SWEET
- ☐ 379. JULIO CRUZ
- ☐ 428. MIKE MOORE
- ☐ 433. MIKE STANTON
- ☐ 478. JIM ESSIAN
- ☐ 505. TODD CRUZ
- ☐ 554. AL COWENS
- ☐ 559. RICHIE ZISK
- ☐ 603. BRYAN CLARK
- ☐ 637. GARY GRAY
- ☐ 649. AL CHAMBERS

TEXAS RANGERS

- ☐ 37. JOHN BUTCHER
- ☐ 69. CHARLIE HOUGH
- ☐ 89. DAVE HOSTETLER
- ☐ 116. GEORGE WRIGHT
- ☐ 142. LAMAR JOHNSON
- ☐ 163. STEVE COMER
- ☐ 195. JON MATLACK
- ☐ 215. BUDDY BELL
- ☐ 242. BILLY SAMPLE
- ☐ 268. MARK WAGNER
- ☐ 289. DANNY DARWIN
- ☐ 321. DAVE J. SCHMIDT
- ☐ 341. JOHN GRUBB
- ☐ 368. MIKE RICHARDT
- ☐ 394. MICKEY RIVERS
- ☐ 415. RICK HONEYCUTT
- ☐ 447. FRANK TANANA
- ☐ 467. LARRY PARRISH
- ☐ 494. BOBBY JOHNSON
- ☐ 520. TERRY BOGENER
- ☐ 541. PAUL MIRABELLA
- ☐ 573. WAYNE TOLLESON
- ☐ 593. DON WERNER
- ☐ 594. BILL STEIN
- ☐ 609. JIM SUNDBERG

TORONTO BLUE JAYS

- ☐ 52. STEVE SENTENEY
- ☐ 54. DAMASO GARCIA
- ☐ 101. JIM CLANCY
- ☐ 129. LUIS LEAL
- ☐ 178. BUCK MARTINEZ
- ☐ 180. ALFREDO GRIFFIN
- ☐ 227. JERRY GARVIN
- ☐ 255. JOEY MCLAUGHLIN
- ☐ 304. ERNIE WHITT
- ☐ 306. GARTH IORG
- ☐ 353. JIM GOTT
- ☐ 381. DALE MURRAY
- ☐ 430. BARRY BONNELL
- ☐ 432. RANCE MULLINIKS
- ☐ 479. ROY LEE JACKSON
- ☐ 507. DAVE STIEB
- ☐ 556. LLOYD MOSEBY
- ☐ 558. WILLIE UPSHAW
- ☐ 595. JESSE BARFIELD
- ☐ 623. GENE PETRALLI
- ☐ 629. ANTHONY JOHNSON
- ☐ 644. HOSKEN POWELL

1984 DONRUSS (660)
2 1/2" X 3 1/2"

ATLANTA BRAVES

- ☐ 36. BRAD KOMMINSK
- ☐ 66. DALE MURPHY
- ☐ 77. BIFF POCOROBA
- ☐ 141. BRETT BUTLER
- ☐ 165. RICK CAMP
- ☐ 188. PHIL NIEKRO
- ☐ 199. KEN DAYLEY
- ☐ 263. GERALD PERRY
- ☐ 287. GENE GARBER
- ☐ 310. CLAUDELL WASHINGTON
- ☐ 321. RANDY JOHNSON
- ☐ 385. PETE FALCONE
- ☐ 409. BRUCE BENEDICT
- ☐ 432. GLENN HUBBARD
- ☐ 443. LEN BARKER
- ☐ 507. PASCUAL PEREZ
- ☐ 531. JERRY ROYSTER
- ☐ 535. BOB HORNER
- ☐ 537. CHRIS CHAMBLISS
- ☐ 565. STEVE BEDROSIAN
- ☐ 589. RAFAEL RAMIREZ*
- ☐ 599. CRAIG MCMURTRY

*RAMIREZ IS SHOWN ON THIS CARD
WITH THE A'S. HOWEVER HE WAS
NEVER WITH THE A'S ORGANIZA-
TION DURING THIS TIME PERIOD.
THEREFORE IT IS THE FEELING OF
THE AUTHORS THAT THIS CARD IS
AN ERROR AND BELONGS IN THE
ATLANTA BRAVES TEAM SET.

BALTIMORE ORIOLES

- ☐ 47. EDDIE MURRAY
- ☐ 88. JOE ALTOBELLI(M)
- ☐ 106. CAL RIPKEN
- ☐ 123. MIKE BODDICKER
- ☐ 148. TODD CRUZ
- ☐ 169. MIKE FLANAGAN
- ☐ 210. AL BUMBRY
- ☐ 228. JOHN LOWENSTEIN
- ☐ 245. TIM STODDARD
- ☐ 270. BENNY AYALA
- ☐ 291. JOHN SHELBY
- ☐ 332. ALLAN RAMIREZ
- ☐ 350. RICH DAUER
- ☐ 367. DAN FORD
- ☐ 392. GARY ROENICKE
- ☐ 413. RICK DEMPSEY

- ☐ 454. JIM DWYER
- ☐ 472. TIPPY MARTINEZ
- ☐ 489. JOE NOLAN
- ☐ 514. SAMMY STEWART
- ☐ 576. JIM PALMER
- ☐ 585. STORM DAVIS
- ☐ 594. SCOTT MCGREGOR
- ☐ 610. KEN SINGLETON
- ☐ 620. LENN SAKATA
- ☐ 621. MIKE YOUNG
- ☐ 622. JOHN STEFERO
- ☐ 633. DENNIS MARTINEZ

BOSTON RED SOX

- ☐ 50. JIM RICE
- ☐ 91. JOHN HENRY JOHNSON
- ☐ 127. ED JURAK
- ☐ 151. WADE BOGGS
- ☐ 172. JERRY REMY
- ☐ 213. BRUCE HURST
- ☐ 249. JEFF NEWMAN
- ☐ 273. DAVE STAPLETON
- ☐ 294. TONY ARMAS
- ☐ 335. GARY ALLENSON
- ☐ 371. LUIS APONTE
- ☐ 395. DWIGHT EVANS
- ☐ 416. JOHN TUDOR
- ☐ 457. DENNIS BOYD
- ☐ 493. RICK MILLER
- ☐ 517. MIKE BROWN
- ☐ 538. BOB OJEDA
- ☐ 579. RICH GEDMAN
- ☐ 606. GLENN HOFFMAN
- ☐ 611. MARK CLEAR
- ☐ 614. REID NICHOLS
- ☐ 639. DENNIS ECKERSLEY
- ☐ 644. BOB STANLEY

CALIFORNIA ANGELS

- ☐ 35. DICK SCHOFIELD
- ☐ 42. MIKE BROWN
- ☐ 57. REGGIE JACKSON
- ☐ 85. RICK ADAMS
- ☐ 108. FRED LYNN
- ☐ 133. RON JACKSON
- ☐ 158. BOB BOONE
- ☐ 179. BOBBY GRICH
- ☐ 207. JUAN BENIQUEZ
- ☐ 230. DOUG DECINCES
- ☐ 255. ANDY HASSLER
- ☐ 280. KEN FORSCH
- ☐ 301. TOMMY JOHN
- ☐ 329. ROB WILFONG
- ☐ 352. ROD CAREW
- ☐ 377. STEVE LUBRATICH
- ☐ 402. GEOFF ZAHN
- ☐ 423. BRIAN DOWNING
- ☐ 451. DARYL SCONIERS
- ☐ 474. TIM FOLI
- ☐ 499. BRUCE KISON
- ☐ 524. BOBBY CLARK
- ☐ 597. LUIS SANCHEZ
- ☐ 647. GARY PETTIS

CHICAGO CUBS

- ☐ 41. JOE CARTER
- ☐ 67. LEON DURHAM
- ☐ 76. CHUCK RAINEY
- ☐ 117. BILL BUCKNER
- ☐ 144. GARY WOODS
- ☐ 167. SCOT THOMPSON
- ☐ 189. FERGUSON JENKINS
- ☐ 198. STEVE LAKE
- ☐ 239. LARRY BOWA
- ☐ 266. DICKIE NOLES
- ☐ 289. LEE SMITH
- ☐ 311. RYNE SANDBERG
- ☐ 320. MIKE PROLY
- ☐ 361. RON CEY
- ☐ 388. CRAIG LEFFERTS
- ☐ 411. MEL HALL
- ☐ 433. JODY DAVIS
- ☐ 442. WARREN BRUSSTAR
- ☐ 483. KEITH MORELAND
- ☐ 510. DICK RUTHVEN
- ☐ 533. STEVE TROUT
- ☐ 540. JAY JOHNSTONE
- ☐ 555. BILL CAMPBELL
- ☐ 623. CARMELO MARTINEZ

CHICAGO WHITE SOX

- [ ] 27. JOEL SKINNER
- [ ] 58. HAROLD BAINES
- [ ] 86. JERRY HAIRSTON
- [ ] 122. GREG LUZINSKI
- [ ] 135. KEVIN HICKEY
- [ ] 160. JERRY DYBZINSKI
- [ ] 180. RICHARD DOTSON
- [ ] 208. JUAN AGOSTO
- [ ] 244. RON KITTLE
- [ ] 257. RUDY LAW
- [ ] 282. TOM PACIOREK
- [ ] 302. CARLTON FISK
- [ ] 330. MARC HILL
- [ ] 366. FLOYD BANNISTER
- [ ] 379. JULIO CRUZ
- [ ] 404. MIKE SQUIRES
- [ ] 424. BRITT BURNS
- [ ] 452. SCOTT FLETCHER
- [ ] 488. LAMARR HOYT
- [ ] 501. JERRY KOOSMAN
- [ ] 526. DENNIS LAMP
- [ ] 546. VANCE LAW
- [ ] 570. SALOME BAROJAS
- [ ] 609. GREG WALKER

CINCINNATI REDS

- [ ] 62. RON OESTER
- [ ] 81. TOM FOLEY
- [ ] 121. DAVE CONCEPCION
- [ ] 140. RICH GALE
- [ ] 164. FRANK PASTORE
- [ ] 184. GARY REDUS
- [ ] 203. BILL SCHERRER
- [ ] 243. DAN DRIESSEN
- [ ] 262. JEFF JONES
- [ ] 286. ALEX TREVINO
- [ ] 306. CESAR CEDENO
- [ ] 325. DUAN WALKER
- [ ] 365. EDDIE MILNER
- [ ] 384. KELLY PARIS
- [ ] 408. DANN BILARDELLO
- [ ] 428. MARIO SOTO
- [ ] 447. TED POWER
- [ ] 487. BRUCE BERENYI
- [ ] 506. JOE PRICE
- [ ] 530. CHARLIE PULEO
- [ ] 550. TOM HUME
- [ ] 569. JEFF RUSSELL
- [ ] 602. NICK ESASKY

CLEVELAND INDIANS

- [ ] 43. MIKE JEFFCOAT
- [ ] 94. ANDRE THORNTON
- [ ] 102. TOM BRENNAN
- [ ] 129. BERT BLYLEVEN
- [ ] 154. ALAN BANNISTER
- [ ] 216. JULIO FRANCO
- [ ] 224. CHRIS BANDO
- [ ] 251. TOBY HARRAH
- [ ] 276. BRODERICK PERKINS
- [ ] 338. RICH SUTCLIFFE
- [ ] 346. RICK BEHENNA
- [ ] 373. NEAL HEATON
- [ ] 398. JUAN EICHELBERGER
- [ ] 460. RON HASSEY
- [ ] 468. GEORGE VUKOVICH
- [ ] 495. MIKE HARGROVE
- [ ] 520. GERRY WILLARD
- [ ] 536. PAT TABLER
- [ ] 542. BROOK JACOBY
- [ ] 574. GORMAN THOMAS
- [ ] 582. DAN SPILLNER
- [ ] 590. BUD ANDERSON
- [ ] 608. RICHARD BARNES
- [ ] 629. JIM ESSIAN
- [ ] 635. LARY SORENSEN

DETROIT TIGERS

- [ ] 49. LANCE PARRISH
- [ ] 90. JOHN GRUBB
- [ ] 105. DAN PETRY
- [ ] 125. JUAN BERENGUER
- [ ] 150. JOHN WOCKENFUSS
- [ ] 171. CHET LEMON
- [ ] 212. HOWARD BAILEY

- [ ] 227. LOU WHITAKER
- [ ] 247. MARTY CASTILLO
- [ ] 272. DAVE ROZEMA
- [ ] 293. ALAN TRAMMELL
- [ ] 334. WAYNE KRENCHICKI
- [ ] 349. LARRY HERNDON
- [ ] 369. DOUG BAIR
- [ ] 394. LARRY PASHNICK
- [ ] 415. JACK MORRIS
- [ ] 456. ENOS CABELL
- [ ] 471. MILT WILCOX
- [ ] 491. MIKE LAGA
- [ ] 516. AURELIO LOPEZ
- [ ] 578. TOM BROOKENS
- [ ] 593. KIRK GIBSON
- [ ] 618. GLENN WILSON

HOUSTON ASTROS

- [ ] 60. NOLAN RYAN
- [ ] 84. BOB LILLIS(M)
- [ ] 110. JOE NIEKRO
- [ ] 136. MIKE SCOTT
- [ ] 161. MIKE MADDEN
- [ ] 182. JOSE CRUZ
- [ ] 206. MIKE LACOSS
- [ ] 232. RAY KNIGHT
- [ ] 258. HARRY SPILMAN
- [ ] 283. FRANK LACORTE
- [ ] 304. DICKIE THON
- [ ] 328. BILL DAWLEY
- [ ] 354. PHIL GARNER
- [ ] 380. JOHN MIZEROCK
- [ ] 405. CRAIG REYNOLDS
- [ ] 426. JERRY MUMPHREY
- [ ] 450. KEVIN BASS
- [ ] 476. TERRY PUHL
- [ ] 502. FRANK DIPINO
- [ ] 527. TONY SCOTT
- [ ] 539. ALAN ASHBY
- [ ] 548. DAVE SMITH
- [ ] 564. VERN RUHLE
- [ ] 572. BOB KNEPPER
- [ ] 580. BILL DORAN
- [ ] 641. DENNY WALLING

KANSAS CITY ROYALS

- [ ] 53. GEORGE BRETT
- [ ] 95. ONIX CONCEPCION
- [ ] 100. LARRY GURA
- [ ] 130. BUD BLACK
- [ ] 155. WILLIE AIKENS
- [ ] 175. WILLIE WILSON
- [ ] 217. MIKE ARMSTRONG
- [ ] 222. FRANK WHITE
- [ ] 252. CESAR GERONIMO
- [ ] 277. BUTCH DAVIS
- [ ] 297. HAL MCRAE
- [ ] 339. MARK HUISMANN
- [ ] 344. DARRYL MOTLEY
- [ ] 374. GREG PRYOR
- [ ] 399. LEON ROBERTS
- [ ] 419. DON SLAUGHT
- [ ] 461. DANNY JACKSON
- [ ] 466. JOHN WATHAN
- [ ] 496. JOE SIMPSON
- [ ] 521. PAUL SPLITTORFF
- [ ] 543. U.L. WASHINGTON
- [ ] 583. DAN QUISENBERRY
- [ ] 588. PAT SHERIDAN

LOS ANGELES DODGERS

- [ ] 44. SID FERNANDEZ
- [ ] 52. FERNANDO VALENZUELA
- [ ] 93. CANDY MALDONADO
- [ ] 104. STEVE SAX
- [ ] 128. TOM NIENDENFUER
- [ ] 153. BOB WELCH
- [ ] 174. PEDRO GUERRERO
- [ ] 215. PAT ZACHRY
- [ ] 226. DUSTY BAKER
- [ ] 250. ALEJANDRO PENA
- [ ] 275. JOSE MORALES
- [ ] 296. GREG BROCK
- [ ] 337. JOE BECKWITH
- [ ] 348. MIKE MARSHALL
- [ ] 372. JACK FIMPLE
- [ ] 397. DERREL THOMAS

- [ ] 418. JERRY REUSS
- [ ] 459. BURT HOOTON
- [ ] 470. KEN LANDREAUX
- [ ] 494. RICK HONEYCUTT
- [ ] 519. DAVE SAX
- [ ] 581. STEVE YEAGER
- [ ] 587. BILL RUSSELL
- [ ] 642. DAVE ANDERSON

MILWAUKEE BREWERS

- [ ] 31. DION JAMES
- [ ] 48. ROBIN YOUNT
- [ ] 89. ED ROMERO
- [ ] 107. PAUL MOLITOR
- [ ] 115. JIM GANTNER
- [ ] 124. PETE LADD
- [ ] 149. TOM TELLMANN
- [ ] 170. RICK MANNING
- [ ] 211. MARK BROUHARD
- [ ] 229. BEN OGLIVIE
- [ ] 237. MIKE CALDWELL
- [ ] 246. BOB GIBSON
- [ ] 271. NED YOST
- [ ] 292. CHARLIE MOORE
- [ ] 333. CHUCK PORTER
- [ ] 351. CECIL COOPER
- [ ] 359. BOB MCCLURE
- [ ] 368. MOOSE HAAS
- [ ] 393. TOM CANDIOTTI
- [ ] 414. DON SUTTON
- [ ] 455. ROB PICCIOLO
- [ ] 473. TED SIMMONS
- [ ] 481. JIM SLATON
- [ ] 490. MARSHALL EDWARDS
- [ ] 515. BILL SCHROEDER

RON DAVIS P

MINNESOTA TWINS

- [ ] 37. TIM TEUFEL
- [ ] 39. GREG GAGNE
- [ ] 70. KENT HRBEK
- [ ] 72. KEN SCHROM
- [ ] 120. JOHN CASTINO
- [ ] 147. MICKEY HATCHER
- [ ] 192. GARY WARD
- [ ] 194. PETE FILSON
- [ ] 242. TOM BRUNANSKY
- [ ] 269. RON DAVIS
- [ ] 314. GARY GAETTI
- [ ] 316. AL WILLIAMS
- [ ] 364. FRANK VIOLA
- [ ] 391. RON WASHINGTON
- [ ] 436. BOBBY CASTILLO
- [ ] 438. SCOTT ULLGER
- [ ] 486. BRYAN OELKERS
- [ ] 513. RANDY BUSH
- [ ] 558. LEN WHITEHOUSE
- [ ] 560. RICK LYSANDER
- [ ] 598. DAVE ENGLE

MONTREAL EXPOS

- [ ] 29. MIKE STENHOUSE
- [ ] 33. ANGEL SALAZAR
- [ ] 40. MIKE FUENTES
- [ ] 55. GARY CARTER
- [ ] 87. BOB JAMES
- [ ] 97. ANDRE DAWSON
- [ ] 132. DAN SCHATZEDER

1984 Donruss

☐ 157. BRYAN LITTLE
☐ 177. AL OLIVER
☐ 209. BOBBY RAMOS
☐ 219. STEVE ROGERS
☐ 254. DOUG FLYNN
☐ 279. JEFF REARDON
☐ 299. TIM RAINES
☐ 331. RAY BURRIS
☐ 341. SCOTT SANDERSON
☐ 376. CHARLIE LEA
☐ 401. BILL GULLICKSON
☐ 421. TIM WALLACH
☐ 453. BRYN SMITH
☐ 463. TERRY FRANCONA
☐ 498. CHRIS WELSH
☐ 523. CHRIS SPEIER
☐ 575. MANNY TRILLO

NEW YORK METS

☐ 30. RON DARLING
☐ 68. DARRYL STRAWBERRY
☐ 75. ED LYNCH
☐ 116. TOM SEAVER
☐ 190. MOOKIE WILSON
☐ 197. JESSE OROSCO
☐ 238. KEITH HERNANDEZ
☐ 312. GEORGE FOSTER
☐ 319. JUNIOR ORTIZ
☐ 360. DAVE KINGMAN
☐ 434. DANNY HEEP
☐ 441. CRAIG SWAN
☐ 482. MIKE FITZGERALD
☐ 554. RUSTY STAUB
☐ 556. MIKE TORREZ
☐ 563. BRIAN GILES
☐ 595. BOB BAILOR
☐ 600. CARLOS DIAZ
☐ 603. RON HODGES
☐ 607. HUBIE BROOKS
☐ 615. DOUG SISK
☐ 640. WALT TERRELL
☐ 643. JOSE OQUENDO

NEW YORK YANKEES

☐ 45. BRIAN DAYETT
☐ 51. DAVE WINFIELD
☐ 92. JUAN ESPINO
☐ 103. DAVE RIGHETTI
☐ 126. JOHN MONTEFUSCO
☐ 152. DON BAYLOR
☐ 173. RON GUIDRY
☐ 214. BOB SHIRLEY
☐ 225. ROY SMALLEY
☐ 248. DON MATTINGLY
☐ 274. LOU PINIELLA
☐ 295. SHANE RAWLEY
☐ 336. BOB MEACHAM
☐ 347. ANDRE ROBERTSON
☐ 370. RAY FONTENOT
☐ 396. RICH GOSSAGE
☐ 417. WILLIE RANDOLPH
☐ 458. BUTCH WYNEGAR
☐ 469. STEVE KEMP
☐ 492. RICK CERONE
☐ 518. GRAIG NETTLES
☐ 577. DALE MURRAY
☐ 591. GEORGE FRAZIER
☐ 613. KEN GRIFFEY
☐ 626. RUDY MAY
☐ 627. MATT KEOUGH
☐ 637. OMAR MORENO

OAKLAND A'S

☐ 54. RICKEY HENDERSON
☐ 96. DON HILL
☐ 101. DWAYNE MURPHY
☐ 131. GORMAN HEIMUELLER
☐ 156. JEFF BURROUGHS
☐ 176. CARNEY LANSFORD
☐ 218. DAVE BEARD
☐ 223. MIKE HEATH
☐ 253. TOM UNDERWOOD
☐ 278. TONY PHILLIPS
☐ 298. MIKE DAVIS
☐ 340. TIM CONROY
☐ 345. CHRIS CODIROLI
☐ 375. WAYNE GROSS
☐ 400. DAVEY LOPES

☐ 420. STEVE MCCATTY
☐ 462. BOB KEARNEY
☐ 467. BILL ALMON
☐ 497. KEITH ATHERTON
☐ 522. TOM BURGMEIER
☐ 631. MIKE WARREN

PHILADELPHIA PHILLIES

☐ 61. PETE ROSE
☐ 82. JOE LEFEBVRE
☐ 111. STEVE CARLTON
☐ 137. BO DIAZ
☐ 163. WILLIE HERNANDEZ
☐ 183. MIKE SCHMIDT
☐ 204. AL HOLLAND
☐ 233. GARY MATTHEWS
☐ 259. MARTY BYSTROM
☐ 285. GREG GROSS
☐ 305. GARRY MADDOX
☐ 326. OZZIE VIRGIL
☐ 355. JOE MORGAN
☐ 381. KEVIN GROSS
☐ 407. JOHN DENNY
☐ 427. IVAN DEJESUS
☐ 448. CHARLIE HUDSON
☐ 477. VON HAYES
☐ 503. TONY PEREZ
☐ 529. RON REED
☐ 541. BOB DERNIER
☐ 545. KIKO GARCIA
☐ 547. TUG MCGRAW
☐ 549. LEN MATUSZEK

PITTSBURGH PIRATES

☐ 38. DOUG FROBEL
☐ 64. JASON THOMPSON
☐ 78. CECILIO GUANTE
☐ 113. BILL MADLOCK
☐ 142. BRIAN HARPER
☐ 166. LEE MAZZILLI
☐ 186. TONY PENA
☐ 200. MANNY SARMIENTO
☐ 235. ROD SCURRY
☐ 264. GENE TENACE
☐ 288. DAVE PARKER
☐ 308. JOHNNY RAY
☐ 322. JIM MORRISON
☐ 357. JOHN CANDELARIA
☐ 386. MILT MAY
☐ 410. KENT TEKULVE
☐ 430. DALE BERRA
☐ 444. MIKE EASLER
☐ 479. LEE LACY
☐ 508. MARVELL WYNNE
☐ 532. DON ROBINSON
☐ 552. RICK RHODEN
☐ 566. LARRY MCWILLIAMS
☐ 592. LEE TUNNELL
☐ 628. JOSE DELEON

ST. LOUIS CARDINALS

☐ 59. OZZIE SMITH
☐ 83. ANDY VAN SLYKE
☐ 109. NEIL ALLEN
☐ 138. GLENN BRUMMER
☐ 168. BOB FORSCH
☐ 181. JOAQUIN ANDUJAR
☐ 205. DAVID VON OHLEN
☐ 231. LONNIE SMITH
☐ 260. DAVE RUCKER
☐ 290. DAVE LAPOINT
☐ 303. DARRELL PORTER
☐ 327. JEFF LAHTI
☐ 353. WILLIE MCGEE
☐ 382. MIKE RAMSEY
☐ 412. JOHN STUPER
☐ 425. DAVID GREEN
☐ 449. DANNY COX
☐ 475. GEORGE HENDRICK
☐ 504. KEN OBERKFELL
☐ 534. BRUCE SUTTER
☐ 571. DANE IORG
☐ 596. TOM HERR

GARRY TEMPLETON SS

SAN DIEGO PADRES

☐ 34. KEVIN MCREYNOLDS
☐ 63. STEVE GARVEY
☐ 80. KURT BEVACQUA
☐ 112. TERRY KENNEDY
☐ 139. SID MONGE
☐ 162. LUIS DELEON
☐ 185. GARRY TEMPLETON
☐ 202. TIM FLANNERY
☐ 234. JUAN BONILLA
☐ 261. RUPPERT JONES
☐ 284. TIM LOLLAR
☐ 307. GARY LUCAS
☐ 324. TONY GWYNN
☐ 356. LUIS SALAZAR
☐ 383. DOUG GWOSDZ
☐ 406. ERIC SHOW
☐ 429. GENE RICHARDS
☐ 446. DENNIS RASMUSSEN
☐ 478. BOBBY BROWN
☐ 505. MARK THURMOND
☐ 528. ED WHITSON
☐ 551. DAVE DRAVECKY
☐ 568. ALAN WIGGINS

SAN FRANCISCO GIANTS

☐ 46. CHRIS SMITH
☐ 65. JACK CLARK
☐ 79. JIM BARR
☐ 114. CHILI DAVIS
☐ 143. JOHN RABB
☐ 187. GREG MINTON
☐ 201. MARK DAVIS
☐ 236. ATLEE HAMMAKER
☐ 265. BRAD WELLMAN
☐ 309. ANDY MCGAFFIGAN
☐ 323. MAX VENABLE
☐ 358. BILL LASKEY
☐ 387. FRED BREINING
☐ 431. DARRELL EVANS
☐ 445. RENIE MARTIN
☐ 480. JOEL YOUNGBLOOD
☐ 509. MIKE KRUKOW
☐ 553. DUAN KUIPER
☐ 567. JEFF LEONARD
☐ 573. GARY LAVELLE
☐ 601. TOM O'MALLEY
☐ 616. BOB BRENLY
☐ 624. DAVE BERGMAN
☐ 646. SCOTT GARRELTS
☐ 649. JOHNNIE LEMASTER

SEATTLE MARINERS

☐ 69. RICHIE ZISK
☐ 74. JOHN MOSES
☐ 118. BILL CAUDILL
☐ 145. PAT PUTNAM
☐ 191. JIM BEATTIE
☐ 196. RICK SWEET
☐ 240. TONY BERNAZARD
☐ 267. JAMIE ALLEN
☐ 313. SPIKE OWEN
☐ 318. ORLANDO MERCADO
☐ 362. MATT YOUNG
☐ 389. STEVE HENDERSON
☐ 435. EDWIN NUNEZ

☐ 440. DOMINGO RAMOS
☐ 484. RON ROENICKE
☐ 511. AL COWENS
☐ 557. DAVE HENDERSON
☐ 562. BRYAN CLARK
☐ 604. ED VANDE BERG
☐ 619. BOB STODDARD
☐ 630. DARNELL COLES
☐ 632. DEL CRANDALL(M)
☐ 634. MIKE MOORE
☐ 636. RICKY NELSON

TEXAS RANGERS

☐ 28. TOM DUNBAR
☐ 56. BUDDY BELL
☐ 98. FRANK TANANA
☐ 99. CURT WILKERSON
☐ 134. TOM HENKE
☐ 159. DAVE HOSTETLER
☐ 178. JIM SUNDBERG
☐ 220. JOHN BUTCHER
☐ 221. MIKE SMITHSON
☐ 256. ODELL JONES
☐ 281. PETE O'BRIEN
☐ 300. BUCKY DENT
☐ 342. LARRY BITTNER
☐ 343. DAVE STEWART
☐ 378. JON MATLACK
☐ 403. BILLY SAMPLE
☐ 422. LARRY PARRISH
☐ 464. WAYNE TOLLESON
☐ 465. MICKEY RIVERS
☐ 500. BOB JOHNSON
☐ 525. GEORGE WRIGHT
☐ 544. DANNY DARWIN
☐ 586. DAVE SCHMIDT
☐ 638. CHARLIE HOUGH

TORONTO BLUE JAYS

☐ 32. TONY FERNANDEZ
☐ 71. DAVE STIEB
☐ 73. GEORGE BELL
☐ 119. JIM CLANCY
☐ 146. JIM ACKER
☐ 193. JESSE BARFIELD
☐ 195. ROY LEE JACKSON
☐ 241. DAMASO GARCIA
☐ 268. JIM GOTT
☐ 315. WILLIE UPSHAW
☐ 317. JORGE ORTA
☐ 363. LLOYD MOSEBY
☐ 390. RANDY MOFFITT
☐ 437. ERNIE WHITT
☐ 439. DOYLE ALEXANDER
☐ 485. LUIS LEAL
☐ 512. CLIFF JOHNSON
☐ 559. BARRY BONNELL
☐ 561. GARTH IORG
☐ 584. RANCE MULLINIKS
☐ 605. ALFREDO GRIFFIN
☐ 612. BUCK MARTINEZ
☐ 617. JOEY MCLAUGHLIN
☐ 645. DAVE GEISEL
☐ 650. DAVE COLLINS

1985 DONRUSS (660)
2 1/2" X 3 1/2"

DAN QUISENBERRY P.

ATLANTA BRAVES

☐ 66. DALE MURPHY
☐ 77. BOB HORNER
☐ 141. RAFAEL RAMIREZ
☐ 165. LEN BARKER
☐ 188. CRAIG MCMURTRY
☐ 199. GLENN HUBBARD
☐ 263. BRUCE BENEDICT
☐ 287. CHRIS CHAMBLISS
☐ 310. CLAUDELL WASHINGTON
☐ 321. BRAD KOMMINSK
☐ 385. RICK MAHLER
☐ 409. RICK CAMP
☐ 432. KEN OBERKFELL
☐ 443. GERALD PERRY
☐ 507. PASCUAL PEREZ
☐ 531. RANDY JOHNSON
☐ 554. JEFF DEDMON
☐ 565. ALEX TREVINO
☐ 628. STEVE BEDROSIAN
☐ 650. DONNIE MOORE

BALTIMORE ORIOLES

☐ 36. LARRY SHEETS
☐ 45. JIM TRABER
☐ 47. EDDIE MURRAY
☐ 88. MIKE FLANAGAN
☐ 106. RICH DAUER
☐ 123. GARY ROENICKE
☐ 148. SAMMY STEWART
☐ 169. CAL RIPKEN
☐ 210. TIPPY MARTINEZ
☐ 228. WAYNE GROSS
☐ 245. JOHN LOWENSTEIN
☐ 270. KEN DIXON
☐ 291. MIKE BODDICKER
☐ 332. RICK DEMPSEY
☐ 350. AL BUMBRY
☐ 367. MIKE YOUNG
☐ 392. BILL SWAGGERTY
☐ 413. SCOTT MCGREGOR
☐ 454. STORM DAVIS
☐ 472. JOHN SHELBY
☐ 489. DAN FORD
☐ 514. DENNIS MARTINEZ
☐ 535. VIC RODRIGUEZ
☐ 576. FLOYD RAYFORD
☐ 594. JOE NOLAN

BOSTON RED SOX

☐ 29. STEVE LYONS
☐ 40. CHARLIE MITCHELL
☐ 50. JIM RICE
☐ 91. BOB STANLEY
☐ 127. MARTY BARRETT
☐ 151. DENNIS BOYD
☐ 172. WADE BOGGS
☐ 213. MIKE EASLER
☐ 249. TONY ARMAS
☐ 273. ROGER CLEMENS
☐ 294. DWIGHT EVANS
☐ 335. JACKIE GUTIERREZ
☐ 371. BOB OJEDA

☐ 395. STEVE CRAWFORD
☐ 416. BILL BUCKNER
☐ 457. RICH GEDMAN
☐ 493. BRUCE HURST
☐ 517. RICK MILLER
☐ 538. MARK CLEAR
☐ 579. ED JURAK
☐ 614. AL NIPPER
☐ 636. REID NICHOLS

CALIFORNIA ANGELS

☐ 57. REGGIE JACKSON
☐ 85. ROD CAREW
☐ 108. MIKE WITT
☐ 133. FRED LYNN
☐ 158. BRIAN DOWNING
☐ 179. DOUG DECINCES
☐ 207. MIKE BROWN
☐ 230. BOB BOONE
☐ 255. DON AASE
☐ 280. BOBBY GRICH
☐ 301. GEOFF ZAHN
☐ 329. DICK SCHOFIELD
☐ 352. LUIS SANCHEZ
☐ 377. BRUCE KISON
☐ 402. ROB WILFONG
☐ 423. TOMMY JOHN
☐ 451. RON ROMANICK
☐ 474. DOUG CORBETT
☐ 499. GARY PETTIS
☐ 524. CURT KAUFMAN
☐ 545. JIM SLATON
☐ 573. JUAN BENIQUEZ
☐ 620. DARYL SCONIERS
☐ 643. JERRY NARRON
☐ 644. DARRELL MILLER

CHICAGO CUBS

☐ 39. SHAWON DUNSTON
☐ 41. BILLY HATCHER
☐ 67. RYNE SANDBERG
☐ 76. JODY DAVIS
☐ 117. KEITH MORELAND
☐ 144. TIM STODDARD
☐ 167. GEORGE FRAZIER
☐ 189. LEON DURHAM
☐ 198. STEVE TROUT
☐ 239. GARY MATTHEWS
☐ 266. SCOTT SANDERSON
☐ 289. RICH BORDI
☐ 311. LEE SMITH
☐ 320. RON CEY
☐ 361. LARRY BOWA
☐ 388. THAD BOSLEY
☐ 411. HENRY COTTO
☐ 433. RICK SUTCLIFFE
☐ 442. DENNIS ECKERSLEY
☐ 483. DAVE OWEN
☐ 510. BOB DERNIER
☐ 533. WARREN BRUSSTAR
☐ 555. GARY WOODS
☐ 564. RICH HEBNER
☐ 604. DAVE LOPES

CHICAGO WHITE SOX

☐ 33. DARYL BOSTON
☐ 58. HAROLD BAINES
☐ 86. LAMARR HOTY
☐ 122. VANCE LAW
☐ 135. JERRY HAIRSTON
☐ 160. MARC HILL
☐ 180. RON KITTLE
☐ 208. CARLTON FISK
☐ 244. RUDY LAW
☐ 257. BRITT BURNS
☐ 282. RON REED
☐ 302. RICH DOTSON
☐ 330. SCOTT FLETCHER
☐ 366. GREG WALKER
☐ 379. FLOYD BANNISTER
☐ 404. AL JONES
☐ 424. TOM SEAVER
☐ 452. JULIO CRUZ
☐ 488. TOM PACIOREK
☐ 501. MIKE SQUIRES
☐ 526. JUAN AGOSTO
☐ 546. GREG LUZINSKI
☐ 574. JOEL SKINNER

☐ 615. GENE NELSON
☐ 622. ROY SMALLEY
☐ 645. TIM HULETT

CINCINNATI REDS

☐ 62. DAVE PARKER
☐ 81. RON OESTER
☐ 121. NICK ESASKY
☐ 140. WAYNE KRENCHICKI
☐ 164. JOHN FRANCO
☐ 184. MARIO SOTO
☐ 203. DAVE CONCEPCION
☐ 243. DANN BILARDELLO
☐ 262. JAY TIBBS
☐ 286. TED POWER
☐ 306. GARY REDUS
☐ 325. ERIC DAVIS
☐ 365. BRAD GULDEN
☐ 384. DAVE VAN GORDER
☐ 408. TOM HUME
☐ 428. EDDIE MILNER
☐ 447. CESAR CEDENO
☐ 487. JEFF RUSSELL
☐ 506. BOB OWCHINKO
☐ 530. SKEETER BARNES
☐ 550. FRANK PASTORE
☐ 569. TOM FOLEY
☐ 608. DUANE WALKER
☐ 627. JOE PRICE
☐ 634. TOM BROWNING
☐ 641. PERE ROSS(M)
☐ 642. WADE ROWDON
☐ 646. ANDY MCGAFFIGAN
☐ 649. RON ROBINSON

CLEVELAND INDIANS

☐ 94. JULIO FRANCO
☐ 102. TONY BERNAZARD
☐ 129. ERNIE CAMACHO
☐ 154. BROOK JACOBY
☐ 216. BRETT BUTLER
☐ 224. BERT BLYLEVEN
☐ 251. MIKE JEFFCOAT
☐ 276. GEORGE VUKOVICH
☐ 338. MEL HALL
☐ 346. JERRY WILLARD
☐ 373. NEAL HEATON
☐ 398. MIKE HARGROVE
☐ 460. PAT TABLER
☐ 468. ANDRE THORNTON
☐ 495. MIKE FISCHLIN
☐ 520. CHRIS BANDO
☐ 582. TOM WADDELL
☐ 590. CARMEN CASTILLO
☐ 611. ROY SMITH
☐ 616. JOE CARTER
☐ 639. DON SCHULZE
☐ 653. STEVE FARR

JULIO FRANCO SS

DETROIT TIGERS

☐ 49. LANCE PARRISH
☐ 90. CHET LEMON
☐ 105. MILT WILCOX
☐ 125. DAVE ROZEMA
☐ 150. LARRY HERNDON
☐ 171. ALAN TRAMMELL
☐ 212. WILLIE HERNANDEZ

☐ 227. DARRELL EVANS
☐ 247. HOWARD JOHNSON
☐ 272. JUAN BERENGUER
☐ 293. LOU WHITAKER
☐ 334. DAN PETRY
☐ 349. AURELIO LOPEZ
☐ 369. DOUG BAIR
☐ 394. MARTY CASTILLO
☐ 415. JACK MORRIS
☐ 456. BARBARO GARBEY
☐ 471. KIRK GIBSON
☐ 491. SCOTTIE EARL
☐ 516. RUSTY KUNTZ
☐ 537. DAVE BERGMAN
☐ 578. JOHN GRUBB
☐ 593. TOM BROOKENS
☐ 612. RUPPERT JONES

HOUSTON ASTROS

☐ 60. NOLAN RYAN
☐ 84. BILL DORAN
☐ 110. ENOS CABELL
☐ 136. KEVIN BASS
☐ 161. PHIL GARNER
☐ 182. JOE NIEKRO
☐ 260. JERRY MUMPHREY
☐ 232. FRANK DIPINO
☐ 258. MIKE SCOTT
☐ 283. ALAN ASHBY
☐ 304. JOSE CRUZ
☐ 328. CRAIG REYNOLDS
☐ 354. BILL DAWLEY
☐ 380. VERN RUHLE
☐ 405. MIKE LACOSS
☐ 426. TERRY PUHL
☐ 450. MARK BAILEY
☐ 476. BOB KNEPPER
☐ 502. JIM PANKOVITZ
☐ 527. DENNY WALLING
☐ 548. DAVE SMITH
☐ 572. JOE SAMBITO

KANSAS CITY ROYALS

☐ 32. JOHN MORRIS
☐ 42. RUSS STEPHANS
☐ 53. GEORGE BRETT
☐ 95. DAN QUISENBERRY
☐ 100. BUD BLACK
☐ 130. JORGE ORTA
☐ 155. ONIX CONCEPCION
☐ 175. FRANK WHITE
☐ 217. LARRY GURA
☐ 222. BRET SABERHAGEN
☐ 252. DANE IORG
☐ 277. GREG PRYOR
☐ 297. WILLIE WILSON
☐ 339. PAT SHERIDAN
☐ 344. MARK GUBICZA
☐ 374. DANNY JACKSON
☐ 399. CHARLIE LEIBRANDT
☐ 419. STEVE BALBONI
☐ 461. DARRYL MOTLEY
☐ 466. JOHN WATHAN
☐ 496. DON SLAUGHT
☐ 521. U.L. WASHINGTON
☐ 541. JOE BECKWITH
☐ 583. MARK HUISMANN
☐ 588. HAL MCRAE
☐ 640. MIKE JONES

LOS ANGELES DODGERS

☐ 31. TONY BREWER
☐ 52. FERNANDO VALENZUELA
☐ 93. BILL RUSSELL
☐ 104. BURT HOOTON
☐ 128. R.J. REYNOLDS
☐ 153. TOM NIEDENFUER
☐ 174. PEDRO GUERRERO
☐ 215. RICK HONEYCUTT
☐ 226. JERRY REUSS
☐ 250. CANDY MALDONADO
☐ 275. DAVE ANDERSON
☐ 296. MIKE MARSHALL
☐ 337. ALEJANDRO PENA
☐ 348. FRANKLIN STUBBS
☐ 372. BOB WELCH
☐ 397. BOB BAILOR

☐ 418. STEVE SAX
☐ 459. MIKE SCIOSCIA
☐ 470. SID BREAM
☐ 494. KEN LANDREAUX
☐ 519. STEVE YEAGER
☐ 540. TERRY WHITFIELD
☐ 581. OREL HERSHISER
☐ 592. KEN HOWELL
☐ 638. GERMAN RIVERA

ALEJANDRO PENA P

MILWAUKEE BREWERS

☐ 46. DOUG LOMAN
☐ 48. ROBIN YOUNT
☐ 89. JIM SUNDBERG
☐ 107. DON SUTTON
☐ 115. CHUCK PORTER
☐ 124. BILL SCHROEDER
☐ 149. MARK BROUHARD
☐ 170. CECIL COOPER
☐ 211. DION JAMES
☐ 229. JIM GANTNER
☐ 237. RICK MANNING
☐ 246. TOM TELLMANN
☐ 271. PETE LADD
☐ 292. ROLLIE FINGERS
☐ 333. BEN OGLIVIE
☐ 351. CHARLIE MOORE
☐ 359. PAUL MOLITOR
☐ 368. RICK WAITS
☐ 393. BOB GIBSON
☐ 414. TED SIMMONS
☐ 455. JAIME COCANOWER
☐ 473. MOOSE HAAS
☐ 481. BOBBY CLARK
☐ 490. MIKE CALDWELL
☐ 515. ED ROMERO
☐ 536. BOB MCCLURE
☐ 577. ROY HOWELL
☐ 595. WILLIE LOZADO

MINNESOTA TWINS

☐ 30. JEFF REED
☐ 70. KENT HRBEK
☐ 72. DAVE ENGLE
☐ 120. RON DAVIS
☐ 147. DAVE MEIER
☐ 192. TIM TEUFEL
☐ 194. MICKEY HATCHER
☐ 242. GARY GAETTI
☐ 269. HOUSTON JIMENEZ
☐ 314. JOHN BUTCHER
☐ 316. MIKE SMITHSON
☐ 364. TOM BRUNANSKY
☐ 391. RON WASHINGTON
☐ 436. FRANK VIOLA
☐ 438. KIRBY PUCKETT
☐ 486. KEN SCHROM
☐ 513. LEN WHITEHOUSE
☐ 558. DARRELL BROWN
☐ 560. RICK LYSANDER
☐ 607. PETE FILSON
☐ 633. RANDY BUSH
☐ 652. TIM LAUDNER

MONTREAL EXPOS

☐ 55. GARY CARTER
☐ 87. TIM WALLACH
☐ 97. BILL GULLICKSON

☐ 132. TERRY FRANCONA
☐ 157. JOE HESKETH
☐ 177. CHARLIE LEA
☐ 209. BRYN SMITH
☐ 219. STEVE ROGERS
☐ 254. PETE ROSE
☐ 279. BOB JAMES
☐ 299. TIM RAINES
☐ 331. JEFF REARDON
☐ 341. DAVID PALMER
☐ 376. MIKE STENHOUSE
☐ 401. RAZOR SHINES
☐ 421. ANDRE DAWSON
☐ 453. MIGUEL DILONE
☐ 463. DOUG FLYNN
☐ 498. GARY LUCAS
☐ 523. ANGEL SALAZAR
☐ 543. DAN SCHATZEDER
☐ 575. RANDY ST. CLAIRE
☐ 585. JIM WOHLFORD
☐ 619. DAN DRIESSEN

NEW YORK METS

☐ 38. CALVIN SCHIRALDI
☐ 68. KEITH HERNANDEZ
☐ 75. JESSE OROSCO
☐ 116. JOHN GIBBONS
☐ 190. DWIGHT GOODEN
☐ 197. HUBIE BROOKS
☐ 238. MIKE FITZGERALD
☐ 312. DARRYL STRAWBERRY
☐ 319. WALLY BACKMAN
☐ 360. RON GARDENHIRE
☐ 434. RON DARLING
☐ 441. DOUG SISK
☐ 482. MOOKIE WILSON
☐ 556. DANNY HEEP
☐ 563. SID FERNANDEZ
☐ 597. WALT TERRELL
☐ 603. GEORGE FOSTER
☐ 610. RAFAEL SANTANA
☐ 617. RAY KNIGHT
☐ 623. ED LYNCH
☐ 625. BRUCE BERENYI
☐ 626. KELVIN CHAPMAN

NEW YORK YANKEES

☐ 37. SCOTT BRADLEY
☐ 51. DAVE WINFIELD
☐ 92. WILLIE RANDOLPH
☐ 103. JAY HOWELL
☐ 126. BOBBY MEACHAM
☐ 152. BRIAN DAYETT
☐ 173. DON BAYLOR
☐ 214. RON GUIDRY
☐ 225. STEVE KEMP
☐ 248. RAY FONTENOT
☐ 274. RICK CERONE
☐ 295. DON MATTINGLY
☐ 336. DAVE RIGHETTI
☐ 347. KEN GRIFFEY
☐ 370. BOB SHIRLEY
☐ 396. CLAY CHRISTIANSEN
☐ 417. BUTCH WYNEGAR
☐ 458. PHIL NIEKRO
☐ 469. REX HUDLER
☐ 492. JOSE RIJO
☐ 518. DENNIS RASMUSSEN
☐ 539. MIKE PAGLIARULO
☐ 580. JOHN MONTEFUSCO
☐ 591. OMAR MORENO
☐ 602. MIKE ARMSTRONG
☐ 613. JOE COWLEY
☐ 629. VIC MATA
☐ 637. DAN PASQUA

OAKLAND A'S

☐ 35. STEVE KIEFER
☐ 54. DAVE KINGMAN
☐ 96. BILL CAUDILL
☐ 101. TONY PHILLIPS
☐ 131. LARY SORENSEN
☐ 156. TIM CONROY
☐ 176. RICKEY HENDERSON
☐ 218. RAY BURRIS
☐ 223. MIKE DAVIS
☐ 253. BRUCE BOCHTE
☐ 278. MIKE WARREN
☐ 298. MIKE HEATH

☐ 340. KEITH ATHERTON
☐ 345. CARNEY LANSFORD
☐ 375. DONNIE HILL
☐ 400. TOM BURGMEIER
☐ 420. DWAYNE MURPHY
☐ 462. CHRIS CODOROLI
☐ 467. BILL KRUEGER
☐ 497. STEVE MCCATTY
☐ 522. CURT YOUNG
☐ 542. JEFF BURROUGHS
☐ 584. JOE MORGAN
☐ 589. BILL ALMON
☐ 618. CHUCK RAINEY

PHILADLEPHIA PHILLIES

☐ 44. STEVE JELTZ
☐ 61. MIKE SCHMIDT
☐ 82. OZZIE VIRGIL
☐ 111. JOHN DENNY
☐ 137. GARRY MADDOX
☐ 163. BILL CAMPBELL
☐ 183. JUAN SAMUEL
☐ 204. IVAN DEJESUS
☐ 233. JERRY KOOSMAN
☐ 259. LEN MATUSZEK
☐ 285. JOE LEFEBVRE
☐ 305. STEVE CARLTON
☐ 326. VON HAYES
☐ 355. CHARLIE HUDSON
☐ 381. TIM CORCORAN
☐ 407. GREG GROSS
☐ 427. AL HOLLAND
☐ 448. RICK SCHU
☐ 477. KEVIN GROSS
☐ 503. LUIS AGUAYO
☐ 529. SIXTO LEZCANO
☐ 549. JOHN WOCKENFUSS
☐ 570. LARRY ANDERSEN
☐ 598. AL OLIVER
☐ 599. SHANE RAWLEY
☐ 609. GLENN WILSON
☐ 624. JEFF STONE
☐ 648. JOHN RUSSELL

PITTSBURGH PIRATES

☐ 28. MIKE BIELECKI
☐ 34. ALFONSO PULIDO
☐ 64. TONY PENA
☐ 78. LARRY MCWILLIAMS
☐ 113. MARVELL WYNNE
☐ 142. ROD SCURRY
☐ 166. BENNY DISTEFANO
☐ 186. JOHNNY RAY
☐ 200. BILL MADLOCK
☐ 235. JOHN TUDOR
☐ 264. DON ROBINSON
☐ 288. LEE TUNNELL
☐ 308. JOSE DELEON
☐ 322. JASON THOMPSON
☐ 357. CECILIO GUANTE
☐ 386. LEE MAZZILLI
☐ 410. MILT MAY
☐ 430. JOHN CANDELARIA
☐ 444. DALE BERRA
☐ 479. KENT TEKULVE
☐ 508. LEE LACY
☐ 532. JIM MORRISON
☐ 552. RICK RHODEN
☐ 566. BRIAN HARPER
☐ 600. DENNY GONZALEZ

ST. LOUIS CARDINALS

☐ 59. OZZIE SMITH
☐ 83. RICKY HORTON
☐ 109. BRUCE SUTTER
☐ 138. DAVE LAPOINT
☐ 168. TITO LANDRUM
☐ 181. GEORGE HENDRICK
☐ 205. NEIL ALLEN
☐ 231. LONNIE SMITH
☐ 260. DAVE RUCKER
☐ 290. GLENN BRUMMER
☐ 303. DAVID GREEN
☐ 327. ANDY VAN SLYKE
☐ 353. DARRELL PORTER
☐ 382. KURT KEPSHIRE
☐ 412. DAVE VON OHLEN
☐ 425. TOM HERR

☐ 449. JOAQUIN ANDUJAR
☐ 475. WILLIE MCGEE
☐ 504. RALPH CITARELLA
☐ 534. TERRY PENDLETON
☐ 547. MARK SALAS
☐ 571. DANNY COX
☐ 596. TOM NIETO

SAN DIEGO PADRES

☐ 63. TONY GWYNN
☐ 80. ALAN WIGGINS
☐ 112. DAVE DRAVECKY
☐ 139. KEVIN MCREYNOLDS
☐ 162. JERRY DAVIS
☐ 185. RICH GOSSAGE
☐ 202. ERIC SHOW
☐ 234. GRAIG NETTLES
☐ 261. CRAIG LEFFERTS
☐ 284. MARK THURMOND
☐ 307. STEVE GARVEY
☐ 324. TIM LOLLAR
☐ 356. GARRY TEMPLETON
☐ 383. BOBBY BROWN
☐ 406. LUIS DELEON
☐ 429. TERRY KENNEDY
☐ 446. ED WHITSON
☐ 478. CARMELO MARTINEZ
☐ 505. BRUCE BOCHY
☐ 528. ANDY HAWKINS
☐ 551. TIM FLANNERY
☐ 568. LUIS SALAZAR
☐ 647. KURT BEVACQUA

SAN FRANCISCO GIANTS

☐ 43. ALEJANDRO SANCHEZ
☐ 65. JACK CLARK
☐ 79. JOEL YOUNGBLOOD
☐ 114. JOHNNIE LEMASTER
☐ 143. GREG MINTO
☐ 187. BOB BRENLY
☐ 201. JEFF ROBINSON
☐ 236. JOHN RABB
☐ 265. GARY LAVELLE
☐ 309. RANDY LERCH
☐ 323. FRANK WILLIAMS
☐ 358. JEFF LEONARD
☐ 387. BILL LASKEY
☐ 431. MANNY TRILLO
☐ 445. DUSTY BAKER
☐ 480. CHILI DAVIS
☐ 509. ATLEE HAMMAKER
☐ 553. MARK DAVIS
☐ 567. DAN GLADDEN
☐ 601. MARK GRANT
☐ 630. MIKE KRUKOW

SEATTLE MARINERS

☐ 27. DANNY TARTABULL
☐ 69. ALVIN DAVIS
☐ 74. JACK PERCONTE
☐ 118. DARNELL COLES
☐ 145. STEVE HENDERSON
☐ 191. BARRY BONNELL
☐ 196. AL COWENS
☐ 240. JIM PRESLEY
☐ 267. MATT YOUNG
☐ 313. JIM BEATTIE
☐ 318. KEN PHELPS
☐ 362. BOB KEARNEY
☐ 389. AL CHAMBERS
☐ 435. SPIKE OWEN
☐ 440. MIKE MOORE
☐ 484. EDWIN NUNEZ
☐ 511. ED VANDE BERG
☐ 557. MARK LANGSTON
☐ 562. MIKE STANTON
☐ 605. SALOME BAROJAS
☐ 631. PHIL BRADLEY

TEXAS RANGERS

☐ 56. BUDDY BELL
☐ 98. DANNY DARWIN
☐ 99. CURTIS WILKERSON
☐ 134. BOBBY JONES
☐ 159. TOMMY DUNBAR
☐ 178. PETE O'BRIEN
☐ 220. FRANK TANANA

☐ 221. NED YOST
☐ 256. GEORGE WRIGHT
☐ 281. MIKE MASON
☐ 300. LARRY PARRISH
☐ 342. GARY WARD
☐ 343. DAVE STEWART
☐ 378. WAYNE TOLLESON
☐ 403. TOM HENKE
☐ 422. CHARLIE HOUGH
☐ 464. BILLY SAMPLE
☐ 465. MICKEY RIVERS
☐ 500. MARVIS FOLEY
☐ 525. ODELL JONES
☐ 544. DONNIE SCOTT
☐ 586. DAVE SCHMIDT
☐ 587. JEFF KUNKEL
☐ 621. BILL STEIN

TORONTO BLUE JAYS

☐ 71. WILLIE UPSHAW
☐ 73. ALFREDO GRIFFIN
☐ 119. DENNIS LAMP
☐ 146. GEORGE BELL
☐ 193. DAVE STIEB
☐ 195. JESSE BARFIELD
☐ 241. DAVE COLLINS
☐ 268. ERNIE WHITT
☐ 315. DAMASO GARCIA
☐ 317. LUIS LEAL
☐ 363. GARTH IORG
☐ 390. TONY FERNANDEZ
☐ 437. LLOYD MOSEBY
☐ 439. JIM CLANCY
☐ 485. RANCE MULLINIKS
☐ 512. CLIFF JOHNSON
☐ 559. JIMMY KEY
☐ 561. DOYLE ALEXANDER
☐ 606. ROY LEE JACKSON
☐ 632. JIM GOTT

1986 DONRUSS (660)
2 1/2 X 3 1/2

ATLANTA BRAVES

☐ 36. MARTY CLARY
☐ 66. DALE MURPHY
☐ 77. RICK MAHLER
☐ 141. GLENN HUBBARD
☐ 165. GERALD PERRY
☐ 188. BOB HORNER
☐ 199. STEVE BEDROSIAN
☐ 263. RAFAEL RAMIREZ
☐ 287. CLAUDELL WASHINGTON
☐ 310. RICK CERONE
☐ 321. BRUCE SUTTER
☐ 385. RICK CAMP
☐ 409. LEN BARKER
☐ 432. TERRY FORSTER
☐ 443. JEFF DEDMON
☐ 507. MILT THOMPSON
☐ 531. KEN OBERKFELL
☐ 554. BRUCE BENEDICT
☐ 565. ZANE SMITH
☐ 618. CHRIS CHAMBLISS
☐ 624. JOE JOHNSON
☐ 627. TERRY HARPER

BALTIMORE ORIOLES

☐ 45. JOHN HABYAN
☐ 47. MIKE BODDICKER
☐ 88. EDDIE MURRAY
☐ 106. RICK DEMPSEY
☐ 123. MIKE YOUNG
☐ 148. KEN DIXON
☐ 169. STORM DAVIS
☐ 210. CAL RIPKEN
☐ 228. LEE LACY
☐ 245. FRED LYNN
☐ 270. SAMMY STEWART
☐ 291. SCOTT MCGREGOR
☐ 332. FLOYD RAYFORD
☐ 350. LARRY SHEETS
☐ 367. NATE SNELL
☐ 392. DON AASE
☐ 413. JIM DWYER
☐ 454. DENNIS MARTINEZ
☐ 472. GARY ROENICKE
☐ 489. AL PARDO
☐ 514. TIPPY MARTINEZ
☐ 535. WAYNE GROSS
☐ 576. MIKE FLANAGAN
☐ 594. BILL SWAGGERTY
☐ 599. BRAD HAVENS
☐ 607. ALAN WIGGINS
☐ 643. JOHN SHELBY

BOSTON RED SOX

☐ 50. OIL CAN BOYD
☐ 91. BOB STANLEY
☐ 127. TONY ARMAS
☐ 151. BILL BUCKNER
☐ 172. ROGER CLEMENS
☐ 213. JIM RICE
☐ 249. DWIGHT EVANS
☐ 273. RICH GEDMAN
☐ 294. MARTY BARRETT
☐ 335. JACKIE GUTIERREZ
☐ 371. WADE BOGGS
☐ 395. MIKE EASLER
☐ 416. STEVE CRAWFORD
☐ 457. GLENN HOFFMAN
☐ 493. MARK CLEAR
☐ 517. BRUCE HURST
☐ 538. AL NIPPER
☐ 579. STEVE LYONS
☐ 614. MARC SULLIVAN
☐ 616. BRUCE KISON
☐ 620. TIM LOLLAR
☐ 636. BOB OJEDA

CALIFORNIA ANGELS

☐ 35. MARK MCLEMORE
☐ 57. DOUG DECINCES
☐ 85. RON ROMANICK
☐ 108. BRIAN DOWNING
☐ 133. DICK SCHOFIELD
☐ 158. GARY PETTIS
☐ 179. MIKE WITT
☐ 207. BOBBY GRICH
☐ 230. BOB BOONE
☐ 255. DONNIE MOORE
☐ 280. ROD CAREW
☐ 301. STU CLIBURN
☐ 329. URBANO LUGO
☐ 352. JUAN BENIQUEZ
☐ 377. REGGIE JACKSON
☐ 402. JIM SLATON
☐ 423. RUPPERT JONES
☐ 451. JERRY NARRON
☐ 474. KIRK MCCASKILL
☐ 499. JOHN CANDELARIA
☐ 524. JACK HOWELL
☐ 545. CRAIG GERBER
☐ 573. AL HOLLAND
☐ 611. DON SUTTON

CHICAGO CUBS

☐ 32. JOHNNY ABREGO
☐ 67. RYNE SANDBERG
☐ 76. GARY MATTHEWS
☐ 117. STEVE TROUT
☐ 144. LEE SMITH
☐ 167. KEITH MORELAND
☐ 189. RICK SUTCLIFFE

☐ 198. RON CEY
☐ 239. DENNIS ECKERSLEY
☐ 266. BOB DERNIER
☐ 289. JODY DAVIS
☐ 311. SHAWON DUNSTON
☐ 320. LEON DURHAM
☐ 361. RAY FONTENOT
☐ 388. DAVEY LOPES
☐ 411. GEORGE FRAZIER
☐ 433. BILLY HATCHER
☐ 442. SCOTT SANDERSON
☐ 483. THAD BOSLEY
☐ 510. STEVE ENGEL
☐ 533. RON MERIDITH
☐ 555. WARREN BRUSSTAR
☐ 564. DICK RUTHVEN
☐ 613. JAY BALLER

CHICAGO WHITE SOX

☐ 58. BRITT BURNS
☐ 86. DARYL BOSTON
☐ 122. DAN SPILLNER
☐ 135. GREG WALKER
☐ 160. RICHARD DOTSON
☐ 180. HAROLD BAINES
☐ 208. OZZIE GUILLEN
☐ 244. FLOYD BANNISTER
☐ 257. JULIO CRUZ
☐ 282. SCOTT FLETCHER
☐ 302. LUIS SALAZAR
☐ 330. JOEL SKINNER
☐ 366. CARLTON FISK
☐ 379. BOB JAMES
☐ 404. TIM HULETT
☐ 424. JERRY HAIRSTON
☐ 452. BRYAN LITTLE
☐ 488. JUAN AGOSTO
☐ 501. GENE NELSON
☐ 526. RON KITTLE
☐ 546. JOE DESA
☐ 574. REID NICHOLS
☐ 609. TOM SEAVER
☐ 623. JOEL DAVIS
☐ 632. RUDY LAW

CINCINNATI REDS

☐ 27. KAL DANIELS
☐ 37. PAUL O'NEILL
☐ 62. PETE ROSE
☐ 81. RON OESTER
☐ 121. RON ROBINSON
☐ 140. WAYNE KRENCHICKI
☐ 164. ERIC DAVIS
☐ 184. MARIO SOTO
☐ 203. DAVE PARKER
☐ 243. DAVE CONCEPCION
☐ 262. JAY TIBBS
☐ 286. NICK ESASKY
☐ 306. GARY REDUS
☐ 325. EDDIE MILNER
☐ 365. TOM HUME
☐ 384. TOM BROWNING
☐ 408. TED POWER
☐ 428. TONY PEREZ
☐ 447. BUDDY BELL
☐ 487. JOHN FRANCO
☐ 506. JOE PRICE
☐ 530. BO DIAZ
☐ 550. DAVE VAN GORDER
☐ 569. TOM RUNNELLS
☐ 650. MAX VENABLE

CLEVELAND INDIANS

☐ 29. CORY SNYDER
☐ 94. TOM WADDELL
☐ 102. BRETT BUTLER
☐ 129. PAT TABLER
☐ 154. BROOK JACOBY
☐ 216. JULIO FRANCO
☐ 224. JOE CARTER
☐ 251. ANDRE THORNTON
☐ 276. MEL HALL
☐ 338. NEAL HEATON
☐ 346. GEORGE VUKOVICH
☐ 373. CHRIS BANDO
☐ 398. JERRY WILLARD
☐ 460. CARMEN CASTILLO

1986 Donruss

- ☐ 468. ROY SMITH
- ☐ 495. RAMON ROMERO
- ☐ 520. TONY BERNAZARD
- ☐ 582. JAMIE EASTERLY
- ☐ 590. MIKE HARGROVE

DETROIT TIGERS

- ☐ 49. LOU WHITAKER
- ☐ 90. CHET LEMON
- ☐ 105. JACK MORRIS
- ☐ 125. KIRK GIBSON
- ☐ 150. CHRIS PITTARO
- ☐ 171. ALAN TRAMMELL
- ☐ 212. DAN PETRY
- ☐ 227. WILLIE HERNANDEZ
- ☐ 247. WALT TERRELL
- ☐ 272. NELSON SIMMONS
- ☐ 293. AURELIO LOPEZ
- ☐ 334. LANCE PARRISH
- ☐ 349. BARBARO GARBEY
- ☐ 369. DARRELL EVANS
- ☐ 394. RANDY O'NEAL
- ☐ 415. ALEJANDRO SANCHEZ
- ☐ 456. BOB MELVIN
- ☐ 471. DAVE BERGMAN
- ☐ 491. FRANK TANANA
- ☐ 516. BILL SCHERRER
- ☐ 537. TOM BROOKENS
- ☐ 578. MIKE LAGA
- ☐ 593. LARRY HERNDON
- ☐ 615. JOHN GRUBB

HOUSTON ASTROS

- ☐ 31. TY GAINEY
- ☐ 60. JOSE CRUZ
- ☐ 84. JERRY MUMPHREY
- ☐ 110. BILL DORAN
- ☐ 136. DENNY WALLING
- ☐ 161. BOB KNEPPER
- ☐ 182. JEFF HEATHCOCK
- ☐ 206. TERRY PUHL
- ☐ 232. CRAIG REYNOLDS
- ☐ 258. NOLAN RYAN
- ☐ 283. BILL DAWLEY
- ☐ 304. FRANK DIPINO
- ☐ 328. DAVE SMITH
- ☐ 354. MARK BAILEY
- ☐ 380. GLENN DAVIS
- ☐ 405. ALAN ASHBY
- ☐ 426. JEFF CALHOUN
- ☐ 450. JIM PANKOVITS
- ☐ 476. MIKE SCOTT
- ☐ 502. JOHN MIZEROCK
- ☐ 527. PHIL GARNER
- ☐ 548. KEVIN BASS
- ☐ 572. DICKIE THON

KANSAS CITY ROYALS

- ☐ 53. GEORGE BRETT
- ☐ 95. DANNY JACKSON
- ☐ 100. BRET SABERHAGEN
- ☐ 130. FRANK WHITE
- ☐ 155. PAT SHERIDAN
- ☐ 175. WILLIE WILSON
- ☐ 217. DARRYL MOTLEY
- ☐ 222. STEVE BALONI
- ☐ 252. ONIX CONCEPCION

- ☐ 277. JIM SUNDBERG
- ☐ 297. CHARLIE LEIBRANDT
- ☐ 339. JORGE ORTA
- ☐ 344. GREG PRYOR
- ☐ 374. BUD BLACK
- ☐ 399. LONNIE SMITH
- ☐ 419. MIKE JONES
- ☐ 461. DAVE LEEPER
- ☐ 466. LYNN JONES
- ☐ 496. JOHN WATHAN
- ☐ 521. HAL MCRAE
- ☐ 541. DAN QUISENBERRY
- ☐ 583. MARK GUBICZA
- ☐ 588. STEVE FARR
- ☐ 605. BUDDY BIANCALANA

LOS ANGELES DODGERS

- ☐ 52. MIKE MARSHALL
- ☐ 93. MIKE SCIOSCIA
- ☐ 104. JERRY REUSS
- ☐ 128. MARIANO DUNCAN
- ☐ 153. BILL RUSSELL
- ☐ 174. PEDRO GUERRERO
- ☐ 215. FERNANDO VALENZUELA
- ☐ 226. OREL HERSHISER
- ☐ 250. DENNIS POWELL
- ☐ 275. KEN HOWELL
- ☐ 296. GREG BROCK
- ☐ 337. TERRY WHITFIELD
- ☐ 348. CARLOS DIAZ
- ☐ 372. RICK HONEYCUTT
- ☐ 397. TOM NIEDENFUER
- ☐ 418. ENOS CABELL
- ☐ 459. BOB WELCH
- ☐ 470. KEN LANDREAUX
- ☐ 494. LEN MATUSZEK
- ☐ 519. STEVE YEAGER
- ☐ 540. STEVE SAX
- ☐ 581. GILBERTO REYES
- ☐ 592. FRANKLIN STUBBS
- ☐ 617. BILL MADLOCK

MILWAUKEE BREWERS

- ☐ 40. JUAN NIEVES
- ☐ 48. ROBIN YOUNT
- ☐ 89. DION JAMES
- ☐ 107. RAY BURRIS
- ☐ 115. JIM GANTNER
- ☐ 124. PAUL MOLITOR
- ☐ 149. DANNY DARWIN
- ☐ 170. CECIL COOPER
- ☐ 211. BILL SCHROEDER
- ☐ 229. ROLLIE FINGERS
- ☐ 237. MOOSE HAAS
- ☐ 246. CHARLIE MOORE
- ☐ 271. BOB GIBSON
- ☐ 292. TED SIMMONS
- ☐ 333. BEN OGLIVIE
- ☐ 351. TED HIGUERA
- ☐ 359. EARNEST RILES
- ☐ 368. RICK MANNING
- ☐ 393. JAIME COCANOWER
- ☐ 414. PAUL HOUSEHOLDER
- ☐ 455. ED ROMERO
- ☐ 473. PETE VUCKOVICH
- ☐ 481. RANDY READY
- ☐ 490. BILL WEGMAN
- ☐ 515. BILLY JO ROBIDOUX
- ☐ 536. RAY SEARAGE
- ☐ 577. TIM LEARY
- ☐ 595. CARLOS PONCE
- ☐ 634. MIKE FELDER

MINNESOTA TWINS

- ☐ 70. KENT HRBEK
- ☐ 72. KIRBY PUCKETT
- ☐ 120. JOHN BUTCHER
- ☐ 147. MIKE SMITHSON
- ☐ 192. TOM BRUNANSKY
- ☐ 194. FRANK VIOLA
- ☐ 242. TIM TEUFEL
- ☐ 269. MICKEY HATCHER
- ☐ 314. GARY GAETTI
- ☐ 316. MARK SALAS
- ☐ 364. RON DAVIS
- ☐ 391. TIM LAUDNER
- ☐ 436. PETE FILSON
- ☐ 438. DAVE ENGLE

- ☐ 486. ROY SMALLEY
- ☐ 513. FRANK EUFEMIA
- ☐ 558. GREG GAGNE
- ☐ 560. RON WASHINGTON
- ☐ 598. STEVE LOMBARDOZZI
- ☐ 630. MARK FUNDERBURK
- ☐ 635. KEN SCHROM
- ☐ 649. BERT BLYLEVEN

MONTREAL EXPOS

- ☐ 33. ANDRES GALARRAGA
- ☐ 55. HUBIE BROOKS
- ☐ 87. ANDRE DAWSON
- ☐ 97. MIKE FITZGERALD
- ☐ 132. VANCE LAW
- ☐ 157. JIM WOHLFORD
- ☐ 177. TIM RAINES
- ☐ 209. JEFF REARDON
- ☐ 219. TIM WALLACH
- ☐ 254. DAVID PALMER
- ☐ 279. HERMAN WINNINGHAM
- ☐ 299. BRYN SMITH
- ☐ 331. BILL GULLICKSON
- ☐ 341. JOE HESKETH
- ☐ 376. CHARLIE LEA
- ☐ 401. TERRY FRANCONA
- ☐ 421. TIM BURKE
- ☐ 453. GARY LUCAS
- ☐ 463. RANDY ST. CLAIRE
- ☐ 498. U.L. WASHINGTON
- ☐ 523. MITCH WEBSTER
- ☐ 543. FLOYD YOUMANS
- ☐ 575. BERT ROBERGE
- ☐ 585. BILL LASKEY

NEW YORK METS

- ☐ 68. GARY CARTER
- ☐ 75. DWIGHT GOODEN
- ☐ 116. GEORGE FOSTER
- ☐ 190. KEITH HERNANDEZ
- ☐ 197. DARRYL STRAWBERRY
- ☐ 238. WALLY BACKMAN
- ☐ 312. HOWARD JOHNSON
- ☐ 319. RAFAEL SANTANA
- ☐ 360. JOHN CHRISTENSEN
- ☐ 434. CLINT HURDLE
- ☐ 441. RICK AGUILERA
- ☐ 482. LENNY DYKSTRA
- ☐ 556. DANNY HEEP
- ☐ 563. RON DARLING
- ☐ 597. RAY KNIGHT
- ☐ 604. MOOKIE WILSON
- ☐ 625. SID FERNANDEZ
- ☐ 629. ROGER MCDOWELL
- ☐ 631. ED LYNCH
- ☐ 646. JESSE OROSCO
- ☐ 647. BILLY BEANE
- ☐ 652. CALVIN SCHIRALDI

NEW YORK YANKEES

- ☐ 51. RICKEY HENDERSON
- ☐ 92. WILLIE RANDOLPH
- ☐ 103. RON GUIDRY
- ☐ 126. KEN GRIFFEY
- ☐ 152. MIKE PAGLIARULO
- ☐ 173. DON MATTINGLY
- ☐ 214. DAVE RIGHETTI
- ☐ 225. ED WHITSON
- ☐ 248. DAVE WINFIELD
- ☐ 274. BUTCH WYNEGAR
- ☐ 295. DALE BERRA
- ☐ 336. DENNIS RASMUSSEN
- ☐ 347. DON BAYLOR
- ☐ 370. RON HASSEY
- ☐ 396. SCOTT BRADLEY
- ☐ 417. DAN PASQUA
- ☐ 458. BOB SHIRLEY
- ☐ 469. ANDRE ROBERTSON
- ☐ 492. BRIAN FISHER
- ☐ 518. RICH BORDI
- ☐ 539. BILLY SAMPLE
- ☐ 580. PHIL NIEKRO
- ☐ 591. MARTY BYSTROM
- ☐ 601. JOE NIEKRO
- ☐ 608. JOE COWLEY
- ☐ 610. NEIL ALLEN
- ☐ 638. BOBBY MEACHAM

1986 Donruss

OAKLAND A'S

- ☐ 39. JOSE CANSECO
- ☐ 54. DAVE KINGMAN
- ☐ 96. MIKE DAVIS
- ☐ 101. ALFREDO GRIFFIN
- ☐ 131. CARNEY LANSFORD
- ☐ 156. MIKE GALLEGO
- ☐ 176. DWAYNE MURPHY
- ☐ 218. DAVE COLLINS
- ☐ 223. JAY HOWELL
- ☐ 253. MIKE HEATH
- ☐ 278. CHRIS CODIROLI
- ☐ 298. BILL KRUEGER
- ☐ 340. DONNIE HILL
- ☐ 345. MICKEY TETTLETON
- ☐ 375. STEVE HENDERSON
- ☐ 400. BRUCE BOCHTE
- ☐ 420. STEVE KIEFER
- ☐ 462. TIM BIRTSAS
- ☐ 467. DUSTY BAKER
- ☐ 497. ROB PICCIOLO
- ☐ 522. JOSE RIJO
- ☐ 542. TONY PHILLIPS
- ☐ 584. STAN JAVIER
- ☐ 589. STEVE ONTIVEROS

PHILADELPHIA PHILLIES

- ☐ 34. DAVE SPIPANOFF
- ☐ 61. MIKE SCHMIDT
- ☐ 82. JOHN RUSSELL
- ☐ 111. KENT TEKULVE
- ☐ 137. OZZIE VIRGIL
- ☐ 163. GREG GROSS
- ☐ 183. STEVE CARLTON
- ☐ 204. JOHN DENNY
- ☐ 233. SHANE RAWLEY
- ☐ 259. JEFF STONE
- ☐ 285. GLENN WILSON
- ☐ 305. VON HAYES
- ☐ 326. JUAN SAMUEL
- ☐ 355. LARRY ANDERSON
- ☐ 381. TIM CORCORAN
- ☐ 407. GARRY MADDOX
- ☐ 427. DON CARMAN
- ☐ 448. DAVE RUCKER
- ☐ 477. DARREN DAULTON
- ☐ 503. LUIS AGUAYO
- ☐ 529. KEVIN GROSS
- ☐ 549. TOM FOLEY
- ☐ 570. RICK SCHU
- ☐ 612. FRED TOLIVER
- ☐ 619. DAVE STEWART
- ☐ 622. CHARLES HUDSON

PITTSBURGH PIRATES

- ☐ 44. BOB KIPPER
- ☐ 64. TONY PENA
- ☐ 78. BENNY DISTEFANO
- ☐ 113. MARVELL WYNNE
- ☐ 142. CECILIO GUANTE
- ☐ 166. RICK RHODEN
- ☐ 186. JOHNNY RAY
- ☐ 200. STEVE KEMP
- ☐ 235. JOSE DELEON
- ☐ 264. LARRY MCWILLIAMS
- ☐ 288. LEE MAZZILLI
- ☐ 308. SAM KHALIFA
- ☐ 322. JASON THOMPSON
- ☐ 357. DON ROBINSON
- ☐ 386. JIM MORRISON
- ☐ 410. DENNY GONZALEZ
- ☐ 430. BOB WALK
- ☐ 444. JOE ORSULAK
- ☐ 479. BILL ALMON
- ☐ 508. JUNIOR ORTIZ
- ☐ 532. RICK REUSCHEL
- ☐ 552. R.J. REYNOLDS
- ☐ 566. SID BREAM
- ☐ 600. PAT CLEMENTS
- ☐ 642. MIKE BROWN

ST. LOUIS CARDINALS

- ☐ 43. TODD WORRELL
- ☐ 59. OZZIE SMITH
- ☐ 83. TOMMY HERR
- ☐ 109. WILLIE MCGEE
- ☐ 138. RICKY HORTON
- ☐ 168. JACK CLARK
- ☐ 181. VINCE COLEMAN
- ☐ 205. TERRY PENDLETON
- ☐ 231. JOAQUIN ANDUJAR
- ☐ 260. JOHN TUDOR
- ☐ 290. DARRELL PORTER
- ☐ 303. KEN DAYLEY
- ☐ 327. TOM NIETO
- ☐ 353. BOB FORSCH
- ☐ 382. DANNY COX
- ☐ 412. ANDY VAN SLYKE
- ☐ 425. TITO LANDRUM
- ☐ 449. IVAN DEJESUS
- ☐ 475. JEFF LAHTI
- ☐ 504. KURT KEPSHIRE
- ☐ 534. STEVE BRAUN
- ☐ 547. BRIAN HARPER
- ☐ 571. BILL CAMPBELL
- ☐ 596. PAT PERRY
- ☐ 648. CESAR CEDENO

SAN DIEGO PADRES

- ☐ 41. LANCE MCCULLERS
- ☐ 63. STEVE GARVEY
- ☐ 80. KEVIN MCREYNOLDS
- ☐ 112. TONY GWYNN
- ☐ 139. LAMARR HOYT
- ☐ 162. DAVE DRAVECKY
- ☐ 185. GOOSE GOSSAGE
- ☐ 202. GARRY TEMPLETON
- ☐ 234. ERIC SHOW
- ☐ 261. MARK THURMOND
- ☐ 284. ANDY HAWKINS
- ☐ 307. CRAIG LEFFERTS
- ☐ 324. CARMELO MARTINEZ
- ☐ 356. TERRY KENNEDY
- ☐ 383. TIM FLANNERY
- ☐ 406. TIM STODDARD
- ☐ 429. JERRY DAVIS
- ☐ 446. JERRY ROYSTER
- ☐ 478. GRAIG NETTLES
- ☐ 505. ED WOJNA
- ☐ 528. KURT BEVACQUA
- ☐ 551. BRUCE BOCHY
- ☐ 568. MARIO RAMIREZ

SAN FRANCISCO GIANTS

- ☐ 46. MIKE WOODARD
- ☐ 65. CHILI DAVIS
- ☐ 79. JEFF LEONARD
- ☐ 114. DAVID GREEN
- ☐ 143. MIKE KRUKOW
- ☐ 187. DAN GLADDEN
- ☐ 201. MANNY TRILLO
- ☐ 236. JOSE URIBE
- ☐ 265. MARK DAVIS
- ☐ 309. SCOTT GARRELTS
- ☐ 323. BOB BRENLY
- ☐ 358. JIM GOTT
- ☐ 387. DAVE LAPOINT
- ☐ 431. BRAD WELLMAN
- ☐ 445. ATLEE HAMMAKER
- ☐ 480. GREG MINTON
- ☐ 509. VIDA BLUE
- ☐ 553. CHRIS BROWN
- ☐ 567. JOEL YOUNGBLOOD
- ☐ 633. ROGER MASON
- ☐ 641. DAN DRIESSEN

SEATTLE MARINERS

- ☐ 38. DANNY TARTABULL
- ☐ 69. ALVIN DAVIS
- ☐ 74. BOB KEARNEY
- ☐ 118. MARK LANGSTON
- ☐ 145. EDWIN NUNEZ
- ☐ 191. PHIL BRADLEY
- ☐ 196. JIM BEATTIE
- ☐ 240. MIKE MOORE
- ☐ 267. MATT YOUNG
- ☐ 313. JIM PRESLEY
- ☐ 318. DAVE HENDERSON
- ☐ 362. SPIKE OWEN
- ☐ 389. AL COWENS
- ☐ 435. IVAN CALDERON
- ☐ 440. GORMAN THOMAS
- ☐ 484. HAROLD REYNOLDS
- ☐ 511. KARL BEST

- ☐ 557. DARNELL COLES
- ☐ 562. BILLY SWIFT
- ☐ 628. JACK LAZORKO
- ☐ 637. ED VANDE BERG

TEXAS RANGERS

- ☐ 30. JOSE GUZMAN
- ☐ 42. RICK SURHOFF
- ☐ 56. ODDIBE MCDOWELL
- ☐ 98. GARY WARD
- ☐ 99. PETE O'BRIEN
- ☐ 134. WAYNE TOLLESON
- ☐ 159. TOBY HARRAH
- ☐ 178. LARRY PARRISH
- ☐ 220. GEORGE WRIGHT
- ☐ 221. TOMMY DUNBAR
- ☐ 256. CURTIS WILKERSON
- ☐ 281. DON SLAUGHT
- ☐ 300. BURT HOOTON
- ☐ 342. CHARLIE HOUGH
- ☐ 343. DAVE ROZEMA
- ☐ 378. DAVE SCHMIDT
- ☐ 403. BILL STEIN
- ☐ 422. MIKE MASON
- ☐ 464. CHRIS WELSH
- ☐ 465. GREG HARRIS
- ☐ 500. DUANE WALKER
- ☐ 525. ALAN BANNISTER
- ☐ 544. STEVE BUECHELE
- ☐ 586. JEFF RUSSELL
- ☐ 587. DICKIE NOLES
- ☐ 603. DWAYNE HENRY

TORONTO BLUE JAYS

- ☐ 28. FRED MCGRIFF
- ☐ 71. GEORGE BELL
- ☐ 73. LLOYD MOSEBY
- ☐ 119. TONY FERNANDEZ
- ☐ 146. DAVE STIEB
- ☐ 193. JESSE BARFIELD
- ☐ 195. WILLIE UPSHAW
- ☐ 241. DAMASO GARCIA
- ☐ 268. JIM CLANCY
- ☐ 315. LUIS LEAL
- ☐ 317. BILL CAUDILL
- ☐ 363. JIM ACKER
- ☐ 390. DOYLE ALEXANDER
- ☐ 437. TOM HENKE
- ☐ 439. TOM FILER
- ☐ 485. AL OLIVER
- ☐ 512. CECIL FIELDER
- ☐ 559. ERNIE WHITT
- ☐ 561. JIMMY KEY
- ☐ 606. RANCE MULLINIKS
- ☐ 621. GARY LAVELLE
- ☐ 626. DENNIS LAMP
- ☐ 639. CLIFF JOHNSON
- ☐ 640. GARTH IORG

1986 DONRUSS ROOKIES (56)
2 1/2 X 3 1/2

ATLANTA BRAVES

☐ 10. ANDRES THOMAS
☐ 28. PAUL ASSENMACHER

BALTIMORE ORIOLES

NO CARDS ISSUED

BOSTON RED SOX

☐ 29. JEFF SELLERS
☐ 48. REY QUINONEZ
☐ 53. ROB WOODWARD

CALIFORNIA ANGELS

☐ 1. WALLY JOYNER

CHICAGO CUBS

NO CARDS ISSUED

CHICAGO WHITE SOX

☐ 30. BOBBY BONILLA
☐ 51. JOHN CANGELOSI
☐ 55. JOE MCKEON

CINCINNATI REDS

☐ 2. TRACY JONES

CLEVELAND INDIANS

☐ 15. CORY SNYDER
☐ 25. SCOTT BAILES
☐ 43. ANDY ALLANSON

DETROIT TIGERS

☐ 27. ERIC KING

HOUSTON ASTROS

☐ 9. CHARLIE KERFELD
☐ 34. JIM DESHAIES

KANSAS CITY ROYALS

☐ 36. SCOTT BANKHEAD
☐ 38. BO JACKSON

LOS ANGELES DODGERS

☐ 5. REGGIE WILLIAMS

MILWAUKEE BREWERS

☐ 12. JUAN NIEVES
☐ 14. DAN PLESAC
☐ 37. DALE SVEUM

MINNESOTA TWINS

☐ 3. ALLAN ANDERSON
☐ 18. STEVE LOMBARDOZZI
☐ 44. MARK PORTUGAL

MONTREAL EXPOS

☐ 7. ANDRES GALARRAGA
☐ 9. AL NEWMAN

NEW YORK METS

☐ 17. KEVIN MITCHELL
☐ 54. ED HEARN

NEW YORK YANKEES

☐ 8. BOB TEWKSBURY
☐ 31. DOUG DRABEK

OAKLAND A'S

☐ 22. JOSE CANSECO
☐ 40. ERIC PLUNK
☐ 41. BILL BATHE
☐ 50. BILL MOONEYHAM

PHILADELPHIA PHILLIES

NO CARDS ISSUED

PITTSBURGH PIRATES

☐ 11. BARRY BONDS
☐ 46. BOB KIPPER

ST. LOUIS CARDINALS

☐ 21. TODD WORRELL
☐ 26. GREG MATHEWS
☐ 35. MIKE LAVALLIERE

SAN DIEGO PADRES

☐ 33. BIP ROBERTS
☐ 42. JOHN KRUK
☐ 47. GENE WALTER

SAN FRANCISCO GIANTS

☐ 32. WILL CLARK
☐ 39. ROB THOMPSON

SEATTLE MARINERS

☐ 45. DANNY TARTABULL

TEXAS RANGERS

☐ 4. ED CORREA
☐ 19. MITCH WILLIAMS
☐ 23. PETE INCAVIGLIA
☐ 24. JOSE GUZMAN
☐ 49. BOBBY WITT
☐ 52. RUBEN SIERRA

TORONTO BLUE JAYS

☐ 13. MARK EICHHORN
☐ 16. KELLY GRUBER
☐ 20. JOHN CERUTTI

1987 DONRUSS (660)
2 1/2 X 3 1/2

ATLANTA BRAVES

☐ 67. OZZIE VIRGIL
☐ 78. DALE MURPHY
☐ 143. BILLY SAMPLE
☐ 167. ZANE SMITH
☐ 190. RICK MAHLER
☐ 202. RAFAEL RAMIREZ
☐ 266. ANDRES THOMAS
☐ 290. PAUL ASSENMACHER
☐ 314. JEFF DEDMON
☐ 325. DAVID PALMER
☐ 389. BOB HORNER
☐ 414. GENE GARBER
☐ 437. KEN OBERKFELL
☐ 448. BRUCE BENEDICT
☐ 513. KEN GRIFFEY
☐ 537. TED SIMMONS
☐ 560. ED OLWINE
☐ 571. CLIFF SPECK
☐ 634. GLENN HUBBARD
☐ 657. DOYLE ALEXANDER
☐ 659. JIM ACKER

BALTIMORE ORIOLES

☐ 30. KEN GERHART
☐ 39. ERIC BELL
☐ 48. EDDIE MURRAY
☐ 89. CAL RIPKEN
☐ 108. FRED LYNN
☐ 125. MIKE BODDICKER
☐ 150. MIKE YOUNG
☐ 171. KEN DIXON
☐ 213. RICH BORDI
☐ 231. DON AASE
☐ 248. LARRY SHEETS
☐ 273. STORM DAVIS
☐ 294. RICK DEMPSEY
☐ 336. LEE LACY
☐ 354. JOHN SHELBY
☐ 371. JUAN BENIQUEZ

☐ 396. NATE SNELL
☐ 418. JIM DWYER
☐ 459. MIKE FLANAGAN
☐ 477. JIM TRABER
☐ 494. JOHN HABYAN
☐ 520. SCOTT MCGREGOR
☐ 541. JOHN STEFERO
☐ 582. ODELL JONES
☐ 601. JACKIE GUTIERREZ

BOSTON RED SOX

☐ 44. PAT DODSON
☐ 51. OIL CAN BOYD
☐ 92. JIM RICE
☐ 129. DWIGHT EVANS
☐ 153. RICH GEDMAN
☐ 174. BRUCE HURST
☐ 216. BOB STANLEY
☐ 252. WADE BOGGS
☐ 276. ROGER CLEMENS
☐ 297. AL NIPPER
☐ 339. DON BAYLOR
☐ 375. TOM SEAVER
☐ 399. STEVE CRAWFORD
☐ 421. JOE SAMBITO
☐ 462. BILL BUCKNER
☐ 498. TONY ARMAS
☐ 523. MARTY BARRETT
☐ 544. JEFF SELLERS
☐ 585. MIKE GREENWELL
☐ 606. ED ROMERO
☐ 622. DAVE HENDERSON
☐ 633. SPIKE OWEN
☐ 641. CALVIN SCHIRALDI
☐ 643. MARC SULLIVAN
☐ 647. DAVE SAX
☐ 652. ROB WOODWARD
☐ 658. SAMMY STEWART

CALIFORNIA ANGELS

☐ 38. DEVON WHITE
☐ 40. WILL FRASER
☐ 58. MIKE WITT
☐ 86. BRIAN DOWNING
☐ 110. DONNIE MOORE
☐ 135. WALLY JOYNER
☐ 160. GARY PETTIS
☐ 181. DON SUTTON
☐ 210. REGGIE JACKSON
☐ 233. BOB BOONE
☐ 258. ROB WILFONG
☐ 283. DICK SCHOFIELD
☐ 305. JACK HOWELL
☐ 333. DOUG CORBETT
☐ 356. DOUG DECINCES
☐ 381. KIRK MCCASKILL
☐ 407. CHUCK FINLEY
☐ 428. RUPPERT JONES
☐ 456. BOBBY GRICH
☐ 479. MARK MCLEMORE
☐ 505. RAY CHADWICK
☐ 530. STU CLIBURN
☐ 551. JOHN CANDELARIA
☐ 579. GUS POLIDOR
☐ 583. MARK RYAL
☐ 603. JERRY NARRON
☐ 618. GARY LUCAS

CHICAGO CUBS

☐ 36. GREG MADDUX
☐ 43. RAFAEL PALMEIRO
☐ 68. RICK SUTCLIFFE
☐ 77. RYNE SANDBERG
☐ 119. SHAWON DUNSTON
☐ 146. BOB DERNIER
☐ 169. KEITH MORELAND
☐ 191. THAD BOSLEY
☐ 201. STEVE TROUT
☐ 242. LEON DURHAM
☐ 269. JODY DAVIS
☐ 292. LEE SMITH
☐ 315. JAMIE MOYER
☐ 324. JERRY MUMPHREY
☐ 365. DENNIS ECKERSLEY
☐ 392. CHRIS SPEIER
☐ 416. FRANK DIPINO
☐ 438. RON DAVIS
☐ 447. SCOTT SANDERSON

☐ 488. DAVE MARTINEZ
☐ 516. ED LYNCH
☐ 539. CHICO WALKER
☐ 570. MANNY TRILLO
☐ 594. DREW HALL

CHICAGO WHITE SOX

☐ 59. GREG WALKER
☐ 87. OZZIE GUILLEN
☐ 124. JOEL DAVIS
☐ 137. DARYL BOSTON
☐ 162. JOHN CANGELOSI
☐ 182. DAVE SCHMIDT
☐ 211. FLOYD BANNISTER
☐ 247. CARLTON FISK
☐ 260. TIM HULETT
☐ 285. JERRY HAIRSTON
☐ 306. RUSS MORMAN
☐ 334. RON KARKOVICE
☐ 370. BOBBY THIGPEN
☐ 383. RICH DOTSON
☐ 409. STEVE LYONS
☐ 429. HAROLD BAINES
☐ 457. JOSE DELEON
☐ 493. BOB JAMES
☐ 507. NEIL ALLEN
☐ 532. RON HASSEY
☐ 552. JOE COWLEY
☐ 580. GENE NELSON
☐ 617. STEVE CARLTON
☐ 628. BILL DAWLEY

JERRY HAIRSTON OF

CINCINNATI REDS

☐ 63. TOM BROWNING
☐ 82. MARIO SOTO
☐ 123. KURT STILLWELL
☐ 142. KAL DANIELS
☐ 166. NICK ESASKY
☐ 186. PETE ROSE(M)
☐ 206. RON OESTER
☐ 246. BO DIAZ
☐ 265. ERIC DAVIS
☐ 289. JOHN FRANCO
☐ 310. RON ROBINSON
☐ 329. JOHN DENNY
☐ 369. BILL GULLICKSON
☐ 388. DAVE PARKER
☐ 413. TRACY JONES
☐ 433. EDDIE MILNER
☐ 452. ROB MURPHY
☐ 492. BARRY LARKIN
☐ 512. TERRY MCGRIFF
☐ 536. TED POWER
☐ 556. BUDDY BELL

CLEVELAND INDIANS

☐ 32. GREG SWINDELL
☐ 95. ANDY ALLANSON
☐ 104. BROOK JACOBY
☐ 131. JULIO FRANCO
☐ 156. JOE CARTER
☐ 219. BRETT BUTLER
☐ 227. SCOTT BAILES
☐ 254. PAT TABLER
☐ 279. ANDRE THORNTON
☐ 342. TOM CANDIOTTI
☐ 350. ERNIE CAMACHO
☐ 377. TONY BERNAZARD

☐ 403. KEN SCHROM
☐ 465. PHIL NIEKRO
☐ 473. MEL HALL
☐ 501. CHRIS BANDO
☐ 526. CORY SNYDER
☐ 588. CARMEN CASTILLO
☐ 596. BRYAN OELKERS
☐ 623. DAVE CLARK

DETROIT TIGERS

☐ 47. BRUCE FIELDS
☐ 50. KIRK GIBSON
☐ 91. LANCE PARRISH
☐ 107. LOU WHITAKER
☐ 127. ALAN TRAMMELL
☐ 152. FRANK TANANA
☐ 173. JACK MORRIS
☐ 215. DAVE COLLINS
☐ 230. DARNELL COLES
☐ 250. ERIC KING
☐ 275. WALT TERRELL
☐ 296. TOM BROOKENS
☐ 338. DWIGHT LOWRY
☐ 353. CHET LEMON
☐ 373. DAN PETRY
☐ 398. DARRELL EVANS
☐ 420. DAVE BERGMAN
☐ 461. CHUCK CARY
☐ 476. JOHNNY GRUBB
☐ 496. MIKE HEATH
☐ 522. WILLIE HERNANDEZ
☐ 543. MARK THURMOND
☐ 584. RANDY O'NEAL

HOUSTON ASTROS

☐ 61. GLENN DAVIS
☐ 85. JOSE CRUZ
☐ 112. BOB KNEPPER
☐ 138. NOLAN RYAN
☐ 163. MIKE SCOTT
☐ 184. JIM DESHAIES
☐ 209. CHARLIE KERFELD
☐ 235. MARK BAILEY
☐ 261. DICKIE THON
☐ 286. BILL DORAN
☐ 308. DAVE SMITH
☐ 332. ALAN ASHBY
☐ 358. PHIL GARNER
☐ 384. CRAIG REYNOLDS
☐ 410. KEVIN BASS
☐ 431. TERRY PUHL
☐ 455. DAVEY LOPES
☐ 481. BILLY HATCHER
☐ 508. DANNY DARWIN
☐ 533. TY GAINEY
☐ 554. DENNY WALLING
☐ 578. JEFF CALHOUN
☐ 605. JIM PANKOVITS
☐ 629. AURELIO LOPEZ
☐ 640. LARRY ANDERSEN
☐ 653. JOHN MIZEROCK

KANSAS CITY ROYALS

☐ 35. BO JACKSON
☐ 54. GEORGE BRETT
☐ 96. WILLIE WILSON
☐ 102. STEVE BALBONI
☐ 132. BRET SABERHAGEN
☐ 157. DANNY JACKSON
☐ 177. DAN QUISENBERRY
☐ 220. CHARLIE LEIBRANDT
☐ 225. LONNIE SMITH
☐ 255. FRANK WHITE
☐ 280. JIM SUNDBERG
☐ 301. STEVE FARR
☐ 343. RUDY LAW
☐ 348. JORGE ORTA
☐ 378. GREG PRYOR
☐ 404. BUD BLACK
☐ 424. MIKE KINGERY
☐ 466. MARK GUBICZA
☐ 471. HAL MCRAE
☐ 502. DAVID CONE
☐ 527. BUDDY BIANCALANA
☐ 624. ANGEL SALAZAR

1987 Donruss

LOS ANGELES DODGERS

- ☐ 53. PEDRO GUERRERO
- ☐ 94. FERNANDO VALENZUELA
- ☐ 106. OREL HERSHISER
- ☐ 130. MIKE SCIOSCIA
- ☐ 155. BILL MADLOCK
- ☐ 176. MIKE MARSHALL
- ☐ 218. TOM NIEDENFUER
- ☐ 229. KEN HOWELL
- ☐ 253. MARIANO DUNCAN
- ☐ 278. STEVE SAX
- ☐ 299. FRANKLIN STUBBS
- ☐ 341. REGGIE WILLIAMS
- ☐ 352. KEN LANDREAUX
- ☐ 376. ED VANDE BERG
- ☐ 402. RICK HONEYCUTT
- ☐ 423. LEN MATUSZEK
- ☐ 464. JEFF HAMILTON
- ☐ 475. BOB WELCH
- ☐ 499. DENNIS POWELL
- ☐ 525. JOSE GONZALEZ
- ☐ 546. ALEX TREVINO
- ☐ 587. RALPH BRYANT
- ☐ 598. BRIAN HOLTON

MILWAUKEE BREWERS

- ☐ 28. B.J. SURHOFF
- ☐ 33. MIKE BIRKBECK
- ☐ 49. TED HIGUERA
- ☐ 90. JUAN NIEVES
- ☐ 109. BILL WEGMAN
- ☐ 117. PAUL MOLITOR
- ☐ 126. ROBIN YOUNT
- ☐ 151. ERNEST RILES
- ☐ 172. JIM GANTNER
- ☐ 214. DAN PLESAC
- ☐ 232. TIM LEARY
- ☐ 240. BILLY JO ROBIDOUX
- ☐ 249. JUAN CASTILLO
- ☐ 274. ROB DEER
- ☐ 295. MIKE FELDER
- ☐ 337. GLENN BRAGGS
- ☐ 355. MARK CLEAR
- ☐ 363. CECIL COOPER
- ☐ 372. CHARLIE MOORE
- ☐ 397. BRYAN CLUTTERBUCK
- ☐ 419. BEN OGLIVIE
- ☐ 460. JOEY MEYER
- ☐ 478. CHRIS BOSIO
- ☐ 486. BILL SCHROEDER
- ☐ 495. JIM ADDUCI
- ☐ 521. RICK MANNING
- ☐ 542. DALE SVEUM

MINNESOTA TWINS

- ☐ 71. BERT BLYLEVEN
- ☐ 73. KENT HRBEK
- ☐ 122. GARY GAETTI
- ☐ 149. KIRBY PUCKETT
- ☐ 194. TOM BRUNANSKY
- ☐ 196. FRANK VIOLA
- ☐ 245. MIKE SMITHSON
- ☐ 272. KEITH ATHERTON
- ☐ 318. STEVE LOMBARDOZZI
- ☐ 320. TIM LAUDNER
- ☐ 368. ALLAN ANDERSON
- ☐ 395. GREG GAGNE
- ☐ 441. RANDY BUSH
- ☐ 443. ROY SMALLEY
- ☐ 491. MICKEY HATCHER
- ☐ 519. ANDRE DAVID
- ☐ 564. GEORGE FRAZIER
- ☐ 566. MARK PORTUGAL
- ☐ 615. NEAL HEATON

MONTREAL EXPOS

- ☐ 56. TIM RAINES
- ☐ 88. HUBIE BROOKS
- ☐ 98. JEFF REARDON
- ☐ 134. JOE HESKETH
- ☐ 159. BRYN SMITH
- ☐ 179. TIM WALLACH
- ☐ 212. VANCE LAW
- ☐ 222. TIM BURKE
- ☐ 257. FLOYD YOUMANS
- ☐ 282. JAY TIBBS
- ☐ 303. ANDRES GALARRAGA

- ☐ 335. MITCH WEBSTER
- ☐ 345. MIKE FITZGERALD
- ☐ 380. ANDY MCGAFFIGAN
- ☐ 406. WAYNE KRENCHICKI
- ☐ 426. AL NEWMAN
- ☐ 458. ANDRE DAWSON
- ☐ 468. BOB SEBRA
- ☐ 504. TOM FOLEY
- ☐ 529. WILFREDO TEJADA
- ☐ 549. CASEY CANDAELE
- ☐ 625. RANDY HUNT

NEW YORK METS

- ☐ 29. RANDY MYERS
- ☐ 69. GARY CARTER
- ☐ 76. KEITH HERNANDEZ
- ☐ 118. DARRYL STRAWBERRY
- ☐ 192. RON DARLING
- ☐ 199. DWIGHT GOODEN
- ☐ 241. ROGER MCDOWELL
- ☐ 316. WALLY BACKMAN
- ☐ 323. SID FERNANDEZ
- ☐ 364. BOB OJEDA
- ☐ 439. JESSE OROSCO
- ☐ 446. ED HEARN
- ☐ 487. MOOKIE WILSON
- ☐ 562. LEE MAZZILLI
- ☐ 569. RAFAEL SANTANA
- ☐ 575. DAVE MAGADAN
- ☐ 581. TIM TEUFEL
- ☐ 586. RAY KNIGHT
- ☐ 599. KEVIN MITCHELL
- ☐ 611. LEN DYKSTRA
- ☐ 620. RICK AGUILERA
- ☐ 626. JOHN GIBBONS
- ☐ 635. KEVIN ELSTER
- ☐ 642. STAN JEFFERSON
- ☐ 646. HOWARD JOHNSON
- ☐ 649. DANNY HEEP

NEW YORK YANKEES

- ☐ 52. DON MATTINGLY
- ☐ 93. RON GUIDRY
- ☐ 105. DAVE WINFIELD
- ☐ 128. DAVE RIGHETTI
- ☐ 154. WILLIE RANDOLPH
- ☐ 175. DENNIS RASMUSSEN
- ☐ 217. JOE NIEKRO
- ☐ 228. RICKEY HENDERSON
- ☐ 251. DOUG DRABEK
- ☐ 277. MIKE EASLER
- ☐ 298. MIKE PAGLIARULO
- ☐ 340. BRIAN FISHER
- ☐ 351. RON KITTLE
- ☐ 374. ROD SCURRY
- ☐ 401. PHIL LOMBARDI
- ☐ 422. BOB TEWKSBURY
- ☐ 463. BOB SHIRLEY
- ☐ 474. DAN PASQUA
- ☐ 497. TIM STODDARD
- ☐ 524. WAYNE TOLLESON
- ☐ 545. JOEL SKINNER
- ☐ 597. SCOTT NIELSEN

OAKLAND A'S

- ☐ 34. TERRY STEINBACH
- ☐ 46. MARK MCGWIRE
- ☐ 55. JOSE RIJO
- ☐ 97. JOSE CANSECO
- ☐ 103. TONY PHILLIPS
- ☐ 133. MIKE DAVIS
- ☐ 158. CARNEY LANSFORD
- ☐ 178. ERIC PLUNK
- ☐ 221. STEVE ONTIVEROS
- ☐ 226. CHRIS CODIROLI
- ☐ 256. ALFREDO GRIFFIN
- ☐ 281. BILL BATHE
- ☐ 302. BILL MOONEYHAM
- ☐ 344. CURT YOUNG
- ☐ 349. MICKEY TETTLETON
- ☐ 379. DWAYNE MURPHY
- ☐ 405. DONNIE HILL
- ☐ 425. DAVE KINGMAN
- ☐ 467. JERRY WILLARD
- ☐ 472. DAVE LEIPER
- ☐ 503. JAY HOWELL
- ☐ 528. MOOSE HAAS
- ☐ 548. JOAQUIN ANDUJAR

- ☐ 590. STAN JAVIER
- ☐ 595. ROB NELSON
- ☐ 648. DAVE STEWART

PHILADELPHIA PHILLIES

- ☐ 42. CHRIS JAMES
- ☐ 62. GLENN WILSON
- ☐ 83. SHANE RAWLEY
- ☐ 113. VON HAYES
- ☐ 139. MIKE SCHMIDT
- ☐ 165. JUAN SAMUEL
- ☐ 185. STEVE BEDROSIAN
- ☐ 207. JOHN RUSSELL
- ☐ 236. KEVIN GROSS
- ☐ 262. DARREN DAULTON
- ☐ 288. GARY REDUS
- ☐ 309. JEFF STONE
- ☐ 330. MILT THOMPSON
- ☐ 359. STEVE JELTZ
- ☐ 385. GREG GROSS
- ☐ 412. RON ROENICKE
- ☐ 432. DON CARMAN
- ☐ 453. KENT TEKULVE
- ☐ 482. DAN SCHATZEDER
- ☐ 509. RICK SCHU
- ☐ 535. MIKE MADDUX
- ☐ 555. BRUCE RUFFIN
- ☐ 576. MARVIN FREEMAN
- ☐ 630. CHARLIE HUDSON

PITTSBURGH PIRATES

- ☐ 65. R.J. REYNOLDS
- ☐ 79. SID BREAM
- ☐ 115. TONY PENA
- ☐ 144. JOHNNY RAY
- ☐ 168. MIKE BROWN
- ☐ 188. RICK REUSCHEL
- ☐ 203. BOB WALK
- ☐ 238. CECILIO GUANTE
- ☐ 267. MIKE DIAZ
- ☐ 291. JOE ORSULAK
- ☐ 312. JIM WINN
- ☐ 326. BILL ALMON
- ☐ 361. BARRY BONDS
- ☐ 390. PAT CLEMENTS
- ☐ 415. MIKE BIELECKI
- ☐ 435. RICK RHODEN
- ☐ 449. JUNIOR ORTIZ
- ☐ 484. JIM MORRISON
- ☐ 514. BENNY DISTEFANO
- ☐ 538. RAFAEL BELLIARD
- ☐ 558. BOBBY BONILLA
- ☐ 572. BOB KIPPER
- ☐ 602. BARRY JONES
- ☐ 608. DON ROBINSON

ST. LOUIS CARDINALS

- ☐ 37. JIM LINDEMAN
- ☐ 60. OZZIE SMITH
- ☐ 84. WILLIE MCGEE
- ☐ 111. JACK CLARK
- ☐ 140. TOMMY HERR
- ☐ 170. JOHN TUDOR
- ☐ 183. TERRY PENDLETON
- ☐ 208. GREG MATHEWS
- ☐ 234. RICKY HORTON
- ☐ 263. VINCE COLEMAN

1987 Donruss

- ☐ 293. MIKE LAGA
- ☐ 307. TODD WORRELL
- ☐ 331. MIKE LAVALLIERE
- ☐ 357. KEN DAYLEY
- ☐ 386. TITO LANDRUM
- ☐ 417. ANDY VAN SLYKE
- ☐ 430. PAT PERRY
- ☐ 454. CURT FORD
- ☐ 480. JOHN MORRIS
- ☐ 510. JOSE OQUENDO
- ☐ 540. BOB FORSCH
- ☐ 553. DANNY COX
- ☐ 577. JEFF LAHTI
- ☐ 604. STEVE LAKE
- ☐ 631. RAY SOFF

SAN DIEGO PADRES

- ☐ 31. BENITO SANTIAGO
- ☐ 64. TONY GWYNN
- ☐ 81. STEVE GARVEY
- ☐ 114. LEON "BIP" ROBERTS
- ☐ 141. GARRY TEMPLETON
- ☐ 164. ERIC SHOW
- ☐ 187. DAVE DRAVECKY
- ☐ 205. TERRY KENNEDY
- ☐ 237. LANCE MCCULLERS
- ☐ 264. ANDY HAWKINS
- ☐ 287. TIM FLANNERY
- ☐ 311. BRUCE BOCHY
- ☐ 328. JOHN KRUK
- ☐ 360. ED WHITSON
- ☐ 387. CRAIG LEFFERTS
- ☐ 411. MARVELL WYNNE
- ☐ 434. LAMARR HOYT
- ☐ 451. KEVIN MCREYNOLDS
- ☐ 483. RICH GOSSAGE
- ☐ 511. GENE WALTER
- ☐ 534. JERRY ROYSTER
- ☐ 557. JIMMY JONES
- ☐ 574. RANDY ASADOOR
- ☐ 589. ED WOJNA
- ☐ 607. DAVE LAPOINT
- ☐ 632. RAY HAYWARD
- ☐ 654. TIM PYZNARSKI

SAN FRANCISCO GIANTS

- ☐ 66. WILL CLARK
- ☐ 80. CHRIS BROWN
- ☐ 116. SCOTT GARRELTS
- ☐ 145. ROB THOMPSON
- ☐ 189. DAN GLADDEN
- ☐ 204. ROGER MASON
- ☐ 239. BOB MELVIN
- ☐ 268. CHILI DAVIS
- ☐ 313. MARK DAVIS
- ☐ 327. CANDY MALDONADO
- ☐ 362. VIDA BLUE
- ☐ 391. JEFF LEONARD
- ☐ 436. JOSE URIBE
- ☐ 450. MIKE ALDRETE
- ☐ 485. BOB BRENLY
- ☐ 515. TERRY MULHOLLAND
- ☐ 547. RANDY KUTCHER
- ☐ 559. JEFF ROBINSON
- ☐ 573. KELLY DOWNS
- ☐ 609. MIKE KRUKOW
- ☐ 616. JUAN BERENGUER
- ☐ 636. MIKE LACOSS
- ☐ 644. MARK GRANT

SEATTLE MARINERS

- ☐ 70. MIKE MOORE
- ☐ 75. ALVIN DAVIS
- ☐ 120. JIM PRESLEY
- ☐ 147. DANNY TARTABULL
- ☐ 193. MATT YOUNG
- ☐ 198. KARL BEST
- ☐ 243. ED NUNEZ
- ☐ 270. PHIL BRADLEY
- ☐ 317. KEN PHELPS
- ☐ 322. LEE GUETTERMAN
- ☐ 366. MIKE MORGAN
- ☐ 393. JOHN MOSES
- ☐ 440. SCOTT BRADLEY
- ☐ 445. BOB KEARNEY
- ☐ 489. HAROLD REYNOLDS
- ☐ 517. BILL SWIFT
- ☐ 563. MIKE BROWN

- ☐ 568. MARK LANGSTON
- ☐ 610. DAVE VALLE
- ☐ 613. MIKE TRUJILLO
- ☐ 638. REY QUINONES
- ☐ 656. MICKEY BRANTLEY
- ☐ 660. PETE LADD

TEXAS RANGERS

- ☐ 41. JERRY BROWNE
- ☐ 57. ED CORREA
- ☐ 99. BOBBY WITT
- ☐ 101. JOSE GUZMAN
- ☐ 136. DON SLAUGHT
- ☐ 161. ODDIBE MCDOWELL
- ☐ 180. STEVE BUECHELE
- ☐ 223. CURTIS WILKERSON
- ☐ 224. PETE INCAVIGLIA
- ☐ 259. PETE O'BRIEN
- ☐ 284. MIKE MASON
- ☐ 304. SCOTT FLETCHER
- ☐ 346. RUBEN SIERRA
- ☐ 347. MITCH WILLIAMS
- ☐ 382. GREG HARRIS
- ☐ 408. TOBY HARRAH
- ☐ 427. GARY WARD
- ☐ 469. LARRY PARRISH
- ☐ 470. CHARLIE HOUGH
- ☐ 506. MIKE LOYND
- ☐ 531. DALE MOHORCIC
- ☐ 550. JEFF RUSSELL
- ☐ 592. MIKE STANLEY
- ☐ 593. DARRELL PORTER
- ☐ 619. GENO PETRALLI
- ☐ 627. KEVIN BROWN
- ☐ 637. DWAYNE HENRY
- ☐ 651. BOB BROWER

TORONTO BLUE JAYS

- ☐ 45. DUANE WARD
- ☐ 72. TONY FERNANDEZ
- ☐ 74. LLOYD MOSEBY
- ☐ 121. JESSE BARFIELD
- ☐ 148. ERNIE WHITT
- ☐ 195. DAVE STIEB
- ☐ 197. TOM HENKE
- ☐ 244. JIMMY KEY
- ☐ 271. GEORGE BELL
- ☐ 319. RANCE MULLINIKS
- ☐ 321. MARK EICHHORN
- ☐ 367. WILLIE UPSHAW
- ☐ 394. GARTH IORG
- ☐ 442. JOHN CERUTTI
- ☐ 444. KELLY GRUBER
- ☐ 490. JEFF HEARRON
- ☐ 518. MANNY LEE
- ☐ 561. GLENALLEN HILL
- ☐ 565. MIKE SHARPERSON
- ☐ 567. RICK LEACH
- ☐ 591. JEFF MUSSELMAN
- ☐ 614. DAMASO GARCIA
- ☐ 621. FRED MCGRIFF
- ☐ 639. JIM CLANCY
- ☐ 645. CLIFF JOHNSON
- ☐ 650. JOE JOHNSON
- ☐ 655. LUIS AQUINO

1987 DONRUSS ROOKIES (56) 2 1/2 X 3 1/2

BILLY RIPKEN 2B

ATLANTA BRAVES

NO CARDS ISSUED

BALTIMORE ORIOLES

- ☐ 2. ERIC BELL
- ☐ 3. MARK WILLIAMSON
- ☐ 16. BILLY RIPKEN
- ☐ 24. KEN GERHART

BOSTON RED SOX

- ☐ 4. MIKE GREENWELL
- ☐ 5. ELLIS BURKS
- ☐ 30. TODD BENZINGER

CALIFORNIA ANGELS

- ☐ 6. DEWAYNE BUICE
- ☐ 7. MARK MCLEMORE
- ☐ 8. DEVON WHITE
- ☐ 9. WILLIE FRASER

CHICAGO CUBS

- ☐ 10. LESTER LANCASTER
- ☐ 47. RAFAEL PALMEIRO
- ☐ 51. PAUL NOCE
- ☐ 52. GREG MADDUX

CHICAGO WHITE SOX

- ☐ 11. KEN WILLIAMS
- ☐ 48. BILL LONG

CINCINNATI REDS

NO CARDS ISSUED

CLEVELAND INDIANS

NO CARDS ISSUED

DETROIT TIGERS

- ☐ 12. MATT NOKES
- ☐ 13. JEFF ROBINSON
- ☐ 32. MIKE HENNEMAN

MATT NOKES C

HOUSTON ASTROS

- ☐ 46. DAVE MEADS
- ☐ 55. CHUCK JACKSON

KANSAS CITY ROYALS

- ☐ 14. BO JACKSON
- ☐ 15. KEVIN SEITZER

LOS ANGELES DODGERS

- ☐ 54. BRIAN HOLTON

MILWAUKEE BREWERS

- ☐ 17. B.J. SURHOFF
- ☐ 18. CHUCK CRIM
- ☐ 19. MIKE BIRKBECK
- ☐ 20. CHRIS BOSIO

MINNESOTA TWINS

- ☐ 21. LES STRAKER
- ☐ 22. MARK DAVIDSON
- ☐ 23. GENE LARKIN

MONTREAL EXPOS

- ☐ 33. CASEY CANDAELE

NEW YORK METS

- ☐ 34. DAVE MAGADAN
- ☐ 35. DAVID CONE
- ☐ 37. JOHN MITCHELL

NEW YORK YANKEES

NO CARDS ISSUED

OAKLAND A'S

- ☐ 1. MARK MCGWIRE
- ☐ 25. LUIS POLONIA
- ☐ 26. TERRY STEINBACH

MARK McGWIRE 1B

PHILADELPHIA PHILLIES

- ☐ 36. MIKE JACKSON

PITTSBURGH PIRATES

- ☐ 38. MIKE DUNNE
- ☐ 39. JOHN SMILEY

ST. LOUIS CARDINALS

- ☐ 40. JOE MAGRANE
- ☐ 41. JIM LINDEMAN

SAN DIEGO PADRES

- ☐ 42. SHANE MACK
- ☐ 43. STAN JEFFERSON
- ☐ 44. BENITO SANTIAGO
- ☐ 50. JAMES STEELS

SAN FRANCISCO GIANTS

- ☐ 45. MATT WILLIAMS

SEATTLE MARINERS

- ☐ 27. MICKEY BRANTLEY

TEXAS RANGERS

- ☐ 28. MIKE STANLEY
- ☐ 29. JERRY BROWNE
- ☐ 49. BOB BROWER

TORONTO BLUE JAYS

- ☐ 31. FRED MCGRIFF
- ☐ 53. JEFF JUSSELMAN

1988 DONRUSS (660)
2 1/2 X 3 1/2

Dale Murphy OF

ATLANTA BRAVES

- ☐ 67. KEN OBERKFELL
- ☐ 78. DALE MURPHY
- ☐ 143. OZZIE VIRGIL
- ☐ 167. ZANE SMITH
- ☐ 190. DION JAMES
- ☐ 202. KEN GRIFFEY
- ☐ 266. DAVID PALMER
- ☐ 290. ALBERT HALL
- ☐ 314. GLENN HUBBARD
- ☐ 325. JEFF DEDMON
- ☐ 389. RICK MAHLER
- ☐ 414. DAMASO GARCIA
- ☐ 437. GERALD PERRY
- ☐ 448. RAFAEL RAMIREZ
- ☐ 513. JEFF BLAUSER
- ☐ 537. CHARLIE PULEO
- ☐ 560. TED SIMMONS
- ☐ 571. PETE SMITH
- ☐ 627. ANDRES THOMAS
- ☐ 644. TOM GLAVINE
- ☐ 654. RON GANT

BALTIMORE ORIOLES

- ☐ 48. KEN DIXON
- ☐ 89. MIKE BODDICKER
- ☐ 108. RAY KNIGHT
- ☐ 125. ERIC BELL
- ☐ 150. TERRY KENNEDY
- ☐ 171. CAL RIPKEN
- ☐ 213. KEN GERHART
- ☐ 231. EDDIE MURRAY
- ☐ 248. FRED LYNN
- ☐ 273. LARRY SHEETS
- ☐ 294. TOM NIEDENFUER
- ☐ 336. BILLY RIPKEN
- ☐ 354. JOHN HABYAN
- ☐ 371. DAVE SCHMIDT
- ☐ 396. MIKE YOUNG
- ☐ 418. MARK WILLIAMSON
- ☐ 459. JIM DWYER
- ☐ 477. CARL NICHOLS
- ☐ 494. MIKE GRIFFIN
- ☐ 520. JEFF BALLARD
- ☐ 541. PETE STANICEK
- ☐ 582. RENE GONZALES
- ☐ 601. JOSE MESA

Bruce Hurst P

BOSTON RED SOX

- ☐ 41. JODY REED
- ☐ 51. ROGER CLEMENS
- ☐ 92. BOB STANLEY
- ☐ 129. RICH GEDMAN
- ☐ 153. WADE BOGGS
- ☐ 174. ELLIS BURKS
- ☐ 216. DWIGHT EVANS
- ☐ 252. BRUCE HURST
- ☐ 276. MARTY BARRETT
- ☐ 297. TODD BENZINGER
- ☐ 339. MIKE GREENWELL
- ☐ 375. CALVIN SCHIRALDI
- ☐ 399. JIM RICE
- ☐ 421. JOHN MARZANO
- ☐ 462. OIL CAN BOYD
- ☐ 498. SAM HORN
- ☐ 523. AL NIPPER
- ☐ 544. SPIKE OWEN
- ☐ 585. JEFF SELLERS
- ☐ 623. ED ROMERO
- ☐ 634. WES GARDNER

CALIFORNIA ANGELS

- ☐ 58. DEWAYNE BUICE
- ☐ 86. MIKE WITT
- ☐ 110. WALLY JOYNER
- ☐ 135. WILLIE FRASER
- ☐ 160. JACK LAZORKO
- ☐ 181. MARK MCLEMORE
- ☐ 210. GARY PETTIS
- ☐ 233. DICK SCHOFIELD
- ☐ 258. BRIAN DOWNING
- ☐ 283. DEVON WHITE
- ☐ 305. BOB BOONE
- ☐ 333. JACK HOWELL
- ☐ 356. GUS POLIDOR
- ☐ 381. KIRK MCCASKILL
- ☐ 407. DON SUTTON
- ☐ 428. JOHNNY RAY
- ☐ 456. BILL BUCKNER
- ☐ 479. GEORGE HENDRICK
- ☐ 505. GREG MINTON
- ☐ 530. CHUCK FINLEY
- ☐ 551. DARRELL MILLER
- ☐ 579. GARY LUCAS
- ☐ 621. DONNIE MOORE

CHICAGO CUBS

- ☐ 40. MARK GRACE
- ☐ 68. RICK SUTCLIFFE
- ☐ 77. ED LYNCH
- ☐ 110. JODY DAVIS
- ☐ 146. SHAWON DUNSTON
- ☐ 169. JAMIE MOYER
- ☐ 191. LEON DURHAM
- ☐ 201. KEITH MORELAND
- ☐ 242. RYNE SANDBERG
- ☐ 269. ANDRE DAWSON
- ☐ 292. LEE SMITH
- ☐ 315. PAUL NOCE
- ☐ 324. RAFAEL PALMEIRO
- ☐ 365. LUIS QUINONES
- ☐ 392. BOB DERNIER
- ☐ 416. BRAIN DAYETT
- ☐ 438. DAVE MARTINEZ
- ☐ 447. JERRY MUMPHREY
- ☐ 488. JIM SUNDBERG
- ☐ 516. MANNY TRILLO
- ☐ 539. GREG MADDUX
- ☐ 561. LESTER LANCASTER
- ☐ 570. FRANK DIPINO
- ☐ 609. MIKE BRUMLEY
- ☐ 639. DAMON BERRYHILL
- ☐ 646. SCOTT SANDERSON

CHICAGO WHITE SOX

- ☐ 47. JACK MCDOWELL
- ☐ 59 JOSE DELEON
- ☐ 87. DONNIE HILL
- ☐ 124. RICHARD DOTSON
- ☐ 137. OZZIE GUILLEN
- ☐ 162. GREG WALKER
- ☐ 182. IVAN CALDERON
- ☐ 211. HAROLD BAINES
- ☐ 247. BOBBY THIGPEN
- ☐ 260. CARLTON FISK

☐ 285. JERRY HAIRSTON
☐ 306. BILL LONG
☐ 334. KEN WILLIAMS
☐ 370. GARY REDUS
☐ 383. FLOYD BANNISTER
☐ 409. JIM WINN
☐ 429. RAY SEARAGE
☐ 457. JOHN PAWLOWSKI
☐ 493. FRED MANRIQUE
☐ 507. BOB JAMES
☐ 532. STEVE LYONS
☐ 552. DAVE LAPOINT
☐ 580. RON HASSEY

CINCINNATI REDS

☐ 29. JEFF TREADWAY
☐ 63. TOM BROWNING
☐ 82. ROB MURPHY
☐ 123. JOHN FRANCO
☐ 142. TED POWER
☐ 166. RON ROBINSON
☐ 186. BO DIAZ
☐ 206. BUDDY BELL
☐ 246. RON OESTER
☐ 265. KURT STILLWELL
☐ 289. KAL DANIELS
☐ 310. TRACY JONES
☐ 329. DAVE CONCEPCION
☐ 369. ERIC DAVIS
☐ 388. DAVE PARKER
☐ 413. NICK ESASKY
☐ 433. PAUL O'NEILL
☐ 452. GUY HOFFMAN
☐ 492. BARRY LARKIN
☐ 512. FRANK WILLIAMS
☐ 536. PAT PACILLO
☐ 556. TERRY MCGRIFF
☐ 575. DENNIS RASMUSSEN
☐ 626. PAT PERRY

CLEVELAND INDIANS

☐ 42. JOHN FARRELL
☐ 46. EDDIE WILLIAMS
☐ 95. CHRIS BANDO
☐ 104. SCOTT BAILES
☐ 131. BROOK JACOBY
☐ 156. JULIO FRANCO
☐ 219. PAT TABLER
☐ 227. GREG SWINDELL
☐ 254. JOE CARTER
☐ 279. BRETT BUTLER
☐ 342. MEL HALL
☐ 350. CORY SNYDER
☐ 377. TOM CONDIOTTI
☐ 403. CARMEN CASTILLO
☐ 465. ANDY ALLANSON
☐ 473. DAVE CLARK
☐ 501. KEN SCHROM
☐ 526. TOMMY HINZO
☐ 588. DOUG JONES
☐ 596. SAMMY STEWART
☐ 637. JAY BELL

DETROIT TIGERS

☐ 50 ERIC KING
☐ 91. WALT TERRELL
☐ 107. TOM BROOKENS
☐ 127. JACK MORRIS
☐ 152. MATT NOKES
☐ 173. LOU WHITAKER
☐ 215. CHET LEMON
☐ 230. ALAN TRAMMELL
☐ 250. DARRELL EVANS
☐ 275. KIRK GIBSON
☐ 296. JEFF ROBINSON
☐ 338. MIKE HEATH
☐ 353. LARRY HERNDON
☐ 373. DAVE BERGMAN
☐ 398. WILLIE HERNANDEZ
☐ 420. MIKE HENNEMAN
☐ 461. FRANK TANANA
☐ 476. DAN PETRY
☐ 496. BILL MADLOCK
☐ 522. PAT SHERIDAN
☐ 543. JIM MORRISON
☐ 584. DOYLE ALEXANDER
☐ 599. MARK THURMOND
☐ 615. SCOTT LUSADER

HOUSTON ASTROS

☐ 61. NOLAN RYAN
☐ 85. JIM DESHAIES
☐ 112. MIKE SCOTT
☐ 138. BOB KNEPPER
☐ 163. ALAN ASHBY
☐ 184. GLENN DAVIS
☐ 209. CRAIG REYNOLDS
☐ 235. BILL DORAN
☐ 261. BILLY HATCHER
☐ 286. KEVIN BASS
☐ 308. KEN CAMINITI
☐ 332. LARRY ANDERSEN
☐ 358. DANNY DARWIN
☐ 384. DENNY WALLING
☐ 410. DAVE SMITH
☐ 431. GERALD YOUNG
☐ 455. DAVE MEADS
☐ 481. MANNY HERNANDEZ
☐ 508. ROBBIE WINE
☐ 533. TERRY PUHL
☐ 554. ROCKY CHILDRESS
☐ 578. TY GAINEY

KANSAS CITY ROYALS

☐ 44. GARY THURMAN
☐ 54. MARK GUBICZA
☐ 96. BRET SABERHAGEN
☐ 102. GEROGE BRETT
☐ 132. DANNY JACKSON
☐ 157. CHARLIE LEIBRANDT
☐ 177. DANNY TARTABULL
☐ 220. BO JACKSON
☐ 225. FRANK WHITE
☐ 255. WILLIE WILSON
☐ 280. KEVIN SEITZER
☐ 301. BUD BLACK
☐ 343. JIM EISENREICH
☐ 348. THAD BOSLEY
☐ 378. STEVE FARR
☐ 404. JAMIE QUIRK
☐ 424. STEVE BALBONI
☐ 466. BILL PECOTA
☐ 471. DAN QUISENBERRY
☐ 502. ANGEL SALAZAR
☐ 527. LONNIE SMITH
☐ 547. JERRY GLEATON
☐ 589. MELIDO PEREZ
☐ 584. JOHN DAVIS
☐ 618. GENE GARBER

LOS ANGELES DODGERS

☐ 35. SHAWN HILLEGAS
☐ 53. FERNANDO VALENZUELA
☐ 94. OREL HERSHIER
☐ 106. MIKE SCIOSCIA
☐ 130. KEN HOWELL
☐ 155. MARIANO DUNCAN
☐ 176. STEVE SAX
☐ 218. FRANKLIN STUBBS
☐ 229. MIKE MARSHALL
☐ 253. BOB WELCH
☐ 278. PEDRO GUERRERO
☐ 299. MICKEY HATCHER
☐ 341. JOSE GONZALEZ
☐ 352. JOHN SHELBY
☐ 376. ALEX TREVINO
☐ 402. BRIAN HOLTON
☐ 423. MATT YOUNG
☐ 464. TIM CREWS
☐ 475. DAVE ANDERSON
☐ 499. TRACY WOODSON
☐ 525. JEFF HAMILTON
☐ 546. MIKE DEVEREAUX
☐ 587. TIM BELCHER
☐ 598. ALEJANDRO PENA

MILWAUKEE BREWERS

☐ 36. JOEY MEYER
☐ 49. MIKE BIRKBECK
☐ 90. TED HIGUERA
☐ 109. DAN PLESAC
☐ 117. CHRIS BOSIO
☐ 126. JUAN NIEVES
☐ 151. BILL WEGMAN
☐ 172. B.J. SURHOFF
☐ 214. JIM GANTNER

☐ 232. DALE SVEUM
☐ 240. GLENN BRAGGS
☐ 249. PAUL MOLITOR
☐ 274. ROB DEER
☐ 295. ROBIN YOUNT
☐ 337. GREG BROCK
☐ 355. CHUCK CRIM
☐ 363. JUAN CASTILLO
☐ 372. MARK CLEAR
☐ 397. MIKE FELDER
☐ 419. BILL SCHROEDER
☐ 460. JAY ALRRICH
☐ 478. ERNEST RILES
☐ 486. RICK MANNING
☐ 495. MARK KNUDSON
☐ 521. DAVE STAPLETON
☐ 542. STEVE KIEFER
☐ 583. BRAD KOMMINSK
☐ 602. DON AUGUST

MINNESOTA TWINS

☐ 71. BERT BLYLEVEN
☐ 73. LES STRAKER
☐ 122. JEFF REARDON
☐ 149. FRANK VIOLA
☐ 194. GARY GAETTI
☐ 196. STEVE LOBARDOZZI
☐ 245. TOM BRUNANSKY
☐ 272. RANDY BUSH
☐ 318. KEITH ATHERTON
☐ 320. KENT HRBEK
☐ 368. KIRBY PUCKETT
☐ 395. JUAN BERENGUER
☐ 441. GREG GAGNE
☐ 443. GEORGE FRAZIER
☐ 491. DAN GLADDEN
☐ 519. MARK DAVISON
☐ 564. GENE LARKIN
☐ 566. ROY SMALLEY
☐ 612. TOM NIETO
☐ 631. TIM LAUDNER
☐ 645. AL NEWMAN

MONTREAL EXPOS

☐ 56. FLOYD YOUMANS
☐ 88. JEFF REED
☐ 98. TIM BURKE
☐ 134. NEAL HEATON
☐ 159. MIKE FITZGERALD
☐ 179. CASEY CANDAELE
☐ 212. VANCE LAW
☐ 222. TIM WALLACH
☐ 257. MITCH WEBSTER
☐ 282. ANDRES GALARRAGA
☐ 303. TOM FOLEY
☐ 335. BRYN SMITH
☐ 345. TIM RAINES
☐ 380. ANDY MCGAFFIGAN
☐ 406. JEFF PARRETT
☐ 426. RANDY ST. CLAIRE
☐ 458. BOB SEBRA
☐ 468. HUBIE BROOKS
☐ 504. JOE HESKETH
☐ 529. ROB MCCLURE
☐ 549. DENNIS MARTINEZ
☐ 581. HERM WINNINGHAM
☐ 591. PASCUAL PEREZ

NEW YORK METS

☐ 37. DEVIN ELSTER
☐ 69. DWIGHT GOODEN
☐ 76. RON DARLING
☐ 118. SID FERNANDEZ
☐ 192. JESSE OROSCO
☐ 199. GARY CARTER
☐ 241. WALLY BACKMAN
☐ 316. KEITH HERNANDEZ
☐ 323. DAVE MAGADAN
☐ 364. LEN DYKSTRA
☐ 439. DARRYL STRAWBERRY
☐ 446. RICH AGUILERA
☐ 487. BILL ALMON
☐ 562. KEITH MILLER
☐ 569. HOWARD JOHNSON
☐ 603. TERRY LEACH
☐ 608. JOHN CANDELARIA
☐ 614. LEE MAZZILLI
☐ 617. KEVIN MCREYNOLDS
☐ 619. BARRY LYONS

- [ ] 620. RANDY MYERS
- [ ] 632. BOB OJEDA
- [ ] 633. RAFAEL SANTANA
- [ ] 642. DOUG SISK
- [ ] 648. TIM TEUFEL
- [ ] 651. ROGER MCDOWELL
- [ ] 652. MOOKIE WILSON
- [ ] 653. DAVID CONE
- [ ] 657. GREGG JEFFERIES

NEW YORK YANKEES

- [ ] 43. AL LEITER
- [ ] 52. PAT CLEMENTS
- [ ] 93. DAVE RIGHETTI
- [ ] 105. MIKE PAGLIARULO
- [ ] 128. RICH RHODEN
- [ ] 154. WAYNE TOLLESON
- [ ] 175. RON GUIDRY
- [ ] 217. DON MATTINGLY
- [ ] 228. WILLIE RANDOLPH
- [ ] 251. GARY WARD
- [ ] 277. RICKEY HENDERSON
- [ ] 298. DAVE WINFIELD
- [ ] 340. CLAUDELL WASHINGTON
- [ ] 351. RICK CERONE
- [ ] 374. CHARLES HUDSON
- [ ] 401. TOMMY JOHN
- [ ] 422. RON KITTLE
- [ ] 463. DAN PASQUA
- [ ] 474. JOEL SKINNER
- [ ] 497. TIM STODDARD
- [ ] 524. STEVE TROUT
- [ ] 545. JAY BUHNER
- [ ] 586. BILL GULLICKSON
- [ ] 597. NEIL ALLEN
- [ ] 616. BOBBY MEACHAM
- [ ] 635. ROBERTO KELLY
- [ ] 660. JERRY ROYSTER

Don Mattingly 1B

OAKLAND A'S

- [ ] 56. JAY HOWELL
- [ ] 97. CURT YOUNG
- [ ] 103. MICKEY TETTLETON
- [ ] 133. GENE NELSON
- [ ] 158. TERRY STEINBACH
- [ ] 178. CARNEY LANSFORD
- [ ] 221. TONY PHILLIPS
- [ ] 226. ALFREDO GRIFFIN
- [ ] 256. MARK MCGWIRE
- [ ] 281. MIKE DAVIS
- [ ] 302. JOSE CANSECO
- [ ] 344. TONY BERNAZARD
- [ ] 349. DENNIS ECKERSLEY
- [ ] 379. MIKE GALLEGO
- [ ] 405. DWAYNE MURPHY
- [ ] 425. LUIS POLONIA
- [ ] 467. STEVE ONTIVEROS
- [ ] 472. DAVE STEWART
- [ ] 503. ERIC PLUNK
- [ ] 528. GREG CARADET
- [ ] 548. JOSE RIJO
- [ ] 590. RICK HONEYCUTT
- [ ] 595. STORM DAVIS

PHILADELPHIA PHILLIES

- [ ] 62. STEVE BEDROSIAN
- [ ] 83. SHANE RAWLEY
- [ ] 113. KEVIN GROSS

- [ ] 139. MIKE JACKSON
- [ ] 165. BRUCE RUFFIN
- [ ] 185. LUIS AGUAYO
- [ ] 207. VON HAYES
- [ ] 236. MILT THOMPSON
- [ ] 262. GLENN WILSON
- [ ] 288. JUAN SAMUEL
- [ ] 309. DARREN DAULTON
- [ ] 330. MIKE SCHMIDT
- [ ] 359. LANCE PARRISH
- [ ] 385. DON CARMAN
- [ ] 412. GREG GROSS
- [ ] 432. RICK SCHU
- [ ] 453. CHRIS JAMES
- [ ] 482. JEFF STONE
- [ ] 509. JEFF CALHOUN
- [ ] 535. KENT TEKULVE
- [ ] 555. WALLY RITCHIE
- [ ] 576. STEVE JELTZ
- [ ] 604. TOM NEWELL
- [ ] 643. KEITH HUGHES

PITTSBURGH PIRATES

- [ ] 28. MACKEY SASSER
- [ ] 38. JOSE LIND
- [ ] 45. VICENTE PALACIOS
- [ ] 65. R. J. REYNOLDS
- [ ] 79. DOUG DRABEK
- [ ] 115. BOB KIPPER
- [ ] 144. FELIX FERMIN
- [ ] 168. JUNIOR ORTIZ
- [ ] 188. SID BREAM
- [ ] 203. TOMMY GREGG
- [ ] 238. BOBBY BONILLA
- [ ] 267. MIKE DIAZ
- [ ] 291. ANDY VAN SLYKE
- [ ] 312. MIKE LAVALLIER
- [ ] 326. BARRY BONDS
- [ ] 361. AL PEDRIQUE
- [ ] 390. MIKE DUNNE
- [ ] 415. BRIAN FISHER
- [ ] 435. JOHN CANGELOSI
- [ ] 449. JOHN SMILEY
- [ ] 484. MIKE BIELECKI
- [ ] 514. BOB WALK
- [ ] 538. TOM PRINCE
- [ ] 558. JEFF ROBINSON
- [ ] 572. DARNELL COLES
- [ ] 606. JIM GOTT

ST. LOUIS CARDINALS

- [ ] 31. LANCE JOHNSON
- [ ] 60. DANNY COX
- [ ] 84. GREG MATHEWS
- [ ] 111. BOB FORSCH
- [ ] 140. JOE MAGRANE
- [ ] 170. TONY PENA
- [ ] 183. JACK CLARK
- [ ] 208. TOMMY HERR
- [ ] 234. JOSE OQUENDO
- [ ] 263. OZZIE SMITH
- [ ] 293. VINCE COLEMAN
- [ ] 307. WILLIE MCGEE
- [ ] 331. BILL DAWLEY
- [ ] 357. KEN DAYLEY
- [ ] 386. TODD WORRELL
- [ ] 417. CURT FORD
- [ ] 430. RICKY HORTON
- [ ] 454. TERRY PENDLETON
- [ ] 480. JOHN MORRIS
- [ ] 510. STEVE LAKE
- [ ] 540. JIM LINDEMAN
- [ ] 553. JOHN TUDOR
- [ ] 577. TOM PAGNOZZI
- [ ] 647. SCOTT TERRY

SAN DIEGO PADRES

- [ ] 33. SHAWN ABNER
- [ ] 34. ROBERTO ALOMAR
- [ ] 64. MARK DAVIS
- [ ] 81. ED WHITSON
- [ ] 114. BENITO SANTIAGO
- [ ] 141. JIMMY JONES
- [ ] 164. TONY GWYNN
- [ ] 187. STAN JEFFERSON
- [ ] 205. JOHN KRUK
- [ ] 237. MARVELL WYNNE
- [ ] 264. RANDY READY
- [ ] 287. CARMELO MARTINEZ

- [ ] 311. GREG BOOKER
- [ ] 328. TIM FLANNERY
- [ ] 360. JAMES STEELS
- [ ] 387. ERIC SHOW
- [ ] 411. SHANE MACK
- [ ] 434. RICH GOSSAGE
- [ ] 451. LANCE MCCULLERS
- [ ] 483. CHRIS BROWN
- [ ] 511. MARK GRANT
- [ ] 534. ERIC NOLTE
- [ ] 557. DAVE LEIPER
- [ ] 574. ROB NELSON
- [ ] 605. RANDALL BYERS
- [ ] 649. GARRY TEMPLETON

SAN FRANCISCO GIANTS

- [ ] 39. KIRT MANWARING
- [ ] 66. KEVIN MITCHELL
- [ ] 80. SCOTT GARRELTS
- [ ] 116. MIKE KRUKOW
- [ ] 145. KELLY DOWNS
- [ ] 189. BOB BRENLY
- [ ] 204. WILL CLARK
- [ ] 239. CHRIS SPEIER
- [ ] 268. ROB THOMPSON
- [ ] 313. CHILI DAVIS
- [ ] 327. JEFFREY LEONARD
- [ ] 362. MIKE ALDRETE
- [ ] 391. CANDY MALDONADO
- [ ] 436. MIKE LACOSS
- [ ] 450. ATLEE HAMMAKER
- [ ] 485. DAVE DRAVECKY
- [ ] 515. CRAIG LEFFERTS
- [ ] 559. JOSE URIBE
- [ ] 573. DON ROBINSON
- [ ] 607. HARRY SPILMAN
- [ ] 613. RICK REUSCHEL
- [ ] 628. MATT WILLIAMS
- [ ] 638. BOB MELVIN
- [ ] 655. JOE PRICE

SEATTLE MARINERS

- [ ] 30. MIKE CAMPBELL
- [ ] 70. SCOTT BANKHEAD
- [ ] 75. MIKE MOORE
- [ ] 120. MIKE MORGAN
- [ ] 147. SCOTT BRADLEY
- [ ] 193. ALVIN DAVIS
- [ ] 198. REY QUINONES
- [ ] 243. PHIL BRADLEY
- [ ] 270. LEE GUETTERMAN
- [ ] 317. MARK LANGSTON
- [ ] 322. MIKE KINGERY
- [ ] 366. JIM PRESLEY
- [ ] 393. DAVE VALLE
- [ ] 440. JOHN MOSES
- [ ] 445. ED NUNEZ
- [ ] 489. KEN PHELPS
- [ ] 517. JERRY REED
- [ ] 563. HAROLD REYNOLDS
- [ ] 568. BILL WILKINSON
- [ ] 610. MICKEY BRANTLEY
- [ ] 622. DOMINGO RAMOS
- [ ] 629. DAVE HENGEL

TEXAS RANGERS

- [ ] 57. ED CORREA
- [ ] 99. CHARLIE HOUGH
- [ ] 101. BOBBY WITT
- [ ] 136. JOSE GUZMAN
- [ ] 161. MITCH WILLIAMS
- [ ] 180. SCOTT FLETCHER
- [ ] 223. RUBEN SIERRA
- [ ] 224. STEVE BUECHELE
- [ ] 259. MIKE STANLEY
- [ ] 284. PETE O'BRIEN
- [ ] 304. PETE INCAVIGLIA
- [ ] 346. BOB BROWER
- [ ] 347. LARRY PARRISH
- [ ] 382. ODDIBE MCDOWELL
- [ ] 408. JERRY BROWNE
- [ ] 427. GREG HARRIS
- [ ] 469. PAUL KILGUS
- [ ] 470. DALE MOHORCIC
- [ ] 506. GENO PETRALLI
- [ ] 531. JEFF RUSSELL
- [ ] 500. MIKE LOYND
- [ ] 592. CURT WILKERSON
- [ ] 593. STEVE HOWE

1988 Donruss

TORONTO BLUE JAYS

- ☐ 32. NELSON LIRIANO
- ☐ 72. JIMMY KEY
- ☐ 74. JIM CLANCY
- ☐ 121. MARK EICHHORN
- ☐ 148. DAVE STIEB
- ☐ 195. FRED MCGRIFF
- ☐ 197. RANCE MULLINIKS
- ☐ 244. KELLY GRUBER
- ☐ 271. WILLIE UPSHAW
- ☐ 319. TONY FERNANDEZ
- ☐ 321. JOHN CERUTTI
- ☐ 367. LLOYD MOSEBY
- ☐ 394. ERNIE WHITT
- ☐ 442. JESSE BARFIELD
- ☐ 444. GARTH IORG
- ☐ 490. TOM HENKE
- ☐ 518. RICK LEACH
- ☐ 565. CECIL FIELDER
- ☐ 567. DUANE WARD
- ☐ 611. JOSE NUNEZ
- ☐ 624. GREG MYERS
- ☐ 630. JEFF MUSSELMAN
- ☐ 636. MIKE FLANAGAN
- ☐ 640. DAVID WELLS
- ☐ 650. MANNY LEE
- ☐ 656. GEORGE BELL
- ☐ 658. TODD STOTTLEMYRE
- ☐ 659. GERONIMO BERROA

1988 DONRUSS ROOKIES (56) 2 1/2 X 3 1/2

Kevin Elster SS

ATLANTA BRAVES

- ☐ 10. PETE SMITH
- ☐ 47. RON GANT
- ☐ 49. KEVIN COFFMAN

BALTIMORE ORIOLES

- ☐ 15. PETE STANICEK
- ☐ 23. CRAIG WORTHINGTON
- ☐ 39. CARL NICHOLS
- ☐ 41. JOSE BAUTISTA

BOSTON RED SOX

- ☐ 14. BRADY ANDERSON
- ☐ 24. JOHN TRAUTWEIN
- ☐ 44. JODY REED
- ☐ 54. STEVE ELLSWORTH

CALIFORNIA ANGELS

- ☐ 53. BRYAN HARVEY

CHICAGO CUBS

- ☐ 1. MARK GRACE
- ☐ 31. DAMON BERRYHILL
- ☐ 45. DARRIN JACKSON
- ☐ 46. MIKE CAPEL

CHICAGO WHITE SOX

- ☐ 7. DAVE GALLAGHER
- ☐ 21. MELIDO PEREZ

- ☐ 40. JACK MCDOWELL
- ☐ 48. JOHN DAVIS

CINNINNATI REDS

- ☐ 17. JEFF TREADWAY
- ☐ 30. CHRIS SABO

CLEVELAND INDIANS

NO CARDS ISSUED

DETROIT TIGERS

- ☐ 19. PAUL GIBSON

HOUSTON ASTROS

NO CARDS ISSUED

KANSAS CITY ROYALS

- ☐ 33. GARY THURMAN
- ☐ 55. MIKE MACFARLANE

LOS ANGELES DODGERS

- ☐ 20. TIM CREWS
- ☐ 28. TIM BELCHER

Tim Belcher P

MILWAUKEE BREWERS

- ☐ 4. DAVE STAPLETON
- ☐ 38. JOEY MEYER

MINNESOTA TWINS

NO CARDS ISSUED

MONTREAL EXPOS

- ☐ 29. JOHNNY PAREDES
- ☐ 43. JOHN DOPSON

NEW YORK METS

- ☐ 34. KEVIN ELSTER
- ☐ 51. MACKEY SASSER

NEW YORK YANKEES

- ☐ 11. JAY BUHNER
- ☐ 16. ROBERTO KELLY
- ☐ 27. AL LEITER

OAKLAND A'S

- ☐ 13. DOUG JENNINGS
- ☐ 18. WALT WEISS

PHILADELPHIA PHILLIES

- ☐ 3. TODD FROHWIRTH

PITTSBURGH PIRATES

- ☐ 32. RANDY MILLIGAN

ST. LOUIS CARDINALS

- ☐ 22. STEVE PETERS
- ☐ 50. CRIS CARPENTER
- ☐ 52. LUIS ALICEA

SAN DIEGO PADRES

- ☐ 5. SHAWN ABNER
- ☐ 8. MARK PARENT
- ☐ 35. ROBERTO ALOMAR

SAN FRANCISCO GIANTS

NO CARDS ISSUED

SEATTLE MARINERS

- ☐ 2. MIKE CAMPBELL
- ☐ 36. EDGAR MARTINEZ

TEXAS RANGERS

- ☐ 6. JOSE CECENA
- ☐ 9. CECIL ESPY
- ☐ 25. DEWAYNE VAUGHN

TORONTO BLUE JAYS

- ☐ 12. PAT BORDERS
- ☐ 26. DAVID WELLS
- ☐ 37. TODD STOTTLEMYRE
- ☐ 42. SIL CAMPUSANO

Todd Stottlemyre P

1989 DONRUSS (660) 2 1/2 X 3 1/2

Chris Sabo 3B

ATLANTA BRAVES

- ☐ 50. RON GANT
- ☐ 104. DALE MURPHY
- ☐ 121. TOMMY GREGG
- ☐ 145. OZZIE VIRGIL
- ☐ 168. JOE BOEVER
- ☐ 222. RICK MAHLER
- ☐ 239. GERALD PERRY
- ☐ 263. PETE SMITH
- ☐ 286. CHARLIE PULEO
- ☐ 340. DION JAMES
- ☐ 357. PAUL ASSENMACHER
- ☐ 381. TOM GLAVINE
- ☐ 405. JOSE ALVAREZ
- ☐ 458. BRUCE SUTTER
- ☐ 475. BRUCE BENEDICT
- ☐ 499. ZANE SMITH

☐ 523. MARK LEMKE
☐ 576. ANDRES THOMAS
☐ 592. JEFF BLAUSER
☐ 616. ANDY NEZELEK
☐ 642. JOHN SMOLTZ
☐ 650. JODY DAVIS
☐ 653. DEREK LILLIQUIST

BALTIMORE ORIOLES

☐ 44. PETE HARNISCH
☐ 46. GREGG OLSON
☐ 51. CAL RIPKEN
☐ 96. EDDIE MURRAY
☐ 141. TERRY KENNEDY
☐ 164. MIKE MORGAN
☐ 169. PETE STANICEK
☐ 215. DAVE SCHMIDT
☐ 259. BILLY RIPKEN
☐ 282. TOM NIEDENFUER
☐ 287. JOEW ORSULAK
☐ 333. LARRY SHEETS
☐ 377. R. C. GONZALES
☐ 401. MICKEY TETTLETON
☐ 406. RICK SCHU
☐ 451. JOSE BAUTISTA
☐ 495. JEFF BALLARD
☐ 519. BRADY ANDERSON
☐ 524. OSWALD PERAZA
☐ 569. CRAIG WORTHINGTON
☐ 635. CURT SCHILLING
☐ 651. BOB MILACKI

BOSTON RED SOX

☐ 37. CARLOS QUINTANA
☐ 66. LEE SMITH
☐ 68. WADE BOGGS
☐ 122. JIM RICE
☐ 162. RICH GEDMAN
☐ 184. MARTY BARRETT
☐ 186. MIKE GREENWELL
☐ 240. DWIGHT EVANS
☐ 280. ROGER CLEMENS
☐ 303. ELLIS BURKS
☐ 305. JODY REED
☐ 358. TODD BENZINGER
☐ 398. RICK CERONE
☐ 421. BOB STANLEY
☐ 423. BRUCE HURST
☐ 476. OIL CAN BOYD
☐ 517. JEFF SELLERS
☐ 539. TOM BOLTON
☐ 541. WES GARDNER
☐ 593. SPIKE OWEN
☐ 612. MIKE BODDICKER
☐ 628. MIKE SMITHSON
☐ 633. DENNIS LAMP
☐ 660. ERIC HETZEL

CALIFORNIA ANGELS

☐ 52. WALLY JOYNER
☐ 94. MARK MCLEMORE
☐ 108. DICK SCHOFIELD
☐ 136. KIRK MCCASKILL
☐ 170. BOB BOONE
☐ 213. DEVON WHITE
☐ 226. CHUCK FINLEY
☐ 254. BRIAN DOWNING
☐ 288. JACK HOWELL
☐ 331. JOHNNY RAY
☐ 344. DAN PETRY
☐ 372. MIKE WITT
☐ 407. SHERMAN CORBETT
☐ 449. CHILI DAVIS
☐ 462. STEW CLIBURN
☐ 490. GREG MINTON
☐ 525. BRYAN HARVEY
☐ 567. WILLIE FRASER
☐ 580. TONY ARMAS
☐ 607. TERRY CLARK
☐ 634. DANTE BICHETTE

CHICAGO CUBS

☐ 43. MIKE HARKEY
☐ 49. RAFAEL PALMEIRO
☐ 105. RYNE SANDBERG
☐ 137. SHAWON DUNSTON
☐ 157. JAMIE MOYER
☐ 158. RICH GOSSAGE

☐ 167. ANDRE DAWSON
☐ 223. RICK SUTCLIFFE
☐ 255. MARK GRACE
☐ 275. DAMON BERRYHILL
☐ 276. VANCE LAW
☐ 285. CALVIN SCHIRALDI
☐ 341. LES LANCASTER
☐ 373. GREG MADDUX
☐ 393. FRANK DIPINO
☐ 384. AL NIPPER
☐ 404. PAT PERRY
☐ 459. MITCH WEBSTER
☐ 491. DOUG DASCENZO
☐ 512. MIKE BIELECKI
☐ 513. JEFF PICO
☐ 522. DREW HALL
☐ 577. ROLANDO ROOMES
☐ 608. MANNY TRILLO
☐ 629. SCOTT SANDERSON
☐ 658. KEVIN BLANKENSHIP

CHICAGO WHITE SOX

☐ 58. MELIDO PEREZ
☐ 101. CARLTON FISK
☐ 135. GREG WALKER
☐ 148. HAROLD BAINES
☐ 176. OZZIE GUILLEN
☐ 219. STEVE ROSENBERG
☐ 253. STEVE LYONS
☐ 266. BOBBY THIGPEN
☐ 294. DAN PASQUA
☐ 337. KEN WILLIAMS
☐ 371. IVAN CALDERON
☐ 384. DAVE GALLAGHER
☐ 413. JERRY REUSS
☐ 455. DARYL BOSTON
☐ 489. FRED MANRIQUE
☐ 503. SHAWN HILLEGAS
☐ 531. JACK MCDOWELL
☐ 573. BILL LONG
☐ 606. LANCE JOHNSON
☐ 619. ADAM PETERSON
☐ 647. BARRY JONES
☐ 655. MIKE DIAZ

CINCINNATI REDS

☐ 71. TOM BROWNING
☐ 80. ERIC DAVIS
☐ 115. KEITH BROWN
☐ 124. DANNY JACKSON
☐ 139. ROB MURPHY
☐ 189. NICK ESASKY
☐ 198. KAL DANIELS
☐ 233. JOHN FRANCO
☐ 242. BO DIAZ
☐ 257. BARRY LARKIN
☐ 308. RON ROBINSON
☐ 317. CHRIS SABO
☐ 351. JEFF TREADWAY
☐ 360. PAUL O'NEILL
☐ 375. JOSE RIJO
☐ 426. ROB DIBBLE
☐ 435. HERM WINNINGHAM
☐ 469. JEFF REED
☐ 478. FRANK WILLIAMS
☐ 493. JACK ARMSTRONG
☐ 544. NORM CHARLTON
☐ 553. RON OESTER
☐ 586. VAN SNIDER
☐ 595. LLOYD MCCLENDON

CLEVELAND INDIANS

☐ 36. LUIS MEDINA
☐ 73. MEL HALL
☐ 83. JOE CARTER
☐ 114. BROOK JACOBY
☐ 138. ANDY ALLANSON
☐ 191. CORY SNYDER
☐ 202. SCOTT BAILES
☐ 232. GREG SWINDELL
☐ 256. TOM CANDIOTTI
☐ 310. JULIO FRANCO
☐ 320. JOHN FARRELL
☐ 350. JAY BELL
☐ 374. CARMEN CASTILLO
☐ 428. RON KITTLE
☐ 438. DOUG JONES
☐ 468. RON WASHINGTON
☐ 492. WILLIE UPSHAW

☐ 546. RICH YETT
☐ 556. BUD BLACK
☐ 585. DAVE CLARK
☐ 609. SCOTT JORDAN
☐ 639. TOM LAMPKIN
☐ 649. ROD NICHOLS

DETROIT TIGERS

☐ 29. STEVE SEARCY
☐ 60. GARY PETTIS
☐ 62. GUILLERMO HERNANDEZ
☐ 90. FRANK TANANA
☐ 116. MATT NOKES
☐ 153. TED POWER
☐ 178. DOYLE ALEXANDER
☐ 180. ALAN TRAMMELL
☐ 209. CHET LEMON
☐ 234. JACK MORRIS
☐ 271. MIKE HEATH
☐ 296. WALT TERRELL
☐ 298. LOU WHITAKER
☐ 327. MIKE HENNEMAN
☐ 352. LUIS SALAZAR
☐ 389. DAVE BERGMAN
☐ 415. JIM WALEWANDER
☐ 417. PAT SHERIDAN
☐ 445. PAUL GIBSON
☐ 470. JEFF ROBINSON
☐ 508. TOM BROOKENS
☐ 533. DARRELL EVANS
☐ 535. ERIC KING
☐ 563. FRED LYNN

HOUSTON ASTROS

☐ 30. CAMERON DREW
☐ 69. MIKE SCOTT
☐ 88. ALAN ASHBY
☐ 118. BOB FORSCH
☐ 123. BOB KNEPPER
☐ 154. NOLAN RYAN
☐ 187. BILLY HATCHER
☐ 207. GERALD YOUNG
☐ 236. GLENN DAVIS
☐ 241. JIM DESHAIES
☐ 272. DAVE SMITH
☐ 306. BILL DORAN
☐ 325. KEVIN BASS
☐ 354. JUAN AGOSTO
☐ 359. LARRY ANDERSEN
☐ 390. DANNY DARWIN
☐ 424. DAVE MEADS
☐ 443. JOHN FISHEL
☐ 472. TERRY PUHL
☐ 477. CRAIG REYNOLDS
☐ 509. RAFAEL RAMIREZ
☐ 542. KEN CAMINITI
☐ 561. CRAIG BIGGIO
☐ 640. BRIAN MEYER

KANSAS CITY ROYALS

☐ 45. TOM GORDON
☐ 61. DANNY TARTABULL
☐ 85. FRANK WHITE
☐ 89. CHARLIE LEIBRANDT
☐ 120. WILLIE WILSON
☐ 144. BRET SABERHAGEN
☐ 179. MARK GUBICZA
☐ 204. GEORGE BRETT
☐ 208. BO JACKSON
☐ 238. KEVIN SEITZER
☐ 262. FLOYD BANNISTER
☐ 297. ED HEARN
☐ 322. KURT STILLWELL
☐ 326. PAT TABLER
☐ 356. STEVE FARR
☐ 380. BRAD WELLMAN
☐ 416. MIKE MACFARLANE
☐ 440. JEFF MONTGOMERY
☐ 444. JERRY DON GLEATON
☐ 474. ISRAEL SANCHEZ
☐ 498. GARY THURMAN
☐ 534. LUIS AQUINO
☐ 558. JOSE DEJESUS
☐ 562. LUIS DE LOS SANTOS

LOS ANGELES DODGERS

☐ 77. MIKE SCIOSCIA
☐ 79. ALFREDO GRIFFIN

☐ 84. STEVE SAX
☐ 110. MIKE MARSHALL
☐ 132. KIRK GIBSON
☐ 195. JOHN TUDOR
☐ 197. OREL HERSHISER
☐ 203. TIM BELCHER
☐ 228. JESSE OROSCO
☐ 250. FERNANDO VALENZUELA
☐ 314. JOHN SHELBY
☐ 316. MIKE DAVIS
☐ 321. FRANKLIN STUBBS
☐ 346. MICKEY HATCHER
☐ 368. DANNY HEEP
☐ 432. RICK DEMPSEY
☐ 434. DAVE ANDERSON
☐ 439. BRIAN HOLTON
☐ 464. RAMON MARTINEZ
☐ 486. TIM CREWS
☐ 550. JEFF HAMILTON
☐ 552. TIM LEARY
☐ 557. ALEJANDRO PENA
☐ 582. RICKY HORTON
☐ 589. WILLIAM BRENNAN
☐ 603. MIKE DEVEREAUX
☐ 610. JAY HOWELL

Robin Yount OF

MILWAUKEE BREWERS

☐ 31. GARY SHEFFIELD
☐ 55. ROBIN YOUNT
☐ 57. GREG BROCK
☐ 103. GLENN BRAGGS
☐ 146. DALE SVEUM
☐ 173. ROB DEER
☐ 175. TED HIGUERA
☐ 221. B. J. SURHOFF
☐ 264. JIM GANTNER
☐ 291. PAUL MOLITOR
☐ 293. BILL WEGMAN
☐ 339. JOEY MEYER
☐ 382. DAN PLESAC
☐ 410. DON AUGUST
☐ 412. CHRIS BOSIO
☐ 457. JEFFREY LEONARD
☐ 501. MIKE BIRKBECK
☐ 528. MARK CLEAR
☐ 530. JUAN CASTILLO
☐ 575. JUAN NIEVES
☐ 617. CHUCK CRIM
☐ 632. MIKE YOUNG
☐ 644. BILL SCHROEDER
☐ 654. PAUL MIRABELLA

MINNESOTA TWINS

☐ 64. GARY GAETTI
☐ 81. JUAN BERENGUER
☐ 119. BERT BLYLEVEN
☐ 155. JEFF REARDON
☐ 182. KIRBY PUCKETT
☐ 199. KENT HRBEK
☐ 237. FRANK VIOLA
☐ 273. KEITH ATHERTON
☐ 301. TOMMY HERR
☐ 318. GREG GAGNE
☐ 355. GENE LARKIN
☐ 391. DAN GLADDEN
☐ 419. ALLAN ANDERSON
☐ 436. AL NEWMAN
☐ 473. CHARLIE LEA
☐ 510. FRED TOLIVER
☐ 537. RANDY BUSH

☐ 554. STEVE LOMBARDOZZI
☐ 590. GERMAN GONZALEZ
☐ 615. TIM LAUDNER
☐ 626. JOHN MOSES
☐ 641. BRIAN HARPER

MONTREAL EXPOS

☐ 42. RANDY JOHNSON
☐ 97. TIM RAINES
☐ 102. DAVE MARTINEZ
☐ 106. DENNIS MARTINEZ
☐ 130. ANDRES GALARRAGA
☐ 156. TIM WALLACH
☐ 216. BRYN SMITH
☐ 220. HUBIE BROOKS
☐ 224. NEAL HEATON
☐ 248. PASCUAL PEREZ
☐ 274. TIM BURKE
☐ 234. JEFF PARRETT
☐ 338. ANDY MCGAFFIGAN
☐ 342. TOM FOLEY
☐ 366. NELSON SANTOVENIA
☐ 392. JOHN DOPSON
☐ 452. REX HUDLER
☐ 456. MIKE FITZGERALD
☐ 460. JOE HESKETH
☐ 484. WALLACE JOHNSON
☐ 511. BRIAN HOLMAN
☐ 570. JOHNNY PAREDES
☐ 574. TRACY JONES
☐ 578. LUIS RIVERA

NEW YORK METS

☐ 35. GREGG JEFFERIES
☐ 41. DAVE WEST
☐ 53. GARY CARTER
☐ 99. KEVIN MCREYNOLDS
☐ 117. KEITH HERNANDEZ
☐ 147. DARRYL STRAWBERRY
☐ 152. MOOKIE WILSON
☐ 171. RON DARLING
☐ 218. BOB OJEDA
☐ 235. HOWARD JOHNSON
☐ 265. ROGER MCDOWELL
☐ 270. DWIGHT GOODEN
☐ 289. KEVIN ELSTER
☐ 336. RANDY MYERS
☐ 353. LENNY DYKSTRA
☐ 383. WALLY BACKMAN
☐ 388. DAVID CONE
☐ 408. DAVE MAGADAN
☐ 454. MACKEY SASSER
☐ 471. SID FERNANDEZ
☐ 502. TERRY LEACH
☐ 507. TIM TEUFEL
☐ 526. RICK AGUILERA
☐ 572. BARRY LYONS
☐ 618. JACK SAVAGE
☐ 623. KEITH MILLER

NEW YORK YANKEES

☐ 72. CLAUDELL WASHINGTON
☐ 74. DON MATTINGLY
☐ 78. DAVE RIGHETTI
☐ 127. MIKE PAGLIARULO
☐ 159. DAVE WINFIELD
☐ 190. DON SLAUGHT
☐ 192. JOHN CANDELARIA
☐ 196. NEIL ALLEN
☐ 245. RICKEY HENDERSON
☐ 277. RICH DOTSON
☐ 309. RAFAEL SANTANA
☐ 311. JACK CLARK
☐ 315. AL LEITER
☐ 363. KEN PHELPS
☐ 395. WILLIE RANDOLPH
☐ 427. JOEL SKINNER
☐ 429. RICK RHODEN
☐ 433. ROBERTO KELLY
☐ 481. DAVE EILAND
☐ 514. CHARLES HUDSON
☐ 545. HAL MORRIS
☐ 547. HENSLEY MEULENS
☐ 551. LOUIS AGUAYO
☐ 598. HIPOLITO PENA
☐ 630. DALE MOHORCIC
☐ 659. WAYNE TOLLESON

OAKLAND A'S

☐ 38. FELIX JOSE
☐ 67. DENNIS ECKERSLEY
☐ 91. JOSE CANSECO
☐ 95. MARK MCGWIRE
☐ 125. ERIC PLUNK
☐ 150. DAVE PARKER
☐ 185. STAN JAVIER
☐ 210. STORM DAVIS
☐ 214. DAVE STEWART
☐ 243. CARNEY LANSFORD
☐ 268. TERRY STEINBACH
☐ 304. CURT YOUNG
☐ 328. RICK HONEYCUTT
☐ 332. BOB WELCH
☐ 361. RON HASSEY
☐ 386. LUIS POLONIA
☐ 422. MIKE GALLEGO
☐ 446. WALT WEISS
☐ 450. DAVE HENDERSON
☐ 479. GREG CADARET
☐ 505. DOUG JENNINGS
☐ 540. GENE NELSON
☐ 564. TODD BURNS
☐ 568. GLENN HUBBARD
☐ 596. STEVE ONTIVEROS
☐ 621. LANCE BLANKENSHIP

PHILADELPHIA PHILLIES

☐ 40. RON JONES
☐ 75. STEVE BEDROSIAN
☐ 76. JUAN SAMUEL
☐ 133. DAVID PALMER
☐ 160. VON HAYES
☐ 193. MIKE SCHMIDT
☐ 194. KEVIN GROSS
☐ 251. SHANE RAWLEY
☐ 278. LANCE PARRISH
☐ 312. CHRIS JAMES
☐ 313. MILT THOMPSON
☐ 369. PHIL BRADLEY
☐ 396. DON CARMAN
☐ 430. BOB DERNIER
☐ 431. STEVE JELTZ
☐ 487. MIKE MADDUX
☐ 515. BRUCE RUFFIN
☐ 548. GREG HARRIS
☐ 549. DARREN DAULTON
☐ 587. TODD FROHWIRTH
☐ 604. ALEX MADRID
☐ 624. RICKY JORDAN
☐ 631. MARVIN FREEMAN

PITTSBURGH PIRATES

☐ 54. ANDY VAN SLYKE
☐ 92. BARRY BONDS
☐ 126. BRIAN FISHER
☐ 134. R. J. REYNOLDS
☐ 151. BOBBY BONILLA
☐ 172. BOB WALK
☐ 211. DOUG DRABEK
☐ 244. MIKE LAVALLIERE
☐ 252. SID BREAM
☐ 269. MIKE DUNNE
☐ 290. JOSE LIND
☐ 329. JOHN SMILEY
☐ 362. JIM GOTT
☐ 370. JEFF ROBINSON
☐ 387. JUNIOR ORTIZ
☐ 409. BOB KIPPER
☐ 447. GLENN WILSON
☐ 480. RANDY KRAMER
☐ 488. DAVE LAPOINT
☐ 506. KEN OBERKFELL
☐ 527. TOM PRINCE
☐ 565. FELIX FERMIN
☐ 597. SCOTT MEDVIN
☐ 605. GARY REDUS
☐ 622. MIGUEL GARCIA

ST. LOUIS CARDINALS

☐ 39. CRIS CARPENTER
☐ 63. OZZIE SMITH
☐ 82. TODD WORRELL
☐ 112. TOM BRUNANSKY
☐ 161. WILLIE MCGEE
☐ 163. TONY PENA
☐ 181. VINCE COLEMAN

1989 Donruss

☐ 201. JOE MAGRANE
☐ 230. TERRY PENDLETON
☐ 279. DENNY WALLING
☐ 281. GREG MATHEWS
☐ 299. KEN DAYLEY
☐ 319. JOSE OQUENDO
☐ 348. DANNY COX
☐ 397. SCOTT TERRY
☐ 399. TOM PAGNOZZI
☐ 418. PEDRO GUERRERO
☐ 437. JOSE DELEON
☐ 466. LOUIS ALICEA
☐ 516. LARRY MCWILLIAMS
☐ 518. JOHN COSTELLO
☐ 536. KEN HILL
☐ 555. TIM JONES

SAN DIEGO PADRES

☐ 28. SANDY ALOMAR JR.
☐ 34. GREG HARRIS
☐ 65. MARK DAVIS
☐ 86. JOHN KRUK
☐ 111. KEITH MORELAND
☐ 128. TONY GWYNN
☐ 129. LANCE MCCULLERS
☐ 183. CHRIS BROWN
☐ 205. BENITO SANTIAGO
☐ 229. ED WHITSON
☐ 246. ROBERTO ALOMAR
☐ 247. JIMMY JONES
☐ 302. MIKE BRUMLEY
☐ 323. SHAWN ABNER
☐ 347. MARVELL WYNNE
☐ 364. TIM FLANNERY
☐ 365. RANDY READY
☐ 420. MARK PARENT
☐ 441. DICKIE THON
☐ 465. DAVE LEIPER
☐ 482. ERIC SHOW
☐ 483. GARRY TEMPLETON
☐ 538. SHANE MACK
☐ 559. DENNIS RASMUSSEN
☐ 583. ANDY HAWKINS
☐ 599. JERALD CLARK
☐ 601. CARMELO MARTINEZ

SAN FRANCISCO GIANTS

☐ 59. CRAIG LEFFERTS
☐ 98. ROB THOMPSON
☐ 131. JOSE URIBE
☐ 140. MIKE ALDRETE
☐ 177. CANDY MALDONADO
☐ 217. BRETT BUTLER
☐ 249. WILL CLARK
☐ 258. MIKE KRUKOW
☐ 295. SCOTT GARRELTS
☐ 335. RICK REUSCHEL
☐ 367. KELLY DOWNS
☐ 376. JOE PRICE
☐ 414. ATLEE HAMMAKER
☐ 453. BOB BRENLY
☐ 485. KEVIN MITCHELL
☐ 494. KIRT MANWARING
☐ 532. CHRIS SPEIER
☐ 571. DON ROBINSON
☐ 594. MATT WILLIAMS
☐ 602. MIKE LACOSS
☐ 611. FRANCISCO MELENDEZ
☐ 625. ERNEST RILES
☐ 646. DENNIS COOK

SEATTLE MARINERS

☐ 32. ERIK HANSON
☐ 33. KEN GRIFFEY
☐ 93. HAROLD REYNOLDS
☐ 109. HENRY COTTO
☐ 143. STEVE BALBONI
☐ 212. MICKEY BRANTLEY
☐ 227. MARK LANGSTON
☐ 261. SCOTT BRADLEY
☐ 330. REY QUINONES
☐ 345. ALVIN DAVIS
☐ 379. JIM PRESLEY
☐ 448. MIKE MOORE
☐ 463. SCOTT BANKHEAD
☐ 497. MIKE CAMPBELL
☐ 566. DARNELL COLES
☐ 581. JAY BUHNER

☐ 614. DAVE VALLE
☐ 637. MIKE SCHOOLER
☐ 645. EDGAR MARTINEZ
☐ 652. MIKE JACKSON
☐ 657. JERRY REED

TEXAS RANGERS

☐ 48. RUBEN SIERRA
☐ 56. PETE INCAVIGLIA
☐ 107. PETE O'BRIEN
☐ 142. SCOTT FLETCHER
☐ 165. CHARLIE HOUGH
☐ 166. MIKE STANLEY
☐ 174. STEVE BUECHELE
☐ 225. MITCH WILLIAMS
☐ 260. CECILIO GUANTE
☐ 283. PAUL KILGUS
☐ 284. JOSE GUZMAN
☐ 292. CECIL ESPY
☐ 343. GENO PETRALLI
☐ 378. ODDIBE MCDOWELL
☐ 402. CURTIS WILKERSON
☐ 403. JEFF RUSSELL
☐ 411. BOB BROWER
☐ 461. BOBBY WITT
☐ 496. JEFF KUNKEL
☐ 520. CRAIG MCMURTRY
☐ 521. RAY HAYWARD
☐ 529. JERRY BROWNE
☐ 579. CHAD KREUTER
☐ 613. KEVIN BROWN
☐ 636. SCOTT MAY

TORONTO BLUE JAYS

☐ 47. ALEX SANCHEZ
☐ 70. FRED MCGRIFF
☐ 87. RANCE MULLINIKS
☐ 113. KELLY GRUBER
☐ 149. GEORGE BELL
☐ 188. JIMMY KEY
☐ 206. TONY FERNANDEZ
☐ 231. LLOYD MOSEBY
☐ 267. JIM CLANCY
☐ 307. DAVID WELLS
☐ 324. MIKE FLANAGAN
☐ 349. DAVE STIEB
☐ 385. TOM HENKE
☐ 425. JESSE BARFIELD
☐ 442. CECIL FIELDER
☐ 467. JOHN CERUTTI
☐ 504. MANNY LEE
☐ 543. DUANE WARD
☐ 560. PAT BORDERS
☐ 584. SIL CAMPUSANO
☐ 591. ERNIE WHITT
☐ 620. TODD STOTTLEMYRE
☐ 627. NELSON LIRIANO
☐ 638. RICK LEACH
☐ 656. JEFF MUSSELMAN

1989 DONRUSS TRADED (56)
2 1/2 X 3 1/2

ATLANTA BRAVES

NO CARDS ISSUED

BALTIMORE ORIOLES

☐ 20T. BRIAN HOLTON
☐ 30T. MIKE DEVEREAUX
☐ 41T. PHIL BRADLEY

BOSTON RED SOX

☐ 7T. JOHN DOPSON
☐ 15T. ROB MURPHY
☐ 18T. NICK ESASKY

CALIFORNIA ANGELS

☐ 35T. BERT BLYLEVEN
☐ 46T. CLAUDELL WASHINGTON

CHICAGO CUBS

☐ 34T. CURT WILKERSON
☐ 38T. MITCH WILLIAMS
☐ 42T. PAUL KILGUS

CHICAGO WHITE SOX

☐ 29T. EDDIE WILLIAMS
☐ 37T. ERIC KING
☐ 51T. RON KITTLE

CINCINNATI REDS

☐ 24T. RICK MAHLER
☐ 47T. TODD BENZINGER

CLEVELAND INDIANS

☐ 16T. PETE O'BRIEN
☐ 22T. JOEL SKINNER
☐ 26T. JESSE OROSCO
☐ 33T. FELIX FERMIN
☐ 44T. JERRY BROWNE
☐ 49T. ODDIBE MCDOWELL

DETROIT TIGERS

☐ 9T. CHRIS BROWN
☐ 17T. KEN WILLIAMS
☐ 50T. CHARLES HUDSON

HOUSTON ASTROS

☐ 32T. JIM CLANCY
☐ 40T. RICK RHODEN

KANSAS CITY ROYALS

☐ 5T. BOB BOONE

LOS ANGELES DODGERS

☐ 8T. WILLIE RANDOLPH
☐ 12T. EDDIE MURRAY

MILWAUKEE BREWERS

NO CARDS ISSUED

MINNESOTA TWINS

☐ 10T. WALLY BACKMAN

MONTREAL EXPOS

☐ 3T. KEVIN GROSS
☐ 14T. SPKIE OWEN
☐ 25T. MIKE ALDRETE

NEW YORK METS

NO CARDS ISSUED

NEW YORK YANKEES

☐ 13T. LANCE MCCULLERS
☐ 23T. STEVE SAX
☐ 27T. DAVE LAPOINT
☐ 36T. MEL HALL
☐ 48T. STEVE BALBONI
☐ 52T. ANDY HAWKINS
☐ 53T. TOM BROOKENS

OAKLAND A'S

☐ 21T. MIKE MOORE

PHILADELPHIA PHILLIES

☐ 4T. TOMMY HERR
☐ 11T. STEVE ONTIVEROS
☐ 55T. JEFF PARRETT

PITTSBURGH PIRATES

NO CARDS ISSUED

ST. LOUIS CARDINALS

☐ 43T. MILT THOMPSON

SAN DIEGO PADRES

☐ 2T. JACK CLARK
☐ 28T. WALT TERRELL
☐ 45T. BRUCE HURST

SAN FRANCISCO GIANTS

NO CARDS ISSUED

SEATTLE MARINERS

☐ 1T. JEFFREY LEONARD
☐ 54T. TOM NIEDENFUER

TEXAS RANGERS

☐ 6T. RAFAEL PALMEIRO
☐ 19T. NOLAN RYAN
☐ 31T. JULIO FRANCO
☐ 39T. JAMIE MOYER

TORONTO BLUE JAYS

NO CARDS ISSUED

1989 DONRUSS ROOKIES (56)
2 1/2 X 3 1/2

ATLANTA BRAVES

☐ 19. GERONIMO BERROA
☐ 54. DEREK LILLIQUIST

BALTIMORE ORIOLES

☐ 22. BOB MILACKI
☐ 25. CRAIG WORTHINGTON
☐ 35. GREGG OLSON
☐ 47. STEVE FINLEY
☐ 51. MIKE DEVEREAUX

BOSTON RED SOX

NO CARDS ISSUED

CALIFORNIA ANGELS

☐ 16. JIM ABBOTT
☐ 29. DANTE BICHETTE

CHICAGO CUBS

☐ 10. STEVE WILSON
☐ 23. JOE GIRARDI
☐ 26. JEROME WALTON
☐ 32. DWIGHT SMITH
☐ 36. PHIL STEPHENSON
☐ 38. RICK WRONA

CHICAGO WHITE SOX

☐ 7. DONN PALL
☐ 14. CARLOS MARTINEZ
☐ 37. KEN PATTERSON
☐ 50. MATT MERULLO

CINCINNATI REDS

NO CARDS ISSUED

CLEVELAND INDIANS

☐ 20. LUIS MEDINA

DETROIT TIGERS

☐ 17. TOREY LOVULLO
☐ 39. MIKE BRUMLEY

HOUSTON ASTROS

☐ 34. ERIC YELDING

KANSAS CITY ROYALS

☐ 4. TOM GORDON
☐ 33. LUIS DE LOS SANTOS

LOS ANGELES DODGERS

☐ 45. RAMON MARTINEZ

MILWAUKEE BREWERS

☐ 1. GARY SHEFFIELD
☐ 5. BILLY SPIERS

MINNESOTA TWINS

☐ 9. FRANCISCO OLIVERAS
☐ 24. GERMAN GONZALEZ
☐ 27. GARY WAYNE

MONTREAL EXPOS

☐ 43. RANDY JOHNSON

NEW YORK METS

☐ 2. GREGG JEFFERIES
☐ 18. MARK CARREON

NEW YORK YANKEES

☐ 6. DEION SANDERS
☐ 11. BOB GEREN
☐ 52. CLAY PARKER

OAKLAND A'S

NO CARDS ISSUED

PHILADELPHIA PHILLIES

☐ 42. RON JONES

PITTSBURGH PIRATES

☐ 8. STEVE CARTER
☐ 48. RANDY KRAMER

ST. LOUIS CARDINALS

☐ 28. TIM JONES
☐ 31. KEN HILL
☐ 40. CRIS CARPENTER

SAN DIEGO PADRES

☐ 21. SANDY ALOMAR, JR.
☐ 46. GREG HARRIS

SAN FRANCISCO GIANTS

☐ 41. JEFF BRANTLEY

SEATTLE MARINERS

☐ 3. KEN GRIFFEY, JR.
☐ 15. EDGAR MARTINEZ
☐ 49. ERIK HANSON
☐ 53. OMAR VIZQUEL

TEXAS RANGERS

☐ 13. KENNY ROGERS
☐ 44. KEVIN BROWN

TORONTO BLUE JAYS

☐ 12. TONY CASTILLO
☐ 30. ALEXIS INFANTE
☐ 55. JUNIOR FELIX

1990 DONRUSS (715)
2 1/2 X 3 1/2

ATLANTA BRAVES

☐ 31. KENT MERCKER
☐ 39. STEVE AVERY
☐ 46. KELLY MANN
☐ 50. JEFF TREADWAY
☐ 104. GERONIMO BERROA
☐ 121. JOHN SMOLTZ
☐ 145. TOM GLAVINE
☐ 153. GERALD PERRY
☐ 168. DALE MURPHY
☐ 222. LONNIE SMITH
☐ 239. TOMMY GREGG
☐ 263. ANDRES THOMAS
☐ 271. JEFF BLAUSER
☐ 286. DEREK LILLIQUIST
☐ 340. ODDIBE MCDOWELL
☐ 357. JOE BOEVER
☐ 381. MARTY CLARY
☐ 389. JOSE ALVAREZ
☐ 405. SERGIO VALDEZ
☐ 458. JOHN RUSSELL
☐ 475. RON GANT
☐ 499. PETE SMITH
☐ 508. MIKE STANTON
☐ 523. ANDY NEZELEK
☐ 576. TOMMY GREENE
☐ 592. TONY CASTILLO
☐ 624. MARK LEMKE
☐ 646. FRANCISCO CABRERA
☐ 704. DAVE JUSTICE
☐ 713. GARY EAVE

BALTIMORE ORIOLES

☐ 32. BEN MCDONALD
☐ 51. JEFF BALLARD
☐ 96. CAL RIPKEN
☐ 141. CRAIG WORTHINGTON
☐ 164. BILLY RIPKEN
☐ 169. MICKEY TETTLETON
☐ 215. STEVE FINLEY
☐ 259. PHIL BRADLEY
☐ 282. MIKE DEVEREAUX
☐ 287. JOE ORSULAK
☐ 333. BOB MILACKI
☐ 377. GREGG OLSON
☐ 401. RENE GONZALES
☐ 406. MARK WILLIAMSON

☐ 451. BOB MELVIN
☐ 495. LARRY SHEETS
☐ 519. RANDY MILLIGAN
☐ 524. DAVE SCHMIDT
☐ 569. JIM TRABER
☐ 583. KEVIN HICKEY
☐ 596. PETE HARNISCH
☐ 612. MARK THURMOND
☐ 635. BRIAN HOLTON
☐ 638. BRADY ANDERSON
☐ 667. CURT SCHILLING
☐ 702. DAVE JOHNSON

BOSTON RED SOX

☐ 66. MIKE GREENWELL
☐ 68. WADE BOGGS
☐ 110. LEE SMITH
☐ 122. DWIGHT EVANS
☐ 162. JOHN DOPSON
☐ 184. ROGER CLEMENS
☐ 186. ROB MURPHY
☐ 228. ELLIS DURKS
☐ 240. MARTY BARRETT
☐ 280. MIKE BODDICKER
☐ 303. NICK ESASKY
☐ 305. RICK CERONE
☐ 346. RICH GEDMAN
☐ 358. DANNY HEEP
☐ 398. JODY REED
☐ 421. LUIS RIVERA
☐ 423. DENNIS LAMP
☐ 464. MIKE SMITHSON
☐ 476. KEVIN ROMINE
☐ 517. CARLOS QUINTANA
☐ 539. ERIC HETZEL
☐ 541. WES GARDNER
☐ 582. GREG HARRIS
☐ 633. OIL CAN BOYD

CALIFORNIA ANGELS

☐ 35. MIKE FETERS
☐ 52. CLAUDELL WASHINGTON
☐ 94. WALLY JOYNER
☐ 108. JIM ABBOTT
☐ 116. GREG MINTON
☐ 136. CHILI DAVIS
☐ 170. KIRK MCCASKILL
☐ 213. LANCE PARRISH
☐ 226. DEVON WHITE
☐ 234. JOHNNY RAY
☐ 254. JACK HOWELL
☐ 288. DICK SCHOFIELD
☐ 331. BERT BLYLEVEN
☐ 344. CHUCK FINLEY
☐ 352. BRIAN DOWNING
☐ 372. BRYAN HARVEY
☐ 407. GLENN HOFFMAN
☐ 449. LEE STEVENS
☐ 462. RICH MONTELEONE
☐ 470. BOB MCCLURE
☐ 490. KENT ANDERSON
☐ 525. TONY ARMAS
☐ 567. BILL SCHROEDER
☐ 580. MIKE WITT
☐ 587. WILLIE FRASER

CHICAGO CUBS

☐ 49. SHAWON DUNSTON
☐ 105. RYNE SANDBERG
☐ 137. MITCH WEBSTER
☐ 157. RICK SUTCLIFFE
☐ 158. GREG MADDUX
☐ 167. DAMON BERRYHILL
☐ 223. ANDRE DAWSON
☐ 255. MARVELL WYNNE
☐ 275. MITCH WILLIAMS
☐ 276. PAUL KILGUS
☐ 285. JEROME WALTON
☐ 341. LLOYD MCCLENDON
☐ 373. MIKE BIELECKI
☐ 393. DWIGHT SMITH
☐ 394. STEVE WILSON
☐ 404. JOE GIRARDI
☐ 459. PAUL ASSENMACHER
☐ 491. DOMINGO RAMOS
☐ 512. RICK WRONA
☐ 513. LUIS SALAZAR
☐ 522. MIKE HARKEY
☐ 577. MARK GRACE

☐ 585. JEFF PICO
☐ 608. CURT WILKERSON
☐ 628. LES LANCASTER
☐ 629. VANCE LAW
☐ 647. SCOTT SANDERSON

CHICAGO WHITE SOX

☐ 28. ROBIN VENTURA
☐ 58. CARLTON FISK
☐ 101. MELIDO PEREZ
☐ 135. OZZIE GUILLEN
☐ 148. RON KITTLE
☐ 176. DAN PASQUA
☐ 219. DAVE GALLAGHER
☐ 253. STEVE ROSENBERG
☐ 266. BOBBY THIGPEN
☐ 294. IVAN CALDERON
☐ 337. ERIC KING
☐ 371. KEN PATTERSON
☐ 384. GREG HIBBARD
☐ 413. RON KARKOVICE
☐ 455. SCOTT FLETCHER
☐ 489. SAMMY SOSA
☐ 503. JERRY KUTZLER
☐ 531. CARLOS MARTINEZ
☐ 573. LANCE JOHNSON
☐ 606. DONN PALL
☐ 619. SHAWN HILLEGAS
☐ 651. STEVE LYONS

CINCINNATI REDS

☐ 71. BARRY LARKIN
☐ 80. DANNY JACKSON
☐ 115. JOSE RIJO
☐ 124. JOHN FRANCO
☐ 139. BO DIAZ
☐ 189. ROB DIBBLE
☐ 198. PAUL O'NEILL
☐ 233. ERIC DAVIS
☐ 242. CHRIS SABO
☐ 257. TODD BENZINGER
☐ 308. TOM BROWNING
☐ 317. RON OESTER
☐ 351. JEFF REED
☐ 360. ROLANDO ROOMES
☐ 375. RICK MAHLER
☐ 426. NORM CHARLTON
☐ 435. SCOTT SCUDDER
☐ 469. KEN GRIFFEY
☐ 478. HERM WINNINGHAM
☐ 493. TIM BIRTSAS
☐ 544. JACK ARMSTRONG
☐ 553. RON ROBINSON
☐ 586. JOE OLIVER
☐ 595. LUIS QUINONES
☐ 670. TIM LEARY
☐ 684. MARIANO DUNCAN

CLEVELAND INDIANS

☐ 73. JOEL SKINNER
☐ 83. BROOK JACOBY
☐ 114. JOE CARTER
☐ 138. JERRY BROWNE
☐ 154. JESSE OROSCO
☐ 191. FELIX FERMIN
☐ 202. PETE O'BRIEN
☐ 232. JOHN FARRELL
☐ 256. TOM CANDIOTTI
☐ 272. CORY SNYDER
☐ 310. GREG SWINDELL
☐ 320. DOUG JONES
☐ 350. BRAD KOMMINSK
☐ 374. TOM MAGRANN
☐ 390. JOEY BELLE
☐ 428. DION JAMES
☐ 438. STEVE OLIN
☐ 468. SCOTT BAILES
☐ 492. DAVE CLARK
☐ 509. RICH YETT
☐ 546. ROD NICHOLS
☐ 556. BUD BLACK
☐ 691. BEAU ALLRED

DETROIT TIGERS

☐ 38. BRIAN DUBOIS
☐ 60. CHET LEMON
☐ 62. DOYLE ALEXANDER
☐ 90. ALAN TRAMMELL

☐ 178. MATT NOKES
☐ 180. FRANK TANANA
☐ 209. MIKE HEATH
☐ 296. MIKE HENNEMAN
☐ 298. LOU WHITAKER
☐ 327. FRANK WILLIAMS
☐ 415. KEVIN RITZ
☐ 417. JEFF ROBINSON
☐ 445. DAVE BERGMAN
☐ 533. MIKE BRUMLEY
☐ 535. DOUG STRANGE
☐ 563. EDWIN NUNEZ
☐ 599. RICK SCHU
☐ 610. GUILLERMO HERNANDEZ
☐ 621. GARY WARD
☐ 636. TRACY JONES
☐ 639. JACK MORRIS
☐ 657. PAUL GIBSON
☐ 661. GARY PETTIS
☐ 696. SCOTT LUSADER

HOUSTON ASTROS

☐ 34. ERIC ANTHONY
☐ 69. JIM CLANCY
☐ 88. DAVE SMITH
☐ 118. GLENN DAVIS
☐ 123. EIRC YELDING
☐ 187. JIM DESHAIES
☐ 207. MIKE SCOTT
☐ 236. BILL DORAN
☐ 241. RAFAEL RAMIREZ
☐ 306. CRAIG BIGGIO
☐ 325. GERALD YOUNG
☐ 354. TERRY PUHL
☐ 359. LARRY ANDERSEN
☐ 424. KEN CAMINITI
☐ 443. ALEX TREVINO
☐ 472. GLENN WILSON
☐ 477. JUAN AGOSTO
☐ 542. MARK PORTUGAL
☐ 561. DANNY DARWIN
☐ 589. KEVIN BASS
☐ 594. DAN SCHATZEDER
☐ 648. BRIAN MEYER
☐ 688. STEVE LOMBARDOZZI

KANSAS CITY ROYALS

☐ 61. BO JACKSON
☐ 85. KEVIN SEITZER
☐ 89. BRET SABERHAGEN
☐ 120. KURT STILLWELL
☐ 144. GEORGE BRETT
☐ 179. LUIS AQUINO
☐ 204. MARK GUBICZA
☐ 208. CHARLIE LEIBRANDT
☐ 238. JIM EISENREICH
☐ 262. FRANK WHITE
☐ 297. TOM GORDON
☐ 322. DANNY TARTABULL
☐ 326. BOB BOONE
☐ 356. STEVE FARR
☐ 380. JEFF MONTGOMERY
☐ 416. GARY THURMAN
☐ 440. WILLIE WILSON
☐ 444. PAT TABLER
☐ 474. BILL BUCKNER
☐ 498. MIKE MACFARLANE
☐ 534. TERRY LEACH
☐ 562. RICK LUECKEN
☐ 709. LARRY MCWILLIAMS

LOS ANGELES DODGERS

☐ 77. EDDIE MURRAY
☐ 79. TIM BELCHER
☐ 84. MIKE MARSHALL
☐ 132. MIKE MORGAN
☐ 195. ALFREDO GRIFFIN
☐ 197. OREL HERSHISER
☐ 203. JAY HOWELL
☐ 250. WILLIE RANDOLPH
☐ 314. JOSE GONZALEZ
☐ 316. MIKE SCIOSCIA
☐ 321. JEFF HAMILTON
☐ 368. KIRK GIBSON
☐ 432. KAL DANIELS
☐ 434. LENNY HARRIS
☐ 439. MICKEY HATCHER
☐ 486. DAVE ANDERSON
☐ 550. TIM CREWS
☐ 552. MIKE DAVIS
☐ 557. RICK DEMPSEY
☐ 603. MIKE SHARPERSON
☐ 615. FRANKLIN STUBBS
☐ 625. FERNANDO VALENZUELA
☐ 649. RAY SEARAGE
☐ 664. ALEJANDRO PENA
☐ 671. JOHN WETTELAND
☐ 685. RAMON MARTINEZ

MILWAUKEE BREWERS

☐ 37. GREG VAUGHN
☐ 55. ROB DEER
☐ 57. CHRIS BOSIO
☐ 103. PAUL MOLITOR
☐ 146. ROBIN YOUNT
☐ 173. B. J. SURHOFF
☐ 175. DAN PLESAC
☐ 221. CHUCK CRIM
☐ 264. GLENN BRAGGS
☐ 291. JIM GANTNER
☐ 293. GREG BROCK
☐ 339. TED HIGUERA
☐ 382. BILL SPIERS
☐ 410. CHARLIE O'BRIEN
☐ 412. GUS POLIDOR
☐ 457. TONY FOSSAS
☐ 501. GARY SHEFFIELD
☐ 528. JERRY REUSS
☐ 530. JEFF PETEREK
☐ 575. MARK KNUDSON
☐ 609. MIKE FELDER
☐ 617. DON AUGUST
☐ 640. JAIME NAVARRO
☐ 687. TOM FILER
☐ 699. GEORGE CANALE

MINNESOTA TWINS

☐ 64. ALLAN ANDERSON
☐ 81. KENT HRBEK
☐ 119. JEFF REARDON
☐ 151. GARY GAETTI
☐ 155. WALLY BACKMAN
☐ 182. DAN GLADDEN
☐ 199. RANDY BUSH
☐ 237. GREG GAGNE
☐ 269. KIRBY PUCKETT
☐ 273. ROY SMITH
☐ 301. JUAN BERENGUER
☐ 318. GARY WAYNE
☐ 355. BRIAN HARPER
☐ 387. DAVE WEST
☐ 391. RICK AGUILERA
☐ 419. TIM LAUDNER
☐ 436. GENE LARKIN
☐ 473. KEVIN TAPANI
☐ 506. AL NEWMAN
☐ 510. TIM DRUMMOND
☐ 537. SHANE RAWLEY
☐ 554. CARMEN CASTILLO
☐ 590. JOHN MOSES
☐ 622. MARK GUTHRIE
☐ 626. PAUL SORRENTO
☐ 642. MIKE DYER
☐ 690. CHIP HALE

MONTREAL EXPOS

☐ 36. MARQUIS GRISSOM
☐ 40. MARK GARDNER
☐ 42. DELINO DESHIELDS

☐ 97. ANDRES GALARRAGA
☐ 102. SPIKE OWEN
☐ 106. BRYN SMITH
☐ 130. HUBIE BROOKS
☐ 156. DENNIS MARTINEZ
☐ 216. TIM RAINES
☐ 220. TIM WALLACH
☐ 224. NELSON SANTOVENIA
☐ 248. KEVIN GROSS
☐ 274. TOM FOLEY
☐ 334. TIM BURKE
☐ 338. MARK LANGSTON
☐ 342. PASCUAL PEREZ
☐ 366. REX HUDLER
☐ 392. MIKE FITZGERALD
☐ 452. DAVE MARTINEZ
☐ 456. OTIS NIXON
☐ 460. ZANE SMITH
☐ 484. JIM DWYER
☐ 511. JOE HESKETH
☐ 570. WALLACE JOHNSON
☐ 574. ANDY MCGAFFIGAN
☐ 578. LARRY WALKER
☐ 693. JEFF HUSON

NEW YORK METS

☐ 47. JULIO MACHADO
☐ 53. JUAN SAMUEL
☐ 99. HOWARD JOHNSON
☐ 117. BOB OJEDA
☐ 147. GARY CARTER
☐ 152. KEVIN ELSTER
☐ 171. DWIGHT GOODEN
☐ 218. KEVIN MCREYNOLDS
☐ 235. DARRYL STRAWBERRY
☐ 265. DAVID CONE
☐ 270. GREGG JEFFERIES
☐ 289. RON DARLING
☐ 336. RANDY MYERS
☐ 353. FRANK VIOLA
☐ 383. DAVE MAGADAN
☐ 388. KEITH HERNANDEZ
☐ 408. JEFF INNIS
☐ 454. MARK CARREON
☐ 471. MACKEY SASSER
☐ 502. TERRY BROSS
☐ 507. KEITH MILLER
☐ 526. BARRY LYONS
☐ 572. SID FERNANDEZ
☐ 618. TIM TEUFEL
☐ 623. JEFF MUSSELMAN

NEW YORK YANKEES

☐ 72. DAVE LAPOINT
☐ 74. JESSE BARFIELD
☐ 78. STEVE SAX
☐ 127. LEE GUETTERMAN
☐ 159. ANDY HAWKINS
☐ 190. DON MATTINGLY
☐ 192. ROBERTO KELLY
☐ 196. ERIC PLUNK
☐ 245. ALVARO ESPINOZA
☐ 277. DON SLAUGHT
☐ 309. WALT TERRELL
☐ 311. DAVE RIGHETTI
☐ 315. STEVE BALBONI
☐ 363. CLAY PARKER
☐ 395. BOB GEREN
☐ 427. DEION SANDERS
☐ 429. CHUCK CARY
☐ 433. LANCE MCCULLERS
☐ 481. KEVIN MMAHAT
☐ 514. HAL MORRIS
☐ 545. GREG CADARET
☐ 547. LUIS POLONIA
☐ 551. DAVE WINFIELD
☐ 598. MEL HALL
☐ 630. RANDY VELARDE
☐ 656. MIKE BLOWERS
☐ 678. GOOSE GOSSAGE
☐ 689. BERNIE WILLIAMS

OAKLAND A'S

☐ 67. WALT WEISS
☐ 91. TONY PHILLIPS
☐ 95. CARNEY LANSFORD
☐ 125. JOSE CANSECO
☐ 150. DAVE STEWART
☐ 185. MARK MCGWIRE

1990 Donruss

- ☐ 210. DENNIS ECKERSLEY
- ☐ 214. MIKE MOORE
- ☐ 243. DAVE HENDERSON
- ☐ 268. TERRY STEINBACH
- ☐ 304. RICKEY HENDERSON
- ☐ 328. DAVE PARKER
- ☐ 332. BOB WELCH
- ☐ 361. MIKE GALLEGO
- ☐ 386. RICK HONEYCUTT
- ☐ 422. JIM CORSI
- ☐ 446. TODD BURNS
- ☐ 450. RON HASSEY
- ☐ 479. STORM DAVIS
- ☐ 505. CURT YOUNG
- ☐ 540. GENE NELSON
- ☐ 564. FELIX JOSE
- ☐ 568. STAN JAVIER
- ☐ 675. KEN PHELPS

PHILADELPHIA PHILLIES

- ☐ 44. PAT COMBS
- ☐ 75. TOMMY HERR
- ☐ 76. RICKY JORDAN
- ☐ 133. STEVE JELTZ
- ☐ 160. JOHN KRUK
- ☐ 193. DENNIS COOK
- ☐ 194. DARREN DAULTON
- ☐ 251. ROGER MCDOWELL
- ☐ 278. VON HAYES
- ☐ 312. MIKE MADDUX
- ☐ 313. LENNY DYKSTRA
- ☐ 369. JEFF PARRETT
- ☐ 396. RANDY READY
- ☐ 430. KEN HOWELL
- ☐ 431. STEVE LAKE
- ☐ 487. RON JONES
- ☐ 515. TERRY MULHOLLAND
- ☐ 548. CHARLIE HAYES
- ☐ 549. DICKIE THON
- ☐ 604. DON CARMAN
- ☐ 631. TODD FROHWIRTH
- ☐ 643. MIKE SCHMIDT
- ☐ 694. CURT FORD

PITTSBURGH PIRATES

- ☐ 54. JOHN SMILEY
- ☐ 92. DOUG DRABEK
- ☐ 126. BARRY BONDS
- ☐ 134. JEFF ROBINSON
- ☐ 172. JOSE LIND
- ☐ 211. MIKE LAVALLIERE
- ☐ 244. ANDY VAN SLYKE
- ☐ 252. RAFAEL BELLIARD
- ☐ 290. BOBBY BONILLA
- ☐ 329. SID BREAM
- ☐ 362. BOB KIPPER
- ☐ 370. BOB WALK
- ☐ 409. RANDY KRAMER
- ☐ 447. R. J. REYNOLDS
- ☐ 480. JEFF KING
- ☐ 488. JAY BELL
- ☐ 527. RICK REED
- ☐ 565. JOHN CANGELOSI
- ☐ 597. GARY REDUS
- ☐ 605. JIM GOTT
- ☐ 616. BILLY HATCHER
- ☐ 658. NEAL HEATON
- ☐ 668. BILL LANDRUM

ST. LOUIS CARDINALS

- ☐ 29. TODD ZEILE
- ☐ 63. PEDRO GUERRERO
- ☐ 82. MILT THOMPSON
- ☐ 161. JOSE OQUENDO
- ☐ 163. JOE MAGRANE
- ☐ 181. TONY PENA
- ☐ 201. OZZIE SMITH
- ☐ 279. VINCE COLEMAN
- ☐ 281. KEN DAYLEY
- ☐ 299. TERRY PENDLETON
- ☐ 319. TODD WORRELL
- ☐ 397. KEN HILL
- ☐ 399. TOM BRUNANSKY
- ☐ 418. SCOTT TERRY
- ☐ 437. DAN QUISENBERRY
- ☐ 516. JOHN MORRIS
- ☐ 518. FRANK DIPINO
- ☐ 536. JOSE DELEON
- ☐ 555. JOHN COSTELLO
- ☐ 591. TOM PAGNOZZI
- ☐ 632. WILLIE MCGEE
- ☐ 634. CRIS CARPENTER
- ☐ 653. TED POWER
- ☐ 666. RICKY HORTON
- ☐ 677. DENNY WALLING
- ☐ 686. TIM JONES
- ☐ 714. BOB TEWKSBURY

SAN DIEGO PADRES

- ☐ 30. SANDY ALOMAR, JR.
- ☐ 41. ANDY BENES
- ☐ 65. GREG HARRIS
- ☐ 86. TONY GWYNN
- ☐ 111. ROBERTO ALOMAR
- ☐ 128. JACK CLARK
- ☐ 183. BRUCE HURST
- ☐ 205. ED WHITSON
- ☐ 229. MARK PARENT
- ☐ 246. GARRY TEMPLETON
- ☐ 302. MARK DAVIS
- ☐ 323. CHRIS JAMES
- ☐ 347. BIP ROBERTS
- ☐ 364. MIKE PAGLIARULO
- ☐ 420. DENNIS RASMUSSEN
- ☐ 441. MARK GRANT
- ☐ 465. BENITO SANTIAGO
- ☐ 482. CARMELO MARTINEZ
- ☐ 538. JOEY CORA
- ☐ 559. ERIC SHOW
- ☐ 593. JERALD CLARK
- ☐ 641. DARRIN JACKSON
- ☐ 672. CALVIN SCHIRALDI

SAN FRANCISCO GIANTS

- ☐ 59. KIRT MANWARING
- ☐ 98. KEVIN MITCHELL
- ☐ 112. RICK REUSCHEL
- ☐ 131. ERNEST RILES
- ☐ 140. ROBBY THOMPSON
- ☐ 177. KELLY DOWNS
- ☐ 217. SCOTT GARRELTS
- ☐ 230. WILL CLARK
- ☐ 249. BRETT BUTLER
- ☐ 258. DON ROBINSON
- ☐ 295. STEVE BEDROSIAN
- ☐ 335. JOSE URIBE
- ☐ 348. MATT WILLIAMS
- ☐ 367. PAT SHERIDAN
- ☐ 376. CRAIG LEFFERTS
- ☐ 414. TREVOR WILSON
- ☐ 453. GREG LITTON
- ☐ 466. JEFF BRANTLEY
- ☐ 485. BOB KNEPPER
- ☐ 494. KEN OBERKFELL
- ☐ 532. ATLEE HAMMAKER
- ☐ 571. DONELL NIXON
- ☐ 602. TERRY KENNEDY
- ☐ 611. CANDY MALDONADO
- ☐ 652. MIKE LACOSS
- ☐ 680. BILL BATHE

SEATTLE MARINERS

- ☐ 93. JEFFREY LEONARD
- ☐ 109. ALVIN DAVIS
- ☐ 129. DAVE VALLE
- ☐ 143. BRIAN HOLMAN

- ☐ 212. DARNELL COLES
- ☐ 227. HAROLD REYNOLDS
- ☐ 247. GENE HARRIS
- ☐ 261. SCOTT BANKHEAD
- ☐ 330. MIKE SCHOOLER
- ☐ 345. ERIK HANSON
- ☐ 365. KEN GRIFFEY, JR.
- ☐ 379. RANDY JOHNSON
- ☐ 448. JAY BUHNER
- ☐ 463. GREG BRILEY
- ☐ 483. OMAR VIZQUEL
- ☐ 497. JIM PRESLEY
- ☐ 566. BILLY SWIFT
- ☐ 581. SCOTT BRADLEY
- ☐ 601. MIKE KINGERY
- ☐ 614. JERRY REED
- ☐ 644. HENRY COTTO
- ☐ 662. CLINT ZAVARAS

TEXAS RANGERS

- ☐ 33. JUAN GONZALEZ
- ☐ 43. SCOTT COOLBAUGH
- ☐ 48. PETE INCAVIGLIA
- ☐ 56. GENO PETRALLI
- ☐ 107. STEVE BUECHELE
- ☐ 142. JULIO FRANCO
- ☐ 165. FRED MANRIQUE
- ☐ 166. NOLAN RYAN
- ☐ 174. RUBEN SIERRA
- ☐ 225. RAFAEL PALMEIRO
- ☐ 260. CECIL ESPY
- ☐ 283. KENNY ROGERS
- ☐ 284. JEFF RUSSELL
- ☐ 292. BOBBY WITT
- ☐ 343. KEVIN BROWN
- ☐ 378. JAMIE MOYER
- ☐ 402. HAROLD BAINES
- ☐ 403. CECILIO GUANTE
- ☐ 411. CHARLIE HOUGH
- ☐ 461. JACK DAUGHERTY
- ☐ 496. JEFF JUNKEL
- ☐ 520. CHAD KREUTER
- ☐ 521. MIKE JEFFCOAT
- ☐ 529. DEAN PALMER
- ☐ 579. MIKE STANLEY
- ☐ 613. RICK LEACH
- ☐ 679. GARY MIELKE

TORONTO BLUE JAYS

- ☐ 45. ALEX SANCHEZ
- ☐ 70. JUNIOR FELIX
- ☐ 87. DAVE STIEB
- ☐ 113. KELLY GRUBER
- ☐ 149. TONY FERNANDEZ
- ☐ 188. FRED MCGRIFF
- ☐ 206. GEORGE BELL
- ☐ 231. JIMMY KEY
- ☐ 267. NELSON LIRIANO
- ☐ 307. DUANE WARD
- ☐ 324. MIKE FLANAGAN
- ☐ 349. TOM HENKE
- ☐ 385. ERNIE WHITT
- ☐ 425. DAVID WELLS
- ☐ 442. MOOKIE WILSON
- ☐ 467. JOSE NUNEZ
- ☐ 504. LLOYD MOSEBY
- ☐ 543. AL LEITER
- ☐ 558. JIM ACKER
- ☐ 560. PAT BORDERS
- ☐ 584. LEE MAZZILLI
- ☐ 607. RANCE MULLINIKS
- ☐ 620. MANNY LEE
- ☐ 627. GLENALLEN HILL
- ☐ 645. JOHN CERUTTI
- ☐ 655. MAURO GOZZO
- ☐ 669. TODD STOTTLEMYRE
- ☐ 681. TOM LAWLESS
- ☐ 682. XAVIER HERNANDEZ
- ☐ 698. STEVE CUMMINGS
- ☐ 706. GREG MYERS
- ☐ 711. JOHN OLERUD

DEN'S COLLECTORS DEN

PLASTIC CARD PROTECTING PAGES
LARGEST SELECTION IN THE HOBBY

FINEST QUALITY PLASTIC SHEETS

Featuring:
- NON—MIGRATING PLASTIC IN ALL SHEETS
- PLASTIC THAT DOES NOT STICK TOGETHER
- STIFFNESS TO RESIST CARD CURLING
- INTELLIGENT DESIGN
- RESISTANCE TO CRACKING
- FULL COVERAGE OF CARDS, PHOTOS, ENVELOPES

DEN'S COLLECTORS DEN — HOME OF SPORT AMERICANA

DEPT. 594
P.O. BOX 606, LAUREL, MD 20725

SEND ONLY $ 1.00 for DEN'S BIG CATALOGUE — CATALOGUE sent FREE with each ORDER

NO MIX & MATCH

STYLE	POCKETS CAPACITY	RECOMMENDED FOR	PRICE EACH (Does not include Post. & Hand.)			
			1–24	25–99	100–299	300 plus
9	9 / 18	TOPPS (1957 to present), FLEER, DONRUSS SCORE, SPORTFLICS, TCMA, LEAF (1960), All standard 2½" X 3½" cards, SIDE LOAD	.25	.23	.21	.19
9T	9 / 18	SAME AS STYLE 9 ABOVE, TOP LOAD	.25	.23	.21	.19
8	8 / 16	TOPPS (1952–1956, 1988 Big), BOWMAN (1953–1955)	.25	.23	.21	.19
12	12 / 24	BOWMAN (1948–1950), TOPPS (1951), TOPPS (Stickers), FLEER (Minis & Stickers)	.25	.23	.21	.19
1	1 / 2	PHOTOGRAPHS (8" X 10")	.25	.23	.21	.19
2	2 / 4	PHOTOGRAPHS (5" X 7"), TOPPS (1984, 1985 & 1986 Supers)	.25	.23	.21	.19
4	4 / 8	POSTCARDS, EXHIBITS, PEREZ—STEELE (Hall of Fame postcards), DONRUSS (1983–1987 All-Stars), TOPPS (1964,70,71 Supers)	.25	.23	.21	.19
6P	6 / 12	POLICE AND SAFETY CARDS (All sports)	.25	.23	.21	.19
18	18 / 36	T206 and most other T CARDS, BAZOOKA (1963–1967 Individual cards), Many 19th Century cards (N Cards)	.40	.40	35	.35
9G	9 / 18	GOUDEY, DIAMOND STARS, LEAF (1948)	.40	.40	.35	.35
9PB	9 / 18	PLAY BALL, BOWMAN (1951-52), All GUM, INC. Cards, TOPPS (Minis), DOUBLE PLAY	.40	.40	.35	.35
1C	1 / 2	TURKEY RED (T3), PRESS GUIDES, PEREZ—STEELE (Greatest Moments), Many WRAPPERS (Sport & non-sport)	.40	.40	.35	.35
3	3 / 6	3—CARD PANELS (Hostess, Star, Zeller's)	.40	.40	.35	.35
6V	6 / 12	TOPPS (Double Headers, Greatest Moments, 1951 Connie Mack, Current All-Stars, Team, 1965 Football and Hockey, Bucks, 1969–1970 Basketball, T201 (Mecca Double folders), T202 (Hassan Triple folders), DADS (Hockey), DONRUSS (1986–87 Pop—Ups)	.40	.40	.35	.35
6D	6 / 12	RED MAN (With or without tabs), DISCS, KAHN'S (1955–1967)	.40	.40	.35	.35
1Y	1 / 1	YEARBOOKS, PROGRAMS, MAGAZINES, Pocket Size is 9" X 12"	.40	.40	.35	.35
1S	1 / 2	MAGAZINE PAGES and PHOTOS, SMALL PROGRAMS, CRACKER JACK (1982 sheets), Pocket Size is 8½" X 11"	.40	.40	.35	.35
10	10 / 10	MATCHBOOK COVERS (Standard 20 match)	.40	.40	.35	.35
3E	3 / 3	FIRST DAY COVERS, BASEBALL COM—MEMORATIVE ENVELOPES	.40	.40	.35	.35
3L	3 / 6	SQUIRT PANELS, PEPSI (1963), FLEER (Stamps in strips)	.40	.40	.35	.35

POSTAGE & HANDLING SCHEDULE
$ .01 to $ 20.00 add $ 2.00
$ 20.01 to $ 29.99 add $ 2.50
$ 30.00 to $ 49.99 add $ 3.00
$ 50.00 or more add $ 4.00

VISA/MASTER CHARGE ACCEPTED

MARYLAND RESIDENTS ADD 5% SALES TAX
CANADIAN ORDERS – BOOKS ONLY
Canadian orders, orders outside the contiguous
United States, APO and FPO add 25% additional
U.S. FUNDS ONLY

1963 FLEER (66)
2 1/2" X 3 1/2"

KEN BOYER
St. Louis Cardinals—Third Base

BALTIMORE ORIOLES

- ☐ 1. STEVE BARBER
- ☐ 2. RON HANSEN
- ☐ 3. MILT PAPPAS
- ☐ 4. BROOKS ROBINSON

BOSTON RED SOX

- ☐ 6. LOU CLINTON
- ☐ 7. BILL MONBOUQUETTE
- ☐ 8. CARL YASTRZEMSKI

CHICAGO CUBS

- ☐ 31. GLEN HOBBIE
- ☐ 32. RON SANTO

CHICAGO WHITE SOX

- ☐ 9. RAY HERBERT
- ☐ 10. JIM LANDIS

CINCINNATI REDS

- ☐ 33. GENE FREESE
- ☐ 34. VADA PINSON
- ☐ 35. BOB PURKEY

CLEVELAND INDIANS

- ☐ 11. DICK DONOVAN
- ☐ 12. TITO FRANCONA
- ☐ 13. JERRY KINDALL
- ☐ 46. JOE ADCOCK

DETROIT TIGERS

- ☐ 14. FRANK LARY

HOUSTON COLT .45'S

- ☐ 37. BOB ASPROMONTE
- ☐ 38. DICK FARRELL
- ☐ 39. AL SPANGLER

KANSAS CITY ATHLETICS

- ☐ 15. DICK HOWSER
- ☐ 16. JERRY LUMPE
- ☐ 17. NORM SIEBERN

LOS ANGELES ANGELS

- ☐ 18. DON LEE
- ☐ 19. ALBIE PEARSON
- ☐ 20. BOB RODGERS
- ☐ 21. LEON WAGNER

LOS ANGELES DODGERS

- ☐ 40. TOMMY DAVIS
- ☐ 41. DON DRYSDALE
- ☐ 42. SANDY KOUFAX
- ☐ 43. MAURY WILLS

WARREN SPAHN
Milwaukee Braves—Pitcher

MILWAUKEE BRAVES

- ☐ 44. FRANK BOLLING
- ☐ 45. WARREN SPAHN

MINNESOTA TWINS

- ☐ 22. JIM KAAT
- ☐ 23. VIC POWER
- ☐ 24. RICH ROLLINS

NEW YORK METS

- ☐ 47. ROGER CRAIG
- ☐ 48. AL JACKSON
- ☐ 49. ROD KANEHL

NEW YORK YANKEES

- ☐ 25. BOBBY RICHARDSON
- ☐ 26. RALPH TERRY

PHILADELPHIA PHILLIES

- ☐ 50. RUBEN AMARO
- ☐ 51. JOHN CALLISON
- ☐ 52. CLAY DALRYMPLE
- ☐ 53. DON DEMETER
- ☐ 54. ART MAHAFFEY

PITTSBURGH PIRATES

- ☐ 55. SMOKY BURGESS
- ☐ 56. ROBERTO CLEMENTE
- ☐ 57. ELROY FACE
- ☐ 58. VERNON LAW
- ☐ 59. BILL MAZEROSKI

ST. LOUIS CARDINALS

- ☐ 60. KEN BOYER
- ☐ 61. BOB GIBSON
- ☐ 62. GENE OLIVER
- ☐ 63. BILL WHITE

WILLIE MAYS
San Francisco Giants—Outfield

SAN FRANCISCO GIANTS

- ☐ 5. WILLIE MAYS
- ☐ 36. JOE AMALFITANO
- ☐ 64. ORLANDO CEPEDA
- ☐ 65. JIMMY DAVENPORT
- ☐ 66. BILLY O'DELL

WASHINGTON SENATORS

- ☐ 27. TOM CHENEY
- ☐ 28. CHUCK COTTIER
- ☐ 29. JIMMY PIERSALL
- ☐ 30. DAVE STENHOUSE

1981 FLEER (660)
2 1/2" X 3 1/2"

CHRIS CHAMBLISS
FIRST BASE

ATLANTA BRAVES

- ☐ 242. PHIL NIEKRO
- ☐ 243. DALE MURPHY
- ☐ 244. BOB HORNER
- ☐ 245. JEFF BURROUGHS
- ☐ 246. RICK CAMP
- ☐ 247. BOBBY COX(M)
- ☐ 248. BRUCE BENEDICT
- ☐ 249. GENE GARBER
- ☐ 250. JERRY ROYSTER
- ☐ 251. GARY MATTHEWS
- ☐ 252. CHRIS CHAMBLISS
- ☐ 253. LUIS GOMEZ
- ☐ 254. BILL NAHORODNY
- ☐ 255. DOYLE ALEXANDER
- ☐ 256. BRIAN ASSELSTINE
- ☐ 257. BIFF POCOROBA
- ☐ 258. MIKE LUM
- ☐ 259. CHARLIE SPIKES
- ☐ 260. GLENN HUBBARD
- ☐ 261. TOMMY BOGGS
- ☐ 262. AL HRABOSKY
- ☐ 263. RICK MATULA
- ☐ 264. PRESTON HANNA
- ☐ 265. LARRY BRADFORD
- ☐ 266. RAFAEL RAMIREZ
- ☐ 267. LARRY MCWILLIAMS
- ☐ 646. TEAM CHECKLIST(B)

BALTIMORE ORIOLES

- ☐ 169. JIM PALMER
- ☐ 170. STEVE STONE
- ☐ 171. MIKE FLANAGAN
- ☐ 172. AL BUMBRY
- ☐ 173. DOUG DECINCES
- ☐ 174. SCOTT MCGREGOR
- ☐ 175. MARK BELANGER
- ☐ 176. TIM STODDARD
- ☐ 177. RICK DEMPSEY
- ☐ 178. EARL WEAVER(M)
- ☐ 179. TIPPY MARTINEZ
- ☐ 180. DENNIS MARTINEZ
- ☐ 181. SAMMY STEWART
- ☐ 182. RICH DAUER
- ☐ 183. LEE MAY
- ☐ 184. EDDIE MURRAY
- ☐ 185. BENNY AYALA
- ☐ 186. JOHN LOWENSTEIN
- ☐ 187. GARY ROENICKE

☐ 188. KEN SINGLETON
☐ 189. DAN GRAHAM
☐ 190. TERRY CROWLEY
☐ 191. KIKO GARCIA
☐ 192. DAVE FORD
☐ 193. MARK COREY
☐ 194. LENN SAKATA
☐ 195. DOUG DECINCES
☐ 644. TEAM CHECKLIST(F)

BOSTON RED SOX

☐ 221. CARL YASTRZEMSKI
☐ 222. JIM RICE
☐ 223. FRED LYNN
☐ 224. CARLTON FISK
☐ 225. RICK BURLESON
☐ 226. DENNIS ECKERSLEY
☐ 227. BUTCH HOBSON
☐ 228. TOM BURGMEIER
☐ 229. GARRY HANCOCK
☐ 230. DON ZIMMER(M)
☐ 231. STEVE RENKO
☐ 232. DWIGHT EVANS
☐ 233. MIKE TORREZ
☐ 234. BOB STANLEY
☐ 235. JIM DWYER
☐ 236. DAVE STAPLETON
☐ 237. GLENN HOFFMAN
☐ 238. JERRY REMY
☐ 239. DICK DRAGO
☐ 240. BILL CAMPBELL
☐ 241. TONY PEREZ
☐ 638. CARL YASTRZEMSKI
☐ 646. TEAM CHECKLIST(F)

CALIFORNIA ANGELS

☐ 268. ROD CAREW
☐ 269. BOBBY GRICH
☐ 270. CARNEY LANSFORD
☐ 271. DON BAYLOR
☐ 272. JOE RUDI
☐ 273. DAN FORD
☐ 274. JIM FREGOSI(M)
☐ 275. DAVE FROST
☐ 276. FRANK TANANA
☐ 277. DICKIE THON
☐ 278. JASON THOMPSON
☐ 279. RICK MILLER
☐ 280. BERT CAMPANERIS
☐ 281. TOM DONOHUE
☐ 282. BRIAN DOWNING
☐ 283. FRED PATEK
☐ 284. BRUCE KISON
☐ 285. DAVE LAROCHE
☐ 286. DON AASE
☐ 287. JIM BARR
☐ 288. ALFREDO MARTINEZ
☐ 289. LARRY HARLOW
☐ 290. ANDY HASSLER
☐ 647. TEAM CHECKLIST(F)

CHICAGO CUBS

☐ 291. DAVE KINGMAN
☐ 292. BILL BUCKNER
☐ 293. RICK REUSCHEL
☐ 294. BRUCE SUTTER
☐ 295. JERRY MARTIN
☐ 296. SCOT THOMPSON
☐ 297. IVAN DEJUSUS
☐ 298. STEVE DILLARD
☐ 299. DICK TIDROW
☐ 300. RANDY MARTZ
☐ 301. LENNY RANDLE
☐ 302. LYNN MCGLOTHEN
☐ 303. CLIFF JOHNSON
☐ 304. TIM BLACKWELL
☐ 305. DENNIS LAMP
☐ 306. BILL CAUDILL
☐ 307. CARLOS LEZCANO
☐ 308. JIM TRACY
☐ 309. DOUG CAPILLA*
☐ 310. WILLIE HERNANDEZ
☐ 311. MIKE VAIL
☐ 312. MIKE KRUKOW
☐ 313. BARRY FOOTE
☐ 314. LARRY BIITTNER
☐ 315. MIKE TYSON
☐ 647. TEAM CHECKLIST(B)

CHICAGO WHITE SOX

☐ 339. ED FARMER
☐ 340. BOB MOLINARO
☐ 341. TODD CRUZ
☐ 342. BRITT BURNS
☐ 343. KEVIN BELL
☐ 344. TONY LARUSSA(M)
☐ 345. STEVE TROUT
☐ 346. HAROLD BAINES
☐ 347. RICH WORTHAM
☐ 348. WAYNE NORDHAGEN
☐ 349. MIKE SQUIRES
☐ 350. LAMAR JOHNSON
☐ 352. FRANCISCO BARRIOS
☐ 353. THAD BOSLEY
☐ 354. CHET LEMON
☐ 355. BRUCE KIMM
☐ 356. RICHARD DOTSON
☐ 357. JIM MORRISON
☐ 358. MIKE PROLY
☐ 359. GREG PRYOR
☐ 648. TEAM CHECKLIST(B)

CINCINNATI REDS

☐ 196. JOHNNY BENCH
☐ 197. DAVE CONCEPCION
☐ 198. RAY KNIGHT
☐ 199. KEN GRIFFEY
☐ 200. TOM SEAVER
☐ 201. DAVE COLLINS
☐ 202. GEORGE FOSTER
☐ 203. JUNIOR KENNEDY
☐ 204. FRANK PASTORE
☐ 205. DAN DRIESSEN
☐ 206. HECTOR CRUZ
☐ 207. PAUL MOSKAU
☐ 208. CHARLIE LEIBRANDT
☐ 209. HARRY SPILMAN
☐ 210. JOE PRICE
☐ 211. TOM HUME
☐ 212. JOE NOLAN
☐ 213. DOUG BAIR
☐ 214. MARIO SOTO
☐ 215. BILL BONHAM
☐ 216. GEORGE FOSTER
☐ 217. PAUL HOUSEHOLDER
☐ 218. RON OESTER
☐ 219. SAM MEJIAS
☐ 220. SHELDON BURNSIDE
☐ 644. TEAM CHECKLIST(B)

CLEVELAND INDIANS

☐ 387. MIKE HARGROVE
☐ 388. JORGE ORTA
☐ 389. TOBY HARRAH
☐ 390. TOM VERYZER
☐ 391. MIGUEL DILONE
☐ 392. DAN SPILLNER
☐ 393. JACK BROHAMER
☐ 394. WAYNE GARLAND
☐ 395. SID MONGE
☐ 396. RICK WAITS
☐ 397. JOE CHARBONEAU
☐ 398. GARY ALEXANDER
☐ 399. JERRY DYBZINSKI
☐ 400. MIKE STANTON
☐ 401. MIKE PAXTON
☐ 402. GARY GRAY
☐ 403. RICK MANNING
☐ 404. BO DIAZ
☐ 405. RON HASSEY
☐ 406. ROSS GRIMSLEY
☐ 407. VICTOR CRUZ
☐ 408. LEN BARKER
☐ 649. TEAM CHECKLIST(B)

DETROIT TIGERS

☐ 459. STEVE KEMP
☐ 460. SPARKY ANDERSON(M)
☐ 461. ALAN TRAMMELL
☐ 462. MARK FIDRYCH
☐ 463. LOU WHITAKER
☐ 464. DAVE ROZEMA
☐ 465. MILT WILCOX
☐ 466. CHAMP SUMMERS
☐ 467. LANCE PARRISH

☐ 468. DAN PETRY
☐ 469. PAT UNDERWOOD
☐ 470. RICK PETERS
☐ 471. AL COWENS
☐ 472. JOHN WOCKENFUSS
☐ 473. TOM BROOKENS
☐ 474. RICHIE HEBNER
☐ 475. JACK MORRIS
☐ 476. JIM LENTINE
☐ 477. BRUCE ROBBINS
☐ 478. MARK WAGNER
☐ 479. TIM CORCORAN
☐ 480. STAN PAPI
☐ 481. KIRK GIBSON
☐ 482. DAN SCHATZEDER
☐ 652. TEAM CHECKLIST(F)

HOUSTON ASTROS

☐ 51. ART HOWE
☐ 52. KEN FORSCH
☐ 53. VERN RUHLE
☐ 54. JOE NIEKRO
☐ 55. FRANK LACORTE
☐ 56. J.R. RICHARD
☐ 57. NOLAN RYAN
☐ 58. ENOS CABELL
☐ 59. CESAR CEDENO
☐ 60. JOSE CRUZ
☐ 61. BILL VIRDON(M)
☐ 62. TERRY PUHL
☐ 63. JOAQUIN ANDUJAR
☐ 64. ALAN ASHBY
☐ 65. JOE SAMBITO
☐ 66. DENNY WALLING
☐ 67. JEFF LEONARD
☐ 68. LUIS PUJOLS
☐ 69. BRUCE BOCHY
☐ 70. RAFAEL LANDESTOY
☐ 71. DAVE SMITH
☐ 72. DANNY HEEP
☐ 73. JULIO GONZALEZ
☐ 74. CRAIG REYNOLDS
☐ 75. GARY WOODS
☐ 76. DAVE BERGMAN
☐ 77. RANDY NIEMANN
☐ 78. JOE MORGAN
☐ 642. TEAM CHECKLIST(F)

KANSAS CITY ROYALS

☐ 28. GEORGE BRETT
☐ 29. WILLIE WILSON
☐ 30. PAUL SPLITTORFF
☐ 31. DAN QUISENBERRY
☐ 32. AMOS OTIS
☐ 33. STEVE BUSBY
☐ 34. U.L. WASHINGTON
☐ 35. DAVE CHALK
☐ 36. DARRELL PORTER
☐ 37. MARTY PATTIN
☐ 38. LARRY GURA
☐ 39. RENIE MARTIN
☐ 40. RICH GALE
☐ 41. HAL MCRAE
☐ 42. DENNIS LEONARD
☐ 43. WILLIE AIKENS
☐ 44. FRANK WHITE
☐ 45. CLINT HURDLE
☐ 46. JOHN WATHAN
☐ 47. PETE LACOCK
☐ 48. RANCE MULLINIKS
☐ 49. JEFF TWITTY
☐ 50. JAMIE QUIRK
☐ 483. AMOS OTIS
☐ 641. TEAM CHECKLIST(B)
☐ 653. WILLIE WILSON
☐ 655. GEORGE BRETT

LOS ANGELES DODGERS

☐ 110. STEVE GARVEY
☐ 111. REGGIE SMITH
☐ 112. DON SUTTON
☐ 113. BURT HOOTON
☐ 114. DAVE LOPES
☐ 115. DUSTY BAKER
☐ 116. TOM LASORDA(M)
☐ 117. BILL RUSSELL
☐ 118. JERRY REUSS
☐ 119. TERRY FORSTER

* Capilla appears with Braves on the back of his card. This notation is in error as Capilla did not play for the Braves. His card is not, therefore, listed with the Braves.

1981 Fleer

- ☐ 120. BOB WELCH
- ☐ 121. DON STANHOUSE
- ☐ 122. RICK MONDAY
- ☐ 123. DERREL THOMAS
- ☐ 124. JOE FERGUSON
- ☐ 125. RICK SUTCLIFFE
- ☐ 126. RON CEY
- ☐ 127. DAVE GOLTZ
- ☐ 128. JAY JOHNSTONE
- ☐ 129. STEVE YEAGER
- ☐ 130. GARY WEISS
- ☐ 131. MIKE SCIOSCIA
- ☐ 132. VIC DAVALILLO
- ☐ 133. DOUG RAU
- ☐ 134. PEPE FRIAS
- ☐ 135. MICKEY HATCHER
- ☐ 136. STEVE HOWE
- ☐ 137. BOBBY CASTILLO
- ☐ 138. GARY THOMASSON
- ☐ 139. RUDY LAW
- ☐ 140. FERNANDO VALENZUELA
- ☐ 141. MANNY MOTA
- ☐ 606. STEVE GARVEY
- ☐ 643. TEAM CHECKLIST(F)

MILWAUKEE BREWERS(23)

- ☐ 507. GORMAN THOMAS
- ☐ 508. BEN OGLIVIE
- ☐ 509. LARRY HISLE
- ☐ 510. SAL BANDO
- ☐ 511. ROBIN YOUNT
- ☐ 512. MIKE CALDWELL
- ☐ 513. SIXTO LEZCANO
- ☐ 514. BILL TRAVERS
- ☐ 515. PAUL MOLITOR
- ☐ 516. MOSSE HAAS
- ☐ 517. BILL CASTRO
- ☐ 518. JIM SLATON
- ☐ 519. LARY SORENSEN
- ☐ 520. BOB MCCLURE
- ☐ 521. CHARLIE MOORE
- ☐ 522. JIM GANTNER
- ☐ 523. REGGIE CLEVELAND
- ☐ 524. DON MONEY
- ☐ 525. BILL TRAVERS
- ☐ 526. BUCK MARTINEZ
- ☐ 527. DICK DAVIS
- ☐ 639. CECIL COOPER
- ☐ 654. TEAM CHECKLIST(F)

MINNESOTA TWINS(22)

- ☐ 551. ROY SMALLEY
- ☐ 552. JERRY KOOSMAN
- ☐ 553. KEN LANDREAUX
- ☐ 554. JOHN CASTINO
- ☐ 555. DOUG CORBETT
- ☐ 556. BOMBO RIVERA
- ☐ 557. RON JACKSON
- ☐ 558. BUTCH WYNEGAR
- ☐ 559. HOSKEN POWELL
- ☐ 560. PETE REDFERN
- ☐ 561. ROGER ERICKSON
- ☐ 562. GLENN ADAMS
- ☐ 563. RICK SOFIELD
- ☐ 564. GEOFF ZAHN
- ☐ 565. PETE MACKANIN
- ☐ 566. MIKE CUBBAGE
- ☐ 567. DARRELL JACKSON
- ☐ 568. DAVE EDWARDS
- ☐ 569. ROB WILFONG
- ☐ 570. SAL BUTERA
- ☐ 571. JOSE MORALES
- ☐ 656. TEAM CHECKLIST(F)

MONTREAL EXPOS(28)

- ☐ 142. GARY CARTER
- ☐ 143. STEVE ROGERS
- ☐ 144. WARREN CROMARTIE
- ☐ 145. ANDRE DAWSON
- ☐ 146. LARRY PARRISH
- ☐ 147. ROWLAND OFFICE
- ☐ 148. ELLIS VALENTINE
- ☐ 149. DICK WILLIAMS(M)
- ☐ 150. BILL GULLICKSON
- ☐ 151. ELIAS SOSA
- ☐ 152. JOHN TAMARGO
- ☐ 153. CHRIS SPEIER
- ☐ 154. RON LEFLORE

- ☐ 155. RODNEY SCOTT
- ☐ 156. STAN BAHNSEN
- ☐ 157. BILL LEE
- ☐ 158. FRED NORMAN
- ☐ 159. WOODIE FRYMAN
- ☐ 160. DAVE PALMER
- ☐ 161. JERRY WHITE
- ☐ 162. ROBERTO RAMOS
- ☐ 163. JOHN D'ACQUISTO
- ☐ 164. TOMMY HUTTON
- ☐ 165. CHARLIE LEA
- ☐ 166. SCOTT SANDERSON
- ☐ 167. KEN MACHA
- ☐ 168. TONY BERNAZARD
- ☐ 643. TEAM CHECKLIST(B)

NEW YORK METS(24)

- ☐ 316. LEE MAZZILLI
- ☐ 317. JOHN STEARNS
- ☐ 318. ALEX TREVINO
- ☐ 319. CRAIG SWAN
- ☐ 320. FRANK TAVERAS
- ☐ 321. STEVE HANDERSON
- ☐ 322. NEIL ALLEN
- ☐ 323. MARK BOMBACK
- ☐ 324. MIKE JORGENSEN
- ☐ 325. JOE TORRE(M)
- ☐ 326. ELLIOTT MADDOX
- ☐ 327. PETE FALCONE
- ☐ 328. RAY BURRIS
- ☐ 329. CLAUDELL WASHINGTON
- ☐ 330. DOUG FLYNN
- ☐ 331. JOEL YOUNGBLOOD
- ☐ 332. BILL ALMON
- ☐ 333. TOM HAUSMAN
- ☐ 334. PAT ZACHRY
- ☐ 335. JEFF REARDON
- ☐ 336. WALLY BACKMAN
- ☐ 337. DAN NORMAN
- ☐ 338. JERRY MORALES
- ☐ 648. TEAM CHECKLIST(F)

NEW YORK YANKEES(33)

- ☐ 79. REGGIE JACKSON
- ☐ 80. BUCKY DENT
- ☐ 81. TOMMY JOHN
- ☐ 82. LUIS TIANT
- ☐ 83. RICK CERONE
- ☐ 84. DICK HOWSER(M)
- ☐ 85. LOU PINIELLA
- ☐ 86. RON DAVIS
- ☐ 87. GRAIG NETTLES
- ☐ 88. RON GUIDRY
- ☐ 89. RICH GOSSAGE
- ☐ 90. RUDY MAY
- ☐ 91. GAYLORD PERRY
- ☐ 92. ERIC SODERHOLM
- ☐ 93. BOB WATSON
- ☐ 94. BOBBY MURCER
- ☐ 95. BOBBY BROWN
- ☐ 96. JIM SPENCER
- ☐ 97. TOM UNDERWOOD
- ☐ 98. OSCAR GAMBLE
- ☐ 99. JOHNNY OATES
- ☐ 100. FRED STANLEY
- ☐ 101. RUPPERT JONES
- ☐ 102. DENNIS WERTH
- ☐ 103. JOE LEFEBVRE
- ☐ 104. BRIAN DOYLE
- ☐ 105. AURELIO RODRIGUEZ
- ☐ 106. DOUG BIRD
- ☐ 107. MIKE GRIFFIN
- ☐ 108. TIM LOLLAR
- ☐ 109. WILLIE RANDOLPH
- ☐ 642. TEAM CHECKLIST(B)
- ☐ 650. REGGIE JACKSON

OAKLAND A'S(24)

- ☐ 351. RICKEY HENDERSON
- ☐ 572. RICK LANGFORD
- ☐ 573. MIKE NORRIS
- ☐ 574. RICKEY HENDERSON
- ☐ 575. TONY ARMAS
- ☐ 576. DAVE REVERING
- ☐ 577. JEFF NEWMAN
- ☐ 578. BOB LACEY
- ☐ 579. BRIAN KINGMAN

- ☐ 580. MITCHELL PAGE
- ☐ 581. BILLY MARTIN(M)
- ☐ 582. ROB PICCIOLO
- ☐ 583. MIKE HEATH
- ☐ 584. MICKEY KLUTTS
- ☐ 585. ORLANDO GONZALEZ
- ☐ 586. MIKE DAVIS
- ☐ 587. WAYNE GROSS
- ☐ 588. MATT KEOUGH
- ☐ 589. STEVE MCCATTY
- ☐ 590. DWAYNE MURPHY
- ☐ 591. MARIO GUERRERO
- ☐ 592. DAVE MCKAY
- ☐ 593. JIM ESSIAN
- ☐ 656. TEAM CHECKLIST(B)

PHILADELPHIA PHILLIES(31)

- ☐ 1. PETE ROSE
- ☐ 2. LARRY BOWA
- ☐ 3. MANNY TRILLO
- ☐ 4. BOB BOONE
- ☐ 5. MIKE SCHMIDT
- ☐ 6. STEVE CARLTON
- ☐ 7. TUG MCGRAW
- ☐ 8. LARRY CHRISTENSON
- ☐ 9. BAKE MCBRIDE
- ☐ 10. GREG LUZINSKI
- ☐ 11. RON REED
- ☐ 12. DICKIE NOLES
- ☐ 13. KEITH MORELAND
- ☐ 14. BOB WALK
- ☐ 15. LONNIE SMITH
- ☐ 16. DICK RUTHVEN
- ☐ 17. SPARKY LYLE
- ☐ 18. GREG GROSS
- ☐ 19. GARRY MADDOX
- ☐ 20. NINO ESPINOSA
- ☐ 21. GEORGE VUKOVICH
- ☐ 22. JOHN VUKOVICH
- ☐ 23. RAMON AVILES
- ☐ 24. KEVIN SAUCIER
- ☐ 25. RANDY LERCH
- ☐ 26. DEL UNSER
- ☐ 27. TIM MCCARVER
- ☐ 640. MIKE SCHMIDT
- ☐ 641. TEAM CHECKLIST(F)
- ☐ 657. TUG MCGRAW
- ☐ 660. STEVE CARLTON

DAVE PARKER
OUTFIELD

PITTSBURGH PIRATES(29)

- ☐ 360. DAVE PARKER
- ☐ 361. OMAR MORENO
- ☐ 362. KENT TEKULVA
- ☐ 363. WILLIE STARGELL
- ☐ 364. PHIL GARNER
- ☐ 365. ED OTT
- ☐ 366. DON ROBINSON
- ☐ 367. CHUCK TANNER(M)
- ☐ 368. JIM ROOKER
- ☐ 369. DALE BERRA
- ☐ 370. JIM BIBBY
- ☐ 371. STEVE NICOSIA
- ☐ 372. MIKE EASLER
- ☐ 373. BILL ROBINSON
- ☐ 374. LEE LACY
- ☐ 375. JOHN CANDELARIA
- ☐ 376. MANNY SANGUILLEN
- ☐ 377. RICK RHODEN
- ☐ 378. GRANT JACKSON

- ☐ 379. TIM FOLI
- ☐ 380. ROD SCURRY
- ☐ 381. BILL MADLOCK
- ☐ 382. KURT BEVACQUA
- ☐ 383. BERT BLYLEVEN
- ☐ 384. EDDIE SOLOMON
- ☐ 385. ENRIQUE ROMO
- ☐ 386. JOHN MILNER
- ☐ 419. JESSE JEFFERSON(B)
- ☐ 649. TEAM CHECKLIST(F)

ST. LOUIS CARDINALS

- ☐ 528. TED SIMMONS
- ☐ 529. GARRY TEMPLETON
- ☐ 530. KEN REITZ
- ☐ 531. TONY SCOTT
- ☐ 532. KEN OBERKFELL
- ☐ 533. BOB SYKES
- ☐ 534. KEITH SMITH
- ☐ 535. JOHN LITTLEFIELD
- ☐ 536. JIM KAAT
- ☐ 537. BOB FORSCH
- ☐ 538. MIKE PHILLIPS
- ☐ 539. TERRY LANDRUM
- ☐ 540. LEON DURHAM
- ☐ 541. TERRY KENNEDY
- ☐ 542. GEORGE HENDRICK
- ☐ 543. DANE IORG
- ☐ 544. MARK LITTELL
- ☐ 545. KEITH HERNANDEZ
- ☐ 546. SILVIO MARTINEZ
- ☐ 547. DON HOOD
- ☐ 548. BOBBY BONDS
- ☐ 549. MIKE RAMSEY
- ☐ 550. TOM HERR
- ☐ 654. TEAM CHECKLIST(B)

SAN DIEGO PADRES

- ☐ 484. DAVE WINFIELD
- ☐ 485. ROLLIE FINGERS
- ☐ 486. GENE RICHARDS
- ☐ 487. RANDY JONES
- ☐ 488. OZZIE SMITH
- ☐ 489. GENE TENACE
- ☐ 490. BILL FAHEY
- ☐ 491. JOHN CURTIS
- ☐ 492. DAVE CASH
- ☐ 493. TIM FLANNERY
- ☐ 494. JERRY MUMPHREY
- ☐ 495. BOB SHIRLEY
- ☐ 496. STEVE MURA
- ☐ 497. ERIC RASMUSSEN
- ☐ 498. BRODERICK PERKINS
- ☐ 499. BARRY EVANS
- ☐ 500. CHUCK BAKER
- ☐ 501. LUIS SALAZAR
- ☐ 502. GARY LUCAS
- ☐ 503. MIKE ARMSTRONG
- ☐ 504. JERRY TURNER
- ☐ 505. DENNIS KINNEY
- ☐ 506. WILLIE MONTANEZ
- ☐ 652. TEAM CHECKLIST(B)

SAN FRANCISCO GIANTS

- ☐ 432. VIDA BLUE
- ☐ 433. JACK CLARK
- ☐ 434. WILLIE MCCOVEY
- ☐ 435. MIKE IVIE
- ☐ 436. DARRELL EVANS
- ☐ 437. TERRY WHITFIELD
- ☐ 438. RENNIE STENNETT
- ☐ 439. JOHN MONTEFUSCO
- ☐ 440. JIM WOHLFORD
- ☐ 441. BILL NORTH
- ☐ 442. MILT MAY
- ☐ 443. MAX VENABLE
- ☐ 444. ED WHITSON
- ☐ 445. AL HOLLAND
- ☐ 446. RANDY MOFFITT
- ☐ 447. BOB KNEPPER
- ☐ 448. GARY LAVELLE
- ☐ 449. GREG MINTON
- ☐ 450. JOHNNIE LEMASTER
- ☐ 451. LARRY HERNDON
- ☐ 452. RICH MURRAY
- ☐ 453. JOE PETTINI
- ☐ 454. ALLEN RIPLEY

- ☐ 455. DENNIS LITTLEJOHN
- ☐ 456. TOM GRIFFIN
- ☐ 457. ALAN HARGESHEIMER
- ☐ 458. JOE STRAIN
- ☐ 651. TEAM CHECKLIST(B)

SEATTLE MARINERS

- ☐ 594. DAVE HEAVERLO
- ☐ 595. MUARY WILLS(M)
- ☐ 596. JUAN BENIQUEZ
- ☐ 597. RODNEY CRAIG
- ☐ 598. JIM ANDERSON
- ☐ 599. FLOYD BANNISTER
- ☐ 600. BRUCE BOCHTE
- ☐ 601. JULIO CRUZ
- ☐ 602. TED COX
- ☐ 603. DAN MEYER
- ☐ 604. LARRY COX
- ☐ 605. BILL STEIN
- ☐ 607. DAVE A. ROBERTS
- ☐ 608. LEON ROBERTS
- ☐ 609. REGGIE WALTON
- ☐ 610. DAVE ELDER
- ☐ 611. LARRY MILBOURNE
- ☐ 612. KIM ALLEN
- ☐ 613. MARIO MENDOZA
- ☐ 614. TOM PACIOREK
- ☐ 615. GLENN ABBOTT
- ☐ 616. JOE SIMPSON
- ☐ 658. TEAM CHECKLIST(F)

TEXAS RANGERS

- ☐ 617. MICKEY RIVERS
- ☐ 618. JIM KERN
- ☐ 619. JIM SUNDBERG
- ☐ 620. RICHIE ZISK
- ☐ 621. JON MATLACK
- ☐ 622. FERGUSON JENKINS
- ☐ 623. PAT CORRALES(M)
- ☐ 624. ED FIGUEROA
- ☐ 625. BUDDY BELL
- ☐ 626. AL OLIVER
- ☐ 627. DOC MEDICH
- ☐ 628. BUMP WILLS
- ☐ 629. RUSTY STAUB
- ☐ 630. PAT PUTNAM
- ☐ 631. JOHN GRUBB
- ☐ 632. DANNY DARWIN
- ☐ 633. KEN CLAY
- ☐ 634. JIM NORRIS
- ☐ 635. JOHN BUTCHER
- ☐ 636. DAVE W. ROBERTS
- ☐ 637. BILLY SAMPLE
- ☐ 658. TEAM CHECKLIST(B)

ALFREDO GRIFFIN
SHORTSTOP

TORONTO BLUE JAYS

- ☐ 409. BOB BAILOR
- ☐ 410. OTTO VELEZ
- ☐ 411. ERNIE WHITT
- ☐ 412. JIM CLANCY
- ☐ 413. BARRY BONNELL
- ☐ 414. DAVE STIEB
- ☐ 415. DAMASO GARCIA
- ☐ 416. JOHN MAYBERRY
- ☐ 417. ROY HOWELL
- ☐ 418. DANNY AINGE
- ☐ 419. JESSE JEFFERSON(F)

- ☐ 420. JOEY MCLAUGHLIN
- ☐ 421. LLOYD MOSEBY
- ☐ 422. AL WOODS
- ☐ 423. GARTH IORG
- ☐ 424. DOUG AULT
- ☐ 425. KEN SCHROM
- ☐ 426. MIKE WILLIS
- ☐ 427. STEVE BRAUN
- ☐ 428. BOB DAVIS
- ☐ 429. JERRY GARVIN
- ☐ 430. ALFREDO GRIFFIN
- ☐ 431. BOB MATTICK(M)
- ☐ 651. TEAM CHECKLIST(F)

1982 FLEER (660)
2 1/2" X 3 1/2"

Mark Brouhard
BREWERS • OUTFIELD

ATLANTA BRAVES

- ☐ 428. BRIAN ASSELSTINE
- ☐ 429. BRUCE BENEDICT
- ☐ 430. TOM BOGGS
- ☐ 431. LARRY BRADFORD
- ☐ 432. RICK CAMP
- ☐ 433. CHRIS CHAMBLISS
- ☐ 434. GENE GARBER
- ☐ 435. PRESTON HANNA
- ☐ 436. BOB HORNER
- ☐ 437. GLENN HUBBARD
- ☐ 438. AL HRABOSKY
- ☐ 439. RUFINO LINARES
- ☐ 440. RICK MAHLER
- ☐ 441. ED MILLER
- ☐ 442. JOHN MONTEFUSCO
- ☐ 443. DALE MURPHY
- ☐ 444. PHIL NIEKRO
- ☐ 445. GAYLORD PERRY
- ☐ 446. BIFF POCOROBA
- ☐ 447. RAFAEL RAMIREZ
- ☐ 448. JERRY ROYSTER
- ☐ 449. CLAUDELL WASHINGTON
- ☐ 655. TEAM CHECKLIST(B)

BALTIMORE ORIOLES

- ☐ 157. BENNY AYALA
- ☐ 158. MARK BELANGER
- ☐ 159. AL BUMBRY
- ☐ 160. TERRY CROWLEY
- ☐ 161. RICH DAUER
- ☐ 162. DOUG DECINCES
- ☐ 163. RICK DEMPSEY
- ☐ 164. JIM DWYER
- ☐ 165. MIKE FLANAGAN
- ☐ 166. DAVE FORD
- ☐ 167. DAN GRAHAM
- ☐ 168. WAYNE KRENCHICKI
- ☐ 169. JOHN LOWENSTEIN
- ☐ 170. DENNIS MARTINEZ
- ☐ 171. TIPPY MARTINEZ
- ☐ 172. SCOTT MCGREGOR
- ☐ 173. JOSE MORALES
- ☐ 174. EDDIE MURRAY
- ☐ 175. JIM PALMER
- ☐ 176. CAL RIPKEN
- ☐ 177. GARY ROENICKE
- ☐ 178. LENN SAKATA
- ☐ 179. KEN SINGLETON
- ☐ 180. SAMMY STEWART

☐ 181. TIM STODDARD
☐ 182. STEVE STONE
☐ 650. TEAM CHECKLIST(F)

BOSTON RED SOX

☐ 287. GARY ALLENSON
☐ 288. TOM BURGMEIER
☐ 289. BILL CAMPBELL
☐ 290. MARK CLEAR
☐ 291. STEVE CRAWFORD
☐ 292. DENNIS ECKERSLEY
☐ 293. DWIGHT EVANS
☐ 294. RICH GEDMAN
☐ 295. GARRY HANCOCK
☐ 296. GLENN HOFFMAN
☐ 297. BRUCE HURST
☐ 298. CARNEY LANSFORD
☐ 299. RICK MILLER
☐ 300. REID NICHOLS
☐ 301. BOB OJEDA
☐ 302. TONY PEREZ
☐ 303. CHUCK RAINEY
☐ 304. JERRY REMY
☐ 305. JIM RICE
☐ 306. JOE RUDI
☐ 307. BOB STANLEY
☐ 308. DAVE STAPLETON
☐ 309. FRANK TANANA
☐ 310. MIKE TORREZ
☐ 311. JOHN TUDOR
☐ 312. CARL YASTRZEMSKI
☐ 652. TEAM CHECKLIST(B)

CALIFORNIA ANGELS

☐ 450. DON AASE
☐ 451. DON BAYLOR
☐ 452. JUAN BENIQUEZ
☐ 453. RICK BURLESON
☐ 454. BERT CAMPANERIS
☐ 455. ROD CAREW
☐ 456. BOB CLARK
☐ 457. BRIAN DOWNING
☐ 458. DAN FORD
☐ 459. KEN FORSCH
☐ 460. DAVE FROST
☐ 461. BOBBY GRICH
☐ 462. LARRY HARLOW
☐ 463. JOHN HARRIS
☐ 464. ANDY HASSLER
☐ 465. BUTCH HOBSON
☐ 466. JESSE JEFFERSON
☐ 467. BRUCE KISON
☐ 468. FRED LYNN
☐ 469. ANGEL MORENO
☐ 470. ED OTT
☐ 471. FRED PATEK
☐ 472. STEVE RENKO
☐ 473. MIKE WITT
☐ 474. GEOFF ZAHN
☐ 656. TEAM CHECKLIST(F)

CHICAGO CUBS

☐ 586. DOUG BIRD
☐ 587. TIM BLACKWELL
☐ 588. BOBBY BONDS
☐ 589. BILL BUCKNER
☐ 590. BILL CAUDILL
☐ 591. HECTOR CRUZ
☐ 592. JODY DAVID
☐ 593. IVAN DEJESUS
☐ 594. STEVE DILLARD
☐ 595. LEON DURHAM
☐ 596. RAWLY EASTWICK
☐ 597. STEVE HENDERSON
☐ 598. MIKE KRUKOW
☐ 599. MIKE LUM
☐ 600. RANDY MARTZ
☐ 601. JERRY MORALES
☐ 602. KEN REITZ
☐ 603. LEE SMITH
☐ 604. DICK TIDROW
☐ 605. JIM TRACY
☐ 606. MIKE TYSON
☐ 607. TY WALLER
☐ 659. TEAM CHECKLIST(F)

CHICAGO WHITE SOX

☐ 335. BILL ALMON
☐ 336. HAROLD BAINES
☐ 337. ROSS BAUMGARTEN
☐ 338. TONY BERNAZARD
☐ 339. BRITT BURNS
☐ 340. RICHARD DOTSON
☐ 341. JIM ESSIAN
☐ 342. ED FARMER
☐ 343. CARLTON FISK
☐ 344. KEVIN HICKEY
☐ 345. LAMARR HOYT
☐ 346. LAMAR JOHNSON
☐ 347. JERRY KOOSMAN
☐ 348. RUSTY KUNTZ
☐ 349. DENNIS LAMP
☐ 350. RON DEFLORE
☐ 351. CHET LEMON
☐ 352. GREG LUZINSKI
☐ 353. BOB MOLINARO
☐ 354. JIM MORRISON
☐ 355. WAYNE NORDHAGEN
☐ 356. GREG PRYOR
☐ 357. MIKE SQUIRES
☐ 358. STEVE TROUT
☐ 653. TEAM CHECKLIST(B)

CINCINNATI REDS

☐ 57. JOHNNY BENCH
☐ 58. BRUCE BERENYI
☐ 59. LARRY BIITTNER
☐ 60. SCOTT BROWN
☐ 61. DAVE COLLINS
☐ 62. GEOFF COMBE
☐ 63. DAVE CONCEPCION
☐ 64. DAN DRIESSEN
☐ 65. JOE EDELEN
☐ 66. GEORGE FÓSTER
☐ 67. KEN GRIFFEY
☐ 68. PAUL HOUSEHOLDER
☐ 69. TOM HUME
☐ 70. JUNIOR KENNEDY
☐ 71. RAY KNIGHT
☐ 72. MIKE LACOSS
☐ 73. RAFAEL LANDESTOY
☐ 74. CHARLIE LEIBRANDT
☐ 75. SAM MEJIAS
☐ 76. PAUL MOSKAU
☐ 77. JOE NOLAN
☐ 78. MIKE O'BERRY
☐ 79. RON OESTER
☐ 80. FRANK PASTORE
☐ 81. JOE PRICE
☐ 82. TOM SEAVER
☐ 83. MARIO SOTO
☐ 84. MIKE VAIL
☐ 648. TEAM CHECKLIST(F)

CLEVELAND INDIANS

☐ 359. ALAN BANNISTER
☐ 360. LEN BARKER
☐ 361. BERT BLYLEVEN
☐ 362. JOE CHARBONEAU
☐ 363. JOHN DENNY
☐ 364. BO DIAZ
☐ 365. MIGUEL DILONE
☐ 366. JERRY DYBZINSKI
☐ 367. WAYNE GARLAND
☐ 368. MIKE HARGROVE
☐ 369. TOBY HARRAH
☐ 370. RON HASSEY
☐ 371. VON HAYES
☐ 372. PAT KELLY
☐ 373. DUANE KUIPER
☐ 374. RICK MANNING
☐ 375. SID MONGE
☐ 376. JORGE ORTA
☐ 377. DAVE ROSELLO
☐ 378. DAN SPILLNER
☐ 379. MIKE STANTON
☐ 380. ANDRE THORNTON
☐ 381. TOM VERYZER
☐ 382. RICK WAITS
☐ 654. TEAM CHECKLIST(F)

DETROIT TIGERS

☐ 263. TOM BROOKENS
☐ 264. GEORGE CAPPUZZELLO
☐ 265. MARTY CASTILLO
☐ 266. AL COWENS
☐ 267. KIRK GIBSON
☐ 268. RICHIE HEBNER
☐ 269. RON JACKSON
☐ 270. LYNN JONES
☐ 271. STEVE KEMP
☐ 272. RICK LEACH
☐ 273. AURELIO LOPEZ
☐ 274. JACK MORRIS
☐ 275. KEVIN SAUCIER
☐ 276. LANCE PARRISH
☐ 277. RICK PETERS
☐ 278. DAN PETRY
☐ 279. DAVID ROZEMA
☐ 280. STAN PAPI
☐ 281. DAN SCHATZEDER
☐ 282. CHAMP SUMMERS
☐ 283. ALAN TRAMMELL
☐ 284. LOU WHITAKER
☐ 285. MILT WILCOX
☐ 286. JOHN WOCKENFUSS
☐ 652. TEAM CHECKLIST(F)

HOUSTON ASTROS

☐ 212. ALAN ASHBY
☐ 213. CESAR CEDENO
☐ 214. JOSE CRUZ
☐ 215. KIKO GARCIA
☐ 216. PHIL GARNER
☐ 217. DANNY HEEP
☐ 218. ART HOWE
☐ 219. BOB KNEPPER
☐ 220. FRANK LACORTE
☐ 221. JOE NIEKRO
☐ 222. JOE PITTMAN
☐ 223. TERRY PUHL
☐ 224. LUIS PUJOLS
☐ 225. CRAIG REYNOLDS
☐ 226. J.R. RICHARD
☐ 227. DAVE W. ROBERTS
☐ 228. VERN RUHLE
☐ 229. NOLAN RYAN
☐ 230. JOE SAMBITO
☐ 231. TONY SCOTT
☐ 232. DAVE SMITH
☐ 233. HARRY SPILMAN
☐ 234. DON SUTTON
☐ 235. DICKIE THON
☐ 236. DENNY WALLING
☐ 237. GARY WOODS
☐ 651. TEAM CHECKLIST(F)

George Brett
ROYALS • THIRD BASE

KANSAS CITY ROYALS

☐ 404. WILLIE AIKENS
☐ 405. GEORGE BRETT
☐ 406. KEN BRETT
☐ 407. DAVE CHALK
☐ 408. RICH GALE
☐ 409. CESAR GERONIMO
☐ 410. LARRY GURA
☐ 411. CLINT HURDLE

☐ 412. MIKE JONES
☐ 413. DENNIS LEONARD
☐ 414. RENIE MARTIN
☐ 415. LEE MAY
☐ 416. HAL MCRAE
☐ 417. DARRYL MOTLEY
☐ 418. RANCE MULLINIKS
☐ 419. AMOS OTIS
☐ 420. KEN PHELPS
☐ 421. JAMIE QUIRK
☐ 422. DAN QUISENBERRY
☐ 423. PAUL SPLITTORFF
☐ 424. U.L. WASHINGTON
☐ 425. JOHN WATHAN
☐ 426. FRANK WHITE
☐ 427. WILLIE WILSON
☐ 655. TEAM CHECKLIST(F)

LOS ANGELES DODGERS

☐   1. DUSTY BAKER
☐   2. BOBBY CASTILLO
☐   3. RON CEY
☐   4. TERRY FORSTER
☐   5. STEVE GARVEY
☐   6. DAVE GOLTZ
☐   7. PEDRO GUERRERO
☐   8. BURT HOOTON
☐   9. STEVE HOWE
☐ 10. JAY JOHNSTONE
☐ 11. KEN LANDREAUX
☐ 12. DAVEY LOPES
☐ 13. MIKE MARSHALL
☐ 14. BOBBY MITCHELL
☐ 15. RICK MONDAY
☐ 16. TOM NIEDENFUER
☐ 17. TED POWER
☐ 18. JERRY REUSS
☐ 19. RON ROENICKE
☐ 20. BILL RUSSELL
☐ 21. STEVE SAX
☐ 22. MIKE SCIOSCIA
☐ 23. REGGIE SMITH
☐ 24. DAVE STEWART
☐ 25. RICK SUTCLIFFE
☐ 26. DERREL THOMAS
☐ 27. FERNANDO VALENZUELA
☐ 28. BOB WELCH
☐ 29. STEVE YEAGER
☐ 647. TEAM CHECKLIST(F)

MILWAUKEE BREWERS

☐ 133. JERRY AUGUSTINE
☐ 134. SAL BANDO
☐ 135. MARK BROUHARD
☐ 136. MIKE CALDWELL
☐ 137. REGGIE CLEVELAND
☐ 138. CECIL COOPER
☐ 139. JAMIE EASTERLY
☐ 140. MARSHALL EDWARDS
☐ 141. ROLLIE FINGERS
☐ 142. JIM GANTNER
☐ 143. MOOSE HAAS
☐ 144. LARRY HISLE
☐ 145. ROY HOWELL
☐ 146. RICKEY KEETON
☐ 147. RANDY LERCH
☐ 148. PAUL MOLITOR
☐ 149. DON MONEY
☐ 150. CHARLIE MOORE
☐ 151. BEN OGLIVIE
☐ 152. TED SIMMONS
☐ 153. JIM SLATON
☐ 154. GORMAN THOMAS
☐ 155 ROBIN YOUNT
☐ 156. PETE VUCKOVICH
☐ 649. TEAM CHECKLIST(B)

MINNESOTA TWINS

☐ 545. GLENN ADAMS
☐ 546. FERNANDO ARROYO
☐ 547. JOHN VERHOEVEN
☐ 548. SAL BUTERA
☐ 549. JOHN CASTINO
☐ 550. DON COOPER
☐ 551. DOUG CORBETT
☐ 552. DAVE ENGLE
☐ 553. ROGER ERICKSON

☐ 554. DANNY GOODWIN
☐ 555. DARRELL JACKSON
☐ 556. PETE MACKANIN
☐ 557. JACK O'CONNOR
☐ 558. HOSKEN POWELL
☐ 559. PETE REDFERN
☐ 560. ROY SMALLEY
☐ 561. CHUCK BAKER
☐ 562. GARY WARD
☐ 563. ROB WILFONG
☐ 564. AL WILLIAMS
☐ 565. BUTCH WYNEGAR
☐ 658. TEAM CHECKLIST(F)

MONTREAL EXPOS

☐ 183. STAN BAHNSEN
☐ 184. RAY BURRIS
☐ 185. GARY CARTER
☐ 186. WARREN CROMARTIE
☐ 187. ANDRE DAWSON
☐ 188. TERRY FRANCONA
☐ 189. WOODIE FRYMAN
☐ 190. BILL GULLICKSON
☐ 191. GRANT JACKSON
☐ 192. WALLACE JOHNSON
☐ 193. CHARLIE LEA
☐ 194. BILL LEE
☐ 195. JERRY MANUEL
☐ 196. BRAD MILLS
☐ 197. JOHN MILNER
☐ 198. ROWLAND OFFICE
☐ 199. DAVID PALMER
☐ 200. LARRY PARRISH
☐ 201. MIKE PHILLIPS
☐ 202. TIM RAINES
☐ 203. BOBBY RAMOS
☐ 204. JEFF REARDON
☐ 205. STEVE ROGERS
☐ 206. SCOTT SANDERSON
☐ 207. RODNEY SCOTT
☐ 208. ELIAS SOSA
☐ 209. CHRIS SPEIER
☐ 210. TIM WALLACH
☐ 211. JERRY WHITE
☐ 630. TEAM CHECKLIST(B)

NEW YORK METS

☐ 520. NEIL ALLEN
☐ 521. BOB BAILOR
☐ 522. HUBIE BROOKS
☐ 523. MIKE CUBBAGE
☐ 524. PETE FALCONE
☐ 525. DOUG FLYNN
☐ 526. TOM HAUSMAN
☐ 527. RON HODGES
☐ 528. RANDY JONES
☐ 529. MIKE JORGENSEN
☐ 530. DAVE KINGMAN
☐ 531. ED LYNCH
☐ 532. MIKE MARSHALL
☐ 533. LEE MAZZILLI
☐ 534. DYAR MILLER
☐ 535. MIKE SCOTT
☐ 536. RUSTY STAUB
☐ 537. JOHN STEARNS
☐ 538. CRAIG SWAN
☐ 539. FRANK TAVERAS
☐ 540. ALEX TREVINO
☐ 541. ELLIS VALENTINE
☐ 542. MOOKIE WILSON
☐ 543. JOEL YOUNGBLOOD
☐ 544. PAT ZACHRY
☐ 657. TEAM CHECKLIST(B)

NEW YORK YANKEES

☐ 30. BOBBY BROWN
☐ 31. RICK CERONE
☐ 32. RON DAVIS
☐ 33. BUCKY DENT
☐ 34. BARRY FOOTE
☐ 35. GEORGE FRAZIER
☐ 36. OSCAR GAMBLE
☐ 37. RICH GOSSAGE
☐ 38. RON GUIDRY
☐ 39. REGGIE JACKSON
☐ 40. TOMMY JOHN
☐ 41. RUDY MAY

☐ 42. LARRY MILBOURNE
☐ 43. JERRY MUMPHREY
☐ 44. BOBBY MURCER
☐ 45. GENE NELSON
☐ 46. GRAIG NETTLES
☐ 47. JOHNNY OATES
☐ 48. LOU PINIELLA
☐ 49. WILLIE RANDOLPH
☐ 50. RICK REUSCHEL
☐ 51. DAVE REVERING
☐ 52. DAVE RIGHETTI
☐ 53. AURELIO RODRIGUEZ
☐ 54. BOB WATSON
☐ 55. DENNIS WERTH
☐ 56. DAVE WINFIELD
☐ 647. TEAM CHECKLIST(B)

OAKLAND A'S

☐ 85. TONY ARMAS
☐ 86. SHOOTY BABBIT
☐ 87. DAVE BEARD
☐ 88. RICK BOSETTI
☐ 89. KEITH DRUMRIGHT
☐ 90. WAYNE GROSS
☐ 91. MIKE HEATH
☐ 92. RICKEY HENDERSON
☐ 93. CLIFF JOHNSON
☐ 94. JEFF JONES
☐ 95. MATT KEOUGH
☐ 96. BRIAN KINGMAN
☐ 97. MICKEY KLUTTS
☐ 98. RICK LANGFORD
☐ 99. STEVE MCCATTY
☐ 100. DAVE MCKAY
☐ 101. DWAYNE MURPHY
☐ 102. JEFF NEWMAN
☐ 103. MIKE NORRIS
☐ 104. BOB OWCHINKO
☐ 105. MITCHELL PAGE
☐ 106. ROB PICCIOLO
☐ 107. JIM SPENCER
☐ 108. FRED STANLEY
☐ 109. TOM UNDERWOOD
☐ 648. TEAM CHECKLIST(B)

Mickey Klutts
A's • THIRD BASE

PHILADELPHIA PHILLIES

☐ 238. LUIS AGUAYO
☐ 239. RAMON AVILES
☐ 240. BOB BOONE
☐ 241. LARRY BOWA
☐ 242. WARREN BRUSSTAR
☐ 243. STEVE CARLTON
☐ 244. LARRY CHRISTENSON
☐ 245. DICK DAVIS
☐ 246. GREG GROSS
☐ 247. SPARKY LYLE
☐ 248. GARRY MADDOX
☐ 249. GARY MATTHEWS
☐ 250. BAKE MCBRIDE
☐ 251. TUG MCGRAW
☐ 252. KEITH MORELAND
☐ 253. DICKIE NOLES
☐ 254. MIKE PROLY
☐ 255. RON REED
☐ 256. PETE ROSE
☐ 257. DICK RUTHVEN
☐ 258. MIKE SCHMIDT
☐ 259. LONNIE SMITH

☐ 260. MANNY TRILLO
☐ 261. DEL UNSER
☐ 262. GEORGE VUKOVICH
☐ 651. TEAM CHECKLIST(B)

PITTSBURGH PIRATES

☐ 475. GARY ALEXANDER
☐ 476. DALE BERRA
☐ 477. KURT BEVACQUA
☐ 478. JIM BIBBY
☐ 479. JOHN CANDELARIA
☐ 480. VICTOR CRUZ
☐ 481. MIKE EASLER
☐ 482. TIM FOLI
☐ 483. LEE LACY
☐ 484. VANCE LAW
☐ 485. BILL MADLOCK
☐ 486. WILLIE MONTANEZ
☐ 487. OMAR MORENO
☐ 488. STEVE NICOSIA
☐ 489. DAVE PARKER
☐ 490. TONY PENA
☐ 491. PASCUAL PEREZ
☐ 492. JOHNNY RAY
☐ 493. RICK RHODEN
☐ 494. BILL ROBINSON
☐ 495. DON ROBINSON
☐ 496. ENRIQUE ROMO
☐ 497. ROD SCURRY
☐ 498. EDDIE SOLOMON
☐ 499. WILLIE STARGELL
☐ 500. KENT TEKULVE
☐ 501. JASON THOMPSON
☐ 656. TEAM CHECKLIST(B)

ST. LOUIS CARDINALS

☐ 110. JOAQUIN ANDUJAR
☐ 111. STEVE BRAUN
☐ 112. BOB FORSCH
☐ 113. GEORGE HENDRICK
☐ 114. KEITH HERNANDEZ
☐ 115. TOM HERR
☐ 116. DANE IORG
☐ 117. JIM KAAT
☐ 118. TITO LANDRUM
☐ 119. SIXTO LEZCANO
☐ 120. MARK LITTELL
☐ 121. JOHN MARTIN
☐ 122. SILVIO MARTINEZ
☐ 123. KEN OBERKFELL
☐ 124. DARRELL PORTER
☐ 125. MIKE RAMSEY
☐ 126. ORLANDO SANCHEZ
☐ 127. BOB SHIRLEY
☐ 128. LARY SORENSEN
☐ 129. BRUCE SUTTER
☐ 130. BOB SYKES
☐ 131. GARRY TEMPLETON
☐ 132. GENE TENACE
☐ 649. TEAM CHECKLIST(F)

SAN FRANCISCO GIANTS

☐ 383. DOYLE ALEXANDER
☐ 384. VIDA BLUE
☐ 385. FRED BREINING
☐ 386. ENOS CABELL
☐ 387. JACK CLARK
☐ 388. DARRELL EVANS
☐ 389. TOM GRIFFIN
☐ 390. LARRY HERNDON
☐ 391. AL HOLLAND
☐ 392. GARY LAVELLE
☐ 393. JOHNNIE LEMASTER
☐ 394. JERRY MARTIN
☐ 395. MILT MAY
☐ 396. GREG MINTON
☐ 397. JOE MORGAN
☐ 398. JOE PETTINI
☐ 399. ALAN RIPLEY
☐ 400. BILLY E. SMITH
☐ 401. RENNIE STENNETT
☐ 402. ED WHITSON
☐ 403. JIM WOHLFORD
☐ 654. TEAM CHECKLIST(B)

SAN DIEGO PADRES

☐ 566. RANDY BASS
☐ 567. JUAN BONILLA
☐ 568. DANNY BOONE
☐ 569. JOHN CURTIS
☐ 570. JUAN EICHELBERGER
☐ 571. BARRY EVANS
☐ 572. TIM FLANNERY
☐ 573. RUPPERT JONES
☐ 574. TERRY KENNEDY
☐ 575. JOE LEFEBVRE
☐ 576. JOHN LITTLEFIELD
☐ 577. GARY LUCAS
☐ 578. STEVE MURA
☐ 579. BRODERICK PERKINS
☐ 580. GENE RICHARDS
☐ 581. LUIS SALAZAR
☐ 582. OZZIE SMITH
☐ 583. JOHN URREA
☐ 584. CHRIS WELSH
☐ 585. RICK WISE
☐ 658. TEAM CHECKLIST

SEATTLE MARINERS

☐ 502. GLENN ABBOTT
☐ 503. JIM ANDERSON
☐ 504. FLOYD BANNISTER
☐ 505. BRUCE BOCHTE
☐ 506. JEFF BURROUGHS
☐ 507. BRYAN CLARK
☐ 508. KEN CLAY
☐ 509. JULIO CRUZ
☐ 510. DICK DRAGO
☐ 511. GARY GRAY
☐ 512. DAN MEYER
☐ 513. JERRY NARRON
☐ 514. TOM PACIOREK
☐ 515. CASEY PARSONS
☐ 516. LENNY RANDLE
☐ 517. SHANE RAWLEY
☐ 518. JOE SIMPSON
☐ 519. RICHIE ZISK
☐ 657. TEAM CHECKLIST(F)

TEXAS RANGERS

☐ 313. BUDDY BELL
☐ 314. STEVE COMER
☐ 315. DANNY DARWIN
☐ 316. JOHN ELLIS
☐ 317. JOHN GRUBB
☐ 318. RICK HONEYCUTT
☐ 319. CHARLIE HOUGH
☐ 320. FERGUSON JENKINS
☐ 321. JOHN HENRY JOHNSON
☐ 322. JIM KERN
☐ 323. JON MATLACK
☐ 324. DOC MEDICH
☐ 325. MARIO MENDOZA
☐ 326. AL OLIVER
☐ 327. PAT PUTNAM
☐ 328. MICKEY RIVERS
☐ 329. LEON ROBERTS
☐ 330. BILLY SAMPLE
☐ 331. BILL STEIN
☐ 332. JIM SUNDBERG
☐ 333. MARK WAGNER
☐ 334. BUMP WILLS
☐ 653. TEAM CHECKLIST(F)

TORONTO BLUE JAYS

☐ 608. DANNY AINGE
☐ 609. JORGE BELL
☐ 610. MARK BOMBACK
☐ 611. BARRY BONNELL
☐ 612. JIM CLANCY
☐ 613. DAMASO GARCIA
☐ 614. JERRY GARVIN
☐ 615. ALFREDO GRIFFIN
☐ 616. GARTH IORG
☐ 617. LUIS LEAL
☐ 618. KEN MACHA
☐ 619. JOHN MAYBERRY
☐ 620. JOEY MCLAUGHLIN
☐ 621. LLOYD MOSEBY
☐ 622. DAVE STIEB
☐ 623. JACKSON TODD

☐ 624. WILLIE UPSHAW
☐ 625. OTTO VELEZ
☐ 626. ERNIE WHITT
☐ 627. AL WOODS
☐ 659. TEAM CHECKLIST(B)

1983 FLEER (660)
2 1/2" X 3 1/2"

Steve Garvey
FIRST BASE

ATLANTA BRAVES

☐ 129. STEVE BEDROSIAN
☐ 130. BRUCE BENEDICT
☐ 131. TOMMY BOGGS
☐ 132. BRETT BUTLER
☐ 133. RICK CAMP
☐ 134. CHRIS CHAMBLISS
☐ 135. KEN DAYLEY
☐ 136. GENE GARBER
☐ 137. TERRY HARPER
☐ 138. BOB HORNER
☐ 139. GLENN HUBBARD
☐ 140. RUFINO LINARES
☐ 141. RICK MAHLER
☐ 142. DALE MURPHY
☐ 143. PHIL NIEKRO
☐ 144. PASCUAL PEREZ
☐ 145. BIFF POCOROBA
☐ 146. RAFAEL RAMIREZ
☐ 147. JERRY ROYSTER
☐ 148. KEN SMITH
☐ 149. BOB WALK
☐ 150. CLAUDELL WASHINGTON
☐ 151. BOB WATSON
☐ 152. LARRY WHISENTON
☐ 649. TEAM CHECKLIST(B)

BALTIMORE ORIOLES

☐ 52. BENNY AYALA
☐ 53. BOB BONNER
☐ 54. AL BUMBRY
☐ 55. TERRY CROWLEY
☐ 56. STORM DAVIS
☐ 57. RICH DAUER
☐ 58. RICK DEMPSEY
☐ 59. JIM DWYER
☐ 60. MIKE FLANAGAN
☐ 61. DAN FORD
☐ 62. GLENN GULLIVER
☐ 63. JOHN LOWENSTEIN
☐ 64. DENNIS MARTINEZ
☐ 65. TIPPY MARTINEZ
☐ 66. SCOTT MCGREGOR
☐ 67. EDDIE MURRAY
☐ 68. JOE NOLAN
☐ 69. JIM PALMER
☐ 70. CAL RIPKEN
☐ 71. GARY ROENICKE
☐ 72. LENN SAKATA
☐ 73. KEN SINGLETON
☐ 74. SAMMY STEWART
☐ 75. TIM STODDARD
☐ 648. TEAM CHECKLIST(F)

BOSTON RED SOX

- ☐ 177. GARY ALLENSON
- ☐ 178. LUIS APONTE
- ☐ 179. WADE BOGGS
- ☐ 180. TOM BURGMEIER
- ☐ 181. MARK CLEAR
- ☐ 182. DENNIS ECKERSLEY
- ☐ 183. DWIGHT EVANS
- ☐ 184. RICH GEDMAN
- ☐ 185. GLENN HOFFMAN
- ☐ 186. BRUCE HURST
- ☐ 187. CARNEY LANSFORD
- ☐ 188. RICK MILLER
- ☐ 189. REID NICHOLS
- ☐ 190. BOB OJEDA
- ☐ 191. TONY PEREZ
- ☐ 192. CHUCK RAINEY
- ☐ 193. JERRY REMY
- ☐ 194. JIM RICE
- ☐ 195. BOB STANLEY
- ☐ 196. DAVE STAPLETON
- ☐ 197. MIKE TORREZ
- ☐ 198. JOHN TUDOR
- ☐ 199. JULIO VALDEZ
- ☐ 200. CARL YASTRZEMSKI
- ☐ 650. TEAM CHECKLIST(B)

CALIFORNIA ANGELS

- ☐ 76. DON AASE
- ☐ 77. DON BAYLOR
- ☐ 78. JUAN BENIQUEZ
- ☐ 79. BOB BOONE
- ☐ 80. RICK BURLESON
- ☐ 81. ROD CAREW
- ☐ 82. BOBBY CLARK
- ☐ 83. DOUG CORBETT
- ☐ 84. JOHN CURTIS
- ☐ 85. DOUG DECINCES
- ☐ 86. BRIAN DOWNING
- ☐ 87. JOE FERGUSON
- ☐ 88. TIM FOLI
- ☐ 89. KEN FORSCH
- ☐ 90. DAVE GOLTZ
- ☐ 91. BOBBY GRICH
- ☐ 92. ANDY HASSLER
- ☐ 93. REGGIE JACKSON
- ☐ 94. RON JACKSON
- ☐ 95. TOMMY JOHN
- ☐ 96. BRUCE KISON
- ☐ 97. FRED LYNN
- ☐ 98. ED OTT
- ☐ 99. STEVE RENKO
- ☐ 100. LUIS SANCHEZ
- ☐ 101. ROB WILFONG
- ☐ 102. MIKE WITT
- ☐ 103. GEOFF ZAHN
- ☐ 648. TEAM CHECKLIST(B)

CHICAGO CUBS

- ☐ 490. DOUG BIRD
- ☐ 491. LARRY BOWA
- ☐ 492. BILL BUCKNER
- ☐ 493. BILL CAMPBELL
- ☐ 494. JODY DAVIS
- ☐ 495. LEON DURHAM
- ☐ 496. STEVE HENDERSON
- ☐ 497. WILLIE HERNANDEZ
- ☐ 498. FERGUSON JENKINS
- ☐ 499. JAY JOHNSTONE
- ☐ 500. JUNIOR KENNEDY
- ☐ 501. RANDY MARTZ
- ☐ 502. JERRY MORALES
- ☐ 503. KEITH MORELAND
- ☐ 504. DICKIE NOLES
- ☐ 505. MIKE PROLY
- ☐ 506. ALLEN RIPLEY
- ☐ 507. RYNE SANDBERG
- ☐ 508. LEE SMITH
- ☐ 509. PAT TABLER
- ☐ 510. DICK TIDROW
- ☐ 511. BUMP WILLS
- ☐ 512. GARY WOODS
- ☐ 657. TEAM CHECKLIST(F)

CHICAGO WHITE SOX

- ☐ 228. BILL ALMON
- ☐ 229. HAROLD BAINES
- ☐ 230. SALOME BAROJAS
- ☐ 231. TONY BERNAZARD
- ☐ 232. BRITT BURNS
- ☐ 233. RICHARD DOTSON
- ☐ 234. ERNESTO ESCARREGA
- ☐ 235. CARLTON FISK
- ☐ 236. JERRY HAIRSTON
- ☐ 237. KEVIN HICKEY
- ☐ 238. LEMARR HOYT
- ☐ 239. STEVE KEMP
- ☐ 240. JIM KERN
- ☐ 241. RON KITTLE
- ☐ 242. JERRY KOOSMAN
- ☐ 243. DENNIS LAMP
- ☐ 244. RUDY LAW
- ☐ 245. VANCE LAW
- ☐ 246. RON LEFLORE
- ☐ 247. GREG LUZINSKI
- ☐ 248. TOM PACIOREK
- ☐ 249. AURELIO RODRIGUEZ
- ☐ 250. MIKE SQUIRES
- ☐ 251. STEVE TROUT
- ☐ 651. TEAM CHECKLIST(B)

CINCINNATI REDS

- ☐ 584. JOHNNY BENCH
- ☐ 585. BRUCE BERENYI
- ☐ 586. LARRY BIITTNER
- ☐ 587. CESAR CEDENO
- ☐ 588. DAVE CONCEPCION
- ☐ 589. DAN DRIESSEN
- ☐ 590. GREG HARRIS
- ☐ 591. BEN HAYES
- ☐ 592. PAUL HOUSEHOLDER
- ☐ 593. TOM HUME
- ☐ 594. WAYNE KRENCHICKI
- ☐ 595. RAFAEL LANDESTOY
- ☐ 596. CHARLIE LEIBRANDT
- ☐ 597. EDDIE MILNER
- ☐ 598. RON OESTER
- ☐ 599. FRANK PASTORE
- ☐ 600. JOE PRICE
- ☐ 601. TOM SEAVER
- ☐ 602. BOB SHIRLEY
- ☐ 603. MARIO SOTO
- ☐ 604. ALEX TREVINO
- ☐ 605. MIKE VAIL
- ☐ 606. DUANE WALKER
- ☐ 659. TEAM CHECKLIST(F)

CLEVELAND INDIANS

- ☐ 400. CHRIS BANDO
- ☐ 401. ALAN BANNISTER
- ☐ 402. LEN BARKER
- ☐ 403. TOM BRENNAN
- ☐ 404. CARMELO CASTILLO
- ☐ 405. MIGUEL DILONE
- ☐ 406. JERRY DYBZINSKI
- ☐ 407. MIKE FISCHLIN
- ☐ 408. ED GLYNN
- ☐ 409. MIKE HARGROVE
- ☐ 410. TOBY HARRAH
- ☐ 411. RON HASSEY
- ☐ 412. VON HAYES
- ☐ 413. RICK MANNING
- ☐ 414. BAKE MCBRIDE
- ☐ 415. LARRY MILBOURNE
- ☐ 416. BILL NAHORODNY
- ☐ 417. JACK PERCONTE
- ☐ 418. LARY SORENSEN
- ☐ 419. DAN SPILLNER
- ☐ 420. RICK SUTCLIFFE
- ☐ 421. ANDRE THORNTON
- ☐ 422. RICK WAITS
- ☐ 423. EDDIE WHITSON
- ☐ 655. TEAM CHECKLIST(F)

DETROIT TIGERS

- ☐ 327. TOM BROOKENS
- ☐ 328. ENOS CABELL
- ☐ 329. KIRK GIBSON
- ☐ 330. LARRY HERNDON
- ☐ 331. MIKE IVIE
- ☐ 332. HOWARD JOHNSON
- ☐ 333. LYNN JONES
- ☐ 334. RICK LEACH
- ☐ 335. CHET LEMON
- ☐ 336. JACK MORRIS
- ☐ 337. LANCE PARRISH
- ☐ 338. LARRY PASHNICK
- ☐ 339. DAN PETRY
- ☐ 340. DAVE ROZEMA
- ☐ 341. DAVE RUCKER
- ☐ 342. ELIAS SOSA
- ☐ 343. DAVE TOBIK
- ☐ 344. ALAN TRAMMELL
- ☐ 345. JERRY TURNER
- ☐ 346. JERRY UJDUR
- ☐ 347. PAT UNDERWOOD
- ☐ 348. LOU WHITAKER
- ☐ 349. MILT WILCOX
- ☐ 350. GLENN WILSON
- ☐ 351. JOHN WOCKENFUSS
- ☐ 653. TEAM CHECKLIST(B)

HOUSTON ASTROS

- ☐ 445. ALAN ASHBY
- ☐ 446. JOSE CRUZ
- ☐ 447. KIKO GARCIA
- ☐ 448. PHIL GARNER
- ☐ 449. DANNY HEEP
- ☐ 450. ART HOWE
- ☐ 451. BOB KNEPPER
- ☐ 452. ALAN KNICELY
- ☐ 453. RAY KNIGHT
- ☐ 454. FRANK LACORTE
- ☐ 455. MIKE LACOSS
- ☐ 456. RANDY MOFFITT
- ☐ 457. JOE NIEKRO
- ☐ 458. TERRY PUHL
- ☐ 459. LUIS PUJOLS
- ☐ 460. CRAIG REYNOLDS
- ☐ 461. BERT ROBERGE
- ☐ 462. VERN RUHLE
- ☐ 463. NOLAN RYAN
- ☐ 464. JOE SAMBITO
- ☐ 465. TONY SCOTT
- ☐ 466. DAVE SMITH
- ☐ 467. HARRY SPILMAN
- ☐ 468. DICKIE THON
- ☐ 469. DENNY WALLING
- ☐ 656. TEAM CHECKLIST(F)

LOS ANGELES DODGERS

- ☐ 201. DUSTY BAKER
- ☐ 202. JOE BECKWITH
- ☐ 203. GREG BROCK
- ☐ 204. RON CEY
- ☐ 205. TERRY FORSTER
- ☐ 206. STEVE GARVEY
- ☐ 207. PEDRO GUERRERO
- ☐ 208. BURT HOOTON
- ☐ 209. STEVE HOWE
- ☐ 210. KEN LANDREAUX
- ☐ 211. MIKE MARSHALL
- ☐ 212. CANDY MALDONADO
- ☐ 213. RICK MONDAY
- ☐ 214. TOM NIEDENFUER
- ☐ 215. JORGE ORTA
- ☐ 216. JERRY REUSS
- ☐ 217. RON ROENICKE
- ☐ 218. VINCENTE ROMO
- ☐ 219. BILL RUSSELL
- ☐ 220. STEVE SAX
- ☐ 221. MIKE SCIOSCIA
- ☐ 222. DAVE STEWART
- ☐ 223. DERREL THOMAS
- ☐ 224. FERNANDO VALENZUELA
- ☐ 225. BOB WELCH
- ☐ 226. RICKY WRIGHT
- ☐ 227. STEVE YEAGER
- ☐ 651. TEAM CHECKLIST(F)

KANSAS CITY ROYALS

- ☐ 104. WILLIE AIKENS
- ☐ 105. MIKE ARMSTRONG
- ☐ 106. VIDA BLUE
- ☐ 107. BUD BLACK
- ☐ 108. GEORGE BRETT
- ☐ 109. BILL CASTRO
- ☐ 110. ONIX CONCEPCION
- ☐ 111. DAVE FROST
- ☐ 112. CESAR GERONIMO
- ☐ 113. LARRY GURA
- ☐ 114. STEVE HAMMOND
- ☐ 115. DON HOOD
- ☐ 116. DENNIS LEONARD
- ☐ 117. JERRY MARTIN

☐ 118. LEE MAY
☐ 119. HAL MCRAE
☐ 120. AMOS OTIS
☐ 121. GREG PRYOR
☐ 122. DAN QUISENBERRY
☐ 123. DON SLAUGHT
☐ 124. PAUL SPLITTORFF
☐ 125. U.L. WASHINGTON
☐ 126. JOHN WATHAN
☐ 127. FRANK WHITE
☐ 128. WILLIE WILSON
☐ 649. TEAM CHECKLIST(F)

Rollie Fingers
PITCHER

MILWAUKEE BREWERS

☐ 26. JERRY AUGUSTINE
☐ 27. DWIGHT BERNARD
☐ 28. MARK BROUHARD
☐ 29. MIKE CALDWELL
☐ 30. CECIL COOPER
☐ 31. JAMIE EASTERLY
☐ 32. MARSHALL EDWARDS
☐ 33. ROLLIE FINGERS
☐ 34. JIM GANTNER
☐ 35. MOOSE HAAS
☐ 36. ROY HOWELL
☐ 37. PETER LADD
☐ 38. BOB MCCLURE
☐ 39. DOC MEDICH
☐ 40. PAUL MOLITOR
☐ 41. DON MONEY
☐ 42. CHARLIE MOORE
☐ 43. BEN OGLIVIE
☐ 44. ED ROMERO
☐ 45. TED SIMMONS
☐ 46. JIM SLATON
☐ 47. DON SUTTON
☐ 48. GORMAN THOMAS
☐ 49. PETE VUCKOVICH
☐ 50. NED YOST
☐ 51. ROBIN YOUNT
☐ 647. TEAM CHECKLIST(B)

MINNESOTA TWINS

☐ 607. TOM BRUNANSKY
☐ 608. BOBBY CASTILLO
☐ 609. JOHN CASTINO
☐ 610. RON DAVIS
☐ 611. LENNY FAEDO
☐ 612. TERRY FELTON
☐ 613. GARY GAETTI
☐ 614. MICKEY HATCHER
☐ 615. BRAD HAVENS
☐ 616. KENT HRBEK
☐ 617. RANDY JOHNSON
☐ 618. TIM LAUDNER
☐ 619. JEFF LITTLE
☐ 620. BOB MITCHELL
☐ 621. JACK O'CONNOR
☐ 622. JOHN PACELLA
☐ 623. PETE REDFERN
☐ 624. JESUS VEGA
☐ 625. FRANK VIOLA
☐ 626. RON WASHINGTON
☐ 627. GARY WARD
☐ 628. AL WILLIAMS
☐ 659. TEAM CHECKLIST(B)

Al Oliver
FIRST BASE

MONTREAL EXPOS

☐ 277. RAY BURRIS
☐ 278. GARY CARTER
☐ 279. WARREN CROMARTIE
☐ 280. ANDRE DAWSON
☐ 281. TERRY FRANCONA
☐ 282. DOUG FLYNN
☐ 283. WOODY FRYMAN
☐ 284. BILL GULLICKSON
☐ 285. WALLACE JOHNSON
☐ 286. CHARLIE LEA
☐ 287. RANDY LERCH
☐ 288. BRAD MILLS
☐ 289. DAN NORMAN
☐ 290. AL OLIVER
☐ 291. DAVID PALMER
☐ 292. TIM RAINES
☐ 293. JEFF REARDON
☐ 294. STEVE ROGERS
☐ 295. SCOTT SANDERSON
☐ 296. DAN SCHATZEDER
☐ 297. BRYN SMITH
☐ 298. CHRIS SPEIER
☐ 299. TIM WALLACH
☐ 300. JERRY WHITE
☐ 301. JOEL YOUNGBLOOD
☐ 652. TEAM CHECKLIST(B)

NEW YORK METS

☐ 536. NEIL ALLEN
☐ 537. WALLY BACKMAN
☐ 538. BOB BAILOR
☐ 539. HUBIE BROOKS
☐ 540. CARLOS DIAZ
☐ 541. PETE FALCONE
☐ 542. GEORGE FOSTER
☐ 543. RON GARDENHIRE
☐ 544. BRIAN GILES
☐ 545. RON HODGES
☐ 546. RANDY JONES
☐ 547. MIKE JORGENSEN
☐ 548. DAVE KINGMAN
☐ 549. ED LYNCH
☐ 550. JESSE OROSCO
☐ 551. RICK OWNBEY
☐ 552. CHARLIE PULEO
☐ 553. GARY RAJSICH
☐ 554. MIKE SCOTT
☐ 555. RUSTY STAUB
☐ 556. JOHN STEARNS
☐ 557. CRAIG SWAN
☐ 558. ELLIS VALENTINE
☐ 559. TOM VERYZER
☐ 560. MOOKIE WILSON
☐ 561. PAT ZACHRY
☐ 658. TEAM CHECKLIST(F)

NEW YORK YANKEES

☐ 376. RICK CERONE
☐ 377. DAVE COLLINS
☐ 378. ROGER ERICKSON
☐ 379. GEORGE FRAZIER
☐ 380. OSCAR GAMBLE
☐ 381. RICH GOSSAGE
☐ 382. KEN GRIFFEY
☐ 383. RON GUIDRY

☐ 384. DAVE LAROCHE
☐ 385. RUDY MAY
☐ 386. JOHN MAYBERRY
☐ 387. LEE MAZZILLI
☐ 388. MIKE MORGAN
☐ 389. JERRY MUMPHREY
☐ 390. BOBBY MURCER
☐ 391. GRAIG NETTLES
☐ 392. LOU PINIELLA
☐ 393. WILLIE RANDOLPH
☐ 394. SHANE RAWLEY
☐ 395. DAVE RIGHETTI
☐ 396. ANDRE ROBERTSON
☐ 397. ROY SMALLEY
☐ 398. DAVE WINFIELD
☐ 399. BUTCH WYNEGAR
☐ 654. TEAM CHECKLIST(B)

OAKLAND A'S

☐ 513. TONY ARMAS
☐ 514. DAVE BEARD
☐ 515. JEFF BURROUGHS
☐ 516. JOHN D'ACQUISTO
☐ 517. WAYNE GROSS
☐ 518. MIKE HEATH
☐ 519. RICKEY HENDERSON
☐ 520. CLIFF JOHNSON
☐ 521. MATT KEOUGH
☐ 522. BRIAN KINGMAN
☐ 523. RICK LANGFORD
☐ 524. DAVEY LOPES
☐ 525. STEVE MCCATTY
☐ 526. DAVE MCKAY
☐ 527. DAN MEYER
☐ 528. DWAYNE MURPHY
☐ 529. JEFF NEWMAN
☐ 530. MIKE NORRIS
☐ 531. BOB OWCHINKO
☐ 532. JOE RUDI
☐ 533. JIMMY SEXTON
☐ 534. FRED STANLEY
☐ 535. TOM UNDERWOOD
☐ 657. TEAM CHECKLIST(B)

PHILADELPHIA PHILLIES

☐ 153. PORFIORIO ALTAMIRANO
☐ 154. MARTY BYSTROM
☐ 155. STEVE CARLTON
☐ 156. LARRY CHRISTENSON
☐ 157. IVAN DEJESUS
☐ 158. JOHN DENNY
☐ 159. BOB DERNIER
☐ 160. BO DIAZ
☐ 161. ED FARMER
☐ 162. GREG GROSS
☐ 163. MIKE KRUKOW
☐ 164. GARRY MADDOX
☐ 165. GARY MATTHEWS
☐ 166. TUG MCGRAW
☐ 167. BOB MOLINARO
☐ 168. SID MONGE
☐ 169. RON REED
☐ 170. BILL ROBINSON
☐ 171. PETE ROSE
☐ 172. DICK RUTHVEN
☐ 173. MIKE SCHMIDT
☐ 174. MANNY TRILLO
☐ 175. OZZIE VIRGIL
☐ 176. GEORGE VUKOVICH
☐ 650. TEAM CHECKLIST(F)

PITTSBURGH PIRATES

☐ 302. ROSS BAUMGARTEN
☐ 303. DALE BERRA
☐ 304. JOHN CANDELARIA
☐ 305. DICK DAVIS
☐ 306. MIKE EASLER
☐ 307. RICHIE HEBNER
☐ 308. LEE LACY
☐ 309. BILL MADLOCK
☐ 310. LARRY MCWILLIAMS
☐ 311. JOHN MILNER
☐ 312. OMAR MORENO
☐ 313. JIM MORRISON
☐ 314. STEVE NICOSIA
☐ 315. DAVE PARKER

☐ 316. TONY PENA
☐ 317. JOHNNY RAY
☐ 318. RICK RHODEN
☐ 319. DON ROBINSON
☐ 320. ENRIQUE ROMO
☐ 321. MANNY SARMIENTO
☐ 322. ROD SCURRY
☐ 323. JIM SMITH
☐ 324. WILLIE STARGELL
☐ 325. JASON THOMPSON
☐ 326. KENT TEKULVE
☐ 653. TEAM CHECKLIST(F)

ST. LOUIS CARDINALS

☐   1. JOAQUIN ANDUJAR
☐   2. DOUG BAIR
☐   3. STEVE BRAUN
☐   4. GLENN BRUMMER
☐   5. BOB FORSCH
☐   6. DAVID GREEN
☐   7. GEORGE HENDRICK
☐   8. KEITH HERNANDEZ
☐   9. TOM HERR
☐ 10. DANE IORG
☐ 11. JIM KAAT
☐ 12. JEFF LAHTI
☐ 13. TITO LANDRUM
☐ 14. DAVE LAPOINT
☐ 15. WILLIE MCGEE
☐ 16. STEVE MURA
☐ 17. KEN OBERKFELL
☐ 18. DARRELL PORTER
☐ 19. MIKE RAMSEY
☐ 20. GENE ROOF
☐ 21. LONNIE SMITH
☐ 22. OZZIE SMITH
☐ 23. JOHN STUPER
☐ 24. BRUCE SUTTER
☐ 25. GENE TENACE
☐ 647. TEAM CHECKLIST(F)

SAN DIEGO PADRES

☐ 352. KURT BEVACQUA
☐ 353. JUAN BONILLA
☐ 354. FLOYD CHIFFER
☐ 355. LUIS DELEON
☐ 356. DAVE DRAVECKY
☐ 357. DAVE EDWARDS
☐ 358. JUAN EICHELBERGER
☐ 359. TIM FLANNERY
☐ 360. TONY GWYNN
☐ 361. RUPPERT JONES
☐ 362. TERRY KENNEDY
☐ 363. JOE LEFEBVRE
☐ 364. SIXTO LEZCANO
☐ 365. TIM LOLLAR
☐ 366. GARY LUCAS
☐ 367. JOHN MONTEFUSCO
☐ 368. BRODERICK PERKINS
☐ 369. JOE PITTMAN
☐ 370. GENE RICHARDS
☐ 371. LUIS SALAZAR
☐ 372. ERIC SHOW
☐ 373. GARRY TEMPLETON
☐ 374. CHRIS WELSH
☐ 375. ALAN WIGGINS
☐ 654. TEAM CHECKLIST(F)

SAN FRANCISCO GIANTS

☐ 252. JIM BARR
☐ 253. DAVE BERGMANN
☐ 254. FRED BREINING
☐ 255. BOB BRENLY
☐ 256. JACK CLARK
☐ 257. CHILI DAVIS
☐ 258. DARRELL EVANS
☐ 259. ALAN FOWLKES
☐ 260. RICH GALE
☐ 261. ATLEE HAMMAKER
☐ 262. AL HOLLAND
☐ 263. DUANE KUIPER
☐ 264. BILL LASKEY
☐ 265. GARY LAVELLE
☐ 266. JOHNNIE LEMASTER
☐ 267. RENIE MARTIN
☐ 268. MILT MAY
☐ 269. GREG MINTO
☐ 270. JOE MORGAN

☐ 271. TOM O'MALLEY
☐ 272. REGGIE SMITH
☐ 273. GUY SULARZ
☐ 274. CHAMP SUMMERS
☐ 275. MAX VENABLE
☐ 276. JIM WOHLFORD
☐ 652. TEAM CHECKLIST(F)

SEATTLE MARINERS

☐ 470. LARRY ANDERSEN
☐ 471. FLOYD BANNISTER
☐ 472. JIM BEATTIE
☐ 473. BRUCE BOCHTE
☐ 474. MANNY CASTILLO
☐ 475. BILL CAUDILL
☐ 476. BRYAN CLARK
☐ 477. AL COWENS
☐ 478. JULIO CRUZ
☐ 479. TODD CRUZ
☐ 480. GARY GRAY
☐ 481. DAVE HENDERSON
☐ 482. MIKE MOORE
☐ 483. GAYLORD PERRY
☐ 484. DAVE REVERING
☐ 485. JOE SIMPSON
☐ 486. MIKE STANTON
☐ 487. RICK SWEET
☐ 488. ED VANDEBERG
☐ 489. RICHIE ZISK
☐ 656. TEAM CHECKLIST(B)

TEXAS RANGERS

☐ 562. BUDDY BELL
☐ 563. JOHN BUTCHER
☐ 564. STEVE COMER
☐ 565. DANNY DARWIN
☐ 566. BUCKY DENT
☐ 567. JOHN GRUBB
☐ 568. RICK HONEYCUTT
☐ 569. DAVE HOSTETLER
☐ 570. CHARLIE HOUGH
☐ 571. LAMAR JOHNSON
☐ 572. JON MATLACK
☐ 573. PAUL MIRABELLA
☐ 574. LARRY PARRISH
☐ 575. MIKE RICHARDT
☐ 576. MICKEY RIVERS
☐ 577. BILLY SAMPLE
☐ 578. DAVE J. SCHMIDT
☐ 579. BILL STEIN
☐ 580. JIM SUNDBERG
☐ 581. FRANK TANANA
☐ 582. MARK WAGNER
☐ 583. GEORGE WRIGHT
☐ 658. TEAM CHECKLIST(B)

TORONTO BLUE JAYS

☐ 424 JESSIE BARFIELD
☐ 425. BARRY BONNELL
☐ 426. JIM CLANCY
☐ 427. DAMASO GARCIA
☐ 428. JERRY GARVIN
☐ 429. ALFREDO GRIFFIN
☐ 430. GARTH IORG
☐ 431. ROY LEE JACKSON
☐ 432. LUIS LEAL
☐ 433. BUCK MARTINEZ
☐ 434. JOE MCLAUGHLIN
☐ 435. LLOYD MOSEBY
☐ 436. RANCE MULLINIKS
☐ 437. DALE MURRAY
☐ 438. WAYNE NORDHAGEN
☐ 439. GENE PETRALLI
☐ 440. HOSKEN POWELL
☐ 441. DAVE STIEB
☐ 442. WILLIE UPSHAW
☐ 443. ERNIE WHITT
☐ 444. AL WOODS
☐ 655 TEAM CHECKLIST(B)

1984 FLEER (660)
2 1/2" X 3 1/2"

ATLANTA BRAVES

☐ 170. LEN BARKER
☐ 171. STEVE BEDROSIAN
☐ 172. BRUCE BENEDICT
☐ 173. BRETT BUTLER
☐ 174. RICK CAMP
☐ 175. CHRIS CHAMBLISS
☐ 176. KEN DAYLEY
☐ 177. PETE FALCONE
☐ 178. TERRY FORSTER
☐ 179. GENE GARBER
☐ 180. TERRY HARPER
☐ 181. BOB HORNER
☐ 182. GLENN HUBBARD
☐ 183. RANDY JOHNSON
☐ 184. CRAIG MCMURTRY
☐ 185. DONNIE MOORE
☐ 186. DALE MURPHY
☐ 187. PHIL NIEKRO
☐ 188. PASCUAL PEREZ
☐ 189. BIFF POCOROBA
☐ 190. RAFAEL RAMIREZ
☐ 191. JERRY ROYSTER
☐ 192. CLAUDELL WASHINGTON
☐ 193. BOB WATSON
☐ 654. TEAM(F) & TORRE(M)

BALTIMORE ORIOLES

☐   1. MIKE BODDICKER
☐   2. AL BUMBRY
☐   3. TODD CRUZ
☐   4. RICH DAUER
☐   5. STORM DAVIS
☐   6. RICK DEMPSEY
☐   7. JIM DWYER
☐   8. MIKE FLANAGAN
☐   9. DAN FORD
☐ 10. JOHN LOWENSTEIN
☐ 11. DENNIS MARTINEZ
☐ 12. TIPPY MARTINEZ
☐ 13. SCOTT MCGREGOR
☐ 14. EDDIE MURRAY
☐ 15. JOE NOLAN
☐ 16. JIM PALMER
☐ 17. CAL RIPKEN
☐ 18. GARY ROENICKE
☐ 19. LENN SAKATA
☐ 20. JOHN SHELBY
☐ 21. KEN SINGLETON
☐ 22. SAMMY STEWARD
☐ 23. TIM STODDARD
☐ 647. TEAM(F) & ALTOBELLI(M)

BOSTON RED SOX

☐ 388. GARY ALLENSON
☐ 389. LUIS APONTE
☐ 390. TONY ARMAS
☐ 391. DOUG BIRD
☐ 392. WADE BOGGS
☐ 393. DENNIS BOYD
☐ 394. MIKE BROWN
☐ 395. MARK CLEAR
☐ 396. DENNIS ECKERSLEY

- □ 397. DWIGHT EVANS
- □ 398. RICH GEDMAN
- □ 399. GLENN HOFFMAN
- □ 400. BRUCE HURST
- □ 401. JOHN HENRY JOHNSON
- □ 402. ED JURAK
- □ 403. RICK MILLER
- □ 404. JEFF NEWMAN
- □ 405. REID NICHOLS
- □ 406. BOB OJEDA
- □ 407. JERRY REMY
- □ 408. JIM RICE
- □ 409. BOB STANELY
- □ 410. DAVE STAPLETON
- □ 411. JOHN TUDOR
- □ 412. CARL YASTRZMESKI
- □ 649. TEAM CHECKLIST(B)

CALIFORNIA ANGELS

- □ 508. JUAN BENIQUEZ
- □ 509. BOB BOONE
- □ 510. RICK BURLESON
- □ 511. ROD CAREW
- □ 512. BOBBY CLARK
- □ 513. JOHN CURTIS
- □ 514. DOUG DECINCES
- □ 515. BRIAN DOWNING
- □ 516. TIM FOLI
- □ 517. KEN FORSCH
- □ 518. BOBBY GRICH
- □ 519. ANDY HASSLER
- □ 520. REGGIE JACKSON
- □ 521. RON JACKSON
- □ 522. TOMMY JOHN
- □ 523. BRUCE KISON
- □ 524. STEVE LUBRATICH
- □ 525. FRED LYNN
- □ 526. GARY PETTIS
- □ 527. LUIS SANCHEZ
- □ 528. DARYL SCONIERS
- □ 529. ELLIS VALENTINE
- □ 530. ROB WILFONG
- □ 531. MIKE WITT
- □ 532. GEOFF ZAHN
- □ 654. TEAM CHECKLIST(B)

CHICAGO CUBS

- □ 486. LARRY BOWA
- □ 487. WARREN BRUSSTAR
- □ 488. BILL BUCKNER
- □ 489. BILL CAMPBELL
- □ 490. RON CEY
- □ 491. JODY DAVIS
- □ 492. LEON DURHAM
- □ 493. MEL HALL
- □ 494. FERGUSON JENKINS
- □ 495. JAY JOHNSTONE
- □ 496. CRAIG LEFFERTS
- □ 497. CARMELO MARTINEZ
- □ 498. JERRY MORALES
- □ 499. KEITH MORELAND
- □ 500. DICKIE NOLES
- □ 501. MIKE PROLY
- □ 502. CHUCK RAINEY
- □ 503. DICK RUTHVEN
- □ 504. RYNE SANDBERY
- □ 505. LEE SMITH
- □ 506. STEVE TROUT
- □ 507. GARY WOODS
- □ 653. TEAM CHECKLIST(B)

CHICAGO WHITE SOX

- □ 50. JUAN AGOSTO
- □ 51. HARROLD BAINES
- □ 52. FLOYD BANNISTER
- □ 53. SALOME BAROJAS
- □ 54. BRITT BURNS
- □ 55. JULIO CRUZ
- □ 56. RICHARD DOTSON
- □ 57. JERRY DYBZINSKI
- □ 58. CARLTON FISK
- □ 59. SCOTT FLETCHER
- □ 60. JERRY HAIRSTON
- □ 61. KEVIN HICKEY
- □ 62. MARC HILL
- □ 63. LA MARR HOYT
- □ 64. RON KITTLE
- □ 65. JERRY KOOSMAN

- □ 66. DENNIS LAMP
- □ 67. RUDY LAW
- □ 68. VANCE LAW
- □ 69. GREG LUZINSKI
- □ 70. TOM PACIOREK
- □ 71. MIKE SQUIRES
- □ 72. DICK TIDROW
- □ 73. GREG WALKER
- □ 649. TEAM(F) & LARUSSA(M)

CINCINNATI REDS

- □ 462. JOHNNY BENCY
- □ 463. BRUCE BERENYI
- □ 464. DANN BILARDELLO
- □ 465. CESAR CEDENO
- □ 466. DAVE CONCEPCION
- □ 467. DAN DRIESSEN
- □ 468. NICK ESASKY
- □ 469. RICH GALE
- □ 470. BEN HAYES
- □ 471. PAUL HOUSEHOLDER
- □ 471. TOM HUME
- □ 473. ALAN KNICELY
- □ 474. EDDIE MILNER
- □ 475. RON OESTER
- □ 476. KELLY PARIS
- □ 477. FRANK PASTORE
- □ 478. TED POWER
- □ 479. JOE PRICE
- □ 480. CHARLIE PULEO
- □ 481. GARY REDUS
- □ 482. BILL SCHERRER
- □ 483. MARIO SOTO
- □ 484. ALEX TREVINO
- □ 485. DUANE WALKER
- □ 652. TEAM CHECKLIST(B)

CLEVELAND INDIANS

- □ 533. BUD ANDERSON
- □ 534. CHRIS BANDO
- □ 535. ALAN BANNISTER
- □ 536. BERT BLYLEVEN
- □ 537. TOM BRENNAN
- □ 538. JAMIE EASTERLY
- □ 539. JUAN EICHELBERGER
- □ 540. JIM ESSIAN
- □ 541. MIKE FISCHLIN
- □ 542. JULIO FRANCO
- □ 543. MIKE HARGROVE
- □ 544. TOBY HARRAH
- □ 545. RON HASSEY
- □ 546. NEAL HEATON
- □ 547. BAKE MCBRIDE
- □ 548. BRODERICK PERKINS
- □ 549. LARY SORENSEN
- □ 550. DAN SPILLNER
- □ 551. RICK SUTCLIFFE
- □ 552. PAT TABLER
- □ 553. GORMAN THOMAS
- □ 554. ANDRE THORNTON
- □ 555. GEORGE VUKOVICH
- □ 655. TEAM CHECKLIST(B)

DETROIT TIGERS

- □ 74. GLENN ABBOTT
- □ 75. HOWARD BAILEY
- □ 76. DOUG BAIR
- □ 77. JUAN BERENGUER
- □ 78. TOM BROOKENS
- □ 79. ENOS CABELL
- □ 80. KIRK GIBSON
- □ 81. JOHN GRUBB
- □ 82. LARRY HERNDON
- □ 83. WAYNE KRENCHICKI
- □ 84. RICK LEACH
- □ 85. CHET LEMON
- □ 86. AURELIO LOPEZ
- □ 87. JACK MORRIS
- □ 88. LANCE PARRISH
- □ 89. DAN PETRY
- □ 90. DAVE ROZEMA
- □ 91. ALAN TRAMMELL
- □ 92. LOU WHITAKER
- □ 93. MILT WILCOX
- □ 94. GLENN WILSON
- □ 95. JOHN WOCKENFUSS
- □ 650. TEAM(F) & ANDERSON(M)

HOUSTON ASTROS

- □ 220. ALAN ASHBY
- □ 221. KEVIN BASS
- □ 222. JOSE CRUZ
- □ 223. BILL DAWLEY
- □ 224. FRANK DIPINO
- □ 225. BILL DORAN
- □ 226. PHIL GARNER
- □ 227. ART HOWE
- □ 228. BOB KNEPPER
- □ 229. RAY KNIGHT
- □ 230. FRANK LACORTE
- □ 231. MIKE LACOSS
- □ 232. MIKE MADDEN
- □ 233. JERRY MUMPHREY
- □ 234. JOE NIEKRO
- □ 235. TERRY PUHL
- □ 236. LUIS PUJOLS
- □ 237. CRAIG REYNOLDS
- □ 238. VERN RUHLE
- □ 239. NOLAN RYAN
- □ 240. MIKE SCOTT
- □ 241. TONY SCOTT
- □ 242. DAVE SMITH
- □ 243. DICKIE THON
- □ 244. DENNY WALLING
- □ 656. TEAM(F) & LILLIS(M)

KANSAS CITY ROYALS

- □ 341. WILLIE AIKENS
- □ 342. MIKE ARMSTRONG
- □ 343. BUD BLACK
- □ 344. GEORGE BRETT
- □ 345. ONIX CONCEPCION
- □ 346. KEITH CREEL
- □ 347. LARRY GURA
- □ 348. DON HOOD
- □ 349. DENNIS LEONARD
- □ 350. HAL MCRAE
- □ 351. AMOS OTIS
- □ 352. GAYLORD PERRY
- □ 353. GREG PRYOR
- □ 354. DAN QUISENBERRY
- □ 355. STEVE RENKO
- □ 356. LEON ROBERTS
- □ 357. PAT SHERIDAN
- □ 358. JOE SIMPSON
- □ 359. DON SLAUGHT
- □ 360. PAUL SPLITTORFF
- □ 361. U.L. WASHINGTON
- □ 362. JOHN WATHAN
- □ 363. FRANKE WHITE
- □ 364. WILLIE WILSON
- □ 647. TEAM CHECKLIST(B)

LOS ANGELES DODGERS

- □ 96. DUSTY BAKER
- □ 97. JOE BECKWITH
- □ 98. GREG BROCK
- □ 99. JACK FIMPLE
- □ 100. PEDRO GUERRERO
- □ 101. RICK HONEYCUTT
- □ 102. BURT HOOTON
- □ 103. STEVE HOWE
- □ 104. KEN LANDREAUX
- □ 105. MIKE MARSHALL
- □ 106. RICK MONDAY
- □ 107. JOSE MORALES
- □ 108. TOM NIENDENFUER
- □ 109. ALEJANDRO PENA
- □ 110. JERRY REUSS
- □ 111. BILL RUSSELL
- □ 112. STEVE SAX
- □ 113. MIKE SCIOSCIA
- □ 114. DERREL THOMAS
- □ 115. FERNANDO VALENZUELA
- □ 116. BOB WELCH
- □ 117. STEVE YEAGER
- □ 118. PAT ZACHRY
- □ 651. TEAM(F) & LASORDA(M)

MILWAUKEE BREWERS

- □ 194. JERRY AUGUSTINE
- □ 195. MARK BROUHARD
- □ 196. MIKE CALDWELL
- □ 197. TOM CANDIOTTI

☐ 198. CECIL COOPER
☐ 199. ROLLIE FINGERS
☐ 200. JIM GANTNER
☐ 201. BOB GIBSON
☐ 202. MOOSE HAAS
☐ 203. ROY HOWELL
☐ 204. PETE LADD
☐ 205. RICK MANNING
☐ 206. BOB MCCLURE
☐ 207. PAUL MOLITOR
☐ 208. DON MONEY
☐ 209. CHARLIE MOORE
☐ 210. BEN OGLIVIE
☐ 211. CHUCK PORTER
☐ 212. ED ROMERO
☐ 213. TED SIMMONS
☐ 214. JIM SLATON
☐ 215. DON SUTTON
☐ 216. TOM TELLMANN
☐ 217. PETE VUCKOVICH
☐ 218. NED YOST
☐ 219. ROBIN YOUNT
☐ 655. TEAM(F) & LACHEMANN(M)

MINNESOTA TWINS

☐ 556. DARRELL BROWN
☐ 557. TOM BRUNANSKY
☐ 558. RANDY BUSH
☐ 559. BOBBY CASTILLO
☐ 560. JOHN CASTINO
☐ 561. RON DAVIS
☐ 562. DAVE ENGLE
☐ 563. LENNY FAEDO
☐ 564. PETE FILSON
☐ 565. GARY GAETTI
☐ 566. MICKEY HATCHER
☐ 567. KENT HRBEK
☐ 568. RUSTY KUNTZ
☐ 569. TIM LAUDNER
☐ 570. RICK LYSANDER
☐ 571. BOBBY MITCHELL
☐ 572. KEN SCHROM
☐ 573. RAY SMITH
☐ 574. TIM TEUFEL
☐ 575. FRANK VIOLA
☐ 576. GARY WARD
☐ 577. RON WASHINGTON
☐ 578. LEN WHITEHOUSE
☐ 579. AL WILLIAMS
☐ 656. TEAM CHECKLIST(B)

MONTREAL EXPOS

☐ 270. RAY BURRIS
☐ 271. GARY CARTER
☐ 272. WARREN CROMARTIE
☐ 273. ANDRE DAWSON
☐ 274. DOUG FLYNN
☐ 275. TERRY FRANCONA
☐ 276. BILL GULLICKSON
☐ 277. BOB JAMES
☐ 278. CHARLIE LEA
☐ 279. BRYAN LITTLE
☐ 280. AL OLIVER
☐ 281. TIM RAINES
☐ 282. BOBBY RAMOS
☐ 283. JEFF REARDON
☐ 284. STEVE ROGERS
☐ 285. SCOTT SANDERSON
☐ 286. DAN SCHATZEDER
☐ 287. BRYN SMITH
☐ 288. CHRIS SPEIER
☐ 289. MANNY TRILLO
☐ 290. MIKE VAIL
☐ 291. TIM WALLACH
☐ 292. CHRIS WELSH
☐ 293. JIM WOHLFORD
☐ 658. TEAM(F) & VIRDON(M)

NEW YORK METS

☐ 580. BOB BAILOR
☐ 581. MARK BRADLEY
☐ 582. HUBIE BROOKS
☐ 583. CARLOS DIAZ
☐ 584. GEORGE FOSTER
☐ 585. BRIAN GILES
☐ 586. DANNY HEEP
☐ 587. KEITH HERNANDEZ
☐ 588. RON HODGES

☐ 589. SCOTT HOLMAN
☐ 590. DAVE KINGMAN
☐ 591. ED LYNCH
☐ 592. JOSE OQUENDO
☐ 593. JESSE OROSCO
☐ 594. JUNIOR ORTIZ
☐ 595. TOM SEAVER
☐ 596. DOUG SISK
☐ 597. RUSTY STAUB
☐ 598. JOHN STEARNS
☐ 599. DARRYL STRAWBERRY
☐ 600. CRAIG SWAN
☐ 601. WALT TERRELL
☐ 602. MIKE TORREZ
☐ 603. MOOKIE WILSON
☐ 657. TEAM CHECKLIST(B)

NEW YORK YANKEES

☐ 119. DON BAYLOR
☐ 120. BERT CAMPANERIS
☐ 121. RICK CERONE
☐ 122. RAY FONTENOT
☐ 123. GEORGE FRAZIER
☐ 124. OSCAR GAMBLE
☐ 125. GOOSE GOSSAGE
☐ 126. KEN GRIFFEY
☐ 127. RON GUIDRY
☐ 128. JAY HOWELL
☐ 129. STEVE KEMP
☐ 130. MATT KEOUGH
☐ 131. DON MATTINGLY
☐ 132. JOHN MONTEFUSCO
☐ 133. OMAR MORENO
☐ 134. DALE MURRAY
☐ 135. GRAIG NETTLES
☐ 136. LOU PINIELLA
☐ 137. WILLIE RANDOLPH
☐ 138. SHANE RAWLEY
☐ 139. DAVE RIGHETTI
☐ 140. ANDRE ROBERTSON
☐ 141. BOB SHIRLEY
☐ 142. ROY SMALLEY
☐ 143. DAVE WINFIELD
☐ 144. BUTCH WYNEGAR
☐ 652. TEAM(F) & MARTIN(M)

OAKLAND A'S

☐ 436. BILL ALMON
☐ 437. KEITH ATHERTON
☐ 438. DAVE BEARD
☐ 439. TOM BURGMEIER
☐ 440. JEFF BURROUGHS
☐ 441. CHRIS CONDIROLI
☐ 442. TIM CONROY
☐ 443. MIKE DAVIS
☐ 444. WAYNE GROSS
☐ 445. GARRY HANCOCK
☐ 446. MIKE HEATH
☐ 447. RICKEY HENDERSON
☐ 448. DON HILL
☐ 449. BOB KEARNEY
☐ 450. BILL KRUEGER
☐ 451. RICK LANGFORD
☐ 452. CARNEY LANSFORD
☐ 453. DAVEY LOPES
☐ 454. STEVE MCCATTY
☐ 455. DAN MEYER
☐ 456. DWAYNE MURPHY
☐ 457. MIKE NORRIS
☐ 458. RICKY PETERS
☐ 459. TONY PHILLIPS
☐ 460. TOM UNDERWOOD
☐ 461. MIKE WARREN
☐ 651. TEAM CHECKLIST(B)

PHILADELPHIA PHILLIES

☐ 24. MARTY BYSTROM
☐ 25. STEVE CARLTON
☐ 26. IVAN DEJESUS
☐ 27. JOHN DENNY
☐ 28. BOB DERNIER
☐ 29. BO DIAZ
☐ 30. KIKO GARCIA
☐ 31. GREG GROSS
☐ 32. KEVIN GROSS
☐ 33. VON HAYES
☐ 34. WILLIE HERNANDEZ

☐ 35. AL HOLLAND
☐ 36. CHARLES HUDSON
☐ 37. JOE LEFEBVRE
☐ 38. SIXTON LEZCANO
☐ 39. GARRY MADDOX
☐ 40. GARY MATTHEWS
☐ 41. LEN MATUSZEK
☐ 42. TUG MCGRAW
☐ 43. JOE MORGAN
☐ 44. TONY PEREZ
☐ 45. RON REED
☐ 46. PETE ROSE
☐ 47. JUAN SAMUEL
☐ 48. MIKE SCHMIDT
☐ 49. OZZIE VIRGIL
☐ 648. TEAM(F) & OWENS(M)

Steve Carlton
PITCHER

PITTSBURGH PIRATES

☐ 245. DALE BERRA
☐ 246. JIM BIBBY
☐ 247. JOHN CANDELARIA
☐ 248. JOSE DELEON
☐ 249. MIKE EASLER
☐ 250. CECILIO GUANTE
☐ 251. RICHIE HEBNER
☐ 252. LEE LACY
☐ 253. BILL MADLOCK
☐ 254. MILT MAY
☐ 255. LEE MAZZILLI
☐ 256. LARRY MCWILLIAMS
☐ 257. JIM MORRISON
☐ 258. DAVE PARKER
☐ 259. TONY PENA
☐ 260. JOHNNY RAY
☐ 261. RICK RHODEN
☐ 262. DON ROBINSON
☐ 263. MANNY SARMIENTO
☐ 264. ROD SCURRY
☐ 265. KENT TEKULVE
☐ 266. GENE TENACE
☐ 267. JASON THOMPSON
☐ 268. LEE TUNNELL
☐ 269. MARVELL WYNNE
☐ 657. TEAM(F) & TANNER(M)

ST. LOUIS CARDINALS

☐ 318. NEIL ALLEN
☐ 319. JOAQUIN ANDUJAR
☐ 320. STEVE BRAUN
☐ 321. GLENN BRUMMER
☐ 322. BOB FORSCH
☐ 323. DAVID GREEN
☐ 324. GEORGE HENDRICK
☐ 325. TOM HERR
☐ 326. DANE IORG
☐ 327. JEFF LAHTI
☐ 328. DAVE LAPOINT
☐ 329. WILLIE MCGEE
☐ 330. KEN OBERKFELL
☐ 331. DARRELL PORTER
☐ 332. JAMIE QUIRK
☐ 333. MIKE RAMSEY
☐ 334. FLOYD RAYFORD
☐ 335. LONNIE SMITH
☐ 336. OZZIE SMITH
☐ 337. JOHN STUPER
☐ 338. BRUCE SUTTER

☐ 339. ANDY VAN SLYKE
☐ 340. DAVE VON OHLEN
☐ 660. TEAM(F) & HERZOG(M)

SAN DIEGO PADRES

☐ 294. KURT BEVACQUA
☐ 295. JUAN BONILLA
☐ 296. BOBBY BROWN
☐ 297. LUIS DELEON
☐ 298. DAVE DRAVECKY
☐ 299. TIM FLANNERY
☐ 300. STEVE GARVEY
☐ 301. TONY GWYNN
☐ 302. ANDY HAWKINS
☐ 303. RUPPERT JONES
☐ 304. TERRY KENNEDY
☐ 305. TIM LOLLAR
☐ 306. GARY LUCAS
☐ 307. KEVIN MCREYNOLDS
☐ 308. SID MONGE
☐ 309. MARIO RAMIREZ
☐ 310. GENE RICHARDS
☐ 311. LUIS SALAZAR
☐ 312. ERIC SHOW
☐ 313. ELIAS SOSA
☐ 314. GARRY TEMPLETON
☐ 315. MARK THURMOND
☐ 316. ED WHITSON
☐ 317. ALAN WIGGINS
☐ 659. TEAM(F) & WILLIAMS(M)

SAN FRANCISCO GIANTS

☐ 365. JIM BARR
☐ 366. DAVE BERGMAN
☐ 367. FRED BREINING
☐ 368. BOB BRENLY
☐ 369. JACK CLARK
☐ 370. CHILI DAVIS
☐ 371. MARK DAVIS
☐ 372. DARRELL EVANS
☐ 373. ATLEE HAMMAKER
☐ 374. MIKE KRUKOW
☐ 375. DUANE KUIPER
☐ 376. BILL LASKEY
☐ 377. GARY LAVELL
☐ 378. JOHNNIE LEMASTER
☐ 379. JEFF LEONARD
☐ 380. RANDY LERCH
☐ 381. RENIE MARTIN
☐ 382. ANDY MCGAFFIGAN
☐ 383. GREG MINTON
☐ 384. TOM O'MALLEY
☐ 385. MAX VENABLE
☐ 386. BRAD WELLMAN
☐ 387. JOEL YOUNGBLOOD
☐ 648. TEAM CHECKLIST(B)

SEATTLE MARINERS

☐ 604. JAMIE ALLEN
☐ 605. JIM BEATTIE
☐ 606. TONY BERNAZARD
☐ 607. MANNY CASTILLO
☐ 608. BILL CAUDILL
☐ 609. BRYAN CLARK
☐ 610. AL COWENS
☐ 611. DAVE HENDERSON
☐ 612. STEVE HENDERSON
☐ 613. ORLANDO MERCADO
☐ 614. MIKE MOORE
☐ 615. RICKY NELSON
☐ 616. SPIKE OWEN
☐ 617. PAT PUTNAM
☐ 618. RON ROENICKE
☐ 619. MIKE STANTON
☐ 620. BOB STODDARD
☐ 621. RICK SWEET
☐ 622. ROY THOMAS
☐ 623. ED VANDEBERG
☐ 624. MATT YOUNG
☐ 625. RICHIE ZISK
☐ 658. TEAM CHECKLIST(B)

TEXAS RANGERS

☐ 413. BUDDY BELL
☐ 414. LARRY BITTNER
☐ 415. JOHN BUTCHER

☐ 416. DANNY DARWIN
☐ 417. BUCKY DENT
☐ 418. DAVE HOSTETLER
☐ 419. CHARLIE HOUGH
☐ 420. BOBBY JOHNSON
☐ 421. ODELL JONES
☐ 422. JON MATLACK
☐ 423. PETE O'BRIEN
☐ 424. LARRY PARRISH
☐ 425. MICKEY RIVERS
☐ 426. BILLY SAMPLE
☐ 427. DAVE SCHMIDT
☐ 428. MIKE SMITHSON
☐ 429. BILL STEIN
☐ 430. DAVE STEWART
☐ 431. JIM SUNDBERG
☐ 432. FRANK TANANA
☐ 433. DAVE TOBIK
☐ 434. WAYNE TOLLESON
☐ 435. GEORGE WRIGHT
☐ 650. TEAM CHECKLIST(B)

Bucky Dent
SHORTSTOP

TORONTO BLUE JAYS

☐ 145. JIM ACKER
☐ 146. DOYLE ALEXANDER
☐ 147. JESSE BARFIELD
☐ 148. JORGE BELL
☐ 149. BARRY BONNELL
☐ 150. JIM CLANCY
☐ 151. DAVE COLLINS
☐ 152. TONY FERNANDEZ
☐ 153. DAMASO GARCIA
☐ 154. DAVE GEISEL
☐ 155. JIM GOTT
☐ 156. ALFREDO GRIFFIN
☐ 157. GARTH IORG
☐ 158. ROY LEE JACKSON
☐ 159. CLIFF JOHNSON
☐ 160. LUIS LEAL
☐ 161. BUCK MARTINEZ
☐ 162. JOEY MCLAUGHLIN
☐ 163. RANDY MOFFIT
☐ 164. LLOYD MOSEBY
☐ 165. RANCE MULLINIKS
☐ 166. JORGE ORTA
☐ 167. DAVE STIEB
☐ 168. WILLIE UPSHAW
☐ 169. ERNIE WHITT
☐ 653. TEAM(F) & COX(M)

1984 FLEER
TRADED (132)
2 1/2" X 3 1/2"

Graig Nettles
THIRD BASE

ATLANTA BRAVES

☐ 63U. BRAD KOMMINSK
☐ 84U. KEN OBERKFELL
☐ 92U. GERALD PERRY
☐ 118U. ALEX TREVINO

BALTIMORE ORIOLES

☐ 45U. WAYNE GROSS
☐ 95U. FLOYD RAYFORD
☐ 121U. TOM UNDERWOOD
☐ 131U. MIKE YOUNG

BOSTON RED SOX

☐ 8U. MARTY BARRETT
☐ 18U. BILL BUCKNER
☐ 27U. ROGER CLEMENS
☐ 33U. MIKE EASLER
☐ 41U. RICH GALE
☐ 47U. JACKIE GUTIERREZ

CALIFORNIA ANGELS

☐ 17U. MIKE BROWN
☐ 67U. FRANK LACORTE
☐ 101U. RON ROMANICK
☐ 105U. DICK SCHOFIELD
☐ 107U. JIM SLATON
☐ 115U. CRAIG SWAN

CHICAGO CUBS

☐ 31U. BOB DERNIER
☐ 34U. DENNIS ECKERSLEY
☐ 40U. GEORGE FRAZIER
☐ 49U. RON HASSEY
☐ 50U. RICHIE HEBNER
☐ 77U. GARY MATTHEWS
☐ 104U. SCOTT SANDERSON
☐ 110U. TIM STODDARD
☐ 114U. RICK SUTCLIFFE

CHICAGO WHITE SOX

☐ 96U. RON REED
☐ 106U. TOM SEAVER

CINCINNATI REDS

☐ 39U. JOHN FRANCO
☐ 65U. WAYNE KRENCHICKI
☐ 88U. BOB OWCHINKO
☐ 89U. DAVE PARKER
☐ 91U. TONY PEREZ

CLEVELAND INDIANS

☐ 2U. LUIS APONTE
☐ 12U. TONY BERNAZARD
☐ 21U. BRETT BUTLER
☐ 56U. BROOK JACOBY
☐ 58U. MIKE JEFFCOAT
☐ 123U. TOM WADDELL

1984 Fleer Traded

Willie Hernandez
PITCHER

Ray Burris
PITCHER

☐ 1U. WILLIE AIKENS
☐ 26U. BRYAN CLARK
☐ 61U. JIMMY KEY
☐ 68U. DENNIS LAMP
☐ 71U. RICH LEACH

1985 FLEER
2 1/2″ X 3 1/2″

DWIGHT GOODEN
PITCHER

FLEER

DETROIT TIGERS

☐ 11U. DAVE BERGMAN
☐ 36U. DARRELL EVANS
☐ 42U. BARBARO GARBEY
☐ 51U. WILLIE HERNANDEZ
☐ 59U. RUPPERT JONES
☐ 66U. RUSTY KUNTZ

HOUSTON ASTROS

☐ 3U. MARK BAILEY
☐ 22U. ENOS CABELL

KANSAS CITY ROYALS

☐ 6U. STEVE BALBONI
☐ 10U. JOE BECKWITH
☐ 46U. MARK GUBICZA
☐ 55U. DANE IORG
☐ 81U. DARRYL MOTLEY
☐ 86U. JORGE ORTA
☐ 103U. BRET SABERHAGEN

LOS ANGELES DODGERS

☐ 4U. BOB BAILOR
☐ 32U. CARLOS DIAZ
☐ 97U. R.J. REYNOLDS
☐ 122U. MIKE VAIL
☐ 125U. TERRY WHITFIELD

MILWAUKEE BREWERS

☐ 25U. BOBBY CLARK
☐ 28U. JAIME COCANOWER
☐ 57U. DION JAMES
☐ 113U. JIM SUNDBERG

MINNESOTA TWINS

☐ 20U. JOHN BUTCHER
☐ 52U. ED HODGE
☐ 93U. KIRBY PUCKETT
☐ 108U. MIKE SMITHSON

MONTREAL EXPOS

☐ 16U. FRED BREINING
☐ 73U. GARY LUCAS
☐ 78U. ANDY MCGAFFIGAN
☐ 102U. PETE ROSE
☐ 116U. DERREL THOMAS

NEW YORK METS

☐ 29U. RON DARLING
☐ 37U. MIKE FITZGERALD
☐ 43U. DWIGHT GOODEN
☐ 74U. JERRY MARTIN

NEW YORK YANKEES

☐ 38U. TIM FOLI
☐ 48U. TOBY HARRAH
☐ 83U. PHIL NIEKRO
☐ 99U. JOSE RIJO

OAKLAND A'S

☐ 13U. BRUCE BOCHTE
☐ 19U. RAY BURRIS
☐ 24U. BILL CAUDILL
☐ 35U. JIM ESSIAN
☐ 62U. DAVE KINGMAN
☐ 80U. JOE MORGAN
☐ 109U. LARY SORENSEN

PHILADELPHIA PHILLIES

☐ 23U. BILL CAMPBELL
☐ 64U. JERRY KOOSMAN
☐ 94U. SHANE RAWLEY
☐ 111U. JEFF STONE
☐ 128U. GLENN WILSON
☐ 129U. JOHN WOCKENFUSS

PITTSBURGH PIRATES

☐ 87U. AMOS OTIS
☐ 120U. JOHN TUDOR

ST. LOUIS CARDINALS

☐ 53U. RICKY HORTON
☐ 54U. ART HOWE
☐ 69U. TITO LANDRUM

SAN DIEGO PADRES

☐ 44U. RICH GOSSAGE
☐ 72U. CRAIG LEFFERTS
☐ 75U. CARMELO MARTINEZ
☐ 82U. GRAIG NETTLES
☐ 112U. CHAMP SUMMERS

SAN FRANCISCO GIANTS

☐ 5U. DUSTY BAKER
☐ 85U. AL OLIVER
☐ 98U. GENE RICHARDS
☐ 100U. JEFF ROBINSON
☐ 119U. MANNY TRILLO
☐ 127U. FRANK WILLIAMS

SEATTLE MARINERS

☐ 9U. DAVE BEARD
☐ 14U. BARRY BONNELL
☐ 15U. PHIL BRADLEY
☐ 30U. ALVIN DAVIS
☐ 60U. BOB KEARNEY
☐ 70U. MARK LANGSTON
☐ 90U. JACK PERCONTE
☐ 117U. GORMAN THOMAS

TEXAS RANGERS

☐ 7U. ALAN BANNISTER
☐ 76U. MIKE MASON
☐ 79U. JOEY MCLAUGHLIN
☐ 124U. CURTIS WILKERSON
☐ 130U. NED YOST

ATLANTA BRAVES

☐ 318. LEN BARKER
☐ 319. STEVE BEDROSIAN
☐ 320. BRUCE BENEDICT
☐ 321. RICK CAMP
☐ 322. CHRIS CHAMBLISS
☐ 323. JEFF DEDMON
☐ 324. TERRY FORSTER
☐ 325. GENE GARBER
☐ 326. ALBERT HALL
☐ 327. TERRY HARPER
☐ 328. BOB HORNER
☐ 329. GLENN HUBBARD
☐ 330. RANDY JOHNSON
☐ 331. BRAD KOMMINSK
☐ 332. RICK MAHLER
☐ 333. CRAIG MCMURTRY
☐ 334. DONNIE MOORE
☐ 335. DALE MURPHY
☐ 336. KEN OBERKFELL
☐ 337. PASCUAL PEREZ
☐ 338. GERALD PERRY
☐ 339. RAFAEL RAMIREZ
☐ 340. JERRY ROYSTER
☐ 341. ALEX TREVINO
☐ 342. CLAUDELL WASHINGTON
☐ 651. ZANE SMITH(P)
☐ 651. PAUL ZUVELLA(P)
☐ 657. TEAM CHECKLIST(F)

BALTIMORE ORIOLES

☐ 170. MIKE BODDICKER
☐ 171. AL BUMBRY
☐ 172. TODD CRUZ
☐ 173. RICH DAUER
☐ 174. STORM DAVIS
☐ 175. RICK DEMPSEY
☐ 176. JIM DWYER
☐ 177. MIKE FLANAGAN
☐ 178. DAN FORD
☐ 179. WAYNE GROSS
☐ 180. JOHN LOWENSTEIN
☐ 181. DENNIS MARTINEZ
☐ 182. TIPPY MARTINEZ
☐ 183. SCOTT MCGREGOR
☐ 184. EDDIE MURRAY
☐ 185. JOE NOLAN
☐ 186. FLOYD RAYFORD
☐ 187. CAL RIPKEN
☐ 188. GARY ROENICKE
☐ 189. LENN SAKATA
☐ 190. JOHN SHELBY
☐ 191. KEN SINGLETON
☐ 192. SAMMY STEWART
☐ 193. BILL SWAGGERTY
☐ 194. TOM UNDERWOOD
☐ 195. MIKE YOUNG
☐ 655. TEAM CHECKLIST(B)

BOSTON RED SOX

- ☐ 148. GARY ALLENSON
- ☐ 149. TONY ARMAS
- ☐ 150. MARTY BARRETT
- ☐ 151. WADE BOGGS
- ☐ 152. DENNIS BOYD
- ☐ 153. BILL BUCKNER
- ☐ 154. MARK CLEAR
- ☐ 155. ROGER CLEMENS
- ☐ 156. STEVE CRAWFORD
- ☐ 157. MIKE EASLER
- ☐ 158. DWIGHT EVANS
- ☐ 159. RICH GEDMAN
- ☐ 160. JACKIE GUTIERREZ
- ☐ 161. BRUCE HURST
- ☐ 162. JOHN HENRY JOHNSON
- ☐ 163. RICK MILLER
- ☐ 164. REID NICHOLS
- ☐ 165. AL NIPPER
- ☐ 166. BOB OJEDA
- ☐ 167. JERRY REMY
- ☐ 168. JIM RICE
- ☐ 169. BOB STANLEY
- ☐ 655. TEAM CHECKLIST(B)

CALIFORNIA ANGELS

- ☐ 293. DON AASE
- ☐ 294. JUAN BENIQUEZ
- ☐ 295. BOB BOONE
- ☐ 296. MIKE BROWN
- ☐ 297. ROD CAREW
- ☐ 298. DOUG CORBETT
- ☐ 299. DOUG DECINCES
- ☐ 300. BRIAN DOWNING
- ☐ 301. KEN FORSCH
- ☐ 302. BOBBY GRICH
- ☐ 303. REGGIE JACKSON
- ☐ 304. TOMMY JOHN
- ☐ 305. CURT KAUFMAN
- ☐ 306. BRUCE KISON
- ☐ 307. FRED LYNN
- ☐ 308. GARY PETTIS
- ☐ 309. RON ROMANICK
- ☐ 310. LUIS SANCHEZ
- ☐ 311. DICK SCHOFIELD
- ☐ 312. DARYL SCONIERS
- ☐ 313. JIM SLATON
- ☐ 314. DERREL THOMAS
- ☐ 315. ROB WILFONG
- ☐ 316. MIKE WITT
- ☐ 317. GEOFF ZAHN
- ☐ 657. TEAM CHECKLIST(F)

CHICAGO CUBS

- ☐ 49. RICH BORDI
- ☐ 50. LARRY BOWA
- ☐ 51. WARREN BRUSSTAR
- ☐ 52. RON CEY
- ☐ 53. HENRY COTTO
- ☐ 54. JODY DAVIS
- ☐ 55. BOB DERNIER
- ☐ 56. LEON DURHAM
- ☐ 57. DENNIS ECKERSLEY
- ☐ 58. GEORGE FRAZIER
- ☐ 59. RICHIE HEBNER
- ☐ 60. DAVE LOPES
- ☐ 61. GARY MATTHEWS
- ☐ 62. KEITH MORELAND
- ☐ 63. RICK REUSCHEL
- ☐ 64. DICK RUTHVEN
- ☐ 65. RYNE SANDBERG
- ☐ 66. SCOTT SANDERSON
- ☐ 67. LEE SMITH
- ☐ 68. TIM STODDARD
- ☐ 69. RICK SUTCLIFFE
- ☐ 70. STEVE TROUT
- ☐ 71. GARY WOODS
- ☐ 649. BILL HATCHER(P)
- ☐ 649. SHAWON DUNSTON(P)
- ☐ 654. TEAM CHECKLIST(B)

CHICAGO WHITE SOX

- ☐ 506. JUAN AGOSTO
- ☐ 507. HAROLD BAINES
- ☐ 508. FLOYD BANNISTER
- ☐ 509. BRITT BURNS

- ☐ 510. JULIO CRUZ
- ☐ 511. RICHARD DOTSON
- ☐ 512. JERRY DYBZINSKI
- ☐ 513. CARLTON FISK
- ☐ 514. SCOTT FLETCHER
- ☐ 515. JERRY HAIRSTON
- ☐ 516. MARC HILL
- ☐ 517. LAMARR HOYT
- ☐ 518. RON KITTLE
- ☐ 519. RUDY LAW
- ☐ 520. VANCE LAW
- ☐ 521. GREG LUZINSKI
- ☐ 522. GENE NELSON
- ☐ 523. TOM PACIOREK
- ☐ 524. RON REED
- ☐ 525. BERT ROBERGE
- ☐ 526. TOM SEAVER
- ☐ 527. ROY SMALLEY
- ☐ 528. DAN SPILLNER
- ☐ 529. MIKE SQUIRES
- ☐ 530. GREG WALKER
- ☐ 646. JOEL SKINNER(P)
- ☐ 659. TEAM CHECKLIST(F)

CINCINNATI REDS

- ☐ 531. CESAR CEDENO
- ☐ 532. DAVE CONCEPCION
- ☐ 533. ERIC DAVIS
- ☐ 534. NICK ESASKY
- ☐ 535. TOM FOLEY
- ☐ 536. JOHN FRANCO
- ☐ 537. BRAD GULDEN
- ☐ 538. TOM HUME
- ☐ 539. WAYNE KRENCHICKI
- ☐ 540. ANDY MCGAFFIGAN
- ☐ 541. EDDIE MILNER
- ☐ 542. RON OESTER
- ☐ 543. BOB OWCHINKO
- ☐ 544. DAVE PARKER
- ☐ 545. FRANK PASTORE
- ☐ 546. TONY PEREZ
- ☐ 547. TED POWER
- ☐ 548. JOE PRICE
- ☐ 549. GARY REDUS
- ☐ 550. PETE ROSE(M)
- ☐ 551. JEFF RUSSELL
- ☐ 552. MARIO SOTO
- ☐ 553. JAY TIBBS
- ☐ 554. DUANE WALKER
- ☐ 650. RON ROBINSON(P)
- ☐ 659. TEAM CHECKLIST(B)

CLEVELAND INDIANS

- ☐ 437. LUIS APONTE
- ☐ 438. CHRIS BANDO
- ☐ 439. TONY BERNAZARD
- ☐ 440. BERT BLYLEVEN
- ☐ 441. BRETT BUTLER
- ☐ 442. ERNIE CAMACHO
- ☐ 443. JOE CARTER
- ☐ 444. CARMELO CASTILLO
- ☐ 445. JAMIE EASTERLY
- ☐ 446. STEVE FARR
- ☐ 447. MIKE FISCHLIN
- ☐ 448. JULIO FRANCO
- ☐ 449. MEL HALL
- ☐ 450. MIKE HARGROVE
- ☐ 451. NEAL HEATON
- ☐ 452. BROOK JACOBY
- ☐ 453. MIKE JEFFCOAT
- ☐ 454. DON SCHULZE
- ☐ 455. ROY SMITH
- ☐ 456. PAT TABLER
- ☐ 457. ANDRE THORNTON
- ☐ 458. GEORGE VUKOVICH
- ☐ 459. TOM WADDELL
- ☐ 460. JERRY WILLARD
- ☐ 646. JOSE ROMAN(P)
- ☐ 658. TEAM CHECKLIST(B)

DETROIT TIGERS

- ☐ 1. DOUG BAIR
- ☐ 2. JUAN BERENGUER
- ☐ 3. DAVE BERGMAN
- ☐ 4. TOM BROOKENS
- ☐ 5. MARTY CASTILLO
- ☐ 6. DARRELL EVANS
- ☐ 7. BARBARO GARBEY

- ☐ 8. KIRK GIBSON
- ☐ 9. JOHN GRUBB
- ☐ 10. WILLIE HERNANDEZ
- ☐ 11. LARRY HERNDON
- ☐ 12. HOWARD JOHNSON
- ☐ 13. RUPPERT JONES
- ☐ 14. RUSTY KUNTZ
- ☐ 15. CHET LEMON
- ☐ 16. AURELIO LOPEZ
- ☐ 17. SID MONGE
- ☐ 18. JACK MORRIS
- ☐ 19. LANCE PARRISH
- ☐ 20. DAN PETRY
- ☐ 21. DAVE ROZEMA
- ☐ 22. BILL SCHERRER
- ☐ 23. ALAN TRAMMELL
- ☐ 24. LOU WHITAKER
- ☐ 25. MILT WILCOX
- ☐ 654. RANDY O'NEAL(P)
- ☐ 654. TEAM CHECKLIST(F)

HOUSTON ASTROS

- ☐ 343. ALAN ASHBY
- ☐ 344. MARK BAILEY
- ☐ 345. KEVIN BASS
- ☐ 346. ENOS CABELL
- ☐ 347. JOSE CRUZ
- ☐ 348. BILL DAWLEY
- ☐ 349. FRANK DIPINO
- ☐ 350. BILL DORAN
- ☐ 351. PHIL GARNER
- ☐ 352. BOB KNEPPER
- ☐ 353. MIKE LACOSS
- ☐ 354. JERRY MUMPHREY
- ☐ 355. JOE NIEKRO
- ☐ 356. TERRY PUHL
- ☐ 357. CRAIG REYNOLDS
- ☐ 358. VERN RUHLE
- ☐ 359. NOLAN RYAN
- ☐ 360. JOE SAMBITO
- ☐ 361. MIKE SCOTT
- ☐ 362. DAVE SMITH
- ☐ 363. JULIO SOLANO
- ☐ 364. DICKIE THON
- ☐ 365. DENNY WALLING
- ☐ 652. GLENN DAVIS(P)
- ☐ 657. TEAM CHECKLIST(B)

KANSAS CITY ROYALS

- ☐ 196. STEVE BALBONI
- ☐ 197. JOE BECKWITH
- ☐ 198. BUD BLACK
- ☐ 199. GEORGE BRETT
- ☐ 200. ONIX CONCEPCION
- ☐ 201. MARK GUBICZA
- ☐ 202. LARRY GURA
- ☐ 203. MARK HUISMANN
- ☐ 204. DANE IORG
- ☐ 205. DANNY JACKSON
- ☐ 206. CHARLIE LEIBRANDT
- ☐ 207. HAL MCRAE
- ☐ 208. DARRYL MOTLEY
- ☐ 209. JORGE ORTA
- ☐ 210. GREG PRYOR
- ☐ 211. DAN QUISENBERRY
- ☐ 212. BRET SABERHAGEN
- ☐ 213. PAT SHERIDAN

1985 Fleer

☐ 214. DON SLAUGHT
☐ 215. U.L. WASHINGTON
☐ 216. JOHN WATHAN
☐ 217. FRANK WHITE
☐ 218. WILLIE WILSON
☐ 656. TEAM CHECKLIST(F)

LOS ANGELES DODGERS

☐ 366. DAVE ANDERSON
☐ 367. BOB BAILOR
☐ 368. GREG BROCK
☐ 369. CARLOS DIAZ
☐ 370. PEDRO GUERRERO
☐ 371. OREL HERSHISER
☐ 372. RICK HONEYCUTT
☐ 373. BURT HOOTON
☐ 374. KEN HOWELL
☐ 375. KEN LANDREQUX
☐ 376. CANDY MALDONADO
☐ 377. MIKE MARSHALL
☐ 378. TOM NIEDENFUER
☐ 379. ALEJANDRO PENA
☐ 380. JERRY REUSS
☐ 381. R.J. REYNOLDS
☐ 382. GERMAN RIVERA
☐ 383. BILL RUSSELL
☐ 384. STEVE SAX
☐ 385. MIKE SCIOSCIA
☐ 386. FRANKLIN STUBBS
☐ 387. FERNANDO VALENZUELA
☐ 388. BOB WELCH
☐ 389. TERRY WHITFIELD
☐ 390. STEVE YEAGER
☐ 391. PAT ZACHRY
☐ 657. TEAM CHECKLIST(B)

MILWAUKEE BREWERS

☐ 576. MARK BROUHARD
☐ 577. MIKE CALDWELL
☐ 578. BOBBY CLARK
☐ 579. JAIME COCANOWER
☐ 580. CECIL COOPER
☐ 581. ROLLIE FINGERS
☐ 582. JIM GANTNER
☐ 583. MOOSE HAAS
☐ 584. DION JAMES
☐ 585. PETE LADD
☐ 586. RICK MANNING
☐ 587. BOB MCCLURE
☐ 588. PAUL MOLITOR
☐ 589. CHARLIE MOORE
☐ 590. BEN OGLIVIE
☐ 591. CHUCK PORTER
☐ 592. RANDY READY
☐ 593. ED ROMERO
☐ 594. BILL SCHROEDER
☐ 595. RAY SEARAGE
☐ 596. TED SIMMONS
☐ 597. JIM SUNDBERG
☐ 598. DON SUTTON
☐ 599. TOM TELLMAN
☐ 600. RICK WAITS
☐ 601. ROBIN YOUNT
☐ 644. WILLIE LOZADO(P)
☐ 660 TEAM CHECKLIST(F)

MINNESOTA TWINS

☐ 270. DARRELL BROWN
☐ 271. TOM BRUNANSKY
☐ 272. RANDY BUSH
☐ 273. JOHN BUTCHER
☐ 274. BOBBY CASTILLO
☐ 275. RON DAVIS
☐ 276. DAVE ENGLE
☐ 277. PETE FILSON
☐ 278. GARY GAETTI
☐ 279. MICKEY HATCHER
☐ 280. ED HODGE
☐ 281. KENT HRBEK
☐ 282. HOUSTON JIMENEZ
☐ 283. TIM LAUDNER
☐ 284. RICK LYSANDER
☐ 285. DAVE MEIER
☐ 286. KIRBY PUCKETT
☐ 287. PAT PUTNAM
☐ 288. KEN SCHROM
☐ 289. MIKE SMITHSON

☐ 290. TIM TEUFEL
☐ 291. FRANK VIOLA
☐ 292. RON WASHINGTON
☐ 656. TEAM CHECKLIST(B)

MONTREAL EXPOS

☐ 392. FRED BREINING
☐ 393. GARY CARTER
☐ 394. ANDRE DAWSON
☐ 395. MIGUEL DILONE
☐ 396. DAN DRIESSEN
☐ 397. DOUG FLYNN
☐ 398. TERRY FRANCONA
☐ 399. BILL GULLICKSON
☐ 400. BOB JAMES
☐ 401. CHARLIE LEA
☐ 402. BRYAN LITTLE
☐ 403. GARY LUCAS
☐ 404. DAVID PALMER
☐ 405. TIM RAINES
☐ 406. MIKE RAMSEY
☐ 407. JEFF REARDON
☐ 408. STEVE ROGERS
☐ 409. DAN SCHATZEDER
☐ 410. BRYN SMITH
☐ 411. MIKE STENHOUSE
☐ 412. TIM WALLACH
☐ 413. JIM WOHLFORD
☐ 652. JOE HESKETH(P)
☐ 658. TEAM CHECKLIST(F)

NEW YORK METS

☐ 72. WALLY BACKMAN
☐ 73. BRUCE BERENYI
☐ 74. HUBIE BROOKS
☐ 75. KELVIN CHAPMAN
☐ 76. RON DARLING
☐ 77. SID FERNANDEZ
☐ 78. MIKE FITZGERALD
☐ 79. GEORGE FOSTER
☐ 80. BRENT GAFF
☐ 81. RON GARDENHIRE
☐ 82. DWIGHT GOODEN
☐ 83. TOM GORMAN
☐ 84. DANNY HEEP
☐ 85. KEITH HERNANDEZ
☐ 86. RAY KNIGHT
☐ 87. ED LYNCH
☐ 88. JOSE OQUENDO
☐ 89. JESSE OROSCO
☐ 90. RAFAEL SANTANA
☐ 91. DOUG SISK
☐ 92. RUSTY STAUB
☐ 93. DARRYL STRAWBERRY
☐ 94. WALT TERRELL
☐ 95. MOOKIE WILSON
☐ 654. TEAM CHECKLIST(B)

NEW YORK YANKEES

☐ 120. MIKE ARMSTRONG
☐ 121. DON BAYLOR
☐ 122. MARTY BYSTROM
☐ 123. RICK CERONE
☐ 124. JOE COWLEY
☐ 125. BRIAN DAYETT
☐ 126. TIM FOLI
☐ 127. RAY FONTENOT

☐ 128. KEN GRIFFEY
☐ 129. RON GUIDRY
☐ 130. TOBY HARRAH
☐ 131. JAY HOWELL
☐ 132. STEVE KEMP
☐ 133. DON MATTINGLY
☐ 134. BOBBY MEACHAM
☐ 135. JOHN MONTEFUSCO
☐ 136. OMAR MORENO
☐ 137. DALE MURRAY
☐ 138. PHIL NIEKRO
☐ 139. MIKE PAGLIARULO
☐ 140. WILLIE RANDOLPH
☐ 141. DENNIS RASMUSSEN
☐ 142. DAVE RIGHETTI
☐ 143. JOSE RIJO
☐ 144. ANDRE ROBERTSON
☐ 145. BOB SHIRLEY
☐ 146. DAVE WINFIELD
☐ 147. BUTCH WYNEGAR
☐ 644. VIC MATA(P)
☐ 655. TEAM CHECKLIST(F)

OAKLAND A'S

☐ 414. BILL ALMON
☐ 415. KEITH ATHERTON
☐ 416. BRUCE BOCHTE
☐ 417. TOM BURGMEIER
☐ 418. RAY BURRIS
☐ 419. BILL CAUDILL
☐ 420. CHRIS CODIROLI
☐ 421. TIM CONROY
☐ 422. MIKE DAVIS
☐ 423. JIM ESSIAN
☐ 424. MIKE HEATH
☐ 425. RICKEY HENDERSON
☐ 426. DONNIE HILL
☐ 427. DAVE KINGMAN
☐ 428. BILL KRUEGER
☐ 429. CARNEY LANSFORD
☐ 430. STEVE MCCATTY
☐ 431. JOE MORGAN
☐ 432. DWAYNE MURPHY
☐ 433. TONY PHILLIPS
☐ 434. LARY SORENSEN
☐ 435. MIKE WARREN
☐ 436. CURT YOUNG
☐ 647. STEVE KIEFER(P)
☐ 658. TEAM CHECKLIST(F)

PHILADELPHIA PHILLIES

☐ 244. LARRY ANDERSON
☐ 245. BILL CAMPBELL
☐ 246. STEVE CARLTON
☐ 247. TIM CORCORAN
☐ 248. IVAN DEJESUS
☐ 249. JOHN DENNY
☐ 250. BO DIAZ
☐ 251. GREG GROSS
☐ 252. KEVIN GROSS
☐ 253. VON HAYES
☐ 254. AL HOLLAND
☐ 255. CHARLES HUDSON
☐ 256. JERRY KOOSMAN
☐ 257. JOE LEFEBVRE
☐ 258. SIXTO LEZCANO
☐ 259. GARRY MADDOX
☐ 260. LEN MATUSZEK
☐ 261. TUG MCGRAW
☐ 262. AL OLVIER
☐ 263. SHANE RAWLEY
☐ 264. JUAN SAMUEL
☐ 265. MIKE SCHMIDT
☐ 266. JEFF STONE
☐ 267. OZZIE VIRGIL
☐ 268. GLENN WILSON
☐ 269. JOHN WOCKENFUSS
☐ 653. JOHN RUSSELL(P)
☐ 653. STEVE JELTZ(P)
☐ 656. TEAM CHECKLIST(B)

PITTSBURGH PIRATES

☐ 461. DALE BERRA
☐ 462. JOHN CANDELARIA
☐ 463. JOSE DELEON
☐ 464. DOUG FROBEL
☐ 465. CECILLIO GUANTE

☐ 466. BRIAN HARPER
☐ 467. LEE LACY
☐ 468. BILL MADLOCK
☐ 469. LEE MAZZILLI
☐ 470. LARRY MCWILLIAMS
☐ 471. JIM MORRISON
☐ 472. TONY PENA
☐ 473. JOHNNY RAY
☐ 474. RICK RHODEN
☐ 475. DON ROBINSON
☐ 476. ROD SCURRY
☐ 477. KENT TEKULVE
☐ 478. JASON THOMPSON
☐ 479. JOHN TUDOR
☐ 480. LEE TUNNELL
☐ 481. MARVELL WYNNE
☐ 650. MIKE BIELECKI(P)
☐ 658. TEAM CHECKLIST(B)

ST. LOUIS CARDINALS

☐ 219. NEIL ALLEN
☐ 220. JOAQUIN ANDUJAR
☐ 221. STEVE BRAUN
☐ 222. DANNY COX
☐ 223. BOB FORSCH
☐ 224. DAVID GREEN
☐ 225. GEORGE HENDRICK
☐ 226. TOM HERR
☐ 227. RICKY HORTON
☐ 228. ART HOWE
☐ 229. MIKE JORGENSEN
☐ 230. KURT KEPSHIRE
☐ 231. JEFF LAHTI
☐ 232. TITO LANDRUM
☐ 233. DAVE LAPOINT
☐ 234. WILLIE MCGEE
☐ 235. TOM NIETO
☐ 236. TERRY PENDLETON
☐ 237. DARRELL PORTER
☐ 238. DAVE RUCKER
☐ 239. LONNIE SMITH
☐ 240. OZZIE SMITH
☐ 241. BRUCE SUTTER
☐ 242. ANDY VAN SLYKE
☐ 243. DAVE VON OHLEN
☐ 656. TEAM CHECKLIST(F)

SAN DIEGO PADRES

☐ 26. KURT BEVACQUA
☐ 27. GREG BOOKER
☐ 28. BOBBY BROWN
☐ 29. LUIS DELEON
☐ 30. DAVE DRAVECKY
☐ 31. TIM FLANNERY
☐ 32. STEVE GARVEY
☐ 33. GOOSE GOSSAGE
☐ 34. TONY GWYNN
☐ 35. GREG HARRIS
☐ 36. ANDY HAWKINS
☐ 37. TERRY KENNEDY
☐ 38. CRAIG LEFFERTS
☐ 39. TIM LOLLAR
☐ 40. CARMELO MARTINEZ
☐ 41. KEVIN MCREYNOLDS
☐ 42. GRAIG NETTLES
☐ 43. LUIS SALAZAR
☐ 44. ERIC SHOW
☐ 45. GARRY TEMPLETON
☐ 46. MARK THURMOND
☐ 47. ED WHITSON
☐ 48. ALAN WIGGINS
☐ 654. TEAM CHECKLIST(F)

SAN FRANCISCO GIANTS

☐ 602. DUSTY BAKER
☐ 603. BOB BRENLY
☐ 604. JACK CLARK
☐ 605. CHILI DAVIS
☐ 606. MARK DAVIS
☐ 607. DAN GLADDEN
☐ 608. ATLEE HAMMAKER
☐ 609. MIKE KRUKOW
☐ 610. DUANE KUIPER
☐ 611. BOB LACEY
☐ 612. BILL LASKEY
☐ 613. GARY LAVELLE
☐ 614. JOHNNIE LEMASTER
☐ 615. JEFF LEONARD

☐ 616. RANDY LERCH
☐ 617. GREG MINTON
☐ 618. STEVE NICOSIA
☐ 619. GENE RICHARDS
☐ 620. JEFF ROBINSON
☐ 621. SCOT THOMPSON
☐ 622. MANNY TRILLO
☐ 623. BRAD WELLMAN
☐ 624. FRANK WILLIAMS
☐ 625. JOEL YOUNGBLOOD
☐ 648. ROB DEER(P)
☐ 648. ALEJANDRO SANCHEZ(P)
☐ 660. TEAM CHECKLIST(F)

SEATTLE MARINERS

☐ 482. SALOME BAROJAS
☐ 483. DAVE BEARD
☐ 484. JIM BEATTIE
☐ 485. BARRY BONNELL
☐ 486. PHIL BRADLEY
☐ 487. AL COWENS
☐ 488. ALVIN DAVIS
☐ 489. DAVE HENDERSON
☐ 490. STEVE HENDERSON
☐ 491. BOB KEARNEY
☐ 492. MARK LANGSTON
☐ 493. LARRY MILBOURNE
☐ 494. PAUL MIRABELLA
☐ 495. MIKE MOORE
☐ 496. EDWIN NUNEZ
☐ 497. SPIKE OWEN
☐ 498. JACK PERCONTE
☐ 499. KEN PHELPS
☐ 500. JIM PRESLEY
☐ 501. MIKE STANTON
☐ 502. BOB STODDARD
☐ 503. GORMAN THOMAS
☐ 504. ED VANDE BERG
☐ 505. MATT YOUNG
☐ 647. DANNY TARTABULL(P)
☐ 659. TEAM CHECKLIST(F)

TEXAS RANGERS

☐ 555. ALAN BANNISTER
☐ 556. BUDDY BELL
☐ 557. DANNY DARWIN
☐ 558. CHARLIE HOUGH
☐ 559. BOBBY JONES
☐ 560. ODELL JONES
☐ 561. JEFF KUNKEL
☐ 562. MIKE MASON
☐ 563. PETE O'BRIEN
☐ 564. LARRY PARRISH
☐ 565. MICKEY RIVERS
☐ 566. BILLY SAMPLE
☐ 567. DAVE SCHMIDT
☐ 568. DONNIE SCOTT
☐ 569. DAVE STEWART
☐ 570. FRANK TANANA
☐ 571. WAYNE TOLLESON
☐ 572. GARY WARD
☐ 573. CURTIS WILKERSON
☐ 574. GEORGE WRIGHT
☐ 575. NED YOST
☐ 659. TEAM CHECKLIST(B)

TORONTO BLUE JAYS

☐ 96. JIM ACKER
☐ 97. WILLIE AIKENS
☐ 98. DOYLE ALEXANDER
☐ 99. JESSE BARFIELD
☐ 100. GEORGE BELL
☐ 101. JIM CLANCY
☐ 102. DAVE COLLINS
☐ 103. TONY FERNANDEZ
☐ 104. DAMASO GARCIA
☐ 105. JIM GOTT
☐ 106. ALFREDO GRIFFIN
☐ 107. GARTH IORG
☐ 108. ROY LEE JACKSON
☐ 109. CLIFF JOHNSON
☐ 110. JIMMY KEY
☐ 111. DENNIS LAMPE
☐ 112. RICK LEACH
☐ 113. LUIS LEAL
☐ 114. BUCK MARTINEZ
☐ 115. LLOYD MOSEBY

☐ 116. RANCE MULLINIKS
☐ 117. DAVE STIEB
☐ 118. WILLIE UPSHAW
☐ 119. ERNIE WHITT
☐ 645. KELLY GRUBER(P)
☐ 655. TEAM CHECKLIST(F)

1985 FLEER
TRADED (132)
2 1/2 X 3 1/2

ATLANTA BRAVES

☐ 24U. RICK CERONE
☐ 114U. BRUCE SUTTER

BALTIMORE ORIOLES

☐ 1U. DON AASE
☐ 30U. FRITZ CONNALLY
☐ 36U. KEN DIXON
☐ 67U. LEE LACY
☐ 75U. FRED LYNN
☐ 101U. LARRY SHEETS
☐ 107U. NATE SNELL

BOSTON RED SOX

☐ 65U. BRUCE KISON
☐ 76U. STEVE LYONS

CALIFORNIA ANGELS

☐ 26U. PAT CLEMENTS
☐ 27U. STEWART CLIBURN
☐ 63U. RUPPERT JONES
☐ 74U. URBANO LUGO
☐ 82U. DONNIE MOORE

CHICAGO CUBS

☐ 35U. BRIAN DAYETT
☐ 42U. RAY FONTENOT
☐ 108U. LARY SORENSEN
☐ 109U. CHRIS SPEIER

CHICAGO WHITE SOX

☐ 9U. DARYL BOSTON
☐ 39U. BOB FALLON
☐ 44U. OSCAR GAMBLE
☐ 48U. OZZIE GUILLEN
☐ 59U. TIM HULETT
☐ 60U. BOB JAMES
☐ 73U. TIM LOLLAR
☐ 95U. LUIS SALAZAR
☐ 116U. BRUCE TANNER

CINCINNATI REDS

☐ 12U. TOM BROWNING
☐ 112U. JOHN STUPER

CLEVELAND INDIANS

☐ 93U. VERN RUHLE
☐ 120U. RICH THOMPSON
☐ 126U. DAVE VON OHLEN

1985 Fleer Traded

DETROIT TIGERS

- ☐ 87U. CHRIS PITTARO
- ☐ 98U. ALEX SANCHEZ
- ☐ 103U. NELSON SIMMONS
- ☐ 118U. WALT TERRELL

HOUSTON ASTROS

- ☐ 18U. JEFF CALHOUN
- ☐ 78U. RON MATHIS

KANSAS CITY ROYALS

- ☐ 66U. MIKE LACOSS
- ☐ 106U. LONNIE SMITH
- ☐ 113U. JIM SUNDBERG

LOS ANGELES DODGERS

- ☐ 22U. BOBBY CASTILLO
- ☐ 38U. MARIANO DUNCAN
- ☐ 84U. AL OLIVER

MILWAUKEE BREWERS

- ☐ 15U. RAY BURRIS
- ☐ 32U. DANNY DARWIN
- ☐ 54U. TEDDY HIGUERA
- ☐ 89U. EARNIE RILES

MINNESOTA TWINS

- ☐ 43U. GREG GAGNE
- ☐ 94U. MARK SALAS
- ☐ 105U. ROY SMALLEY
- ☐ 110U. MIKE STENHOUSE
- ☐ 127U. CURT WARDLE
- ☐ 131U. RICH YETT

MONTREAL EXPOS

- ☐ 10U. HUBIE BROOKS
- ☐ 14U. TIM BURKE
- ☐ 41U. MIKE FITZGERALD
- ☐ 70U. VANCE LAW
- ☐ 77U. MICKEY MAHLER
- ☐ 128U. U.L. WASHINGTON
- ☐ 130U. HERM WINNINGHAM

NEW YORK METS

- ☐ 21U. GARY CARTER
- ☐ 62U. HOWARD JOHNSON
- ☐ 81U. ROGER MCDOWELL
- ☐ 96U. JOE SAMBITO
- ☐ 99U. CALVIN SCHIRALDI

NEW YORK YANKEES

- ☐ 4U. DALE BERRA
- ☐ 8U. RICH BORDI
- ☐ 31U. HENRY COTTO
- ☐ 40U. BRIAN FISHER
- ☐ 50U. RON HASSEY
- ☐ 51U. RICKEY HENDERSON
- ☐ 86U. DAN PASQUA
- ☐ 97U. BILLY SAMPLE
- ☐ 129U. ED WHITSOM

OAKLAND A'S

- ☐ 3U. DUSTY BAKER
- ☐ 6U. TIM BIRTSAS
- ☐ 29U. DAVE COLLINS
- ☐ 47U. ALFREDO GRIFFIN
- ☐ 52U. STEVE HENDERSON
- ☐ 57U. JAY HOWELL
- ☐ 115U. DON SUTTON
- ☐ 119U. MICKEY TETTLETON

PHILADELPHIA PHILLIES

- ☐ 20U. DON CARMAN
- ☐ 33U. DARREN DAULTON
- ☐ 92U. DAVE RUCKER
- ☐ 100U. RICK SCHU
- ☐ 117U. KENT TEKULVE

PITTSBURGH PIRATES

- ☐ 2U. BILL ALMON
- ☐ 53U. GEORGE HENDRICK
- ☐ 55U. AL HOLLAND
- ☐ 64U. STEVE KEMP
- ☐ 72U. SIXTO LEZCANO
- ☐ 85U. JOE ORSULAK
- ☐ 88U. RICK REUSCHEL

ST. LOUIS CARDINALS

- ☐ 19U. BILL CAMPBELL
- ☐ 25U. JACK CLARK
- ☐ 28U. VINCE COLEMAN
- ☐ 123U. JOHN TUDOR

SAN DIEGO PADRES

- ☐ 13U. AL BUMBRY
- ☐ 34U. JERRY DAVIS
- ☐ 58U. LAMARR HOYT
- ☐ 90U. JERRY ROYSTER
- ☐ 111U. TIM STODDARD

SAN FRANCISCO GIANTS

- ☐ 7U. VIDA BLUE
- ☐ 11U. CHRIS BROWN
- ☐ 45U. JIM GOTT
- ☐ 46U. DAVID GREEN
- ☐ 68U. DAVE LAPOINT
- ☐ 122U. ALEX TREVINO
- ☐ 124U. JOSE URIBE

SEATTLE MARINERS

- ☐ 5U. KARL BEST
- ☐ 17U. IVAN CALDERON
- ☐ 125U. DAVE VALLE

TEXAS RANGERS

- ☐ 37U. TOMMY DUNBAR
- ☐ 49U. TOBY HARRAH
- ☐ 56U. BURT HOOTON
- ☐ 61U. CLIFF JOHNSON
- ☐ 80U. ODDIBE MCDOWELL
- ☐ 91U. DAVE ROZEMA
- ☐ 104U. DON SLAUGHT

TORONTO BLUE JAYS

- ☐ 16U. JEFF BURROUGHS
- ☐ 23U. BILL CAUDILL
- ☐ 69U. GARY LAVELLE
- ☐ 71U. MANNY LEE
- ☐ 79U. LEN MATUSZEK
- ☐ 83U. RON MUSSELMAN
- ☐ 102U. RON SHEPHERD
- ☐ 121U. LOUIS THORNTON

1986 FLEER (660)
2 1/2 X 3 1/2

ATLANTA BRAVES

- ☐ 507. LEN BARKER
- ☐ 508. STEVE BEDROSIAN
- ☐ 509. BRUCE BENEDICT
- ☐ 510. RICK CAMP
- ☐ 511. RICK CERONE
- ☐ 512. CHRIS CHAMBLISS
- ☐ 513. JEFF DEDMON
- ☐ 514. TERRY FORSTER
- ☐ 515. GENE GARBER
- ☐ 516. TERRY HARPER
- ☐ 517. BOB HORNER
- ☐ 518. GLENN HUBBARD
- ☐ 519. JOE JOHNSON
- ☐ 520. BRAD KOMMINSK
- ☐ 521. RICK MAHLER
- ☐ 522. DALE MURPHY
- ☐ 523. KEN OBERKFELL
- ☐ 524. PASCUAL PEREZ
- ☐ 525. GERALD PERRY
- ☐ 526. RAFAEL RAMIREZ
- ☐ 527. STEVE SHIELDS
- ☐ 528. ZANE SMITH
- ☐ 529. BRUCE SUTTER
- ☐ 530. MILT THOMPSON
- ☐ 531. CLAUDELL WASHINGTON
- ☐ 532. PAUL ZUVELLA
- ☐ 659. TEAM CHECKLIST(F)

BALTIMORE ORIOLES

- ☐ 268. DON AASE
- ☐ 269. MIKE BODDICKER
- ☐ 270. RICH DAUER
- ☐ 271. STORM DAVIS
- ☐ 272. RICK DEMPSEY
- ☐ 273. KEN DIXON
- ☐ 274. JIM DWYER
- ☐ 275. MIKE FLANAGAN
- ☐ 276. WAYNE GROSS
- ☐ 277. LEE LACY
- ☐ 278. FRED LYNN
- ☐ 279. DENNIS MARTINEZ
- ☐ 280. TIPPY MARTINEZ
- ☐ 281. SCOTT MCGREGOR
- ☐ 282. EDDIE MURRAY
- ☐ 283. FLOYD RAYFORD
- ☐ 284. CAL RIPKEN
- ☐ 285. GARY ROENICKE
- ☐ 286. LARRY SHEETS
- ☐ 287. JOHN SHELBY
- ☐ 288. NATE SNELL
- ☐ 289. SAMMY STEWART
- ☐ 290. ALAN WIGGINS
- ☐ 291. MIKE YOUNG
- ☐ 656. TEAM CHECKLIST(B)

BOSTON RED SOX

- ☐ 339. TONY ARMAS
- ☐ 340. MARTY BARRETT
- ☐ 341. WADE BOGGS
- ☐ 342. DENNIS BOYD
- ☐ 343. BILL BUCKNER
- ☐ 344. MARK CLEAR
- ☐ 345. ROGER CLEMENS
- ☐ 346. STEVE CRAWFORD
- ☐ 347. MIKE EASLER
- ☐ 348. DWIGHT EVANS
- ☐ 349. RICH GEDMAN
- ☐ 350. JACKIE GUTIERREZ
- ☐ 351. GLENN HOFFMAN
- ☐ 352. BRUCE HURST
- ☐ 353. BRUCE KISON
- ☐ 354. TIM LOLLAR
- ☐ 355. STEVE LYONS
- ☐ 356. AL NIPPER
- ☐ 357. BOB OJEDA
- ☐ 358. JIM RICE
- ☐ 359. BOB STANLEY
- ☐ 360. MIKE TRUJILLO
- ☐ 651. ROB WOODWARD(P)
- ☐ 657. TEAM CHECKLIST(B)

CALIFORNIA ANGELS

- ☐ 148. JUAN BENIQUEZ
- ☐ 149. BOB BOONE
- ☐ 150. JOHN CANDELARIA
- ☐ 151. ROD CAREW
- ☐ 152. STEWARD CLIBURN
- ☐ 153. DOUG DECINCES
- ☐ 154. BRIAN DOWNING
- ☐ 155. KEN FORSCH
- ☐ 156. CRAIG GERBER
- ☐ 157. BOBBY GRICH
- ☐ 158. GEORGE HENDRICK
- ☐ 159. AL HOLLAND
- ☐ 160. REGGIE JACKSON
- ☐ 161. RUPPERT JONES
- ☐ 162. URBANO LUGO
- ☐ 163. KIRK MCCASKILL
- ☐ 164. DONNIE MOORE
- ☐ 165. GARY PETTIS
- ☐ 166. RON ROMANICK

CALIFORNIA ANGELS

- ☐ 148. JUAN BENIQUEZ
- ☐ 149. BOB BOONE
- ☐ 150. JOHN CANDELARIA
- ☐ 151. ROD CAREW
- ☐ 152. STEWART CLIBURN
- ☐ 153. DOUG DECINCES
- ☐ 154. BRIAN DOWNING
- ☐ 155. KEN FORSCH
- ☐ 156. CRAIG GERBER
- ☐ 157. BOBBY GRICH
- ☐ 158. GEORGE HENDRICK
- ☐ 159. AL HOLLAND
- ☐ 160. REGGIE JACKSON
- ☐ 161. RUPPERT JONES
- ☐ 162. URBANO LUGO
- ☐ 163. KIRK MCCASKILL
- ☐ 164. DONNIE MOORE
- ☐ 165. GARY PETTIS
- ☐ 166. RON ROMANICK
- ☐ 167. DICK SCHOFIELD
- ☐ 168. DARYL SCONIERS
- ☐ 169. JIM SLATON
- ☐ 170. DON SUTTON
- ☐ 171. MIKE WITT
- ☐ 650. GUS POLIDOR(P)
- ☐ 650. MARK MCLEMORE(P)
- ☐ 655. TEAM CHECKLIST(B)

CHICAGO CUBS

- ☐ 361. THAD BOSLEY
- ☐ 362. WARREN BRUSSTAR
- ☐ 363. RON CEY
- ☐ 364. JODY DAVIS
- ☐ 365. BOB DERNIER
- ☐ 366. SHAWON DUNSTON
- ☐ 367. LEON DURHAM
- ☐ 368. DENNIS ECKERSLEY
- ☐ 369. RAY FONTENOT
- ☐ 370. GEORGE FRAZIER

- ☐ 371. BILL HATCHER
- ☐ 372. DAVE LOPES
- ☐ 373. GARY MATTHEWS
- ☐ 374. RON MEREDITH
- ☐ 375. KEITH MORELAND
- ☐ 376. REGGIE PATTERSON
- ☐ 377. DICK RUTHVEN
- ☐ 378. RYNE SANDBERG
- ☐ 379. SCOTT SANDERSON
- ☐ 380. LEE SMITH
- ☐ 381. LARY SORENSEN
- ☐ 382. CHRIS SPEIER
- ☐ 383. RICK SUTCLIFFE
- ☐ 384. STEVE TROUT
- ☐ 385. GARY WOODS
- ☐ 657. TEAM CHECKLIST(B)

CHICAGO WHITE SOX

- ☐ 197. JUAN AGOSTO
- ☐ 198. HAROLD BAINES
- ☐ 199. FLOYD BANNISTER
- ☐ 200. BRITT BURNS
- ☐ 201. JULIO CRUZ
- ☐ 202. JOEL DAVIS
- ☐ 203. RICHARD DOTSON
- ☐ 204. CARLTON FISK
- ☐ 205. SCOTT FLETCHER
- ☐ 206. OZZIE GUILLEN
- ☐ 207. JERRY HAIRSTON
- ☐ 208. TIM HULETT
- ☐ 209. BOB JAMES
- ☐ 210. RON KITTLE
- ☐ 211. RUDY LAW
- ☐ 212. BRYAN LITTLE
- ☐ 213. GENE NELSON
- ☐ 214. REID NICHOLS
- ☐ 215. LUIS SALAZAR
- ☐ 216. TOM SEAVER
- ☐ 217. DAN SPILLNER
- ☐ 218. BRUCE TANNER
- ☐ 219. GREG WALKER
- ☐ 220. DAVE WEHRMEISTER
- ☐ 656. TEAM CHECKLIST(F)

CINCINNATI REDS

- ☐ 172. BUDDY BELL
- ☐ 173. TOM BROWNING
- ☐ 174. DAVE CONCEPCION
- ☐ 175. ERIC DAVIS
- ☐ 176. BO DIAZ
- ☐ 177. NICK ESASKY
- ☐ 178. JOHN FRANCO
- ☐ 179. TOM HUME
- ☐ 180. WAYNE KRENCHICKI
- ☐ 181. ANDY MCGAFFIGAN
- ☐ 182. EDDIE MILNER
- ☐ 183. RON OESTER
- ☐ 184. DAVE PARKER
- ☐ 185. FRANK PASTORE
- ☐ 186. TONY PEREZ
- ☐ 187. TED POWER
- ☐ 188. JOE PRICE
- ☐ 189. GARY REDUS
- ☐ 190. RON ROBINSON
- ☐ 191. PETE ROSE(M)
- ☐ 192. MARIO SOTO
- ☐ 193. JOHN STUPER
- ☐ 194. JAY TIBBS
- ☐ 195. DAVE VAN GORDER
- ☐ 196. MAX VENABLE
- ☐ 646. KAL DANIELS(P)
- ☐ 646. PAUL O'NEILL(P)
- ☐ 655. TEAM CHECKLIST(B)

CLEVELAND INDIANS

- ☐ 579. CHRIS BANDO
- ☐ 580. TONY BERNAZARD
- ☐ 581. BRETT BUTLER
- ☐ 582. ERNIE CAMACHO
- ☐ 583. JOE CARTER
- ☐ 584. CARMEN CASTILLO
- ☐ 585. JAMIE EASTERLY
- ☐ 586. JULIO FRANCO
- ☐ 587. MEL HALL
- ☐ 588. MIKE HARGROVE
- ☐ 589. NEAL HEATON
- ☐ 590. BROOK JACOBY

- ☐ 591. OTIS NIXON
- ☐ 592. JERRY REED
- ☐ 593. VERN RUHLE
- ☐ 594. PAT TABLER
- ☐ 595. RICH THOMPSON
- ☐ 596. ANDRE THORNTON
- ☐ 597. DAVE VON OHLEN
- ☐ 598. GEORGE VUKOVICH
- ☐ 599. TOM WADDELL
- ☐ 600. CURT WARDLE
- ☐ 601. JERRY WILLARD
- ☐ 653. CORY SNYDER(P)
- ☐ 660. TEAM CHECKLIST(F)

DETROIT TIGERS

- ☐ 221. JUAN BERENGUER
- ☐ 222. DAVE BERGMAN
- ☐ 223. TOM BROOKENS
- ☐ 224. DARRELL EVANS
- ☐ 225. BARBARO GARBEY
- ☐ 226. KIRK GIBSON
- ☐ 227. JOHN GRUBB
- ☐ 228. WILLIE HERNANDEZ
- ☐ 229. LARRY HERNDON
- ☐ 230. CHET LEMON
- ☐ 231. AURELIO LOPEZ
- ☐ 232. JACK MORRIS
- ☐ 233. RANDY O'NEAL
- ☐ 234. LANCE PARRISH
- ☐ 235. DAN PETRY
- ☐ 236. ALEX SANCHEZ
- ☐ 237. BILL SCHERRER
- ☐ 238. NELSON SIMMONS
- ☐ 239. FRANK TANANA
- ☐ 240. WALT TERRELL
- ☐ 241. ALAN TRAMMELL
- ☐ 242. LOU WHITAKER
- ☐ 243. MILT WILCOX
- ☐ 656. TEAM CHECKLIST(F)

HOUSTON ASTROS

- ☐ 292. ALAN ASHBY
- ☐ 293. MARK BAILEY
- ☐ 294. KEVIN BASS
- ☐ 295. JEFF CALHOUN
- ☐ 296. JOSE CRUZ
- ☐ 297. GLENN DAVIS
- ☐ 298. BILL DAWLEY
- ☐ 299. FRANK DIPINO
- ☐ 300. BILL DORAN
- ☐ 301. PHIL GARNER
- ☐ 302. JEFF HEATHCOCK
- ☐ 303. CHARLIE KERFELD
- ☐ 304. BOB KNEPPER
- ☐ 305. RON MATHIS
- ☐ 306. JERRY MUMPHREY
- ☐ 307. JIM PANKOVITS
- ☐ 308. TERRY PUHL
- ☐ 309. CRAIG REYNOLDS
- ☐ 310. NOLAN RYAN
- ☐ 311. MIKE SCOTT
- ☐ 312. DAVE SMITH
- ☐ 313. DICKIE THON
- ☐ 314. DENNY WALLING
- ☐ 657. TEAM CHECKLIST(F)

KANSAS CITY ROYALS

- ☐ 1. STEVE BALBONI
- ☐ 2. JOE BECKWITH
- ☐ 3. BUDDY BIANCALANA
- ☐ 4. BUD BLACK
- ☐ 5. GEORGE BRETT
- ☐ 6. ONIX CONCEPCION
- ☐ 7. STEVE FARR
- ☐ 8. MARK GUBICZA
- ☐ 9. DANE IORG
- ☐ 10. DANNY JACKSON
- ☐ 11. LYNN JONES
- ☐ 12. MIKE JONES
- ☐ 13. CHARLIE LEIBRANDT
- ☐ 14. HAL MCRAE
- ☐ 15. OMAR MORENO
- ☐ 16. DARRYL MOTLEY
- ☐ 17. JORGE ORTA
- ☐ 18. DAN QUISENBERRY
- ☐ 19. BRET SABERHAGEN
- ☐ 20. PAT SHERIDAN
- ☐ 21. LONNIE SMITH
- ☐ 22. JIM SUNDBERG
- ☐ 23. JOHN WATHAN
- ☐ 24. FRANK WHITE
- ☐ 25. WILLIE WILSON
- ☐ 654. TEAM CHECKLIST(F)

LOS ANGELES DODGERS

- ☐ 123. DAVE ANDERSON
- ☐ 124. BOB BAILOR
- ☐ 125. GREG BROCK
- ☐ 126. ENOS CABELL
- ☐ 127. BOBBY CASTILLO
- ☐ 128. CARLOS DIAZ
- ☐ 129. MARIANO DUNCAN
- ☐ 130. PEDRO GUERRERO
- ☐ 131. OREL HERSHISER
- ☐ 132. RICK HONEYCUTT
- ☐ 133. KEN HOWELL
- ☐ 134. KEN LANDREAUX
- ☐ 135. BILL MADLOCK
- ☐ 136. CANDY MALDONADO
- ☐ 137. MIKE MARSHALL
- ☐ 138. LEN MATUSZEK
- ☐ 139. TOM NIEDENFUER
- ☐ 140. ALEJANDRO PENA
- ☐ 141. JERRY REUSS
- ☐ 142. BILL RUSSELL
- ☐ 143. STEVE SAX
- ☐ 144. MIKE SCIOSCIA
- ☐ 145. FERNANDO VALENZUELA
- ☐ 146. BOB WELCH
- ☐ 147. TERRY WHITFIELD
- ☐ 655. TEAM CHECKLIST(F)

MILWAUKEE BREWERS

- ☐ 482. RAY BURRIS
- ☐ 483. JAIME COCANOWER
- ☐ 484. CECIL COOPER
- ☐ 485. DANNY DARWIN
- ☐ 486. ROLLIE FINGERS
- ☐ 487. JIM GANTNER
- ☐ 488. BOB GIBSON
- ☐ 489. MOOSE HAAS
- ☐ 490. TEDDY HIGUERA
- ☐ 491. PAUL HOUSEHOLDER
- ☐ 492. PETE LADD
- ☐ 493. RICK MANNING
- ☐ 494. BOB MCCLURE
- ☐ 495. PAUL MOLITOR
- ☐ 496. CHARLIE MOORE
- ☐ 497. BEN OGLIVIE
- ☐ 498. RANDY READY
- ☐ 499. EARNIE RILES
- ☐ 500. ED ROMERO
- ☐ 501. BILL SCHROEDER
- ☐ 502. RAY SEARAGE
- ☐ 503. TED SIMMONS
- ☐ 504. PETE VUCKOVICH
- ☐ 505. RICK WAITS
- ☐ 506. ROBIN YOUNT
- ☐ 652. BILLY JOE ROBIDOUX(P)
- ☐ 659. TEAM CHECKLIST(F)

MINNESOTA TWINS

- ☐ 386. BERT BLYLEVEN
- ☐ 387. TOM BRUNANSKY
- ☐ 388. RANDY BUSH
- ☐ 389. JOHN BUTCHER
- ☐ 390. RON DAVIS
- ☐ 391. DAVE ENGLE
- ☐ 392. FRANK EUFEMIA
- ☐ 393. PETE FILSON
- ☐ 394. GARY GAETTI
- ☐ 395. GREG GAGNE
- ☐ 396. MICKEY HATCHER
- ☐ 397. KENT HRBEK
- ☐ 398. TIM LAUDNER
- ☐ 399. RICK LYSANDER
- ☐ 400. DAVE MEIER
- ☐ 401. KIRBY PUCKETT
- ☐ 402. MARK SALAS
- ☐ 403. KEN SCHROM
- ☐ 404. ROY SMALLEY
- ☐ 405. MIKE SMITHSON
- ☐ 406. MIKE STENHOUSE
- ☐ 407. TIM TEUFEL
- ☐ 408. FRANK VIOLA
- ☐ 409. RON WASHINGTON
- ☐ 652. MARK FUNDERBURK(P)
- ☐ 658. TEAM CHECKLIST(F)

MONTREAL EXPOS

- ☐ 244. HUBIE BROOKS
- ☐ 245. TIM BURKE
- ☐ 246. ANDRE DAWSON
- ☐ 247. MIKE FITZGERALD
- ☐ 248. TERRY FRANCONA
- ☐ 249. BILL GULLICKSON
- ☐ 250. JOE HESKETH
- ☐ 251. BILL LASKEY
- ☐ 252. VANCE LAW
- ☐ 253. CHARLIE LEA
- ☐ 254. GARY LUCAS
- ☐ 255. DAVID PALMER
- ☐ 256. TIM RAINES
- ☐ 257. JEFF REARDON
- ☐ 258. BERT ROBERGE
- ☐ 259. DAN SCHATZEDER
- ☐ 260. BRYN SMITH
- ☐ 261. RANDY ST. CLAIRE
- ☐ 262. SCOT THOMPSON
- ☐ 263. TIM WALLACH
- ☐ 264. U.L. WASHINGTON
- ☐ 265. MITCH WEBSTER
- ☐ 266. HERM WINNINGHAM
- ☐ 267. FLOYD YOUMANS
- ☐ 647. ANDRES GALARRAGA(P)
- ☐ 656. TEAM CHECKLIST(B)

NEW YORK METS

- ☐ 74. RICK AGUILERA
- ☐ 75. WALLY BACKMAN
- ☐ 76. GARY CARTER
- ☐ 77. RON DARLING
- ☐ 78. LEN DYKSTRA
- ☐ 79. SID FERNANDEZ
- ☐ 80. GEORGE FOSTER
- ☐ 81. DWIGHT GOODEN
- ☐ 82. TOM GORMAN
- ☐ 83. DANNY HEEP

- ☐ 84. KEITH HERNANDEZ
- ☐ 85. HOWARD JOHNSON
- ☐ 86. RAY KNIGHT
- ☐ 87. TERRY LEACH
- ☐ 88. ED LYNCH
- ☐ 89. ROGER MCDOWELL
- ☐ 90. JESSE OROSCO
- ☐ 91. TOM PACIOREK
- ☐ 92. RONN REYNOLDS
- ☐ 93. RAFAEL SANTANA
- ☐ 94. DOUG SISK
- ☐ 95. RUSTY STAUB
- ☐ 96. DARRYL STRAWBERRY
- ☐ 97. MOOKIE WILSON
- ☐ 654. TEAM CHECKLIST

NEW YORK YANKEES

- ☐ 98. NEIL ALLEN
- ☐ 99. DON BAYLOR
- ☐ 100. DALE BERRA
- ☐ 101. RICH BORDI
- ☐ 102. MARTY BYSTROM
- ☐ 103. JOE COWLEY
- ☐ 104. BRIAN FISHER
- ☐ 105. KEN GRIFFEY
- ☐ 106. RON GUIDRY
- ☐ 107. RON HASSEY
- ☐ 108. RICKEY HENDERSON
- ☐ 109. DON MATTINGLY
- ☐ 110. BOBBY MEACHAM
- ☐ 111. JOHN MONTEFUSCO
- ☐ 112. PHIL NIEKRO
- ☐ 113. MIKE PAGLIARULO
- ☐ 114. DAN PASQUA
- ☐ 115. WILLIE RANDOLPH
- ☐ 116. DAVE RIGHETTI
- ☐ 117. ANDRE ROBERTSON
- ☐ 118. BILLY SAMPLE
- ☐ 119. BOB SHIRLEY
- ☐ 120. ED WHITSON
- ☐ 121. DAVE WINFIELD
- ☐ 122. BUTCH WYNEGAR
- ☐ 655. TEAM CHECKLIST(F)

OAKLAND A'S

- ☐ 410. KEITH ATHERTON
- ☐ 411. DUSTY BAKER
- ☐ 412. TIM BIRTSAS
- ☐ 413. BRUCE BOCHTE
- ☐ 414. CHRIS CODIROLLI
- ☐ 415. DAVE COLLINS
- ☐ 416. MIKE DAVIS
- ☐ 417. ALFREDO GRIFFIN
- ☐ 418. MIKE HEATH
- ☐ 419. STEVE HENDERSON
- ☐ 420. DONNIE HILL
- ☐ 421. JAY HOWELL
- ☐ 422. TOMMY JOHN
- ☐ 423. DAVE KINGMAN
- ☐ 424. BILL KRUEGER
- ☐ 425. RICK LANGFORD
- ☐ 426. CARNEY LANSFORD
- ☐ 427. STEVE MCCATTY
- ☐ 428. DWAYNE MURPHY
- ☐ 429. STEVE ONTIVEROS
- ☐ 430. TONY PHILLIPS
- ☐ 431. JOSE RIJO
- ☐ 432. MICKEY TETTLETON
- ☐ 649. ERIC PLUNK(P)
- ☐ 649. JOSE CANSECO(P)
- ☐ 658. TEAM CHECKLIST(F)

PHILADELPHIA PHILLIES

- ☐ 433. LUIS AGUAYO
- ☐ 434. LARRY ANDERSEN
- ☐ 435. STEVE CARLTON
- ☐ 436. DON CARMAN
- ☐ 437. TIM CORCORAN
- ☐ 438. DARREN DAULTON
- ☐ 439. JOHN DENNY
- ☐ 440. TOM FOLEY
- ☐ 441. GREG GROSS
- ☐ 442. KEVIN GROSS
- ☐ 443. VON HAYES
- ☐ 444. CHARLES HUDSON
- ☐ 445. GARRY MADDOX
- ☐ 446. SHANE RAWLEY

☐ 447. DAVE RUCKER
☐ 448. JOHN RUSSELL
☐ 449. JUAN SAMUEL
☐ 450. MIKE SCHMIDT
☐ 451. RICH SCHU
☐ 452. DAVE SHIPANOFF
☐ 453. DAVE STEWART
☐ 454. JEFF STONE
☐ 455. KENT TEKULVE
☐ 456. OZZIE VIRGIL
☐ 457. GLENN WILSON
☐ 647. FRED TOLIVER(P)
☐ 658. TEAM CHECKLIST(B)

PITTSBURGH PIRATES

☐ 602. BILL ALMON
☐ 603. MIKE BIELECKI
☐ 604. SID BREAM
☐ 605. MIKE BROWN
☐ 606. PAT CLEMENTS
☐ 607. JOSE DELEON
☐ 608. DENNY GONZALEZ
☐ 609. CECILIO GUANTE
☐ 610. STEVE KEMP
☐ 611. SAM KHALIFA
☐ 612. LEE MAZZILLI
☐ 613. LARRY MCWILLIAMS
☐ 614. JIM MORRISON
☐ 615. JOE ORSULAK
☐ 616. TONY PENA
☐ 617. JOHNNY RAY
☐ 618. RICK REUSCHEL
☐ 619. R.J. REYNOLDS
☐ 620. RICK RHODEN
☐ 621. DON ROBINSON
☐ 622. JASON THOMPSON
☐ 623. LEE TUNNELL
☐ 624. JIM WINN
☐ 625. MARVELL WYNNE
☐ 648. BOB KIPPER(P)
☐ 660. TEAM CHECKLIST(F)

ST. LOUIS CARDINALS

☐ 26. JOAQUIN ANDUJAR
☐ 27. STEVE BRAUN
☐ 28. BILL CAMPBELL
☐ 29. CESAR CEDENO
☐ 30. JACK CLARK
☐ 31. VINCE COLEMAN
☐ 32. DANNY COX
☐ 33. KEN DAYLEY
☐ 34. IVAN DEJESUS
☐ 35. BOB FORSCH
☐ 36. BRIAN HARPER
☐ 37. TOM HERR
☐ 38. RICKY HORTON
☐ 39. KURT KEPSHIRE
☐ 40. JEFF LAHTI
☐ 41. TITO LANDRUM
☐ 42. WILLIE MCGEE
☐ 43. TOM NIETO
☐ 44. TERRY PENDLETON
☐ 45. DARRELL PORTER
☐ 46. OZZIE SMITH
☐ 47. JOHN TUDOR
☐ 48. ANDY VAN SLYKE
☐ 49. TODD WORRELL
☐ 648. CURT FORD(P)
☐ 654. TEAM CHECKLIST(F)

SAN DIEGO PADRES

☐ 315. KURT BEVACQUA
☐ 316. AL BUMBRY
☐ 317. JERRY DAVIS
☐ 318. LUIS DELEON
☐ 319. DAVE DRAVECKY
☐ 320. TIM FLANNERY
☐ 321. STEVE GARVEY
☐ 322. GOOSE GOSSAGE
☐ 323. TONY GWYNN
☐ 324. ANDY HAWKINS
☐ 325. LAMARR HOYT
☐ 326. ROY LEE JACKSON
☐ 327. TERRY KENNEDY
☐ 328. CRAIG LEFFERTS
☐ 329. CARMELO MARTINEZ
☐ 330. LANCE MCCULLERS
☐ 331. KEVIN MCREYNOLDS

☐ 332. GRAIG NETTLES
☐ 333. JERRY ROYSTER
☐ 334. ERIC SHOW
☐ 335. TIM STODDARD
☐ 336. GARRY TEMPLETON
☐ 337. MARK THURMOND
☐ 338. ED WOJNA
☐ 644. BENITO SANTIAGO(P)
☐ 644. GENE WALTER(P)
☐ 651. TEAM CHECKLIST(F)

SAN FRANCISCO GIANTS

☐ 533. VIDA BLUE
☐ 534. BOB BRENLEY
☐ 535. CHRIS BROWN
☐ 536. CHILI DAVIS
☐ 537. MARK DAVIS
☐ 538. ROB DEER
☐ 539. DAN DRIESSEN
☐ 540. SCOTT GARRELTS
☐ 541. DAN GLADDEN
☐ 542. JIM GOTT
☐ 543. DAVID GREEN
☐ 544. ATLEE HAMMAKER
☐ 545. MIKE JEFFCOAT
☐ 546. MIKE KRUKOW
☐ 547. DAVE LAPOINT
☐ 548. JEFF LEONARD
☐ 549. GREG MINTON
☐ 550. ALEX TREVINO
☐ 551. MANNY TRILLO
☐ 552. JOSE URIBE
☐ 553. BRAD WELLMAN
☐ 554. FRANK WILLIAMS
☐ 555. JOEL YOUNGBLOOD
☐ 645. MIKE WOODARD(P)
☐ 645. COLIN WARD(P)
☐ 659. TEAM CHECKLIST(B)

SEATTLE MARINERS

☐ 458. JIM BEATTIE
☐ 459. KARL BEST
☐ 460. BARRY BONNELL
☐ 461. PHIL BRADLEY
☐ 462. IVAN CALDERON
☐ 463. AL COWENS
☐ 464. ALVIN DAVIS
☐ 465. DAVE HENDERSON
☐ 466. BOB KEARNEY
☐ 467. MARK LANGSTON
☐ 468. BOB LONG
☐ 469. MIKE MOORE
☐ 470. EDWIN NUNEZ
☐ 471. SPIKE OWEN
☐ 472. JACK PERCONTE
☐ 473. JIM PRESLEY
☐ 474. DONNIE SCOTT
☐ 475. BILL SWIFT
☐ 476. DANNY TARTABULL
☐ 477. GORMAN THOMAS
☐ 478. ROY THOMAS
☐ 479. ED VANDE BERG
☐ 480. FRANK WILLS
☐ 481. MATT YOUNG
☐ 651. MICKEY BRANTLEY(P)
☐ 658. TEAM CHECKLIST(B)

TEXAS RANGERS

☐ 556. ALAN BANNISTER
☐ 557. GLENN BRUMMER
☐ 558. STEVE BUECHELE
☐ 559. JOSE GUZMAN
☐ 560. TOBY HARRAH
☐ 561. GREG HARRIS
☐ 562. DWAYNE HENRY
☐ 563. BURT HOOTON
☐ 564. CHARLIE HOUGH
☐ 565. MIKE MASON
☐ 566. ODDIBE MCDOWELL
☐ 567. DICKIE NOLES
☐ 568. PETE O'BRIEN
☐ 569. LARRY PARRISH
☐ 570. DAVE ROZEMA
☐ 571. DAVE SCHMIDT
☐ 572. DON SLAUGHT
☐ 573. WAYNE TOLLESON
☐ 574. DUANE WALKER

☐ 575. GARY WARD
☐ 576. CHRIS WELSH
☐ 577. CURTIS WILKERSON
☐ 578. GEORGE WRIGHT
☐ 659. TEAM CHECKLIST(B)

TORONTO BLUE JAYS

☐ 50. JIM ACKER
☐ 51. DOYLE ALEXANDER
☐ 52. JESSE BARFIELD
☐ 53. GEORGE BELL
☐ 54. JEFF BURROUGHS
☐ 55. BILL CAUDILL
☐ 56. JIM CLANCY
☐ 57. TONY FERNANDEZ
☐ 58. TOM FILER
☐ 59. DAMASO GARCIA
☐ 60. TOM HENKE
☐ 61. GARTH IORG
☐ 62. CLIFF JOHNSON
☐ 63. JIMMY KEY
☐ 64. DENNIS LAMP
☐ 65. GARY LAVELLE
☐ 66. BUCK MARTINEZ
☐ 67. LLOYD MOSEBY
☐ 68. RANCE MULLINIKS
☐ 69. AL OLIVER
☐ 70. DAVE STIEB
☐ 71. LOUIS THORNTON
☐ 72. WILLIE UPSHAW
☐ 73. ERNIE WHITT
☐ 653. CECIL FIELDER(P)
☐ 654. TEAM CHECKLIST(B)

1986 FLEER TRADED (132) 2 1/2 X 3 1/2

TED SIMMONS CATCHER #3/1

ATLANTA BRAVES

☐ 5U. PAUL ASSENMACHER
☐ 78U. OMAR MORENO
☐ 87U. DAVID PALMER
☐ 102U. BILLY SAMPLE
☐ 106U. TED SIMMONS
☐ 112U. ANDRES THOMAS
☐ 122U. OZZIE VIRGIL
☐ 125U. DUANE WARD

BALTIMORE ORIOLES

☐ 13U. JUAN BENIQUEZ
☐ 16U. RICH BORDI
☐ 47U. JACKIE GUTIERREZ

BOSTON RED SOX

☐ 10U. DON BAYLOR
☐ 93U. REY QUINONES
☐ 101U. JOE SAMBITO
☐ 107U. SAMMY STEWART

CALIFORNIA ANGELS

☐ 42U. TERRY FORSTER
☐ 59U. WALLY JOYNER

1986 Fleer Traded

CHICAGO CUBS

- ☐ 7U. JAY BALLER
- ☐ 43U. TERRY FRANCONA
- ☐ 51U. GUY HOFFMAN
- ☐ 79U. JERRY MUMPHREY
- ☐ 120U. MANNY TRILLO

CHICAGO WHITE SOX

- ☐ 3U. NEIL ALLEN
- ☐ 15U. BOBBY BONILLA
- ☐ 19U. JOHN CANGELOSI
- ☐ 31U. JOE COWLEY
- ☐ 32U. BILL DAWLEY
- ☐ 75U. JOEL MCKEON
- ☐ 103U. DAVE SCHMIDT
- ☐ 118U. WAYNE TOLLESON

CINCINNATI REDS

- ☐ 34U. JOHN DENNY
- ☐ 46U. BILL GULLICKSON
- ☐ 58U. TRACY JONES
- ☐ 108U. KURT STILLWELL

CLEVELAND INDIANS

- ☐ 2U. ANDY ALLANSON
- ☐ 6U. SCOTT BAILES
- ☐ 18U. TOM CANDIOTTI
- ☐ 81U. PHIL NIEKRO
- ☐ 104U. KEN SCHROM

DETROIT TIGERS

- ☐ 17U. BILL CAMPBELL
- ☐ 21U. CHUCK CARY
- ☐ 28U. DAVE COLLINS
- ☐ 27U. DARNELL COLES
- ☐ 39U. DAVE ENGLE
- ☐ 64U. DAVE LAPOINT

HOUSTON ASTROS

- ☐ 35U. JIM DESHAIES
- ☐ 49U. BILLY HATCHER
- ☐ 69U. AURELIO LOPEZ
- ☐ 123U. TONY WALKER

KANSAS CITY ROYALS

- ☐ 8U. SCOTT BANKHEAD
- ☐ 66U. RUDY LAW
- ☐ 67U. DENNIS LEONARD
- ☐ 100U. ANGEL SALAZAR

LOS ANGELS DODGERS

- ☐ 119U. ALEX TREVINO
- ☐ 121U. ED VANDE BERG
- ☐ 128U. REGGIE WILLIAMS

ROB DEER
OUTFIELD

MILWAUKEE BREWERS

- ☐ 22U. JUAN CASTILLO
- ☐ 23U. RICK CERONE
- ☐ 26U. MARK CLEAR
- ☐ 33U. ROB DEER
- ☐ 83U. JUAN NIEVES

- ☐ 90U. DAN PLASAC
- ☐ 97U. BILLY JOE ROBIDOUX
- ☐ 109U. DALE SVEUM

MINNESOTA TWINS

- ☐ 11U. BILLY BEANE
- ☐ 68U. STEVE LOMBARDOZZI
- ☐ 95U. JEFF REED

MONTREAL EXPOS

- ☐ 44U. ANDRES GALARRAGA
- ☐ 60U. WAYNE KRENCHICKI
- ☐ 74U. ANDY MCGAFFIGAN
- ☐ 80U. AL NEWMAN
- ☐ 88U. JEFF PARRETT
- ☐ 113U. JASON THOMPSON
- ☐ 116U. JAY TIBBS

NEW YORK METS

- ☐ 76U. KEVIN MITCHELL
- ☐ 82U. RANDY NIEMANN
- ☐ 84U. BOB OJEDA
- ☐ 110U. TIM TEUFEL

NEW YORK YANKEES

- ☐ 36U. DOUG DRABEK
- ☐ 37U. MIKE EASLER
- ☐ 40U. MIKE FISCHLIN
- ☐ 57U. TOMMY JOHN
- ☐ 98U. GARY ROENICKE
- ☐ 111U. BOB TEWKSBURY

OAKLAND A'S

- ☐ 4U. JOAQUIN ANDUJAR
- ☐ 9U. BILL BATHE
- ☐ 20U. JOSE CANSECO
- ☐ 48U. MOOSE HAAS
- ☐ 56U. STAN JAVIER
- ☐ 77U. BILL MOONEYHAM
- ☐ 126U. JERRY WILLARD

PHILADELPHIA PHILLIES

- ☐ 12U. STEVE BEDROSIAN
- ☐ 52U. TOM HUME
- ☐ 55U. CHRIS JAMES
- ☐ 94U. GARY REDUS
- ☐ 99U. RON ROENICKE
- ☐ 114U. MILT THOMPSON
- ☐ 117U. FRED TOLIVER

PITTSBURGH PIRATES

- ☐ 14U. BARRY BONDS

ST. LOUIS CARDINALS

- ☐ 29U. TIM CONROY
- ☐ 50U. MIKE HEATH
- ☐ 65U. MIKE LA VALLIERE
- ☐ 73U. GREG MATHEWS
- ☐ 85U. RICK OWNBEY
- ☐ 89U. PAT PERRY

SAN DIEGO PADRES

- ☐ 54U. DANE IORG
- ☐ 61U. JOHN KRUK
- ☐ 96U. BIP ROBERTS
- ☐ 124U. GENE WALTER
- ☐ 130U. MARVELL WYNNE

SAN FRANCISCO GIANTS

- ☐ 1U. MIKE ALDRETE
- ☐ 25U. WILL CLARK
- ☐ 62U. MIKE LACOSS
- ☐ 71U. CANDY MALDONADO
- ☐ 72U. ROGER MASON
- ☐ 92U. LUIS QUINONES
- ☐ 115U. ROB THOMPSON

SEATTLE MARINERS

- ☐ 45U. LEE GUETTERMAN
- ☐ 63U. PETER LADD
- ☐ 131U. STEVE YEAGER

PETE LADD
PITCHER

TEXAS RANGERS

- ☐ 30U. ED CORREA
- ☐ 41U. SCOTT FLETCHER
- ☐ 53U. PETE INCAVIGLIA
- ☐ 70U. MICKEY MAHLER
- ☐ 86U. TOM PACIOREK
- ☐ 91U. DARRELL PORTER
- ☐ 105U. RUBEN SIERRA
- ☐ 127U. MITCH WILLIAMS
- ☐ 129U. BOBBY WITT

TORONTO BLUE JAYS

- ☐ 24U. JOHN CERUTTI
- ☐ 38U. MARK EICHHORN

1987 FLEER (660)
2 1/2 X 3 1/2

Jimmy Key

ATLANTA BRAVES

- ☐ 509. JIM ACKER
- ☐ 510. DOYLE ALEXANDER
- ☐ 511. PAUL ASSENMACHER
- ☐ 512. BRUCE BENEDICT
- ☐ 513. CHRIS CHAMBLISS
- ☐ 514. JEFF DEDMON
- ☐ 515. GENE GARBER
- ☐ 516. KEN GRIFFEY
- ☐ 517. TERRY HARPER
- ☐ 518. BOB HORNER
- ☐ 519. GLENN HUBBARD
- ☐ 520. RICK MAHLER
- ☐ 521. OMAR MORENO
- ☐ 522. DALE MURPHY
- ☐ 523. KEN OBERKFELL
- ☐ 524. ED OLWINE
- ☐ 525. DAVID PALMER
- ☐ 526. RAFAEL RAMIREZ
- ☐ 527. BILLY SAMPLE
- ☐ 528. TED SIMMONS
- ☐ 529. ZANE SMITH
- ☐ 530. BRUCE SUTTER
- ☐ 531. ANDRES THOMAS
- ☐ 532. OZZIE VIRGIL
- ☐ 659. TEAM CHECKLIST(F)

BALTIMORE ORIOLES

- ☐ 461. DON AASE
- ☐ 462. JUAN BENIQUEZ
- ☐ 463. MIKE BODDICKER
- ☐ 464. JUAN BONILLA
- ☐ 465. RICH BORDI
- ☐ 466. STORM DAVIS
- ☐ 467. RICK DEMPSEY
- ☐ 468. KEN DIXON
- ☐ 469. JIM DWYER
- ☐ 470. MIKE FLANAGAN
- ☐ 471. JACKIE GUTIERREZ
- ☐ 472. BRAD HAVENS
- ☐ 473. LEE LACY
- ☐ 474. FRED LYNN
- ☐ 475. SCOTT MCGREGOR
- ☐ 476. EDDIE MURRAY
- ☐ 477. TOM O'MALLEY
- ☐ 478. CAL RIPKEN
- ☐ 479. LARRY SHEETS
- ☐ 480. JOHN SHELBY
- ☐ 481. NATE SNELL
- ☐ 482. JIM TRABER
- ☐ 483. MIKE YOUNG
- ☐ 652. JOHN STEFERO(P)
- ☐ 658. TEAM CHECKLIST(B)

BOSTON RED SOX

- ☐ 26. TONY ARMAS
- ☐ 27. MARTY BARRETT
- ☐ 28. DON BAYLOR
- ☐ 29. WADE BOGGS
- ☐ 30. OIL CAN BOYD
- ☐ 31. BILL BUCKNER
- ☐ 32. ROGER CLEMENS
- ☐ 33. STEVE CRAWFORD
- ☐ 34. DWIGHT EVANS
- ☐ 35. RICH GEDMAN
- ☐ 36. DAVE HENDERSON
- ☐ 37. BRUCE HURST
- ☐ 38. TIM LOLLAR
- ☐ 39. AL NIPPER
- ☐ 40. SPIKE OWEN
- ☐ 41. JIM RICE
- ☐ 42. ED ROMERO
- ☐ 43. JOE SAMBITO
- ☐ 44. CALVIN SCHIRALDI
- ☐ 45. TOM SEAVER
- ☐ 46. JEFF SELLERS
- ☐ 47. BOB STANLEY
- ☐ 48. SAMMY STEWART
- ☐ 654. TEAM CHECKLIST(F)

CALIFORNIA ANGELS

- ☐ 73. BOB BOONE
- ☐ 74. RICK BURLESON
- ☐ 75. JOHN CANDELARIA
- ☐ 76. DOUG CORBETT
- ☐ 77. DOUG DECINCES
- ☐ 78. BRIAN DOWNING
- ☐ 79. CHUCK FINLEY
- ☐ 80. TERRY FORSTER
- ☐ 81. BOBBY GRICH
- ☐ 82. GEORGE HENDRICK
- ☐ 83. JACK HOWELL
- ☐ 84. REGGIE JACKSON
- ☐ 85. RUPPERT JONES
- ☐ 86. WALLY JOYNER
- ☐ 87. GARY LUCAS
- ☐ 88. KIRK MCCASKILL
- ☐ 89. DONNIE MOORE
- ☐ 90. GARY PETTIS
- ☐ 91. VERN RUHLE
- ☐ 92. DICK SCHOFIELD
- ☐ 93. DON SUTTON
- ☐ 94. ROB WILFONG
- ☐ 95. MIKE WITT
- ☐ 646. WILLIE FRASER(P)
- ☐ 646. DEVON WHITE(P)
- ☐ 654. TEAM CHECKLIST(B)

CINCINNATI REDS

- ☐ 193. BUDDY BELL
- ☐ 194. TOM BROWNING
- ☐ 195. SAL BUTERA
- ☐ 196. DAVE CONCEPCION
- ☐ 197. KAL DANIELS
- ☐ 198. ERIC DAVIS
- ☐ 199. JOHN DENNY
- ☐ 200. BO DIAZ
- ☐ 201. NICK ESASKY
- ☐ 202. JOHN FRANCO
- ☐ 203. BILL GULLICKSON
- ☐ 204. BARRY LARKIN
- ☐ 205. EDDIE MILNER
- ☐ 206. ROB MURPHY
- ☐ 207. RON OESTER
- ☐ 208. DAVE PARKER
- ☐ 209. TONY PEREZ
- ☐ 210. TED POWER
- ☐ 211. JOE PRICE
- ☐ 212. RON ROBINSON
- ☐ 213. PETE ROSE(M)
- ☐ 214. MARIO SOTO
- ☐ 215. KURT STILLWELL
- ☐ 216. MAX VENABLE
- ☐ 217. CHRIS WELSH
- ☐ 218. CARL WILLIS
- ☐ 651. TRACY JONES(P)
- ☐ 656. TEAM CHECKLIST(F)

Cory Snyder

CLEVELAND INDIANS

- ☐ 241. ANDY ALLANSON
- ☐ 242. SCOTT BAILES
- ☐ 243. CHRIS BANDO
- ☐ 244. TONY BERNAZARD
- ☐ 245. JOHN BUTCHER
- ☐ 246. BRETT BUTLER
- ☐ 247. ERNIE CAMACHO
- ☐ 248. TOM CANDIOTTI
- ☐ 249. JOE CARTER
- ☐ 250. CARMEN CASTILLO
- ☐ 251. JULIO FRANCO
- ☐ 252. MEL HALL
- ☐ 253. BROOK JACOBY
- ☐ 254. PHIL NIEKRO
- ☐ 255. OTIS NIXON
- ☐ 256. DICKIE NOLES
- ☐ 257. BRYAN OELKERS
- ☐ 258. KEN SCHROM
- ☐ 259. DON SCHULZE
- ☐ 260. CORY SNYDER
- ☐ 261. PAT TABLER
- ☐ 262. ANDRE THORNTON
- ☐ 263. RICH YETT
- ☐ 644. DAVE CLARK(P)
- ☐ 644. GREG SWINDELL(P)
- ☐ 656. TEAM CHECKLIST(B)

CHICAGO CUBS

- ☐ 555. THAD BOSLEY
- ☐ 556. RON CEY
- ☐ 557. JODY DAVIS
- ☐ 558. RON DAVIS
- ☐ 559. BOB DERNIER
- ☐ 560. FRANK DIPINO
- ☐ 561. SHAWON DUNSTON
- ☐ 562. LEON DURHAM
- ☐ 563. DENNIS ECKERSLEY
- ☐ 564. TERRY FRANCONA
- ☐ 565. DAVE GUMPERT
- ☐ 566. GUY HOFFMAN
- ☐ 567. ED LYNCH
- ☐ 568. GARY MATTHEWS
- ☐ 569. KEITH MORELAND
- ☐ 570. JAMIE MOYER

- ☐ 571. JERRY MUMPHREY
- ☐ 572. RYNE SANDBERG
- ☐ 573. SCOTT SANDERSON
- ☐ 574. LEE SMITH
- ☐ 575. CHRIS SPEIER
- ☐ 576. RICK SUTCLIFFE
- ☐ 577. MANNY TRILLO
- ☐ 578. STEVE TROUT
- ☐ 659. TEAM CHECKLIST(B)

CHICAGO WHITE SOX

- ☐ 484. NEIL ALLEN
- ☐ 485. HAROLD BAINES
- ☐ 486. FLOYD BANNISTER
- ☐ 487. DARYL BOSTON
- ☐ 488. IVAN CALDERON
- ☐ 489. JOHN CANGELOSI
- ☐ 490. STEVE CARLTON
- ☐ 491. JOE COWLEY
- ☐ 492. JULIO CRUZ
- ☐ 493. BILL DAWLEY
- ☐ 494. JOSE DELEON
- ☐ 495. RICHARD DOTSON
- ☐ 496. CARLTON FISK
- ☐ 497. OZZIE GUILLEN
- ☐ 498. JERRY HAIRSTON
- ☐ 499. RON HASSEY
- ☐ 500. TIM HULETT
- ☐ 501. BOB JAMES
- ☐ 502. STEVE LYONS
- ☐ 503. JOEL MCKEON
- ☐ 504. GENE NELSON
- ☐ 505. DAVE SCHMIDT
- ☐ 506. RAY SEARAGE
- ☐ 507. BOBBY THIGPEN
- ☐ 508. GREG WALKER
- ☐ 645. RUSS MORMAN(P)
- ☐ 645. RON KARKOVICE(P)
- ☐ 659. TEAM CHECKLIST(F)

DETROIT TIGERS

- ☐ 144. DAVE BERGMAN
- ☐ 145. TOM BROOKENS
- ☐ 146. BILL CAMPBELL
- ☐ 147. CHUCK CARY
- ☐ 148. DARNELL COLES
- ☐ 149. DAVE COLLINS
- ☐ 150. DARRELL EVANS
- ☐ 151. KIRK GIBSON
- ☐ 152. JOHN GRUBB
- ☐ 153. WILLIE HERNANDEZ
- ☐ 154. LARRY HERNDON
- ☐ 155. ERIC KING
- ☐ 156. CHET LEMON
- ☐ 157. DWIGHT LOWRY
- ☐ 158. JACK MORRIS
- ☐ 159. RANDY O'NEAL
- ☐ 160. LANCE PARRIS
- ☐ 161. DAN PETRY
- ☐ 162. PAT SHERIDAN
- ☐ 163. JIM SLATON
- ☐ 164. FRANK TANANA
- ☐ 165. WALT TERRELL
- ☐ 166. MARK THURMOND
- ☐ 167. ALLAN TRAMMELL
- ☐ 168. LOU WHITAKER
- ☐ 655. TEAM CHECKLIST(B)

HOUSTON ASTROS

- ☐ 49. LARRY ANDERSON
- ☐ 50. ALAN ASHBY
- ☐ 51. KEVIN BASS
- ☐ 52. JEFF CALHOUN
- ☐ 53. JOSE CRUZ
- ☐ 54. DANNY DARWIN
- ☐ 55. GLENN DAVIS
- ☐ 56. JIM DESHAIES
- ☐ 57. BILL DORAN
- ☐ 58. PHIL GARNER
- ☐ 59. BILLY HATCHER
- ☐ 60. CHARLIE KERFELD
- ☐ 61. BOB KNEPPER
- ☐ 62. DAVE LOPES
- ☐ 63. AURELIO LOPEZ
- ☐ 64. JIM PANKOVITS
- ☐ 65. TERRY PUHL
- ☐ 66. CRAIG REYNOLDS
- ☐ 67. NOLAN RYAN

☐ 68. MIKE SCOTT
☐ 69. DAVE SMITH
☐ 70. DICKIE THON
☐ 71. TONY WALKER
☐ 72. DENNY WALLING
☐ 654. TEAM CHECKLIST(B)

KANSAS CITY ROYALS

☐ 362. STEVE BALBONI
☐ 363. SCOTT BANKHEAD
☐ 364. BUDDY BIANCALANA
☐ 365. BUD BLACK
☐ 366. GEORGE BRETT
☐ 367. STEVE FARR
☐ 368. MARK GUBICZA
☐ 369. BO JACKSON
☐ 370. DANNY JACKSON
☐ 371. MIKE KINGERY
☐ 372. RUDY LAW
☐ 373. CHARLIE LEIBRANDT
☐ 374. DENNIS LEONARD
☐ 375. HAL MCRAE
☐ 376. JORE ORTA
☐ 377. JAMIE QUIRK
☐ 378. DAN QUISENBERRY
☐ 379. BRET SABERHAGEN
☐ 380. ANGEL SALAZAR
☐ 381. LONNIE SMITH
☐ 382. JIM SUNDBERG
☐ 383. FRANK WHITE
☐ 384. WILLIE WILSON
☐ 652. KEVIN SEITZER(P)
☐ 657. TEAM CHECKLIST(B)

LOS ANGELES DODGERS

☐ 436. DAVE ANDERSON
☐ 437. GREG BROCK
☐ 438. ENOS CABELL
☐ 439. MARIANO DUNCAN
☐ 440. PEDRO GUERRERO
☐ 441. OREL HERSHISER
☐ 442. RICK HONEYCUTT
☐ 443. KEN HOWELL
☐ 444. KEN LANDREAUX
☐ 445. BILL MADLOCK
☐ 446. MIKE MARSHALL
☐ 447. LEN MATUSZEK
☐ 448. TOM NIEDENFUER
☐ 449. AJEJANDRO PENA
☐ 450. DENNIS POWELL
☐ 451. JERRY REUSS
☐ 452. BUD RUSSELL
☐ 453. STEVE SAX
☐ 454. MIKE SCIOSCIA
☐ 455. FRANKLIN STUBBS
☐ 456. ALEX TREVINO
☐ 457. FERNANDO VALENZUELA
☐ 458. ED VANDE BERG
☐ 459. BOB WELCH
☐ 460. REGGIE WILLIAMS
☐ 649. RALPH BRYANT(P)
☐ 649. JOSE GONZALEZ(P)
☐ 658. TEAM CHECKLIST(B)

MILWAUKEE BREWERS

☐ 338. CHRIS BOSIO
☐ 339. GLENN BRAGGS
☐ 340. RICK CERONE
☐ 341. MARK CLEAR
☐ 342. BRYAN CLUTTERBUCK
☐ 343. CECIL COOPER
☐ 344. ROB DEER
☐ 345. JIM GANTNER
☐ 346. TED HIGUERA
☐ 347. JOHN HENRY JOHNSON
☐ 348. TIM LEARY
☐ 349. RICK MANNING
☐ 350. PAUL MOLITOR
☐ 351. CHARLIE MOORE
☐ 352. JUAN NIEVES
☐ 353. BEN OGLIVIE
☐ 354. DAN PLESAC
☐ 355. ERNEST RILES
☐ 356. BILLY JOE ROBIDOUX
☐ 357. BILL SCHROEDER
☐ 358. DALE SVEUM
☐ 359. GORMAN THOMAS

☐ 360. BILL WEGMAN
☐ 361. ROBIN YOUNT
☐ 657. TEAM CHECKLIST(B)

MINNESOTA TWINS

☐ 533. ALLAN ANDERSON
☐ 534. KEITH ATHERTON
☐ 535. BILLY BEANE
☐ 536. BERT BLYLEVEN
☐ 537. TOM BRUNANSKY
☐ 538. RANDY BUSH
☐ 539. GEORGE FRAZIER
☐ 540. GARY GAETTI
☐ 541. GREG GAGNE
☐ 542. MICKEY HATCHER
☐ 543. NEAL HEATON
☐ 544. KENT HRBEK
☐ 545. ROY LEE JACKSON
☐ 546. TIM LAUDNER
☐ 547. STEVE LOMBARDOZZI
☐ 548. MARK PORTUGAL
☐ 549. KIRBY PUCKETT
☐ 550. JEFF REED
☐ 551. MARK SALAS
☐ 552. ROY SMALLEY
☐ 553. MIKE SMITHSON
☐ 554. FRANK VIOLA
☐ 659. TEAM CHECKLIST(B)

MONTREAL EXPOS

☐ 313. DANN BILARDELLO
☐ 314. HUBIE BROOKS
☐ 315. TIM BURKE
☐ 316. ANDRE DAWSON
☐ 317. MIKE FITZGERALD
☐ 318. TOM FOLEY
☐ 319. ANDRES GALARRAGA
☐ 320. JOE HESKETH
☐ 321. WALLACE JOHNSON
☐ 322. WAYNE KRENCHICKI
☐ 323. VANCE LAW
☐ 324. DENNIS MARTINEZ
☐ 325. BOB MCCLURE
☐ 326. ANDY MCGAFFIGAN
☐ 327. AL NEWMAN
☐ 328. TIM RAINES
☐ 329. JEFF REARDON
☐ 330. LUIS RIVERA
☐ 331. BOB SEBRA
☐ 332. BRYN SMITH
☐ 333. JAY TIBBS
☐ 334. TIM WALLACH
☐ 335. MITCH WEBSTER
☐ 336. JIM WOHLFORD
☐ 337. FLOYD YOUMANS
☐ 657. TEAM CHECKLIST(F)

NEW YORK METS

☐ 1. RICK AGUILERA
☐ 2. RICHARD ANDERSON
☐ 3. WALLY BACKMAN
☐ 4. GARY CARTER
☐ 5. RON DARLING
☐ 6. LEN DYKSTRA
☐ 7. KEVIN ELSTER
☐ 8. SID FERNANDEZ
☐ 9. DWIGHT GOODEN
☐ 10. ED HEARN
☐ 11. DANNY HEEP
☐ 12. KEITH HERNANDEZ
☐ 13. HOWARD JOHNSON
☐ 14. RAY KNIGHT
☐ 15. LEE MAZZILLI
☐ 16. ROGER MCDOWELL
☐ 17. KEVIN MITCHELL
☐ 18. RANDY NIEMANN
☐ 19. BOB OJEDA
☐ 20. JESSE OROSCO
☐ 21. RAFAEL SANTANA
☐ 22. DOUG SISK
☐ 23. DARRYL STRAWBERRY
☐ 24. TIM TEUFEL
☐ 25. MOOKIE WILSON
☐ 648. DAVE MAGADAN(P)
☐ 654. TEAM CHECKLIST(F)

NEW YORK YANKEES

☐ 96. DOUG DRABEK
☐ 97. MIKE EASLER
☐ 98. MIKE FISCHLIN
☐ 99. BRIAN FISHER
☐ 100. RON GUIDRY
☐ 101. RICKEY HENDERSON
☐ 102. TOMMY JOHN
☐ 103. RON KITTLE
☐ 104. DON MATTINGLY
☐ 105. BOBBY MEACHAM
☐ 106. JOE NIEKRO
☐ 107. MIKE PAGLIARULO
☐ 108. DAN PASQUA
☐ 109. WILLIE RANDOLPH
☐ 110. DENNIS RASMUSSEN
☐ 111. DAVE RIGHETTI
☐ 112. GARY ROENICKE
☐ 113. ROD SCURRY
☐ 114. BOB SHIRLEY
☐ 115. JOEL SKINNER
☐ 116. TIM STODDARD
☐ 117. BOB TEWKSBURY
☐ 118. WAYNE TOLLESON
☐ 119. CLAUDELL WASHINGTON
☐ 120. DAVE WINFIELD
☐ 648. PHIL LOMBARDI(P)
☐ 655. TEAM CHECKLIST(F)

OAKLAND A'S

☐ 385. JOAQUIN ANDUJAR
☐ 386. DOUG BAIR
☐ 387. DUSTY BAKER
☐ 388. BRUCE BOCHTE
☐ 389. JOSE CANSECO
☐ 390. CHRIS CONDIROLI
☐ 391. MIKE DAVIS
☐ 392. ALFREDO GRIFFIN
☐ 393. MOOSE HAAS
☐ 394. DONNIE HILL
☐ 395. JAY HOWELL
☐ 396. DAVE KINGMAN
☐ 397. CARNEY LANSFORD
☐ 398. DAVID LEIPER
☐ 399. BILL MOONEYHAM
☐ 400. DWAYNE MURPHY
☐ 401. STEVE ONTIVEROS
☐ 402. TONY PHILLIPS
☐ 403. ERIC PLUNK
☐ 404. JOSE RIJO
☐ 405. TERRY STEINBACH
☐ 406. DAVE STEWART
☐ 407. MICKEY TETTLETON
☐ 408. DAVE VON OHLEN
☐ 409. JERRY WILLARD
☐ 410. CURT YOUNG
☐ 653. ROB NELSON(P)
☐ 658. TEAM CHECKLIST(F)

PHILADELPHIA PHILLIES

☐ 169. LUIS AGUAYO
☐ 170. STEVE BEDROSIAN
☐ 171. DON CARMAN
☐ 172. DARREN DAULTON
☐ 173. GREG GROSS
☐ 174. KEVIN GROSS
☐ 175. VON HAYES

☐ 176. CHARLES HUDSON
☐ 177. TOM HUME
☐ 178. STEVE JELTZ
☐ 179. MIKE MADDUX
☐ 180. SHANE RAWLEY
☐ 181. GARY REDUS
☐ 182. RON ROENICKE
☐ 183. BRUCE RUFFIN
☐ 184. JOHN RUSSELL
☐ 185. JUAN SAMUEL
☐ 186. DAN SCHATZEDER
☐ 187. MIKE SCHMIDT
☐ 188. RICK SCHU
☐ 189. JEFF STONE
☐ 190. KENT TEKULVE
☐ 191. MILT THOMPSON
☐ 192. GLENN WILSON
☐ 651. MARVIN FREEMAN(P)
☐ 655 TEAM CHECKLIST(B)

PITTSBURGH PIRATES

☐ 601. BILL ALMON
☐ 602. RAFAEL BELLIARD
☐ 603. MIKE BIELECKI
☐ 604. BARRY BONDS
☐ 605. BOBBY BONILLA
☐ 606. SID BREAM
☐ 607. MIKE BROWN
☐ 608. PAT CLEMENTS
☐ 609. MIKE DIAZ
☐ 610. CECILIO GUANTE
☐ 611. BARRY JONES
☐ 612. BOB KIPPER
☐ 613. LARRY MCWILLIAMS
☐ 614. JIM MORRISON
☐ 615. JOE ORSULAK
☐ 616. JUNIOR ORTIZ
☐ 617. TONY PENA
☐ 618. JOHNNY RAY
☐ 619. RICK REUSCHEL
☐ 620. R. J. REYNOLDS
☐ 621. RICK RHODEN
☐ 622. DON ROBINSON
☐ 623. BOB WALK
☐ 624. JIM WINN
☐ 660. TEAM CHECKLIST(F)

ST. LOUIS CARDINALS

☐ 289. JACK CLARK
☐ 290. VINCE COLEMAN
☐ 291. TIM CONROY
☐ 292. DANNY COX
☐ 293. KEN DAYLEY
☐ 294. CURT FORD
☐ 295. BOB FORSCH
☐ 296. TOM HERR
☐ 297. RICKY HORTON
☐ 298. CLINT HURDLE
☐ 299. JEFF LAHTI
☐ 300. STEVE LAKE
☐ 301. TITO LANDRUM
☐ 302. MIKE LAVALLIERE
☐ 303. GREG MATHEWS
☐ 304. WILLIE MCGEE
☐ 305. JOSE OQUENDO
☐ 306. TERRY PENDLETON
☐ 307. PAT PERRY
☐ 308. OZZIE SMITH
☐ 309. RAY SOFF
☐ 310. JOHN TUDOR
☐ 311. ANDY VAN SLYKE
☐ 312. TODD WORRELL
☐ 657. TEAM CHECKLIST(F)

SAN DIEGO PADRES

☐ 411. BRUCE BOCHY
☐ 412. DAVE DRAVECKY
☐ 413. TIM FLANNERY
☐ 414. STEVE GARVEY
☐ 415. GOOSE GOSSAGE
☐ 416. TONY GWYNN
☐ 417. ANDY HAWKINS
☐ 418. LAMARR HOYT
☐ 419. TERRY KENNEDY
☐ 420. JOHN KRUK
☐ 421. DAVE LAPOINT
☐ 422. CRAIG LEFFERTS
☐ 423. CARMELO MARTINEZ

☐ 424. LANCE MCCULLERS
☐ 425. KEVIN MCREYNOLDS
☐ 426. GRAIG NETTLES
☐ 427. BIP ROBERTS
☐ 428. JERRY ROYSTER
☐ 429. BENITO SANTIAGO
☐ 430. ERIC SHOW
☐ 431. BOB STODDARD
☐ 432. GARRY TEMPLETON
☐ 433. GENE WALTER
☐ 434. ED WHITSON
☐ 435. MARVELL WYNNE
☐ 650. JIMMY JONES(P)
☐ 650. RANDY ASADOOR(P)
☐ 658. TEAM CHECKLIST(F)

SAN FRANCISCO GIANTS

☐ 264. MIKE ALDRETE
☐ 265. JUAN BERENGUER
☐ 266. VIDA BLUE
☐ 267. BOB BRENLY
☐ 268. CHRIS BROWN
☐ 269. WILL CLARK
☐ 270. CHILI DAVIS
☐ 271. MARK DAVIS
☐ 272. KELLY DOWNS
☐ 273. SCOTT GARRELTS
☐ 274. DAN GLADDEN
☐ 275. MIKE KRUKOW
☐ 276. RANDY KUTCHER
☐ 277. MIKE LACOSS
☐ 278. JEFF LEONARD
☐ 279. CANDY MALDONADO
☐ 280. ROGER MASON
☐ 281. BOB MELVIN
☐ 282. GREG MINTON
☐ 283. JEFF ROBINSON
☐ 284. HARRY SPILMAN
☐ 285. ROB THOMPSON
☐ 286. JOSE URIBE
☐ 287. FRANK WILLIAMS
☐ 288. JOEL YOUNGBLOOD
☐ 656. TEAM CHECKLIST(B)

SEATTLE MARINERS

☐ 579. KARL BEST
☐ 580. PHIL BRADLEY
☐ 581. SCOTT BRADLEY
☐ 582. MICKEY BRANTLEY
☐ 583. MIKE BROWN
☐ 584. ALVIN DAVIS
☐ 585. LEE GUETTERMAN
☐ 586. MARK HUISMANN
☐ 587. BOB KEARNEY
☐ 588. PETE LADD
☐ 589. MARK LANGSTON
☐ 590. MIKE MOORE
☐ 591. MIKE MORGAN
☐ 592. JOHN MOSES
☐ 593. KEN PHELPS
☐ 594. JIM PRESLEY
☐ 595. REY QUINONEZ
☐ 596. HAROLD REYNOLDS
☐ 597. BILLY SWIFT
☐ 598. DANNY TARTABULL
☐ 599. STEVE YEAGER
☐ 600. MATT YOUNG
☐ 653. STEVE FIREOVID(P)
☐ 660. TEAM CHECKLIST(F)

TEXAS RANGERS

☐ 121. STEVE BUECHELE
☐ 122. ED CORREA
☐ 123. SCOTT FLETCHER
☐ 124. JOSE GUZMAN
☐ 125. TOBY HARRAH
☐ 126. GREG HARRIS
☐ 127. CHARLIE HOUGH
☐ 128. PETE INCAVIGLIA
☐ 129. MIKE MASON
☐ 130. ODDIBE MCDOWELL
☐ 131. DALE MOHORCIC
☐ 132. PETE O'BRIEN
☐ 133. TOM PACIOREK
☐ 134. LARRY PARRISH
☐ 135. GENO PETRALLI
☐ 136. DARRELL PORTER

☐ 137. JEFF RUSSELL
☐ 138. RUBEN SIERRA
☐ 139. DON SLAUGHT
☐ 140. GARY WARD
☐ 141. CURTIS WILKERSON
☐ 142. MITCH WILLIAMS
☐ 143. BOBBY WITT
☐ 647. JERRY BROWNE(P)
☐ 647. MIKE STANLEY(P)
☐ 655. TEAM CHECKLIST(F)

TORONTO BLUE JAYS

☐ 219. JESSE BARFIELD
☐ 220. GEORGE BELL
☐ 221. BILL CAUDILL
☐ 222. JOHN CERUTTI
☐ 223. CLANCY
☐ 224. MARK EICHHORN
☐ 225. TONY FERNANDEZ
☐ 226. DAMASO GARCIA
☐ 227. KELLY GRUBER
☐ 228. TOM HENKE
☐ 229. GARTH IORG
☐ 230. CLIFF JOHNSON
☐ 231. JOE JOHNSON
☐ 232. JIMMY KEY
☐ 233. DENNIS LAMP
☐ 234. RICK LEACH
☐ 235. BUCK MARTINEZ
☐ 236. LLOYD MOSEBY
☐ 237. RANCE MULLINIKS
☐ 238. DAVE STIEB
☐ 239. WILLIE UPSHAW
☐ 240. ERNIE WHITT
☐ 656. TEAM CHECKLIST(F)

1987 FLEER
TRADED (132)
2 1/2 X 3 1/2

ATLANTA BRAVES

☐ 39U. ALBERT HALL
☐ 51U. DION JAMES

BALTIMORE ORIOLES

☐ 2U. ERIC BELL
☐ 34U. KEN GERHART
☐ 56U. TERRY KENNEDY
☐ 58U. RAY KNIGHT
☐ 107U. DAVE SCHMIDT
☐ 124U. ALAN WIGGINS

BOSTON RED SOX

☐ 15U. ELLIS BURKS
☐ 37U. MIKE GREENWELL

CALIFORNIA ANGELS

☐ 14U. DEWAYNE BUICE
☐ 33U. WILLIE FRASER
☐ 61U. JACK LAZORKO
☐ 77U. MARK LEMORE
☐ 80U. GREG MINTON
☐ 123U. DEVON WHITE

1987 Fleer Traded

CHICAGO CUBS

- [ ] 24U. ANDRE DAWSON
- [ ] 25U. BRIAN DAYETT
- [ ] 68U. GREG MADDUX
- [ ] 73U. MIKE MASON
- [ ] 91U. DICKIE NOLES
- [ ] 114U. JIM SUNDBERG

CHICAGO WHITE SOX

- [ ] 66U. BILL LONG
- [ ] 72U. FRED MANRIQUE
- [ ] 102U. GARY REDUS
- [ ] 126U. JIM WINN
- [ ] 128U. KEN WILLIAMS

CINCINNATI REDS

- [ ] 45U. GUY HOFFMAN
- [ ] 55U. TRACY JONES
- [ ] 74U. LLOYD MCCLENDON
- [ ] 94U. PAUL O'NEILL
- [ ] 127U. FRANK WILLIAMS

CLEVELAND INDIANS

- [ ] 17U. STEVE CARLTON
- [ ] 26U. RICK DEMPSEY
- [ ] 116U. GREG SWINDELL
- [ ] 120U. ED VANDEBERG

DETROIT TIGERS

- [ ] 42U. MIKE HEATH
- [ ] 44U. MIKE HENNEMAN
- [ ] 69U. BILL MADLOCK
- [ ] 90U. MATT NOKES
- [ ] 105U. JEFF ROBINSON

HOUSTON ASTROS

- [ ] 47U. CHUCK JACKSON
- [ ] 79U. DAVE MEADS

KANSAS CITY ROYALS

- [ ] 3U. JUAN BENIQUEZ
- [ ] 8U. THAD BOSLEY
- [ ] 97U. BILL PECOTA
- [ ] 108U. KEVIN SEITZER
- [ ] 117U. DANNY TARTABULL

LOS ANGELES DODGERS

- [ ] 13U. RALPH BRYANT
- [ ] 41U. MICKEY HATCHER
- [ ] 109U. JOHN SHELBY
- [ ] 131U. MATT YOUNG

MILWAUKEE BREWERS

- [ ] 5U. MIKE BIRKBECK
- [ ] 9U. GREG BROCK
- [ ] 18U. JUAN CASTILLO
- [ ] 19U. CHUCK CRIM
- [ ] 95U. JIM PACIOREK
- [ ] 115U. B. J. SURHOFF

MINNESOTA TWINS

- [ ] 4U. JUAN BERENGUER
- [ ] 20U. MARK DAVIDSON
- [ ] 36U. DAN GLADDEN
- [ ] 59U. GENE LARKIN
- [ ] 87U. JOE NIEKRO
- [ ] 88U. TOM NIETO
- [ ] 101U. JEFF REARDON

MONTREAL EXPOS

- [ ] 16U. CASEY CANDAELE
- [ ] 43U. NEAL HEATON
- [ ] 89U. REID NICHOLS
- [ ] 111U. LARY SORENSEN
- [ ] 113U. RANDY ST. CLAIRE
- [ ] 130U. HERM WINNINGHAM

NEW YORK METS

- [ ] 62U. TERRY LEACH
- [ ] 70U. DAVE MAGADAN
- [ ] 78U. KEVIN MCREYNOLDS
- [ ] 81U. JOHN MITCHELL
- [ ] 85U. RANDY MYERS

NEW YORK YANKEES

- [ ] 38U. CECILIO GUANTE
- [ ] 46U. CHARLES HUDSON
- [ ] 103U. RICK RHODEN
- [ ] 106U. MARK SALAS
- [ ] 122U. GARY WARD

OAKLAND A'S

- [ ] 30U. DENNIS ECKERSLEY
- [ ] 49U. REGGIE JACKSON
- [ ] 52U. STAN JAVIER
- [ ] 76U. MARK MCGWIRE
- [ ] 86U. GENE NELSON
- [ ] 99U. LUIS POLONIA

PHILADELPHIA PHILLIES

- [ ] 27U. KEN DOWELL
- [ ] 48U. MIKE JACKSON
- [ ] 50U. CHRIS JAMES
- [ ] 96U. LANCE PARRISH
- [ ] 104U. WALLY RITCHIE

PITTSBURGH PIRATES

- [ ] 29U. MIKE DUNNE
- [ ] 32U. BRIAN FISHER
- [ ] 60U. MIKE LAVALLIERE
- [ ] 110U. JOHN SMILEY
- [ ] 118U. DORN TAYLOR
- [ ] 121U. ANDY VAN SLYKE

ST. LOUIS CARDINALS

- [ ] 7U. ROD BOOKER
- [ ] 23U. BILL DAWLEY
- [ ] 65U. JIM LINDEMAN
- [ ] 71U. JOE MAGRANE
- [ ] 83U. JOHN MORRIS
- [ ] 98U. TONY PENA
- [ ] 119U. LEE TUNNELL

SAN DIEGO PADRES

- [ ] 11U. CHRIS BROWN
- [ ] 21U. MARK DAVIS
- [ ] 22U. STORM DAVIS
- [ ] 53U. STAN JEFFERSON
- [ ] 54U. JIMMY JONES
- [ ] 100U. RANDY READY

SAN FRANCISCO GIANTS

- [ ] 6U. RANDY BOCKUS
- [ ] 28U. DAVE DRAVECKY
- [ ] 35U. JIM GOTT
- [ ] 40U. ATLEE HAMMAKER
- [ ] 64U. CRAIG LEFFERTS
- [ ] 82U. KEVIN MITCHELL
- [ ] 112U. CHRIS SPEIER
- [ ] 129U. MATT WILLIAMS

SEATTLE MARINERS

- [ ] 1U. SCOTT BANKHEAD
- [ ] 57U. MIKE KINGERY
- [ ] 92U. EDWIN NUNEZ
- [ ] 125U. BILL WILKINSON

TEXAS RANGERS

- [ ] 10U. BOB BROWER
- [ ] 12U. JERRY BROWNE
- [ ] 67U. MIKE LOYND

TORONTO BLUE JAYS

- [ ] 31U. CECIL FIELDER
- [ ] 63U. RICK LEACH
- [ ] 75U. FRED MCGRIFF
- [ ] 84U. JEFF MUSSELMAN
- [ ] 93U. JOSE NUNEZ

1988 FLEER (660)
2 1/2 X 3 1/2

ATLANTA BRAVES

- [ ] 531. JIM ACKER
- [ ] 532. PAUL ASSENMACHER
- [ ] 533. JEFF BLAUSER
- [ ] 534. JOE BOEVER
- [ ] 535. MARTIN CLARY
- [ ] 536. KEVIN COFFMAN
- [ ] 537. JEFF DEDMON
- [ ] 538. RON GANT
- [ ] 539. TOM GLAVINE
- [ ] 540. KEN GRIFFEY
- [ ] 541. AL HALL
- [ ] 542. GLENN HUBBARD
- [ ] 543. DION JAMES
- [ ] 544. DALE MURPHY
- [ ] 545. KEN OBERKFELL
- [ ] 546. DAVID PALMER
- [ ] 547. GERALD PERRY
- [ ] 548. CHARLIE PULEO
- [ ] 549. TED SIMMONS
- [ ] 550. ZANE SMITH
- [ ] 551. ANDRES THOMAS
- [ ] 552. OZZIE VIRGIL
- [ ] 647. PETER SMITH (P)
- [ ] 659. TEAM CHECKLIST (B)

BALTIMORE ORIOLES

- ☐ 553. DON AASE
- ☐ 554. JEFF BALLARD
- ☐ 555. ERIC BELL
- ☐ 556. MIKE BODDICKER
- ☐ 557. KEN DIXON
- ☐ 558. JIM DWYER
- ☐ 559. KEN GERHART
- ☐ 560. RENE GONZALES
- ☐ 561. MIKE GRIFFIN
- ☐ 562. JOHN HAYBAN
- ☐ 563. TERRY KENNEDY
- ☐ 564. RAY KNIGHT
- ☐ 565. LEE LACY
- ☐ 566. FRED LYNN
- ☐ 567. EDDIE MURRAY
- ☐ 568. TOM NIEDENFUER
- ☐ 569. BILL RIPKEN
- ☐ 570. CAL RIPKEN, JR.
- ☐ 571. DAVE SCHMIDT
- ☐ 572. LARRY SHEETS
- ☐ 573. PETE STANICEK
- ☐ 574. MARK WILLIAMSON
- ☐ 575. MIKE YOUNG
- ☐ 659. TEAM CHECKLIST (B)

BOSTON RED SOX

- ☐ 343. MARTY BARRETT
- ☐ 344. TODD BENZINGER
- ☐ 345. WADE BOGGS
- ☐ 346. TOM BOLTON
- ☐ 347. OIL CAN BOYD
- ☐ 348. ELLIS BURKS
- ☐ 349. ROGER CLEMENS
- ☐ 350. STEVE CRAWFORD
- ☐ 351. DWIGHT EVANS
- ☐ 352. WES GARDNER
- ☐ 353. RICH GEDMAN
- ☐ 354. MIKE GREENWELL
- ☐ 355. SAM HORN
- ☐ 356. BRUCE HURST
- ☐ 357. JOHN MARZANO
- ☐ 358. AL NIPPER
- ☐ 359. SPIKE OWEN
- ☐ 360. JODY REED
- ☐ 361. JIM RICE
- ☐ 362. ED ROMERO
- ☐ 363. KEVIN ROMINE
- ☐ 364. JOE SAMBITO
- ☐ 365. CALVIN SCHIRALDI
- ☐ 366. JEFF SELLERS
- ☐ 367. BOB STANLEY
- ☐ 657. TEAM CHECKLIST (B)

CALIFORNIA ANGELS

- ☐ 484. TONY ARMAS
- ☐ 485. BOB BOONE
- ☐ 486. BILL BUCKNER
- ☐ 487. DEWAYNE BUICE
- ☐ 488. BRIAN DOWNING
- ☐ 489. CHUCK FINLEY
- ☐ 490. WILLIE FRASER
- ☐ 491. JACK HOWELL
- ☐ 492. RUPPERT JONES
- ☐ 493. WALLY JOYNER
- ☐ 494. JACK LAZORKO
- ☐ 495. GARY LUCAS
- ☐ 496. KIRK MCCASKILL
- ☐ 497. MARK MCLEMORE
- ☐ 498. DARRELL MILLER
- ☐ 499. GREG MINTON
- ☐ 500. DONNIE MOORE
- ☐ 501. GUS POLIDOR
- ☐ 502. JOHNNY RAY
- ☐ 503. MARK RYAL
- ☐ 504. DICK SCHOFIELD
- ☐ 505. DON SUTTON
- ☐ 506. DEVON WHITE
- ☐ 507. MIKE WITT
- ☐ 645. JIM EPPARD (P)
- ☐ 659. TEAM CHECKLIST (F)

CHICAGO CUBS

- ☐ 414. JODY DAVIS
- ☐ 415. ANDRE DAWSON
- ☐ 416. BRIAN DAYETT
- ☐ 417. BOB DERNIER
- ☐ 418. FRANK DIPINO
- ☐ 419. SHAWON DUNSTON
- ☐ 420. LEON DURHAM
- ☐ 421. LES LANCASTER
- ☐ 422. ED LYNCH
- ☐ 423. GREG MADDUX
- ☐ 424. DAVE MARTINEZ
- ☐ 425. KEITH MORELAND
- ☐ 426. JAMIE MOYER
- ☐ 427. JERRY MUMPHREY
- ☐ 428. PAUL NOCE
- ☐ 429. RAFAEL PALMEROI
- ☐ 430. WADE ROWDON
- ☐ 431. RYNE SANDBERG
- ☐ 432. SCOTT SANDERSON
- ☐ 433. LEE SMITH
- ☐ 434. JIM SUNDBERG
- ☐ 435. RICK SUTCLIFFE
- ☐ 436. MANNY TRILLO
- ☐ 641. MARK GRACE (P)
- ☐ 641. DARRIN JACKSON (P)
- ☐ 642. DAMON BERRYHILL (P)
- ☐ 658. TEAM CHECKLIST (F)

CHICAGO WHITE SOX

- ☐ 391. HAROLD BAINES
- ☐ 392. FLOYD BANNISTER
- ☐ 393. DARYL BOSTON
- ☐ 394. IVAN CALDERON
- ☐ 395. JOSE DELEON
- ☐ 396. RICHARD DOTSON
- ☐ 397. CARLTON FISK
- ☐ 398. OZZIE GUILLEN
- ☐ 399. RON HASSEY
- ☐ 400. DONNIE HILL
- ☐ 401. BOB JAMES
- ☐ 402. DAVE LAPOINT
- ☐ 403. BILL LINDSEY
- ☐ 404. BILL LONG
- ☐ 405. STEVE LYONS
- ☐ 406. FRED MANRIQUE
- ☐ 407. JACK MCDOWELL
- ☐ 408. GARY REDUS
- ☐ 409. RAY SEARAGE
- ☐ 410. BOBBY THIGPEN
- ☐ 411. GREG WALKER
- ☐ 412. KENNY WILLIAMS
- ☐ 413. JIM WINN
- ☐ 646. ADAM PETERSON (P)
- ☐ 658. TEAM CHECKLIST (F)

CINCINNATI REDS

- ☐ 227. BUDDY BELL
- ☐ 228. TOM BROWNING
- ☐ 229. DAVE CONCEPCION
- ☐ 230. KAL DANIELS
- ☐ 231. ERIC DAVIS
- ☐ 232. BO DIAZ
- ☐ 233. NICK ESASKY
- ☐ 234. JOHN FRANCO
- ☐ 235. GUY HOFFMAN
- ☐ 236. TOM HUME
- ☐ 237. TRACY JONES
- ☐ 238. BILL LANDRUM
- ☐ 239. BARRY LARKIN
- ☐ 240. TERRY MCGRIFF
- ☐ 241. ROB MURPHY
- ☐ 242. RON OESTER
- ☐ 243. DAVE PARKER
- ☐ 244. PAT PERRY
- ☐ 245. TED POWER
- ☐ 246. DENNIS RASMUSSEN
- ☐ 247. RON ROBINSON
- ☐ 248. KURT STILLWELL
- ☐ 249. JEFF TREADWAY
- ☐ 250. FRANK WILLIAMS
- ☐ 642. JEFF MONTGOMERY (P)
- ☐ 656. TEAM CHECKLIST (F)

CLEVELAND INDIANS

- ☐ 600. SCOTT BAILES
- ☐ 601. CHRIS BANDO
- ☐ 602. JAY BELL
- ☐ 603. BRETT BUTLER
- ☐ 604. TOM CANDIOTTI
- ☐ 605. JOE CARTER
- ☐ 606. CARMEN CASTILLO
- ☐ 607. BRIAN DORSETT
- ☐ 608. JOHN FARRELL
- ☐ 609. JULIO FRANCO
- ☐ 610. MEL HALL
- ☐ 611. TOMMY HINZO
- ☐ 612. BROOK JACOBY
- ☐ 613. DOUG JONES
- ☐ 614. KEN SCHROM
- ☐ 615. CORY SNYDER
- ☐ 616. SAMMY STEWART
- ☐ 617. GREG SWINDELL
- ☐ 618. PAT TABLER
- ☐ 619. ED VANDEBERG
- ☐ 620. EDDIE WILLIAMS
- ☐ 621. RICH YETT
- ☐ 660. TEAM CHECKLIST (F)

DETROIT TIGERS

- ☐ 51. DOYLE ALEXANDER
- ☐ 52. DAVE BERGMAN
- ☐ 53. TOM BROOKENS
- ☐ 54. DARRELL EVANS
- ☐ 55. KIRK GIBSON
- ☐ 56. MIKE HEATH
- ☐ 57. MIKE HENNEMAN
- ☐ 58. WILLIE HERNANDEZ
- ☐ 59. LARRY HERNDON
- ☐ 60. ERIC KING
- ☐ 61. CHET LEMON
- ☐ 62. SCOTT LUSADER
- ☐ 63. BILL MADLOCK
- ☐ 64. JACK MORRIS
- ☐ 65. JIM MORRISON
- ☐ 66. MATT NOKES
- ☐ 67. DAN PETRY
- ☐ 68. JEFF ROBINSON
- ☐ 69. PAT SHERIDAN
- ☐ 70. NATE SNELL
- ☐ 71. FRANK TANANA
- ☐ 72. WALT TERRELL
- ☐ 73. MARK THURMOND
- ☐ 74. ALAN TRAMMELL
- ☐ 75. LOU WHITAKER
- ☐ 654. TEAM CHECKLIST (B)

HOUSTON ASTROS

- ☐ 437. JUAN AGOSTO
- ☐ 438. LARRY ANDERSEN
- ☐ 439. ALAN ASHBY
- ☐ 440. KEVIN BASS
- ☐ 441. KEN CAMINITI
- ☐ 442. ROCKY CHILDRESS
- ☐ 443. JOSE CRUZ
- ☐ 444. DANNY DARWIN
- ☐ 445. GLENN DAVIS
- ☐ 446. JIM DESHAIES
- ☐ 447. BILL DORAN
- ☐ 448. TY GAINEY
- ☐ 449. BILLY HATCHER
- ☐ 450. JEFF HEATHCOCK
- ☐ 451. BOB KNEPPER
- ☐ 452. ROB MALLICOAT
- ☐ 453. DAVE MEADS
- ☐ 454. CRAIG REYNOLDS
- ☐ 455. NOLAN RYAN
- ☐ 456. MIKE SCOTT
- ☐ 457. DAVE SMITH
- ☐ 458. DENNY WALLING
- ☐ 459. ROBBIE WINE
- ☐ 460. GERALD YOUNG
- ☐ 658. TEAM CHECKLIST (B)

KANSAS CITY ROYALS

- [ ] 251. STEVE BALBONI
- [ ] 252. BUD BLACK
- [ ] 253. THAD BOSLEY
- [ ] 254. GEORGE BRETT
- [ ] 255. JOHN DAVIS
- [ ] 256. STEVE FARR
- [ ] 257. GENE GARBER
- [ ] 258. JERRY GLEATON
- [ ] 259. MARK GUBICZA
- [ ] 260. BO JACKSON
- [ ] 261. DANNY JACKSON
- [ ] 262. ROSS JONES
- [ ] 263. CHARLIE LEIBRANDT
- [ ] 264. BILL PECOTA
- [ ] 265. MELIDO PEREZ
- [ ] 266. JAMIE QUIRK
- [ ] 267. DAN QUISENBERRY
- [ ] 268. BRET SABERHAGEN
- [ ] 269. ANGEL SALAZAR
- [ ] 270. KEVIN SEITZER
- [ ] 271. DANNY TARTABULL
- [ ] 272. GARY THURMAN
- [ ] 273. FRANK WHITE
- [ ] 274. WILLIE WILSON
- [ ] 656. TEAM CHECKLIST

LOS ANGELES DODGERS

- [ ] 508. DAVE ANDERSON
- [ ] 509. TIM BELCHER
- [ ] 510. RALPH BRYANT
- [ ] 511. TIM CREWS
- [ ] 512. MIKE DEVEREAUX
- [ ] 513. MARIANO DUNCAN
- [ ] 514. PEDRO GUERRERO
- [ ] 515. JEFF HAMILTON
- [ ] 516. MICKEY HATCHER
- [ ] 517. BRAD HAVENS
- [ ] 518. OREL HERSHISER
- [ ] 519. SHAWN HILLEGAS
- [ ] 520. KEN HOWELL
- [ ] 521. TIM LEARY
- [ ] 522. MIKE MARSHALL
- [ ] 523. STEVE SAX
- [ ] 524. MIKE SCIOSCIA
- [ ] 525. MIKE SHARPERSON
- [ ] 526. JOHN SHELBY
- [ ] 527. FRANKLIN STUBBS
- [ ] 528. FERNANDO VALENZUELA
- [ ] 529. BOB WELCH
- [ ] 530. MATT YOUNG
- [ ] 647. CHRIS GWYNN (P)
- [ ] 650. JACK SAVAGE (P)
- [ ] 659. TEAM CHECKLIST (P)

MILWAUKEE BREWERS

- [ ] 155. JAY ALDRICH
- [ ] 156. CHRIS BOSIO
- [ ] 157. GLENN BRAGGS
- [ ] 158. GREG BROCK
- [ ] 159. JUAN CASTILLO
- [ ] 160. MARK CLEAR
- [ ] 161. CECIL COOPER
- [ ] 162. CHUCK CRIM
- [ ] 163. ROB DEER
- [ ] 164. RICK FELDER
- [ ] 165. JIM GANTNER
- [ ] 166. TED HIGUERA
- [ ] 167. STEVE KIEFER
- [ ] 168. RICK MANNING
- [ ] 169. PAUL MOLITOR
- [ ] 170. JUAN NIEVES
- [ ] 171. DAN PLESAC
- [ ] 172. EARNEST RILES
- [ ] 173. BILL SCHROEDER
- [ ] 174. STEVE STANICEK
- [ ] 175. B. J. SURHOFF
- [ ] 176. DALE SVEUM
- [ ] 177. BILL WEGMAN
- [ ] 178. ROBIN YOUNT
- [ ] 645. JOEY MEYER (P)
- [ ] 655. TEAM CHECKLIST (B)

MINNESOTA TWINS

- [ ] 1. KEITH ATHERTON
- [ ] 2. DON BAYLOR
- [ ] 3. JUAN BERENGUER
- [ ] 4. BERT BLYLEVEN
- [ ] 5. TOM BRUNANSKY
- [ ] 6. RANDY BUSH
- [ ] 7. STEVE CARLTON
- [ ] 8. MARK DAVIDSON
- [ ] 9. GEORGE FRAZIER
- [ ] 10. GARY GAETTI
- [ ] 11. GREG GAGNE
- [ ] 12. DAN GLADDEN
- [ ] 13. KENT HRBEK
- [ ] 14. GENE LARKIN
- [ ] 15. TIM LAUDNER
- [ ] 16. STEVE LOMBARDOZZI
- [ ] 17. AL NEWMAN
- [ ] 18. JOE NIEKRO
- [ ] 19. KIRBY PUCKETT
- [ ] 20. JEFF REARDON
- [ ] 21. DAN SCHATZADER
- [ ] 22. ROY SMALLEY
- [ ] 23. MIKE SMITHSON
- [ ] 24. LES STRAKER
- [ ] 25. FRANK VIOLA
- [ ] 654. TEAM CHECKLIST (F)

MONTREAL EXPOS

- [ ] 179. HUBIE BROOKS
- [ ] 180. TIM BURKE
- [ ] 181. CASEY CANDAELE
- [ ] 182. MIKE FITZGERALD
- [ ] 183. TOM FOLEY
- [ ] 184. ANDRES GALARRAGA
- [ ] 185. NEAL HEATON
- [ ] 186. WALLACE JOHNSON
- [ ] 187. VANCE LAW
- [ ] 188. DENNIS MARTINEZ
- [ ] 189. BOB MCCLURE
- [ ] 190. ANDY MCGAFFIGAN
- [ ] 191. REID NICHOLS
- [ ] 192. PASCUAL PEREZ
- [ ] 193. TIM RAINES
- [ ] 194. JEFF REED
- [ ] 195. BOB SEBRA
- [ ] 196. BRYN SMITH
- [ ] 197. RANDY ST. CLAIRE
- [ ] 198. TIM WALLACH
- [ ] 199. MITCH WEBSTER
- [ ] 200. HERM WINNINGHAM
- [ ] 201. FLOYD YOUMANS
- [ ] 655. TEAM CHECKLIST (B)

NEW YORK METS

- [ ] 127. RICK AGUILERA
- [ ] 128. WALLY BACKMAN
- [ ] 129. MARK CARREON
- [ ] 130. GARY CARTER
- [ ] 131. DAVID CONE
- [ ] 132. RON DARLING
- [ ] 133. LEN DYKSTRA
- [ ] 134. SID FERNANDEZ
- [ ] 135. DWIGHT GOODEN
- [ ] 136. KEITH HERNANDEZ
- [ ] 137. GREGG JEFFERIES
- [ ] 138. HOWARD JOHNSON
- [ ] 139. TERRY LEACH
- [ ] 140. BARRY LYONS
- [ ] 141. DAVE MAGADAN
- [ ] 142. ROGER MCDOWELL
- [ ] 143. KEVIN MCREYNOLDS
- [ ] 144. KEITH MILLER
- [ ] 145. JOHN MITCHELL
- [ ] 146. RANDY MYERS
- [ ] 147. BOB OJEDA
- [ ] 148. JESSE OROSCO
- [ ] 149. RAFAEL SANTANA
- [ ] 150. DOUG SISK
- [ ] 151. DARRYL STRAWBERRY
- [ ] 152. TIM TEUFEL
- [ ] 153. GENE WALTER
- [ ] 154. MOOKIE WILSON
- [ ] 655. TEAM CHECKLIST (F)

NEW YORK YANKEES

- [ ] 202. BRAD ARNSBERG
- [ ] 203. RICK CERONE
- [ ] 204. PAT CLEMENTS
- [ ] 205. HENRY COTTO
- [ ] 206. MIKE EASLER
- [ ] 207. RON GUIDRY
- [ ] 208. BILL GULLICKSON
- [ ] 209. RICKEY HENDERSON
- [ ] 210. CHARLES HUDSON
- [ ] 211. TOMMY JOHN
- [ ] 212. ROBERTO KELLY
- [ ] 213. RON KITTLE
- [ ] 214. DON MATTINGLY
- [ ] 215. BOBBY MEACHAM
- [ ] 216. MIKE PAGLIARULO
- [ ] 217. DAN PASQUA
- [ ] 218. WILLIE RANDOLPH
- [ ] 219. RICK RHODEN
- [ ] 220. DAVE RIGHETTI
- [ ] 221. JERRY ROYSTER
- [ ] 222. TIM STODDARD
- [ ] 223. WAYNE TOLLESON
- [ ] 224. GARY WARD
- [ ] 225. CLAUDELL WASHINGTON
- [ ] 226. DAVE WINFIELD
- [ ] 646. RANDY VELARDE (P)
- [ ] 656. TEAM CHECKLIST (F)

OAKLAND A'S

- [ ] 275. TONY BERNAZARD
- [ ] 276. JOSE CANSECO
- [ ] 277. MIKE DAVIS
- [ ] 278. STORM DAVIS
- [ ] 279. DENNIS ECKERSLEY
- [ ] 280. ALFREDO GRIFFIN
- [ ] 281. RICK HONEYCUTT
- [ ] 282. JAY HOWELL
- [ ] 283. REGGIE JACKSON
- [ ] 284. DENNIS LAMP
- [ ] 285. CARNEY LANSFORD
- [ ] 286. MARK MCGWIRE
- [ ] 287. DWAYNE MURPHY
- [ ] 288. GENE NELSON
- [ ] 289. STEVE ONTIVEROS
- [ ] 290. TONY PHILLIPS
- [ ] 291. ERIC PLUNK
- [ ] 292. LUIS POLONIA
- [ ] 293. RICK RODRIGUEZ
- [ ] 294. TERRY STEINBACH
- [ ] 295. DAVE STEWART
- [ ] 296. CURT YOUNG
- [ ] 652. WALT WEISS (P)
- [ ] 652. DAVE OTTO (P)
- [ ] 656. TEAM CHECKLIST (B)

PHILADELPHIA PHILLIES

- [ ] 297. LUIS AGUAYO
- [ ] 298. STEVE BEDROSIAN
- [ ] 299. JEFF CALHOUN
- [ ] 300. DON CARMAN
- [ ] 301. TODD FROHWIRTH
- [ ] 302. GREG GROSS
- [ ] 303. KEVIN GROSS
- [ ] 304. VON HAYES
- [ ] 305. KEITH HUGHES
- [ ] 306. MIKE JACKSON
- [ ] 307. CHRIS JAMES
- [ ] 308. STEVE JELTZ
- [ ] 309. MIKE MADDUX
- [ ] 310. LANCE PARRISH
- [ ] 311. SHANE RAWLEY
- [ ] 312. WALLY RITCHIE
- [ ] 313. BRUCE RUFFIN
- [ ] 314. JUAN SAMUEL
- [ ] 315. MIKE SCHMIDT
- [ ] 316. RICK SCHU
- [ ] 317. JEFF STONE
- [ ] 318. KENT TEKULVE
- [ ] 319. MILT THOMPSON
- [ ] 320. GLENN WILSON
- [ ] 648. GREG JELKS (P)
- [ ] 648. TOM NEWELL (P)
- [ ] 657. TEAM CHECKLIST (F)

PITTSBURGH PIRATES

- [ ] 321. RAFAEL BELLIARD
- [ ] 322. BARRY BONDS
- [ ] 323. BOBBY BONILLA
- [ ] 324. SID BREAM
- [ ] 325. JOHN CANGELOSI
- [ ] 326. MIKE DIAZ
- [ ] 327. DOUG DRABEK
- [ ] 328. MIKE DUNNE
- [ ] 329. BRIAN FISHER
- [ ] 330. BRETT GIDEON

☐ 331. TERRY HARPER
☐ 332. BOB KIPPER
☐ 333. MIKE LAVALLIERE
☐ 334. JOSE LIND
☐ 335. JUNIOR ORTIZ
☐ 336. VINCENTE PALACIOS
☐ 337. BOB PATTERSON
☐ 338. AL PEDRIQUE
☐ 339. R. J. REYNOLDS
☐ 340. JOHN SMILEY
☐ 341. ANDY VAN SLYKE
☐ 342. BOB WALK
☐ 643. FELIX FERMIN (P)
☐ 653. JEFF KING (P)
☐ 657. TEAM CHECKLIST (F)

ST. LOUIS CARDINALS

☐ 26. JACK CLARK
☐ 27. VINCE COLEMAN
☐ 28. DANNY COX
☐ 29. BILL DAWLEY
☐ 30. KEN DAYLEY
☐ 31. DOUG DECINCES
☐ 32. CURT FORD
☐ 33. BOB FORSCH
☐ 34. DAVID GREEN
☐ 35. TOM HERR
☐ 36. RICKY HORTON
☐ 37. LANCE JOHNSON
☐ 38. STEVE LAKE
☐ 39. JIM LINDEMAN
☐ 40. JOE MAGRANE
☐ 41. GREG MATHEWS
☐ 42. WILLIE MCGEE
☐ 43. JOHN MORRIS
☐ 44. JOSE OQUENDO
☐ 45. TONY PENA
☐ 46. TERRY PENDLETON
☐ 47. OZZIE SMITH
☐ 48. JOHN TUDOR
☐ 49. LEE TUNNELL
☐ 50. TODD WORRELL
☐ 654. TEAM CHECKLIST (F)

SAN DIEGO PADRES

☐ 576. SHAWN ABNER
☐ 577. GREG BOOKER
☐ 578. CHRIS BROWN
☐ 579. KEITH COMSTOCK
☐ 580. JOEY CORA
☐ 581. MARK DAVIS
☐ 582. TIM FLANNERY
☐ 583. GOOSE GOSSAGE
☐ 584. MARK GRANT
☐ 585. TONY GWYNN
☐ 586. ANDY HAWKINS
☐ 587. STAN JEFFERSON
☐ 588. JIMMY JONES
☐ 589. JOHN KRUK
☐ 590. SHANE MACK
☐ 591. CARMELO MARTINEZ
☐ 592. LANCE MCCULLERS
☐ 593. ERIC NOLTE
☐ 594. RANDY READY
☐ 595. LUIS SALAZAR
☐ 596. BENITO SANTIAGO
☐ 597. ERIC SHOW
☐ 598. GARRY TEMPLETON
☐ 599. ED WHITSON
☐ 650. TODD SIMMONS (P)
☐ 653. RANDELL BYERS (P)
☐ 660. TEAM CHECKLIST (F)

SAN FRANCISCO GIANTS

☐ 76. MIKE ALDRETE
☐ 77. BOB BRENLY
☐ 78. WILL CLARK
☐ 79. CHILI DAVIS
☐ 80. KELLY DOWNS
☐ 81. DAVE DRAVECKY
☐ 82. SCOTT GARRELTS
☐ 83. ATLEE HAMMAKER
☐ 84. DAVE HENDERSON
☐ 85. MIKE KRUKOW
☐ 86. MIKE LACOSS
☐ 87. CRAIG LEFFERTS
☐ 88. JEFF LEONARD
☐ 89. CANDY MALDONADO
☐ 90. BOB MELVIN

☐ 91. ED MILNER
☐ 92. KEVIN MITCHELL
☐ 93. JON PERLMAN
☐ 94. RICK REUSCHEL
☐ 95. DON ROBINSON
☐ 96. CHRIS SPEIER
☐ 97. HARRY SPILMAN
☐ 98. ROBBIE THOMPSON
☐ 99. JOSE URIBE
☐ 100. MARK WASINGER
☐ 101. MATT WILLIAMS
☐ 643. JESSIE REID (P)
☐ 651. KIRT MANWARING (P)
☐ 651. JOHN BURKETT (P)
☐ 654. TEAM CHECKLIST (B)

SEATTLE MARINERS

☐ 368. SCOTT BANKHEAD
☐ 369. PHIL BRADLEY
☐ 370. SCOTT BRADLEY
☐ 371. MICKEY BRANTLEY
☐ 372. MIKE CAMPBELL
☐ 373. ALVIN DAVIS
☐ 374. LEE GUETTERMAN
☐ 375. DAVE HENGEL
☐ 376. MIKE KINGERY
☐ 377. MARK LANGSTON
☐ 378. EDGAR MARTINEZ
☐ 379. MIKE MOORE
☐ 380. MIKE MORGAN
☐ 381. JOHN MOSES
☐ 382. DONNELL NIXON
☐ 383. EDWIN NUNEZ
☐ 384. KEN PHELPS
☐ 385. JIM PRESLEY
☐ 386. REY QUINONES
☐ 387. JERRY REED
☐ 388. HAROLD REYNOLDS
☐ 389. DAVE VALLE
☐ 390. BILL WILKINSON
☐ 649. MARIO DIAZ (P)
☐ 649. CLAY PARKER (P)
☐ 657. TEAM CHECKLIST (B)

TEXAS RANGERS

☐ 461. BOB BROWER
☐ 462. JERRY BROWNE
☐ 463. STEVE BUECHELE
☐ 464. EDWIN CORREA
☐ 465. CECIL ESPY
☐ 466. SCOTT FLETCHER
☐ 467. JOSE GUZMAN
☐ 468. GREG HARRIS
☐ 469. CHARLIE HOUGH
☐ 470. PETE INCAVIGLIA
☐ 471. PAUL KILGUS
☐ 472. MIKE LOYND
☐ 473. ODDIBE MCDOWELL
☐ 474. DALE MOHORCIC
☐ 475. PETE O'BRIEN
☐ 476. LARRY PARRISH
☐ 477. GENO PETRALLI
☐ 478. JEFF RUSSELL
☐ 479. RUBEN SIERRA
☐ 480. MIKE STANLEY
☐ 481. CURTIS WILKERSON
☐ 482. MITCH WILLIAMS
☐ 483. BOBBY WITT
☐ 644. GREG TABOR (P)
☐ 658. TEAM CHECKLIST (B)

TORONTO BLUE JAYS

☐ 102. JESSE BARFIELD
☐ 103. GEORGE BELL
☐ 104. JUAN BENIQUEZ
☐ 105. JOHN CERUTTI
☐ 106. JIM CLANCY
☐ 107. ROB DUCEY
☐ 108. MARK EICHHORN
☐ 109. TONY FERNANDEZ
☐ 110. CECIL FIELDER
☐ 111. KELLY GRUBER
☐ 112. TOM HENKE
☐ 113. GARTH IORG
☐ 114. JIMMY KEY
☐ 115. RICK LEACH
☐ 116. MANNY LEE
☐ 117. NELSON LIRIANO
☐ 118. FRED MCGRIFF
☐ 119. LLOYD MOSEBY
☐ 120. RANCE MULLINIKS
☐ 121. JEFF MUSSELMAN
☐ 122. JOSE NUNEZ
☐ 123. DAVE STIEB
☐ 124. WILLIE UPSHAW
☐ 125. DUANE WARD
☐ 126. ERNIE WHITT
☐ 644. GREG MYERS (P)
☐ 655. TEAM CHECKLIST (F)

1988 FLEER TRADED (132) 2 1/2 X 3 1/2

ATLANTA BRAVES

☐ 70U. JOSE ALVAREZ
☐ 71U. PAUL RUNGE
☐ 72U. CESAR JIMENEZ
☐ 73U. PETE SMITH
☐ 74U. JOHN SMOLTZ

BALTIMORE ORIOLES

☐ 1U. JOSE BAUTISTA
☐ 2U. JOE ORSULAK
☐ 3U. DOUG SISK
☐ 4U. CRAIG WORTHINGTON

BOSTON RED SOX

☐ 5U. MIKE BODDICKER
☐ 6U. RICK CERONE
☐ 7U. LARRY PARRISH
☐ 8U. LEE SMITH
☐ 9U. MIKE SMITHSON
☐ 10U. JOHN TRAUTWEIN

CALIFORNIA ANGELS

☐ 11U. SHERMAN CORBETT
☐ 12U. CHILI DAVIS
☐ 13U. JIM EPPARD
☐ 14U. BRYAN HARVEY

CHICAGO CUBS

☐ 75U. DAMON BERRYHILL
☐ 76U. GOOSE GOSSAGE
☐ 77U. MARK GRACE

☐ 78U. DARRIN JACKSON
☐ 79U. VANCE LAW
☐ 80U. JEFF PICO
☐ 81U. GARY VARSHO

CHICAGO WHITE SOX

☐ 15U. JOHN DAVIS
☐ 16U. DAVE GALLAGHER
☐ 17U. RICKY HORTON
☐ 18U. DAN PASQUA
☐ 19U. MELIDO PEREZ
☐ 20U. JOSE SEGURA

CINCINNATI REDS

☐ 82U. TIM BIRTSAS
☐ 83U. ROB DIBBLE
☐ 84U. DANNY JACKSON
☐ 85U. PAUL O'NEILL
☐ 86U. JOSE RIJO
☐ 87U. CHRIS SABO

CLEVELAND INDIANS

☐ 21U. ANDY ALLANSON
☐ 22U. JON PERLMAN
☐ 23U. DOMINGO RAMOS
☐ 24U. RICK RODRIGUEZ
☐ 25U. WILLIE UPSHAW

DETROIT TIGERS

☐ 26U. PAUL GIBSON
☐ 27U. DON HEINKEL
☐ 28U. RAY KNIGHT
☐ 29U. GARY PETTIS
☐ 30U. LUIS SALAZAR

HOUSTON ASTROS

☐ 88U. JOHN FISHEL
☐ 89U. CRAIG BIGGIO
☐ 90U. TERRY PUHL
☐ 91U. RAFAEL RAMIREZ
☐ 92U. LOUIE MEADOWS

KANSAS CITY ROYALS

☐ 31U. MIKE MACFARLANE
☐ 32U. JEFF MONTGOMERY
☐ 33U. TED POWER
☐ 34U. ISRAEL SANCHEZ
☐ 35U. KURT STILLWELL
☐ 36U. PAT TABLER

LOS ANGELES DODGERS

☐ 93U. KIRK GIBSON
☐ 94U. ALFREDO GRIFFIN
☐ 95U. JAY HOWELL
☐ 96U. JESSE OROSCO
☐ 97U. ALEJANDRO PENA
☐ 98U. TRACY WOODSON

MILWAUKEE BREWERS

☐ 37U. DON AUGUST
☐ 38U. DARRYL HAMILTON
☐ 39U. JEFF LEONARD
☐ 40U. JOEY MEYER

MINNESOTA TWINS

☐ 41U. ALLAN ANDERSON
☐ 42U. BRIAN HARPER
☐ 43U. TOM HERR
☐ 44U. CHARLIE LEA
☐ 45U. JOHN MOSES

MONTREAL EXPOS

☐ 99U. JOHN DOPSON
☐ 100U. BRIAN HOLMAN
☐ 101U. REX HUDLER
☐ 102U. JEFF PARRETT
☐ 103U. NELSON SANTOVENIA

NEW YORK METS

☐ 104U. KEVIN ELSTER
☐ 105U. JEFF INNIS
☐ 106U. MACKEY SASSER

NEW YORK YANKEES

☐ 46U. JOHN CANDELARIA
☐ 47U. JACK CLARK
☐ 48U. RICHARD DOTSON
☐ 49U. AL LEITER
☐ 50U. RAFAEL SANTANA
☐ 51U. DON SLAUGHT

OAKLAND A'S

☐ 52U. TODD BURNS
☐ 53U. DAVE HENDERSON
☐ 54U. DOUG JENNINGS
☐ 55U. DAVE PARKER
☐ 56U. WALT WEISS
☐ 57U. BOB WELCH

PHILADELPHIA PHILLIES

☐ 107U. PHIL BRADLEY
☐ 108U. DANNY CLAY
☐ 109U. GREG HARRIS
☐ 110U. RICKY JORDAN
☐ 111U. DAVID PALMER

PITTSBURGH PIRATES

☐ 112U. JIM GOTT
☐ 113U. TOMMY GREGG
☐ 114U. BARRY JONES
☐ 115U. RANDY MILLIGAN

ST. LOUIS CARDINALS

☐ 116U. LUIS ALICEA
☐ 117U. TOM BRUNANSKY
☐ 118U. JOHN COSTELLO
☐ 119U. JOSE DELEON
☐ 120U. BOB HORNER
☐ 121U. SCOTT TERRY

SAN DIEGO PADRES

☐ 122U. ROBERTO ALOMAR
☐ 123U. DAVE LEIPER
☐ 124U. KEITH MORELAND
☐ 125U. MARK PARENT
☐ 126U. DENNIS RASMUSSEN

SAN FRANCISCO GIANTS

☐ 127U. RANDY BOCKUS
☐ 128U. BRETT BUTLER
☐ 129U. DONELL NIXON
☐ 130U. EARNEST RILES
☐ 131U. ROGER SAMUELS

SEATTLE MARINERS

☐ 58U. HENRY COTTO
☐ 59U. MARIO DIAZ
☐ 60U. MIKE JACKSON
☐ 61U. BILL SWIFT

TEXAS RANGERS

☐ 62U. JOSE CECENA
☐ 63U. RAY HAYWARD
☐ 64U. JIM STEELE

TORONTO BLUE JAYS

☐ 65U. PAT BORDERS
☐ 66U. SIL CAMPUSANO
☐ 67U. MIKE FLANAGAN
☐ 68U. TODD STOTTLEMYRE
☐ 69U. DAVID WELLS

1989 FLEER (660)
2 1/2 X 3 1/2

ATLANTA BRAVES

☐ 585. JOSE ALVAREZ
☐ 586. PAUL ASSENMACHER
☐ 587. BRUCE BENEDICT
☐ 588. JEFF BLAUSER
☐ 589. TERRY BLOCKER
☐ 590. RON GANT
☐ 591. TOM GLAVINE
☐ 592. TOMMY GREGG
☐ 593. ALBERT HALL
☐ 594. DION JAMES
☐ 595. RICH MAHLER
☐ 596. DALE MURPHY
☐ 597. GERALD PERRY
☐ 598. CHARLIE PULEO
☐ 599. TED SIMMONS
☐ 600. PETE SMITH
☐ 601. ZANE SMITH
☐ 602. JOHN SMOLTZ
☐ 603. BRUCE SUTTER
☐ 604. ANDRES THOMAS
☐ 605. OZZIE VIRGIL
☐ 660. TEAM CHECKLIST (F)

BALTIMORE ORIOLES

☐ 606. BRADY ANDERSON
☐ 607. JEFF BALLARD
☐ 608. JOSE BAUTISTA
☐ 609. KEN GERHART
☐ 610. TERRY KENNEDY
☐ 611. EDDIE MURRAY
☐ 612. CARL NICHOLS
☐ 613. TOM NIEDENFUER
☐ 614. JOE ORSULAK
☐ 615. OSWALDO PERAZA
☐ 616. BILL RIPKEN

- ☐ 617. CAL RIPKEN, JR.
- ☐ 618. DAVE SCHMIDT
- ☐ 619. RICH SCHU
- ☐ 620. LARRY SHEETS
- ☐ 621. DOUGH SISK
- ☐ 622. PETE STANICEK
- ☐ 623. MICKEY TETTLETON
- ☐ 624. JAY TIBBS
- ☐ 625. JIM TRABER
- ☐ 626. MARK WILLIAMSON
- ☐ 627. CRAIG WORTHINGTON
- ☐ 649. BOB MILACKI (P)
- ☐ 660. TEAM CHECKLIST (F)

BOSTON RED SOX

- ☐ 78. MARTY BARRETT
- ☐ 79. TODD BENZINGER
- ☐ 80. MIKE BODDICKER
- ☐ 81. WADE BOGGS
- ☐ 82. OIL CAN BOYD
- ☐ 83. ELLIS BURKS
- ☐ 84. RICK CERONE
- ☐ 85. ROGER CLEMENS
- ☐ 86. STEVE CURRY
- ☐ 87. DWIGHT EVANS
- ☐ 88. WES GARDNER
- ☐ 89. RICH GEDMAN
- ☐ 90. MIKE GREENWELL
- ☐ 91. BRUCE HURST
- ☐ 92. DENNIS LAMP
- ☐ 93. SPIKE OWEN
- ☐ 94. LARRY PARRISH
- ☐ 95. CARLOS QUINTANA
- ☐ 96. JODY REED
- ☐ 97. JIM RICE
- ☐ 98. KEVIN ROMINE
- ☐ 99. LEE SMITH
- ☐ 100. MIKE SMITHSON
- ☐ 101. BOB STANLEY
- ☐ 650. MIKE ROCHFORD (P)
- ☐ 654. TEAM CHECKLIST (B)

GREG MINTON
PITCHER

CALIFORNIA ANGELS

- ☐ 467. TONY ARMAS
- ☐ 468. DANTE BICHETTE
- ☐ 469. BOB BOONE
- ☐ 470. TERRY CLARK
- ☐ 471. STEW CLIBURN
- ☐ 472. MIKE COOK
- ☐ 473. SHERMAN CORBETT
- ☐ 474. CHILI DAVIS
- ☐ 475. BRIAN DOWNING
- ☐ 476. JIM EPPARD
- ☐ 477. CHUCK FINLEY
- ☐ 478. WILLIE FRASER
- ☐ 479. BRYAN HARVEY
- ☐ 480. JACK HOWELL
- ☐ 481. WALLY JOYNER
- ☐ 482. JACK LAZORKO
- ☐ 483. KIRK MCCASKILL
- ☐ 484. MARK MCLEMORE
- ☐ 485. GREG MINTON
- ☐ 486. DAN PETRY
- ☐ 487. JOHNNY RAY
- ☐ 488. DICK SCHOFIELD
- ☐ 489. DEVON WHITE
- ☐ 490. MIKE WITT
- ☐ 651. VANCE LOVELACE (P)
- ☐ 658. TEAM CHECKLIST (B)

CHICAGO CUBS

- ☐ 418. DAMON BERRYHILL
- ☐ 419. MIKE BIELECKI
- ☐ 420. DOUG DASCENZO
- ☐ 421. JODY DAVIS
- ☐ 422. ANDRE DAWSON
- ☐ 423. FRANK DIPINO
- ☐ 424. SHAWON DUNSTON
- ☐ 425. GOOSE GOSSAGE
- ☐ 426. MARK GRACE
- ☐ 427. MIKE HARKEY
- ☐ 428. DARRIN JACKSON
- ☐ 429. LES LANCASTER
- ☐ 430. VANCE LAW
- ☐ 431. GREG MADDUX
- ☐ 432. JAMIE MOYER
- ☐ 433. AL NIPPER
- ☐ 434. RAFAEL PALMEIRO
- ☐ 435. PAT PERRY
- ☐ 436. JEFF PICO
- ☐ 437. RYNE SANDBERG
- ☐ 438. CALVIN SCHIRALDI
- ☐ 439. RICK SUTCLIFFE
- ☐ 440. MANNY TRILLO
- ☐ 441. GARY VARSHO
- ☐ 442. MITCH WEBSTER
- ☐ 643. MIKE CAPEL (P)
- ☐ 643. DREW HALL (P)
- ☐ 644. JOE GIRARDI (P)
- ☐ 644. ROLANDO ROOMES (P)
- ☐ 658. TEAM CHECKLIST (F)

CHICAGO WHITE SOX

- ☐ 491. HAROLD BAINES
- ☐ 492. DARYL BOSTON
- ☐ 493. IVAN CALDERON
- ☐ 494. MIKE DIAZ
- ☐ 495. CARLTON FISK
- ☐ 496. DAVE GALLAGHER
- ☐ 497. OZZIE GUILLEN
- ☐ 498. SHAWN HILLEGAS
- ☐ 499. LANCE JOHNSON
- ☐ 500. BARRY JONES
- ☐ 501. BILL LONG
- ☐ 502. STEVE LYONS
- ☐ 503. FRED MANRIQUE
- ☐ 504. JACK MCDOWELL
- ☐ 505. DONN PALL
- ☐ 506. KELLY PARIS
- ☐ 507. DAN PASQUA
- ☐ 508. KEN PATTERSON
- ☐ 509. MELIDO PEREZ
- ☐ 510. JERRY REUSS
- ☐ 511. MARK SALAS
- ☐ 512. BOBBY THIGPEN
- ☐ 513. MIKE WOODARD
- ☐ 650. GRADY HALL (P)
- ☐ 659. TEAM CHECKLIST (F)

CINCINNATI REDS

- ☐ 152. TIM BIRTSAS
- ☐ 153. TOM BROWNING
- ☐ 154. KEITH BROWN
- ☐ 155. NORM CHARLTON
- ☐ 156. DAVE CONCEPCION
- ☐ 157. KAL DANIELS
- ☐ 158. ERIC DAVIS
- ☐ 159. BO DIAZ
- ☐ 160. ROB DIBBLE
- ☐ 161. NICK ESASKY
- ☐ 162. JOHN FRANCO
- ☐ 163. DANNY JACKSON
- ☐ 164. BARRY LARKIN
- ☐ 165. ROB MURPHY
- ☐ 166. PAUL O'NEILL
- ☐ 167. JEFF REED
- ☐ 168. JOSE RIJO
- ☐ 169. RON ROBINSON
- ☐ 170. CHRIS SABO
- ☐ 171. CANDY SIERRA
- ☐ 172. VAN SNIDER
- ☐ 173. JEFF TREADWAY
- ☐ 174. FRANK WILLIAMS
- ☐ 175. HERM WINNINGHAM
- ☐ 645. LENNY HARRIS (P)
- ☐ 645. MARTY BROWN (P)
- ☐ 655. TEAM CHECKLIST (B)

CLEVELAND INDIANS

- ☐ 396. ANDY ALLANSON
- ☐ 397. ROD ALLEN
- ☐ 398. SCOTT BAILES
- ☐ 399. TOM CANDIOTTI
- ☐ 400. JOE CARTER
- ☐ 401. CARMEN CASTILLO
- ☐ 402. DAVE CLARK
- ☐ 403. JOHN FARRELL
- ☐ 404. JULIO FRANCO
- ☐ 405. DON GORDON
- ☐ 406. MEL HALL
- ☐ 407. BRAD HAVENS
- ☐ 408. BROOK JACOBY
- ☐ 409. DOUG JONES
- ☐ 410. JEFF KAISER
- ☐ 411. LUIS MEDINA
- ☐ 412. CORY SNYDER
- ☐ 413. GREG SWINDELL
- ☐ 414. RON TINGLEY
- ☐ 415. WILLIE UPSHAW
- ☐ 416. RON WASHINGTON
- ☐ 417. RICH YETT
- ☐ 658. TEAM CHECKLIST (F)

DETROIT TIGERS

- ☐ 128. DOYLE ALEXANDER
- ☐ 129. DAVE BERGMAN
- ☐ 130. TOM BROOKENS
- ☐ 131. PAUL GIBSON
- ☐ 132. MIKE HEATH
- ☐ 133. DON HEINKEL
- ☐ 134. MIKE HENNEMAN
- ☐ 135. GUILLERMO HERNANDEZ
- ☐ 136. ERIC KING
- ☐ 137. CHET LEMON
- ☐ 138. FRED LYNN
- ☐ 139. JACK MORRIS
- ☐ 140. MATT NOKES
- ☐ 141. GARY PETTIS
- ☐ 142. TED POWER
- ☐ 143. JEFF M. ROBINSON
- ☐ 144. LUIS SALAZAR
- ☐ 145. STEVE SEARCY
- ☐ 146. PAT SHERIDAN
- ☐ 147. FRANK TANANA
- ☐ 148. ALAN TRAMMELL
- ☐ 149. WALT TERRELL
- ☐ 150. JIM WALEWANDER
- ☐ 151. LOU WHITAKER
- ☐ 648. TOREY LOVULLO (P)
- ☐ 655. TEAM CHICKLIST (F)

HOUSTON ASTROS

- ☐ 348. JUAN AGOSTO
- ☐ 349. LARRY ANDERSEN
- ☐ 350. ALAN ASHBY
- ☐ 351. KEVIN BASS
- ☐ 352. BUDDY BELL
- ☐ 353. CRAIG BIGGIO
- ☐ 354. DANNY DARWIN
- ☐ 355. GLENN DAVIS
- ☐ 356. JIM DESHAIES
- ☐ 357. BILL DORAN
- ☐ 358. JOHN FISHEL
- ☐ 359. BILLY HATCHER
- ☐ 360. BOB KNEPPER
- ☐ 361. LOUIE MEADOWS
- ☐ 362. DAVE MEADS
- ☐ 363. JIM PANKOVITS
- ☐ 364. TERRY PUHL
- ☐ 365. RAFAEL RAMIREZ
- ☐ 366. CRAIG REYNOLDS
- ☐ 367. NOLAN RYAN
- ☐ 368. MIKE SCOTT
- ☐ 369. DAVE SMITH
- ☐ 370. GERALD YOUNG
- ☐ 640. CAMERON DREW (P)
- ☐ 657. TEAM CHECKLIST (B)

KANSAS CITY ROYALS

- ☐ 275. LUIS AQUINO
- ☐ 276. FLOYD BANNISTER
- ☐ 277. GEORGE BRETT
- ☐ 278. BILL BUCKNER
- ☐ 279. NICK CAPRA
- ☐ 280. JOSE DEJESUS

□ 281. STEVE FARR
□ 282. JERRY GLEATON
□ 283. MARK GUBICZA
□ 284. TOM GORDON
□ 285. BO JACKSON
□ 286. CHARLIE LEIBRANDT
□ 287. MIKE MACFARLANE
□ 288. JEFF MONTGOMERY
□ 289. BILL PECOTA
□ 290. JAMIE QUIRK
□ 291. BRET SABERHAGEN
□ 292. KEVIN SEITZER
□ 293. KURT STILLWELL
□ 294. PAT TABLER
□ 295. DANNY TARTABULL
□ 296. GARY THURMAN
□ 297. FRANK WHITE
□ 298. WILLIE WILSON
□ 646. LUIS DELOS SANTOS (P)
□ 646. JIM CAMPBELL (P)
□ 648. ROBERT PALACIOS (P)
□ 656. TEAM CHECKLIST (B)

LOS ANGELES DODGERS

□ 53. DAVE ANDERSON
□ 54. TIM BELCHER
□ 55. MIKE DAVIS
□ 56. MIKE DEVEREAUX
□ 57. KIRK GIBSON
□ 58. ALFREDO GRIFFIN
□ 59. CHRIS GWYNN
□ 60. JEFF HAMILTON
□ 61. DANNY HEEP
□ 62. OREL HERSHISER
□ 63. BRIAN HOLTON
□ 64. JAY HOWELL
□ 65. TIM LEARY
□ 66. MIKE MARSHALL
□ 67. RAMON MARTINEZ
□ 68. JESS OROSCO
□ 69. ALEJANDRO PENA
□ 70. STEVE SAX
□ 71. MIKE SCIOSCIA
□ 72. MIKE SHARPERSON
□ 73. JOHN SHELBY
□ 74. FRANKLIN STUBBS
□ 75. JOHN TUDOR
□ 76. FERNANDO VALENZUELA
□ 77. TRACY WOODSON
□ 654. TEAM CHECKLIST (B)

MILWAUKEE BREWERS

□ 176. JIM ADDUCI
□ 177. DON AUGUST
□ 178. MIKE BIRKBECK
□ 179. CHRIS BOSLO
□ 180. GLENN BRAGGS
□ 181. GREG BROCK
□ 182. MARK CLEAR
□ 183. CHUCK CRIM
□ 184. ROB DEER
□ 185. TOM FILER
□ 186. JIM GANTNER
□ 187. DARRYL HAMILTON
□ 188. TED HIGUERA
□ 189. ODELL JONES
□ 190. JEFFREY LEONARD
□ 191. JOEY MEYER
□ 192. PAUL MIRABELLA

□ 193. PAUL MOLITOR
□ 194. CHARLIE O'BRIEN
□ 195. DAN PLESAC
□ 196. GARY SHEFFIELD
□ 197. B. J. SURHOFF
□ 198. DALE SVEUM
□ 199. BILL WEGMAN
□ 200. ROBIN YOUNT
□ 655. TEAM CHECKLIST (B)

MINNESOTA TWINS

□ 102. ALLAN ANDERSON
□ 103. KEITH ATHERTON
□ 104. JUAN BERENGUER
□ 105. BERT BLYLEVEN
□ 106. ERIC BULLOCK
□ 107. RANDY BUSH
□ 108. JOHN CHRISTENSEN
□ 109. MARK DAVIDSON
□ 110. GARY GAETTI
□ 111. GREG GAGNE
□ 112. DAN GLADDEN
□ 113. GERMAN GONZALEZ
□ 114. BRIAN HARPER
□ 115. TOM HERR
□ 116. KENT HRBEK
□ 117. GENE LARKIN
□ 118. TIM LAUDNER
□ 119. CHARLIE LEA
□ 120. STEVE LOMBARDOZZI
□ 121. JOHN MOSES
□ 122. AL NEWMAN
□ 123. MARK PORTUGAL
□ 124. KIRBY PUCKETT
□ 125. JEFF REARDON
□ 126. FRED TOLIVER
□ 127. FRANK VIOLA
□ 655. TEAM CHECKLIST(F)

MONTREAL EXPOS

□ 371. HUBIE BROOKS
□ 372. TIM BURKE
□ 373. JOHN DOPSON
□ 374. MIKE FITZGERALD
□ 375. TOM FOLEY
□ 376. ANDRES GALARRAGA
□ 377. NEAL HEATON
□ 378. JOE HESKETH
□ 379. BRIAN HOLMAN
□ 380. REX HUDLER
□ 381. RANDY JOHNSON
□ 382. WALLACE JOHNSON
□ 383. TRACY JONES
□ 384. DAVE MARTINEZ
□ 385. DENNIS MARTINEZ
□ 386. ANDY MCGAFFIGAN
□ 387. OTIS NIXON
□ 388. JOHNNY PAREDES
□ 389. JEFF PARRETT
□ 390. PASCUAL PEREZ
□ 391. TIM RAINES
□ 392. LUIS RIVERA
□ 393. NELSON SANTOVENIA
□ 394. BRYN SMITH
□ 395. TIM WALLACH
□ 657. TEAM CHECKLIST (B)

NEW YORK METS

□ 27. RICK AGUILERA
□ 28. WALLY BACKMAN
□ 29. MARK CARREON
□ 30. GARY CARTER
□ 31. DAVID CONE
□ 32. RON DARLING
□ 33. LEN DYKSTRA
□ 34. KEVIN ELSTER
□ 35. SID FERNANDEZ
□ 36. DWIGHT GOODEN
□ 37. KEITH HERNANDEZ
□ 38. GREGG JEFFERIES
□ 39. HOWARD JOHNSON
□ 40. TERRY LEACH
□ 41. DAVE MAGADAN
□ 42. BOB MCCLURE
□ 43. ROGER MCDOWELL
□ 44. KEVIN MCREYNOLDS
□ 45. KEITH MILLER
□ 46. RANDY MYERS
□ 47. BOB OJEDA

□ 48. MACKEY SASSER
□ 49. DARRYL STRAWBERRY
□ 50. TIM TEUFEL
□ 51. DAVE WEST
□ 52. MOOKIE WILSON
□ 654. TEAM CHECKLIST (F)

NEW YORK YANKEES

□ 249. LUIS AGUAYO
□ 250. NEIL ALLEN
□ 251. JOHN CANDELARIA
□ 252. JACK CLARK
□ 253. RICHARD DOTSON
□ 254. RICKEY HENDERSON
□ 255. TOMMY JOHN
□ 256. ROBERTO KELLY
□ 257. AL LEITER
□ 258. DON MATTINGLY
□ 259. DALE MOHORCIC
□ 260. HAL MORRIS
□ 261. SCOTT NIELSEN
□ 262. MIKE PAGLIARULO
□ 263. HIPOLITO PENA
□ 264. KEN PHELPS
□ 265. WILLIE RANDOLPH
□ 266. RICK RHODEN
□ 267. DAVE RIGHETTI
□ 268. RAFAEL SANTANA
□ 269. STEVE SHIELDS
□ 270. JOEL SKINNER
□ 271. DON SLAUGHT
□ 272. CLAUDELL WASHINGTON
□ 273. GARY WARD
□ 274. DAVE WINFIELD
□ 656. TEAM CHECKLIST (B)

OAKLAND A'S

□ 1. DON BAYLOR
□ 2. LANCE BLANKENSHIP
□ 3. TODD BURNS
□ 4. GREG CADARET
□ 5. JOSE CANSECO
□ 6. STORM DAVIS
□ 7. DENNIS ECKERSLEY
□ 8. MIKE GALLEGO
□ 9. RON HASSEY
□ 10. DAVE HENDERSON
□ 11. RICK HONEYCUTT
□ 12. GLENN HUBBARD
□ 13. STAN JAVIER
□ 14. DOUG JENNINGS
□ 15. FELIX JOSE
□ 16. CARNEY LANSFORD
□ 17. MARK MCGWIRE
□ 18. GENE NELSON
□ 19. DAVE PARKER
□ 20. ERIC PLUNK
□ 21. LUIS POLONIA
□ 22. TERRY STEINBACH
□ 23. DAVE STEWART
□ 24. WALT WEISS
□ 25. BOB WELCH
□ 26. CURT YOUNG
□ 649. JIM CORSI (P)
□ 654. TEAM CHECKLIST (F)

PHILADELPHIA PHILLIES

□ 562. STEVE BEDROSIAN
□ 563. PHIL BRADLEY
□ 564. DON CARMAN
□ 565. BOB DERNIER
□ 566. MARVIN FREEMAN
□ 567. TODD FROHWIRTH
□ 568. GREG GROSS
□ 569. KEVIN GROSS
□ 570. GREG HARRIS
□ 571. VON HAYES
□ 572. CHRIS JAMES
□ 573. STEVE JELTZ
□ 574. RON JONES
□ 575. RICKY JORDAN
□ 576. MIKE MADDUX
□ 577. DAVID PALMER
□ 578. LANCE PARRISH
□ 579. SHANE RAWLEY
□ 580. BRUCE RUFFIN
□ 581. JUAN SAMUEL
□ 582. MIKE SCHMIDT
□ 583. KENT TEKULVE

□ 584. MILT THOMPSON
□ 653. SCOTT SERVICE (P)
□ 653. SHANE TURNER (P)
□ 659. TEAM CHECKLIST (B)

PITTSBURGH PIRATES

□ 201. RAFAEL BELLIARD
□ 202. BARRY BONDS
□ 203. BOBBY BONILLA
□ 204. SID BREAM
□ 205. BENNY DISTEFANO
□ 206. DOUG DRABEK
□ 207. MIKE DUNNE
□ 208. FELIX FERMIN
□ 209. BRIAN FISHER
□ 210. JIM GOTT
□ 211. BOB KIPPER
□ 212. DAVE LAPOINT
□ 213. MIKE LAVALLIERE
□ 214. JOSE LIND
□ 215. JUNIOR ORIZ
□ 216. VICENTE PALACIOS
□ 217. TOM PRINCE
□ 218. GARY REDUS
□ 219. R. J. REYNOLDS
□ 220. JEFF ROBINSON
□ 221. JOHN SMILEY
□ 222. ANDY VAN SLYKE
□ 223. BOB WALK
□ 224. GLENN WILSON
□ 647. RANDY KRAMER (P)
□ 647. MIGUEL GARCIA (P)
□ 656. TEAM CHECKLIST (F)

ST. LOUIS CARDINALS

□ 443. LUIS ALICEA
□ 444. TOM BRUNANSKY
□ 445. VINCE COLEMAN
□ 446. JOHN COSTELLO
□ 447. DANNY COX
□ 448. KEN DAYLEY
□ 449. JOSE DELEON
□ 450. CURT FORD
□ 451. PEDRO GUERRERO
□ 452. BOB HORNER
□ 453. TIM JONES
□ 454. STEVE LAKE
□ 455. JOE MAGRANE
□ 456. GREG MATHEWS
□ 457. WILLIE MCGEE
□ 458. LARRY MCWILLIAMS
□ 459. JOSE OQUENDO
□ 460. TONY PENA
□ 461. TERRY PENDLETQN
□ 462. STEVE PETERS
□ 463. OZZIE SMITH
□ 464. SCOTT TERRY
□ 465. DENNY WALLING
□ 466. TODD WORRELL
□ 652. KEN HILL (P)
□ 658. TEAM CHECKLIST (B)

SAN DIEGO PADRES

□ 299. ROBERTO ALOMAR
□ 300. SANDY ALOMAR, JR.
□ 301. CHRIS BROWN
□ 302. MIKE BRUMLEY
□ 303. MARK DAVIS
□ 304. MARK GRANT
□ 305. TONY GWYNN
□ 306. GREG W. HARRIS
□ 307. ANDY HAWKINS
□ 308. JIMMY JONES
□ 309. JOHN KRUK
□ 310. DAVE LEIPER
□ 311. CARMELO MARTINEZ
□ 312. LANCE MCCULLERS
□ 313. KEITH MORELAND
□ 314. DENNIS RASMUSSEN
□ 315. RANDY READY
□ 316. BENITO SANTIAGO
□ 317. ERIC SHOW
□ 318. TODD SIMMONS
□ 319. GARRY TEMPLETON
□ 320. DICKIE THON
□ 321. ED WHITSON
□ 322. MARVELL WYNNE
□ 642. BRAD POUNDERS (P)
□ 642. JERALD CLARK (P)
□ 657. TEAM CHECKLIST (F)

SAN FRANCISCO GIANTS

□ 323. MIKE ALDRETE
□ 324. BRETT BUTLER
□ 325. WILL CLARK
□ 326. KELLY DOWNS
□ 327. DAVE DRAVECKY
□ 328. SCOTT GARRELTS
□ 329. ATLEE HAMMAKER
□ 330. CHARLIE HAYES
□ 331. MIKE KRUKOW
□ 332. CRAIG LEFFERTS
□ 333. CANDY MALDONADO
□ 334. KIRT MANWARING
□ 335. BOB MELVIN
□ 336. KEVIN MITCHELL
□ 337. DONELL NIXON
□ 338. TONY PEREZCHICA
□ 339. JOE PRICE
□ 340. RICK REUSCHEL
□ 341. EARNEST RILES
□ 342. DON ROBINSON
□ 343. CHRIS SPEIER
□ 344. ROBBY THOMPSON
□ 345. JOSE URIBE
□ 346. MATT WILLIAMS
□ 347. TREVOR WILSON
□ 652. DENNIS COOK (P)
□ 657. TEAM CHECKLIST (F)

SEATTLE MARINERS

□ 538. STEVE BALBONI
□ 539. SCOTT BANKHEAD
□ 540. SCOTT BRADLEY
□ 541. MICKEY BRANTLEY
□ 542. JAY BUHNER
□ 543. MIKE CAMPBELL
□ 544. DARNELL COLES
□ 545. HENRY COTTO
□ 546. ALVIN DAVIS
□ 547. MARIO DIAZ
□ 548. KEN GRIFFEY, JR.
□ 549. ERIK HANSON
□ 550. MIKE JACKSON
□ 551. MARK LANGSTON
□ 552. EDGAR MARTINEZ
□ 553. BILL MCGUIRE
□ 554. MIKE MOORE
□ 555. JIM PRESLEY
□ 556. REY QUINONES
□ 557. JERRY REED
□ 558. HAROLD REYNOLDS
□ 559. MIKE SCHOOLER
□ 560. BILL SWIFT
□ 561. DAVE VALLE
□ 651. TERRY TAYLOR (P)
□ 659. TEAM CHECKLIST (B)

TEXAS RANGERS

□ 514. BOB BROWER
□ 515. STEVE BUECHELE
□ 516. JOSE CECENA
□ 517. CECIL ESPY
□ 518. SCOTT FLETCHER
□ 519. CECILIO GUANTE
□ 520. JOSE GUZMAN
□ 521. RAY HAYWARD
□ 522. CHARLIE HOUGH
□ 523. PETE INCAVIGLIA
□ 524. MIKE JEFFCOAT
□ 525. PAUL KILGUS
□ 526. CHAD KREUTER
□ 527. JEFF KUNKEL
□ 528. ODDIBE MCDOWELL
□ 529. PETE O'BRIEN
□ 530. GENO PETRALLI
□ 531. JEFF RUSSELL
□ 532. RUBEN SIERRA
□ 533. MIKE STANLEY
□ 534. ED VANDEBERG
□ 535. CURTIS WILKERSON
□ 536. MITCH WILLIAMS
□ 537. BOBBY WITT
□ 640. STEVE WILSON (P)
□ 641. KEVIN BROWN (P)
□ 641. KEVIN REIMER (P)
□ 659. TEAM CHECKLIST (F)

TORONTO BLUE JAYS

□ 225. JESS BARFIELD
□ 226. GEORGE BELL
□ 227. PAT BORDERS
□ 228. JOHN CERUTTI
□ 229. JIM CLANCY
□ 230. MARK EICHHORN
□ 231. TONY FERNANDEZ
□ 232. CECIL FIELDER
□ 233. MIKE FLANAGAN
□ 234. KELLY GRUBER
□ 235. TOM HENKE
□ 236. JIMMY KEY
□ 237. RICK LEACH
□ 238. MANNY LEE
□ 239. NELSON LIRIANO
□ 240. FRED MCGRIFF
□ 241. LLOYD MOSEBY
□ 242. RANCE MULLINIKS
□ 243. JEFF MUSSELMAN
□ 244. DAVE STIEB
□ 245. TODD STOTTLEMYRE
□ 246. DUANE WARD
□ 247. DAVID WELLS
□ 248. ERNIE WHITT
□ 656. TEAM CHECKLIST (F)

1989 FLEER TRADED (132)
2 1/2 X 3 1/2

ATLANTA BRAVES

□   72U. GERONIMO BERROA
□   73U. DEREK LILLIQUIST
□   74U. LONNIE SMITH
□   75U. JEFF TREADWAY

BALTIMORE ORIOLES

□   1U. PHIL BRADLEY
□   2U. MIKE DEVEREAUX
□   3U. STEVE FINLEY
□   4U. KEVIN HICKEY
□   5U. BRIAN HOLTON
□   6U. BOB MILACKI
□   7U. RANDY MILLIGAN

BOSTON RED SOX

□   8U. JOHN DOPSON
□   9U. NICK ESASKY
□   10U. ROB MURPHY

CALIFORNIA ANGELS

□   11U. JIM ABBOTT
□   12U. BERT BLYLEVEN
□   13U. JEFF MANTO
□   14U. BOB MCCLURE
□   15U. LANCE PARRISH
□   16U. LEE STEVENS
□   17U. CLAUDELL WASHINGTON

1989 Fleer Traded

CHICAGO CUBS

- 76U. PAUL KILGUS
- 77U. LLOYD MCCLENDON
- 78U. SCOTT SANDERSON
- 79U. DWIGHT SMITH
- 80U. JEROME WALTON
- 81U. MITCH WILLIAMS
- 82U. STEVE WILSON

CHICAGO WHITE SOX

- 18U. MARK DAVIS
- 19U. ERIC KING
- 20U. RON KITTLE
- 21U. MATT MERULLO
- 22U. STEVE ROSENBERG
- 23U. ROBIN VENTURA

CINCINNATI REDS

- 83U. TODD BENZINGER
- 84U. KEN GRIFFEY
- 85U. RICK MAHLER
- 86U. ROLANDO ROOMES
- 87U. SCOTT SCUDDER

CLEVELAND INDIANS

- 24U. KEITH ATHERTON
- 25U. JOEY BELLE
- 26U. JERRY BROWNE
- 27U. FELIX FERMIN
- 28U. BRAD KOMMINSK
- 29U. PETE O'BRIEN

DETROIT TIGERS

- 30U. MIKE BRUMLEY
- 31U. TRACY JONES
- 32U. MIKE SCHWABE
- 33U. GARY WARD
- 34U. FRANK WILLIAMS

HOUSTON ASTROS

- 88U. JIM CLANCY
- 89U. RICH RHODEN
- 90U. DAN SCHATZEDER

KANSAS CITY ROYALS

- 35U. KEVIN APPIER
- 36U. BOB BOONE
- 37U. LUIS DE LOS SANTOS
- 38U. JIM EISENREICH

LOS ANGELES DODGERS

- 91U. MIKE MORGAN
- 92U. EDDIE MURRAY
- 93U. WILLIE RANDOLPH
- 94U. RAY SEARAGE

MILWAUKEE BREWERS

- 39U. JAIME NAVARRO
- 40U. BILL SPIERS
- 41U. GREG VAUGHN
- 42U. RANDY VERES

BILL SPIERS
INFIELD
FLEER

MINNESOTA TWINS

- 43U. WALLY BACKMAN
- 44U. SHANE RAWLEY

MONTREAL EXPOS

- 95U. MIKE ALDRETE
- 96U. KEVIN GROSS
- 97U. MARK LANGSTON
- 98U. SPIKE OWEN
- 99U. ZANE SMITH

NEW YORK METS

- 100U. DON AASE
- 101U. BARRY LYONS
- 102U. JUAN SAMUEL
- 103U. WALLY WHITEHURST

NEW YORK YANKEES

- 45U. STEVE BALBONI
- 46U. JESSE BARFIELD
- 47U. ALVARO ESPINOZA
- 48U. BOB GEREN
- 49U. MEL HALL
- 50U. ANDY HAWKINS
- 51U. HENSLEY MEULENS
- 52U. STEVE SAX
- 53U. DEION SANDERS

OAKLAND A'S

- 54U. RICKEY HENDERSON
- 55U. MIKE MOORE
- 56U. TONY PHILLIPS

PHILADELPHIA PHILLIES

- 104U. DENNIS COOK
- 105U. LENNY DYKSTRA
- 106U. CHARLIE HAYES
- 107U. TOMMY HERR
- 108U. KEN HOWELL
- 109U. JOHN KRUK
- 110U. ROGER MCDOWELL
- 111U. TERRY MULHOLLAND
- 112U. JEFF PARRETT
- 131U. MIKE SCHMIDT

PITTSBURGH PIRATES

- 113U. NEAL HEATON
- 114U. JEFF KING
- 115U. RANDY KRAMER
- 116U. BILL LANDRUM

DAN QUISENBERRY
PITCHER
FLEER

ST. LOUIS CARDINALS

- 117U. CRIS CARPENTER
- 118U. FRANK DIPINO
- 119U. KEN HILL
- 120U. DAN QUISENBERRY
- 121U. MILT THOMPSON
- 122U. TODD ZEILE

SAN DIEGO PADRES

- 123U. JACK CLARK
- 124U. BRUCE HURST
- 125U. MARK PARENT
- 126U. BIP ROBERTS

SAN FRANCISCO GIANTS

- 127U. JEFF BRANTLEY
- 128U. TERRY KENNEDY
- 129U. MIKE LACOSS
- 130U. GREG LITTON

SEATTLE MARINERS

- 57U. GREG BRILEY
- 58U. GENE HARRIS
- 59U. RANDY JOHNSON
- 60U. JEFFREY LWONARD
- 61U. DENNIS POWELL
- 62U. OMAR VIZQUEL

TEXAS RANGERS

- 63U. KEVIN BROWN
- 64U. JULIO FRANCO
- 65U. JAMIE MOYER
- 66U. RAFAEL PALMEIRO
- 67U. NOLAN RYAN

TORONTO BLUE JAYS

- 68U. FRANCISCO CABRERA
- 69U. JUNIOR FELIX
- 70U. AL LEITER
- 71U. ALEX SANCHEZ

1990 FLEER (660)
2 1/2 X 3 1/2

FLEER'90
Orioles
Gregg Olson PITCHER

ATLANTA BRAVES

- 574. JOSE ALVAREZ
- 575. GERONIMO BERROA
- 576. JEFF BLAUSER
- 577. JOE BOEVER
- 578. MARTY CLARY
- 579. JODY DAVIS
- 580. MARK EICHHORN
- 581. DARRELL EVANS
- 582. RON GANT
- 583. TOM GLAVINE
- 584. TOMMY GREENE
- 585. TOMMY GREGG
- 586. DAVID JUSTICE
- 587. MARK LEMKE
- 588. DEREK LILLIQUIST
- 589. ODDIBE MCDOWELL
- 590. KENT MERCKER
- 591. DALE MURPHY
- 592. GERALD PERRY
- 593. LONNIE SMITH
- 594. PETE SMITH
- 595. JOHN SMOLTZ
- 596. MIKE STANTON
- 597. ANDRES THOMAS
- 598. JEFF TREADWAY
- 642. KELLY MANN (P)
- 660. TEAM CHECKLIST (F)

BALTIMORE ORIOLES

- [ ] 172. BRADY ANDERSON
- [ ] 173. JEFF BALLARD
- [ ] 174. PHIL BRADLEY
- [ ] 175. MIKE DEVEREAUX
- [ ] 176. STEVE FINLEY
- [ ] 177. PETE HARNISCH
- [ ] 178. KEVIN HICKEY
- [ ] 179. BRIAN HOLTON
- [ ] 180. BEN MCDONALD
- [ ] 181. BOB MELVIN
- [ ] 182. BOB MILACKI
- [ ] 183. RANDY MILLIGAN
- [ ] 184. GREGG OLSON
- [ ] 185. JOE ORSULAK
- [ ] 186. BILL RIPKEN
- [ ] 187. CAL RIPKEN, JR.
- [ ] 188. DAVE SCHMIDT
- [ ] 189. LARRY SHEETS
- [ ] 190. MICKEY TETTLETON
- [ ] 191. MARK THURMOND
- [ ] 192. JAY TIBBS
- [ ] 193. JIM TRABER
- [ ] 194. MARK WILLIAMSON
- [ ] 195. CRAIG WORTHINGTON
- [ ] 655. TEAM CHECKLIST (B)

BOSTON RED SOX

- [ ] 266. MARTY BARRETT
- [ ] 267. MIKE BODDICKER
- [ ] 268. WADE BOGGS
- [ ] 269. ELLIS BURKS
- [ ] 270. RICK CERONE
- [ ] 271. ROGER CLEMENS
- [ ] 272. JOHN DOPSON
- [ ] 273. NICK ESASKY
- [ ] 274. DWIGHT EVANS
- [ ] 275. WES GARDNER
- [ ] 276. RICH GEDMAN
- [ ] 277. MIKE GREENWELL
- [ ] 278. DANNY HEEP
- [ ] 279. ERIC HETZEL
- [ ] 280. DENNIS LAMP
- [ ] 281. ROB MURPHY
- [ ] 282. JOE PRICE
- [ ] 283. CARLOS QUINTANA
- [ ] 284. JODY REED
- [ ] 285. LUIS RIVERA
- [ ] 286. KEVIN ROMINE
- [ ] 287. LEE SMITH
- [ ] 288. MIKE SMITHSON
- [ ] 289. BOB STANLEY
- [ ] 648. DANA WILLIAMS (P)
- [ ] 656. TEAM CHECKLIST (B)

CALIFORNIA ANGELS

- [ ] 125. JIM ABBOTT
- [ ] 126. TONY ARMAS
- [ ] 127. DANTE BICHETTE
- [ ] 128. BERT BLYLEVEN
- [ ] 129. CHILI DAVIS
- [ ] 130. BRIAN DOWNING
- [ ] 131. MIKE FETTERS
- [ ] 132. CHUCK FINLEY
- [ ] 133. WILLIE FRASER
- [ ] 134. BRYAN HARVEY
- [ ] 135. JACK HOWELL
- [ ] 136. WALLY JOYNER
- [ ] 137. JEFF MANTO
- [ ] 138. KIRK MCCASKILL
- [ ] 139. BOB MCCLURE
- [ ] 140. GREG MINTON
- [ ] 141. LANCE PARRISH
- [ ] 142. DAN PETRY
- [ ] 143. JOHNNY RAY
- [ ] 144. DICK SCHOFIELD
- [ ] 145. LEE STEVENS
- [ ] 146. CLAUDELL WASHINGTON
- [ ] 147. DEVON WHITE
- [ ] 148. MIKE WITT
- [ ] 640. COLIN CHARLAND (P)
- [ ] 647. JOHN ORTON (P)
- [ ] 648. RICH MONTELEONE (P)
- [ ] 651. BOBBY ROSE (P)
- [ ] 655. TEAM CHECKLIST (F)

CHICAGO CUBS

- [ ] 25. PAUL ASSENMACHER
- [ ] 26. DAMON BERRYHILL
- [ ] 27. MIKE BIELECKI
- [ ] 28. KEVIN BLANKENSHIP
- [ ] 29. ANDRE DAWSON
- [ ] 30. SHAWON DUNSTON
- [ ] 31. JOE GIRARDI
- [ ] 32. MARK GRACE
- [ ] 33. MIKE HARKEY
- [ ] 34. PAUL KILGUS
- [ ] 35. LES LANCASTER
- [ ] 36. VANCE LAW
- [ ] 37. GREG MADDUX
- [ ] 38. LLOYD MCCLENDON
- [ ] 39. JEFF PICO
- [ ] 40. RYNE SANDBERG
- [ ] 41. SCOTT SANDERSON
- [ ] 42. DWIGHT SMITH
- [ ] 43. RICK SUTCLIFFE
- [ ] 44. JEROME WALTON
- [ ] 45. MITCH WEBSTER
- [ ] 46. CURT WILKERSON
- [ ] 47. DEAN WILKINS
- [ ] 48. MITCH WILLIAMS
- [ ] 49. STEVE WILSON
- [ ] 643. GREG SMITH (P)
- [ ] 645. DERRICK MAY (P)
- [ ] 654. TEAM CHECKLIST (F)

CHICAGO WHITE SOX

- [ ] 529. IVAN CALDERON
- [ ] 530. CARLTON FISK
- [ ] 531. SCOTT FLETCHER
- [ ] 532. DAVE GALLAGHER
- [ ] 533. OZZIE GUILLEN
- [ ] 534. GREG HIBBARD
- [ ] 535. SHAWN HILLEGAS
- [ ] 536. LANCE JOHNSON
- [ ] 537. ERIC KING
- [ ] 538. RON KITTLE
- [ ] 539. STEVE LYONS
- [ ] 540. CARLOS MARTINEZ
- [ ] 541. TOM MCCARTHY
- [ ] 542. MATT MERULLO
- [ ] 543. DONN PALL
- [ ] 544. DAN PASQUA
- [ ] 545. KEN PATTERSON
- [ ] 546. MELIDO PEREZ
- [ ] 547. STEVE ROSENBERG
- [ ] 548. SAMMY SOSA
- [ ] 549. BOBBY THIGPEN
- [ ] 550. ROBIN VENTURA
- [ ] 551. GREG WALKER
- [ ] 644. TOM DREES (P)
- [ ] 652. WAYNE EDWARDS (P)
- [ ] 659. TEAM CHECKLIST (B)

CINCINNATI REDS

- [ ] 412. JACK ARMSTRONG
- [ ] 413. TODD BENZINGER
- [ ] 414. TIM BIRTSAS
- [ ] 415. TOM BROWNING
- [ ] 416. NORM CHARLTON
- [ ] 417. ERIC DAVIS
- [ ] 418. ROB DIBBLE
- [ ] 419. JOHN FRANCO
- [ ] 420. KEN GRIFFEY
- [ ] 421. CHRIS HAMMOND
- [ ] 422. DANNY JACKSON
- [ ] 423. BARRY LARKIN
- [ ] 424. TIM LEARY
- [ ] 425. RICK MAHLER
- [ ] 426. JOE OLIVER
- [ ] 427. PAUL O'NEILL
- [ ] 428. LUIS QUINONES
- [ ] 429. JEFF REED
- [ ] 430. JOSE RIJO
- [ ] 431. RON ROBINSON
- [ ] 432. ROLANDO ROOMES
- [ ] 433. CHRIS SABO
- [ ] 434. SCOTT SCUDDER
- [ ] 435. HERM WINNINGHAM
- [ ] 645. MIKE ROESLER (P)
- [ ] 658. TEAM CHECKLIST (F)

CLEVELAND INDIANS

- [ ] 483. ANDY ALLANSON
- [ ] 484. SCOTT BAILES
- [ ] 485. JOEY BELLE
- [ ] 486. BUD BLACK
- [ ] 487. JERRY BROWNE
- [ ] 488. TOM CANDIOTTI
- [ ] 489. JOE CARTER
- [ ] 490. DAVID CLARK
- [ ] 491. JOHN FARRELL
- [ ] 492. FELIX FERMIN
- [ ] 493. BROOK JACOBY
- [ ] 494. DION JAMES
- [ ] 495. DOUG JONES
- [ ] 496. BRAD KOMMINSK
- [ ] 497. ROD NICHOLS
- [ ] 498. PETE O'BRIEN
- [ ] 499. STEVE OLIN
- [ ] 500. JESSE OROSCO
- [ ] 501. JOEL SKINNER
- [ ] 502. CORY SNYDER
- [ ] 503. GREG SWINDELL
- [ ] 504. RICH YETT
- [ ] 640. RUDY SEANEZ (P)
- [ ] 659. TEAM CHECKLIST (F)

DETROIT TIGERS

- [ ] 599. DOYLE ALEXANDER
- [ ] 600. DAVE BERGMAN
- [ ] 601. BRIAN DUBOIS
- [ ] 602. PAUL GIBSON
- [ ] 603. MIKE HEATH
- [ ] 604. MIKE HENNEMAN
- [ ] 605. GUILLERMO HERNANDEZ
- [ ] 606. SHAWN HOLMAN
- [ ] 607. TRACY JONES
- [ ] 608. CHET LEMON
- [ ] 609. FRED LYNN
- [ ] 610. JACK MORRIS
- [ ] 611. MATT NOKES
- [ ] 612. GARY PETTIS
- [ ] 613. KEVIN RITZ
- [ ] 614. JEFF ROBINSON
- [ ] 615. STEVE SEARCY
- [ ] 616. FRANK TANANA
- [ ] 617. ALAN TRAMMELL
- [ ] 618. GARY WARD
- [ ] 619. LOU WHITAKER
- [ ] 620. FRANK WILLIAMS
- [ ] 660. TEAM CHECKLIST (F)

HOUSTON ASTROS

- [ ] 220. JUAN AGOSTO
- [ ] 221. LARRY ANDERSEN
- [ ] 222. ERIC ANTHONY
- [ ] 223. KEVIN BASS
- [ ] 224. CRAIG BIGGIO
- [ ] 225. KEN CAMINITI
- [ ] 226. JIM CLANCY
- [ ] 227. DANNY DARWIN
- [ ] 228. GLENN DAVIS
- [ ] 229. JIM DESHAIES
- [ ] 230. BILL DORAN
- [ ] 231. BOB FORSCH
- [ ] 232. BRIAN MEYER
- [ ] 233. TERRY PUHL
- [ ] 234. RAFAEL RAMIREZ
- [ ] 235. RICK RHODEN
- [ ] 236. DAN SCHATZEDER
- [ ] 237. MIKE SCOTT
- [ ] 238. DAVE SMITH
- [ ] 239. ALEX TREVINO
- [ ] 240. GLENN WILSON
- [ ] 241. GERALD YOUNG
- [ ] 656. TEAM CHECKLIST (F)

KANSAS CITY ROYALS

- [ ] 100. KEVIN APPIER
- [ ] 101. LUIS AQUINO
- [ ] 102. BOB BOONE
- [ ] 103. GEORGE BRETT
- [ ] 104. JOSE DEJESUS
- [ ] 105. LUIS DE LOS SANTOS
- [ ] 106. JIM EISENREICH
- [ ] 107. STEVE FARR
- [ ] 108. TOM GORDON

☐ 109. MARK GUBICZA
☐ 110. BO JACKSON
☐ 111. TERRY LEACH
☐ 112. CHARLIE LEIBRANDT
☐ 113. RICH LUECKEN
☐ 114. MIKE MACFARLANE
☐ 115. JEFF MONTGOMERY
☐ 116. BRET SABERHAGEN
☐ 117. KEVIN SEITZER
☐ 118. KURT STILLWELL
☐ 119. PAT TABLER
☐ 120. DANNY TARTABULL
☐ 121. GARY THURMAN
☐ 122. FRANK WHITE
☐ 123. WILLIE WILSON
☐ 124. MATT WINTERS
☐ 655. TEAM CHECKLIST (F)

LOS ANGELES DODGERS

☐ 389. TIM BELCHER
☐ 390. TIM CREWS
☐ 391. MIKE DAVIS
☐ 392. RICK DEMPSEY
☐ 393. KIRK GIBSON
☐ 394. JOSE GONZALEZ
☐ 395. ALFREDO GRIFFIN
☐ 396. JEFF HAMILTON
☐ 397. LENNY HARRIS
☐ 398. MICKEY HATCHER
☐ 399. OREL HERSHISER
☐ 400. JAY HOWELL
☐ 401. MIKE MARSHALL
☐ 402. RAMON MARTINEZ
☐ 403. MIKE MORGAN
☐ 404. EDDIE MURRAY
☐ 405. ALEJANDRO PENA
☐ 406. WILLIE RANDOLPH
☐ 407. MIKE SCIOSCIA
☐ 408. RAY SEARAGE
☐ 409. FERNANDO VALENZUELA
☐ 410. JOSE VIZCAINO
☐ 411. JOHN WETTELAND
☐ 642. DAVE HANSEN (P)
☐ 649. MIKE HUFF (P)
☐ 651. MIKE HARTLEY (P)
☐ 658. TEAM CHECKLIST (F)

MILWAUKEE BREWERS

☐ 316. CHRIS BOSIO
☐ 317. GLENN BRAGGS
☐ 318. GREG BROCK
☐ 319. CHUCK CRIM
☐ 320. ROB DEER
☐ 321. MIKE FELDER
☐ 322. TOM FILER
☐ 323. TONY FOSSAS
☐ 324. JIM GANTNER
☐ 325. DARRYL HAMILTON
☐ 326. TED HIGUERA
☐ 327. MARK KNUDSON
☐ 328. BILL KRUEGER
☐ 329. TIM MCINTOSH
☐ 330. PAUL MOLITOR
☐ 331. JAIME NAVARRO
☐ 332. CHARLIE O'BRIEN
☐ 333. JEFF PETEREK
☐ 334. DAN PLESAC
☐ 335. JERRY REUSS
☐ 336. GARY SHEFFIELD
☐ 337. BILL SPIERS
☐ 338. B. J. SURHOFF
☐ 339. GREG VAUGHN
☐ 340. ROBIN YOUNT
☐ 641. GEORGE CANALE (P)
☐ 651. TEAM CHECKLIST (F)

MINNESOTA TWINS

☐ 365. RICK AGUILERA
☐ 366. ALLAN ANDERSON
☐ 367. WALLY BACKMAN
☐ 368. DOUG BAKER
☐ 369. JUAN BERENGUER
☐ 370. RANDY BUSH
☐ 371. CARMEN CASTILLO
☐ 372. MIKE DYER
☐ 373. GARY GAETTI
☐ 374. GREG GAGNE
☐ 375. DAN GLADDEN

☐ 376. GERMAN GONZALEZ
☐ 377. BRIAN HARPER
☐ 378. KENT HRBEK
☐ 379. GENE LARKIN
☐ 380. TIM LAUDNER
☐ 381. JOHN MOSES
☐ 382. AL NEWMAN
☐ 383. KIRBY PUCKETT
☐ 384. SHANE RAWLEY
☐ 385. JEFF REARDON
☐ 386. ROY SMITH
☐ 387. GARY WAYNE
☐ 388. DAVE WEST
☐ 647. SCOTT LEIUS (P)
☐ 657. TEAM CHECKLIST (B)

MONTREAL EXPOS

☐ 341. HUBIE BROOKS
☐ 342. TIM BURKE
☐ 343. MIKE FITZGERALD
☐ 344. TOM FOLEY
☐ 345. ANDRES GALARRAGA
☐ 346. DAMASO GARCIA
☐ 347. MARQUIS GRISSOM
☐ 348. KEVIN GROSS
☐ 349. JOE HESKETH
☐ 350. JEFF HUSON
☐ 351. WALLACE JOHNSON
☐ 352. MARK LANGSTON
☐ 353. DAVE MARTINEZ
☐ 354. DENNIS MARTINEZ
☐ 355. ANDY MCGAFFIGAN
☐ 356. OTIS NIXON
☐ 357. SPIKE OWEN
☐ 358. PASCUAL PEREZ
☐ 359. TIM RAINES
☐ 360. NELSON SANTOVENIA
☐ 361. BRYN SMITH
☐ 362. ZANE SMITH
☐ 363. LARRY WALKER
☐ 364. TIM WALLACH
☐ 646. MARK GARDNER (P)
☐ 649. STEVE FREY (P)
☐ 653. DELINO DESHIELDS (P)
☐ 657. TEAM CHECKLIST (B)

NEW YORK METS

☐ 196. DON AASE
☐ 197. BLAINE BEATTY
☐ 198. MARK CARREON
☐ 199. GARY CARTER
☐ 200. DAVID CONE
☐ 201. RON DARLING
☐ 202. KEVIN ELSTER
☐ 203. SID FERNANDEZ
☐ 204. DWIGHT GOODEN
☐ 205. KEITH HERNANDEZ
☐ 206. JEFF INNIS
☐ 207. GREGG JEFFERIES
☐ 208. HOWARD JOHNSON
☐ 209. BARRY LYONS
☐ 210. DAVE MAGADAN
☐ 211. KEVIN MCREYNOLDS
☐ 212. JEFF MUSSELMAN
☐ 213. RANDY MYERS
☐ 214. BOB OJEDA
☐ 215. JUAN SAMUEL
☐ 216. MACKEY SASSER
☐ 217. DARRYL STRAWBERRY
☐ 218. TIM TEUFEL
☐ 219. FRANK VIOLA
☐ 656. TEAM CHECKLIST (F)

NEW YORK YANKEES

☐ 436. STEVE BALBONI
☐ 437. JESSE BARFIELD
☐ 438. MIKE BLOWERS
☐ 439. TOM BROOKENS
☐ 440. GREG CADARET
☐ 441. ALVARO ESPINOZA
☐ 442. BOB GEREN
☐ 443. LEE GUETTERMAN
☐ 444. MEL HALL
☐ 445. ANDY HAWKINS
☐ 446. ROBERTO KELLY
☐ 447. DON MATTINGLY
☐ 448. LANCE MCCULLERS
☐ 449. HENSLEY MEULENS
☐ 450. DALE MOHORCIC

☐ 451. CLAY PARKER
☐ 452. ERIC PLUNK
☐ 453. DAVE RIGHETTI
☐ 454. DEION SANDERS
☐ 455. STEVE SAX
☐ 456. DON SLAUGHT
☐ 457. WALT TERRELL
☐ 458. DAVE WINFIELD
☐ 641. KEVIN MAAS (P)
☐ 658. TEAM CHECKLIST (B)

OAKLAND A'S

☐   1. LANCE BLANKENSHIP
☐   2. TODD BURNS
☐   3. JOSE CANSECO
☐   4. JIM CORSI
☐   5. STORM DAVIS
☐   6. DENNIS ECKERSLEY
☐   7. MIKE GALLEGO
☐   8. RON HASSEY
☐   9. DAVE HENDERSON
☐ 10. RICKEY HENDERSON
☐ 11. RICK HONEYCUTT
☐ 12. STAN JAVIER
☐ 13. FELIX JOSE
☐ 14. CARNEY LANSFORD
☐ 15. MARK MCGWIRE
☐ 16. MIKE MOORE
☐ 17. GENE NELSON
☐ 18. DAVE PARKER
☐ 19. TONY PHILLIPS
☐ 20. TERRY STEINBACH
☐ 21. DAVE STEWART
☐ 22. WALT WEISS
☐ 23. BOB WELCH
☐ 24. CURT YOUNG
☐ 644. DANN HOWITT (P)
☐ 646. SCOTT HEMOND (P)
☐ 654. TEAM CHECKLIST (F)

PHILADELPHIA PHILLIES

☐ 552. DON CARMAN
☐ 553. PAT COMBS
☐ 554. DENNIS COOK
☐ 555. DARREN DAULTON
☐ 556. LENNY DYKSTRA
☐ 557. CURT FORD
☐ 558. CHARLIE HAYES
☐ 559. VON HAYES
☐ 560. TOM HERR
☐ 561. KEN HOWELL
☐ 562. STEVE JELTZ
☐ 563. RON JONES
☐ 564. RICKY JORDAN
☐ 565. JOHN KRUK
☐ 566. STEVE LAKE
☐ 567. ROGER MCDOWELL
☐ 568. TERRY MULHOLLAND
☐ 569. DWAYNE MURPHY
☐ 570. JEFF PARRETT
☐ 571. RANDY READY
☐ 572. BRUCE RUFFIN
☐ 573. DICKIE THON
☐ 650. CHUCK MCELROY (P)
☐ 653. JASON GRIMSLEY (P)
☐ 659. TEAM CHECKLIST (B)

1990 Fleer

PITTSBURGH PIRATES

- ☐ 459. JAY BELL
- ☐ 460. RAFAEL BELLIARD
- ☐ 461. BARRY BONDS
- ☐ 462. BOBBY BONILLA
- ☐ 463. SID BREAM
- ☐ 464. BENNY DISTEFANO
- ☐ 465. DOUG DRABEK
- ☐ 466. JIM GOTT
- ☐ 467. BILLY HATCHER
- ☐ 468. NEAL HEATON
- ☐ 469. JEFF KING
- ☐ 470. BOB KIPPER
- ☐ 471. RANDY KRAMER
- ☐ 472. BILL LANDRUM
- ☐ 473. MIKE LAVALLIERE
- ☐ 474. JOSE LIND
- ☐ 475. JUNIOR ORTIZ
- ☐ 476. GARY REDUS
- ☐ 477. RICK REED
- ☐ 478. R. J. REYNOLDS
- ☐ 479. JEFF ROBINSON
- ☐ 480. JOHN SMILEY
- ☐ 481. ANDY VAN SLYKE
- ☐ 482. BOB WALK
- ☐ 650. MOISES ALOU (P)
- ☐ 658. TEAM CHECKLIST (B)

ST. LOUIS CARDINALS

- ☐ 242. TOM BRUNANSKY
- ☐ 243. CRIS CARPENTER
- ☐ 244. ALEX COLE
- ☐ 245. VINCE COLEMAN
- ☐ 246. JOHN COSTELLO
- ☐ 247. KEN DAYLEY
- ☐ 248. JOSE DELEON
- ☐ 249. FRANK DIPINO
- ☐ 250. PEDRO GUERRERO
- ☐ 251. KEN HILL
- ☐ 252. JOE MAGRANE
- ☐ 253. WILLIE MCGEE
- ☐ 254. JOHN MORRIS
- ☐ 255. JOSE OQUENDO
- ☐ 256. TONY PENA
- ☐ 257. TERRY PENDLETON
- ☐ 258. TED POWER
- ☐ 259. DAN QUISENBERRY
- ☐ 260. OZZIE SMITH
- ☐ 261. SCOTT TERRY
- ☐ 262. MILT THOMPSON
- ☐ 263. DENNY WALLING
- ☐ 264. TODD WORRELL
- ☐ 265. TODD ZEILE
- ☐ 652. MATT KINZER (P)
- ☐ 656. TEAM CHECKLIST (B)

SAN DIEGO PADRES

- ☐ 149. ROBERTO ALOMAR
- ☐ 150. SANDY ALOMAR, JR.
- ☐ 151. ANDY BENES
- ☐ 152. JACK CLARK
- ☐ 153. PAT CLEMENTS
- ☐ 154. JOEY CORA
- ☐ 155. MARK DAVIS
- ☐ 156. MARK GRANT
- ☐ 157. TONY GWYNN
- ☐ 158. GREG HARRIS
- ☐ 159. BRUCE HURST
- ☐ 160. DARRIN JACKSON
- ☐ 161. CHRIS JAMES
- ☐ 162. CARMELO MARTINEZ
- ☐ 163. MIKE PAGLIARULO
- ☐ 164. MARK PARENT
- ☐ 165. DENNIS RASMUSSEN
- ☐ 166. BIP ROBERTS
- ☐ 167. BENITO SANTIAGO
- ☐ 168. CALVIN SCHIRALDI
- ☐ 169. ERIC SHOW
- ☐ 170. GARRY TEMPLETON
- ☐ 171. ED WHITSON
- ☐ 655. TEAM CHECKLIST (B)

SAN FRANCISCO GIANTS

- ☐ 50. STEVE BEDROSIAN
- ☐ 51. MIKE BENJAMIN
- ☐ 52. JEFF BRANTLEY
- ☐ 53. BRETT BUTLER

- ☐ 54. WILL CLARK
- ☐ 55. KELLY DOWNS
- ☐ 56. SCOTT GARRELTS
- ☐ 57. ATLEE HAMMAKER
- ☐ 58. TERRY KENNEDY
- ☐ 59. MIKE LACOSS
- ☐ 60. CRAIG LEFFERTS
- ☐ 61. GREG LITTON
- ☐ 62. CANDY MALDONADO
- ☐ 63. KIRT MANWARING
- ☐ 64. RANDY MCCAMENT
- ☐ 65. KEVIN MITCHELL
- ☐ 66. DONELL NIXON
- ☐ 67. KEN OBERKFELL
- ☐ 68. RICK REUSCHEL
- ☐ 69. ERNEST RILES
- ☐ 70. DON ROBINSON
- ☐ 71. PAT SHERIDAN
- ☐ 72. CHRIS SPEIER
- ☐ 73. ROBBY THOMPSON
- ☐ 74. JOSE URIBE
- ☐ 75. MATT WILLIAMS
- ☐ 643. STU TATE (P)
- ☐ 654. TEAM CHECKLIST (B)

SEATTLE MARINERS

- ☐ 505. SCOTT BANKHEAD
- ☐ 506. SCOTT BRADLEY
- ☐ 507. GREG BRILEY
- ☐ 508. JAY BUHNER
- ☐ 509. DARNELL COLES
- ☐ 510. KEITH COMSTOCK
- ☐ 511. HENRY COTTO
- ☐ 512. ALVIN DAVIS
- ☐ 513. KEN GRIFFEY, JR.
- ☐ 514. ERIK HANSON
- ☐ 515. GENE HARRIS
- ☐ 516. BRIAN HOLMAN
- ☐ 517. MIKE JACKSON
- ☐ 518. RANDY JOHNSON
- ☐ 519. JEFFREY LEONARD
- ☐ 520. EDGAR MARTINEZ
- ☐ 521. DENNIS POWELL
- ☐ 522. JIM PRESLEY
- ☐ 523. JERRY REED
- ☐ 524. HAROLD REYNOLDS
- ☐ 525. MIKE SCHOOLER
- ☐ 526. BILL SWIFT
- ☐ 527. DAVID VALLE
- ☐ 528. OMAR VIZQUEL
- ☐ 659. TEAM CHECKLIST (F)

TEXAS RANGERS

- ☐ 290. HAROLD BAINES
- ☐ 291. KEVIN BROWN
- ☐ 292. STEVE BUECHELE
- ☐ 293. SCOTT COOLBAUGH
- ☐ 294. JACK DAUGHERTY
- ☐ 295. CECIL ESPY
- ☐ 296. JULIO FRANCO
- ☐ 297. JUAN GONZALEZ
- ☐ 298. CECILIO GUANTE
- ☐ 299. DREW HALL
- ☐ 300. CHARLIE HOUGH
- ☐ 301. PETE INCAVIGLIA
- ☐ 302. MIKE JEFFCOAT
- ☐ 303. CHAD KREUTER
- ☐ 304. JEFF KUNKEL
- ☐ 305. RICK LEACH
- ☐ 306. FRED MANRIQUE
- ☐ 307. JAMIE MOYER
- ☐ 308. RAFAEL PALMEIRO
- ☐ 309. GENO PETRALLI
- ☐ 310. KEVIN REIMER
- ☐ 311. KENNY ROGERS
- ☐ 312. JEFF RUSSELL
- ☐ 313. NOLAN RYAN
- ☐ 314. RUBEN SIERRA
- ☐ 315. BOBBY WITT
- ☐ 657. TEAM CHECKLIST (F)

1st Full Time Dealer - Starting May 1, 1970

1982 & 1983 MIDWEST LEAGUE CARDS PRINTED AND DISTRIBUTED BY FRITSCH CARDS

Jose Canseco 40-40 Special

1983 Madison Muskie set contains Jose Canseco, baseball's only 40-40 man ever, 1987 Rookie of the Year, and Oakland Bash Brother. Canseco's first card.

l set	$30.00
5 sets	$125.00
l0 sets	$200.00

Kirby Puckett Special

1983 Visalia Oaks set contains Kirby Puckett. Puckett has proven himself as a constant threat both offensively and defensively. Was voted major leagues best all around player by Major League Baseball Players Association in 1989. Puckett's first card.

1 set	$60.00
5 sets	$275.00
10 sets	$500.00

Devon White Special

Both the 1982 Danville Suns and 1983 Peoria Suns sets contain Angel's surprising young star, Devon White. Take advantage of this Devon White special and collect his first two cards.

1 set each	$19.00
5 sets each	$90.00
10 sets each	$175.00

White Sox Special

Two more solid big-leaguers to come from the midwest league farms. The 1982 Appleton set contains White Sox's Daryl Boston while the 1983 Appleton set contains White Sox's Ron Karkovice. A must for a White Sox fan.

1 set	$12.00
5 sets each	$57.50
10 sets each	$100.00

Other 1982 and 1983 Midwest League Teams

1982 Teams		Each	10 sets	25 sets
Clinton Giants (32)	Grant, Nokes, Ouellette	$15.00	$120.00	$262.50
Springfield Cardinals (24)	Cox, Hunt, Lyons	$ 8.00	$ 52.00	$114.00
Wausau Timbers (Mariners-31)	Calderon, Nixon	$ 7.50	$ 40.00	$ 87.50
All 10 1982 Teams		$ 60.00	$350.00	$750.00

1983 Teams		Each	10 sets	25 sets
Burlington Rangers (30)	Brower, Guzman, Buckley, Cook	$ 6.00	$ 38.00	$ 79.00
Cedar Rapids Reds (26)	Murphy, Daniels	$15.00	$ 80.00	$175.00
Clinton Giants (30)	Powell	$10.00	$ 60.00	$131.00
WI Rapids Twins (28)	Anderson	$10.00	$ 60.00	$131.00
All 12 1983 Teams		$140.00	$1000.00	NA

A complete checklist of the 1982 and 1983 Midwest League Teams is available for 50¢ each year and a SASE (self-addressed stamped envelope).

Brewer Special

Both the 1982 and 1983 Beloit teams have proven to be very beneficial to the Milwaukee Brewers. In all six players have at one time played for Milwaukee. Two of the best to come from these teams are Bill Wegman from the 1982 set and Chris Bosio from the 1983.

l set each	$16.50
5 sets each	$77.50
10 sets each	$150.00

Sleeper Special

Included in our Sleeper Special are 5 teams which have few players to have proven themselves in the Big Leagues as of late. Who knows there could be another Canseco or Puckett in one of these sets!!

	Each	10 Sets	25 Sets
1982 Burlington Rangers (30)	$5.00	$30.00	$66.00
1982 Madison Muskies (A's) (34)	$5.00	$30.00	$66.00
1982 Waterloo Indians (28)	$5.00	$30.00	$66.00
1983 Waterloo Indians (29)	$5.00	$24.00	$52.50
1983 Wausau Timbers (Mariners) (31)	$5.00	$24.00	$52.50

New York Yankee Special

The 1982 Wisconsin Rapids set contains Yankee shortstop Alvaro Espinoza while the 1983 Springfield set contains Yankee catcher Bob Geren. Both Espinoza and Geren have proven themselves as solid Major Leaguers and should contribute much to the Yankee line-up.

1 set each	$11.00
5 sets each	$50.00
10 sets each	$95.00

MILWAUKEE BRAVES HISTORY BOOK

No one has ever recorded the history of the Milwaukee Braves in a book—UNTIL NOW! **The Milwaukee Braves: A Baseball Eulogy** revives the Milwaukee Miracle, 1953-1965, in 415 pages, including 125 Vintage photographs and a foreword by Hall of Fame third baseman Eddie Mathews.

The Braves, ugly ducklings in Boston in 1952, were transformed into beautiful swans the moment they donned Milwaukee uniforms. In a new stadium, in a new city, they established new attendance records and brought excitement to a National League pennant race that had become the private domain of New York City.

In their thirteen-year Milwaukee existence, the Braves won two pennants, one World Series, and the hearts of baseball fans everywhere. They sent three of their players to the Hall of Fame and produced:

Four no-hitters, the man who smashed Babe Ruth's career home run record, the greatest left-handed pitcher of all time, the NL's sluggingest third baseman and the greatest single-game home run performance by one hitter.

Twice they were the victim of no-hitters, one a 12-inning perfect game, yet they won both contests. And amazingly, unique among professional sports franchises, they never suffered a losing season.

This book brings back the golden days when baseball immortals strode the basepaths—legendary figures like Stan Musial, Warren Spahn, Duke Snider, Jackie Robinson, Hank Aaron, Mickey Mantle, and many more.

If you're a baseball fan, you will never forget this book. The book is available in both hard and soft cover editions.

Braves Book (soft cover) $12.95
Braves Book (hard cover) $19.95

CHECK POLICY:
All personal checks will be held 15 working days for clearance. For faster service, please send postal money orders.

CANADA CUSTOMERS:
Please send Postal Money Order in U.S. Funds only, and an additional $6.00 per set for sets over 250 cards, $3.00 per set for sets under 250 cards for shipping your sets.

ALASKA, HAWAII, PUERTO RICO, APO, FPO & P.O. CUSTOMERS:
Add an additional $4.00 per set for sets over 250 cards and $2.50 per set for sets under 250 cards for shipping your sets. (If you have a P.O. Box and want your order shipped via UPS, please include your UPS shipping address).

SHIPPING AND INSURANCE TABLE

$ .01 To $25.00	add $2.95
$25.01 To $50.00	add $3.95
$50.01 And Over	add $4.95

Canada, Alaska, Hawaii, Puerto Rico,
APO, FPO and P.O. Box Customers
see to left for additional fee.

LARRY FRITSCH CARDS

OUR 43nd YEAR IN CARDS

735 Old Wausau Road
P.O. Box 863, DEPT. 594
Stevens Point, WI 54481
(715) 344-8687 (cards issued 1981-present)
(715) 344-0821 (cards issued prior to 1981)
See our inside front cover ad for other items we have in stock.

WITH OVER 35 MILLION CARDS IN STOCK...WE HAVE AMERICA'S MOST COMPLETE STOCK OF SPORTS TRADING CARDS. Full money back guarantee if you are not completely satisfied with our service and products. YOU, the customers are always NO 1 to us!

To receive Super Service it is necessary to send a POSTAL MONEY ORDER with your order.
(All personal checks are held 15 days for clearance)
(Charge orders add 5% to total)
Minimum charge order $20.00.

Krause Publications

35,000,000 cards in stock!

1933 GOUDEY (240)
2 3/8" X 2 7/8"

BOSTON BRAVES

- ☐ 24. HORACE FORD
- ☐ 30. FRANK HOGAN
- ☐ 50. ED BRANDT
- ☐ 69. RANDY MOORE
- ☐ 91. TOM ZACHARY
- ☐ 98. WALTER BERGER
- ☐ 117. RABBIT MARANVILLE
- ☐ 131. FRED FRANKHOUSE
- ☐ 139. BEN CANTWELL
- ☐ 161. AL SPOHRER
- ☐ 162. LEO MANGUM
- ☐ 172. BILLY HARGRAVE
- ☐ 179. FRED LEACH
- ☐ 185. BOB SMITH
- ☐ 212. BILLY URBANSKI

BOSTON RED SOX

- ☐ 8. ROY JOHNSON
- ☐ 14. HENRY JOHNSON
- ☐ 42. EDDIE COLLINS
- ☐ 48. MARTY MCMANUS
- ☐ 93. JOHN WELCH
- ☐ 105. BERNIE FRIBERG
- ☐ 197. RICK FERRELL
- ☐ 221. DALE ALEXANDER

BROOKLYN DODGERS

- ☐ 2. DAZZY VANCE(F)
- ☐ 13. LAFAYETTE THOMPSON
- ☐ 17. WATSON CLARK
- ☐ 32. JOHN CLANCY
- ☐ 58. LEFTY O'DOUL
- ☐ 72. OWEN CARROLL
- ☐ 78. JACK QUINN
- ☐ 99. TONY CUCCINELLO
- ☐ 118. VAL PICINICH
- ☐ 141. RAY BENGE
- ☐ 143. GLENN WRIGHT
- ☐ 151. JAKE FLOWERS
- ☐ 155. JOE JUDGE
- ☐ 211. HACK WILSON

CHICAGO CUBS

- ☐ 5. BABE HERMAN
- ☐ 23. KIKI CUYLER
- ☐ 39. MARK KOENIG
- ☐ 51. CHARLIE GRIMM
- ☐ 55. PAT MALONE
- ☐ 64. BURLEIGH GRIMES
- ☐ 67. GUY BUSH
- ☐ 135. WOODY ENGLISH
- ☐ 152. ZACK TAYLOR
- ☐ 186. JOHN SCHULTE(C)
- ☐ 202. GABBY HARTNETT
- ☐ 203. LON WARNEKE
- ☐ 204. RIGGS STEPHENSON
- ☐ 224. FRANK DEMAREE
- ☐ 225. BILL JURGES
- ☐ 226. CHARLEY ROOT
- ☐ 227. BILL HERMAN

CHICAGO WHITE SOX

- ☐ 6. JIMMY DYKES
- ☐ 7. TED LYONS
- ☐ 33. RALPH KRESS
- ☐ 35. AL SIMMONS
- ☐ 43. LEW FONSECA
- ☐ 65. MILTON GASTON
- ☐ 79. RED FABER
- ☐ 81. SAM JONES
- ☐ 184. CHARLEY BERRY
- ☐ 195. EVAR SWANSON
- ☐ 219. MULE HAAS

CINCINNATI REDS

- ☐ 40. TAYLOR DOUTHIT
- ☐ 44. JIM BOTTOMLEY
- ☐ 45. LARRY BENTON
- ☐ 66. GEORGE GRANTHAM
- ☐ 74. EPPA RIXEY
- ☐ 80. CLYDE MANION
- ☐ 97. JOE MORRISSEY
- ☐ 137. FRED LUCAS
- ☐ 150. RAY KOLP
- ☐ 213. EARL ADAMS

CLEVELAND INDIANS

- ☐ 10. GLENN MYATT
- ☐ 26. CHALMER CISSELL
- ☐ 27. GEORGE CONNALLY
- ☐ 75. WILLIE KAMM
- ☐ 96. WILLIS HUDLIN
- ☐ 116. EDDIE MORGAN
- ☐ 171. CHARLEY JAMIESON
- ☐ 194. EARL AVERILL
- ☐ 218. WESLEY FERRELL

DETROIT TIGERS

- ☐ 4. HEINIE SCHUBLE
- ☐ 11. BILLY ROGELL
- ☐ 15. VICTOR SORRELL
- ☐ 100. GEORGE UHLE
- ☐ 104. FRED MARBERRY
- ☐ 199. TOM BRIDGES
- ☐ 222. CHARLEY GEHRINGER

NEW YORK GIANTS

- ☐ 3. HUGH GRITZ
- ☐ 20. BILLY TERRY
- ☐ 41. GUS MANCUSO
- ☐ 52. ANDY COHEN
- ☐ 84. GLENN SPENCER
- ☐ 102. TRAVIS JACKSON
- ☐ 125. BILL TERRY (M)
- ☐ 126. JOE MOORE
- ☐ 127. MEL OTT
- ☐ 129. HAROLD SCHUMACHER
- ☐ 130. FRED FITZSIMMONS
- ☐ 142. PAUL RICHARDS

- ☐ 207. MEL OTT
- ☐ 208. BERNIE JAMES
- ☐ 209. ADOLFO LUQUE
- ☐ 230. CARL HUBBELL
- ☐ 231. JOE MOORE
- ☐ 232. LEFTY O'DOUL
- ☐ 233. JOHNNY VERGEZ
- ☐ 234. CARL HUBBELL
- ☐ 235. FRED FITZSIMMONS
- ☐ 236. GEORGE DAVIS
- ☐ 237. GUS MANCUSO
- ☐ 238. HUGH CRITZ
- ☐ 239. LEROY PARMELEE
- ☐ 240. HAROLD SCHUMACHER

NEW YORK YANKEES

- ☐ 12. GEORGE PIPGRAS
- ☐ 19. BILL DICKEY
- ☐ 31. TONY LAZZERI
- ☐ 53. BABE RUTH
- ☐ 56. RED RUFFING
- ☐ 83. PETE JABLONOWSKI
- ☐ 92. LOU GEHRIG
- ☐ 103. EARLE COMBS
- ☐ 138. HERB PENNOCK
- ☐ 144. BABE RUTH
- ☐ 148. EDDIE FARRELL
- ☐ 149. BABE RUTH
- ☐ 156. DANNY MACFAYDEN
- ☐ 157. SAM BYRD
- ☐ 160. LOU GEHRIG
- ☐ 165. JOE SEWELL
- ☐ 181. BABE RUTH
- ☐ 191. BEN CHAPMAN
- ☐ 192. WALTER BROWN
- ☐ 193. LYNFORD LARY
- ☐ 215. RUSSELL VAN ATTA
- ☐ 216. LEFTY GOMEZ
- ☐ 217. FRANK CROSETTI

PHILADELPHIA ATHLETICS

- ☐ 29. JIMMY FOXX
- ☐ 59. BING MILLER
- ☐ 61. MAX BISHOP
- ☐ 76. MICKEY COCHRANE
- ☐ 82. DIB WILLIAMS
- ☐ 145. GEORGE WALBERT
- ☐ 154. JIMMY FOXX
- ☐ 183. GEORGE WALBERG
- ☐ 196. LEROY MAHAFFEY
- ☐ 220. LEFTY GROVE

PHILADELPHIA PHILLIES

- ☐ 21. PHIL COLLINS
- ☐ 28. DICK BARTELL
- ☐ 38. FRED BRICKELL
- ☐ 115. CLIFF HEATHCOTE
- ☐ 128. CHUCK KLEIN
- ☐ 132. JIM ELLIOTT
- ☐ 136. FLINT RHEM
- ☐ 170. HARRY MCCURDY
- ☐ 178. JACKIE WARNER
- ☐ 210. VIRGIL DAVIS

PITTSBURGH PIRATES

- ☐ 22. PIE TRAYNOR
- ☐ 25. PAUL WANER
- ☐ 36. TOMMY THEVENOW
- ☐ 54. RAY KREMER
- ☐ 60. WAITE HOYT
- ☐ 77. ADAM COMOROSKY
- ☐ 133. FRED LINDSTROM
- ☐ 164. LLOYD WANER
- ☐ 205. HEINIE MEINE
- ☐ 206. GUS SUHR
- ☐ 228. TONY PIET
- ☐ 229. FLOYD VAUGHAN

ST. LOUIS BROWNS

- ☐ 1. BENNY BENGOUGH
- ☐ 16. GEORGE BLAEHOLDER
- ☐ 18. MUDDY RUEL
- ☐ 101. DICK COFFMAN
- ☐ 120. CARL REYNOLDS
- ☐ 140. IRVING HADLEY
- ☐ 166. SAM WEST
- ☐ 188. ROGERS HORNSBY(M)
- ☐ 198. IRVING BURNS

ST. LOUIS CARDINALS

- ☐ 2. DAZZY VANCE(B)
- ☐ 34. BOB O'FARRELL
- ☐ 37. JIMMY WILSON
- ☐ 46. ETHAN ALLEN
- ☐ 49. FRANK FRISCH
- ☐ 62. PEPPER MARTIN
- ☐ 73. JESSE HAINES
- ☐ 94. BILL WALKER
- ☐ 119. ROGERS HORNSBY
- ☐ 147. LEO DUROCHER
- ☐ 173. ROSCOE HOLM
- ☐ 200. BILL HALLAHAN
- ☐ 201. ERNIE ORSATTI
- ☐ 223. DIZZY DEAN

WASHINGTON SENATORS

- ☐ 9. DAVE HARRIS
- ☐ 47. HEINIE MANUSH
- ☐ 63. JOE CRONIN(M)
- ☐ 71. ROBERT BURKE
- ☐ 95. ALVIN CROWDER
- ☐ 107. HEINIE MANUSH
- ☐ 108. JOE KUHEL
- ☐ 109. JOE CRONIN(M)
- ☐ 110. GOOSE GOSLIN
- ☐ 111. MONTE WEAVER
- ☐ 112. FRED SCHULTE
- ☐ 113. OSWALD BLUEGE
- ☐ 114. LUKE SEWELL
- ☐ 121. WALTER STEWART
- ☐ 122. ALVIN CROWDER
- ☐ 123. JACK RUSSELL
- ☐ 124. EARL WHITEHILL
- ☐ 134. SAM RICE
- ☐ 146. WALTER STEWART
- ☐ 153. BUDDY MYER
- ☐ 158. MOE BERG
- ☐ 159. OSWALD BLUEGE
- ☐ 163. LUKE SEWELL
- ☐ 167. JACK RUSSELL
- ☐ 168. GOOSE GOSLIN
- ☐ 169. AL THOMAS
- ☐ 187. HEINIE MANUSH
- ☐ 189. JOE CRONIN(M)
- ☐ 190. FRED SCHULTE
- ☐ 214. JOHN KERR

1934 GOUDEY (96)
2 3/8" X 2 7/8"

BOSTON BRAVES

- ☐ 5. ED BRANDT
- ☐ 20. FRANK HOGAN
- ☐ 31. BAXTER JORDAN
- ☐ 36. WALTER BETTS
- ☐ 59. JOE MOWRY
- ☐ 80. MARTY MCMANUS
- ☐ 81. BOB BROWN

BOSTON RED SOX

- ☐ 19. LEFTY GROVE
- ☐ 30. JULIUS SOLTERS
- ☐ 75. BILL WERBER
- ☐ 93. FRED OSTERMUELLER

BROOKLYN DODGERS

- ☐ 24. RAY BENGE
- ☐ 46. JOE STRIPP
- ☐ 47. JOHN FREDERICK

- ☐ 49. SAM LESLIE
- ☐ 50. WALTER BECK
- ☐ 89. LINUS FREY

CHICAGO CUBS

- ☐ 3. CHARLIE GRIMM(M)
- ☐ 4. WOODY ENGLISH
- ☐ 10. CHUCK KLEIN
- ☐ 60. LYNN NELSON
- ☐ 71. LYLE TINNING
- ☐ 90. KI KI CUYLER

CHICAGO WHITE SOX

- ☐ 27. LUKE APPLING
- ☐ 41. GEORGE EARNSHAW(B)
- ☐ 63. MINTER HAYES
- ☐ 74. BOB BOKEN
- ☐ 79. EDDIE DURHAM

CINCINNATI REDS

- ☐ 8. TONY PIET
- ☐ 34. CHICK HAFEY
- ☐ 35. ERNIE LOMBARDI
- ☐ 54. WESLEY SCHULMERICH(B)
- ☐ 56. MARK KOENIG
- ☐ 84. PAUL DERRINGER
- ☐ 85. ADAM COMOROSKY

CLEVELAND INDIANS

- ☐ 14. WILLIE KAMM
- ☐ 38. ORAL HILDEBRAND
- ☐ 43. DICK PORTER
- ☐ 66. MEL HARDER
- ☐ 67. BOB WEILAND
- ☐ 76. HAL TROSKY
- ☐ 77. JOE VOSMIK

DETROIT TIGERS

- ☐ 2. MICKEY COCHRANE(M)
- ☐ 23. CHARLEY GEHRINGER
- ☐ 26. GERALD WALKER
- ☐ 44. TOM BRIDGES
- ☐ 62. HANK GREENBERG
- ☐ 70. PETE FOX
- ☐ 92. STEVE LARKIN

NEW YORK GIANTS

- ☐ 12. CARL HUBBELL
- ☐ 17. HUGH CRITZ
- ☐ 21. BILL TERRY(M)
- ☐ 32. BLONDY RYAN
- ☐ 52. HERMAN BELL
- ☐ 53. GEORGE WATKINS
- ☐ 88. HOMER PEEL

NEW YORK YANKEES

- ☐ 9. BEN CHAPMAN
- ☐ 37. LOU GEHRIG
- ☐ 39. FRED WALKER
- ☐ 42. JOHN ALLEN
- ☐ 61. LOU GEHRIG
- ☐ 72. ARNDT JORGENS
- ☐ 94. RED ROLFE
- ☐ 95. MYRIL HOAG
- ☐ 96. JIM DESHONG

PHILADELPHIA ATHLETICS

- ☐ 1. JIMMY FOXX
- ☐ 25. ROGER CRAMER
- ☐ 28. ED COLEMAN
- ☐ 41. GEORGE EARNSHAW(F)
- ☐ 68. BOB JOHNSON
- ☐ 69. JOHN MARCUM
- ☐ 78. PINKEY HIGGINS

PHILADELPHIA PHILLIES

- ☐ 33. FRANK HURST
- ☐ 54. WESLEY SCHULMERICH(F)
- ☐ 55. ED HOLLEY
- ☐ 87. GEORGE DARROW
- ☐ 91. DOLPH CAMILLI

PITTSBURGH PIRATES

- ☐ 11. PAUL WANER
- ☐ 22. FLOYD VAUGHAN
- ☐ 29. LARRY FRENCH
- ☐ 57. BILL SWIFT
- ☐ 58. EARL GRACE
- ☐ 86. LLOYD JOHNSON

ST. LOUIS BROWNS

- ☐ 45. OSCAR MELILLO
- ☐ 64. FRANK GRUBE
- ☐ 73. ED WELLS

ST. LOUIS CARDINALS

- ☐ 6. DIZZY DEAN
- ☐ 7. LEO DUROCHER
- ☐ 13. FRANK FRISCH
- ☐ 48. TEX CARLETON
- ☐ 51. RIP COLLINS
- ☐ 82. BILL HALLAHAN
- ☐ 83. JIM MOONEY

WASHINGTON SENATORS

- ☐ 15. ALVIN CROWDER
- ☐ 16. JOE KUHEL
- ☐ 18. HEINIE MANUSH
- ☐ 40. JOHN STONE
- ☐ 65. CLIFF BOLTON

1935 GOUDEY
PUZZLE (36)
2 3/8" X 2 7/8"

Each of the 1935 Goudey cards has four players depicted on the card. While most cards portray four players from the same team, several cards portray players from different teams. Players in parentheses are not on the same team as the subject player(s), but are on the same card.

1935 Goudey

BOSTON BRAVES

- MOORE, HOGAN, FRANKHOUSE, BRANDT
- RUTH, MCMANUS, BRANDT, MARANVILLE
- SPOHRER, RHEM, CANTWELL, BENTON

BOSTON RED SOX

- CRONIN, REYNOLDS, BISHOP, CISSELL
- WERBER, R. FERRELL, W. FERRELL, OSTERMUELLER

BROOKLYN DODGERS

- LESLIE, FREY, STRIPP, W. CLARK
- BENGE, ZACHARY (KOENIG, FITZSIMMONS)
- VANCE (BERRY, BURKE, KRESS)

CHICAGO CUBS

- GRIMES, KLEIN, CUYLER, ENGLISH

CHICAGO WHITE SOX

- EARNSHAW, DYKES, L. SEWELL, APPLINE
- HAYES, LYONS, HAAS, BONURA
- RUEL, SIMMONS (KAMM, COCHRANE)
- WRIGHT (TRAYNOR, LUCAS, THEVENOW

CINCINNATI REDS

- CAMPBELL, MEYERS, GOODMAN, KAMPOURIS
- PIET, COMORDSKY, BOTTOMLEY, ADAMS
- BYRD, MACFAYDEN (MARTIN, O'FARRELL)
- COMOROSKY, BOTTOMLEY (HUDLIN, MYATT)

CLEVELAND INDIANS

- KAMM, HILDEBRAND, AVERILL, TROSKY
- VOSMIK, KNICKERBOCKER, HARDER, STEWART
- HUDLIN, MYATT (COMOROSKY, BOTTOMLEY
- KAMM (RUEL, SIMMONS, COCHRANE)

DETROIT TIGERS

- COCHRANE, GEHRINGER, BRIDGES, ROGELL
- FOX, GREENBERG, WALKER, ROWE
- SCHUBLE, MARBERRY, GOSLIN, CROWDER
- COCHRANE (RUEL, SIMMONS, KAMM)

NEW YORK GIANTS

- CRITZ, BARTELL, OTT, MANCUSO
- TERRY, SCHUMACHER, MANCUSO, JACKSON
- KOENIG FITZSIMMONS (BENGE, ZACHARY)

NEW YORK YANKEES

- DESHONG, ALLEN, ROLFE, WALKER
- RUFFING, MALONE, LAZZERI, DICKEY

PHILADELPHIA ATHLETICS

- JOHNSON, COLEMAN, MARCUM, CRAMER
- MAHAFFEY, FOXX, WILLIAMS, HIGGINS
- BERRY (VANCE, BURKE, KRESS)

PHILADELPHIA PHILLIES

- WILSON, ALLEN, JONNARD, BRICKELL

PITTSBURGH PIRATES

- HERMAN, SUHR, PADDEN, BLANTON
- P. WANER, BUSH, W. HOYT, L. WANER
- TRAYNOR, LUCAS, THE VENOW (WRIGHT)

ST. LOUIS BROWNS

- BURNS, HEMSLEY, GRUBE, WEILAND
- WEST, MELILLO, BLAEHOLDER, COFFMAN

ST. LOUIS CARDINALS

- FRISCH, J. DEAN, ORSATTI, TEX CARLETON
- MARTIN, O'FARRELL (BYRD, MACFAYDEN)

WASHINGTON SENATORS

- KUHEL, WHITEHILL, MEYER, STONE
- MANUSH, LARY, M. WEAVER, HADLEY
- BURKE, KRESS (BERRY, VANCE)

1936 GOUDEY GAME (25)
2 3/8" X 2 7/8"
BLACK & WHITE

BOSTON BRAVES

- 1. WALLY BERGER
- 8. JOE COSCARART

BOSTON RED SOX

- 13. RICK FERRELL
- 25. BILL WERBER

BROOKLYN DODGERS

- 3. FRENCHI BORDAGARAY

CHICAGO CUBS

- 20. CHUCK KLEIN

CHICAGO WHITE SOX

- 2. ZEKE BONURA
- 12. JIMMY DYKES

CINCINNATI REDS

- 10. KIKI CUYLER
- 11. PAUL DERRINGER

CLEVELAND INDIANS

- 19. ORAL HILDEBRAND
- 23. JOE VOSMIK

DETROIT TIGERS

- 7. MICKEY COCHRANE
- 15. HANK GREENBERG

NEW YORK GIANTS

- 6. CLYDE CASTLEMAN

NEW YORK YANKEES

- 9. FRANK CROSETTI
- 14. LEFTY GOMEZ

PHILADELPHIA ATHLETICS

- 18. PINKY HIGGINS

PHILADELPHIA PHILLIES

- 5. DOLPH CAMILLI

PITTSBURGH PIRATES

- 4. BILL BRUBAKER
- 24. PAUL WANER

ST. LOUIS BROWNS

- 17. ROLLIE HEMSLEY

ST. LOUIS CARDINALS

☐ 21. PEPPER MARTIN

WASHINGTON SENATORS

☐ 16. BUCKY HARRIS
☐ 22. BOBO NEWSOM

1938 GOUDEY HEADS UP (48)
2 3/8" X 2 7/8"

BOSTON BEES

☐ 257. AL LOPEZ
☐ 281. AL LOPEZ

JOE VOSMIK, Red Sox

BOSTON RED SOX

☐ 247. JOE VOSMIK
☐ 249. JIMMIE FOXX
☐ 258. BOBBY DOERR
☐ 271. JOE VOSMIK
☐ 273. JIMMIE FOXX
☐ 282. BOBBY DOERR

BROOKLYN DODGERS

☐ 254. VAN LINGLE MUNGO
☐ 278. VAN LINGLE MUNGO

CHICAGO CUBS

☐ 244. FRANK DEMAREE
☐ 268. FRANK DEMAREE

CHICAGO WHITE SOX

☐ 243. JOE KUHEL
☐ 261. RIP RADCLIFF
☐ 263. MARVIN OWEN
☐ 267. JOE KUHEL
☐ 285. RIP RADCLIFF
☐ 287. MARVIN OWEN

CINCINNATI REDS

☐ 246. ERNIE LOMBARDI
☐ 270. ERNIE LOMBARDI

CLEVELAND INDIANS

☐ 245. FRANK PYTLAK
☐ 255. MOOSE SOLTERS
☐ 264. BOB FELLER

☐ 269. FRANK PYTLAK
☐ 279. MOOSE SOLTERS
☐ 288. BOB FELLER

DETROIT TIGERS

☐ 241. CHARLIE GEHRINGER
☐ 242. PETE FOX
☐ 253. HANK GREENBERG
☐ 256. VERNON KENNEDY
☐ 260. RUDY YORK
☐ 265. CHARLIE GEHRINGER
☐ 266. PETE FOX
☐ 277. HANK GREENBERG
☐ 280. VERNON KENNEDY
☐ 284. RUDY YORK

ERVIN FOX, Tigers

NEW YORK GIANTS

☐ 248. DICK BARTELL
☐ 272. DICK BARTELL

NEW YORK YANKEES

☐ 250. JOE DIMAGGIO
☐ 251. BUMP HADLEY
☐ 274. JOE DIMAGGIO
☐ 275. BUMP HADLEY

PHILADELPHIA ATHLETICS

☐ 259. BILL WERBER
☐ 283. BILL WERBER

PHILADELPHIA PHILLIES

NO CARDS ISSUED

PITTSBURGH PIRATES

NO CARDS ISSUED

ST. LOUIS BROWNS

NO CARDS ISSUED

ST. LOUIS CARDINALS

☐ 262. JOE MEDWICK
☐ 286. JOE MEDWICK

WASHINGTON SENATORS

☐ 252. ZEKE BONURA
☐ 276. ZEKE BONURA

1941 GOUDEY (33)
2 3/8" X 2 7/8"

BILL POSEDEL
BEES-PITCHER

BOSTON BEES

☐ 19. BILL POSEDEL
☐ 22. JOE SULLIVAN
☐ 24. STANLEY ANDREWS
☐ 30. JIM TOBIN
☐ 31. CHESTER ROSS

EMERSON DICKMAN
RED SOX—PITCHER

BOSTON RED SOX

☐ 6. EMERSON DICKMAN

BROOKLYN DODGERS

☐ 18. WHITLOW WYATT

CHICAGO CUBS

☐ 21. HAROLD WARSTLER
☐ 28. AL TODD

CHICAGO WHITE SOX

☐ 9. BILL DIETRICH
☐ 10. TAFT WRIGHT
☐ 15. DARIO LODIGIANI

DARIO LODIGIANI
WHITE SOX—INFIELDER

CINCINNATI REDS

☐ 7. WAYNE AMBLER

CLEVELAND INDIANS

NO CARDS ISSUED

DETROIT TIGERS

☐ 32. GEORGE COFFMAN

NEW YORK GIANTS

☐ 3. LOUIS CHIOZZA
☐ 20. CARL HUBBELL
☐ 23. BABE YOUNG
☐ 25. MORRIS ARNOVICH
☐ 33. MELT OTT

NEW YORK YANKEES

☐ 4. BUDDY ROSAR

PHILADELPHIA ATHLETICS

☐ 13. FRANK HAYES

PHILADELPHIA PHILLIES

☐ 1. HUGH MULCAHY
☐ 17. VITO TAMULIS
☐ 27. BILL CROUCH

PITTSBURGH PIRATES

- ☐ 26. ELBERT FLETCHER
- ☐ 29. DEBS GARMS

ST. LOUIS BROWNS

- ☐ 2. HARLAND CLIFT
- ☐ 5. GEORGE MCQUINN
- ☐ 8. BOB MUNCRIEF
- ☐ 11. DON HEFFNER
- ☐ 12. FRITZ OSTERMUELLER
- ☐ 14. JACK KRAMER

ST. LOUIS CARDINALS

NO CARDS ISSUED

WASHINGTON SENATORS

- ☐ 16. GEORGE CASE

1939 PLAY BALL AMERICA (162) 2 1/2" X 3 1/8" BLACK & WHITE

BOSTON BEES

- ☐ 49. EDDIE MILLER
- ☐ 57. BUDDY HASSETT
- ☐ 61. TONY CUCCINELLO
- ☐ 69. ELBIE FLETCHER
- ☐ 70. FRED FRANKHOUSE
- ☐ 72. DEBS GARMS
- ☐ 85. JOHN COONEY
- ☐ 87. MILBURN SHOFFNER
- ☐ 120. RABBIT WARSTLER
- ☐ 121. BILL POSEDEL
- ☐ 149. MAX WEST
- ☐ 155. JIM OUTLAW

BOSTON RED SOX

- ☐ 4. ELDEN AUKER
- ☐ 7. BOBBY DOERR
- ☐ 14. JIM TABOR
- ☐ 16. JOHN PEACOCK
- ☐ 17. EMERSON DICKMAN
- ☐ 20. JOE HEVING
- ☐ 27. FRED OSTERMUELLER
- ☐ 29. JACK WILSON
- ☐ 40. JIM BAGBY
- ☐ 62. TOM CAREY
- ☐ 92. TED WILLIAMS
- ☐ 101. ROGER CRAMER
- ☐ 103. MOE BERG
- ☐ 107. JOE VOSMIK
- ☐ 116. GENE DESAUTELS

BROOKLYN DODGERS

- ☐ 6. LEO DUROCHER(M)
- ☐ 13. LUKE HAMLIN
- ☐ 68. FRED SINGTON
- ☐ 74. COOKIE LAVAGETTO
- ☐ 76. GOODY ROSEN
- ☐ 86. DOLPH CAMILLI
- ☐ 95. WHIT WYATT
- ☐ 96. BABE PHELPS

- ☐ 110. FRED FITZSIMMONS
- ☐ 111. VAN LINGLE MUNGO
- ☐ 134. FORREST PRESSNELL
- ☐ 139. VITO TAMULIS
- ☐ 140. RAY HAYWORTH
- ☐ 141. PETE COSCARART
- ☐ 142. IRA HUTCHINSON
- ☐ 151. HUGH CASEY
- ☐ 154. JOHN HUDSON
- ☐ 159. RED EVANS
- ☐ 160. GENE MOORE

CHICAGO CUBS

NO CARDS ISSUED

CHICAGO WHITE SOX

- ☐ 91. JOHN KNOTT
- ☐ 105. ERIC MCNAIR

CINCINNATI REDS

- ☐ 2. LEE GRISSOM
- ☐ 15. PAUL DERRINGER
- ☐ 22. BUCKY WALTERS
- ☐ 36. FRANK MCCORMICK
- ☐ 38. BILL MYERS
- ☐ 65. HARRY CRAFT
- ☐ 67. ED JOOST
- ☐ 75. STAN BORDAGARAY
- ☐ 77. LEW RIGGS
- ☐ 99. WALLY BERGER
- ☐ 119. BILL HERSHBERGER
- ☐ 123. RAY DAVIS
- ☐ 161. LONNIE FREY
- ☐ 162. WHITEY MOORE

CLEVELAND INDIANS

- ☐ 5. LUKE SEWELL
- ☐ 78. JAKE SOLTERS
- ☐ 143. EARL AVERILL
- ☐ 152. ROY WEATHERLY

DETROIT TIGERS

- ☐ 50. CHARLIE GEHRINGER
- ☐ 56. HANK GREENBERG
- ☐ 60. SCHOOLBOY ROWE
- ☐ 80. PETE FOX
- ☐ 104. TOM BRIDGES
- ☐ 115. RALPH KRESS

- ☐ 136. ROY BELL
- ☐ 147. GEORGE COFFMAN
- ☐ 150. JIM WALKUP
- ☐ 153. DIZZY TROUT
- ☐ 158. BUD THOMAS

NEW YORK GIANTS

- ☐ 18. HARRY DANNING
- ☐ 23. BURGESS WHITEHEAD
- ☐ 24. RICHARD COFFMAN
- ☐ 32. BOB SEEDS
- ☐ 34. FRANK DEMAREE
- ☐ 35. BILL JURGES
- ☐ 51. MEL OTT
- ☐ 53. CARL HUBBELL
- ☐ 54. HARRY GUMBERT
- ☐ 58. LOU CHIOZZA
- ☐ 66. JIM RIPPLE
- ☐ 73. HAL SCHUMACHER
- ☐ 79. JOJO MOORE
- ☐ 124. WALTER BROWN
- ☐ 125. CLIFF MELTON
- ☐ 144. ZEKE BONURA

NEW YORK YANKEES

- ☐ 1. JAKE POWELL
- ☐ 3. RED RUFFING
- ☐ 25. GEORGE SELKIRK
- ☐ 26. JOE DIMAGGIO
- ☐ 30. BILL DICKEY
- ☐ 42. ARNDT JORGENS
- ☐ 48. LEFTY GOMEZ
- ☐ 52. TOMMY HENRICH
- ☐ 71. MONTE PEARSON
- ☐ 81. BABE DAHLGREN
- ☐ 88. CHARLIE KELLER

PHILADELPHIA PHILLIES

- ☐ 12. HERSHEL MARTIN
- ☐ 28. SYLVESTER JOHNSON
- ☐ 33. DEL YOUNG
- ☐ 37. VIRGIL DAVIS
- ☐ 45. MERRILL MAY
- ☐ 46. MORRIS ARNOVICH
- ☐ 63. EMMETT MUELLER
- ☐ 82. CHUCK KLEIN(F)
- ☐ 98. PINKEY WHITNEY
- ☐ 127. GIL BRACK
- ☐ 145. HUGH MULCAHY

PHILADELPHIA ATHLETCS

- ☐ 8. HENRY PIPPEN
- ☐ 64. WALLY MOSES
- ☐ 84. SKEETER NEWSOME
- ☐ 97. BOB JOHNSON
- ☐ 108. FRANK HAYES
- ☐ 117. WAYNE AMBLER
- ☐ 118. LYNN NELSON

PITTSBURGH PIRATES

- ☐ 9. JIM TOBIN
- ☐ 11. JOHN RIZZO
- ☐ 55. ARKIE VAUGHAN
- ☐ 82. CHUCK KLEIN(B)
- ☐ 83. GUS SUHR
- ☐ 89. LLOYD WANER
- ☐ 90. BOB KLINGER
- ☐ 94. HEINIE MANUSH
- ☐ 102. PEP YOUNG
- ☐ 112. PAUL WANER
- ☐ 128. JOE BOWMAN
- ☐ 129. BILL SWIFT
- ☐ 130. BILL BRUBAKER
- ☐ 156. RAY BERRES

ST. LOUIS BROWNS

- ☐ 43. MELO ALMADA
- ☐ 44. DON HEFFNER
- ☐ 109. MYRIL HOAG
- ☐ 122. GEORGE MCQUINN
- ☐ 148. BILL TROTTER

ST. LOUIS CARDINALS

- ☐ 19. DAFFY DEAN
- ☐ 41. LON WARNEKE
- ☐ 131. MORT COOPER

☐ 132. JIM BROWN
☐ 133. LYNN MYERS
☐ 135. MICKEY OWEN
☐ 146. TOM SUNKEL
☐ 157. DON PADGETT

WASHINGTON SENATORS

☐ 10. JIM DESHONG
☐ 21. DUTCH LEONARD
☐ 31. SAM WEST
☐ 39. RICK FERRELL
☐ 47. BUDDY LEWIS
☐ 59. KEN CHASE
☐ 93. CHARLIE GELBERT
☐ 100. BUDDY MYER
☐ 114. CECIL TRAVIS
☐ 137. PETE APPLETON
☐ 138. GEORGE CASE

1940 PLAY BALL (240)
2 1/2" X 3 1/8"
BLACK & WHITE

"TWINKLETOES" SELKIRK

BOSTON BEES

☐ 56. EDDIE MILLER
☐ 57. MAX WEST
☐ 58. BILL POSEDEL
☐ 59. RABBITT WARTSLER
☐ 60. JOHN COONEY
☐ 61. TONY CUCCINELLO
☐ 62. BUDDY HASSETT
☐ 140. DICK COFFMAN
☐ 141. CASEY STENGEL(M)
☐ 142. GEORGE KELLY(C)
☐ 143. GENE MOORE(B)

BOSTON RED SOX

☐ 27. TED WILLIAMS
☐ 28. GENE DESAUTELS
☐ 29. ROGER CRAMER
☐ 30. MOE BERG(C)
☐ 31. JACK WILSON
☐ 32. JIM BAGBY
☐ 33. FRED OSTERMUELLER
☐ 34. JOHN PEACOCK
☐ 35. JOE HEVING
☐ 36. JIM TABOR
☐ 37. EMERSON DICKMAN
☐ 38. BOBBY DOERR
☐ 39. TOM CAREY
☐ 133. JIMMIE FOXX
☐ 134. JOE CRONIN(M)
☐ 196. LEO NONNENKAMP
☐ 197. LOU FINNEY
☐ 198. DENNY GALEHOUSE

BROOKLYN DODGERS

☐ 63. PETE COSCARART
☐ 64. VAN LINGO MUNGO
☐ 65. FRED FITZSIMMONS
☐ 66. BABE PHELPS
☐ 67. WHIT WYATT
☐ 68. DOLPH CAMILLI
☐ 69. COOKIE LAVAGETTO
☐ 70. LUKE HAMLIN
☐ 71. MELO ALMADA
☐ 72. CHUCK DRESSEN(C)
☐ 143. GENE MOORE(F)

☐ 144. JOE VOSMIK
☐ 145. VITO TAMULIS
☐ 146. FORREST PRESSNELL
☐ 147. JOHN HUDSON
☐ 148. HUGH CASEY
☐ 207. GUS MANCUSO

"CHUCK" DRESSEN

CHICAGO CUBS

☐ 239. GEORGE UHLE(C)

CHICAGO WHITE SOX

☐ 13. JOHN KNOTT
☐ 14. ERIC MCNAIR
☐ 126. JAKE SOLTERS
☐ 127. MUDDY RUEL(C)
☐ 128. PETE APPLETON
☐ 184. MULE HAAS(C)
☐ 185. JOE JUHEL
☐ 186. TAFT WRIGHT
☐ 187. JIMMY DYKES(M)

"WILDFIRE" CRAFT

CINCINNATI REDS

☐ 73. BUCKY WALTERS
☐ 74. PAUL DERRINGER
☐ 75. FRANK MCCORMICK
☐ 76. LONNIE FREY
☐ 77. BILL HERSHBERGER
☐ 78. LEW RIGGS
☐ 79. HARRY CRAFT
☐ 80. BILL MYERS
☐ 81. WALLY BERGER
☐ 82. HANK GOWDY(C)
☐ 149. MILBURN SHOFFNER
☐ 150. WHITEY MOORE
☐ 151. ED JOOST
☐ 152. JIMMY WILSON(C)
☐ 153. BILL MCKECHNIE(M)
☐ 208. LEE GAMBLE

CLEVELAND INDIANS

☐ 47. OSCAR VITT(M)
☐ 48. LUKE SEWELL(C)
☐ 49. ROY WEATHERLY
☐ 50. HAL TROSKY
☐ 138. BEAU BELL
☐ 202. AL MILNAR
☐ 203. ODELL HALE
☐ 204. HARRY EISENSTAT
☐ 205. ROLLIE HEMSLEY

DETROIT TIGERS

☐ 40. HANK GREENBERG
☐ 41. CHARLIE GEHRINGER
☐ 42. BUD THOMAS
☐ 43. PETE FOX
☐ 44. DIZZY TROUT
☐ 45. RALPH KRESS
☐ 46. EARL AVERILL
☐ 135. LYNN NELSON
☐ 136. COTTON PIPPEN
☐ 137. BING MILLER(C)
☐ 199. PINKY HIGGINS
☐ 200. BRUCE CAMPBELL
☐ 201. BARNEY MCCOSKY

NEW YORK GIANTS

☐ 83. CLIFF MELTON
☐ 84. JOJO MOORE
☐ 85. HAL SCHUMACHER
☐ 86. HARRY GUMBERT
☐ 87. CARL HUBBELL
☐ 88. MEL OTT
☐ 89. BILL JURGES
☐ 90. FRANK DEMAREE
☐ 91. BOB SEEDS
☐ 92. BURGESS WHITEHEAD
☐ 93. HARRY DANNING
☐ 154. WALTER BROWN
☐ 155. RAY HAYWORTH
☐ 156. DAFFY DEAN
☐ 157. LOU CHIOZZA
☐ 158. TRAVIS JACKSON(C)
☐ 159. FRANK SNYDER(C)
☐ 209. HY VANDENBERG
☐ 210. BILL LOHRMAN
☐ 211. ROY JOINER
☐ 212. BABE YOUNG
☐ 213. JOHN RUCKER
☐ 214. KEN O'DEA
☐ 215. JOHNNIE MCCARTHY

NEW YORK YANKEES

☐ 1. JOE DIMAGGIO
☐ 2. ARNDT JORGENS
☐ 3. BABE DAHLGREN
☐ 4. TOMMY HENRICH
☐ 5. MONTE PEARSON
☐ 6. LEFTY GOMEZ
☐ 7. BILL DICKEY
☐ 8. GEORGE SELKIRK
☐ 9. CHARLIE KELLER
☐ 10. RED RUFFING
☐ 11. JAKE POWELL
☐ 12. JOHNNY SCHULTE(C)
☐ 121. ATLEY DONALD
☐ 122. STEVE SUNDRA
☐ 123. ORAL HILDEBRAND
☐ 124. EARLE COMBS(C)
☐ 125. ART FLETCHER(C)
☐ 181. SPUD CHANDLER
☐ 182. BILL KNICKERBOCKER
☐ 183. MARVIN BREUER

PHILADELPHIA ATHLETICS

☐ 24. FRANK HAYES
☐ 25. BOB JOHNSON
☐ 26. WALLY MOSES
☐ 132. CONNIE MACK(M)
☐ 190. CHARLEY BERRY(C)
☐ 191. JOHNNY BABICH
☐ 192. DICK SIEBERT
☐ 193. CHUBBY DEAN
☐ 194. SAM CHAPMAN
☐ 195. DEE MILES

PHIADELPHIA PHILLIES

☐ 94. GUS SUHR
☐ 95. HUGH MULCAHY
☐ 96. EMMETT MUELLER
☐ 97. MORRIS ARNOVICH
☐ 98. MERRILL MAY
☐ 99. SYLVESTER JOHNSON
☐ 100. HERSHEL MARTIN
☐ 101. DEL YOUNG
☐ 102. CHUCK KLEIN
☐ 160. HANS LOBERT(C)
☐ 216. JOE MARTY

☐ 217. WALTER BECK
☐ 218. WALTER MILLIES
☐ 240. BILL ATWOOD

PITTSBURGH PIRATES

☐ 103. ELBIE FLETCHER
☐ 104. PAUL WANER
☐ 105. LLOYD WANER
☐ 106. PEP YOUNG
☐ 107. ARKY VAUGHAN
☐ 108. JOHN RIZZO
☐ 161. DEBS GARMS
☐ 162. JOE BOWMAN
☐ 163. SPUD DAVIS
☐ 164. RAY BERRES
☐ 165. BOB KLINGER
☐ 166. BILL BRUBAKER
☐ 167. FRANK FRISCH(M)
☐ 168. HONUS WAGNER(C)
☐ 219. RUSS BAUERS
☐ 220. MACE BROWN
☐ 221. LEE HANDLEY
☐ 222. MAX BUTCHER

ST. LOUIS BROWNS

☐ 51. DON HEFFNER
☐ 52. MYRIL HOAG
☐ 53. GEORGE MCQUINN
☐ 54. BILL TROTTER
☐ 55. GEORGE COFFMAN
☐ 139. ELDEN AUKER
☐ 206. CHET LAABS

ST. LOUIS CARDINALS

☐ 109. DON PADGETT
☐ 110. TOM SUNKEL
☐ 111. MICKEY OWEN
☐ 112. JIM BROWN
☐ 113. MORT COOPER
☐ 114. LON WARNEKE
☐ 115. MIKE GONZALES(C)

WASHINGTON SENATORS

☐ 15. GEORGE CASE
☐ 16. CECIL TRAVIS
☐ 17. BUDDY MYER
☐ 18. CHARLIE GELBERT
☐ 19. KEN CHASE
☐ 20. BUDDY LEWIS
☐ 21. RICK FERRELL
☐ 22. SAM WEST
☐ 23. DUTCH LEONARD
☐ 129. BUCKY HARRIS(M)
☐ 130. CLYDE MILAN(C)
☐ 131. ZEKE BONURA
☐ 188. JOE KRAKAUSKAS
☐ 189. JIM BLOODWORTH

1941 PLAY BALL SPORTS HALL OF FAME (72) 2 1/2" X 3 1/8"

BARNEY McCOSKY

BOSTON BRAVES

☐ 1. EDDIE MILLER*
☐ 2. MAX WEST*
☐ 25. GENE MOORE

* Nos. 1 and 2 appear with Boston Bees on the back of the card.

☐ 49. BABE DAHLGREN
☐ 50. JOHN COONEY
☐ 58. FRANK DEMAREE

BOSTON RED SOX

☐ 13. JIMMIE FOXX
☐ 14. TED WILLIAMS
☐ 15. JOE CRONIN(M)
☐ 29. JACK WILSON
☐ 30. LOU FINNEY
☐ 63. DOM DIMAGGIO
☐ 64. BOBBY DOERR

BROOKLYN DODGERS

☐ 51. DOLPH CAMILLI
☐ 52. KIRBY HIGBE
☐ 53. LUKE HAMLIN
☐ 54. PEE WEE REESE
☐ 55. WHIT WYATT

CHICAGO CUBS

NO CARDS ISSUED

CHICAGO WHITE SOX

☐ 31. JOE KUHEL
☐ 32. TAFT WRIGHT

CLEVELAND INDIANS

☐ 16. HAL TROSKY
☐ 17. ROY WEATHERLY
☐ 33. AL MILNAR
☐ 34. ROLLIE HEMSLEY

DETROIT TIGERS

☐ 18. HANK GREENBERG
☐ 19. CHARLIE GEHRINGER
☐ 35. PINKY HIGGINS
☐ 36. BARNEY MCCOSKY
☐ 37. BRUCE CAMPBELL
☐ 65. TOMMY BRIDGES

CARL HUBBELL

NEW YORK GIANTS

☐ 6. CARL HUBBELL
☐ 7. HARRY DANNING
☐ 8. MEL OTT
☐ 26. HARRY GUMBERT
☐ 27. BABE YOUNG
☐ 57. MORRIS ARNOVICH
☐ 59. BILL JURGES

NEW YORK YANKEES

☐ 20. RED RUFFING
☐ 21. CHARLIE KELLER
☐ 38. ATLEY DONALD
☐ 39. TOMMY HENRICH
☐ 70. BILL DICKEY
☐ 71. JOE DIMAGGIO
☐ 72. LEFTY GOMEZ

PHILADELPHIA ATHLETICS

☐ 22. BOB JOHNSON
☐ 40. JOHN BABICH
☐ 41. FRANK HAYES
☐ 42. WALLY MOSES

☐ 43. AL BRANCATO
☐ 44. SAM CHAPMAN
☐ 68. JOHN KNOTT

"PINKY" MAY

PHILADELPHIA PHILLIES

☐ 9. MERRILL MAY
☐ 28. JOE MARTY
☐ 60. CHUCK KLEIN

PITTSBURGH PIRATES

☐ 10. ARKY VAUGHAN
☐ 11. DEBS GARMS
☐ 61. VINCE DIMAGGIO
☐ 62. ELBIE FLETCHER

ST. LOUIS BROWNS

☐ 23. GEORGE MCQUINN
☐ 45. ELDEN AUKER
☐ 66. HARLAND CLIFT
☐ 67. WALT JUDNICH

ST. LOUIS CARDINALS

☐ 12. JIM BROWN

WASHINGTON SENATORS

☐ 24. DUTCH LEONARD
☐ 46. SID HUDSON
☐ 47. BUDDY LEWIS
☐ 48. CECIL TRAVIS*
☐ 69. GEORGE CASE

1988 SCORE (660)
2 1/2 X 3 1/2

JIM DWYER

★★★

ATLANTA BRAVES

- ☐ 111. GLENN HUBBARD
- ☐ 129. OZZIE VIRGIL
- ☐ 136. GERALD PERRY
- ☐ 148. ALBERT HALL
- ☐ 245. KEN OBERKFELL
- ☐ 285. TED SIMMONS
- ☐ 299. ANDRES THOMAS
- ☐ 319. RICK MAHLER
- ☐ 379. ED OLWINE
- ☐ 390. KEN GRIFFEY
- ☐ 395. DION JAMES
- ☐ 410. ZANE SMITH
- ☐ 423. BRUCE BENEDICT
- ☐ 426. RAFAEL RAMIREZ
- ☐ 440. GRAIG NETTLES
- ☐ 450. DALE MURPHY
- ☐ 454. CHARLIE PULEO
- ☐ 457. DAVID PALMER
- ☐ 482. GARY ROENICKE
- ☐ 498. JEFF DEDMON
- ☐ 542. JOE BOEVER
- ☐ 555. PHIL NIEKRO
- ☐ 562. JEFF BLAUSER
- ☐ 576. JIM ACKER
- ☐ 638. TOM GLAVINE
- ☐ 647. RON GANT

BALTIMORE ORIOLES

- ☐ 18. EDDIE MURRAY
- ☐ 42. FRED LYNN
- ☐ 58. KEN GERHART
- ☐ 67. MIKE BODDICKER
- ☐ 96. RAY KNIGHT
- ☐ 101. ERIC BELL
- ☐ 103. DAVE SCHMIDT
- ☐ 123. TERRY KENNEDY
- ☐ 173. LEE LACY
- ☐ 200. BILL RIPKEN
- ☐ 219. LARRY SHEETS
- ☐ 229. JIM DWYER
- ☐ 261. TOM NIEDENFUER
- ☐ 291. ALAN WIGGINS
- ☐ 315. SCOTT MCGREGOR
- ☐ 353. JOHN HABYAN
- ☐ 359. FLOYD RAYFORD
- ☐ 393. MIKE YOUNG
- ☐ 411. KEN DIXON
- ☐ 427. MIKE FLANAGAN (F)
- ☐ 434. JACK O'CONNOR
- ☐ 518. DON AASE
- ☐ 550. CAL RIPKEN
- ☐ 628. PETE STANICEK

BOSTON RED SOX

- ☐ 2. WADE BOGGS
- ☐ 14. JIM RICE
- ☐ 65. DWIGHT EVANS
- ☐ 110. ROGER CLEMENS
- ☐ 121. DENNIS BOYD
- ☐ 155. MARTY BARRETT
- ☐ 175. MIKE GREENWELL
- ☐ 201. SAME HORN
- ☐ 218. CALVIN SCHIRALDI

- ☐ 228. DAVE HENDERSON (F)
- ☐ 241. RICH GEDMAN
- ☐ 250. DON BAYLOR (F)
- ☐ 259. ED ROMERO
- ☐ 271. MARC SULLIVAN
- ☐ 289. STEVE CRAWFORD
- ☐ 300. BOB STANLEY
- ☐ 314. JOE SAMBITO
- ☐ 352. PAT DODSON
- ☐ 372. SPIKE OWEN
- ☐ 380. BRUCE HURST
- ☐ 403. ROB WOODWARD
- ☐ 472. ELLIS BURKS
- ☐ 527. AL NIPPER
- ☐ 541. JEFF SELLERS
- ☐ 546. TODD BENZINGER
- ☐ 584. JOHN MARZANO
- ☐ 625. JODY REED
- ☐ 644. KEVIN ROMINE

CALIFORNIA ANGELS

- ☐ 7. WALLY JOYNER
- ☐ 44. BRIAN DOWNING
- ☐ 63. BOB BOONE
- ☐ 81. MIKE WITT
- ☐ 105. DON SUTTON
- ☐ 124. JACK HOWELL
- ☐ 152. MARK MCLEMORE
- ☐ 176. GREG MINTON
- ☐ 195. DONNIE MOORE
- ☐ 212. DEVON WHITE
- ☐ 239. DOUG DECINCES
- ☐ 254. JOHNNY RAY
- ☐ 255. GARY PETTIS
- ☐ 270. JERRY REUSS
- ☐ 274. DICK SCHOFIELD
- ☐ 293. JOHN CANDELARIA
- ☐ 308. GEORGE HENDRICK
- ☐ 333. RUPPERT JONES
- ☐ 341. GUS POLIDOR
- ☐ 355. BUTCH WYNEGAR
- ☐ 376. DEWAYNE BUICE
- ☐ 394. WILLIE FRASER
- ☐ 437. JACK LAZORKO
- ☐ 463. DARRELL MILLER
- ☐ 487. TONY ARMAS
- ☐ 552. KIRK MCCASKILL
- ☐ 591. BILL BUCKNER

CHICAGO CUBS

- ☐ 4. ANDRE DAWSON
- ☐ 26. RYNE SANDBERG
- ☐ 31. LEE SMITH
- ☐ 50. RICK SUTCLIFFE
- ☐ 71. KEITH MORELAND
- ☐ 186. RAFAEL PALMEIRO
- ☐ 205. BRIAN DAYETT
- ☐ 223. DAVE MARTINEZ
- ☐ 244. JIM SUNDBERG
- ☐ 329. PAUL NOCE
- ☐ 378. LEON DURHAM
- ☐ 413. FRANK DIPINO
- ☐ 451. BOB DERNIER
- ☐ 467. JERRY MUMPHREY
- ☐ 506. ED LYNCH
- ☐ 524. MANNY TRILLO
- ☐ 529. SHAWON DUNSTON
- ☐ 544. SCOTT SANDERSON
- ☐ 551. JODY DAVIS
- ☐ 573. JAMIE MOYER
- ☐ 602. LES LANCASTER

CHICAGO WHITE SOX

- ☐ 93. GREG WALKER
- ☐ 112. KEN WILLIAMS
- ☐ 139. FRED MANRIQUE
- ☐ 307. BOBBY THIGPEN
- ☐ 374. RON KARKOVICE
- ☐ 443. GARY REDUS
- ☐ 462. JIM WINN
- ☐ 480. RICHARD DOTSON
- ☐ 508. JOSE DELEON
- ☐ 539. BILL LONG
- ☐ 572. DONNIE HILL
- ☐ 582. DARYL BOSTON
- ☐ 589. DAVE LAPOINT
- ☐ 590. HAROLD BAINES
- ☐ 592. CARLTON FISK
- ☐ 603. OZZIE GUILLEN

- ☐ 607. IVAN CALDERON
- ☐ 622. FLOYD BANNISTER

CINNINNATI REDS

- ☐ 10. ERIC DAVIS
- ☐ 17. DAVE PARKER
- ☐ 72. BARRY LARKIN
- ☐ 86. KAL DANIELS
- ☐ 99. BUDDY BELL
- ☐ 132. TOM BROWNING
- ☐ 163. NICK ESASKY
- ☐ 183. RON OESTER
- ☐ 206. BO DIAZ
- ☐ 210. DAVE CONCEPCION
- ☐ 221. KURT STILLWELL
- ☐ 242. TED POWER
- ☐ 281. TERRY MCGRIFF
- ☐ 297. TERRY FRANCONA
- ☐ 304. PAUL O'NEILL
- ☐ 317. FRANK WILLIAMS
- ☐ 326. TRACY JONES
- ☐ 371. DAVE COLLINS
- ☐ 476. RON ROBINSON
- ☐ 494. TOM HUME (B)
- ☐ 497. JEFF MONTGOMERY
- ☐ 535. JOHN FRANCO
- ☐ 557. PAT PERRY
- ☐ 559. ROB MURPHY
- ☐ 560. DENNIS RASMUSSEN
- ☐ 609. GUY HOFFMAN
- ☐ 646. JEFF TREADWAY

CLEVELAND INDIANS

- ☐ 23. PAT TABLER
- ☐ 39. BROOK JACOBY
- ☐ 60. JULIO FRANCO
- ☐ 80. JOE CARTER
- ☐ 92. CORY SNYDER
- ☐ 122. BRETT BUTLER
- ☐ 154. GREG SWINDELL
- ☐ 172. CHRIS BANDO
- ☐ 231. ANDRE THORNTON
- ☐ 262. RICK DEMPSEY
- ☐ 441. MEL HALL
- ☐ 484. RICH YETT
- ☐ 567. TOMMY HINZO
- ☐ 574. KEN SCHROM
- ☐ 581. CARMEN CASTILLO
- ☐ 586. ANDY ALLANSON
- ☐ 594. DOUG JONES
- ☐ 595. TOM CANDIOTTI
- ☐ 620. JOHN FARRELL
- ☐ 623. DARRELL AKERFELDS
- ☐ 633. DAVE CLARK

DETROIT TIGERS

- ☐ 15. MATT NOKES
- ☐ 37. ALAN TRAMMELL
- ☐ 56. LOU WHITAKER
- ☐ 75. DARRELL EVANS
- ☐ 119. CHET LEMON
- ☐ 138. LARRY HERNDON
- ☐ 156. MIKE HEATH
- ☐ 171. PAT SHERIDAN
- ☐ 199. JOHN GRUBB
- ☐ 217. DAVE BERGMAN
- ☐ 233. TOM BROOKENS
- ☐ 272. JIM MORRISON
- ☐ 382. MARK THURMOND
- ☐ 445. BILL MADLOCK
- ☐ 461. DAN PETRY
- ☐ 471. ERIC KING
- ☐ 490. FRANK TANANA
- ☐ 507. WILLIE HERNANDEZ
- ☐ 620. MIKE HENNEMAN
- ☐ 525. KIRK GIBSON
- ☐ 538. WALT TERRELL
- ☐ 545. JACK MORRIS
- ☐ 549. JEFF ROBINSON
- ☐ 571. JIM WALEWANDER
- ☐ 610. DOYLE ALEXANDER

HOUSTON ASTROS

- ☐ 28. JOSE CRUZ
- ☐ 33. KEVIN BASS
- ☐ 52. BILL DORAN
- ☐ 73. ALAN ASHBY
- ☐ 133. LARRY ANDERSEN

☐ 145. DENNIS WALLING
☐ 164. KEN CAMINITI
☐ 184. DANNY DARWIN
☐ 207. CRAIG REYNOLDS
☐ 222. CHUCK JACKSON
☐ 243. DAVE MEADS
☐ 282. TERRY PUHL
☐ 335. MIKE SCOTT
☐ 344. BOB KNEPPER
☐ 354. JIM DESHAIES
☐ 365. DAVE SMITH
☐ 383. BUDDY BIANCALANA
☐ 442. GERALD YOUNG
☐ 460. GLENN DAVIS
☐ 479. CHARLIE KERFELD
☐ 489. DAVEY LOPES
☐ 496. ROBBIE WINE
☐ 505. BILLY HATCHER
☐ 558. JUAN AGOSTO
☐ 575. NOLAN RYAN

KANSAS CITY ROYALS

☐   6. KEVIN SEITZER
☐ 11. GEORGE BRETT
☐ 61. CHARLIE LEIBRANDT
☐ 79. FRANK WHITE
☐ 89. BRET SABERHAGEN
☐ 102. WILLIE WILSON
☐ 106. DANNY TARTABULL
☐ 180. BO JACKSON
☐ 230. LARRY OWEN
☐ 263. LONNIE SMITH
☐ 273. STEVE BALBONI
☐ 290. DAN QUISENBERRY
☐ 313. BUD BLACK
☐ 330. ANGEL SALAZAR
☐ 343. JERRY DON GLEATON
☐ 377. BILL PECOTA
☐ 398. DANNY JACKSON
☐ 456. JIM EISENREICH
☐ 466. STEVE FARR
☐ 516. MARK GUBICZA
☐ 565. GENE GARBER
☐ 569. ED HEARN
☐ 577. JAMIE QUIRK
☐ 598. ROSS JONES
☐ 631. GARY THURMAN
☐ 636. JOHN DAVIS

LOS ANGELES DODGERS

☐   9. PEDRO GUERRERO
☐ 35. STEVE SAX
☐ 53. MIKE SCIOSCIA
☐ 87. RICK HONEYCUTT (F)
☐ 135. MIKE MARSHALL
☐ 147. FRANKLIN STUBBS
☐ 166. DAVE ANDERSON
☐ 182. ALEX TREVINO
☐ 208. BRIAN HOLTON
☐ 224. TIM LEARY
☐ 247. KEN LANDREAUX
☐ 267. MIKE RAMSEY
☐ 286. JOHN SHELBY
☐ 298. MICKEY HATCHER
☐ 321. MARIANO DUNCAN
☐ 357. MATT YOUNG
☐ 364. JOSE GONZALEZ
☐ 406. KEN HOWELL
☐ 417. DANNY HEEP
☐ 424. LEN MATUSZEK
☐ 431. PHIL GARNER
☐ 470. OREL HERSHISER
☐ 510. BOB WELCH
☐ 600. FERNANDO VALENZUELA
☐ 612. SHAWN HILLEGAS
☐ 637. MIKE DEVEREAUX
☐ 640. CHRIS GWYNN
☐ 641. TIM CREWS

MILWAUKEE BREWERS

☐ 22. B. J. SURHOFF
☐ 38. CHRIS BOSIO
☐ 59. GLENN BRAGGS
☐ 77. DAN PLESAC
☐ 95. ROB DEER
☐ 120. DALE SVEUM
☐ 160. ROBIN YOUNT
☐ 169. CECIL COOPER
☐ 197. JIM GANTNER

☐ 234. GREG BROCK
☐ 280. TEDDY HIGUERA
☐ 296. BILL WEGMAN
☐ 311. BILL SCHROEDER
☐ 334. BILLY JO ROBIDOUX
☐ 340. PAUL MOLITOR
☐ 349. ERNEST RILES
☐ 369. MIKE BIRKBECK
☐ 388. MIKE FELDER
☐ 402. CHUCK CRIM
☐ 429. JUAN CASTILLO
☐ 446. MARK CLEAR
☐ 513. JUAN NIEVES
☐ 578. JAY ALDRICH
☐ 593. RICK MANNING
☐ 630. STEVE KIEFER

MINNESOTA TWINS

☐ 24. KIRBY PUCKETT
☐ 43. KENT HRBEK
☐ 62. GARY GAETTI
☐ 90. BERT BLYLEVEN
☐ 91. JEFF REARDON
☐ 108. LES STRAKER
☐ 153. TOM LAUDNER
☐ 174. STEVE LOMBARDOZZI
☐ 194. TOM BRUNANSKY
☐ 214. GREG GAGNE
☐ 237. JOE NIEKRO
☐ 250. DON BAYLOR (B)
☐ 252. AL NEWMAN
☐ 276. GENE LARKIN
☐ 292. RANDY BUSH
☐ 324. DAN GLADDEN
☐ 332. GEORGE FRAZIER
☐ 361. SAL BUTERA
☐ 475. FRANK VIOLA
☐ 570. MARK DAVIDSON
☐ 606. ROY SMALLEY
☐ 613. KEITH ATHERTON

MONTREAL EXPOS

☐   3. TIM RAINES
☐ 19. ANDRES GALARRAGA
☐ 70. TIM WALLACH
☐ 85. VANCE LAW
☐ 97. CASEY CANDAELE
☐ 142. HERM WINNINGHAM
☐ 159. TOM FOLEY
☐ 187. TIM BURKE
☐ 305. HUBIE BROOKS
☐ 318. MIKE FITZGERALD
☐ 327. FLOYD YOUMANS
☐ 337. BOB SEBRA
☐ 345. MITCH WEBSTER
☐ 356. BRYN SMITH
☐ 366. ANDY MCGAFFIGAN
☐ 381. BOB MCCLURE
☐ 397. RANDY ST. CLAIRE
☐ 408. JEFF REED
☐ 430. NEAL HEATON
☐ 433. WALLACE JOHNSON
☐ 459. PASCUAL PEREZ
☐ 601. DENNIS MARTINEZ
☐ 608. JAY TIBBS
☐ 617. DAVE ENGLE

OAKLAND A'S

☐   5. MARK MCGWIRE
☐ 45. JOSE CANSECO
☐ 64. LUIS POLONIA
☐ 82. TERRY STEINBACH
☐ 87. RICK HONEYCUTT (B)
☐ 88. ALFREDO GRIFFIN
☐ 104. DENNIS ECKERSLEY
☐ 125. CURT YOUNG
☐ 177. MOOSE HAAS
☐ 193. JOAQUIN ANDUJAR
☐ 211. MIKE DAVIS
☐ 253. CARNEY LANSFORD
☐ 269. MICKEY TETTLETON
☐ 294. TONY PHILLIPS
☐ 348. DAVE LEIPER (F)
☐ 367. STAN JAVIER
☐ 392. JOSE RIJO
☐ 428. MIKE GALLEGO
☐ 455. DWAYNE MURPHY
☐ 458. DAVE STEWART
☐ 504. REGGIE JACKSON

☐ 511. STEVE ONTIVEROS
☐ 522. JAY HOWELL
☐ 547. STEVE HENDERSON
☐ 588. GENE NELSON
☐ 604. TONY BERNAZARD
☐ 614. ERIC PLUNK
☐ 616. DENNIS LAMP

PHILADELPHIA PHILLIES

☐ 16. MIKE SCHMIDT
☐ 32. JUAN SAMUEL
☐ 115. MILT THOMPSON
☐ 131. LANCE PARRISH
☐ 144. MIKE JACKSON
☐ 161. STEVE BEDROSIAN
☐ 375. SHANE RAWLEY
☐ 386. GREG GROSS
☐ 401. DAN CARMAN
☐ 405. GLENN WILSON
☐ 409. CHRIS JAMES
☐ 425. KENT TEKULVE
☐ 435. STEVE JELTZ
☐ 448. RICK SCHU
☐ 468. KEVIN GROSS
☐ 473. DARREN DAULTON
☐ 492. BRUCE RUFFIN
☐ 494. TOM HUME (F)
☐ 499. LUIS AGUAYO
☐ 515. VON HAYES
☐ 526. WALLY RITCHIE
☐ 566. RON ROENICKE
☐ 635. KEITH HUGHES

PITTSBURGH PIRATES

☐ 34. R. J. REYNOLDS
☐ 51. DOUG DRABEK
☐ 116. BOBBY BONILLA
☐ 130. BRIAN FISHER
☐ 143. MIKE DIAZ
☐ 162. BOB WALK
☐ 260. SID BREAM
☐ 265. BARRY BONDS
☐ 287. JOHN SMILEY
☐ 301. AL PEDRIQUE
☐ 320. JIM GOTT
☐ 404. JUNIOR ORTIZ
☐ 416. ANDY VAN SLYKE
☐ 418. JOHN CANGELOSI
☐ 421. MIKE LAVALLIERE
☐ 432. MIKE DUNNE
☐ 439. JEFF ROBINSON
☐ 453. RAFAEL BELLIARD
☐ 554. DARNELL COLES
☐ 597. JOSE LIND
☐ 611. MIKE BIELECKI
☐ 642. MACKEY SASSER
☐ 643. VINCENTE PALACIOS

NEW YORK METS

☐ 21. KEVIN MCREYNOLDS
☐ 41. DAVE MAGADAN
☐ 49. DAVID CONE
☐ 69. HOWARD JOHNSON
☐ 128. TIM TEUFEL
☐ 141. RON DARLING
☐ 158. LEE MAZZILLI
☐ 188. ROGER MCDOWELL
☐ 203. TERRY LEACH
☐ 227. DOUG SISK

☐ 249. JOHN MITCHELL
☐ 303. WALLY BACKMAN
☐ 316. RAFAEL SANTANA
☐ 325. GARY CARTER
☐ 336. RANDY MYERS
☐ 350. DWIGHT GOODEN
☐ 360. DARRYL STRAWBERRY
☐ 370. LEN DYKSTRA
☐ 387. BARRY LYONS
☐ 400. KEITH HERNANDEZ
☐ 474. MOOKIE WILSON
☐ 495. JESSE OROSCO
☐ 521. RICK AGUILERA
☐ 563. BOB OJEDA
☐ 615. SID FERNANDEZ
☐ 623. RANDY MILLIGAN
☐ 624. KEVIN ELSTER
☐ 639. KEITH MILLER
☐ 645. GREGG JEFFERIES

NEW YORK YANKEES

☐   1. DON MATTINGLY
☐ 13. RICKEY HENDERSON
☐ 55. DAVE WINFIELD
☐ 74. RICK RHODEN
☐ 117. WAYNE TOLLESON
☐ 137. BOBBY MEACHAM
☐ 157. GARY WARD
☐ 170. MIKE PAGLIARULO
☐ 196. DAN PASQUA
☐ 220. MIKE EASLER
☐ 232. MARK SALAS
☐ 240. TOMMY JOHN
☐ 258. TIM STODDARD
☐ 266. WILLIE RANDOLPH
☐ 310. RON GUIDRY
☐ 342. STEVE TROUT
☐ 351. DAVE RIGHETTI
☐ 368. HENRY COTTO
☐ 389. PAT CLEMENTS
☐ 449. RON KITTLE
☐ 486. RICK CERONE
☐ 532. JOEL SKINNER
☐ 579. CLAUDELL WASHINGTON
☐ 585. BILL GULLICKSON
☐ 634. ROBERTO KELLY

ST. LOUIS CARDINALS

☐ 12. OZZIE SMITH
☐ 40. WILLIE MCGEE
☐ 48. TONY PENA
☐ 68. VINCE COLEMAN
☐ 84. TOM HERR
☐ 94. JOE MAGRANE
☐ 100. JACK CLARK
☐ 190. TERRY PENDLETON
☐ 202. TODD WORRELL
☐ 226. GREG MATHEWS
☐ 248. JOSE OQUENDO
☐ 264. BOB FORSCH
☐ 275. JOHN TUDOR
☐ 288. CURT FORD
☐ 302. JIM LINDEMAN
☐ 328. BILL DAWLEY
☐ 346. JOHN MORRIS
☐ 358. TOM PAGNOZZI
☐ 384. TIM CONROY
☐ 412. RICK HORTON
☐ 415. DANNY COX
☐ 517. KEN DAYLEY
☐ 587. LEE TUNNELL
☐ 596. STEVE LAKE

SAN DIEGO PADRES

☐ 26. BENNY SANTIAGO
☐ 36. JOHN KRUK
☐ 114. STAN JEFFERSON
☐ 150. LANCE MCCULLERS
☐ 167. ED WHITSON
☐ 181. CARMELO MARTINEZ
☐ 189. GARRY TEMPLETON
☐ 209. MARVELL WYNNE
☐ 225. STEVE GARVEY
☐ 246. JIMMY JONES
☐ 284. LUIS SALAZAR
☐ 331. GOOSE GOSSAGE
☐ 338. ERIC SHOW
☐ 347. ANDY HAWKINS
☐ 348. DAVE LEIPER (B)

☐ 363. CHRIS BROWN
☐ 385. TONY GWYNN
☐ 391. MARK DAVIS
☐ 414. SHANE MACK
☐ 420. JOEY CORA
☐ 438. KEITH COMSTOCK
☐ 447. GREG BOOKER
☐ 469. BRUCE BOCHY
☐ 483. TIM FLANNERY
☐ 512. RANDY READY
☐ 568. ERIC NOLTE
☐ 626. SHAWN ABNER

SHANE MACK

SAN FRANCISCO GIANTS

☐ 27. KELLY DOWNS
☐ 54. CANDY MALDONADO
☐ 78. WILL CLARK
☐ 118. MATT WILLIAMS
☐ 134. BOB BRENLY
☐ 146. ROBBY THOMPSON
☐ 165. JOSE URIBE
☐ 185. MIKE KRUKOW
☐ 228. DAVE HENDERSON (B)
☐ 283. MARK WASINGER
☐ 465. MIKE LACOSS
☐ 477. BOB MELVIN
☐ 481. KEVIN MITCHELL
☐ 493. CHRIS SPEIER
☐ 509. JOEL YOUNGBLOOD
☐ 519. RICK REUSCHEL
☐ 528. ATLEE HAMMAKER
☐ 533. SCOTT GARRELTS
☐ 548. EDDIE MILNER
☐ 553. CRAIG LEFFERTS
☐ 556. MIKE ALDRETE
☐ 564. DAVE DRAVECKY
☐ 580. JEFFREY LEONARD
☐ 605. CHILI DAVIS
☐ 618. HARRY SPILMAN
☐ 619. DON ROBINSON
☐ 627. KIRT MANWARING

SEATTLE MARINERS

☐ 30. MARK LANGSTON
☐ 46. JIM PRESLEY
☐ 66. PHIL BRADLEY
☐ 83. ALVIN DAVIS
☐ 126. DAVE VALLE
☐ 151. SCOTT BRADLEY
☐ 178. MIKE KINGERY
☐ 192. REY QUINONES
☐ 213. MICKEY BRANTLEY
☐ 238. SCOTT BANKHEAD
☐ 256. KEN PHELPS
☐ 277. HAROLD REYNOLDS
☐ 295. MIKE MORGAN
☐ 309. JOHN MOSES
☐ 323. LEE GUETTERMAN
☐ 362. DOMINGO RAMOS
☐ 396. STEVE SHIELDS
☐ 419. JOHN CHRISTENSEN
☐ 436. DONELL NIXON
☐ 464. MIKE MOORE
☐ 488. JERRY REED
☐ 599. GARY MATTHEWS

TEXAS RANGERS

☐ 29. PETE O'BRIEN
☐ 47. MIKE STANLEY

☐ 113. RUBEN SIERRA
☐ 127. CURT WILKERSON
☐ 140. CHARLIE HOUGH
☐ 149. BOBBY WITT
☐ 179. GREG HARRIS
☐ 191. LARRY PARRISH
☐ 215. ODDIBE MCDOWELL
☐ 236. BOB BROWER
☐ 251. SCOTT FLETCHER
☐ 268. DON SLAUGHT
☐ 278. JERRY BROWNE
☐ 306. STEVE BUECHELE
☐ 322. JOSE GUZMAN
☐ 339. MITCH WILLIAMS
☐ 373. GENO PETRALLI
☐ 407. JEFF KUNKEL
☐ 452. DALE MOHORCIC
☐ 485. PETE INCAVIGLIA
☐ 491. MIKE LOYND
☐ 514. JEFF RUSSELL
☐ 523. ED CORREA
☐ 531. TOM PACIOREK
☐ 534. TOM O'MALLEY
☐ 536. PAUL KILGUS
☐ 537. DARRELL PORTER
☐ 543. STEVE HOWE

TORONTO BLUE JAYS

☐   8. JESSE BARFIELD
☐ 20. TONY FERNANDEZ
☐ 57. TOM HENKE
☐ 76. DAVE STIEB
☐ 98. JOHN CERUTTI
☐ 107. FRED MCGRIFF
☐ 109. LLOYD MOSEBY
☐ 168. ERNIE WHITT
☐ 198. MARK EICHHORN
☐ 204. GARTH IORG
☐ 216. JIMMY KEY
☐ 235. RANCE MULLINIKS
☐ 257. RICK LEACH
☐ 279. WILLIE UPSHAW
☐ 312. JOSE NUNEZ
☐ 399. CECIL FIELDER
☐ 422. KELLY GRUBER
☐ 427. MIKE FLANAGAN (B)
☐ 444. CHARLIE MOORE
☐ 478. JEFF MUSSELMAN
☐ 530. JIM CLANCY
☐ 540. GEORGE BELL
☐ 561. MANNY LEE
☐ 583. JEFF DEWILLIS
☐ 621. NELSON LIRIANO
☐ 629. ROB DUCEY

1988 SCORE
ROOKIE & TRADED (110)
2 1/2 X 3 1/2

BRETT BUTLER

ATLANTA BRAVES

☐ 84T. PETE SMITH

BALTIMORE ORIOLES

☐ 31T. MICKEY TETTLETON
☐ 41T. JOE ORSULAK
☐ 70T. BRADY ANDERSON
☐ 77T. OSWALD PERAZA

BOSTON RED SOX

- ☐ 6T. DENNIS LAMP
- ☐ 20T. LEE SMITH
- ☐ 21T. RICK CERONE
- ☐ 59T. MIKE SMITHSON
- ☐ 65T. LARRY PARRISH
- ☐ 81T. STEVE CURRY
- ☐ 83T. STEVE ELLSWORTH

CALIFORNIA ANGELS

- ☐ 26T. DAN PETRY
- ☐ 28T. CHILI DAVIS
- ☐ 87T. BRYAN HARVEY

CHICAGO CUBS

- ☐ 14T. GOOSE GOSSAGE
- ☐ 16T. VANCE LAW
- ☐ 39T. CALVIN SCHIRALDI
- ☐ 80T. MARK GRACE
- ☐ 82T. DAMON BERRYHILL
- ☐ 94T. JEFF PICO
- ☐ 109T. DARRIN JACKSON

CHICAGO WHITE SOX

- ☐ 24T. RICK HORTON
- ☐ 52T. MARK SALAS
- ☐ 56T. DAN PASQUA
- ☐ 61T. JERRY REUSS
- ☐ 66T. JEFF BITTIGER
- ☐ 85T. JACK MCDOWELL
- ☐ 89T. DAVE GALLAGHER
- ☐ 108T. MELIDO PEREZ

CINCINNATI REDS

- ☐ 2T. DANNY JACKSON
- ☐ 27T. JOSE RIJO
- ☐ 43T. HERM WINNINGHAM
- ☐ 78T. JACK ARMSTRONG
- ☐ 86T. ROB DIBBLE
- ☐ 100T. CHRIS SABO

CLEVELAND INDIANS

- ☐ 11T. BUD BLACK
- ☐ 42T. WILLIE UPSHAW
- ☐ 44T. RON KITTLE
- ☐ 92T. DON GORDON

DETROIT TIGERS

- ☐ 13T. LUIS SALAZAR
- ☐ 17T. RAY KNIGHT
- ☐ 38T. GARY PETTIS
- ☐ 79T. DON HEINKEL

HOUSTON ASTROS

- ☐ 12T. RAFAEL RAMIREZ
- ☐ 103T. CRAIG BIGGIO

KANSAS CITY ROYALS

- ☐ 4T. KURT STILLWELL
- ☐ 22T. PAT TABLER
- ☐ 36T. BILL BUCKNER
- ☐ 63T. FLOYD BANNISTER
- ☐ 71T. JEFF MONTGOMERY
- ☐ 76T. MIKE MACFARLANE

KIRK GIBSON

LOS ANGELES DODGERS

- ☐ 10T. KIRK GIBSON
- ☐ 32T. RICK DEMPSEY
- ☐ 35T. JAY HOWELL
- ☐ 37T. ALFREDO GRIFFIN
- ☐ 53T. MIKE DAVIS
- ☐ 64T. JESSE OROSCO
- ☐ 101T. TIM BELCHER

MILWAUKEE BREWERS

- ☐ 72T. DARRYL HAMILTON
- ☐ 75T. JOEY MEYER
- ☐ 104T. DON AUGUST

MINNESOTA TWINS

- ☐ 8T. TOM HERR

MONTREAL EXPOS

- ☐ 25T. GRAIG NETTLES
- ☐ 88T. JOHN DOPSON
- ☐ 96T. NELSON SANTOVENIA

NEW YORK METS

- ☐ 30T. MACKEY SASSER

NEW YORK YANKEES

- ☐ 1T. JACK CLARK
- ☐ 19T. DON SLAUGHT
- ☐ 40T. JOHN CANDELARIA
- ☐ 47T. STEVE SHIELDS
- ☐ 54T. RAFAEL SANTANA
- ☐ 60T. RICHARD DOTSON
- ☐ 97T. AL LEITER

OAKLAND A'S

- ☐ 15T. BOB WELCH
- ☐ 33T. RON HASSEY
- ☐ 49T. DAVE HENDERSON
- ☐ 50T. DAVE PARKER
- ☐ 55T. DON BAYLOR
- ☐ 58T. GLENN HUBBARD
- ☐ 102T. WALT WEISS
- ☐ 106T. TODD BURNS

PHILADELPHIA PHILLIES

- ☐ 34T. PHIL BRADLEY
- ☐ 45T. BOB DERNIER
- ☐ 51T. MIKE YOUNG
- ☐ 68T. RICKY JORDAN

PITTSBURGH PIRATES

- ☐ 69T. TOMMY GREGG
- ☐ 110T. ORESTES DESTRADE

TOM BRUNANSKY

ST. LOUIS CARDINALS

- ☐ 5T. TOM BRUNANSKY
- ☐ 7T. JOSE DELEON
- ☐ 18T. DAN QUISENBERRY
- ☐ 23T. LARRY MCWILLIAMS
- ☐ 98T. LUIS ALICEA
- ☐ 107T. JOHN COSTELLO

SAN DIEGO PADRES

- ☐ 9T. KEITH MORELAND
- ☐ 29T. DICKIE THON
- ☐ 105T. ROBERTO ALOMAR

SAN FRANCISCO GIANTS

- ☐ 3T. BRETT BUTLER
- ☐ 57T. ERNEST RILES

SEATTLE MARINERS

- ☐ 46T. STEVE BALBONI
- ☐ 48T. HENRY COTTO
- ☐ 62T. MIKE JACKSON
- ☐ 74T. GREG BRILEY
- ☐ 91T. MIKE SCHOOLER
- ☐ 95T. JAY BUHNER

TEXAS RANGERS

- ☐ 67T. RAY HAYWARD
- ☐ 73T. CECIL ESPY

TORONTO BLUE JAYS

- ☐ 90T. TODD STOTTLEMYRE
- ☐ 93T. SIL CAMPUSANO
- ☐ 99T. PAT BORDERS

1989 SCORE (660)
2 1/2 X 3 1/2

BERT BLYLEVEN

ATLANTA BRAVES

- ☐ 30. DALE MURPHY
- ☐ 74. ALBERT HALL
- ☐ 101. GERALD PERRY
- ☐ 111. OZZIE VIRGIL
- ☐ 139. KEN OBERKFELL
- ☐ 163. DION JAMES
- ☐ 207. PETE SMITH
- ☐ 229. RICK MAHLER
- ☐ 372. RON GANT
- ☐ 373. PAUL ASSENMACHER
- ☐ 406. ANDRES THOMAS
- ☐ 425. BRUCE SUTTER
- ☐ 442. TOM GLAVINE
- ☐ 448. CHARLIE PULEO
- ☐ 492. ZANE SMITH
- ☐ 502. BRUCE BENEDICT
- ☐ 589. JEFF BLAUSER
- ☐ 605. TERRY BLOCKER
- ☐ 611. TED SIMMONS
- ☐ 616. JOHN SMOLTZ
- ☐ 631. DEREK LILLIQUIST

BALTIMORE ORIOLES

- ☐ 15. CAL RIPKEN, JR.
- ☐ 18. BILL RIPKEN
- ☐ 81. LARRY SHEETS
- ☐ 94. EDDIE MURRAY
- ☐ 123. TERRY KENNEDY
- ☐ 126. FRED LYNN
- ☐ 236. PETE STANICEK
- ☐ 247. JOE ORSULAK
- ☐ 252. TOM NIEDENFUER
- ☐ 262. JAY TIBBS
- ☐ 264. DOUG SISK

☐ 292. DAVE SCHMIDT
☐ 358. MICKEY TETTLETON
☐ 452. RICK SCHU
☐ 506. KEN GERHART
☐ 524. DON AASE
☐ 551. JEFF BALLARD
☐ 563. BRADY ANDERSON
☐ 571. OSWALD PERAZA
☐ 573. JOSE BAUTISTA
☐ 585. RENE GONZALES
☐ 590. JIM TRABER
☐ 592. MARK WILLIAMSON
☐ 636. CRAIG WORTHINGTON
☐ 651. BOB MILACKI

BOSTON RED SOX

☐ 9. ELLIS BURKS
☐ 63. MARTY BARRETT
☐ 66. MIKE GREENWELL
☐ 85. JIM RICE
☐ 150. LEE SMITH
☐ 175. WADE BOGGS
☐ 193. DWIGHT EVANS
☐ 218. SPIKE OWEN
☐ 238. DENNIS BOYD
☐ 325. BRUCE HURST
☐ 345. RICH GEDMAN
☐ 350. ROGER CLEMENS
☐ 371. TODD BENZINGER
☐ 383. BOB STANLEY
☐ 396. RICK CERONE
☐ 403. MIKE SMITHSON
☐ 412. WES GARDNER
☐ 486. JODY REED
☐ 491. JEFF SELLERS
☐ 495. LARRY PARRISH
☐ 508. DENNIS LAMP
☐ 531. TOM BOLTON
☐ 541. KEVIN ROMINE
☐ 549. MIKE BODDICKER
☐ 623. CARLOS QUINTANA

CALIFORNIA ANGELS

☐ 14. JOHNNY RAY
☐ 16. DICK SCHOFIELD
☐ 54. CHILI DAVIS
☐ 65. WALLY JOYNER
☐ 76. BRIAN DOWNING
☐ 122. DAN PETRY
☐ 140. BUTCH WYNEGAR
☐ 153. DEWAYNE BUICE
☐ 157. WILLIS FRASER
☐ 181. KIRK MCCASKILL
☐ 182. TONY ARMAS
☐ 185. BRYAN HARVEY
☐ 208. MARK MCLEMORE
☐ 233. BOB BOONE
☐ 261. JACK HOWELL
☐ 298. MIKE WITT
☐ 323. DEVON WHITE
☐ 445. STEWART CLIBURN
☐ 499. DARRELL MILLER
☐ 503. CHUCK FINLEY
☐ 535. DONNIE MOORE
☐ 543. GREG MINTON
☐ 566. TERRY CLARK

CHICAGO CUBS

☐ 2. ANDRE DAWSON
☐ 13. JEFF PICO
☐ 35. RYNE SANDBERG
☐ 60. LES LANCASTER
☐ 71. MITCH WEBSTER
☐ 77. DAVE MARTINEZ
☐ 102. VANCE LAW
☐ 119. GREG MADDUX
☐ 146. FRANK DIPINO
☐ 173. JODY DAVIS
☐ 199. RAFAEL PALMEIRO
☐ 223. RICH GOSSAGE
☐ 235. SHAWON DUNSTON
☐ 263. JAMIE MOYER
☐ 288. JERRY MUMPHREY
☐ 321. CALVIN SCHIRALDI
☐ 336. DAMON BERRYHILL
☐ 360. DARRIN JACKSON
☐ 362. MARK GRACE
☐ 364. PAT PERRY
☐ 407. RICK SUTCLIFFE

☐ 446. MANNY TRILLO
☐ 527. ANGEL SALAZAR
☐ 532. AL NIPPER
☐ 604. GARY VARSHO
☐ 621. DOUG DASCENZO
☐ 624. MIKE HARKEY
☐ 642. DWIGHT SMITH

CHICAGO WHITE SOX

☐ 37. GREG WALKER
☐ 67. KEN WILLIAMS
☐ 128. HAROLD BAINES
☐ 145. RICK HORTON
☐ 177. GARY REDUS
☐ 289. JACK MCDOWELL
☐ 331. IVAN CALDERON
☐ 338. DAN PASQUA
☐ 351. BILL LONG
☐ 384. DAVE LAPOINT
☐ 386. MELIDO PEREZ
☐ 388. STEVE LYONS
☐ 399. BOBBY THIGPEN
☐ 433. OZZIE GUILLEN
☐ 443. DARYL BOSTON
☐ 449. CARLTON FISK
☐ 455. DAVE GALLAGHER
☐ 457. FRED MANRIQUE
☐ 489. JERRY REUSS
☐ 512. JEFF BITTIGER
☐ 542. MARK SALAS
☐ 583. DONNIE HILL
☐ 603. MIKE DIAZ
☐ 607. JIM EPPARD
☐ 608. JOHN DAVIS

CARLTON FISK

CINCINNATI REDS

☐ 7. KAL DANIELS
☐ 31. BARRY LARKIN
☐ 64. NICK ESASKY
☐ 86. JEFF TREADWAY
☐ 104. CHRIS SABO
☐ 109. ERIC DAVIS
☐ 141. ROB MURPHY
☐ 166. DAVE CONCEPCION
☐ 187. BO DIAZ
☐ 206. PAUL O'NEILL
☐ 267. DAVE COLLINS
☐ 454. TIM BIRTSAS
☐ 462. JACK ARMSTRONG
☐ 485. FRANK WILLIAMS
☐ 496. HERM WINNINGHAM
☐ 521. LLOYD MCCLENDON
☐ 552. JOSE RIJO
☐ 554. TOM BROWNING
☐ 555. DANNY JACKSON
☐ 559. RON ROBINSON
☐ 575. JOHN FRANCO
☐ 609. KEN GRIFFEY, SR.
☐ 615. RON OESTER
☐ 618. ROB DIBBLE
☐ 640. VAN SNIDER
☐ 646. NORM CHARLTON

CLEVELAND INDIANS

☐ 11. JULIO FRANCO
☐ 17. MEL HALL
☐ 19. BROOK JACOBY
☐ 46. ANDY ALLANSON

☐ 52. CORY SNYDER
☐ 96. RON KITTLE
☐ 188. WILLIE UPSHAW
☐ 213. JOE CARTER
☐ 239. TOM CANDIOTTI
☐ 266. JOHN FARRELL
☐ 282. GREG SWINDELL
☐ 352. JAY BELL
☐ 387. DOUG JONES
☐ 404. BUD BLACK
☐ 424. SCOTT BAILES
☐ 467. RICH YETT
☐ 497. CARMEN CASTILLO
☐ 547. DON GORDON
☐ 591. JON PERLMAN
☐ 597. TERRY FRANCONA
☐ 598. PAUL ZUVELLA
☐ 633. LUIS MEDINA

DETROIT TIGERS

☐ 43. MATT NOKES
☐ 26. GARY PETTIS
☐ 44. CHET LEMON
☐ 110. ALAN TRAMMELL
☐ 112. FRANK TANANA
☐ 129. DOYLE ALEXANDER
☐ 131. MIKE HEATH
☐ 135. RAY KNIGHT
☐ 168. DON HEINKEL
☐ 171. DARRELL EVANS
☐ 204. PAT SHERIDAN
☐ 230. LOU WHITAKER
☐ 250. JACK MORRIS
☐ 269. TOM BROOKENS
☐ 275. GUILLERMO HERNANDEZ
☐ 279. LARRY HERNDON
☐ 284. JEFF ROBINSON
☐ 293. MIKE HENNEMAN
☐ 311. JIM WALEWANDER
☐ 314. WALT TERRELL
☐ 316. LUIS SALAZAR
☐ 469. DAVE BERGMAN
☐ 471. ERIC KING
☐ 545. DWAYNE MURPHY
☐ 595. PAUL GIBSON
☐ 627. STEVE SEARCY

HOUSTON ASTROS

☐ 12. BILL DORAN
☐ 49. DENNY WALLING
☐ 61. BILLY HATCHER
☐ 97. GERALD YOUNG
☐ 113. RAFAEL RAMIREZ
☐ 164. GLENN DAVIS
☐ 192. JIM PANKOVITS
☐ 226. KEVIN BASS
☐ 237. CRAIG BIGGIO
☐ 245. DAVE SMITH
☐ 273. BOB KNEPPER
☐ 283. JUAN AGOSTO
☐ 300. NOLAN RYAN
☐ 366. ALAN ASHBY
☐ 468. CRAIG REYNOLDS
☐ 472. JOAQUIN ANDUJAR
☐ 523. LARRY ANDERSEN
☐ 546. JIM DESHAIES
☐ 550. MIKE SCOTT
☐ 553. DANNY DARWIN
☐ 567. TERRY PUHL
☐ 574. ALEX TREVINO
☐ 584. CHUCK JACKSON
☐ 593. DAVE MEADS
☐ 610. BUDDY BELL
☐ 643. CAMERON DREW

KANSAS CITY ROYALS

☐ 28. WILLIE WILSON
☐ 55. KEVIN SEITZER
☐ 75. GEORGE BRETT
☐ 105. DANNY TARTABULL
☐ 133. CHARLIE LEIBRANDT
☐ 162. KURT STILLWELL
☐ 183. STEVE FARR
☐ 214. BILL BUCKNER
☐ 249. FLOYD BANNISTER
☐ 251. BRET SABERHAGEN
☐ 291. MARK GUBICZA
☐ 319. MIKE MACFARLANE
☐ 330. BO JACKSON

☐ 339. BILL PECOTA
☐ 348. TED POWER
☐ 367. JEFF MONTGOMERY
☐ 390. FRANK WHITE
☐ 391. PAT TABLER
☐ 423. JERRY DON GLEATON
☐ 441. RICK ANDERSON
☐ 461. JAMIE QUIRK
☐ 504. BRAD WELLMAN
☐ 594. JIM EISENREICH
☐ 634. TOM GORDON
☐ 648. LUIS DE LOS SANTOS

LOS ANGELES DODGERS

☐ 69. STEVE SAX
☐ 103. JOHN SHELBY
☐ 121. MIKE SCIOSCIA
☐ 167. ALFREDO GRIFFIN
☐ 186. MIKE MARSHALL
☐ 210. KIRK GIBSON
☐ 332. MICKEY HATCHER
☐ 343. DANNY HEEP
☐ 356. JESSE OROSCO
☐ 370. OREL HERSHISER
☐ 376. MIKE DAVIS
☐ 378. JAY HOWELL
☐ 389. ALEJANDRO PENA
☐ 400. DON SUTTON
☐ 418. TIM BELCHER
☐ 429. TIM LEARY
☐ 437. FERNANDO VALENZUELA
☐ 478. DAVE ANDERSON
☐ 488. SHAWN HILLEGAS
☐ 505. TIM CREWS
☐ 507. BRIAN HOLTON
☐ 556. RICK DEMPSEY
☐ 560. JOHN TUDOR
☐ 570. JEFF HAMILTON
☐ 586. TRACY WOODSON
☐ 588. MARIO SOTO
☐ 599. FRANKLIN STUBBS
☐ 602. MIKE SHARPERSON
☐ 622. BILL BRENNAN
☐ 635. RAMON MARTINEZ

MILWAUKEE BREWERS

☐ 72. ROB DEER
☐ 132. TEDDY HIGUERA
☐ 147. GLENN BRAGGS
☐ 151. ROBIN YOUNT
☐ 154. B. J. SURHOFF
☐ 243. CHRIS BOSIO
☐ 256. DALE SVEUM
☐ 272. CHUCK CRIM
☐ 307. GREG BROCK
☐ 313. JIM GANTNER
☐ 320. DAN PLESAC
☐ 335. BILL WEGMAN
☐ 374. JOEY MEYER
☐ 410. JUAN NIEVES
☐ 419. DON AUGUST
☐ 430. MARK CLEAR
☐ 557. JEFFREY LEONARD
☐ 565. PAUL MOLITOR
☐ 569. PAUL MIRABELLA
☐ 579. ODELL JONES
☐ 581. DAVE STAPLETON
☐ 587. JIM ADDUCI
☐ 596. MIKE BIRKBECK
☐ 606. CHARLIE O'BRIEN
☐ 625. GARY SHEFFIELD

MINNESOTA TWINS

☐ 8. GARY GAETTI
☐ 20. KIRBY PUCKETT
☐ 62. DAN GLADDEN
☐ 107. MARK DAVIDSON
☐ 134. TIM LAUDNER
☐ 159. GREG GAGNE
☐ 191. TOMMY HERR
☐ 212. RANDY BUSH
☐ 215. BERT BLYLEVEN
☐ 244. LES STRAKER
☐ 280. GENE LARKIN
☐ 290. FRANK VIOLA
☐ 305. JEFF REARDON
☐ 381. KEITH ATHERTON
☐ 382. KENT HRBEK
☐ 394. ALLAN ANDERSON

☐ 408. BRIAN HARPER
☐ 414. JUAN BERENGUER
☐ 421. STEVE LOMBARDOZZI
☐ 432. JOHN MOSES
☐ 479. FRED TOLIVER
☐ 482. MARK PORTUGAL
☐ 493. AL NEWMAN
☐ 501. CHARLIE LEA

MONTREAL EXPOS

☐ 40. TIM RAINES
☐ 53. HUBIE BROOKS
☐ 99. JEFF REED
☐ 114. DENNIS MARTINEZ
☐ 138. ANDY MCGAFFIGAN
☐ 144. ANDRES GALARRAGA
☐ 169. LUIS RIVERA
☐ 196. WALLACE JOHNSON
☐ 220. TIM WALLACH
☐ 228. TIM BURKE
☐ 253. NEAL HEATON
☐ 277. GRAIG NETTLES
☐ 299. PASCUAL PEREZ
☐ 346. NELSON SANTOVENIA
☐ 377. JEFF PARRETT
☐ 405. TOM FOLEY
☐ 428. BRYN SMITH
☐ 451. OTIS NIXON
☐ 466. JOHN DOPSON
☐ 470. REX HUDLER
☐ 498. JOE HESKETH
☐ 510. TRACY JONES
☐ 511. MIKE FITZGERALD
☐ 645. RANDY JOHNSON

NEW YORK METS

☐ 10. DARRYL STRAWBERRY
☐ 41. KEITH HERNANDEZ
☐ 58. TIM TEUFEL
☐ 84. LEN DYKSTRA
☐ 93. KEVIN MCREYNOLDS
☐ 116. BOB OJEDA
☐ 130. KEVIN ELSTER
☐ 136. HOWARD JOHNSON
☐ 180. RON DARLING
☐ 200. DOC GOODEN
☐ 217. LEE MAZZILLI
☐ 221. DAVID CONE
☐ 240. GARY CARTER
☐ 268. SID FERNANDEZ
☐ 281. ROGER MCDOWELL
☐ 302. MOOKIE WILSON
☐ 303. MACKEY SASSER
☐ 306. RANDY MYERS
☐ 312. DAVE MAGADAN
☐ 315. WALLY BACKMAN
☐ 327. RICK AGUILERA
☐ 431. TERRY LEACH
☐ 456. BARRY LYONS
☐ 464. KEITH MILLER
☐ 572. BOB MCCLURE
☐ 600. GREGG JEFFERIES
☐ 650. DAVE WEST

NEW YORK YANKEES

☐ 25. JACK CLARK
☐ 45. WILLIE RANDOLPH
☐ 50. DAVE WINFIELD
☐ 70. RICKEY HENDERSON
☐ 100. DON MATTINGLY
☐ 189. MIKE PAGLIARULO
☐ 211. CLAUDELL WASHINGTON
☐ 225. DAVE RIGHETTI
☐ 246. JOHN CANDELARIA
☐ 278. RICH DOTSON
☐ 296. RAFAEL SANTANA
☐ 317. RICK RHODEN
☐ 342. RON GUIDRY
☐ 375. NEIL ALLEN
☐ 415. CHARLES HUDSON
☐ 435. GARY WARD
☐ 436. LUIS AGUAYO
☐ 439. CECILIO GUANTE
☐ 447. JOEL SKINNER
☐ 477. TOMMY JOHN
☐ 487. ROBERTO KELLY
☐ 509. BOBBY MEACHAM
☐ 561. DON SLAUGHT
☐ 578. STEVE SHIELDS

☐ 580. AL LEITER
☐ 582. WAYNE TOLLESON

OAKLAND A'S

☐ 1. JOSE CANSECO
☐ 3. MARK MCGWIRE
☐ 29. CURT YOUNG
☐ 32. DAVE STEWART
☐ 34. GLENN HUBBARD
☐ 108. DAVE PARKER
☐ 156. TONY PHILLIPS
☐ 165. WALT WEISS
☐ 179. CARNEY LANSFORD
☐ 205. DON BAYLOR
☐ 248. STORM DAVIS
☐ 276. DENNIS ECKERSLEY
☐ 308. BOB WELCH
☐ 322. STAN JAVIER
☐ 334. RON HASSEY
☐ 337. STEVE ONTIVEROS
☐ 340. GREG CADARET
☐ 365. TERRY STEINBACH
☐ 380. LUIS POLONIA
☐ 392. ERIC PLUNK
☐ 416. RICK HONEYCUTT
☐ 434. GENE NELSON
☐ 459. DOUG JENNINGS
☐ 465. TODD BURNS
☐ 533. DAVE HENDERSON
☐ 537. MIKE GALLEGO
☐ 629. FELIX JOSE
☐ 641. LANCE BLANKENSHIP

PHILADELPHIA PHILLIES

☐ 39. VON HAYES
☐ 79. PHIL BRADLEY
☐ 92. MILT THOMPSON
☐ 95. LANCE PARRISH
☐ 125. GREG GROSS
☐ 149. MIKE SCHMIDT
☐ 170. SHANE RAWLEY
☐ 202. CHRIS JAMES
☐ 222. DON CARMAN
☐ 227. KEVIN GROSS
☐ 255. JUAN SAMUEL
☐ 260. STEVE BEDROSIAN
☐ 287. KENT TEKULVE
☐ 328. BRUCE RUFFIN
☐ 355. STEVE JELTZ
☐ 357. BOB DERNIER
☐ 393. MIKE MADDUX
☐ 413. DARREN DAULTON
☐ 476. GREG HARRIS
☐ 494. MIKE YOUNG
☐ 544. DAVE PALMER
☐ 548. RICKY JORDAN
☐ 639. RON JONES
☐ 647. TODD FROHWIRTH

PITTSBURGH PIRATES

☐ 24. BRIAN FISHER
☐ 33. MIKE LAVALLIERE
☐ 48. SID BREAM
☐ 83. DARNELL COLES
☐ 87. JOSE LIND
☐ 91. R. J. REYNOLDS
☐ 117. DOUG DRABEK
☐ 127. BARRY BONDS
☐ 174. ANDY VAN SLYKE
☐ 195. BOBBY BONILLA
☐ 224. BOB WALK
☐ 257. JIM GOTT
☐ 285. MIKE DUNNE
☐ 309. JEFF ROBINSON
☐ 333. BARRY JONES
☐ 354. BOB KIPPER
☐ 379. RAFAEL BELLIARD
☐ 402. JUNIOR ORTIZ
☐ 409. JOHN SMILEY
☐ 601. JOHN CANGELOSI
☐ 614. AL PEDRIQUE
☐ 620. FELIX FERMIN
☐ 626. TOM PRINCE

ST. LOUIS CARDINALS

☐ 36. TONY PENA
☐ 68. BOB HORNER
☐ 80. OZZIE SMITH

☐ 88. WILLIE MCGEE
☐ 115. JOSE DELEON
☐ 137. TERRY PENDLETON
☐ 155. VINCE COLEMAN
☐ 184. TOM BRUNANSKY
☐ 231. LUIS ALICEA
☐ 259. LARRY MCWILLIAMS
☐ 265. TODD WORRELL
☐ 286. GREG MATHEWS
☐ 363. STEVE LAKE
☐ 397. SCOTT TERRY
☐ 460. JOE MARGRANE
☐ 483. TOM PAGNOZZI
☐ 520. DAN QUISENBERRY
☐ 525. BOB FORSCH
☐ 529. JOSE OQUENDO
☐ 534. JOHN COSTELLO
☐ 536. MIKE LAGA
☐ 564. PEDRO GUERRERO
☐ 613. DANNY COX
☐ 649. TIM JONES

SAN DIEGO PADRES

☐ 4. BENNY SANTIAGO
☐ 42. KEITH MORELAND
☐ 90. TONY GWYNN
☐ 118. ANDY HAWKINS
☐ 148. JOHN KRUK
☐ 158. LANCE MCCULLERS
☐ 176. GARRY TEMPLETON
☐ 203. MARVELL WYNNE
☐ 232. ROBERTO ALOMAR
☐ 234. DICKIE THON
☐ 254. ERIC SHOW
☐ 270. SHANE MACK
☐ 294. JIMMY JONES
☐ 329. ED WHITSON
☐ 349. MARK GRANT
☐ 369. CHRIS BROWN
☐ 411. SHAWN ABNER
☐ 417. GREG BOOKER
☐ 426. RANDY READY
☐ 490. MARK DAVIS
☐ 513. TIM FLANNERY
☐ 515. DAVE LEIPER
☐ 517. CARMELO MARTINEZ
☐ 519. STAN JEFFERSON
☐ 562. DENNIS RASMUSSEN
☐ 576. MARK PARENT
☐ 630. SANDY ALOMAR
☐ 644. JERALD CLARK

SAN FRANCISCO GIANTS

☐ 5. RICK REUSCHEL
☐ 39. KEVIN MITCHELL
☐ 47. CANDY MALDONADO
☐ 56. JOSE URIBE
☐ 82. MIKE ALDRETE
☐ 124. KELLY DOWNS
☐ 172. ROBBY THOMPSON
☐ 178. CRAIG LEFFERTS
☐ 190. MIKE KRUKOW
☐ 216. BRETT BUTLER
☐ 258. SCOTT GARRELTS
☐ 297. CHRIS SPEIER
☐ 395. BOB BRENLY
☐ 422. ATLEE HAMMAKER
☐ 440. DON ROBINSON
☐ 444. JOE PRICE

☐ 450. WILL CLARK
☐ 458. ERNEST RILES
☐ 474. TERRY MULHOLLAND
☐ 481. DONELL NIXON
☐ 500. MIKE LACOSS
☐ 539. JOEL YOUNGBLOOD
☐ 612. MATT WILLIAMS
☐ 617. BOB MELVIN
☐ 619. KIRT MANWARING
☐ 628. CHARLIE HAYES

SEATTLE MARINERS

☐ 27. DAVE VALLE
☐ 51. ALVIN DAVIS
☐ 73. JIM PRESLEY
☐ 89. MICKEY BRANTLEY
☐ 106. GLENN WILSON
☐ 142. RICH RENTERIA
☐ 161. MARK LANGSTON
☐ 209. HENRY COTTO
☐ 219. BILL SWIFT
☐ 242. KEN PHELPS
☐ 274. MIKE MOORE
☐ 310. HAROLD REYNOLDS
☐ 324. SCOTT BRADLEY
☐ 341. SCOTT BANKHEAD
☐ 353. STEVE BALBONI
☐ 361. REY QUINONES
☐ 398. MIKE JACKSON
☐ 427. JERRY REED
☐ 516. ROD SCURRY
☐ 522. STEVE TROUT
☐ 528. MIKE SCHOOLER
☐ 530. JAY BUHNER
☐ 568. MIKE CAMPBELL
☐ 637. EDGAR MARTINEZ

TEXAS RANGERS

☐ 22. PETE O'BRIEN
☐ 43. RUBEN SIERRA
☐ 59. ODDIBE MCDOWELL
☐ 78. SCOTT FLETCHER
☐ 143. JOSE GUZMAN
☐ 201. PETE INCAVIGLIA
☐ 241. MIKE STANLEY
☐ 271. PAUL KILGUS
☐ 295. CHARLIE HOUGH
☐ 301. MITCH WILLIAMS
☐ 344. BOB BROWER
☐ 368. STEVE BUECHELE
☐ 401. CECIL ESPY
☐ 420. DALE MOHORCIC
☐ 438. JEFF RUSSELL
☐ 463. BOBBY WITT
☐ 484. JEFF KUNKEL
☐ 514. RAY HAYWARD
☐ 518. CURTIS WILKERSON
☐ 526. GENO PETRALLI
☐ 638. CHAD KRUETER

TORONTO BLUE JAYS

☐ 6. FRED MCGRIFF
☐ 12. LLOYD MOSEBY
☐ 57. TONY FERNANDEZ
☐ 98. ERNIE WHITT
☐ 120. CECIL FIELDER
☐ 152. MARK EICHHORN
☐ 160. JESSE BARFIELD
☐ 194. KELLY GRUBER
☐ 197. DAVE STIEB
☐ 198. PAT BORDERS
☐ 304. JOHN CERUTTI
☐ 318. TOM HENKE
☐ 326. MANNY LEE
☐ 347. GEORGE BELL
☐ 359. DUANE WARD
☐ 385. RANCE MULLINIKS
☐ 453. TODD STOTTLEMYRE
☐ 473. SIL CAMPUSANO
☐ 475. MIKE FLANAGAN
☐ 480. JIMMY KEY
☐ 538. JIM CLANCY
☐ 540. RICK LEACH
☐ 558. JEFF MUSSELMAN
☐ 577. NELSON LIRIANO
☐ 632. GERONIMO BERROA

1989 SCORE
ROOKIE & TRADED (110)
2 1/2 X 3 1/2

ATLANTA BRAVES

☐ 18T. JEFF TREADWAY
☐ 64T. JODY DAVIS
☐ 65T. DARRELL EVANS
☐ 72T. ODDIBE MCDOWELL

BALTIMORE ORIOLES

☐ 29T. KEITH MORELAND
☐ 44T. PHIL BRADLEY
☐ 59T. BRIAN HOLTON
☐ 61T. BOB MELVIN
☐ 95T. STEVE FINLEY
☐ 96T. GREGG OLSON
☐ 110T. PETE HARNISCH

BOSTON RED SOX

☐ 8T. ROB MURPHY
☐ 37T. NICK ESASKY
☐ 40T. JOHN DOPSON
☐ 57T. DANNY HEEP

CALIFORNIA ANGELS

☐ 10T. CLAUDELL WASHINGTON
☐ 17T. BERT BLYLEVEN
☐ 36T. LANCE PARRISH
☐ 58T. BOB MCCLURE
☐ 88T. JIM ABBOTT
☐ 92T. RICH MONTELEONE

CHICAGO CUBS

☐ 32T. MITCH WILLIAMS
☐ 84T. JOE GIRARDI
☐ 85T. JEROME WALTON

CHICAGO WHITE SOX

☐ 26T. ERIC KING
☐ 47T. SCOTT FLETCHER
☐ 80T. RICHARD DOTSON
☐ 97T. KEN PATTERSON
☐ 102T. DONN PALL
☐ 103T. CARLOS MARTINEZ

CINCINNATI REDS

☐ 15T. TODD BENZINGER
☐ 52T. TIM LEARY
☐ 66T. JOEL YOUNGBLOOD
☐ 79T. RICK MAHLER
☐ 99T. SCOTT SCUDDER
☐ 104T. JOE OLIVER
☐ 109T. ROLANDO ROOMES

CLEVELAND INDIANS

☐ 6T. PETE O'BRIEN
☐ 51T. DION JAMES
☐ 76T. JOEL SKINNER
☐ 78T. FELIX FERMIN
☐ 106T. JOEY BELLE

DETROIT TIGERS

☐ 43T. TRACY JONES

HOUSTON ASTROS

☐ 42T. JIM CLANCY

KANSAS CITY ROYALS

☐ 24T. TERRY LEACH
☐ 74T. BOB BOONE

LOS ANGELES DODGERS

☐ 31T. EDDIE MURRAY
☐ 41T. WILLIE RANDOLPH
☐ 48T. KAL DANIELS
☐ 90T. JOHN WETTELAND

MILWAUKEE BREWERS

☐ 82T. BILL SPIERS

MINNESOTA TWINS

☐ 23T. CARMELO CASTILLO
☐ 34T. WALLY BACKMAN
☐ 91T. GARY WAYNE

MONTREAL EXPOS

☐ 13T. SPIKE OWEN
☐ 25T. MARK LANGSTON
☐ 39T. KEVIN GROSS
☐ 56T. ZANE SMITH
☐ 68T. MIKE ALDRETE

NEW YORK METS

☐ 21T. JUAN SAMUEL
☐ 67T. FRANK VIOLA
☐ 108T. MARK CARREON

NEW YORK YANKEES

☐ 4T. DAVE LAPOINT
☐ 14T. ANDY HAWKINS
☐ 20T. STEVE SAX
☐ 22T. JESSE BARFIELD
☐ 27T. STEVE BALBONI
☐ 38T. LUIS POLONIA
☐ 54T. MEL HALL
☐ 63T. LANCE MCCULLERS
☐ 69T. GREG CADARET
☐ 73T. TOM BROOKENS
☐ 75T. WALT TERRELL
☐ 93T. BOB GEREN
☐ 94T. CLAY PARKER

OAKLAND A'S

☐ 5T. MIKE MOORE
☐ 50T. RICKEY HENDERSON

PHILADELPHIA PHILLIES

☐ 9T. TOM HERR
☐ 12T. STEVE LAKE
☐ 28T. LENNY DYKSTRA
☐ 33T. JEFF PARRETT
☐ 53T. ROGER MCDOWELL
☐ 55T. DICKIE THON
☐ 60T. RANDY READY
☐ 70T. JOHN KRUK

TOM HERR

PITTSBURGH PIRATES

NO CARDS ISSUED

ST. LOUIS CARDINALS

☐ 45T. MILT THOMPSON
☐ 81T. CRIS CARPENTER
☐ 98T. KEN HILL

SAN DIEGO PADRES

☐ 3T. JACK CLARK
☐ 11T. MIKE PAGLIARULO
☐ 19T. BRUCE HURST
☐ 46T. CHRIS JAMES
☐ 87T. GREG HARRIS

SAN FRANCISCO GIANTS

☐ 30T. TERRY KENNEDY
☐ 49T. STEVE BEDROSIAN
☐ 71T. PAT SHERIDAN
☐ 86T. GREG LITTON
☐ 101T. JEFF BRANTLEY

SEATTLE MARINERS

☐ 7T. JEFFREY LEONARD
☐ 77T. RANDY JOHNSON
☐ 100T. KEN GRIFFEY, JR.
☐ 105T. OMAR VIZQUEL

TEXAS RANGERS

☐ 1T. RAFAEL PALMEIRO
☐ 2T. NOLAN RYAN
☐ 35T. JULIO FRANCO
☐ 62T. HAROLD BAINES
☐ 89T. KEVIN BROWN
☐ 107T. KENNY ROGERS

RAFAEL PALMEIRO

TORONTO BLUE JAYS

☐ 16T. MOOKIE WILSON
☐ 83T. JUNIOR FELIX

1990 SCORE (704)
2 1/2 X 3 1/2

KEVIN MITCHELL LF

ATLANTA BRAVES

☐ 66. DALE MURPHY
☐ 78. TOMMY GREGG
☐ 81. JOE BOEVER
☐ 95. JEFF TREADWAY
☐ 99. ANDRES THOMAS
☐ 148. JOSE ALVAREZ
☐ 151. GERONIMO BERROA
☐ 178. JEFF BLAUSER
☐ 225. PETE SMITH
☐ 243. DEREK LILLIQUIST
☐ 249. GERALD PERRY
☐ 302. DARRELL EVANS
☐ 328. JODY DAVIS
☐ 370. JOHN SMOLTZ
☐ 399. LONNIE SMITH
☐ 476. ODDIBE MCDOWELL
☐ 481. TOM GLAVINE
☐ 540. JEFF WETHERBY
☐ 593. MARK LEMKE
☐ 609. MIKE STANTON
☐ 621. GARY EAVE
☐ 627. KELLY MANN
☐ 640. TOMMY GREENE
☐ 644. ED WHITED
☐ 650. DAVE JUSTICE
☐ 677. TYLER HOUSTON

BALTIMORE ORIOLES

☐ 2. CAL RIPKEN
☐ 24. PHIL BRADLEY
☐ 30. DAVE SCHMIDT
☐ 33. BRADY ANDERSON
☐ 41. JOE ORSULAK
☐ 63. GREGG OLSON
☐ 111. LARRY SHEETS
☐ 118. RENE GONZALES
☐ 174. BILL RIPKEN
☐ 177. BRIAN HOLTON
☐ 214. KEVIN HICKEY
☐ 232. MIKE DEVEREAUX
☐ 234. CRAIG WORTHINGTON
☐ 239. BOB MILACKI
☐ 252. RANDY MILLIGAN
☐ 322. MICKEY TETTLETON
☐ 332. MARK WILLIAMSON
☐ 339. STEVE FINLEY
☐ 349. JEFF BALLARD
☐ 350. MARK THURMOND
☐ 355. PETE HARNISCH
☐ 444. KEITH MORELAND
☐ 453. BOB MELVIN
☐ 480. JAY TIBBS
☐ 528. DAVE JOHNSON
☐ 581. CURT SCHILLING
☐ 603. JUAN BELL
☐ 616. MICKEY WESTON
☐ 635. MIKE SMITH
☐ 680. BEN MCDONALD

BOSTON RED SOX

☐ 3. DWIGHT EVANS
☐ 11. JODY REED
☐ 15. MARTY BARRETT
☐ 31. MIKE BODDICKER
☐ 37. LEE SMITH
☐ 91. NICK ESASKY
☐ 113. DANNY HEEP
☐ 137. DENNIS BOYD
☐ 139. RICK CERONE
☐ 173. RICH GEDMAN
☐ 181. ROB MURPHY
☐ 245. WADE BOGGS
☐ 310. ROGER CLEMENS
☐ 331. JOHN DOPSON
☐ 340. ELLIS BURKS
☐ 345. MIKE GREENWELL
☐ 348. WES GARDNER
☐ 458. KEVIN ROMINE
☐ 471. DENNIS LAMP
☐ 512. MIKE SMITHSON
☐ 543. ERIC HETZEL
☐ 551. RANDY KUTCHER
☐ 651. SCOTT COOPER
☐ 658. CARLOS QUINTANA
☐ 675. MAURICE VAUGHN
☐ 681. GREG BLOSSER

CALIFORNIA ANGELS

- ☐ 8. BRYAN HARVEY
- ☐ 26. BRIAN DOWNING
- ☐ 35. LANCE PARRISH
- ☐ 44. DICK SCHOFIELD
- ☐ 48. GREG MINTON
- ☐ 117. BOB MCCLURE
- ☐ 120. WALLY JOYNER
- ☐ 180. BERT BLYLEVEN
- ☐ 206. JACK HOWELL
- ☐ 211. DAN PETRY
- ☐ 217. KIRK MCCASKILL
- ☐ 226. MIKE WITT
- ☐ 293. JOHNNY RAY
- ☐ 298. CLAUDELL WASHINGTON
- ☐ 312. DEVON WHITE
- ☐ 326. CHILI DAVIS
- ☐ 330. JIM ABBOTT
- ☐ 358. WILLIE FRASER
- ☐ 362. BILL SCHROEDER
- ☐ 378. TONY ARMAS
- ☐ 380. CHUCK FINLEY
- ☐ 412. KENT ANDERSON
- ☐ 565. RICH MONTELEONE
- ☐ 582. JOHN ORTON
- ☐ 604. BOBBY ROSE
- ☐ 673. KYLE ABBOTT

CHICAGO CUBS

- ☐ 73. VANCE LAW
- ☐ 85. MITCH WEBSTER
- ☐ 90. RYNE SANDBERG
- ☐ 92. LUIS SALAZAR
- ☐ 150. MARK GRACE
- ☐ 163. DAMON BERRYHILL
- ☐ 169. SHAWON DUNSTON
- ☐ 176. LLOYD MCCLENDON
- ☐ 196. PAUL KILGUS
- ☐ 229. JEROME WALTON
- ☐ 240. DWIGHT SMITH
- ☐ 262. MITCH WILLIAMS
- ☐ 265. ANDRE DAWSON
- ☐ 337. MARVELL WYNNE
- ☐ 403. GRED MADDUX
- ☐ 413. LES LANCASTER
- ☐ 428. JEFF PICO
- ☐ 436. PAT PERRY
- ☐ 450. RICK SUTCLIFFE
- ☐ 474. CURTIS WILKERSON
- ☐ 484. MIKE BIELECKI
- ☐ 488. SCOTT SANDERSON
- ☐ 489. DOMINGO RAMOS
- ☐ 531. STEVE WILSON
- ☐ 535. JOE GIRARDI
- ☐ 557. RICK WRONA
- ☐ 614. GREG SMITH
- ☐ 630. DEAN WILKINS
- ☐ 646. KEVIN BLANKENSHIP
- ☐ 670. EARL CUNNINGHAM

CHICAGO WHITE SOX

- ☐ 6. OZZIE GUILLEN
- ☐ 19. RICHARD DOTSON
- ☐ 22. RON KARKOVICE
- ☐ 28. ERIC KING
- ☐ 58. SCOTT FLETCHER
- ☐ 88. STEVE LYONS
- ☐ 94. IVAN CALDERON

- ☐ 115. DAVE GALLAGHER
- ☐ 152. BARRY JONES
- ☐ 207. KEN PATTERSON
- ☐ 213. DARYL BOSTON
- ☐ 290. CARLTON FISK
- ☐ 304. DONN PALL
- ☐ 306. DAN PASQUA
- ☐ 311. MELIDO PEREZ
- ☐ 314. CARLOS MARTINEZ
- ☐ 329. SHAWN HILLEGAS
- ☐ 335. BOBBY THIGPEN
- ☐ 354. GREG WALKER
- ☐ 369. GREG HIBBARD
- ☐ 523. STEVE ROSENBERG
- ☐ 526. BILL LONG
- ☐ 529. RON KITTLE
- ☐ 558. SAMMY SOSA
- ☐ 570. LANCE JOHNSON
- ☐ 595. ROBIN VENTURA
- ☐ 605. MATT MERULLO
- ☐ 617. JOHN PAWLOWSKI
- ☐ 663. FRANK THOMAS

CINCINNATI REDS

- ☐ 38. HERM WINNINGHAM
- ☐ 59. RON OESTER
- ☐ 65. TODD BENZINGER
- ☐ 70. CHRIS SABO
- ☐ 87. RICK MAHLER
- ☐ 147. JEFF REED
- ☐ 155. BARRY LARKIN
- ☐ 165. TOM BROWNING
- ☐ 185. ERIC DAVIS
- ☐ 248. NORM CHARLTON
- ☐ 273. JOHN FRANCO
- ☐ 277. ROB DIBBLE
- ☐ 289. DANNY JACKSON
- ☐ 295. PAUL O'NEILL
- ☐ 338. KEN GRIFFEY
- ☐ 344. JOEL YOUNGBLOOD
- ☐ 408. TIM BIRTSAS
- ☐ 417. ROLANDO ROOMES
- ☐ 434. BO DIAZ
- ☐ 495. RON ROBINSON
- ☐ 499. LUIS QUINONES
- ☐ 504. TIM LEARY
- ☐ 506. MARIANO DUNCAN
- ☐ 511. JOSE RIJO
- ☐ 518. SCOTT SCUDDER
- ☐ 576. JOE OLIVER
- ☐ 629. CHRIS HAMMOND
- ☐ 648. MIKE ROESLER
- ☐ 667. SCOTT BRYANT

CLEVELAND INDIANS

- ☐ 10. CORY SNYDER
- ☐ 52. JERRY BROWNE
- ☐ 56. BROOK JACOBY
- ☐ 103. JOHN FARRELL
- ☐ 130. DOUG JONES
- ☐ 141. DAVE CLARK
- ☐ 175. PETE O'BRIEN
- ☐ 187. STEVE DAVIS
- ☐ 197. BUD BLACK
- ☐ 218. SCOTT BAILES
- ☐ 230. GREG SWINDELL
- ☐ 256. FELIX FERMIN
- ☐ 269. TOM CANDIOTTI
- ☐ 274. RICH YETT
- ☐ 319. JOE CARTER
- ☐ 353. JESSE OROSCO
- ☐ 452. ANDY ALLANSON
- ☐ 496. BRAD KOMMINSK
- ☐ 508. JOEY BELLE
- ☐ 514. DION JAMES
- ☐ 590. STEVE OLIN
- ☐ 611. CHARLES NAGY
- ☐ 618. JOE SKALSKI

DETROIT TIGERS

- ☐ 9. ALAN TRAMMELL
- ☐ 55. MATT NOKES
- ☐ 57. FRANK TANANA
- ☐ 75. LOU WHITAKER
- ☐ 106. CHET LEMON
- ☐ 131. FRED LYNN
- ☐ 136. GARY PETTIS
- ☐ 172. MIKE HEATH

- ☐ 184. MIKE HENNEMAN
- ☐ 203. JACK MORRIS
- ☐ 237. DOYLE ALEXANDER
- ☐ 254. DAVE BERGMAN
- ☐ 261. PAUL GIBSON
- ☐ 267. GUILLERMO HERNANDEZ
- ☐ 291. TRACY JONES
- ☐ 333. JEFF ROBINSON
- ☐ 341. FRANK WILLIAMS
- ☐ 513. GARY WARD
- ☐ 572. KEVIN RITZ
- ☐ 575. SCOTT LUSADER
- ☐ 583. MILT CUYLER
- ☐ 607. RANDY NOSEK
- ☐ 620. SHAWN HOLMAN
- ☐ 626. PAT AUSTIN
- ☐ 657. BRIAN DUBOIS
- ☐ 679. GREG GOHR

HOUSTON ASTROS

- ☐ 40. MIKE SCOTT
- ☐ 42. RAFAEL RAMIREZ
- ☐ 43. GERALD YOUNG
- ☐ 45. DAVE SMITH
- ☐ 76. KEN CAMINITI
- ☐ 154. JIM DESHAIES
- ☐ 182. BILL DORAN
- ☐ 219. BOB FORSCH
- ☐ 272. GLENN DAVIS
- ☐ 275. CRAIG BIGGIO
- ☐ 279. KEVIN BASS
- ☐ 282. LARRY ANDERSEN
- ☐ 284. JUAN AGOSTO
- ☐ 346. GLENN WILSON
- ☐ 402. DANNY DARWIN
- ☐ 411. ERIC YELDING
- ☐ 418. DAN SCHATZEDER
- ☐ 424. JIM CLANCY
- ☐ 473. TERRY PUHL
- ☐ 552. MARK PORTUGAL
- ☐ 584. ERIC ANTHONY

KANSAS CITY ROYALS

- ☐ 60. BOB BOONE
- ☐ 82. CHARLIE LEIBRANDT
- ☐ 96. KURT STILLWELL
- ☐ 104. WILLIE WILSON
- ☐ 121. MARK GUBICZA
- ☐ 140. GEORGE BRETT
- ☐ 179. JIM EISENREICH
- ☐ 195. BRET SABERHAGEN
- ☐ 199. KEVIN SEITZER
- ☐ 242. PAT TABLER
- ☐ 244. DANNY TARTABULL
- ☐ 280. BO JACKSON
- ☐ 356. STEVE FARR
- ☐ 365. JEFF MONTGOMERY
- ☐ 372. FRANK WHITE
- ☐ 396. BILL BUCKNER
- ☐ 432. LUIS AQUINO
- ☐ 472. TOM GORDON
- ☐ 502. TERRY LEACH
- ☐ 587. JOSE DEJESUS
- ☐ 625. KEVIN APPIER
- ☐ 659. LUIS DE LOS SANTOS
- ☐ 664. BRENT MAYNE

LOS ANGELES DODGERS

- ☐ 23. LENNY HARRIS
- ☐ 39. ALEJANDRO PENA
- ☐ 50. OREL HERSHISER
- ☐ 54. FERNANDO VALENZUELA
- ☐ 80. EDDIE MURRAY
- ☐ 126. TIM BELCHER
- ☐ 132. JEFF HAMILTON
- ☐ 156. ALFREDO GRIFFIN
- ☐ 164. TIM CREWS
- ☐ 227. JAY HOWELL
- ☐ 238. DAVE ANDERSON
- ☐ 342. MIKE MORGAN
- ☐ 359. MICKEY HATCHER
- ☐ 368. JOSE GONZALEZ
- ☐ 384. MIKE MARSHALL
- ☐ 388. JOHN WETTELAND
- ☐ 395. WILLIE RANDOLPH
- ☐ 398. MIKE SCIOSCIA
- ☐ 414. RICK DEMPSEY
- ☐ 437. MIKE DAVIS
- ☐ 461. RAMON MARTINEZ

1990 Score

☐ 478. FRANKLIN STUBBS
☐ 487. KIRK GIBSON
☐ 490. KAL DANIELS
☐ 597. MIKE HUFF
☐ 613. JOSE VIZCAINO
☐ 622. DARRIN FLETCHER
☐ 641. MIKE HARTLEY
☐ 653. MIKE MUNOZ
☐ 654. JEFF FISCHER
☐ 668. TOM GOODWIN
☐ 676. KEITH JONES

MILWAUKEE BREWERS

☐ 74. B. J. SURHOFF
☐ 86. DAN PLESAC
☐ 97. GARY SHEFFIELD
☐ 105. GLENN BRAGGS
☐ 108. CHUCK CRIM
☐ 144. DON AUGUST
☐ 188. BILL WEGMAN
☐ 216. TERRY FRANCONA
☐ 268. MIKE FELDER
☐ 283. CHRIS BOSIO
☐ 305. TEDDY HIGUERA
☐ 320. ROBIN YOUNT
☐ 366. BILL KRUEGER
☐ 382. JIM GANTNER
☐ 390. ROB DEER
☐ 449. BILL SPIERS
☐ 460. PAUL MOLITOR
☐ 485. GREG BROCK
☐ 532. JOEY MEYER
☐ 539. MARK KNUDSON
☐ 567. TONY FOSSAS
☐ 569. JAIME NAVARRO
☐ 585. GREG VAUGHN
☐ 608. BILLY BATES
☐ 656. GEORGE CANALE
☐ 669. CAL ELDRED

MINNESOTA TWINS

☐ 61. DAN GLADDEN
☐ 71. SHANE RAWLEY
☐ 102. GREG GAGNE
☐ 123. CARMELO CASTILLO
☐ 128. AL NEWMAN
☐ 133. GERMAN GONZALEZ
☐ 145. GARY GAETTI
☐ 189. BRIAN HARPER
☐ 223. JUAN BERENGUER
☐ 276. GENE LARKIN
☐ 278. RANDY BUSH
☐ 281. WALLY BACKMAN
☐ 292. ALLAN ANDERSON
☐ 318. TIM LAUDNER
☐ 381. KENT HRBEK
☐ 391. JOHN MOSES
☐ 400. KIRBY PUCKETT
☐ 519. RICK AGUILERA
☐ 522. JEFF REARDON
☐ 527. GARY WAYNE
☐ 568. ROY SMITH
☐ 571. MIKE DYER
☐ 573. DAVE WEST
☐ 588. CHIP HALE
☐ 638. LENNY WEBSTER
☐ 647. PAUL SORRENTO
☐ 655. TERRY JORGENSEN
☐ 672. CHUCK KNOBLAUCH

MONTREAL EXPOS

☐ 25. ANDRES GALARRAGA
☐ 27. DAVE MARTINEZ
☐ 32. TOM FOLEY
☐ 47. DENNIS MARTINEZ
☐ 127. TIM BURKE
☐ 192. TIM WALLACH
☐ 220. MIKE ALDRETE
☐ 224. ANDY MCGAFFIGAN
☐ 241. OTIS NIXON
☐ 247. SPIKE OWEN
☐ 251. KEVIN GROSS
☐ 287. REX HUDLER
☐ 299. HUBIE BROOKS
☐ 361. MIKE FITZGERALD
☐ 401. MARK LANGSTON
☐ 409. TIM RAINES
☐ 419. BRYN SMITH

☐ 451. NELSON SANTOVENIA
☐ 477. ZANE SMITH
☐ 479. WALLACE JOHNSON
☐ 483. JOE HESKETH
☐ 486. PASCUAL PEREZ
☐ 591. MARQUIS GRISSOM
☐ 615. JEFF HUSON
☐ 631. LARRY WALKER
☐ 639. MARK GARDNER
☐ 645. DELINO DESHIELDS

NEW YORKS METS

☐ 5. KEVIN MCREYNOLDS
☐ 18. SID FERNANDEZ
☐ 29. BARRY LYONS
☐ 46. DAVE MAGADAN
☐ 53. BOB OJEDA
☐ 124. HOWARD JOHNSON
☐ 193. KEITH HERNANDEZ
☐ 198. JUAN SAMUEL
☐ 200. DARRYL STRAWBERRY
☐ 313. DWIGHT GOODEN
☐ 351. RANDY MYERS
☐ 363. MARK CARREON
☐ 377. DON AASE
☐ 416. GARY CARTER
☐ 430. DAVID CONE
☐ 443. KEVIN ELSTER
☐ 446. RON DARLING
☐ 468. GREGG JEFFERIES
☐ 500. FRANK VIOLA
☐ 501. TIM TEUFEL
☐ 510. MACKEY SASSER
☐ 525. JEFF MUSSELMAN
☐ 559. KEITH MILLER
☐ 599. WALLY WHITEHURST
☐ 632. BLAINE BEATTY
☐ 671. ALAN ZINTER

NEW YORK YANKEES

☐ 1. DON MATTINGLY
☐ 79. DON SLAUGHT
☐ 100. ROBERTO KELLY
☐ 101. ALVARO ESPINOZA
☐ 125. STEVE SAX
☐ 186. LANCE MCCULLERS
☐ 191. DALE MOHORCIC
☐ 194. DAVE RIGHETTI
☐ 222. JESSE BARFIELD
☐ 294. LEE GUETTERMAN
☐ 297. TOM BROOKENS
☐ 307. DAVE WINFIELD
☐ 316. CLAY PARKER
☐ 327. STEVE BALBONI
☐ 357. DAVE LAPOINT
☐ 383. MEL HALL
☐ 386. WAYNE TOLLESON
☐ 393. CHUCK CARY
☐ 442. LUIS POLONIA
☐ 463. WALT TERRELL
☐ 464. BOB GEREN
☐ 524. RANDY VELARDE
☐ 586. DEION SANDERS
☐ 602. HAL MORRIS
☐ 606. KEVIN MAAS
☐ 619. BERNIE WILLIAMS
☐ 624. MIKE BLOWERS
☐ 636. HENSLEY MEULENS
☐ 643. KEVIN MMAHAT
☐ 652. DAVE EILAND

OAKLAND A'S

☐ 64. TODD BURNS
☐ 84. TONY PHILLIPS
☐ 110. WALT WEISS
☐ 135. DAVE PARKER
☐ 159. BOB WELCH
☐ 162. TERRY STEINBACH
☐ 168. RON HASSEY
☐ 190. MIKE MOORE
☐ 266. STORM DAVIS
☐ 296. CARNEY LANSFORD
☐ 315. DENNIS ECKERSLEY
☐ 317. RICK HONEYCUTT
☐ 321. FELIX JOSE
☐ 323. MIKE GALLEGO
☐ 325. DAVE HENDERSON
☐ 360. RICKEY HENDERSON
☐ 375. JOSE CANSECO
☐ 385. MARK MCGWIRE
☐ 394. STAN JAVIER
☐ 410. DAVE STEWART
☐ 441. GENE NELSON
☐ 533. CURT YOUNG
☐ 536. LANCE BLANKENSHIP
☐ 553. JIM CORSI
☐ 598. SCOTT HEMOND

PHILADELPHIA PHILLIES

☐ 16. RICKY JORDAN
☐ 36. VON HAYES
☐ 142. DICKIE THON
☐ 171. TOM HERR
☐ 183. CURT FORD
☐ 364. RON JONES
☐ 376. RANDY READY
☐ 389. DARREN DAULTON
☐ 421. STEVE JELTZ
☐ 427. LENNY DYKSTRA
☐ 435. STEVE LAKE
☐ 445. ROGER MCDOWELL
☐ 467. JOHN KRUK
☐ 507. CHARLIE HAYES
☐ 542. TERRY MULHOLLAND
☐ 545. DENNIS COOK
☐ 623. PAT COMBS
☐ 633. TOM BARRETT
☐ 649. JASON GRIMSLEY
☐ 678. JEFF JACKSON

PITTSBURGH PIRATES

☐ 4. BARRY BONDS
☐ 14. GARY REDUS
☐ 21. BOB WALK
☐ 83. JOSE LIND
☐ 116. MIKE LAVALLIERE
☐ 143. JUNIOR ORTIZ
☐ 170. BOBBY BONILLA
☐ 334. JOHN SMILEY
☐ 367. JOHN CANGELOSI
☐ 423. SID BREAM
☐ 440. ANDY VAN SLYKE
☐ 456. BILL LANDRUM
☐ 469. R. J. REYNOLDS
☐ 505. DOUG DRABEK
☐ 515. JIM GOTT
☐ 517. DOUG BAIR
☐ 520. RAFAEL BELLIARD
☐ 544. RICK REED
☐ 547. BRIAN FISHER
☐ 549. JEFF KING
☐ 562. BILLY HATCHER
☐ 563. JAY BELL
☐ 592. MOISES ALOU
☐ 634. STAN BELINDA
☐ 682. WILLIE GREEN

ST. LOUIS CARDINALS

☐ 13. PEDRO GUERRERO
☐ 17. JOE MAGRANE
☐ 49. MILT THOMPSON
☐ 68. JOSE OQUENDO
☐ 72. TOM BRUNANSKY
☐ 122. TONY PENA
☐ 134. JOHN MORRIS
☐ 208. TERRY PENDLETON
☐ 233. KEN HILL
☐ 235. SCOTT TERRY

1990 Score

☐ 260. VINCE COLEMAN
☐ 285. OZZIE SMITH
☐ 309. JOSE DELEON
☐ 347. JOHN COSTELLO
☐ 374. WILLIE MCGEE
☐ 392. TODD WORRELL
☐ 462. FRANK DIPINO
☐ 475. DAN QUISENBERRY
☐ 537. GREG MATHEWS
☐ 556. KEN DAYLEY
☐ 579. TIM JONES
☐ 600. TODD ZEILE
☐ 628. MATT KINZER
☐ 662. PAUL COLEMAN

SAN DIEGO PADRES

☐ 12. ROBERTO ALOMAR
☐ 20. JACK CLARK
☐ 51. BIP ROBERTS
☐ 114. CARMELO MARTINEZ
☐ 119. MARK PARENT
☐ 129. DENNIS RASMUSSEN
☐ 212. DAVE LEIPER
☐ 255. TONY GWYNN
☐ 257. GREG HARRIS
☐ 259. MARK DAVIS
☐ 270. BRUCE HURST
☐ 336. GARRY TEMPLETON
☐ 352. SHAWN ABNER
☐ 373. ED WHITSON
☐ 434. BENNY SANTIAGO
☐ 466. MARK GRANT
☐ 493. ERIC SHOW
☐ 494. MIKE PAGLIARULO
☐ 498. CHRIS JAMES
☐ 541. DARRIN JACKSON
☐ 577. SANDY ALOMAR, JR.
☐ 578. ANDY BENES
☐ 642. PHIL STEPHENSON
☐ 660. JERALD CLARK

SAN FRANCISCO GIANTS

☐ 7. TERRY KENNEDY
☐ 112. DON ROBINSON
☐ 138. CANDY MALDONADO
☐ 146. KIRT MANWARING
☐ 209. CRAIG LEFFERTS
☐ 215. MIKE KRUKOW
☐ 231. ATLEE HAMMAKER
☐ 236. BRETT BUTLER
☐ 246. SCOTT GARRELTS
☐ 253. MIKE LACOSS
☐ 300. WILL CLARK
☐ 343. KEVIN MITCHELL
☐ 371. JEFF BRANTLEY
☐ 379. STEVE BEDROSIAN
☐ 397. ROBBY THOMPSON
☐ 422. KEN OBERKFELL
☐ 447. ERNEST RILES
☐ 455. JOSE URIBE
☐ 465. RICK REUSCHEL
☐ 497. GREG LITTON
☐ 503. MATT WILLIAMS
☐ 509. PAT SHERIDAN
☐ 534. KELLY DOWNS
☐ 538. DONELL NIXON
☐ 550. DAVE DRAVECKY
☐ 580. RANDY MCCAMENT
☐ 666. STEVE HOSEY

SEATTLE MARINERS

☐ 34. JIM PRESLEY
☐ 62. DARNELL COLES
☐ 98. JEFFREY LEONARD
☐ 109. DAVE VALLE
☐ 149. MIKE SCHOOLER
☐ 161. HERNY COTTO
☐ 167. HAROLD REYNOLDS
☐ 205. ALVIN DAVIS
☐ 228. SCOTT BRADLEY
☐ 264. OMAR VIZQUEL
☐ 303. GREG BRILEY
☐ 308. DENNIS POWELL
☐ 324. EDGAR MARTINEZ
☐ 387. BRIAN HOLMAN
☐ 415. RANDY JOHNSON
☐ 492. JERRY REED
☐ 521. JAY BUHNER
☐ 530. ERIK HANSON
☐ 546. MIKE JACKSON
☐ 548. GENE HARRIS
☐ 555. SCOTT BANKHEAD
☐ 560. KEN GRIFFEY, JR.
☐ 596. TINO MARTINEZ
☐ 674. ROGER SALKELD

TEXAS RANGERS

☐ 69. CECIL ESPY
☐ 93. PETE INCAVIGLIA
☐ 107. JAMIE MOYER
☐ 153. GENO PETRALLI
☐ 158. MIKE JEFFCOAT
☐ 160. JULIO FRANCO
☐ 166. FRED MANRIQUE
☐ 202. CHARLIE HOUGH
☐ 210. KEVIN BROWN
☐ 221. STEVE BUECHELE
☐ 250. NOLAN RYAN
☐ 263. JEFF RUSSELL
☐ 301. KENNY ROGERS
☐ 405. RAFAEL PALMEIRO
☐ 406. CHAD KREUTER
☐ 420. RUBEN SIERRA
☐ 426. RICK LEACH
☐ 431. JEFF KUNKEL
☐ 438. CECILIO GUANTE
☐ 457. BOBBY WITT
☐ 470. HAROLD BAINES
☐ 516. DREW HALL
☐ 564. JACK DAUGHERTY
☐ 574. GARY MIELKE
☐ 594. DEAN PALMER
☐ 612. SCOTT COOLBAUGH
☐ 637. JUAN GONZALEZ
☐ 661. DONALD HARRIS

TORONTO BLUE JAYS

☐ 67. MIKE FLANAGAN
☐ 77. NELSON LIRIANO
☐ 89. TONY FERNANDEZ
☐ 157. TOM HENKE
☐ 201. DAVE STIEB
☐ 204. RANCE MULLINIKS
☐ 258. JUNIOR FELIX
☐ 271. FRED MCGRIFF
☐ 286. GEORGE BELL
☐ 288. PAT BORDERS
☐ 404. LLOYD MOSEBY
☐ 407. JIMMY KEY
☐ 425. KELLY GRUBER
☐ 429. JOHN CERUTTI
☐ 433. ERNIE WHITT
☐ 439. DUANE WARD
☐ 448. MOOKIE WILSON
☐ 459. LEE MAZZILLI
☐ 482. MANNY LEE
☐ 491. DAVID WELLS
☐ 554. TODD STOTTLEMYRE
☐ 589. JOHN OLERUD
☐ 601. GLENALLEN HILL
☐ 610. GOOSE GOZZO
☐ 665. EDDIE ZOSKY

SPORTFLICS

The technology of the Sportflics cards allows them to portray more than one player per card. Because the purpose of this team checklist is to account for the cards of all players on a particular team in a particular year, it is necessary to list the card numbers more than once if more than one player is on a given card. The conventions below are used to denote a card with more than one player on it.

BS — Big Six Card
TS — Tri-Star Card
BT — Big Twelve Card

1986 SPORTFLICS (200)
2 1/2 X 3 1/2

ATLANTA BRAVES

- [ ] 5. DALE MURPHY
- [ ] 47. BRUCE SUTTER
- [ ] 62. DALE MURPHY(TS)
- [ ] 65. BRUCE SUTTER(TS)
- [ ] 66. BOB HORNER(TS)
- [ ] 115. BOB HORNER
- [ ] 135. PHIL NIEKRO(TS)
- [ ] 179. DALE MURPHY(BS)
- [ ] 183. DALE MURPHY(BS)

BALTIMORE ORIOLES

- [ ] 4. EDDIE MURRAY
- [ ] 8. CAL RIPKEN
- [ ] 38. FRED LYNN
- [ ] 54. CAL RIPKEN(TS)
- [ ] 57. CAL RIPKEN(TS)
- [ ] 59. MIKE FLANAGAN(TS)
- [ ] 63. FRED LYNN(TS)
- [ ] 69. CAL RIPKEN(TS)
- [ ] 71. FRED LYNN(TS)
- [ ] 73. FRED LYNN(TS)
- [ ] 73. EDDIE MURRAY(TS)
- [ ] 73. CAL RIPKEN(TS)
- [ ] 87. LEE LACY
- [ ] 104. MIKE BODDICKER
- [ ] 128. CAL RIPKEN(TS)
- [ ] 137. FRED LYNN(TS)
- [ ] 145. EDDIE MURRAY(TS)
- [ ] 147. RICK DEMPSEY(TS)
- [ ] 149. MIKE BODDICKER(TS)
- [ ] 150. FRED LYNN(TS)
- [ ] 177. LARRY SHEETS(BS)
- [ ] 199. MIKE YOUNG

BOSTON RED SOX

- [ ] 3. WADE BOGGS
- [ ] 17. JIM RICE
- [ ] 32. DWIGHT EVANS
- [ ] 52. JIM RICE(TS)
- [ ] 61. JIM RICE(TS)
- [ ] 61. TONY ARMAS(TS)
- [ ] 75. WADE BOGGS(TS)
- [ ] 81. BILL BUCKNER
- [ ] 84. RICH GEDMAN
- [ ] 139. JIM RICE(TS)
- [ ] 140. BILL BUCKNER(TS)
- [ ] 145. TONY ARMAS(TS)
- [ ] 146. JIM RICE(TS)
- [ ] 152. DENNIS BOYD
- [ ] 169. BOB STANLEY
- [ ] 178. MIKE GREENWELL(BS)
- [ ] 180. WADE BOGGS(BS)
- [ ] 183. WADE BOGGS(BS)
- [ ] 184. WADE BOGGS(BS)

CALIFORNIA ANGELS

- [ ] 37. REGGIE JACKSON
- [ ] 53. MIKE WITT(TS)
- [ ] 57. REGGIE JACKSON(TS)
- [ ] 61. REGGIE JACKSON(TS)
- [ ] 69. ROD CAREW(TS)
- [ ] 71. REGGIE JACKSON(TS)
- [ ] 74. ROD CAREW(TS)
- [ ] 106. ROD CAREW
- [ ] 129. JOHN CANDELARIA(TS)
- [ ] 135. DON SUTTON(TS)
- [ ] 146. ROD CAREW(TS)
- [ ] 147. REGGIE JACKSON(TS)
- [ ] 150. REGGIE JACKSON(TS)
- [ ] 154. BRIAN DOWNING
- [ ] 173. DOUG DECINCES
- [ ] 175. DON SUTTON
- [ ] 177. STEWART CLIBURN(BS)
- [ ] 180. ROD CAREW(BS)
- [ ] 182. ROD CAREW(BS)

CHICAGO CUBS

- [ ] 20. RYNE SANDBERG
- [ ] 45. LEE SMITH
- [ ] 46. RICK SUTCLIFFE
- [ ] 51. RYNE SANDBERG(TS)
- [ ] 55. LEE SMITH(TS)
- [ ] 60. RICK SUTCLIFFE(TS)
- [ ] 66. GARY MATTHEWS(TS)
- [ ] 70. RICK SUTCLIFFE(TS)
- [ ] 72. RICK SUTCLIFFE(TS)
- [ ] 90. KEITH MORELAND
- [ ] 111. LEON DURHAM
- [ ] 127. RYNE SANDBERG(TS)
- [ ] 129. DENNIS ECKERSLEY(TS)
- [ ] 130. RON CEY(TS)
- [ ] 134. RICK SUTCLIFFE(TS)
- [ ] 144. DAVEY LOPES(TS)
- [ ] 149. RICK SUTCLIFFE(TS)
- [ ] 155. SHAWON DUNSTON
- [ ] 194. DAVEY LOPES

CHICAGO WHITE SOX

- [ ] 7. HAROLD BAINES
- [ ] 22. OZZIE GUILLEN
- [ ] 25. TOM SEAVER
- [ ] 52. HAROLD BAINES(TS)
- [ ] 60. TOM SEAVER(TS)
- [ ] 67. RON KITTLE(TS)
- [ ] 67. CARLTON FISK(TS)
- [ ] 67. TOM SEAVER(TS)
- [ ] 70. TOM SEAVER(TS)
- [ ] 86. RON KITTLE
- [ ] 105. BRITT BURNS
- [ ] 125. CARLTON FISK
- [ ] 133. RICHARD DOTSON(TS)
- [ ] 134. TOM SEAVER(TS)
- [ ] 135. TOM SEAVER(TS)
- [ ] 142. TOM SEAVER(TS)
- [ ] 158. BOB JAMES
- [ ] 174. GREG WALKER
- [ ] 176. OZZIE GUILLEN(BS)
- [ ] 182. TOM SEAVER(BS)

CINCINNATI REDS

- [ ] 23. DAVE PARKER
- [ ] 50. PETE ROSE
- [ ] 51. PETE ROSE(TS)
- [ ] 56. PETE ROSE(TS)
- [ ] 58. DAVE PARKER(TS)
- [ ] 58. PETE ROSE(TS)
- [ ] 69. PETE ROSE(TS)
- [ ] 79. TOM BROWNING
- [ ] 130. PETE ROSE(TS)
- [ ] 131. DAVE CONCEPCION(TS)
- [ ] 138. TONY PEREZ(TS)
- [ ] 138. PETE ROSE(TS)
- [ ] 151. BUDDY BELL
- [ ] 153. DAVE CONCEPCION
- [ ] 156. JOHN FRANCO
- [ ] 166. TED POWER
- [ ] 168. MARIO SOTO
- [ ] 181. DAVE PARKER(BS)
- [ ] 181. PETE ROSE(BS)
- [ ] 182. PETE ROSE(BS)
- [ ] 183. DAVE PARKER(BS)
- [ ] 185. TOM BROWNING(BS)

CLEVELAND INDIANS

- [ ] 26. BRETT BUTLER
- [ ] 33. JULIO FRANCO
- [ ] 171. ANDRE THORNTON

DETROIT TIGERS

- [ ] 21. KIRK GIBSON
- [ ] 48. LOU WHITAKER
- [ ] 65. WILLIE HERNANDEZ(TS)
- [ ] 74. LOU WHITAKER(TS)
- [ ] 85. WILLIE HERNANDEZ
- [ ] 92. LANCE PARRISH
- [ ] 117. JACK MORRIS
- [ ] 141. JACK MORRIS(TS)
- [ ] 147. ALAN TRAMMELL(TS)
- [ ] 172. ALAN TRAMMELL
- [ ] 183. DARRELL EVANS(BS)
- [ ] 189. DARRELL EVANS

HOUSTON ASTROS

- [ ] 30. JOSE CRUZ
- [ ] 43. NOLAN RYAN
- [ ] 141. NOLAN RYAN(TS)
- [ ] 143. NOLAN RYAN(TS)
- [ ] 182. NOLAN RYAN(BS)
- [ ] 188. GLENN DAVIS
- [ ] 195. MIKE SCOTT

KANSAS CITY ROYALS

- [ ] 1. GEORGE BRETT
- [ ] 10. BRET SABERHAGEN
- [ ] 52. GEORGE BRETT(TS)
- [ ] 55. DAN QUISENBERRY(TS)
- [ ] 63. GEORGE BRETT(TS)
- [ ] 118. DAN QUISENBERRY
- [ ] 124. WILLIE WILSON
- [ ] 128. WILLIE WILSON(TS)
- [ ] 144. WILLIE WILSON(TS)

☐ 159. CHARLIE LEIBRANDT
☐ 176. BRET SABERHAGEN(BS)
☐ 179. GEORGE BRETT(BS)
☐ 180. GEORGE BRETT(BS)
☐ 180. WILLIE WILSON(BS)
☐ 185. BRET SABERHAGEN(BS)
☐ 186. BRET SABERHAGEN(BT)
☐ 186. LONNIE SMITH(BT)
☐ 186. DANNY JACKSON(BT)
☐ 186. DANE IORG(BT)
☐ 186. JIM SUNDBERG(BT)
☐ 186. CHARLIE LEIBRANDT(BT)
☐ 186. DAN QUISENBERRY(BT)
☐ 186. DARRYL MOTLEY(BT)
☐ 186. GEORGE BRETT(BT)
☐ 186. STEVE BALBONI(BT)
☐ 186. WILLIE WILSON(BT)
☐ 186. FRANK WHITE(BT)
☐ 200. BUDDY BIANCALANA

LOS ANGELES DODGERS

☐ 9. OREL HERSHISER
☐ 12. FERNANDO VALENZUELA
☐ 14. PEDRO GUERRERO
☐ 53. JERRY REUSS(TS)
☐ 56. STEVE SAX(TS)
☐ 58. BILL MADLOCK(TS)
☐ 60. FERNANDO VALENZUELA(TS)
☐ 72. FERNANDO VALENZUELA(TS)
☐ 88. BILL MADLOCK
☐ 89. MIKE MARSHALL
☐ 95. STEVE SAX
☐ 131. BILL MADLOCK(TS)
☐ 132. FERNANDO VALENZUELA(TS)
☐ 143. FERNANDO VALENZUELA(TS)
☐ 148. PEDRO GUERRERO(TS)
☐ 167. MIKE SCIOSCIA
☐ 181. BILL MADLOCK(BS)
☐ 181. PEDRO GUERRERO(BS)
☐ 198. BOB WELCH

MILWAUKEE BREWERS

☐ 16. ERNEST RILES
☐ 29. CECIL COOPER
☐ 39. PAUL MOLITOR
☐ 42. ROBIN YOUNT
☐ 54. ROBIN YOUNT(TS)
☐ 63. ROBIN YOUNT(TS)
☐ 65. ROLLIE FINGERS(TS)
☐ 71. ROBIN YOUNT(TS)
☐ 114. TEDDY HIGUERA
☐ 128. PAUL MOLITOR(TS)
☐ 130. ROLLIE FINGERS(TS)
☐ 145. CECIL COOPER(TS)
☐ 146. ROLLIE FINGERS(TS)
☐ 178. BILLY JO ROBIDOUX(BS)
☐ 180. CECIL COOPER(BS)
☐ 196. TED SIMMONS

MINNESOTA TWINS

☐ 36. KENT HRBEK
☐ 64. BERT BLYLEVEN(TS)
☐ 80. TOM BRUNANSKY
☐ 93. KIRBY PUCKETT
☐ 99. FRANK VIOLA
☐ 103. BERT BLYLEVEN
☐ 142. BERT BLYLEVEN(TS)
☐ 177. MARK SALAS(BS)
☐ 178. MARK FUNDERBURK(BS)
☐ 178. STEVE LOMBARDOZZI(BS)

MONTREAL EXPOS

☐ 11. TIM RAINES
☐ 66. ANDRE DAWSON(TS)
☐ 110. ANDRE DAWSON
☐ 119. JEFF REARDON
☐ 120. BRYN SMITH
☐ 123. TIM WALLACH
☐ 127. TIM RAINES(TS)
☐ 144. TIM RAINES(TS)
☐ 177. JOE HESKETH(BS)
☐ 187. HUBIE BROOKS

NEW YORK METS

☐ 15. KEITH HERNANDEZ
☐ 28. GARY CARTER
☐ 56. DARRYL STRAWBERRY(TS)

☐ 62. KEITH HERNANDEZ(TS)
☐ 68. GEORGE FOSTER(TS)
☐ 97. DARRYL STRAWBERRY
☐ 100. DWIGHT GOODEN
☐ 109. RON DARLING
☐ 126. GARY CARTER(TS)
☐ 126. GEORGE FOSTER(TS)
☐ 127. KEITH HERNANDEZ(TS)
☐ 131. GEORGE FOSTER(TS)
☐ 136. DWIGHT GOODEN(TS)
☐ 137. GARY CARTER(TS)
☐ 138. RUSTY STAUB(TS)
☐ 139. GEORGE FOSTER(TS)
☐ 143. DWIGHT GOODEN(TS)
☐ 161. ROGER MCDOWELL
☐ 176. DWIGHT GOODEN(BS)
☐ 179. KEITH HERNANDEZ(BS)
☐ 181. KEITH HERNANDEZ(BS)
☐ 184. DWIGHT GOODEN(BS)
☐ 185. DWIGHT GOODEN(BS)

NEW YORK YANKEES

☐ 2. DON MATTINGLY
☐ 6. RICKEY HENDERSON
☐ 18. RON GUIDRY
☐ 41. DAVE RIGHETTI
☐ 49. DAVE WINFIELD
☐ 53. PHIL NIEKRO(TS)
☐ 54. DON MATTINGLY(TS)
☐ 57. DON BAYLOR(TS)
☐ 59. RON GUIDRY(TS)
☐ 72. DAVE RIGHETTI(TS)
☐ 75. DON MATTINGLY(TS)
☐ 141. DAVE RIGHETTI(TS)
☐ 149. RON GUIDRY(TS)
☐ 163. PHIL NIEKRO
☐ 176. DON MATTINGLY(BS)
☐ 177. BRIAN FISHER(BS)
☐ 179. RON GUIDRY(BS)
☐ 179. DON MATTINGLY(BS)
☐ 180. DON MATTINGLY(BS)
☐ 182. PHIL NIEKRO(BS)
☐ 183. DON MATTINGLY(BS)
☐ 184. RICKEY HENDERSON(BS)
☐ 184. DON MATTINGLY(BS)
☐ 185. RON GUIDRY(BS)

OAKLAND A'S

☐ 68. DAVE KINGMAN(TS)
☐ 75. CARNEY LANSFORD(TS)
☐ 83. MIKE DAVIS
☐ 116. DAVE KINGMAN
☐ 136. ALFREDO GRIFFIN(TS)
☐ 150. DAVE KINGMAN(TS)
☐ 178. JOSE CANSECO(BS)
☐ 192. JAY HOWELL

PHILADELPHIA PHILLIES

☐ 27. STEVE CARLTON
☐ 44. MIKE SCHMIDT
☐ 62. MIKE SCHMIDT(TS)
☐ 64. JERRY KOOSMAN(TS)
☐ 64. JOHN DENNY(TS)
☐ 68. MIKE SCHMIDT(TS)
☐ 70. STEVE CARLTON(TS)
☐ 94. JUAN SAMUEL
☐ 132. JOHN DENNY(TS)

☐ 134. JOHN DENNY(TS)
☐ 139. MIKE SCHMIDT(TS)
☐ 148. MIKE SCHMIDT(TS)

PITTSBURGH PIRATES

☐ 165. TONY PENA
☐ 177. JOE ORSULAK(BS)

ST. LOUIS CARDINALS

☐ 19. WILLIE MCGEE
☐ 24. VINCE COLEMAN
☐ 101. JOAQUIN ANDUJAR
☐ 107. JACK CLARK
☐ 108. DANNY COX
☐ 113. TOM HERR
☐ 121. OZZIE SMITH
☐ 122. JOHN TUDOR
☐ 129. BOB FORSCH(TS)
☐ 133. JOAQUIN ANDUJAR(TS)
☐ 136. VINCE COLEMAN(TS)
☐ 148. DARRELL PORTER(TS)
☐ 176. VINCE COLEMAN(BS)
☐ 176. WILLIE MCGEE(BS)
☐ 179. WILLIE MCGEE(BS)
☐ 183. WILLIE MCGEE(BS)
☐ 184. WILLIE MCGEE(BS)
☐ 184. JOHN TUDOR(BS)
☐ 185. JOHN TUDOR(BS)
☐ 185. JOAQUIN ANDUJAR(BS)

SAN DIEGO PADRES

☐ 13. TONY GWYNN
☐ 35. STEVE GARVEY
☐ 51. STEVE GARVEY(TS)
☐ 55. GOOSE GOSSAGE(TS)
☐ 59. LAMARR HOYT(TS)
☐ 91. GRAIG NETTLES
☐ 137. STEVE GARVEY(TS)
☐ 140. TONY GWYNN(TS)
☐ 170. GARRY TEMPLETON
☐ 181. TONY GWYNN(BS)
☐ 190. GOOSE GOSSAGE
☐ 191. ANDY HAWKINS
☐ 193. LAMARR HOYT

SAN FRANCISCO GIANTS

☐ 78. CHRIS BROWN
☐ 82. CHILI DAVIS
☐ 132. VIDA BLUE(TS)
☐ 142. VIDA BLUE(TS)
☐ 157. SCOTT GARRELTS

SEATTLE MARINERS

☐ 31. ALVIN DAVIS
☐ 40. JIM PRESLEY
☐ 74. ALVIN DAVIS(TS)
☐ 77. PHIL BRADLEY
☐ 162. MIKE MOORE
☐ 178. DAN TARTABULL(BS)

TEXAS RANGERS

☐ 160. ODDIBE MCDOWELL
☐ 197. GARY WARD

TORONTO BLUE JAYS

☐ 34. DAMASO GARCIA
☐ 76. JESSE BARFIELD
☐ 96. DAVE STIEB
☐ 98. WILLIE UPSHAW
☐ 102. GEORGE BELL
☐ 112. TONY FERNANDEZ
☐ 126. AL OLIVER(TS)
☐ 133. DOYLE ALEXANDER(TS)
☐ 140. AL OLIVER(TS)
☐ 164. AL OLIVER

1986 SPORTFLICS
ROOKIES (50)
2 1/2 X 3 1/2

ATLANTA BRAVES

☐ 14. ANDRES THOMAS
☐ 24. PAUL ASSENMACHER

BALTIMORE ORIOLES

☐ 32. JIM TRABER
☐ 46. FRED LYNN(TS)
☐ 48. EDDIE MURRAY(BS)
☐ 48. CAL RIPKEN(BS)

BOSTON RED SOX

☐ 44. CALVIN SCHIRALDI

CALIFORNIA ANGELS

☐ 7. WALLY JOYNER

CHICAGO CUBS

NO CARDS ISSUED

CHICAGO WHITE SOX

☐ 31. JOHN CANGELOSI
☐ 33. RUSS MORMAN

CINCINNATI REDS

☐ 34. BARRY LARKIN
☐ 43. KAL DANIELS
☐ 46. PETE ROSE(TS)

CLEVELAND INDIANS

☐ 9. SCOTT BAILES
☐ 18. CORY SNYDER
☐ 30. GREG SWINDELL

DETROIT TIGERS

☐ 42. ERIC KING
☐ 48. LOU WHITAKER(BS)

HOUSTON ASTROS

☐ 15. JIM DESHAIES
☐ 23. CHARLIE KERFELD

KANSAS CITY ROYALS

☐ 37. MIKE KINGERY
☐ 39. SCOTT BANKHEAD
☐ 40. BO JACKSON

LOS ANGELES DODGERS

☐ 19. REGGIE WILLIAMS
☐ 47. FERNANDO VALENZUELA(TS)
☐ 48. STEVE SAX(BS)

MILWAUKEE BREWERS

☐ 4. DALE SVEUM
☐ 5. JUAN NIEVES
☐ 10. DAN PLESAC
☐ 21. GLENN BRAGGS
☐ 28. BILLY JO ROBIDOUX

MINNESOTA TWINS

☐ 17. STEVE LOMBARDOZZI

MONTREAL EXPOS

☐ 27. ANDRES GALARRAGA

NEW YORK METS

☐ 47. TOM SEAVER(TS)
☐ 47. DWIGHT GOODEN(TS)
☐ 48. DARRYL STRAWBERRY(BS)
☐ 49. KEVIN MITCHELL

NEW YORK YANKEES

☐ 48. DAVE RIGHETTI(BS)

OAKLAND A'S

☐ 11. JOSE CANSECO

PHILADELPHIA PHILLIES

☐ 29. BRUCE RUFFIN

PITTSBURGH PIRATES

☐ 13. BARRY BONDS
☐ 26. BOBBY BONILLA
☐ 50. MIKE DIAZ

ST. LOUIS CARDINALS

☐ 35. TODD WORRELL
☐ 41. GREG MATHEWS

SAN DIEGO PADRES

☐ 1. JOHN KRUK
☐ 8. LANCE MCCULLERS

SAN FRANCISCO GIANTS

☐ 6. WILL CLARK
☐ 25. ROBBY THOMPSON
☐ 46. WILLIE MAYS(TS)

SEATTLE MARINERS

☐ 22. DANNY TARTABULL
☐ 45. MICKEY BRANTLEY

TEXAS RANGERS

☐ 2. EDWIN CORREA
☐ 3. PETE INCAVIGLIA
☐ 12. BOBBY WITT
☐ 16. RUBEN SIERRA
☐ 20. MITCH WILLIAMS

TORONTO BLUE JAYS

☐ 36. JOHN CERUTTI
☐ 38. MARK EICHHORN

1987 SPORTFLICS (200)
2 1/2 X 3 1/2

ATLANTA BRAVES

☐ 3. DALE MURPHY
☐ 73. BOB HORNER
☐ 155. DALE MURPHY(TS)
☐ 159. DALE MURPHY(BS)
☐ 196. BOB HORNER(TS)

BALTIMORE ORIOLES

☐ 6. EDDIE MURRAY
☐ 9. CAL RIPKEN
☐ 49. FRED LYNN
☐ 56. MIKE BODDICKER
☐ 75. EDDIE MURRAY(TS)
☐ 86. LEE LACY
☐ 113. CAL RIPKEN(TS)
☐ 159. EDDIE MURRAY(BS)
☐ 165. DON AASE
☐ 194. DON AASE(TS)
☐ 198. FRED LYNN(TS)

BOSTON RED SOX

☐ 2. WADE BOGGS
☐ 10. ROGER CLEMENS
☐ 28. TOM SEAVER
☐ 38. BRUCE HURST
☐ 47. DENNIS BOYD
☐ 70. BILL BUCKNER
☐ 80. JIM RICE(TS)
☐ 97. JIM RICE
☐ 111. ROGER CLEMENS(TS)
☐ 112. MARTY BARRETT(TS)
☐ 114. WADE BOGGS(TS)
☐ 118. PAT DODSON(BS)
☐ 128. DWIGHT EVANS
☐ 149. RICH GEDMAN
☐ 154. RICH GEDMAN(TS)
☐ 159. ROGER CLEMENS(BS)
☐ 163. DON BAYLOR
☐ 182. MARTY BARRETT
☐ 196. ROGER CLEMENS(TS)
☐ 197. WADE BOGGS(BS)

CALIFORNIA ANGELS

- □ 26. WALLY JOYNER
- □ 44. REGGIE JACKSON
- □ 59. MIKE WITT
- □ 75. WALLY JOYNER(TS)
- □ 99. DON SUTTON
- □ 106. DOUG DECINCES
- □ 127. KIRK MCCASKILL
- □ 148. JOHN CANDELARIA
- □ 156. DON SUTTON(TS)
- □ 157. GARY PETTIS(TS)
- □ 161. BRIAN DOWNING
- □ 184. BOBBY GRICH

CHICAGO CUBS

- □ 8. RYNE SANDBERG
- □ 79. SHAWON DUNSTON(TS)
- □ 98. SHAWON DUNSTON
- □ 104. LEE SMITH
- □ 116. RYNE SANDBERG(TS)
- □ 122. KEITH MORELAND
- □ 158. RAFAEL PALMEIRO(BS)
- □ 170. JODY DAVIS
- □ 185. LEON DURHAM
- □ 197. RYNE SANDBERG(BS)

CHICAGO WHITE SOX

- □ 140. CARLTON FISK
- □ 153. HAROLD BAINES(TS)
- □ 157. JOHN CANGELOSI(TS)
- □ 158. DAVE COCHRANE(BS)
- □ 171. HAROLD BAINES
- □ 186. OZZIE GUILLEN
- □ 196. JOE COWLEY(TS)
- □ 200. STEVE CARLTON

CINCINNATI REDS

- □ 22. ERIC DAVIS
- □ 25. PETE ROSE
- □ 35. DAVE PARKER
- □ 117. DAVE PARKER(TS)
- □ 141. BUDDY BELL
- □ 155. ERIC DAVIS(TS)
- □ 192. JOHN FRANCO
- □ 199. ERIC DAVIS(TS)

CLEVELAND INDIANS

- □ 24. CORY SNYDER
- □ 60. TONY BERNAZARD
- □ 66. PAT TABLER
- □ 69. BRETT BUTLER
- □ 84. JULIO FRANCO
- □ 107. KEN SCHROM
- □ 109. BROOK JACOBY
- □ 112. TONY BERNAZARD(TS)
- □ 118. DAVID CLARK(BS)
- □ 147. PHIL NIEKRO
- □ 176. JOE CARTER
- □ 180. MEL HALL

DETROIT TIGERS

- □ 48. KIRK GIBSON
- □ 87. JACK MORRIS
- □ 101. LANCE PARRISH
- □ 105. WILLIE HERNANDEZ
- □ 111. JACK MORRIS(TS)
- □ 112. LOU WHITAKER(TS)
- □ 132. DARRELL EVANS
- □ 137. LOU WHITAKER
- □ 154. LANCE PARRISH(TS)
- □ 188. ALAN TRAMMELL

HOUSTON ASTROS

- □ 17. GLENN DAVIS
- □ 19. MIKE SCOTT
- □ 29. BOB KNEPPER
- □ 42. JOSE CRUZ
- □ 77. DAVE SMITH(TS)
- □ 94. DAVE SMITH
- □ 116. BILL DORAN(TS)
- □ 117. KEVIN BASS(TS)
- □ 118. TY GAINEY(BS)
- □ 119. MIKE SCOTT(TS)

- □ 120. MIKE SCOTT(TS)
- □ 125. NOLAN RYAN
- □ 146. CHARLIE KERFELD
- □ 152. JOSE CRUZ(TS)
- □ 156. JIM DESHAIES(TS)
- □ 162. BILL DORAN
- □ 175. KEVIN BASS
- □ 195. GLENN DAVIS(TS)

KANSAS CITY ROYALS

- □ 5. GEORGE BRETT
- □ 85. WILLIE WILSON
- □ 114. GEORGE BRETT(TS)
- □ 145. BRET SABERHAGEN
- □ 158. KEVIN SEITZER(BS)
- □ 167. DAN QUISENBERRY
- □ 168. FRANK WHITE
- □ 190. BO JACKSON
- □ 197. GEORGE BRETT(BS)

LOS ANGELES DODGERS

- □ 12. STEVE SAX
- □ 27. PEDRO GUERRERO
- □ 43. OREL HERSHISER
- □ 67. MIKE SCIOSCIA
- □ 82. MIKE MARSHALL
- □ 119. FERNANDO VALENZUELA(TS)
- □ 120. FERNANDO VALENZUELA(TS)
- □ 130. BILL MADLOCK
- □ 150. FERNANDO VALENZUELA
- □ 151. MIKE SCIOSCIA(TS)

MILWAUKEE BREWERS

- □ 11. TEDDY HIGUERA
- □ 16. ROBIN YOUNT
- □ 54. PAUL MOLITOR
- □ 111. TEDDY HIGUERA(TS)
- □ 169. CECIL COOPER
- □ 172. ROB DEER

MINNESOTA TWINS

- □ 7. KIRBY PUCKETT
- □ 15. KENT HRBEK
- □ 64. GARY GAETTI
- □ 81. BERT BLYLEVEN
- □ 114. GARY GAETTI(TS)
- □ 134. TOM BRUNANSKY
- □ 198. KIRBY PUCKETT(TS)

MONTREAL EXPOS

- □ 18. HUBIE BROOKS
- □ 34. TIM RAINES
- □ 72. TIM WALLACH
- □ 77. JEFF REARDON(TS)
- □ 79. HUBIE BROOKS(TS)
- □ 103. FLOYD YOUMANS
- □ 115. TIM WALLACH(TS)
- □ 139. ANDRE DAWSON
- □ 152. TIM RAINES(TS)
- □ 158. CASEY CANDAELE(BS)
- □ 177. MITCH WEBSTER
- □ 197. HUBIE BROOKS(BS)
- □ 197. TIM RAINES(BS)
- □ 199. TIM RAINES(TS)

NEW YORK METS

- □ 20. DARRYL STRAWBERRY
- □ 36. BOB OJEDA
- □ 50. GARY CARTER
- □ 53. RON DARLING
- □ 58. LEN DYKSTRA
- □ 63. SID FERNANDEZ
- □ 76. JESSIE OROSCO
- □ 88. RAY KNIGHT
- □ 100. DWIGHT GOODEN
- □ 120. DWIGHT GOODEN(TS)
- □ 124. WALLY BACKMAN
- □ 133. KEITH HERNANDEZ
- □ 144. KEVIN MITCHELL
- □ 151. GARY CARTER(TS)
- □ 159. DWIGHT GOODEN(BS)
- □ 160. ROGER MCDOWELL
- □ 195. KEITH HERNANDEZ(TS)

NEW YORK YANKEES

- □ 1. DON MATTINGLY
- □ 4. RICKEY HENDERSON
- □ 41. DAVE WINFIELD
- □ 55. MIKE PAGLIARULO
- □ 57. DAVE RIGHETTI
- □ 71. DENNIS RASMUSSEN
- □ 75. DON MATTINGLY(TS)
- □ 83. RON GUIDRY
- □ 92. MIKE EASLER
- □ 118. PHIL LOMBARDI(BS)
- □ 119. DAVE RIGHETTI(TS)
- □ 143. DAN PASQUA
- □ 153. DAVE WINFIELD(TS)
- □ 157. RICKEY HENDERSON(TS)
- □ 159. DON MATTINGLY(BS)
- □ 159. RICKEY HENDERSON(BS)
- □ 194. DAVE RIGHETTI(TS)
- □ 198. RICKEY HENDERSON(TS)

OAKLAND A'S

- □ 80. JOSE CANSECO(TS)
- □ 90. JOSE CANSECO
- □ 118. TERRY STEINBACH(BS)
- □ 138. CARNEY LANSFORD
- □ 164. ALFREDO GRIFFIN
- □ 178. DAVE KINGMAN

PHILADELPHIA PHILLIES

- □ 30. MIKE SCHMIDT
- □ 108. DON CARMAN
- □ 110. STEVE BEDROSIAN
- □ 115. MIKE SCHMIDT(TS)
- □ 123. JUAN SAMUEL
- □ 156. MIKE SCHMIDT(TS)
- □ 166. GLENN WILSON
- □ 181. SHANE RAWLEY
- □ 193. VON HAYES

PITTSBURGH PIRATES

- □ 93. TONY PENA
- □ 116. JOHNNY RAY(TS)
- □ 121. JOHNNY RAY
- □ 129. RICK RHODEN
- □ 151. TONY PENA(TS)

ST. LOUIS CARDINALS

- □ 33. TODD WORRELL
- □ 65. VINCE COLEMAN
- □ 74. WILLIE MCGEE
- □ 77. TODD WORRELL(TS)
- □ 79. OZZIE SMITH(TS)
- □ 142. OZZIE SMITH
- □ 152. VINCE COLEMAN(TS)
- □ 173. JOHN TUDOR
- □ 191. BOB FORSCH
- □ 199. VINCE COLEMAN(TS)

SAN DIEGO PADRES

- □ 31. TONY GWYNN
- □ 40. STEVE GARVEY
- □ 61. JOHN KRUK
- □ 117. TONY GWYNN(TS)
- □ 118. BENITO SANTIAGO(BS)
- □ 135. KEVIN MCREYNOLDS

□ 155. KEVIN MCREYNOLDS(TS)
□ 158. RANDY ASADOOR(BS)
□ 158. TIM PYZNARSKI(BS)
□ 197. TONY GWYNN(BS)

SAN FRANCISCO GIANTS

□ 13. CHRIS BROWN
□ 45. CHILI DAVIS
□ 46. ROBBY THOMPSON
□ 62. MIKE KRUKOW
□ 68. SCOTT GARRELTS
□ 78. CANDY MALDONADO
□ 95. WILL CLARK
□ 115. CHRIS BROWN(TS)
□ 195. WILL CLARK(TS)

SEATTLE MARINERS

□ 21. ALVIN DAVIS
□ 23. DANNY TARTABULL
□ 89. PHIL BRADLEY
□ 102. MARK LANGSTON
□ 179. JIM PRESLEY

TEXAS RANGERS

□ 32. DON SLAUGHT
□ 37. PETE INCAVIGLIA
□ 39. BOBBY WITT
□ 52. PETE O'BRIEN
□ 91. GARY WARD
□ 113. SCOTT FLETCHER(TS)
□ 126. GREG HARRIS
□ 131. ODDIBE MCDOWELL
□ 136. SCOTT FLETCHER
□ 154. DON SLAUGHT(TS)
□ 174. LARRY PARRISH

TORONTO BLUE JAYS

□ 14. JESSE BARFIELD
□ 51. GEORGE BELL
□ 80. GEORGE BELL(TS)
□ 96. LLOYD MOSEBY
□ 113. TONY FERNANDEZ(TS)
□ 153. JESSE BARFIELD(TS)
□ 183. DAMASO GARCIA
□ 187. TONY FERNANDEZ
□ 189. JIM CLANCY
□ 194. MARK EICHHORN(TS)

1987 SPORTFLICS
ROOKIES (25 + 25)
2 1/2 X 3 1/2

ATLANTA BRAVES

□ 48. JEFF BLAUSER

BALTIMORE ORIOLES

□ 1. ERIC BELL
□ 7. KEN GERHART
□ 28. BILL RIPKEN

BOSTON RED SOX

□ 5. ELLIS BURKS
□ 8. MIKE GREENWELL
□ 38. SAM HORN
□ 47. TODD BENZINGER
□ 49. JOHN MARZANO

CALIFORNIA ANGELS

□ 14. MARK MCLEMORE
□ 24. DEVON WHITE
□ 26. DEWAYNE BUICE
□ 27. WILLIE FRASER

CHICAGO CUBS

□ 32. RAFAEL PALMEIRO

CHICAGO WHITE SOX

□ 41. KEN WILLIAMS

CINCINNATI REDS

□ 17. PAUL O'NEILL

CLEVELAND INDIANS

NO CARDS ISSUED

DETROIT TIGERS

□ 16. MATT NOKES
□ 29. MIKE HENNEMAN
□ 46. JEFF ROBINSON

HOUSTON ASTROS

□ 36. GERALD YOUNG
□ 37. KEN CAMINITI

KANSAS CITY ROYALS

□ 20. KEVIN SEITZER

LOS ANGELES DODGERS

□ 30. SHAWN HILLEGAS

MILWAUKEE BREWERS

□ 2. CHRIS BOSIO
□ 23. B. J. SURHOFF

MINNESOTA TWINS

□ 34. GENE LARKIN
□ 45. LES STRAKER

MONTREAL EXPOS

□ 6. CASEY CANDAELE

NEW YORK METS

□ 10. DAVE MAGADAN
□ 39. DAVID CONE
□ 50. KEITH MILLER

NEW YORK YANKEES

NO CARDS ISSUED

OAKLAND A'S

□ 13. MARK MCGWIRE
□ 18. LUIS POLONIA
□ 22. TERRY STEINBACH

PHILADELPHIA PHILLIES

□ 33. MIKE JACKSON

PITTSBURGH PIRATES

□ 21. JOHN SMILEY
□ 40. MIKE DUNNE

ST. LOUIS CARDINALS

□ 11. JOE MAGRANE
□ 42. JOHN MORRIS
□ 43. JIM LINDEMAN

SAN DIEGO PADRES

□ 9. STAN JEFFERSON
□ 19. BENNY SANTIAGO
□ 31. SHANE MACK
□ 35. JIMMY JONES

SAN FRANCISCO GIANTS

□ 25. MATT WILLIAMS

SEATTLE MARINERS

NO CARDS ISSUED

TEXAS RANGERS

- ☐ 3. BOB BROWER
- ☐ 4. JERRY BROWNE
- ☐ 44. MIKE STANLEY

TORONTO BLUE JAYS

- ☐ 12. FRED MCGRIFF
- ☐ 15. JEFF MUSSELMAN

1988 SPORTFLICS (225)
2 1/2 X 3 1/2

JULIO FRANCO 14   SHORTSTOP

ATLANTA BRAVES

- ☐ 36. DION JAMES
- ☐ 134. ZANE SMITH
- ☐ 165. KEN OBERKFELL
- ☐ 170. DALE MURPHY
- ☐ 178. KEN GRIFFEY
- ☐ 217. OZZIE VIRGIL

BALTIMORE ORIOLES

- ☐ 23. FRED LYNN
- ☐ 59. EDDIE MURRAY
- ☐ 94. TERRY KENNEDY
- ☐ 115. RAY KNIGHT
- ☐ 146. MIKE BODDICKER
- ☐ 152. CAL RIPKEN
- ☐ 161. LARRY SHEETS
- ☐ 216. BILL RIPKEN

BOSTON RED SOX

- ☐ 50. WADE BOGGS
- ☐ 114. SAM HORN
- ☐ 118. MIKE GREENWELL
- ☐ 137. DWIGHT EVANS
- ☐ 144. ELLIS BURKS
- ☐ 157. MARTY BARRETT
- ☐ 158. JIM RICE
- ☐ 197. BRUCE HURST
- ☐ 207. ROGER CLEMENS
- ☐ 225. JODY REED (TS)

CALIFORNIA ANGELS

- ☐ 32. MIKE WITT
- ☐ 75. WALLY JOYNER
- ☐ 78. KIRK MCCASKILL
- ☐ 99. DEVON WHITE
- ☐ 181. BRIAN DOWNING
- ☐ 185. DOUG DECINCES (F)
- ☐ 186. JOHNNY RAY (B)
- ☐ 212. BOB BOONE
- ☐ 213. DON SUTTON

CHICAGO CUBS

- ☐ 3. ANDRE DAWSON
- ☐ 12. RYNE SANDBERG
- ☐ 27. RICK SUTCLIFFE
- ☐ 60. JODY DAVIS
- ☐ 163. SHAWON DUNSTON
- ☐ 164. KEITH MORELAND
- ☐ 179. LEE SMITH

CHICAGO WHITE SOX

- ☐ 14. OZZIE GUILLEN
- ☐ 33. HAROLD BAINES
- ☐ 43. CARLTON FISK
- ☐ 69. KEN WILLIAMS
- ☐ 103. GREG WALKER
- ☐ 166. IVAN CALDERON

CINCINNATI REDS

- ☐ 10. ERIC DAVIS
- ☐ 38. TRACY JONES
- ☐ 101. DAVE PARKER
- ☐ 112. KAL DANIELS
- ☐ 117. BO DIAZ
- ☐ 147. BUDDY BELL
- ☐ 195. JOHN FRANCO
- ☐ 218. DAVE CONCEPCION
- ☐ 225. JEFF TREADWAY (TS)

CLEVELAND INDIANS

- ☐ 5. JOE CARTER
- ☐ 29. CORY SNYDER
- ☐ 37. TOM CANDIOTTI
- ☐ 58. JULIO FRANCO
- ☐ 72. BROOK JACOBY
- ☐ 132. JOHN FARRELL
- ☐ 153. BRETT BUTLER
- ☐ 189. MEL HALL
- ☐ 205. PAT TABLER

DETROIT TIGERS

- ☐ 6. MATT NOKES
- ☐ 25. ALAN TRAMMELL
- ☐ 30. LOU WHITAKER
- ☐ 111. KIRK GIBSON
- ☐ 123. BILL MADLOCK
- ☐ 129. MIKE HENNEMAN
- ☐ 133. FRANK TANANA
- ☐ 176. JACK MORRIS
- ☐ 188. DARRELL EVANS

HOUSTON ASTROS

- ☐ 39. NOLAN RYAN
- ☐ 48. BILL DORAN
- ☐ 55. KEVIN BASS
- ☐ 63. BILLY HATCHER
- ☐ 66. MIKE SCOTT
- ☐ 102. GLENN DAVIS
- ☐ 124. KEN CAMINITI
- ☐ 190. JIM DESHAIES
- ☐ 208. DAVE SMITH
- ☐ 219. ALAN ASHBY

KANSAS CITY ROYALS

- ☐ 15. BRET SABERHAGEN
- ☐ 17. KEVIN SEITZER
- ☐ 19. DANNY TARTABULL
- ☐ 21. CHARLIE LEIBRANDT
- ☐ 76. DAN QUISENBERRY
- ☐ 88. GENE GARBER
- ☐ 148. BO JACKSON
- ☐ 149. FRANK WHITE
- ☐ 150. GEORGE BRETT
- ☐ 192. WILLIE WILSON
- ☐ 223. GARY THURMAN (TS)
- ☐ 224. JOHN DAVIS (TS)

LOS ANGELES DODGERS

- ☐ 40. FERNANDO VALENZUELA
- ☐ 97. PEDRO GUERRERO
- ☐ 110. MIKE SCIOSCIA
- ☐ 160. OREL HERSHISER
- ☐ 167. BOB WELCH
- ☐ 220. MIKE MARSHALL
- ☐ 224. TIM CREWS (TS)

MILWAUKEE BREWERS

- ☐ 20. TEDDY HIGUERA
- ☐ 34. ROBIN YOUNT
- ☐ 57. B. J. SURHOFF
- ☐ 79. PAUL MOLITOR
- ☐ 130. JIM GANTNER
- ☐ 180. JUAN NIEVES (TS)
- ☐ 183. ROB DEER

- ☐ 184. GREG BROCK
- ☐ 191. DAN PLESAC
- ☐ 211. JUAN NIEVES
- ☐ 221. PAUL MOLITOR (TS)

MINNESOTA TWINS

- ☐ 8. KIRBY PUCKETT
- ☐ 53. JEFF REARDON
- ☐ 92. BERT BLYLEVEN
- ☐ 95. KENT HRBEK
- ☐ 107. GENE LARKIN
- ☐ 154. GARY GAETTI
- ☐ 180. KIRBY PUCKETT (TS)
- ☐ 194. TOM BRUNANSKY
- ☐ 196. FRANK VIOLA

JEFF REARDON 41   RELIEF PITCHER

MONTREAL EXPOS

- ☐ 2. TIM RAINES
- ☐ 41. VANCE LAW
- ☐ 81. NEAL HEATON
- ☐ 105. MITCH WEBSTER
- ☐ 108. FLOYD YOUMANS
- ☐ 140. CASEY CANDAELE
- ☐ 151. TIM WALLACH
- ☐ 182. ANDRES GALARRAGA
- ☐ 187. HUBIE BROOKS

NEW YORK METS

- ☐ 28. GARY CARTER
- ☐ 31. KEITH HERNANDEZ
- ☐ 42. ROGER MCDOWELL
- ☐ 56. KEVIN MCREYNOLDS
- ☐ 73. RON DARLING
- ☐ 83. DAVE MAGADAN
- ☐ 89. JESSE OROSCO
- ☐ 106. LEN DYKSTRA
- ☐ 138. HOWARD JOHNSON
- ☐ 139. TERRY LEACH
- ☐ 155. DARRYL STRAWBERRY
- ☐ 177. SID FERNANDEZ
- ☐ 200. DWIGHT GOODEN
- ☐ 225. KEITH MILLER (TS)

NEW YORK YANKEES

- ☐ 1. DON MATTINGLY
- ☐ 7. DAVE WINFIELD
- ☐ 11. RICKEY HENDERSON
- ☐ 47. WILLIE RANDOLPH
- ☐ 104. RICK RHODEN
- ☐ 121. MIKE PAGLIARULO
- ☐ 122. TOMMY JOHN
- ☐ 125. GARY WARD
- ☐ 135. DAVE RIGHETTI
- ☐ 222. DON MATTINGLY (TS)
- ☐ 223. JAY BUHNER (TS)

OAKLAND A'S

- ☐ 71. LUIS POLONIA
- ☐ 86. JAY HOWELL
- ☐ 100. MARK MCGWIRE
- ☐ 120. REGGIE JACKSON
- ☐ 156. ALFREDO GRIFFIN
- ☐ 162. DAVE STEWART
- ☐ 174. TERRY STEINBACH
- ☐ 201. JOSE CANSECO
- ☐ 202. CARNEY LANSFORD
- ☐ 206. MIKE DAVIS

☐ 209. CURT YOUNG
☐ 221. MARK MCGWIRE (TS)

PHILADELPHIA PHILLIES

☐ 35. MIKE SCHMIDT
☐ 51. SHANE RAWLEY
☐ 62. VON HAYES
☐ 70. STEVE BEDROSIAN
☐ 96. JUAN SAMUEL
☐ 143. LANCE PARRISH
☐ 173. MILT THOMPSON
☐ 180. MIKE SCHMIDT (TS)
☐ 204. GLENN WILSON
☐ 222. STEVE BEDROSIAN (TS)

PITTSBURGH PIRATES

☐ 98. SID BREAM
☐ 109. ANDY VAN SLYKE
☐ 119. BARRY BONDS
☐ 131. BOBBY BONILLA
☐ 136. RICK REUSCHEL
☐ 171. MIKE DUNNE
☐ 186. JOHNNY RAY (F)
☐ 193. MIKE LAVALLIER
☐ 224. VINCENTE PALACIOS (TS)

ST. LOUIS CARDINALS

☐ 18. JACK CLARK
☐ 61. TODD WORRELL
☐ 67. VINCE COLEMAN
☐ 68. OZZIE SMITH
☐ 84. DANNY COX
☐ 91. WILLIE MCGEE
☐ 128. JOE MAGRANE
☐ 141. TOM HERR
☐ 142. TONY PENA
☐ 159. TERRY PENDLETON
☐ 185. DOUG DECINCES (B)
☐ 198. JOHN TUDOR
☐ 199. BOB FORSCH
☐ 221. VINCE COLEMAN (TS)

SAN DIEGO PADRES

☐ 16. TONY GWYNN
☐ 22. BENNY SANTIAGO
☐ 64. JOHN KRUK
☐ 85. LANCE MCCULLERS
☐ 222. BENNY SANTIAGO (TS)
☐ 223. SHAWN ABNER (TS)

SAN FRANCISCO GIANTS

☐ 9. WILL CLARK
☐ 24. ROBBY THOMPSON
☐ 44. SCOTT GARRELTS
☐ 80. MIKE ALDRETE
☐ 82. JEFFREY LEONARD
☐ 90. DON ROBINSON
☐ 126. CANDY MALDONADO
☐ 172. CHILI DAVIS
☐ 203. KELLY DOWNS

SEATTLE MARINERS

☐ 45. LEE GUETTERMAN
☐ 46. MARK LANGSTON
☐ 52. ALVIN DAVIS

☐ 54. JIM PRESLEY
☐ 93. PHIL BRADLEY
☐ 127. HAROLD REYNOLDS

TEXAS RANGERS

☐ 49. LARRY PARRISH
☐ 77. SCOTT FLETCHER
☐ 87. CHARLIE HOUGH
☐ 113. RUBEN SIERRA
☐ 145. PETE O'BRIEN
☐ 169. PETE INCAVIGLIA
☐ 175. ODDIBE MCDOWELL

TORONTO BLUE JAYS

☐ 4. GEORGE BELL
☐ 13. JESSE BARFIELD
☐ 26. TONY FERNANDEZ
☐ 65. TOM HENKE
☐ 74. LLOYD MOSEBY
☐ 116. JIMMY KEY
☐ 168. FRED MCGRIFF
☐ 210. MARK EICHHORN
☐ 214. WILLIE UPSHAW
☐ 215. JIM CLANCY

1989 SPORTFLICS (225)
2 1/2 X 3 1/2

ROGER CLEMENS
BOSTON RED SOX

ATLANTA BRAVES

☐ 28. RON GANT
☐ 94. OZZIE VIRGIL
☐ 110. DALE MURPHY
☐ 164. GERALD PERRY

BALTIMORE ORIOLES

☐ 66. CAL RIPKEN, JR.
☐ 68. FRED LYNN
☐ 134. CRAIG WORTHINGTON
☐ 147. EDDIE MURRAY
☐ 224. BOB MILACKI (TS)

BOSTON RED SOX

☐ 3. ROGER CLEMENS
☐ 100. WADE BOGGS
☐ 122. MIKE BODDICKER
☐ 143. MIKE GREENWELL
☐ 148. LEE SMITH
☐ 173. JIM RICE
☐ 175. BRUCE HURST
☐ 191. ELLIS BURKS
☐ 198. MARTY BARRETT
☐ 204. DWIGHT EVANS
☐ 210. JODY REED
☐ 221. WADE BOGGS (TS)
☐ 221. MIKE GREENWELL (TS)

CALIFORNIA ANGELS

☐ 2. WALLY JOYNER
☐ 16. DEVON WHITE
☐ 40. BOB BOONE
☐ 117. BRIAN DOWNING
☐ 129. CHILI DAVIS
☐ 130. BRYAN HARVEY
☐ 195. JOHNNY RAY

☐ 197. MIKE WITT
☐ 214. KIRK MCCASKILL

CHICAGO CUBS

☐ 15. MARK GRACE
☐ 30. RAFAEL PALMEIRO
☐ 42. DOUG DASCENZO
☐ 67. MITCH WEBSTER
☐ 95. ANDRE DAWSON
☐ 108. GREG MADDUX
☐ 132. MIKE HARKEY
☐ 162. VANCE LAW
☐ 187. JODY DAVIS
☐ 190. SHAWON DUNSTON
☐ 201. RYNE SANDBERG
☐ 216. DAMON BERRYHILL
☐ 217. RICK SUTCLIFFE

CHICAGO WHITE SOX

☐ 19. GREG WALKER
☐ 85. OZZIE GUILLEN
☐ 88. DAVE GALLAGHER
☐ 118. MELIDO PEREZ
☐ 157. HAROLD BAINES
☐ 207. BOBBY THIGPEN
☐ 219. CARLTON FISK

CINCINNATI REDS

☐ 13. CHRIS DABO
☐ 69. ERIC DAVIS
☐ 80. DANNY JACKSON
☐ 107. JEFF TREADWAY
☐ 136. BARRY LARKIN
☐ 176. JOHN FRANCO
☐ 177. VAN SNIDER
☐ 180. TOM BROWNING
☐ 222. TOM BROWNING (TS)

CLEVELAND INDIANS

☐ 4. GREG SWINDELL
☐ 37. JOHN FARRELL
☐ 38. DOUG JONES
☐ 104. JOE CARTER
☐ 144. MEL HALL
☐ 149. JULIO FRANCO
☐ 192. BROOK JACOBY
☐ 196. CORY SNYDER

DETROIT TIGERS

☐ 5. JACK MORRIS
☐ 18. LOU WHITAKER
☐ 56. MIKE HENNEMAN
☐ 103. FRANK TANANA
☐ 171. CHET LEMON
☐ 193. JEFF ROBINSON
☐ 203. MATT NOKES
☐ 211. DOYLE ALEXANDER
☐ 215. ALAN TRAMMELL

HOUSTON ASTROS

☐ 11. KEVIN BASS
☐ 57. BILL DORAN
☐ 115. NOLAN RYAN
☐ 120. MIKE SCOTT
☐ 125. GERALD YOUNG
☐ 137. GLENN DAVIS
☐ 174. BILLY HATCHER
☐ 225. CAMERON DREW (TS)

KANSAS CITY ROYALS

☐ 46. DANNY TARTABULL
☐ 55. KEVIN SEITZER
☐ 64. GEORGE BRETT
☐ 70. BO JACKSON
☐ 102. MARK GUBICZA
☐ 109. BRET SABERHAGEN
☐ 154. FLOYD BANNISTER
☐ 172. PAT TABLER
☐ 186. WILLIE WILSON

LOS ANGELES DODGERS

☐ 36. OREL HERSHISER
☐ 54. MIKE MARSHALL
☐ 58. STEVE SAX

1989 Sportflics

☐ 65. KIRK GIBSON
☐ 81. TIM LEARY
☐ 86. JOHN TUDOR
☐ 121. TIM BELCHER
☐ 124. FERNANDO VALENZUELA
☐ 138. MIKE SCIOSCIA
☐ 222. OREL HERSHISER (TS)
☐ 224. RAMON MARTINEZ (TS)

MILWAUKEE BREWERS

☐ 29. GLENN BRAGGS
☐ 41. GARY SHEFFIELD
☐ 47. TEDDY HIGUERA
☐ 111. ROB DEER
☐ 128. DAN PLESAC
☐ 131. DON AUGUST
☐ 135. JOEY MEYER
☐ 199. ROBIN YOUNT
☐ 208. B. J. SURHOFF
☐ 209. PAUL MOLITOR
☐ 223. GARY SHEFFIELD (TS)

MINNESOTA TWINS

☐ 10. FRANK VIOLA
☐ 48. GARY GAETTI
☐ 152. TIM LAUDNER
☐ 156. KIRBY PUCKETT
☐ 168. JEFF REARDON
☐ 188. KENT HRBEK
☐ 220. ALLAN ANDERSON

MONTREAL EXPOS

☐ 73. TIM BURKE
☐ 96. HUBIE BROOKS
☐ 106. DENNIS MARTINEZ
☐ 114. TIM WALLACH
☐ 139. ANDRES GALARRAGA
☐ 150. TIM RAINES
☐ 224. RANDY JOHNSON (TS)

ANDRES GALARRAGA
1ST BASE • 14

NEW YORK METS

☐ 32. RON DARLING
☐ 45. DAVE WEST
☐ 51. DAVID CONE
☐ 60. KEITH HERNANDEZ
☐ 71. KEVIN ELSTER
☐ 79. ROGER MCDOWELL
☐ 90. GREGG JEFFERIES
☐ 97. KEVIN MCREYNOLDS
☐ 123. LEN DYKSTRA
☐ 140. DOC GOODEN
☐ 155. GARY CARTER
☐ 205. DARRYL STRAWBERRY
☐ 223. GREGG JEFFERIES (TS)

NEW YORK YANKEES

☐ 24. DAVE WINFIELD
☐ 26. JACK CLARK
☐ 50. DON MATTINGLY
☐ 75. CLAUDELL WASHINGTON
☐ 145. RICKEY HENDERSON
☐ 153. MIKE PAGLIARULO
☐ 158. DAVE RIGHETTI
☐ 194. RICH DOTSON
☐ 202. JOHN CANDELARIA
☐ 218. DON SLAUGHT

OAKLAND A'S

☐ 1. JOSE CANSECO
☐ 23. DAVE STEWART
☐ 49. DAVE PARKER
☐ 52. KAL DANIELS
☐ 53. CARNEY LANSFORD
☐ 87. TODD BURNS
☐ 91. BOB WELCH
☐ 101. DENNIS ECKERSLEY
☐ 116. WALT WEISS
☐ 119. TERRY STEINBACH
☐ 127. DAVE HENDERSON
☐ 133. LUIS POLONIA
☐ 200. MARK MCGWIRE
☐ 221. JOSE CANSECO (TS)
☐ 222. DENNIS ECKERSLEY (TS)

PHILADELPHIA PHILLIES

☐ 17. JUAN SAMUEL
☐ 21. MIKE SCHMIDT
☐ 44. RICKY JORDAN
☐ 59. LANCE PARRISH
☐ 63. STEVE BEDROSIAN
☐ 169. MILT THOMPSON
☐ 178. RON JONES
☐ 181. VON HAYES
☐ 213. KEVIN GROSS
☐ 225. RON JONES (TS)

BOBBY BONILLA
THIRD BASE • 25

PITTSBURGH PIRATES

☐ 27. DOUG DRABEK
☐ 34. BOB WALK
☐ 62. JOSE LIND
☐ 83. JIM GOTT
☐ 98. MIKE LAVALLIERE
☐ 146. BARRY BONDS
☐ 166. ANDY VAN SLYKE
☐ 182. BOBBY BONILLA

ST. LOUIS CARDINALS

☐ 99. TERRY PENDLETON
☐ 105. OZZIE SMITH
☐ 113. VINCE COLEMAN
☐ 161. TOM BRUNANSKY
☐ 183. TODD WORRELL
☐ 206. WILLIE MCGEE

SAN DIEGO PADRES

☐ 20. ROBERTO ALOMAR
☐ 22. BENNY SANTIAGO
☐ 74. MARK DAVIS
☐ 76. LANCE MCCULLERS
☐ 84. ANDY HAWKINS
☐ 141. KEITH MORELAND
☐ 160. TONY GWYNN
☐ 179. JERALD CLARK
☐ 184. JOHN KRUK
☐ 212. DENNIS RASMUSSEN
☐ 223. SANDY ALOMAR (TS)

SAN FRANCISCO GIANTS

☐ 31. BRETT BUTLER
☐ 39. KELLY DOWNS
☐ 61. JOSE URIBE
☐ 72. RICK REUSCHEL

☐ 78. ROBBY THOMPSON
☐ 142. KEVIN MITCHELL
☐ 170. WILL CLARK

SEATTLE MARINERS

☐ 6. MICKEY BRANTLEY
☐ 7. JIM PRESLEY
☐ 12. GLENN WILSON
☐ 33. ALVIN DAVIS
☐ 77. MIKE MOORE
☐ 89. JAY BUHNER
☐ 159. MARK LANGSTON
☐ 165. HAROLD REYNOLDS

TEXAS RANGERS

☐ 8. PETE O'BRIEN
☐ 43. CHAD KRUETER
☐ 82. BOBBY WITT
☐ 92. CHARLIE HOUGH
☐ 112. PETE INCAVIGLIA
☐ 151. MITCH WILLIAMS
☐ 185. SCOTT FLETCHER
☐ 189. RUBEN SIERRA

TORONTO BLUE JAYS

☐ 9. JESSE BARFIELD
☐ 14. FRED MCGRIFF
☐ 25. GEORGE BELL
☐ 35. DAVE STIEB
☐ 93. TONY FERNANDEZ
☐ 126. TOM HENKE
☐ 163. KELLY GRUBER
☐ 167. JIMMY KEY
☐ 225. GERONIMO BERROA (TS)

1990 SPORTFLICS (225)
2 1/2 X 3 1/2

ATLANTA BRAVES

☐ 24. DEREK LILLIQUIST
☐ 34. TOM GLAVINE
☐ 61. JOHN SMOLTZ
☐ 65. LONNIE SMITH
☐ 189. DALE MURPHY
☐ 207. ODDIBE MCDOWELL
☐ 219. JEFF TREADWAY
☐ 224. TOMMY GREENE

BALTIMORE ORIOLES

☐ 38. JOE ORSULAK
☐ 95. PHIL BRADLEY
☐ 100. CAL RIPKEN
☐ 114. MIKE DEVEREAUX
☐ 117. CRAIG WORTHINGTON
☐ 123. JEFF BALLARD
☐ 133. CURT SCHILLING
☐ 139. KEITH MORELAND
☐ 171. MICKEY TETTLETON
☐ 215. GREGG OLSON

BOSTON RED SOX

☐ 2. WADE BOGGS
☐ 50. MIKE GREENWELL
☐ 72. NICK ESASKY

☐ 80. ELLIS BURKS
☐ 149. ROGER CLEMENS
☐ 217. DWIGHT EVANS

CALIFORNIA ANGELS

☐ 21. CHILI DAVIS
☐ 31. BRYAN HARVEY
☐ 49. WALLY JOYNER
☐ 77. BRIAN DOWNING
☐ 82. JOHNNY RAY
☐ 99. JIM ABBOTT
☐ 132. JOHN ORTON
☐ 169. KIRK MCCASKILL
☐ 172. CHUCK FINLEY
☐ 193. BERT BLYLEVEN
☐ 210. DEVON WHITE

CHICAGO CUBS

☐ 15. MARK GRACE
☐ 54. RYNE SANDBERG
☐ 67. JEROME WALTON
☐ 108. ANDRE DAWSON
☐ 152. DWIGHT SMITH
☐ 164. DAMON BERRYHILL
☐ 181. RICK SUTCLIFFE
☐ 196. MITCH WILLIAMS
☐ 211. GREG MADDUX

CHICAGO WHITE SOX

☐ 27. BOBBY THIGPEN
☐ 48. OZZIE GUILLEN
☐ 81. SAMMY SOSA
☐ 105. DAVE GALLAGHER
☐ 167. IVAN CALDERON
☐ 204. CARLTON FISK
☐ 213. CARLOS MARTINEZ
☐ 220. SCOTT FLETCHER
☐ 222. ROBIN VENTURA

CINCINNATI REDS

☐ 4. PAUL O'NEILL
☐ 56. TODD BENZINGER
☐ 71. JOE OLIVER
☐ 89. DANNY JACKSON
☐ 91. TOM BROWNING
☐ 97. ERIC DAVIS
☐ 138. JOHN FRANCO
☐ 160. BARRY LARKIN

CLEVELAND INDIANS

☐ 3. CORY SNYDER
☐ 92. PETE O'BRIEN
☐ 96. DOUG JONES
☐ 111. JERRY BROWNE
☐ 120. JOE CARTER
☐ 126. TOM CANDIOTTI
☐ 155. BROOK JACOBY
☐ 159. JOEY BELLE
☐ 178. STEVE OLIN

DETROIT TIGERS

☐ 29. KEVIN RITZ
☐ 103. LOU WHITAKER
☐ 144. MIKE HENNEMAN
☐ 154. ALAN TRAMMELL
☐ 202. GARY PETTIS

HOUSTON ASTROS

☐ 19. GLENN DAVIS
☐ 22. CRAIG BIGGIO
☐ 32. JIM DESHAIES
☐ 55. MIKE SCOTT
☐ 83. DANNY DARWIN
☐ 140. DAVE SMITH
☐ 179. ERIC ANTHONY
☐ 198. KEVIN BASS
☐ 209. KEN CAMINITI

KANSAS CITY ROYALS

☐ 30. TOM GORDON
☐ 40. BOB BOONE
☐ 46. KEVIN SEITZER
☐ 94. BRET SABERHAGEN
☐ 129. DANNY TARTABULL
☐ 131. JOSE DEJESUS
☐ 166. JIM EISENREICH
☐ 200. BO JACKSON
☐ 214. GEORGE BRETT
☐ 218. PAT TABLER

LOS ANGELES DODGERS

☐ 68. RAMON MARTINEZ
☐ 78. JAY HOWELL
☐ 163. MIKE SCIOSCIA
☐ 175. WILLIE RANDOLPH
☐ 197. OREL HERSHISER

MILWAUKEE BREWERS

☐ 18. ROBIN YOUNT
☐ 25. CHRIS BOSIO
☐ 44. TEDDY HIGUERA
☐ 52. GARY SHEFFIELD
☐ 102. DAN PLESAC
☐ 135. GREG VAUGHN
☐ 137. ROB DEER
☐ 183. PAUL MOLITOR
☐ 206. BILL SPIERS

MINNESOTA TWINS

☐ 11. KIRBY PUCKETT
☐ 37. JEFF REARDON
☐ 51. GARY GAETTI
☐ 59. ALLAN ANDERSON
☐ 121. BRIAN HARPER
☐ 190. DAN GLADDEN
☐ 203. KENT HRBEK
☐ 223. CHIP HALE

MONTREAL EXPOS

☐ 53. DENNIS MARTINEZ
☐ 69. TIM RAINES
☐ 110. MARK LANGSTON
☐ 134. MARQUIS GRISSOM
☐ 148. ANDRES GALARRAGA
☐ 162. NELSON SANTOVENIA
☐ 176. JEFF HUSON
☐ 182. TIM WALLACH
☐ 199. TIM BURKE

NEW YORK METS

☐ 14. GREGG JEFFERIES
☐ 106. KEITH HERNANDEZ
☐ 109. HOWARD JOHNSON
☐ 113. SID FERNANDEZ
☐ 118. KEVIN ELSTER
☐ 122. FRANK VIOLA
☐ 127. KEVIN MCREYNOLDS
☐ 145. DWIGHT GOODEN
☐ 146. DARRYL STRAWBERRY
☐ 173. DAVE MAGADAN
☐ 201. DAVID CONE

NEW YORK YANKEES

☐ 10. JESSE BARFIELD
☐ 12. STEVE SAX
☐ 87. DAVE WINFIELD
☐ 88. DAVE RIGHETTI
☐ 150. DON MATTINGLY

☐ 184. ROBERTO KELLY
☐ 205. BOB GEREN
☐ 221. DEION SANDERS

OAKLAND A'S

☐ 23. JOSE CANSECO
☐ 33. TERRY STEINBACH
☐ 35. BOB WELCH
☐ 74. WALT WEISS
☐ 84. CARNEY LANSFORD
☐ 141. MARK MCGWIRE
☐ 170. DENNIS ECKERSLEY
☐ 185. MIKE MOORE
☐ 194. DAVE STEWART
☐ 208. RICKEY HENDERSON

PHILADELPHIA PHILLIES

☐ 36. CHARLIE HAYES
☐ 63. TOM HERR
☐ 75. ROGER MCDOWELL
☐ 124. JOHN KRUK
☐ 147. VON HAYES
☐ 153. RICKY JORDAN
☐ 156. LENNY DYKSTRA

PITTSBURGH PIRATES

☐ 58. JOSE LIND
☐ 101. ANDY VAN SLYKE
☐ 143. BARRY BONDS
☐ 157. MIKE LAVALLIERE
☐ 191. JOHN SMILEY
☐ 195. BOBBY BONILLA

ST. LOUIS CARDINALS

☐ 16. OZZIE SMITH
☐ 66. PEDRO GUERRERO
☐ 76. JOSE DELEON
☐ 85. JOSE OQUENDO
☐ 142. VINCE COLEMAN
☐ 151. JOE MAGRANE
☐ 165. TODD WORRELL
☐ 174. TERRY PENDLETON
☐ 177. TODD ZEILE

SAN DIEGO PADRES

☐ 28. JACK CLARK
☐ 47. BRUCE HURST
☐ 62. MARK DAVIS
☐ 90. ANDY BENES
☐ 93. ROBERTO ALOMAR
☐ 98. TONY GWYNN
☐ 115. BENNY SANTIAGO
☐ 116. BIP ROBERTS
☐ 212. ED WHITSON

SAN FRANCISCO GIANTS

☐ 1. KEVIN MITCHELL
☐ 5. WILL CLARK
☐ 39. SCOTT GARRELTS
☐ 60. ROBBY THOMPSON
☐ 70. MATT WILLIAMS
☐ 79. JOSE URIBE
☐ 104. STEVE BEDROSIAN
☐ 130. CRAIG LEFFERTS
☐ 136. BRETT BUTLER
☐ 161. RICK REUSCHEL

1990 Sportflics

SEATTLE MARINERS

- ☐ 7. KEN GRIFFEY, JR.
- ☐ 20. JEFFREY LEONARD
- ☐ 41. SCOTT BANKHEAD
- ☐ 43. GREG BRILEY
- ☐ 64. RANDY JOHNSON
- ☐ 112. ALVIN DAVIS
- ☐ 119. HAROLD REYNOLDS
- ☐ 187. MIKE SCHOOLER

TEXAS RANGERS

- ☐ 8. NOLAN RYAN
- ☐ 9. RAFAEL PALMEIRO
- ☐ 73. KEVIN BROWN
- ☐ 125. HAROLD BAINES
- ☐ 158. JULIO FRANCO
- ☐ 180. SCOTT COOLBAUGH
- ☐ 188. RUBEN SIERRA
- ☐ 192. JEFF RUSSELL
- ☐ 216. KENNY ROGERS
- ☐ 225. DEAN PALMER

TORONTO BLUE JAYS

- ☐ 6. TONY FERNANDEZ
- ☐ 13. FRED MCGRIFF
- ☐ 17. GEORGE BELL
- ☐ 26. DAVE STIEB
- ☐ 42. TOM HENKE
- ☐ 45. PAT BORDERS
- ☐ 57. KELLY GRUBER
- ☐ 86. JOHN CERUTTI
- ☐ 107. DUANE WARD
- ☐ 128. MOOKIE WILSON
- ☐ 168. GOOSE GOZZO
- ☐ 186. JUNIOR FELIX

1951 TOPPS
TEAM CARDS
DATED (9)
2 1/16" X 5 1/4"

1951 TOPPS
TEAM CARDS
UNDATED (9)
2 1/16" X 5 1/4"

☐ BOSTON RED SOX
☐ BROOKLYN DODGERS
☐ CHICAGO WHITE SOX
☐ CINCINNATI REDS
☐ NEW YORK GIANTS
☐ PHILADELPHIA ATHLETICS
☐ PHILADELPHIA PHILLIES
☐ ST. LOUIS CARDINALS
☐ WASHINGTON SENATORS

☐ BOSTON RED SOX
☐ BROOKLYN DODGERS
☐ CHICAGO WHITE SOX
☐ CINCINNATI REDS
☐ NEW YORK GIANTS
☐ PHILADELPHIA ATHLETICS
☐ PHILADELPHIA PHILLIES
☐ ST. LOUIS CARDINALS
☐ WASHINGTON SENATORS

1951 TOPPS
RED BACKS (52)
2" X 2 5/8"

BOSTON BRAVES

☐ 2. SID GORDON
☐ 30. WARREN SPAHN
☐ 52. TOMMY HOLMES

BOSTON RED SOX

☐ 4. VERN STEPHENS
☐ 10. MEL PARNELL
☐ 20. DOM DIMAGGIO

☐ 42. RAY SCARBOROUGH
☐ 43. MICKEY MCDERMOTT
☐ 46. BILLY GOODMAN

BROOKLYN DODGERS

☐ 11. GENE HERMANSKI
☐ 16. PREACHER ROE
☐ 31. GIL HODGES
☐ 38. DUKE SNIDER

CHICAGO CUBS

☐ 14. WAYNE TERWILLIGER

CHICAGO WHITE SOX

☐ 36. GUS ZERNIAL
☐ 49. AL ZARILLA
☐ 51. EDDIE ROBINSON

CINCINNATI REDS

☐ 34. GRADY HATTON
☐ 39. TED KLUSZEWSKI

CLEVELAND INDIANS

☐ 8. EARLY WYNN
☐ 12. JIM HEGAN
☐ 13. DALE MITCHELL
☐ 22. BOB FELLER
☐ 23. RAY BOONE

☐ 26. LUKE EASTER
☐ 29. BOB KENNEDY
☐ 35. AL ROSEN
☐ 40. MIKE GARCIA

DETROIT TIGERS

NO CARDS ISSUED

NEW YORK GIANTS

☐ 21. LARRY JANSEN
☐ 32. HENRY THOMPSON
☐ 37. WES WESTRUM
☐ 41. WHITEY LOCKMAN
☐ 48. EDDIE STANKY
☐ 50. MONTE IRVIN

NEW YORK YANKEES

- ☐ 1. YOGI BERRA
- ☐ 5. PHIL RIZZUTO
- ☐ 6. ALLIE REYNOLDS
- ☐ 18. GERRY COLEMAN
- ☐ 24. HANK BAUER

PHILADELPHIA ATHLETICS

- ☐ 3. FERRIS FAIN
- ☐ 28. ELMER VALO
- ☐ 36. GUS ZERNIAL

PHILADELPHIA PHILLIES

- ☐ 45. ANDY SEMINICK

PITTSBURGH PIRATES

- ☐ 15. RALPH KINER
- ☐ 17. GUS BELL
- ☐ 25. CLIFF CHAMBERS
- ☐ 27. WALLY WESTLAKE
- ☐ 33. BILL WERLE

ST. LOUIS BROWNS

- ☐ 9. ROY SIEVERS
- ☐ 19. DICK KOKOS

ST. LOUIS CARDINALS

- ☐ 7. HOWIE POLLET
- ☐ 47. TOMMY GLAVIANO

WASHINGTON SENATORS

- ☐ 44. SID HUDSON

1951 TOPPS
BLUE BACKS (52)
2″ X 2 5/8″

BOSTON BRAVES

- ☐ 9. JOHNNY SAIN
- ☐ 12. SAM JETHROE
- ☐ 32. BOB ELLIOTT
- ☐ 34. EARL TORGESON

BOSTON RED SOX

- ☐ 5. JOHNNY PESKY
- ☐ 37. BOBBY DOERR

BROOKLYN DODGERS

- ☐ 20. RALPH BRANCA
- ☐ 42. BRUCE EDWARDS
- ☐ 48. BILLY COX

CHICAGO CUBS

- ☐ 17. ROY SMALLEY
- ☐ 27. ANDY PAFKO
- ☐ 41. JOHNNY SCHMITZ
- ☐ 49. HANK SAUER

CHICAGO WHITE SOX

- ☐ 2. HANK MAJESKI
- ☐ 19. PHIL MASI
- ☐ 26. CHICO CARRASQUEL
- ☐ 45. BILLY PIERCE

CINCINNATI REDS

- ☐ 44. JOHNNY WYROSTEK
- ☐ 47. HERM WEHMEIER

CLEVELAND INDIANS

- ☐ 31. LOU BRISSIE
- ☐ 52. SAM CHAPMAN

DETROIT TIGERS

- ☐ 11. JOHNNY GROTH
- ☐ 23. DIZZY TROUT
- ☐ 40. VIC WERTZ
- ☐ 46. GERRY PRIDDY

NEW YORK GIANTS

NO CARDS ISSUED

NEW YORK YANKEES

- ☐ 10. JOE PAGE
- ☐ 35. TOMMY BYRNE
- ☐ 39. ED LOPAT
- ☐ 50. JOHNNY MIZE

PHILADELPHIA ATHLETICS

- ☐ 15. EDDIE JOOST

PHILADELPHIA PHILLIES

- ☐ 3. RICHIE ASHBURN
- ☐ 4. DEL ENNIS
- ☐ 8. DICK SISLER
- ☐ 29. GRANNY HAMNER
- ☐ 43. WILLIE JONES
- ☐ 51. EDDIE WAITKUS

PITTSBURGH PIRATES

- ☐ 16. MURRY DICKSON

ST. LOUIS BROWNS

- ☐ 18. NED GARVER
- ☐ 24. SHERMAN LOLLAR
- ☐ 33. DON LENHARDT
- ☐ 36. CLIFF FANNIN

ST. LOUIS CARDINALS

- ☐ 6. RED SCHOENDIENST
- ☐ 7. GERRY STALEY
- ☐ 14. GEORGE MUNGER
- ☐ 21. BILLY JOHNSON
- ☐ 28. HARRY BRECHEEN
- ☐ 30. ENOS SLAUGHTER

WASHINGTON SENATORS

- ☐ 1. EDDIE YOST
- ☐ 13. MICKEY VERNON
- ☐ 22. BOB KUZAVA
- ☐ 25. SAM MELE
- ☐ 38. IRV NOREN

1952 TOPPS (407)
2 5/8″ X 3 3/4″

BOSTON BRAVES

- ☐ 14. BOB ELLIOTT
- ☐ 27. SAM JETHROE
- ☐ 33. WARREN SPAHN
- ☐ 96. WILLARD MARSHALL
- ☐ 97. EARL TORGESON
- ☐ 140. JOHN ANTONELLI
- ☐ 162. DEL CRANDALL
- ☐ 252. VERN BICKFORD
- ☐ 264. ROY HARTSFIELD
- ☐ 267. SID GORDON
- ☐ 276. JIM WILSON
- ☐ 288. CHET NICHOLS
- ☐ 289. TOMMY HOLMES(M)
- ☐ 293. SIBBY SISTI
- ☐ 294. WALKER COOPER
- ☐ 302. MAX SURKONT
- ☐ 360. GEORGE CROWE
- ☐ 367. BOB THORPE
- ☐ 388. BOB CHIPMAN
- ☐ 393. EBBA ST. CLAIRE
- ☐ 407. ED MATHEWS

BOSTON RED SOX

- ☐ 4. DON LENHARDT
- ☐ 15. JOHNNY PESKY
- ☐ 22. DOM DIMAGGIO
- ☐ 23. BILLY GOODMAN
- ☐ 30. MEL PARNELL
- ☐ 43. RAY SCARBOROUGH
- ☐ 54. LEO KIELY
- ☐ 72. KARL OLSON
- ☐ 78. ELLIS KINDER
- ☐ 84. VERN STEPHENS
- ☐ 119. MICKEY MCDERMOTT
- ☐ 121. GUS NIARHOS
- ☐ 139. KEN WOOD
- ☐ 152. AL EVANS

☐ 177. BILL WIGHT
☐ 180. CHARLEY MAXWELL
☐ 186. WALT MASTERSON
☐ 235. WALT DROPO
☐ 247. RANDY GUMPERT
☐ 255. CLYDE VOLLMER
☐ 269. WILLARD NIXON
☐ 327. ARCHIE WILSON
☐ 329. IVAN DELOCK
☐ 335. TED LEPCIO
☐ 343. DICK GERNERT
☐ 345. SAM WHITE
☐ 374. AL BENTON
☐ 376. FAYE THRONEBERRY
☐ 383. DEL WILBER
☐ 404. DICK BRODOWSKI

BROOKLYN DODGERS

☐   1. ANDY PAFKO
☐   7. WAYNE TERWILLIGER
☐ 20. BILLY LOES
☐ 36. GIL HODGES
☐ 37. DUKE SNIDER
☐ 51. JIM RUSSEL
☐ 53. CHRIS VAN CUYK
☐ 66. PREACHER ROE
☐ 136. JOHNNY SCHMITZ
☐ 188. CLARENCE PODBIELAN
☐ 198. PHIL HAUGSTAD
☐ 205. CLYDE KING
☐ 232. BILLY COX
☐ 239. ROCKY BRIDGES
☐ 250. CARL ERSKINE
☐ 273. ERV PALICA
☐ 274. RALPH BRANCA
☐ 312. JACKIE ROBINSON
☐ 314. ROY CAMPANELLA
☐ 319. RUBE WALKER
☐ 320. JOHN RUTHERFORD
☐ 321. JOE BLACK
☐ 326. GEORGE SHUBA
☐ 333. PEE WEE REESE
☐ 342. CLEM LABINE
☐ 355. BOBBY MORGAN
☐ 365. COOKIE LAVAGETTO(C)
☐ 377. CHUCK DRESSEN(M)
☐ 389. BEN WADE
☐ 390. ROCKY NELSON
☐ 394. BILLY HERMAN(C)
☐ 395. JAKE PITLER(C)
☐ 396. DICK WILLIAMS

CHICAGO CUBS

☐ 16. GENE HERMANSKI
☐ 35. HANK SAUER
☐ 105. JOHN PRAMESA
☐ 110. DUTCH LEONARD
☐ 114. WILLARD RAMSDELL
☐ 127. PAUL MINNER
☐ 148. JOHNNY KLIPPSTEIN
☐ 153. BOB RUSH
☐ 157. BOB USHER
☐ 164. WALT DUBIEL
☐ 172. EDDIE MIKSIS
☐ 173. ROY SMALLEY
☐ 184. BOB RAMAZZOTTI
☐ 194. JOE HATTEN
☐ 204. RON NORTHEY
☐ 224. BRUCE EDWARDS
☐ 225. FRANK BAUMHOLTZ
☐ 259. BOB ADDIS
☐ 295. PHIL CAVARRETTA(M)
☐ 322. RANDY JACKSON
☐ 324. WARREN HACKER
☐ 325. BILL SERENA
☐ 330. TURK LOWN
☐ 341. HAL JEFFCOAT
☐ 348. BOB KELLY
☐ 356. TOBY ATWELL
☐ 359. DEE FONDY
☐ 401. BOB SCHULTZ

CHICAGO WHITE SOX

☐ 32. EDDIE ROBINSON
☐ 42. LOU KRETLOW
☐ 50. MARV RICKERT
☐ 62. CHUCK STOBBS
☐ 70. AL ZARILLA
☐ 95. KEN HOLCOMBE
☐ 98. BILL PIERCE
☐ 102. BILL KENNEDY(B)
☐ 117. SHERMAN LOLLAR
☐ 133. AL WIDMAR
☐ 159. SAUL ROGOVIN
☐ 169. HOWIE JUDSON
☐ 195. MINNIE MINOSO
☐ 211. RAY COLEMAN
☐ 251. CHICO CARRASQUEL

☐ 254. JOE DOBSON
☐ 279. ED STEWART
☐ 283. PHIL MASI
☐ 303. HARRY DORISH
☐ 304. SAM DENTE
☐ 305. PAUL RICHARDS(M)
☐ 308. LUIS ALOMA

CINCINNATI REDS

☐   6. GRADY HATTON
☐ 13. JOHNNY WYROSTEK
☐ 29. TED KLUSZEWSKI
☐ 69. VIRGIL STALLCUP
☐ 80. HERM WEHMEIER
☐ 113. DICK SISLER
☐ 118. KEN RAFFENSBERGER
☐ 135. DIXIE HOWELL
☐ 137. ROY MCMILLAN
☐ 142. HARRY PERKOWSKI
☐ 144. ED BLAKE
☐ 151. WALLY POST
☐ 156. FRANK HILLER
☐ 161. BUD BYERLY
☐ 171. ED ERAUTT
☐ 176. HANK EDWARDS
☐ 179. FRANK SMITH
☐ 249. BOBBY ADAMS
☐ 297. ANDY SEMINICK
☐ 323. BUBBA CHURCH
☐ 328. BOB BORKOWSKI
☐ 344. EWELL BLACKWELL
☐ 347. JOE ADCOCK
☐ 350. CAL ABRAMS
☐ 379. JOE ROSSI
☐ 391. BEN CHAPMAN(C)
☐ 405. ED PELLAGRINI
☐ 406. JOE NUXHALL

CLEVELAND INDIANS

☐ 10. AL ROSEN
☐ 17. JIM HEGAN
☐ 18. MERRILL COMBS
☐ 24. LUKE EASTER
☐ 55. RAY BOONE
☐ 77. BOB KENNEDY
☐ 88. BOB FELLER
☐ 92. DALE MITCHELL
☐ 120. BOB CHAKALES
☐ 189. PETE REISER
☐ 193. HARRY SIMPSON
☐ 199. GEORGE ZUVERINK
☐ 207. MICKEY HARRIS
☐ 217. GEORGE STIRNWEISS
☐ 243. LARRY DOBY
☐ 253. JOHN BERARDINO
☐ 257. BOBBY AVILA
☐ 258. STEVE GROMEK
☐ 268. BOB LEMON
☐ 270. LOU BRISSIE
☐ 272. MIKE GARCIA
☐ 277. EARLY WYNN
☐ 282. BIRDIE TEBBETTS
☐ 300. BARNEY MCCOSKY
☐ 363. DICK ROZEK
☐ 382. SAM JONES
☐ 399. JIM FRIDLEY

DETROIT TIGERS

☐ 25. JOHN GROTH
☐ 28. JERRY PRIDDY
☐ 39. DIZZY TROUT
☐ 86. TED GRAY
☐ 89. JOHNNY LIPON
☐ 103. CLIFF MAPES
☐ 104. DON KOLLOWAY
☐ 126. FRED HUTCHINSON
☐ 146. FRANK HOUSE
☐ 181. BOB SWIFT
☐ 192. MYRON GINSBERG
☐ 208. MARLIN STUART
☐ 222. HOOT EVERS
☐ 230. MATT BATTS
☐ 234. STEVE SOUCHOCK
☐ 238. ART HOUTTEMAN
☐ 244. VIC WERTZ
☐ 246. GEORGE KELL
☐ 262. VIRGIL TRUCKS
☐ 275. PAT MULLIN
☐ 296. RED ROLFE(M)
☐ 354. FRED HATFIELD
☐ 370. BILLY HOEFT

NEW YORK GIANTS

☐   3. HANK THOMPSON
☐   5. LARRY JANSEN
☐ 26. MONTY IRVIN
☐ 52. DON MUELLER

☐ 61. TOOKIE GILBERT
☐ 75. WES WESTRUM
☐ 101. MAX LANIER
☐ 124. MONTE KENNEDY
☐ 125. BILL RIGNEY
☐ 130. SHELDON JONES
☐ 141. CLINT HARTUNG
☐ 261. WILLIE MAYS
☐ 265. CHUCK DIERING
☐ 313. BOBBY THOMSON
☐ 315. LEO DUROCHER(M)
☐ 316. DAVEY WILLIAMS
☐ 318. HAL GREGG
☐ 336. DAVE KOSLO
☐ 337. JIM HEARN
☐ 338. SAL YVARS
☐ 346. GEORGE SPENCER
☐ 351. AL DARK
☐ 371. BOB HOFMAN
☐ 385. HERMAN FRANKS(C)
☐ 392. HOYT WILHELM

BILL RIGNEY

NEW YORK YANKEES

☐   9. BOB HOGUE
☐ 11. PHIL RIZZUTO
☐ 48. JOE PAGE
☐ 49. JOHNNY SAIN
☐ 57. ED LOPAT
☐ 67. ALLIE REYNOLDS
☐ 85. BOB KUZAVA
☐ 99. GENE WOODLING
☐ 122. JACK JENSEN
☐ 128. DON BOLLWEG
☐ 129. JOHNNY MIZE
☐ 155. FRANK OVERMIRE
☐ 168. CHARLIE SILVERA
☐ 175. BILLY MARTIN
☐ 191. YOGI BERRA
☐ 200. RALPH HOUK
☐ 202. JOE COLLINS
☐ 206. JOE OSTROWSKI
☐ 214. JOHNNY HOPP
☐ 215. HANK BAUER
☐ 237. JERRY COLEMAN
☐ 248. FRANK SHEA(F)
☐ 311. MICKEY MANTLE
☐ 331. TOM MORGAN
☐ 372. GIL MCDOUGALD
☐ 373. JIM TURNER(C)
☐ 384. FRANK CROSETTI(C)
☐ 400. BILL DICKEY(C)
☐ 403. BILL MILLER

PHILADELPHIA ATHLETICS

☐ 21. FERRIS FAIN
☐ 31. GUS ZERNIAL
☐ 34. ELMER VALO
☐ 41. BOB WELLMAN
☐ 45. EDDIE JOOST
☐ 112. HENRY MAJESKI
☐ 116. CARL SCHEIB
☐ 131. MORRIE MARTIN
☐ 134. JOE TIPTON
☐ 182. BILLY HITCHCOCK
☐ 201. ALEX KELLNER
☐ 210. DICK FOWLER
☐ 219. BOBBY SHANTZ
☐ 226. DAVE PHILLEY
☐ 231. SAM ZOLDAK
☐ 256. PETE SUDER
☐ 278. AL CLARK
☐ 290. JOE ASTROTH
☐ 299. RAY MURRAY
☐ 340. BOB HOOPER
☐ 358. JOHN KUCAB
☐ 368. ED WRIGHT

PHILADELPHIA PHILLIES

- [ ] 44. CON DEMPSEY
- [ ] 47. WILLIE JONES
- [ ] 59. ROBIN ROBERTS
- [ ] 74. ANDY HANSEN
- [ ] 107. CONNIE RYAN
- [ ] 108. JIM KONSTANTY
- [ ] 158. EDDIE WAITKUS
- [ ] 185. BILL NICHOLSON
- [ ] 187. BOB J. MILLER
- [ ] 203. CURT SIMMONS
- [ ] 209. HOWIE FOX
- [ ] 213. NIPPY JONES
- [ ] 216. RICHIE ASHBURN
- [ ] 221. GRANNY HAMNER
- [ ] 223. DEL ENNIS
- [ ] 281. TOMMY BROWN
- [ ] 339. RUSS MEYER
- [ ] 352. KARL DREWS
- [ ] 357. SMOKY BURGESS
- [ ] 362. KEN HEINTZELMAN

DALE COOGAN

PITTSBURGH PIRATES

- [ ] 12. MONTY BASGALL
- [ ] 63. HOWIE POLLET
- [ ] 73. BILL WERLE
- [ ] 81. VERNON LAW
- [ ] 87. DALE COOGAN
- [ ] 109. TED WILKS
- [ ] 138. BILL MACDONALD
- [ ] 150. TED BEARD
- [ ] 154. JOE MUIR
- [ ] 166. PAUL LEPALME
- [ ] 167. BILL HOWERTON
- [ ] 170. GUS BELL
- [ ] 183. ERV DUSAK
- [ ] 197. GEORGE STRICKLAND
- [ ] 218. CLYDE MCCULLOUGH
- [ ] 227. JOE GARAGIOLA
- [ ] 233. BOB FRIEND
- [ ] 236. ED FITZ GERALD
- [ ] 240. JACK PHILLIPS
- [ ] 260. PETE CASTIGLIONE
- [ ] 266. MURRY DICKSON
- [ ] 310. GEORGE METKOVICH
- [ ] 332. TONY BARTIROME
- [ ] 353. BOBBY DEL GRECO
- [ ] 361. BILL POSEDEL(C)
- [ ] 364. CLYDE SUKEFORTH(C)
- [ ] 369. DICK GROAT
- [ ] 375. JACK MERSON
- [ ] 380. CLEM KOSHOREK
- [ ] 381. MILT STOCK(C)
- [ ] 387. BILLY MEYER(M)
- [ ] 397. FORREST MAIN

ST. LOUIS BROWNS

- [ ] 8. FRED MARSH
- [ ] 46. GORDON GOLDSBERRY
- [ ] 58. BOB MAHONEY
- [ ] 64. ROY SIEVERS
- [ ] 82. DUANE PILLETTE
- [ ] 102. BILLY KENNEDY(F)
- [ ] 143. LES MOSS
- [ ] 147. BOB YOUNG
- [ ] 149. DICK KRYHOSKI
- [ ] 160. OWEN FRIEND
- [ ] 163. STAN ROJEK
- [ ] 174. CLARENCE MARSHALL
- [ ] 212. NED GARVER
- [ ] 229. GENE BEARDEN
- [ ] 241. TOMMY BYRNE
- [ ] 271. JIM DELSING

- [ ] 284. HANK ARFT
- [ ] 285. CLIFF FANNIN
- [ ] 286. JOE DEMAESTRI
- [ ] 349. BOB CAIN
- [ ] 366. DAVE MADISON
- [ ] 402. EARL HARRIST

ST. LOUIS CARDINALS

- [ ] 19. JOHNNY BUCHA
- [ ] 38. WALLY WESTLAKE
- [ ] 56. TOMMY GLAVIANO
- [ ] 65. ENOS SLAUGHTER
- [ ] 68. CLIFF CHAMBERS
- [ ] 76. EDDIE STANKY
- [ ] 79. GERRY STALEY
- [ ] 83. BILLY JOHNSON
- [ ] 91. RED SCHOENDIENST
- [ ] 100. DEL RICE
- [ ] 111. HARRY LOWREY
- [ ] 115. GEORGE MUNGER
- [ ] 165. EDDIE KAZAK
- [ ] 196. SOLLY HEMUS
- [ ] 220. JOE PRESKO
- [ ] 228. AL BRAZLE
- [ ] 242. TOM POHOLSKY
- [ ] 263. HARRY BRECHEEN
- [ ] 280. CLOYD BOYER
- [ ] 287. STEVE BILKO
- [ ] 334. WILMER MIZELL
- [ ] 378. LES FUSSELMAN
- [ ] 386. EDDIE YUHAS
- [ ] 398. HAL RICE

WASHINGTON SENATORS

- [ ] 2. PETE RUNNELS
- [ ] 40. IRV NOREN
- [ ] 60. SID HUDSON
- [ ] 71. TOM UPTON
- [ ] 90. MICKEY GRASSO
- [ ] 93. AL SIMA
- [ ] 94. SAM MELE
- [ ] 106. MICKEY VERNON
- [ ] 123. EDDIE YOST
- [ ] 132. CLYDE KLUTTZ
- [ ] 145. JOE HAYNES
- [ ] 178. CASS MICHAELS
- [ ] 190. DON JOHNSON
- [ ] 245. SHERRY ROBERTSON
- [ ] 248. FRANK SHEA(B)
- [ ] 291. GIL COAN
- [ ] 292. FLOYD BAKER
- [ ] 298. BOB ROSS
- [ ] 301. BOB PORTERFIELD
- [ ] 306. LOU SLEATER
- [ ] 307. FRANK CAMPOS
- [ ] 309. JIM BUSBY
- [ ] 317. CONNIE MARRERO

1953 TOPPS (274)
2 5/8" X 3 3/4"

ED MATHEWS
Third base
BOSTON BRAVES

BOSTON RED SOX

- [ ] 18. TED LEPCIO
- [ ] 19. MEL PARNELL
- [ ] 30. WILLARD NIXON
- [ ] 32. CLYDE VOLLMER
- [ ] 40. JOHN LIPON
- [ ] 44. ELLIS KINDER
- [ ] 49. FAYE THRONEBERRY
- [ ] 55. MICKEY MCDERMOTT

- [ ] 63. GUS NIARHOS
- [ ] 69. DICK BRODOWSKI
- [ ] 94. BILL KENNEDY
- [ ] 138. GEORGE KELL
- [ ] 139. SAMMY WHITE
- [ ] 149. DOM DIMAGGIO
- [ ] 169. DIZZY TROUT
- [ ] 170. BILL WERLE
- [ ] 181. AL ZARILLA
- [ ] 184. HAL BROWN
- [ ] 248. GENE STEPHENS
- [ ] 251. SID HUDSON
- [ ] 280. MILT BOLLING

BROOKLYN DODGERS

- [ ] 1. JACKIE ROBINSON
- [ ] 4. BEN WADE
- [ ] 14. CLEM LABINE
- [ ] 27. ROY CAMPANELLA
- [ ] 34. GEORGE SHUBA
- [ ] 50. CHUCK DRESSEN(M)
- [ ] 76. PEE WEE REESE
- [ ] 81. JOE BLACK
- [ ] 85. BOBBY MORGAN
- [ ] 125. DICK WILLIAMS
- [ ] 134. RUBE WALKER
- [ ] 137. JOHN RUTHERFORD
- [ ] 174. BILLY LOES
- [ ] 176. DON HOAK
- [ ] 216. JIM HUGHES
- [ ] 221. BOB MILLIKEN
- [ ] 254. PREACHER ROE
- [ ] 255. DIXIE HOWELL
- [ ] 258. JIM GILLIAM
- [ ] 263. JOHN PODRES
- [ ] 272. BILL ANTONELLO

CHICAGO CUBS

- [ ] 23. TOBY ATWELL
- [ ] 29. HAL JEFFCOAT
- [ ] 39. EDDIE MIKSIS
- [ ] 46. JOHNNY KLIPPSTEIN
- [ ] 92. PAUL MINNER
- [ ] 111. HANK SAUER
- [ ] 130. TURK LOWN
- [ ] 144. BOB SCHULTZ
- [ ] 155. DUTCH LEONARD
- [ ] 157. BOB ADDIS
- [ ] 173. PRESTON WARD
- [ ] 179. GENE HERMANSKI
- [ ] 202. CARL SAWATSKI

CHICAGO WHITE SOX

- [ ] 5. JOE DOBSON
- [ ] 53. SHERMAN LOLLAR
- [ ] 66. MINNIE MINOSO
- [ ] 73. EDDIE ROBINSON
- [ ] 123. TOMMY BYRNE
- [ ] 143. BILLY PIERCE
- [ ] 156. JIM RIVERA
- [ ] 196. BOB KEEGAN
- [ ] 229. ROCKY KRSNICH
- [ ] 240. FRED MARSH
- [ ] 250. BOB WILSON
- [ ] 257. BOB BOYD
- [ ] 270. VERN STEPHENS

CINCINNATI REDS

- [ ] 7. BOB BORKOWSKI
- [ ] 12. HOWIE JUDSON
- [ ] 28. EDDIE PELLAGRINI
- [ ] 45. GRADY HATTON
- [ ] 47. BUBBA CHURCH
- [ ] 95. WILLARD MARSHALL
- [ ] 105. JOE NUXHALL
- [ ] 110. HERM WEHMEIER
- [ ] 116. FRANK SMITH
- [ ] 118. GUS BELL
- [ ] 152. BOB ADAMS
- [ ] 153. ANDY SEMINICK
- [ ] 162. TED KLUSZEWSKI
- [ ] 206. ED BAILEY
- [ ] 209. JIM GREENGRASS
- [ ] 226. ED ERAUTT
- [ ] 236. HARRY PERKOWSKI
- [ ] 237. BUD PODBIELAN
- [ ] 252. HANK FOILES
- [ ] 259. ROY MCMILLAN
- [ ] 276. KEN RAFFENSBERGER

CLEVELAND INDIANS

- [ ] 2. LUKE EASTER
- [ ] 6. SAM JONES
- [ ] 25. RAY BOONE
- [ ] 26. DALE MITCHELL

☐ 33. BOB KENNEDY
☐ 54. BOB FELLER
☐ 61. EARLY WYNN
☐ 75. MIKE GARCIA
☐ 80. JIM HEGAN
☐ 84. BOB HOOPER
☐ 101. TED WILKS
☐ 135. AL ROSEN
☐ 150. HARRY SIMPSON
☐ 171. BILL GLYNN
☐ 187. JIM FRIDLEY
☐ 192. WALLY WESTLAKE
☐ 233. AL ABER

DETROIT TIGERS

☐ 52. TED GRAY
☐ 72. FRED HUTCHINSON(M)
☐ 99. DAVE MADISON
☐ 112. NED GARVER
☐ 113. JERRY PRIDDY
☐ 121. WALT DROPO
☐ 163. FRED HATFIELD
☐ 165. BILLY HOEFT
☐ 194. EDDIE KAZAK
☐ 211. J. W. PORTER
☐ 228. HAL NEWHOUSER
☐ 239. JIM DELSING
☐ 277. DON LUND

MILWAUKEE BRAVES

☐ 3. GEORGE CROWE★
☐ 37. ED MATHEWS★
☐ 91. EBBA ST. CLAIRE★
☐ 106. JOHNNY ANTONELLI★
☐ 117. SID GORDON★
☐ 124. SIBBY SISTI★
☐ 147. WARREN SPAHN★
☐ 158. JOHN LOGAN★
☐ 161. VERN BICKFORD★
☐ 185. JIM PENDLETON
☐ 197. DEL CRANDALL
☐ 208. JIM WILSON
☐ 212. JACK DITTMER
☐ 214. BILL BRUTON
☐ 215. GENE CONLEY
☐ 217. MURRAY WALL

NEW YORK GIANTS

☐ 11. SAL YVARS
☐ 20. HANK THOMPSON
☐ 38. JIM HEARN
☐ 62. MONTE IRVIN
☐ 109. AL DARK
☐ 115. GEORGE SPENCER
☐ 120. DAVEY WILLIAMS
☐ 126. BILL CONNELLY
☐ 151. HOYT WILHELM
☐ 182. BOBBY HOFMAN
☐ 244. WILLIE MAYS
☐ 260. SAM CALDERONE

NEW YORK YANKEES

☐ 9. JOE COLLINS
☐ 31. EWELL BLACKWELL
☐ 35. IRV NOREN
☐ 43. GIL MCDOUGALD
☐ 77. JOHNNY MIZE
☐ 82. MICKEY MANTLE
☐ 86. BILLY MARTIN
☐ 87. ED LOPAT
☐ 100. BILL MILLER

☐ 104. YOGI BERRA
☐ 114. PHIL RIZZUTO
☐ 119. JOHNNY SAIN
☐ 132. TOM MORGAN
☐ 141. ALLIE REYNOLDS
☐ 167. ART SCHULT
☐ 188. ANDY CAREY
☐ 207. WHITEY FORD
☐ 210. BOB CERV
☐ 213. RAY SCARBOROUGH
☐ 242. CHARLIE SILVERA
☐ 264. GENE WOODLING

PHILADELPHIA ATHLETICS

☐ 15. BOBO NEWSOM
☐ 17. BILLY HITCHCOCK
☐ 24. FERRIS FAIN
☐ 42. GUS ZERNIAL
☐ 57. CARL SCHEIB
☐ 64. DAVE PHILLEY
☐ 97. DON KOLLOWAY
☐ 103. JOE ASTROTH
☐ 122. ELMER VALO
☐ 129. KEITH THOMAS
☐ 131. HARRY BYRD
☐ 186. CHARLIE BISHOP
☐ 195. ED MCGHEE
☐ 199. MARION FRICANO
☐ 225. BOBBY SHANTZ
☐ 227. MORRIS MARTIN
☐ 234. RAY MURRAY
☐ 279. JOE COLEMAN

PHILADELPHIA PHILLIES

☐ 10. SMOKY BURGESS
☐ 22. HOWIE FOX
☐ 59. KARL DREWS
☐ 79. JOHNNY WYROSTEK
☐ 88. WILLIE JONES
☐ 102. CONNIE RYAN
☐ 136. KEN HEINTZELMAN
☐ 140. TOMMY GLAVIANO
☐ 146. GRANNY HAMNER

PITTSBURGH PIRATES

☐ 8. CLEM KOSHOREK
☐ 48. BOB DEL GRECO
☐ 58. GEORGE METKOVICH
☐ 71. TONY BARTIROME
☐ 74. JOE ROSSI
☐ 83. HOWIE POLLET
☐ 98. CAL ABRAMS
☐ 107. DANNY O'CONNELL
☐ 154. DICK GROAT
☐ 175. RON KLINE
☐ 178. JIM WAUGH
☐ 191. RALPH KINER
☐ 198. FORREST MAIN
☐ 201. PAUL LA PALME
☐ 222. VIC JANOWICZ
☐ 223. JOHN O'BRIEN
☐ 230. JOHNNY LINDELL
☐ 235. JOHN HETKI
☐ 238. CAL HOGUE
☐ 243. CARLOS BERNIER
☐ 246. ROY FACE
☐ 247. MIKE SANDLOCK
☐ 249. ED O'BRIEN

ST. LOUIS BROWNS

☐ 36. JOHNNY GROTH
☐ 65. EARL HARRIST
☐ 67. ROY SIEVERS
☐ 90. HANK EDWARDS
☐ 96. VIRGIL TRUCKS
☐ 127. CLINT COURTNEY
☐ 142. VIC WERTZ
☐ 160. BOB YOUNG
☐ 166. BILL HUNTER
☐ 177. JIM DYCK
☐ 200. GORDON GOLDSBERRY
☐ 203. CLIFF FANNIN
☐ 220. SATCHEL PAIGE
☐ 232. DICK KOKOS
☐ 245. BILL NORMAN(C)
☐ 266. BOB CAIN
☐ 269. DUANE PILLETTE
☐ 278. WILLIE MIRANDA

ST. LOUIS CARDINALS

☐ 16. HARRY LOWREY
☐ 21. BILLY JOHNSON
☐ 41. ENOS SLAUGHTER
☐ 56. GERALD STALEY
☐ 60. CLOYD BOYER

☐ 68. DEL RICE
☐ 70. ED YUHAS
☐ 78. RED SCHOENDIENST
☐ 93. HAL RICE
☐ 128. WILMER MIZELL
☐ 168. WILLARD SCHMIDT
☐ 172. RIP REPULSKI
☐ 180. VIRGIL STALLCUP
☐ 183. STU MILLER
☐ 189. RAY JABLONSKI
☐ 190. DIXIE WALKER(C)
☐ 193. MIKE CLARK
☐ 204. DICK BOKELMANN
☐ 205. VERN BENSON
☐ 218. LES FUSSELMAN
☐ 231. SOLLY HEMUS
☐ 273. HARVEY HADDIX
☐ 274. JOHN RIDDLE(C)

WASHINGTON SENATORS

☐ 13. CONNIE MARRERO
☐ 51. FRANK CAMPOS
☐ 89. CHUCK STOBBS
☐ 108. BOB PORTERFIELD
☐ 133. GIL COAN
☐ 148. MICKEY GRASSO
☐ 159. WAYNE TERWILLIGER
☐ 164. FRANK SHEA
☐ 219. PETE RUNNELS
☐ 224. LOU SLEATER
☐ 241. AL SIMA
☐ 256. LES PEDEN
☐ 262. BOB OLDIS
☐ 265. JACKIE JENSEN

1954 TOPPS (250)
2 5/8" X 3 3/4"

BALTIMORE ORIOLES

☐ 8. BOB YOUNG
☐ 19. JOHNNY LIPON(F)
☐ 48. BILLY HUNTER
☐ 54. VERN STEPHENS
☐ 85. BOB TURLEY
☐ 106. DICK KOKOS
☐ 107. DUANE PILLETTE
☐ 150. DICK KRYHOSKI

* Nos. 3, 37, 91, 106, 117, 124, 147, 158 & 161 appear with Boston Braves on the front of the card.

1954 Topps

CLEVELAND INDIANS

DETROIT TIGERS

MILWAUKEE BRAVES

NEW YORK GIANTS

NEW YORK YANKEES

PHILADELPHIA ATHLETICS

PHILADELPHIA PHILLIES

PITTSBURGH PIRATES

ST. LOUIS CARDINALS

- ☐ 9. HARVEY HADDIX
- ☐ 26. RAY JABLONSKI
- ☐ 38. EDDIE STANKY(M)
- ☐ 115. RIP REPULSKI
- ☐ 116. STEVE BILKO
- ☐ 117. SOLLY HEMUS
- ☐ 135. JOE PRESKO
- ☐ 137. WALLY MOON
- ☐ 142. TOM POHOLSKY
- ☐ 147. JOHN RIDDLE(C)
- ☐ 151. ALEX GRAMMAS
- ☐ 158. PEANUTS LOWREY
- ☐ 164. STU MILLER
- ☐ 191. DICK SCHOFIELD
- ☐ 192. COT DEAL
- ☐ 194. BILL SARNI
- ☐ 237. MIKE RYBA(C)
- ☐ 249. WILMER MIZELL

WASHINGTON SENATORS

- ☐ 6. PETE RUNNELS
- ☐ 33. JOHNNY SCHMITZ
- ☐ 73. WAYNE TERWILLIGER
- ☐ 91. BOB OLDIS
- ☐ 97. JERRY LANE
- ☐ 114. DEAN STONE
- ☐ 140. TOM WRIGHT
- ☐ 185. CHUCK STOBBS
- ☐ 187. HEINIE MANUSH(C)
- ☐ 189. BOB ROSS
- ☐ 204. ANGEL SCULL
- ☐ 223. JOE HAYNES(C)
- ☐ 245. ROY SIEVERS

1955 TOPPS (206)
2 5/8" X 3 3/4"

BALTIMORE ORIOLES

- ☐ 8. HAL W. SMITH
- ☐ 13. FRED MARSH
- ☐ 48. BOB KENNEDY
- ☐ 57. BILLY O'DELL
- ☐ 64. GUS TRIANDOS
- ☐ 105. CHUCK DIERING
- ☐ 113. HARRY BRECHEEN(C)
- ☐ 154. WILLIE MIRANDA
- ☐ 162. JOE COLEMAN
- ☐ 165. DON JOHNSON
- ☐ 168. DUANE PILLETTE
- ☐ 185. DON FERRARESE
- ☐ 190. GENE WOODLING
- ☐ 208. RAY MOORE

BOSTON RED SOX

- ☐ 2. TED WILLIAMS
- ☐ 18. RUSS KEMMERER
- ☐ 36. LEO KIELY
- ☐ 72. KARL OLSON
- ☐ 83. TOM BREWER
- ☐ 91. MILT BOLLING
- ☐ 106. FRANK SULLIVAN
- ☐ 115. ELLIS KINDER
- ☐ 116. TOM HURD
- ☐ 128. TED LEPCIO
- ☐ 131. GRADY HATTON
- ☐ 140. MEL PARNELL
- ☐ 148. HAL BROWN
- ☐ 150. MIKE HIGGINS(M)
- ☐ 152. HARRY AGGANIS
- ☐ 163. FAYE THRONEBERRY
- ☐ 171. DICK BRODOWSKI
- ☐ 176. NORM ZAUCHIN
- ☐ 200. JACK JENSEN
- ☐ 206. PETE DALEY
- ☐ 207. BILL CONSOLO

BROOKLYN DODGERS

- ☐ 5. JIM GILLIAM
- ☐ 19. BILLY HERMAN(C)
- ☐ 25. JOHNNY PODRES
- ☐ 40. DON HOAK
- ☐ 50. JACKIE ROBINSON
- ☐ 51. JIM HUGHES
- ☐ 75. SANDY AMOROS
- ☐ 90. KARL SPOONER
- ☐ 92. DON ZIMMER
- ☐ 108. RUBE WALKER
- ☐ 111. BOB MILLIKEN
- ☐ 123. SANDY KOUFAX
- ☐ 156. JOE BLACK
- ☐ 180. CLEM LABINE
- ☐ 187. GIL HODGES
- ☐ 195. ED ROEBUCK
- ☐ 199. BERT HAMRIC
- ☐ 210. DUKE SNIDER

CHICAGO CUBS

- ☐ 6. STAN HACK(M)
- ☐ 28. ERNIE BANKS
- ☐ 45. HANK SAUER
- ☐ 52. BILL TREMEL
- ☐ 68. JIM DAVIS
- ☐ 76. HOWIE POLLET
- ☐ 93. STEVE BILKO
- ☐ 129. ELVIN TAPPE
- ☐ 172. FRANK BAUMHOLTZ
- ☐ 179. JIM BOLGER
- ☐ 184. HARRY PERKOWSKI
- ☐ 196. GALE WADE

CHICAGO WHITE SOX

- ☐ 10. BOB KEEGAN
- ☐ 32. ED MCGHEE
- ☐ 58. JIM RIVERA
- ☐ 66. RON JACKSON
- ☐ 104. JACK HARSHMAN
- ☐ 122. CARL SAWATSKI
- ☐ 146. DICK DONOVAN
- ☐ 201. SHERM LOLLAR

CINCINNATI REDS

- ☐ 3. ART FOWLER
- ☐ 44. CORKY VALENTINE
- ☐ 56. RAY JABLONSKI
- ☐ 69. ED BAILEY
- ☐ 74. BOB BORKOWSKI
- ☐ 82. CHUCK HARMON
- ☐ 120. TED KLUSZEWSKI
- ☐ 153. BUD PODBIELAN
- ☐ 170. JIM PEARCE
- ☐ 174. RUDY MINARCIN
- ☐ 178. BOBBY ADAMS
- ☐ 181. ROY MCMILLAN

CLEVELAND INDIANS

- ☐ 7. JIM HEGAN
- ☐ 24. HAL NEWHOUSER
- ☐ 39. BILLY GLYNN
- ☐ 70. AL ROSEN
- ☐ 85. DON MOSSI
- ☐ 102. WALLY WESTLAKE
- ☐ 133. DAVE HOSKINS
- ☐ 151. RED KRESS(C)
- ☐ 160. RAY NARLESKI
- ☐ 197. AL SMITH

DETROIT TIGERS

- ☐ 4. AL KALINE
- ☐ 9. BOB G. MILLER
- ☐ 11. FERRIS FAIN
- ☐ 49. J.W. PORTER
- ☐ 65. RAY BOONE

KANSAS CITY ATHLETICS

- ☐ 14. JIM FINIGAN
- ☐ 30. VIC POWER
- ☐ 54. LOU LIMMER
- ☐ 61. SPOOK JACOBS
- ☐ 77. ARNOLD PORTOCARRERO
- ☐ 86. BILL WILSON
- ☐ 96. CHARLIE BISHOP
- ☐ 101. JOHNNY GRAY
- ☐ 110. GUS ZERNIAL
- ☐ 121. BILL RENNA
- ☐ 132. BOB TRICE
- ☐ 145. ELMER VALO
- ☐ 177. JIM ROBERTSON

MILWAUKEE BRAVES

- ☐ 15. JIM PENDLETON
- ☐ 23. JACK PARKS
- ☐ 31. WARREN SPAHN
- ☐ 35. DAVE JOLLY
- ☐ 47. HANK AARON
- ☐ 81. GENE CONLEY
- ☐ 103. CHARLIE WHITE
- ☐ 117. MEL ROACH
- ☐ 134. JOE JAY
- ☐ 149. RAY CRONE
- ☐ 155. ED MATHEWS
- ☐ 161. CHUCK TANNER
- ☐ 182. HUMBERTO ROBINSON

NEW YORK GIANTS

- ☐ 1. DUSTY RHODES
- ☐ 17. BOBBY HOFMAN
- ☐ 27. BILLY GARDNER
- ☐ 42. WINDY MCCALL
- ☐ 53. BILL TAYLOR
- ☐ 71. RUBEN GOMEZ
- ☐ 100. MONTE IRVIN
- ☐ 119. BOB LENNON
- ☐ 144. JOE AMALFITANO
- ☐ 194. WILLIE MAYS

NEW YORK YANKEES

- ☐ 20. ANDY CAREY
- ☐ 22. BILL SKOWRON
- ☐ 38. BOB TURLEY
- ☐ 63. JOE COLLINS
- ☐ 80. BOB GRIM
- ☐ 99. FRANK LEJA
- ☐ 109. ED LOPAT
- ☐ 139. STEVE KRALY
- ☐ 158. TOM CARROLL
- ☐ 166. HANK BAUER
- ☐ 188. CHARLIE SILVERA
- ☐ 189. PHIL RIZZUTO
- ☐ 193. JOHNNY SAIN
- ☐ 198. YOGI BERRA

PHILADELPHIA PHILLIES

- ☐ 29. HERMAN WEHMEIER
- ☐ 33. TOM QUALTERS
- ☐ 46. TED KAZANSKI
- ☐ 62. THORNTON KIPPER
- ☐ 79. DANNY SCHELL
- ☐ 114. LOU ORTIZ
- ☐ 130. MAYO SMITH(M)
- ☐ 157. BOB J. MILLER
- ☐ 167. TOM CASAGRANDE
- ☐ 202. JIM OWENS

PITTSBURGH PIRATES

- ☐ 12. JAKE THIES
- ☐ 26. DICK GROAT
- ☐ 59. GAIR ALLIE
- ☐ 73. JACK SHEPARD
- ☐ 88. BOB SKINNER
- ☐ 95. PRESTON WARD
- ☐ 107. CURT ROBERTS
- ☐ 112. NELSON KING
- ☐ 118. BOB PURKEY
- ☐ 126. DICK HALL
- ☐ 127. DALE LONG
- ☐ 135. JOHNNY O'BRIEN
- ☐ 142. JERRY LYNCH
- ☐ 147. LAURIN PEPPER
- ☐ 164. ROBERTO CLEMENTE
- ☐ 205. GENE FREESE

Inside the top card image: JACKIE ROBINSON

Inside the bottom card image: AL KALINE outfield DETROIT TIGERS

ST. LOUIS CARDINALS

- ☐ 21. ALEX GRAMMAS
- ☐ 37. JOE CUNNINGHAM
- ☐ 43. HARVEY HADDIX
- ☐ 55. RIP REPULSKI
- ☐ 67. WALLY MOON
- ☐ 78. GORDON JONES
- ☐ 89. JOE FRAZIER
- ☐ 98. JOHNNY RIDDLE(C)
- ☐ 125. KEN BOYER
- ☐ 137. HARRY ELLIOTT
- ☐ 143. DICK SCHOFIELD
- ☐ 183. TONY JACOBS
- ☐ 191. ED STANKY(M)
- ☐ 204. FRANK SMITH

ROY SIEVERS *outfield* **WASHINGTON NATIONALS**

WASHINGTON SENATORS

- ☐ 16. ROY SIEVERS
- ☐ 34. WAYNE TERWILLIGER
- ☐ 41. CHUCK STOBBS
- ☐ 60. DEAN STONE
- ☐ 84. CAMILO PASCUAL
- ☐ 97. CARLOS PAULA
- ☐ 124. HARMON KILLEBREW
- ☐ 136. BUNKY STEWART
- ☐ 141. TOM WRIGHT
- ☐ 159. JOHNNY SCHMITZ
- ☐ 169. BOB OLDIS
- ☐ 173. BOB KLINE

1956 TOPPS (340)
2 5/8″ X 3 3/4″

GUS TRIANDOS

BALTIMORE ORIOLES

- ☐ 19. CHUCK DIERING
- ☐ 23. FRED MARSH
- ☐ 43. RAY MOORE
- ☐ 62. HAL W. SMITH
- ☐ 80. GUS TRIANDOS
- ☐ 100. TEAM CARD
- ☐ 103. WILLIE MIRANDA
- ☐ 154. DAVE POPE
- ☐ 167. HARRY DORISH
- ☐ 169. BOB NELSON
- ☐ 171. JIM WILSON
- ☐ 206. ERV PALICA
- ☐ 222. DAVE PHILLEY
- ☐ 229. HARRY BRECHEEN(C)
- ☐ 231. BOB HALE
- ☐ 266. DON FERRARESE
- ☐ 276. GEORGE ZUVERINK
- ☐ 286. BILL WIGHT
- ☐ 287. BOBBY ADAMS
- ☐ 303. JIM DYCK

BOSTON RED SOX

- ☐ 5. TED WILLIAMS
- ☐ 26. GRADY HATTON
- ☐ 34. TOM BREWER
- ☐ 71. FRAMK SULLIVAN

- ☐ 89. NORM ZAUCHIN
- ☐ 93. GEORGE SUSCE
- ☐ 111. TEAM CARD
- ☐ 115. JACKIE JENSEN
- ☐ 122. WILLARD NIXON
- ☐ 143. JIM PIERSALL
- ☐ 168. SAMMY WHITE
- ☐ 217. BILLY KLAUS
- ☐ 228. MICKEY VERNON
- ☐ 245. BILLY GOODMAN
- ☐ 248. BOB PORTERFIELD
- ☐ 256. TOM HURD
- ☐ 284. IKE DELOCK
- ☐ 298. JOHNNY SCHMITZ
- ☐ 304. FRANK MALZONE
- ☐ 313. GENE STEPHENS
- ☐ 315. MILT BOLLING

BROOKLYN DODGERS

- ☐ 8. WALTER ALSTON(M)
- ☐ 30. JACKIE ROBINSON
- ☐ 42. SANDY AMOROS
- ☐ 58. ED ROEBUCK
- ☐ 63. ROGER CRAIG
- ☐ 79. SANDY KOUFAX
- ☐ 83. KARL SPOONER
- ☐ 99. DON ZIMMER
- ☐ 101. ROY CAMPANELLA
- ☐ 145. GIL HODGES
- ☐ 150. DUKE SNIDER
- ☐ 166. TEAM CARD
- ☐ 173. JOHNNY PODRES
- ☐ 184. DON BESSENT
- ☐ 190. CARL FURILLO
- ☐ 223. RANDY JACKSON
- ☐ 233. CARL ERSKINE
- ☐ 235. DON NEWCOMBE
- ☐ 260. PEE WEE REESE
- ☐ 270. BILLY LOES
- ☐ 280. JIM GILLIAM
- ☐ 295. CLEM LABINE
- ☐ 299. CHARLEY NEAL
- ☐ 333. RUBE WALKER

CHICAGO CUBS

- ☐ 11. TEAM CARD
- ☐ 15. ERNIE BANKS
- ☐ 41. HANK SAUER
- ☐ 66. BOB SPEAKE
- ☐ 74. JIM KING
- ☐ 96. BILL TREMEL
- ☐ 102. JIM DAVIS
- ☐ 112. DEE FONDY
- ☐ 124. DON KAISER
- ☐ 142. GENE BAKER
- ☐ 179. HARRY CHITI
- ☐ 182. PAUL MINNER
- ☐ 194. MONTE IRVIN
- ☐ 214. BOB RUSH
- ☐ 227. RUSS MEYER
- ☐ 259. SAM JONES
- ☐ 282. WARREN HACKER
- ☐ 285. EDDIE MIKSIS
- ☐ 291. FRANK KELLERT
- ☐ 314. HOBIE LANDRITH
- ☐ 335. DON HOAK

CHICAGO WHITE SOX

- ☐ 18. DICK DONOVAN
- ☐ 29. JACK HARSHMAN
- ☐ 38. BOB KENNEDY
- ☐ 54. BOB KEEGAN
- ☐ 70. JIM RIVERA
- ☐ 118. NELLIE FOX
- ☐ 125. MINNIE MINOSO
- ☐ 144. BOB POWELL
- ☐ 149. DIXIE HOWELL
- ☐ 160. BILLY PIERCE
- ☐ 186. RON JACKSON
- ☐ 188. TEAM CARD
- ☐ 195. GEORGE KELL
- ☐ 238. WALT DROPO
- ☐ 243. SHERM LOLLAR
- ☐ 250. LARRY DOBY
- ☐ 262. HOWIE POLLET
- ☐ 265. SANDY CONSUEGRA
- ☐ 267. BOB NIEMAN
- ☐ 292. LUIS APARICIO
- ☐ 326. CONNIE JOHNSON

CINCINNATI REDS

- ☐ 25. TED KLUSZEWSKI
- ☐ 36. RUDY MINARCIN
- ☐ 47. ART FOWLER
- ☐ 86. RAY JABLONSKI
- ☐ 90. TEAM CARD

- ☐ 123. ROY MCMILLAN
- ☐ 137. AL SILVERA
- ☐ 158. WALLY POST
- ☐ 162. GUS BELL
- ☐ 178. JOE BLACK
- ☐ 192. SMOKY BURGESS
- ☐ 212. JOHNNY TEMPLE
- ☐ 218. JOE NUXHALL
- ☐ 224. BUD PODBIELAN
- ☐ 242. HERSHELL FREEMAN
- ☐ 249. JOHNNY KLIPPSTEIN
- ☐ 289. HAL JEFFCOAT
- ☐ 305. BROOKS LAWRENCE
- ☐ 308. CHUCK HARMON
- ☐ 324. ROCKY BRIDGES

CLEVELAND INDIANS

- ☐ 35. AL ROSEN
- ☐ 39. DON MOSSI
- ☐ 48. JIM HEGAN
- ☐ 59. JOSE SANTIAGO
- ☐ 85. TEAM CARD
- ☐ 105. AL SMITH
- ☐ 132. BOBBY AVILA
- ☐ 133. RAY NARLESKI
- ☐ 140. HERB SCORE
- ☐ 163. GENE WOODLING
- ☐ 187. EARLY WYNN
- ☐ 200. BOB FELLER
- ☐ 210. MIKE GARCIA
- ☐ 230. CHICO CARRASQUEL
- ☐ 255. BOB LEMON
- ☐ 268. DALE MITCHELL
- ☐ 281. ART HOUTTEMAN
- ☐ 300. VIC WERTZ
- ☐ 311. HAL NARAGON
- ☐ 330. JIM BUSBY

DETROIT TIGERS

- ☐ 6. RAY BOONE
- ☐ 20. AL KALINE
- ☐ 32. FRANK HOUSE
- ☐ 57. DUKE MAAS
- ☐ 84. BABE BIRRER
- ☐ 92. RED WILSON
- ☐ 117. VIRGIL TRUCKS
- ☐ 126. JIM BRADY
- ☐ 147. EARL TORGESON
- ☐ 152. BILLY HOEFT
- ☐ 155. HARVEY KUENN
- ☐ 189. NED GARVER
- ☐ 191. FRANK LARY
- ☐ 203. BILL TUTTLE
- ☐ 207. JIM SMALL
- ☐ 213. TEAM CARD
- ☐ 263. BOB G. MILLER
- ☐ 310. STEVE GROMEK
- ☐ 317. AL ABER
- ☐ 318. FRED HATFIELD
- ☐ 338. JIM DELSING

GUS ZERNIAL
outfield KANSAS CITY ATHLETICS

KANSAS CITY ATHLETICS

- ☐ 3. ELMER VALO
- ☐ 16. HECTOR LOPEZ
- ☐ 22. JIM FINIGAN
- ☐ 45. GUS ZERNIAL
- ☐ 53. ARNOLD PORTOCARRERO
- ☐ 67. VIC POWER
- ☐ 82. BILL RENNA
- ☐ 106. JOE ASTROTH
- ☐ 109. ENOS SLAUGHTER
- ☐ 151. SPOOK JACOBS
- ☐ 161. JOE DEMAESTRI
- ☐ 176. ALEX KELLNER
- ☐ 236. TEAM CARD
- ☐ 239. HARRY SIMPSON
- ☐ 246. TOM GORMAN
- ☐ 258. ART DITMAR
- ☐ 261. BOBBY SHANTZ
- ☐ 279. JOHNNY GROTH
- ☐ 319. JACK CRIMIAN
- ☐ 339. RANCE PLESS

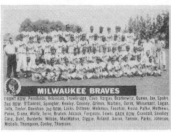

MILWAUKEE BRAVES

FRONT ROW: Pendleton, Roberson, Trowbridge, Cavo, Vargas, Brankewitz, Queen, Jay, Spahn. 2nd ROW: O'Connell, Spangler, Keeley, Conner, Grimm, Walters, Gorin, Whisenant, Logan, Jolly, Taylor, Davidson. 3rd ROW: Locks, Dittmer, Malkmus, Facchini, Krsnic, Pafko, Mathews, Paine, Crone, White, Torre, Bruton, Adcock, Ferguson, Lewis. BACK ROW: Crandall, Smalley, Cole, Buhl, Burdette, Wilson, MacMahon, Diggle, Roland, Aaron, Tanner, Parks, Johnson, Nichols, Thompson, Conley, Thomson.

MILWAUKEE BRAVES

- ☐ 10. WARREN SPAHN
- ☐ 17. GENE CONLEY
- ☐ 31. HANK AARON
- ☐ 69. CHUCK TANNER
- ☐ 76. RAY CRONE
- ☐ 95. TEAM CARD
- ☐ 107. ED MATHEWS
- ☐ 131. BOB ROSELLI
- ☐ 136. JOHNNY LOGAN
- ☐ 172. FRANK TORRE
- ☐ 175. DEL CRANDALL
- ☐ 185. BILL BRUTON
- ☐ 219. LEW BURDETTE
- ☐ 244. BOB BUHL
- ☐ 254. GEORGE CROWE
- ☐ 257. BOBBY THOMSON
- ☐ 272. DANNY O'CONNELL
- ☐ 278. CHET NICHOLS
- ☐ 294. ERNIE JOHNSON
- ☐ 312. ANDY PAFKO
- ☐ 320. JOE ADCOCK

NEW YORK GIANTS

- ☐ 9. RUBEN GOMEZ
- ☐ 28. BOBBY HOFMAN
- ☐ 44. WINDY MCCALL
- ☐ 50. DUSTY RHODES
- ☐ 73. WAYNE TERWILLIGER
- ☐ 91. GAIL HARRIS
- ☐ 104. BOB LENNON
- ☐ 130. WILLIE MAYS
- ☐ 138. JOHNNY ANTONELLI
- ☐ 148. ALVIN DARK
- ☐ 156. WES WESTRUM
- ☐ 199. HANK THOMPSON
- ☐ 202. JIM HEARN
- ☐ 205. WHITEY LOCKMAN
- ☐ 226. TEAM CARD
- ☐ 241. DON MUELLER
- ☐ 264. RAY MONZANT
- ☐ 271. FOSTER CASTLEMAN
- ☐ 277. DARYL SPENCER
- ☐ 301. MARV GRISSOM
- ☐ 307. HOYT WILHELM
- ☐ 325. DON LIDDLE

NEW YORK YANKEES

- ☐ 12. ANDY CAREY
- ☐ 21. JOE COLLINS
- ☐ 40. BOB TURLEY
- ☐ 52. BOB GRIM
- ☐ 61. BILL SKOWRON
- ☐ 88. JOHNNY KUCKS
- ☐ 110. YOGI BERRA
- ☐ 113. PHIL RIZZUTO
- ☐ 135. MICKEY MANTLE
- ☐ 139. TOMMY CARROLL
- ☐ 177. HANK BAUER
- ☐ 181. BILLY MARTIN
- ☐ 208. ELSTON HOWARD
- ☐ 215. TOMMY BYRNE
- ☐ 225. GIL MCDOUGALD
- ☐ 240. WHITEY FORD
- ☐ 251. TEAM CARD
- ☐ 253. IRV NOREN
- ☐ 288. BOB CERV
- ☐ 302. EDDIE ROBINSON
- ☐ 316. JERRY COLEMAN
- ☐ 321. JIM KONSTANTY
- ☐ 332. DON LARSEN
- ☐ 340. MICKEY MCDERMOTT

PHILADELPHIA PHILLIES

- ☐ 7. RON NEGRAY
- ☐ 60. MAYO SMITH(M)
- ☐ 72. TEAM CARD
- ☐ 78. HERM WEHMEIER
- ☐ 81. WALLY WESTLAKE

- ☐ 114. JIM OWENS
- ☐ 120. RICHIE ASHBURN
- ☐ 127. WILLIE JONES
- ☐ 174. GLEN GORBOUS
- ☐ 180. ROBIN ROBERTS
- ☐ 183. STAN LOPATA
- ☐ 197. GRANNY HAMNER
- ☐ 211. MURRY DICKSON
- ☐ 220. DEL ENNIS
- ☐ 269. JACK MEYER
- ☐ 274. FRANK BAUMHOLTZ
- ☐ 275. JIM GREENGRASS
- ☐ 290. CURT SIMMONS
- ☐ 296. ANDY SEMINICK
- ☐ 334. BOB J. MILLER
- ☐ 337. BOBBY MORGAN

PITTSBURGH PIRATES

- ☐ 13. ROY FACE
- ☐ 24. DICK GROAT
- ☐ 33. ROBERTO CLEMENTE
- ☐ 46. GENE FREESE
- ☐ 56. DALE LONG
- ☐ 65. JOHNNY O'BRIEN
- ☐ 94. RON KLINE
- ☐ 97. JERRY LYNCH
- ☐ 108. LAURIN PEPPER
- ☐ 116. EDDIE O'BRIEN
- ☐ 121. TEAM CARD
- ☐ 129. JAKE MARTIN
- ☐ 153. FRANK THOMAS
- ☐ 204. ART SWANSON
- ☐ 209. MAX SURKONT
- ☐ 221. BOB FRIEND
- ☐ 232. TOBY ATWELL
- ☐ 252. VERNON LAW
- ☐ 297. BOB SKINNER
- ☐ 306. CURT ROBERTS
- ☐ 328. PRESTON WARD
- ☐ 331. DICK HALL

ST. LOUIS CARDINALS

- ☐ 14. KEN BOYER
- ☐ 27. NELSON BURBRINK
- ☐ 37. ALEX GRAMMAS
- ☐ 55. WALLY MOON
- ☐ 64. LUIS ARROYO
- ☐ 77. HARVEY HADDIX
- ☐ 119. LARRY JACKSON
- ☐ 134. TEAM CARD
- ☐ 141. JOE FRAZIER
- ☐ 165. RED SCHOENDIENST
- ☐ 170. BILL VIRDON
- ☐ 193. WILMER MIZELL
- ☐ 196. TOM POHOLSKY
- ☐ 201. RIP REPULSKI
- ☐ 247. BILL SARNI
- ☐ 273. WALKER COOPER
- ☐ 283. HAL R. SMITH
- ☐ 293. STU MILLER
- ☐ 309. DON BLASINGAME
- ☐ 323. WILLARD SCHMIDT
- ☐ 336. ELLIS KINDER

WASHINGTON SENATORS

- ☐ 4. CARLOS PAULA
- ☐ 49. PEDRO RAMOS
- ☐ 51. ERNIE ORAVETZ
- ☐ 68. CHUCK STOBBS
- ☐ 75. ROY SIEVERS
- ☐ 87. DEAN STONE
- ☐ 98. CAMILO PASCUAL
- ☐ 128. EDDIE YOST
- ☐ 146. TEAM CARD
- ☐ 157. DICK BRODOWSKI
- ☐ 159. CLINT COURTNEY
- ☐ 164. HARMON KILLEBREW
- ☐ 198. ED FITZ GERALD
- ☐ 216. JERRY SCHOONMAKER
- ☐ 234. PETE RUNNELS
- ☐ 237. JOSE VALDIVIELSO
- ☐ 322. KARL OLSON
- ☐ 327. BOB WIESLER
- ☐ 329. LOU BERBERET

1957 TOPPS (407)
2 1/2" X 3 1/2"

BILL Mazeroski
PITTSBURGH PIRATES 2nd BASE

BALTIMORE ORIOLES

- ☐ 11. GEORGE ZUVERINK
- ☐ 14. BOB NIEMAN
- ☐ 17. BILLY GARDNER
- ☐ 26. BOB BOYD
- ☐ 43. CONNIE JOHNSON
- ☐ 59. DICK WILLIAMS
- ☐ 106. RAY MOORE
- ☐ 116. MIKE FORNIELES
- ☐ 146. DON FERRARESE
- ☐ 151. WILLIE MIRANDA
- ☐ 156. GUS TRIANDOS
- ☐ 184. TITO FRANCONA
- ☐ 194. HAL BROWN
- ☐ 230. GEORGE KELL
- ☐ 236. JOE GINSBERG
- ☐ 244. BILLY LOES
- ☐ 251. TEAM CARD
- ☐ 276. JIM PYBURN
- ☐ 311. AL PILARCIK
- ☐ 316. BILLY O'DELL
- ☐ 328. BROOKS ROBINSON
- ☐ 340. BILL WIGHT
- ☐ 382. JIM BRIDEWESER
- ☐ 406. BOB HALE

BOSTON RED SOX

- ☐ 1. TED WILLIAMS
- ☐ 21. FRANK SULLIVAN
- ☐ 56. DAVE SISLER
- ☐ 63. IKE DELOCK
- ☐ 75. JIM PIERSALL
- ☐ 92. MICKEY VERNON
- ☐ 112. TOM BREWER
- ☐ 118. BOB PORTERFIELD
- ☐ 131. MILT BOLLING
- ☐ 163. SAMMY WHITE
- ☐ 171. TEAM CARD
- ☐ 189. WILLARD NIXON
- ☐ 202. DICK GERNERT
- ☐ 217. GENE STEPHENS
- ☐ 220. JACKIE JENSEN
- ☐ 229. GEORGE SUSCE
- ☐ 288. TED LEPCIO
- ☐ 292. BILLY KLAUS
- ☐ 303. BILLY GOODMAN
- ☐ 313. MEL PARNELL
- ☐ 336. HAYWOOD SULLIVAN
- ☐ 342. GENE MAUCH
- ☐ 355. FRANK MALZONE
- ☐ 372. NORM ZAUCHIN
- ☐ 381. DEAN STONE
- ☐ 388. PETE DALEY
- ☐ 399. BILLY CONSOLO

BROOKLYN DODGERS

- ☐ 5. SAL MAGLIE
- ☐ 18. DON DRYSDALE
- ☐ 30. PEE WEE REESE
- ☐ 45. CARL FURILLO
- ☐ 53. CLEM LABINE
- ☐ 80. GIL HODGES
- ☐ 115. JIM GILLIAM
- ☐ 130. DON NEWCOMBE
- ☐ 147. AL WALKER
- ☐ 170. DUKE SNIDER
- ☐ 173. ROGER CRAIG
- ☐ 178. DON BESSENT
- ☐ 190. RANDY JACKSON

☐ 201. SANDY AMOROS
☐ 210. ROY CAMPANELLA
☐ 242. CHARLEY NEAL
☐ 252. CARL ERSKINE
☐ 277. JOHNNY PODRES
☐ 284. DON ZIMMER
☐ 302. SANDY KOUFAX
☐ 319. GINO CIMOLI
☐ 324. TEAM CARD
☐ 337. RENE VALDES
☐ 366. KEN LEHMAN
☐ 376. DON ELSTON

CHICAGO CUBS

☐ 16. WALT MORYN
☐ 42. DEE FONDY
☐ 55. ERNIE BANKS
☐ 74. VITO VALENTINETTI
☐ 84. MOE DRABOWSKY
☐ 134. DON KAISER
☐ 137. BOB RUSH
☐ 155. JIM BROSNAN
☐ 159. SOLLY DRAKE
☐ 176. GENE BAKER
☐ 183. TEAM CARD
☐ 186. JIM KING
☐ 218. RAY JABLONSKI
☐ 235. TOM POHOLSKY
☐ 247. TURK LOWN
☐ 255. CHARLIE SILVERA
☐ 268. JACKIE COLLUM
☐ 289. JIM BOLGER
☐ 339. BOB SPEAKE
☐ 346. DICK LITTLEFIELD
☐ 351. DAVE HILLMAN
☐ 353. CAL NEEMAN
☐ 371. BOB LENNON
☐ 378. ELMER SINGLETON
☐ 396. CASEY WISE

LUIS **Aparicio**
CHICAGO WHITE SOX S.S.

CHICAGO WHITE SOX

☐ 7. LUIS APARICIO
☐ 23. SHERM LOLLAR
☐ 31. RON NORTHEY
☐ 38. NELLIE FOX
☐ 85. LARRY DOBY
☐ 99. BOB KEEGAN
☐ 107. JIM RIVERA
☐ 124. DAVE PHILLEY
☐ 138. MINNIE MINOSO
☐ 152. JACK HARSHMAN
☐ 160. BILL PIERCE
☐ 181. DICK DONOVAN
☐ 213. LES MOSS
☐ 221. DIXIE HOWELL
☐ 227. JERRY STALEY
☐ 257. WALT DROPO
☐ 278. FRED HATFIELD
☐ 301. SAM ESPOSITO
☐ 329. TEAM CARD
☐ 330. JIM WILSON
☐ 344. PAUL LAPALME
☐ 352. ELLIS KINDER
☐ 375. JIM LANDIS
☐ 395. BUBBA PHILLIPS
☐ 401. EARL BATTEY

CINCINNATI REDS

☐ 9. JOHNNY TEMPLE
☐ 32. HERSH FREEMAN
☐ 35. FRANK ROBINSON
☐ 66. BROOKS LAWRENCE
☐ 69. ROY MCMILLAN
☐ 73. GEORGE CROWE

☐ 93. HAL JEFFCOAT
☐ 103. JOE NUXHALL
☐ 128. ED BAILEY
☐ 157. WALLY POST
☐ 165. TED KLUSZEWSKI
☐ 180. GUS BELL
☐ 219. TOM ACKER
☐ 222. ALEX GRAMMAS
☐ 228. SMOKY BURGESS
☐ 233. ART FOWLER
☐ 274. DON HOAK
☐ 279. BOB THURMAN
☐ 294. ROCKY BRIDGES
☐ 296. JOHNNY KLIPPSTEIN
☐ 322. TEAM CARD
☐ 341. DON GROSS
☐ 358. JERRY LYNCH
☐ 370. WARREN HACKER
☐ 373. PETE WHISENANT
☐ 393. RAUL SANCHEZ

CLEVELAND INDIANS

☐ 8. DON MOSSI
☐ 40. EARLY WYNN
☐ 50. HERB SCORE
☐ 67. CHICO CARRASQUEL
☐ 78. VIC WERTZ
☐ 96. HANK AGUIRRE
☐ 120. BOB LEMON
☐ 136. JIM HEGAN
☐ 144. RAY NARLESKI
☐ 145. AL SMITH
☐ 172. GENE WOODLING
☐ 195. BOBBY AVILA
☐ 212. ROCKY COLAVITO
☐ 226. PRESTON WARD
☐ 249. DAVE POPE
☐ 263. GEORGE STRICKLAND
☐ 266. KEN KUHN
☐ 275. TEAM CARD
☐ 300. MIKE GARCIA
☐ 309. JIM BUSBY
☐ 347. HAL NARAGON
☐ 364. CAL MCLISH
☐ 385. ART HOUTTEMAN

DETROIT TIGERS

☐ 19. BOB WILSON
☐ 33. JIM SMALL
☐ 60. BILLY HOEFT
☐ 72. BILL TUTTLE
☐ 77. PAUL FOYTACK
☐ 88. HARVEY KUENN
☐ 102. RAY BOONE
☐ 125. AL KALINE
☐ 141. AL ABER
☐ 149. BOB KENNEDY
☐ 168. FRANK LARY
☐ 198. TEAM CARD
☐ 205. CHARLEY MAXWELL
☐ 223. FRANK HOUSE
☐ 238. EDDIE ROBINSON
☐ 248. JIM FINIGAN
☐ 258. STEVE GROMEK
☐ 282. JACK DITTMER
☐ 297. JACK CRIMIAN
☐ 307. JACK PHILLIPS
☐ 325. FRANK BOLLING
☐ 338. JIM BUNNING
☐ 357. EARL TORGESON
☐ 379. DON LEE
☐ 390. RENO BERTOIA
☐ 405. DUKE MAAS

KANSAS CITY ATHLETICS

☐ 6. HECTOR LOPEZ
☐ 13. WALLY BURNETTE
☐ 41. HAL W. SMITH
☐ 44. JOE DEMAESTRI
☐ 83. LOU SKIZAS
☐ 87. TOM GORMAN
☐ 121. CLETE BOYER
☐ 139. LOU KRETLOW
☐ 142. CHARLEY THOMPSON
☐ 167. VIC POWER
☐ 187. VIRGIL TRUCKS
☐ 204. TEAM CARD
☐ 207. BILLY HUNTER
☐ 225. HARRY SIMPSON
☐ 239. TOM MORGAN
☐ 253. GUS ZERNIAL
☐ 269. BOB CERV
☐ 280. ALEX KELLNER
☐ 285. NED GARVER
☐ 298. IRV NOREN
☐ 318. MICKEY MCDERMOTT
☐ 354. RIP COLEMAN

☐ 360. JOHNNY GROTH
☐ 369. MILT GRAFF
☐ 402. JIM PISONI

JOHNNY Logan
MILWAUKEE BRAVES

MILWAUKEE BRAVES

☐ 4. JOHNNY LOGAN
☐ 20. HANK AARON
☐ 28. GENE CONLEY
☐ 37. FRANK TORRE
☐ 48. BILL BRUTON
☐ 68. RAY CRONE
☐ 90. WARREN SPAHN
☐ 114. TEAM CARD
☐ 117. JOE ADCOCK
☐ 127. BOB BUHL
☐ 133. DEL CRANDALL
☐ 143. ANDY PAFKO
☐ 188. FELIX MANTILLA
☐ 193. DEL RICE
☐ 208. LEW BURDETTE
☐ 250. ED METHEWS
☐ 262. BOBBY THOMSON
☐ 271. DANNY O'CONNELL
☐ 283. WES COVINGTON
☐ 321. RED MURFF
☐ 333. ERNIE JOHNSON
☐ 343. TAYLOR PHILLIPS
☐ 383. JUAN PIZARRO
☐ 389. DAVE JOLLY
☐ 392. CHUCK TANNER

NEW YORK GIANTS

☐ 10. WILLIE MAYS
☐ 39. AL WORTHINGTON
☐ 49. DARYL SPENCER
☐ 58. RUBEN GOMEZ
☐ 61. DUSTY RHODES
☐ 86. BILL SARNI
☐ 105. JOHNNY ANTONELLI
☐ 109. HANK THOMPSON
☐ 123. STEVE RIDZIK
☐ 148. DON MUELLER
☐ 154. RED SCHOENDIENST
☐ 191. JOE MARGONERI
☐ 197. HANK SAUER
☐ 216. MARV GRISSOM
☐ 232. WHITEY LOCKMAN
☐ 237. FOSTER CASTLEMAN
☐ 281. GAIL HARRIS
☐ 291. WINDY MCCALL
☐ 310. MAX SURKONT
☐ 317. TEAM CARD
☐ 323. WES WESTRUM
☐ 331. RAY KATT
☐ 361. CURT BARCLAY
☐ 365. OSSIE VIRGIL
☐ 377. ANDRE RODGERS

NEW YORK YANKEES

☐ 2. YOGI BERRA
☐ 25. WHITEY FORD
☐ 34. TOM STURDIVANT
☐ 36. BOB GRIM
☐ 62. BILLY MARTIN
☐ 82. ELSTON HOWARD
☐ 95. MICKEY MANTLE
☐ 97. TEAM CARD
☐ 108. TOMMY BYRNE
☐ 132. ART DITMAR
☐ 135. BILL SKOWRON
☐ 164. TOMMY CARROLL
☐ 175. DON LARSEN
☐ 185. JOHNNY KUCKS
☐ 192. JERRY COLEMAN

1957 Topps

- ☐ 200. GIL MCDOUGALD
- ☐ 215. ENOS SLAUGHTER
- ☐ 240. HANK BAUER
- ☐ 264. BOB TURLEY
- ☐ 272. BOBBY SHANTZ
- ☐ 286. BOBBY RICHARDSON
- ☐ 290. ANDY CAREY
- ☐ 295. JOE COLLINS
- ☐ 306. DARRELL JOHNSON
- ☐ 312. TONY KUBEK
- ☐ 391. RALPH TERRY
- ☐ 398. AL CICOTTE

PHILADELPHIA PHILLIES

- ☐ 15. ROBIN ROBERTS
- ☐ 27. TED KAZANSKI
- ☐ 46. BOB J. MILLER
- ☐ 54. ELMER VALO
- ☐ 70. RICHIE ASHBURN
- ☐ 91. MACK BURK
- ☐ 119. STAN LOPATA
- ☐ 129. SAUL ROGOVIN
- ☐ 158. CURT SIMMONS
- ☐ 162. JACK MEYER
- ☐ 174. WILLIE JONES
- ☐ 214. TEAM CARD
- ☐ 224. MARV BLAYLOCK
- ☐ 231. SOLLY HEMUS
- ☐ 241. JOE LONNETT
- ☐ 245. RIP REPULSKI
- ☐ 254. RON NEGRAY
- ☐ 265. HARVEY HADDIX
- ☐ 305. CHICO FERNADEZ
- ☐ 314. ED BOUCHEE
- ☐ 332. BOB BOWMAN
- ☐ 335. GRANNY HAMNER
- ☐ 348. JIM HEARN
- ☐ 374. DON CARDWELL
- ☐ 387. JACK SANFORD
- ☐ 397. ROY SMALLEY
- ☐ 404. HARRY ANDERSON

PITTSBURGH PIRATES

- ☐ 3. DALE LONG
- ☐ 12. DICK GROAT
- ☐ 24. BILL MAZEROSKI
- ☐ 52. LEE WALLS
- ☐ 76. BOB CLEMENTE
- ☐ 104. HANK FOILES
- ☐ 110. BILL VIRDON
- ☐ 140. FRANK THOMAS
- ☐ 150. BOB FRIEND
- ☐ 161. TEAM CARD
- ☐ 166. ROY FACE
- ☐ 199. VERNON LAW
- ☐ 209. BOB SKINNER
- ☐ 234. DICK COLE
- ☐ 256. RON KLINE
- ☐ 259. EDDIE O'BRIEN
- ☐ 267. DANNY KRAVITZ
- ☐ 308. DICK HALL
- ☐ 327. JIM PENDLETON
- ☐ 345. PAUL SMITH
- ☐ 349. NELSON KING
- ☐ 362. ROMAN MEJIAS
- ☐ 368. BOB PURKEY
- ☐ 394. LUIS ARROYO

ST. LOUIS CARDINALS

- ☐ 47. DON BLASINGAME
- ☐ 65. WALLY MOON
- ☐ 71. MURRY DICKSON
- ☐ 79. LINDY MCDANIEL
- ☐ 81. HERM WEHMEIER
- ☐ 94. BOBBY DEL GRECO
- ☐ 98. AL DARK
- ☐ 111. HAL R. SMITH
- ☐ 113. WILMER MIZELL
- ☐ 122. KEN BOYER
- ☐ 182. HOBIE LANDRITH
- ☐ 196. LARRY JACKSON
- ☐ 203. HOYT WILHELM
- ☐ 206. WILLARD SCHMIDT
- ☐ 243. TEAM CARD
- ☐ 260. DEL ENNIS
- ☐ 273. JIM DAVIS
- ☐ 287. SAM JONES
- ☐ 299. CHUCK HARMON
- ☐ 304. JOE CUNNINGHAM
- ☐ 350. EDDIE MIKSIS
- ☐ 359. TOM CHENEY
- ☐ 363. EDDIE KASKO
- ☐ 380. WALKER COOPER
- ☐ 384. BOBBY GENE SMITH

WASHINGTON SENATORS

- ☐ 22. JERRY SNYDER
- ☐ 29. WHITEY HERZOG
- ☐ 51. CLINT COURTNEY
- ☐ 57. JIM LEMON
- ☐ 64. PETE RUNNELS
- ☐ 89. ROY SIEVERS
- ☐ 101. CHUCK STOBBS
- ☐ 126. BOB WIESLER
- ☐ 153. KARL OLSON
- ☐ 169. HERB PLEWS
- ☐ 177. EDDIE YOST
- ☐ 179. ERNIE ORAVETZ
- ☐ 211. CAMILO PASCUAL
- ☐ 246. JOSE VALDIVIELSO
- ☐ 261. BOB CHAKALES
- ☐ 270. TEAM CARD
- ☐ 293. TED ABERNATHY
- ☐ 315. LOU BERBERET
- ☐ 320. NEIL CHRISLEY
- ☐ 326. PEDRO RAMOS
- ☐ 334. JERRY SCHOONMAKER
- ☐ 356. FAYE THRONEBERRY
- ☐ 367. ED FITZ GERALD
- ☐ 386. LYLE LUTTRELL
- ☐ 403. DICK HYDE

1958 TOPPS (494)
2 1/2" X 3 1/2"

Ossie Virgil

3rd B. SAN FRANCISCO GIANTS

BALTIMORE ORIOLES

- ☐ 6. GEORGE ZUVERINK
- ☐ 28. JIM BUSBY
- ☐ 40. GEORGE KELL
- ☐ 67. JOE GINSBERG
- ☐ 84. BILLY O'DELL
- ☐ 96. JOE DURHAM
- ☐ 105. BILLY GARDNER
- ☐ 113. JERRY WALKER
- ☐ 121. EDDIE MIKSIS
- ☐ 141. KEN LEHMAN
- ☐ 165. BOB NIEMAN
- ☐ 179. WILLIE MIRANDA
- ☐ 191. ART CECCARELLI
- ☐ 217. JACK HARSHMAN
- ☐ 229. FRANK ZUPO
- ☐ 259. AL PILARCIK
- ☐ 266. CONNIE JOHNSON
- ☐ 279. BOB BOYD
- ☐ 307. BROOKS ROBINSON
- ☐ 336. BERT HAMRIC
- ☐ 359. BILLY LOES
- ☐ 381. HAL BROWN
- ☐ 398. GENE WOODLING
- ☐ 408. TEAM CARD
- ☐ 416. FOSTER CASTLEMAN
- ☐ 429. GUS TRIANDOS
- ☐ 441. JIM MARSHALL
- ☐ 457. MILT PAPPAS
- ☐ 465. ARNIE PORTOCARRERO
- ☐ 471. LENNY GREEN

BOSTON RED SOX

- ☐ 1. TED WILLIAMS
- ☐ 18. FRANK SULLIVAN
- ☐ 29. TED LEPCIO
- ☐ 38. DICK GERNERT
- ☐ 59. DAVE SISLER
- ☐ 73. PETE DALEY
- ☐ 89. BILLY KLAUS
- ☐ 130. JACKIE JENSEN
- ☐ 148. BILLY CONSOLO

- ☐ 167. FRANK BAUMANN
- ☐ 189. GEORGE SUSCE
- ☐ 197. HAYWOOD SULLIVAN
- ☐ 204. LEO KIELY
- ☐ 220. TOM BREWER
- ☐ 227. GENE STEPHENS
- ☐ 260. FRANK MALZONE
- ☐ 265. PETE RUNNELS
- ☐ 280. JIM PIERSALL
- ☐ 297. DON BUDDIN
- ☐ 312. TEAM CARD
- ☐ 328. IKE DELOCK
- ☐ 344. BOB PORTERFIELD
- ☐ 361. MIKE FORNIELES
- ☐ 371. MARTY KEOUGH
- ☐ 383. LOU BERBERET
- ☐ 395. WILLARD NIXON
- ☐ 410. MURRAY WALL
- ☐ 414. SAMMY WHITE
- ☐ 445. BOB W. SMITH
- ☐ 473. BILL RENNA

CHICAGO CUBS

- ☐ 7. DALE LONG
- ☐ 33. CAL NEEMAN
- ☐ 41. DAVE HILLMAN
- ☐ 66. LEE WALLS
- ☐ 80. DICK DROTT
- ☐ 91. CHUCK TANNER
- ☐ 99. BOBBY ADAMS
- ☐ 122. WALT MORYN
- ☐ 135. MOE BRABOWSKY
- ☐ 144. BOBBY MORGAN
- ☐ 159. TAYLOR PHILLIPS
- ☐ 184. ELVIN TAPPE
- ☐ 201. JIM BOLGER
- ☐ 209. BOB ANDERSON
- ☐ 221. JERRY KINDALL
- ☐ 241. DICK LITTLEFIELD
- ☐ 261. TURK LOWN
- ☐ 281. SAM TAYLOR
- ☐ 310. ERNIE BANKS
- ☐ 327. TEAM CARD
- ☐ 342. JIM BROSNAN
- ☐ 363. DON ELSTON
- ☐ 384. JOHN GORYL
- ☐ 411. TONY TAYLOR
- ☐ 430. BOBBY THOMSON
- ☐ 449. GENE FODGE
- ☐ 461. ED MAYER
- ☐ 467. GLEN HOBBIE

CHICAGO WHITE SOX

- ☐ 11. JIM RIVERA
- ☐ 26. RON JACKSON
- ☐ 50. BILLY PIERCE
- ☐ 56. BILL FISCHER
- ☐ 85. LUIS APARICIO
- ☐ 100. EARLY WYNN
- ☐ 108. JIM LANDIS
- ☐ 129. JIM DERRINGTON
- ☐ 138. EARL TORGESON
- ☐ 153. LES MOSS
- ☐ 163. JIM WILSON
- ☐ 177. AL SMITH
- ☐ 200. BOB KEEGAN
- ☐ 212. BUBBA PHILLIPS
- ☐ 225. BILLY GOODMAN
- ☐ 249. RAY MOORE
- ☐ 256. TEAM CARD
- ☐ 267. SHERM LOLLAR
- ☐ 290. DICK DONOVAN
- ☐ 316. TITO FRANCONA
- ☐ 338. WALT DROPO
- ☐ 347. DON RUDOLPH
- ☐ 364. EARL BATTEY
- ☐ 400. NELLIE FOX
- ☐ 412. JERRY STALEY
- ☐ 421. DIXIE HOWELL
- ☐ 425. SAM ESPOSITO
- ☐ 453. TOM QUALTERS

CINCINNATI REDS

- ☐ 12. GEORGE CROWE
- ☐ 27. BUD FREEMAN
- ☐ 34. BOB THURMAN
- ☐ 49. SMOKY BURGESS
- ☐ 63. JOE NUXHALL
- ☐ 75. GUS BELL
- ☐ 103. JERRY LYNCH
- ☐ 118. HARVEY HADDIX
- ☐ 126. STAN PALYS
- ☐ 131. BOB HENRICH
- ☐ 149. TOM ACKER
- ☐ 157. DEE FONDY
- ☐ 160. DON HOAK
- ☐ 205. JOHNNY TEMPLE
- ☐ 214. WILLARD SCHMIDT

☐ 237. BILL WIGHT
☐ 242. JOHNNY KLIPPSTEIN
☐ 254. ALEX GRAMMAS
☐ 285. FRANK ROBINSON
☐ 294. HAL JEFFCOAT
☐ 311. BOB PURKEY
☐ 330. ED BAILEY
☐ 346. STEVE BILKO
☐ 360. ROY MCMILLAN
☐ 374. BROOKS LAWRENCE
☐ 376. CHARLEY RABE
☐ 396. DUTCH DOTTERER
☐ 420. VADA PINSON
☐ 428. TEAM CARD
☐ 466. PETE WHISENANT

CLEVELAND INDIANS

☐   2. BOB LEMON
☐ 22. HAL NARAGON
☐ 35. DON MOSSI
☐ 47. ROGER MARIS
☐ 55. CHICO CARRASQUEL
☐ 79. DICK WILLIAMS
☐ 102. GEORGE STRICKLAND
☐ 123. DICK TOMANEK
☐ 133. RUSS NIXON
☐ 158. TEAM CARD
☐ 170. VIC WERTZ
☐ 182. JOE CAFFIE
☐ 196. MIKE GARCIA
☐ 208. CAL MCLISH
☐ 222. BUD DALEY
☐ 233. MICKEY VERNON
☐ 243. LARRY RAINES
☐ 276. BOBBY AVILA
☐ 295. MINNIE MINOSO
☐ 324. HOYT WILHELM
☐ 339. FRED HATFIELD
☐ 352. HERB SCORE
☐ 368. ROCKY COLAVITO
☐ 388. BILLY MORAN
☐ 394. JIM GRANT
☐ 424. LARRY DOBY
☐ 439. RAY NARLESKI
☐ 443. BILLY HARRELL
☐ 446. CARROLL HARDY
☐ 456. DICK BROWN
☐ 462. GARY GEIGER
☐ 469. DON FERRARESE

DETROIT TIGERS

☐ 13. BILLY HOEFT
☐ 32. J.W. PORTER
☐ 46. LOU SLEATER
☐ 57. TIM THOMPSON
☐ 70. AL KALINE
☐ 81. STEVE BOROS
☐ 95. FRANK BOLLING
☐ 112. GUS ZERNIAL
☐ 115. JIM BUNNING
☐ 154. HARRY BYRD
☐ 185. RAY BOONE
☐ 206. BOB SHAW
☐ 213. RED WILSON
☐ 232. RENO BERTOIA
☐ 245. FRANK LARY
☐ 262. JOHNNY GROTH
☐ 271. BILLY MARTIN
☐ 282. PAUL FOYTACK
☐ 309. GAIL HARRIS
☐ 319. LOU SKIZAS
☐ 337. HANK AGUIRRE
☐ 345. JIM HEGAN
☐ 365. TOM MORGAN
☐ 380. CHARLEY MAXWELL
☐ 389. BILL TAYLOR
☐ 397. TEAM CARD
☐ 434. HARVEY KUENN
☐ 448. CHARLIE LAU
☐ 463. VITO VALENTINETTI

KANSAS CITY ATHLETICS

☐   3. ALEX KELLNER
☐ 23. BILL TUTTLE
☐ 39. BOB MARTYN
☐ 62. JOE DEMAESTRI
☐ 69. WALLY BURNETTE
☐ 98. BILLY HUNTER
☐ 119. HARRY CHITI
☐ 139. GEORGE BRUNET
☐ 155. HECTOR LOPEZ
☐ 169. RALPH TERRY
☐ 174. TEAM CARD
☐ 192. MILT GRAFF
☐ 202. WOODY HELD
☐ 228. DUKE MAAS
☐ 235. TOM GORMAN

☐ 257. HAL W. SMITH
☐ 277. VIRGIL TRUCKS
☐ 292. NED GARVER
☐ 302. MIKE BAXES
☐ 318. FRANK HOUSE
☐ 329. BOB CERV
☐ 349. MURRY DICKSON
☐ 367. JACK URBAN
☐ 379. RAY HERBERT
☐ 391. DAVE MELTON
☐ 406. VIC POWER
☐ 450. PRESTON WARD

Sandy Koufax

LOS ANGELES DODGERS

☐ 16. CHARLEY NEAL
☐ 25. DON DRYSDALE
☐ 42. JOHN ROSEBORO
☐ 71. TEAM CARD
☐ 77. DON ZIMMER
☐ 88. DUKE SNIDER
☐ 93. SANDY AMOROS
☐ 120. JOHNNY PODRES
☐ 146. DICK GRAY
☐ 162. GIL HODGES
☐ 187. SANDY KOUFAX
☐ 194. ROGER CRAIG
☐ 203. AL WALKER
☐ 215. JIM GILLIAM
☐ 244. DON DEMETER
☐ 258. CARL ERSKINE
☐ 286. GINO CIMOLI
☐ 301. RANDY JACKSON
☐ 305. CLEM LABINE
☐ 323. ELMER VALO
☐ 340. DON NEWCOMBE
☐ 357. DANNY MCDEVITT
☐ 373. JOE PIGNATANO
☐ 375. PEE WEE REESE
☐ 401. DON BESSENT
☐ 417. CARL FURILLO
☐ 435. ED ROEBUCK

MILWAUKEE BRAVES

☐ 10. LEW BURDETTE
☐ 17. FELIX MANTILLA
☐ 30. HANK AARON
☐ 51. DEL RICE
☐ 78. ERNIE JOHNSON
☐ 83. BOB HAZLE
☐ 110. JOHNNY LOGAN
☐ 117. FRANK TORRE
☐ 140. WES COVINGTON

☐ 147. DON MCMAHON
☐ 164. BOB TAYLOR
☐ 176. BOB BUHL
☐ 190. RED SCHOENDIENST
☐ 223. ANDY PAFKO
☐ 234. CARL SAWATSKI
☐ 247. CASEY WISE
☐ 252. BOB TROWBRIDGE
☐ 270. WARREN SPAHN
☐ 283. RAY SHEARER
☐ 313. BOB RUSH
☐ 325. JOE ADCOCK
☐ 355. BILL BRUTON
☐ 377. TEAM CARD
☐ 390. DEL CRANDALL
☐ 407. CARLTON WILLEY
☐ 431. GENE CONLEY
☐ 440. ED MATHEWS
☐ 454. HARRY HANEBRINK
☐ 472. JOE JAY

NEW YORK YANKEES

☐   9. HANK BAUER
☐ 20. GIL MCDOUGALD
☐ 43. SAL MAGLIE
☐ 54. NORM SIEBERN
☐ 61. DARRELL JOHNSON
☐ 87. JOHNNY KUCKS
☐ 101. BOBBY RICHARDSON
☐ 127. TOM STURDIVANT
☐ 142. ENOS SLAUGHTER
☐ 150. MICKEY MANTLE
☐ 161. DON LARSEN
☐ 175. MARV THRONEBERRY
☐ 193. JERRY LUMPE
☐ 224. BOB GRIM
☐ 240. BILL SKOWRON
☐ 246. TEAM CARD
☐ 255. BOB TURLEY
☐ 275. ELSTON HOWARD
☐ 296. RYNE DUREN
☐ 299. HARRY SIMPSON
☐ 320. WHITEY FORD
☐ 333. ANDY CAREY
☐ 354. ART DITMAR
☐ 370. YOGI BERRA
☐ 382. AL CICOTTE
☐ 393. TONY KUBEK
☐ 419. BOBBY SHANTZ

PHILADELPHIA PHILLIES

☐ 14. RIP REPULSKI
☐ 36. TED KAZANSKI
☐ 48. CHUCK HARMON
☐ 64. JOE LONNETT
☐ 76. DICK FARRELL
☐ 90. ROBIN ROBERTS
☐ 116. DAVE PHILLEY
☐ 134. TEAM CARD
☐ 171. HARRY ANDERSON
☐ 181. WILLIE JONES
☐ 186. JACK MEYER
☐ 207. SOLLY HEMUS
☐ 230. RICHIE ASHBURN
☐ 251. WARREN HACKER
☐ 264. JACK SANFORD
☐ 268. GRANNY HAMNER
☐ 278. MACK BURK
☐ 291. DON LANDRUM
☐ 298. JIM HEARN
☐ 326. BOB J. MILLER
☐ 348. CHICO FERNANDEZ
☐ 353. STAN LOPATA
☐ 372. DON CARDWELL
☐ 387. WALLY POST
☐ 404. CURT SIMMONS
☐ 415. BOB BOWMAN
☐ 433. PANCHO HERRERA
☐ 460. CHUCK ESSEGIAN
☐ 474. ROMAN SEMPROCH

PITTSBURGH PIRATES

☐   4. HANK FOILES
☐ 45. DICK GROAT
☐ 52. BOB CLEMENTE
☐ 74. ROY FACE
☐ 82. RON KLINE
☐ 94. BOB SKINNER
☐ 104. JIM PENDLETON
☐ 132. VERN LAW
☐ 151. BUDDY PRITCHARD
☐ 172. DON GROSS
☐ 178. TED KLUSZEWSKI
☐ 198. BILL VIRDON
☐ 218. DICK RAND
☐ 226. BOB G. SMITH
☐ 238. BILL MAZEROSKI

☐ 269. PAUL SMITH
☐ 293. GENE FREESE
☐ 306. WHAMMY DOUGLAS
☐ 315. BOB FRIEND
☐ 322. HARDING PETERSON
☐ 341. TEAM CARD
☐ 358. GENE BAKER
☐ 392. BENNIE DANIELS
☐ 409. FRANK THOMAS
☐ 426. JOHNNY O'BRIEN
☐ 432. JOHN POWERS
☐ 444. DANNY KRAVITZ
☐ 452. ROMAN MEJIAS
☐ 459. RON BLACKBURN
☐ 470. R.C. STEVENS

ST. LOUIS CARDINALS

☐ 8. EDDIE KASKO
☐ 24. HOBIE LANDRITH
☐ 53. MORRIE MARTIN
☐ 60. DEL ENNIS
☐ 65. VON MCDANIEL
☐ 97. LARRY JACKSON
☐ 106. DICK SCHOFIELD
☐ 114. IRV NOREN
☐ 125. AL DARK
☐ 143. BILLY MUFFETT
☐ 168. JOE CUNNINGHAM
☐ 180. LINDY MCDANIEL
☐ 199. DON BLASINGAME
☐ 210. WALLY MOON
☐ 216. TEAM CARD
☐ 231. LLOYD MERRITT
☐ 248. HERM WEHMEIER
☐ 273. HAL R. SMITH
☐ 287. SAM JONES
☐ 350. KEN BOYER
☐ 366. GENE GREEN
☐ 385. WILMER MIZELL
☐ 402. BOBBY GENE SMITH
☐ 423. PHIL CLARK
☐ 442. PHIL PAINE
☐ 451. JOE TAYLOR
☐ 464. CURT FLOOD

SAN FRANCISCO GIANTS

☐ 5. WILLIE MAYS
☐ 19. TEAM CARD
☐ 21. CURT BARCLAY
☐ 37. MIKE MCCORMICK
☐ 68. DARYL SPENCER
☐ 86. VALMY THOMAS
☐ 107. OSSIE VIRGIL
☐ 111. STU MILLER
☐ 128. WILLIE KIRKLAND
☐ 136. JIM FINIGAN
☐ 152. JOHNNY ANTONELLI
☐ 166. DANNY O'CONNELL
☐ 183. DAVE JOLLY
☐ 195. WHITEY LOCKMAN
☐ 211. PETE BURNSIDE
☐ 253. DON MUELLER
☐ 263. EDDIE BRESSOUD
☐ 272. RAY CRONE
☐ 284. RAY KATT
☐ 308. PAUL GIEL
☐ 332. JIM KING
☐ 335. RUBEN GOMEZ
☐ 343. ORLANDO CEPEDA
☐ 362. RAY JABLONSKI
☐ 378. HANK SAUER
☐ 399. MARV GRISSOM
☐ 413. JIM DAVENPORT
☐ 427. AL WORTHINGTON
☐ 437. BOB SPEAKE
☐ 447. RAY MONZANT
☐ 468. BOB SCHMIDT

WASHINGTON SENATORS

☐ 15. JIM LEMON
☐ 31. TEX CLEVENGER
☐ 44. TEAM CARD
☐ 58. ART SCHULT
☐ 72. BUD BYERLY
☐ 92. CLINT COURTNEY
☐ 109. HERB PLEWS
☐ 124. BOBBY USHER
☐ 137. RUSS KEMMERER
☐ 156. DICK HYDE
☐ 173. EDDIE YOST
☐ 188. MILT BOLLING
☐ 219. CAMILO PASCUAL
☐ 236. ED FITZ GERALD
☐ 239. CHUCK STOBBS
☐ 250. ROY SIEVERS
☐ 274. ROCKY BRIDGES
☐ 288. HARMON KILLEBREW
☐ 303. NEIL CHRISLEY

☐ 317. ALBIE PEARSON
☐ 331. PEDRO RAMOS
☐ 356. BOB MALKMUS
☐ 369. RALPH LUMENTI
☐ 403. STEVE KORCHECK
☐ 405. KEN ASPROMONTE
☐ 422. NORM ZAUCHIN
☐ 438. WHITEY HERZOG
☐ 455. HAL GRIGGS
☐ 458. JULIO BECQUER

1959 TOPPS (572)
2 1/2" X 3 1/2"

BALTIMORE ORIOLES

☐ 7. AL PILARCIK
☐ 21. CONNIE JOHNSON
☐ 47. JIM FINIGAN
☐ 48. TEAM CARD
☐ 66. JOE GINSBERG
☐ 82. BOB BOYD
☐ 89. BILLY GARDNER
☐ 98. ARNIE PORTOCARRERO
☐ 143. WILLIE TASBY
☐ 144. JERRY WALKER
☐ 170. GENE WOODLING
☐ 192. CHARLEY BEAMON
☐ 209. LENNY GREEN
☐ 219. GEORGE ZUVERINK
☐ 250. BILLY O'DELL
☐ 264. CHICO CARRASQUEL
☐ 279. ERNIE JOHNSON
☐ 299. BILLY KLAUS
☐ 330. GUS TRIANDOS
☐ 336. BILLY LOES
☐ 349. HOYT WILHELM
☐ 363. BOBBY AVILA
☐ 375. BOB NIEMAN
☐ 391. MILT PAPPAS
☐ 411. WHITEY LOCKMAN
☐ 439. BROOKS ROBINSON
☐ 444. RON HANSEN
☐ 475. JACK HARSHMAN
☐ 487. HAL BROWN
☐ 507. BOB HALE
☐ 529. GEORGE BAMBERGER
☐ 540. WILLY MIRANDA

BOSTON RED SOX

☐ 13. DICK GERNERT
☐ 32. DON BUDDING
☐ 42. MURRAY WALL
☐ 55. TOM BREWER
☐ 72. BILL RENNA
☐ 91. HERB MOFORD
☐ 112. BILLY CONSOLO
☐ 139. ED SADOWSKI
☐ 146. JERRY ZIMMERMAN
☐ 161. FRANK BAUMANN
☐ 173. BILL MONBOUQUETTE
☐ 185. JIM BUSBY
☐ 199. LEO KIELY
☐ 220. FRANK MALZONE
☐ 236. TED BOWSFIELD
☐ 248. TEAM CARD
☐ 261. GENE STEPHENS
☐ 276. PETE DALEY
☐ 286. DEAN STONE
☐ 303. MARTY KEOUGH
☐ 323. FRANK SULLIVAN
☐ 348. TED LEPCIO
☐ 361. WILLARD NIXON
☐ 370. PETE RUNNELS
☐ 384. DAVE SISLER
☐ 400. JACKIE JENSEN

☐ 416. HAYWOOD SULLIVAN
☐ 437. IKE DELOCK
☐ 456. JERRY CASALE
☐ 473. MIKE FORNIELES
☐ 486. SAMMY WHITE
☐ 500. VIC WERTZ
☐ 521. GARY GEIGER

CHICAGO CUBS

☐ 15. DICK DROTT
☐ 29. JIM BOLGER
☐ 46. BILL R. HENRY
☐ 62. TONY TAYLOR
☐ 77. JOHN GORYL
☐ 105. LEE WALLS
☐ 113. TAYLOR PHILLIPS
☐ 118. JOHN BUZHARDT
☐ 130. LOU JACKSON
☐ 153. JIM MARSHALL
☐ 177. JOHNNY BRIGGS
☐ 193. SAMMY TAYLOR
☐ 214. MARCELINO SOLIS
☐ 226. ART CECCARELLI
☐ 234. CHUCK TANNER
☐ 249. BOBBY ADAMS
☐ 274. JERRY KINDALL
☐ 301. EARL AVERILL
☐ 304. TEAM CARD
☐ 319. DAVE HILLMAN
☐ 334. GLEN HOBBIE
☐ 350. ERNIE BANKS
☐ 362. DOLAN NICHOLS
☐ 367. CAL NEEMAN
☐ 388. BOB WILL
☐ 407. MOE DRABOWSKY
☐ 414. DALE LONG
☐ 429. BOBBY THOMSON
☐ 447. BOB ANDERSON
☐ 474. MOE THACKER
☐ 488. WALT MORYN
☐ 502. AL DARK
☐ 512. GEORGE ALTMAN
☐ 520. DON ELSTON
☐ 538. CHICK KING
☐ 548. ELMER SINGLETON

CHICAGO WHITE SOX

☐ 5. DICK DONOVAN
☐ 22. AL SMITH
☐ 30. NELLIE FOX
☐ 73. RON JACKSON
☐ 86. BOB KEEGAN
☐ 94. TEAM CARD
☐ 103. BILLY GOODMAN
☐ 114. EARL BATTEY
☐ 119. JOHN CALLISON
☐ 138. JOHN ROMANO
☐ 159. BOB SHAW
☐ 179. DON RUDOLPH
☐ 187. BUBBA PHILLIPS
☐ 213. JIM RIVERA
☐ 252. RAY BOONE
☐ 260. EARLY WYNN
☐ 277. TURK LOWN
☐ 293. RAY MOORE
☐ 310. LUIS APARICIO
☐ 328. LOU SKIZAS
☐ 341. TOM QUALTERS
☐ 351. EARL TORGESON
☐ 368. DON MUELLER
☐ 385. SHERM LOLLAR
☐ 410. BILLY PIERCE
☐ 426. JERRY STALEY
☐ 438. SAM ESPOSITO
☐ 453. LES MOSS
☐ 477. BARRY LATMAN
☐ 493. JIM LANDIS
☐ 509. NORM CASH
☐ 537. RODOLFO ARIAS

CINCINNATI REDS

☐ 14. PETE WHISENANT
☐ 25. DON HOAK
☐ 58. EDDIE MIKSIS
☐ 67. BROOKS LAWRENCE
☐ 81. HAL JEFFCOAT
☐ 97. JERRY LYNCH
☐ 111. TEAM CARD
☐ 120. CHUCK COLES
☐ 136. JIM O'TOOLE
☐ 158. WALT DROPO
☐ 171. WILLARD SCHMIDT
☐ 184. HARVEY HADDIX
☐ 201. TOM ACKER
☐ 210. ED BAILEY
☐ 224. CLAUDE OSTEEN
☐ 232. EDDIE KASKO
☐ 255. DEL ENNIS

- ☐ 271. ORLANDO PENA
- ☐ 288. DUTCH DOTTERER
- ☐ 312. DON NEWCOMBE
- ☐ 335. JOHNNY TEMPLE
- ☐ 356. BOB MABE
- ☐ 365. GUS BELL
- ☐ 389. JOE NUXHALL
- ☐ 405. ROY MCMILLAN
- ☐ 431. WHAMMY DOUGLAS
- ☐ 435. FRANK ROBINSON
- ☐ 448. VADA PINSON
- ☐ 489. JOHN POWERS
- ☐ 490. FRANK THOMAS
- ☐ 494. DON PAVLETICH
- ☐ 506. BOB PURKEY
- ☐ 518. MIKE CUELLER
- ☐ 541. BOB THURMAN

CLEVELAND INDIANS

- ☐ 11. BILLY HUNTER
- ☐ 38. MORRIE MARTIN
- ☐ 57. AL CICOTTE
- ☐ 61. DICK BROWN
- ☐ 80. MINNIE MINOSO
- ☐ 88. HERB SCORE
- ☐ 106. HAL WOODESHICK
- ☐ 115. MICKEY VERNON
- ☐ 123. DON DILLARD
- ☐ 142. DICK STIGMAN
- ☐ 168. CARROLL HARDY
- ☐ 186. JIM GRANT
- ☐ 196. BILLY MORAN
- ☐ 207. GEORGE STRICKLAND
- ☐ 229. VIC POWER
- ☐ 247. DON FERRARESE
- ☐ 266. WOODY HELD
- ☐ 283. RUSS HEMAN
- ☐ 295. BILLY MARTIN
- ☐ 327. GARY BELL
- ☐ 344. RUSS NIXON
- ☐ 355. JIM PIERSALL
- ☐ 371. DICK BRODOWSKI
- ☐ 376. HAL NARAGON
- ☐ 394. RANDY JACKSON
- ☐ 420. HECTOR LOPEZ
- ☐ 445. CAL MCLISH
- ☐ 476. TEAM CARD
- ☐ 501. BOBBY TIEFENAUER
- ☐ 516. MIKE GARCIA
- ☐ 531. RAY WEBSTER
- ☐ 542. JIM PERRY

DETROIT TIGERS

- ☐ 2. EDDIE YOST
- ☐ 24. RED WILSON
- ☐ 36. HANK AGUIRRE
- ☐ 52. COOT VEAL
- ☐ 70. HARVEY KUENN
- ☐ 96. LOU BERBERET
- ☐ 132. DON LEE
- ☐ 149. JIM BUNNING
- ☐ 164. JOHNNY GROTH
- ☐ 189. NEIL CHRISLEY
- ☐ 203. OSSIE VIRGIL
- ☐ 233. PAUL FOYTACK
- ☐ 256. JERRY DAVIE
- ☐ 268. TITO FRANCONA
- ☐ 280. FRANK BOLLING
- ☐ 302. DON MOSSIE
- ☐ 318. ROCKY BRIDGES
- ☐ 329. TEAM CARD
- ☐ 331. STEVE BOROS
- ☐ 343. BILLY HOEFT
- ☐ 354. PETE BURNSIDE
- ☐ 360. AL KALINE
- ☐ 378. GAIL HARRIS
- ☐ 393. FRANK LARY
- ☐ 409. GUS ZERNIAL
- ☐ 421. HERM WEHMEIER
- ☐ 442. RAY NARLESKI
- ☐ 455. LARRY DOBY
- ☐ 481. CHARLEY MAXWELL
- ☐ 504. OSSIE ALVAREZ
- ☐ 511. GEORGE SUSCE
- ☐ 524. LARRY OSBORNE
- ☐ 545. TOM MORGAN

KANSAS CITY ATHLETICS

- ☐ 18. JACK URBAN
- ☐ 41. BOB MARTYN
- ☐ 51. RIP COLEMAN
- ☐ 64. JOE DEMAESTRI
- ☐ 79. HARRY CHITI
- ☐ 100. BOB CERV
- ☐ 127. KENT HADLEY
- ☐ 140. CHARLIE SECREST
- ☐ 154. RAY HERBERT

- ☐ 172. TEAM CARD
- ☐ 176. PRESTON WARD
- ☐ 182. MILT GRAFF
- ☐ 202. ROGER MARIS
- ☐ 227. HAL W. SMITH
- ☐ 245. NED GARVER
- ☐ 254. ZEKE BELLA
- ☐ 263. BUDDY DALEY
- ☐ 281. WALT CRADDOCK
- ☐ 292. DICK WILLIAMS
- ☐ 313. FRANK HOUSE
- ☐ 333. HARRY SIMPSON
- ☐ 358. RALPH TERRY
- ☐ 369. DICK TOMANEK
- ☐ 381. MIKE BAXES
- ☐ 392. WHITEY HERZOG
- ☐ 402. HECTOR LOPEZ
- ☐ 423. BOB GRIM
- ☐ 449. TOM GORMAN
- ☐ 459. BILL TUTTLE
- ☐ 482. RUSS MEYER
- ☐ 496. WAYNE TERWILLIGER
- ☐ 513. TOM CARROLL
- ☐ 532. MARK FREEMAN

LOS ANGELES DODGERS

- ☐ 16. JOE PIGNATANO
- ☐ 20. DUKE SNIDER
- ☐ 43. STEVE BILKO
- ☐ 53. STAN WILLIAMS
- ☐ 71. DON BESSENT
- ☐ 107. NORM LARKER
- ☐ 125. RON FAIRLY
- ☐ 133. BOB LILLIS
- ☐ 152. JOHNNY KLIPPSTEIN
- ☐ 163. SANDY KOUFAX
- ☐ 195. RIP REPULSKI
- ☐ 206. CARL FURILLO
- ☐ 217. CARL ERSKINE
- ☐ 244. DICK GRAY
- ☐ 258. FRED KIPP
- ☐ 270. GIL HODGES
- ☐ 287. DON ZIMMER
- ☐ 306. JIM GILLIAM
- ☐ 321. BOB GIALLOMBARDO
- ☐ 324. DON DEMETER
- ☐ 364. DANNY MCDEVITT
- ☐ 387. DON DRYSDALE
- ☐ 403. CLEM LABINE
- ☐ 406. SOLLY DRAKE
- ☐ 427. CHARLIE NEAL
- ☐ 441. JOHN ROSEBORO
- ☐ 457. TEAM CARD
- ☐ 495. JOHNNY PODRES
- ☐ 508. ART FOWLER
- ☐ 522. GENE SNYDER
- ☐ 530. WALLY MOON
- ☐ 547. JIM BAXES

MILWAUKEE BRAVES

- ☐ 3. DON MCMAHON
- ☐ 27. ANDY PAFKO
- ☐ 40. WARREN SPAHN
- ☐ 54. MEL ROACH
- ☐ 65. FRANK TORRE
- ☐ 95. CARL WILLEY
- ☐ 104. DEL RICE
- ☐ 126. EDDIE HAAS
- ☐ 128. BOB HARTMAN
- ☐ 157. FELIX MANTILLA
- ☐ 165. BILL BRUTON
- ☐ 188. JUAN PIZARRO
- ☐ 204. CASEY WISE
- ☐ 225. JOHNNY LOGAN
- ☐ 239. BOB TROWBRIDGE

- ☐ 259. JIM PISONI
- ☐ 273. JOE JAY
- ☐ 290. WES COVINGTON
- ☐ 315. JOE ADCOCK
- ☐ 322. HARRY HANEBRINK
- ☐ 347. BOB BUHL
- ☐ 366. HUMBERTO ROBINSON
- ☐ 380. HANK AARON
- ☐ 396. BOB RUSH
- ☐ 419. TEAM CARD
- ☐ 425. DEL CRANDALL
- ☐ 440. LOU BURDETTE
- ☐ 450. ED MATHEWS
- ☐ 480. RED SCHOENDIENST
- ☐ 499. JOHNNY O'BRIEN

NEW YORK YANKEES

- ☐ 10. MICKEY MANTLE
- ☐ 23. MURRY DICKSON
- ☐ 45. ANDY CAREY
- ☐ 60. BOB TURLEY
- ☐ 76. BOBBY RICHARDSON
- ☐ 90. BILL SKOWRON
- ☐ 108. ZACK MONROE
- ☐ 117. JOHN BLANCHARD
- ☐ 131. DERON JOHNSON
- ☐ 155. ENOS SLAUGHTER
- ☐ 167. DUKE MAAS
- ☐ 180. YOGI BERRA
- ☐ 205. DON LARSEN
- ☐ 222. BOBBY SHANTZ
- ☐ 240. HANK BAUER
- ☐ 251. CLETIS BOYER
- ☐ 272. JERRY LUMPE
- ☐ 289. JOHNNY KUCKS
- ☐ 308. NORM SIEBERN
- ☐ 326. MARV THRONEBERRY
- ☐ 345. GIL MCDOUGALD
- ☐ 374. ART DITMAR
- ☐ 395. ELSTON HOWARD
- ☐ 417. VIRGIL TRUCKS
- ☐ 430. WHITEY FORD
- ☐ 471. TOM STURDIVANT
- ☐ 485. RYNE DUREN
- ☐ 505. TONY KUBEK
- ☐ 510. TEAM CARD
- ☐ 525. JIM COATES
- ☐ 533. DARRELL JOHNSON

PHILIADELPHIA PHILLIES

- ☐ 8. TEAM CARD
- ☐ 31. KEN LEHMAN
- ☐ 39. ED BOUCHEE
- ☐ 56. CARL SAWATSKI
- ☐ 63. JIM HEARN
- ☐ 85. HARRY ANDERSON
- ☐ 92. DAVE PHILLEY
- ☐ 99. TED KAZANSKI
- ☐ 121. BOB CONLEY
- ☐ 129. FRANK HERRERA
- ☐ 175. DICK FARRELL
- ☐ 178. RUBEN AMARO
- ☐ 197. RAY SEMPROCH
- ☐ 208. WILLIE JONES
- ☐ 221. BOB BOWMAN
- ☐ 235. VALMY THOMAS
- ☐ 253. SETH MOREHEAD
- ☐ 269. JACK MEYER
- ☐ 300. RICHIE ASHBURN
- ☐ 314. DON CARDWELL
- ☐ 338. SPARKY ANDERSON
- ☐ 352. ROBIN ROBERTS
- ☐ 372. JIM HEGAN
- ☐ 382. CURT SIMMONS
- ☐ 398. WALLY POST
- ☐ 412. STAN LOPATA
- ☐ 436. GRANNY HAMNER
- ☐ 452. CHICO FERNANDEZ
- ☐ 472. GENE FREESE
- ☐ 492. GENE CONLEY
- ☐ 503. JIM OWENS
- ☐ 517. JOE KOPPE
- ☐ 535. RUBEN GOMEZ
- ☐ 546. AL SCHROLL

PITTSBURGH PIRATES

- ☐ 12. VERN LAW
- ☐ 35. TED KLUSZEWSKI
- ☐ 49. BILL HALL
- ☐ 68. DICK SCHOFIELD
- ☐ 83. BOB G. SMITH
- ☐ 110. GEORGE WITT
- ☐ 122. BENNIE DANIELS
- ☐ 134. JIM MCDANIEL
- ☐ 160. DICK GROAT
- ☐ 174. JIM PENDLETON

☐ 181. BOB PORTERFIELD
☐ 190. BILL VIRDON
☐ 218. ROMAN MEJIAS
☐ 228. DON GROSS
☐ 238. GENE BAKER
☐ 265. RON KLINE
☐ 282. R.C. STEVENS
☐ 294. HANK FOILES
☐ 305. CURT RAYDON
☐ 320. BOB SKINNER
☐ 339. ROY FACE
☐ 357. DICK STUART
☐ 401. RON BLACKBURN
☐ 415. BILL MAZEROSKI
☐ 432. SMOKY BURGESS
☐ 446. ROCKY NELSON
☐ 460. BOB FRIEND
☐ 478. BOB CLEMENTE
☐ 523. HARRY BRIGHT
☐ 528. TEAM CARD
☐ 536. DAN KRAVITZ

ST. LOUIS CARDINALS

☐ 6. ALEX GRAMMAS
☐ 26. CHUCK STOBBS
☐ 37. GENE GREEN
☐ 59. IRV NOREN
☐ 75. SAM JONES
☐ 101. ALEX KELLNER
☐ 135. GENE OLIVER
☐ 137. DICK RICKETTS
☐ 150. STAN MUSIAL
☐ 162. BOBBY GENE SMITH
☐ 194. JIM BROSNAN
☐ 211. BOB BLAYLOCK
☐ 223. TEAM CARD
☐ 231. ELLIS BURTON
☐ 243. MARV GRISSOM
☐ 278. CHUCK ESSEGIAN
☐ 285. JOE CUNNINGHAM
☐ 296. ERNIE BROGLIO
☐ 309. SAL MAGLIE
☐ 325. KEN BOYER
☐ 337. GEORGE CROWE
☐ 353. CURT FLOOD
☐ 379. BOB J. MILLER
☐ 399. LARRY JACKSON
☐ 418. GINO CIMOLI
☐ 433. BILLY HARRELL
☐ 454. PHIL CLARK
☐ 479. LINDY MCDANIEL
☐ 491. DON BLASINGAME
☐ 497. HAL R. SMITH
☐ 514. BOB GIBSON
☐ 527. SOLLY HEMUS(M)
☐ 539. GARY BLAYLOCK
☐ 544. LEE TATE
☐ 549. HOWIE NUNN

willie mays

SAN FRANCISCO GIANTS
OUTFIELD

SAN FRANCISCO GIANTS

☐ 9. PAUL GIEL
☐ 19. ED BRESSOUD
☐ 28. RED WORTHINGTON
☐ 50. WILLIE MAYS
☐ 69. TEAM CARD
☐ 87. DANNY O'CONNELL
☐ 102. FELIPE ALOU
☐ 109. BOB SCHMIDT
☐ 141. JOE SHIPLEY
☐ 145. DOM ZANNI
☐ 148. MIKE MCCORMICK
☐ 183. STU MILLER
☐ 198. JIM DAVENPORT
☐ 216. ANDRE RODGERS
☐ 241. BILLY MUFFETT

☐ 257. LEON WAGNER
☐ 275. JACK SANFORD
☐ 297. JACKIE BRANDT
☐ 307. CURT BARCLAY
☐ 332. RAY MONZANT
☐ 342. RAY JABLONSKI
☐ 359. BILL WHITE
☐ 377. JOHNNY ANTONELLI
☐ 390. ORLANDO CEPEDA
☐ 404. HANK SAUER
☐ 422. HOBIE LANDRITH
☐ 443. DARYL SPENCER
☐ 458. GORDON JONES
☐ 484. WILLIE KIRKLAND
☐ 526. BOB SPEAKE

WASHINGTON SENATORS

☐ 4. ALBIE PEARSON
☐ 33. ED FITZ GERALD
☐ 44. VITO VALENTINETTI
☐ 78. PEDRO RAMOS
☐ 84. RENO BERTOIA
☐ 93. JULIO BECQUER
☐ 116. BOB ALLISON
☐ 124. DAN DOBBEK
☐ 151. BOB MALKMUS
☐ 169. TED ABERNATHY
☐ 191. RUSS KEMMERER
☐ 215. JIM LEMON
☐ 230. BILL FISCHER
☐ 242. RON SAMFORD
☐ 246. J.W. PORTER
☐ 267. JOHN ROMONOSKY
☐ 284. STEVE KORCHECK
☐ 298. TEX CLEVENGER
☐ 311. NORM ZAUCHIN
☐ 316. RALPH LUMENTI
☐ 340. ROY SIEVERS
☐ 373. HERB PLEWS
☐ 386. JIM DELSING
☐ 397. TEAM CARD
☐ 413. CAMILO PASCUAL
☐ 424. KEN ASPROMONTE
☐ 434. HAL GRIGGS
☐ 451. JIMMY CONSTABLE
☐ 483. CLINT COURTNEY
☐ 498. DICK HYDE
☐ 515. HARMON KILLEBREW
☐ 534. FAYE THRONEBERRY

1960 TOPPS (572)
2 1/2" X 3 1/2"

ELIO CHACON
CINCINNATI REDS

BALTIMORE ORIOLES

☐ 12. MILT PAPPAS
☐ 28. BROOKS ROBINSON
☐ 46. JACK FISHER
☐ 53. JACKIE BRANDT
☐ 60. GUS TRIANDOS
☐ 79. WALT DROPO
☐ 89. HAL BROWN
☐ 98. GORDON JONES
☐ 106. BILLY GARDNER
☐ 126. CHUCK ESTRADA
☐ 127. RON HANSEN
☐ 179. RIP COLEMAN
☐ 190. GENE WOODLING
☐ 207. BOB BOYD
☐ 224. PAUL RICHARDS(M)
☐ 241. ALBIE PEARSON
☐ 254. ARNIE PORTOCARRERO
☐ 269. GENE GREEN
☐ 288. BOB MABE
☐ 304. JOE GINSBERG
☐ 322. WILLIE TASBY
☐ 348. BARRY SHETRONE
☐ 369. BILLY HOEFT
☐ 395. HOYT WILHELM
☐ 406. BILLY KLAUS
☐ 422. JOHNNY POWERS

☐ 448. JIM GENTILE
☐ 455. COACHES CARD
☐ 481. WES STOCK
☐ 494. TEAM CARD
☐ 498. AL PILARCIK
☐ 514. STEVE BARBER
☐ 525. MARV BREEDING
☐ 540. JERRY WALKER

BOSTON RED SOX

☐ 15. PETE RUNNELS
☐ 38. JERRY CASALE
☐ 54. MIKE FORNIELES
☐ 68. DAVE HILLMAN
☐ 71. MARTY KEOUGH
☐ 94. LEO KIELY
☐ 111. VIC WERTZ
☐ 117. TOM BORLAND
☐ 148. CARL YASTRZEMSKI
☐ 153. BOBBY THOMSON
☐ 184. GARY GEIGER
☐ 203. SAMMY WHITE
☐ 220. BILLY JURGES(M)
☐ 232. JIM BUSBY
☐ 249. EARL WILSON
☐ 267. JIM MARSHALL
☐ 280. FRANK SULLIVAN
☐ 296. NELSON CHITTUM
☐ 310. FRANK MALZONE
☐ 317. PUMPSIE GREEN
☐ 336. IKE DELOCK
☐ 363. GENE STEPHENS
☐ 382. TED BOWSFIELD
☐ 403. ED SADOWSKI
☐ 426. RON JACKSON
☐ 439. TOM BREWER
☐ 452. RAY WEBSTER
☐ 456. COACHES CARD
☐ 474. HAYWOOD SULLIVAN
☐ 487. TOM STURDIVANT
☐ 520. DON BUDDIN
☐ 533. LU CLINTON
☐ 537. TEAM CARD
☐ 544. BILL MONBOUQUETTE

CHICAGO CUBS

☐ 10. ERNIE BANKS
☐ 27. DICK DROTT
☐ 39. EARL AVERILL
☐ 74. WALT MORYN
☐ 86. DICK GERNERT
☐ 93. ART SCHULT
☐ 95. FRANK THOMAS
☐ 125. DICK ELLSWORTH
☐ 147. BOB WILL
☐ 156. ART CECCARELLI
☐ 162. SAMMY TAYLOR
☐ 182. GLEN HOBBIE
☐ 217. CHARLEY GRIMM(M)
☐ 233. DON ELSTON
☐ 248. DEL RICE
☐ 259. GEORGE ALTMAN
☐ 277. HARRY BRIGHT
☐ 294. TONY TAYLOR
☐ 305. RICHIE ASHBURN
☐ 337. CAL NEEMAN
☐ 349. MOE DRABOWSKY
☐ 357. AL SCHROLL
☐ 375. DALE LONG
☐ 412. BOB ANDERSON
☐ 433. IRV NOREN
☐ 444. JERRY KINDALL
☐ 457. COACHES CARD
☐ 476. LOU JOHNSON
☐ 489. STEVE RIDZIK
☐ 504. SETH MOREHEAD
☐ 513. TEAM CARD
☐ 528. BEN JOHNSON

CHICAGO WHITE SOX

☐ 1. EARLY WYNN
☐ 31. SAMMY ESPOSITO
☐ 41. BARRY LATMAN
☐ 69. BILLY GOODMAN
☐ 100. NELLIE FOX
☐ 116. JIM RIVERA
☐ 121. CAMILO CARREON
☐ 131. ED HOBAUGH
☐ 150. BILLY PIERCE
☐ 169. JAKE STRIKER
☐ 180. HARRY SIMPSON
☐ 199. DICK DONOVAN
☐ 208. TEAM CARD
☐ 222. AL LOPEZ(M)
☐ 240. LUIS APARICIO
☐ 256. DICK BROWN
☐ 276. KEN MCBRIDE

☐ 299. EARL TORGESON
☐ 306. FRANK BAUMANN
☐ 313. TURK LOWN
☐ 328. EARL BATTEY
☐ 346. J.C. MARTIN
☐ 365. MINNIE MINOSO
☐ 380. BOB SHAW
☐ 407. GARY PETERS
☐ 428. AL SMITH
☐ 435. GENE FREESE
☐ 447. RAY MOORE
☐ 458. COACHES CARD
☐ 477. DON FERRARESE
☐ 495. SHERM LOLLAR
☐ 505. TED KLUSZEWSKI
☐ 510. JERRY STALEY
☐ 532. MIKE GARCIA
☐ 538. FRANK BARNES
☐ 550. JIM LANDIS

CINCINNATI REDS

☐ 4. BOB PURKEY
☐ 21. DUTCH DOTTERER
☐ 45. ROY MCMILLAN
☐ 61. EDDIE KASKO
☐ 110. CAL MCLISH
☐ 119. CHICO CARDENAS
☐ 146. TED WIEAND
☐ 164. TEAM CARD
☐ 173. BILLY MARTIN
☐ 176. VADA PINSON
☐ 187. JAY HOOK
☐ 198. JERRY LYNCH
☐ 206. CLAUDE OSTEEN
☐ 219. FRED HUTCHINSON(M)
☐ 235. GUS BELL
☐ 257. GORDY COLEMAN
☐ 282. JOE NUXHALL
☐ 289. WILLIE JONES
☐ 311. RAUL SANCHEZ
☐ 325. JIM O'TOOLE
☐ 345. DON NEWCOMBE
☐ 359. BUDDY GILBERT
☐ 372. FRANK HOUSE
☐ 398. MIKE CUELLAR
☐ 411. ED BAILEY
☐ 424. PETE WHISENANT
☐ 434. BROOKS LAWRENCE
☐ 449. JIM BROSNAN
☐ 459. COACHES CARD
☐ 490. FRANK ROBINSON
☐ 506. LEE WALLS
☐ 518. TONY GONZALEZ
☐ 524. BILL R. HENRY
☐ 535. WHITEY LOCKMAN
☐ 543. ELIO CHACON

CLEVELAND INDIANS

☐ 14. JIM GRANT
☐ 30. TITO FRANCONA
☐ 36. RUSS NIXON
☐ 44. BOBBY LOCKE
☐ 63. GEORGE STRICKLAND
☐ 75. VIC POWER
☐ 112. JACK HARSHMAN
☐ 122. DON DILLARD
☐ 139. CARL MATHIAS
☐ 159. JIM PIERSALL
☐ 174. TEAM CARD
☐ 178. WOODY HELD
☐ 216. JOE GORDON
☐ 228. ERNIE JOHNSON
☐ 243. BUBBA PHILLIPS
☐ 279. CHUCK TANNER
☐ 309. BOB HALE
☐ 318. JIM BAXES
☐ 323. JOHNNY ROMANO
☐ 324. JIM PERRY
☐ 341. CARROLL HARDY
☐ 360. HERBY SCORE
☐ 376. JOHNNY BRIGGS
☐ 400. ROCKY COLAVITO
☐ 423. ED FITZ GERALD
☐ 441. GARY BELL
☐ 460. COACHES CARD
☐ 473. AL CICOTTE
☐ 500. JOHNNY TEMPLE
☐ 507. DICK STIGMAN
☐ 521. MIKE LEE
☐ 536. WYNN HAWKINS
☐ 552. WALT BOND

DETROIT TIGERS

☐ 6. LOU BERBERET
☐ 22. ROCKY BRIDGES
☐ 33. TOM MORGAN
☐ 50. AL KALINE
☐ 72. TEAM CARD
☐ 85. FRANK LARY
☐ 118. BOB BRUCE
☐ 141. JIM PROCTOR
☐ 152. GAIL HARRIS
☐ 161. RAY NARLESKI
☐ 171. JOHNNY GROTH
☐ 186. DAVE SISLER
☐ 201. LARRY OSBORNE
☐ 214. JIMMIE DYKES(M)
☐ 245. EDDIE YOST
☐ 261. PETE BURNSIDE

☐ 273. NEIL CHRISLEY
☐ 286. RAY SEMPROCH
☐ 301. JERRY DAVIE
☐ 314. CHICO FERNADEZ
☐ 330. HARVEY KUENN
☐ 342. CASEY WISE
☐ 364. PAUL FOYTACK
☐ 379. RED WILSON
☐ 396. STEVE BILKO
☐ 418. DON MOSSI
☐ 443. CHARLIE MAXWELL
☐ 461. COACHES CARD
☐ 482. FRANK BOLING
☐ 488. NORM CASH
☐ 502. JIM BUNNING
☐ 531. SANDY AMOROS
☐ 546. HANK AGUIRRE

KANSAS CITY ATHLETICS

☐ 8. BUD DALEY
☐ 11. NORM SIEBERN
☐ 26. WAYNE TERWILLIGER
☐ 66. BOB TROWBRIDGE
☐ 77. HANK FOILES
☐ 78. BOB GRIM
☐ 81. RUSS SNYDER
☐ 92. WHITEY HERZOG
☐ 108. PETE DALEY
☐ 135. KEN JOHNSON
☐ 137. LOU KLIMCHOCK
☐ 177. JOHNNY KUCKS
☐ 188. DICK WILLIAMS
☐ 215. BOB ELLIOTT(M)
☐ 229. JOE MORGAN
☐ 252. RAY HERBERT
☐ 262. HANK BAUER
☐ 274. TOM ACKER
☐ 290. JERRY LUMPE
☐ 308. DICK HALL
☐ 339. HARRY CHITI
☐ 353. DON LARSEN
☐ 367. BILL TUTTLE
☐ 413. TEAM CARD
☐ 415. BOB CERV
☐ 427. AL GRUNWALD
☐ 436. MARV THRONEBERRY
☐ 462. COACHES CARD
☐ 471. NED GARVER
☐ 497. JOHN TSITOURIS
☐ 516. MARTY KUTYNA
☐ 542. KEN HAMLIN

LOS ANGELES DODGERS

☐ 5. WALLY MOON
☐ 18. TEAM CARD
☐ 29. CLEM LABINE
☐ 47. DON ZIMMER
☐ 62. ROGER CRAIG
☐ 88. JOHN ROSEBORO
☐ 105. LARRY SHERRY
☐ 128. BILL HARRIS
☐ 132. FRANK HOWARD
☐ 155. CHARLIE NEAL
☐ 166. CHUCK ESSEGIAN
☐ 191. JOHNNY KLIPPSTEIN
☐ 202. FRED KIPP
☐ 212. WALT ALSTON(M)
☐ 234. DON DEMETER
☐ 255. JIM GILLIAM
☐ 265. RIP REPULSKI
☐ 278. STAN WILLIAMS
☐ 295. GIL HODGES
☐ 321. RON FAIRLY
☐ 333. DANNY MCDEVITT
☐ 343. SANDY KOUFAX
☐ 354. BOB LILLIS
☐ 394. NORM LARKER
☐ 408. CARL FURILLO
☐ 425. JOHNNY PODRES
☐ 442. JOE PIGNATANO
☐ 463. COACHES CARD
☐ 475. DON DRYSDALE
☐ 493. DUKE SNIDER
☐ 509. TOMMY DAVIS
☐ 519. ED ROEBUCK
☐ 529. NORM SHERRY
☐ 547. BOB ASPROMONTE
☐ 551. ED RAKOW

MILWAUKEE BRAVES

☐ 3. JOE ADCOCK
☐ 19. FELIX MANTILLA
☐ 37. BILL BRUTON

☐ 59. JUAN PIZARRO
☐ 70. LOU BURDETTE
☐ 90. BOBBY AVILA
☐ 107. CARL WILLEY
☐ 129. BOB HARTMAN
☐ 143. AL SPANGLER
☐ 158. WES COVINGTON
☐ 170. DEL CRANDALL
☐ 189. DON MCMAHON
☐ 205. JOHNNY LOGAN
☐ 213. CHUCK DRESSEN(M)
☐ 246. LEE MAYE
☐ 266. JOE JAY
☐ 281. RAY BOONE
☐ 300. HANK AARON
☐ 312. CHARLIE LAU
☐ 335. RED SCHOENDIENST
☐ 351. DON NOTTEBART
☐ 374. BOB BUHL
☐ 381. TEAM CARD
☐ 404. BOB RUSH
☐ 417. CHUCK COTTIER
☐ 420. ED MATHEWS
☐ 445. WARREN SPAHN
☐ 464. COACHES CARD
☐ 478. FRANK TORRE
☐ 491. MEL ROACH
☐ 515. STAN LOPATA
☐ 534. KEN MACKENZIE

NEW YORK YANKEES

☐ 35. WHITEY FORD
☐ 51. JIM COATES
☐ 65. ELSTON HOWARD
☐ 83. TONY KUBEK
☐ 96. RALPH TERRY
☐ 102. KENT HADLEY
☐ 109. CLETIS BOYER
☐ 134. DERON JOHNSON
☐ 142. BILL SHORT
☐ 163. HECTOR LOPEZ
☐ 183. ELI GRBA
☐ 196. ANDY CAREY
☐ 204. RYNE DUREN
☐ 227. CASEY STENGEL(M)
☐ 237. ELMER VALO
☐ 247. GIL MCDOUGALD
☐ 270. BOB TURLEY
☐ 283. JOHN BLANCHARD
☐ 315. BOBBY SHANTZ
☐ 329. ZACK MONROE
☐ 332. TEAM CARD
☐ 350. MICKEY MANTLE
☐ 358. JOE DEMAESTRI
☐ 370. BILL SKOWRON
☐ 377. ROGER MARIS
☐ 405. BOBBY RICHARDSON
☐ 421. DUKE MAAS
☐ 430. ART DITMAR
☐ 465. COACHES CARD
☐ 480. YOGI BERRA
☐ 499. JOHNNY JAMES
☐ 522. KEN L. HUNT

PHILADELPHIA PHILLIES

☐ 13. WALLY POST
☐ 17. JOHNNY CALLISON
☐ 34. SPARKY ANDERSON
☐ 52. DAVE PHILLEY
☐ 64. JACK MEYER
☐ 82. RUBEN GOMEZ
☐ 97. TED LEPCIO
☐ 103. DICK FARRELL
☐ 130. FRANK HERRERA
☐ 138. ART MAHAFFEY
☐ 167. VALMY THOMAS
☐ 185. JIM OWENS
☐ 194. BOBBY GENE SMITH
☐ 211. TAYLOR PHILLIPS
☐ 226. EDDIE SAWYER(M)
☐ 251. BOBBY MALKMUS
☐ 264. ROBIN ROBERTS
☐ 285. HARRY ANDERSON
☐ 293. GENE CONLEY
☐ 302. TEAM CARD
☐ 319. JOE KOPPE
☐ 331. HENRY MASON
☐ 347. ED BOUCHEE
☐ 366. DALLAS GREEN
☐ 384. DON CARDWELL
☐ 416. HUMBERTO ROBINSON
☐ 438. JIM COKER
☐ 451. CURT SIMMONS
☐ 466. COACHES CARD
☐ 472. AL DARK
☐ 486. BOBBY DEL GRECO
☐ 511. KEN WALTERS
☐ 523. CLAY DALRYMPLE
☐ 541. TONY CURRY
☐ 549. JOHN BUZHARDT

PITTSBURGH PIRATES

☐ 2. ROMAN MEJIAS
☐ 20. ROY FACE
☐ 48. HAL W. SMITH
☐ 49. CURT RAYDON
☐ 55. BILL MAZEROSKI
☐ 58. GINO CIMOLI

1960 Topps

- ☐ 91. BENNIE DANIELS
- ☐ 104. DICK SCHOFIELD
- ☐ 113. BOB SKINNER
- ☐ 133. JULIAN JAVIER
- ☐ 145. JIM UMBRICHT
- ☐ 157. ROCKY NELSON
- ☐ 209. RON BLACKBURN
- ☐ 223. DANNY MURTAUGH(M)
- ☐ 238. DANNY KRAVITZ
- ☐ 258. DICK GROAT
- ☐ 272. FRED GREEN
- ☐ 284. DON GROSS
- ☐ 298. GEORGE WITT
- ☐ 326. BOB CLEMENTE
- ☐ 340. HARVEY HADDIX
- ☐ 361. BOB OLDIS
- ☐ 373. DON HOAK
- ☐ 393. SMOKY BURGESS
- ☐ 402. DICK STUART
- ☐ 414. DON WILLIAMS
- ☐ 437. BOB FRIEND
- ☐ 453. VERN LAW
- ☐ 467. COACHES CARD
- ☐ 484. TEAM CARD
- ☐ 496. BILL VIRDON
- ☐ 512. JOE GIBBON
- ☐ 526. PAUL GIEL
- ☐ 539. GENE BAKER

ST. LOUIS CARDINALS

- ☐ 16. ERNIE BROGLIO
- ☐ 24. DICK GRAY
- ☐ 40. JOE CUNNINGHAM
- ☐ 73. BOB GIBSON
- ☐ 84. HAL R. SMITH
- ☐ 101. BOB L. MILLER
- ☐ 120. DUKE CARMEL
- ☐ 124. JIM DONOHUE
- ☐ 149. BOB NIEMAN
- ☐ 168. ALEX GRAMMAS
- ☐ 195. LINDY MCDANIEL
- ☐ 197. RON KLINE
- ☐ 218. SOLLY HEMUS(M)
- ☐ 236. DICK RICKETTS
- ☐ 242. TEAM CARD
- ☐ 250. STAN MUSIAL
- ☐ 263. DARRELL JOHNSON
- ☐ 275. CURT FLOOD
- ☐ 291. BOB KEEGAN
- ☐ 307. GENE OLIVER
- ☐ 327. RAY SADECKI
- ☐ 355. BILL WHITE
- ☐ 368. DARYL SPENCER
- ☐ 383. LEON WAGNER
- ☐ 401. BOB DULIBA
- ☐ 419. GEORGE CROWE
- ☐ 446. ELLIS BURTON
- ☐ 468. COACHES CARD
- ☐ 485. KEN BOYER
- ☐ 492. LARRY JACKSON
- ☐ 517. CHARLEY JAMES
- ☐ 545. CARL SAWATSKI

JIM DAVENPORT
SAN FRANCISCO GIANTS   THIRD BASE

SAN FRANCISCO GIANTS

- ☐ 23. EDDIE FISHER
- ☐ 42. HOBIE LANDRITH
- ☐ 67. JOSE PAGAN
- ☐ 80. JOHNNY ANTONELLI
- ☐ 140. JULIO NAVARRO
- ☐ 144. AL STIEGLITZ
- ☐ 151. TEAM CARD
- ☐ 154. JIM DAVENPORT
- ☐ 165. JACK SANFORD
- ☐ 172. WILLIE KIRKLAND
- ☐ 181. BILLY LOES
- ☐ 192. DANNY O'CONNELL
- ☐ 200. WILLIE MAYS
- ☐ 225. BILL RIGNEY(M)
- ☐ 239. JOE SHIPLEY
- ☐ 253. EDDIE BRESSOUD
- ☐ 268. AL WORTHINGTON

- ☐ 287. FELIPE ALOU
- ☐ 303. BILLY O'DELL
- ☐ 316. WILLIE MCCOVEY
- ☐ 338. RAY MONZANT
- ☐ 356. JOE AMALFITANO
- ☐ 371. BUD BYERLY
- ☐ 378. STU MILLER
- ☐ 397. DON BLASINGAME
- ☐ 410. SAM JONES
- ☐ 431. ANDRE RODGERS
- ☐ 450. ORLANDO CEPEDA
- ☐ 469. COACHES CARD
- ☐ 479. GEORGES MARANDA
- ☐ 501. BOB SCHMIDT
- ☐ 530. MIKE MCCORMICK

WASHINGTON SENATORS

- ☐ 9. FAYE THRONEBERRY
- ☐ 25. ROY SIEVERS
- ☐ 43. TEAM CARD
- ☐ 56. STEVE KORCHECK
- ☐ 76. BILL FISCHER
- ☐ 87. JOHN ROMONOSKY
- ☐ 99. LENNY GREEN
- ☐ 114. KEN ASPROMONTE
- ☐ 123. DAN DOBBEK
- ☐ 136. JIM KAAT
- ☐ 175. PEDRO RAMOS
- ☐ 193. DICK HYDE
- ☐ 210. HARMON KILLEBREW
- ☐ 221. COOKIE LAVAGETTO(M)
- ☐ 231. HAL NARAGON
- ☐ 244. HAL GRIGGS
- ☐ 271. JULIO BECQUER
- ☐ 297. RENO BERTOILA
- ☐ 320. BOB ALLISON
- ☐ 334. TED ABERNATHY
- ☐ 344. CLINT COURTNEY
- ☐ 362. RUSS KEMMERER
- ☐ 392. TEX CLEVENGER
- ☐ 409. RON SAMFORD
- ☐ 432. CHUCK STOBBS
- ☐ 440. JIM LEMON
- ☐ 454. HAL WOODESHICK
- ☐ 470. COACHES CARD
- ☐ 483. CAMILO PASCUAL
- ☐ 503. DON LEE
- ☐ 508. BILLY CONSOLO
- ☐ 527. JOSE VALDIVIELSO
- ☐ 548. DON MINCHER

1961 TOPPS (587)
2 1/2" X 3 1/2"

HANK AARON
Outfield

BALTIMORE ORIOLES

- ☐ 10. BROOKS ROBINSON
- ☐ 26. WES STOCK
- ☐ 62. AL PILARCIK
- ☐ 71. JERRY ADAIR
- ☐ 85. JERRY WALKER
- ☐ 102. GENE STEPHENS
- ☐ 125. STEVE BARBER
- ☐ 131. PAUL RICHARDS
- ☐ 140. GUS TRIANDOS
- ☐ 143. RUSS SNYDER(B)
- ☐ 159. TEAM CARD
- ☐ 182. DAVE NICHOLSON
- ☐ 218. HAL BROWN
- ☐ 240. RON HANSEN
- ☐ 256. BILLY HOEFT
- ☐ 277. HANK FOILES
- ☐ 295. MILT PAPPAS
- ☐ 321. MARV BREEDING

- ☐ 343. EARL ROBINSON
- ☐ 369. DAVE PHILLEY
- ☐ 395. CHUCK ESTRADA
- ☐ 428. RAY BARKER
- ☐ 442. GORDON JONES
- ☐ 463. JACK FISHER
- ☐ 489. WALT DROPO
- ☐ 515. JACKIE BRANDT
- ☐ 545. HOYT WILHELM
- ☐ 559. JIM GENTILE

BOSTON RED SOX

- ☐ 16. BILLY MUFFETT
- ☐ 33. GARY GEIGER
- ☐ 53. RUSS NIXON
- ☐ 69. EARL WILSON
- ☐ 81. TRACY STALLARD
- ☐ 99. DON BUDDIN
- ☐ 113. MIKE FORNIELES
- ☐ 128. RIP REPULSKI
- ☐ 193. GENE CONLEY
- ☐ 210. PETE RUNNELS
- ☐ 221. MIKE HIGGINS(M)
- ☐ 236. DON GILE
- ☐ 257. CARROLL HARDY
- ☐ 268. IKE DELOCK
- ☐ 287. CARL YASTRZEMSKI
- ☐ 301. CHET NICHOLS
- ☐ 326. DAVE HILLMAN
- ☐ 340. VIC WERTZ
- ☐ 354. BILLY HARRELL
- ☐ 373. TEAM CARD
- ☐ 419. TOM BORLAND
- ☐ 434. TOM BREWER
- ☐ 445. FRANK MALZONE
- ☐ 454. PUMPSIE GREEN
- ☐ 499. CHUCK SCHILLING
- ☐ 519. JIM PAGLIARONI
- ☐ 540. JACKIE JENSEN
- ☐ 548. TED WILLS
- ☐ 562. BILL MONBOUQUETTE

CHICAGO CUBS

- ☐ 12. MOE THACKER
- ☐ 27. JERRY KINDALL
- ☐ 35. RON SANTO
- ☐ 58. JOE SCHAFFERNOTH
- ☐ 88. RICHIE ASHBURN
- ☐ 107. SETH MOREHEAD
- ☐ 122. TEAM CARD
- ☐ 141. BILLY WILLIAMS
- ☐ 169. DON ELSTON
- ☐ 196. ED BOUCHEE
- ☐ 214. DANNY MURPHY
- ☐ 231. DICK DROTT
- ☐ 253. SAMMY TAYLOR
- ☐ 264. GLEN HOBBIE
- ☐ 283. BOB ANDERSON
- ☐ 302. AL HEIST
- ☐ 317. JIM BREWER
- ☐ 350. ERNIE BANKS
- ☐ 364. MOE DRABOWSKY
- ☐ 382. FRANK THOMAS
- ☐ 427. DICK ELLSWORTH
- ☐ 441. DICK BERTELL
- ☐ 493. DON ZIMMER
- ☐ 512. BOB WILL
- ☐ 533. JACK CURTIS
- ☐ 551. GEORGE ALTMAN
- ☐ 564. DON CARDWELL

CHICAGO WHITE SOX

- ☐ 7. TEAM CARD
- ☐ 30. NELLIE FOX
- ☐ 56. RUSS KEMMERER
- ☐ 79. JOE GINSBERG
- ☐ 90. JERRY STALEY
- ☐ 124. J.C. MARTIN
- ☐ 132. AL LOPEZ(M)
- ☐ 152. EARL TORGESON
- ☐ 157. CAL MCLISH
- ☐ 170. AL SMITH
- ☐ 185. HERB SCORE
- ☐ 205. BILL PIERCE
- ☐ 227. JUAN PIZARRO
- ☐ 247. BILLY GOODMAN
- ☐ 271. JIM LANDIS
- ☐ 285. SHERM LOLLAR
- ☐ 303. GARY PETERS
- ☐ 323. SAMMY ESPOSITO
- ☐ 352. BOB SHAW
- ☐ 367. JIM RIVERA
- ☐ 380. MINNIE MINOSO
- ☐ 391. WINSTON BROWN
- ☐ 424. TURK LOWN
- ☐ 440. LUIS APARICIO
- ☐ 455. EARLY WYNN

☐ 470. ROY SIEVERS
☐ 509. CAMILO CARREON
☐ 529. BOB ROSELLI
☐ 550. FRANK BAUMANN

CINCINNATI REDS

☐ 9. BOB PURKEY
☐ 66. BILL R. HENRY
☐ 76. HARRY ANDERSON
☐ 97. JERRY LYNCH
☐ 110. VADA PINSON
☐ 135. FRED HUTCHINSON(M)
☐ 162. JAY HOOK
☐ 166. DANNY KRAVITZ
☐ 175. GENE FREESE
☐ 194. GORDY COLEMAN
☐ 215. GUS BELL
☐ 233. JOE JAY
☐ 244. CHICO CARDENAS
☐ 249. TEAM CARD
☐ 276. RAY RIPPELMEYER
☐ 292. JIM BAUMER
☐ 328. JIM O'TOOLE
☐ 346. HOWIE NUNN
☐ 360. FRANK ROBINSON
☐ 378. WALLY POST
☐ 399. CLIFF COOK
☐ 418. ED BAILEY
☐ 436. JIM MALONEY
☐ 456. HAL BEVAN
☐ 497. WILLIE JONES
☐ 513. JIM BROSNAN
☐ 534. EDDIE KASKO
☐ 556. KEN R. HUNT

CLEVELAND INDIANS

☐ 5. JOHN ROMANO
☐ 15. WILLIE KIRKLAND
☐ 18. JIM GRANT
☐ 34. WYNN HAWKINS
☐ 60. WOODIE HELD
☐ 77. DICK STIGMAN
☐ 101. BUBBA PHILLIPS
☐ 115. JOHNNY ANTONELLI
☐ 155. JOHNNY TEMPLE
☐ 172. DON DILLARD
☐ 191. MIKE DE LA HOZ
☐ 222. JIMMIE DYKES(M)
☐ 255. VIC POWER
☐ 274. GARY BELL
☐ 319. VALMY THOMAS
☐ 334. WALT BOND
☐ 345. JIM PIERSALL
☐ 362. FRANK FUNK
☐ 385. JIM PERRY
☐ 421. TY CLINE
☐ 452. BOB ALLEN
☐ 467. TEAM CARD
☐ 503. TITO FRANCONA
☐ 511. JOE MORGAN
☐ 532. BOB HALE
☐ 537. BOBBY LOCKE
☐ 560. BARRY LATMAN

DETROIT TIGERS

☐ 13. CHUCK COTTIER
☐ 14. DON MOSSI
☐ 37. CHARLIE MAXWELL
☐ 51. TEAM CARD
☐ 67. OSSIE VIRGIL
☐ 83. BOB BRUCE
☐ 95. NORM CASH
☐ 112. CHICO FERNANDEZ
☐ 151. JIM DONOHUE
☐ 171. PAUL FOYTACK
☐ 192. DICK BROWN
☐ 208. LARRY OSBORNE
☐ 223. BOB SCHEFFING(M)
☐ 239. DAVE SISLER(B)
☐ 243. FRANK LARY
☐ 251. BILL BRUTON
☐ 269. HARRY CHITI
☐ 284. DICK GERNERT
☐ 324. HANK AGUIRRE
☐ 330. ROCKY COLAVITO
☐ 348. STEVE BOROS
☐ 376. MIKE ROARKE
☐ 429. AL KALINE
☐ 439. PHIL REGAN
☐ 459. TERRY FOX
☐ 490. JIM BUNNING
☐ 514. JAKE WOOD
☐ 544. GEORGE THOMAS
☐ 553. BILL FISCHER

KANSAS CITY ATHLETICS

☐ 8. DICK WILLIAMS
☐ 24. KEN JOHNSON
☐ 39. LEO POSADA
☐ 57. MARV THRONEBERRY
☐ 94. JOHNNY KUCKS
☐ 106. WHITEY HERZOG
☐ 143. RUSS SNYDER(F)
☐ 177. DON LARSEN
☐ 197. DICK HALL
☐ 199. BOB BOYD
☐ 212. HAYWOOD SULLIVAN
☐ 224. JOE GORDON(M)
☐ 248. ED KEEGAN
☐ 267. NORM SIEBERN
☐ 297. TEAM CARD
☐ 322. BILL KUNKEL
☐ 342. CLINT COURTNEY
☐ 365. JERRY LUMPE
☐ 381. DAVE WICKERSHAM
☐ 384. CHUCK ESSEGIAN
☐ 398. HANK BAUER
☐ 416. DICK HOWSER
☐ 422. BUD DALEY
☐ 444. JOE NUXHALL
☐ 462. LOU KLIMCHOCK
☐ 498. RAY HERBERT
☐ 518. ANDY CAREY
☐ 536. BILL TUTTLE(F)
☐ 552. JIM ARCHER

ROCKY BRIDGES
Shortstop — Los Angeles Angels

LOS ANGELES ANGELS

☐ 65. TED KLUSZEWSKI
☐ 121. ELI GRBA
☐ 156. KEN L. HUNT
☐ 163. ED SADOWSKI
☐ 176. KEN ASPROMONTE
☐ 184. STEVE BILKO
☐ 195. JERRY CASALE
☐ 209. KEN MCBRIDE
☐ 216. TED BOWSFIELD
☐ 225. BILL RIGNEY(M)
☐ 246. BOB DAVIS
☐ 263. KEN HAMLIN
☐ 272. TOM MORGAN
☐ 282. FAYE THRONEBERRY
☐ 288. ALBIE PEARSON
☐ 291. TEX CLEVENGER
☐ 329. JULIO BECQUER
☐ 331. NED GARVER
☐ 358. EARL AVERILL
☐ 413. EDDIE YOST
☐ 448. DEL RICE
☐ 457. JOHNNY JAMES
☐ 464. LEROY THOMAS
☐ 466. RON MOELLER
☐ 508. ROCKY BRIDGES
☐ 527. GENE LEEK
☐ 547. LEON WAGNER

LOS ANGELES DODGERS

☐ 6. ED ROEBUCK
☐ 23. DON DEMETER
☐ 38. BOB LILLIS
☐ 74. JOE PIGNATANO
☐ 86. TEAM CARD
☐ 109. JOHNNY PODRES
☐ 130. NORM LARKER
☐ 136. WALT ALSTON(M)
☐ 147. ED RAKOW
☐ 168. TOMMY DAVIS
☐ 190. STAN WILLIAMS
☐ 238. JIM GILLIAM
☐ 260. DON DRYSDALE
☐ 280. FRANK HOWARD

☐ 298. JIM GOLDEN
☐ 325. WALLY MOON
☐ 344. SANDY KOUFAX
☐ 363. JOHN ROSEBORO
☐ 396. BOB ASPROMONTE
☐ 412. LARRY SHERRY
☐ 423. CHARLIE NEAL
☐ 443. DUKE SNIDER
☐ 460. GIL HODGES
☐ 492. RON FAIRLY
☐ 506. WILLIE DAVIS
☐ 522. DICK FARRELL
☐ 525. RON PERRANOSKI
☐ 543. ROGER CRAIG

MILWAUKEE BRAVES

☐ 29. DON NOTTEBART
☐ 61. RON PICHE
☐ 73. AL SPANGLER
☐ 84. LEE MAYE
☐ 89. BILLY MARTIN
☐ 105. CARL WILLEY
☐ 120. ED MATHEWS
☐ 137. CHUCK DRESSEN(M)
☐ 145. BOB BUHL
☐ 164. FELIX MANTILLA
☐ 183. ANDRE RODGERS
☐ 200. WARREN SPAHN
☐ 217. MEL ROACH
☐ 245. JOE ADCOCK
☐ 261. CHARLIE LAU
☐ 278. DON MCMAHON
☐ 296. WES COVINGTON
☐ 320. LOU BURDETTE
☐ 335. FRANK BOLLING
☐ 353. HOWIE BEDELL
☐ 372. BOB HENDLEY
☐ 390. DEL CRANDALL
☐ 415. HANK AARON
☐ 446. BOB TAYLOR
☐ 463. TEAM CARD
☐ 465. ROY MCMILLAN
☐ 496. KEN MACKENZIE
☐ 501. JOHN DEMERIT
☐ 524. JOHNNY LOGAN

MINNESOTA TWINS

☐ 4. LENNY GREEN
☐ 21. ZORRO VERSALLES
☐ 36. JACK KRALICK
☐ 63. JIM KAAT
☐ 80. HARMON KILLEBREW
☐ 92. HAL NARAGON
☐ 108. DAN DOBBEK
☐ 123. BILLY GARDNER
☐ 153. DON LEE
☐ 186. ELMER VALO
☐ 201. PETE WHISENANT
☐ 226. COOKIE LAVAGETTO(M)
☐ 235. CAMILO PASCUAL
☐ 254. TED SADOWSKI
☐ 289. RAY MOORE
☐ 315. EARL BATTEY
☐ 336. DON MINCHER
☐ 355. BOB ALLISON
☐ 374. PAUL GIEL
☐ 392. RENO BERTOIA
☐ 431. CHUCK STOBBS
☐ 450. JIM LEMON
☐ 469. RALPH LUMENTI
☐ 504. BILLY CONSOLO
☐ 528. PEDRO RAMOS
☐ 536. BILL TUTTLE(B)
☐ 542. TEAM CARD
☐ 557. JOSE VALDIVIELSO

NEW YORK YANKEES

☐ 2. ROGER MARIS
☐ 19. CLETIS BOYER
☐ 28. HECTOR LOPEZ
☐ 40. BOB TURLEY
☐ 68. DERON JOHNSON
☐ 104. JOHN BLANCHARD
☐ 116. JOE DEMAESTRI
☐ 133. RALPH HOUK(M)
☐ 142. LUIS ARROYO
☐ 160. WHITEY FORD
☐ 180. BOBBY RICHARDSON
☐ 213. BILL STAFFORD
☐ 228. TEAM CARD
☐ 252. BILL SHORT
☐ 265. TONY KUBEK
☐ 300. MICKEY MANTLE
☐ 333. FRITZ BRICKELL
☐ 349. DANNY MCDEVITT
☐ 356. RYNE DUREN

□ 371. BILL SKOWRON
□ 387. DUKE MAAS
□ 389. RALPH TERRY
□ 425. YOGI BERRA
□ 495. ELSTON HOWARD
□ 510. ART DITMAR
□ 531. JIM COATES
□ 541. ROLAND SHELDON
□ 563. BOB CERV

PHILADELPHIA PHILLIES

□ 3. JOHN BUZHARDT
□ 20. ROBIN ROBERTS
□ 59. JIM WOODS
□ 78. LEE WALLS
□ 93. TONY GONZALEX
□ 103. RUBEN AMARO
□ 111. JACK MEYER
□ 144. JIM COKER
□ 154. BOBBY DEL GRECO
□ 179. JOE KOPPE
□ 202. AL NEIGER
□ 219. GENE MAUCH(M)
□ 234. TED LEPCIO
□ 262. TONY CURRY
□ 281. FRANK SULLIVAN
□ 299. CLAY DALRYMPLE
□ 316. BOBBY GENE SMITH
□ 341. JIM OWENS
□ 359. DALLAS GREEN
□ 377. RUBEN GOMEZ
□ 394. KEN WALTERS
□ 411. TONY TAYLOR
□ 433. ART MAHAFFEY
□ 468. JOHNNY CALLISON
□ 491. TEAM CARD
□ 502. CLARENCE COLEMAN
□ 530. BOBBY MALKMUS
□ 558. DON FERRARESE

PITTSBURGH PIRATES

□ 1. DICK GROAT
□ 22. CLEM LABINE
□ 54. EARL FRANCIS
□ 70. BILL VIRDON
□ 82. JOE CHRISTOPHER
□ 100. HARVEY HADDIX
□ 126. DICK STUART
□ 138. DANNY MURTAUGH(M)
□ 149. BOB OLDIS
□ 165. GINO CIMOLI
□ 181. FRED GREEN
□ 204. BOB SKINNER
□ 230. DON HOAK
□ 242. HAL W. SMITH
□ 270. BOB FRIEND
□ 286. GEORGE WITT
□ 304. ROCKY NELSON
□ 339. GENE BAKER
□ 370. ROY FACE
□ 379. BOBBY SHANTZ
□ 388. BOB CLEMENTE
□ 400. VERN LAW
□ 430. BILL MAZEROSKI
□ 453. DICK SCHOFIELD
□ 461. SMOKY BURGESS
□ 494. TOM CHENEY
□ 523. JOE GIBBON
□ 554. TEAM CARD

ST. LOUIS CARDINALS

□ 11. CURT SIMMONS
□ 32. RAY SADECKI
□ 52. GEORGE CROWE
□ 64. ALEX GRAMMAS
□ 91. WALT MORYN
□ 118. CHRIS CANNIZZARO
□ 127. RON KLINE
□ 139. SOLLY HEMUS(M)
□ 148. JULIAN JAVIER
□ 178. BOB NIEMAN
□ 198. CARL SAWATSKI
□ 211. BOB GIBSON
□ 232. BILL WHITE
□ 241. AL CICOTTE
□ 266. LINDY MCDANIEL
□ 290. STAN MUSIAL
□ 314. BOB L. MILLER
□ 338. DON LANDRUM
□ 347. TEAM CARD
□ 357. DARYL SPENCER
□ 375. KEN BOYER
□ 420. ERNIE BROGLIO
□ 438. CURT FLOOD
□ 487. GENE OLIVER
□ 505. RED SCHOENDIENST

□ 520. JOE CUNNINGHAM
□ 535. LARRY JACKSON
□ 549. HAL R. SMITH
□ 561. CHARLEY JAMES

BILL WHITE
First Base

SAN FRANCISCO GIANTS

□ 31. BOB SCHMIDT
□ 55. JIM DAVENPORT
□ 72. STU MILLER
□ 87. JOE AMALFITANO
□ 96. BILLY O'DELL
□ 114. HOBIE LANDRITH
□ 150. WILLIE MAYS
□ 161. SHERMAN JONES
□ 167. TEAM CARD
□ 188. JIM MARSHALL
□ 203. EDDIE BRESSOUD
□ 220. AL DARK(M)
□ 237. BILLY LOES
□ 258. JACK SANFORD
□ 279. JOSE PAGAN
□ 294. DON BLASINGAME
□ 305. MIKE MCCORMICK
□ 327. MATTY ALOU
□ 366. EDDIE FISHER
□ 417. JUAN MARICHAL
□ 435. ORLANDO CEPEDA
□ 449. BOBBY BOLIN
□ 500. HARVEY KUEEN
□ 517. WILLIE MCCOVEY
□ 538. CHUCK HILLER
□ 555. SAM JONES
□ 565. FELIPE ALOU

WASHINGTON SENATORS

□ 117. DALE LONG
□ 129. ED HOBAUGH
□ 134. MICKEY VERNON(M)
□ 146. MARTY KEOUGH
□ 158. PETE DALEY
□ 174. RAY SEMPROCH
□ 187. BILLY KLAUS
□ 206. GENE GREEN
□ 229. RUDY HERNANDEX
□ 239. DAVE SISLER(F)
□ 259. JOHN SCHAIVE
□ 275. GENE WOODLING
□ 293. TOM STURDIVANT
□ 318. DANNY O'CONNELL
□ 332. DUTCH DOTTERER
□ 351. JIM KING
□ 368. BENNIE DANIELS
□ 386. JOE HICKS
□ 397. HAL WOODESHICK
□ 414. DICK DONOVAN
□ 432. COOT VEAL
□ 447. HARRY BRIGHT
□ 458. WILLIE TASBY
□ 488. JOE MCCLAIN
□ 507. PETE BURNSIDE
□ 526. R.C. STEVENS
□ 539. JOHNNY KLIPPSTEIN
□ 546. MARTY KUTYNA

1962 TOPPS (598)
2 1/2" X 3 1/2"

ERNIE BANKS
CHICAGO CUBS SS

BALTIMORE ORIOLES

□ 6. MARV BREEDING
□ 34. JOHNNY TEMPLE
□ 45. BROOKS ROBINSON
□ 64. RUSS SNYDER
□ 75. MILT PAPPAS
□ 99. BOOG POWELL
□ 112. HANK FOILES
□ 121. BILLY HITCHCOCK(M)
□ 134. BILLY HOEFT
□ 165. JACKIE BRANDT
□ 189. DICK HALL
□ 203. JACK FISHER
□ 221. BILL SHORT
□ 245. RON HANSEN
□ 272. EARL ROBINSON
□ 290. JIM GENTILE
□ 327. OSSIE VIRGIL
□ 355. STEVE BARBER
□ 382. DICK WILLIAMS
□ 420. GUS TRIANDOS
□ 442. WES STOCK
□ 449. JERRY ADAIR
□ 476. TEAM CARD
□ 488. HAL BROWN
□ 513. WHITEY HERZOG
□ 533. CHARLEY LAU
□ 545. HOYT WILHELM
□ 560. CHUCK ESTRADA
□ 577. DAVE NICHOLSON
□ 591. ART QUIRK(R)

BOSTON RED SOX

□ 3. PETE RUNNELS
□ 35. DON SCHWALL
□ 81. JIM PAGLIARONI
□ 101. CARROLL HARDY
□ 117. GARY GEIGER
□ 153. PUMPSIE GREEN
□ 187. GENE CONLEY
□ 201. IKE DELOCK
□ 225. FRANK MALZONE
□ 244. DON GILE
□ 276. HAL KOLSTAD
□ 301. GALEN CISCO
□ 334. TEAM CARD
□ 336. BILLY MUFFETT
□ 345. CHUCK SCHILLING
□ 368. BOB TILLMAN
□ 403. CHET NICHOLS
□ 425. CARL YASTRZEMSKI
□ 444. TED WILLS
□ 457. LOU CLINTON
□ 504. EDDIE BRESSOUD
□ 512. MIKE FORNIELES
□ 523. RUSS NIXON
□ 542. DAVE PHILLEY
□ 559. MIKE HIGGINS(M)
□ 567. TRACY STALLARD
□ 580. BILL MONBOUQUETTE
□ 591. DICK RADATZ(R)

CHICAGO CUBS

□ 25. ERNIE BANKS
□ 47. BOB WILL
□ 66. CUNO BARRAGON
□ 89. BARNEY SCHULTZ
□ 119. DANNY MURPHY

☐ 170. RON SANTO
☐ 191. JIM BREWER
☐ 240. GEORGE ALTMAN
☐ 264. DICK ELLSWORTH
☐ 274. SAMMY TAYLOR
☐ 288. BILLY WILLIAMS
☐ 309. MOE MORHARDT
☐ 359. BOBBY LOCKE
☐ 372. JACK CURTIS
☐ 387. LOU BROCK
☐ 446. DON ELSTON
☐ 458. BOB BUHL
☐ 461. KEN HUBBS
☐ 477. ANDRE RODGERS
☐ 495. DON CARDWELL
☐ 546. MOE THACKER
☐ 552. TEAM CARD
☐ 557. BOB ANDERSON
☐ 585. GLEN HOBBIE
☐ 597. JIM MCKNIGHT(R)

CHICAGO WHITE SOX

☐ 8. RAY HERBERT
☐ 73. NELLIE FOX
☐ 91. J.C. MARTIN
☐ 113. TEAM CARD
☐ 116. HERB SCORE
☐ 161. FRANK BAUMANN
☐ 178. CAMILO CARREON
☐ 195. JOE CUNNINGHAM
☐ 214. DOM ZANNI
☐ 255. JUAN PIZARRO
☐ 283. CHARLIE SMITH
☐ 286. AL LOPEZ(M)
☐ 325. LUIS APARICIO
☐ 341. MIKE HERSHBERGER
☐ 363. BOB ROSELLI
☐ 385. EARLY WYNN
☐ 410. AL SMITH
☐ 426. BOB FARLEY
☐ 454. FLOYD ROBINSON
☐ 479. JOEL HORLEN
☐ 514. SHERM LOLLAR
☐ 528. TURK LOWN
☐ 540. JIM LANDIS
☐ 555. JOHN BUZHARDT
☐ 576. RUSS KEMMERER
☐ 586. SAMMY ESPOSITO
☐ 595. BOB FRANK SADOWSKI(R)

CINCINNATI REDS

☐ 2. JIM BROSNAN
☐ 16. DARRELL JOHNSON
☐ 41. CLIFF COOK
☐ 80. VADA PINSON
☐ 103. DON BLASINGAME
☐ 120. BOB PURKEY
☐ 148. WALLY POST
☐ 151. JOHNNY KLIPPSTEIN
☐ 171. DAVE SISLER
☐ 172. FRED HUTCHINSON(M)
☐ 193. EDDIE KASKO
☐ 205. GENE FREESE
☐ 258. MARTY KEOUGH
☐ 267. DAN DOBBEK
☐ 282. DAVE HILLMAN
☐ 302. JOHN EDWARDS
☐ 331. MOE DRABOWSKY
☐ 350. FRANK ROBINSON
☐ 364. KEN R. HUNT
☐ 381. CHICO CARDENAS
☐ 414. JOE GAINES
☐ 440. JOE JAY
☐ 450. JIM O'TOOLE
☐ 465. TEAM CARD
☐ 478. DON ZIMMER
☐ 487. JERRY LYNCH
☐ 508. GORDY COLEMAN
☐ 524. HOWIE NUNN
☐ 562. BILL R. HENRY
☐ 594. DON PAVLETICH(R)

CLEVELAND INDIANS

☐ 15. DICK DONOVAN
☐ 49. HAL JONES
☐ 78. GENE GREEN
☐ 97. TITO FRANCONA
☐ 123. MIKE DE LA HOZ
☐ 145. BARRY LATMAN
☐ 182. BOB NIEMAN
☐ 215. WOODY HELD
☐ 224. DON RUDOLPH
☐ 242. MEL MCGAHA(M)
☐ 253. HARRY CHITI
☐ 273. GARY BELL
☐ 292. JERRY KINDALL
☐ 307. JIM GRANT

☐ 330. JOHNNY ROMANO
☐ 362. TY CLINE
☐ 379. CHUCK ESSEGIAN
☐ 405. JIM PERRY
☐ 447. WILLIE KIRKLAND
☐ 462. WILLIE TASBY
☐ 485. PEDRO RAMOS
☐ 511. BUBBA PHILLIPS
☐ 537. TEAM CARD
☐ 543. BOB ALLEN
☐ 563. KEN ASPROMONTE
☐ 587. FRANK FUNK
☐ 591. SAM MCDOWELL(R)
☐ 591. RON TAYLOR(R)
☐ 594. DOC EDWARDS(R)
☐ 598. AL LUPLOW(R)

DETROIT TIGERS

☐ 20. ROCKY COLAVITO
☐ 24. TEAM CARD
☐ 62. STEVE BOROS
☐ 87. MIKE ROARKE
☐ 92. SAM JONES
☐ 105. DON MOSSI
☐ 114. HOWIE KOPLITZ
☐ 150. AL KALINE
☐ 173. CHICO FERNANDEZ
☐ 196. TERRY FOX
☐ 216. RON KLINE
☐ 250. NORM CASH
☐ 261. GEORGE ALUSIK
☐ 299. DON WERT
☐ 335. BILL BRUTON
☐ 349. PAUL FOYTACK
☐ 366. PHIL REGAN
☐ 407. HANK AGUIRRE
☐ 416. BOB SCHEFFING(M)
☐ 427. JAKE WOOD
☐ 438. DICK BROWN
☐ 460. JIM BUNNING
☐ 481. VIC WERTZ
☐ 506. CHARLIE MAXWELL
☐ 527. DICK MCAULIFFE
☐ 554. BUBBA MORTON
☐ 583. LARRY OSBORNE
☐ 591. RON NISCHWITZ(R)

HOUSTON COLT .45'S

☐ 12. HARRY CRAFT(M)
☐ 23. NORM LARKER
☐ 44. DON TAUSSIG
☐ 74. BOB LILLIS
☐ 126. AL CICOTTE
☐ 156. MERRITT RANEW
☐ 177. BOBBY SHANTZ
☐ 204. JOHNNY WEEKLY
☐ 227. BOBBY TIEFENAUER
☐ 248. BOB ASPROMONTE
☐ 278. KEN JOHNSON
☐ 304. DICK FARRELL
☐ 332. DON BUDDIN
☐ 354. ROMAN MEJIAS
☐ 373. AL HEIST
☐ 419. BOB BRUCE
☐ 432. JIM PENDLETON
☐ 456. JOE AMALFITANO
☐ 483. DON MCMAHON(B)
☐ 492. HAL W. SMITH
☐ 509. DAVE GIUSTI
☐ 526. HAL WOODESHICK
☐ 536. DICK GERNERT
☐ 556. AL SPANGLER
☐ 568. JIM GOLDEN
☐ 574. DEAN STONE
☐ 598. ED OLIVARES(R)

KANSAS CITY ATHLETICS

☐ 13. DICK HOWSER
☐ 38. GENE STEPHENS
☐ 82. DERON JOHNSON
☐ 122. NORM BASS
☐ 147. BILL KUNKEL
☐ 168. LEO POSADA
☐ 184. HAYWOOD SULLIVAN
☐ 246. ART DITMAR
☐ 254. GORDON WINDHORN
☐ 275. NORM SIEBERN
☐ 305. JERRY LUMPE
☐ 333. FRANK CIPRIANI
☐ 342. ED RAKOW
☐ 357. JERRY WALKER
☐ 384. TEAM CARD
☐ 402. GINO CIMOLI
☐ 417. JOE AZCUE
☐ 433. JIM ARCHER
☐ 451. JOSE TARTABULL
☐ 463. HANK BAUER(M)
☐ 493. DANNY MCDEVITT
☐ 496. WAYNE CAUSEY
☐ 517. DAVE WICKERSHAM
☐ 548. BOBBY DEL GRECO
☐ 564. BOB GRIM
☐ 592. DAN PFISTER(R)
☐ 595. MARLAN COUGHTRY(R)
☐ 598. MANNY JIMENEZ(R)

LOS ANGELES ANGELS

☐ 11. TOM MORGAN
☐ 39. JOE KOPPE
☐ 68. KEN L. HUNT
☐ 96. ELI GRBA
☐ 128. ART FOWLER
☐ 132. TEAM CARD
☐ 154. LEE THOMAS
☐ 176. EDDIE YOST
☐ 194. DEAN CHANCE
☐ 209. JIM FREGOSI
☐ 257. JACK SPRING
☐ 268. KEN MCBRIDE
☐ 287. GEORGE WITT
☐ 343. ALBIE PEARSON
☐ 369. TED BOWSFIELD
☐ 388. RYNE DUREN
☐ 422. STEVE BILKO
☐ 431. BOB RODGERS
☐ 452. EARL AVERILL
☐ 491. LEON WAGNER
☐ 498. JIM DONOHUE
☐ 525. GEORGE THOMAS
☐ 539. BILLY MORAN
☐ 549. BILL RIGNEY(M)
☐ 569. ED SADOWSKI
☐ 592. BO BELINSKY(R)
☐ 595. FELIX TORRES(R)

LOS ANGELES DODGERS

☐ 5. SANDY KOUFAX
☐ 32. JOHN ROSEBORO
☐ 43. TEAM CARD
☐ 69. PHIL ORTEGA
☐ 108. WILLIE DAVIS
☐ 129. LEE WALLS
☐ 131. PETE RICHERT
☐ 175. FRANK HOWARD
☐ 190. WALLY MOON
☐ 197. DARYL SPENCER
☐ 217. WALT ALSTON(M)
☐ 238. NORM SHERRY
☐ 280. JOHNNY PODRES
☐ 297. RON PERRANOSKI
☐ 340. DON DRYSDALE
☐ 348. LARRY BURRIGHT
☐ 358. TOMMY DAVIS
☐ 375. RON FAIRLY
☐ 404. TIM HARKNESS
☐ 418. ANDY CAREY
☐ 435. LARRY SHERRY
☐ 486. JIM GILLIAM
☐ 500. DUKE SNIDER
☐ 515. STAN WILLIAMS
☐ 535. ED ROEBUCK
☐ 594. DOUG CAMILLI(R)

MILWAUKEE BRAVES

☐ 30. ED MATHEWS
☐ 63. TONY CLONINGER
☐ 76. HOWIE BEDELL
☐ 100. WARREN SPAHN
☐ 109. BOB SHAW
☐ 130. FRANK BOLLING
☐ 158. TEAM CARD
☐ 174. CARL WILLEY

☐ 186. MACK JONES
☐ 218. JOE TORRE
☐ 239. CECIL BUTLER
☐ 259. LOU KLIMCHOCK
☐ 265. JOE ADCOCK
☐ 289. MIKE KRSNICH
☐ 320. HANK AARON
☐ 361. BOB HENDLEY
☐ 380. LOU BURDETTE
☐ 406. BOB TAYLOR
☐ 443. DEL CRANDALL
☐ 483. DON MCMAHON(F)
☐ 518. LEE MAVE
☐ 541. DON NOTTEBART
☐ 582. RON PICHE
☐ 588. BIRDIE TEBBETTS(M)
☐ 594. BOB UECKER(R)
☐ 597. DENIS MENKE(R)
☐ 597. AMADO SAMUEL(R)

MINNESOTA TWINS

☐ 21. JIM KAAT
☐ 70. HARMON KILLEBREW
☐ 84. LENNY GREEN
☐ 102. AL SCHROLL
☐ 124. BILL PLEIS
☐ 164. HAL NARAGON
☐ 166. DON LEE
☐ 180. BOB ALLISON
☐ 208. BILLY MARTIN
☐ 222. JERRY ZIMMERMAN
☐ 230. CAMILO PASCUAL
☐ 298. BILL TUTTLE
☐ 321. LEE STANGE
☐ 339. JOSE VALDIVIELSO
☐ 346. JACK KRALICK
☐ 371. EARL BATTEY
☐ 386. DON MINCHER
☐ 437. RAY MOORE
☐ 445. VIC POWER
☐ 482. SAM MELE(M)
☐ 499. ZOILO VERSALLES
☐ 510. JIM LEMON
☐ 532. DICK STIGMAN
☐ 558. JOHN GORYL
☐ 584. TEAM CARD
☐ 592. JOE BONIKOWSKI(R)
☐ 596. BERNIE ALLEN(R)
☐ 596. RICH ROLLINS(R)

NEW YORK METS

☐ 4. JOHN DEMERIT
☐ 7. FRANK THOMAS
☐ 26. CHRIS CANNIZZARO
☐ 29. CASEY STENGEL(M)
☐ 85. GIL HODGES
☐ 94. JAY HOOK
☐ 162. SAMMY DRAKE
☐ 183. ROGER CRAIG
☐ 213. RICHIE ASHBURN
☐ 256. ELIO CHACON
☐ 279. HOBIE LANDRITH
☐ 293. BOB L. MILLER
☐ 308. NEIL CHRISLEY
☐ 337. JIM MARSHALL
☐ 365. CHARLEY NEAL
☐ 408. GUS BELL
☐ 421. KEN MACKENZIE
☐ 436. FELIX MANTILLA
☐ 464. AL JACKSON
☐ 497. ED BOUCHEE
☐ 572. BOB G. MILLER
☐ 593. CRAIG ANDERSON(R)
☐ 593. BOB MOORHEAD(R)
☐ 597. ROD KANEHL(R)
☐ 598. JIM HICKMAN(R)

NEW YORK YANKEES

☐ 1. ROGER MARIS
☐ 31. TOM TRESH
☐ 48. RALPH TERRY
☐ 65. BOBBY RICHARDSON
☐ 88. RALPH HOUK(M)
☐ 93. JOHN BLANCHARD
☐ 110. BILL SKOWRON
☐ 159. HAL RENIFF
☐ 169. BOB CERV
☐ 185. ROLAND SHELDON
☐ 200. MICKEY MANTLE
☐ 219. AL DOWNING
☐ 243. ROBIN ROBERTS
☐ 251. TEAM CARD
☐ 281. JAKE GIBBS
☐ 291. HAL STOWE
☐ 310. WHITEY FORD
☐ 338. BILLY GARDNER
☐ 360. YOGI BERRA

☐ 376. BUD DALEY
☐ 400. ELSTON HOWARD
☐ 430. TONY KUBEK
☐ 455. LUIS ARROYO
☐ 490. CLETE BOYER
☐ 502. HECTOR LOPEZ
☐ 553. JIM COATES
☐ 570. BILL STAFFORD
☐ 589. BOB TURLEY
☐ 592. JIM BOUTON(R)
☐ 596. PHIL LINZ(R)
☐ 596. JOE PEPITONE(R)

PHILADELPHIA PHILLIES

☐ 17. JOHN CALLISON
☐ 46. JACK BALDSCHUN
☐ 77. TONY TAYLOR
☐ 104. TED SAVAGE
☐ 111. DALLAS GREEN
☐ 146. DON DEMETER
☐ 157. WES COVINGTON
☐ 181. PAUL BROWN
☐ 212. JIM OWENS
☐ 220. ROY SIEVERS
☐ 249. ED KEEGAN
☐ 269. BOB OLDIS
☐ 284. RUBEN AMARO
☐ 294. TEAM CARD
☐ 303. FRANK TORRE
☐ 328. KEN WALTERS
☐ 352. FRANK SULLIVAN
☐ 374. GENE MAUCH(M)
☐ 434. CLAY DALRYMPLE
☐ 453. CAL MCLISH
☐ 494. SAMMY WHITE
☐ 521. JACKIE DAVIS
☐ 534. TONY GONZALEZ
☐ 550. ART MAHAFFEY
☐ 571. BILLY KLAUS
☐ 581. MEL ROACH
☐ 593. JACK HAMILTON(R)

PITTSBURGH PIRATES

☐ 10. ROBERTO CLEMENTE
☐ 36. DON LEPPERT
☐ 67. HARVEY HADDIX
☐ 86. DONN CLENDENON
☐ 95. DON HOAK
☐ 115. BOB SKINNER
☐ 160. DICK STUART
☐ 179. TOM STURDIVANT
☐ 210. ROY FACE
☐ 229. JESUS MCFARLANE
☐ 252. EARL FRANCIS
☐ 270. DICK GROAT
☐ 295. VERN LAW
☐ 326. TOM PARSONS
☐ 353. BILL MAZEROSKI
☐ 389. SMOKY BURGESS
☐ 409. TEAM CARD
☐ 415. BILL VIRDON
☐ 424. AL MCBEAN
☐ 448. JOE GIBBON
☐ 484. DICK SCHOFIELD
☐ 503. DANNY MURTAUGH(M)
☐ 520. BOB FRIEND
☐ 573. JOHNNY LOGAN
☐ 593. JACK LAMABE(R)
☐ 593. BOB VEALE(R)
☐ 598. HOWIE GOSS(R)

ST. LOUIS CARDINALS

☐ 14. BILL WHITE
☐ 19. RAY WASHBURN
☐ 28. MINNIE MINOSO
☐ 50. STAN MUSIAL
☐ 61. TEAM CARD
☐ 83. LARRY JACKSON
☐ 106. CARL SAWATSKI
☐ 118. JULIAN JAVIER
☐ 149. BOB DULIBA
☐ 167. TIM MCCARVER
☐ 198. JOHNNY KEANE(M)
☐ 202. CARL WARWICK
☐ 223. ALEX GRAMMAS
☐ 241. JOHNNY KUCKS
☐ 266. JOHN ANDERSON
☐ 285. CURT SIMMONS
☐ 323. DON LANDRUM
☐ 344. ED BAUTA
☐ 370. KEN BOYER
☐ 383. RAY SADECKI
☐ 412. CHARLIE JAMES
☐ 439. JERRY BUCHEK
☐ 489. JULIO GOTAY
☐ 507. ERNIE BROGLIO

☐ 522. LINDY MCDANIEL
☐ 530. BOB GIBSON
☐ 531. BOBBY GENE SMITH
☐ 547. DON FERRARESE
☐ 561. GENE OLIVER
☐ 575. RED SCHOENDIENST
☐ 579. JIM SCHAFFER
☐ 590. CURT FLOOD

SAN FRANCISCO GIANTS

☐ 9. JIM DAVENPORT
☐ 33. DON LARSEN
☐ 40. ORLANDO CEPEDA
☐ 71. DICK LEMAY
☐ 107. MIKE MCCORMICK
☐ 133. FELIPE ALOU
☐ 155. STU MILLER
☐ 188. CHUCK HILLER
☐ 199. GAYLORD PERRY
☐ 226. TEAM CARD
☐ 231. ERNIE BOWMAN
☐ 247. JOE PIGNATANO
☐ 260. BILL PIERCE
☐ 300. WILLIE MAYS
☐ 322. AL DARK(M)
☐ 329. BOB BOLIN
☐ 356. TOM HALLER
☐ 377. JOHNNY ORSINO
☐ 413. MATTY ALOU
☐ 429. BILLY O'DELL
☐ 459. ED BAILEY
☐ 480. HARVEY KUENN
☐ 505. JUAN MARICHAL
☐ 538. JACK SANFORD
☐ 544. WILLIE MCCOVEY
☐ 565. JOSE PAGAN
☐ 578. JIM DUFFALO

WASHINGTON SENATORS

☐ 27. CHUCK COTTIER
☐ 42. JIM KING
☐ 79. ED HOBAUGH
☐ 90. JIM PIERSALL
☐ 125. GENE WOODLING
☐ 152. MICKEY VERNON(M)
☐ 206. TEAM CARD
☐ 207. PETE BURNSIDE
☐ 228. DALE LONG
☐ 262. BOB SCHMIDT
☐ 271. RAY RIPPELMEYER
☐ 296. KEN HAMLIN
☐ 324. JOE MCCLAIN
☐ 347. CHUCK HINTON
☐ 378. BENNIE DANIELS
☐ 411. DANNY O'CONNELL
☐ 428. JOE HICKS
☐ 501. CLAUDE OSTEEN
☐ 519. BOB W. JOHNSON
☐ 529. JOHN SCHAIVE
☐ 551. HARRY BRIGHT
☐ 566. MARTY KUTYNA
☐ 592. DAVE STENHOUSE(R)
☐ 594. KEN RETZER(R)

1963 TOPPS (576)
2 1/2" X 3 1/2"

BALTIMORE ORIOLES

- [ ] 12. STEVE BARBER
- [ ] 19. PETE BURNSIDE
- [ ] 41. CHARLIE LAU
- [ ] 65. JACKIE BRANDT
- [ ] 88. RON HANSEN
- [ ] 108. HOYT WILHELM
- [ ] 112. DICK BROWN
- [ ] 125. ROBIN ROBERTS
- [ ] 158. BOB SAVERINE(R)
- [ ] 205. LUIS APARICIO
- [ ] 208. JOHN MILLER(R)
- [ ] 209. HOBIE LANDRITH
- [ ] 213. BILLY HITCHCOCK(M)
- [ ] 260. JIM GENTILE
- [ ] 286. STU MILLER
- [ ] 319. JOE GAINES
- [ ] 345. BROOKS ROBINSON
- [ ] 358. MILT PAPPAS
- [ ] 377. TEAM CARD
- [ ] 398. BOOG POWELL
- [ ] 418. JOHNNY ORSINO
- [ ] 438. WES STOCK
- [ ] 465. CHUCK ESTRADA
- [ ] 488. JERRY ADAIR
- [ ] 496. STEVE DALKOWSKI(R)
- [ ] 504. BOB W. JOHNSON
- [ ] 526. DICK HALL
- [ ] 543. RUSS SNYDER
- [ ] 562. DAVE MCNALLY(R)
- [ ] 563. MIKE MCCORMICK

BOSTON RED SOX

- [ ] 28. MIKE FORNIELES
- [ ] 52. CHUCK SCHILLING
- [ ] 76. EARL WILSON
- [ ] 96. LOU CLINTON
- [ ] 115. CARL YASTRZEMSKI
- [ ] 136. IKE DELOCK
- [ ] 168. RUSS NIXON
- [ ] 188. EDDIE BRESSOUD
- [ ] 202. TEAM CARD
- [ ] 216. GENE CONLEY
- [ ] 232. FRANK MALZONE
- [ ] 251. JACK LAMABE
- [ ] 253. PETE JERNIGAN(R)
- [ ] 285. DICK STUART
- [ ] 299. DAVE MOREHEAD(R)
- [ ] 307. CHET NICHOLS
- [ ] 328. DICK WILLIAMS
- [ ] 343. JOHNNY PESKY(M)
- [ ] 363. DICK RADATZ
- [ ] 384. BOB TILLMAN
- [ ] 408. BILLY GARDNER
- [ ] 432. ROMAN MEJIAS
- [ ] 447. FELIX MANTILLA
- [ ] 480. BILL MONBOUQUETTE
- [ ] 513. GARY GEIGER
- [ ] 553. JIM GOSGER(R)
- [ ] 574. HAL KOLSTAD

CHICAGO CUBS

- [ ] 15. KEN HUBBS
- [ ] 31. CAL KOONCE
- [ ] 54. NELSON MATHEWS(R)
- [ ] 58. BOB WILL
- [ ] 81. JIMMIE SCHAFFER
- [ ] 95. LARRY JACKSON
- [ ] 113. DON LANDRUM
- [ ] 175. BOB BUHL
- [ ] 193. ANDRE RODGERS
- [ ] 212. GLEN HOBBIE
- [ ] 222. TEAM CARD
- [ ] 252. RON SANTO
- [ ] 272. DANNY MURPHY
- [ ] 287. DICK BERTELL
- [ ] 309. JIM BREWER
- [ ] 329. LINDY MCDANIEL
- [ ] 353. BILLY WILLIAMS
- [ ] 380. ERNIE BANKS
- [ ] 399. DICK ELLSWORTH
- [ ] 416. ALEX GRAMMAS
- [ ] 452. BARNEY SCHULTZ
- [ ] 459. DICK LEMAY
- [ ] 464. KEN ASPROMONTE
- [ ] 472. LOU BROCK
- [ ] 489. PAUL TOTH
- [ ] 515. DON ELSTON
- [ ] 532. STEVE BOROS
- [ ] 557. CUNO BARRAGAN

CHICAGO WHITE SOX

- [ ] 16. AL SMITH
- [ ] 35. JOHN BUZHARDT
- [ ] 54. DAVE DEBUSSCHERE(R)
- [ ] 66. MIKE JOYCE
- [ ] 86. CHARLEY MAXWELL
- [ ] 100. JOE CUNNINGHAM
- [ ] 118. SHERM LOLLAR
- [ ] 160. JUAN PIZARRO
- [ ] 181. SAMMY ESPOSITO
- [ ] 223. EDDIE FISHER
- [ ] 234. DAVE NICHOLSON
- [ ] 253. DEACON JONES(R)
- [ ] 254. MIKE HERSHBERGER
- [ ] 271. DEAN STONE
- [ ] 288. TEAM CARD
- [ ] 308. CAMILO CARREON
- [ ] 324. PETE WARD(R)
- [ ] 332. JOEL HORLEN
- [ ] 354. DOM ZANNI
- [ ] 381. FRANK BAUMANN
- [ ] 405. FLOYD ROBINSON
- [ ] 424. CHARLEY SMITH
- [ ] 458. AL LOPEZ(M)
- [ ] 485. JIM LANDIS
- [ ] 499. J.C. MARTIN
- [ ] 522. GARY PETERS(R)
- [ ] 525. NELLIE FOX
- [ ] 537. AL WEIS(R)
- [ ] 560. RAY HERBERT

CINCINNATI REDS

- [ ] 21. MARTY KEOUGH
- [ ] 29. SAMMY ELLIS(R)
- [ ] 29. JESSE GONDER(R)
- [ ] 37. JERRY LYNCH
- [ ] 63. TEAM CARD
- [ ] 70. JIM O'TOOLE
- [ ] 90. GORDY COLEMAN
- [ ] 116. JIM BROSNAN
- [ ] 133. GENE FREESE
- [ ] 158. TOMMY HARPER(R)
- [ ] 178. JOHNNY EDWARDS
- [ ] 194. JOE NUXHALL
- [ ] 203. CHICO CARDENAS
- [ ] 225. JOE JAY
- [ ] 244. JOHN TSITOURIS
- [ ] 265. VADA PINSON
- [ ] 284. DAVE SISLER
- [ ] 304. HARRY BRIGHT
- [ ] 326. HANK FOILES
- [ ] 350. BOB PURKEY
- [ ] 378. BILL R. HENRY
- [ ] 400. FRANK ROBINSON
- [ ] 407. CHICO RUIZ(R)
- [ ] 422. FRED HUTCHINSON(M)
- [ ] 444. JIM MALONEY
- [ ] 462. WALLY POST
- [ ] 483. JIM OWENS
- [ ] 498. EDDIE KASKO
- [ ] 518. DON BLASINGAME
- [ ] 534. KEN WALTERS
- [ ] 537. PETE ROSE(R)
- [ ] 556. AL WORTHINGTON

CLEVELAND INDIANS

- [ ] 14. PEDRO RAMOS
- [ ] 36. JERRY KINDALL
- [ ] 48. BIRDIE TEBBETTS(M)
- [ ] 72. JOHNNY ROMANO
- [ ] 103. CHUCK ESSEGIAN
- [ ] 129. GARY BELL
- [ ] 152. RON NISCHWITZ
- [ ] 170. JOE ADCOCK
- [ ] 187. WILLIE KIRKLAND
- [ ] 211. FRED WHITFIELD
- [ ] 227. JIM GRANT
- [ ] 228. MAX ALVIS(R)
- [ ] 248. TITO FRANCONA
- [ ] 266. BOB ALLEN
- [ ] 296. DOC EDWARDS
- [ ] 317. SAM MCDOWELL
- [ ] 324. VIC DAVALILLO(R)
- [ ] 351. AL LUPLOW
- [ ] 370. DICK DONOVAN
- [ ] 391. BILL DAILEY
- [ ] 413. JERRY WALKER
- [ ] 426. BARRY LATMAN
- [ ] 435. WOODY HELD
- [ ] 451. TEAM CARD
- [ ] 463. JOE SCHAFFERNOTH
- [ ] 466. TONY MARTINEZ(R)
- [ ] 493. WALT BOND
- [ ] 506. GENE GREEN
- [ ] 558. BOB LIPSKI(R)
- [ ] 561. MIKE DE LA HOZ

DETROIT TIGERS

- [ ] 25. AL KALINE
- [ ] 44. TERRY FOX
- [ ] 64. DICK MCAULIFFE
- [ ] 84. RON KLINE
- [ ] 134. BOB SCHEFFING(M)
- [ ] 140. FRANK LARY
- [ ] 164. BUBBA MORTON
- [ ] 169. DICK EGAN(R)
- [ ] 177. BUBBA PHILLIPS
- [ ] 224. MIKE ROARKE
- [ ] 240. ROCKY COLAVITO
- [ ] 257. HANK AGUIRRE
- [ ] 278. CHICO FERNANDEZ
- [ ] 299. BOB DUSTAL(R)
- [ ] 302. WHITEY HERZOG
- [ ] 327. PAUL FOYTACK
- [ ] 348. VIC WERTZ
- [ ] 365. JIM BUNNING
- [ ] 379. BOB ANDERSON
- [ ] 406. HOWIE KOPLITZ
- [ ] 407. FRANK KOSTRO(R)
- [ ] 437. BILL BRUTON
- [ ] 445. NORM CASH
- [ ] 453. JAKE WOOD
- [ ] 466. BILL FREEHAN(R)
- [ ] 475. GUS TRIANDOS
- [ ] 494. PHIL REGAN
- [ ] 516. PURNAL GOLDY
- [ ] 530. DON MOSSI
- [ ] 552. TEAM CARD
- [ ] 558. BILL FAUL(R)
- [ ] 573. COOT VEAL

HOUSTON COLT .45'S

- [ ] 24. BOB BRUCE
- [ ] 45. BOB ASPROMONTE
- [ ] 77. AL SPANGLER
- [ ] 99. JIM UMBRICHT
- [ ] 119. BOB LILLIS
- [ ] 141. MANNY MOTA
- [ ] 153. HAL W. SMITH
- [ ] 158. DAVE L. ROBERTS(R)
- [ ] 189. DAVE GIUSTI
- [ ] 204. DON NOTTEBART
- [ ] 208. WALLY WOLF(R)
- [ ] 230. PETE RUNNELS
- [ ] 262. ELLIS BURON
- [ ] 277. DICK FARRELL

□ 297. JIM GOLDEN
□ 312. TEAM CARD
□ 324. GEORGE WILLIAMS(R)
□ 333. CARL WARWICK
□ 338. RUSS KEMMERER
□ 352. KEN JOHNSON
□ 373. JIM CAMPBELL
□ 386. JOHN BATEMAN(R)
□ 395. DON MCMAHON
□ 442. J.C. HARTMAN
□ 468. CARROLL HARDY
□ 491. HARRY CRAFT(M)
□ 517. HAL WOODESHICK
□ 538. GEORGE BRUNET
□ 544. RUSTY STAUB(R)
□ 553. BROCK DAVIS(R)
□ 562. RANDY CARDINAL(R)
□ 576. JOHNNY TEMPLE

KANSAS CITY ATHLETICS

□ 23. ED LOPAT(M)
□ 51. GEORGE ALUSIK
□ 67. ED CHARLES
□ 82. ED RAKOW
□ 104. LEW KRAUSSE
□ 124. DICK HOWSER
□ 157. DIEGO SEGUI
□ 195. MANNY JIMENEZ
□ 214. ORLANDO PENA
□ 236. BILL BRYAN
□ 253. JOHN WOJCIK(R)
□ 256. JERRY LUMPE
□ 282. BOB DEL GRECO
□ 301. BILL FISCHER
□ 321. GINO CIMOLI
□ 339. TED BOWSFIELD
□ 359. HAYWOOD SULLIVAN
□ 376. JOHNNIE WYATT
□ 397. TEAM CARD
□ 430. NORM SIEBERN
□ 449. JOSE TARTABULL
□ 461. NORM BASS
□ 492. DAVE WICKERSHAM
□ 501. JOE AZCUE
□ 521. DAN PFISTER
□ 539. WAYNE CAUSEY
□ 549. PETE LOVRICH(R)

BO
BELINSKY

LOS ANGELES ANGELS

□ 17. RYNE DUREN
□ 33. BO BELINSKY
□ 39. TEAM CARD
□ 57. BILLY MORAN
□ 98. GEORGE THOMAS
□ 114. DAN OSINSKI
□ 117. JACKE DAVIS
□ 167. JIM FREGOSI
□ 169. JULIO NAVARRO(R)
□ 182. ALBIE PEARSON
□ 207. KEN L. HUNT
□ 231. ELI GRBA
□ 249. LEO BURKE
□ 280. BOB RODGERS
□ 294. BILL RIGNEY(M)
□ 322. BOB TURLEY
□ 335. LEON WAGNER
□ 355. DEAN CHANCE
□ 372. DON LEE

□ 386. ED KIRKPATRICK(R)
□ 396. JOE KOPPE
□ 407. DICK SIMPSON(R)
□ 421. TOM MORGAN
□ 441. LEE THOMAS
□ 454. ART FOWLER
□ 482. FELIX TORRES
□ 496. FRED NEWMAN(R)
□ 510. KEN MCBRIDE
□ 522. MEL NELSON(R)
□ 527. ED SADOWSKI
□ 541. RON MOELLER
□ 548. TOM SATRIANO
□ 568. BOB FRANK SADOWSKI
□ 572. JACK SPRING

LOS ANGELES DODGERS

□ 11. LEE WALLS
□ 53. JOE MOELLER
□ 80. JIM GILLIAM
□ 105. RON FAIRLY
□ 123. FRANK HOWARD
□ 150. JOHNNY PODRES
□ 154. WALTER ALSTON(M)
□ 180. BILL SKOWRON
□ 196. DOUG CAMILLI
□ 210. SANDY KOUFAX
□ 229. WILLIE DAVIS
□ 261. BOB L. MILLER
□ 279. WALLY MOON
□ 295. ED ROEBUCK
□ 310. TOMMY DAVIS
□ 337. TEAM CARD
□ 360. DON DRYSDALE
□ 383. PETE RICHERT
□ 403. RON PERRANOSKI
□ 439. DON ZIMMER
□ 466. NATE OLIVER(R)
□ 467. PHIL ORTEGA
□ 487. JOHN ROSEBORO
□ 496. JACK SMITH(R)
□ 502. DARYL SPENCER
□ 537. KEN MCMULLEN(R)
□ 544. BILL HAAS(R)
□ 562. KEN ROWE(R)
□ 565. LARRY SHERRY

MILWAUKEE BRAVES

□ 46. TOMMIE AARON
□ 62. BOB HENDLEY
□ 73. BOBBY BRAGAN(M)
□ 74. DENVER LEMASTER
□ 109. LEE MAYE
□ 126. BOB UECKER
□ 137. MACK JONES
□ 156. ROY MCMILLAN
□ 179. RON PICHE
□ 201. CECIL BUTLER
□ 238. LOU JOHNSON
□ 253. LEN GABRIELSON(R)
□ 255. BOB SHAW
□ 275. ED MATHEWS
□ 298. DON DILLARD
□ 299. DAN SCHNEIDER(R)
□ 320. WARREN SPAHN
□ 324. PHILL ROOF(R)
□ 347. JOE TORRE
□ 367. TONY CLONINGER
□ 390. HANK AARON
□ 411. JIM CONSTABLE
□ 414. TY CLINE
□ 429. LOU BURDETTE
□ 433. DENIS MENKE
□ 460. DEL CRANDALL
□ 476. FRANK FUNK
□ 481. BOB TAYLOR
□ 503. TEAM CARD
□ 519. CLAUDE RAYMOND
□ 536. NORM LARKER
□ 547. GUS BELL
□ 554. HANK FISCHER
□ 570. FRANK BOLLING

MINNESOTA TWINS

□ 26. RAY MOORE
□ 40. VIC POWER
□ 75. BOB ALLISON

□ 89. DICK STIGMAN
□ 110. RICH ROLLINS
□ 127. BILL TUTTLE
□ 162. TEAM CARD
□ 165. JIM KAAT
□ 186. JERRY ZIMMERMAN
□ 198. LENNY GREEN
□ 220. CAMILO PASCUAL
□ 228. TONY OLIVA(R)
□ 246. LEE STANGE
□ 269. DON MINCHER
□ 293. BILL PLEIS
□ 314. JOHN GORYL
□ 349. ZOILO VERSALLES
□ 369. JIM LEMON
□ 386. GARRY ROGGENBURK(R)
□ 389. FRANK SULLIVAN
□ 410. EARL BATTEY
□ 427. BERNIE ALLEN
□ 448. JACK KRALICK
□ 500. HARMON KILLEBREW
□ 522. JIM ROLAND(R)
□ 531. SAM MELE(M)
□ 535. JIM PERRY
□ 549. PAUL RATLIFF(R)
□ 564. GEORGE BANKS

NEW YORK METS

□ 27. CHOO CHOO COLEMAN
□ 59. CRAIG ANDERSON
□ 78. MARV THRONEBERRY
□ 93. GALEN CISCO
□ 107. JIM HICKMAN
□ 111. AL JACKSON
□ 135. RICHIE ASHBURN
□ 174. LARRY BURRIGHT
□ 197. ROGER CRAIG
□ 217. JOE CHRISTOPHER
□ 228. ED KRANEPOOL(R)
□ 233. CASEY STENGEL(M)
□ 245. GIL HODGES
□ 273. SAMMY TAYLOR
□ 292. PUMPSIE GREEN
□ 316. NORM SHERRY
□ 334. WYNN HAWKINS
□ 342. GENE WOODLING
□ 371. ROD KANEHL
□ 386. LARRY BEARNARTH(R)
□ 393. KEN MACKENZIE
□ 419. TRACY STALLARD
□ 436. TIM HARKNESS
□ 469. JAY HOOK
□ 473. TEAM CARD
□ 495. FRANK THOMAS
□ 511. CHARLIE NEAL
□ 528. CARL WILLEY
□ 550. DUKE SNIDER
□ 558. AL MORAN(R)
□ 558. RON HUNT(R)
□ 562. DON ROWE(R)
□ 566. CLIFF COOK

NEW YORK YANKEES

□ 20. TONY KUBEK
□ 38. BUD DALEY
□ 42. STAN WILLIAMS
□ 54. JACK CULLEN(R)
□ 60. ELSTON HOWARD
□ 92. HECTOR LOPEZ
□ 120. ROGER MARIS
□ 155. BILL STAFFORD
□ 183. JOE PEPITONE
□ 200. MICKEY MANTLE
□ 237. JIM COATES
□ 247. TEAM CARD
□ 264. PHIL LINZ
□ 289. HAL BROWN
□ 315. RALPH TERRY
□ 340. YOGI BERRA
□ 361. CLETE BOYER
□ 382. RALPH HOUK(M)
□ 401. JIM BOUTON
□ 420. BOBBY RICHARDSON
□ 446. WHITEY FORD
□ 457. TEX CLEVENGER
□ 470. TOM TRESH
□ 484. DALE LONG
□ 507. ROLAND SHELDON

☐ 523. BILL KUNKEL
☐ 537. PEDRO GONZALEZ(R)
☐ 546. HAL RENIFF
☐ 555. JOHN BLANCHARD
☐ 569. LUIS ARROYO

PHILADELPHIA PHILLIES

☐ 13. TEAM CARD
☐ 29. JOHN BOOZER(R)
☐ 29. RAY CULP(R)
☐ 32. TONY GONZALEZ
☐ 56. DENNIS BENNETT
☐ 71. BOBBY WINE
☐ 91. DALLAS GREEN
☐ 132. JACK HAMILTON
☐ 139. EARL AVERILL
☐ 161. FRANK TORRE
☐ 192. CLAY DALRYMPLE
☐ 221. COOKIE ROJAS
☐ 241. BILLY SMITH
☐ 268. DON DEMETER
☐ 283. ROY SIEVERS
☐ 305. DON HOAK
☐ 318. GENE MAUCH(M)
☐ 341. JACK BALDSCHUN
☐ 366. TONY TAYLOR
☐ 385. ART MAHAFFEY
☐ 404. BOB OLDIS
☐ 434. JOHNNY CALLISON
☐ 455. RUBEN AMARO
☐ 478. PAUL BROWN
☐ 512. CAL MCLISH
☐ 529. WES COVINGTON
☐ 549. MARCELINO LOPEZ(R)
☐ 551. BILLY KLAUS
☐ 553. JOHN HERNSTEIN(R)
☐ 571. JOHNNY KLIPPSTEIN

PITTSBURGH PIRATES

☐ 34. DICK SCHOFIELD
☐ 55. BILL VIRDON
☐ 87. BOB VEALE
☐ 101. JOE GIBBON
☐ 122. JULIO GOTAY
☐ 151. TEAM CARD
☐ 159. JIM PAGLIARONI
☐ 169. TOMMIE SISK(R)
☐ 184. VERNON LAW
☐ 215. BOB SKINNER
☐ 228. BOB BAILEY(R)
☐ 239. HARVEY HADDIX
☐ 259. JOHNNY LOGAN
☐ 281. TOM STURDIVANT
☐ 299. TOM BUTTERS(R)
☐ 303. EARL FRANCIS
☐ 323. BILL MAZEROSKI
☐ 344. DON SCHWALL
☐ 364. HOWIE GOSS
☐ 387. AL MCBEAN
☐ 407. LARRY ELLIOT(R)
☐ 409. ROY FACE
☐ 425. SMOKY BURGESS
☐ 450. BOB FRIEND
☐ 477. DONN CLENDENON
☐ 508. TED SAVAGE
☐ 540. BOB CLEMENTE
☐ 549. ELMO PLASKETT(R)
☐ 553. WILLIE STARGELL(R)
☐ 559. DANNY MURTAUGH(M)
☐ 575. DON CARDWELL

ST. LOUIS CARDINALS

☐ 22. CURT SIMMONS
☐ 49. DAL MAXVILL
☐ 54. HARRY FANOK(R)
☐ 83. CHARLEY JAMES
☐ 97. BOB DULIBA
☐ 130. DICK GROAT
☐ 166. JOHNNY KEANE(M)
☐ 172. GENE OLIVER
☐ 190. MINNIE MINOSO
☐ 206. RAY WASHBURN
☐ 208. RON TAYLOR(R)
☐ 226. JULIAN JAVIER
☐ 250. STAN MUSIAL
☐ 267. CARL SAWATSKI
☐ 290. BILL WHITE

☐ 313. ERNIE BROGLIO
☐ 336. ED BAUTA
☐ 357. GEORGE ALTMAN
☐ 375. KEN BOYER
☐ 394. TIM MCCARVER
☐ 415. BOB GIBSON
☐ 486. RAY SADECKI
☐ 505. CURT FLOOD
☐ 524. TEAM CARD
☐ 533. BOBBY SHANTZ
☐ 544. DUKE CARMEL(R)

SAN FRANCISCO GIANTS

☐ 30. HARVEY KUEEN
☐ 50. BILL PIERCE
☐ 61. ERNIE BOWMAN
☐ 85. TOM HALLER
☐ 106. BOB BOLIN
☐ 128. MATTY ALOU
☐ 163. DON LARSEN
☐ 169. GAYLORD PERRY(R)
☐ 185. CHUCK HILLER
☐ 199. JOE AMALFITANO
☐ 208. RON HERBEL(R)
☐ 235. BILLY O'DELL
☐ 258. ALVIN DARK(M)
☐ 270. FELIPE ALOU
☐ 300. WILLIE MAYS
☐ 325. JACK SANFORD
☐ 346. BILLY HOEFT
☐ 368. ED BAILEY
☐ 388. JIM DAVENPORT
☐ 417. TEAM CARD
☐ 428. CARL BOLES
☐ 440. JUAN MARICHAL
☐ 456. JIM COKER
☐ 466. JERRY ROBINSON(R)
☐ 474. JACK FISHER
☐ 490. WILLIE MCCOVEY
☐ 520. ORLANDO CEPEDA
☐ 545. JOSE PAGAN
☐ 567. JIM DUFFALO

WASHINGTON SENATORS

☐ 47. DON LOCK
☐ 69. BUD ZIPFEL
☐ 94. BOB SCHMIDT
☐ 121. JIM HANNAN
☐ 131. TEAM CARD
☐ 149. MARV BREEDING
☐ 158. ROGELIO ALVAREZ(R)
☐ 171. STEVE HAMILTON
☐ 176. JIM KING
☐ 219. CHUCK COTTIER
☐ 243. DON LEPPERT
☐ 263. DAVE STENHOUSE
☐ 276. BARRY SHETRONE
☐ 291. DON RUDOLPH
☐ 311. JOE MCCLAIN
☐ 330. CHUCK HINTON
☐ 356. JOHN SCHAIVE
☐ 374. CLAUDE OSTEEN
☐ 402. MICKEY VERNON(M)
☐ 423. ED HOBAUGH
☐ 443. JIM PIERSALL
☐ 471. KEN RETZER
☐ 479. ED BRINKMAN
☐ 496. CARL BOULDIN(R)
☐ 497. BENNIE DANIELS
☐ 514. LARRY OSBORNE
☐ 522. ART QUIRK(R)
☐ 542. LOU KLIMCHOCK
☐ 544. DICK PHILLIPS(R)

1964 TOPPS (587)
2 1/2" X 3 1/2"

BALTIMORE ORIOLES

☐ 17. WILLIE KIRKLAND
☐ 22. JERRY ADAIR
☐ 45. MILT PAPPAS
☐ 63. JOHNNY ORSINO
☐ 89. BOOG POWELL
☐ 126. RUSS SNYDER
☐ 145. NORM SIEBERN
☐ 161. DAVE MCNALLY
☐ 178. HANK BAUER(M)
☐ 201. SAM BOWENS(R)
☐ 201. WALLY BUNKER(R)
☐ 221. BOB SAVERINE
☐ 230. BROOKS ROBINSON
☐ 239. HERM STARRETTE
☐ 263. CHUCK ESTRADA
☐ 285. ROBIN ROBERTS
☐ 304. BOB W. JOHNSON
☐ 322. GEORGE BRUNET
☐ 364. JOE GAINES
☐ 382. WES STOCK
☐ 399. JACKIE BRANDT
☐ 418. DAROLD KNOWLES(R)
☐ 418. LES NARUM(R)
☐ 439. HARVEY HADDIX
☐ 450. STEVE BARBER
☐ 473. TEAM CARD
☐ 487. MIKE MCCORMICK
☐ 511. LOU JACKSON
☐ 540. LUIS APARICIO
☐ 565. STU MILLER

BOSTON RED SOX

☐ 25. BILL MONBOUQUETTE
☐ 60. FRANK MALZONE
☐ 79. BOB HEFFNER
☐ 93. GARY GEIGER
☐ 112. BOB TILLMAN
☐ 153. DICK WILLIAMS
☐ 170. DICK RADATZ
☐ 186. ROMAN MEJIAS
☐ 210. CARL YASTRZEMSKI
☐ 228. FELIX MANTILLA
☐ 248. JOHNNY PESKY(M)
☐ 267. WILBUR WOOD
☐ 287. TONY CONIGLIARO(R)
☐ 287. BILL SPANSWICK(R)
☐ 305. JACK LAMABE
☐ 329. RUSS NIXON
☐ 352. ED BRESSOUD
☐ 376. DAVE MOREHEAD
☐ 410. DICK STUART
☐ 428. ARCHIE SKEEN(R)
☐ 428. PETE SMITH(R)
☐ 459. PETE CHARTON(R)
☐ 459. DALTON JONES(R)
☐ 481. CHUCK SCHILLING
☐ 503. EARL WILSON
☐ 526. LOU CLINTON
☐ 572. DAVE GRAY(R)
☐ 579. TEAM CARD

CHICAGO CUBS

- [ ] 29. LOU BROCK
- [ ] 55. ERNIE BANKS
- [ ] 78. MERRITT RANEW
- [ ] 96. BOB BUHL
- [ ] 111. DON ELSTON
- [ ] 131. STEVE BOROS
- [ ] 175. BILLY WILLIAMS
- [ ] 192. JOHN BOCCABELLA(R)
- [ ] 192. BILLY COWAN(R)
- [ ] 220. DICK ELLSWORTH
- [ ] 237. TEAM CARD
- [ ] 252. KEN ASPROMONTE
- [ ] 269. ELLIS BURTON
- [ ] 286. DON LANDRUM
- [ ] 309. PAUL TOTH
- [ ] 336. ANDRE RODGERS
- [ ] 359. JIM SCHAFFER
- [ ] 375. RON SANTO
- [ ] 408. JIM STEWART(R)
- [ ] 408. FRED BURDETTE(R)
- [ ] 424. DICK BERTELL
- [ ] 444. LARRY JACKSON
- [ ] 451. JOE AMALFITANO
- [ ] 469. FRED NORMAN(R)
- [ ] 469. STERLING SLAUGHTER(R)
- [ ] 486. BOB KENNEDY(HC)
- [ ] 510. LINDY MCDANIEL
- [ ] 548. WAYNE SCHURR(R)
- [ ] 557. LEO BURKE
- [ ] 578. GLEN HOBBIE

CHICAGO WHITE SOX

- [ ] 13. HOYT WILHELM
- [ ] 31. DAVE NICHOLSON
- [ ] 66. EDDIE FISHER
- [ ] 85. PETE WARD
- [ ] 107. BRUCE HOWARD
- [ ] 107. FRANK KREUTZER(R)
- [ ] 130. GARY PETERS
- [ ] 148. J.C. MARTIN
- [ ] 168. AL WEIS
- [ ] 195. FLOYD ROBINSON
- [ ] 215. RAY HERBERT
- [ ] 232. AL LOPEZ(M)
- [ ] 247. DAVE DEBUSSCHERE
- [ ] 264. JIM LANDIS
- [ ] 283. TOMMY MCCRAW
- [ ] 308. GENE STEPHENS
- [ ] 323. JOHN BUZHARDT
- [ ] 340. JOE CUNNINGHAM
- [ ] 368. FRITZ ACKLEY(R)
- [ ] 368. DON BUFORD(R)
- [ ] 384. RON HANSEN
- [ ] 401. CHARLIE MAXWELL
- [ ] 421. CAMILO CARREON
- [ ] 430. JUAN PIZARRO
- [ ] 453. FRANK BAUMANN
- [ ] 465. MIKE HERSHBERGER
- [ ] 496. TEAM CARD
- [ ] 538. MINNIE MINOSO
- [ ] 564. JERRY MCNERTNEY(R)
- [ ] 584. JOEL HORLEN

CINCINNATI REDS

- [ ] 33. SAMMY ELLIS(R)
- [ ] 33. MEL QUEEN(R)
- [ ] 49. BILL R. HENRY
- [ ] 72. CHICO CARDENAS
- [ ] 80. VADA PINSON
- [ ] 106. JOE NUXHALL
- [ ] 125. PETE ROSE
- [ ] 144. AL WORTHINGTON
- [ ] 166. MARTY KEOUGH
- [ ] 185. JIM O'TOOLE
- [ ] 207. FRED HUTCHINSON(M)
- [ ] 233. HAL W. SMITH
- [ ] 260. FRANK ROBINSON
- [ ] 275. JOHN TSITOURIS
- [ ] 303. JIM CAMPBELL
- [ ] 330. TOMMY HARPER
- [ ] 346. JOE JAY
- [ ] 356. BILL MCCOOL(R)
- [ ] 356. CHICO RUIZ(R)
- [ ] 377. BOB SKINNER
- [ ] 403. TEAM CARD

- [ ] 420. JIM MALONEY
- [ ] 436. CHARLIE NEAL
- [ ] 449. DERON JOHNSON
- [ ] 480. BOB PURKEY
- [ ] 507. JOHN EDWARDS
- [ ] 524. JIM DICKSON(R)
- [ ] 524. BOBBY KLAUS(R)
- [ ] 577. GORDY COLEMAN

CLEVELAND INDIANS

- [ ] 64. TED ABERNATHY
- [ ] 77. JERRY WALKER
- [ ] 105. WOODY HELD
- [ ] 122. DON MCMAHON
- [ ] 133. JIM GRANT
- [ ] 146. TOMMY JOHN(R)
- [ ] 146. BOB CHANCE(R)
- [ ] 172. TEAM CARD
- [ ] 184. AL LUPLOW
- [ ] 199. JOSE AZCUE
- [ ] 216. MIKE DE LA HOZ
- [ ] 234. GARY BELL
- [ ] 253. WALLY POST
- [ ] 301. LARRY BROWN
- [ ] 317. AL SMITH
- [ ] 338. JACK KRALICK
- [ ] 367. FRED WHITFIELD
- [ ] 391. SAM MCDOWELL
- [ ] 404. TONY MARTINEZ
- [ ] 435. VIC DAVALILLO
- [ ] 462. BIRDIE TEBBETTS(M)
- [ ] 478. DICK HOWSER
- [ ] 499. CHICO SALMON(R)
- [ ] 499. GORDON SEYFRIED(R)
- [ ] 515. JOHN ROMANO
- [ ] 530. LEON WAGNER
- [ ] 545. MAX ALVIS
- [ ] 552. TOM KELLEY(R)
- [ ] 552. SONNY SIEBERT(R)
- [ ] 562. PEDRO RAMOS
- [ ] 571. GENE CONLEY
- [ ] 583. TITO FRANCONA

DETROIT TIGERS

- [ ] 19. DON WERT
- [ ] 39. HANK AGUIRRE
- [ ] 58. DON DEMETER
- [ ] 67. TEAM CARD
- [ ] 98. BILL BRUTON
- [ ] 128. MICKEY LOLICH
- [ ] 143. BUBBA PHILLIPS
- [ ] 165. JERRY LUMPE
- [ ] 181. DAVE WICKERSHAM
- [ ] 197. FRANK LARY
- [ ] 236. BILL FAUL
- [ ] 250. AL KALINE
- [ ] 272. JAKE WOOD
- [ ] 292. MIKE ROARKE
- [ ] 312. FRITZ FISHER(R)
- [ ] 312. FRED GLADDING(R)
- [ ] 335. DON MOSSI
- [ ] 363. DICK MCAULIFFE
- [ ] 387. TERRY FOX
- [ ] 407. BILL FREEHAN
- [ ] 425. NORM CASH
- [ ] 443. CHARLIE DRESSEN(M)
- [ ] 461. GEORGE THOMAS
- [ ] 471. GATES BROWN
- [ ] 474. LARRY SHERRY
- [ ] 489. JULIO NAVARRO
- [ ] 491. ED RAKOW
- [ ] 512. WILLIE HORTON(R)
- [ ] 512. JOE SPARMA(R)
- [ ] 535. PHIL REGAN
- [ ] 572. DICK EGAN(R)

HOUSTON COLT .45'S

- [ ] 23. CHRIS ZACHARY
- [ ] 38. JIM WYNN
- [ ] 56. HAL BROWN
- [ ] 109. RUSTY STAUB
- [ ] 121. PETE RUNNELS
- [ ] 142. JOHN BATEMAN
- [ ] 158. KEN JOHNSON
- [ ] 179. CARL WARWICK
- [ ] 205. NELLIE FOX

- [ ] 226. JERRY GROTE(R)
- [ ] 226. LARRY YELLEN(R)
- [ ] 241. JIM OWENS
- [ ] 256. JOHNNY WEEKLY
- [ ] 282. BOB BRUCE
- [ ] 298. HARRY CRAFT(M)
- [ ] 321. BOB LILLIS
- [ ] 339. WALT BOND
- [ ] 354. DAVE GIUSTI
- [ ] 370. HAL WOODESHICK
- [ ] 389. JIM UMBRICHT
- [ ] 406. AL SPANGLER
- [ ] 434. DON NOTTEBART
- [ ] 467. BOB ASPROMONTE
- [ ] 492. JIM BEAUCHAMP(R)
- [ ] 492. MIKE WHITE(R)
- [ ] 504. CLAUDE RAYMOND
- [ ] 544. STEVE HERTZ(R)
- [ ] 544. JOE HOERNER(R)
- [ ] 560. DICK FARRELL

ATHLETICS

ORLANDO PENA   pitcher

KANSAS CITY ATHLETICS

- [ ] 26. GINO CIMOLI
- [ ] 42. MOE DRABOWSKY
- [ ] 75. WAYNE CAUSEY
- [ ] 108. JOHN WYATT
- [ ] 124. ORLANDO PENA
- [ ] 151. TEAM CARD
- [ ] 174. DOC EDWARDS
- [ ] 196. JIM GENTILE
- [ ] 212. PETE LOVRICH
- [ ] 229. CHARLEY LAU
- [ ] 244. TONY LARUSSA
- [ ] 276. JOSE TARTABULL
- [ ] 302. DAN PFISTER
- [ ] 320. ROCKY COLAVITO
- [ ] 334. LEW KRAUSSE
- [ ] 348. ED LOPAT(M)
- [ ] 366. NELSON MATHEWS
- [ ] 388. JOHN O'DONOGHUE(R)
- [ ] 388. GEORGE WILLIAMS(R)
- [ ] 402. TOM STURDIVANT
- [ ] 419. KEN HARRELSON
- [ ] 431. GEORGE ALUSIK
- [ ] 447. TED BOWSFIELD
- [ ] 466. DICK GREEN(R)
- [ ] 466. AURELIO MONTEAGUDO(R)
- [ ] 475. ED CHARLES
- [ ] 508. DIEGO SEGUI
- [ ] 528. DAVE DUNCAN(R)
- [ ] 528. TOM REYNOLDS(R)
- [ ] 574. MANNY JIMENEZ

LOS ANGELES ANGELS

- [ ] 32. DEAN CHANCE
- [ ] 48. BOB PERRY
- [ ] 71. JACK SPRING
- [ ] 97. JIM FREGOSI
- [ ] 110. ALBIE PEARSON
- [ ] 127. AUBREY GATEWOOD(R)
- [ ] 127. DICK SIMPSON(R)
- [ ] 149. PAUL FOYTACK
- [ ] 159. CHARLIE DEES
- [ ] 213. TEAM CARD
- [ ] 227. BARRY LATMAN
- [ ] 255. LEE THOMAS
- [ ] 273. MEL NELSON

☐ 279. JOE KOPPE
☐ 296. ED KIRKPATRICK
☐ 315. BO BELINSKY
☐ 333. BILLY MORAN
☐ 349. ART FOWLER
☐ 383. BILL RIGNEY
☐ 405. KEN MCBRIDE
☐ 426. BOB RODGERS
☐ 441. BOB DULIBA
☐ 493. DON LEE
☐ 502. BOBBY KNOOP(R)
☐ 502. BOB LEE(R)
☐ 521. TOM SATRIANO
☐ 537. DAN OSINSKI
☐ 554. HANK FOILES
☐ 569. FRED NEWMAN
☐ 586. JIM PIERSALL

LOS ANGELES DODGERS

☐ 14. DICK NEN(R)
☐ 14. NICK WILLHITE(R)
☐ 30. RON PERRANOSKI
☐ 51. PETE RICHERT
☐ 68. WILLIE DAVIS
☐ 88. JOHN ROSEBORO
☐ 101. WALT ALSTON(M)
☐ 120. DON DRYSDALE
☐ 154. DICK TRACEWSKI
☐ 180. TOMMY DAVIS
☐ 200. SANDY KOUFAX
☐ 214. KEN MCMULLEN
☐ 231. DICK CALMUS
☐ 249. DOUG CAMILLI
☐ 291. PHIL ORTEGA
☐ 310. JIM GILLIAM
☐ 337. AL FERRARA(R)
☐ 337. JEFF TORBORG(R)
☐ 353. WALLY MOON
☐ 371. FRANK HOWARD
☐ 394. BOB L. MILLER
☐ 411. LEE WALLS
☐ 456. WES PARKER(R)
☐ 456. JOHN WERHAS(R)
☐ 490. RON FAIRLY
☐ 531. TEAM CARD
☐ 548. PAUL SPECKENBACH(R)
☐ 549. JOE MOELLER
☐ 553. JIM BREWER
☐ 580. JOHNNY PODRES

MILWAUKEE BRAVES

☐ 35. ED MATHEWS
☐ 53. DENIS MENKE
☐ 65. FELIPE ALOU
☐ 70. JOE TORRE
☐ 94. JIM BRITTON(R)
☐ 94. LARRY MAXIE(R)
☐ 115. FRANK BOLLING
☐ 132. TEAM CARD
☐ 152. DENVER LEMASTER
☐ 171. TY CLINE
☐ 198. LEN GABRIELSON
☐ 218. HANK FISCHER
☐ 238. ROY MCMILLAN
☐ 271. BOB SADOWSKI
☐ 289. FRANK FUNK
☐ 300. HANK AARON
☐ 316. GENE OLIVER
☐ 351. DAN SCHNEIDER
☐ 378. WOODY WOODWARD(R)
☐ 378. JACK SMITH(R)
☐ 400. WARREN SPAHN
☐ 416. LEE MAYE
☐ 437. ED BAILEY
☐ 454. TOMMIE AARON
☐ 476. RICO CARTY(R)
☐ 476. DICK KELLEY(R)
☐ 506. BOBBY BRAGAN(M)
☐ 522. BOB TIEFENAUER
☐ 534. GUS BELL
☐ 541. PHIL ROOF(R)
☐ 541. PHIL NIEKRO(R)
☐ 551. BILLY HOEFT
☐ 575. TONY CLONINGER

MINNESOTA TWINS

☐ 15. ZOILO VERSALLES
☐ 34. JIM PERRY
☐ 54. SAM MELE(M)
☐ 73. JIMMIE HALL
☐ 90. EARL BATTEY
☐ 116. JAY WARD(R)
☐ 116. TONY OLIVA(R)
☐ 156. BILL DAILEY
☐ 177. HARMON KILLEBREW
☐ 194. JOHN GORYL
☐ 223. GEORGE BANKS
☐ 245. DICK STIGMAN
☐ 258. GARRY ROGGENBURK
☐ 270. RICH ROLLINS
☐ 290. BOB ALLISON
☐ 318. TEAM CARD
☐ 341. JIM ROLAND
☐ 355. VIC POWER
☐ 369. JERRY ZIMMERMAN
☐ 386. LENNY GREEN
☐ 409. BILL FISCHER
☐ 455. BERNIE ALLEN
☐ 484. BILL PLEIS
☐ 500. CAMILO PASCUAL
☐ 516. JERRY ARRIGO(R)
☐ 516. DWIGHT SIEBLER(R)
☐ 532. BUD BLOOMFIELD(R)
☐ 532. JOE NOSSEK(R)
☐ 542. DON MINCHER
☐ 555. LEE STANGE
☐ 564. JOE MCCABE(R)
☐ 567. JIM KAAT

NEW YORK METS

☐ 27. TEAM CARD
☐ 44. DUKE CARMEL
☐ 57. TIM HARKNESS
☐ 84. CARL WILLEY
☐ 95. GEORGE ALTMAN
☐ 113. GROVER POWELL
☐ 129. AMADO SAMUEL
☐ 155. DUKE SNIDER
☐ 176. TRACY STALLARD
☐ 202. GALEN CISCO
☐ 235. RON HUNT
☐ 251. CHOO CHOO COLEMAN
☐ 288. AL MORAN
☐ 324. CASEY STENGEL(M)
☐ 345. FRANK THOMAS
☐ 361. JAY HOOK
☐ 381. BOB TAYLOR
☐ 398. BILL HAAS(R)
☐ 398. DICK SMITH(R)
☐ 422. JACK FISHER
☐ 442. PUMPSIE GREEN
☐ 457. JESSE GONDER
☐ 477. MIKE JOYCE
☐ 494. AL JACKSON
☐ 514. JIM HICKMAN
☐ 519. CHARLIE SMITH
☐ 527. LARRY BEARNARTH
☐ 536. LARRY ELLIOT(R)
☐ 536. JOHN STEPHENSON(R)
☐ 546. JOE CHRISTOPHER
☐ 556. STEVE DILLON(R)
☐ 556. RON LOCKE(R)
☐ 566. ED KRANEPOOL
☐ 576. JERRY HINSLEY(R)
☐ 576. BILL WAKEFIELD
☐ 582. ROD KANEHL

NEW YORK YANKEES

☐ 21. YOGI BERRA(M)
☐ 36. HAL RENIFF
☐ 50. MICKEY MANTLE
☐ 69. CLETE BOYER
☐ 86. AL DOWNING
☐ 100. ELSTON HOWARD
☐ 118. JOHN BLANCHARD
☐ 164. BUD DALEY
☐ 190. BOBBY RICHARDSON
☐ 206. STEVE HAMILTON
☐ 225. ROGER MARIS
☐ 259. HARRY BRIGHT
☐ 281. JAKE GIBBS(R)
☐ 281. TOM METCALF(R)

☐ 299. BILL STAFFORD
☐ 325. HECTOR LOPEZ
☐ 344. PHIL LINZ
☐ 360. JOE PEPITONE
☐ 380. WHITEY FORD
☐ 395. TOM TRESH
☐ 415. TONY KUBEK
☐ 433. TEAM CARD
☐ 458. RALPH TERRY
☐ 470. JIM BOUTON
☐ 488. PETE MIKKELSEN(R)
☐ 488. BOB MEYER(R)
☐ 505. STAN WILLIAMS
☐ 581. PEDRO GONZALEZ(R)
☐ 581. ARCHIE MOORE(R)

PHILADELPHIA PHILLIES

☐ 16. JOHN BOOZER
☐ 43. ROY SIEVERS
☐ 83. GUS TRIANDOS
☐ 104. ART MAHAFFEY
☐ 135. JOHNNY CALLISON
☐ 157. GENE MAUCH(M)
☐ 173. RYNE DUREN
☐ 191. CLAY DALRYMPLE
☐ 208. WES COVINGTON
☐ 243. RICHIE ALLEN
☐ 243. JOHN HERRNSTEIN(R)
☐ 254. DON HOAK
☐ 265. JIM BUNNING
☐ 293. TEAM CARD
☐ 319. PAUL BROWN
☐ 347. BOBBY WINE
☐ 365. CAL MCLISH
☐ 379. TONY GONZALEZ
☐ 396. DENNIS BENNETT
☐ 412. RAY CULP
☐ 432. RUBEN AMARO
☐ 448. COOKIE ROJAS
☐ 464. DALLAS GREEN
☐ 482. JOHN BRIGGS(R)
☐ 482. DANNY CARTER(R)
☐ 520. JACK BALDSCHUN
☐ 533. JOHNNY KLIPPSTEIN
☐ 561. DAVE BENNETT(R)
☐ 561. RICK WISE(R)
☐ 585. TONY TAYLOR

PITTSBURGH PIRATES

☐ 20. BOB FRIEND
☐ 37. SMOKY BURGESS
☐ 62. TED SAVAGE
☐ 74. BOB PRIDDY(R)
☐ 74. TOM BUTTERS(R)
☐ 91. BOB BAILEY
☐ 117. EARL FRANCIS
☐ 141. DANNY MURTAUGH(M)
☐ 163. DONN CLENDENON
☐ 193. JERRY LYNCH
☐ 209. BOB ALLEN
☐ 224. TOMMIE SISK
☐ 246. MANNY MOTA
☐ 266. GENE FREESE
☐ 284. DICK SCHOFIELD
☐ 307. JOE GIBBON
☐ 326. RON BRAND
☐ 342. WILLIE STARGELL
☐ 373. TEAM CARD
☐ 392. JIM PAGLIARONI
☐ 417. DON CARDWELL
☐ 440. BOB CLEMENTE
☐ 472. VERNON LAW
☐ 495. BILL VIRDON
☐ 501. BOB VEALE
☐ 509. GENE ALLEY(R)
☐ 509. ORLANDO MCFARLANE(R)
☐ 525. AL MCBEAN
☐ 539. ROY FACE
☐ 558. DON SCHWALL
☐ 570. BILL MAZEROSKI

ST. LOUIS CARDINALS

☐ 24. CARL SAWATSKI
☐ 40. DICK GROAT
☐ 59. ERNIE BROGLIO
☐ 87. TEAM CARD
☐ 103. CURT FLOOD

1964 Topps

- ☐ 119. GARY KOLB
- ☐ 147. RAY SADECKI
- ☐ 160. KEN BOYER
- ☐ 183. RON TAYLOR
- ☐ 211. JIM COKER
- ☐ 240. BILL WHITE
- ☐ 262. MIKE SHANNON(R)
- ☐ 262. HARRY FANOK(R)
- ☐ 278. BOBBY SHANTZ
- ☐ 295. ROGER CRAIG
- ☐ 314. JERRY BUCHEK
- ☐ 332. RAY WASHBURN
- ☐ 357. CHARLIE JAMES
- ☐ 385. CURT SIMMONS
- ☐ 413. JOHNNY KEANE(M)
- ☐ 429. TIM MCCARVER
- ☐ 446. JULIAN JAVIER
- ☐ 460. BOB GIBSON
- ☐ 479. DAVE BAKENHASTER(R)
- ☐ 479. JOHNNY LEWIS(R)
- ☐ 497. JEOFF LONG
- ☐ 523. LOU BURDETTE
- ☐ 543. BOB UECKER
- ☐ 563. DAL MAXVILL
- ☐ 568. PHIL GAGLIANO(R)

SAN FRANCISCO GIANTS

- ☐ 18. BILLY O'DELL
- ☐ 47. JESUS ALOU(R)
- ☐ 47. RON HERBEL(R)
- ☐ 82. JIM DAVENPORT
- ☐ 99. AL STANEK
- ☐ 123. JOSE PAGAN
- ☐ 150. WILLIE MAYS
- ☐ 169. DEL CRANDALL
- ☐ 189. BOB HENDLEY
- ☐ 204. MATTY ALOU
- ☐ 222. BILL PIERCE
- ☐ 242. HARVEY KUENN
- ☐ 257. TEAM CARD
- ☐ 280. JUAN MARICHAL
- ☐ 297. KEN MACKENZIE
- ☐ 313. CHUCK HILLER
- ☐ 328. BOB SHAW
- ☐ 350. WILLIE MCCOVEY
- ☐ 374. BOBBY BOLIN
- ☐ 390. ORLANDO CEPEDA
- ☐ 414. JACK SANFORD
- ☐ 452. GIL GARRIDO(R)
- ☐ 452. JIM HART(R)
- ☐ 468. GAYLOR PERRY
- ☐ 485. TOM HALLER
- ☐ 513. DON LARSEN
- ☐ 529. AL DARK(M)
- ☐ 568. CAP PETERSON(R)
- ☐ 573. JIM DUFFALO

DON ZIMMER   3rd base

WASHINGTON SENATORS

- ☐ 28. CLAUDE OSTEEN
- ☐ 46. ED BRINKMAN
- ☐ 52. CHUCK HINTON
- ☐ 92. STEVE RIDZIK
- ☐ 114. DON LOCK
- ☐ 134. DON ZIMMER
- ☐ 167. MIKE BRUMLEY(R)
- ☐ 167. LOU PINIELLA(R)
- ☐ 187. ED ROEBUCK
- ☐ 203. JOHN KENNEDY

- ☐ 217. JIM KING
- ☐ 261. JIM HANNAN
- ☐ 277. KEN RETZER
- ☐ 294. KEN L. HUNT
- ☐ 311. TOM BROWN
- ☐ 327. DON BLASINGAME
- ☐ 343. TEAM CARD
- ☐ 358. RON KLINE
- ☐ 372. HOWIE KOPLITZ
- ☐ 397. CHUCK COTTIER
- ☐ 427. DON RUDOLPH
- ☐ 445. BILL SKOWRON
- ☐ 463. DON LEPPERT
- ☐ 483. FRED VALENTINE
- ☐ 498. DAVE STENHOUSE
- ☐ 518. CARL BOULDIN
- ☐ 547. GIL HODGES(M)
- ☐ 559. DICK PHILLIPS
- ☐ 587. BENNIE DANIELS

1965 TOPPS (598)
2 1/2" X 3 1/2"

PITCHER
ROBIN ROBERTS

BALTIMORE ORIOLES

- ☐ 15. ROBIN ROBERTS
- ☐ 33. JACKIE BRANDT
- ☐ 49. CURT BLEFARY(R)
- ☐ 49. JOHN MILLER()(R)
- ☐ 67. HARVEY HADDIX
- ☐ 94. CHARLIE LAU
- ☐ 113. STEVE BARBER
- ☐ 150. BROOKS ROBINSON
- ☐ 169. DAVE VINEYARD
- ☐ 188. SAM BOWENS
- ☐ 204. RUSS SNYDER
- ☐ 231. JERRY ADAIR
- ☐ 249. DAVE MCNALLY
- ☐ 270. MILT PAPPAS
- ☐ 290. WALLY BUNKER
- ☐ 303. JOHNNY ORSINO
- ☐ 323. HANK BAUER
- ☐ 343. MIKE MCCORMICK
- ☐ 363. BOB W. JOHNSON
- ☐ 378. CHUCK ESTRADA
- ☐ 396. FRANK BERTAINA
- ☐ 410. LUIS APARICIO
- ☐ 427. BOB SAVERINE
- ☐ 455. NORM SIEBERN
- ☐ 473. PAUL BLAIR(R)
- ☐ 473. DAVE A. JOHNSON(R)
- ☐ 499. STU MILLER
- ☐ 518. KEN ROWE
- ☐ 539. HERM STARRETTE
- ☐ 560. BOOG POWELL
- ☐ 572. TEAM CARD
- ☐ 577. DAROLD KNOWLES(R)

BOSTON RED SOX

- ☐ 29. FELIX MANTILLA
- ☐ 42. EARL WILSON
- ☐ 55. TONY CONIGLIARO
- ☐ 74. RICO PETROCELLI(R)
- ☐ 74. JERRY STEPHENSON(R)
- ☐ 88. JACK LAMABE
- ☐ 111. LEE THOMAS
- ☐ 142. BILL MONBOUQUETTE

- ☐ 147. DENNIS BENNETT
- ☐ 162. RUSS NIXON
- ☐ 178. DALTON JONES
- ☐ 199. BOB HEFFNER
- ☐ 222. BOB TILLMAN
- ☐ 251. BILLY HERMAN(M)
- ☐ 272. CHUCK SCHILLING
- ☐ 295. DICK RADATZ
- ☐ 315. FRANK MALZONE
- ☐ 356. BILL SPANSWICK
- ☐ 385. CARL YASTRZEMSKI
- ☐ 403. TEAM CARD
- ☐ 434. DAVE MOREHEAD
- ☐ 452. GARY GEIGER
- ☐ 494. JAY RITCHIE
- ☐ 509. BOB GUINDON(R)
- ☐ 509. GERRY VEZENDY(R)
- ☐ 525. ED BRESSOUD
- ☐ 543. ED CONNOLLY
- ☐ 573. JIM LONBORG(R)
- ☐ 573. GERRY MOSES(R)
- ☐ 573. MIKE RYAN(R)
- ☐ 573. BILL SCHLESINGER(R)
- ☐ 588. LENNY GREEN

CALIFORNIA ANGELS*

- ☐ 26. BOBBY KNOOP
- ☐ 46. BOB LEE
- ☐ 66. BILL RIGNEY(M)
- ☐ 85. WILLIE SMITH
- ☐ 101. FRED NEWMAN
- ☐ 124. TOM SATRIANO
- ☐ 140. DEAN CHANCE
- ☐ 172. JIM PIERSALL
- ☐ 194. BILL KELSO(R)
- ☐ 194. RICK REICHARDT(R)
- ☐ 210. JIM FREGOSI
- ☐ 229. LOU CLINTON
- ☐ 242. GEORGE BRUNET
- ☐ 268. KEN MCBRIDE
- ☐ 293. TEAM CARD
- ☐ 307. BARRY LATMAN
- ☐ 324. BOBBY LOCKE
- ☐ 342. BOB RODGERS
- ☐ 358. ALBIE PEARSON
- ☐ 374. JOSE CARDENAL(R)
- ☐ 374. DICK SIMPSON
- ☐ 393. ED KIRKPATRICK
- ☐ 422. AUBREY GATEWOOD
- ☐ 442. VIC POWER
- ☐ 464. RON PICHE
- ☐ 486. TOM EGAN(R)
- ☐ 486. PAT ROGAN(R)
- ☐ 517. PAUL SCHAAL(R)
- ☐ 517. JACKIE J. WARNER(R)
- ☐ 537. MARCELINO LOPEZ(R)
- ☐ 537. RUDY MAY(R)
- ☐ 537. PHIL ROOF(R)
- ☐ 552. JULIO GOTAY
- ☐ 569. GINO CIMOLI
- ☐ 595. DON LEE

CHICAGO CUBS

- ☐ 14. LEN GABRIELSON
- ☐ 27. DICK BERTELL
- ☐ 34. CAL KOONCE
- ☐ 64. LOU BURDETTE
- ☐ 91. TEAM CARD
- ☐ 110. RON SANTO
- ☐ 149. WAYNE SCHURR
- ☐ 161. FRANK BAUMANN
- ☐ 165. DICK ELLSWORTH
- ☐ 186. BILLY COWAN
- ☐ 202. LEO BURKE
- ☐ 220. BILLY WILLIAMS
- ☐ 244. LINDY MCDANIEL
- ☐ 264. BOB BUHL
- ☐ 298. JIM STEWART
- ☐ 314. STERLING SLAUGHTER
- ☐ 334. VIC ROZNOVSKY
- ☐ 354. BILLY OTT(R)
- ☐ 354. JACK D. WARNER(R)
- ☐ 386. PAUL JAECKEL(R)
- ☐ 386. FRED NORMAN(R)
- ☐ 402. JOE AMALFITANO
- ☐ 420. LARRY JACKSON
- ☐ 436. DON ELSTON
- ☐ 457. BOB KENNEDY(HC)

142

* All of the cards appear as Los Angeles Angels.

☐ 510. ERNIE BANKS
☐ 528. GEORGE ALTMAN
☐ 549. ROBERTA PENA(R)
☐ 549. GLENN BECKERT(R)
☐ 565. ERNIE BROGLIO
☐ 584. HARRY BRIGHT
☐ 596. DON LANDRUM

CHICAGO WHITE SOX

☐ 41. BRUCE HOWARD(R)
☐ 41. MARV STAEHLE(R)
☐ 58. FRED TALBOT
☐ 70. BILL SKOWRON
☐ 81. DON BUFORD
☐ 89. MIKE HERSHBERGER
☐ 125. JUAN PIZARRO
☐ 146. RON HANSEN
☐ 183. DAVE NICHOLSON
☐ 198. SMOKY BURGESS
☐ 208. TOMMY JOHN
☐ 215. PETE WARD
☐ 234. TEAM CARD
☐ 253. DANNY CATER
☐ 276. HOYT WILHELM
☐ 297. DAVE DEBUSSCHERE
☐ 313. JIMMIE SCHAFFTER
☐ 328. EDDIE FISHER
☐ 345. FLOYD ROBINSON
☐ 368. KEN BERRY
☐ 368. JOEL GIBSON(R)
☐ 382. J.C. MARTIN
☐ 414. AL LOPEZ(M)
☐ 430. GARY PETERS
☐ 458. JOHN BUZHARDT
☐ 480. JOEL HORLEN
☐ 498. GENE STEPHENS
☐ 516. AL WEIS
☐ 541. GREG BOLLO(R)
☐ 541. BOB LOCKER(R)
☐ 586. TOMMY MCCRAW

CINCINNATI REDS

☐ 18. BILL MCCOOL
☐ 47. TOMMY HARPER
☐ 60. JIM O'TOOLE
☐ 75. DERON JOHNSON
☐ 102. STEVE BOROS
☐ 120. FRANK ROBINSON
☐ 141. CHARLIE JAMES
☐ 158. DICK SISLER(M)
☐ 174. JOE JAY
☐ 192. JIM COKER
☐ 207. PETE ROSE
☐ 221. JOHN TSITOURIS
☐ 243. TED DAVIDSON(R)
☐ 243. TOMMY HELMS(R)
☐ 263. MARTY KEOUGH
☐ 289. GORDY COLEMAN
☐ 312. JOE NUXHALL
☐ 316. TEAM CARD
☐ 339. RYNE DUREN
☐ 355. VADA PINSON
☐ 398. DAN NEVILLE(R)
☐ 398. ART SHAMSKY(R)
☐ 411. ROGER CRAIG
☐ 418. JOHNNY EDWARDS
☐ 437. CHICO CARDENAS
☐ 456. BILL R. HENRY
☐ 472. DON PAVLETICH
☐ 488. TED WILLS
☐ 507. SAMMY ELLIS
☐ 530. JIM MALONEY
☐ 554. CHICO RUIZ
☐ 581. TONY PEREZ(R)

CLEVELAND INDIANS

☐ 17. JOHNNY ROMANO
☐ 76. SAM MCDOWELL
☐ 92. DICK HOWSER
☐ 96. SONNY SIEBERT
☐ 105. CHICO SALMON
☐ 128. VIC DAVALILLO
☐ 145. LUIS TIANT
☐ 166. GEORGE CULVER(R)
☐ 166. TOMMIE AGEE
☐ 185. MAX ALVIS

☐ 235. CHUCK HINTON
☐ 262. BUD DALEY
☐ 283. FRED WHITFIELD
☐ 301. BIRDIE TEBBETTS(M)
☐ 317. DON MCMAHON
☐ 332. TED ABERNATHY
☐ 348. GEORGE BANKS
☐ 367. LEON WAGNER
☐ 380. ROCKY COLAVITO
☐ 404. STAN WILLIAMS
☐ 406. RALPH TERRY
☐ 424. GARY BELL
☐ 448. LEE STANGE
☐ 468. LARRY BROWN
☐ 481. TEAM CARD
☐ 501. RALPH GAGLIANO(R)
☐ 501. JIM RITTWAGE(R)
☐ 514. JOE AZCUE
☐ 535. JACK KRALICK
☐ 546. BILL DAVIS(R)
☐ 546. MIKE HEDLUND(R)
☐ 546. FLOYD WEAVER(R)
☐ 546. RAY BARKER(R)
☐ 562. BILLY MORAN
☐ 577. RICHIE SCHEINBLUM(R)
☐ 578. CAMILO CARREON

DETROIT TIGERS

☐ 19. GATES BROWN
☐ 37. FRED GLADDING
☐ 53. DICK MCAULIFFE
☐ 83. GEORGE THOMAS
☐ 130. AL KALINE
☐ 153. NORM CASH
☐ 173. TEAM CARD
☐ 191. PHIL REGAN
☐ 206. WILLIE HORTON
☐ 236. DENNIS MCLAIN
☐ 259. JIM NORTHRUP(R)
☐ 259. RAY OYLER(R)
☐ 271. DON WERT
☐ 288. JACK HAMILTON
☐ 306. BUBBA PHILLIPS
☐ 335. MICKEY LOLICH
☐ 353. JERRY LUMPE
☐ 375. DAVE WICKERSHAM
☐ 390. BILL FREEHAN
☐ 408. LARRY SHERRY
☐ 429. DON DEMETER
☐ 454. ED RAKOW
☐ 471. BILLY HOEFT
☐ 483. GEORGE SMITH
☐ 493. BILL ROMAN(R)
☐ 493. BRUCE BRUBAKER(R)
☐ 522. HANK AGUIRRE
☐ 538. CHUCK DRESSEN(M)
☐ 547. JAKE WOOD
☐ 563. JULIO NAVARRO
☐ 576. TERRY FOX
☐ 587. JOE SPARMA
☐ 593. JACKIE MOORE(R)
☐ 593. JOHN SULLIVAN(R)

HOUSTON ASTROS

☐ 16. JOE MORGAN(R)
☐ 16. SONNY JACKSON(R)
☐ 31. MIKE WHITE
☐ 48. CLAUDE RAYMOND
☐ 80. TURK FARRELL
☐ 109. WALT BOND
☐ 164. AL SPANGLER
☐ 175. BOB ASPROMONTE
☐ 179. HAL WOODESHICK
☐ 212. RON BRAND
☐ 240. BOB BRUCE
☐ 257. JIM WYNN
☐ 274. LUM HARRIS(M)
☐ 292. LARRY YELLEN
☐ 321. RUSTY STAUB
☐ 359. KEN JOHNSON
☐ 389. DON LARSEN
☐ 409. JIM BEAUCHAMP(R)
☐ 409. LARRY DIERKER(R)
☐ 433. JOHN BATEMAN
☐ 451. JIM OWENS
☐ 469. DON NOTTEBART
☐ 485. NELLIE FOX
☐ 504. JERRY GROTE

☐ 524. DAVE GIUSTI
☐ 553. DAN COOMBS(R)
☐ 553. JACK MCCLURE(R)
☐ 553. GENE RATLIFF(R)
☐ 594. JOE GAINES

KANSAS CITY ATHLETICS

☐ 35. ED CHARLES
☐ 51. BILLY BRYAN
☐ 71. JOHN O'DONOGHUE
☐ 87. NELSON MATHEWS
☐ 117. WES STOCK
☐ 151. TEAM CARD
☐ 168. DICK GREEN
☐ 197. DIEGO SEGUI
☐ 219. BOB MEYER
☐ 239. DOC EDWARDS
☐ 266. BERT CAMPANERIS
☐ 286. JIM DICKSON
☐ 286. AURELIO MONTEAGUDO(R)
☐ 311. ORLANDO PENA
☐ 333. TOMMIE REYNOLDS
☐ 365. JIM GENTILE
☐ 376. JIM LANDIS
☐ 391. MEL MCGAHA(M)
☐ 425. WAYNE CAUSEY
☐ 439. MOE DRABOWSKY
☐ 462. LEW KRAUSSE
☐ 479. KEN HARRELSON
☐ 526. RENE LACHEMANN(R)
☐ 526. JOHN ODOM(R)
☐ 526. SKIP LOCKWOOD(R)
☐ 526. JIM HUNTER(R)
☐ 557. JOSE SANTIAGO
☐ 577. DON BUSCHHORN(R)
☐ 590. JOHN WYATT

LOS ANGELES DODGERS

☐ 40. FRANK HOWARD
☐ 59. NATE OLIVER
☐ 77. DOUG CAMILLI
☐ 98. BOB L. MILLER
☐ 112. DERRELL GRIFFITH
☐ 119. JOHN KENNEDY
☐ 126. TEAM CARD
☐ 196. RON FAIRLY
☐ 217. WALT ALSTON(M)
☐ 238. JOE MOELLER
☐ 247. WALLY MOON
☐ 260. DON DRYSDALE
☐ 279. DICK TRACEWSKI
☐ 300. SANDY KOUFAX
☐ 331. AL FERRARA(R)
☐ 331. JOHN PURDIN(R)
☐ 344. WES PARKER
☐ 370. TOMMY DAVIS
☐ 387. JOHNNY PODRES
☐ 405. JOHN ROSEBORO
☐ 416. JIM BREWER
☐ 435. WILLIE DAVIS
☐ 453. WILLIE CRAWFORD(R)
☐ 453. JOHN WERHAS(R)
☐ 484. RON PERRANOSKI
☐ 527. JEFF TORBORG
☐ 544. HOWIE REED
☐ 561. DENNIS DABOLL(R)
☐ 561. MIKE KEKICH(R)

□ 561. JIM LEFEBVRE(R)
□ 561. HECTOR VALLE(R)
□ 570. CLAUDE OSTEEN
□ 579. DICK SMITH

MILWAUKEE BRAVES

□ 23. BOB TIEFENAUER
□ 44. WADE BLASINGAME
□ 63. TY CLINE
□ 82. SANDY ALOMAR(R)
□ 82. JOHN BRAUN(R)
□ 106. GENE OLIVER
□ 127. FRANK LARY
□ 156. BOB SADOWSKI
□ 170. HANK AARON
□ 182. MIKE DE LA HOZ
□ 200. JOE TORRE
□ 223. DAN OSINSKI
□ 241. MACK JONES
□ 269. FRANK BOLLING
□ 287. GARY KOLB
□ 305. RICO CARTY
□ 327. DENIS MENKE
□ 346. BOBBY BRAGAN(M)
□ 366. DAN SCHNEIDER
□ 383. FELIPE ALOU
□ 407. LEE MAYE
□ 426. TEAM CARD
□ 441. DENNY LEMASTER
□ 461. CLAY CARROLL(R)
□ 461. PHIL NIEKRO(R)
□ 476. BILLY O'DELL
□ 487. WOODY WOODWARD
□ 500. EDDIE MATHEWS
□ 520. TONY CLONINGER
□ 542. LOU KLIMCHOCK
□ 567. TOMMIE AARON
□ 585. HANK FISCHER

MINNESOTA TWINS

□ 24. TEAM CARD
□ 39. GERRY ARRIGO
□ 62. JIM KAAT
□ 90. RICH ROLLINS
□ 108. DON MINCHER
□ 122. BILL PLEIS
□ 157. ZOILO VERSALLES
□ 171. JIM ROLAND
□ 180. BOB ALLISON
□ 201. SANDY VALDESPINO(R)
□ 201. CESAR TOVAR(R)
□ 216. AL WORTHINGTON
□ 237. BERNIE ALLEN
□ 255. CAMILO PASCUAL
□ 278. KEN RETZER
□ 299. JERRY ZIMMERMAN
□ 326. DWIGHT SIEBLER
□ 340. TONY OLIVA
□ 351. JIM PERRY
□ 384. JOHNNY KLIPPSTEIN
□ 400. HARMON KILLEBREW
□ 421. GARY DOTTER(R)
□ 421. JAY WARD(R)
□ 432. JIM GRANT
□ 459. FRANK KOSTRO
□ 490. EARL BATTEY
□ 506. SAM MELE(M)
□ 529. JERRY FOSNOW
□ 548. DICK STIGMAN
□ 564. MEL NELSON
□ 580. JIMMIE HALL
□ 597. JOE NOSSEK(R)
□ 597. RICH REESE(R)
□ 597. JOHN SEVCIK(R)

NEW YORK METS

□ 22. CHARLIE SMITH
□ 45. ROY MCMILLAN
□ 61. CHRIS CANNIZZARO
□ 73. DENNIS RIBANT
□ 93. JACK FISHER
□ 114. JIM HICKMAN
□ 144. ED KRANEPOOL
□ 167. BILLY WAKEFIELD
□ 187. CASEY STENGEL(M)
□ 205. WARREN SPAHN
□ 227. BOBBY KLAUS

□ 258. LARRY BEARNARTH
□ 277. JOHNNY LEWIS
□ 285. RON HUNT
□ 308. CLEON JONES(R)
□ 308. TOM PARSONS(R)
□ 329. HAWK TAYLOR
□ 349. LARRY MILLER
□ 364. GALEN CISCO
□ 381. AL JACKSON
□ 401. CARL WILLEY
□ 423. JESSE GONDER
□ 449. JERRY HINSLEY(R)
□ 449. GARY KROLL(R)
□ 470. YOGI BERRA
□ 495. JOE CHRISTOPHER
□ 511. RON LOCKE
□ 533. DAN NAPOLEON(R)
□ 533. RON SWOBODA(R)
□ 533. JIM BETHKE(R)
□ 533. TUG MCGRAW(R)
□ 551. TEAM CARD
□ 581. KEVIN COLLINS(R)

NEW YORK YANKEES

□ 13. PEDRO RAMOS
□ 30. JIM BOUTON
□ 65. TONY KUBEK
□ 97. PEDRO GONZALEZ
□ 115. BOBBY RICHARDSON
□ 131. JOHNNY KEANE(M)
□ 155. ROGER MARIS
□ 177. PETE MIKKELSEN
□ 226. ELVIO JIMENEZ(R)
□ 226. JAKE GIBBS(R)
□ 245. JOE PEPITONE
□ 254. ROLAND SHELDON
□ 261. DUKE CARMEL
□ 281. BILL STAFFORD
□ 309. STEVE HAMILTON
□ 330. WHITEY FORD
□ 350. MICKEY MANTLE
□ 369. PHIL LINZ
□ 388. JOHN BLANCHARD
□ 413. HAL RENIFF
□ 440. TOM TRESH
□ 450. ELSTON HOWARD
□ 475. CLETE BOYER
□ 513. TEAM CARD
□ 532. HECTOR LOPEZ
□ 550. MEL STOTTLEMYRE
□ 566. GIL BLANCO(R)
□ 566. ART LOPEZ(R)
□ 566. ROSS MOSCHITTO(R)
□ 582. BOB SCHMIDT
□ 598. AL DOWNING

PHILADELPHIA PHILLIES

□ 20. JIM BUNNING
□ 36. BOBBY WINE
□ 52. ED ROEBUCK
□ 72. TONY GONZALEZ
□ 107. PAT CORRALES(R)
□ 107. COSTEN SHOCKLEY(R)
□ 123. FRANK THOMAS
□ 163. JOHN BRIGGS
□ 184. JOHN BOOZER
□ 203. DALLAS GREEN
□ 225. BOB BELINSKY
□ 248. GUS TRIANDOS
□ 280. DICK STUART
□ 296. TONY TAYLOR
□ 310. JOHNNY CALLISON
□ 322. RICK WISE
□ 338. TEAM CARD
□ 352. ALEX JOHNSON
□ 372. CLAY DALRYMPLE
□ 399. RAY HERBERT
□ 419. RUBEN AMARO
□ 446. ART MAHAFFEY
□ 460. RICHIE ALLEN
□ 474. COOKIE ROJAS
□ 489. GENE MAUCH(M)
□ 505. RAY CULP
□ 521. DAVE BENNETT(R)
□ 521. MORRIE STEEVENS(R)
□ 534. JOHN HERRNSTEIN
□ 555. JACK BALDSCHUN
□ 583. WES COVINGTON

PITTSBURGH PIRATES

□ 25. AL MCBEAN
□ 54. JOE GIBBON
□ 69. BILL VIRDON
□ 95. BILL MAZEROSKI
□ 121. GENE ALLEY
□ 143. JOHN GELNAR(R)
□ 143. JERRY MAY(R)
□ 160. BOB CLEMENTE
□ 195. BOB VEALE
□ 209. TEAM CARD
□ 218. DICK SCHOFIELD
□ 232. STEVE BLASS
□ 246. TOM BUTTERS
□ 265. JIM PAGLIARONI
□ 291. JERRY LYNCH
□ 325. DONN CLENDENON
□ 347. ROY FACE
□ 362. DON SCHWALL
□ 377. WILLIE STARGELL
□ 392. BOB FRIEND
□ 412. BOB BAILEY
□ 438. HARRY WALKER(M)
□ 463. MANNY MOTA
□ 478. WILBUR WOOD
□ 492. GENE FREESE
□ 502. DON CARDWELL
□ 515. VERN LAW
□ 536. ANDRE RODGERS
□ 558. TOMMIE SISK
□ 571. OSSIE VIRGIL
□ 592. FRANK BORK

ST. LOUIS CARDINALS

□ 28. BARNEY SCHULTZ
□ 43. MIKE SHANNON
□ 57. TEAM CARD
□ 78. DAL MAXVILL
□ 100. KEN BOYER
□ 116. DAVE DOWLING(R)
□ 116. BOB TOLAN(R)
□ 154. BOB HUMPHREYS
□ 190. BILL WHITE
□ 214. BOB PURKEY
□ 230. RAY SADECKI
□ 256. TITO FRANCONA
□ 275. DICK GROAT
□ 294. TIM MCCARVER
□ 320. BOB GIBSON
□ 337. MIKE CUELLAR
□ 357. CARL WARWICK
□ 373. CURT SIMMONS
□ 397. JERRY BUCHEK
□ 415. CURT FLOOD
□ 431. NELSON BRILES(R)
□ 431. ED SPIEZIO(R)
□ 447. JULIAN JAVIER
□ 467. RAY WASHBURN
□ 477. FRITZ ACKLEY(R)
□ 477. STEVE CARLTON(R)
□ 491. TRACY STALLARD
□ 503. PHIL GAGLIANO
□ 519. BOB UECKER
□ 540. LOU BROCK
□ 556. RED SCHOENDIENST(M)
□ 568. RON TAYLOR
□ 581. DAVE RICKETTS(R)
□ 591. BOB SKINNER

SAN FRANCISCO GIANTS

□ 32. HERMAN FRANKS(M)
□ 50. JUAN MARICHAL
□ 68. DEL CRANDALL
□ 84. RON HERBEL
□ 103. HARVEY KUENN
□ 118. HAL LANIER
□ 159. JIM DUFFALO
□ 176. WILLIE MCCOVEY
□ 193. GAYLORD PERRY
□ 213. JIM DAVENPORT
□ 228. JACK SANFORD
□ 250. WILLIE MAYS
□ 282. DICK ESTELLE(R)
□ 282. MASANORI MURAKAMI(R)
□ 302. AL STANEK
□ 318. MATTY ALOU
□ 341. BOBBY BOLIN

□ 360. ORLANDO CEPEDA
□ 379. TEAM CARD
□ 395. JIM HART
□ 428. BOB SHAW
□ 444. BOB HENDLEY
□ 465. TOM HALLER
□ 482. BOB PRIDDY
□ 497. KEN HENDERSON(R)
□ 497. JACK HIATT(R)
□ 512. CAP PETERSON
□ 531. CHUCK HILLER
□ 545. JESUS ALOU
□ 559. ED BAILEY
□ 575. JOSE PAGAN
□ 589. FRANK LINZY(R)
□ 589. BOB SCHRODER(R)

WASHINGTON SENATORS

□ 21. DON BLASINGAME
□ 38. JIM KING
□ 56. RON KLINE
□ 86. LES NARUM
□ 99. GIL HODGES(M)
□ 129. BENNIE DANIELS
□ 148. WILLIE KIRKLAND
□ 152. PHIL ORTEGA
□ 181. DON LOUN(R)
□ 181. JOE MCCABE(R)
□ 211. STEVE RIDZIK
□ 224. BOB CHANCE
□ 233. DON ZIMMER
□ 252. PETE RICHERT
□ 267. TEAM CARD
□ 284. NICK WILLHITE
□ 304. DAVE STENHOUSE
□ 319. KEN MCMULLEN
□ 336. WOODY HELD
□ 371. FRANK KREUTZER
□ 394. JIM HANNAN
□ 417. ED BRINKMAN
□ 445. DON LOCK
□ 466. PETE CRAIG(R)
□ 466. DICK NEN(R)
□ 496. JOE CUNNINGHAM
□ 523. MIKE BRUMLEY
□ 574. ROY SIEVERS

1966 TOPPS (598)
2 1/2″ X 3 1/2″

JOE TORRE   catcher-1b

ATLANTA BRAVES

□ 10. TONY CLONINGER
□ 28. PHIL NIEKRO
□ 49. WOODY WOODWARD
□ 84. JIM BEAUCHAMP(R)
□ 84. DICK KELLEY(R)
□ 96. FELIPE ALOU
□ 130. JOE TORRE
□ 153. RICO CARTY
□ 168. DAN OSINSKI
□ 184. DENIS MENKE
□ 200. EDDIE MATHEWS
□ 237. BILLY O'DELL
□ 252. DENVER LEMASTER
□ 268. JOHN BLANCHARD
□ 286. GARY GEIGER
□ 307. CLAY CARROLL
□ 326. TEAM CARD
□ 346. MIKE DE LA HOZ
□ 355. WADE BLASINGAME
□ 381. HANK FISCHER
□ 408. LEE THOMAS
□ 428. SANDY ALOMAR
□ 446. MACK JONES
□ 466. KEN JOHNSON
□ 476. BOBBY BRAGAN(M)
□ 497. CHRIS CANNIZZARO
□ 500. HANK AARON
□ 518. HERB HIPPAUF(R)
□ 518. ARNIE UMBACH(R)
□ 541. GENE OLIVER
□ 553. PAT GARRETT(R)
□ 578. CHI CHI OLIVO

BALTIMORE ORIOLES

□ 14. NORM SIEBERN
□ 27. DAROLD KNOWLES(R)
□ 27. ANDY ETCHEBARREN(R)
□ 48. PAUL BLAIR
□ 90. LUIS APARICIO
□ 105. MILT PAPPAS
□ 126. JIM PALMER
□ 136. WOODY HELD
□ 148. BOB W. JOHNSON
□ 167. BOOG POWELL
□ 193. DAVE MCNALLY
□ 229. HANK BAUER(M)
□ 247. CARL WARWICK
□ 265. STU MILLER
□ 291. MOE DRABOWSKY
□ 310. FRANK ROBINSON
□ 348. TEAM CARD
□ 368. CHARLIE LAU
□ 390. BROOKS ROBINSON
□ 412. SAM BOWENS
□ 427. JOHN MILLER
□ 442. EDDIE BARNOWSKI(R)
□ 442. EDDIE WATT(R)
□ 460. CURT BLEFARY
□ 467. VIC ROZNOVSKY
□ 477. STEVE BARBER
□ 499. WALLY BUNKER

□ 513. CAMILO CARREON
□ 533. JERRY ADAIR
□ 562. RUSS SNYDER
□ 579. FRANK BERTAINA(R)
□ 579. GENE BRABENDER(R)
□ 579. DAVE A. JOHNSON

BOSTON RED SOX

□ 6. CHUCK SCHILLING
□ 37. BILLY HERMAN(M)
□ 53. BOB DULIBA
□ 70. CARL YASTRZEMSKI
□ 93. JIM LONBORG
□ 114. JIM GOSGER
□ 135. DAVE MOREHEAD
□ 178. BOB TILLMAN
□ 203. JOSE SANTIAGO
□ 227. RUSS NIXON
□ 259. TEAM CARD
□ 277. GEORGE THOMAS
□ 298. RICO PETROCELLI
□ 317. DALTON JONES
□ 329. PETE CHARTON
□ 343. JOE CHRISTOPHER
□ 356. OWEN JOHNSON(R)
□ 356. KEN SANDERS(R)
□ 380. TONY CONIGLIARO
□ 396. JERRY STEPHENSON
□ 419. MIKE RYAN
□ 456. DARRELL BRANDON(R)
□ 456. JOE FOY(R)
□ 475. DICK RADATZ
□ 491. DENNIS BENNETT
□ 502. LENNY GREEN
□ 512. DICK STIGMAN(F)
□ 523. BOB SADOWSKI
□ 542. GEORGE SMITH
□ 558. GUIDO GRILLI(R)
□ 558. PETE MAGRINI(R)
□ 558. GEORGE SCOTT(R)
□ 575. EARL WILSON

CALIFORNIA ANGELS

□ 5. JIM FREGOSI
□ 23. JACK SANFORD
□ 42. AUBREY GATEWOOD
□ 62. MERRITT RANEW
□ 83. ALBIE PEARSON
□ 102. ED KIRKPATRICK
□ 131. TEAM CARD
□ 152. FRANK MALZONE
□ 155. MARCELINO LOPEZ
□ 173. AL SPANGLER
□ 192. VIC POWER
□ 213. FRED NEWMAN
□ 249. BILL RIGNEY(M)
□ 263. TOM EGAN
□ 280. BOBBY KNOOP
□ 299. LOU BURDETTE
□ 321. RICK REICHARDT
□ 340. DEAN CHANCE
□ 361. TOM SATRIANO
□ 376. PAUL SCHAAL
□ 393. GEORGE BRUNET
□ 417. ED SUKLA(R)
□ 417. JIM MCGLOTHLIN(R)
□ 438. WILLIE SMITH
□ 462. BOB RODGERS
□ 481. BOB LEE
□ 505. JOSE CARDENAL
□ 536. DICK EGAN
□ 553. JACKIE J. WARNER(R)
□ 565. JIMMY PIERSALL

CHICAGO CUBS

□ 2. TED ABERNATHY
□ 24. DON KESSINGER
□ 43. DON LANDRUM
□ 63. JIM STEWART
□ 82. BOB HENDLEY
□ 110. ERNIE BANKS
□ 139. BYRON BROWNE(R)
□ 139. DON YOUNG(R)
□ 146. GEORGE ALTMAN
□ 166. CHRIS KRUG
□ 185. BUB BUHL

☐ 204. TEAM CARD
☐ 232. GLENN BECKERT
☐ 246. ED BAILEY
☐ 278. CALVIN KOONCE
☐ 290. RON SANTO
☐ 306. TY CLINE
☐ 322. BILL FAUL
☐ 342. BOB HUMPHREYS
☐ 372. HARVEY KUENN
☐ 392. BILL HANDS(R)
☐ 392. RANDY HUNDLEY(R)
☐ 409. BILLY HOEFT
☐ 423. ERNIE BROGLIO
☐ 447. DICK ELLSWORTH
☐ 482. JOHN BOCCABELLA(R)
☐ 482. DAVE DOWLING(R)
☐ 484. WES COVINGTON
☐ 559. ROBERTO PENA
☐ 580. BILLY WILLIAMS

CHICAGO WHITE SOX

☐   8. FLOYD ROBINSON
☐ 25. PETE WARD
☐ 47. J.C. MARTIN
☐ 66. AL WEIS
☐ 85. EDDIE FISHER
☐ 111. GARY PETERS
☐ 127. KEN BERRY
☐ 141. TOM MCCRAW
☐ 164. TOMMY AGEE(R)
☐ 164. MARV STAEHLE(R)
☐ 245. JOHN BUZHARDT
☐ 261. RON HANSEN
☐ 281. BRUCE HOWARD
☐ 301. GREG BOLLO
☐ 319. GENE FREESE
☐ 335. JUAN PIZARRO
☐ 354. SMOKY BURGESS
☐ 374. BOB LOCKER
☐ 398. DANNY CATER
☐ 413. JOHN ROMANO
☐ 426. TEAM CARD
☐ 448. EDDIE STANKY(M)
☐ 465. DON BUFORD
☐ 486. TOMMY JOHN
☐ 510. HOYT WILHELM
☐ 529. LEE ELIA
☐ 529. DENNIS HIGGINS(R)
☐ 529. BILL VOSS(R)
☐ 560. JOEL HORLEN
☐ 577. JACK LAMABE
☐ 590. BILL SKOWRON

CINCINNATI REDS

☐ 12. JOHN TSITOURIS
☐ 30. PETE ROSE
☐ 59. TEAM CARD
☐ 72. TONY PEREZ
☐ 89. TED DAVIDSON
☐ 119. ART SHAMSKY
☐ 140. JIM MALONEY
☐ 159. CHICO RUIZ
☐ 180. VADA PINSON
☐ 196. DON PAVLETICH
☐ 214. TOMMY HARPER
☐ 233. DOM ZANNI
☐ 250. SAM ELLIS
☐ 269. DON HEFFNER(M)
☐ 272. JACK BALDSCHUN
☐ 292. JIM COKER
☐ 311. TOMMY HELMS(R)
☐ 311. DICK SIMPSON(R)
☐ 334. MARTY KEOUGH
☐ 357. GERRY ARRIGO
☐ 370. LEO CARDENAS
☐ 389. JIM O'TOOLE
☐ 406. JOE JAY
☐ 424. LEE MAY(R)
☐ 424. DARRELL OSTEEN(R)
☐ 440. DERON JOHNSON
☐ 459. BILL MCCOOL
☐ 483. JOE NUXHALL
☐ 494. GORDY COLEMAN
☐ 507. JOHN EDWARDS
☐ 556. MEL QUEEN

CLEVELAND INDIANS

☐ 16. LARRY BROWN
☐ 44. BILL DAVIS(R)
☐ 44. TOM KELLEY(R)
☐ 65. LEON WAGNER
☐ 88. FRED WHITFIELD
☐ 109. RALPH TERRY
☐ 128. JIM LANDIS
☐ 129. JACK KRALICK
☐ 133. DON MCMAHON
☐ 150. ROCKY COLAVITO
☐ 169. DUKE SIMS
☐ 197. SONNY SIEBERT
☐ 231. FLOYD WEAVER
☐ 266. PEDRO GONZALES
☐ 285. LUIS TIANT
☐ 303. TEAM CARD
☐ 325. VIC DAVALILLO
☐ 339. DEL CRANDALL
☐ 371. LEE STANGE
☐ 391. CHUCK HINTON
☐ 415. MAX ALVIS
☐ 432. BOB HEFFNER
☐ 452. JOE AZCUE
☐ 470. SAM MCDOWELL
☐ 488. GEORGE BANKS
☐ 501. JOHN O'DONOGHUE
☐ 508. STEVE HARGAN
☐ 525. GARY BELL
☐ 538. BOB ALLEN
☐ 552. BIRDIE TEBBETTS
☐ 567. DICK HOWSER
☐ 581. TONY MARTINEZ
☐ 594. CHICO SALMON

DETROIT TIGERS

☐ 20. WILLIE HORTON
☐ 38. RON NISCHWITZ
☐ 58. DAVE WICKERSHAM
☐ 81. RAY OYLER
☐ 98. DON DEMETER
☐ 113. HANK AGUIRRE
☐ 145. BILL FREEHAN
☐ 161. JERRY LUMPE
☐ 187. CHUCK DRESSEN(M)
☐ 198. MICKEY STANLEY
☐ 209. FRITZ FISHER(R)
☐ 209. JOHN HILLER(R)
☐ 239. ORLANDO PENA
☐ 253. DON WERT
☐ 267. JOE SPARMA
☐ 289. LARRY SHERRY
☐ 315. NORM CASH
☐ 337. FRED GLADDING
☐ 362. GATES BROWN
☐ 378. DICK TRACEWSKI
☐ 410. AL KALINE
☐ 429. BILL MONBOUQUETTE
☐ 455. MICKEY LOLICH
☐ 472. TERRY FOX
☐ 495. DICK MCAULIFFE
☐ 509. JAKE WOOD
☐ 527. JULIO NAVARRO
☐ 540. DENNY MCLAIN
☐ 554. JIM NORTHRUP
☐ 569. ORLANDO MCFARLANE
☐ 583. TEAM CARD
☐ 597. JOHN SULLIVAN

HOUSTON ASTROS

☐ 21. DON NOTTEBART
☐ 45. JIM GENTILE
☐ 64. BOB BRUCE
☐ 86. JOHN BATEMAN
☐ 106. RUSTY STAUB
☐ 122. JOE GAINES
☐ 147. LUM HARRIS(M)
☐ 162. LEE MAYE
☐ 174. RON TAYLOR
☐ 195. JOE MORGAN
☐ 228. LARRY DIERKER
☐ 244. CHUCK HARRISON(R)
☐ 244. SONNY JACKSON(R)
☐ 258. DAVE GIUSTI
☐ 297. JIM OWENS
☐ 313. CHRIS ZACHARY

☐ 352. BOB ASPROMONTE
☐ 377. TURK FARRELL
☐ 394. RON BRAND
☐ 414. DAN COOMBS
☐ 431. WALT BOND
☐ 451. BARRY LATMAN
☐ 504. GRADY HATTON(M)
☐ 520. JIM WYNN
☐ 530. ROBIN ROBERTS
☐ 539. BILL HEATH(R)
☐ 539. CARROLL SEMBERA(R)
☐ 548. GARY KROLL
☐ 557. FELIX MANTILLA
☐ 566. MIKE CUELLAR
☐ 576. DAVE NICHOLSON
☐ 586. CLAUDE RAYMOND
☐ 596. NATE COLBERT(R)
☐ 596. GREG SIMS(R)

JIM HUNTER   pitcher

KANSAS CITY ATHLETICS

☐ 18. ROLAND SHELDON
☐ 36. JIM HUNTER
☐ 55. KEN HARRELSON
☐ 74. DON MOSSI
☐ 107. LARRY STAHL(R)
☐ 107. RON TOMPKINS(R)
☐ 143. JOSE TARTABULL
☐ 157. RENE LACHEMANN
☐ 175. BERT CAMPANERIS
☐ 201. JIM DICKSON
☐ 236. MIKE HERSHBERGER
☐ 256. LEW KRAUSSE
☐ 287. JACK AKER
☐ 309. DIEGO SEGUI
☐ 332. BILLY BRYAN
☐ 366. WAYNE CAUSEY
☐ 382. PHIL ROOF
☐ 403. FRED TALBOT
☐ 422. ED CHARLES
☐ 433. ALVIN DARK(M)
☐ 458. MANNY JIMENEZ
☐ 492. TEAM CARD
☐ 521. JOHN WYATT
☐ 532. AURELIO MONTEAGUDO
☐ 545. DICK GREEN
☐ 568. PAUL LINDBLAD(R)
☐ 568. RON STONE(R)
☐ 588. CHUCK DOBSON(R)
☐ 588. KEN SUAREZ(R)

LOS ANGELES DODGERS

☐ 13. LOU JOHNSON
☐ 41. DON LE JOHN
☐ 57. JIM LEFEBVRE
☐ 75. TOMMY DAVIS
☐ 100. SANDY KOUFAX
☐ 116. WALTER ALSTON(M)
☐ 134. WES PARKER
☐ 158. JIM BREWER
☐ 171. NICK WILLHITE
☐ 189. JOHN ROSEBORO
☐ 208. BOB L. MILLER
☐ 238. TEAM CARD
☐ 257. JEFF TORBORG
☐ 270. CLAUDE OSTEEN
☐ 288. BILL SINGER(R)

☐ 288. DON SUTTON(R)
☐ 314. HECTOR VALLE
☐ 330. RON FAIRLY
☐ 347. PHIL REGAN
☐ 364. NATE OLIVER
☐ 387. HOWIE REED
☐ 407. JOHN KENNEDY
☐ 430. DON DRYSDALE
☐ 449. JOE MOELLER
☐ 468. JOHNNY PODRES
☐ 487. AL FERRARA
☐ 535. WILLIE DAVIS
☐ 555. RON PERRANOSKI
☐ 573. DERRELL GRIFFITH
☐ 591. BART SHIRLEY(R)

MINNESOTA TWINS

☐   3. SAM MELE(M)
☐ 22. JOE NOSSEK
☐ 40. JIM GRANT
☐ 56. SANDY VALDESPINO
☐ 73. JERRY ZIMMERMAN
☐ 97. JIM MERRITT
☐ 120. HARMON KILLEBREW
☐ 181. AL WORTHINGTON
☐ 190. JIMMIE HALL
☐ 207. FRANK QUILICI
☐ 240. EARL BATTEY
☐ 264. ANDY KOSCO(R)
☐ 264. TED UHLAENDER(R)
☐ 283. JIM PERRY
☐ 305. CAMILO PASCUAL
☐ 327. BERNIE ALLEN
☐ 345. BOB ALLISON
☐ 367. MEL NELSON
☐ 388. DON MINCHER
☐ 400. ZOILO VERSALLES
☐ 445. JIM KAAT
☐ 450. TONY OLIVA
☐ 473. RICH ROLLINS
☐ 493. JOHN KLIPPSTEIN
☐ 512. DICK STIGMAN(B)
☐ 526. TEAM CARD
☐ 546. DWIGHT SIEBLER
☐ 563. PETE CIMINO(R)
☐ 563. CESAR TOVAR(R)
☐ 582. GARRY ROGGENBURK

NEW YORK METS

☐ 17. JOHN STEPHENSON
☐ 35. RON SWOBODA
☐ 51. GORDON RICHARDSON
☐ 67. CLEON JONES(R)
☐ 67. DICK SELMA(R)
☐ 87. DAN NAPOLEON
☐ 108. BOBBY KLAUS
☐ 124. TUG MCGRAW
☐ 154. CHUCK HILLER
☐ 172. TEAM CARD
☐ 188. AL LUPLOW
☐ 191. DARRELL SUTHERLAND
☐ 212. ED KRANEPOOL
☐ 241. DENNIS RIBANT
☐ 262. JACK HAMILTON
☐ 282. JOHNNY LEWIS
☐ 302. ERNIE BOWMAN
☐ 316. JACK FISHER
☐ 328. JERRY GROTE
☐ 341. WES WESTRUM(M)
☐ 360. RON HUNT
☐ 385. KEN BOYER
☐ 402. JIM HICKMAN
☐ 421. ROY MCMILLAN
☐ 443. BILL WAKEFIELD
☐ 464. LARRY BEARNARTH
☐ 480. DICK STUART
☐ 516. EDDIE BRESSOUD
☐ 534. DAVE EILERS(R)
☐ 534. ROB GARDNER(R)
☐ 561. CHOO CHOO COLEMAN
☐ 574. BILL HELPER(R)
☐ 574. BILL MURPHY(R)
☐ 589. LOU KLIMCHOCK

NEW YORK YANKEES

☐   9. CLETE BOYER
☐ 31. JACK CULLEN
☐ 50. MICKEY MANTLE
☐ 68. HAL RENIFF
☐ 79. JOE PEPITONE
☐ 92. TEAM CARD
☐ 117. JAKE GIBBS
☐ 138. ROGER REPOZ
☐ 160. WHITEY FORD
☐ 177. HECTOR LOPEZ
☐ 186. RUBEN AMARO
☐ 205. TOM TRESH
☐ 234. RICH BECK(R)
☐ 234. ROY WHITE(R)
☐ 276. JIM BOUTON
☐ 296. JOHNNY KEANE(M)
☐ 323. RAY BARKER
☐ 350. MEL STOTTLEMYRE
☐ 365. ROGER MARIS
☐ 384. AL DOWNING
☐ 405. ELSTON HOWARD
☐ 439. PEDRO RAMOS
☐ 469. BOBBY MURCER(R)
☐ 469. DOOLEY WOMACK(R)
☐ 490. BOBBY RICHARDSON
☐ 503. STEVE HAMILTON
☐ 519. BOB FRIEND
☐ 547. HORACE CLARKE
☐ 584. FRANK FERNANDEZ(R)
☐ 584. FRITZ PETERSON(R)

PHILADELPHIA PHILLIES

☐   4. RAY CULP
☐ 32. ADOLFO PHILLIPS
☐ 80. RICHIE ALLEN
☐ 104. ALEX JOHNSON
☐ 121. RAY HERBERT
☐ 151. GARY WAGNER
☐ 170. COOKIE ROJAS
☐ 202. CLAY DALRYMPLE
☐ 230. JOHNNY CALLISON
☐ 254. FERGUSON JENKINS(R)
☐ 254. BILL SORRELL(R)
☐ 284. BOBBY WINE
☐ 304. JOHN HERRNSTEIN
☐ 324. JOHN BOOZER
☐ 359. JOHN BRIGGS
☐ 383. JACKIE BRANDT
☐ 397. BILL WHITE
☐ 411. GENE MAUCH(M)
☐ 435. JIM BUNNING
☐ 463. TEAM CARD
☐ 478. TONY GONZALEZ
☐ 506. BO BELINSKY
☐ 522. PHIL LINZ
☐ 543. ROGER CRAIG
☐ 585. TONY TAYLOR
☐ 591. GRANT JACKSON(R)
☐ 595. LARRY JACKSON

PITTSBURGH PIRATES

☐ 15. VERN LAW
☐ 33. JIM PAGLIARONI
☐ 54. JOSE PAGAN
☐ 71. FRANK CARPIN
☐ 112. MANNY MOTA
☐ 123. FRANK BORK(R)
☐ 123. JERRY MAY(R)
☐ 144. DON SCHWALL
☐ 182. JERRY LYNCH
☐ 210. BILL MAZEROSKI
☐ 235. DON CARDWELL
☐ 248. PETE MIKKELSEN
☐ 255. WILLIE STARGELL
☐ 300. BOB CLEMENTE
☐ 318. HARRY WALKER(M)
☐ 336. GENE ALLEY
☐ 344. STEVE BLASS
☐ 353. AL MCBEAN
☐ 375. DONN CLENDENON
☐ 404. TEAM CARD
☐ 425. BOB VEALE
☐ 441. TOMMIE SISK
☐ 461. ROY FACE
☐ 485. BOB BAILEY

☐ 498. LUKE WALKER(R)
☐ 498. WOODY FRYMAN(R)
☐ 528. JESSE GONDER
☐ 551. BOB PURKEY
☐ 571. DAVE L. ROBERTS
☐ 592. ANDRE RODGERS

ST. LOUIS CARDINALS

☐   7. TRACY STALLARD
☐ 26. RAY SADECKI
☐ 60. CURT FLOOD
☐ 76. RED SCHOENDIENST(M)
☐ 91. BOB UECKER
☐ 103. DICK GROAT
☐ 125. LOU BROCK
☐ 137. PAT CORRALES
☐ 142. DON DENNIS
☐ 163. TITO FRANCONA
☐ 179. DENNIS AUST(R)
☐ 179. BOB TOLAN
☐ 206. ALVIN JACKSON
☐ 243. NELSON BRILES
☐ 275. TIM MCCARVER
☐ 293. MIKE SHANNON
☐ 320. BOB GIBSON
☐ 338. DAL MAXVILL
☐ 358. CHARLIE SMITH
☐ 379. TEAM CARD
☐ 399. RAY WASHBURN
☐ 418. PHIL GAGLIANO
☐ 436. JULIAN JAVIER
☐ 454. JERRY BUCHEK
☐ 471. BOB SKINNER
☐ 489. CURT SIMMONS
☐ 514. HAL WOODESHICK
☐ 544. JOE HOERNER(R)
☐ 544. GEORGE KERNEK(R)
☐ 544. JIMMY WILLIAMS(R)
☐ 570. ART MAHAFFEY

SAN FRANCISCO GIANTS

☐   1. WILLIE MAYS
☐ 19. TEAM CARD
☐ 39. KEN HENDERSON
☐ 61. BOB BOLIN
☐ 78. FRANK LINZY
☐ 94. MATTY ALOU
☐ 115. BILL R. HENRY
☐ 132. ORLANDO CEPEDA
☐ 176. JIM DAVENPORT
☐ 242. JESUS ALOU
☐ 260. BOB SHAW
☐ 271. HAL LANIER
☐ 295. JIM HART
☐ 308. TOM HALLER
☐ 331. RON HERBEL
☐ 349. CAP PETERSON
☐ 373. JACK HIATT(R)
☐ 373. DICK ESTELLE(R)
☐ 395. LEN GABRIELSON
☐ 420. JUAN MARICHAL
☐ 437. AL STANEK
☐ 457. JOE GIBBON
☐ 474. DICK SCHOFIELD
☐ 496. LINDY MCDANIEL
☐ 511. BOB BARTON(R)
☐ 511. TITO FUENTES(R)
☐ 524. OLLIE BROWN(R)
☐ 524. DON MASON(R)
☐ 537. HERMAN FRANKS(M)
☐ 550. WILLIE MCCOVEY
☐ 572. BOB PRIDDY
☐ 587. DICK BERTELL
☐ 598. GAYLORD PERRY

WASHINGTON SENATORS

☐ 11. BRANT ALYEA(R)
☐ 11. PETE CRAIG(R)
☐ 29. MIKE BRUMLEY
☐ 46. HOWIE KOPLITZ
☐ 69. KEN HAMLIN
☐ 77. JOHNNY ORSINO
☐ 95. PETE RICHERT
☐ 118. MIKE MCCORMICK
☐ 149. DICK NEN
☐ 165. DON LOCK

1966 Topps

- ☐ 194. TEAM CARD
- ☐ 211. FRANK KREUTZER
- ☐ 251. ED BRINKMAN
- ☐ 274. BUSTER NARUM
- ☐ 294. STEVE RIDZIK
- ☐ 312. BOB SAVERINE
- ☐ 333. JOE COLEMAN
- ☐ 333. JIM FRENCH(R)
- ☐ 351. FRED VALENTINE
- ☐ 369. JIM KING
- ☐ 386. GIL HODGES(M)
- ☐ 401. KEN MCMULLEN
- ☐ 416. PHIL ORTEGA
- ☐ 434. WILLIE KIRKLAND
- ☐ 453. RON KLINE
- ☐ 479. JIM HANNAN
- ☐ 515. FRANK HOWARD
- ☐ 531. JOE CUNNINGHAM
- ☐ 549. AL CLOSTER(R)
- ☐ 549. CASEY COX(R)
- ☐ 564. BOB CHANCE
- ☐ 593. DOUG CAMILLI

FRED VALENTINE   outfield

1967 TOPPS (609)
2 1/2" X 3 1/2"

BOB ASPROMONTE • 3B

ASTROS

ATLANTA BRAVES

- ☐ 18. GENE OLIVER
- ☐ 35. RICO CARTY
- ☐ 57. PAT JARVIS
- ☐ 89. FELIX MILLAN
- ☐ 101. KEN JOHNSON
- ☐ 113. DAVE NICHOLSON
- ☐ 119. WADE BLASINGAME
- ☐ 138. DICK KELLEY
- ☐ 179. CHARLEY VAUGHN(R)
- ☐ 179. CECIL UPSHAW(R)
- ☐ 199. BILLY HITCHCOCK(M)
- ☐ 219. CLAY CARROLL
- ☐ 250. HANK AARON
- ☐ 267. DON SCHWALL
- ☐ 288. DENVER LEMASTER
- ☐ 307. JIM BEAUCHAMP
- ☐ 328. CLETE BOYER
- ☐ 350. JOE TORRE

- ☐ 372. MIKE DE LA HOZ
- ☐ 417. BOB BRUCE
- ☐ 435. MACK JONES
- ☐ 456. PHIL NIEKRO
- ☐ 477. TEAM CARD
- ☐ 490. TONY CLONINGER
- ☐ 504. ORLANDO MARTINEZ
- ☐ 518. DENIS MENKE
- ☐ 530. FELIPE ALOU
- ☐ 546. WOODY WOODWARD
- ☐ 566. GARY GEIGER
- ☐ 576. RAMON HERNANDEZ(R)
- ☐ 591. TY CLINE

BALTIMORE ORIOLES

- ☐ 22. GENE BRABENDER
- ☐ 38. BOB W. JOHNSON
- ☐ 60. LUIS APARICIO
- ☐ 82. STEVE BARBER
- ☐ 100. FRANK ROBINSON
- ☐ 125. MOE DRABOWSKY
- ☐ 141. JOHN MILLER
- ☐ 163. VIC ROZNOVSKY
- ☐ 180. CURT BLEFARY
- ☐ 204. MIKE EPSTEIN(R)
- ☐ 204. TOM PHOEBUS(R)
- ☐ 230. BOOG POWELL
- ☐ 251. WOODY HELD
- ☐ 271. EDDIE WATT
- ☐ 302. TEAM CARD
- ☐ 319. PAUL BLAIR
- ☐ 329. CHARLEY LAU
- ☐ 345. STU MILLER
- ☐ 363. DAVE A. JOHNSON
- ☐ 382. DAVE MCNALLY
- ☐ 405. RUSS SNYDER
- ☐ 434. EDDIE FISHER
- ☐ 457. ANDY ETCHEBARREN
- ☐ 475. JIM PALMER
- ☐ 491. SAM BOWENS
- ☐ 507. ED BARNOWSKI(R)
- ☐ 507. LARRY HANEY(R)
- ☐ 534. HANK BAUER(M)
- ☐ 558. MARK BELANGER(R)
- ☐ 558. BILL DILLMAN(R)
- ☐ 585. WALLY BUNKER
- ☐ 600. BROOKS ROBINSON

BOSTON RED SOX

- ☐ 7. DON MCMAHON
- ☐ 36. BOB TILLMAN
- ☐ 56. JOSE TARTABULL
- ☐ 75. GEORGE SCOTT
- ☐ 99. LEE STANGE
- ☐ 117. DARRELL BRANDON
- ☐ 139. DALTON JONES
- ☐ 161. DICK WILLIAMS(M)
- ☐ 184. GEORGE THOMAS
- ☐ 206. DENNIS BENNETT
- ☐ 223. MIKE RYAN
- ☐ 261. JOHN WYATT
- ☐ 280. TONY CONIGLIARO
- ☐ 297. DAVE MOREHEAD
- ☐ 314. MIKE ANDREWS(R)
- ☐ 314. REGGIE SMITH(R)
- ☐ 331. JOE FOY
- ☐ 342. HANK FISCHER
- ☐ 355. CARL YASTRZEMSKI
- ☐ 371. JIM LONBORG
- ☐ 429. GARRY ROGGENBURK
- ☐ 444. GEORGE SMITH
- ☐ 473. JOSE SANTIAGO
- ☐ 528. RICO PETROCELLI
- ☐ 547. RUSS GIBSON(R)
- ☐ 547. BILL ROHR(R)
- ☐ 572. DON DEMETER
- ☐ 594. DAN OSINSKI
- ☐ 596. GALEN CISCO
- ☐ 604. TEAM CARD

CALIFORNIA ANGELS

- ☐ 19. JIM MCGLOTHLIN
- ☐ 34. PETE CIMINO
- ☐ 40. RICK REICHARDT
- ☐ 58. PAUL SCHAAL
- ☐ 79. BUBBA MORTON
- ☐ 104. MINNIE ROJAS

- ☐ 122. GEORGE BRUNET
- ☐ 147. TOM EGAN
- ☐ 175. BOBBY KNOOP
- ☐ 193. JOSE CARDENAL
- ☐ 213. JAY JOHNSTONE
- ☐ 249. NICK WILLHITE
- ☐ 265. LOU BURDETTE
- ☐ 281. BOB RODGERS
- ☐ 293. ED KIRKPATRICK
- ☐ 312. DON MINCHER
- ☐ 327. TEAM CARD
- ☐ 343. TOM SATRIANO
- ☐ 367. BILL KELSO(R)
- ☐ 367. DON WALLACE(R)
- ☐ 385. JIM FREGOSI
- ☐ 401. JIM COATES
- ☐ 432. JIMMIE HALL
- ☐ 451. FRED NEWMAN
- ☐ 469. LEN GABRIELSON
- ☐ 494. BILL RIGNEY(M)
- ☐ 496. ORLANDO MCFARLANE
- ☐ 513. MARCELINO LOPEZ
- ☐ 549. JACK SANFORD
- ☐ 584. JIM PIERSALL

CHICAGO CUBS

- ☐ 16. BILL HANDS
- ☐ 39. CURT SIMMONS
- ☐ 70. RON SANTO
- ☐ 87. GEORGE ALTMAN
- ☐ 106. RANDY HUNDLEY
- ☐ 124. JIM STEWART
- ☐ 148. ADOLFO PHILLIPS
- ☐ 168. RAY CULP
- ☐ 171. CAL KOONCE
- ☐ 185. KEN HOLTZMAN
- ☐ 215. ERNIE BANKS
- ☐ 256. BOB HENDLEY
- ☐ 272. BILL CONNORS(R)
- ☐ 272. DAVE DOWLING(R)
- ☐ 296. GLENN BECKERT
- ☐ 315. BILLY WILLIAMS
- ☐ 333. FERGUSON JENKINS
- ☐ 354. TEAM CARD
- ☐ 388. ARNOLD EARLEY
- ☐ 419. DON KESSINGER
- ☐ 439. BYRON BROWNE
- ☐ 458. LEE THOMAS
- ☐ 481. LEO DUROCHER(M)
- ☐ 497. RON CAMPBELL
- ☐ 524. FELIX MANTILLA
- ☐ 536. JOE NIEKRO(R)
- ☐ 536. PAUL POPOVICH(R)
- ☐ 552. TED SAVAGE
- ☐ 576. NORM GIGON(R)
- ☐ 578. JOHN BOCCABELLA
- ☐ 608. RICH NYE(R)
- ☐ 608. JOHN UPHAM(R)

CHICAGO WHITE SOX

- ☐ 9. RON HANSEN
- ☐ 29. TOMMY MCCRAW
- ☐ 52. DENNIS HIGGINS
- ☐ 67. KEN BERRY
- ☐ 81. EDDIE STANKY(M)
- ☐ 107. JOEL HORLEN
- ☐ 159. BRUCE HOWARD
- ☐ 178. JOHN BUZHARDT.
- ☐ 208. JACK LAMABE
- ☐ 232. DON BUFORD
- ☐ 259. DON DENNIS
- ☐ 286. WAYNE CAUSEY
- ☐ 310. GARY PETERS
- ☐ 338. BOB LOCKER
- ☐ 357. BILL SKOWRON
- ☐ 373. DUANE JOSEPHSON(R)
- ☐ 373. FRED KLAGES(R)
- ☐ 391. WILBUR WOOD
- ☐ 406. LEE ELIA
- ☐ 422. HOYT WILHELM
- ☐ 436. PETE WARD
- ☐ 455. TOMMIE AGEE
- ☐ 467. JIM O'TOOLE
- ☐ 484. JERRY ADAIR
- ☐ 506. SMOKY BURGESS
- ☐ 532. JIM HICKS
- ☐ 538. J.C. MARTIN

☐ 556. AL WEIS
☐ 573. TEAM CARD
☐ 598. WALT WILLIAMS(R)
☐ 598. ED STROUD(R)
☐ 609. TOMMY JOHN

CINCINNATI REDS

☐ 6. DICK SIMPSON
☐ 21. DAVE BRISTOL(M)
☐ 44. JOE NUXHALL
☐ 61. GORDY COLEMAN
☐ 80. JIM MALONEY
☐ 96. ART SHAMSKY
☐ 114. JACK BALDSCHUN
☐ 120. FLOYD ROBINSON
☐ 135. DERON JOHNSON
☐ 158. JIMMIE COKER
☐ 176. SAMMY ELLIS
☐ 202. JOHNNY EDWARDS
☐ 222. DARRELL OSTEEN(R)
☐ 222. LEE MAY(R)
☐ 254. MILT PAPPAS
☐ 269. DON NOTTEBART
☐ 292. DON PAVLETICH
☐ 325. CHICO CARDENAS
☐ 339. CHICO RUIZ
☐ 353. BILL MCCOOL
☐ 374. MEL QUEEN
☐ 392. TOMMY HARPER
☐ 407. TEAM CARD
☐ 430. PETE ROSE
☐ 453. AURELIO MONTEAGUDO
☐ 476. TONY PEREZ
☐ 488. GERRY ARRIGO
☐ 505. TOMMY HELMS
☐ 519. TED DAVIDSON
☐ 550. VADA PINSON
☐ 597. TED ABERNATHY

CLEVELAND INDIANS

☐ 3. DUKE SIMS
☐ 24. BOB ALLEN
☐ 43. CHICO SALMON
☐ 69. VIC DAVALILLO
☐ 95. SONNY SIEBERT
☐ 127. JOHN O'DONOGHUE
☐ 145. LARRY BROWN
☐ 174. DICK RADATZ
☐ 189. CHUCK HINTON
☐ 214. TOM KELLEY
☐ 253. BILL DAVIS(R)
☐ 253. GUS GIL(R)
☐ 258. LEE MAYE
☐ 275. FRED WHITFIELD
☐ 295. SAM MCDOWELL
☐ 316. JACK KRALICK
☐ 336. JOE AZCUE
☐ 360. LEON WAGNER
☐ 377. LUIS TIANT
☐ 397. WILLIE SMITH
☐ 424. PEDRO GONZALEZ
☐ 440. STEVE HARGAN
☐ 479. GARY BELL
☐ 499. GEORGE CULVER(R)
☐ 499. JOSE VIDAL(R)
☐ 520. MAX ALVIS
☐ 544. TEAM CARD
☐ 563. JOE ADCOCK
☐ 580. ROCKY COLAVITO

DETROIT TIGERS

☐ 13. JOE SPARMA
☐ 30. AL KALINE
☐ 48. BILL FREEHAN
☐ 72. GEORGE KORINCE(R)
☐ 72. JOHN MATCHICK(R)
☐ 88. MICKEY LOLICH
☐ 112. DAVE WICKERHAM
☐ 134. GATES BROWN
☐ 170. DICK MCAULIFFE
☐ 192. FRED GLADDING
☐ 247. JERRY LUMPE
☐ 263. HANK AGUIRRE
☐ 284. JOHNNY PODRES
☐ 305. EARL WILSON
☐ 321. MAYO SMITH(M)

☐ 352. RAY OYLER
☐ 378. TEAM CARD
☐ 394. JAKE WOOD
☐ 408. JIM NORTHRUP
☐ 420. DENNIS MCLAIN
☐ 449. ORLANDO PENA
☐ 465. WILLIE HORTON
☐ 482. BILL MONBOUQUETTE
☐ 511. DON WERT
☐ 526. PAT DOBSON(R)
☐ 526. GEORGE KORINCE(R)
☐ 540. NORM CASH
☐ 559. DICK TRACEWSKI
☐ 571. LARRY SHERRY
☐ 588. JOHNNY KLIPPSTEIN
☐ 607. MICKEY STANLEY

DICK McAULIFFE • SS

TIGERS

HOUSTON ASTROS

☐ 8. CHUCK HARRISON
☐ 28. BARRY LATMAN
☐ 51. DAVE ADLESH(R)
☐ 51. WES BALES(R)
☐ 73. RUSTY STAUB
☐ 97. MIKE CUELLAR
☐ 136. CARROLL SEMBERA
☐ 166. ED MATHEWS
☐ 172. BILL HEATH
☐ 190. TURK FARRELL
☐ 212. CHRIS ZACHARY
☐ 231. JOHN BATEMAN
☐ 274. BOB ASPROMONTE
☐ 298. RON DAVIS
☐ 318. DAVE GUISTI
☐ 337. JOE MORGAN
☐ 347. GRADY HATTON(M)
☐ 364. CLAUDE RAYMOND
☐ 390. JIM WYNN
☐ 412. NORM MILLER(R)
☐ 412. DOUG RADER(R)
☐ 415. SONNY JACKSON
☐ 447. BOB BELINSKY
☐ 464. DAN COOMBS
☐ 483. JIM LANDIS
☐ 498. LARRY DIERKER
☐ 502. DERRELL GRIFFITH
☐ 543. DAN SCHNEIDER
☐ 564. ALONZO HARRIS(R)
☐ 564. AARON POINTER(R)
☐ 582. JIM OWENS

KANSAS CITY ATHLETICS

☐ 17. JIM GOSGER
☐ 33. SAL BANDO(R)
☐ 33. RANDY SCHWARTZ(R)
☐ 54. DICK GREEN
☐ 74. WES STOCK
☐ 90. JIM NASH
☐ 110. JACK AKER
☐ 129. PHIL ROOF
☐ 157. DANNY CATER
☐ 182. ED CHARLES
☐ 209. JOE NOSSEK
☐ 227. PAUL LINDBLAD
☐ 262. TEAM CARD
☐ 282. JOHNNY ODOM
☐ 303. GIL BLANCO

☐ 323. MIKE HERSHBERGER
☐ 344. OSSIE CHAVARRIA
☐ 369. JIM HUNTER
☐ 389. AL DARK(M)
☐ 416. ROGER REPOZ
☐ 438. CHUCK DOBSON
☐ 471. RENE LACHEMANN
☐ 515. BERT CAMPANERIS
☐ 542. RICK MONDAY(R)
☐ 542. TONY PIERCE(R)
☐ 565. LEW KRAUSSE
☐ 599. BOB DULIBA
☐ 603. TIM TALTON(R)
☐ 603. RAMON WEBSTER(R)

LOS ANGELES DODGERS

☐ 12. JIMMY CAMPANIS(R)
☐ 12. BILL SINGER(R)
☐ 31. JIM BREWER
☐ 32. BOB BAILEY
☐ 55. DON DRYSDALE
☐ 76. JIM BARBIERI
☐ 94. RON FAIRLY
☐ 111. JOHN KENNEDY
☐ 130. PHIL REGAN
☐ 149. JOE MOELLER
☐ 160. WILLIE DAVIS
☐ 197. RON PERRANOSKI
☐ 218. WES PARKER
☐ 260. JIM LEFEBVRE
☐ 276. BRUCE BRUBAKER
☐ 294. WALT ALSTON(M)
☐ 313. BOB LEE
☐ 330. CLAUDE OSTEEN
☐ 346. JIM HICKMAN
☐ 365. JOHN ROSEBORO
☐ 381. DICK SCHOFIELD
☐ 398. JEFF TORBORG
☐ 410. LOU JOHNSON
☐ 428. TOM HUTTON(R)
☐ 428. GENE MICHAEL(R)
☐ 445. DON SUTTON
☐ 461. BOB L. MILLER
☐ 503. TEAM CARD
☐ 514. JOHN WERHAS
☐ 525. RON HUNT
☐ 539. DICK EGAN
☐ 557. AL FERRARA

MINNESOTA TWINS

☐ 15. EARL BATTEY
☐ 50. TONY OLIVA
☐ 98. RICH ROLLINS
☐ 133. RON KLINE
☐ 137. RON CLARK(R)
☐ 137. JIM OLLOM(R)
☐ 164. DWIGHT SIEBLER
☐ 194. BOB ALLISON
☐ 211. TEAM CARD
☐ 224. WALT BOND
☐ 246. JIM PERRY
☐ 270. ZOILO VERSALLES
☐ 300. JIM KAAT
☐ 317. CESAR TOVAR
☐ 366. ANDY KOSCO
☐ 380. DEAN CHANCE
☐ 399. AL WORTHINGTON
☐ 418. SAM MELE(M)
☐ 431. TEN UHLAENDER
☐ 446. RUSS NIXON
☐ 460. HARMON KILLEBREW
☐ 486. RICH REESE(R)
☐ 486. BILL WHITBY(R)
☐ 501. JERRY ZIMMERMAN
☐ 523. JIM MERRITT
☐ 545. JIM GRANT
☐ 569. ROD CAREW(R)
☐ 575. DAVE BOSWELL

NEW YORK METS

☐ 2. JACK HAMILTON
☐ 23. LARRY ELLIOT
☐ 42. TEAM CARD
☐ 59. RALPH TERRY
☐ 91. JOHNNY LEWIS
☐ 105. KEN BOYER

□ 121. ED BRESSOUD
□ 144. BILL HEPLER
□ 165. CLEON JONES
□ 198. CHUCK HILLER
□ 217. ROB GARDNER
□ 264. RON SWOBODA
□ 287. GREG GOOSSEN(R)
□ 287. BART SHIRLEY(R)
□ 306. BUD HARRELSON
□ 348. TUG MCGRAW
□ 370. TOMMY DAVIS
□ 386. DICK SELMA
□ 413. JERRY GROTE
□ 433. AL LUPLOW
□ 452. ED KRANEPOOL
□ 470. BOB SHAW
□ 487. TOMMIE REYNOLDS
□ 522. JOHN STEPHENSON
□ 533. JACK FISHER
□ 537. CHUCK ESTRADA
□ 555. DON CARDWELL
□ 561. SANDY ALOMAR
□ 568. JACKIE SULLIVAN
□ 574. JERRY BUCHEK
□ 581. BILL DENEHY(R)
□ 581. TOM SEAVER(R)
□ 587. DON SHAW(R)
□ 593. WES WESTRUM(M)
□ 606. RON TAYLOR

NEW YORK YANKEES

□   5. WHITEY FORD
□ 25. ELSTON HOWARD
□ 77. DOOLEY WOMACK
□ 93. STAN BAHNSEN(R)
□ 93. BOBBY MURCER(R)
□ 131. TEAM CARD
□ 150. MICKEY MANTLE
□ 169. HORACE CLARKE
□ 201. HAL RENIFF
□ 225. MEL STOTTLEMYRE
□ 257. CHARLEY SMITH
□ 277. STEVE WHITAKER
□ 289. TOM TRESH
□ 308. AL DOWNING
□ 340. JOE PEPITONE
□ 358. RUBEN AMARO
□ 375. JAKE GIBBS
□ 393. JIM BOUTON
□ 411. DICK HOWSER
□ 426. LOU CLINTON
□ 442. BILL ROBINSON(R)
□ 442. JOE VERBANIC(R)
□ 468. RALPH HOUK(M)
□ 495. FRITZ PETERSON
□ 517. FRED TALBOT
□ 553. MIKE HEGAN(R)
□ 553. THAD TILLOTSON(R)
□ 567. STEVE HAMILTON
□ 583. RAY BARKER
□ 601. BILL BRYAN

PHILADELPHIA PHILLIES

□ 14. PHIL LINZ
□ 37. RICK WISE
□ 53. CLAY DALRYMPLE
□ 68. BOB BUHL
□ 85. JOHNNY CALLISON
□ 102. TEAM CARD
□ 126. TONY TAYLOR
□ 142. JACKIE BRANDT
□ 181. TERRY FOX
□ 187. PEDRO RAMOS
□ 205. DICK GROAT
□ 229. LARRY JACKSON
□ 248. GENE MAUCH(M)
□ 268. JOHN BRIGGS
□ 290. BILL WHITE
□ 326. BOB UECKER
□ 359. DICK ELLSWORTH
□ 376. DON LOCK
□ 395. CHRIS SHORT
□ 402. GRANT JACKSON(R)
□ 402. BILLY WILSON(R)
□ 427. RUBEN GOMEZ
□ 443. TITO FRANCONA
□ 450. RICHIE ALLEN

□ 466. BOBBY WINE
□ 489. DOUG CLEMENS
□ 508. DICK HALL
□ 529. GARY WAGNER
□ 548. TONY GONZALEZ
□ 560. JIM BUNNING
□ 587. GARY SUTHERLAND(R)
□ 595. COOKIE ROJAS

PITTSBURGH PIRATES

□ 10. MATTY ALOU
□ 49. ROY FACE
□ 66. MANNY MOTA
□ 84. TOMMIE SISK
□ 123. JIMMIE PRICE(R)
□ 123. LUKE WALKER(R)
□ 140. WILLIE STARGELL
□ 162. BILLY O'DELL
□ 183. JIM PAGLIARONI
□ 203. AL MCBEAN
□ 221. WOODY FRYMAN
□ 283. GENE ALLEY
□ 301. JESSE GONDER
□ 322. JOSE PAGAN
□ 335. BOB VEALE
□ 351. VERN LAW
□ 379. JERRY MAY
□ 400. BOB CLEMENTE
□ 425. PETE MIKKELSON
□ 448. HARRY WALKER(M)
□ 472. JOHN GELNAR(R)
□ 472. GEORGE SPRIGGS(R)
□ 492. TEAM CARD
□ 510. BILL MAZEROSKI
□ 527. DENNIS RIBANT
□ 535. DONN CLENDENON
□ 554. ANDRE RODGERS
□ 562. STEVE BLASS
□ 570. MAURY WILLS
□ 577. BILL SHORT
□ 586. MANNY JIMENEZ
□ 592. JIM SHELLENBACK(R)
□ 602. JUAN PIZARRO

ST. LOUIS CARDINALS

□ 20. ORLANDO CEPEDA
□ 41. JOE HOERNER
□ 45. ROGER MARIS
□ 78. PAT CORRALES
□ 92. RAY WASHBURN
□ 108. ALEX JOHNSON
□ 128. ED SPIEZIO
□ 146. STEVE CARLTON
□ 173. TEAM CARD
□ 195. AL JACKSON
□ 196. JOHN ROMANO
□ 210. BOB GIBSON
□ 226. JULIAN JAVIER
□ 245. CURT FLOOD
□ 285. LOU BROCK
□ 304. PHIL GAGLIANO
□ 324. HAL WOODESHICK
□ 356. LARRY JASTER
□ 384. JIM COSMAN(R)
□ 384. DICK HUGHES(R)
□ 404. NELSON BRILES
□ 421. DAL MAXVILL
□ 474. BOB TOLAN
□ 485. TIM MCCARVER
□ 512. RED SCHOENDIENST(M)
□ 589. DAVE RICKETTS
□ 592. RON WILLIS(R)
□ 605. MIKE SHANNON

SAN FRANCISCO GIANTS

□   4. HAL LANIER
□ 26. BOB PRIDDY(R)
□ 46. LINDY MCDANIEL
□ 65. TOM HALLER
□ 83. OLLIE BROWN
□ 86. MIKE MCCORMICK(B)
□ 116. HERMAN FRANKS(M)
□ 132. OSSIE VIRGIL
□ 156. RON HERBEL
□ 177. TITO FUENTES

□ 200. WILLIE MAYS
□ 220. JIM HART
□ 252. BOB BOLIN
□ 279. FRANK LINZY
□ 299. NORM SIEBERN
□ 320. GAYLORD PERRY
□ 332. JESUS ALOU
□ 341. DICK DIETZ(R)
□ 341. BILL SORRELL(R)
□ 368. JACK HIATT
□ 383. KEN HENDERSON
□ 409. RAY SADECKI
□ 441. JIM DAVENPORT
□ 462. BOB BARTON
□ 480. WILLIE MCCOVEY
□ 500. JUAN MARICHAL
□ 516. TEAM CARD
□ 541. JOE GIBBON
□ 579. BILL R. HENRY

WASHINGTON SENATORS

□ 11. BARRY MOORE
□ 26. BOB PRIDDY
□ 27. BOB SAVERINE
□ 47. KEN MCMULLEN
□ 64. FRED VALENTINE
□ 71. CAMILO PASCUAL
□ 86. MIKE MCCORMICK(R)
□ 115. PAUL CASANOVA
□ 118. BERNIE ALLEN
□ 167. JOE COLEMAN
□ 167. TIM CULLEN(R)
□ 188. KEN HARRELSON
□ 207. JOHN ORSINO
□ 228. GIL HODGES(M)
□ 255. FRANK HOWARD
□ 273. DICK LINES
□ 291. JIM HANNAN
□ 311. ED BRINKMAN
□ 349. BOB CHANCE
□ 362. DAROLD KNOWLES
□ 387. CAP PETERSON
□ 403. DICK NEN
□ 414. CASEY COX
□ 437. TEAM CARD
□ 459. DICK BOSMAN(R)
□ 459. PETE CRAIG(R)
□ 478. BOB HUMPHREYS
□ 493. PHIL ORTEGA
□ 509. JIM NEN
□ 551. DOUG CAMILLI
□ 569. HANK ALLEN(R)
□ 590. PETE RICHERT

1968 TOPPS (598)
2 1/2" X 3 1/2"

TOMMIE
AARON

ATLANTA BRAVES

- [ ] 30. JOE TORRE
- [ ] 55. FELIPE ALOU
- [ ] 76. JIM BRITTON(R)
- [ ] 76. RON REED(R)
- [ ] 93. TONY CLONINGER
- [ ] 110. HANK AARON
- [ ] 134. PAT JARVIS
- [ ] 166. CLAUDE RAYMOND
- [ ] 174. BOB TILLMAN
- [ ] 187. SONNY JACKSON
- [ ] 203. DICK KELLEY
- [ ] 221. TEAM CARD
- [ ] 241. FELIX MILLAN
- [ ] 257. PHIL NIEKRO
- [ ] 286. CECIL UPSHAW
- [ ] 304. SANDY VALDESPINO
- [ ] 323. DERON JOHNSON
- [ ] 342. KEN JOHNSON
- [ ] 394. TOMMIE AARON
- [ ] 412. CLAY CARROLL
- [ ] 439. LUMAN HARRIS(M)
- [ ] 455. RICO CARTY
- [ ] 476. WOODY WOODWARD
- [ ] 527. TITO FRANCONA
- [ ] 550. CLETE BOYER
- [ ] 578. ORLANDO MARTINEZ
- [ ] 579. MIKE LUM(R)

BALTIMORE ORIOLES

- [ ] 20. BROOKS ROBINSON
- [ ] 42. LARRY HANEY
- [ ] 56. DAVE LEONHARD(R)
- [ ] 56. DAVE MAY(R)
- [ ] 82. SAM BOWENS
- [ ] 97. TOM PHOEBUS
- [ ] 118. MARK BELANGER
- [ ] 135. PAUL BLAIR
- [ ] 163. GENE BRABENDER
- [ ] 186. EDDIE WATT
- [ ] 194. DON BUFORD
- [ ] 204. ANDY ETCHEBARREN
- [ ] 222. JIM HARDIN
- [ ] 242. MOE DRABOWSKY
- [ ] 273. DAVE A. JOHNSON
- [ ] 293. BRUCE HOWARD
- [ ] 312. CURT BLEFARY
- [ ] 334. TEAM CARD
- [ ] 354. PETE RICHERT
- [ ] 381. BOOG POWELL
- [ ] 409. FRANK PETERS(R)
- [ ] 409. RON STONE(R)
- [ ] 428. VIC ROZNOVSKY
- [ ] 456. JOHN O'DONOGHUE
- [ ] 466. BILL DILLMAN
- [ ] 478. DAVE MCNALLY
- [ ] 489. WALLY BUNKER
- [ ] 500. FRANK ROBINSON
- [ ] 513. HANK BAUER(M)
- [ ] 549. CURT MOTTON(R)
- [ ] 549. ROGER NELSON(R)
- [ ] 575. JIM PALMER

BOSTON RED SOX

- [ ] 26. DARRELL BRANDON
- [ ] 43. GARY BELL
- [ ] 61. REGGIE SMITH
- [ ] 87. DICK WILLIAMS(M)
- [ ] 106. DALTON JONES
- [ ] 123. JOSE SANTIAGO
- [ ] 140. TONY CONIGLIARO
- [ ] 167. ELSTON HOWARD
- [ ] 189. BILL LANDIS
- [ ] 212. DAVE MOREHEAD
- [ ] 233. GEORGE SCOTT
- [ ] 250. CARL YASTRZEMSKI
- [ ] 272. RAY CULP
- [ ] 297. RUSS GIBSON
- [ ] 314. BILL ROHR(R)
- [ ] 314. GEORGE SPRIGGS(R)
- [ ] 331. DAN OSINSKI
- [ ] 346. JERRY ADAIR
- [ ] 387. JOE FOY
- [ ] 406. DICK ELLSWORTH
- [ ] 430. RICO PETROCELLI
- [ ] 449. GENE OLIVER
- [ ] 460. JIM LONBORG
- [ ] 481. JOHN WYATT
- [ ] 502. MIKE ANDREWS
- [ ] 519. JERRY STEPHENSON
- [ ] 537. NORM SIEBERN
- [ ] 555. JOSE TARTABULL
- [ ] 566. KEN HARRELSON
- [ ] 581. GARRY ROGGENBURK
- [ ] 593. LEE STANGE

CALIFORNIA ANGELS

- [ ] 24. BOBBY LOCKE
- [ ] 52. HAWK TAYLOR
- [ ] 75. DON MINCHER
- [ ] 102. JOSE CARDENAL
- [ ] 121. JIMMIE HALL
- [ ] 143. PETE CIMINO
- [ ] 170. JIM FREGOSI
- [ ] 193. JACK HAMILTON
- [ ] 216. BUBBA MORTON
- [ ] 238. TOM SATRIANO
- [ ] 252. TEAM CARD
- [ ] 271. BOBBY KNOOP
- [ ] 289. WOODY HELD
- [ ] 305. MINNIE ROJAS
- [ ] 328. CHUCK VINSON(R)
- [ ] 328. JIM WEAVER(R)
- [ ] 347. GEORGE BRUNET
- [ ] 389. JAY JOHNSTONE
- [ ] 416. BILL RIGNEY(M)
- [ ] 433. BOB RODGERS
- [ ] 453. SAMMY ELLIS
- [ ] 474. PAUL SCHAAL
- [ ] 493. JIM MCGLOTHLIN
- [ ] 531. CHUCK HINTON
- [ ] 552. ED KIRKPATRICK
- [ ] 570. RICK REICHARDT
- [ ] 587. ROGER REPOZ

BILLY
WILLIAMS

CHICAGO CUBS

- [ ] 13. CHUCK HARTENSTEIN
- [ ] 37. BILLY WILLIAMS
- [ ] 60. KEN HOLTZMAN
- [ ] 83. JOHN STEPHENSON

- [ ] 101. GLENN BECKERT
- [ ] 119. TED SAVAGE
- [ ] 136. RANDY HUNDLEY
- [ ] 159. DON KESSINGER
- [ ] 179. BILL STONEMAN
- [ ] 184. LOU JOHNSON
- [ ] 202. ADOLFO PHILLIPS
- [ ] 219. ROB GARDNER
- [ ] 235. RON SANTO
- [ ] 258. JOSE ARCIA(R)
- [ ] 258. BILL SCHLESINGER(R)
- [ ] 279. BILL HANDS
- [ ] 296. BYRON BROWNE
- [ ] 321. LEO DUROCHER(M)
- [ ] 339. RICH NYE
- [ ] 355. ERNIE BANKS
- [ ] 382. RAMON HERNANDEZ
- [ ] 410. FERGUSON JENKINS
- [ ] 427. DICK CALMUS
- [ ] 451. AL SPANGLER
- [ ] 475. JOE NIEKRO
- [ ] 506. CLARENCE JONES
- [ ] 516. PETE MIKKELSON
- [ ] 542. JOHN BOCCABELLA
- [ ] 561. LEE ELIA
- [ ] 591. DICK NEN

CHICAGO WHITE SOX

- [ ] 14. JERRY MCNERTNEY
- [ ] 33. PETE WARD
- [ ] 51. BOB LOCKER
- [ ] 72. TOMMY JOHN
- [ ] 99. ROCKY COLAVITO
- [ ] 125. JOE HORLEN
- [ ] 142. BUDDY BRADFORD(R)
- [ ] 142. BILL VOSS(R)
- [ ] 172. WALT WILLIAMS
- [ ] 210. GARY PETERS
- [ ] 229. FRED KLAGES
- [ ] 259. KEN BOYER
- [ ] 265. TOMMY DAVIS
- [ ] 287. MICKEY ABARBANEL(R)
- [ ] 287. CISCO CARLOS(R)
- [ ] 310. LUIS APARICIO
- [ ] 329. DUANE JOSEPHSON
- [ ] 350. HOYT WILHELM
- [ ] 391. BOB PRIDDY
- [ ] 413. TOMMY MCCRAW
- [ ] 424. TEAM CARD
- [ ] 444. JACK FISHER
- [ ] 464. DON MCMAHON
- [ ] 485. KEN BERRY
- [ ] 504. RUSS SNYDER
- [ ] 522. WAYNE CAUSEY
- [ ] 541. SANDY ALOMAR
- [ ] 564. EDDIE STANKY(M)
- [ ] 585. WILBUR WOOD

CINCINNATI REDS

- [ ] 23. CHICO CARDENAS
- [ ] 48. TED DAVIDSON
- [ ] 74. MILT PAPPAS
- [ ] 90. VADA PINSON
- [ ] 108. DON PAVLETICH
- [ ] 130. TONY PEREZ
- [ ] 133. FRED WHITFIELD
- [ ] 148. DAVE BRISTOL(M)
- [ ] 171. DON NOTTEBART
- [ ] 196. GARY NOLAN
- [ ] 213. CHICO RUIZ
- [ ] 230. PETE ROSE
- [ ] 247. JOHNNY BENCH(R)
- [ ] 247. RON TOMPKINS(R)
- [ ] 264. TED ABERNATHY
- [ ] 283. MEL QUEEN
- [ ] 302. GERRY ARRIGO
- [ ] 319. GEORGE CULVER
- [ ] 338. BOB W. JOHNSON
- [ ] 353. MACK JONES
- [ ] 384. BILL F. HENRY(R)
- [ ] 384. HAL MCRAE(R)
- [ ] 405. TOMMY HELMS
- [ ] 425. JIM MALONEY
- [ ] 441. ALEX JOHNSON
- [ ] 463. JIMMIE SCHAFFER
- [ ] 487. LEE MAY
- [ ] 511. BILL KELSO
- [ ] 523. JOHN TSITOURIS

☐ 543. BOB LEE
☐ 574. TEAM CARD
☐ 597. BILL MCCOOL

CLEVELAND INDIANS

☐ 16. LOU PINIELLA(R)
☐ 16. RICHIE SCHEINBLUM(R)
☐ 35. STEVE HARGAN
☐ 54. STAN WILLIAMS
☐ 71. VERN FULLER
☐ 94. LEE MAYE
☐ 115. SAM MCDOWELL
☐ 176. BOB ALLEN
☐ 197. LARRY BROWN
☐ 218. KEN SUAREZ
☐ 237. ALVIN DARK(M)
☐ 269. BOB TIEFENAUER
☐ 295. SONNY SIEBERT
☐ 318. CHICO SALMON
☐ 340. MAX ALVIS
☐ 397. VIC DAVALILLO
☐ 418. EDDIE FISHER
☐ 432. BILL DAVIS(R)
☐ 432. JOSE VIDAL(R)
☐ 443. JOE AZCUE
☐ 471. ORLANDO PENA
☐ 495. LEON WAGNER
☐ 508. DUKE SIMS
☐ 532. LUIS TIANT
☐ 551. DARRELL SUTHERLAND
☐ 568. WILLIE SMITH
☐ 590. TOMMY HARPER

DETROIT TIGERS

☐ 22. PAT DOBSON
☐ 40. DENNY MCLAIN
☐ 58. ED MATHEWS
☐ 78. JIM NORTHRUP
☐ 113. TOM MATCHICK(R)
☐ 113. DARYL PATTERSON(R)
☐ 129. MICKEY STANLEY
☐ 160. EARL WILSON
☐ 178. DON WERT
☐ 201. MIKE MARSHALL
☐ 226. JIMMIE PRICE
☐ 240. AL KALINE
☐ 256. NORM CASH
☐ 285. DICK MCAULIFFE
☐ 307. JOHN HILLER
☐ 326. DENNIS RIBANT
☐ 360. WILLIE HORTON
☐ 399. RAY OYLER
☐ 414. MICKEY LOLICH
☐ 447. GEORGE KORINCE(R)
☐ 447. FRED LASHER(R)
☐ 470. BILL FREEHAN
☐ 488. DICK TRACEWSKI
☐ 505. JOE SPARMA
☐ 528. TEAM CARD
☐ 544. MAYO SMITH(M)
☐ 583. GATES BROWN

HOUSTON ASTROS

☐ 21. RON DAVIS
☐ 41. JULIO GOTAY
☐ 57. DAN SCHNEIDER
☐ 77. DON WILSON
☐ 95. BOB ASPROMONTE
☐ 128. TOM DUKES(R)
☐ 128. ALONZO HARRIS(R)
☐ 144. JOE MORGAN
☐ 161. NORM MILLER
☐ 182. DAVE GIUSTI
☐ 207. CARROLL SEMBERA
☐ 232. DENIS MENKE
☐ 260. JIM WYNN
☐ 274. MIKE CUELLAR
☐ 300. RUSTY STAUB
☐ 317. RON BRAND
☐ 332. DOUG RADER
☐ 359. JOE MOELLER
☐ 392. GRADY HATTON(M)
☐ 403. JOHN BUZHARDT
☐ 423. FRED GLADDING
☐ 438. LEE THOMAS
☐ 468. LARRY SHERRY

☐ 491. DENNY LEMASTER
☐ 507. WADE BLASINGAME
☐ 529. BRUCE VON HOFF
☐ 539. JIM RAY(R)
☐ 547. DAN COOMBS
☐ 565. LARRY DIERKER
☐ 569. IVAN MURRELL(R)
☐ 576. DAVE ADLESH
☐ 592. JOHN BATEMAN

LOS ANGELES DODGERS

☐ 15. RON HUNT
☐ 34. AL FERRARA
☐ 65. JOHN ROSEBORO
☐ 88. PHIL REGAN
☐ 103. DON SUTTON
☐ 124. NATE OLIVER
☐ 145. DON DRYSDALE
☐ 168. TEAM CARD
☐ 208. WILLIE DAVIS
☐ 228. JACK BILLINGHAM(R)
☐ 228. JIM FAIREY(R)
☐ 249. BILL SINGER
☐ 266. PAUL POPOVICH
☐ 281. JIM CAMPANIS
☐ 298. JIM BREWER
☐ 315. ZOILO VERSALLES
☐ 336. JOHN PURDIN
☐ 357. LEN GABRIELSON
☐ 398. JIM GRANT
☐ 417. WILLIE CRAWFORD
☐ 440. CLAUDE OSTEEN
☐ 457. JIM LEFEBVRE
☐ 472. WALT ALSTON(M)
☐ 492. JEFF TORBORG
☐ 510. RON FAIRLY
☐ 533. WES PARKER
☐ 553. HANK AGUIRRE
☐ 580. BOB BAILEY

TED UHLAENDER
OUTFIELD TWINS

MINNESOTA TWINS

☐ 28. TED UHLAENDER
☐ 44. FRANK KOSTRO
☐ 64. JIM MERRITT
☐ 80. ROD CAREW
☐ 91. JIM OLLOM
☐ 111. RICH REESE
☐ 137. TEAM CARD
☐ 165. TONY OLIVA
☐ 181. JERRY ZIMMERMAN
☐ 206. CAL ERMER(M)
☐ 220. HARMON KILLEBREW
☐ 243. RICH ROLLINS
☐ 255. DEAN CHANCE
☐ 276. JIM ROLAND
☐ 301. GEORGE MITTERWALD(R)
☐ 301. RICH RENICK(R)
☐ 322. DAVE BOSWELL
☐ 335. BOB ALLISON
☐ 352. JACKIE HERNANDEZ
☐ 393. JIM PERRY
☐ 420. CESAR TOVAR
☐ 435. RON PERRANOSKI
☐ 450. JIM KAAT
☐ 473. AL WORTHINGTON
☐ 515. RUSS NIXON

☐ 534. BOB L. MILLER
☐ 557. FRANK QUILICI
☐ 589. RON CLARK(R)
☐ 589. MOE OGIER(R)

NEW YORK METS

☐ 27. GIL HODGES(M)
☐ 45. TOM SEAVER
☐ 63. DICK KENWORTHY
☐ 92. ED KRANEPOOL
☐ 114. RON SWOBODA
☐ 132. BUD HARRELSON
☐ 177. JERRY KOOSMAN(R)
☐ 177. NOLAN RYAN(R)
☐ 191. DAN FRISELLA
☐ 211. J.C. MARTIN
☐ 236. TUG MCGRAW
☐ 254. CLEON JONES
☐ 277. JERRY BUCHEK
☐ 292. ART SHAMSKY
☐ 313. AL WEIS
☐ 345. BOB HENDLEY
☐ 386. GREG GOOSSEN
☐ 401. TEAM CARD
☐ 421. RON TAYLOR
☐ 437. DON CARDWELL
☐ 465. TOMMIE AGEE
☐ 486. CAL KOONCE
☐ 503. AL JACKSON
☐ 521. DON SHAW
☐ 536. BILL SHORT
☐ 556. DICK SELMA
☐ 563. ED CHARLES
☐ 569. LESS ROHR(R)
☐ 572. DON BOSCH
☐ 582. JERRY GROTE
☐ 594. PHIL LINZ

NEW YORK YANKEES

☐ 29. JOE VERBANIC
☐ 47. RALPH HOUK(M)
☐ 69. TOM TRESH
☐ 89. JAKE GIBBS
☐ 105. AL DOWNING
☐ 120. MEL STOTTLEMYRE
☐ 138. RUBEN AMARO
☐ 195. JOE PEPITONE
☐ 214. STAN BAHNSEN(R)
☐ 214. FRANK FERNANDEZ(R)
☐ 234. BILL MONBOUQUETTE
☐ 246. FRITZ PETERSON
☐ 263. HORACE CLARKE
☐ 280. MICKEY MANTLE
☐ 299. GENE MICHAEL
☐ 316. STEVE BARBER
☐ 337. BILL ROBINSON
☐ 383. STEVE WHITAKER
☐ 402. MIKE HEGAN
☐ 431. DOOLEY WOMACK
☐ 467. DICK HOWSER
☐ 496. STEVE HAMILTON
☐ 524. ANDY KOSCO
☐ 539. MIKE FERRARO(R)
☐ 546. ROY WHITE
☐ 562. JIM BOUTON
☐ 577. FRED TALBOT
☐ 596. CHARLIE SMITH

OAKLAND A'S

☐ 18. MIKE HERSHBERGER
☐ 38. TONY PIERCE
☐ 62. CHUCK DOBSON
☐ 79. TED KUBIAK
☐ 109. BERT CAMPANERIS
☐ 127. PAUL LINDBLAD
☐ 146. SAL BANDO
☐ 164. RAMON WEBSTER
☐ 183. BOB KENNEDY(M)
☐ 199. ROBERTO RODRIQUEZ(R)
☐ 199. DARRELL OSTEEN(R)
☐ 224. JACK AKER
☐ 244. JOHN DONALDSON
☐ 261. DAVE DUNCAN
☐ 282. RICK MONDAY
☐ 303. DICK GREEN
☐ 324. JIM NASH

☐ 343. JIM GOSGER
☐ 385. JIM HUNTER
☐ 404. FLOYD ROBINSON
☐ 422. RENE LACHEMANN
☐ 458. LEW KRAUSSE
☐ 484. PHIL ROOF
☐ 501. JOHN ODOM
☐ 517. DIEGO SEGUI
☐ 535. DANNY CATER
☐ 554. TEAM CARD
☐ 571. TONY LARUSSA
☐ 586. JIM PAGLIARONI

PHILADELPHIA PHILLIES

☐ 17. DICK HALL
☐ 39. COOKIE ROJAS
☐ 59. DON LOCK
☐ 81. LARRY JACKSON
☐ 98. GARY SUTHERLAND
☐ 112. WOODY FRYMAN
☐ 122. GENE MAUCH(M)
☐ 139. CHRIS SHORT
☐ 173. JOHN BOOZER
☐ 190. BILL WHITE
☐ 217. TURK FARRELL
☐ 225. RICHIE ALLEN
☐ 245. TONY GONZALEZ
☐ 262. RICK WISE
☐ 284. JOHN BRIGGS
☐ 306. MIKE RYAN
☐ 327. TONY TAYLOR
☐ 348. LARRY COLTON(R)
☐ 348. DICK THOENEN(R)
☐ 396. BOBBY WINE
☐ 415. JOHNNY CALLISON
☐ 434. RICK JOSEPH
☐ 448. GARY WAGNER
☐ 477. TEAM CARD
☐ 512. GRANT JACKSON
☐ 567. CLAY DALRYMPLE
☐ 579. LARRY HISLE(R)

PITTSBURGH PIRATES

☐ 19. JUAN PIZARRO
☐ 36. BOB MOOSE(R)
☐ 36. BOB ROBERTSON(R)
☐ 53. GENE ALLEY
☐ 70. BOB VEALE
☐ 86. WILLIE STARGELL
☐ 150. BOB CLEMENTE
☐ 175. MAURY WILLS
☐ 198. ROY FACE
☐ 215. JIM BUNNING
☐ 251. MANNY SANGUILLEN
☐ 270. MATTY ALOU
☐ 288. DAVE WICKERSHAM
☐ 308. TEAM CARD
☐ 325. MANNY MOTA
☐ 344. DONN CLENDENON
☐ 390. BILL MAZEROSKI
☐ 407. GARY KOLB
☐ 429. TOMMIE SISK
☐ 446. RON KLINE
☐ 461. CHUCK HILLER
☐ 482. JOSE PAGAN
☐ 499. STEVE BLASS
☐ 514. AL MCBEAN
☐ 538. MANNY JIMENEZ
☐ 559. CARL TAYLOR(R)
☐ 559. LUKE WALKER(R)
☐ 584. LARRY SHEPARD(M)
☐ 598. JERRY MAY

ST. LOUIS CARDINALS

☐ 25. JULIAN JAVIER
☐ 46. DAVE RICKETTS
☐ 68. RON WILLIS
☐ 84. BOB TOLAN
☐ 100. BOB GIBSON
☐ 117. LARRY JASTER
☐ 141. DAL MAXVILL
☐ 162. HAL GILSON(R)
☐ 162. MIKE TORREZ(R)
☐ 180. CURT FLOOD
☐ 200. ORLANDO CEPEDA
☐ 227. JOE HOERNER

☐ 253. DICK HUGHES
☐ 275. TIM MCCARVER
☐ 294. RED SCHOENDIENST(M)
☐ 311. JACK LAMABE
☐ 330. ROGER MARIS
☐ 349. ED SPIEZIO
☐ 388. RAY WASHBURN
☐ 408. STEVE CARLTON
☐ 445. MIKE SHANNON
☐ 459. DICK SIMPSON
☐ 479. PHIL GAGLIANO
☐ 497. TEAM CARD
☐ 520. LOU BROCK
☐ 540. NELSON BRILES
☐ 558. JOHN EDWARDS
☐ 588. DICK SCHOFIELD

SAN FRANCISCO GIANTS

☐ 32. JOE GIBBON
☐ 50. WILLIE MAYS
☐ 73. JIM HART
☐ 85. GAYLORD PERRY
☐ 104. DICK DIETZ
☐ 126. BOBBY ETHERIDGE
☐ 147. FRANK LINZY
☐ 169. BOB BOLIN
☐ 185. TOM HALLER
☐ 205. JUAN MARICAHL
☐ 223. OLLIE BROWN
☐ 239. BILL R. HENRY
☐ 267. HERMAN FRANKS(M)
☐ 290. WILLIE MCCOVEY
☐ 309. KEN HENDERSON
☐ 333. RON HERBEL
☐ 351. BOB BARTON
☐ 400. MIKE MCCORMICK
☐ 419. JACK HIATT
☐ 436. HAL LANIER
☐ 452. JESUS ALOU
☐ 469. TY CLINE
☐ 494. RAY SADECKI
☐ 525. JIM DAVENPORT
☐ 545. LINDY MCDANIEL

WASHINGTON SENATORS

☐ 31. ED STROUD
☐ 49. ED BRINKMAN
☐ 66. CASEY COX
☐ 96. FRANK COGGINS(R)
☐ 96. DICK NOLD(R)
☐ 116. KEN MCMULLEN
☐ 131. FRANK BERTAINA
☐ 149. BOB SAVERINE
☐ 188. CAP PETERSON
☐ 209. TIM CULLEN
☐ 231. DAVE BALDWIN
☐ 248. FRED VALENTINE
☐ 268. BOB HUMPHREYS
☐ 291. DICK LINES
☐ 320. FRANK HOWARD
☐ 341. JIM LEMON(M)
☐ 358. MIKE EPSTEIN
☐ 395. CAMILO PASCUAL
☐ 411. RON HANSEN
☐ 426. HANK ALLEN
☐ 442. DICK BOSMAN
☐ 462. BARRY MOORE
☐ 483. DAROLD KNOWLES
☐ 498. BILL BRYAN
☐ 509. DENNIS HIGGINS
☐ 526. BILL DENEHY
☐ 548. BERNIE ALLEN
☐ 560. PAUL CASANOVA
☐ 573. JOE COLEMAN
☐ 595. PHIL ORTEGA

1969 TOPPS (664)
2 1/2" X 3 1/2"

ATLANTA BRAVES

☐ 33. WAYNE CAUSEY
☐ 53. SONNY JACKSON
☐ 79. MILT PAPPAS
☐ 100. HANK AARON
☐ 128. TOMMIE AARON
☐ 154. JIM BRITTON
☐ 177. RON REED
☐ 196. LUM HARRIS(M)
☐ 210. FELIX MILLAN
☐ 238. KEN JOHNSON
☐ 261. BOB W. JOHNSON
☐ 282. PAT JARVIS
☐ 300. FELIPE ALOU
☐ 331. GIL GARRIDO(R)
☐ 331. TOM HOUSE(R)
☐ 355. PHIL NIEKRO
☐ 374. BOB TILLMAN
☐ 385. ORLANDO CEPEDA
☐ 398. TITO FRANCONA
☐ 446. CLAUDE RAYMOND
☐ 489. CLETE BOYER
☐ 514. MIKE LUM
☐ 542. BOB ASPROMONTE
☐ 568. CECIL UPSHAW
☐ 590. RICO CARTY
☐ 611. BOB DIDIER(R)
☐ 611. WALT HRINIAK(R)
☐ 611. GARY NEIBAUER(R)
☐ 627. GEORGE STONE

BALTIMORE ORIOLES

☐ 15. BOOG POWELL
☐ 37. CURT MOTTON
☐ 66. MIKE ADAMSON(R)
☐ 66. MERV RETTENMUND(R)
☐ 86. PETE RICHERT
☐ 113. DAVE MAY
☐ 141. BILL DILLMAN
☐ 151. CLAY DALRYMPLE
☐ 185. TOM PHOEBUS
☐ 203. DAVE A. JOHNSON
☐ 228. DAVE LEONHARD
☐ 250. FRANK ROBINSON
☐ 277. ELROD HENDRICKS
☐ 299. MARK BELANGER
☐ 323. LARRY MILLER
☐ 340. DAVE MCNALLY
☐ 368. VIC ROZNOVSKY
☐ 393. GENE BRABENDER
☐ 453. MIKE CUELLAR
☐ 478. DON BUFORD
☐ 506. PAUL BLAIR
☐ 516. EARL WEAVER(M)
☐ 550. BROOKS ROBINSON
☐ 573. JIM PALMER
☐ 597. BOBBY FLOYD(R)
☐ 610. JIM HARDIN
☐ 634. ANDY ETCHEBARREN
☐ 652. EDDIE WATT

BOSTON RED SOX

- ☐ 21. JOSE SANTIAGO
- ☐ 52. MIKE ANDREWS
- ☐ 89. RUSS GIBSON
- ☐ 109. JIM LONBORG
- ☐ 130. CARL YASTRZEMSKI
- ☐ 148. LEE STANGE
- ☐ 172. JERRY STEPHENSON
- ☐ 189. JOE LAHOUD(R)
- ☐ 189. JOHN THIBDEAU(R)
- ☐ 215. RICO PETROCELLI
- ☐ 240. KEN HARRELSON
- ☐ 264. BILL LANDIS
- ☐ 287. JOSE TARTABULL
- ☐ 311. SPARKY LYLE
- ☐ 330. TONY CONIGLIARO
- ☐ 349. DICK WILLIAMS(M)
- ☐ 391. RAY CULP
- ☐ 457. DALTON JONES
- ☐ 476. KEN BRETT(R)
- ☐ 476. GERRY MOSES(R)
- ☐ 498. JUAN PIZARRO
- ☐ 521. GEORGE THOMAS
- ☐ 543. FRED NEWMAN
- ☐ 574. GEORGE SCOTT
- ☐ 628. BILL CONIGLIARO(R)
- ☐ 628. SYD O'BRIEN(R)
- ☐ 628. FRED WENZ(R)
- ☐ 660. REGGIE SMITH

CALIFORNIA ANGELS

- ☐ 32. SAMMY ELLIS
- ☐ 59. JAY JOHNSTONE
- ☐ 78. TOM SATRIANO
- ☐ 103. ROGER REPOZ
- ☐ 134. JIM WEAVER
- ☐ 157. BOB RODGERS
- ☐ 182. BILL RIGNEY(M)
- ☐ 205. RICK REICHARDT
- ☐ 224. BILL HARRELSON(R)
- ☐ 224. STEVE KEALEY(R)
- ☐ 252. CHUCK COTTIER
- ☐ 275. VIC DAVALILLO
- ☐ 296. ANDY MESSERSMITH
- ☐ 315. EDDIE FISHER
- ☐ 342. BUBBA MORTON
- ☐ 365. JIM FREGOSI
- ☐ 386. JIM MCGLOTHLIN
- ☐ 407. TOM EGAN
- ☐ 445. BOBBY KNOOP
- ☐ 474. TOM MURPHY
- ☐ 502. MINNIE ROJAS
- ☐ 523. BOB CHANCE
- ☐ 565. HOYT WILHELM
- ☐ 583. CLYDE WRIGHT
- ☐ 598. RUBEN AMARO
- ☐ 621. BILL VOSS
- ☐ 645. GEORGE BRUNET
- ☐ 653. AURELIO RODRIGUEZ

CHICAGO CUBS

- ☐ 20. ERNIE BANKS
- ☐ 43. JOE NIEKRO
- ☐ 63. JIM HICKMAN
- ☐ 88. RICH NYE
- ☐ 115. BILL HANDS
- ☐ 147. LEO DUROCHER(M)
- ☐ 171. GLENN BECKERT
- ☐ 198. WILLIE SMITH
- ☐ 225. DON KESSINGER
- ☐ 247. GENE OLIVER
- ☐ 268. AL SPANGLER
- ☐ 288. KEN HOLTZMAN
- ☐ 312. LEE ELIA
- ☐ 347. RANDY HUNDLEY
- ☐ 372. ADOLFO PHILLIPS
- ☐ 404. VIC LAROSE(R)
- ☐ 404. GARY ROSS(R)
- ☐ 450. BILLY WILLIAMS
- ☐ 483. TED ABERNATHY
- ☐ 535. PHIL REGAN
- ☐ 538. CHARLIE SMITH
- ☐ 570. RON SANTO
- ☐ 593. DON NOTTEBART
- ☐ 602. ALEC DISTASO(R)
- ☐ 602. DON YOUNG(R)
- ☐ 602. JIM QUALLS(R)
- ☐ 640. FERGIE JENKINS

CHICAGO WHITE SOX

- ☐ 34. GARY PETERS
- ☐ 54. CISCO CARLOS
- ☐ 75. LUIS APARICIO
- ☐ 97. BUDDY BRADFORD
- ☐ 123. WILBUR WOOD
- ☐ 155. PETE WARD
- ☐ 173. BOB CHRISTIAN(R)
- ☐ 173. GERRY NYMAN(R)
- ☐ 179. DON PAVLETICH
- ☐ 222. DUANE JOSEPHSON
- ☐ 248. BOB PRIDDY
- ☐ 283. SANDY ALOMAR
- ☐ 309. WALT WILLIAMS
- ☐ 328. JOE HORLEN
- ☐ 363. RUSS NIXON
- ☐ 388. TOM MCCRAW
- ☐ 439. ED HERRMANN(R)
- ☐ 439. DAN LAZAR(R)
- ☐ 465. TOMMY JOHN
- ☐ 481. BILL MELTON
- ☐ 494. KEN BERRY
- ☐ 527. AL LOPEZ(M)
- ☐ 548. BOB LOCKER
- ☐ 566. RON HANSEN
- ☐ 622. DAN OSINSKI
- ☐ 636. WOODIE HELD
- ☐ 654. CARLOS MAY(R)
- ☐ 654. DON SECRIST(R)
- ☐ 654. RICH MORALES(R)

CINCINNATI REDS

- ☐ 26. CLAY CARROLL
- ☐ 70. TOMMY HELMS
- ☐ 81. MEL QUEEN
- ☐ 95. JOHNNY BENCH
- ☐ 120. PETE ROSE
- ☐ 142. WOODY WOODWARD
- ☐ 187. LEON WAGNER
- ☐ 213. GERRY ARRIGO
- ☐ 234. DAVE BRISTOL(M)
- ☐ 259. BILL SHORT
- ☐ 280. ALEX JOHNSON
- ☐ 295. TONY PEREZ
- ☐ 318. JACK FISHER
- ☐ 339. STEVE MINGORI(R)
- ☐ 339. JOE PENA(R)
- ☐ 362. JIM MALONEY
- ☐ 382. PAT CORRALES
- ☐ 405. LEE MAY
- ☐ 448. BOB TOLAN
- ☐ 469. CHICO RUIZ
- ☐ 492. TONY CLONINGER
- ☐ 518. FRED WHITFIELD
- ☐ 551. WAYNE GRANGER
- ☐ 581. GARY NOLAN
- ☐ 613. JIM BEAUCHAMP
- ☐ 624. DARREL CHANEY(R)
- ☐ 635. GEORGE CULVER
- ☐ 661. JIM MERRITT

CLEVELAND INDIANS

- ☐ 19. KEN SUAREZ
- ☐ 61. JIMMIE HALL
- ☐ 91. ALVIN DARK(M)
- ☐ 118. STAN WILLIAMS
- ☐ 145. MAX ALVIS
- ☐ 176. JOE AZCUE
- ☐ 201. RUSS SNYDER
- ☐ 220. SAM MCDOWELL
- ☐ 244. RAY FOSSE(R)
- ☐ 244. GEORGE WOODSON(R)
- ☐ 267. VICENTE ROMO
- ☐ 291. VERN FULLER
- ☐ 325. JOSE CARDENAL
- ☐ 348. STEVE HARGAN
- ☐ 367. LOU JOHNSON
- ☐ 414. DUKE SIMS
- ☐ 455. SONNY SIEBERT
- ☐ 479. RICHIE SCHEINBLUM
- ☐ 503. LARRY BROWN
- ☐ 537. MIKE PAUL
- ☐ 560. LUIS TIANT
- ☐ 571. CAP PETERSON
- ☐ 579. DAVE NELSON
- ☐ 595. LEE MAYE
- ☐ 597. LARRY BURCHART(R)

- ☐ 605. DICK ELLSWORTH
- ☐ 629. JACK HAMILTON
- ☐ 644. CHUCK HINTON

DETROIT TIGERS

- ☐ 13. MICKEY STANLEY
- ☐ 40. MAYO SMITH(M)
- ☐ 80. NORM CASH
- ☐ 101. DARYL PATTERSON
- ☐ 126. DICK TRACEWSKI
- ☐ 150. DENNY MCLAIN
- ☐ 180. WILLIE HORTON
- ☐ 207. ROY FACE
- ☐ 231. PAT DOBSON
- ☐ 256. GATES BROWN
- ☐ 270. MICKEY LOLICH
- ☐ 305. DICK MCAULIFFE
- ☐ 324. LES CAIN(R)
- ☐ 324. DAVE CAMPBELL(R)
- ☐ 344. TOM MATCHICK
- ☐ 373. FRED LASHER
- ☐ 390. BILL FREEHAN
- ☐ 410. AL KALINE
- ☐ 443. DON WERT
- ☐ 472. JIM PRICE
- ☐ 488. JOE SPARMA
- ☐ 525. EARL WILSON
- ☐ 544. MIKE KILKENNEY(R)
- ☐ 544. RON WOODS(R)
- ☐ 580. JIM NORTHRUP
- ☐ 616. DON MCMAHON
- ☐ 642. JOHN HILLER
- ☐ 663. DICK RADATZ

HOUSTON ASTROS

- ☐ 35. JOE MORGAN
- ☐ 58. FRED GLADDING
- ☐ 76. NORM MILLER
- ☐ 96. DENVER LEMASTER
- ☐ 119. DOUG RADER
- ☐ 156. HAL GILSON(R)
- ☐ 156. LEON MCFADDEN(R)
- ☐ 186. JOHN EDWARDS
- ☐ 202. DON WILSON
- ☐ 208. DONN CLENDENON
- ☐ 257. JIM RAY
- ☐ 278. GARY GEIGER
- ☐ 308. WADE BLASINGAME
- ☐ 337. MARTY MARTINEZ
- ☐ 360. JIM WYNN
- ☐ 389. DAN COOMBS
- ☐ 411. LARRY DIERKER
- ☐ 458. CURT BLEFARY
- ☐ 487. DENIS MENKE
- ☐ 499. DON BRYANT(R)
- ☐ 499. STEVE SHEA(R)
- ☐ 526. HECTOR TORRES
- ☐ 562. BOB WATSON
- ☐ 594. DOOLEY WOMACK
- ☐ 614. TOM GRIFFIN(R)
- ☐ 614. SKIP GUINN(R)
- ☐ 633. HARRY WALKER(M)
- ☐ 656. DAN SCHNEIDER

KANSAS CITY ROYALS

- ☐ 29. DAVE MOREHEAD
- ☐ 49. STEVE JONES
- ☐ 49. ELLIE RODRIGUEZ(R)
- ☐ 71. STEVE WHITAKER
- ☐ 93. JOE FOY
- ☐ 116. CHUCK HARRISON
- ☐ 137. WALLY BUNKER
- ☐ 159. JERRY ADAIR
- ☐ 211. GALEN CISCO
- ☐ 239. BOB TAYLOR
- ☐ 258. JACKIE HERNANDEZ
- ☐ 279. ROGER NELSON
- ☐ 298. DAVE NICHOLSON
- ☐ 352. PAUL SCHAAL
- ☐ 376. MIKE FIORE(R)
- ☐ 376. JIM ROOKER(R)
- ☐ 396. JIM CAMPANIS
- ☐ 437. LUIS ALCARAZ
- ☐ 463. DENNIS RIBANT
- ☐ 484. JOE GORDON(M)
- ☐ 508. MOE DRABOWSKY
- ☐ 529. ED KIRKPATRICK

☐ 558. TOM BURGMEIER
☐ 569. BILLY HARRIS
☐ 591. MIKE HEDLUND
☐ 603. JOE KEOUGH
☐ 619. BILL BUTLER(R)
☐ 619. H. PAT KELLY(R)
☐ 619. JUAN RIOS(R)
☐ 632. JON WARDEN
☐ 647. DAVE WICKERSHAM
☐ 662. DICK DRAGO(R)
☐ 662. GEORGE SPRIGGS(R)
☐ 662. BOB OLIVER(R)

LOS ANGELES DODGERS

☐ 24. WALTER ALSTON(M)
☐ 47. PAUL POPOVICH
☐ 65. WILLIE DAVIS
☐ 94. HANK AGUIRRE
☐ 122. RON FAIRLY
☐ 139. ANDY KOSCO
☐ 140. JIM LEFEBVRE
☐ 161. JOHN PURDIN
☐ 216. DON SUTTON
☐ 241. JIM BREWER
☐ 266. TOM HUTTON(R)
☐ 266. ALAN FOSTER(R)
☐ 289. BART SHIRLEY
☐ 310. TOM HALLER
☐ 327. WILLIE CRAWFORD
☐ 353. JEFF TORBORG
☐ 379. KEN BOYER
☐ 400. DON DRYSDALE
☐ 444. JOE MOELLER
☐ 471. TED SAVAGE
☐ 493. WES PARKER
☐ 528. CLAUDE OSTEEN
☐ 552. TED SIZEMORE(R)
☐ 552. BILL SUDAKIS(R)
☐ 575. BILL SINGER
☐ 615. LEN GABRIELSON
☐ 641. BOBBY DARWIN(R)
☐ 641. JOHN MILLER(R)

MINNESOTA TWINS

☐ 30. BOB ALLISON
☐ 56. RICH REESE
☐ 77. RON PERRANOSKI
☐ 99. DANNY MORRIS(R)
☐ 99. GRAIG NETTLES(R)
☐ 121. JOE GRZENDA
☐ 146. JIM PERRY
☐ 194. TED UHLAENDER
☐ 218. JOHN ROSEBORO
☐ 242. FRANK KOSTRO
☐ 265. CHICO CARDENAS
☐ 290. JIM KAAT
☐ 317. BRUCE LOOK
☐ 336. JIM ROLAND
☐ 356. FRANK QUILICI
☐ 375. HARMON KILLEBREW
☐ 403. BOB L. MILLER
☐ 459. DAVE BOSWELL
☐ 491. JERRY CRIDER(R)
☐ 491. GEORGE MITTERWALD(R)
☐ 510. ROD CAREW
☐ 530. CESAR TOVAR
☐ 547. BILLY MARTIN(M)
☐ 561. RON CLARK
☐ 600. TONY OLIVA
☐ 620. DEAN CHANCE
☐ 658. TOM HALL(R)

MONTREAL EXPOS

☐ 22. JESUS ALOU
☐ 45. MAURY WILLS
☐ 67. BILL STONEMAN
☐ 92. JACK BILLINGHAM
☐ 117. JIM FAIREY
☐ 138. JOHN BATEMAN
☐ 183. DON SHAW
☐ 230. RUSTY STAUB
☐ 236. MANNY MOTA
☐ 284. JERRY ROBERTSON(R)
☐ 284. MIKE WEGENER(R)
☐ 306. JIM GRANT
☐ 326. GARY SUTHERLAND
☐ 351. CARROLL SEMBERA

☐ 378. JOSE HERRERA
☐ 399. BOB BAILEY
☐ 442. TY CLINE
☐ 466. JOHN BOCCABELLA
☐ 496. LARRY JASTER
☐ 524. JOSE LABOY(R)
☐ 524. FLOYD WICKER(R)
☐ 549. RON BRAND
☐ 578. DON BOSCH
☐ 606. GENE MAUCH(M)
☐ 625. MACK JONES
☐ 646. DAN MCGINN(R)
☐ 646. CARL MORTON(R)
☐ 648. BOBBY WINE

NEW YORK METS

☐ 31. GARY GENTRY(R)
☐ 31. AMOS OTIS(R)
☐ 55. JERRY GROTE
☐ 72. RON TAYLOR
☐ 90. JERRY KOOSMAN
☐ 112. J.C. MARTIN
☐ 127. KEVIN COLLINS
☐ 144. BOB HENDLEY
☐ 193. DON CARDWELL
☐ 221. ART SHAMSKY
☐ 245. ED CHARLES
☐ 269. AL WEIS
☐ 303. CAL KOONCE
☐ 321. JIM MCANDREW
☐ 343. DAN FRISELLA
☐ 364. TOMMIE AGEE
☐ 381. ED KRANEPOOL
☐ 402. KEN BOSWELL
☐ 456. BUD HARRELSON
☐ 480. TOM SEAVER
☐ 512. CLEON JONES
☐ 533. NOLAN RYAN
☐ 564. GIL HODGES(M)
☐ 585. RON SWOBODA
☐ 601. TUG MCGRAW
☐ 624. DUFFY DYER(R)
☐ 649. AL JACKSON

NEW YORK YANKEES

☐ 25. ROY WHITE
☐ 46. FRITZ PETERSON
☐ 69. STEVE HAMILTON
☐ 87. HORACE CLARKE
☐ 114. ALAN CLOSTER(R)
☐ 114. JOHN CUMBERLAND(R)
☐ 191. LINDY MCDANIEL
☐ 212. TOM TRESH
☐ 237. BOBBY COX
☐ 262. MIKE KEKICH
☐ 292. AL DOWNING
☐ 313. BILL ROBINSON
☐ 332. FRED TALBOT
☐ 354. NATE OLIVER
☐ 380. STAN BAHNSEN
☐ 401. JAKE GIBBS
☐ 447. RALPH HOUK(M)
☐ 470. MEL STOTTLEMYRE
☐ 500. MICKEY MANTLE
☐ 519. GERRY KENNEY(R)
☐ 519. LEN BOEHMER(R)
☐ 541. JOE VERBANIC
☐ 557. FRANK FERNANDEZ
☐ 589. JOE PEPITONE
☐ 608. DICK SIMPSON
☐ 626. GENE MICHAEL
☐ 643. BILLY COWAN
☐ 657. BOBBY MURCER
☐ 658. BILL BURBACH(R)

OAKLAND A'S

☐ 23. LEW KRAUSSE
☐ 44. DANNY CATER
☐ 68. DAVE DUNCAN
☐ 105. RICK MONDAY
☐ 124. HANK BAUER(M)
☐ 143. JOE NOSSEK
☐ 195. JOHN ODOM
☐ 217. JOHN DONALDSON
☐ 235. JIM HUNTER
☐ 260. REGGIE JACKSON

☐ 281. TED KUBIAK
☐ 302. JIM PAGLIARONI
☐ 334. PHIL ROOF
☐ 358. GEORGE LAUZERIQUE(R)
☐ 358. ROBERTO RODRIQUEZ(R)
☐ 371. SAL BANDO
☐ 397. CHUCK DOBSON
☐ 449. PAUL LINDBLAD
☐ 467. TOM REYNOLDS
☐ 495. BERT CAMPANERIS
☐ 515. DICK GREEN
☐ 546. JIM NASH
☐ 587. JOE RUDI
☐ 597. ROLLIE FINGERS(R)
☐ 618. RAMON WEBSTER
☐ 638. ED SPRAGUE
☐ 655. MIKE HERSHBERGER

PHILADELPHIA PHILLIES

☐ 28. MIKE RYAN
☐ 51. WOODY FRYMAN
☐ 73. JOHNNY BRIGGS
☐ 108. TONY TAYLOR
☐ 133. JOHNNY CALLISON
☐ 174. GRANT JACKSON
☐ 188. RICK WISE
☐ 206. LARRY HISLE(R)
☐ 206. BARRY LERSCH(R)
☐ 229. DON LOCK
☐ 253. JERRY JOHNSON
☐ 276. GARY WAGNER
☐ 297. DERON JOHNSON
☐ 329. RICK JOSEPH
☐ 350. RICHIE ALLEN
☐ 369. BOB SKINNER
☐ 395. CHRIS SHORT
☐ 454. LARRY COLTON(R)
☐ 454. DON MONEY(R)
☐ 477. JEFF JAMES
☐ 507. COOKIE ROJAS
☐ 531. DICK FARRELL
☐ 576. RON STONE(R)
☐ 576. BILL WILSON(R)
☐ 599. JOHN BOOZER
☐ 624. TERRY HARMON(R)

PITTSBURGH PIRATES

☐ 36. LUKE WALKER
☐ 50. BOB CLEMENTE
☐ 82. RICH HEBNER(R)
☐ 82. AL OLIVER(R)
☐ 104. STEVE BLASS
☐ 131. CHRIS CANNIZZARO
☐ 152. TOMMIE SISK
☐ 175. JIM BUNNING
☐ 192. JOSE PAGAN
☐ 219. FREDDIE PATEK
☐ 243. RON KLINE
☐ 263. JERRY MAY
☐ 286. DOCK ELLIS
☐ 307. GARY KOLB
☐ 335. BILL MAZEROSKI
☐ 357. CARL TAYLOR
☐ 384. LARRY SHEPARD(M)
☐ 409. BOB MOOSE
☐ 436. GENE ALLEY
☐ 468. BRUCE DAL CANTON(R)
☐ 468. BOB ROBERTSON(R)
☐ 490. MATTY ALOU
☐ 509. MANNY SANGUILLEN
☐ 520. BOB VEALE
☐ 545. WILLIE STARGELL
☐ 553. RON DAVIS
☐ 567. ELVIO JIMENEZ(R)
☐ 567. JIM SHELLENBACK(R)
☐ 596. CHUCK HARTENSTEIN

ST. LOUIS CARDINALS

☐ 18. DICK SCHOFIELD
☐ 39. DICK HUGHES
☐ 60. NELSON BRILES
☐ 85. LOU BROCK
☐ 110. MIKE SHANNON
☐ 136. STEVE HUNTZ(R)
☐ 136. MIKE TORREZ(R)
☐ 160. VADA PINSON

□ 181. MEL NELSON
□ 200. BOB GIBSON
□ 232. DAVE RICKETTS
□ 255. STEVE CARLTON
□ 273. RON WILLIS
□ 320. DAL MAXVILL
□ 341. DAVE ADLESH
□ 366. BO BELINSKY
□ 415. RAY WASHBURN
□ 438. GARY WASLEWSKI
□ 460. JOE TORRE
□ 462. RED SCHOENDIENST(M)
□ 475. TIM MCCARVER
□ 497. JULIAN JAVIER
□ 522. JOE HOERNER
□ 540. CURT FLOOD
□ 559. JOE HAGUE(R)
□ 559. JIM HICKS(R)
□ 588. BILL WHITE
□ 609. PHIL GAGLIANO

SAN DIEGO PADRES

□ 14. AL MCBEAN
□ 38. ZOILO VERSALLES
□ 74. PRESTON GOMEZ(M)
□ 98. DAVE GIUSTI
□ 129. BILL MCCOOL
□ 149. OLLIE BROWN
□ 184. ROBERTO PENA
□ 197. DICK SELMA
□ 223. TOM DUKES
□ 249. ED SPIEZIO
□ 271. LARRY STAHL
□ 304. BILL DAVIS(R)
□ 304. CLARENCE GASTON(R)
□ 333. IVAN MURRELL
□ 359. DICK KELLEY
□ 387. BOBBY KLAUS
□ 408. NATE COLBERT
□ 452. AL FERRARA
□ 473. JOSE ARCIA
□ 501. TONY GONZALEZ
□ 536. DANNY BREEDEN(R)
□ 536. DAVE A. ROBERTS(R)
□ 592. RAFAEL ROBLES(R)
□ 592. AL SANTORINI(R)
□ 617. JESSE GONDER
□ 637. JERRY DAVANON(R)
□ 637. FRANK REBERGER(R)
□ 637. CLAY KIRBY(R)
□ 641. TOMMY DEAN(R)
□ 659. JOHNNY PODRES

SAN FRANCISCO GIANTS

□ 16. CESAR GUTIERREZ(R)
□ 16. RICH ROBERTSON(R)
□ 41. BOB BARTON
□ 64. BILL MONBOUQUETTE
□ 102. JIM DAVENPORT
□ 125. RAY SADECKI
□ 158. JOE GIBBON
□ 190. WILLIE MAYS
□ 204. JACK HIATT
□ 227. FRANK JOHNSON
□ 251. RON HERBEL
□ 274. CLYDE KING(M)
□ 293. DICK DIETZ
□ 316. HAL LANIER
□ 345. FRANK LINZY
□ 370. JUAN MARICHAL
□ 392. BOB BURDA
□ 440. WILLIE MCCOVEY
□ 464. DAVE MARSHALL
□ 485. GAYLOR PERRY
□ 505. BOBBY BOLIN
□ 517. MIKE MCCORMICK
□ 555. JIM HART
□ 584. DON MASON
□ 604. BOBBY ETHERIDGE
□ 630. BOBBY BONDS
□ 664. RON HUNT

SEATTLE PILOTS

□ 17. MIKE MARSHALL
□ 42. TOMMY HARPER
□ 62. CHICO SALMON
□ 83. MIKE FERRARO
□ 111. JOHNNY MORRIS
□ 135. TOMMY DAVIS
□ 178. RAY OYLER
□ 209. LARRY HANEY
□ 233. STEVE BARBER
□ 254. JOE SCHULTZ(M)
□ 285. DON MINCHER
□ 301. DARRELL BRANDON
□ 322. JOSE VIDAL
□ 346. WAYNE COMER
□ 377. GARY BELL
□ 394. LOU PINIELLA(R)
□ 394. MARV STAEHLE(R)
□ 413. ROLAND SHELDON
□ 451. RICH ROLLINS
□ 482. JIM GOSGER
□ 511. DIEGO SEGUI
□ 534. JERRY MCNERTNEY
□ 563. MARTY PATTIN
□ 577. MIKE HEGAN
□ 612. JACK AKER
□ 631. JOHN KENNEDY
□ 651. GUS GIL

WASHINGTON SENATORS

□ 27. BERNIE ALLEN
□ 48. BRANT ALYEA
□ 84. BOB HUMPHREYS
□ 106. JIM HANNAN
□ 132. DAVE BALDWIN
□ 153. ED BRINKMAN
□ 170. FRANK HOWARD
□ 199. JIM FRENCH
□ 226. BRUCE HOWARD
□ 246. JOE COLEMAN
□ 272. ED STROUD
□ 294. JIM LEMON(M)
□ 319. KEN MCMULLEN
□ 338. DEL UNSER
□ 361. GARY HOLMAN
□ 383. CASEY COX

□ 406. PHIL ORTEGA
□ 441. DENNIS HIGGINS
□ 461. MIKE EPSTEIN
□ 486. PAUL CASANOVA
□ 513. CAMILO PASCUAL
□ 554. FRANK BERTAINA
□ 586. TIM CULLEN
□ 607. DICK BOSMAN
□ 623. HANK ALLEN
□ 639. BARRY MOORE
□ 650. TED WILLIAMS(M)
□ 658. JIM MILES(R)

1970 TOPPS (720)
2 1/2" X 3 1/2"

ATLANTA BRAVES

□ 17. HOYT WILHELM
□ 48. GIL GARRIDO
□ 86. LUM HARRIS(M)
□ 105. TONY GONZALEZ
□ 122. GEORGE STONE
□ 145. RICO CARTY
□ 160. PHIL NIEKRO
□ 171. JIM NASH
□ 172. GARRY HILL(R)
□ 172. RALPH GARR(R)
□ 206. CLETE BOYER
□ 232. BOB DIDIER
□ 278. TOMMIE AARON
□ 295. CECIL UPSHAW
□ 327. HAL KING
□ 367. MIKE LUM
□ 384. GARY NEIBAUER
□ 413. SONNY JACKSON
□ 438. PAT JARVIS
□ 472. TEAM CARD
□ 500. HANK AARON
□ 529. BOB ASPROMONTE
□ 546. RON REED
□ 555. ORLANDO CEPEDA
□ 576. MILT PAPPAS
□ 621. MIKE MCQUEEN(R)
□ 621. DARRELL EVANS(R)
□ 621. RICK KESTER(R)
□ 668. BOB TILLMAN
□ 687. BOB PRIDDY
□ 710. FELIX MILLAN

BALTIMORE ORIOLES

□ 20. DAVE MCNALLY
□ 45. DAVE A. JOHNSON
□ 81. DAVE MAY
□ 101. BOBBY FLOYD
□ 121. FRED BEENE(R)
□ 121. TERRY CROWLEY(R)
□ 148. EARL WEAVER(M)
□ 182. DICK HALL
□ 213. ANDY ETCHEBARREN
□ 230. BROOKS ROBINSON
□ 261. CURT MOTTON
□ 285. PAUL BLAIR
□ 301. CHICO SALMON
□ 319. CLAYTON DALRYMPLE
□ 344. MARCELINO LOPEZ

- ☐ 363. TOMY SHOPAY
- ☐ 387. TEAM CARD
- ☐ 410. BOOG POWELL
- ☐ 428. DON BUFORD
- ☐ 449. JIM PALMER
- ☐ 477. AL SEVERINSEN(R)
- ☐ 477. ROGER FREED(R)
- ☐ 497. EDDIE WATT
- ☐ 528. ELROD HENDRICKS
- ☐ 590. MIKE CUELLAR
- ☐ 601. PETE RICHERT
- ☐ 615. MARK BELANGER
- ☐ 629. MERV RETTENMUND
- ☐ 638. FRANK BERTAINA
- ☐ 656. JIM HARDIN
- ☐ 674. DAVE LEONHARD
- ☐ 700. FRANK ROBINSON
- ☐ 717. TOM PHOEBUS

BOSTON RED SOX

- ☐ 10. CARL YASTRZEMSKI
- ☐ 39. MIKE NAGY
- ☐ 78. JOE LAHOUD
- ☐ 104. GERRY MOSES
- ☐ 116. SPARKY LYLE
- ☐ 144. RAY CULP
- ☐ 163. SYD O'BRIEN
- ☐ 191. VICENTE ROMO
- ☐ 215. REGGIE SMITH
- ☐ 237. RUSS GIBSON
- ☐ 251. DICK SCHOFIELD
- ☐ 279. BILL LEE
- ☐ 317. BILL CONIGLIARO(R)
- ☐ 317. LUIS ALVARADO(R)
- ☐ 340. TONY CONIGLIARO
- ☐ 361. RAY JARVIS
- ☐ 385. GEORGE SCOTT
- ☐ 406. MIKE ANDREWS
- ☐ 447. LEE STANGE
- ☐ 489. EDDIE KASKO(M)
- ☐ 504. DON PAVLETICH
- ☐ 540. GARY PETERS
- ☐ 563. TEAM CARD
- ☐ 581. TOM SATRIANO
- ☐ 597. SONNY SIEBERT
- ☐ 627. GARY WAGNER
- ☐ 647. TOM MATCHICK
- ☐ 665. JIM LONBORG
- ☐ 680. RICO PETROCELLI
- ☐ 708. JOSE SANTIAGO

CALIFORNIA ANGELS

- ☐ 4. TOM EGAN
- ☐ 29. SANDY ALOMAR
- ☐ 74. GREG WASHBURN(R)
- ☐ 74. WALLY WOLF(R)
- ☐ 132. JIM MCGLOTHLIN
- ☐ 156. EDDIE FISHER
- ☐ 173. JIM HICKS
- ☐ 203. RUDY MAY
- ☐ 228. AURELIO RODRIGUEZ
- ☐ 255. JIM SPENCER
- ☐ 277. PAUL DOYLE
- ☐ 294. JOSE AZCUE
- ☐ 326. BILL VOSS
- ☐ 351. TOM MURPHY
- ☐ 376. LEFTY PHILLIPS(M)
- ☐ 397. ROGER REPOZ
- ☐ 430. ANDY MESSERSMITH
- ☐ 485. JAY JOHNSTONE
- ☐ 522. TEAM CARD
- ☐ 543. CLYDE WRITHT
- ☐ 570. JIM FREGOSI
- ☐ 586. RICKEY CLARK
- ☐ 606. CHICO RUIZ
- ☐ 642. GREG GARRETT(R)
- ☐ 642. GORDON LUND(R)
- ☐ 642. JARVIS TATUM(R)
- ☐ 658. KEN TATUM
- ☐ 684. JACK FISHER
- ☐ 720. RICK REICHARDT

CHICAGO CUBS

- ☐ 46. KEN RUDOLPH
- ☐ 80. DON KESSINGER
- ☐ 117. DON YOUNG
- ☐ 170. BILLY WILLIAMS

- ☐ 192. JIM QUALLS
- ☐ 223. NATE OLIVER
- ☐ 240. FERGIE JENKINS
- ☐ 258. PAUL POPOVICH
- ☐ 265. RANDY HUNDLEY
- ☐ 291. LEO DUROCHER(M)
- ☐ 318. WILLIE SMITH
- ☐ 334. PHIL REGAN
- ☐ 375. JOHNNY CALLISON
- ☐ 405. BILL HANDS
- ☐ 429. RANDY BOBB(R)
- ☐ 429. JIM COSMAN(R)
- ☐ 480. GLENN BECKERT
- ☐ 505. KEN HOLTZMAN
- ☐ 541. BILL HEATH
- ☐ 562. TED ABERNATHY
- ☐ 593. TEAM CARD
- ☐ 612. JIM HICKMAN
- ☐ 630. ERNIE BANKS
- ☐ 649. JIMMIE HALL
- ☐ 654. BOOTS DAY(R)
- ☐ 670. RON SANTO
- ☐ 699. HANK AGUIRRE
- ☐ 714. AL SPANGLER

CHICAGO WHITE SOX

- ☐ 18. CARLOS MAY
- ☐ 35. JOE HORLEN
- ☐ 51. BOB CHRISTIAN
- ☐ 91. RICH MORALES
- ☐ 123. DON GUTTERIDGE(M)
- ☐ 146. DANNY MURPHY
- ☐ 180. TOMMY JOHN
- ☐ 217. RON HANSEN
- ☐ 239. KEN BERRY
- ☐ 263. DUANE JOSEPHSON
- ☐ 274. GERRY ARRIGO
- ☐ 299. BUDDY BRADFORD
- ☐ 315. LUIS APARICIO
- ☐ 342. WILBUR WOOD
- ☐ 368. ED HERRMANN
- ☐ 395. WALT WILLIAMS
- ☐ 414. PAUL EDMONDSON
- ☐ 444. BILLY FARMER(R)
- ☐ 444. JOHN MATIAS(R)
- ☐ 483. GAIL HOPKINS
- ☐ 501. TEAM CARD
- ☐ 518. BILL MELTON
- ☐ 561. TOM MCCRAW
- ☐ 618. BILLY WYNNE
- ☐ 669. BART JOHNSON(R)
- ☐ 669. DAN LAZAR(R)
- ☐ 669. MICKEY SCOTT(R)
- ☐ 695. BOBBY KNOOP

CINCINNATI REDS

- ☐ 3. DARRELL CHANEY
- ☐ 22. RAY WASHBURN
- ☐ 36. DANNY BREEDEN(R)
- ☐ 36. BERNIE CARBO(R)
- ☐ 73. WAYNE GRANGER
- ☐ 115. ALEX JOHNSON
- ☐ 133. CLAY CARROLL
- ☐ 159. TOMMY HELMS
- ☐ 181. SPARKY ANDERSON(M)
- ☐ 225. LEE MAY
- ☐ 254. CAMILO PASCUAL
- ☐ 283. ANGEL BRAVO
- ☐ 296. WOOODY WOODWARD
- ☐ 320. JIM MALONEY
- ☐ 358. PEDRO BORBON
- ☐ 380. TONY PEREZ
- ☐ 409. BOB TOLAN
- ☐ 443. AL JACKSON
- ☐ 484. GARY NOLAN
- ☐ 507. PAT CORRALES
- ☐ 544. TEAM CARD
- ☐ 580. PETE ROSE
- ☐ 602. TED SAVAGE
- ☐ 616. JIM MERRITT
- ☐ 636. JIM STEWART
- ☐ 660. JOHNNY BENCH
- ☐ 683. VERN GEISHERT(R)
- ☐ 683. HAL MCRAE(R)
- ☐ 683. WAYNE SIMPSON(R)
- ☐ 705. TONY CLONINGER

CLEVELAND INDIANS

- ☐ 7. GARY BOYD(R)
- ☐ 7. RUSS NAGELSON(R)
- ☐ 27. CHUCK HINTON
- ☐ 59. DICK ELLSWORTH
- ☐ 85. MAX ALVIS
- ☐ 112. DAVE NELSON
- ☐ 136. STEVE HARGAN
- ☐ 161. RICHIE SCHEINBLUM
- ☐ 184. RAY FOSSE
- ☐ 209. KEN SUAREZ
- ☐ 247. LOU KLIMCHOCK
- ☐ 257. DENNIS HIGGINS
- ☐ 275. DUKE SIMS
- ☐ 292. EDDIE LEON
- ☐ 347. RUSS SNYDER
- ☐ 366. BARRY MOORE
- ☐ 391. LARRY BROWN
- ☐ 412. LARRY BURCHART
- ☐ 445. VADA PINSON
- ☐ 491. GRAIG NETTLES
- ☐ 524. ALVIN DARK(M)
- ☐ 545. KEN HARRELSON
- ☐ 558. VERN FULLER
- ☐ 582. MIKE PAUL
- ☐ 625. DEAN CHANCE
- ☐ 637. TEAM CARD
- ☐ 650. SAM MCDOWELL
- ☐ 673. TED UHLAENDER
- ☐ 704. FRANK BAKER

DETROIT TIGERS

- ☐ 12. JOHN HILLER
- ☐ 33. DON WERT
- ☐ 95. EARL WILSON
- ☐ 98. GATES BROWN
- ☐ 129. JIMMIE PRICE
- ☐ 152. IKE BROWN
- ☐ 177. JIM NORTHRUP
- ☐ 207. NORMAN MCRAE(R)
- ☐ 207. BOB REED(R)
- ☐ 269. CESAR GUTIERREZ
- ☐ 313. MAYO SMITH(M)
- ☐ 335. BILL FREEHAN
- ☐ 356. FRED LASHER
- ☐ 383. MICKEY STANLEY
- ☐ 400. DENNY MCLAIN
- ☐ 424. MIKE KILKENNY
- ☐ 475. DICK MCAULIFFE
- ☐ 508. JOE NIEKRO
- ☐ 520. WILLIE HORTON
- ☐ 554. TOM TIMMERMANN
- ☐ 579. TEAM CARD
- ☐ 592. DARYL PATTERSON
- ☐ 611. NORM CASH
- ☐ 640. AL KALINE
- ☐ 661. JERRY ROBERTSON
- ☐ 682. DALTON JONES
- ☐ 698. TOM TRESH
- ☐ 715. MICKEY LOLICH

HOUSTON ASTROS

- ☐ 15. LARRY DIERKER
- ☐ 32. HARRY WALKER(M)
- ☐ 60. JIM WYNN
- ☐ 113. JIM RAY
- ☐ 126. MARTY MARTINEZ
- ☐ 155. DENIS MENKE
- ☐ 178. DENNY LEMASTER
- ☐ 208. FRED GLADDING
- ☐ 227. JOHN MAYBERRY(R)
- ☐ 227. BOB WATKINS(R)
- ☐ 248. JESUS ALOU
- ☐ 272. HECTOR TORRES
- ☐ 316. SKIP GUINN
- ☐ 339. JOHNNY EDWARDS
- ☐ 355. DOUG RADER
- ☐ 382. JACK DILAURO
- ☐ 407. BOB WATSON
- ☐ 448. TEAM CARD
- ☐ 492. KEITH LAMPARD(R)
- ☐ 492. SCIPIO SPINKS(R)
- ☐ 515. DON WILSON
- ☐ 537. JOE MORGAN
- ☐ 559. TOMMY DAVIS
- ☐ 578. TOM GRIFFIN
- ☐ 598. JOE PEPITONE
- ☐ 619. NORM MILLER
- ☐ 672. LEON MCFADDEN
- ☐ 701. JACK BILLINGHAM

1970 Topps

Ed Kirkpatrick OUTFIELD

KANSAS CITY ROYALS

- ☐ 16. CHARLIE METRO(M)
- ☐ 37. DICK DRAGO
- ☐ 57. H. PAT KELLY
- ☐ 89. JUAN RIOS
- ☐ 108. TOM BURGMEIER
- ☐ 165. ED KIRKPATRICK
- ☐ 187. MIKE HEDLUND
- ☐ 222. JIM ROOKER
- ☐ 241. AL FITZMORRIS(R)
- ☐ 241. SCOTT NORTHEY(R)
- ☐ 266. WALLY BUNKER
- ☐ 321. LOU PINIELLA
- ☐ 338. PAUL SCHAAL
- ☐ 354. AMOS OTIS
- ☐ 377. BILL BUTLER
- ☐ 402. ELLIE RODRIGUEZ
- ☐ 422. TEAM CARD
- ☐ 471. CHRIS ZACHARY
- ☐ 495. DAVE MOREHEAD
- ☐ 512. BILLY HARRIS
- ☐ 525. JERRY ADAIR
- ☐ 552. DON O'RILEY(R)
- ☐ 552. DENNIS PAEPKE(R)
- ☐ 552. FRED RICO(R)
- ☐ 567. BOB OLIVER
- ☐ 589. JOE KEOUGH
- ☐ 609. BUCK MARTINEZ
- ☐ 633. ROGER NELSON
- ☐ 653. MOE DRABOWSKY
- ☐ 671. JIM CAMPANIS
- ☐ 686. JACKIE HERNANDEZ
- ☐ 702. BOB D. JOHNSON(R)
- ☐ 709. MIKE FIORE

LOS ANGELES DODGERS

- ☐ 5. WES PARKER
- ☐ 34. WILLIE CRAWFORD
- ☐ 54. JEFF TORBORG
- ☐ 97. JOE MOELLER
- ☐ 131. RAY LAMB(R)
- ☐ 131. BOB STINSON(R)
- ☐ 157. MANNY MOTA
- ☐ 174. TED SIZEMORE
- ☐ 204. LEN GABRIELSON
- ☐ 242. WALTER ALSTON(M)
- ☐ 260. CLAUDE OSTEEN
- ☐ 286. JACK JENKINS(R)
- ☐ 286. BILL BUCKNER(R)
- ☐ 304. BILL RUSSELL
- ☐ 341. BILL SUDAKIS
- ☐ 369. ALAN FOSTER
- ☐ 390. WILLIE DAVIS
- ☐ 411. TEAM CARD
- ☐ 427. FRED NORMAN
- ☐ 446. BILL GRABARKEWITZ
- ☐ 490. BILL SINGER
- ☐ 523. JOSE PENA
- ☐ 535. ANDY KOSCO
- ☐ 553. JIM LEFEBVRE
- ☐ 571. JIM BREWER
- ☐ 595. MAURY WILLS
- ☐ 622. DON SUTTON
- ☐ 641. AL MCBEAN
- ☐ 685. TOM HALLER

MILWAUKEE BREWERS*

- ☐ 2. DIEGO SEGUI
- ☐ 31. MARTY PATTIN
- ☐ 53. JOHN KENNEDY
- ☐ 88. MIGUEL FUENTES(R)
- ☐ 88. DICK BANEY(R)
- ☐ 111. MIKE HEGAN
- ☐ 134. DANNY WALTON
- ☐ 158. JERRY MCNERTNEY
- ☐ 185. DON MINCHER
- ☐ 224. STEVE BARBER
- ☐ 249. BOB LOCKER
- ☐ 271. GREG GOOSSEN
- ☐ 289. GENE BRABENDER
- ☐ 323. WAYNE COMER
- ☐ 359. PHIL ROOF
- ☐ 370. TOMMY HARPER
- ☐ 393. JOHN GELNAR
- ☐ 418. JOHN DONALDSON
- ☐ 441. JOHN O'DONOGHUE
- ☐ 473. DON BRYANT
- ☐ 499. SKIP LOCKWOOD
- ☐ 514. STEVE HOVLEY
- ☐ 533. BUZZ STEPHEN
- ☐ 556. DAVE BRISTOL(M)
- ☐ 574. BOBBY BOLIN
- ☐ 596. MIKE HERSHBERGER
- ☐ 613. DAVE BALDWIN
- ☐ 652. RICH ROLLINS
- ☐ 667. BOB MEYER
- ☐ 688. TED KUBIAK
- ☐ 713. TEAM CARD

Dave Boswell PITCHER

MINNESOTA TWINS

- ☐ 25. CESAR TOVAR
- ☐ 47. BOB L. MILLER
- ☐ 75. JIM KAAT
- ☐ 93. RICK RENICK
- ☐ 118. GEORGE MITTERWALD
- ☐ 150. HARMON KILLEBREW
- ☐ 169. TOM HALL
- ☐ 194. CHUCK MANUEL
- ☐ 226. RON PERRANOSKI
- ☐ 231. LUIS TIANT
- ☐ 245. LEO CARDENAS
- ☐ 267. HERMAN HILL(R)
- ☐ 267. PAUL RATLIFF(R)
- ☐ 290. ROD CAREW
- ☐ 325. DAVE BOSWELL
- ☐ 353. STAN WILLIAMS
- ☐ 379. TOM TISCHINSKI
- ☐ 404. RICH REESE
- ☐ 426. BILL RIGNEY(M)
- ☐ 479. DICK WOODSON
- ☐ 510. TONY OLIVA
- ☐ 534. TEAM CARD
- ☐ 572. FRANK QUILICI
- ☐ 620. JIM PERRY
- ☐ 635. BOB ALLISON
- ☐ 702. BILL ZEPP(R)

MONTREAL EXPOS

- ☐ 19. JOHN BOCCABELLA
- ☐ 38. MACK JONES
- ☐ 87. STEVE RENKO
- ☐ 109. GARRY JESTADT(R)
- ☐ 109. CARL MORTON(R)

- ☐ 124. LARRY JASTER
- ☐ 147. ANGEL HERMOSO
- ☐ 164. TY CLINE
- ☐ 193. MIKE WEGENER
- ☐ 221. RON BRAND
- ☐ 238. JOSE LABOY
- ☐ 243. JOE SPARMA
- ☐ 268. CLAUDE RAYMOND
- ☐ 293. BOB BAILEY
- ☐ 332. BOBBY WINE
- ☐ 364. DAN MCGINN
- ☐ 398. BILL STONEMAN
- ☐ 417. JOHN BATEMAN
- ☐ 442. GENE MAUCH(M)
- ☐ 476. DON SHAW
- ☐ 509. TEAM CARD
- ☐ 527. DON BOSCH
- ☐ 548. HOWIE REED
- ☐ 585. RUSTY STAUB
- ☐ 607. GARY WASLEWSKI
- ☐ 632. GARY SUTHERLAND
- ☐ 646. JIM BRITTON
- ☐ 666. ADOLFO PHILLIPS
- ☐ 690. RON FAIRLY
- ☐ 707. KEVIN COLLINS

NEW YORK METS

- ☐ 1. TEAM CARD
- ☐ 26. TUG MCGRAW
- ☐ 50. TOMMIE AGEE
- ☐ 83. DON CARDWELL
- ☐ 99. BOBBY PFEIL
- ☐ 137. ART SHAMSKY
- ☐ 138. JOE FOY
- ☐ 153. GARY GENTRY
- ☐ 183. JERRY GROTE
- ☐ 214. KEN BOSWELL
- ☐ 246. JIM MCANDREW
- ☐ 280. DONN CLENDENON
- ☐ 300. TOM SEAVER
- ☐ 348. MIKE JORGENSEN(R)
- ☐ 348. JESSE HUDSON(R)
- ☐ 371. ROD GASPAR
- ☐ 394. GIL HODGES(M)
- ☐ 419. RON TAYLOR
- ☐ 431. RON SWOBODA
- ☐ 488. J.C. MARTIN
- ☐ 498. AL WEIS
- ☐ 521. CAL KOONCE
- ☐ 557. ED KRANEPOOL
- ☐ 575. CLEON JONES
- ☐ 610. JERRY KOOSMAN
- ☐ 628. WAYNE GARRETT
- ☐ 634. BUD HARRELSON
- ☐ 679. RAY SADECKI
- ☐ 692. DUFFY DYER
- ☐ 712. NOLAN RYAN

NEW YORK YANKEES

- ☐ 23. BILL ROBINSON
- ☐ 43. JACK AKER
- ☐ 82. FRANK FERNANDEZ
- ☐ 100. MEL STOTTLEMYRE
- ☐ 114. GENE MICHAEL
- ☐ 142. FRITZ PETERSON
- ☐ 167. BILL BURBACH
- ☐ 189. THURMAN MUNSON(R)
- ☐ 189. DAVE MCDONALD(R)
- ☐ 219. JERRY KENNEY
- ☐ 253. RON WOODS
- ☐ 273. RALPH HOUK(M)
- ☐ 297. CURT BLEFARY
- ☐ 333. BOBBY MURCER
- ☐ 349. STEVE HAMILTON
- ☐ 373. ROY WHITE
- ☐ 399. TEAM CARD
- ☐ 416. JOE VERBANIC
- ☐ 437. DANNY CATER
- ☐ 493. LINDY MCDANIEL
- ☐ 516. JOHN ELLIS(R)
- ☐ 516. JIM LYTTLE(R)
- ☐ 536. MIKE KEKICH
- ☐ 568. STAN BAHNSEN
- ☐ 594. JAKE GIBBS
- ☐ 623. HORACE CLARKE
- ☐ 659. PETE WARD
- ☐ 689. FRANK TEPEDINO
- ☐ 702. RON KLIMKOWSKI(R)

* All cards appear as Seattle Pilots.

OAKLAND A'S

- ☐ 21. VIDA BLUE(R)
- ☐ 21. GENE TENACE(R)
- ☐ 41. GEORGE LAUZERIQUE
- ☐ 55. JOHN ODOM
- ☐ 102. JOE RUDI
- ☐ 120. SAL BANDO
- ☐ 140. REGGIE JACKSON
- ☐ 205. BERT CAMPENERIS
- ☐ 233. LEW KRAUSSE
- ☐ 259. TOMMIE REYNOLDS
- ☐ 287. FRED TALBOT
- ☐ 311. DICK GREEN
- ☐ 331. CHUCK DOBSON
- ☐ 381. BOBBY BROOKS(R)
- ☐ 381. MIKE OLIVO(R)
- ☐ 408. PAUL LINDBLAD
- ☐ 434. FELIPE ALOU
- ☐ 481. JOSE TARTABULL
- ☐ 502. ROLLIE FINGERS
- ☐ 531. RON CLARK
- ☐ 547. RICK MONDAY
- ☐ 565. JIM HUNTER
- ☐ 584. AL DOWNING
- ☐ 603. RAY OYLER
- ☐ 631. TEAM CARD
- ☐ 648. LARRY HANEY
- ☐ 663. TITO FRANCONA
- ☐ 678. DAVE DUNCAN
- ☐ 693. BOB W. JOHNSON
- ☐ 706. JOHN MCNAMARA(M)
- ☐ 719. JIM ROLAND

PHILADELPHIA PHILLIES

- ☐ 6. GRANT JACKSON
- ☐ 24. DICK SELMA
- ☐ 28. BILLY WILSON
- ☐ 56. JOE LIS(R)
- ☐ 56. SCOTT REID(R)
- ☐ 90. TIM MCCARVER
- ☐ 125. DERON JOHNSON
- ☐ 149. BILLY CHAMPION
- ☐ 168. DAVE WATKINS
- ☐ 186. RICK JOSEPH
- ☐ 218. RON STONE
- ☐ 252. LOWELL PALMER
- ☐ 270. CHRIS SHORT
- ☐ 288. LARRY HISLE
- ☐ 302. JEFF JAMES
- ☐ 324. TONY TAYLOR
- ☐ 360. CURT FLOOD
- ☐ 388. BYRON BROWNE
- ☐ 403. JIM BUNNING
- ☐ 436. TEAM CARD
- ☐ 486. TERRY HARMON
- ☐ 511. JOE HOERNER
- ☐ 539. DENNY DOYLE(R)
- ☐ 539. LARRY BOWA(R)
- ☐ 564. JOHNNY BRIGGS
- ☐ 591. MIKE RYAN
- ☐ 605. RICK WISE
- ☐ 645. DON MONEY
- ☐ 654. OSCAR GAMBLE(R)
- ☐ 662. FRANK LUCCHESI(M)
- ☐ 677. WOODIE FRYMAN

PITTSBURGH PIRATES

- ☐ 8. JOSE MARTINEZ
- ☐ 30. MATTY ALOU
- ☐ 52. BRUCE DAL CANTON
- ☐ 94. FRED PATEK
- ☐ 110. BOB MOOSE
- ☐ 141. DAVE CASH(R)
- ☐ 141. JOHNNY JETER(R)
- ☐ 166. AL OLIVER
- ☐ 188. MANNY SANGUILLEN
- ☐ 216. CHUCK HARTENSTEIN
- ☐ 236. BOB VEALE
- ☐ 264. RICH HEBNER
- ☐ 322. LUKE WALKER
- ☐ 350. ROBERTO CLEMENTE
- ☐ 372. DAVE GIUSTI
- ☐ 396. STEVE BLASS
- ☐ 423. JERRY MAY
- ☐ 440. BILL MAZEROSKI
- ☐ 470. WILLIE STARGELL
- ☐ 517. JOE GIBBON

- ☐ 532. DANNY MURTAUGH(M)
- ☐ 551. DOCK ELLIS
- ☐ 566. GENE ALLEY
- ☐ 608. TEAM CARD
- ☐ 626. DAVE RICKETTS
- ☐ 643. JOSE PAGAN
- ☐ 654. ANGEL MANGUAL(R)
- ☐ 664. BOB ROBERTSON
- ☐ 703. LOU MARONE

ST. LOUIS CARDINALS

- ☐ 40. RICH ALLEN
- ☐ 76. CARL TAYLOR
- ☐ 92. GEORGE CULVER
- ☐ 96. LERON LEE(R)
- ☐ 96. JERRY REUSS(R)
- ☐ 119. CHUCK TAYLOR
- ☐ 139. RICH NYE
- ☐ 143. PHIL GAGLIANO
- ☐ 162. JERRY JOHNSON
- ☐ 190. JOE TORRE
- ☐ 220. STEVE CARLTON
- ☐ 256. VIC DAVALILLO
- ☐ 282. STEVE HUNTZ
- ☐ 312. MIKE TORREZ
- ☐ 330. LOU BROCK
- ☐ 346. RED SCHOENDIENST(M)
- ☐ 362. JOE HAGUE
- ☐ 386. BILL DILLMAN
- ☐ 415. JULIAN JAVIER
- ☐ 435. NELSON BRILES
- ☐ 482. TOM HILGENDORF
- ☐ 503. DAL MAXVILL
- ☐ 530. BOB GIBSON
- ☐ 549. TEAM CARD
- ☐ 569. COOKIE ROJAS
- ☐ 614. MIKE SHANNON
- ☐ 675. JOSE CARDENAL
- ☐ 716. SAL CAMPISI(R)
- ☐ 716. REGGIE CLEVELAND(R)
- ☐ 716. SANTIAGO GUZMAN(R)

SAN DIEGO PADRES

- ☐ 11. NATE COLBERT
- ☐ 44. ROBERTO PENA
- ☐ 79. CLAY KIRBY
- ☐ 103. FRANK REBERGER
- ☐ 130. OLLIE BROWN
- ☐ 151. DAVE A. ROBERTS
- ☐ 179. IVAN MURRELL
- ☐ 212. AL SANTORINI
- ☐ 234. TOMMY DEAN
- ☐ 262. JERRY MORALES(R)
- ☐ 262. JIM WILLIAMS(R)
- ☐ 284. JACK BALDSCHUN
- ☐ 314. BILL MCCOOL
- ☐ 329. CHRIS CANNIZZARO
- ☐ 345. AL FERRARA
- ☐ 352. BOB BARTON
- ☐ 374. TOMMIE SISK
- ☐ 392. WALT HRINIAK
- ☐ 421. PAT DOBSON
- ☐ 474. DICK KELLEY
- ☐ 494. LARRY STAHL
- ☐ 513. PRESTON GOMEZ(M)
- ☐ 526. RON HERBEL
- ☐ 573. MIKE CORKINS(R)
- ☐ 573. RAFAEL ROBLES(R)
- ☐ 573. RON SLOCUM(R)
- ☐ 587. JOSE ARCIA
- ☐ 604. CLARENCE GASTON
- ☐ 639. DAVE CAMPBELL
- ☐ 644. GERRY NYMAN
- ☐ 657. TEAM CARD
- ☐ 694. GARY ROSS
- ☐ 718. ED SPIEZIO

SAN FRANCISCO GIANTS

- ☐ 13. JACK HIATT
- ☐ 42. TITO FUENTES
- ☐ 58. DAVE MARSHALL
- ☐ 77. FRANK LINZY
- ☐ 107. BOBBY ETHERIDGE
- ☐ 135. DICK DIETZ
- ☐ 176. JIM HART
- ☐ 210. JUAN MARICHAL
- ☐ 229. RICH ROBERTSON

- ☐ 250. WILLIE MCCOVEY
- ☐ 276. RON HUNT
- ☐ 298. KEN HENDERSON
- ☐ 337. MIKE MCCORMICK
- ☐ 357. BOB BURDA
- ☐ 378. JIM DAVENPORT
- ☐ 401. JOHN HARRELL(R)
- ☐ 401. BERNIE WILLIAMS(R)
- ☐ 425. BOBBY BONDS
- ☐ 433. RON BRYANT
- ☐ 478. BOB HEISE
- ☐ 496. STEVE WHITAKER
- ☐ 519. DON MCMAHON
- ☐ 560. GAYLORD PERRY
- ☐ 583. HAL LANIER
- ☐ 600. WILLIE MAYS
- ☐ 624. CLYDE KING(M)
- ☐ 651. JIM GOSGER
- ☐ 681. BOB GARIBALDI
- ☐ 696. TEAM CARD

WASHINGTON SENATORS

- ☐ 14. HANK ALLEN
- ☐ 49. TIM CULLEN
- ☐ 84. PAUL CASANOVA
- ☐ 106. DAROLD KNOWLES
- ☐ 127. JOE COLEMAN
- ☐ 154. JIM MILES(R)
- ☐ 154. JAN DUKES(R)
- ☐ 175. DICK BOSMAN
- ☐ 211. TED WILLIAMS(M)
- ☐ 235. MIKE EPSTEIN
- ☐ 281. CASEY COX
- ☐ 303. BRANT ALYEA
- ☐ 328. GEORGE BRUNET
- ☐ 336. DEL UNSER
- ☐ 365. ZOILO VERSALLES
- ☐ 389. JIM SHELLENBACK
- ☐ 420. KEN MCMULLEN
- ☐ 439. LEE MAYE
- ☐ 487. CISCO CARLOS
- ☐ 506. ED STROUD
- ☐ 538. BOB HUMPHREYS
- ☐ 550. FRANK HOWARD
- ☐ 577. BERNIE ALLEN
- ☐ 599. DICK STELMASZEK(R)
- ☐ 599. GENE MARTIN(R)
- ☐ 599. DICK SUCH(R)
- ☐ 617. JIM FRENCH
- ☐ 655. JOHN ROSEBORO
- ☐ 676. TEAM CARD
- ☐ 691. JOE GRZENDA
- ☐ 697. JIM HANNAN
- ☐ 711. ED BRINKMAN

1971 TOPPS (752)
2 1/2" X 3 1/2"

ATLANTA BRAVES

- ☐ 8. MIKE MCQUEEN
- ☐ 30. PHIL NIEKRO
- ☐ 52. OSCAR BROWN(R)
- ☐ 52. EARL WILLIAMS(R)
- ☐ 81. FELIX MILLAN
- ☐ 88. HAL KING

- ☐ 147. BOB PRIDDY
- ☐ 173. GIL GARRIDO
- ☐ 194. MIKE LUM
- ☐ 223. CECIL UPSHAL
- ☐ 244. BOB TILLMAN
- ☐ 270. RICO CARTY
- ☐ 306. JIM NASH
- ☐ 346. LUM HARRIS(M)
- ☐ 359. RON REED
- ☐ 374. CLETE BOYER
- ☐ 387. RON HERBEL
- ☐ 400. HANK AARON
- ☐ 432. BOB DIDIER
- ☐ 463. TOM KELLEY
- ☐ 494. RALPH GARR(R)
- ☐ 494. RICK KESTER(R)
- ☐ 507. GEORGE STONE
- ☐ 529. MARTY PEREZ(R)
- ☐ 587. SONNY JACKSON
- ☐ 605. ORLANDO CEPEDA
- ☐ 623. PAT JARVIS
- ☐ 652. TEAM CARD
- ☐ 663. MARV STAEHLE
- ☐ 668. GARY NEIBAUER
- ☐ 709. DUSTY BAKER(R)
- ☐ 717. TOMMIE AARON

BALTIMORE ORIOLES

- ☐ 1. TEAM CARD
- ☐ 29. DON BUFORD
- ☐ 53. PAUL BLAIR
- ☐ 99. MARK BELANGER
- ☐ 122. EDDIE WATT
- ☐ 137. MARCELINO LOPEZ
- ☐ 170. MIKE CUELLAR
- ☐ 193. BOB GRICH
- ☐ 219. ELROD HENDRICKS
- ☐ 249. CHICO SALMON
- ☐ 273. PETE RICHERT
- ☐ 300. BROOKS ROBINSON
- ☐ 320. DAVE MCNALLY
- ☐ 362. MIKE ADAMSON(R)
- ☐ 362. ROGER FREED(R)
- ☐ 392. GRANT JACKSON
- ☐ 393. MERV RETTENMUND
- ☐ 417. DICK HALL
- ☐ 453. TERRY CROWLEY
- ☐ 477. EARL WEAVER(M)
- ☐ 491. JIM HARDIN
- ☐ 501. ANDY ETCHEBARREN
- ☐ 547. PAT DOBSON
- ☐ 570. JIM PALMER
- ☐ 595. DAVE A. JOHNSON
- ☐ 617. CLAY DALRYMPLE
- ☐ 640. FRANK ROBINSON
- ☐ 684. CURT MOTTON
- ☐ 700. BOOG POWELL
- ☐ 709. DON BAYLOR(R)
- ☐ 716. DAVE LEONHARD

BOSTON RED SOX

- ☐ 9. GEORGE SCOTT
- ☐ 31. EDDIE KASKO(M)
- ☐ 58. BILL LEE
- ☐ 89. KEN BRETT
- ☐ 114. BILLY CONIGLIARO
- ☐ 159. JARVIS TATUM
- ☐ 176. BOB MONTGOMERY(R)
- ☐ 176. DOUG GRIFFIN(R)
- ☐ 191. MIKE ANDREWS
- ☐ 225. GARY PETERS
- ☐ 254. CAL KOONCE
- ☐ 287. MIKE FIORE
- ☐ 302. PHIL GAGLIANO
- ☐ 305. REGGIE SMITH
- ☐ 340. RICO PETROCELLI
- ☐ 363. MIKE NAGY
- ☐ 386. TEAM CARD
- ☐ 409. DON PAVLETICH
- ☐ 446. BOBBY BOLIN
- ☐ 473. GARY WAGNER
- ☐ 498. JOHN KENNEDY
- ☐ 512. DICK MILLS(R)
- ☐ 512. MIKE GARMAN(R)
- ☐ 530. CARL YASTRZEMSKI
- ☐ 557. TOM SATRIANO
- ☐ 577. JIM LONBORG
- ☐ 601. KEN TATUM

- ☐ 622. JOE LAHOUD
- ☐ 649. SPARKY LYLE
- ☐ 660. RAY CULP
- ☐ 678. GEORGE THOMAS
- ☐ 692. ROGELIO MORET(R)
- ☐ 710. SONNY SIEBERT
- ☐ 740. LUIS APARICIO

CALIFORNIA ANGELS

- ☐ 15. ANDY MESSERSMITH
- ☐ 43. STEVE KEALEY
- ☐ 78. JIM SPENCER
- ☐ 105. TONY CONIGLIARO
- ☐ 152. LLOYD ALLEN(R)
- ☐ 152. WINSTON LLENAS(R)
- ☐ 174. DAVE LAROCHE
- ☐ 205. GERRY MOSES
- ☐ 240. CLYDE WRITHT
- ☐ 256. TONY GONZALEZ
- ☐ 279. LEFTY PHILLIPS(M)
- ☐ 318. RUDY MAY
- ☐ 360. JIM FREGOSI
- ☐ 401. TOM MURPHY
- ☐ 421. JOHN STEPHENSON
- ☐ 442. TEAM CARD
- ☐ 466. KEN BERRY
- ☐ 485. KEN MCMULLEN
- ☐ 508. ROGER REPOZ
- ☐ 526. RAY JARVIS
- ☐ 559. TERRY COX(R)
- ☐ 561. SYD O'BRIEN
- ☐ 590. ALEX JOHNSON
- ☐ 614. BILLY COWAN
- ☐ 631. EDDIE FISHER
- ☐ 645. JIM MALONEY
- ☐ 657. JOSE AZCUE
- ☐ 664. ARCHIE REYNOLDS(R)
- ☐ 666. GENE BRABENDER
- ☐ 676. TOMMIE REYNOLDS
- ☐ 686. CHICO RUIZ
- ☐ 697. RICKEY CLARK
- ☐ 707. FRED LASHER
- ☐ 718. BILLY WYNNE
- ☐ 736. MEL QUEEN
- ☐ 745. SANDY ALOMAR

CHICAGO CUBS

- ☐ 12. JOHNNY CALLISON
- ☐ 38. JIM COLBORN
- ☐ 90. JOE PEPITONE
- ☐ 98. JOE DECKER
- ☐ 121. JIM DUNEGAN(R)
- ☐ 121. ROE SKIDMORE(R)
- ☐ 151. TOMMY DAVIS
- ☐ 175. JIM HICKMAN
- ☐ 203. LARRY GURA
- ☐ 220. RON SANTO
- ☐ 248. HOYT WILHELM
- ☐ 280. FERGIE JENKINS
- ☐ 350. BILLY WILLIAMS
- ☐ 390. GLENN BECKERT
- ☐ 410. KEN HOLTZMAN
- ☐ 424. ROBERTO RODRIQUEZ
- ☐ 441. MILT PAPPAS
- ☐ 455. DON KESSINGER
- ☐ 472. KEN RUDOLPH
- ☐ 502. TEAM CARD
- ☐ 525. ERNIE BANKS
- ☐ 542. BOB L. MILLER
- ☐ 558. HECTOR TORRES
- ☐ 576. ADRIAN GARRETT(R)
- ☐ 576. BROCK DAVIS(R)
- ☐ 576. GARRY JESTADT(R)
- ☐ 592. RANDY HUNDLEY
- ☐ 609. LEO DUROCHER(M)
- ☐ 634. PHIL REGAN
- ☐ 647. JUAN PIZARRO
- ☐ 670. BILL HANDS
- ☐ 704. J.C. MARTIN
- ☐ 726. PAUL POPOVICH

CHICAGO WHITE SOX

- ☐ 13. CHARLIE BRINKMAN(R)
- ☐ 13. DICK MOLONEY(R)
- ☐ 37. RICH MCKINNEY
- ☐ 56. DUANE JOSEPHSON

- ☐ 80. BILL MELTON
- ☐ 113. JERRY CRIDER
- ☐ 156. BART JOHNSON
- ☐ 169. ED HERRMAN
- ☐ 186. BOB SPENCE
- ☐ 227. FLOYD WEAVER
- ☐ 243. CARLOS MAY
- ☐ 267. RICH MORALES
- ☐ 289. TEAM CARD
- ☐ 292. JAY JOHNSTONE
- ☐ 311. LEE STANGE
- ☐ 345. JOE HORLEN
- ☐ 373. TOM MCCRAW
- ☐ 413. H. PAT KELLY
- ☐ 436. WILBUR WOOD
- ☐ 458. RON LOLICH(R)
- ☐ 458. DAVE LEMONDS(R)
- ☐ 489. LUIS ALVARADO
- ☐ 506. BOBBY KNOOP
- ☐ 520. TOMMY JOHN
- ☐ 537. TOM EGAN
- ☐ 555. WALT WILLIAMS
- ☐ 588. TOM BRADLEY
- ☐ 627. STEVE HAMILTON
- ☐ 643. RICK REICHARDT
- ☐ 661. CHUCK TANNER(M)
- ☐ 679. DON O'RILEY
- ☐ 723. VICENTE ROMO
- ☐ 733. LEE MAYE
- ☐ 748. JOHN PURDIN

CINCINNATI REDS

- ☐ 14. DAVE CONCEPCION
- ☐ 40. LEE MAY
- ☐ 75. GARY NOLAN
- ☐ 100. PETE ROSE
- ☐ 124. DON GULLETT
- ☐ 164. FRANK DUFFY(R)
- ☐ 164. MILT WILCOX(R)
- ☐ 177. HAL MCRAE
- ☐ 190. BOB TOLAN
- ☐ 218. TONY CLONINGER
- ☐ 250. JOHNNY BENCH
- ☐ 272. TOMMY HELMS
- ☐ 293. PAT CORRALES
- ☐ 319. TY CLINE
- ☐ 339. WAYNE SIMPSON
- ☐ 357. TEAM CARD
- ☐ 377. GREG GARRETT
- ☐ 379. WAYNE GRANGER
- ☐ 394. CLAY CARROLL
- ☐ 420. JIM MERRITT
- ☐ 457. WILLIE SMITH
- ☐ 478. BERNIE CARBO
- ☐ 496. WOODY WOODWARD
- ☐ 538. ANGEL BRAVO
- ☐ 556. JIM MCGLOTHLIN
- ☐ 580. TONY PEREZ
- ☐ 613. PEDRO BORBON
- ☐ 632. DARREL CHANEY
- ☐ 644. JIM STEWART
- ☐ 688. SPARKY ANDERSON(M)
- ☐ 731. JIM QUALLS

CLEVELAND INDIANS

- ☐ 24. RICH HAND
- ☐ 41. RICK AUSTIN
- ☐ 87. JACK HEIDEMANN
- ☐ 107. ROY FOSTER
- ☐ 125. RAY FOSSE
- ☐ 150. SAM MCDOWELL
- ☐ 172. DUKE SIMS
- ☐ 211. PHIL HENNIGAN
- ☐ 231. VINCE COLBERT(R)
- ☐ 231. JOHN LOWENSTEIN(R)
- ☐ 252. EDDIE LEON
- ☐ 275. VADA PINSON
- ☐ 294. STEVE DUNNING
- ☐ 324. GRAIG NETTLES
- ☐ 347. TED UHLAENDER
- ☐ 375. STEVE HARGAN
- ☐ 397. ALVIN DARK(M)
- ☐ 429. CHUCK HINTON
- ☐ 454. MIKE PAUL
- ☐ 479. DENNIS HIGGINS
- ☐ 510. KEN HARRELSON
- ☐ 539. LARRY BROWN
- ☐ 552. BUDDY BRADFORD

1971 Topps

☐ 584. TEAM CARD
☐ 597. KEN SUAREZ
☐ 612. LOU CAMILLI(R)
☐ 612. TED FORD(R)
☐ 612. STEVE MINGORI(R)
☐ 689. FRANK BAKER
☐ 727. RAY LAMB

DETROIT TIGERS

☐   3. DICK MCAULIFFE
☐ 39. LERRIN LAGROW(R)
☐ 39. GENE LAMONT(R)
☐ 86. MIKE KILKENNY
☐ 101. LES CAIN
☐ 120. WILLIE HORTON
☐ 133. MICKEY LOLICH
☐ 154. CESAR GUTIERREZ
☐ 180. AL KALINE
☐ 208. BILLY MARTIN
☐ 229. JIM HANNAN
☐ 265. JIM NORTHRUP
☐ 296. TOM TIMMERMANN
☐ 316. FRED SCHERMAN
☐ 336. TEAM CARD
☐ 367. DALTON JONES
☐ 389. ED BRINKMAN
☐ 403. JOE COLEMAN
☐ 423. DENNIS SAUNDERS(R)
☐ 423. TIM MARTING(R)
☐ 444. JIMMIE PRICE
☐ 464. AURELIO RODRIGUEZ
☐ 481. DARYL PATTERSON
☐ 503. GATES BROWN
☐ 524. MICKEY STANLEY
☐ 553. KEVIN COLLINS
☐ 575. BILL FREEHAN
☐ 599. NORM CASH
☐ 629. JOHN HILLER
☐ 669. IKE BROWN
☐ 695. JOE NIEKRO
☐ 708. RUSS NAGELSON
☐ 732. BOB REED
☐ 749. KEN SZOTKIEWICZ

HOUSTON ASTROS

☐ 18. NORM MILLER
☐ 44. JOHNNY EDWARDS
☐ 79. WADE BLASINGAME
☐ 102. KEN FORSCH(R)
☐ 102. LARRY HOWARD(R)
☐ 130. DENIS MENKE
☐ 148. JOHN MAYBERRY
☐ 162. JACK BILLINGHAM
☐ 222. BOB WATSON
☐ 237. CESAR CEDENO
☐ 242. JIM RAY
☐ 264. JOE MORGAN
☐ 291. GEORGE CULVER
☐ 312. HARRY WALKER(M)
☐ 337. JESUS ALOU
☐ 371. JACK HIATT
☐ 381. FRED GLADDING
☐ 404. BUDDY HARRIS(R)
☐ 404. ROGER METZGER(R)
☐ 425. DOUG RADER
☐ 447. CESAR GERONIMO
☐ 471. TOM GRIFFIN
☐ 484. DON WILSON
☐ 540. LARRY DIERKER
☐ 565. JIM WYNN
☐ 583. RON COOK
☐ 602. MARTY MARTINEZ
☐ 636. DENNY LEMASTER
☐ 677. JACK DILAURO
☐ 722. TEAM CARD
☐ 728. KEITH LAMPARD(R)
☐ 741. SKIP GUINN
☐ 747. SCIPIO SPINKS(R)

KANSAS CITY ROYALS

☐ 17. BILLY SORRELL
☐ 35. LOU PINIELLA
☐ 91. BOB LEMON(M)
☐ 103. RICH SEVERSON
☐ 118. COOKIE ROJAS
☐ 129. AURELIO MONTEAGUDO
☐ 144. JACKIE HERNANDEZ

☐ 163. BUCK MARTINEZ
☐ 187. TED ABERNATHY
☐ 221. DAVE MOREHEAD
☐ 247. JERRY CRAM(R)
☐ 247. PAUL SPLITTORFF(R)
☐ 269. GAIL HOPKINS
☐ 299. ED KIRKPATRICK
☐ 321. TOM MATCHICK
☐ 344. ELLIE RODRIGUEZ
☐ 411. GEORGE SPRIGGS
☐ 431. TOM BURGMEIER
☐ 451. JOE KEOUGH
☐ 470. BOB OLIVER
☐ 487. PAUL SCHAAL
☐ 504. KEN WRIGHT
☐ 528. WALLY BUNKER
☐ 546. JOHN MATIAS
☐ 564. AL FITZMORRIS
☐ 581. ROGER NELSON
☐ 610. AMOS OTIS
☐ 626. FREEDIE PATEK
☐ 633. SCOTT NORTHEY(R)
☐ 646. BOBBY FLOYD
☐ 662. MIKE HEDLUND
☐ 681. BILL BUTLER
☐ 701. BOB GARIBALDI
☐ 719. JERRY MAY
☐ 730. JIM ROOKER
☐ 742. TEAM CARD
☐ 752. DICK DRAGO

LOS ANGELES DODGERS

☐ 10. CLAUDE OSTEEN
☐ 34. SANDY VANCE
☐ 57. VON JOSHUA
☐ 85. BILLY GRABARKEWITZ
☐ 112. MANNY MOTA
☐ 145. BILL SINGER
☐ 188. BOB VALENTINE(R)
☐ 188. MIKE STRAHLER(R)
☐ 207. ALAN FOSTER
☐ 226. BILL RUSSELL
☐ 253. BILL SUDAKIS
☐ 288. JOE MOELLER
☐ 314. JEFF TORBORG
☐ 341. STEVE GARVEY
☐ 361. DON SUTTON
☐ 385. MAURY WILLS
☐ 402. TEAM CARD
☐ 430. WES PARKER
☐ 459. JIM LEFEBVRE
☐ 488. JERRY STEPHENSON
☐ 519. WILLIE CRAWFORD
☐ 529. BILL BUCKNER(R)
☐ 549. JIM BREWER
☐ 567. WALT ALSTON(M)
☐ 585. WILLIE DAVIS
☐ 639. TOM HALLER
☐ 650. RICH ALLEN
☐ 693. JOSE PENA
☐ 709. TOM PACIOREK(R)

MILWAUKEE BREWERS

☐ 22. PHIL ROOF
☐ 48. DAVE BALDWIN
☐ 76. TED SAVAGE
☐ 97. FLOYD WICKER

☐ 116. KEN SANDERS
☐ 149. MIKE HERSHBERGER
☐ 182. AL DOWNING
☐ 204. BERNIE SMITH(R)
☐ 204. GEORGE KOPACZ(R)
☐ 236. BOB HUMPHREYS
☐ 260. TOMMY HARPER
☐ 281. DANNY WALTON
☐ 309. DICK ELLSWORTH
☐ 334. ROBERTO PENA
☐ 353. CARL TAYLOR
☐ 372. LEW KRAUSSE
☐ 415. MIKE HEGAN
☐ 433. SKIP LOCKWOOD
☐ 456. BOB MEYER
☐ 493. DAVE MAY
☐ 516. TED KUBIAK
☐ 579. MARTY PATTIN
☐ 604. JOHN GELNAR
☐ 633. PETE KOEGEL(R)
☐ 637. DAVE BRISTOL(M)
☐ 653. RUSS SNYDER
☐ 671. BILL VOSS
☐ 692. WAYNE TWITCHELL(R)
☐ 698. TEAM CARD
☐ 721. JOHN MORRIS
☐ 746. ANDY KOSCO

MINNESOTA TWINS

☐   7. JIM HOLT
☐ 26. BERT BLYLEVEN
☐ 74. PETE HAMM(R)
☐ 74. JIM NETTLES(R)
☐ 95. LUIS TIANT
☐ 127. DANNY THOMPSON
☐ 141. FRANK QUILICI
☐ 165. CESAR TOVAR
☐ 189. GEORGE MITTERWALD
☐ 210. ROD CAREW
☐ 245. JIM KATT
☐ 271. BILL ZEPP
☐ 290. TONY OLIVA
☐ 313. TOM HALL
☐ 349. RICH REESE
☐ 391. STEVE BRYE(R)
☐ 391. COTTON NASH(R)
☐ 405. LEO CARDENAS
☐ 449. BRANT ALYEA
☐ 475. RON PERRANOSKI
☐ 500. JIM PERRY
☐ 522. TEAM CARD
☐ 532. BILL RIGNEY(M)
☐ 550. HARMON KILLEBREW
☐ 568. SAL CAMPISI
☐ 586. DICK WOODSON
☐ 607. PAUL RATLIFF
☐ 638. STAN WILLIAMS
☐ 675. DAVE BOSWELL
☐ 692. HAL HAYDEL(R)
☐ 694. RICK RENICK
☐ 724. TOM TISCHINSKI
☐ 744. CHUCK MANUEL

MONTREAL EXPOS

☐ 21. DAN MCGINN
☐ 42. BOOTS DAY
☐ 59. GENE MAUCH(M)
☐ 94. DON HAHN
☐ 132. JOSE LABOY
☐ 142. MACK JONES
☐ 157. BOB BAILEY
☐ 171. BOBBY WINE
☐ 209. STEVE RENKO
☐ 232. JOHN STROHMAYER
☐ 266. BILL STONEMAN
☐ 284. JIM GOSGER
☐ 304. RON BRAND
☐ 315. RON FAIRLY
☐ 376. CLYDE MASHORE(R)
☐ 376. ERNIE MCANALLY(R)
☐ 398. HOWIE REED
☐ 418. ADOLFO PHILLIPS
☐ 434. GARY SUTHERLAND
☐ 452. JOHN BOCCABELLA
☐ 474. JIM FAIREY
☐ 515. CARL MORTON
☐ 536. CLAUDE RAYMOND

☐ 560. RUSTY STAUB
☐ 578. RON HUNT
☐ 608. MIKE WEGENER
☐ 628. JOHN BATEMAN
☐ 664. BOB REYNOLDS(R)
☐ 665. RON SWOBODA
☐ 674. TEAM CARD
☐ 699. JIM BRITTON
☐ 713. MIKE MARSHALL
☐ 743. JOHN O'DONOGHUE
☐ 747. BALOR MOORE(R)

NEW YORK METS

☐ 16. KEN SINGLETON
☐ 36. DEAN CHANCE
☐ 83. TIM FOLI(R)
☐ 83. RANDY BOBB(R)
☐ 104. DAN FRISELLA
☐ 115. DONN CLENDENON
☐ 136. DUFFY DYER
☐ 160. TOM SEAVER
☐ 183. GIL HODGES(M)
☐ 228. WAYNE GARRETT
☐ 259. DAVE MARSHALL
☐ 278. JERRY GROTE
☐ 310. TOMMIE AGEE
☐ 335. JERRY KOOSMAN
☐ 355. BUD HARRELSON
☐ 406. RAY SADECKI
☐ 428. JIM MCANDREW
☐ 445. ART SHAMSKY
☐ 469. BOB ASPROMONTE
☐ 492. KEN BOSWELL
☐ 513. NOLAN RYAN
☐ 527. CLEON JONES
☐ 573. ED KRANEPOOL
☐ 596. MIKE JORGENSEN
☐ 618. TUG MCGRAW
☐ 641. TEAM CARD
☐ 648. RICH FOLKERS(R)
☐ 648. TED MARTINEZ(R)
☐ 648. JON MATLACK(R)
☐ 651. JERRY ROBERTSON
☐ 687. RON TAYLOR
☐ 725. GARY GENTRY
☐ 751. AL WEIS

NEW YORK YANKEES

☐ 5. THURMAN MUNSON
☐ 28. RON KLIMKOWSKI
☐ 51. STEVE KLINE
☐ 111. LOYD COLSON(R)
☐ 111. BOBBY MITCHELL(R)
☐ 131. CURT BLEFARY
☐ 146. RALPH HOUK(M)
☐ 184. STAN BAHNSEN
☐ 213. FRANK W. BAKER
☐ 234. JIM LYTTLE
☐ 263. JOHN ELLIS
☐ 277. GARY WASLEWSKI
☐ 303. LINDY MCDANIEL
☐ 342. FRANK TEPEDINO
☐ 358. DANNY CATER
☐ 382. JAKE GIBBS
☐ 395. ROY WHITE
☐ 419. RON HANSEN
☐ 438. MIKE MCCORMICK
☐ 460. FRITZ PETERSON
☐ 483. GENE MICHAEL
☐ 514. RON WOODS
☐ 543. TEAM CARD
☐ 559. GARY JONES(R)
☐ 572. JERRY KENNEY
☐ 593. JACK AKER
☐ 615. MEL STOTTLEMYRE
☐ 635. BOBBY MURCER
☐ 667. PETE WARD
☐ 683. BILL BURBACH
☐ 703. MIKE KEKICH
☐ 715. HORACE CLARKE
☐ 734. ROB GARDNER

OAKLAND A'S

☐ 20. REGGIE JACKSON
☐ 45. JIM HUNTER
☐ 84. MARCEL LACHEMANN
☐ 109. STEVE HOVLEY

☐ 135. RICK MONDAY
☐ 178. DAVE DUNCAN
☐ 215. DIEGO SEGUI
☐ 238. CHUCK DOBSON
☐ 258. DICK GREEN
☐ 285. SAL BANDO
☐ 317. JIM DRISCOLL(R)
☐ 317. ANGEL MANGUAL(R)
☐ 338. GENE TENACE
☐ 356. BOB LOCKER
☐ 384. ROLLIE FINGERS
☐ 407. JOE RUDI
☐ 440. BERT CAMPANERIS
☐ 468. FRANK FERNANDEZ
☐ 495. FELIPE ALOU
☐ 523. JOHN ODOM
☐ 544. VIDA BLUE
☐ 624. TEAM CARD
☐ 633. BOBBY BROOKS(R)
☐ 642. JIM ROLAND
☐ 658. PAUL LINDBLAD
☐ 680. DON MINCHER
☐ 714. DICK WILLIAMS(M)

PHILADELPHIA PHILLIES

☐ 23. OSCAR GAMBLE
☐ 49. DON MONEY
☐ 77. MIKE COMPTON
☐ 92. FRED WENZ
☐ 119. FRANK LUCCHESI(M)
☐ 138. JOE LIS(R)
☐ 138. WILLIE MONTANEZ(R)
☐ 166. JOE HOERNER
☐ 192. BILLY WILSON
☐ 233. LARRY BOWA
☐ 246. TONY TAYLOR
☐ 268. TEAM CARD
☐ 297. JOHNNY BRIGGS
☐ 323. BILLY CHAMPION
☐ 352. DENNY DOYLE
☐ 366. RON STONE
☐ 414. WOODIE FRYMAN
☐ 439. GREG LUZINSKI(R)
☐ 439. SCOTT REID(R)
☐ 465. TIM MCCARVER
☐ 490. DERON JOHNSON
☐ 511. CHRIS SHORT
☐ 533. MIKE RYAN
☐ 554. LOWELL PALMER
☐ 574. JIM BUNNING
☐ 598. RICK WISE
☐ 616. LARRY HISLE
☐ 659. BYRON BROWNE
☐ 664. KEN REYNOLDS(R)
☐ 682. TERRY HARMON
☐ 705. DICK SELMA
☐ 728. WAYNE REDMOND(R)
☐ 739. BARRY LERSCH

PITTSBURGH PIRATES

☐ 2. DOCK ELLIS
☐ 27. FRED CAMBRIA(R)
☐ 27. GENE CLINES(R)
☐ 47. JOHNNY JETER
☐ 73. GEORGE BRUNET
☐ 110. BILL MAZEROSKI
☐ 143. STEVE BLASS
☐ 168. BRUCE DAL CANTON
☐ 212. RICH HEBNER
☐ 230. WILLIE STARGELL
☐ 255. BOB ROBERTSON
☐ 282. JOSE PAGAN
☐ 298. JIM NELSON
☐ 343. ED ACOSTA(R)
☐ 343. MILT MAY(R)
☐ 365. BOB D. JOHNSON
☐ 368. BOB VEALE
☐ 388. AL OLIVER
☐ 416. GENE ALLEY
☐ 437. DANNY MURTAUGH(M)
☐ 480. MANNY SANGUILLEN
☐ 509. JIM GRANT
☐ 534. LUKE WALKER
☐ 562. DAVE GIUSTI
☐ 582. DAVE CASH
☐ 603. TEAM CARD
☐ 630. ROBERTO CLEMENTE
☐ 690. BOB MOOSE
☐ 712. JOSE MARTINEZ

ST. LOUIS CARDINALS

☐ 4. VIC DAVALILLO
☐ 32. JERRY DAVANON
☐ 55. STEVE CARLTON
☐ 96. JOE HAGUE
☐ 117. TED SIMMONS
☐ 158. JERRY REUSS
☐ 185. JULIAN JAVIER
☐ 216. REGGIE CLEVELAND(R)
☐ 216. LUIS MELENDEZ(R)
☐ 239. RED SCHOENDIENST(M)
☐ 257. NELSON BRILES
☐ 286. JERRY MCNERTNEY
☐ 308. TEAM CARD
☐ 322. JIM BEAUCHAMP
☐ 348. FRED NORMAN
☐ 370. JOE TORRE
☐ 396. DICK SCHOFIELD
☐ 422. FRANK BERTAINA
☐ 435. JOSE CARDENAL
☐ 450. BOB GIBSON
☐ 476. DAL MAXVILL
☐ 521. LERON LEE
☐ 531. MIKE TORREZ
☐ 541. BOB BURDA
☐ 551. FRANK LINZY
☐ 571. TED SIZEMORE
☐ 594. BOB CHLUPSA(R)
☐ 594. BOB STINSON(R)
☐ 594. AL HRABOSKY(R)
☐ 606. CHUCK TAYLOR
☐ 625. LOU BROCK
☐ 654. DON SHAW
☐ 672. ED CROSBY
☐ 685. MOE DRABOWSKY
☐ 702. MILT RAMIREZ
☐ 720. MATTY ALOU
☐ 735. MIKE SHANNON

SAN DIEGO PADRES

☐ 6. ED SPIEZIO
☐ 25. CLARENCE GASTON
☐ 46. DAVE CAMPBELL
☐ 106. TOM DUKES
☐ 126. DANNY COOMBS
☐ 134. JOSE ARCIA
☐ 153. GARY ROSS
☐ 179. MIKE CORKINS
☐ 214. AL FERRARA
☐ 235. NATE COLBERT
☐ 262. JIM WILLIAMS(R)
☐ 262. DAVE ROBINSON(R)
☐ 274. RON SLOCUM
☐ 301. EARL WILSON
☐ 333. CLAY KIRBY
☐ 364. TOMMY DEAN
☐ 383. ROD GASPAR
☐ 408. RAFAEL ROBLES
☐ 426. CHRIS CANNIZZARO
☐ 448. DAVE A. ROBERTS
☐ 467. AL SANTORINI
☐ 482. TEAM CARD
☐ 505. OLLIE BROWN
☐ 529. ENZO HERNANDEZ(R)
☐ 548. DON MASON
☐ 569. IVAN MURRELL
☐ 589. BOB BARTON
☐ 611. TOM PHOEBUS

□ 656. GERRY NYMAN
□ 696. JERRY MORALES
□ 711. LARRY STAHL
□ 737. PRESTON GOMEZ(M)
□ 747. AL SEVERINSEN(R)

SAN FRANCISCO GIANTS

□ 19. SKIP PITLOCK
□ 50. WILLIE MCCOVEY
□ 108. JOHN CUMBERLAND
□ 128. FRANK JOHNSON
□ 140. GAYLORD PERRY
□ 155. KEN HENDERSON
□ 181. HAL LANIER
□ 224. ALAN GALLAGHER
□ 251. FRANK REBERGER
□ 276. MIKE DAVISON(R)
□ 276. GEORGE FOSTER(R)
□ 295. BOBBY BONDS
□ 325. JUAN MARICHAL
□ 354. DON MCMAHON
□ 378. TITO FUENTES
□ 412. JERRY JOHNSON
□ 443. RICH ROBERTSON
□ 461. JIM HART
□ 486. STEVE HUNTZ
□ 517. CHARLIE FOX(M)
□ 545. DICK DIETZ
□ 563. TEAM CARD
□ 600. WILLIE MAYS
□ 621. RON BRYANT
□ 691. BOB HEISE
□ 728. BERNIE WILLIAMS(R)
□ 738. RUSS GIBSON

WASHINGTON SENATORS

□ 11. ELLIOTT MADDOX
□ 33. DEL UNSER
□ 60. DICK BOSMAN
□ 82. CASEY COX
□ 93. NORM MCRAE(R)
□ 93. DENNY RIDDLEBERGER(R)
□ 139. PAUL CASANOVA
□ 167. TOM GRIEVE
□ 217. ED STROUD
□ 241. DAVE NELSON
□ 261. DAROLD KNOWLES
□ 283. DICK SUCH
□ 307. DON WERT
□ 326. RICHIE SCHEINBLUM
□ 351. JIM SHELLENBACK
□ 380. TED WILLIAMS(M)
□ 399. JIM FRENCH
□ 427. BERNIE ALLEN
□ 462. TEAM CARD
□ 497. HORACIO PINA
□ 518. JOE GRZENDA
□ 535. CURT FLOOD
□ 559. BILL GOGOLEWSKI
□ 566. TIM CULLEN
□ 591. JACKIE BROWN
□ 620. FRANK HOWARD
□ 655. MIKE EPSTEIN
□ 673. GERRY JANESKI
□ 706. JOE FOY
□ 729. DICK BILLINGS
□ 750. DENNY MCLAIN

1972 TOPPS (787)
2 1/2" X 3 1/2"

ROD CAREW

ATLANTA BRAVES

□ 21. TEAM CARD
□ 74. CECIL UPSHAW
□ 97. TOM KELLEY
□ 119. MARTY PEREZ
□ 149. GARY NEIBAUER
□ 171. DARRELL EVANS
□ 195. ORLANDO CEPEDA
□ 214. MIKE MCQUEEN
□ 260. RALPH GARR
□ 299. HANK AARON
□ 318. SONNY JACKSON
□ 333. STEVE BARBER
□ 351. TOM HOUSE(R)
□ 351. RICK KESTER(R)
□ 351. JIMMY BRITTON(R)
□ 380. EARL WILLIAMS
□ 401. JIM NASH
□ 451. TONY LARUSSA
□ 469. RON HERBEL
□ 484. LUM HARRIS(M)
□ 516. OSCAR BROWN
□ 540. FELIX MILLAN
□ 591. PAUL CASANOVA
□ 601. GEORGE STONE
□ 620. PHIL NIEKRO
□ 641. MIKE LUM
□ 675. PAT JARVIS
□ 740. RICO CARTY
□ 758. GIL GARRIDO
□ 764. DUSTY BAKER
□ 787. RON REED

BALTIMORE ORIOLES

□ 26. ANDY ETCHEBARREN
□ 70. MIKE CUELLAR
□ 100. FRANK ROBINSON
□ 128. EDDIE WATT
□ 140. PAT DOBSON
□ 212. GRANT JACKSON
□ 235. MERV RETTENMUND
□ 250. BOOG POWELL
□ 270. JIM PALMER
□ 323. EARL WEAVER(M)
□ 338. BOB GRICH
□ 370. DON BUFORD
□ 418. TOM SHOPAY
□ 456. MARK BELANGER
□ 474. DON BAYLOR(R)
□ 474. RORIC HARRISON(R)
□ 474. JOHNNY OATES(R)
□ 490. DAVE MCNALLY
□ 508. ELLIE HENDRICKS
□ 527. DAVE LEONHARD
□ 550. BROOKS ROBINSON
□ 579. DOYLE ALEXANDER
□ 628. TERRY CROWLEY
□ 646. CHICO SALMON
□ 660. PAUL BLAIR
□ 680. DAVE A. JOHNSON
□ 724. MICKEY SCOTT(R)
□ 731. TEAM CARD

BOSTON RED SOX

□ 2. RAY CULP
□ 30. RICO PETROCELLI
□ 37. CARL YASTRZEMSKI
□ 79. MIKE GARMAN(R)
□ 79. CECIL COOPER(R)
□ 79. CARLTON FISK(R)
□ 113. ROGELIO MORET
□ 144. MARTY PATTIN
□ 199. MIKE FIORE
□ 218. EDDIE KASKO(M)
□ 259. SPARKY LYLE
□ 266. BOBBY BOLIN
□ 290. SONNY SIEBERT
□ 313. LUIS APARICIO
□ 328. TEAM CARD
□ 411. BOB MONTGOMERY
□ 455. TOMMY HARPER
□ 472. PHIL GAGLIANO
□ 488. MIKE NAGY
□ 503. GARY PETERS
□ 543. DUANE JOSEPHSON
□ 565. REGGIE SMITH
□ 592. LEW KRAUSSE
□ 636. BILL LEE
□ 674. JOHN KENNEDY
□ 676. DANNY CATER
□ 681. BOBBY PFEIL
□ 703. DOUG GRIFFIN
□ 724. JOHN CURTIS(R)
□ 734. BOB BURDA
□ 741. RICK MILLER(R)
□ 761. BEN OGLIVIE(R)
□ 772. KEN TATUM

CALIFORNIA ANGELS

□ 19. BILLY COWAN
□ 55. CLYDE WRIGHT
□ 71. TEAM CARD
□ 102. LLOYD ALLEN
□ 115. JIM FREGOSI
□ 135. VADA PINSON
□ 160. ANDY MESSERSMITH
□ 196. MEL QUEEN
□ 213. BILL PARKER(R)
□ 213. ART KUSNYER(R)
□ 213. TOM SILVERIO(R)
□ 253. SANDY ALOMAR
□ 272. MICKEY RIVERS
□ 289. SYD O'BRIEN
□ 354. TOM MURPHY
□ 379. KEN BERRY
□ 404. JEFF TORBORG
□ 419. JIM SPENCER
□ 462. RICKEY CLARK
□ 521. ALAN FOSTER
□ 541. ROGER REPOZ
□ 561. LEO CARDENAS
□ 595. NOLAN RYAN
□ 629. PAUL DOYLE
□ 656. RUDY MAY
□ 672. ARCHIE REYNOLDS
□ 689. EDDIE FISHER
□ 718. DEL RICE(M)
□ 765. KEN MCMULLEN

CHICAGO CUBS

□ 18. JUAN PIZARRO
□ 29. BILL BONHAM
□ 45. GLENN BECKERT
□ 61. BURT HOOTON(R)
□ 61. GENE HISER(R)
□ 61. EARL STEPHENSON(R)
□ 117. CLEO JAMES
□ 145. DON KESSINGER
□ 192. TEAM CARD
□ 208. MILT PAPPAS
□ 258. RANDY HUNDLEY
□ 271. KEN RUDOLPH
□ 303. JOE PEPITONE
□ 335. BILL HANDS
□ 364. JOHNNY CALLISON
□ 410. FERGIE JENKINS
□ 439. BILLY WILLIAMS
□ 485. PHIL REGAN
□ 512. PAUL POPOVICH

1972 Topps

☐ 534. JIM HICKMAN
☐ 555. RON SANTO
☐ 576. LEO DUROCHER(M)
☐ 612. JOE DECKER
☐ 639. J.C. MARTIN
☐ 666. HECTOR TORRES
☐ 667. RAY NEWMAN
☐ 684. HAL BREEDEN
☐ 730. RICK MONDAY
☐ 766. STEVE HAMILTON

CHICAGO WHITE SOX

☐ 15. WALT WILLIAMS
☐ 73. STEVE HUNTZ
☐ 98. CHUCK TANNER(M)
☐ 126. BART JOHNSON
☐ 146. STEVE KEALEY
☐ 183. BILL MELTON
☐ 207. TOM EGAN
☐ 233. JAY JOHNSTONE
☐ 240. RICH ALLEN
☐ 248. TOM BRADLEY
☐ 326. H. PAT KELLY
☐ 361. MIKE ANDREWS
☐ 381. TEAM CARD
☐ 413. DON EDDY(R)
☐ 413. DAVE LEMONDS(R)
☐ 452. ED HERRMANN
☐ 476. LEE RICHARD
☐ 499. VICENTE ROMO
☐ 525. CARLOS MAY
☐ 539. TERRY FORSTER
☐ 553. WILBUR WOOD
☐ 593. RICH MORALES
☐ 618. RICH ROBERTSON
☐ 648. JIM LYTTLE
☐ 662. STAN BAHNSEN
☐ 685. JOE HORLEN
☐ 746. LOWELL PALMER
☐ 774. LUIS ALVARADO
☐ 786. CHUCK BRINKMAN

CINCINNATI REDS

☐   3. BOB TOLAN
☐ 80. TONY PEREZ
☐ 99. ROSS GRIMSLEY
☐ 121. ED SPRAGUE
☐ 136. DARREL CHANEY
☐ 157. DON GULLETT
☐ 236. JIM MCGLOTHLIN
☐ 256. GEORGE FOSTER
☐ 267. DAVE CONCEPCION
☐ 291. HAL MCRAE
☐ 311. CLAY CARROLL
☐ 358. SPARKY ANDERSON(M)
☐ 382. JOE GIBBON
☐ 417. TOM HALL
☐ 433. JOHNNY BENCH
☐ 463. BERNIE CARBO
☐ 475. GARY NOLAN
☐ 524. ED ARMBRISTER(R)
☐ 524. MEL BEHNEY(R)
☐ 542. JACK BILLINGHAM
☐ 559. PETE ROSE
☐ 586. DENIS MENKE
☐ 614. TED UHLAENDER
☐ 651. TEAM CARD
☐ 659. BOB ASPROMONTE
☐ 705. PAT CORRALES
☐ 719. CESAR GERONIMO
☐ 738. JIM MERRITT
☐ 745. JULIAN JAVIER
☐ 762. WAYNE SIMPSON

CLEVELAND INDIANS

☐ 24. TED FORD
☐ 59. FRED STANLEY
☐ 84. VINCE COLBERT
☐ 116. ED FARMER
☐ 142. CHRIS CHAMBLISS
☐ 193. KURT BEVACQUA
☐ 215. ALEX JOHNSON
☐ 261. STEVE MINGORI
☐ 285. GAYLORD PERRY
☐ 356. GERRY MOSES
☐ 374. JACK HEIDEMANN
☐ 399. MILT WILCOX

☐ 422. RAY LAMB
☐ 470. RAY FOSSE
☐ 486. JOHN LOWENSTEIN
☐ 506. TERRY LEY(R)
☐ 506. JIM MOYER(R)
☐ 506. DICK TIDROW(R)
☐ 547. TEAM CARD
☐ 590. GRAIG NETTLES
☐ 607. FRANK DUFFY
☐ 615. STEVE HARGAN
☐ 642. DENNY RIDDLEBERGER
☐ 658. STEVE DUNNING
☐ 687. DEL UNSER
☐ 721. EDDIE LEON
☐ 748. PHIL HENNIGAN
☐ 784. KEN ASPROMONTE(M)

DETROIT TIGERS

☐   6. FRED SCHERMAN
☐ 33. BILLY MARTIN(M)
☐ 83. DALTON JONES
☐ 120. BILL FREEHAN
☐ 150. NORM CASH
☐ 175. TOM HALLER
☐ 187. GATES BROWN
☐ 216. JOE NIEKRO
☐ 239. TOM TIMMERMANN
☐ 257. JIM FOOR(R)
☐ 257. TIM HOSLEY(R)
☐ 257. PAUL JATA(R)
☐ 284. IKE BROWN
☐ 319. AURELIO RODRIGUEZ
☐ 337. MIKE KILKENNY
☐ 367. RON PERRANOSKI
☐ 385. MICKEY STANLEY
☐ 408. JIM NORTHRUP
☐ 450. MICKEY LOLICH
☐ 487. TEAM CARD
☐ 511. TONY TAYLOR
☐ 535. ED BRINKMAN
☐ 600. AL KALINE
☐ 640. JOE COLEMAN
☐ 725. DICK MCAULIFFE
☐ 750. WILLIE HORTON
☐ 783. LES CAIN

HOUSTON ASTROS

☐ 20. DON WILSON
☐ 56. RICH CHILES
☐ 65. CESAR CEDENO
☐ 101. BILL GREIF(R)
☐ 101. J.R. RICHARD(R)
☐ 101. RAY BUSSE(R)
☐ 132. JOE MORGAN
☐ 155. LARRY DIERKER
☐ 202. SCIPIO SPINKS
☐ 204. TOMMY HELMS
☐ 217. ROGER METZGER
☐ 249. HARRY WALKER(M)
☐ 282. TEAM CARD
☐ 339. RON COOK
☐ 355. BOB WATSON
☐ 360. DAVE A. ROBERTS
☐ 394. KEN FORSCH
☐ 416. JOHNNY EDWARDS
☐ 466. NORM MILLER
☐ 480. LEE MAY
☐ 507. FRED GLADDING
☐ 536. DOUG RADER
☐ 581. WADE BLASINGAME
☐ 603. JIM RAY
☐ 633. JACK HIATT
☐ 679. BOB FENWICK(R)
☐ 679. BOB STINSON(R)
☐ 716. JESUS ALOU
☐ 732. GEORGE CULVER
☐ 747. JIM STEWART
☐ 770. JIM WYNN

KANSAS CITY ROYALS

☐ 10. AMOS OTIS
☐ 57. BOB OLIVER
☐ 68. JIM YORK
☐ 81. MIKE HEDLUND
☐ 109. JERRY MAY
☐ 133. JOE KEOUGH

☐ 177. PAUL SCHAAL
☐ 205. DICK DRAGO
☐ 246. TOM BURGMEIER
☐ 273. BOBBY FLOYD
☐ 315. PAUL SPLITTORFF
☐ 332. BUCK MARTINEZ
☐ 349. AL FITZMORRIS
☐ 372. LANCE CLEMONS(R)
☐ 372. MONTY MONTGOMERY(R)
☐ 373. JOHN MAYBERRY
☐ 415. COOKIE ROJAS
☐ 449. BOB LEMON(M)
☐ 468. RICHIE SCHEINBLUM
☐ 519. TED ABERNATHY
☐ 531. FREDDIE PATEK
☐ 569. ED KIRKPATRICK
☐ 580. LOU PINIELLA
☐ 617. TEAM CARD
☐ 638. KEN WRIGHT
☐ 664. BOBBY KNOOP
☐ 683. STEVE HOVLEY
☐ 717. BRUCE DAL CANTON
☐ 728. GAIL HOPKINS
☐ 742. JIM ROOKER
☐ 763. RON HANSEN

LOS ANGELES DODGERS

☐ 11. BOBBY VALENTINE
☐ 25. BILL SINGER
☐ 63. DUKE SIMS
☐ 114. BILL BUCKNER
☐ 151. JIM BREWER
☐ 198. CHARLIE HOUGH(R)
☐ 198. BOB O'BRIEN(R)
☐ 198. MIKE STRAHLER(R)
☐ 264. TOMMY JOHN
☐ 265. WES PARKER
☐ 297. CLAUDE OSTEEN
☐ 322. JOSE PENA
☐ 369. JIM LEFEBVRE
☐ 390. WILLIE DAVIS
☐ 398. LARRY HISLE
☐ 437. MAURY WILLS
☐ 460. AL DOWNING
☐ 522. TEAM CARD
☐ 530. DON SUTTON
☐ 578. BILLY GRABARKEWITZ
☐ 596. MANNY MOTA
☐ 616. JOE FERGUSON
☐ 649. PETE RICHERT
☐ 669. WILLIE CRAWFORD
☐ 686. STEVE GARVEY
☐ 736. BILL RUSSELL
☐ 749. WALTER ALSTON(M)
☐ 759. CHRIS CANNIZZARO
☐ 761. RON CEY(R)
☐ 777. HOYT WILHELM

MILWAUKEE BREWERS

☐ 12. JOSE CARDENAL
☐ 77. RON THEOBALD
☐ 106. TEAM CARD
☐ 118. SKIP LOCKWOOD
☐ 153. RICK AUERBACK
☐ 161. BROCK DAVIS
☐ 162. JERRY BELL(R)
☐ 162. DARRELL PORTER(R)
☐ 162. BOB REYNOLDS(R)
☐ 197. JOHNNY BRIGGS
☐ 255. JIM LONBORG
☐ 281. BILL PARSONS
☐ 321. JOE LAHOUD
☐ 359. DON PAVLETICH
☐ 376. ANDY KOSCO
☐ 386. JIM COLBORN
☐ 391. KEN SANDERS
☐ 393. CURT MOTTON
☐ 402. BOBBY HEISE
☐ 421. ELLIE RODRIGUEZ
☐ 458. AURELIO MONTEAGUDO
☐ 481. BILLY CONIGLIARO
☐ 517. KEN BRETT
☐ 549. DAVE MAY
☐ 585. GEORGE SCOTT
☐ 602. DAVE BRISTOL(M)
☐ 613. MIKE FERRARO
☐ 652. MARCELINO LOPEZ
☐ 744. JIM SLATON
☐ 776. BILL VOSS

1972 Topps

MINNESOTA TWINS

- ☐ 28. BOB GEBHARD(R)
- ☐ 28. STEVE BRYE(R)
- ☐ 28. HAL HAYDEL(R)
- ☐ 51. HARMON KILLEBREW
- ☐ 66. RAY CORBIN
- ☐ 131. JIM NETTLES
- ☐ 156. TEAM CARD
- ☐ 201. PHIL ROOF
- ☐ 220. JIM PERRY
- ☐ 244. STEVE BRAUN
- ☐ 275. CESAR TOVAR
- ☐ 301. GEORGE MITTERWALD
- ☐ 352. DAVE LAROCHE
- ☐ 368. DANNY THOMPSON
- ☐ 389. BILL RIGNEY(M)
- ☐ 400. TONY OLIVA
- ☐ 459. RICK RENICK
- ☐ 501. PETE HAMM
- ☐ 515. BERT BLYLEVEN
- ☐ 545. WAYNE GRANGER
- ☐ 588. JIM HOLT
- ☐ 611. RICH REESE
- ☐ 634. DICK WOODSON
- ☐ 678. STEVE LUEBBER
- ☐ 695. ROD CAREW
- ☐ 709. JIM KAAT
- ☐ 778. VIC ALBURY(R)
- ☐ 778. RICK DEMPSEY(R)
- ☐ 778. JIM STRICKLAND(R)

JOHN BOCCABELLA

MONTREAL EXPOS

- ☐ 5. JOHN BATEMAN
- ☐ 58. ERNIE MCANALLY
- ☐ 82. RON WOODS
- ☐ 110. RON HUNT
- ☐ 134. CARL MORTON
- ☐ 159. JOHN BOCCABELLA
- ☐ 211. GARY SUTHERLAND
- ☐ 234. RON TAYLOR
- ☐ 254. BOOTS DAY
- ☐ 276. GENE MAUCH(M)
- ☐ 307. STEVE RENKO
- ☐ 331. STAN SWANSON
- ☐ 371. DENNY LEMASTER
- ☐ 405. RON FAIRLY
- ☐ 473. DAN MCGINN
- ☐ 489. TERRY HUMPHREY(R)
- ☐ 489. KEITH LAMPARD(R)
- ☐ 505. MIKE MARSHALL
- ☐ 526. BOB BAILEY
- ☐ 582. TEAM CARD
- ☐ 610. BILL STONEMAN
- ☐ 631. JOHN STROHMAYER
- ☐ 653. JIM FAIREY
- ☐ 657. BOBBY WINE
- ☐ 727. JOSE LABOY
- ☐ 743. CESAR GUTIERREZ
- ☐ 773. RON BRAND

NEW YORK METS

- ☐ 16. MIKE JORGENSEN
- ☐ 31. CLEON JONES
- ☐ 53. BUD HARRELSON
- ☐ 105. GARY GENTRY
- ☐ 127. DUFFY DYER
- ☐ 141. BUZZ CAPRA(R)
- ☐ 141. LEROY STANTON(R)
- ☐ 141. JON MATLACK(R)
- ☐ 163. TUG MCGRAW
- ☐ 181. ED KRANEPOOL
- ☐ 245. TOMMIE AGEE
- ☐ 269. DON HAHN
- ☐ 293. DANNY FRISELLA
- ☐ 305. KEN BOSWELL
- ☐ 362. TEAM CARD
- ☐ 388. CHARLIE WILLIAMS
- ☐ 407. CHUCK TAYLOR
- ☐ 425. KEN SINGLETON
- ☐ 445. TOM SEAVER
- ☐ 465. GIL HODGES(M)
- ☐ 518. WAYNE GARRETT
- ☐ 544. TED MARTINEZ
- ☐ 563. RAY SADECKI
- ☐ 594. JIM BEAUCHAMP
- ☐ 655. JERRY GROTE
- ☐ 673. DAVE MARSHALL
- ☐ 697. JERRY KOOSMAN
- ☐ 707. TIM FOLI
- ☐ 722. BILL SUDAKIS
- ☐ 741. JOHN MILNER(R)
- ☐ 781. JIM MCANDREW

NEW YORK YANKEES

- ☐ 8. RON SWOBODA
- ☐ 22. ROB GARDNER
- ☐ 47. JOHN ELLIS
- ☐ 108. GARY WASLEWSKI
- ☐ 124. ALAN CLOSTER(R)
- ☐ 124. RUSTY TORRES(R)
- ☐ 124. ROGER HAMBRIGHT(R)
- ☐ 138. MIKE KEKICH
- ☐ 158. JERRY KENNEY
- ☐ 203. RON BLOMBERG
- ☐ 237. TEAM CARD
- ☐ 263. FELIPE ALOU
- ☐ 287. JIM HARDIN
- ☐ 325. MEL STOTTLEMYRE
- ☐ 340. ROY WHITE
- ☐ 387. HORACE CLARKE
- ☐ 409. FRANK W. BAKER
- ☐ 441. THURMAN MUNSON
- ☐ 467. STEVE KLINE
- ☐ 513. LINDY MCDANIEL
- ☐ 533. RALPH HOUK(M)
- ☐ 573. FRITZ PETERSON
- ☐ 589. HAL LANIER
- ☐ 597. JIM MAGNUSON
- ☐ 619. RICH MCKINNEY
- ☐ 644. BERNIE ALLEN
- ☐ 699. BOBBY MURCER
- ☐ 713. GENE MICHAEL
- ☐ 724. RICH HINTON(R)
- ☐ 769. JACK AKER

OAKLAND A'S

- ☐ 17. DAVE DUNCAN
- ☐ 41. TOMMY DAVIS
- ☐ 62. ANGEL MANGUAL
- ☐ 75. BERT CAMPANERIS
- ☐ 111. JIM GRANT
- ☐ 137. DICK WILLIAMS(M)
- ☐ 169. VIDA BLUE
- ☐ 189. GENE TENACE
- ☐ 209. JOE RUDI
- ☐ 241. ROLLIE FINGERS
- ☐ 268. DWAIN ANDERSON(R)
- ☐ 268. CHRIS FLOETHE(R)
- ☐ 279. LARRY BROWN
- ☐ 330. JIM HUNTER
- ☐ 363. RON KLIMKOWSKI
- ☐ 383. BRANT ALYEA
- ☐ 406. GEORGE HENDRICK
- ☐ 435. REGGIE JACKSON
- ☐ 454. TEAM CARD
- ☐ 464. JIM ROLAND
- ☐ 523. CHUCK DOBSON
- ☐ 537. BOB LOCKER
- ☐ 557. JOHN ODOM
- ☐ 583. DAROLD KNOWLES
- ☐ 632. MIKE HEGAN
- ☐ 650. SAL BANDO
- ☐ 670. KEN HOLTZMAN
- ☐ 691. CURT BLEFARY
- ☐ 715. MIKE EPSTEIN
- ☐ 735. DIEGO SEGUI
- ☐ 780. DICK GREEN

PHILADELPHIA PHILLIES

- ☐ 14. PETE KOEGEL(R)
- ☐ 14. MIKE ANDERSON(R)
- ☐ 14. WAYNE TWITCHELL(R)
- ☐ 43. RICK WISE
- ☐ 69. ROGER FREED
- ☐ 112. GREG LUZINSKI
- ☐ 139. TIM MCCARVER
- ☐ 167. DERON JOHNSON
- ☐ 188. FRANK LUCCHESI(M)
- ☐ 252. KEN REYNOLDS
- ☐ 283. DARRELL BRANDON
- ☐ 324. MIKE RYAN
- ☐ 357. WOODIE FRYMAN
- ☐ 377. TERRY HARMON
- ☐ 397. TEAM CARD
- ☐ 423. OSCAR GAMBLE
- ☐ 453. BARRY LERSCH
- ☐ 482. JOE HOERNER
- ☐ 520. LARRY BOWA
- ☐ 528. RON STONE
- ☐ 587. BILLY WILSON
- ☐ 599. BILLY CHAMPION
- ☐ 635. DON MONEY
- ☐ 665. CHRIS SHORT
- ☐ 690. WILLIE MONTANEZ
- ☐ 726. DICK SELMA
- ☐ 741. TOM HUTTON(R)
- ☐ 768. DENNY DOYLE

PITTSBURGH PIRATES

- ☐ 1. TEAM CARD
- ☐ 27. BOB D. JOHNSON
- ☐ 60. MANNY SANGUILLEN
- ☐ 72. BRUCE KISON
- ☐ 125. DAVE CASH
- ☐ 152. GENE CLINES
- ☐ 179. DOCK ELLIS
- ☐ 190. DAVE GIUSTI
- ☐ 219. RENNIE STENNETT
- ☐ 247. MILT MAY
- ☐ 286. GENE ALLEY
- ☐ 309. ROBERTO CLEMENTE
- ☐ 320. STEVE BLASS
- ☐ 392. FRED CAMBRIA(R)
- ☐ 392. RICHIE ZISK(R)
- ☐ 414. BOB L. MILLER
- ☐ 429. BOB ROBERTSON
- ☐ 447. WILLIE STARGELL
- ☐ 471. LUKE WALKER
- ☐ 502. JACKIE HERNANDEZ
- ☐ 538. CHARLIE SANDS
- ☐ 575. AL OLIVER
- ☐ 605. NELSON BRILES
- ☐ 630. RICH HEBNER
- ☐ 647. BOB MOOSE
- ☐ 661. BILL VIRDON(M)
- ☐ 701. JOSE PAGAN
- ☐ 729. BOB VEALE
- ☐ 760. BILL MAZEROSKI
- ☐ 785. VIC DAVALILLO

ST. LOUIS CARDINALS

- ☐ 9. STAN WILLIAMS
- ☐ 13. JOE GRZENDA
- ☐ 67. RED SCHOENDIENST(M)
- ☐ 107. JOSE CRUZ
- ☐ 130. BOB GIBSON
- ☐ 154. TED SIMMONS
- ☐ 200. LOU BROCK
- ☐ 206. DAL MAXVILL
- ☐ 243. FRANK LINZY
- ☐ 278. DENNIS HIGGINS
- ☐ 316. JIM BIBBY(R)
- ☐ 316. JORGE ROQUE(R)
- ☐ 316. SANTIAGO GUZMAN(R)
- ☐ 336. MARTY MARTINEZ
- ☐ 353. ART SHAMSKY
- ☐ 375. REGGIE CLEVELAND
- ☐ 395. MATTY ALOU
- ☐ 420. STEVE CARLTON
- ☐ 479. DON SHAW
- ☐ 500. JOE TORRE
- ☐ 514. TED SIZEMORE
- ☐ 546. JOE HAGUE
- ☐ 584. JERRY MCNERTNEY
- ☐ 606. LUIS MELENDEZ

165

☐ 627. MOE DRABOWSKY
☐ 645. JIM MALONEY
☐ 671. DONN CLENDENON
☐ 688. TEAM CARD
☐ 723. AL SANTORINI
☐ 775. JERRY REUSS
☐ 779. TONY CLONINGER

SAN DIEGO PADRES

☐ 7. ENZO HERNANDEZ
☐ 39. BOB BARTON
☐ 78. STEVE ARLIN
☐ 123. ED ACOSTA
☐ 143. GARRY JESTADT
☐ 173. CLAY KIRBY
☐ 194. FRED NORMAN
☐ 238. LERON LEE
☐ 262. TEAM CARD
☐ 274. AL SEVERINSEN
☐ 288. JOHNNY JETER
☐ 384. DAVE CAMPBELL
☐ 412. DICK KELLEY
☐ 431. CLARENCE GASTON
☐ 457. DARCY FAST(R)
☐ 457. DERREL THOMAS(R)
☐ 457. MIKE IVIE(R)
☐ 477. TOM PHOEBUS
☐ 504. ED SPIEZIO
☐ 532. FRED KENDALL
☐ 551. OLLIE BROWN
☐ 571. NATE COLBERT
☐ 608. MIKE CORKINS
☐ 637. PRESTON GOMEZ(M)
☐ 677. IVAN MURRELL
☐ 739. DON MASON
☐ 782. LARRY STAHL

SAN FRANCISCO GIANTS

☐ 35. JERRY JOHNSON
☐ 49. WILLIE MAYS
☐ 76. DON CARRITHERS
☐ 129. CHARLIE FOX(M)
☐ 147. DAVE KINGMAN
☐ 165. CHRIS SPEIER
☐ 185. RON BRYANT
☐ 232. CHRIS ARNOLD(R)
☐ 232. JIM BARR(R)
☐ 232. DAVE RADER(R)
☐ 280. WILLIE MCCOVEY
☐ 295. DICK DIETZ
☐ 327. STEVE STONE
☐ 366. JIMMY ROSARIO
☐ 403. JOHN CUMBERLAND
☐ 427. TITO FUENTES
☐ 443. KEN HENDERSON
☐ 509. DON MCMAHON
☐ 548. FRANK REBERGER
☐ 567. JUAN MARICHAL
☐ 643. RUSS GIBSON
☐ 663. FRAN HEALY
☐ 682. MIKE MCCORMICK
☐ 693. ALAN GALLAGHER
☐ 711. BOBBY BONDS
☐ 720. SAM MCDOWELL
☐ 733. JIM HART
☐ 761. BERNIE WILLIAMS(R)
☐ 771. TEAM CARD

TEXAS RANGERS

☐ 23. TED KUBIAK
☐ 64. PETE BROBERG
☐ 104. TOBY HARRAH
☐ 122. LARRY BIITTNER
☐ 148. DICK BILLINGS
☐ 191. JEFF BURROUGHS
☐ 210. DENNY MCLAIN
☐ 231. CASEY COX
☐ 242. DON MINCHER
☐ 277. ELLIOTT MADDOX
☐ 317. RICH HAND
☐ 329. ROY FOSTER
☐ 334. BILL FAHEY(R)
☐ 334. JIM MASON(R)
☐ 334. TOM RAGLAND(R)
☐ 350. FRANK HOWARD
☐ 365. DICK BOSMAN
☐ 396. PAUL LINDBLAD

☐ 424. BILL GOGOLEWSKI
☐ 461. TIM CULLEN
☐ 483. KEN SUAREZ
☐ 510. TED WILLIAMS(M)
☐ 529. DAVE NELSON
☐ 577. MIKE PAUL
☐ 598. HAL KING
☐ 609. TOM GRIEVE
☐ 654. HORACIO PINA
☐ 668. TEAM CARD
☐ 737. LENNY RANDLE
☐ 767. TOM MCCRAW

PETE BROBERG

1973 TOPPS (660)
2 1/2″ X 3 1/2″

DON SUTTON
PITCHER

ATLANTA BRAVES

☐ 15. RALPH GARR
☐ 33. JIM BREAZEALE
☐ 72. RON REED
☐ 100. HANK AARON
☐ 124. JIM HARDIN
☐ 144. MARTY PEREZ
☐ 169. RON SCHUELER
☐ 192. PAT JARVIS
☐ 215. DUSTY BAKER
☐ 237. MATHEWS(M) & COACHES
☐ 266. MIKE LUM
☐ 288. GARY GENTRY
☐ 312. OSCAR BROWN
☐ 359. CECIL UPSHAW
☐ 374. DARRELL EVANS
☐ 403. SONNY JACKSON
☐ 432. DAN FRISELLA
☐ 452. PAUL CASANOVA
☐ 503. PHIL NIEKRO
☐ 521. TEAM CARD
☐ 550. DAVE A. JOHNSON
☐ 574. BOB DIDIER
☐ 609. LARVELL BLANKS(R)
☐ 610. JIMMY FREEMAN(R)
☐ 630. DENNY MCLAIN
☐ 653. JOE HOERNER

BALTIMORE ORIOLES

☐ 9. JOHNNY OATES
☐ 34. PAT DOBSON
☐ 56. MERV RETTENMUND
☐ 90. BROOKS ROBINSON
☐ 109. DOYLE ALEXANDER
☐ 136. WEAVER(M) & COACHES
☐ 160. JIM PALMER
☐ 183. DON BUFORD
☐ 229. RORIC HARRISON
☐ 253. MARK BELANGER
☐ 278. TEAM CARD
☐ 302. TERRY CROWLEY
☐ 325. BOOG POWELL
☐ 362. EDDIE WATT
☐ 384. DON BAYLOR
☐ 396. GRANT JACKSON
☐ 418. BOBBY GRICH
☐ 470. MIKE CUELLAR
☐ 504. EARL WILLIAMS
☐ 528. PAUL BLAIR
☐ 553. MICKEY SCOTT
☐ 600. DAVE MCNALLY
☐ 601. SERGIO ROBLES(R)
☐ 604. JESSE JEFFERSON(R)
☐ 605. ENOS CABELL(R)
☐ 611. RICH COGGINS(R)
☐ 612. BOB REYNOLDS(R)
☐ 614. AL BUMBRY(R)
☐ 618. ANDY ETCHEBARREN
☐ 631. TOM MATCHICK

BOSTON RED SOX

☐ 14. SONNY SIEBERT
☐ 40. REGGIE SMITH
☐ 69. PHIL GAGLIANO
☐ 96. DOUG GRIFFIN
☐ 114. LYNN MCGLOTHEN
☐ 131. KASKO(M) & COACHES
☐ 143. JOHN CURTIS
☐ 165. LUIS APARICIO
☐ 193. CARLTON FISK
☐ 224. BILL LEE
☐ 245. CARL YASTRZEMSKI
☐ 270. LUIS TIANT
☐ 291. ROGELIO MORET
☐ 317. DANNY CATER
☐ 365. RICO PETROCELLI
☐ 388. BEN OGLIVIE
☐ 415. MARTY PATTIN
☐ 437. JOHN KENNEDY
☐ 463. KEN TATUM
☐ 491. BOB MONTGOMERY
☐ 518. BOB VEALE
☐ 541. BOB BOLIN
☐ 566. LEW KRAUSSE
☐ 596. TEAM CARD
☐ 607. MARIO GUERRERO(R)
☐ 614. DWIGHT EVANS(R)
☐ 616. MIKE GARMAN(R)
☐ 620. TOMMY HARPER

CALIFORNIA ANGELS

☐ 18. LEROY STANTON
☐ 36. STEVE BARBER
☐ 75. VADA PINSON
☐ 102. RUDY MAY
☐ 123. SANDY ALOMAR
☐ 154. JEFF TORBORG
☐ 175. FRANK ROBINSON
☐ 178. DON ROSE
☐ 220. NOLAN RYAN
☐ 243. TEAM CARD
☐ 267. LLOYD ALLEN
☐ 279. MIKE STRAHLER
☐ 289. BOB OLIVER
☐ 301. BILLY GRABARKEWITZ
☐ 319. JIM SPENCER
☐ 354. BILLY PARKER
☐ 373. CLYDE WRIGHT
☐ 402. JACK HIATT
☐ 421. WINKLES(M) & COACHES
☐ 445. KEN BERRY
☐ 502. BOBBY VALENTINE
☐ 522. LEO CARDENAS
☐ 543. ALAN FOSTER
☐ 570. BILL SINGER
☐ 597. MICKEY RIVERS
☐ 636. RICK CLARK

1973 Topps

CHICAGO CUBS

- ☐ 21. RANDY HUNDLEY
- ☐ 44. RICK MONDAY
- ☐ 70. MILT PAPPAS
- ☐ 81. LOCKMAN(M) & COACHES
- ☐ 115. RON SANTO
- ☐ 139. CARMEN FANZONE
- ☐ 180. FERGIE JENKINS
- ☐ 200. BILLY WILLIAMS
- ☐ 262. JACK AKER
- ☐ 285. DON KESSINGER
- ☐ 309. PAUL POPOVICH
- ☐ 328. BILL BONHAM
- ☐ 367. BURT HOOTON
- ☐ 393. JOSE CARDENAL
- ☐ 414. KEN RUDOLPH
- ☐ 426. DAVE LAROCHE
- ☐ 440. GLENN BECKERT
- ☐ 464. TEAM CARD
- ☐ 482. RICK REUSCHEL
- ☐ 501. LARRY GURA
- ☐ 527. DAN MCGINN
- ☐ 552. J.C. MARTIN
- ☐ 565. JIM HICKMAN
- ☐ 580. JOE PEPITONE
- ☐ 603. TERRY HUGHES(R)
- ☐ 605. PAT BOURQUE(R)
- ☐ 645. BOB LOCKER

CHICAGO WHITE SOX

- ☐ 20. STAN BAHNSEN
- ☐ 42. MIKE ANDREWS
- ☐ 73. ED HERRMANN
- ☐ 105. CARLOS MAY
- ☐ 129. TERRY FORSTER
- ☐ 150. WILBUR WOOD
- ☐ 174. RICH GOSSAGE
- ☐ 194. JORGE ORTA
- ☐ 238. TONY MUSER
- ☐ 261. H. PAT KELLY
- ☐ 287. EDDIE LEON
- ☐ 310. DICK ALLEN
- ☐ 356. TANNER(M) & COACHES
- ☐ 379. CY ACOSTA
- ☐ 404. CHUCK BRINKMAN
- ☐ 423. JOHNNY JETER
- ☐ 439. EDDIE FISHER
- ☐ 455. BILL MELTON
- ☐ 481. TEAM CARD
- ☐ 494. RICH MORALES
- ☐ 506. BART JOHNSON
- ☐ 534. DAVE LEMONDS
- ☐ 561. JIM GEDDES
- ☐ 581. STEVE KEALEY
- ☐ 604. DENNIS O'TOOLE(R)
- ☐ 627. LUIS ALVARADO
- ☐ 648. TOM EGAN

CINCINNATI REDS

- ☐ 8. TOM HALL
- ☐ 28. HAL MCRAE
- ☐ 52. DENIS MENKE
- ☐ 89. JACK BILLINGHAM
- ☐ 130. PETE ROSE
- ☐ 156. CESAR GERONIMO
- ☐ 177. BILL PLUMMER
- ☐ 195. CLAY CARROLL
- ☐ 230. JOE MORGAN
- ☐ 260. GARY NOLAN
- ☐ 275. TONY PEREZ
- ☐ 296. ANDERSON(M) & COACHES
- ☐ 318. JIM MCGLOTHLIN
- ☐ 335. BOB TOLAN
- ☐ 357. ROSS GRIMSLEY
- ☐ 380. JOHNNY BENCH
- ☐ 399. GEORGE FOSTER
- ☐ 447. JOE HAGUE
- ☐ 492. PEDRO BORBON
- ☐ 507. DARREL CHANEY
- ☐ 533. LARRY STAHL
- ☐ 554. DAVE CONCEPCION
- ☐ 595. DON GULLETT
- ☐ 602. MEL BEHNEY(R)
- ☐ 626. BOB BARTON
- ☐ 641. TEAM CARD

CLEVELAND INDIANS

- ☐ 11. CHRIS CHAMBLISS
- ☐ 31. BUDDY BELL
- ☐ 53. STEVE DUNNING
- ☐ 86. TOM MCCRAW
- ☐ 134. MILT WILCOX
- ☐ 157. DENNY RIDDLEBERGER
- ☐ 181. JACK BROHAMER
- ☐ 226. RAY FOSSE
- ☐ 247. DEL UNSER
- ☐ 272. ED FARMER
- ☐ 297. WALT WILLIAMS
- ☐ 327. JOHN LOWENSTEIN
- ☐ 339. DICK TIDROW
- ☐ 372. OSCAR GAMBLE
- ☐ 376. FRANK DUFFY
- ☐ 400. GAYLORD PERRY
- ☐ 425. ALEX JOHNSON
- ☐ 449. ASPROMONTE(M) & CHS.
- ☐ 496. RAY LAMB
- ☐ 514. JERRY KENNEY
- ☐ 532. STEVE MINGORI
- ☐ 551. MIKE KILKENNY
- ☐ 571. RUSTY TORRES
- ☐ 591. MIKE HEDLUND
- ☐ 601. GEORGE PENA(R)
- ☐ 608. DICK COLPAERT(R)
- ☐ 612. BRENT STROM(R)
- ☐ 614. CHARLIE SPIKES(R)
- ☐ 629. TEAM CARD
- ☐ 644. JACK HEIDEMANN
- ☐ 656. JOHN ELLIS

DETROIT TIGERS

- ☐ 5. ED BRINKMAN
- ☐ 29. TONY TAYLOR
- ☐ 51. CHUCK SEELBACH
- ☐ 88. MICKEY STANLEY
- ☐ 120. JOE COLEMAN
- ☐ 146. WOODIE FRYMAN
- ☐ 168. JIM NORTHRUP
- ☐ 191. TEAM CARD
- ☐ 218. AURELIO RODRIGUEZ
- ☐ 256. CHRIS ZACHARY
- ☐ 280. AL KALINE
- ☐ 304. DUKE SIMS
- ☐ 323. MARTIN(M) & COACHES
- ☐ 349. DICK MCAULIFFE
- ☐ 369. LERRIN LAGROW
- ☐ 390. MICKEY LOLICH
- ☐ 413. TOM TIMMERMANN
- ☐ 433. WILLIE HORTON
- ☐ 448. JOHN HILLER
- ☐ 460. BILL FREEHAN
- ☐ 485. NORM CASH
- ☐ 508. GATES BROWN
- ☐ 537. BILL SLAYBACK
- ☐ 560. FRANK HOWARD
- ☐ 585. JOE NIEKRO
- ☐ 604. BOB STRAMPE(R)
- ☐ 633. IKE BROWN
- ☐ 660. FRED SCHERMAN

HOUSTON ASTROS

- ☐ 17. FRED GLADDING
- ☐ 39. DAVE A. ROBERTS
- ☐ 76. DOUG RADER
- ☐ 93. JESUS ALOU
- ☐ 110. BOB WATSON
- ☐ 135. LEE MAY
- ☐ 158. TEAM CARD
- ☐ 185. JIM WYNN
- ☐ 217. DON WILSON
- ☐ 242. GEORGE CULVER
- ☐ 290. CESAR CEDENO
- ☐ 313. JIM RAY
- ☐ 351. JIMMY STEWART
- ☐ 375. LARRY DIERKER
- ☐ 395. ROGER METZGER
- ☐ 420. TOMMIE AGEE
- ☐ 446. JERRY REUSS
- ☐ 468. TOM GRIFFIN
- ☐ 495. TOMMY HELMS
- ☐ 519. JOHN EDWARDS
- ☐ 546. JIM YORK
- ☐ 572. GARY SUTHERLAND
- ☐ 589. KEN FORSCH
- ☐ 613. SKIP JUTZE(R)
- ☐ 624. DUROCHER(M) & COACHES
- ☐ 637. NORM MILLER

KANSAS CITY ROYALS

- ☐ 22. TED ABERNATHY
- ☐ 48. PAUL SPLITTORFF
- ☐ 78. RICHIE SCHEINBLUM
- ☐ 99. CARL TAYLOR
- ☐ 118. JOHN MAYBERRY
- ☐ 140. LOU PINIELLA
- ☐ 164. MONTY MONTGOMERY
- ☐ 188. COOKIE ROJAS
- ☐ 233. ED KIRKPATRICK
- ☐ 251. ROGER NELSON
- ☐ 282. STEVE HOVLEY
- ☐ 306. TOM BURGMEIER
- ☐ 334. FREDDIE PATEK
- ☐ 347. TEAM CARD
- ☐ 392. DICK DRAGO
- ☐ 416. PAUL SCHAAL
- ☐ 428. WAYNE SIMPSON
- ☐ 441. GAIL HOPKINS
- ☐ 466. JOSE ARCIA
- ☐ 487. BRUCE DAL CANTON
- ☐ 510. AMOS OTIS
- ☐ 539. TOM MURPHY
- ☐ 558. JERRY MAY
- ☐ 578. KEN WRIGHT
- ☐ 593. MCKEON(M) & COACHES
- ☐ 608. STEVE BUSBY(R)
- ☐ 611. JIM WOHLFORD(R)
- ☐ 616. NORM ANGELINI(R)
- ☐ 643. AL FITZMORRIS

LOS ANGELES DODGERS

- ☐ 10. DON SUTTON
- ☐ 35. WILLIE DAVIS
- ☐ 59. STEVE YEAGER
- ☐ 91. TEAM CARD
- ☐ 108. BILL RUSSELL
- ☐ 126. JIM BREWER
- ☐ 151. WES PARKER
- ☐ 196. KEN MCMULLEN
- ☐ 213. STEVE GARVEY
- ☐ 239. PETE RICHERT
- ☐ 258. TOMMY JOHN
- ☐ 324. AL DOWNING
- ☐ 368. BILL BUCKNER
- ☐ 391. LEE LACY
- ☐ 412. MANNY MOTA
- ☐ 442. DICK DIETZ
- ☐ 490. CLAUDE OSTEEN
- ☐ 515. ANDY MESSERSMITH
- ☐ 544. VON JOSHUA
- ☐ 569. ALSTON(M) & COACHES
- ☐ 602. DOUG RAU(R)
- ☐ 606. TOM PACIOREK(R)
- ☐ 609. DAVE LOPES(R)
- ☐ 610. CHARLIE HOUGH(R)
- ☐ 615. RON CEY(R)
- ☐ 621. JOE FERGUSON
- ☐ 639. WILLIE CRAWFORD

MILWAUKEE BREWERS

- ☐ 45. ELLIE RODRIGUEZ
- ☐ 71. JOHNNY BRIGGS
- ☐ 74. BILLY CHAMPION
- ☐ 92. TEAM CARD
- ☐ 127. TEAM CARD
- ☐ 152. DAVE MAY
- ☐ 176. CHUCK TAYLOR
- ☐ 212. JOE LAHOUD
- ☐ 231. BILL PARSONS
- ☐ 263. GEORGE SCOTT
- ☐ 286. FRANK LINZY
- ☐ 308. SKIP LOCKWOOD
- ☐ 332. JOHN FELSKE
- ☐ 366. BROCK DAVIS
- ☐ 386. DON MONEY
- ☐ 408. JIM COLBORN
- ☐ 427. RICK AUERBACH
- ☐ 451. JOHN VUKOVICH
- ☐ 526. OLLIE BROWN
- ☐ 547. BOBBY HEISE
- ☐ 568. RAY NEWMAN
- ☐ 582. DARRELL PORTER
- ☐ 609. PEDRO GARCIA(R)
- ☐ 628. JIM SLATON
- ☐ 646. CRANDALL(M) & COACHES

MINNESOTA TWINS

- ☐ 16. STEVE BRAUN
- ☐ 49. QUILICI(M) & COACHES
- ☐ 80. TONY OLIVA
- ☐ 98. DICK WOODSON
- ☐ 122. JIM STRICKLAND
- ☐ 148. DAVE GOLTZ
- ☐ 170. HARMON KILLEBREW
- ☐ 199. BERT BLYLEVEN
- ☐ 228. BOBBY DARWIN
- ☐ 259. JIM HOLT
- ☐ 284. GLENN BORGMANN
- ☐ 311. JOE DECKER
- ☐ 330. ROD CAREW
- ☐ 353. STEVE BRYE
- ☐ 358. JIM NETTLES
- ☐ 385. JIM PERRY
- ☐ 411. RAY CORBIN
- ☐ 443. DANNY THOMPSON
- ☐ 469. DAN MONZON
- ☐ 516. DANNY WALTON
- ☐ 530. JIM KAAT
- ☐ 555. BILL HANDS
- ☐ 577. ERIC SODERHOLM
- ☐ 598. PHIL ROOF
- ☐ 622. LARRY HISLE
- ☐ 638. KEN REYNOLDS
- ☐ 654. TEAM CARD

MONTREAL EXPOS

- ☐ 19. TIM FOLI
- ☐ 41. TOM WALKER
- ☐ 77. MIKE TORREZ
- ☐ 106. TERRY HUMPHREY
- ☐ 125. RON FAIRLY
- ☐ 149. RON HUNT
- ☐ 173. HAL BREEDEN
- ☐ 211. BALOR MOORE
- ☐ 232. KEN SINGLETON
- ☐ 254. BILL STONEMAN
- ☐ 281. MIKE JORGENSEN
- ☐ 307. BOOTS DAY
- ☐ 331. CARL MORTON
- ☐ 355. MIKE MARSHALL
- ☐ 377. MAUCH(M) & COACHES
- ☐ 401. CLYDE MASHORE
- ☐ 429. JIM FAIREY
- ☐ 457. JOHN STROHMAYER
- ☐ 484. ERNIE MCANALLY
- ☐ 505. BOB BAILEY
- ☐ 531. RON WOODS
- ☐ 576. TEAM CARD
- ☐ 592. JOHN BOCCABELLA
- ☐ 606. JORGE ROQUE(R)
- ☐ 607. PEPE FRIAS(R)
- ☐ 623. STEVE RENKO
- ☐ 642. JOSE LABOY

TUG
McGRAW
NEW YORK METS   PITCHER

NEW YORK METS

- ☐ 4. JOHN MILNER
- ☐ 30. TUG MCGRAW
- ☐ 55. JON MATLACK
- ☐ 87. KEN BOSWELL
- ☐ 107. PHIL HENNIGAN
- ☐ 113. JERRY GROTE
- ☐ 137. JIM BEAUCHAMP

- ☐ 161. TED MARTINEZ
- ☐ 184. JERRY KOOSMAN
- ☐ 223. BUD HARRELSON
- ☐ 257. BERRA(M) & COACHES
- ☐ 283. RAY SADECKI
- ☐ 305. WILLIE MAYS
- ☐ 329. ED KRANEPOOL
- ☐ 350. TOM SEAVER
- ☐ 389. TEAM CARD
- ☐ 407. FELIX MILLAN
- ☐ 436. JIM MCANDREW
- ☐ 493. DUFFY DYER
- ☐ 525. JIM FREGOSI
- ☐ 540. CLEON JONES
- ☐ 562. WAYNE GARRETT
- ☐ 586. BILL SUDAKIS
- ☐ 610. HANK WEBB(R)
- ☐ 617. RICH CHILES
- ☐ 647. GEORGE STONE

NEW YORK YANKEES

- ☐ 25. ROY WHITE
- ☐ 46. LINDY MCDANIEL
- ☐ 82. FRITZ PETERSON
- ☐ 103. CELERINO SANCHEZ
- ☐ 116. HOUK(M) & COACHES
- ☐ 132. MATTY ALOU
- ☐ 142. THURMAN MUNSON
- ☐ 172. STEVE KLINE
- ☐ 198. HORACE CLARKE
- ☐ 240. BOBBY MURCER
- ☐ 265. GENE MICHAEL
- ☐ 293. BERNIE ALLEN
- ☐ 314. RON SWOBODA
- ☐ 371. MIKE KEKICH
- ☐ 394. SPARKY LYLE
- ☐ 419. CASEY COX
- ☐ 431. GERRY MOSES
- ☐ 462. RON BLOMBERG
- ☐ 479. HAL LANIER
- ☐ 498. GRAIG NETTLES
- ☐ 520. MEL STOTTLEMYRE
- ☐ 535. JOHN CALLISON
- ☐ 556. TEAM CARD
- ☐ 573. FRED BEENE
- ☐ 608. GEORGE MEDICH(R)
- ☐ 616. STEVE BLATERIC(R)
- ☐ 634. ALAN CLOSTER
- ☐ 650. FELIPE ALOU

OAKLAND A'S

- ☐ 13. GEORGE HENDRICK
- ☐ 38. MIKE EPSTEIN
- ☐ 60. KEN HOLTZMAN
- ☐ 84. ROLLIE FINGERS
- ☐ 155. SAL BANDO
- ☐ 179. WILLIAMS(M) & COACHES
- ☐ 214. DAVE HAMILTON
- ☐ 222. ROB GARDNER
- ☐ 234. BILL NORTH
- ☐ 235. JIM HUNTER
- ☐ 255. REGGIE JACKSON
- ☐ 274. DAROLD KNOWLES
- ☐ 295. BERT CAMPANERIS
- ☐ 315. JOHN ODOM
- ☐ 337. DAVE DUNCAN
- ☐ 360. JOE RUDI
- ☐ 382. MIKE HEGAN
- ☐ 406. PAUL LINDBLAD
- ☐ 430. VIDA BLUE
- ☐ 456. DICK GREEN
- ☐ 483. DAL MAXVILL
- ☐ 500. TEAM CARD
- ☐ 524. GENE TENACE
- ☐ 545. ORLANDO CEPEDA
- ☐ 563. LARRY HANEY
- ☐ 587. RICH MCKINNEY
- ☐ 605. GONZALO MARQUEZ(R)
- ☐ 625. ANGEL MANGUAL
- ☐ 652. TED KUBIAK

PHILADELPHIA PHILLIES

- ☐ 3. JIM LONBORG
- ☐ 6. MAC SCARCE
- ☐ 37. BILL ROBINSON
- ☐ 97. WILLIE MONTANEZ
- ☐ 119. LARRY BOWA

- ☐ 147. MIKE ANDERSON
- ☐ 166. TERRY HARMON
- ☐ 189. GREG LUZINSKI
- ☐ 227. WAYNE TWITCHELL
- ☐ 246. KEN SANDERS
- ☐ 271. TOM HUTTON
- ☐ 300. STEVE CARLTON
- ☐ 326. DARRELL BRANDON
- ☐ 405. CESAR TOVAR
- ☐ 424. DENNY DOYLE
- ☐ 444. KEN BRETT
- ☐ 454. TOM HALLER
- ☐ 467. MIKE RYAN
- ☐ 486. OZARK(M) & COACHES
- ☐ 509. JIM NASH
- ☐ 536. TEAM CARD
- ☐ 559. BARRY LERSCH
- ☐ 590. DERON JOHNSON
- ☐ 613. BOB BOONE(R)
- ☐ 615. MIKE SCHMIDT(R)
- ☐ 619. BILLY WILSON
- ☐ 632. DICK SELMA
- ☐ 659. JOSE PAGAN

PITTSBURGH PIRATES

- ☐ 2. RICH HEBNER
- ☐ 26. TEAM CARD
- ☐ 50. ROBERTO CLEMENTE
- ☐ 95. STEVE BLASS
- ☐ 117. RAMON HERNANDEZ
- ☐ 141. BRUCE KISON
- ☐ 163. VIC DAVALILLO
- ☐ 187. LUKE WALKER
- ☐ 225. AL OLIVER
- ☐ 250. MANNY SANGUILLEN
- ☐ 277. BOB L. MILLER
- ☐ 303. NELSON BRILES
- ☐ 333. GENE CLINES
- ☐ 348. RENNIE STENNETT
- ☐ 363. JACKIE HERNANDEZ
- ☐ 370. WILLIE STARGELL
- ☐ 397. DAVE CASH
- ☐ 422. BOB ROBERTSON
- ☐ 465. DAVE GIUSTI
- ☐ 499. BOB MOOSE
- ☐ 517. VIRDON(M) & COACHES
- ☐ 529. MILT MAY
- ☐ 575. DOCK ELLIS
- ☐ 611. RICHIE ZISK(R)
- ☐ 635. GENE ALLEY
- ☐ 657. BOB D. JOHNSON

ST. LOUIS CARDINALS

- ☐ 24. AL SANTORINI
- ☐ 47. LUIS MELENDEZ
- ☐ 85. TED SIMMONS
- ☐ 104. REGGIE CLEVELAND
- ☐ 128. TED SIZEMORE
- ☐ 153. AL HRABOSKY
- ☐ 171. BERNIE CARBO
- ☐ 190. BOB GIBSON
- ☐ 219. TEAM CARD
- ☐ 241. DWAIN ANDERSON
- ☐ 269. TIM MCCARVER
- ☐ 292. JOSE CRUZ
- ☐ 320. LOU BROCK
- ☐ 364. RICK WISE
- ☐ 383. DIEGO SEGUI
- ☐ 417. SCIPIO SPINKS
- ☐ 450. JOE TORRE
- ☐ 497. SCHOENDIENST(M) & CHS.
- ☐ 523. WAYNE GRANGER
- ☐ 548. DON DURHAM
- ☐ 567. BOB FENWICK
- ☐ 599. ED CROSBY
- ☐ 603. KEN REITZ(R)
- ☐ 607. RAY BUSSE(R)
- ☐ 649. RICH FOLKERS

SAN DIEGO PADRES

- ☐ 12. ZIMMER(M) & COACHES
- ☐ 32. FRED NORMAN
- ☐ 57. DERREL THOMAS
- ☐ 83. LERON LEE
- ☐ 112. GARY ROSS
- ☐ 133. DAVE W. ROBERTS
- ☐ 159. CLARENCE GASTON

- ☐ 182. MIKE CALDWELL
- ☐ 221. FRED KENDALL
- ☐ 244. ED ACOSTA
- ☐ 268. JERRY MORALES
- ☐ 294. STEVE ARLIN
- ☐ 316. TEAM CARD
- ☐ 340. NATE COLBERT
- ☐ 381. VICENTE ROMO
- ☐ 409. IVAN MURRELL
- ☐ 438. ENZO HERNANDEZ
- ☐ 461. MIKE CORKINS
- ☐ 488. DAVE CAMPBELL
- ☐ 513. DAVE MARSHALL
- ☐ 542. PAT CORRALES
- ☐ 583. BILL GREIF
- ☐ 602. RALPH GARCIA(R)
- ☐ 613. MIKE IVIE(R)
- ☐ 615. JOHN HILTON(R)
- ☐ 655. CLAY KIRBY

SAN FRANCISCO GIANTS

- ☐ 23. DAVE KINGMAN
- ☐ 43. RANDY MOFFITT
- ☐ 79. JIM WILLOUGHBY
- ☐ 101. KEN HENDERSON
- ☐ 121. DAVE RADER
- ☐ 145. BOBBY BONDS
- ☐ 167. STEVE STONE
- ☐ 197. ED GOODSON
- ☐ 236. TITO FUENTES
- ☐ 248. JERRY JOHNSON
- ☐ 252. FOX(M) & COACHES
- ☐ 273. CHRIS SPEIER
- ☐ 298. RON BRYANT
- ☐ 322. GARRY MADDOX
- ☐ 336. TOM BRADLEY
- ☐ 361. FRAN HEALY
- ☐ 387. JIM BARR
- ☐ 410. WILLIE MCCOVEY
- ☐ 434. TEAM CARD
- ☐ 459. JIMMY HOWARTH
- ☐ 480. JUAN MARICHAL
- ☐ 511. SAM MCDOWELL
- ☐ 538. JIM HART
- ☐ 557. BERNIE WILLIAMS
- ☐ 584. CHRIS ARNOLD
- ☐ 606. GARY MATTHEWS(R)
- ☐ 651. DON CARRITHERS

DAVE
NELSON
TEXAS RANGERS 3rd BASE

TEXAS RANGERS

- ☐ 7. TEAM CARD
- ☐ 27. BILL GOGOLEWSKI
- ☐ 58. MIKE PAUL
- ☐ 94. DICK BILLINGS
- ☐ 111. DAVE NELSON
- ☐ 138. HORACIO PINA
- ☐ 162. PETE BROBERG
- ☐ 186. BILL FAHEY
- ☐ 216. TOBY HARRAH
- ☐ 249. LARRY BIITTNER
- ☐ 276. JOE LOVITTO
- ☐ 299. TED FORD
- ☐ 321. RICH HINTON
- ☐ 352. DON STANHOUSE
- ☐ 378. LENNY RANDLE
- ☐ 398. RICH HAND
- ☐ 435. RICO CARTY

- ☐ 458. JIM MASON
- ☐ 489. JEFF BURROUGHS
- ☐ 512. DALTON JONES
- ☐ 549. HERZOG(M) & COACHES
- ☐ 564. MIKE THOMPSON
- ☐ 579. TOM GRIEVE
- ☐ 594. VIC HARRIS
- ☐ 601. RICK STELMASZEK(R)
- ☐ 603. BILL MCNULTY(R)
- ☐ 612. STEVE LAWSON(R)
- ☐ 640. DICK BOSMAN
- ☐ 658. ELLIOTT MADDOX

1974 TOPPS (660)
2 1/2" X 3 1/2"

BALTIMORE PITCHER
JIM PALMER ORIOLES

ATLANTA BRAVES

- ☐ 1. HANK AARON
- ☐ 29. PHIL NIEKRO
- ☐ 45. DAVE A. JOHNSON
- ☐ 71. DANNY FRISELLA
- ☐ 93. ROD GILBREATH
- ☐ 140. DARRELL EVANS
- ☐ 164. TOM HOUSE
- ☐ 183. JOHNNY OATES
- ☐ 227. MIKE LUM
- ☐ 244. CARL MORTON
- ☐ 272. PAUL CASANOVA
- ☐ 298. RORIC HARRISON
- ☐ 320. DUSTY BAKER
- ☐ 346. RON REED
- ☐ 374. MARTY PEREZ
- ☐ 415. GARY GENTRY
- ☐ 439. NORM MILLER
- ☐ 457. CHUCK GOGGIN
- ☐ 483. TEAM CARD
- ☐ 504. JOE NIEKRO
- ☐ 526. FRANK TEPEDINO
- ☐ 544. RON SCHUELER
- ☐ 570. RALPH GARR
- ☐ 591. SONNY JACKSON
- ☐ 607. LEO FOSTER(R)
- ☐ 614. ADRIAN DEVINE
- ☐ 634. MATHEWS(M) & COACHES

BALTIMORE ORIOLES

- ☐ 16. TEAM CARD
- ☐ 40. JIM PALMER
- ☐ 68. GRANT JACKSON
- ☐ 92. PAUL BLAIR
- ☐ 109. BOB GRICH
- ☐ 137. AL BUMBRY
- ☐ 160. BROOKS ROBINSON
- ☐ 187. DON BAYLOR
- ☐ 235. DAVE MCNALLY
- ☐ 259. BOB REYNOLDS
- ☐ 282. DOYLE ALEXANDER
- ☐ 306. WEAVER(M) & COACHES
- ☐ 329. MARK BELANGER
- ☐ 353. RICH COGGINS
- ☐ 375. EARL WILLIAMS
- ☐ 396. TOMMY DAVIS
- ☐ 411. FRANK W. BAKER
- ☐ 436. DON HOOD
- ☐ 460. BOOG POWELL
- ☐ 488. ANDY ETCHEBARREN

- ☐ 509. JESSE JEFFERSON
- ☐ 534. EDDIE WATT
- ☐ 560. MIKE CUELLAR
- ☐ 585. MERV RETTENMUND
- ☐ 596. WAYNE GARLAND(R)
- ☐ 603. SERGIO ROBLES(R)
- ☐ 606. JIM FULLER(R)
- ☐ 648. TERRY CROWLEY

BOSTON RED SOX

- ☐ 33. DON NEWHAUSER
- ☐ 61. LUIS APARICIO
- ☐ 83. ORLANDO CEPEDA
- ☐ 84. RICK WISE
- ☐ 105. CARLTON FISK
- ☐ 113. DICK DRAGO
- ☐ 118. BILL LEE
- ☐ 167. LUIS TIANT
- ☐ 192. MARIO GUERRERO
- ☐ 219. DOUG GRIFFIN
- ☐ 247. RICK MILLER
- ☐ 280. CARL YASTRZEMSKI
- ☐ 301. BOB MONTGOMERY
- ☐ 325. TOMMY HARPER
- ☐ 351. DWIGHT EVANS
- ☐ 373. JOHN CURTIS
- ☐ 403. JOHNSON(M) & COACHES
- ☐ 427. BOBBY BOLIN
- ☐ 495. DICK MCAULIFFE
- ☐ 523. CECIL COOPER
- ☐ 543. DANNY CATER
- ☐ 567. TEAM CARD
- ☐ 590. ROGELIO MORET
- ☐ 596. DICK POLE(R)
- ☐ 609. RICO PETROCELLI
- ☐ 621. BERNIE CARBO
- ☐ 647. JUAN BENIQUEZ

CALIFORNIA ANGELS

- ☐ 20. NOLAN RYAN
- ☐ 37. DAVE SELLS
- ☐ 55. FRANK ROBINSON
- ☐ 76. MICKEY RIVERS
- ☐ 101. BOBBY VALENTINE
- ☐ 114. TEAM CARD
- ☐ 139. AURELIO MONTEAGUDO
- ☐ 188. RUDY MEOLI
- ☐ 210. BILL SINGER
- ☐ 243. BOB OLIVER
- ☐ 276. WINKLES(M) & COACHES
- ☐ 302. RUDY MAY
- ☐ 323. RICHIE SCHEINBLUM
- ☐ 347. SANDY ALOMAR
- ☐ 381. CHARLIE SANDS
- ☐ 405. ELLIE RODRIGUEZ
- ☐ 429. DICK LANGE
- ☐ 449. TOM MCCRAW
- ☐ 467. WINSTON LLENAS
- ☐ 490. VADA PINSON
- ☐ 512. JOE LAHOUD
- ☐ 532. SKIP LOCKWOOD
- ☐ 552. DENNY DOYLE
- ☐ 571. RICH HAND
- ☐ 594. LEROY STANTON
- ☐ 597. DAVE CHALK(R)
- ☐ 605. FRANK TANANA(R)
- ☐ 611. RICK STELMASZEK
- ☐ 625. OLLIE BROWN
- ☐ 650. MIKE EPSTEIN

CHICAGO CUBS

- ☐ 14. PAUL POPOVICH
- ☐ 38. DON KESSINGER
- ☐ 62. BOB LOCKER
- ☐ 110. BILLY WILLIAMS
- ☐ 136. RICK REUSCHEL
- ☐ 157. VIC HARRIS
- ☐ 161. RAY BURRIS
- ☐ 185. JOSE CARDENAL
- ☐ 211. TEAM CARD
- ☐ 258. JERRY MORALES
- ☐ 270. RON SANTO
- ☐ 295. RICK MONDAY
- ☐ 319. RANDY HUNDLEY
- ☐ 354. LOCKMAN(M) & COACHES
- ☐ 378. BURT HOOTON
- ☐ 399. MIKE PAUL

☐ 422. GONZALO MARQUEZ
☐ 452. GENE HISER
☐ 484. CARMEN FANZONE
☐ 502. DAVE LAROCHE
☐ 528. BILL BONHAM
☐ 562. JACK AKER
☐ 584. KEN RUDOLPH
☐ 598. JIM TYRONE(R)
☐ 600. BILL MADLOCK(R)
☐ 603. TOM LUNDSTEDT(R)
☐ 604. ANDY THORNTON(R)
☐ 607. DAVE ROSELLO(R)
☐ 616. LARRY GURA
☐ 640. MILT PAPPAS
☐ 656. ADRIAN GARRETT

CHICAGO WHITE SOX

☐ 22. CY ACOSTA
☐ 46. H. PAT KELLY
☐ 70. DICK ALLEN
☐ 96. JERRY HAIRSTON
☐ 120. WILBUR WOOD
☐ 147. BART JOHNSON
☐ 170. BILL MELTON
☐ 195. CARLOS MAY
☐ 221. TANNER(M) & COACHES
☐ 254. STAN BAHNSEN
☐ 286. TONY MUSER
☐ 310. TERRY FORSTER
☐ 357. BUDDY BRADFORD
☐ 376. JORGE ORTA
☐ 394. KEN HENDERSON
☐ 416. TEAM CARD
☐ 438. ED HERRMANN
☐ 440. JIM KAAT
☐ 462. LUIS ALVARADO
☐ 486. STEVE STONE
☐ 501. EDDIE LEON
☐ 519. BILL SHARP
☐ 542. RICH GOSSAGE
☐ 557. JIM MCGLOTHLIN
☐ 582. BUCKY DENT
☐ 601. BRIAN DOWNING(R)
☐ 605. KEN FRAILING(R)
☐ 615. JOHNNY JETER
☐ 641. CHUCK BRINKMAN

CINCINNATI REDS

☐ 10. JOHNNY BENCH
☐ 34. ANDY KOSCO
☐ 59. ROSS GRIMSLEY
☐ 85. JOE MORGAN
☐ 111. CLAY CARROLL
☐ 134. DENIS MENKE
☐ 158. JACK BILLINGHAM
☐ 181. CESAR GERONIMO
☐ 230. TONY PEREZ
☐ 248. TOM HALL
☐ 277. GARY NOLAN
☐ 287. CLAY KIRBY
☐ 300. PETE ROSE
☐ 326. ANDERSON(M) & CHS.
☐ 341. DAN DRIESSEN
☐ 362. HAL KING
☐ 385. DON GULLETT
☐ 410. PEDRO BORBON
☐ 435. DAVE CONCEPCION
☐ 459. TEAM CARD
☐ 491. ROGER NELSON
☐ 507. LARRY STAHL
☐ 524. BILL PLUMMER
☐ 559. DARREL CHANEY
☐ 581. FRED NORMAN
☐ 598. KEN GRIFFEY(R)
☐ 601. ED ARMBRISTER(R)
☐ 608. DICK BANEY(R)
☐ 622. PHIL GAGLIANO
☐ 646. GEORGE FOSTER

CLEVELAND INDIANS

☐ 13. TOM HILGENDORF
☐ 35. GAYLORD PERRY
☐ 58. CHARLIE SPIKES
☐ 81. FRANK DUFFY
☐ 128. JOHN ELLIS
☐ 152. OSCAR GAMBLE
☐ 176. JOHN LOWENSTEIN

☐ 199. MIKE KEKICH
☐ 231. DICK TIDROW
☐ 257. BUDDY BELL
☐ 284. DAVE DUNCAN
☐ 303. GEORGE HENDRICK
☐ 327. TOM TIMMERMANN
☐ 359. BRENT STROM
☐ 384. CHRIS CHAMBLISS
☐ 418. WALT WILLIAMS
☐ 441. TOM RAGLAND
☐ 465. DICK BOSMAN
☐ 499. RUSTY TORRES
☐ 521. ASPROMONTE(M) & CHS.
☐ 541. TEAM CARD
☐ 565. MILT WILCOX
☐ 586. JACK BROHAMER
☐ 606. TOMMY SMITH(R)
☐ 617. TED FORD
☐ 638. KEN SANDERS

DETROIT TIGERS

☐ 9. MICKEY LOLICH
☐ 24. JOHN HILLER
☐ 48. DICK SHARON
☐ 72. AURELIO RODRIGUEZ
☐ 94. TEAM CARD
☐ 115. WILLIE HORTON
☐ 138. ED BRINKMAN
☐ 162. BILL FREEHAN
☐ 186. FRED SCHERMAN
☐ 215. AL KALINE
☐ 240. JOE COLEMAN
☐ 256. JIM NORTHRUP
☐ 292. CHUCK SEELBACH
☐ 316. JIM PERRY
☐ 367. NORM CASH
☐ 389. GATES BROWN
☐ 409. IKE BROWN
☐ 433. LERRIN LAGROW
☐ 482. BOB DIDIER
☐ 506. ED FARMER
☐ 530. MICKEY STANLEY
☐ 555. WOODIE FRYMAN
☐ 578. RALPH HOUK(M)
☐ 596. FRED HOLDSWORTH(R)
☐ 597. JOHN GAMBLE(R)
☐ 600. RON CASH(R)
☐ 600. REGGIE SANDERS(R)
☐ 604. JOHN KNOX(R)

HOUSTON ASTROS

☐ 21. BOB GALLAGHER
☐ 31. GOMEZ(M) & COACHES
☐ 43. JIM WYNN
☐ 67. TOMMY HELMS
☐ 91. KEN FORSCH
☐ 154. TEAM CARD
☐ 177. DAVE A. ROBERTS
☐ 200. CESAR CEDENO
☐ 224. ROGER METZGER
☐ 256. TOM GRIFFIN
☐ 279. JIM CRAWFORD
☐ 293. MILT MAY
☐ 304. DON WILSON
☐ 328. SKIP JUTZE
☐ 370. BOB WATSON
☐ 395. DOUG RADER

☐ 428. GARY SUTHERLAND
☐ 458. JIM RAY
☐ 500. LEE MAY
☐ 522. J.R. RICHARD
☐ 556. DAVE CAMPBELL
☐ 579. CECIL UPSHAW
☐ 635. JOHN EDWARDS
☐ 660. LARRY DIERKER

KANSAS CITY ROYALS

☐ 17. DOUG BIRD
☐ 41. BOBBY FLOYD
☐ 65. AMOS OTIS
☐ 88. FREDDIE PATEK
☐ 150. JOHN MAYBERRY
☐ 166. MCKEON(M) & COACHES
☐ 191. AL FITZMORRIS
☐ 225. PAUL SPLITTORFF
☐ 238. FRAN HEALY
☐ 262. ED KIRKPATRICK
☐ 278. COOKIE ROJAS
☐ 308. BRUCE DAL CANTON
☐ 343. TEAM CARD
☐ 365. STEVE BUSBY
☐ 390. LOU PINIELLA
☐ 407. JIM WOHLFORD
☐ 431. GENE GARBER
☐ 454. KURT BEVACQUA
☐ 493. JOE HOERNER
☐ 514. PAUL SCHAAL
☐ 537. STEVE MINGORI
☐ 563. HAL MCRAE
☐ 583. MARTY PATTIN
☐ 596. MARK LITTELL(R)
☐ 604. FRANK WHITE(R)
☐ 627. CARL TAYLOR
☐ 652. GAIL HOPKINS

LOS ANGELES DODGERS

☐ 42. CLAUDE OSTEEN
☐ 64. DOUG RAU
☐ 86. JOE FERGUSON
☐ 112. DAVE LOPES
☐ 127. TOM PACIOREK
☐ 144. ALSTON(M) & COACHES
☐ 165. WILLIE DAVIS
☐ 189. JIM BREWER
☐ 220. DON SUTTON
☐ 239. BILL RUSSEL
☐ 267. ANDY MESSERSMITH
☐ 289. RICK AUERBACH
☐ 315. RON CEY
☐ 348. PETE RICHERT
☐ 368. MANNY MOTA
☐ 408. CHARLIE HOUGH
☐ 434. KEN MCMULLEN
☐ 451. TOMMY JOHN
☐ 480. WILLIE CRAWFORD
☐ 505. BILL BUCKNER
☐ 551. VON JOSHUA
☐ 575. STEVE GARVEY
☐ 593. STEVE YEAGER
☐ 599. GREG SHANAHAN(R)
☐ 620. AL DOWNING
☐ 643. TEAM CARD
☐ 658. LEE LACY

MILWAUKEE BREWERS

☐ 12. DAVE MAY
☐ 27. GEORGE SCOTT
☐ 51. BOBBY HEISE
☐ 75. JIM COLBORN
☐ 99. CRANDALL(M) & COACHES
☐ 124. BOB COLUCCIO
☐ 142. PEDRO GARCIA
☐ 163. KEN BERRY
☐ 171. EDUARDO RODRIGUEZ
☐ 194. DARRELL PORTER
☐ 218. JOHNNY BRIGGS
☐ 261. JERRY BELL
☐ 288. GORMAN THOMAS
☐ 314. TEAM CARD
☐ 349. JOHN VUKOVICH
☐ 371. JIM SLATON
☐ 391. BILLY CHAMPION
☐ 413. DON MONEY

☐ 497. BOBBY MITCHELL
☐ 525. CLYDE WRIGHT
☐ 554. TIM JOHNSON
☐ 574. BILL PARSONS
☐ 603. CHARLIE MOORE(R)
☐ 605. KEVIN KOBEL(R)
☐ 606. WILBUR HOWARD(R)
☐ 631. STEVE BARBER

MINNESOTA TWINS

☐ 26. BILL CAMPBELL
☐ 50. ROD CAREW
☐ 74. TEAM CARD
☐ 98. BERT BLYLEVEN
☐ 122. JIM HOLT
☐ 143. DICK WOODSON
☐ 168. DANNY THOMPSON
☐ 190. TONY OLIVA
☐ 232. STEVE BRYE
☐ 249. GEORGE MITTERWALD
☐ 271. BILL HANDS
☐ 296. RAY CORBIN
☐ 321. STEVE BRAUN
☐ 366. LARRY HISLE
☐ 388. PHIL ROOF
☐ 400. HARMON KILLEBREW
☐ 421. DAN FIFE
☐ 447. QUILICI(M) & COACHES
☐ 469. JOE DECKER
☐ 481. JERRY TERRELL
☐ 503. ERIC SODERHOLM
☐ 527. BOBBY DARWIN
☐ 547. GLENN BORGMANN
☐ 573. MIKE ADAMS
☐ 592. ED BANE
☐ 602. DAN VOSSLER(R)
☐ 605. VIC ALBURY(R)
☐ 613. DAN MONZON
☐ 636. DAVE GOLTZ
☐ 659. JOE LIS

MONTREAL EXPOS

☐ 25. KEN SINGLETON
☐ 49. STEVE RENKO
☐ 73. MIKE MARSHALL
☐ 97. BOB BAILEY
☐ 121. LARRY LINTZ
☐ 146. RON FAIRLY
☐ 169. STEVE ROGERS
☐ 193. TOM WALKER
☐ 217. TIM FOLI
☐ 253. JOHN BOCCABELLA
☐ 275. RON HUNT
☐ 297. HAL BREEDEN
☐ 322. ERNIE MCANALLY
☐ 352. BILL STONEMAN
☐ 377. RON WOODS
☐ 412. CHUCK TAYLOR
☐ 437. JIM LYTTLE
☐ 453. BALOR MOORE
☐ 468. PEPE FRIAS
☐ 485. FELIPE ALOU
☐ 508. TEAM CARD
☐ 531. MAUCH(M) & COACHES
☐ 549. MIKE JORGENSEN
☐ 568. MIKE TORREZ
☐ 589. BOOTS DAY
☐ 600. JIM COX(R)
☐ 603. BARRY FOOTE(R)
☐ 653. BOB STINSON

NEW YORK METS

☐ 8. GEORGE THEODORE
☐ 56. TEAM CARD
☐ 80. TOM SEAVER
☐ 106. HARRY PARKER
☐ 132. FELIX MILLAN
☐ 153. JON MATLACK
☐ 179. BERRA(M) & COACHES
☐ 216. RAY SADECKI
☐ 234. JOHN MILNER
☐ 245. CLEON JONES
☐ 265. TUG MCGRAW
☐ 291. DON HAHN
☐ 311. JERRY GROTE
☐ 356. JERRY KOOSMAN
☐ 380. BUD HARRELSON

☐ 397. GEORGE STONE
☐ 424. JIM BEAUCHAMP
☐ 448. RON HODGES
☐ 487. TED MARTINEZ
☐ 510. WAYNE GARRETT
☐ 536. DUFFY DYER
☐ 561. ED KRANEPOOL
☐ 602. CRAIG SWAN(R)
☐ 608. BOB APODACA(R)
☐ 624. BOB L. MILLER
☐ 629. RUSTY STAUB
☐ 645. KEN BOSWELL

NEW YORK YANKEES

☐ 19. GERRY MOSES
☐ 44. MEL STOTTLEMYRE
☐ 66. SPARKY LYLE
☐ 90. BOBBY MURCER
☐ 117. RON BLOMBERG
☐ 135. ROY WHITE
☐ 159. JIM HART
☐ 182. LINDY MCDANIEL
☐ 229. FRITZ PETERSON
☐ 251. GRAIG NETTLES
☐ 274. FRED BEENE
☐ 299. GENE MICHAEL
☐ 324. STEVE KLINE
☐ 340. THURMAN MUNSON
☐ 363. TEAM CARD
☐ 398. DUKE SIMS
☐ 423. FRED STANLEY
☐ 445. GEORGE MEDICH
☐ 463. PAT DOBSON
☐ 517. MIKE HEGAN
☐ 529. HORACE CLARKE
☐ 550. SAM MCDOWELL
☐ 569. RICK DEMPSEY
☐ 588. HAL LANIER
☐ 601. RICH BLADT(R)
☐ 606. OTTO VELEZ(R)
☐ 623. CELERINO SANCHEZ
☐ 644. WAYNE GRANGER

OAKLAND A'S

☐ 7. JIM HUNTER
☐ 57. DAROLD KNOWLES
☐ 79. GENE TENACE
☐ 103. SAL BANDO
☐ 130. REGGIE JACKSON
☐ 141. PAT BOURQUE
☐ 155. BERT CAMPANERIS
☐ 180. KEN HOLTZMAN
☐ 212. ROLLIE FINGERS
☐ 228. TED KUBIAK
☐ 246. TEAM CARD
☐ 264. JOE RUDI
☐ 290. VIDA BLUE
☐ 312. DERON JOHNSON
☐ 345. BILL NORTH
☐ 369. PAUL LINDBLAD
☐ 392. DICK GREEN
☐ 420. RAY FOSSE
☐ 444. VIC DAVALILLO
☐ 461. JOHN ODOM
☐ 516. HORACIO PINA
☐ 545. BILLY CONIGLIARO
☐ 597. MANNY TRILLO(R)
☐ 602. GLENN ABBOTT(R)
☐ 633. DAVE HAMILTON
☐ 654. JESUS ALOU

PHIADELPHIA PHILLIES

☐ 23. CRAIG ROBINSON
☐ 47. DICK RUTHVEN
☐ 69. DEL UNSER
☐ 95. STEVE CARLTON
☐ 119. OZARK(M) & COACHES
☐ 131. BOB BOONE
☐ 149. MAC SCARCE
☐ 174. BILL ROBINSON
☐ 198. DAVE CASH
☐ 214. BILLY GRABARKEWITZ
☐ 255. LARRY BOWA
☐ 283. MIKE SCHMIDT
☐ 313. BARRY LERSCH
☐ 342. JIM LONBORG
☐ 360. GREG LUZINSKI

☐ 383. TEAM CARD
☐ 419. WAYNE TWITCHELL
☐ 443. TOM HUTTON
☐ 492. MIKE ROGODZINSKI
☐ 515. WILLIE MONTANEZ
☐ 538. CESAR TOVAR
☐ 564. MIKE RYAN
☐ 587. LARRY CHRISTENSON
☐ 599. RON DIORIO(R)
☐ 608. MIKE WALLACE(R)
☐ 619. MIKE ANDERSON
☐ 632. GEORGE CULVER
☐ 642. TERRY HARMON

PITTSBURGH PIRATES

☐ 28. MANNY SANGUILLEN
☐ 52. AL OLIVER
☐ 82. DAVE GIUSTI
☐ 100. WILLIE STARGELL
☐ 116. JERRY REUSS
☐ 123. NELSON BRILES
☐ 145. DOCK ELLIS
☐ 172. GENE CLINES
☐ 222. RAMON HERNANDEZ
☐ 237. KEN BRETT
☐ 252. DAVE PARKER
☐ 269. BOB D. JOHNSON
☐ 317. RICHIE ZISK
☐ 358. DAL MAXVILL
☐ 382. BOB MOOSE
☐ 402. JIM ROOKER
☐ 426. RENNIE STENNETT
☐ 450. RICH HEBNER
☐ 489. MURTAUGH(M) & COACHES
☐ 513. JIM CAMPANIS
☐ 540. BOB ROBERTSON
☐ 566. JACKIE HERNANDEZ
☐ 595. STEVE BLASS
☐ 598. DAVE AUGUSTINE(R)
☐ 607. FRANK TAVERAS(R)
☐ 612. LUKE WALKER
☐ 626. TEAM CARD
☐ 649. FERNANDO GONZALEZ

ST. LOUIS CARDINALS

☐ 15. JOE TORRE
☐ 36. TEAM CARD
☐ 60. LOU BROCK
☐ 108. AL HRABOSKY
☐ 151. DIEGO SEGUI
☐ 175. REGGIE CLEVELAND
☐ 209. TED SIZEMORE
☐ 236. SCHOENDIENST(M) & CHS.
☐ 260. TED SIMMONS
☐ 285. REGGIE SMITH
☐ 307. LUIS MELENDEZ
☐ 350. BOB GIBSON
☐ 372. KEN REITZ
☐ 393. ORLANDO PENA
☐ 417. RICH FOLKERS
☐ 442. ALAN FOSTER
☐ 464. JOSE CRUZ
☐ 496. TOM MURPHY
☐ 520. TIM MCCARVER
☐ 548. SONNY SIEBERT
☐ 576. SCIPIO SPINKS
☐ 601. BAKE MCBRIDE(R)
☐ 604. TERRY HUGHES(R)
☐ 607. TOM HEINTZELMAN(R)
☐ 630. TOMMIE AGEE
☐ 655. MIKE TYSON

SAN DIEGO PADRES

☐ 32. JOHN GRUBB*
☐ 53. FRED KENDALL*
☐ 77. RICH TROEDSON*
☐ 102. BILL GREIF*
☐ 125. NATE COLBERT*
☐ 148. DAVE HILTON*
☐ 173. RANDY JONES*
☐ 197. VICENTE ROMO*
☐ 226. TEAM CARD*
☐ 241. GLENN BECKERT*
☐ 250. WILLIE MCCOVEY*
☐ 309. DAVE W. ROBERTS*
☐ 364. CLARENCE GASTON*
☐ 387. RICH MORALES*

* Cards appear with both San Diego Padres and Washington National League Identifications.

1974 Topps

☐ 406. STEVE ARLIN
☐ 430. MATTY ALOU
☐ 456. DAVE WINFIELD
☐ 498. PAT CORRALES
☐ 518. DERREL THOMAS
☐ 535. BOB TOLAN
☐ 546. MIKE CORKINS
☐ 572. ENZO HERNANDEZ
☐ 599. DAVE FREISLEBEN(R)*
☐ 628. IVAN MURRELL
☐ 651. LERON LEE

SAN FRANCISCO GIANTS

☐ 18. GARY THOMASSON
☐ 30. BOBBY BONDS
☐ 54. ELIAS SOSA
☐ 78. FOX(M) & COACHES
☐ 104. RON BRYANT
☐ 129. CHRIS SPEIER
☐ 156. RANDY MOFFITT
☐ 178. GARRY MADDOX
☐ 213. DAVE RADER
☐ 233. JIM BARR
☐ 281. TEAM CARD
☐ 305. TITO FUENTES
☐ 330. JUAN MARICHAL
☐ 344. MIKE CALDWELL
☐ 361. DON CARRITHERS
☐ 386. GARY MATTHEWS
☐ 404. JIM HOWARTH
☐ 432. CHRIS ARNOLD
☐ 455. TOM BRADLEY
☐ 494. ED GOODSON
☐ 533. MIKE PHILLIPS
☐ 553. JIM WILLOUGHBY
☐ 577. MIKE SADEK
☐ 598. STEVE ONTIVEROS(R)
☐ 599. FRANK RICELLI(R)
☐ 608. JOHN D'ACQUISTO(R)
☐ 610. DAVE KINGMAN

TEXAS RANGERS

☐ 11. JIM BIBBY
☐ 39. KEN SUAREZ
☐ 63. BILL SUDAKIS
☐ 87. FERGIE JENKINS
☐ 89. JACKIE BROWN
☐ 107. ALEX JOHNSON
☐ 133. DAVID CLYDE
☐ 184. TEAM CARD
☐ 196. JIM FREGOSI
☐ 223. JEFF BURROUGHS
☐ 242. BILL GOGOLEWSKI
☐ 268. TOM GRIEVE
☐ 294. STEVE FOUCAULT
☐ 318. JIM MERRITT
☐ 355. DAVE NELSON
☐ 379. MARTIN(M) & COACHES
☐ 401. ELLIOTT MADDOX
☐ 425. PETE BROBERG
☐ 446. LEN RANDLE
☐ 466. DICK BILLINGS
☐ 511. TOBY HARRAH
☐ 539. LLOYD ALLEN
☐ 558. BILL FAHEY
☐ 580. JIM SPENCER

☐ 597. PETE MACKANIN(R)
☐ 602. RICK HENNINGER(R)
☐ 618. JIM MASON
☐ 639. JOE LOVITTO
☐ 657. JIM SHELLENBACK

1974 TOPPS TRADED (44) 2 1/2" X 3 1/2"

ATLANTA BRAVES

☐ 23T. CRAIG ROBINSON
☐ 313T. BARRY LERSCH

BALTIMORE ORIOLES

☐ 59T. ROSS GRIMSLEY

BOSTON RED SOX

☐ 151T. DIEGO SEGUI
☐ 175T. REGGIE CLEVELAND
☐ 330T. JUAN MARICHAL

CALIFORNIA ANGELS

NO CARDS ISSUED

CHICAGO CUBS

☐ 249T. GEORGE MITTERWALD
☐ 486T. STEVE STONE
☐ 516T. HORACIO PINA

CHICAGO WHITE SOX

☐ 270T. RON SANTO

CINCINNATI REDS

☐ 585T. MERV RETTENMUND

CLEVELAND INDIANS

☐ 269T. BOB JOHNSON
☐ 579T. CECIL UPSHAW

DETROIT TIGERS

☐ 428T. GARY SUTHERLAND
☐ 458T. JIM RAY
☐ 612T. LUKE WALKER

HOUSTON ASTROS

☐ 42T. CLAUDE OSTEEN
☐ 186T. FRED SCHERMAN

KANSAS CITY ROYALS

☐ 123T. NELSON BRILES
☐ 182T. LINDY MCDANIEL
☐ 649T. FERNANDO GONZALEZ

LOS ANGELES DODGERS

☐ 43T. JIM WYNN
☐ 73T. MIKE MARSHALL
☐ 630T. TOMMIE AGEE

MILWAUKEE BREWERS

☐ 485T. FELIPE ALOU
☐ 496T. TOM MURPHY

MINNESOTA TWINS

☐ 319T. RANDY HUNDLEY

MONTREAL EXPOS

☐ 165T. WILLIE DAVIS

NEW YORK METS

NO CARDS ISSUED

NEW YORK YANKEES

☐ 63T. BILL SUDAKIS
☐ 390T. LOU PINIELLA
☐ 618T. JIM MASON

OAKLAND A'S

☐ 62T. BOB LOCKER

PHILADELPHIA PHILLIES

☐ 139T. AURELIO MONTEAGUDO
☐ 534T. EDDIE WATT
☐ 544T. RON SCHUELER

PITTSBURGH PIRATES

☐ 262T. ED KIRKPATRICK
☐ 454T. KURT BEVACQUA

ST. LOUIS CARDINALS

☐ 51T. BOBBY HEISE
☐ 348T. PETE RICHERT
☐ 373T. JOHN CURTIS

172

SAN DIEGO PADRES

NO CARDS ISSUED

SAN FRANCISCO GIANTS

NO CARDS ISSUED

TEXAS RANGERS

☐ 538T. CESAR TOVAR
☐ 616T. LARRY GURA
☐ 648T. TERRY CROWLEY

1975 TOPPS (660)
2 1/2" X 3 1/2"

1975 TOPPS
MINIS (660)
2 1/4" X 3 1/8"

ROBIN YOUNT

ATLANTA BRAVES

☐   9. FRANK TEPEDINO
☐ 33. DUSTY BAKER
☐ 57. DAVE A. JOHNSON
☐ 81. RON REED
☐ 105. BUZZ CAPRA
☐ 130. PHIL NIEKRO
☐ 154. MIKE LUM
☐ 177. VIC CORRELL
☐ 237. CARL MORTON
☐ 262. ROWLAND OFFICE
☐ 287. RORIC HARRISON
☐ 319. JOHNNY OATES
☐ 367. CRAIG ROBINSON
☐ 393. GARY GENTRY
☐ 394. LARVELL BLANKS
☐ 418. LEO FOSTER
☐ 427. CLARENCE GASTON
☐ 431. ROD GILBREATH
☐ 442. MAXIMINO LEON
☐ 475. DARRELL EVANS
☐ 499. MARTY PEREZ
☐ 525. TOM HOUSE
☐ 550. RALPH GARR
☐ 589. TEAM & KING(M)
☐ 595. JOE NIEKRO
☐ 603. LEW KRAUSSE
☐ 618. JAMIE EASTERLY(R)
☐ 633. PAUL CASANOVA
☐ 650. DAVE MAY

BALTIMORE ORIOLES

☐ 26. DAVE MCNALLY
☐ 50. BROOKS ROBINSON
☐ 74. MARK BELANGER
☐ 97. EARL WILLIAMS
☐ 117. TEAM & WEAVER(M)
☐ 142. BOB REYNOLDS
☐ 167. RICH COGGINS
☐ 225. BOB GRICH

☐ 247. ENOS CABELL
☐ 275. PAUL BLAIR
☐ 303. GRANT JACKSON
☐ 335. JIM PALMER
☐ 358. AL BUMBRY
☐ 382. DON BAYLOR
☐ 410. MIKE CUELLER
☐ 458. ROSS GRIMSLEY
☐ 491. DOYLE ALEXANDER
☐ 516. DON HOOD
☐ 539. JESSE JERRERSON
☐ 564. TOMMY DAVIS
☐ 583. ANDY ETCHEBARREN
☐ 594. JIM FULLER
☐ 609. ELLIE HENDRICKS
☐ 614. DYAR MILLER(R)
☐ 617. DOUG DECINCES(R)
☐ 625. BOOG POWELL
☐ 641. JIM NORTHRUP
☐ 657. BOB OLIVER

BOSTON RED SOX

☐   8. ROGELIO MORET
☐   32. REGGIE CLEVELAND
☐   56. RICK WISE
☐   80. CARLTON FISK
☐ 103. RICK MILLER
☐ 128. BILL LEE
☐ 152. MARIO GUERRERO
☐ 172. TEAM & JOHNSON(M)
☐ 232. DIEGO SEGUI
☐ 255. DWIGHT EVANS
☐ 280. CARL YASTRZEMSKI
☐ 302. RICK BURLESON
☐ 333. DICK DRAGO
☐ 356. RICO PETROCELLI
☐ 379. BERNIE CARBO
☐ 430. LUIS TIANT
☐ 454. DOUG GRIFFIN
☐ 489. CECIL COOPER
☐ 513. DICK POLE
☐ 537. TOMMY HARPER
☐ 559. BOB MONTGOMERY
☐ 586. TIM MCCARVER
☐ 601. JUAN BENIQUEZ
☐ 612. TERRY HUGHES
☐ 616. JIM RICE(R)
☐ 622. FRED LYNN(R)
☐ 645. DANNY CATER

CALIFORNIA ANGELS

☐   16. FRANK TANANA
☐   40. BILL SINGER
☐   64. DAVE CHALK
☐   88. TOM EGAN
☐ 114. DICK LANGE
☐ 139. HORACIO PINA
☐ 164. MICKEY RIVERS
☐ 187. DENNY DOYLE
☐ 215. BOBBY VALENTINE
☐ 236. TEAM & WILLIAMS(M)
☐ 261. ANDY HASSLER
☐ 285. ELLIE RODRIGUEZ
☐ 317. JOE LAHOUD
☐ 342. LEROY STANTON
☐ 366. KEN SANDERS
☐ 392. BRUCE BOCHTE
☐ 417. SKIP LOCKWOOD
☐ 441. BOBBY HEISE
☐ 476. ED FIGUEROA
☐ 500. NOLAN RYAN
☐ 524. JOHN DOHERTY
☐ 533. RUDY MEOLI
☐ 548. CHARLIE SANDS
☐ 573. ORLANDO PENA
☐ 597. WINSTON LLENAS
☐ 632. MORRIS NETTLES
☐ 635. CHUCK DOBSON

CHICAGO CUBS

☐   15. JOSE CARDENAL
☐   39. ANDY THRONTON
☐   63. STEVE SWISHER
☐   85. BILL BONHAM
☐ 104. BILL MADLOCK
☐ 129. RICK MONDAY

☐ 153. RICK REUSCHEL
☐ 176. BURT HOOTON
☐ 233. BILLY GRABARKEWITZ
☐ 258. DAVE LAROCHE
☐ 282. JERRY MORALES
☐ 315. DON KESSINGER
☐ 338. RICK STELMASZEK
☐ 352. DAROLD KNOWLES
☐ 363. CARMEN FANZONE
☐ 388. STEVE STONE
☐ 411. GEORGE MITTERWALD
☐ 434. BOB LOCKER
☐ 436. KEN FRAILING
☐ 469. TOM DETTORE
☐ 494. PETE LACOCK
☐ 519. JIM TODD
☐ 566. RAY BURRIS
☐ 587. CHRIS WARD
☐ 604. OSCAR ZAMORA
☐ 617. MANNY TRILLO(R)
☐ 638. TEAM & MARSHALL(M)
☐ 658. VIC HARRIS

CHICAGO WHITE SOX

☐ 11. BILL MELTON
☐ 35. RON SANTO
☐ 59. KEN HENDERSON
☐ 82. H. PAT KELLY
☐ 110. WILBUR WOOD
☐ 137. TERRY FORSTER
☐ 161. STAN BAHNSEN
☐ 184. JORGE ORTA
☐ 219. ED HERRMANN
☐ 243. JIM KAAT
☐ 276. TEAM & TANNER(M)
☐ 299. BUCKY DENT
☐ 327. JERRY HAIRSTON
☐ 348. TONY MUSER
☐ 373. BILL SHARP
☐ 400. DICK ALLEN
☐ 422. BRIAN DOWNING
☐ 446. BART JOHNSON
☐ 480. CARLOS MAY
☐ 504. BUDDY BRADFORD
☐ 528. EDDIE LEON
☐ 554. RICH GOSSAGE
☐ 572. ROGER NELSON
☐ 579. SKIP PITLOCK
☐ 614. JACK KUCEK(R)
☐ 619. NYLS NYMAN(R)
☐ 624. JIM OTTEN(R)
☐ 634. CY ACOSTA
☐ 653. LEE RICHARD

CINCINNATI REDS

☐ 17. DAVE CONCEPCION
☐ 41. CESAR GERONIMO
☐ 65. DON GULLETT
☐ 87. GEORGE FOSTER
☐ 108. TOM HALL
☐ 133. DAN DRIESSEN
☐ 157. PEDRO BORBON
☐ 180. JOE MORGAN
☐ 235. JACK BILLINGHAM
☐ 260. JOHNNY BENCH
☐ 284. KEN GRIFFEY
☐ 320. PETE ROSE
☐ 345. CLAY CARROLL
☐ 369. MERV RETTENMUND
☐ 396. FRED NORMAN
☐ 423. CLAY KIRBY
☐ 447. TERRY CROWLEY
☐ 481. WILL MCENANEY
☐ 507. TOM CARROLL
☐ 531. TEAM & ANDERSON(M)
☐ 560. TONY PEREZ
☐ 562. GARY NOLAN
☐ 581. DARREL CHANEY
☐ 602. JOHN VUKOVICH
☐ 615. PAT DARCY(R)
☐ 621. RAWLY EASTWICK(R)
☐ 622. ED ARMBRISTER(R)
☐ 656. BILL PLUMMER

CLEVELAND INDIANS

☐ 14. MILT WILCOX
☐ 38. BUDDY BELL
☐ 62. FRITZ PETERSON

- ☐ 86. JOE LIS
- ☐ 109. GEORGE HENDRICK
- ☐ 135. CHARLIE SPIKES
- ☐ 159. STEVE ARLIN
- ☐ 181. FRED BEENE
- ☐ 213. OSCAR GAMBLE
- ☐ 238. DAVE DUNCAN
- ☐ 263. JIM PERRY
- ☐ 288. BRUCE ELLINGSEN
- ☐ 331. TEAM & ROBINSON(M)
- ☐ 354. DICK BOSMAN
- ☐ 377. TOM HILGENDORF
- ☐ 403. TOM BUSKEY
- ☐ 424. JOHN LOWENSTEIN
- ☐ 448. FRANK DUFFY
- ☐ 482. TOM MCCRAW
- ☐ 506. LERON LEE
- ☐ 530. GAYLORD PERRY
- ☐ 552. JACK BROHAMER
- ☐ 580. FRANK ROBINSON
- ☐ 605. JOHN ELLIS
- ☐ 619. TOMMY SMITH(R)
- ☐ 621. JIM KERN(R)
- ☐ 639. STEVE KLINE
- ☐ 655. RICO CARTY

DETROIT TIGERS

- ☐ 18. TEAM & HOUK(M)
- ☐ 42. JOE COLEMAN
- ☐ 66. WILLIE HORTON
- ☐ 89. JIM RAY
- ☐ 116. LERRIN LAGROW
- ☐ 141. MICKEY STANLEY
- ☐ 166. WOODIE FRYMAN
- ☐ 221. AURELIO RODRIGUEZ
- ☐ 245. MICKEY LOLICH
- ☐ 271. JERRY MOSES
- ☐ 293. DICK SHARON
- ☐ 323. FRED HOLDSWORTH
- ☐ 344. BEN OGLIVIE
- ☐ 371. GATES BROWN
- ☐ 397. BILL FREEHAN
- ☐ 415. JOHN HILLER
- ☐ 439. ED BRINKMAN
- ☐ 474. LUKE WALDER
- ☐ 497. JIM NETTLES
- ☐ 522. GARY SUTHERLAND
- ☐ 546. JOHN KNOX
- ☐ 571. DAVE LEMANCZYK
- ☐ 593. GENE LAMONT
- ☐ 599. NATE COLBERT
- ☐ 614. VERN RUHLE(R)
- ☐ 617. REGGIE SANDERS(R)
- ☐ 620. DANNY MEYER(R)
- ☐ 620. LEON ROBERTS(R)
- ☐ 623. TOM VERYZER(R)
- ☐ 628. RON LEFLORE

HOUSTON ASTROS

- ☐ 25. LEE MAY
- ☐ 49. LARRY DIERKER
- ☐ 73. J.R. RICHARD
- ☐ 96. MIKE COSGROVE
- ☐ 119. TOMMY HELMS
- ☐ 143. CLIFF JOHNSON
- ☐ 165. DOUG RADER
- ☐ 188. TOM GRIFFIN
- ☐ 218. JERRY JOHNSON
- ☐ 227. BOB WATSON
- ☐ 252. FRED SCHERMAN
- ☐ 279. MILT MAY
- ☐ 301. DAVE A. ROBERTS
- ☐ 334. GREG GROSS
- ☐ 357. KEN FORSCH
- ☐ 383. JIM YORK
- ☐ 455. DON WILSON
- ☐ 479. KEN BOSWELL
- ☐ 487. TEAM & GOMEZ(M)
- ☐ 512. LARRY MILBOURNE
- ☐ 514. JOSE CRUZ
- ☐ 541. ROGER METZGER
- ☐ 563. WILBUR HOWARD
- ☐ 590. CESAR CEDENO
- ☐ 614. PAUL SIEBERT(R)
- ☐ 624. DOUG KONIECZNY(R)

GEORGE BRETT

KANSAS CITY ROYALS

- ☐ 24. AL FITZMORRIS
- ☐ 48. FREDDIE PATEK
- ☐ 72. TEAM & MCKEON(M)
- ☐ 95. JOHN MAYBERRY
- ☐ 120. STEVE BUSBY
- ☐ 144. JIM WOHLFORD
- ☐ 169. COOKIE ROJAS
- ☐ 228. GEORGE BRETT
- ☐ 251. FRAN HEALY
- ☐ 268. HAL MCRAE
- ☐ 295. VADA PINSON
- ☐ 314. BUCK MARTINEZ
- ☐ 340. PAUL SPLITTORFF
- ☐ 364. DOUG BIRD
- ☐ 389. TONY SOLAITA
- ☐ 413. MARTY PATTIN
- ☐ 437. AL COWENS
- ☐ 472. BRUCE DAL CANTON
- ☐ 495. NELSON BRILES
- ☐ 520. AMOS OTIS
- ☐ 544. STEVE MINGORI
- ☐ 569. FRANK WHITE
- ☐ 615. DENNIS LEONARD(R)
- ☐ 622. TOM POQUETTE(R)
- ☐ 629. JOE HOERNER
- ☐ 652. LINDY MCDANIEL

LOS ANGELES DODGERS

- ☐ 23. BILL RUSSELL
- ☐ 47. TOMMY JOHN
- ☐ 71. CHARLIE HOUGH
- ☐ 93. DAVE LOPES
- ☐ 115. JOE FERGUSON
- ☐ 140. STEVE GARVEY
- ☐ 163. JIM BREWER
- ☐ 186. WILLIE CRAWFORD
- ☐ 220. DON SUTTON
- ☐ 244. BILL BUCKNER
- ☐ 269. DOUG RAU
- ☐ 294. GEOFF ZAHN
- ☐ 330. MIKE MARSHALL
- ☐ 361. TEAM & ALSTON(M)
- ☐ 376. STEVE YEAGER
- ☐ 390. RON CEY
- ☐ 414. MANNY MOTA
- ☐ 440. ANDY MESSERSMITH
- ☐ 473. KEN MCMULLEN
- ☐ 498. AL DOWNING
- ☐ 523. TOM PACIOREK
- ☐ 547. VON JOSHUA
- ☐ 570. JIM WYNN
- ☐ 588. RICK AUERBACH
- ☐ 618. RICK RHODEN(R)
- ☐ 624. EDDIE SOLOMON(R)
- ☐ 631. LEE LACY

MILWAUKEE BREWERS

- ☐ 28. TOM MURPHY
- ☐ 52. DARRELL PORTER
- ☐ 76. ED SPRAGUE
- ☐ 99. MIKE HEGAN
- ☐ 123. JOHNNY BRIGGS
- ☐ 147. PEDRO GARCIA
- ☐ 175. DON MONEY

- ☐ 223. ROBIN YOUNT
- ☐ 256. BILLY CHAMPION
- ☐ 281. JIM SLATON
- ☐ 305. JIM COLBORN
- ☐ 337. KEVIN KOBEL
- ☐ 360. GEORGE SCOTT
- ☐ 384. TEAM & CRANDALL(M)
- ☐ 408. CLYDE WRIGHT
- ☐ 432. KEN BERRY
- ☐ 456. BOB COLUCCIO
- ☐ 468. BOBBY MITCHELL
- ☐ 488. BILL TRAVERS
- ☐ 508. BOB HANSEN
- ☐ 532. GORMAN THOMAS
- ☐ 556. TIM JOHNSON
- ☐ 582. EDUARDO RODRIGUEZ
- ☐ 623. BOB SHELDON(R)
- ☐ 636. CHARLIE MOORE
- ☐ 660. HANK AARON

MINNESOTA TWINS

- ☐ 30. BERT BLYLEVEN
- ☐ 54. ERIC SODERHOLM
- ☐ 78. RAY CORBIN
- ☐ 102. JOE DECKER
- ☐ 127. GLENN BORGMANN
- ☐ 151. STEVE BRYE
- ☐ 226. BILL CAMPBELL
- ☐ 249. DANNY THOMPSON
- ☐ 273. STEVE BRAUN
- ☐ 297. CRAIG KUSICK
- ☐ 325. TONY OLIVA
- ☐ 346. BOBBY DARWIN
- ☐ 368. VIC ALBURY
- ☐ 419. DAVE GOLTZ
- ☐ 443. TEAM & QUILICI(M)
- ☐ 478. TOM BURGMEIER
- ☐ 526. LARRY HISLE
- ☐ 549. BILL BUTLER
- ☐ 576. PHIL ROOF
- ☐ 600. ROD CAREW
- ☐ 618. TOM JOHNSON(R)
- ☐ 621. JUAN VEINTIDOS(R)
- ☐ 640. HARMON KILLEBREW
- ☐ 654. JERRY TERRELL

WILLIE DAVIS

MONTREAL EXPOS

- ☐ 10. WILLIE DAVIS
- ☐ 34. STEVE RENKO
- ☐ 58. CHUCK TAYLOR
- ☐ 101. TEAM & MAUCH(M)
- ☐ 125. KEN SINGLETON
- ☐ 149. TIM FOLI
- ☐ 173. STEVE ROGERS
- ☐ 229. BARRY FOOTE
- ☐ 254. MIKE TORREZ
- ☐ 270. RON FAIRLY
- ☐ 286. MIKE JORGENSON
- ☐ 318. ERNIE MCANALLY
- ☐ 341. HAL BREEDEN
- ☐ 365. BOB BAILEY
- ☐ 391. DON DEMOLA
- ☐ 405. JOHN MONTAGUE
- ☐ 416. LARRY LINTZ
- ☐ 438. DON CARRITHERS
- ☐ 471. BOB STINSON
- ☐ 496. PEPE FRIAS
- ☐ 521. DENNIS BLAIR

1975 Topps

□ 543. LARRY BIITTNER
□ 568. DALE MURRAY
□ 592. BALOR MOORE
□ 616. PEPE MANGUAL(R)
□ 620. GARY CARTER(R)
□ 627. TOM WALKER

NEW YORK METS

□ 19. JERRY KOOSMAN
□ 43. CLEON JONES
□ 67. TUG MCGRAW
□ 90. RUSTY STAUB
□ 111. WAYNE GARETT
□ 134. RON HODGES
□ 158. JERRY GROTE
□ 182. DON HAHN
□ 214. HARRY PARKER
□ 239. GEORGE STONE
□ 264. JOHN MILNER
□ 290. JON MATLACK
□ 324. ED KRANEPOOL
□ 370. TOM SEAVER
□ 395. BUD HARRELSON
□ 406. BOB GALLAGHER
□ 421. TEAM & BERRA(M)
□ 445. FELIX MILLAN
□ 565. JOE TORRE
□ 575. GENE CLINES
□ 615. HANK WEBB(R)
□ 619. BENNY AYALA(R)
□ 637. TED MARTINEZ
□ 659. BOB APODACA

NEW YORK YANKEES

□ 20. THURMAN MUNSON
□ 44. PAT DOBSON
□ 55. BOBBY BONDS
□ 68. RON BLOMBERG
□ 92. CECIL UPSHAW
□ 113. ELLIOTT MADDOX
□ 136. JIM MASON
□ 160. GRAIG NETTLES
□ 183. MEL STOTTLEMYRE
□ 217. LOU PINIELLA
□ 241. DICK TIDROW
□ 266. SANDY ALOMAR
□ 291. BILL SUDAKIS
□ 321. RUDY MAY
□ 375. ROY WHITE
□ 401. MIKE WALLACE
□ 426. GEORGE MEDICH
□ 451. RICK DEMPSEY
□ 485. SPARKY LYLE
□ 503. FRED STANLEY
□ 534. ALEX JOHNSON
□ 557. LARRY GURA
□ 585. CHRIS CHAMBLISS
□ 608. GENE MICHAEL
□ 611. TEAM & VIRDON(M)
□ 618. SCOTT MCGREGOR(R)
□ 622. TERRY WHITFIELD(R)
□ 648. DAVE PAGAN

OAKLAND A'S

□ 21. ROLLIE FINGERS
□ 45. JOE RUDI
□ 69. JOHNNY ODOM
□ 91. DICK GREEN
□ 121. BILL NORTH
□ 145. KEN HOLTZMAN
□ 170. BERT CAMPANERIS
□ 230. JIM HUNTER
□ 253. JESUS ALOU
□ 278. PAUL LINDBLAD
□ 300. REGGIE JACKSON
□ 329. TED KUBIAK
□ 380. SAL BANDO
□ 407. HERB WASHINGTON
□ 428. DAVE HAMILTON
□ 452. ANGEL MANGUAL
□ 486. RAY FOSSE
□ 502. PAT BOURQUE
□ 510. VIDA BLUE
□ 535. GENE TENACE
□ 545. BILLY WILLIAMS
□ 561. TEAM & DARK(M)
□ 591. GLENN ABBOTT

□ 607. JIM HOLT
□ 613. BILL PARSONS
□ 623. PHIL GARNER(R)
□ 626. LARRY HANEY
□ 647. CLAUDELL WASHINGTON

PHILADELPHIA PHILLIES

□ 22. DAVE CASH
□ 46. TEAM & OZARK(M)
□ 70. MIKE SCHMIDT
□ 94. JIM LONBORG
□ 118. MIKE ANDERSON
□ 138. DEL UNSER
□ 162. WILLIE MONTANEZ
□ 185. STEVE CARLTON
□ 242. JAY JOHNSTONE
□ 267. DICK RUTHVEN
□ 292. RON SCHUELER
□ 326. WAYNE TWITCHELL
□ 351. BOB BOONE
□ 374. EDDIE WATT
□ 399. TERRY HARMON
□ 420. LARRY BOWA
□ 444. GENE GARBER
□ 477. TOM HUTTON
□ 501. BILL ROBINSON
□ 527. MAC SCARCE
□ 551. LARRY CHRISTENSON
□ 574. TONY TAYLOR
□ 596. OLLIE BROWN
□ 615. TOM UNDERWOOD(R)
□ 630. GREG LUZINSKI

PITTSBURGH PIRATES

□ 29. DAVE PARKER
□ 53. DAVE GIUSTI
□ 77. RICHIE ZISK
□ 100. WILLIE STARGELL
□ 124. JERRY REUSS
□ 148. JIM ROOKER
□ 171. ED KIRKPATRICK
□ 224. RAMON HERNANDEZ
□ 250. KEN BRETT
□ 277. FRANK TAVERAS
□ 304. TEAM & MURTAUGH(M)
□ 336. RENNIE STENNETT
□ 359. PAUL POPOVICH
□ 385. DOCK ELLIS
□ 409. BOB ROBERTSON
□ 433. LARRY DEMEREY
□ 457. MARIO MENDOZA
□ 492. RICH HEBNER
□ 515. MANNY SANGUILLEN
□ 536. BOB MOOSE
□ 538. DUFFY DYER
□ 555. AL OLIVER
□ 598. BRUCE KISON
□ 616. DAVE AUGUSTINE(R)
□ 651. JOHN MORLAN

ST. LOUIS CARDINALS

□ 27. KEN REITZ
□ 51. BOB FORSCH
□ 75. TED SIMMONS
□ 98. RICH FOLKERS
□ 122. AL HRABOSKY
□ 150. BOB GIBSON
□ 174. BAKE MCBRIDE
□ 231. MIKE TYSON
□ 246. TEAM & SCHOENDIENST(M)
□ 272. LYNN MCGLOTHEN
□ 289. KEN RUDOLPH
□ 296. ALAN FOSTER
□ 328. SONNY SIEBERT
□ 349. RAY SADECKI
□ 353. LUIS MELENDEZ
□ 381. JOHN CURTIS
□ 398. ELIAS SOSA
□ 404. TED SIZEMORE
□ 429. JIM DWYER
□ 453. CLAUDE OSTEEN
□ 490. REGGIE SMITH
□ 540. LOU BROCK
□ 584. MIKE GARMAN
□ 610. RON HUNT
□ 621. JOHN DENNY(R)
□ 623. KEITH HERNANDEZ(R)
□ 649. JACK HEIDEMANN

SAN DIEGO PADRES

□ 13. GENE LOCKLEAR
□ 37. DAVE FREISLEBEN
□ 61. DAVE WINFIELD
□ 84. ENZO HERNANDEZ
□ 112. LARRY HARDY
□ 146. TEAM & MCNAMARA(M)
□ 168. BILL GREIF
□ 222. DAN SPILLNER
□ 248. RANDY JONES
□ 274. VICENTE ROMO
□ 298. JOHNNY GRUBB
□ 332. FRED KENDALL
□ 343. DANNY FRIESELLA
□ 355. CHRIS CANNIZZARO
□ 378. DERREL THOMAS
□ 402. BOB TOLAN
□ 450. WILLIE MCCOVEY
□ 484. GLENN BECKERT
□ 509. DAVE HILTON
□ 558. DAVE W. ROBERTS
□ 578. DAVE TOMLIN
□ 616. JOHN SCOTT(R)
□ 619. JERRY TURNER(R)
□ 643. BRENT STROM

SAN FRANCISCO GIANTS

□ 31. DAVE RADER
□ 79. GARY MATTHEWS
□ 107. JIM BARR
□ 132. RANDY MOFFITT
□ 156. DAVE KINGMAN
□ 179. TOM BRADLEY
□ 216. TEAM & WESTRUM(M)
□ 240. GARRY MADDOX
□ 265. RON BRYANT
□ 322. ED GOODSON
□ 347. MIKE CALDWELL
□ 350. BOBBY MURCER
□ 372. JOHN D'ACQUISTO
□ 425. TITO FUENTES
□ 449. CHARLIE WILLIAMS
□ 467. ED HALICKI
□ 483. STEVE ONTIVEROS
□ 505. CHRIS SPEIER
□ 529. GARY THOMASSON
□ 553. JOHN BOCCABELLA
□ 577. JOHN MORRIS
□ 606. BRUCE MILLER
□ 620. MARC HILL(R)
□ 624. GARY LAVELLE(R)
□ 642. MIKE PHILLIPS

TEXAS RANGERS

□ 12. DAVID CLYDE
□ 36. JOE LOVITTO
□ 60. FERGIE JENKINS
□ 83. JIM MERRITT
□ 106. MIKE HARGROVE
□ 131. TOBY HARRAH
□ 155. JIM BIBBY
□ 178. CESAR TOVAR
□ 234. TOM GRIEVE
□ 259. LEN RANDLE
□ 283. STEVE FOUCAULT
□ 316. JACKIE BROWN
□ 339. JIM FREGOSI
□ 362. STEVE HARGAN
□ 387. JIM SPENCER
□ 412. BILL HANDS
□ 435. DAVE NELSON
□ 470. JEFF BURROUGHS
□ 493. DON STANHOUSE
□ 511. TEAM & MARTIN(M)
□ 518. LEO CARDENAS
□ 542. PETE BROBERG
□ 567. JIM SUNDBERG
□ 617. MIKE CUBBAGE(R)
□ 644. BILL FAHEY

1976 TOPPS (660)
2 1/2" X 3 1/2"

DON BAYLOR
ORIOLES

ATLANTA BRAVES

- [ ] 28. DUSTY BAKER
- [ ] 53. MIKE BEARD
- [ ] 81. DARRELL EVANS
- [ ] 103. BIFF POCOROBA
- [ ] 127. LARVELL BLANKS
- [ ] 153. BUZZ CAPRA
- [ ] 177. MARTY PEREZ
- [ ] 208. MIKE LUM
- [ ] 231. TOM HOUSE
- [ ] 256. ROWLAND OFFICE
- [ ] 281. DAVE MAY
- [ ] 306. ROD GILBREATH
- [ ] 328. CARL MORTON
- [ ] 364. ELIAS SOSA
- [ ] 395. JIM WYNN
- [ ] 410. RALPH GARR
- [ ] 435. PHIL NIEKRO
- [ ] 458. EARL WILLIAMS
- [ ] 486. BRUCE DAL CANTON
- [ ] 511. JAMIE EASTERLY
- [ ] 536. MIKE THOMPSON
- [ ] 558. CLARENCE GASTON
- [ ] 576. MAXIMINO LEON
- [ ] 589. PABLO TORREALBA(R)
- [ ] 592. JERRY ROYSTER(R)
- [ ] 597. FRANK LACORTE(R)
- [ ] 608. VIC CORRELL
- [ ] 631. TEAM & BRISTOL(M)
- [ ] 641. TOM PACIOREK
- [ ] 651. JOHN ODOM

BALTIMORE ORIOLES

- [ ] 25. MIKE TORREZ
- [ ] 49. DAVE DUNCAN
- [ ] 73. TEAM & WEAVER(M)
- [ ] 95. BROOKS ROBINSON
- [ ] 125. DON BAYLOR
- [ ] 149. TOMMY DAVIS
- [ ] 175. KEN SINGLETON
- [ ] 210. LEE MAY
- [ ] 233. GRANT JACKSON
- [ ] 252. TIM NORDBROOK
- [ ] 257. ROSS GRIMSLEY
- [ ] 285. MIKE CUELLAR
- [ ] 307. AL BUMBRY
- [ ] 335. BOB GRICH
- [ ] 371. ELLIE HENDRICKS
- [ ] 393. PAUL MITCHELL
- [ ] 414. WAYNE GARLAND
- [ ] 438. DOUG DECINCES
- [ ] 450. JIM PALMER
- [ ] 473. PAUL BLAIR
- [ ] 505. MARK BELANGER
- [ ] 537. TONY MUSER
- [ ] 555. DYAR MILLER
- [ ] 589. MIKE FLANAGAN(R)
- [ ] 594. ROYLE STILLMAN(R)
- [ ] 638. DOYLE ALEXANDER

BOSTON RED SOX

- [ ] 29. RICK BURLESON
- [ ] 50. FRED LYNN
- [ ] 78. CECIL COOPER
- [ ] 102. JIM WILLOUGHBY
- [ ] 118. TEAM & JOHNSON(M)
- [ ] 130. LUIS TIANT
- [ ] 142. DICK DRAGO
- [ ] 170. RICK WISE
- [ ] 230. CARL YASTRZEMSKI
- [ ] 278. BERNIE CARBO
- [ ] 302. RICK MILLER
- [ ] 326. DICK POLE
- [ ] 340. JIM RICE
- [ ] 365. CARLTON FISK
- [ ] 381. DENNY DOYLE
- [ ] 396. BILL LEE
- [ ] 419. REGGIE CLEVELAND
- [ ] 445. RICO PETROCELLI
- [ ] 471. JIM BURTON
- [ ] 523. BOB MONTGOMERY
- [ ] 529. DERON JOHNSON
- [ ] 575. DWIGHT EVANS
- [ ] 594. ANDY MERCHANT(R)
- [ ] 597. DON AASE(R)
- [ ] 632. ROGELIO MORET
- [ ] 654. DOUG GRIFFIN

CALIFORNIA ANGELS

- [ ] 27. ED FIGUEROA
- [ ] 52. DAVE CHALK
- [ ] 85. MICKEY RIVERS
- [ ] 108. DON KIRKWOOD
- [ ] 129. ANDY ETCHEBARREN
- [ ] 152. LEROY STANTON
- [ ] 176. DICK LANGE
- [ ] 207. ANDY HASSLER
- [ ] 229. JERRY REMY
- [ ] 254. RUDY MEOLI(F)
- [ ] 276. MICKEY SCOTT
- [ ] 304. TEAM & WILLIAMS(M)
- [ ] 330. NOLAN RYAN
- [ ] 363. DAVE COLLINS
- [ ] 387. MIKE MILEY
- [ ] 411. BILL SINGER
- [ ] 434. MORRIS NETTLES
- [ ] 459. JIM BREWER
- [ ] 490. FRANK TANANA
- [ ] 512. ELLIE RODRIGUEZ
- [ ] 539. JOHN BALEZ
- [ ] 562. ADRIAN GARRETT
- [ ] 589. JOE PACTWA(R)
- [ ] 595. SID MONGE(R)
- [ ] 612. JOE LAHOUD
- [ ] 623. BOB ALLIETTA
- [ ] 637. BRUCE BOCHTE

CHICAGO CUBS

- [ ] 26. ANDY THORNTON
- [ ] 34. MIKE GARMAN
- [ ] 51. RAY BURRIS
- [ ] 79. JERRY MORALES
- [ ] 101. PETE LACOCK
- [ ] 126. TOM DETTORE
- [ ] 151. BILL BONHAM
- [ ] 173. STEVE SWISHER
- [ ] 206. MANNY TRILLO
- [ ] 227. OSCAR ZAMORA
- [ ] 251. RICK MONDAY
- [ ] 277. TEAM & MARSHALL(M)
- [ ] 299. CHAMP SUMMERS
- [ ] 323. BOB SPERRING
- [ ] 359. RICK REUSCHEL
- [ ] 378. STEVE STONE
- [ ] 403. GEOFF ZAHN
- [ ] 430. JOSE CARDENAL
- [ ] 482. TIM HOSLEY
- [ ] 506. GEORGE MITTERWALD
- [ ] 546. DAVE ROSELLO
- [ ] 593. KEN CROSBY(R)
- [ ] 598. JOE WALLIS(R)
- [ ] 617. DAROLD KNOWLES
- [ ] 640. BILL MADLOCK

CHICAGO WHITE SOX

- [ ] 23. BRIAN DOWNING
- [ ] 47. JESSE JEFFERSON
- [ ] 80. JIM KAAT
- [ ] 110. CARLOS MAY
- [ ] 131. BILL STEIN
- [ ] 154. BUCKY DENT
- [ ] 180. RICH GOSSAGE
- [ ] 212. H. PAT KELLY
- [ ] 237. DAVE HAMILTON
- [ ] 258. NYLS NYMAN
- [ ] 282. DAN OSBORN
- [ ] 309. BILL MELTON
- [ ] 333. BOB COLUCCIO
- [ ] 368. WILBUR WOOD
- [ ] 391. JERRY HAIRSTON
- [ ] 413. PETE VARNEY
- [ ] 437. TERRY FORSTER
- [ ] 464. KEN HENDERSON
- [ ] 488. CLAUDE OSTEEN
- [ ] 513. BART JOHNSON
- [ ] 533. LEE RICHARD
- [ ] 560. JORGE ORTA
- [ ] 590. CHET LEMON(R)
- [ ] 596. LAMAR JOHNSON(R)
- [ ] 597. JACK KUCEK(R)
- [ ] 607. RICH HINTON
- [ ] 656. TEAM & TANNER(M)

CINCINNATI REDS

- [ ] 24. CESAR GERONIMO
- [ ] 48. DAVE CONCEPCION
- [ ] 77. PEDRO BORBON
- [ ] 104. TEAM & ANDERSON(M)
- [ ] 128. KEN GRIFFEY
- [ ] 155. JACK BILLINGHAM
- [ ] 179. GEORGE FOSTER
- [ ] 211. CLAY CARROLL
- [ ] 240. PETE ROSE
- [ ] 259. DARRELL CHANEY
- [ ] 283. MERV RETTENMUND
- [ ] 300. JOHNNY BENCH
- [ ] 325. TONY PEREZ
- [ ] 362. WILL MCENANEY
- [ ] 390. DON GULLETT
- [ ] 420. JOE MORGAN
- [ ] 444. GARY NOLAN
- [ ] 469. RAWLY EASTWICK
- [ ] 491. TERRY CROWLEY
- [ ] 514. DAN DRIESSEN
- [ ] 518. DOUG FLYNN
- [ ] 538. PAT DARCY
- [ ] 561. TOM CARROLL
- [ ] 579. CLAY KIRBY
- [ ] 589. SANTO ALCALA(R)
- [ ] 599. PAT ZACHRY(R)
- [ ] 609. FRED NORMAN
- [ ] 627. BILL PLUMMER
- [ ] 652. ED ARMBRISTER

CLEVELAND INDIANS

- [ ] 21. DAVE LAROCHE
- [ ] 45. BOOG POWELL
- [ ] 74. OSCAR GAMBLE
- [ ] 98. DENNIS ECKERSLEY
- [ ] 132. DON HOOD
- [ ] 156. RICO CARTY
- [ ] 178. TOM BUSKEY
- [ ] 209. ALAN ASHBY
- [ ] 232. FRANK DUFFY
- [ ] 255. FRITZ PETERSON
- [ ] 275. RICK MANNING
- [ ] 301. JACKIE BROWN
- [ ] 324. JIM BIBBY
- [ ] 358. BUDDY BELL
- [ ] 383. JOHN ELLIS
- [ ] 408. CHARLIE SPIKES
- [ ] 433. RICK WAITS
- [ ] 457. ED CROSBY
- [ ] 477. TEAM & ROBINSON(M)
- [ ] 484. ERIC RAICH
- [ ] 508. DUANE KUIPER
- [ ] 547. RORIC HARRISON
- [ ] 570. GEORGE HENDRICK
- [ ] 618. JACK BROHAMER
- [ ] 646. JOHN LOWENSTEIN

1976 Topps

DETROIT TIGERS

- 13. JOHNNY WOCKENFUSS
- 37. JOHN HILLER
- 61. RON LEFLORE
- 89. VERN RUHLE
- 113. GARY SUTHERLAND
- 138. LERRIN LAGROW
- 162. JACK PIERCE
- 186. TOM WALKER
- 218. JOHN KNOX
- 242. DAN MEYER
- 267. AURELIO RODRIGUEZ
- 292. LEON ROBERTS
- 320. WILLIE HORTON
- 361. TEAM & HOUK(M)
- 385. MICKEY LOLICH
- 409. DAVE LEMANCZYK
- 432. TOM VERYZER
- 456. JOE COLEMAN
- 483. MICKEY STANLEY
- 507. RAY BARE
- 540. BILL FREEHAN
- 552. TERRY HUMPHREY
- 591. STEVE GRILLI(R)
- 596. JERRY MANUEL(R)
- 614. FERNANDO ARROYO
- 659. BEN OGLIVIE

HOUSTON ASTROS

- 20. BOB WATSON
- 44. DOUG RADER
- 75. LARRY DIERKER
- 97. WILBUR HOWARD
- 122. MIKE COSGROVE
- 147. TEAM & VIRDON(M)
- 171. GREG GROSS
- 224. JIM YORK
- 249. CLIFF JOHNSON
- 273. JOE NIEKRO
- 297. ROGER METZGER
- 321. JOSE CRUZ
- 357. KEN FORSCH
- 379. KEN BOSWELL
- 404. ENOS CABELL
- 428. JIM CRAWFORD
- 454. TOM GRIFFIN
- 460. CESAR CEDENO
- 489. SKIP JUTZE
- 516. WAYNE GRANGER
- 532. MILT MAY
- 551. JERRY DAVANON
- 568. ROB ANDREWS
- 583. TOMMY HELMS
- 591. JOSE SOSA(R)
- 602. DOUG KONIECZNY
- 625. J.R. RICHARD
- 649. DAVE A. ROBERTS

KANSAS CITY ROYALS

- 19. GEORGE BRETT
- 43. PAUL SPLITTORFF
- 72. HAL MCRAE
- 96. DOUG BIRD
- 121. TONY SOLAITA
- 144. AL FITZMORRIS
- 167. FREDDIE PATEK
- 236. TEAM & HERZOG(M)
- 260. STEVE BUSBY
- 286. JIM WOHLFORD
- 311. COOKIE ROJAS
- 334. DENNIS LEONARD
- 369. FRANK WHITE
- 394. FRAN HEALY
- 415. VADA PINSON
- 440. JOHN MAYBERRY
- 466. BOB STINSON
- 492. MARTY PATTIN
- 510. AMOS OTIS
- 535. DAVE NELSON
- 541. STEVE MINGORI
- 591. GEORGE THROOP(R)
- 593. MARK LITTELL(R)
- 598. JAMIE QUIRK(R)
- 599. BOB MCCLURE(R)
- 616. BUCK MARTINEZ
- 648. AL COWENS

LOS ANGELES DODGERS

- 22. BILL RUSSELL
- 46. TEAM & ALSTON(M)
- 76. WILLIE CRAWFORD
- 99. LEE LACY
- 124. DOUG RAU
- 150. STEVE GARVEY
- 174. CHARLIE HOUGH
- 228. JOHN HALE
- 253. BILL BUCKNER
- 280. BURT HOOTON
- 305. ANDY MESSERSMITH
- 329. JOE FERGUSON
- 370. RON CEY
- 386. ED GOODSON
- 416. TOMMY JOHN
- 439. RICK RHODEN
- 465. MIKE MARSHALL
- 487. LERON LEE
- 515. STEVE YEAGER
- 530. DON SUTTON
- 548. MANNY MOTA
- 566. KEN MCMULLEN
- 584. STAN WALL
- 590. HENRY CRUZ(R)
- 605. AL DOWNING
- 622. RICK AUERBACH
- 660. DAVE LOPES

MILWAUKEE BREWERS

- 15. GEORGE SCOTT
- 39. PETE BROBERG
- 63. BOBBY DARWIN
- 92. EDUARDO RODRIGUEZ
- 116. CHARLIE MOORE
- 139. GORMAN THOMAS
- 163. JIM SLATON
- 187. PEDRO GARCIA
- 219. TOM MURPHY
- 244. BILL SHARP
- 269. RICK AUSTIN
- 293. BILL CASTRO
- 316. ROBIN YOUNT
- 353. SIXTO LEZCANO
- 377. MIKE HEGAN
- 402. DON MONEY
- 427. KURT BEVACQUA
- 452. TOM HAUSMAN
- 479. ROBBY MITCHELL
- 501. BILLY CHAMPION
- 521. JIM COLBORN
- 550. HANK AARON
- 573. BILL TRAVERS
- 588. KEVIN KOBEL
- 593. LARRY ANDERSON(R)
- 606. TEAM & GRAMMAS(M)
- 613. TIM JOHNSON
- 626. BOB SHELDON
- 645. DARRELL PORTER

MINNESOTA TWINS

- 11. JIM HUGHES
- 35. TONY OLIVA
- 59. LARRY HISLE
- 87. TOM BURGMEIER
- 111. DANNY THOMPSON
- 136. DAVE GOLTZ
- 159. JERRY TERRELL
- 183. STEVE BRAUN
- 214. ERIC SODERHOLM
- 235. BERT BLYLEVEN
- 263. LYMAN BOSTOCK
- 288. BILL CAMBELL
- 313. DAN FORD
- 336. VIC ALBURY
- 373. JOHNNY BRIGGS
- 400. ROD CAREW
- 424. PHIL ROOF
- 448. TOM JOHNSON
- 474. RAY CORBIN
- 498. GLENN BORGMANN
- 519. STEVE BRYE
- 556. TEAM & MAUCH(M)
- 592. DAVE MCKAY(R)
- 597. MIKE PAZIK(R)
- 619. BILL BUTLER
- 636. JOE DECKER

MONTREAL EXPOS

- 18. DALE MURRAY
- 42. BARRY FOOTE
- 71. STEVE ROGERS
- 94. JIM DWYER
- 117. MIKE JORGENSEN
- 141. LARRY PARRISH
- 164. PEPE MANGUAL
- 188. FRED SCHERMAN
- 216. TEAM & KUEHL(M)
- 238. LARRY BIITTNER
- 264. STEVE RENKO
- 287. PETE MACKANIN
- 312. DON CARRITHERS
- 338. BOB BAILEY
- 374. DAN WARTHEN
- 397. TIM FOLI
- 418. JOSE MORALES
- 441. GARY CARTER
- 467. WOODIE FRYMAN
- 495. NATE COLBERT
- 544. PEPE FRIAS
- 571. DON DEMOLA
- 590. ELLIS VALENTINE(R)
- 594. JERRY WHITE(R)
- 642. DENNIS BLAIR

NEW YORK METS

- 16. BOB APODACA
- 40. DAVE KINGMAN
- 64. JERRY KOOSMAN
- 93. MIKE PHILLIPS
- 120. RUSTY STAUB
- 143. JERRY GROTE
- 166. SKIP LOCKWOOD
- 190. JON MATLACK
- 222. WAYNE GARRETT
- 245. FELIX MILLAN
- 268. DEL UNSER
- 291. KEN SANDERS
- 314. ED KRANEPOOL
- 337. BUD HARRELSON
- 372. RICK BALDWIN
- 417. GENE CLINES
- 442. HANK WEBB
- 468. JESUS ALOU
- 494. CRAIG SWAN
- 517. JOHN MILNER
- 531. TEAM & FRAZIER(M)
- 549. RANDY TATE
- 567. GEORGE STONE
- 585. JOE TORRE
- 592. ROY STAIGER(R)
- 600. TOM SEAVER
- 621. TOM HALL
- 633. JOHN STEARNS
- 655. MIKE VAIL

NEW YORK YANKEES

- 17. TEAM & MARTIN(M)
- 41. TIPPY MARTINEZ
- 65. CHRIS CHAMBLISS
- 100. JIM HUNTER
- 123. WALT WILLIAMS
- 146. GEORGE MEDICH
- 169. GRAIG NETTLES
- 225. ROY WHITE
- 248. DICK TIDROW
- 272. RICK DEMPSEY
- 296. PAT DOBSON
- 319. LARRY GURA
- 354. RON BLOMBERG
- 380. BOBBY BONDS
- 406. ED HERRMANN
- 429. FRED STANLEY
- 453. LOU PINIELLA
- 481. RUDY MAY
- 503. ELLIOTT MADDOX
- 545. SPARKY LYLE
- 572. RICH COGGINS
- 590. TERRY WHITFIELD(R)
- 599. RON GUIDRY(R)
- 629. SANDY ALOMAR
- 650. THURMAN MUNSON

1976 Topps

MIKE NORRIS
PITCHER A's

OAKLAND A'S

- [ ] 9. PAUL LINDBLAD
- [ ] 33. BILL NORTH
- [ ] 57. PHIL GARNER
- [ ] 90. SAL BANDO
- [ ] 109. LARRY LINTZ
- [ ] 115. KEN HOLTZMAN
- [ ] 140. VIDA BLUE
- [ ] 165. GENE TENACE
- [ ] 189. CLAUDELL WASHINGTON
- [ ] 221. JIM TODD
- [ ] 246. CESAR TOVAR
- [ ] 274. TOMMY HARPER
- [ ] 298. DICK BOSMAN
- [ ] 322. GLENN ABBOTT
- [ ] 356. TED MARTINEZ
- [ ] 382. MATT ALEXANDER
- [ ] 405. ROLLIE FINGERS
- [ ] 421. TEAM CARD
- [ ] 446. LARRY HANEY
- [ ] 475. JOE RUDI
- [ ] 500. REGGIE JACKSON
- [ ] 525. BILLY WILLIAMS
- [ ] 534. STAN BAHNSEN
- [ ] 554. RAY FOSSE
- [ ] 580. BERT CAMPANERIS
- [ ] 591. CRAIG MITCHELL(R)
- [ ] 603. JIM HOLT
- [ ] 653. MIKE NORRIS

PHIALDELPHIA PHILLIES

- [ ] 14. GENE GARBER
- [ ] 38. GARRY MADDOX
- [ ] 62. JOHNNY OATES
- [ ] 91. TOM HUTTON
- [ ] 114. JAY JOHNSTONE
- [ ] 145. LARRY BOWA
- [ ] 168. TOM HILGENDORF
- [ ] 223. OLLIE BROWN
- [ ] 247. TERRY HARMON
- [ ] 271. JIM LONBORG
- [ ] 295. DAVE CASH
- [ ] 318. BOB BOONE
- [ ] 355. STEVE CARLTON
- [ ] 384. TEAM & OZARK(M)
- [ ] 407. TOM UNDERWOOD
- [ ] 431. DICK RUTHVEN
- [ ] 455. DICK ALLEN
- [ ] 480. MIKE SCHMIDT
- [ ] 502. TIM MCCARVER
- [ ] 527. MIKE ANDERSON
- [ ] 543. WAYNE TWITCHELL
- [ ] 565. TUG MCGRAW
- [ ] 586. RON SCHUELER
- [ ] 595. RANDY LERCH(R)
- [ ] 610. GREG LUZINSKI
- [ ] 624. TONY TAYLOR
- [ ] 634. LARRY CHRISTENSON

PITTSBURGH PIRATES

- [ ] 12. RICHIE ZISK
- [ ] 36. FRANK TAVERAS
- [ ] 60. JERRY REUSS
- [ ] 88. DUFFY DYER
- [ ] 112. KENT TEKULVE
- [ ] 137. BILL ROBINSON
- [ ] 161. BRUCE KISON
- [ ] 185. DAVE PARKER
- [ ] 220. MANNY SANGUILLEN
- [ ] 243. JIM ROOKER
- [ ] 270. WILLIE STARGELL
- [ ] 294. ED KIRKPATRICK
- [ ] 317. JOHN CANDELARIA
- [ ] 352. DAVE GIUSTI
- [ ] 376. RICH HEBNER
- [ ] 401. KEN BRETT
- [ ] 425. RENNIE STENNETT
- [ ] 449. BOB ROBERTSON
- [ ] 476. BOB MOOSE
- [ ] 504. TEAM & MURTAUGH(M)
- [ ] 528. DOCK ELLIS
- [ ] 563. LARRY DEMERY
- [ ] 592. WILLIE RANDOLPH(R)
- [ ] 594. ED OTT(R)
- [ ] 596. CRAIG REYNOLDS(R)
- [ ] 620. AL OLIVER
- [ ] 647. RAMON HERNANDEZ

ST. LOUIS CARDINALS

- [ ] 10. LOU BROCK
- [ ] 58. RON REED
- [ ] 86. MIKE TYSON
- [ ] 135. BAKE MCBRIDE
- [ ] 158. KEN REITZ
- [ ] 182. ERIC RASMUSSEN
- [ ] 215. REGGIE SMITH
- [ ] 239. JOHN CURTIS
- [ ] 290. TED SIMMONS
- [ ] 315. AL HRABOSKY
- [ ] 339. JOHN DENNY
- [ ] 375. RON FAIRLY
- [ ] 399. LUIS MELENDEZ
- [ ] 426. BOB FORSCH
- [ ] 451. BUDDY BRADFORD
- [ ] 478. LYNN MCGLOTHEN
- [ ] 499. MARIO GUERRERO
- [ ] 522. TED SIZEMORE
- [ ] 542. KEITH HERNANDEZ
- [ ] 574. DON KESSINGER
- [ ] 581. TEAM & SCHOENDIENST(M)
- [ ] 598. HECTOR CRUZ(R)
- [ ] 601. KEN RUDOLPH

BOBBY VALENTINE
OUTFIELD PADRES

SAN DIEGO PADRES

- [ ] 8. TITO FUENTES
- [ ] 32. DANNY FRISELLA
- [ ] 56. BOB TOLAN
- [ ] 84. BRENT STROM
- [ ] 107. DAVE W. ROBERTS
- [ ] 134. MIKE IVIE
- [ ] 160. DAVE WINFIELD
- [ ] 184. BILL GREIF
- [ ] 217. DAVE FREISLEBEN
- [ ] 241. HECTOR TORRES
- [ ] 254. RUDY MEOLI(B)
- [ ] 265. WILLIE DAVIS
- [ ] 266. ALAN FOSTER
- [ ] 289. ENZO HERNANDEZ
- [ ] 310. RANDY JONES
- [ ] 331. TEAM & MCNAMARA(M)
- [ ] 351. RANDY HUNDLEY
- [ ] 366. BOBBY VALENTINE
- [ ] 398. DAVE TOMLIN
- [ ] 422. JOHNNY GRUBB
- [ ] 447. GENE LOCKLEAR
- [ ] 472. BOB DAVIS
- [ ] 497. JOE MCINTOSH
- [ ] 520. WILLIE MCCOVEY
- [ ] 557. DAN SPILLNER
- [ ] 578. TED KUBIAK
- [ ] 593. BUTCH METZGER(R)
- [ ] 598. JERRY TURNER(R)
- [ ] 611. RICH FOLKERS
- [ ] 639. FRED KENDALL
- [ ] 658. JERRY JOHNSON

SAN FRANCISCO GIANTS

- [ ] 30. JOHN MONTEFUSCO
- [ ] 54. DAVE RADER
- [ ] 82. VON JOSHUA
- [ ] 105. GARY LAVELLE
- [ ] 133. GARY MATTHEWS
- [ ] 157. MIKE CALDWELL
- [ ] 181. WILLIE MONTANEZ
- [ ] 213. DAVE HEAVERLO
- [ ] 234. MIKE SADEK
- [ ] 261. GARY THOMASSON
- [ ] 283. STEVE ONTIVEROS
- [ ] 308. JIM BARR
- [ ] 332. CHARLIE WILLIAMS
- [ ] 367. BRUCE MILLER
- [ ] 389. GLENN ADAMS
- [ ] 423. ED HALICKI
- [ ] 443. TEAM CARD
- [ ] 470. BOBBY MURCER
- [ ] 493. DERREL THOMAS
- [ ] 524. PETE FALCONE
- [ ] 553. RANDY MOFFITT
- [ ] 577. MARC HILL
- [ ] 596. JOHNNIE LEMASTER(R)
- [ ] 599. ROB DRESSLER(R)
- [ ] 628. JOHN D'ACQUISTO
- [ ] 630. CHRIS SPEIER
- [ ] 644. TOM BRADLEY

TEXAS RANGERS

- [ ] 7. JIM UMBARGER
- [ ] 31. LEN RANDLE
- [ ] 55. GAYLORD PERRY
- [ ] 83. JIM SPENCER
- [ ] 106. TOM GRIEVE
- [ ] 148. STAN THOMAS
- [ ] 172. TEAM & LUCCHESI(M)
- [ ] 226. JIM SUNDBERG
- [ ] 250. FERGIE JENKINS
- [ ] 279. ROY HOWELL
- [ ] 303. STEVE FOUCAULT
- [ ] 327. DAVE MOATES
- [ ] 360. JEFF BURROUGHS
- [ ] 388. STAN PERZANOWSKI
- [ ] 412. TOBY HARRAH
- [ ] 436. BILL FAHEY
- [ ] 463. STEVE HARGAN
- [ ] 485. MIKE HARGROVE
- [ ] 496. JUAN BENIQUEZ
- [ ] 509. BILL HANDS
- [ ] 559. CLYDE WRIGHT
- [ ] 569. NELSON BRILES
- [ ] 582. MIKE KEKICH
- [ ] 587. LEO CARDENAS
- [ ] 595. ART DEFILIPPIS(R)
- [ ] 595. STEVE BARR(R)
- [ ] 604. JOE LOVITTO
- [ ] 615. MIKE CUBBAGE
- [ ] 635. JIM FREGOSI
- [ ] 657. ROY SMALLEY

1976 TOPPS TRADED (44)
2 1/2" X 3 1/2"

ATLANTA BRAVES

- ☐ 99T. LEE LACY
- ☐ 259T. DARREL CHANEY
- ☐ 464T. KEN HENDERSON
- ☐ 632T. ROGELIO MORET

BALTIMORE ORIOLES

NO CARDS ISSUED

BOSTON RED SOX

- ☐ 231T. TOM HOUSE
- ☐ 250T. FERGIE JENKINS

CALIFORNIA ANGELS

- ☐ 309T. BILL MELTON
- ☐ 380T. BOBBY BONDS

CHICAGO CUBS

NO CARDS ISSUED

CHICAGO WHITE SOX

- ☐ 83T. JIM SPENCER
- ☐ 211T. CLAY CARROLL
- ☐ 410T. RALPH GARR
- ☐ 434T. MORRIS NETTLES
- ☐ 618T. JACK BROHAMER

CINCINNATI REDS

- ☐ 208T. MIKE LUM
- ☐ 338T. BOB BAILEY

CLEVELAND INDIANS

- ☐ 127T. LARVELL BLANKS
- ☐ 296T. PAT DOBSON
- ☐ 554T. RAY FOSSE

DETROIT TIGERS

- ☐ 120T. RUSTY STAUB
- ☐ 428T. JIM CRAWFORD
- ☐ 532T. MILT MAY
- ☐ 649T. DAVE A. ROBERTS

HOUSTON ASTROS

- ☐ 292T. LEON ROBERTS
- ☐ 497T. JOE MCINTOSH

KANSAS CITY ROYALS

NO CARDS ISSUED

LOS ANGELES DODGERS

- ☐ 28T. DUSTY BAKER

MILWAUKEE BREWERS

NO CARDS ISSUED

MINNESOTA TWINS

NO CARDS ISSUED

MONTREAL TWINS

NO CARDS ISSUED

MONTREAL EXPOS

- ☐ 579T. CLAY KIRBY

NEW YORK METS

- ☐ 358T. MICKEY LOLICH

NEW YORK YANKEES

- ☐ 27T. ED FIGUEROA
- ☐ 74T. OSCAR GAMBLE
- ☐ 85T. MICKEY RIVERS
- ☐ 401T. KEN BRETT
- ☐ 528T. DOCK ELLIS
- ☐ 592T. WILLIE RANDOLPH

OAKLAND A'S

NO CARDS ISSUED

PHILADELPHIA PHILLIES

- ☐ 58T. RON REED
- ☐ 80T. JIM KAAT

PITTSBURGH PIRATES

- ☐ 146T. GEORGE MEDICH
- ☐ 583T. TOMMY HELMS

ST. LOUIS CARDINALS

- ☐ 524T. PETE FALCONE
- ☐ 527T. MIKE ANDERSON

SAN DIEGO PADRES

- ☐ 44T. DOUG RADER

SAN FRANCISCO GIANTS

- ☐ 158T. KEN REITZ

TEXAS RANGERS

- ☐ 383T. JOHN ELLIS
- ☐ 411T. BILL SINGER

1977 TOPPS (660)
2 1/2" X 3 1/2"

ATLANTA BRAVES

- ☐ 24. CARL MORTON
- ☐ 48. TOM PACIOREK
- ☐ 80. ANDY MESSERSMITH
- ☐ 114. BRUCE DAL CANTON
- ☐ 126. ROD GILBREATH
- ☐ 165. JIM WYNN
- ☐ 192. CLARENCE GASTON
- ☐ 194. GARY MATTHEWS
- ☐ 213. MAXIMINO LEON
- ☐ 242. KEN HENDERSON
- ☐ 263. MIKE MARSHALL
- ☐ 292. ROGELIO MORET
- ☐ 312. ROB BELLOIR
- ☐ 339. ADRIAN DEVINE
- ☐ 364. VIC CORRELL
- ☐ 384. DARREL CHANEY
- ☐ 410. WILLIE MONTANEZ
- ☐ 432. BUZZ CAPRA
- ☐ 442. TEAM & BRISTOL(M)
- ☐ 475. RICK CAMP(R)
- ☐ 476. DALE MURPHY(R)
- ☐ 479. BRIAN ASSELSTINE(R)
- ☐ 499. PABLO TORREALBA
- ☐ 524. ROWLAND OFFICE
- ☐ 549. JERRY ROYSTER
- ☐ 575. DICK RUTHVEN
- ☐ 594. BIFF POCOROBA
- ☐ 615. PHIL NIEKRO

BALTIMORE ORIOLES

- ☐ 56. RUDY MAY
- ☐ 77. DYAR MILLER
- ☐ 106. MIKE FLANAGAN
- ☐ 135. MARK BELANGER
- ☐ 162. MIKE CUELLAR
- ☐ 189. RICK DEMPSEY
- ☐ 216. DOUG DECINCES
- ☐ 238. TIPPY MARTINEZ
- ☐ 251. TONY MUSER
- ☐ 285. BROOKS ROBINSON
- ☐ 313. PAUL BLAIR
- ☐ 380. LEE MAY
- ☐ 414. TOMMY HARPER
- ☐ 445. KEN SINGLETON
- ☐ 466. FRED HOLDSWORTH
- ☐ 469. H. PAT KELLY
- ☐ 474. KIKO GARCIA(R)
- ☐ 475. SCOTT MCGREGOR(R)
- ☐ 477. RICH DAUER(R)
- ☐ 491. DENNY MARTINEZ(R)

1977 Topps

- [ ] 546. TEAM & WEAVER(M)
- [ ] 572. ROSS GRIMSLEY
- [ ] 600. JIM PALMER
- [ ] 626. AL BUMBRY
- [ ] 646. ANDRES MORA

BOSTON RED SOX

- [ ] 25. DWIGHT EVANS
- [ ] 60. JIM RICE
- [ ] 89. BUTCH HOBSON
- [ ] 111. RICO PETROCELLI
- [ ] 142. STEVE DILLARD
- [ ] 166. BILL CAMPBELL
- [ ] 191. DOUG GRIFFIN
- [ ] 210. FRED LYNN
- [ ] 235. CECIL COOPER
- [ ] 258. LUIS TIANT
- [ ] 288. BOB MONTGOMERY
- [ ] 309. TEAM & ZIMMER(M)
- [ ] 336. DENNY DOYLE
- [ ] 358. TOM HOUSE
- [ ] 396. TOM MURPHY
- [ ] 430. FERGIE JENKINS
- [ ] 455. RICK WISE
- [ ] 472. DON AASE(R)
- [ ] 480. CARL YASTRZEMSKI
- [ ] 503. BILL LEE
- [ ] 532. JIM WILLOUGHBY
- [ ] 566. RICK MILLER
- [ ] 585. RICK BURLESON
- [ ] 613. REGGIE CLEVELAND
- [ ] 617. BOBBY DARWIN
- [ ] 640. CARLTON FISK

CALIFORNIA ANGELS

- [ ] 16. BOB JONES
- [ ] 34. TEAM & SHERRY(M)
- [ ] 68. BRUCE BOCHTE
- [ ] 91. JOHN VERHOEVEN
- [ ] 107. BILL MELTON
- [ ] 131. ORLANDO RAMIREZ
- [ ] 153. RON JACKSON
- [ ] 155. JOE RUDI
- [ ] 179. PAUL HARTZELL
- [ ] 200. FRANK TANANA
- [ ] 224. RUSTY TORRES
- [ ] 257. MIKE MILEY
- [ ] 282. SID MONGE
- [ ] 315. DAVE CHALK
- [ ] 342. JERRY REMY
- [ ] 369. TERRY HUMPHREY
- [ ] 401. MICKEY SCOTT
- [ ] 426. DICK DRAGO
- [ ] 454. ANDY ETCHEBARREN
- [ ] 462. DON BAYLOR
- [ ] 482. TONY SOLAITA
- [ ] 489. MIKE OVERY(R)
- [ ] 519. DON KIRKWOOD
- [ ] 521. BOB GRICH
- [ ] 544. GARY ROSS
- [ ] 570. BOBBY BONDS
- [ ] 592. DAN BRIGGS
- [ ] 628. MARIO GUERRERO
- [ ] 650. NOLAN RYAN

CHICAGO CUBS

- [ ] 64. LARRY BIITTNER
- [ ] 92. DAVE ROSELLO
- [ ] 124. GEORGE MITTERWALD
- [ ] 144. BRUCE SUTTER
- [ ] 169. DAROLD KNOWLES
- [ ] 190. RAY BURRIS
- [ ] 219. JOE COLEMAN
- [ ] 250. BILL MADLOCK
- [ ] 279. JOE WALLIS
- [ ] 302. MIKE GARMAN
- [ ] 333. PAUL REUSCHEL
- [ ] 360. RICK MONDAY
- [ ] 395. MANNY TRILLO
- [ ] 419. STEVE SWISHER
- [ ] 446. BILL BONHAM
- [ ] 468. RAMON HERNANDEZ
- [ ] 493. MIKE KRUKOW(R)
- [ ] 502. RANDY HUNDLEY
- [ ] 518. TEAM & FRANKS(M)
- [ ] 530. RICK REUSCHEL

- [ ] 561. PETE LACOCK
- [ ] 586. STEVE RENKO
- [ ] 610. JOSE CARDENAL
- [ ] 639. JERRY MORALES
- [ ] 657. MICK KELLEHER

CHICAGO WHITE SOX

- [ ] 17. STEVE STONE
- [ ] 29. BUCKY DENT
- [ ] 58. CHET LEMON
- [ ] 83. KEVIN BELL
- [ ] 109. JORGE ORTA
- [ ] 133. RALPH GARR
- [ ] 157. KEN BRETT
- [ ] 177. BART JOHNSON
- [ ] 198. WILBUR WOOD
- [ ] 222. FRANCISCO BARRIOS
- [ ] 247. CHRIS KNAPP
- [ ] 271. TERRY FORSTER
- [ ] 273. ERIC SODERHOLM
- [ ] 293. JACK BROHAMER
- [ ] 319. RICH GOSSAGE
- [ ] 338. DAVE DUNCAN
- [ ] 344. BRIAN DOWNING
- [ ] 367. DAVE HAMILTON
- [ ] 389. KEN KRAVEC
- [ ] 418. TEAM & LEMON(M)
- [ ] 443. LAMAR JOHNSON
- [ ] 487. GREG TERLECKY(R)
- [ ] 493. JIM OTTEN(R)
- [ ] 497. CLAY CARROLL
- [ ] 529. JIM ESSIAN
- [ ] 559. ALAN BANNISTER
- [ ] 623. JACK KUCEK
- [ ] 648. JIM SPENCER

CINCINNATI REDS

- [ ] 23. DAN DRIESSEN
- [ ] 45. RAWLY EASTWICK
- [ ] 70. JOHNNY BENCH
- [ ] 86. PAT ZACHRY
- [ ] 100. JOE MORGAN
- [ ] 121. GARY NOLAN
- [ ] 139. FRED NORMAN
- [ ] 160. WILL MCENANEY
- [ ] 186. DOUG FLYNN
- [ ] 203. ED ARMBRISTER
- [ ] 221. BOB BAILEY
- [ ] 239. BILL PLUMMER
- [ ] 287. TEAM & ANDERSON(M)
- [ ] 320. KEN GRIFFEY
- [ ] 347. GEORGE FOSTER
- [ ] 450. PETE ROSE
- [ ] 475. MANNY SARMIENTO(R)
- [ ] 487. JOE HENDERSON(R)
- [ ] 512. JACK BILLINGHAM
- [ ] 535. CESAR GERONIMO
- [ ] 548. JOEL YOUNGBLOOD
- [ ] 560. DAVE CONCEPCION
- [ ] 581. PEDRO BORBON
- [ ] 601. MIKE LUM
- [ ] 636. SANTO ALCALA
- [ ] 655. TONY PEREZ

CLEVELAND INDIANS

- [ ] 18. TEAM & ROBINSON(M)
- [ ] 33. WAYNE GARLAND
- [ ] 41. JIM KERN
- [ ] 62. ERIC RAICH
- [ ] 85. DUANE KUIPER
- [ ] 115. RICK MANNING
- [ ] 147. JACKIE BROWN
- [ ] 168. CHARLIE SPIKES
- [ ] 206. BOOG POWELL
- [ ] 236. TOM BUSKEY
- [ ] 267. RAY FOSSE
- [ ] 296. DON HOOD
- [ ] 306. RICK WAITS
- [ ] 330. GEORGE HENDRICK
- [ ] 385. DAVE LAROCHE
- [ ] 393. JOHN LOWENSTEIN
- [ ] 441. LARVELL BLANKS
- [ ] 449. AL FITZMORRIS
- [ ] 476. RICK CERONE(R)
- [ ] 477. ORLANDO GONZALEZ(R)
- [ ] 501. JIM BIBBY
- [ ] 525. DENNIS ECKERSLEY

- [ ] 542. FRANK DUFFY
- [ ] 590. BUDDY BELL
- [ ] 618. PAT DOBSON
- [ ] 654. RON PRUITT

DETROIT TIGERS

- [ ] 22. BILL FREEHAN
- [ ] 43. RAY BARE
- [ ] 69. JIM CRAWFORD
- [ ] 98. MILT MAY
- [ ] 122. BEN OGLIVIE
- [ ] 145. TOM VERYZER
- [ ] 173. CHUCK SCRIVENER
- [ ] 240. RON LEFLORE
- [ ] 265. MARK FIDRYCH
- [ ] 291. JASON THOMPSON
- [ ] 311. VERN RUHLE
- [ ] 363. DAVE A. ROBERTS
- [ ] 420. RUSTY STAUB
- [ ] 453. PEDRO GARCIA
- [ ] 477. PHIL MANKOWSKI(R)
- [ ] 487. ED GLYNN(R)
- [ ] 490. MARK WAGNER(R)
- [ ] 491. BOB SYKES(R)
- [ ] 492. STEVE KEMP(R)
- [ ] 506. STEVE GRILLI
- [ ] 533. MICKEY STANLEY
- [ ] 554. BRUCE KIMM
- [ ] 574. AURELIO RODRIGUEZ
- [ ] 595. JOHN HILLER
- [ ] 621. TEAM & HOUK(M)
- [ ] 637. ALEX JOHNSON
- [ ] 660. WILLIE HORTON

HOUSTON ASTROS

- [ ] 21. KEN FORSCH
- [ ] 42. JOSE CRUZ
- [ ] 67. JOAQUIN ANDUJAR
- [ ] 90. CESAR CEDENO
- [ ] 116. JOE NIEKRO
- [ ] 143. ED HERRMANN
- [ ] 184. BO MCLAUGHLIN
- [ ] 209. ROB ANDREWS
- [ ] 227. JOE SAMBITO
- [ ] 248. WILBUR HOWARD
- [ ] 260. J.R. RICHARD
- [ ] 283. JERRY DAVANON
- [ ] 308. GENE PENTZ
- [ ] 327. TEAM & VIRDON(M)
- [ ] 350. LARRY DIERKER
- [ ] 429. KEN BOSWELL
- [ ] 456. LEON ROBERTS
- [ ] 474. ALEX TAVERAS(R)
- [ ] 478. MARK LEMONGELLO(R)
- [ ] 481. ROGER METZGER
- [ ] 514. CLIFF JOHNSON
- [ ] 540. BOB WATSON
- [ ] 567. ENOS CABELL
- [ ] 589. MIKE COSGROVE
- [ ] 614. GREG GROSS
- [ ] 641. DAN LARSON

KANSAS CITY ROYALS

- [ ] 46. BUCK MARTINEZ
- [ ] 75. DENNIS LEONARD
- [ ] 93. TOM POQUETTE

☐ 117. FRANK WHITE
☐ 141. MARK LITTELL
☐ 171. KEN SANDERS
☐ 193. LARRY GURA
☐ 218. JOHN WATHAN
☐ 244. JOHN MAYBERRY
☐ 262. AL COWENS
☐ 290. AMOS OTIS
☐ 314. STEVE MINGORI
☐ 340. HAL MCRAE
☐ 362. TOMMY DAVIS
☐ 371. TEAM & HERZOG(M)
☐ 422. FREDDIE PATEK
☐ 463. JAMIE QUIRK
☐ 472. BOB MCCLURE(R)
☐ 509. COOKIE ROJAS
☐ 534. PAUL SPLITTORFF
☐ 556. DOUG BIRD
☐ 580. GEORGE BRETT
☐ 602. ANDY HASSLER
☐ 622. JIM WOHLFORD
☐ 658. MARTY PATTIN

LOS ANGELES DODGERS

☐ 27. BILL BUCKNER
☐ 50. RON CEY
☐ 88. STAN WALL
☐ 105. STEVE YEAGER
☐ 128. TOMMY JOHN
☐ 146. DUSTY BAKER
☐ 180. DAVE LOPES
☐ 245. RICK RHODEN
☐ 253. JOHN HALE
☐ 272. LEE LACY
☐ 298. CHARLIE HOUGH
☐ 322. BILL RUSSELL
☐ 345. REGGIE SMITH
☐ 366. TED SIZEMORE
☐ 386. MANNY MOTA
☐ 400. STEVE GARVEY
☐ 421. DOUG RAU
☐ 448. ELLIE RODRIGUEZ
☐ 476. KEVIN PASLEY(R)
☐ 484. BURT HOOTON
☐ 504. TEAM & LASORDA(M)
☐ 558. ELIAS SOSA
☐ 584. ED GOODSON
☐ 620. DON SUTTON

MILWAUKEE BREWERS

☐ 26. RAY SADECKI
☐ 51. TEAM & GRAMMAS(M)
☐ 79. DON MONEY
☐ 99. TOM HAUSMAN
☐ 125. BILL TRAVERS
☐ 159. BERNIE CARBO
☐ 185. SIXTO LEZCANO
☐ 214. DARRELL PORTER
☐ 255. GEORGE SCOTT
☐ 278. DANNY FRISELLA
☐ 307. GARY SUTHERLAND
☐ 331. JIM COLBORN
☐ 361. EDUARDO RODRIGUEZ
☐ 382. CHARLIE MOORE
☐ 406. TIM JOHNSON
☐ 439. GORMAN THOMAS
☐ 488. DAN THOMAS(R)
☐ 494. JIM GANTNER(R)
☐ 498. SAL BANDO
☐ 507. MIKE HEGAN
☐ 528. BILL CASTRO
☐ 553. JACK HEIDEMANN
☐ 577. JERRY AUGUSTINE
☐ 604. JIM SLATON
☐ 635. ROBIN YOUNT
☐ 651. VON JOSHUA

MINNESOTA TWINS

☐ 13. LUIS GOMEZ
☐ 38. CRAIG KUSICK
☐ 66. ROY SMALLEY
☐ 87. GLENN BORGMANN
☐ 120. ROD CAREW
☐ 149. MIKE CUBBAGE
☐ 175. BUTCH WYNEGAR
☐ 202. TOM JOHNSON
☐ 228. TEAM & MAUCH(M)

☐ 249. PETE REDFERN
☐ 304. JIM HUGHES
☐ 321. DAVE GOLTZ
☐ 375. LARRY HISLE
☐ 398. TOM BURGMEIER
☐ 424. STEVE BRYE
☐ 457. STEVE LUEBBER
☐ 478. JIM GIDEON(R)
☐ 486. ED BANE
☐ 513. JERRY TERRELL
☐ 531. LYMAN BOSTOCK
☐ 536. VIC ALBURY
☐ 555. DAN FORD
☐ 578. BOB RANDALL
☐ 643. MIKE PAZIK

MONTREAL EXPOS

☐ 28. WOODIE FRYMAN
☐ 52. ELLIS VALENTINE
☐ 76. TIM FOLI
☐ 102. JOSE MORALES
☐ 112. BILL GREIF
☐ 132. CHIP LANG
☐ 156. PETE MACKANIN
☐ 178. BOMBO RIVERA
☐ 199. PEPE FRIAS
☐ 223. EARL WILLIAMS
☐ 252. DALE MURRAY
☐ 274. DON STANHOUSE
☐ 295. GARY CARTER
☐ 316. STEVE ROGERS
☐ 341. JOE KERRIGAN
☐ 368. MIKE JORGENSEN
☐ 391. DAN WARTHEN
☐ 417. WAYNE GARRETT
☐ 471. DEL UNSER
☐ 473. ANDRE DAWSON(R)
☐ 479. SAM MEJIAS(R)
☐ 526. LARRY PARRISH
☐ 557. JERRY WHITE
☐ 579. DON CARRITHERS
☐ 593. DENNIS BLAIR
☐ 612. BARRY FOOTE
☐ 647. TEAM & WILLIAMS(M)
☐ 649. DAVE CASH

NEW YORK METS

☐ 44. BUD HARRELSON
☐ 65. SKIP LOCKWOOD
☐ 94. CRAIG SWAN
☐ 119. JOHN STEARNS
☐ 150. TOM SEAVER
☐ 172. JOHN MILNER
☐ 201. ED KRANEPOOL
☐ 225. BOB APODACA
☐ 246. MIKE VAIL
☐ 259. TEAM & FRAZIER(M)
☐ 281. ROY STAIGER
☐ 300. JERRY KOOSMAN
☐ 329. RON HODGES
☐ 352. MIKE PHILLIPS
☐ 376. NINO ESPINOSA
☐ 399. BRUCE BOISCLAIR
☐ 425. JOE TORRE
☐ 440. JON MATLACK
☐ 458. LEO FOSTER
☐ 488. LEE MAZZILLI(R)
☐ 500. DAVE KINGMAN
☐ 552. PEPE MANGUAL
☐ 565. MICKEY LOLICH
☐ 587. RICK BALDWIN
☐ 605. FELIX MILLAN
☐ 627. BOB MYRICK

NEW YORK YANKEES

☐ 10. REGGIE JACKSON
☐ 15. DON GULLETT
☐ 20. GRAIG NETTLES
☐ 54. SANDY ALOMAR
☐ 71. DOCK ELLIS
☐ 96. LOU PINIELLA
☐ 123. FRED STANLEY
☐ 148. FRAN HEALY
☐ 170. THURMAN MUNSON
☐ 195. ED FIGUEROA
☐ 220. CHRIS CHAMBLISS

☐ 280. JIM HUNTER
☐ 305. MICKEY RIVERS
☐ 332. ELLIOTT MADDOX
☐ 359. WILLIE RANDOLPH
☐ 387. TEAM & MARTIN(M)
☐ 408. CESAR TOVAR
☐ 461. DICK TIDROW
☐ 472. GIL PATTERSON(R)
☐ 485. ROY WHITE
☐ 490. MICKEY KLUTTS(R)
☐ 505. OSCAR GAMBLE
☐ 543. RON BLOMBERG
☐ 568. CARLOS MAY
☐ 598. SPARKY LYLE
☐ 625. KEN HOLTZMAN
☐ 656. RON GUIDRY

OAKLAND A'S

☐ 12. LARRY HANEY
☐ 31. JIM TODD
☐ 53. PAUL MITCHELL
☐ 61. MANNY SANGUILLEN
☐ 74. TEAM & MCKEON(M)
☐ 101. DICK BOSMAN
☐ 127. RON FAIRLY
☐ 181. KEN MCMULLEN
☐ 204. JEFF NEWMAN
☐ 230. VIDA BLUE
☐ 261. PHIL GARNER
☐ 284. MIKE NORRIS
☐ 323. LARRY LINTZ
☐ 349. JIM HOLT
☐ 365. MIKE TORREZ
☐ 383. STAN BAHNSEN
☐ 402. TOMMY HELMS
☐ 405. CLAUDELL WASHINGTON
☐ 473. DENNY WALLING(R)
☐ 475. CHRIS BATTON(R)
☐ 479. WAYNE GROSS(R)
☐ 491. CRAIG MITCHELL(R)
☐ 551. BILL NORTH
☐ 583. PAUL LINDBLAD
☐ 616. TOMMY SANDT
☐ 644. MATT ALEXANDER

PHILADELPHIA PHILLIES

☐ 30. GREG LUZINSKI
☐ 59. LARRY CHRISTENSON
☐ 84. OLLIE BROWN
☐ 110. STEVE CARLTON
☐ 140. MIKE SCHMIDT
☐ 164. TUG MCGRAW
☐ 188. BOB TOLAN
☐ 217. TOM UNDERWOOD
☐ 243. RON REED
☐ 264. TOM HUTTON
☐ 289. GENE GARBER
☐ 310. LARRY BOWA
☐ 337. RON SCHUELER
☐ 357. TIM MCCARVER
☐ 388. TERRY HARMON
☐ 415. JAY JOHNSTONE
☐ 444. WAYNE TWITCHELL
☐ 467. TEAM & OZARK(M)
☐ 489. RANDY LERCH(R)
☐ 520. GARRY MADDOX
☐ 545. BOB BOONE

1977 Topps

- [ ] 569. JIM LONBORG
- [ ] 596. JERRY MARTIN
- [ ] 619. JOHNNY OATES
- [ ] 638. JIM KAAT

PITTSBURGH PIRATES

- [ ] 35. RENNIE STENNETT
- [ ] 82. JIM ROOKER
- [ ] 104. OMAR MORENO
- [ ] 130. AL OLIVER
- [ ] 154. DAVE GIUSTI
- [ ] 167. RICH HEBNER
- [ ] 176. BOB ROBERTSON
- [ ] 197. ED OTT
- [ ] 270. DAVE PARKER
- [ ] 294. DOC MEDICH
- [ ] 318. DUFFY DYER
- [ ] 335. BILL ROBINSON
- [ ] 354. TEAM & TANNER(M)
- [ ] 374. KENT TEKULVE
- [ ] 460. WILLIE STARGELL
- [ ] 474. CRAIG REYNOLDS(R)
- [ ] 483. RICHIE ZISK
- [ ] 492. TONY ARMAS(R)
- [ ] 510. JOHN CANDELARIA
- [ ] 538. FRANK TAVERAS
- [ ] 563. BRUCE KISON
- [ ] 582. ED KIRKPATRICK
- [ ] 607. LARRY DEMERY
- [ ] 645. JERRY REUSS

ST. LOUIS CARDINALS

- [ ] 19. JOHN D'ACQUISTO
- [ ] 47. LYNN MCGLOTHEN
- [ ] 72. MIKE ANDERSON
- [ ] 95. KEITH HERNANDEZ
- [ ] 136. JERRY MUMPHREY
- [ ] 161. GARRY TEMPLETON
- [ ] 183. TEAM & RAPP(M)
- [ ] 205. PETE FALCONE
- [ ] 229. DON KESSINGER
- [ ] 355. LOU BROCK
- [ ] 381. BOB FORSCH
- [ ] 404. ERIC RASMUSSEN
- [ ] 427. DAVE RADER
- [ ] 452. MIKE CALDWELL
- [ ] 470. TED SIMMONS
- [ ] 495. AL HRABOSKY
- [ ] 516. BAKE MCBRIDE
- [ ] 541. JOHN DENNY
- [ ] 573. JOE FERGUSON
- [ ] 599. MIKE TYSON
- [ ] 624. HECTOR CRUZ
- [ ] 652. TOM WALKER

SAN DIEGO PADRES

- [ ] 9. DOUG RADER
- [ ] 39. TOM GRIFFIN
- [ ] 63. TITO FUENTES
- [ ] 78. BOB DAVIS
- [ ] 108. ALAN FOSTER
- [ ] 134. TEAM & MCNAMARA(M)
- [ ] 158. TED KUBIAK
- [ ] 182. DAN SPILLNER
- [ ] 215. BUTCH METZGER
- [ ] 241. DAVE TOMLIN
- [ ] 268. RICK SAWYER
- [ ] 286. JOHNNY GRUBB
- [ ] 303. GENE TENACE
- [ ] 325. MIKE IVIE
- [ ] 348. BRENT STROM
- [ ] 372. RICH FOLKERS
- [ ] 390. DAVE WINFIELD
- [ ] 407. DAVE FREISLEBEN
- [ ] 447. JERRY TURNER
- [ ] 472. DAVE WEHRMEISTER(R)
- [ ] 473. GENE RICHARDS(R)
- [ ] 490. BILLY ALMON(R)
- [ ] 491. MIKE DUPREE(R)
- [ ] 494. MIKE CHAMPION(R)
- [ ] 522. ENZO HERNANDEZ
- [ ] 523. ROLLIE FINGERS
- [ ] 550. RANDY JONES
- [ ] 576. FRED KENDALL
- [ ] 603. WILLIE DAVIS
- [ ] 629. BOBBY VALENTINE
- [ ] 659. MERV TETTENMUND

SAN FRANCISCO GIANTS

- [ ] 11. ROB DRESSLER
- [ ] 40. BOBBY MURCER
- [ ] 57. MARC HILL
- [ ] 73. CHARLIE WILLIAMS
- [ ] 97. DAVE HEAVERLO
- [ ] 129. MIKE SADEK
- [ ] 151. JOHNNIE LEMASTER
- [ ] 211. TEAM & ALTOBELLI(M)
- [ ] 266. DERRELL THOMAS
- [ ] 297. KEN REITZ
- [ ] 324. JOHN CURTIS
- [ ] 343. ED HALICKI
- [ ] 370. JOHN MONTEFUSCO
- [ ] 397. LARRY HERNDON
- [ ] 423. GARY LAVELLE
- [ ] 438. MARTY PEREZ
- [ ] 464. RANDY MOFFITT
- [ ] 476. GARY ALEXANDER(R)
- [ ] 488. JACK CLARK(R)
- [ ] 489. GREG MINTON(R)
- [ ] 496. GARY THOMASSON
- [ ] 515. CHRIS SPEIER
- [ ] 547. WILLIE MCCOVEY
- [ ] 571. DARRELL EVANS
- [ ] 591. CHRIS ARNOLD
- [ ] 609. JIM BARR
- [ ] 642. WILLIE CRAWFORD

SEATTLE MARINERS

- [ ] 14. TOMMY SMITH
- [ ] 49. GRANT JACKSON
- [ ] 118. RICK JONES
- [ ] 138. BOB STINSON
- [ ] 187. DICK POLE
- [ ] 207. GLENN ABBOTT
- [ ] 226. LEROY STANTON
- [ ] 269. JOE LIS
- [ ] 317. KURT BEVACQUA
- [ ] 334. BILL STEIN
- [ ] 353. STAN THOMAS
- [ ] 379. LARRY COX
- [ ] 394. BILL LAXTON
- [ ] 409. PETE BROBERG
- [ ] 431. DAVE COLLINS
- [ ] 478. DAVE C. JOHNSON(R)
- [ ] 488. RUPPERT JONES(R)
- [ ] 490. TOMMY MCMILLAN(R)
- [ ] 492. CARLOS LOPEZ(R)
- [ ] 493. GARY WHEELOCK(R)
- [ ] 494. JUAN BERNHARDT(R)
- [ ] 508. DAVE PAGAN
- [ ] 527. DAN MEYER
- [ ] 597. JOHNSON(M) & COACHS
- [ ] 606. STEVE BRAUN
- [ ] 653. DIEGO SEGUI

TEXAS RANGERS

- [ ] 36. JOHN ELLIS
- [ ] 55. JEFF BURROUGHS
- [ ] 81. JUAN BENIQUEZ
- [ ] 103. MIKE BACSIK
- [ ] 137. JEFF TERPKO
- [ ] 152. GAYLORD PERRY
- [ ] 174. NELSON BRILES
- [ ] 196. LEN RANDLE
- [ ] 237. GENE CLINES
- [ ] 254. DOYLE ALEXANDER
- [ ] 256. JOE HOERNER
- [ ] 275. MIKE HARGROVE
- [ ] 301. TOBY HARRAH
- [ ] 328. TOMMY BOGGS
- [ ] 351. JIM SUNDBERG
- [ ] 373. BERT CAMPANERIS
- [ ] 378. JIM UMBARGER
- [ ] 403. TOM GRIEVE
- [ ] 428. TEAM & LUCCHESI(M)
- [ ] 459. STEVE FOUCAULT
- [ ] 489. LEN BARKER(R)
- [ ] 494. BUMP WILLS(R)
- [ ] 511. BILL FAHEY
- [ ] 539. MIKE WALLACE
- [ ] 588. DAVE MOATES
- [ ] 608. ROY HOWELL
- [ ] 630. BERT BLYLEVEN

TORONTO BLUE JAYS

- [ ] 37. STEVE HARGAN
- [ ] 113. HARTSFIELD(M) & CHS.
- [ ] 163. DAVE HILTON
- [ ] 212. JIM MASON
- [ ] 299. OTTO VELEZ
- [ ] 326. JESSE JEFFERSON
- [ ] 346. BILL SINGER
- [ ] 377. DAVE MCKAY
- [ ] 392. PHIL ROOF
- [ ] 416. CHUCK HARTENSTEIN
- [ ] 465. RICO CARTY
- [ ] 473. JOHN SCOTT(R)
- [ ] 474. BOB BAILOR(R)
- [ ] 477. DOUG AULT(R)
- [ ] 478. LEON HOOTEN(R)
- [ ] 479. ALVIS WOODS(R)
- [ ] 487. LARRY ANDERSON(R)
- [ ] 492. GARY WOODS(R)
- [ ] 493. MIKE WILLIS(R)
- [ ] 517. PETE VUCKOVICH
- [ ] 537. DAVE W. ROBERTS
- [ ] 564. ALAN ASHBY
- [ ] 611. DAVE LEMANCZYK

1978 TOPPS (726)
2 1/2" X 3 1/2"

JORGE ORTA

ATLANTA BRAVES

- [ ] 10. PHIL NIEKRO
- [ ] 38. WILLIE MONTANEZ
- [ ] 75. DICK RUTHVEN
- [ ] 93. BOBBY COX(M)
- [ ] 130. JEFF BURROUGHS
- [ ] 156. ANDY MESSERSMITH
- [ ] 187. JERRY ROYSTER
- [ ] 217. ROD GILBREATH
- [ ] 242. BARRY BONNELL
- [ ] 264. JAMIE EASTERLY
- [ ] 296. BIFF POCOROBA
- [ ] 322. TOM PACIOREK
- [ ] 349. RICK CAMP
- [ ] 372. BRIAN ASSELSTINE
- [ ] 402. DAVE CAMPBELL
- [ ] 443. DARREL CHANEY
- [ ] 475. GARY MATTHEWS
- [ ] 502. PAT ROCKETT
- [ ] 527. VIC CORRELL
- [ ] 551. TEAM CARD
- [ ] 578. BUZZ CAPRA
- [ ] 598. EDDIE SOLOMON
- [ ] 617. JOE NOLAN
- [ ] 632. ROWLAND OFFICE
- [ ] 681. ROB BELLOIR
- [ ] 703. MICKEY MAHLER(R)
- [ ] 708. DALE MURPHY(R)
- [ ] 716. CLARENCE GASTON

BALTIMORE ORIOLES

- [ ] 9. DOUG DECINCES
- [ ] 36. EDDIE MURRAY
- [ ] 65. KEN SINGLETON
- [ ] 96. TEAM CARD
- [ ] 119. DENNY MARTINEZ
- [ ] 160. JIM PALMER

- ☐ 188. AL BUMBRY
- ☐ 211. EARL WEAVER(M)
- ☐ 237. RICH DAUER
- ☐ 262. RUDY MAY
- ☐ 287. KIKO GARCIA
- ☐ 315. MARK BELANGER
- ☐ 341. MIKE FLANAGAN
- ☐ 367. RICK DEMPSEY
- ☐ 393. TIPPY MARTINEZ
- ☐ 418. TONY MUSER
- ☐ 466. DENNIS BLAIR
- ☐ 491. SCOTT MCGREGOR
- ☐ 517. ANDRES MORA
- ☐ 543. LARRY HARLOW
- ☐ 593. DAVE SKAGGS
- ☐ 616. H. PAT KELLY
- ☐ 640. LEE MAY
- ☐ 666. BILLY SMITH
- ☐ 691. ROSS GRIMSLEY
- ☐ 717. NELSON BRILES

BOSTON RED SOX

- ☐ 12. DON AASE
- ☐ 40. CARL YASTRZEMSKI
- ☐ 63. DON ZIMMER(M)
- ☐ 83. BOB MONTGOMERY
- ☐ 105. REGGIE CLEVELAND
- ☐ 125. GEORGE SCOTT
- ☐ 155. BUTCH HOBSON
- ☐ 186. BOB STANLEY
- ☐ 216. MIKE PAXTON
- ☐ 245. RICK BURLESON
- ☐ 270. CARLTON FISK
- ☐ 295. BILL LEE
- ☐ 320. FRED LYNN
- ☐ 345. LUIS TIANT
- ☐ 373. JIM WILLOUGHBY
- ☐ 416. JACK BROHAMER
- ☐ 424. TEAM CARD
- ☐ 457. BOB BAILEY
- ☐ 482. RICK MILLER
- ☐ 524. BERNIE CARBO
- ☐ 545. BILL CAMPBELL
- ☐ 567. DICK DRAGO
- ☐ 572. RICK WISE
- ☐ 597. STEVE DILLARD
- ☐ 618. TOMMY HELMS
- ☐ 642. DENNY DOYLE
- ☐ 645. MIKE TORREZ
- ☐ 670. JIM RICE
- ☐ 695. DWIGHT EVANS
- ☐ 706. TED COX(R)
- ☐ 708. BO DIAZ(R)
- ☐ 720. FERGIE JENKINS

CALIFORNIA ANGELS

- ☐ 18. BOB GRICH
- ☐ 48. DON BAYLOR
- ☐ 71. TERRY HUMPHREY
- ☐ 115. GARY NOLAN
- ☐ 150. BOBBY BONDS
- ☐ 178. DAVE CHALK
- ☐ 214. TEAM CARD
- ☐ 239. DYAR MILLER
- ☐ 268. GIL FLORES
- ☐ 291. GARY ROSS
- ☐ 313. ANDY ETCHEBARREN
- ☐ 339. MARIO GUERRERO
- ☐ 368. BALOR MOORE
- ☐ 400. NOLAN RYAN
- ☐ 429. MIKE BARLOW
- ☐ 454. DAVE LAROCHE
- ☐ 478. JERRY REMY
- ☐ 503. IKE HAMPTON
- ☐ 529. PAUL HARTZELL
- ☐ 557. TONY SOLAITA
- ☐ 579. RANCE MULLINIKS
- ☐ 600. FRANK TANANA
- ☐ 619. THAD BOSLEY
- ☐ 635. JOE RUDI
- ☐ 655. LYMAN BOSTOCK
- ☐ 656. DAVE GARCIA(M)
- ☐ 682. KEN BRETT
- ☐ 718. RON JACKSON

CHICAGO CUBS

- ☐ 17. MIKE KRUKOW
- ☐ 50. RICK REUSCHEL
- ☐ 76. STEVE ONTIVEROS
- ☐ 99. WILLIE HERNANDEZ
- ☐ 123. MANNY TRILLO
- ☐ 152. IVAN DEJESUS
- ☐ 175. JERRY MORALES
- ☐ 234. HERMAN FRANKS(M)
- ☐ 252. STEVE SWISHER
- ☐ 302. TEAM CARD
- ☐ 325. BRUCE SUTTER
- ☐ 346. LARRY BIITTNER
- ☐ 371. RAY BURRIS
- ☐ 397. GREG GROSS
- ☐ 423. DAVE ROSELLO
- ☐ 473. BILL BUCKNER
- ☐ 489. RUDY MEOLI
- ☐ 501. DAVE A. ROBERTS
- ☐ 523. DONNIE MOORE
- ☐ 541. LARRY COX
- ☐ 564. MICK KELLEHER
- ☐ 570. DAVE KINGMAN
- ☐ 585. WOODIE FRYMAN
- ☐ 590. BOBBY MURCER
- ☐ 614. JOE WALLIS
- ☐ 639. GENE CLINES
- ☐ 663. PAUL REUSCHEL
- ☐ 688. GEORGE MITTERWALD
- ☐ 711. DENNIS LAMP(R)
- ☐ 722. PETE BROBERG

CHICAGO WHITE SOX

- ☐ 14. LERRIN LAGROW
- ☐ 42. JORGE ORTA
- ☐ 66. TEAM CARD
- ☐ 98. JIM ESSIAN
- ☐ 127. CHET LEMON
- ☐ 153. STEVE STONE
- ☐ 182. JIM SPENCER
- ☐ 213. ALAN BANNISTER
- ☐ 231. WAYNE NORDHAGEN
- ☐ 251. DON KIRKWOOD
- ☐ 272. ROYLE STILLMAN
- ☐ 288. DAVE HAMILTON
- ☐ 316. HENRY CRUZ
- ☐ 329. JOHN VERHOEVEN
- ☐ 361. CHRIS KNAPP
- ☐ 395. JIM HUGHES
- ☐ 409. RON SCHUELER
- ☐ 421. JUNIOR MOORE
- ☐ 439. KEN KRAVEC
- ☐ 463. KEVIN BELL
- ☐ 493. STEVE RENKO
- ☐ 506. RON BLOMBERG
- ☐ 519. BRIAN DOWNING
- ☐ 552. FRANCISCO BARRIOS
- ☐ 574. BOB LEMON(M)
- ☐ 602. ERIC SODERHOLM
- ☐ 615. CLAY CARROLL
- ☐ 628. RALPH GARR
- ☐ 672. DON KESSINGER
- ☐ 693. LAMAR JOHNSON
- ☐ 702. BILL NAHORODNY(R)
- ☐ 726. WILBUR WOOD

CINCINNATI REDS

- ☐ 20. PETE ROSE
- ☐ 47. JACK BILLINGHAM
- ☐ 80. KEN GRIFFEY
- ☐ 106. BILL PLUMMER
- ☐ 126. PAUL MOSKAU
- ☐ 149. DALE MURRAY
- ☐ 180. DAVE CONCEPCION
- ☐ 220. PEDRO BORBON
- ☐ 246. DAN DRIESSEN
- ☐ 273. FRED NORMAN
- ☐ 276. BILL BONHAM
- ☐ 300. JOE MORGAN
- ☐ 326. MIKE LUM
- ☐ 354. CESAR GERONIMO
- ☐ 377. MANNY SARMIENTO
- ☐ 401. SPARKY ANDERSON(M)
- ☐ 427. MARIO SOTO
- ☐ 450. TOM SEAVER
- ☐ 477. DOUG CAPILLA
- ☐ 500. GEORGE FOSTER

- ☐ 526. TEAM CARD
- ☐ 556. ED ARMBRISTER
- ☐ 622. CHAMP SUMMERS
- ☐ 646. RICK AUERBACH
- ☐ 674. RAY KNIGHT
- ☐ 700. JOHNNY BENCH
- ☐ 701. TOM HUME(R)
- ☐ 702. DON WERNER(R)
- ☐ 706. DAVE REVERING(R)

CLEVELAND INDIANS

- ☐ 11. RICK MANNING
- ☐ 37. RICK WAITS
- ☐ 61. LARVELL BLANKS
- ☐ 87. JOHN LOWENSTEIN
- ☐ 101. SID MONGE
- ☐ 122. DENNIS ECKERSLEY
- ☐ 148. ANDRE THORNTON
- ☐ 174. WAYNE GARLAND
- ☐ 198. RON PRUITT
- ☐ 227. AL FITZMORRIS
- ☐ 253. JIM KERN
- ☐ 280. BUDDY BELL
- ☐ 305. RICO CARTY
- ☐ 332. DUANE KUIPER
- ☐ 351. JEFF TORBORG(M)
- ☐ 398. DON HOOD
- ☐ 426. FRED KENDALL
- ☐ 459. CHARLIE SPIKES
- ☐ 484. JIM NORRIS
- ☐ 511. FRANK DUFFY
- ☐ 537. BRUCE BOCHTE
- ☐ 575. PAT DOBSON
- ☐ 608. JOHNNY GRUBB
- ☐ 636. JIM BIBBY
- ☐ 662. PAUL DADE
- ☐ 689. TEAM CARD
- ☐ 703. LARRY ANDERSEN(R)
- ☐ 704. DAVE OLIVER(R)
- ☐ 706. WAYNE CAGE(R)
- ☐ 711. CARDELL CAMPER(R)

DETROIT TIGERS

- ☐ 21. STEVE KEMP
- ☐ 45. MARK FIDRYCH
- ☐ 68. STEVE FOUCAULT
- ☐ 94. CHUCK SCRIVENER
- ☐ 124. DAVE ROZEMA
- ☐ 151. MILT WILCOX
- ☐ 176. MILT MAY
- ☐ 232. MICKEY STANLEY
- ☐ 258. JOHN HILLER
- ☐ 286. BEN OGLIVIE
- ☐ 342. AURELIO RODRIGUEZ
- ☐ 370. RUSTY STAUB
- ☐ 385. TITO FUENTES
- ☐ 404. TEAM CARD
- ☐ 456. VERN RUHLE
- ☐ 480. RON LEFLORE
- ☐ 515. TIM CORCORAN
- ☐ 536. RORIC HARRISON
- ☐ 559. PHIL MANKOWSKI
- ☐ 607. FERNANDO ARROYO
- ☐ 633. TOM VERYZER
- ☐ 660. JASON THOMPSON
- ☐ 684. RALPH HOUK(M)
- ☐ 701. BRUCE TAYLOR(R)
- ☐ 703. JACK MORRIS(R)
- ☐ 704. LOU WHITAKER(R)
- ☐ 707. ALAN TRAMMELL(R)
- ☐ 708. LANCE PARRISH(R)
- ☐ 723. JOHN WOCKENFUSS

HOUSTON ASTROS

- ☐ 13. ART HOWE
- ☐ 39. FLOYD BANNISTER
- ☐ 64. GENE PENTZ
- ☐ 91. OSCAR ZAMORA
- ☐ 112. TEAM CARD
- ☐ 132. ENOS CABELL
- ☐ 158. JOAQUIN ANDUJAR
- ☐ 181. KEN FORSCH
- ☐ 226. JOE FERGUSON
- ☐ 263. DANNY WALTON
- ☐ 279. BILL VIRDON(M)
- ☐ 306. JOE NIEKRO
- ☐ 330. BOB WATSON

☐ 358. MARK LEMONGELLO
☐ 389. JULIO GONZALEZ
☐ 437. BO MCLAUGHLIN
☐ 470. J.R. RICHARD
☐ 498. JOE SAMBITO
☐ 514. ROB SPERRING
☐ 534. WILBUR HOWARD
☐ 553. TERRY PUHL
☐ 625. JOSE CRUZ
☐ 650. CESAR CEDENO
☐ 677. ED HERRMANN
☐ 697. ROGER METZGER
☐ 705. DAVE BERGMAN(R)
☐ 711. ROY THOMAS(R)

KANSAS CITY ROYALS

☐ 19. DARRELL PORTER
☐ 46. AL COWENS
☐ 73. ANDY HASSLER
☐ 100. GEORGE BRETT
☐ 129. JIM COLBORN
☐ 157. PETE LACOCK
☐ 183. DOUG BIRD
☐ 218. MARTY PATTIN
☐ 248. FRANK WHITE
☐ 274. FRED PATEK
☐ 299. WHITEY HERZOG(M)
☐ 331. MARK LITTELL
☐ 336. STEVE BUSBY
☐ 343. JOHN WATHAN
☐ 357. TOM POQUETTE
☐ 382. JOE LAHOUD
☐ 408. JOE ZDEB
☐ 441. LARRY GURA
☐ 465. HAL MCRAE
☐ 490. AMOS OTIS
☐ 525. JERRY TERRELL
☐ 550. JOHN MAYBERRY
☐ 571. BUCK MARTINEZ
☐ 638. PAUL SPLITTORFF
☐ 665. DENNIS LEONARD
☐ 696. STEVE MINGORI
☐ 705. CLINT HURDLE(R)
☐ 707. U.L. WASHINGTON(R)
☐ 724. TEAM CARD

LOS ANGELES DODGERS

☐ 22. CHARLIE HOUGH
☐ 41. BURT HOOTON
☐ 104. LEE LACY
☐ 128. BILL RUSSELL
☐ 145. RICK MONDAY
☐ 168. REGGIE SMITH
☐ 189. TOM LASORDA(M)
☐ 228. MANNY MOTA
☐ 259. TEAM CARD
☐ 285. STEVE YEAGER
☐ 310. DON SUTTON
☐ 347. TERRY FORSTER
☐ 350. STEVE GARVEY
☐ 375. TOMMY JOHN
☐ 417. MIKE GARMAN
☐ 440. DAVE LOPES
☐ 464. JERRY GROTE
☐ 508. JOHNNY OATES
☐ 539. VIC DAVALILLO
☐ 546. TED MARTINEZ
☐ 562. GLENN BURKE
☐ 586. ED GOODSON
☐ 605. RICK RHODEN
☐ 630. RON CEY
☐ 641. DOUG RAU
☐ 668. DUSTY BAKER
☐ 694. ELIAS SOSA
☐ 709. LANCE RAUTZHAN(R)

MILWAUKEE BREWERS

☐ 24. DON MONEY
☐ 51. CHARLIE MOORE
☐ 77. ED KIRKPATRICK
☐ 95. JAMIE QUIRK
☐ 108. VON JOSHUA
☐ 133. JERRY AUGUSTINE
☐ 154. CECIL COOPER
☐ 173. ROBIN YOUNT
☐ 212. MIKE CALDWELL
☐ 243. BOB MCCLURE

☐ 265. SAL BANDO
☐ 303. SAM HINDS
☐ 328. TEAM CARD
☐ 355. BILL TRAVERS
☐ 376. JIM WOHLFORD
☐ 391. LARRY HANEY
☐ 415. RAY FOSSE
☐ 448. BILL CASTRO
☐ 474. JIM SLATON
☐ 516. GARY BEARE
☐ 520. LARRY HISLE
☐ 542. TIM JOHNSON
☐ 569. LARY SORENSEN
☐ 595. SIXTO LEZCANO
☐ 623. EDUARDO RODRIGUEZ
☐ 649. MOOSE HAAS
☐ 673. STEVE BRYE
☐ 707. PAUL MOLITOR(R)

DON MONEY

MINNESOTA TWINS

☐ 27. GEOFF ZAHN
☐ 54. TOM JOHNSON
☐ 81. PETE REDFERN
☐ 113. DON CARRITHERS
☐ 137. CRAIG KUSICK
☐ 162. PAUL THORMODSGARD
☐ 193. RICH CHILES
☐ 219. MIKE CUBBAGE
☐ 249. DAVE GOLTZ
☐ 275. DAN FORD
☐ 307. GLENN BORGMANN
☐ 363. BOB RANDALL
☐ 386. BOB GORINSKI
☐ 432. TERRY BULLING
☐ 451. TEAM CARD
☐ 471. ROY SMALLEY
☐ 497. GLENN ADAMS
☐ 555. BUTCH WYNEGAR
☐ 580. ROD CAREW
☐ 601. GENE MAUCH(M)
☐ 627. DAVE C. JOHNSON
☐ 657. BOMBO RIVERA
☐ 678. TOM BURGMEIER
☐ 704. SAM PERLOZZO(R)
☐ 705. WILLIE NORWOOD(R)

MONTREAL EXPOS

☐ 15. TONY PEREZ
☐ 43. BILL ATKINSON
☐ 72. ANDRE DAWSON
☐ 97. STAN BAHNSEN
☐ 120. GARY CARTER
☐ 185. ELLIS VALENTINE
☐ 221. CHRIS SPEIER
☐ 244. TEAM CARD
☐ 269. WAYNE TWITCHELL
☐ 294. LARRY PARRISH
☐ 321. SANTO ALCALA
☐ 348. DEL UNSER
☐ 374. JOSE MORALES
☐ 399. PETE MACKANIN
☐ 414. DAROLD KNOWLES
☐ 425. STEVE ROGERS
☐ 449. TIM BLACKWELL
☐ 468. WARREN CROMARTIE
☐ 495. DAVE CASH
☐ 522. DICK WILLIAMS(M)

☐ 549. JOE KERRIGAN
☐ 576. SAM MEJIAS
☐ 603. WILL MCENANEY
☐ 629. DON STANHOUSE
☐ 654. PEPE FRIAS
☐ 679. WAYNE GARRETT
☐ 699. JACKIE BROWN
☐ 701. LARRY LANDRETH(R)
☐ 709. DAN SCHATZEDER(R)

NEW YORK METS

☐ 25. JON MATLACK
☐ 49. ED KRANEPOOL
☐ 69. MIKE VAIL
☐ 109. JOE TORRE
☐ 134. STEVE HENDERSON
☐ 147. LEE MAZZILLI
☐ 171. PAT ZACHRY
☐ 197. NINO ESPINOSA
☐ 229. LEO FOSTER
☐ 277. BRUCE BOISCLAIR
☐ 304. JOHN MILNER
☐ 334. JOHN STEARNS
☐ 356. TEAM CARD
☐ 379. SKIP LOCKWOOD
☐ 403. BUD HARRELSON
☐ 428. JOEL YOUNGBLOOD
☐ 442. ELLIOTT MADDOX
☐ 453. DOUG FLYNN
☐ 481. JACKSON TODD
☐ 505. FELIX MILLAN
☐ 544. LEN RANDLE
☐ 565. JERRY KOOSMAN
☐ 592. BOB APODACA
☐ 621. CRAIG SWAN
☐ 653. RON HODGES
☐ 676. BOB MYRICK
☐ 712. BOBBY VALENTINE

NEW YORK YANKEES

☐ 16. ROY WHITE
☐ 35. SPARKY LYLE
☐ 60. THURMAN MUNSON
☐ 70. RICH GOSSAGE
☐ 89. KEN CLAY
☐ 114. PAUL BLAIR
☐ 135. RON GUIDRY
☐ 159. LOU PINIELLA
☐ 179. DICK TIDROW
☐ 200. REGGIE JACKSON
☐ 225. DON GULLETT
☐ 250. GRAIG NETTLES
☐ 282. TEAM CARD
☐ 309. CLIFF JOHNSON
☐ 335. BUCKY DENT
☐ 365. ED FIGUEROA
☐ 387. KEN HOLTZMAN
☐ 460. JIM HUNTER
☐ 485. CHRIS CHAMBLISS
☐ 582. FRAN HEALY
☐ 591. GEORGE ZEBER
☐ 620. WILLIE RANDOLPH
☐ 664. FRED STANLEY
☐ 690. MICKEY RIVERS
☐ 707. MICKEY KLUTTS(R)
☐ 710. DELL ALSTON(R)
☐ 721. BILLY MARTIN(M)

OAKLAND A'S

☐ 29. BOB LACEY
☐ 55. MITCHELL PAGE
☐ 78. PABLO TORREALBA
☐ 102. MATT ALEXANDER
☐ 139. WAYNE GROSS
☐ 163. BILL NORTH
☐ 191. RODNEY SCOTT
☐ 224. JERRY TABB
☐ 261. TIM HOSLEY
☐ 298. TONY ARMAS
☐ 327. RICK LANGFORD
☐ 353. DOUG BAIR
☐ 378. BOBBY WINKLES(M)
☐ 406. MIKE JORGENSEN
☐ 434. MIKE NORRIS
☐ 458. JEFF NEWMAN
☐ 487. JIM TYRONE
☐ 507. WILLIE CRAWFORD

☐ 528. ROB PICCIOLO
☐ 554. JOE COLEMAN
☐ 577. TEAM CARD
☐ 604. EARL WILLIAMS
☐ 613. MARTY PEREZ
☐ 647. STEVE DUNNING
☐ 658. MANNY SANGUILLEN
☐ 680. VIDA BLUE
☐ 701. STEVE MCCATTY(R)
☐ 709. MATT KEOUGH(R)
☐ 711. CRAIG MITCHELL(R)

PHILADELPHIA PHILLIES

☐ 26. RICH HEBNER
☐ 52. JIM LONBORG
☐ 90. LARRY BOWA
☐ 118. TERRY HARMON
☐ 136. TED SIZEMORE
☐ 161. BOB BOONE
☐ 177. GENE GARBER
☐ 210. JOSE CARDENAL
☐ 222. JERRY MARTIN
☐ 235. TIM MCCARVER
☐ 247. LARRY CHRISTENSON
☐ 271. RANDY LERCH
☐ 297. WARREN BRUSSTAR
☐ 317. DAVE A. JOHNSON
☐ 340. BAKE MCBRIDE
☐ 360. MIKE SCHMIDT
☐ 381. TEAM CARD
☐ 420. GREG LUZINSKI
☐ 446. TUG MCGRAW
☐ 472. RON REED
☐ 513. BARRY FOOTE
☐ 540. STEVE CARLTON
☐ 568. TOM HUTTON
☐ 610. GARRY MADDOX
☐ 631. DANNY OZARK(M)
☐ 675. JAY JOHNSTONE
☐ 715. JIM KAAT

PITTSBURGH PIRATES

☐ 28. ED OTT
☐ 53. PHIL GARNER
☐ 84. KENT TEKULVE
☐ 138. LARRY DEMERY
☐ 165. RENNIE STENNETT
☐ 190. JOHN CANDELARIA
☐ 223. BRUCE KISON
☐ 255. JERRY REUSS
☐ 283. OMAR MORENO
☐ 308. JIM ROOKER
☐ 323. JIM FREGOSI
☐ 383. MARIO MENDOZA
☐ 407. ODELL JONES
☐ 430. AL OLIVER
☐ 433. FERNANDO GONZALEZ
☐ 455. BILL ROBINSON
☐ 483. KEN MACHA
☐ 494. CHUCK TANNER(M)
☐ 510. WILLIE STARGELL
☐ 560. DAVE PARKER
☐ 606. TEAM CARD
☐ 637. DUFFY DYER
☐ 661. GRANT JACKSON
☐ 685. FRANK TAVERAS
☐ 703. TIM JONES(R)
☐ 705. MIGUEL DILONE(R)
☐ 710. MIKE EASLER(R)

ST. LOUIS CARDINALS

☐ 32. GARRY TEMPLETON
☐ 58. BOB FORSCH
☐ 88. MIKE PHILLIPS
☐ 111. MIKE TYSON
☐ 143. KEITH HERNANDEZ
☐ 170. LOU BROCK
☐ 195. LARRY DIERKER
☐ 230. AL HRABOSKY
☐ 257. HECTOR CRUZ
☐ 281. ERIC RASMUSSEN
☐ 301. BUDDY SCHULTZ
☐ 324. VERN RAPP(M)
☐ 352. TONY SCOTT
☐ 380. TED SIMMONS
☐ 405. RAWLY EASTWICK

☐ 431. BUTCH METZGER
☐ 452. JERRY MUMPHREY
☐ 479. TEAM CARD
☐ 504. ROGER FREED
☐ 531. TOM UNDERWOOD
☐ 563. DAVE RADER
☐ 587. JOHN URREA
☐ 609. JOHN DENNY
☐ 644. JIM DWYER
☐ 669. PETE FALCONE
☐ 692. KEN REITZ
☐ 710. RICK BOSETTI(R)
☐ 714. MIKE ANDERSON

ROLLIE FINGERS

SAN DIEGO PADRES

☐ 30. GEORGE HENDRICK
☐ 56. RANDY JONES
☐ 86. DAVE TOMLIN
☐ 116. TUCKER ASHFORD
☐ 140. ROLLIE FINGERS
☐ 164. BOB OWCHINKO
☐ 192. TEAM CARD
☐ 240. GENE TENACE
☐ 266. BOB SHIRLEY
☐ 292. GENE RICHARDS
☐ 318. TOM GRIFFIN
☐ 364. JERRY TURNER
☐ 390. OSCAR GAMBLE
☐ 392. BILLY ALMON
☐ 445. MIKE IVIE
☐ 467. ALVIN DARK(M)
☐ 488. DAN SPILLNER
☐ 509. BRENT STROM
☐ 530. DAVE WINFIELD
☐ 566. MERV RETTENMUND
☐ 594. DAVE FREISLEBEN
☐ 611. PAT SCANLON
☐ 683. MIKE CHAMPION
☐ 702. RICK SWEET(R)
☐ 713. BOB DAVIS

SAN FRANCISCO GIANTS

☐   8. MIKE SADEK
☐ 34. WILLIE MCCOVEY
☐ 62. JIM BARR
☐ 82. TEAM CARD
☐ 107. ED HALICKI
☐ 142. JOHN MONTEFUSCO
☐ 167. TIM FOLI
☐ 194. DERREL THOMAS
☐ 215. DARRELL EVANS
☐ 236. TERRY WHITFIELD
☐ 256. JOE ALTOBELLI(M)
☐ 284. RANDY MOFFITT
☐ 312. GREG MINTON
☐ 338. DAVE HEAVERLO
☐ 359. MARC HILL
☐ 384. JACK CLARK
☐ 410. BILL MADLOCK
☐ 436. VIC HARRIS
☐ 461. ROB ANDREWS
☐ 486. JOHN CURTIS
☐ 512. LARRY HERNDON
☐ 538. JOHNNIE LEMASTER
☐ 561. CHARLIE WILLIAMS
☐ 581. LYNN MCGLOTHEN

☐ 589. BOB KNEPPER
☐ 624. GARY ALEXANDER
☐ 648. GARY THOMASSON
☐ 671. GARY LAVELLE
☐ 719. RANDY ELLIOTT

SEATTLE MARINERS

☐ 31. GLENN ABBOTT
☐ 57. DAN MEYER
☐ 79. DARRELL JOHNSON(M)
☐ 117. JOHN MONTAGUE
☐ 141. RUPPERT JONES
☐ 166. CARLOS LOPEZ
☐ 199. CRAIG REYNOLDS
☐ 233. DICK POLE
☐ 254. DAVE COLLINS
☐ 278. ENRIQUE ROMO
☐ 311. JOSE BAEZ
☐ 333. JIM TODD
☐ 366. LARRY MILBOURNE
☐ 396. BOB STINSON
☐ 422. STEVE BRAUN
☐ 447. LEROY STANTON
☐ 476. BILL STEIN
☐ 499. TEAM CARD
☐ 532. SKIP JUTZE
☐ 558. PAUL MITCHELL
☐ 584. JOHN HALE
☐ 596. GARY WHEELOCK
☐ 643. TOM HOUSE
☐ 687. JULIO CRUZ
☐ 698. JUAN BERNHARDT
☐ 702. KEVIN PASLEY(R)
☐ 709. STEVE BURKE(R)

TEXAS RANGERS

☐ 23. BUMP WILLS
☐ 44. TOBY HARRAH
☐ 67. CLAUDELL WASHINGTON
☐ 92. ADRIAN DEVINE
☐ 110. RICHIE ZISK
☐ 131. BERT BLYLEVEN
☐ 146. DOYLE ALEXANDER
☐ 172. MIKE HARGROVE
☐ 209. DOCK ELLIS
☐ 238. JUAN BENIQUEZ
☐ 260. BERT CAMPANERIS
☐ 290. WILLIE HORTON
☐ 314. PAUL LINDBLAD
☐ 337. TOM GRIEVE
☐ 362. DAVE MAY
☐ 388. BILL FAHEY
☐ 438. JOHN ELLIS
☐ 462. ROGELIO MORET
☐ 492. JIM SUNDBERG
☐ 518. TOMMY BOGGS
☐ 533. SANDY ALOMAR
☐ 548. BILLY HUNTER(M)
☐ 583. DOC MEDICH
☐ 588. JIM MASON
☐ 612. KEN HENDERSON
☐ 634. LEN BARKER
☐ 659. TEAM CARD
☐ 686. GAYLORD PERRY
☐ 706. PAT PUTNAM(R)
☐ 710. KEITH SMITH(R)
☐ 725. KURT BEVACQUA

TORONTO BLUE JAYS

☐ 33. DAVE LEMANCZYK
☐ 59. OTTO VELEZ
☐ 85. RON FAIRLY
☐ 103. TOM MURPHY
☐ 121. ALVIS WOODS
☐ 144. JESSE JEFFERSON
☐ 169. JERRY JOHNSON
☐ 196. BOB BAILOR
☐ 241. PETE VUCKOVICH
☐ 267. DOUG AULT
☐ 293. MIKE WILLIS
☐ 319. ALAN ASHBY
☐ 344. SAM EWING
☐ 369. TIM NORDBROOK
☐ 394. ROY HOWELL
☐ 419. JERRY GARVIN
☐ 444. ROY HARTSFIELD(M)
☐ 469. RICK CERONE

☐ 496. JIM CLANCY
☐ 521. STEVE STAGGS
☐ 547. JOHN SCOTT
☐ 573. LUIS GOMEZ
☐ 599. GARY WOODS
☐ 626. TEAM CARD
☐ 651. DOUG RADER
☐ 667. JEFF BYRD
☐ 704. GARTH IORG(R)
☐ 708. ERNIE WHITT(R)

1979 TOPPS (726)
2 1/2" X 3 1/2"

PAUL MOLITOR SS
BREWERS

ATLANTA BRAVES

☐   9. DAVE CAMPBELL
☐ 39. DALE MURPHY
☐ 85. GARY MATTHEWS
☐ 105. RICK CAMP
☐ 132. ROWLAND OFFICE
☐ 156. BUDDY SOLOMON
☐ 184. DARREL CHANEY
☐ 222. BOB BEALL
☐ 245. JEFF BURROUGHS
☐ 257. ADRIAN DEVINE
☐ 296. PRESTON HANNA
☐ 302. TEAM & COX(M)
☐ 331. MICKEY MAHLER
☐ 344. JERRY ROYSTER
☐ 363. CRAIG SKOK
☐ 384. TOMMY BOGGS
☐ 464. JOE NOLAN
☐ 496. BARRY BONNELL
☐ 504. LARRY MCWILLIAMS
☐ 529. BRIAN ASSELSTINE
☐ 555. BIFF POCOROBA
☐ 572. ROD GILBREATH
☐ 586. BOB HORNER
☐ 595. PHIL NIEKRO
☐ 629. GENE GARBER
☐ 684. JAMIE EASTERLY
☐ 715. BRUCE BENEDICT(P)
☐ 715. GLENN HUBBARD(P)
☐ 715. LARRY WHISENTON(P)

BALTIMORE ORIOLES

☐ 10. LEE MAY
☐ 37. JOE KERRIGAN
☐ 65. MARK BELANGER
☐ 91. TERRY CROWLEY
☐ 102. MIKE ANDERSON
☐ 119. DON STANHOUSE
☐ 160. MIKE FLANAGAN
☐ 188. H. PAT KELLY
☐ 211. DENNY MARTINEZ
☐ 237. BILLY SMITH
☐ 262. NELSON BRILES
☐ 287. ANDRES MORA
☐ 314. LARRY HARLOW
☐ 340. JIM PALMER
☐ 367. DAVE SKAGGS
☐ 393. SCOTT MCGREGOR
☐ 421. DOUG DECINCES
☐ 491. TIPPY MARTINEZ
☐ 517. AL BUMBRY
☐ 543. KIKO GARCIA

☐ 568. CARLOS LOPEZ
☐ 593. RICK DEMPSEY
☐ 615. KEN SINGLETON
☐ 640. EDDIE MURRAY
☐ 666. RICH DAUER
☐ 689. TEAM & WEAVER(M)
☐ 701. MARK COREY(P)
☐ 701. JOHN FLINN(P)
☐ 701. SAMMY STEWART(P)

BOSTON RED SOX

☐ 12. DICK DRAGO
☐ 40. DENNIS ECKERSLEY
☐ 63. JACK BROHAMER
☐ 83. FRED KENDALL
☐ 106. FRANK DUFFY
☐ 125. RICK BURLESON
☐ 155. DWIGHT EVANS
☐ 185. MIKE TOREZ
☐ 214. TEAM & ZIMMER(M)
☐ 270. BUTCH HOBSON
☐ 320. CARL YASTRZEMSKI
☐ 349. JIM C. WRIGHT
☐ 375. BILL CAMPBELL
☐ 400. JIM RICE
☐ 423. BOB MONTGOMERY
☐ 455. BILL LEE
☐ 480. FRED LYNN
☐ 524. TOM BURGMEIER
☐ 549. BOB BAILEY
☐ 575. LUIS TIANT
☐ 597. BOB STANLEY
☐ 618. JERRY REMY
☐ 645. GEORGE SCOTT
☐ 680. CARLTON FISK
☐ 696. ANDY HASSLER
☐ 702. JOEL FINCH(P)
☐ 702. GARRY HANCOCK(P)
☐ 702. ALLEN RIPLEY(P)

CALIFORNIA ANGELS

☐ 18. TONY SOLAITA
☐ 48. MERV RETTENMUND
☐ 71. BRIAN DOWNING
☐ 115. NOLAN RYAN
☐ 212. CARNEY LANSFORD
☐ 267. JOE RUDI
☐ 291. TOM GRIFFIN
☐ 313. DYAR MILLER
☐ 322. DANNY GOODWIN
☐ 339. RON JACKSON
☐ 368. DON AASE
☐ 402. PAUL HARTZELL
☐ 424. TEAM & FREGOSI(M)
☐ 453. CHRIS KNAPP
☐ 477. BOB GRICH
☐ 503. TERRY HUMPHREY
☐ 530. FRANK TANANA
☐ 557. KEN BRETT
☐ 580. RON FAIRLY
☐ 601. DAVE LAROCHE
☐ 619. KEN LANDREAUX
☐ 635. DON BAYLOR
☐ 638. AL FITZMORRIS
☐ 654. RICK MILLER
☐ 682. DAVE CHALK
☐ 703. JIM ANDERSON(P)
☐ 703. DAVE FROST(P)
☐ 703. BOB SLATER(P)

CHICAGO CUBS

☐ 17. DONNIE MOORE
☐ 53. MICK KELLEHER
☐ 86. RODNEY SCOTT
☐ 98. RAY BURRIS
☐ 135. BOBBY MURCER
☐ 153. DENNIS LAMP
☐ 171. GENE CLINES
☐ 240. RICK REUSCHEL
☐ 299. STEVE ONTIVEROS
☐ 323. LYNN MCGLOTHEN
☐ 346. BILL BUCKNER
☐ 370. DAVE KINGMAN
☐ 398. IVAN DEJESUS
☐ 433. LARRY BIITTNER
☐ 457. BRUCE SUTTER

☐ 473. DAVE A. ROBERTS
☐ 489. LARRY COX
☐ 494. JERRY WHITE
☐ 513. DAVE A. JOHNSON
☐ 522. KEN HOLTZMAN
☐ 551. TEAM & FRANKS(M)
☐ 579. GREG GROSS
☐ 592. MIKE KRUKOW
☐ 614. WILLIE HERNANDEZ
☐ 639. MANNY TRILLO
☐ 663. MIKE VAIL
☐ 693. DAVE RADER
☐ 716. DAVE GEISEL(P)
☐ 716. KARL PAGEL(P)
☐ 716. SCOT THOMPSON(P)

CHICAGO WHITE SOX

☐ 42. RON BLOMBERG
☐ 88. BOB MOLINARO
☐ 127. THAD BOSLEY
☐ 134. ALAN BANNISTER
☐ 169. BILL NAHORODNY
☐ 186. ERIC SODERHOLM
☐ 216. WILBUR WOOD
☐ 227. STEVE STONE
☐ 242. PABLO TORREALBA
☐ 266. JIM WILLOUGHBY
☐ 275. JUNIOR MOORE
☐ 283. KEN KRAVEC
☐ 309. RALPH GARR
☐ 333. CHET LEMON
☐ 351. WAYNE NORDHAGEN
☐ 372. LAMAR JOHNSON
☐ 386. FRANCISCO BARRIOS
☐ 404. TEAM & KESSINGER(M)
☐ 467. DON KESSINGER
☐ 514. MIKE PROLY
☐ 527. LERRIN LAGROW
☐ 559. GREG PRYOR
☐ 574. CLAUDELL WASHINGTON
☐ 631. JORGE ORTA
☐ 662. KEVIN BELL
☐ 686. RON SCHUELER
☐ 704. ROSS BAUMGARTEN(P)
☐ 704. MIKE COLBERN(P)
☐ 704. MIKE SQUIRES(P)

CINCINNATI REDS

☐ 20. JOE MORGAN
☐ 47. FRED NORMAN
☐ 73. KEN HENDERSON
☐ 100. TOM SEAVER
☐ 126. DOUG BAIR
☐ 149. MANNY SARMIENTO
☐ 174. RICK AUERBACH
☐ 200. JOHNNY BENCH
☐ 220. CESAR GERONIMO
☐ 259. TEAM & ANDERSON(M)
☐ 281. VIC CORRELL
☐ 301. TOM HUME
☐ 326. PEDRO BORBON
☐ 354. BILL BONHAM
☐ 377. PAUL MOSKAU
☐ 401. RAY KNIGHT
☐ 420. KEN GRIFFEY
☐ 450. DAVE CONCEPCION
☐ 475. DAN DRIESSEN
☐ 501. JUNIOR KENNEDY
☐ 516. CHAMP SUMMERS
☐ 556. MIKE LUM
☐ 600. GEORGE FOSTER
☐ 622. DAVE COLLINS
☐ 650. PETE ROSE
☐ 674. DAVE TOMLIN
☐ 717. MIKE LACOSS(P)
☐ 717. RON OESTER(P)
☐ 717. HARRY SPILMAN(P)

CLEVELAND INDIANS

☐ 13. PAUL DADE
☐ 38. BERNIE CARBO
☐ 61. BO DIAZ
☐ 77. DAN BRIGGS
☐ 79. TED COX
☐ 96. TEAM & TORBORG(M)
☐ 122. MIKE PAXTON
☐ 146. DUANE KUIPER

☐ 150. WAYNE CAGE
☐ 168. DAVE FREISLEBEN
☐ 226. RON PRUITT
☐ 253. RICK WISE
☐ 280. ANDRE THORNTON
☐ 307. LARVELL BLANKS
☐ 332. GARY ALEXANDER
☐ 359. DAN SPILLNER
☐ 399. DAVID CLYDE
☐ 425. RICK MANNING
☐ 438. HORACE SPEED
☐ 459. SID MONGE
☐ 484. RICK WAITS
☐ 511. PAUL REUSCHEL
☐ 537. TOM VERYZER
☐ 573. JIM KERN
☐ 611. JIM NORRIS
☐ 636. WAYNE GARLAND
☐ 667. DON HOOD
☐ 690. BUDDY BELL
☐ 705. ALFREDO GRIFFIN(P)
☐ 705. TIM NORRID(P)
☐ 705. DAVE OLIVER(P)

DETROIT TIGERS

☐ 33. DAVE ROZEMA
☐ 66. TEAM & MOSS(M)
☐ 80. JASON THOMPSON
☐ 93. PHIL MANKOWSKI
☐ 123. LOU WHITAKER
☐ 151. JOHN HILLER
☐ 176. AURELIO RODRIGUEZ
☐ 196. STEVE KEMP
☐ 217. STEVE DILLARD
☐ 231. JOHNNY WOCKENFUSS
☐ 251. JACK MORRIS
☐ 272. TIM CORCORAN
☐ 288. MILT WILCOX
☐ 316. MILT MAY
☐ 343. ED GLYNN
☐ 358. ALAN TRAMMELL
☐ 388. JACK BILLINGHAM
☐ 440. RUSTY STAUB
☐ 469. LANCE PARRISH
☐ 541. JIM SLATON
☐ 569. BOB SYKES
☐ 598. MARK WAGNER
☐ 625. MARK FIDRYCH
☐ 660. RON LEFLORE
☐ 692. MICKEY STANLEY
☐ 706. DAVE STEGMAN(P)
☐ 706. DAVE TOBIK(P)
☐ 706. KIP YOUNG(P)

HOUSTON ASTROS

☐ 14. RAFAEL LANDESTORY
☐ 49. VERN RUHLE
☐ 68. JOE NIEKRO
☐ 107. JESUS ALOU
☐ 130. BOB WATSON
☐ 139. LUIS PUJOLS
☐ 158. JOE SAMBITO
☐ 187. MARK LEMONGELLO
☐ 232. JIMMY SEXTON
☐ 268. JULIO GONZALEZ
☐ 289. JOSE CRUZ
☐ 306. FLOYD BANNISTER
☐ 327. ART HOWE
☐ 361. TOM DIXON
☐ 381. TEAM & VIRDON(M)
☐ 437. RICK WILLIAMS
☐ 471. JOAQUIN ANDUJAR
☐ 515. ENOS CABELL
☐ 534. KEN FORSCH
☐ 553. DENNY WALLING
☐ 570. CESAR CEDENO
☐ 590. J.R. RICHARD
☐ 617. TERRY PUHL
☐ 642. WILBUR HOWARD
☐ 697. DAVE BERGMAN
☐ 718. BRUCE BOCHY(P)
☐ 718. MIKE FISCHLIN(P)
☐ 718. DON PISKER(P)

KANSAS CITY ROYALS

☐ 19. LARRY GURA
☐ 26. JAMIE QUIRK
☐ 45. AL HRABOSKY

☐ 72. STEVE MINGORI
☐ 99. JOHN WATHAN
☐ 129. MARTY PATTIN
☐ 157. U.L. WASHINGTON
☐ 183. PAUL SPLITTORFF
☐ 218. DENNIS LEONARD
☐ 248. PETE LACOCK
☐ 273. JERRY TERRELL
☐ 298. RICH GALE
☐ 330. GEORGE BRETT
☐ 360. AMOS OTIS
☐ 389. JOE ZDEB
☐ 409. WILLIE WILSON
☐ 439. FRANK WHITE
☐ 451. TEAM & HERZOG(M)
☐ 476. TOM POQUETTE
☐ 490. AL COWENS
☐ 502. STEVE BRAUN
☐ 525. FREDDIE PATEK
☐ 547. CLINT HURDLE
☐ 571. DARRELL PORTER
☐ 585. HAL MCRAE
☐ 664. DOUG BIRD
☐ 707. RANDY BASS(P)
☐ 707. JIM GAUDET(P)
☐ 707. RANDY MCGILBERRY(P)

LOS ANGELES DODGERS

☐ 23. TERRY FORSTER
☐ 50. STEVE GARVEY
☐ 75. STEVE YEAGER
☐ 104. JOHNNY OATES
☐ 128. TED MARTINEZ
☐ 145. RICK RHODEN
☐ 170. DON SUTTON
☐ 190. RON CEY
☐ 228. VIC DAVALILLO
☐ 255. TOMMY JOHN
☐ 279. JERRY GROTE
☐ 290. DAVE LOPES
☐ 318. BOB WELCH
☐ 347. DOUG RAU
☐ 373. LANCE RAUTZHAN
☐ 441. LEE LACY
☐ 465. REGGIE SMITH
☐ 508. CHARLIE HOUGH
☐ 526. TEAM & LASORDA(M)
☐ 546. BILL RUSSELL
☐ 562. DUSTY BAKER
☐ 605. RICK MONDAY
☐ 641. BOBBY CASTILLO
☐ 644. MANNY MOTA
☐ 668. BILL NORTH
☐ 671. JOE FERGUSON
☐ 694. BURT HOOTON
☐ 719. PEDRO GUERRERO(P)
☐ 719. RUDY LAW(P)
☐ 719. JOE SIMPSON(P)

MILWAUKEE BREWERS

☐ 24. PAUL MOLITOR
☐ 51. RAY FOSSE
☐ 95. ROBIN YOUNT
☐ 108. EDUARDO RODRIGUEZ
☐ 133. BILL CASTRO
☐ 154. JIM GANTNER
☐ 180. LARRY HISLE
☐ 213. BILL TRAVERS
☐ 243. BUCK MARTINEZ
☐ 265. DON MONEY

☐ 303. LARY SORENSEN
☐ 325. CECIL COOPER
☐ 357. JERRY AUGUSTINE
☐ 376. GORMAN THOMAS
☐ 394. RANDY STEIN
☐ 408. CHARLIE MOORE
☐ 427. ANDY REPLOGLE
☐ 448. MOOSE HAAS
☐ 474. DICK DAVIS
☐ 519. BEN OGLIVIE
☐ 550. SAL BANDO
☐ 577. TEAM & BAMBERGER(M)
☐ 596. JIM WOHLFORD
☐ 623. BOB MCCLURE
☐ 651. MIKE CALDWELL
☐ 685. SIXTO LEZCANO
☐ 708. KEVIN BASS(P)
☐ 708. EDDIE ROMERO(P)
☐ 708. NED YOST(P)

MINNESOTA TWINS

☐ 27. DAVE GOLTZ
☐ 41. TEAM & MAUCH(M)
☐ 58. BOB RANDALL
☐ 81. ROGER ERICKSON
☐ 113. PETE REDFERN
☐ 137. LARRY WOLFE
☐ 162. TOM JOHNSON
☐ 193. GLENN ADAMS
☐ 219. ROY SMALLEY
☐ 246. DARRELL JACKSON
☐ 249. PAUL THORMODSGARD
☐ 274. WILLIE NORWOOD
☐ 300. ROD CAREW
☐ 362. MIKE CUBBAGE
☐ 371. JEFF HOLLY
☐ 385. DAN FORD
☐ 405. BUTCH WYNEGAR
☐ 431. GLENN BORGMANN
☐ 449. BOMBO RIVERA
☐ 472. CRAIG KUSICK
☐ 498. RICH CHILES
☐ 552. JOSE MORALES
☐ 627. GARY SERUM
☐ 633. ROB WILFONG
☐ 656. HOSKEN POWELL
☐ 676. JOHNNY SUTTON
☐ 678. GEOFF ZAHN
☐ 709. SAM PERLOZZO(P)
☐ 709. RICK SOFIELD(P)
☐ 709. KEVIN STANFIELD(P)

MONTREAL EXPOS

☐ 15. ROSS GRIMSLEY
☐ 43. WAYNE TWITCHELL
☐ 76. WARREN CROMARTIE
☐ 97. SAM MEJIAS
☐ 124. DAN SCHATZEDER
☐ 181. MIKE GARMAN
☐ 235. STEVE ROGERS
☐ 269. WOODIE FRYMAN
☐ 294. PEPE FRIAS
☐ 348. ANDRE DAWSON
☐ 374. ED HERRMANN
☐ 395. DAVE CASH
☐ 426. CHRIS SPEIER
☐ 468. STAN BAHNSEN
☐ 495. TONY PEREZ
☐ 520. GARY CARTER
☐ 535. ELLIS VALENTINE
☐ 581. DAROLD KNOWLES
☐ 603. RUDY MAY
☐ 606. TEAM & WILLIAMS(M)
☐ 628. DEL UNSER
☐ 652. STAN PAPI
☐ 673. TOM HUTTON
☐ 677. LARRY PARRISH
☐ 699. HAL DUES
☐ 720. JERRY FRY(P)
☐ 720. JERRY PIRTLE(P)
☐ 720. SCOTT SANDERSON(P)

NEW YORK METS

☐ 21. KEVIN KOBEL
☐ 46. RON HODGES
☐ 69. ELLIOTT MADDOX
☐ 82. TEAM & TORRE(M)
☐ 109. JOEL YOUNGBLOOD
☐ 148. BRUCE BOISCLAIR
☐ 172. MIKE BRUHERT
☐ 197. BOB APODACA
☐ 229. DOUG FLYNN
☐ 277. TOM GRIEVE

- ☐ 305. WILLIE MONTANEZ
- ☐ 334. CRAIG SWAN
- ☐ 355. LEE MAZZILLI
- ☐ 379. DALE MURRAY
- ☐ 397. SERGIO FERRER
- ☐ 403. TIM FOLI
- ☐ 428. BOBBY VALENTINE
- ☐ 445. STEVE HENDERSON
- ☐ 454. LEN RANDLE
- ☐ 481. SKIP LOCKWOOD
- ☐ 505. ED KRANEPOOL
- ☐ 545. JOHN STEARNS
- ☐ 566. NINO ESPINOSA
- ☐ 621. PAT ZACHRY
- ☐ 643. TOM HAUSMAN
- ☐ 655. JERRY KOOSMAN
- ☐ 721. JUAN BERENGUER(P)
- ☐ 721. DWIGHT BERNARD(P)
- ☐ 721. DAN NORMAN(P)

NEW YORK YANKEES

- ☐ 16. FRED STANLEY
- ☐ 35. ED FIGUEROA
- ☐ 60. MICKEY RIVERS
- ☐ 89. DICK TIDROW
- ☐ 114. CLIFF JOHNSON
- ☐ 140. DON GULLETT
- ☐ 159. ROY WHITE
- ☐ 179. JIM BEATTIE
- ☐ 225. RICH GOSSAGE
- ☐ 250. WILLIE RANDOLPH
- ☐ 278. ANDY MESSERSMITH
- ☐ 310. THURMAN MUNSON
- ☐ 335. CHRIS CHAMBLISS
- ☐ 365. SPARKY LYLE
- ☐ 387. GARY THOMASSON
- ☐ 434. KEN CLAY
- ☐ 460. GRAIG NETTLES
- ☐ 485. BUCKY DENT
- ☐ 500. RON GUIDRY
- ☐ 558. JAY JOHNSTONE
- ☐ 582. PAUL BLAIR
- ☐ 599. JIM SPENCER
- ☐ 626. TEAM & LEMON(M)
- ☐ 634. PAUL LINDBLAD
- ☐ 648. LOU PINIELLA
- ☐ 670. JIM HUNTER
- ☐ 700. REGGIE JACKSON
- ☐ 710. BRIAN DOYLE(P)
- ☐ 710. MIKE HEATH(P)
- ☐ 710. DAVE RAJSICH(P)

OAKLAND A'S

- ☐ 29. RICK LANGFORD
- ☐ 54. DELL ALSTON
- ☐ 78. ELIAS SOSA
- ☐ 163. GLENN BURKE
- ☐ 191. MIKE NORRIS
- ☐ 224. DAVE REVERING
- ☐ 261. MARIO GUERRERO
- ☐ 295. MITCHELL PAGE
- ☐ 328. TEAM & MCKEON(M)
- ☐ 352. STEVE RENKO
- ☐ 378. ROB PICCIOLO
- ☐ 406. JOE WALLIS
- ☐ 432. DAVE HEAVERLO
- ☐ 458. JIM ESSIAN
- ☐ 487. MIGUEL DILONE
- ☐ 507. TONY ARMAS
- ☐ 528. WAYNE GROSS
- ☐ 554. MATT KEOUGH
- ☐ 565. RICO CARTY
- ☐ 578. PETE BROBERG
- ☐ 604. JEFF NEWMAN
- ☐ 613. MIKE EDWARDS
- ☐ 647. BOB LACEY
- ☐ 658. TAYLOR DUNCAN
- ☐ 681. JOHN HENRY JOHNSON
- ☐ 711. DWAYNE MURPHY(P)
- ☐ 711. BRUCE ROBINSON(P)
- ☐ 711. ALAN WIRTH(P)

PHILADELPHIA PHILLIES

- ☐ 25. STEVE CARLTON
- ☐ 52. RANDY LERCH
- ☐ 90. BOB BOONE
- ☐ 112. TEAM & OZARK(M)

- ☐ 118. BUD HARRELSON
- ☐ 136. JIM KAAT
- ☐ 161. BARRY FOOTE
- ☐ 177. RON REED
- ☐ 210. LARRY BOWA
- ☐ 271. RAWLY EASTWICK
- ☐ 297. TED SIZEMORE
- ☐ 317. JOSE CARDENAL
- ☐ 345. TUG MCGRAW
- ☐ 382. JERRY MARTIN
- ☐ 419. DICK RUTHVEN
- ☐ 446. JIM LONBORG
- ☐ 470. GARRY MADDOX
- ☐ 493. LARRY CHRISTENSON
- ☐ 540. GREG LUZINSKI
- ☐ 567. RICH HEBNER
- ☐ 610. MIKE SCHMIDT
- ☐ 630. BAKE MCBRIDE
- ☐ 653. WARREN BRUSSTAR
- ☐ 675. TIM MCCARVER
- ☐ 722. JIM MORRISON(P)
- ☐ 722. LONNIE SMITH(P)
- ☐ 722. JIM L. WRIGHT(P)

PITTSBURGH PIRATES

- ☐ 28. STEVE BRYE
- ☐ 55. WILLIE STARGELL
- ☐ 70. JOHN CANDELARIA
- ☐ 92. JIM BIBBY
- ☐ 117. GRANT JACKSON
- ☐ 147. DAVE HAMILTON
- ☐ 165. FRANK TAVERAS
- ☐ 189. EDDIE WHITSON
- ☐ 208. CLARENCE GASTON
- ☐ 223. KENT TEKULVE
- ☐ 244. TEAM & TANNER(M)
- ☐ 264. DON ROBINSON
- ☐ 286. DUFFY DYER
- ☐ 308. BERT BLYLEVEN
- ☐ 383. PHIL GARNER
- ☐ 430. DAVE PARKER
- ☐ 447. MANNY SANGUILLEN
- ☐ 509. MARIO MENDOZA
- ☐ 523. JOHN MILNER
- ☐ 536. JERRY REUSS
- ☐ 561. ED OTT
- ☐ 584. JIM ROOKER
- ☐ 607. OMAR MORENO
- ☐ 637. BILL ROBINSON
- ☐ 661. BRUCE KISON
- ☐ 687. RENNIE STENNETT
- ☐ 723. DALE BERRA(P)
- ☐ 723. EUGENIO COTES(P)
- ☐ 723. BEN WILTBANK(P)

ST. LOUIS CARDINALS

- ☐ 32. JERRY MUMPHREY
- ☐ 59. JOHN DENNY
- ☐ 87. PETE FALCONE
- ☐ 111. ROGER FREED
- ☐ 143. TONY SCOTT
- ☐ 175. GEORGE HENDRICK
- ☐ 192. TEAM & BOYER(M)
- ☐ 230. BOB FORSCH
- ☐ 258. MIKE PHILLIPS
- ☐ 304. STEVE SWISHER
- ☐ 319. WAYNE GARRETT
- ☐ 324. MIKE TYSON
- ☐ 350. GARRY TEMPLETON
- ☐ 407. PETE VUCKOVICH
- ☐ 429. JOHN URREA
- ☐ 444. AURELIO LOPEZ
- ☐ 452. JERRY MORALES
- ☐ 466. MARK LITTELL
- ☐ 510. TED SIMMONS
- ☐ 532. BUDDY SCHULTZ
- ☐ 563. ROY THOMAS
- ☐ 587. KEN REITZ
- ☐ 609. SILVIO MARTINEZ
- ☐ 665. LOU BROCK
- ☐ 695. KEITH HERNANDEZ
- ☐ 724. TOM BRUNO(P)
- ☐ 724. GEORGE FRAZIER(P)
- ☐ 724. TERRY KENNEDY(P)

SAN DIEGO PADRES

- ☐ 30. DAVE WINFIELD
- ☐ 57. ERIC RASMUSSEN
- ☐ 116. OZZIE SMITH

- ☐ 138. MARK LEE
- ☐ 164. MICKEY LOLICH
- ☐ 194. RANDY JONES
- ☐ 247. TUCKER ASHFORD
- ☐ 263. OSCAR GAMBLE
- ☐ 292. DON REYNOLDS
- ☐ 321. GAYLORD PERRY
- ☐ 342. DAVE W. ROBERTS
- ☐ 364. GENE RICHARDS
- ☐ 390. ROLLIE FINGERS
- ☐ 435. GENE TENACE
- ☐ 456. CHUCK BAKER
- ☐ 479. TEAM & CRAIG(M)
- ☐ 488. BOB OWCHINKO
- ☐ 506. JOHN D'ACQUISTO
- ☐ 531. FERNANDO GONZALEZ
- ☐ 564. JERRY TURNER
- ☐ 594. BOB SHIRLEY
- ☐ 616. BILLY ALMON
- ☐ 646. RICK SWEET
- ☐ 679. DERREL THOMAS
- ☐ 725. JIM BESWICK(P)
- ☐ 725. STEVE MURA(P)
- ☐ 725. BRODERICK PERKINS(P)

SAN FRANCISCO GIANTS

- ☐ 11. MARC HILL
- ☐ 34. ROB ANDREWS
- ☐ 62. RANDY MOFFITT
- ☐ 84. GREG MINTON
- ☐ 110. VIDA BLUE
- ☐ 142. CHARLIE WILLIAMS
- ☐ 167. ROGER METZGER
- ☐ 195. BILL MADLOCK
- ☐ 215. WILLIE MCCOVEY
- ☐ 236. JIM DWYER
- ☐ 256. MIKE SADEK
- ☐ 284. JOHNNIE LEMASTER
- ☐ 311. GARY LAVELLE
- ☐ 338. VIC HARRIS
- ☐ 356. TEAM & ALTOBELLI(M)
- ☐ 410. DARRELL EVANS
- ☐ 436. HECTOR CRUZ
- ☐ 461. JIM BARR
- ☐ 486. BOB KNEPPER
- ☐ 512. JACK CLARK
- ☐ 538. MIKE IVIE
- ☐ 560. JOHN MONTEFUSCO
- ☐ 589. TERRY WHITFIELD
- ☐ 624. LARRY HERNDON
- ☐ 649. JOHN CURTIS
- ☐ 672. ED HALICKI
- ☐ 726. GREG JOHNSTON(P)
- ☐ 726. JOE STRAIN(P)
- ☐ 726. JOHN TAMARGO(P)

SEATTLE MARINERS

- ☐ 31. TOM HOUSE
- ☐ 56. JOHN HALE
- ☐ 74. SHANE RAWLEY
- ☐ 103. JIM TODD
- ☐ 141. TOM PACIOREK
- ☐ 166. LEON ROBERTS
- ☐ 199. LARRY MILBOURNE
- ☐ 233. PAUL MITCHELL
- ☐ 252. BOB STINSON
- ☐ 276. JIM COLBORN
- ☐ 312. BOB ROBERTSON
- ☐ 337. JOHN MONTAGUE
- ☐ 366. JUAN BERNHARDT
- ☐ 396. BILL PLUMMER
- ☐ 422. RUPPERT JONES
- ☐ 443. BRUCE BOCHTE
- ☐ 482. CRAIG REYNOLDS
- ☐ 497. GLENN ABBOTT
- ☐ 533. LEROY STANTON
- ☐ 548. ENRIQUE ROMO
- ☐ 576. MIKE PARROTT
- ☐ 583. JULIO CRUZ
- ☐ 612. RICK HONEYCUTT
- ☐ 659. TEAM & JOHNSON(M)
- ☐ 683. DAN MEYER
- ☐ 698. BILL STEIN
- ☐ 712. BUD ANDERSON(P)
- ☐ 712. GREG BIERCEVICZ(P)
- ☐ 712. BYRON MCLAUGHLIN(P)

TEXAS RANGERS

- 22. MIKE JORGENSEN
- 44. KURT BEVACQUA
- 67. JIM MASON
- 94. LEN BARKER
- 120. JIM SUNDBERG
- 144. SANDY ALOMAR
- 173. JOHN LOWENSTEIN
- 198. JOHNNY GRUBB
- 209. REGGIE CLEVELAND
- 234. TOBY HARRAH
- 260. RICHIE ZISK
- 285. BOBBY BONDS
- 315. JON MATLACK
- 336. BOBBY THOMPSON
- 369. BUMP WILLS
- 391. AL OLIVER
- 442. DOYLE ALEXANDER
- 463. STEVE COMER
- 478. JUAN BENIQUEZ
- 499. TEAM & CORRALES(M)
- 518. JIM UMBARGER
- 539. JOHN ELLIS
- 544. FERGIE JENKINS
- 591. MIKE HARGROVE
- 620. BERT CAMPANERIS
- 657. GEORGE MEDICH
- 691. DOCK ELLIS
- 713. DANNY DARWIN(P)
- 713. PAT PUTNAM(P)
- 713. BILLY SAMPLE(P)

TORONTO BLUE JAYS

- 36. ALAN ASHBY
- 64. TOM UNDERWOOD
- 101. ROY HOWELL
- 131. JIM CLANCY
- 152. RICK CERONE
- 178. ALVIS WOODS
- 182. TIM JOHNSON
- 207. DAVE LEMANCZYK
- 221. JESSE JEFFERSON
- 238. BALOR MOORE
- 239. WILLIE HORTON
- 254. LUIS GOMEZ
- 282. TEAM & HARTSFIELD(M)
- 293. JERRY GARVIN
- 329. JOE COLEMAN
- 341. WILLIE UPSHAW
- 380. JOHN MAYBERRY
- 392. DOUG AULT
- 462. OTTO VELEZ
- 492. BOB BAILOR
- 521. SAM EWING
- 542. RICK BOSETTI
- 588. TOM MURPHY
- 608. DAVE MCKAY
- 632. DON KIRKWOOD
- 688. MIKE WILLIS
- 714. VICTOR CRUZ(P)
- 714. D. PAT KELLY(P)
- 714. ERNIE WHITT(P)

1980 TOPPS (726) 2 1/2" X 3 1/2"

ATLANTA BRAVES

- 7. MIKE LUM
- 39. ROWLAND OFFICE
- 64. JOE NOLAN
- 87. PEPE FRIAS
- 108. BOB HORNER
- 132. BIFF POCOROBA
- 156. TONY BRIZZOLARA
- 192. TEAM & COX(M)
- 245. PHIL NIEKRO
- 274. DALE MURPHY
- 294. CHARLIE SPIKES
- 309. LARRY MCWILLIAMS
- 326. BO MCLAUGHLIN
- 346. BUDDY SOLOMON
- 355. GARY MATTHEWS
- 384. JOEY MCLAUGHLIN
- 463. JERRY ROYSTER
- 489. PRESTON HANNA
- 504. GENE GARBER
- 528. ADRIAN DEVINE
- 545. JEFF BURROUGHS
- 596. RICK MATULA
- 632. BARRY BONNELL
- 675. BRUCE BENEDICT(FS)
- 675. LARRY BRADFORD(FS)
- 675. EDDIE MILLER(FS)

BALTIMORE ORIOLES

- 10. DENNY MARTINEZ
- 37. KIKO GARCIA
- 65. AL BUMBRY
- 91. RICK DEMPSEY
- 102. RICH DAUER
- 119. SAMMY STEWART
- 160. EDDIE MURRAY
- 188. TERRY CROWLEY
- 211. DAVE SKAGGS
- 237. SCOTT MCGREGOR
- 262. BENNY AYALA
- 287. JOHN LOWENSTEIN
- 314. TIM STODDARD
- 340. KEN SINGLETON
- 367. BILLY SMITH
- 404. TEAM & WEAVER(M)
- 425. MARK BELANGER
- 490. LEE MAY
- 517. DON STANHOUSE
- 543. H. PAT KELLY
- 568. GARY ROENICKE
- 590. JIM PALMER
- 615. DOUG DECINCES
- 640. MIKE FLANAGAN
- 661. MARK COREY(FS)
- 661. DAVE FORD(FS)
- 661. WAYNE KRENCHICKI(FS)
- 688. STEVE STONE
- 706. TIPPY MARTINEZ

BOSTON RED SOX

- 15. BILL CAMPBELL
- 40. CARLTON FISK
- 63. BOB STANLEY

- 81. TED SIZEMORE
- 110. FRED LYNN
- 128. TOM BURGMEIER
- 155. JERRY REMY
- 184. STEVE RENKO
- 200. JIM RICE
- 271. DICK DRAGO
- 320. DENNIS ECKERSLEY
- 349. JACK BROHAMER
- 376. GARY ALLENSON
- 405. DWIGHT EVANS
- 413. ALLEN RIPLEY
- 420. BUTCH HOBSON
- 455. MIKE TORREZ
- 480. BOB WATSON
- 524. JIM C. WRIGHT
- 549. LARRY WOLFE
- 576. JIM DWYER
- 597. TOM POQUETTE
- 618. BOB MONTGOMERY
- 645. RICK BURLESON
- 662. JOEL FINCH(FS)
- 662. MIKE O'BERRY(FS)
- 662. CHUCK RAINEY(FS)
- 689. TEAM & ZIMMER(M)
- 720. CARL YASTRZEMSKI

CALIFORNIA ANGELS

- 20. DAN FORD
- 48. RICK MILLER
- 68. LARRY HARLOW
- 105. FRANK TANANA
- 183. JIM ANDERSON
- 214. TEAM & FREGOSI(M)
- 239. DON AASE
- 253. JOHN MONTAGUE
- 263. DAVE LAROCHE
- 285. DON BAYLOR
- 312. MIKE BARLOW
- 337. CARNEY LANSFORD
- 368. WILLIE AIKENS
- 402. MERV RETTENMUND
- 423. DAVE FROST
- 454. TOM DONOHUE
- 505. BERT CAMPANERIS
- 529. JIM BARR
- 556. JOE RUDI
- 580. NOLAN RYAN
- 602. BRIAN DOWNING
- 621. BOB GRICH
- 638. MARK CLEAR
- 658. CHRIS KNAPP
- 663. RALPH BOTTING(FS)
- 663. BOB CLARK(FS)
- 663. DICKIE THON(FS)
- 700. ROD CAREW

CHICAGO CUBS

- 17. BRUCE SUTTER
- 54. DENNIS LAMP
- 103. BILL CAUDILL
- 135. BILL BUCKNER
- 153. TIM BLACKWELL
- 175. RICK REUSCHEL
- 240. DAVE KINGMAN
- 298. KEN HOLTZMAN
- 232. MICK KELLEHER
- 343. MIKE VAIL
- 381. TEAM & GOMEZ(M)
- 398. BARRY FOOTE
- 431. MIKE KRUKOW
- 452. STEVE DILLARD
- 472. WILLIE HERNANDEZ
- 493. JERRY MARTIN
- 514. STEVE ONTIVEROS
- 523. KEN HENDERSON
- 541. MIGUEL DILONE
- 574. SCOT THOMPSON
- 594. DICK TIDROW
- 628. DOUG CAPILLA
- 639. LARRY BIITTNER
- 676. DAVE GEISEL(FS)
- 676. STEVE MACKO(FS)
- 676. KARL PAGEL(FS)
- 691. IVAN DEJESUS
- 716. LYNN MCGLOTHEN

CHICAGO WHITE SOX

- ☐ 36. RUSTY TORRES
- ☐ 72. FRED HOWARD
- ☐ 83. STEVE TROUT
- ☐ 107. FRANCISCO BARRIOS
- ☐ 112. TEAM & LARUSSA(M)
- ☐ 138. ROSS BAUMGARTEN
- ☐ 164. GREG PRYOR
- ☐ 186. JUNIOR MOORE
- ☐ 242. LAMAR JOHNSON
- ☐ 272. RALPH GARR
- ☐ 291. RANDY SCARBERY
- ☐ 322. CLAUDELL WASHINGTON
- ☐ 347. HARRY CHAPPAS
- ☐ 379. KEVIN BELL
- ☐ 399. MIKE PROLY
- ☐ 412. THAD BOSLEY
- ☐ 442. JORGE ORTA
- ☐ 466. MIKE SQUIRES
- ☐ 487. WAYNE NORDHAGEN
- ☐ 502. RICH WORTHAM
- ☐ 522. JIM MORRISON
- ☐ 552. BILL NAHORODNY
- ☐ 575. KEN KRAVEC
- ☐ 589. CHET LEMON
- ☐ 608. ALAN BANNISTER
- ☐ 647. MILT MAY
- ☐ 664. MIKE COLBERN(FS)
- ☐ 664. GUY HOFFMAN(FS)
- ☐ 664. DEWEY ROBINSON(FS)
- ☐ 702. ED FARMER

CINCINNATI REDS

- ☐ 21. MANNY SARMIENTO
- ☐ 47. BILL BONHAM
- ☐ 73. DAVE COLLINS
- ☐ 100. JOHNNY BENCH
- ☐ 126. DAVE TOMLIN
- ☐ 149. TOM HUME
- ☐ 174. RAY KNIGHT
- ☐ 199. MIKE LACOSS
- ☐ 220. DAVE CONCEPCION
- ☐ 258. PAUL MOSKAU
- ☐ 281. PAUL BLAIR
- ☐ 325. DAN DRIESSEN
- ☐ 354. RICK AUERBACH
- ☐ 377. JUNIOR KENNEDY
- ☐ 400. GEORGE FOSTER
- ☐ 419. VIC CORRELL
- ☐ 449. DOUG BAIR
- ☐ 475. CESAR GERONIMO
- ☐ 500. TOM SEAVER
- ☐ 516. HECTOR CRUZ
- ☐ 550. KEN GRIFFEY
- ☐ 606. TEAM & MCNAMARA(M)
- ☐ 622. MARIO SOTO
- ☐ 650. JOE MORGAN
- ☐ 677. ART DEFREITES(FS)
- ☐ 677. FRANK PASTORE(FS)
- ☐ 677. HARRY SPILMAN(FS)
- ☐ 714. FRED NORMAN

CLEVELAND INDIANS

- ☐ 13. RON PRUITT
- ☐ 38. DAN SPILLNER
- ☐ 74. SID MONGE
- ☐ 99. VICTOR CRUZ
- ☐ 122. DAVE ROSELLO
- ☐ 141. GARY ALEXANDER
- ☐ 168. RICK WAITS
- ☐ 198. DELL ALSTON
- ☐ 208. WAYNE CAGE
- ☐ 222. RON HASSEY
- ☐ 227. LEN BARKER
- ☐ 252. TED COX
- ☐ 276. TOM VERYZER
- ☐ 308. MIKE HARGROVE
- ☐ 333. JIM NORRIS
- ☐ 361. WAYNE GARLAND
- ☐ 388. MIKE PAXTON
- ☐ 410. BOBBY BONDS
- ☐ 429. DUANE KUIPER
- ☐ 451. TEAM & GARCIA(M)
- ☐ 483. BO DIAZ
- ☐ 511. ERIC WILKINS
- ☐ 534. ANDRE THORNTON
- ☐ 564. RICK MANNING
- ☐ 612. CLIFF JOHNSON

- ☐ 636. TOBY HARRAH
- ☐ 665. LARRY ANDERSEN(FS)
- ☐ 665. BOBBY CUELLAR(FS)
- ☐ 665. SANDY WIHTOL(FS)
- ☐ 697. DAVID CLYDE
- ☐ 725. RICK WISE

DETROIT TIGERS

- ☐ 29. MARK WAGNER
- ☐ 59. EDDY PUTMAN
- ☐ 80. RON LEFLORE
- ☐ 101. AURELIO LOPEZ
- ☐ 123. LYNN JONES
- ☐ 150. JASON THOMPSON
- ☐ 176. CHAMP SUMMER
- ☐ 196. LANCE PARRISH
- ☐ 216. PHIL MANKOWSKI
- ☐ 232. ALAN TRAMMELL
- ☐ 251. KIP YOUNG
- ☐ 269. DAVE TOBIK
- ☐ 288. DAVE ROZEMA
- ☐ 315. STEVE KEMP
- ☐ 338. JOHNNY WOCKENFUSS
- ☐ 358. LOU WHITAKER
- ☐ 371. JACK MORRIS
- ☐ 373. DAN PETRY
- ☐ 392. MILT WILCOX
- ☐ 416. TOM BROOKENS
- ☐ 445. MARK FIDRYCH
- ☐ 468. AURELIO RODRIGUEZ
- ☐ 572. JERRY MORALES
- ☐ 603. JACK BILLINGHAM
- ☐ 614. JOHN HILLER
- ☐ 626. TEAM & ANDERSON(M)
- ☐ 666. MIKE CHRIS(FS)
- ☐ 666. AL GREENE(FS)
- ☐ 666. BRUCE ROBBINS(FS)
- ☐ 709. PAT UNDERWOOD

HOUSTON ASTROS

- ☐ 11. JIMMY SEXTON
- ☐ 50. J.R. RICHARD
- ☐ 69. RICK WILLIAMS
- ☐ 82. TEAM & VIRDON(M)
- ☐ 106. JEFF LEONARD
- ☐ 129. CRAIG REYNOLDS
- ☐ 147. TERRY PUHL
- ☐ 187. ALAN ASHBY
- ☐ 234. VERN RUHLE
- ☐ 247. FRANK RICCELLI
- ☐ 268. RAFAEL LANDESTOY
- ☐ 289. BRUCE BOCHY
- ☐ 306. DENNY WALLING
- ☐ 329. BERT ROBERGE
- ☐ 370. CESAR CEDENO
- ☐ 385. ENOS CABELL
- ☐ 411. FRANK LACORTE
- ☐ 437. JOE NIEKRO
- ☐ 469. RANDY NIEMANN
- ☐ 513. TOM DIXON
- ☐ 554. ART HOWE
- ☐ 571. JOE SAMBITO
- ☐ 593. JESUS ALOU
- ☐ 617. JOAQUIN ANDUJAR
- ☐ 642. KEN FORSCH
- ☐ 678. REGGIE BALDWIN(FS)
- ☐ 678. ALAN KNICELY(FS)
- ☐ 678. PETE LADD(FS)
- ☐ 696. JULIO GONZALEZ
- ☐ 722. JOSE CRUZ

KANSAS CITY ROYALS

- ☐ 9. STEVE BRAUN
- ☐ 26. MARTY PATTIN
- ☐ 45. FRANK WHITE
- ☐ 66. TEAM CARD
- ☐ 98. JERRY TERRELL
- ☐ 130. AMOS OTIS
- ☐ 157. WILLIE WILSON
- ☐ 185. HAL MCRAE
- ☐ 219. STEVE MINGORI
- ☐ 248. JAMIE QUIRK
- ☐ 273. EDUARDO RODRIGUEZ
- ☐ 295. LARRY GURA
- ☐ 330. AL COWENS
- ☐ 360. DARRELL PORTER
- ☐ 389. PETE LACOCK
- ☐ 409. PAUL SPLITTORFF

- ☐ 417. CRAIG CHAMBERLAIN
- ☐ 433. RICH GALE
- ☐ 450. GEORGE BRETT
- ☐ 474. STEVE BUSBY
- ☐ 492. TODD CRUZ
- ☐ 508. U.L. WASHINGTON
- ☐ 525. CLINT HURDLE
- ☐ 547. JOHN WATHAN
- ☐ 565. DENNIS LEONARD
- ☐ 585. AL HRABOSKY
- ☐ 667. RENIE MARTIN(FS)
- ☐ 667. BILL PASCHALL(FS)
- ☐ 667. DAN QUISENBERRY(FS)
- ☐ 705. FREDDIE PATEK

LOS ANGELES DODGERS

- ☐ 23. DERREL THOMAS
- ☐ 51. JOE FERGUSON
- ☐ 75. BILL RUSSELL
- ☐ 104. MANNY MOTA
- ☐ 127. GARY THOMASSON
- ☐ 146. BOB WELCH
- ☐ 170. BURT HOOTON
- ☐ 191. TED MARTINEZ
- ☐ 209. VON JOSHUA
- ☐ 228. JOHNNY OATES
- ☐ 255. DUSTY BAKER
- ☐ 290. STEVE GARVEY
- ☐ 302. TEAM & LASORDA(M)
- ☐ 318. JERRY REUSS
- ☐ 440. DON SUTTON
- ☐ 465. RICK MONDAY
- ☐ 510. RON CEY
- ☐ 521. KEN BRETT
- ☐ 527. DOUG RAU
- ☐ 544. RICK SUTCLIFFE
- ☐ 560. DAVE LOPES
- ☐ 605. TERRY FORSTER
- ☐ 624. LERRIN LAGROW
- ☐ 644. CHARLIE HOUGH
- ☐ 679. JOE BECKWITH(FS)
- ☐ 679. MICKEY HATCHER(FS)
- ☐ 679. DAVE PATTERSON(FS)
- ☐ 695. REGGIE SMITH
- ☐ 726. STEVE YEAGER

MILWAUKEE BREWERS

- ☐ 24. JIM SLATON
- ☐ 53. BEN OGLIVIE
- ☐ 95. CECIL COOPER
- ☐ 109. BILL TRAVERS
- ☐ 131. PAUL MITCHELL
- ☐ 154. LARY SORENSEN
- ☐ 181. MOOSE HAAS
- ☐ 215. SIXTO LEZCANO
- ☐ 243. JERRY AUGUSTINE
- ☐ 265. ROBIN YOUNT
- ☐ 303. BILL CASTRO
- ☐ 327. RAY FOSSE
- ☐ 357. BOB MCCLURE
- ☐ 374. JIM GANTNER
- ☐ 394. REGGIE CLEVELAND
- ☐ 406. PAUL MOLITOR
- ☐ 430. LARRY HISLE
- ☐ 448. JIM WOHLFORD
- ☐ 477. BUCK MARTINEZ
- ☐ 515. MIKE CALDWELL
- ☐ 553. DICK DAVIS
- ☐ 579. CHARLIE MOORE
- ☐ 595. DON MONEY
- ☐ 623. GORMAN THOMAS
- ☐ 659. TEAM & BAMBERGER(M)
- ☐ 668. DANNY BOITANO(FS)
- ☐ 668. WILLIE MUELLER(FS)
- ☐ 668. LENN SAKATA(FS)
- ☐ 711. BOB GALASSO
- ☐ 715. SAL BANDO

MINNESOTA TWINS

- ☐ 18. RON JACKSON
- ☐ 43. BOMBO RIVERA
- ☐ 61. GARY SERUM
- ☐ 88. KEN LANDREAUX
- ☐ 113. GEOFF ZAHN
- ☐ 137. JOHN CASTINO
- ☐ 162. BOB RANDALL
- ☐ 193. DAVE GOLTZ

☐ 218. JOSE MORALES
☐ 238. ROB WILFONG
☐ 256. ROGER ERICKSON
☐ 275. JERRY KOOSMAN
☐ 304. BUTCH WYNEGAR
☐ 328. TEAM & MAUCH(M)
☐ 362. DANNY GOODWIN
☐ 386. DARRELL JACKSON
☐ 403. PETE REDFERN
☐ 432. WILLIE NORWOOD
☐ 453. MIKE BACSIK
☐ 471. HOSKEN POWELL
☐ 503. MIKE CUBBAGE
☐ 570. ROY SMALLEY
☐ 604. GLENN ADAMS
☐ 634. GLENN BORGMANN
☐ 657. DAVE EDWARDS
☐ 669. DAN GRAHAM(FS)
☐ 669. RICK SOFIELD(FS)
☐ 669. GARY WARD(FS)
☐ 721. PAUL HARTZELL

MONTREAL EXPOS

☐ 14. DAVE CASH
☐ 42. DAVE PALMER
☐ 70. GARY CARTER
☐ 97. BILL LEE
☐ 125. TONY PEREZ
☐ 180. WARREN CROMARTIE
☐ 235. ANDRE DAWSON
☐ 267. DAN SCHATZEDER
☐ 293. ELIAS SOSA
☐ 319. CHRIS SPEIER
☐ 345. LARRY PARRISH
☐ 375. ROSS GRIMSLEY
☐ 395. ELLIS VALENTINE
☐ 415. BILL ATKINSON
☐ 427. TOM HUTTON
☐ 446. DUFFY DYER
☐ 479. TEAM & WILLIAMS(M)
☐ 497. JIM MASON
☐ 520. STEVE ROGERS
☐ 539. RUDY MAY
☐ 559. DALE MURRAY
☐ 578. SCOTT SANDERSON
☐ 607. WOODIE FRYMAN
☐ 653. STAN BAHNSEN
☐ 660. RUSTY STAUB
☐ 680. TONY BERNAZARD(FS)
☐ 680. RANDY MILLER(FS)
☐ 680. JOHN TAMARGO(FS)
☐ 712. RODNEY SCOTT
☐ 724. JERRY WHITE

NEW YORK METS

☐ 8. CRAIG SWAN
☐ 25. LEE MAZZILLI
☐ 58. DOUG FLYNN
☐ 76. JOHN STEARNS
☐ 94. NEIL ALLEN
☐ 117. DOCK ELLIS
☐ 151. TOM HAUSMAN
☐ 172. RON HODGES
☐ 189. KEVIN KOBEL
☐ 259. TEAM & TORRE(M)
☐ 299. STEVE HENDERSON
☐ 331. RICH HEBNER
☐ 353. ANDY HASSLER
☐ 364. RAY BURRIS

☐ 372. JOEL YOUNGBLOOD
☐ 401. PETE FALCONE
☐ 428. PAT ZACHRY
☐ 456. FRANK TAVERAS
☐ 478. GIL FLORES
☐ 509. ED GLYNN
☐ 512. JOSE CARDENAL
☐ 537. ALEX TREVINO
☐ 567. SKIP LOCKWOOD
☐ 619. SERGIO FERRER
☐ 633. BOB APODACA
☐ 641. ED KRANEPOOL
☐ 654. BRUCE BOISCLAIR
☐ 681. DAN NORMAN(FS)
☐ 681. JESSE OROSCO(FS)
☐ 681. MIKE SCOTT(FS)
☐ 707. ELLIOTT MADDOX

NEW YORK YANKEES

☐ 16. JERRY NARRON
☐ 35. LUIS TIANT
☐ 60. BUCKY DENT
☐ 89. DON HOOD
☐ 114. JUAN BENIQUEZ
☐ 140. RICH GOSSAGE
☐ 159. KEN CLAY
☐ 179. RON DAVIS
☐ 225. LOU PINIELLA
☐ 250. JIM KAAT
☐ 278. JIM SPENCER
☐ 300. RON GUIDRY
☐ 334. JIM BEATTIE
☐ 365. BOBBY MURCER
☐ 387. FRED STANLEY
☐ 414. GEORGE SCOTT
☐ 424. TEAM & HOWSER(M)
☐ 435. DON GULLETT
☐ 460. WILLIE RANDOLPH
☐ 555. ED FIGUEROA
☐ 582. BRAIN DOYLE
☐ 600. REGGIE JACKSON
☐ 625. CHRIS CHAMBLISS
☐ 648. ROY WHITE
☐ 670. BOBBY BROWN(FS)
☐ 670. BRAD GULDEN(FS)
☐ 670. DARRYL JONES(FS)
☐ 690. TOMMY JOHN
☐ 698. OSCAR GAMBLE
☐ 710. GRAIG NETTLES

OAKLAND A'S

☐ 34. JEFF NEWMAN
☐ 49. MARIO GUERRERO
☐ 86. DAVE HAMILTON
☐ 96. TEAM & MARSHALL(M)
☐ 134. MATT KEOUGH
☐ 158. ROB PICCIOLO
☐ 177. DAVE HEAVERLO
☐ 231. STEVE MCCATTY
☐ 261. DAVE CHALK
☐ 284. LARRY MURRAY
☐ 301. MIKE EDWARDS
☐ 316. BOB LACEY
☐ 341. JIM ESSIAN
☐ 363. WAYNE GROSS
☐ 391. TONY ARMAS
☐ 438. DAVE REVERING
☐ 461. DWAYNE MURPHY
☐ 482. RICKEY HENDERSON
☐ 494. CRAIG MINETTO
☐ 546. RICK LANGFORD
☐ 562. JOE WALLIS
☐ 586. MITCHELL PAGE
☐ 599. MIKE NORRIS
☐ 629. JIM TODD
☐ 671. DEREK BRYANT(FS)
☐ 671. BRIAN KINGMAN(FS)
☐ 671. MIKE MORGAN(FS)
☐ 687. MIKE HEATH
☐ 717. MICKEY KLUTTS

PHILADELPHIA PHILLIES

☐ 27. DEL UNSER
☐ 52. WARREN BRUSSTAR
☐ 90. MANNY TRILLO
☐ 120. GREG LUZINSKI
☐ 136. DICK RUTHVEN
☐ 161. LARRY CHRISTENSON

☐ 178. TIM MCCARVER
☐ 210. STEVE CARLTON
☐ 270. MIKE SCHMIDT
☐ 296. DAVE RADER
☐ 317. MIKE ANDERSON
☐ 344. RANDY LERCH
☐ 380. GARRY MADDOX
☐ 421. DOUG BIRD
☐ 447. NINO ESPINOSA
☐ 470. BOB BOONE
☐ 495. BAKE MCBRIDE
☐ 526. TEAM & GREEN(M)
☐ 540. PETE ROSE
☐ 566. BUD HARRELSON
☐ 609. RON REED
☐ 630. LARRY BOWA
☐ 655. TUG MCGRAW
☐ 682. RAMON AVILES(FS)
☐ 682. DICKIE NOLES(FS)
☐ 682. KEVIN SAUCIER(FS)
☐ 692. RAWLY EASTWICK
☐ 718. GREG GROSS

PITTSBURGH PIRATES

☐ 28. BRUCE KISON
☐ 55. BILL MADLOCK
☐ 71. JOHN MILNER
☐ 92. RICK RHODEN
☐ 118. PHIL GARNER
☐ 148. MANNY SANGUILLEN
☐ 165. OMAR MORENO
☐ 194. MIKE EASLER
☐ 212. DAVE A. ROBERTS
☐ 229. JIM BIBBY
☐ 246. TIM FOLI
☐ 264. BILL ROBINSON
☐ 292. DALE BERRA
☐ 310. DAVE PARKER
☐ 332. ENRIQUE ROMO
☐ 383. ED OTT
☐ 426. GRANT JACKSON
☐ 457. BERT BLYLEVEN
☐ 501. RENNIE STENNETT
☐ 519. STEVE NICOSIA
☐ 536. LEE LACY
☐ 542. JOE COLEMAN
☐ 551. TEAM & TANNER(M)
☐ 573. KENT TEKULVE
☐ 610. WILLIE STARGELL
☐ 635. JOHN CANDELARIA
☐ 683. DORIAN BOYLAND(FS)
☐ 683. ALBERTO LOIS(FS)
☐ 683. HERRY SAFERIGHT(FS)
☐ 694. JIM ROOKER
☐ 719. DON ROBINSON

ST. LOUIS CARDINALS

☐ 33. TONY SCOTT
☐ 57. PETE VUCKOVICH
☐ 85. TED SIMMONS
☐ 139. DANE IORG
☐ 152. JOHN FULGHAM
☐ 163. STEVE SWISHER
☐ 182. KEN REITZ
☐ 223. BOB SYKES
☐ 244. TEAM & BOYER(M)
☐ 266. BERNIE CARBO
☐ 286. DAROLD KNOWLES
☐ 321. KEITH HERNANDEZ
☐ 350. GEORGE HENDRICK
☐ 378. JERRY MUMPHREY
☐ 397. ROY THOMAS
☐ 418. ROGER FREED
☐ 439. MIKE PHILLIPS
☐ 464. JOHN DENNY
☐ 486. MIKE TYSON
☐ 496. SILVIO MARTINEZ
☐ 535. BOB FORSCH
☐ 563. WILL MCEANEY
☐ 569. TERRY KENNEDY
☐ 587. GARRY TEMPLETON
☐ 601. BUDDY SCHULTZ
☐ 631. MARK LITTELL
☐ 684. GEORGE FRAZIER(FS)
☐ 684. TOM HERR(FS)
☐ 684. DAN O'BRIEN(FS)
☐ 701. KEN OBERKFELL

1980 Topps

OZZIE SMITH

SAN DIEGO PADRES

- [ ] 31. JAY JOHNSTONE
- [ ] 44. BILL FAHEY
- [ ] 79. BOB OWCHINKO
- [ ] 133. JERRY TURNER
- [ ] 171. FERNANDO GONZALEZ
- [ ] 230. DAVE WINFIELD
- [ ] 254. PAUL DADE
- [ ] 280. GAYLORD PERRY
- [ ] 305. RANDY JONES
- [ ] 339. JOHN D'ACQUISTO
- [ ] 352. DAN BRIGGS
- [ ] 356. TEAM & COLEMAN(M)
- [ ] 393. OZZIE SMITH
- [ ] 436. BILLY ALMON
- [ ] 459. MICKEY LOLICH
- [ ] 476. BOB SHIRLEY
- [ ] 491. STEVE MURA
- [ ] 531. ERIC RASMUSSEN
- [ ] 557. MARK LEE
- [ ] 584. KURT BEVACQUA
- [ ] 598. FRED KENDALL
- [ ] 616. GENE RICHARDS
- [ ] 651. ROLLIE FINGERS
- [ ] 685. TIM FLANNERY(FS)
- [ ] 685. BRIAN GREER(FS)
- [ ] 685. JIM WILHELM(FS)
- [ ] 704. GENE TENACE
- [ ] 708. BOB TOLAN

SAN FRANCISCO GIANTS

- [ ] 12. JOHN CURTIS
- [ ] 30. VIDA BLUE
- [ ] 62. MIKE IVIE
- [ ] 84. GARY LAVELLE
- [ ] 111. BOB KNEPPER
- [ ] 145. DARRELL EVANS
- [ ] 167. JACK CLARK
- [ ] 195. JOHN MONTEFUSCO
- [ ] 217. ED HALICKI
- [ ] 236. MARC HILL
- [ ] 257. LARRY HERNDON
- [ ] 279. ROB ANDREWS
- [ ] 311. ROGER METZGER
- [ ] 335. WILLIE MCCOVEY
- [ ] 359. RANDY MOFFITT
- [ ] 408. BILL NORTH
- [ ] 434. JOHNNIE LEMASTER
- [ ] 462. MIKE SADEK
- [ ] 499. TEAM & BRISTOL(M)
- [ ] 538. JOE STRAIN
- [ ] 561. EDDIE WHITSON
- [ ] 588. GREG MINTON
- [ ] 627. PEDRO BORBON
- [ ] 649. TOM GRIFFIN
- [ ] 686. GREG JOHNSTON(FS)
- [ ] 686. DENNIS LITTLEJOHN(FS)
- [ ] 686. PHIL NASTU(FS)
- [ ] 713. TERRY WHITFIELD

SEATTLE MARINERS

- [ ] 32. JULIO CRUZ
- [ ] 56. BOBBY VALENTINE
- [ ] 78. RUPPERT JONES
- [ ] 116. LARRY COX
- [ ] 143. BRUCE BOCHTE

- [ ] 166. GLENN ABBOTT
- [ ] 197. BYRON MCLAUGHLIN
- [ ] 226. BILL STEIN
- [ ] 282. TEAM & JOHNSON(M)
- [ ] 307. RICK HONEYCUTT
- [ ] 342. ODELL JONES
- [ ] 366. ROB DRESSLER
- [ ] 396. DAN MEYER
- [ ] 422. LARRY MILBOURNE
- [ ] 443. MIKE PARROTT
- [ ] 481. TOM PACIOREK
- [ ] 507. LEON ROBERTS
- [ ] 532. WILLIE HORTON
- [ ] 583. BOB STINSON
- [ ] 613. RANDY STEIN
- [ ] 637. JOE SIMPSON
- [ ] 652. MARIO MENDOZA
- [ ] 672. CHARLIE BEAMON(FS)
- [ ] 672. RODNEY CRAIG(FS)
- [ ] 672. RAFAEL VASQUEZ(FS)
- [ ] 699. FLOYD BANNISTER
- [ ] 723. SHANE RAWLEY

TEXAS RANGERS

- [ ] 22. PAT PUTNAM
- [ ] 41. TEAM & CORRALES(M)
- [ ] 67. DOYLE ALEXANDER
- [ ] 93. DAVE W. ROBERTS
- [ ] 115. SPARKY LYLE
- [ ] 144. STEVE COMER
- [ ] 173. JOHN HENRY JOHNSON
- [ ] 190. BUDDY BELL
- [ ] 213. MIKE JORGENSEN
- [ ] 224. WILLIE MONTANEZ
- [ ] 233. LARUE WASHINGTON
- [ ] 260. AL OLIVER
- [ ] 283. JOHN ELLIS
- [ ] 313. JOHNNY GRUBB
- [ ] 336. GEORGE MEDICH
- [ ] 369. JIM KERN
- [ ] 390. FERGIE JENKINS
- [ ] 441. ERIC SODERHOLM
- [ ] 458. BILLY SAMPLE
- [ ] 473. BUMP WILLS
- [ ] 485. MICKEY RIVERS
- [ ] 498. DANNY DARWIN
- [ ] 518. NELSON NORMAN
- [ ] 530. JIM SUNDBERG
- [ ] 548. DAVE RAJSICH
- [ ] 592. JON MATLACK
- [ ] 620. RICHIE ZISK
- [ ] 656. LARVELL BLANKS
- [ ] 673. BRIAN ALLARD(FS)
- [ ] 673. JERRY DON GLEATON(FS)
- [ ] 673. GREG MAHLBERG(FS)

TORONTO BLUE JAYS

- [ ] 19. BALOR MOORE
- [ ] 46. RICO CARTY
- [ ] 77. DAVE STIEB
- [ ] 124. DAVE LEMANCZYK
- [ ] 142. PHIL HUFFMAN
- [ ] 169. LUIS GOMEZ
- [ ] 221. JOE CANNON
- [ ] 249. JIM CLANCY
- [ ] 277. RICK BOSETTI
- [ ] 297. TIM JOHNSON
- [ ] 324. TOM UNDERWOOD
- [ ] 351. BOB DAVIS
- [ ] 382. DAVE FREISLEBEN
- [ ] 407. TONY SOLAITA
- [ ] 444. ALVIS WOODS
- [ ] 467. JESSE JEFFERSON
- [ ] 488. ROY HOWELL
- [ ] 506. TOM BUSKEY
- [ ] 558. ALFREDO GRIFFIN
- [ ] 577. TEAM CARD
- [ ] 581. BOB BAILOR
- [ ] 591. RICK CERONE
- [ ] 611. JERRY GARVIN
- [ ] 643. JOHN MAYBERRY
- [ ] 674. BUTCH EDGE(FS)
- [ ] 674. D. PAT KELLY(FS)
- [ ] 674. TED WILBORN(FS)
- [ ] 693. CRAIG KUSICK
- [ ] 703. OTTO VELEZ

1981 TOPPS (726)
2 1/2" X 3 1/2"

OUTFIELD
WHITE SOX
CHET LEMON

ATLANTA BRAVES

- [ ] 20. JEFF BURROUGHS
- [ ] 44. LARRY MCWILLIAMS
- [ ] 64. BRIAN ASSELSTINE
- [ ] 87. RICK CAMP
- [ ] 108. BRUCE BENEDICT
- [ ] 132. TOMMY BOGGS
- [ ] 155. CHRIS CHAMBLISS
- [ ] 192. TERRY HARPER(FS)
- [ ] 192. ED MILLER(FS)
- [ ] 192. RAFAEL RAMIREZ(FS)
- [ ] 247. GLENN HUBBARD
- [ ] 268. JERRY ROYSTER
- [ ] 296. BILL NAHORODNY
- [ ] 307. GENE GARBER
- [ ] 326. BIFF POCOROBA
- [ ] 355. BOB HORNER
- [ ] 387. PHIL NIEKRO
- [ ] 457. MIKE LUM
- [ ] 477. LUIS GOMEZ
- [ ] 504. DALE MURPHY
- [ ] 528. GARY MATTHEWS
- [ ] 542. LARRY BRADFORD
- [ ] 594. PRESTON HANNA
- [ ] 611. RICK MATULA
- [ ] 636. AL HRABOSKY
- [ ] 675. TEAM & COX(M)
- [ ] 708. DOYLE ALEXANDER

BALTIMORE ORIOLES

- [ ] 10. MIKE FLANAGAN
- [ ] 37. GARY ROENICKE
- [ ] 65. SCOTT MCGREGOR
- [ ] 91. TIM STODDARD
- [ ] 101. BENNY AYALA
- [ ] 119. TIPPY MARTINEZ
- [ ] 161. DAN GRAHAM
- [ ] 188. DOUG DECINCES
- [ ] 210. JIM PALMER
- [ ] 262. SAMMY STEWART
- [ ] 287. LENN SAKATA
- [ ] 314. RICH DAUER
- [ ] 367. DENNY MARTINEZ
- [ ] 399. MIKE BODDICKER(FS)
- [ ] 399. MARK COREY(FS)
- [ ] 399. FLOYD RAYFORD(FS)
- [ ] 425. AL BUMBRY
- [ ] 490. EDDIE MURRAY
- [ ] 520. STEVE STONE
- [ ] 543. TERRY CROWLEY
- [ ] 570. KEN SINGLETON
- [ ] 591. JOHN LOWENSTEIN
- [ ] 615. RICK DEMPSEY
- [ ] 641. MARK BELANGER
- [ ] 661. TEAM & WEAVER(M)
- [ ] 688. KIKO GARCIA
- [ ] 706. DAVE FORD

BOSTON RED SOX

- [ ] 14. JOHN TUDOR
- [ ] 38. WIN REMMERSWAAL
- [ ] 63. STEVE RENKO
- [ ] 81. DAVE STAPLETON

☐ 110. CARL YASTRZEMSKI
☐ 128. GARY ALLENSON
☐ 153. TOM POQUETTE
☐ 184. JIM DWYER
☐ 199. CHUCK RAINEY
☐ 233. SKIP LOCKWOOD
☐ 275. DWIGHT EVANS
☐ 320. TOM BURGMEIER
☐ 349. GLENN HOFFMAN
☐ 378. DAVE RADER
☐ 396. BILL CAMPBELL
☐ 421. BOB STANLEY
☐ 455. RICK BURLESON
☐ 480. CARLTON FISK
☐ 500. JIM RICE
☐ 525. MIKE TORREZ
☐ 549. JERRY REMY
☐ 575. TONY PEREZ
☐ 595. BUTCH HOBSON
☐ 620. DENNIS ECKERSLEY
☐ 647. DICK DRAGO
☐ 662. TEAM & HOUK(M)
☐ 689. BRUCE HURST(FS)
☐ 689. KEITH MACWHORTER(FS)
☐ 689. REID NICHOLS(FS)
☐ 720. FRED LYNN

CALIFORNIA ANGELS

☐ 12. MARK CLEAR
☐ 48. DAVE SKAGGS
☐ 69. ED HALICKI
☐ 100. ROD CAREW
☐ 121. LARRY HARLOW
☐ 182. BOB GRICH
☐ 209. DICKIE THON
☐ 214. RALPH BOTTING(FS)
☐ 214. JIM DORSEY(FS)
☐ 214. JOHN HARRIS(FS)
☐ 227. FRED MARTINEZ
☐ 239. RICK MILLER
☐ 263. BRIAN DOWNING
☐ 286. DAVE FROST
☐ 288. BOB CLARK
☐ 311. FREDDIE PATEK
☐ 340. BRUCE KISON
☐ 369. FRANK TANANA
☐ 391. DAVE LEMANCZYK
☐ 410. BERT CAMPANERIS
☐ 422. DAN FORD
☐ 454. ANDY HASSLER
☐ 505. JASON THOMPSON
☐ 529. DAVE LAROCHE
☐ 557. CHRIS KNAPP
☐ 580. DON BAYLOR
☐ 601. DON AASE
☐ 621. TOM DONOHUE
☐ 639. CARNEY LANSFORD
☐ 652. JOHN MONTAGUE
☐ 663. TEAM & FREGOSI(M)
☐ 701. JOE RUDI
☐ 717. JIM BARR

PITCHER
CUBS
MIKE
KRUKOW
TOPPS

CHICAGO CUBS

☐ 17. CLIFF JOHNSON
☐ 54. IVAN DEJESUS
☐ 78. STEVE DILLARD
☐ 103. JERRY MARTIN
☐ 136. DOUG CAPILLA
☐ 176. MIKE KRUKOW

☐ 238. WILLIE HERNANDEZ
☐ 294. MIKE TYSON
☐ 331. DENNIS LAMP
☐ 352. DICK TIDROW
☐ 381. CARLOS LEZCANO(FS)
☐ 381. STEVE MACKO(FS)
☐ 381. RANDY MARTZ(FS)
☐ 395. SCOT THOMPSON
☐ 429. MICK KELLEHER
☐ 450. DAVE KINGMAN
☐ 471. MIKE VAIL
☐ 492. BARRY FOOTE
☐ 514. GEORGE RILEY
☐ 533. JESUS FIGUEROA
☐ 553. TIM BLACKWELL
☐ 574. BILL CAUDILL
☐ 590. BRUCE SUTTER
☐ 609. LYNN MCGLOTHEN
☐ 625. BILL BUCKNER
☐ 645. RICK REUSCHEL
☐ 676. TEAM & AMALFITANO(M)
☐ 692. LENNY RANDLE
☐ 718. LARRY BIITTNER

CHICAGO WHITE SOX

☐ 36. ED FARMER
☐ 67. KEN KRAVEC
☐ 83. MIKE PROLY
☐ 107. RICH WORTHAM
☐ 112. RUSTY KUNTZ(FS)
☐ 112. FRAN MULLINS(FS)
☐ 112. LEO SUTHERLAND(FS)
☐ 138. RICH DOTSON
☐ 164. LAMARR HOYT
☐ 186. WAYNE NORDHAGEN
☐ 242. CHET LEMON
☐ 272. BRUCE KIMM
☐ 292. MIKE SQUIRES
☐ 323. JIM MORRISON
☐ 347. HAROLD BAINES
☐ 398. ROSS BAUMGARTEN
☐ 412. BRITT BURNS
☐ 442. RON PRUITT
☐ 466. BOB MOLINARO
☐ 487. DEWEY ROBINSON
☐ 522. MIKE COLBERN
☐ 552. STEVE TROUT
☐ 571. TODD CRUZ
☐ 589. LAMAR JOHNSON
☐ 608. GREG PRYOR
☐ 646. MARVIS FOLEY
☐ 664. TEAM & LARUSSA(M)
☐ 716. GLENN BORGMANN

CINCINNATI REDS

☐ 21. RON OESTER
☐ 52. HECTOR CRUZ
☐ 73. DOUG BAIR
☐ 94. HARRY SPILMAN
☐ 126. CHARLIE LEIBRANDT
☐ 149. JOE NOLAN
☐ 175. DAVE COLLINS
☐ 200. GEORGE FOSTER
☐ 220. TOM SEAVER
☐ 258. JOE PRICE
☐ 280. KEN GRIFFEY
☐ 325. RAY KNIGHT
☐ 354. MARIO SOTO
☐ 375. DAVE CONCEPCION
☐ 390. CESAR GERONIMO
☐ 419. TOM HUME
☐ 447. JUNIOR KENNEDY
☐ 474. MIKE LACOSS
☐ 499. FRANK PASTORE
☐ 521. SAM MEJIAS
☐ 546. PAUL MOSKAU
☐ 600. JOHNNY BENCH
☐ 606. BRUCE BERENYI(FS)
☐ 606. GEOFF COMBE(FS)
☐ 606. PAUL HOUSEHOLDER(FS)
☐ 628. VIC CORRELL
☐ 655. DAN DRIESSEN
☐ 677. TEAM & MCNAMARA(M)
☐ 712. BILL BONHAM

CLEVELAND INDIANS

☐ 13. JOE CHARBONEAU
☐ 39. TOM VERYZER
☐ 74. MIKE HARGROVE

☐ 99. ERIC WILKINS
☐ 122. JOHN DENNY
☐ 141. MIGUEL DILONE
☐ 170. ROSS GRIMSLEY
☐ 198. JERRY DYBZINSKI
☐ 222. JORGE ORTA
☐ 252. VICTOR CRUZ
☐ 276. DAN SPILLNER
☐ 308. RICK MANNING
☐ 333. SID MONGE
☐ 362. BO DIAZ
☐ 388. ANDRE THORNTON
☐ 416. GARY ALEXANDER
☐ 432. LEN BARKER
☐ 451. CHRIS BANDO(FS)
☐ 451. TOM BRENNAN(FS)
☐ 451. SANDY WIHTOL(FS)
☐ 462. JACK BROHAMER
☐ 511. WAYNE GARLAND
☐ 536. BOB OWCHINKO
☐ 564. RON HASSEY
☐ 612. DUANE KUIPER
☐ 632. ALAN BANNISTER
☐ 665. TEAM & GARCIA(M)
☐ 697. RICK WAITS
☐ 721. TOBY HARRAH

DETROIT TIGERS

☐ 27. CHAMP SUMMERS
☐ 59. DAN PETRY
☐ 79. BRUCE ROBBINS
☐ 102. DAVE TOBIK
☐ 123. AL COWENS
☐ 150. MARK FIDRYCH
☐ 177. RICK PETERS
☐ 196. DUFFY DYER
☐ 217. RICH HEBNER
☐ 234. LOU WHITAKER
☐ 251. TOM BROOKENS
☐ 273. STAN PAPI
☐ 291. AURELIO LOPEZ
☐ 315. KIRK GIBSON
☐ 337. LYNN JONES
☐ 358. MARK WAGNER
☐ 373. PAT UNDERWOOD
☐ 392. LANCE PARRISH
☐ 417. DAN SCHATZEDER
☐ 448. TIM CORCORAN
☐ 468. JOHNNY WOCKENFUSS
☐ 572. JACK MORRIS
☐ 593. STEVE KEMP
☐ 614. DAVE ROZEMA
☐ 626. DAVE STEFFEN(FS)
☐ 626. JERRY UJDUR(FS)
☐ 626. ROGER WEAVER(FS)
☐ 658. MILT WILCOX
☐ 666. TEAM & ANDERSON(M)
☐ 709. ALAN TRAMMELL

HOUSTON ASTROS

☐ 45. ENOS CABELL
☐ 82. DANNY HEEP(FS)
☐ 82. ALAN KNICELY(FS)
☐ 82. BOBBY SPROWL(FS)
☐ 105. JOSE CRUZ
☐ 129. ART HOWE
☐ 148. RANDY NIEMANN
☐ 172. GARY WOODS
☐ 190. CESAR CEDENO
☐ 240. NOLAN RYAN
☐ 253. DAVE BERGMAN
☐ 269. KEN FORSCH
☐ 313. LUIS PUJOLS
☐ 329. JOAQUIN ANDUJAR
☐ 350. J.R. RICHARD
☐ 385. JOE SAMBITO
☐ 411. TERRY PUHL
☐ 439. DENNY WALLING
☐ 469. JEFF LEONARD
☐ 491. GORDY PLADSON
☐ 513. FRANK LACORTE
☐ 534. DAVE SMITH
☐ 560. JOE MORGAN
☐ 597. RAFAEL LANDESTOY
☐ 617. CRAIG REYNOLDS
☐ 642. VERN RUHLE
☐ 678. TEAM & VIRDON(M)
☐ 696. ALAN ASHBY
☐ 722. JOE NIEKRO

KANSAS CITY ROYALS

- ☐ 9. PETE LACOCK
- ☐ 26. U.L. WASHINGTON
- ☐ 47. KEN BRETT
- ☐ 66. MANNY CASTILLO(FS)
- ☐ 66. TIM IRELAND(FS)
- ☐ 66. MIKE JONES(FS)
- ☐ 98. CLINT HURDLE
- ☐ 130. LARRY GURA
- ☐ 157. JOHN WATHAN
- ☐ 185. DENNIS LEONARD
- ☐ 218. PAUL SPLITTORFF
- ☐ 274. CRAIG CHAMBERLAIN
- ☐ 295. HAL MCRAE
- ☐ 330. FRANK WHITE
- ☐ 360. WILLIE WILSON
- ☐ 389. MARTY PATTIN
- ☐ 433. RANCE MULLINIKS
- ☐ 452. RENIE MARTIN
- ☐ 473. JOSE CARDENAL
- ☐ 493. DAN QUISENBERRY
- ☐ 507. JAMIE QUIRK
- ☐ 524. WILLIE AIKENS
- ☐ 544. RICH GALE
- ☐ 585. AMOS OTIS
- ☐ 610. DARRELL PORTER
- ☐ 667. TEAM & FREY(M)
- ☐ 700. GEORGE BRETT

LOS ANGELES DODGERS

- ☐ 24. DON STANHOUSE
- ☐ 50. DAVE LOPES
- ☐ 75. REGGIE SMITH
- ☐ 104. TERRY FORSTER
- ☐ 127. RUDY LAW
- ☐ 146. BOBBY CASTILLO
- ☐ 174. DOUG RAU
- ☐ 191. RICK SUTCLIFFE
- ☐ 211. DERREL THOMAS
- ☐ 231. JOE BECKWITH
- ☐ 260. RON CEY
- ☐ 289. MICKEY HATCHER
- ☐ 302. JACK PERCONTE(FS)
- ☐ 302. MIKE SCIOSCIA(FS)
- ☐ 302. FERNANDO VALENZUELA(FS)
- ☐ 318. STEVE YEAGER
- ☐ 372. JAY JOHNSTONE
- ☐ 440. JERRY REUSS
- ☐ 465. BILL RUSSELL
- ☐ 495. DUSTY BAKER
- ☐ 512. GARY THOMASSON
- ☐ 530. STEVE GARVEY
- ☐ 548. DAVE GOLTZ
- ☐ 565. BURT HOOTON
- ☐ 605. DON SUTTON
- ☐ 624. BOB WELCH
- ☐ 651. PEDRO GUERRERO
- ☐ 679. TEAM & LA SORDA(M)
- ☐ 693. STEVE HOWE
- ☐ 711. JOE FERGUSON
- ☐ 726. RICK MONDAY

MILWAUKEE BREWERS

- ☐ 25. SIXTO LEZCANO
- ☐ 56. BUCK MARTINEZ
- ☐ 85. MIKE CALDWELL
- ☐ 106. DON MONEY
- ☐ 135. GORMAN THOMAS
- ☐ 156. BOB MCCLURE
- ☐ 183. DICK DAVIS
- ☐ 215. LARRY HISLE
- ☐ 237. CHARLIE MOORE
- ☐ 271. BILL CASTRO
- ☐ 300. PAUL MOLITOR
- ☐ 327. MOOSE HAAS
- ☐ 357. JIM SLATON
- ☐ 379. LARY SORENSEN
- ☐ 415. BEN OGLIVIE
- ☐ 449. PAUL MITCHELL
- ☐ 482. JIM GANTNER
- ☐ 515. ROBIN YOUNT
- ☐ 555. CECIL COOPER
- ☐ 576. REGGIE CLEVELAND
- ☐ 596. JERRY AUGUSTINE
- ☐ 623. SAL BANDO
- ☐ 659. JOHN FLINN(FS)
- ☐ 659. ED ROMERO(FS)

- ☐ 659. NED YOST(FS)
- ☐ 668. TEAM & RODGERS(M)
- ☐ 704. BILL TRAVERS

MINNESOTA TWINS

- ☐ 18. GLENN ADAMS
- ☐ 43. JOSE MORALES
- ☐ 61. BUTCH WYNEGAR
- ☐ 89. DARRELL JACKSON
- ☐ 115. ROY SMALLEY
- ☐ 137. HOSKEN POWELL
- ☐ 162. DOUG CORBETT
- ☐ 219. KEN LANDREAUX
- ☐ 243. SAL BUTERA
- ☐ 256. BOMBO RIVERA
- ☐ 278. RICK SOFIELD
- ☐ 304. JOHN CASTINO
- ☐ 328. DAVE ENGLE(FS)
- ☐ 328. GREG JOHNSTON(FS)
- ☐ 328. GARY WARD(FS)
- ☐ 363. GEOFF ZAHN
- ☐ 386. DAVE EDWARDS
- ☐ 408. FERNANDO ARROYO
- ☐ 434. ROGER ERICKSON
- ☐ 453. ROB WILFONG
- ☐ 476. JERRY KOOSMAN
- ☐ 509. PETE MACKANIN
- ☐ 527. DANNY GOODWIN
- ☐ 569. AL WILLIAMS
- ☐ 603. JOHN VERHOEVEN
- ☐ 631. RON JACKSON
- ☐ 657. MIKE CUBBAGE
- ☐ 669. TEAM & GORYL(M)
- ☐ 714. PETE REDFERN

MONTREAL EXPOS

- ☐ 15. LARRY PARRISH
- ☐ 42. JERRY WHITE
- ☐ 71. HAL DUES
- ☐ 97. CHRIS SPEIER
- ☐ 125. ANDRE DAWSON
- ☐ 181. ELIAS SOSA
- ☐ 235. SCOTT SANDERSON
- ☐ 267. STAN BAHNSEN
- ☐ 293. CHARLIE LEA
- ☐ 319. ROWLAND OFFICE
- ☐ 345. WARREN CROMARTIE
- ☐ 374. TOM HUTTON
- ☐ 394. WOODIE FRYMAN
- ☐ 413. TONY BERNAZARD
- ☐ 427. JOHN D'ACQUISTO
- ☐ 445. ELLIS VALENTINE
- ☐ 479. BOBBY PATE(FS)
- ☐ 479. TIM RAINES(FS)
- ☐ 479. ROBERTO RAMOS(FS)
- ☐ 497. FRED NORMAN
- ☐ 519. JOHN TAMARGO
- ☐ 539. RODNEY SCOTT
- ☐ 559. WILLIE MONTANEZ
- ☐ 578. BILL GULLICKSON
- ☐ 607. DAVE PALMER
- ☐ 633. BILL LEE
- ☐ 660. GARY CARTER
- ☐ 680. TEAM & WILLIAMS(M)
- ☐ 710. RON LEFLORE
- ☐ 725. STEVE ROGERS

NEW YORK METS

- ☐ 23. ALEX TREVINO
- ☐ 58. JOEL YOUNGBLOOD
- ☐ 93. ED GLYNN
- ☐ 109. MIKE SCOTT
- ☐ 117. PETE FALCONE
- ☐ 151. CLAUDELL WASHINGTON
- ☐ 163. BILLY ALMON
- ☐ 189. CRAIG SWAN
- ☐ 223. ROY LEE JACKSON
- ☐ 224. PAT ZACHRY
- ☐ 259. JUAN BERENGUER(FS)
- ☐ 259. HUBIE BROOKS(FS)
- ☐ 259. MOOKIE WILSON(FS)
- ☐ 299. ELLIOTT MADDOX
- ☐ 322. NEIL ALLEN
- ☐ 343. FRANK TAVERAS
- ☐ 359. TOM HAUSMAN
- ☐ 377. JERRY MORALES
- ☐ 414. JOHN PACELLA
- ☐ 428. JOHN STEARNS

- ☐ 456. JEFF REARDON
- ☐ 472. DYAR MILLER
- ☐ 510. LEE MAZZILLI
- ☐ 537. ROD HODGES
- ☐ 567. MARK BOMBACK
- ☐ 619. STEVE HENDERSON
- ☐ 634. DOUG FLYNN
- ☐ 654. RAY BURRIS
- ☐ 681. TEAM & TORRE(M)
- ☐ 698. MIKE JORGENSEN

NEW YORK YANKEES

- ☐ 16. RON DAVIS
- ☐ 34. AURELIO RODRIGUEZ
- ☐ 60. WILLIE RANDOLPH
- ☐ 88. JOE LEFEBVRE
- ☐ 114. TOM UNDERWOOD
- ☐ 139. OSCAR GAMBLE
- ☐ 159. BRIAN DOYLE
- ☐ 179. RUDY MAY
- ☐ 225. RUPPERT JONES
- ☐ 250. RON GUIDRY
- ☐ 281. FRED STANLEY
- ☐ 303. JOHNNY OATES
- ☐ 335. RICK CERONE
- ☐ 365. GRAIG NETTLES
- ☐ 383. ERIC SODERHOLM
- ☐ 400. REGGIE JACKSON
- ☐ 418. BOBBY BROWN
- ☐ 424. TIM LOLLAR(FS)
- ☐ 424. BRUCE ROBINSON(FS)
- ☐ 424. DENNIS WERTH(FS)
- ☐ 435. JIM SPENCER
- ☐ 460. RICH GOSSAGE
- ☐ 483. MIKE GRIFFIN
- ☐ 516. DOUG BIRD
- ☐ 550. TOMMY JOHN
- ☐ 582. GAYLORD PERRY
- ☐ 602. BOBBY MURCER
- ☐ 627. LUIS TIANT
- ☐ 650. BUCKY DENT
- ☐ 670. TEAM & MICHAEL(M)
- ☐ 690. BOB WATSON
- ☐ 724. LOU PINIELLA

OAKLAND A'S

- ☐ 35. MITCHELL PAGE
- ☐ 55. MIKE NORRIS
- ☐ 86. WAYNE GROSS
- ☐ 96. DAVE BEARD(FS)
- ☐ 96. ERNIE CAMACHO(FS)
- ☐ 96. PAT DEMPSEY(FS)
- ☐ 133. JEFF COX
- ☐ 154. RICK LANGFORD
- ☐ 178. JIM ESSIAN
- ☐ 232. MICKEY KLUTTS
- ☐ 261. RICKEY HENDERSON
- ☐ 284. BRIAN KINGMAN
- ☐ 301. MATT KEOUGH
- ☐ 316. CRAIG MINETTO
- ☐ 341. DWAYNE MURPHY
- ☐ 364. MIKE DAVIS
- ☐ 437. MIKE HEATH
- ☐ 461. DAVE MCKAY
- ☐ 481. BOB LACEY
- ☐ 503. STEVE MCCATTY
- ☐ 547. MARIO GUERRERO
- ☐ 568. DAVE REVERING
- ☐ 587. JEFF NEWMAN
- ☐ 604. ROB PICCIOLO
- ☐ 629. TONY ARMAS
- ☐ 671. TEAM & MARTIN(M)
- ☐ 687. JEFF JONES

PHILADELPHIA PHILLIES

- ☐ 40. TUG MCGRAW
- ☐ 53. KEVIN SAUCIER
- ☐ 90. BAKE MCBRIDE
- ☐ 120. LARRY BOWA
- ☐ 131. KEITH MORELAND
- ☐ 160. GARRY MADDOX
- ☐ 180. PETE ROSE
- ☐ 270. GREG LUZINSKI
- ☐ 290. BOB BOONE
- ☐ 317. LONNIE SMITH
- ☐ 346. LARRY CHRISTENSON
- ☐ 376. RON REED

☐ 405. NINO ESPINOSA
☐ 406. DICKIE NOLES
☐ 426. WARREN BRUSSTAR
☐ 459. GREG GROSS
☐ 470. MANNY TRILLO
☐ 494. BOB WALK
☐ 526. MARTY BYSTROM(FS)
☐ 526. JAY LOVIGLIO(FS)
☐ 526. JIM L. WRGHT(FS)
☐ 540. MIKE SCHMIDT
☐ 566. DEL UNSER
☐ 584. RANDY LERCH
☐ 598. GEORGE VUKOVICH
☐ 630. STEVE CARLTON
☐ 644. RAMON AVILES
☐ 682. TEAM & GREEN(M)
☐ 691. DICK RUGHVEN
☐ 719. SPARKY LYLE

PITTSBURGH PIRATES

☐ 28. ENRIQUE ROMO
☐ 51. BILL ROBINSON
☐ 68. MATT ALEXANDER
☐ 92. MIKE EASLER
☐ 118. KURT BEVACQUA
☐ 147. DALE BERRA
☐ 168. DON ROBINSON
☐ 194. ROD SCURRY
☐ 212. STEVE NICOSIA
☐ 226. MANNY SANGUILLEN
☐ 246. ED OTT
☐ 265. JOHN CANDELARIA
☐ 298. BUDDY SOLOMON
☐ 312. RICK RHODEN
☐ 332. LEE LACY
☐ 380. WILLIE STARGELL
☐ 430. JIM BIBBY
☐ 501. TIM FOLI
☐ 518. GRANT JACKSON
☐ 535. OMAR MORENO
☐ 551. VANCE LAW(FS)
☐ 551. TONY PENA(FS)
☐ 551. PASCUAL PEREZ(FS)
☐ 554. BERT BLYLEVEN
☐ 573. PHIL GARNER
☐ 618. JOHN MILNER
☐ 640. DAVE PARKER
☐ 683. TEAM & TANNER(M)
☐ 695. KENT TEKULVE
☐ 715. BILL MADLOCK

ST. LOUIS CARDINALS

☐ 32. KEN OBERKFELL
☐ 113. MIKE PHILLIPS
☐ 140. BOB FORSCH
☐ 152. JOHN URREA
☐ 165. TONY SCOTT
☐ 193. PETE VUCKOVICH
☐ 230. GEORGE HENDRICK
☐ 244. TITO LANDRUM(FS)
☐ 244. AL OLMSTED(FS)
☐ 244. ANDY RINCON(FS)
☐ 255. MARK LITTELL
☐ 266. TOM HERR
☐ 321. LEON DURHAM
☐ 334. DANE IORG
☐ 348. BOB SYKES
☐ 353. TERRY KENNEDY
☐ 366. MIKE RAMSEY
☐ 420. KEITH HERNANDEZ
☐ 441. KEN REITZ
☐ 485. GARRY TEMPLETON
☐ 489. JOHN LITTLEFIELD
☐ 523. JOHN FULGHAM
☐ 541. STEVE SWISHER
☐ 563. JIM KAAT
☐ 586. SILVIO MARTINEZ
☐ 635. BOBBY BONDS
☐ 684. TEAM & HERZOG(M)
☐ 705. TED SIMMONS

SAN DIEGO PADRES

☐ 29. GENE TENACE
☐ 49. BOB SHIRLEY
☐ 72. BARRY EVANS
☐ 134. STEVE MURA
☐ 171. GENE RICHARDS
☐ 229. ROLLIE FINGERS

☐ 254. OZZIE SMITH
☐ 285. JERRY TURNER
☐ 309. LUIS SALAZAR
☐ 342. ERIC RASMUSSEN
☐ 356. GEORGE STABLEIN(FS)
☐ 356. CRAIG STIMAC(FS)
☐ 356. TOM TELLMAN(FS)
☐ 370. DAVE WINFIELD
☐ 393. BRODERICK PERKINS
☐ 436. GARY LUCAS
☐ 458. RANDY JONES
☐ 478. JUAN EICHELBERGER
☐ 496. PAUL DADE
☐ 531. JOHN CURTIS
☐ 556. JERRY MUMPHREY
☐ 579. TIM FLANNERY
☐ 579. DENNIS KINNEY
☐ 616. RICK WISE
☐ 653. BILL FAHEY
☐ 685. TEAM & HOWARD(M)
☐ 707. DAVE CASH

SAN FRANCISCO GIANTS

☐ 11. JIM WOHLFORD
☐ 30. JACK CLARK
☐ 62. JOE PETTINI
☐ 84. JOHNNIE LEMASTER
☐ 111. GREG MINTON
☐ 144. ALLEN RIPLEY
☐ 167. TERRY WHITFIELD
☐ 195. RICH MURRAY
☐ 213. AL HOLLAND
☐ 236. MIKE IVIE
☐ 257. RENNIE STENNETT
☐ 279. BOB KNEPPER
☐ 310. VIDA BLUE
☐ 336. EDDIE WHITSON
☐ 361. JOE STRAIN
☐ 384. MIKE SADEK
☐ 409. LARRY HERNDON
☐ 438. JOHN MONTEFUSCO
☐ 463. MILT MAY
☐ 484. MAX VENABLE
☐ 502. CHRIS BOURJOS(FS)
☐ 502. AL HARGESHEIMER(FS)
☐ 502. MIKE ROWLAND(FS)
☐ 538. TOM GRIFFIN
☐ 561. DENNIS LITTLEJOHN
☐ 588. GARY LAVELLE
☐ 622. RANDY MOFFITT
☐ 648. DARRELL EVANS
☐ 686. TEAM & BRISTOL(M)
☐ 713. BILL NORTH

SEATTLE MARINERS

☐ 33. RICK HONEYCUTT
☐ 57. DAVE A. ROBERTS
☐ 76. MARIO MENDOZA
☐ 116. JOE SIMPSON
☐ 143. DAN MEYER
☐ 166. FLOYD BANNISTER
☐ 187. MIKE PARROTT
☐ 228. TOM PACIOREK
☐ 249. LARRY COX
☐ 282. RICK ANDERSON(FS)
☐ 282. GREG BIERCEVICZ(FS)
☐ 282. RODNEY CRAIG(FS)
☐ 306. JUAN BENIQUEZ
☐ 344. BYRON MCLAUGHLIN

☐ 368. LEON ROBERTS
☐ 397. JULIO CRUZ
☐ 423. SHANE RAWLEY
☐ 443. JIM BEATTIE
☐ 486. MARC HILL
☐ 508. ROB DRESSLER
☐ 532. BILL STEIN
☐ 583. LARRY MILBOURNE
☐ 613. JIM ANDERSON
☐ 637. JERRY NARRON
☐ 649. MANNY SARMIENTO
☐ 672. TEAM & WILLS(M)
☐ 699. GLENN ABBOTT
☐ 723. BRUCE BOCHTE

TEXAS RANGERS

☐ 22. DANNY DARWIN
☐ 41. BOB BABCOCK(FS)
☐ 41. JOHN BUTCHER(FS)
☐ 41. JERRY DON GLEATON(FS)
☐ 70. AL OLIVER
☐ 80. RUSTY STAUB
☐ 95. JIM SUNDBERG
☐ 145. MICKEY RIVERS
☐ 158. FERGIE JENKINS
☐ 173. BUMP WILLS
☐ 197. JIM KERN
☐ 216. JOHN HENRY JOHNSON
☐ 245. ED FIGUEROA
☐ 264. JIM NORRIS
☐ 283. BILLY SAMPLE
☐ 305. KEN CLAY
☐ 339. JOHN ELLIS
☐ 371. CHARLIE HOUGH
☐ 431. DAVE W. ROBERTS
☐ 464. ADRIAN DEVINE
☐ 475. BUDDY BELL
☐ 498. PAT PUTNAM
☐ 517. RICHIE ZISK
☐ 545. JOHNNY GRUBB
☐ 592. STEVE COMER
☐ 656. JON MATLACK
☐ 673. TEAM & ZIMMER(M)
☐ 694. BUD HARRELSON
☐ 702. GEORGE MEDICH

TORONTO BLUE JAYS

☐ 19. JIM CLANCY
☐ 46. RICK BOSETTI
☐ 77. MIKE BARLOW
☐ 124. JERRY GARVIN
☐ 142. JACKSON TODD
☐ 169. JOHN MAYBERRY
☐ 221. BOB DAVIS
☐ 248. JOEY MCLAUGHLIN
☐ 277. ALFREDO GRIFFIN
☐ 297. BOB BAILOR
☐ 324. MIKE WILLIS
☐ 351. OTTO VELEZ
☐ 382. PAUL MIRABELLA
☐ 407. ERNIE WHITT
☐ 444. GARTH IORG
☐ 467. DAVE STIEB
☐ 488. DAMASO GARCIA
☐ 506. PHIL HUFFMAN
☐ 558. BARRY BONNELL
☐ 577. LUIS LEAL(FS)
☐ 577. BRIAN MILNER(FS)
☐ 577. KEN SCHROM(FS)
☐ 581. ROY HOWELL
☐ 643. LLOYD MOSEBY
☐ 674. TEAM & MATTICK(M)
☐ 703. ALVIS WOODS

1981 TOPPS TRADED (132)
2 1/2" X 3 1/2"

ATLANTA BRAVES

- ☐ 804. JOHN MONTEFUSCO
- ☐ 812. GAYLORD PERRY
- ☐ 853. BOB WALK
- ☐ 854. CLAUDELL WASHINGTON

BALTIMORE ORIOLES

- ☐ 757. JIM DWYER
- ☐ 806. JOSE MORALES

BOSTON RED SOX

- ☐ 748. MARK CLEAR
- ☐ 788. CARNEY LANSFORD
- ☐ 803. RICK MILLER
- ☐ 826. JOE RUDI
- ☐ 841. FRANK TANANA

CALIFORNIA ANGELS

- ☐ 733. JUAN BENIQUEZ
- ☐ 743. RICK BURLESON
- ☐ 764. KEN FORSCH
- ☐ 771. BUTCH HOBSON
- ☐ 797. FRED LYNN
- ☐ 810. ED OTT
- ☐ 818. DOUG RAU
- ☐ 821. STEVE RENKO
- ☐ 845. BILL TRAVERS
- ☐ 856. GEOFF ZAHN

CHICAGO CUBS

- ☐ 737. DOUG BIRD
- ☐ 740. BOBBY BONDS
- ☐ 750. HECTOR CRUZ
- ☐ 756. LEON DURHAM
- ☐ 769. STEVE HENDERSON
- ☐ 783. KEN KRAVEC
- ☐ 795. MIKE LUM
- ☐ 805. JERRY MORALES
- ☐ 820. KEN REITZ
- ☐ 837. JOE STRAIN

CHICAGO WHITE SOX

- ☐ 730. BILLY ALMON
- ☐ 735. TONY BERNAZARD
- ☐ 759. JOM ESSIAN
- ☐ 762. CARLTON FISK
- ☐ 770. MARC HILL
- ☐ 785. DENNIS LAMP
- ☐ 791. RON LEFLORE
- ☐ 796. GREG LUZINSKI

CINCINNATI REDS

- ☐ 736. LARRY BIITTNER
- ☐ 786. RAFAEL LANDESTOY
- ☐ 848. MIKE VAIL

CLEVELAND INDIANS

- ☐ 738. BERT BLYLEVEN
- ☐ 784. BOB LACEY

DETROIT TIGERS

- ☐ 760. BILL FAHEY
- ☐ 779. MICK KELLEHER
- ☐ 827. KEVIN SAUCIER

HOUSTON ASTROS

- ☐ 765. KIKO GARCIA
- ☐ 774. MIKE IVIE
- ☐ 782. BOB KNEPPER
- ☐ 824. DAVE W. ROBERTS
- ☐ 828. TONY SCOTT
- ☐ 833. HARRY SPILMAN
- ☐ 839. DON SUTTON
- ☐ 844. DICKIE THON

KANSAS CITY ROYALS

- ☐ 766. CESAR GERONIMO

LOS ANGELES DODGERS

- ☐ 787. KEN LANDREAUX
- ☐ 850. FERNANDO VALENZUELA

MILWAUKEE BREWERS

- ☐ 761. ROLLIE FINGERS
- ☐ 773. ROY HOWELL
- ☐ 792. RANDY LERCH
- ☐ 830. TED SIMMONS
- ☐ 851. PETE VUCKOVICH

MINNESOTA TWINS

- ☐ 768. MICKEY HATCHER

MONTREAL EXPOS

- ☐ 744. RAY BURRIS
- ☐ 813. MIKE PHILLIPS
- ☐ 816. TIM RAINES
- ☐ 819. JEFF REARDON

NEW YORK METS

- ☐ 732. BOB BAILOR
- ☐ 742. HUBIE BROOKS
- ☐ 752. MIKE CUBBAGE
- ☐ 777. RANDY JONES
- ☐ 781. DAVE KINGMAN
- ☐ 835. RUSTY STAUB
- ☐ 849. ELLIS VALENTINE

NEW YORK YANKEES

- ☐ 763. BARRY FOOTE
- ☐ 789. DAVE LAROCHE
- ☐ 802. LARRY MILBOURNE
- ☐ 808. JERRY MUMPHREY
- ☐ 809. GENE NELSON
- ☐ 822. RICK REUSCHEL
- ☐ 823. DAVE REVERING
- ☐ 855. DAVE WINFIELD

OAKLAND A'S

- ☐ 741. RICK BOSETTI
- ☐ 754. BRIAN DOYLE
- ☐ 776. CLIFF JOHNSON
- ☐ 811. BOB OWCHINKO
- ☐ 832. JIM SPENCER
- ☐ 834. FRED STANLEY
- ☐ 846. TOM UNDERWOOD

PHILADELPHIA PHILLIES

- ☐ 753. DICK DAVIS
- ☐ 800. GARY MATTHEWS
- ☐ 815. MIKE PROLY

PITTSBURGH PIRATES

- ☐ 729. GARY ALEXANDER
- ☐ 751. VICTOR CRUZ
- ☐ 843. JASON THOMPSON

ST. LOUIS CARDINALS

- ☐ 731. JOAQUIN ANDUJAR
- ☐ 793. SIXTO LEZCANO
- ☐ 814. DARRELL PORTER
- ☐ 829. BOB SHIRLEY
- ☐ 831. LARY SORENSEN
- ☐ 838. BRUCE SUTTER
- ☐ 842. GENE TENACE

SAN DIEGO PADRES

- ☐ 758. DAVE EDWARDS
- ☐ 778. RUPPERT JONES
- ☐ 780. TERRY KENNEDY
- ☐ 790. JOE LEFEVRE
- ☐ 794. JOHN LITTLEFIELD
- ☐ 840. STEVE SWISHER
- ☐ 847. JOHN URREA

SAN FRANCISCO GIANTS

- ☐ 728. DOYLE ALEXANDER
- ☐ 734. DAVE BERGMAN
- ☐ 746. ENOS CABELL
- ☐ 798. JERRY MARTIN
- ☐ 807. JOE MORGAN

SEATTLE MARINERS

- ☐ 745. JEFF BURROUGHS
- ☐ 747. KEN CLAY
- ☐ 755. DICK DRAGO
- ☐ 767. GARY GRAY
- ☐ 817. LENNY RANDLE
- ☐ 857. RICHIE ZISK

TEXAS RANGERS

- ☐ 749. LARRY COX
- ☐ 772. RICK HONEYCUTT
- ☐ 801. MARIO MENDOZA
- ☐ 825. LEON ROBERTS
- ☐ 836. BILL STEIN
- ☐ 852. MARK WAGNER

TORONTO BLUE JAYS

- ☐ 727. DANNY AINGE
- ☐ 739. MARK BOMBACK
- ☐ 775. ROY LEE JACKSON
- ☐ 799. BUCK MARTINEZ

1982 TOPPS (792)
2 1/2'' X 3 1/2''

ASTROS
PITCHER DON SUTTON

ATLANTA BRAVES

- [ ] 32. GENE GARBER
- [ ] 61. TOMMY BOGGS
- [ ] 88. BIFF POCOROBA
- [ ] 115. GAYLORD PERRY
- [ ] 126. TEAM LEADER CARD
- [ ] 145. BOB HORNER
- [ ] 185. PHIL NIEKRO
- [ ] 214. BRIAN ASSELSTINE
- [ ] 244. RUFINO LINARES
- [ ] 271. LARRY BRADFORD
- [ ] 296. BOB WALK
- [ ] 320. CHRIS CHAMBLISS
- [ ] 372. LUIS GOMEZ
- [ ] 393. AL HRABOSKY
- [ ] 424. BRUCE BENEDICT
- [ ] 451. ED MILLIER
- [ ] 482. GLENN HUBBARD
- [ ] 502. STEVE BEDROSIAN(FS)
- [ ] 502. BRETT BUTLER(FS)
- [ ] 502. LARRY OWEN(FS)
- [ ] 507. TERRY HARPER
- [ ] 536. RAFAEL RAMIREZ
- [ ] 579. RICK MAHLER
- [ ] 608. JERRY ROYSTER
- [ ] 637. RICK CAMP
- [ ] 668. DALE MURPHY
- [ ] 697. JOHN MONTEFUSCO
- [ ] 733. LARRY MCWILLIAMS
- [ ] 758. CLAUDELL WASHINGTON

BALTIMORE ORIOLES

- [ ] 8. RICH DAUER
- [ ] 21. BOB BONNER(FS)
- [ ] 21. CAL RIPKEN(FS)
- [ ] 21. JEFF SCHNEIDER(FS)
- [ ] 37. DAN GRAHAM
- [ ] 80. JIM PALMER
- [ ] 107. WAYNE KRENCHICKI
- [ ] 136. LENN SAKATA
- [ ] 174. DAVE FORD
- [ ] 204. GARY ROENICKE
- [ ] 232. TERRY CROWLEY
- [ ] 265. AL BUMBRY
- [ ] 290. KEN SINGLETON
- [ ] 331. BENNY AYALA
- [ ] 359. JIM DWYER
- [ ] 390. EDDIE MURRAY
- [ ] 419. STEVE STONE
- [ ] 426. TEAM LEADER CARD
- [ ] 457. TIM STODDARD
- [ ] 489. RICK DEMPSEY
- [ ] 520. MIKE FLANAGAN
- [ ] 564. DOUG DECINCES
- [ ] 583. TIPPY MARTINEZ
- [ ] 617. SCOTT MCGREGOR
- [ ] 648. JOSE MORALES
- [ ] 679. SAMMY STEWART
- [ ] 712. DENNY MARTINEZ
- [ ] 747. JOHN LOWENSTEIN
- [ ] 776. MARK BELANGER

BOSTON RED SOX

- [ ] 25. JERRY REMY
- [ ] 59. RICH GEDMAN
- [ ] 91. CARNEY LANSFORD
- [ ] 124. REID NICHOLS
- [ ] 157. STEVE CRAWFORD
- [ ] 189. GLENN HOFFMAN
- [ ] 225. MIKE TORREZ
- [ ] 255. TONY PEREZ
- [ ] 274. BOB OJEDA
- [ ] 289. BOB STANLEY
- [ ] 322. GARRY HANCOCK
- [ ] 355. DWIGHT EVANS
- [ ] 361. BRUCE HURST(FS)
- [ ] 381. DAVE F. SCHMIDT(FS)
- [ ] 381. JULIO VALDEZ(FS)
- [ ] 388. JOE RUDI
- [ ] 421. MARK CLEAR
- [ ] 455. TOM BURGMEIER
- [ ] 490. DENNIS ECKERSLEY
- [ ] 522. CHUCK RAINEY
- [ ] 558. JOHN TUDOR
- [ ] 589. DAVE STAPLETON
- [ ] 619. BILL CAMPBELL
- [ ] 650. CARL YASTRZEMSKI
- [ ] 686. GARY ALLENSON
- [ ] 717. RICK MILLER
- [ ] 750. JIM RICE
- [ ] 786. TEAM LEADER CARD
- [ ] 792. FRANK TANANA

CALIFORNIA ANGELS

- [ ] 24. DAVE FROST
- [ ] 55. RICK BURLESON
- [ ] 58. JOHN D'ACQUISTO
- [ ] 74. BOB CLARK
- [ ] 94. ANDY HASSLER
- [ ] 134. DAN FORD
- [ ] 158. BRIAN DOWNING
- [ ] 199. DON AASE
- [ ] 229. GEOFF ZAHN
- [ ] 251. FRED LYNN
- [ ] 257. LARRY HARLOW
- [ ] 276. TEAM LEADER CARD
- [ ] 284. BOB GRICH
- [ ] 313. JOHN HARRIS
- [ ] 357. BUTCH HOBSON
- [ ] 385. KEN FORSCH
- [ ] 415. DON BAYLOR
- [ ] 442. BRUCE KISON
- [ ] 469. ED OTT
- [ ] 500. ROD CAREW
- [ ] 514. JOE FERGUSON
- [ ] 572. JUAN BENIQUEZ
- [ ] 602. FREDDIE PATEK
- [ ] 628. BILL TRAVERS
- [ ] 653. TOM BRUNANSKY(FS)
- [ ] 653. LUIS SANCHEZ(FS)
- [ ] 653. DARYL SCONIERS(FS)
- [ ] 659. FRED MARTINEZ
- [ ] 682. JESSE JEFFERSON
- [ ] 702. STEVE RENKO
- [ ] 744. MIKE WITT
- [ ] 772. BERT CAMPANERIS

CHICAGO CUBS

- [ ] 23. WILLIE HERNANDEZ
- [ ] 33. JERRY MORALES
- [ ] 51. JAY HOWELL(FS)
- [ ] 51. CARLOS LEZCANO(FS)
- [ ] 51. TY WALLER(FS)
- [ ] 62. MIKE TYSON
- [ ] 89. STEVE HENDERSON
- [ ] 117. RAWLY EASTWICK
- [ ] 146. MIKE GRIFFIN
- [ ] 188. RANDY MARTZ
- [ ] 215. MIKE KRUKOW
- [ ] 245. KEN REITZ
- [ ] 273. DOUG GIRD
- [ ] 303. BILL CAUDILL
- [ ] 324. STEVE DILLARD
- [ ] 374. TIM BLACKWELL
- [ ] 403. JIM TRACY
- [ ] 436. JOE STRAIN
- [ ] 452. LEE SMITH
- [ ] 456. TEAM LEADER CARD
- [ ] 484. IVAN DEJESUS
- [ ] 508. JODY DAVIS

CHICAGO WHITE SOX

- [ ] 537. DOUG CAPILLA
- [ ] 580. BOBBY BONDS
- [ ] 607. LEON DURHAM
- [ ] 639. KEN DRAVEC
- [ ] 663. HECTOR CRUZ
- [ ] 699. DICK TIDROW
- [ ] 732. MIKE LUM
- [ ] 760. BILL BUCKNER

CHICAGO WHITE SOX

- [ ] 13. LAMAR JOHNSON
- [ ] 44. BRITT BURNS
- [ ] 76. GREG PRYOR
- [ ] 85. LYNN MCGLOTHEN
- [ ] 110. CARLTON FISK
- [ ] 140. RON LEFLORE
- [ ] 176. DEWEY ROBINSON
- [ ] 206. TONY BERNAZARD
- [ ] 216. TEAM LEADER CARD
- [ ] 237. RUSTY KUNTZ
- [ ] 269. JIM ESSIAN
- [ ] 299. STEVE TROUT
- [ ] 328. ED FARMER
- [ ] 363. BOB MOLINARO
- [ ] 398. MIKE SQUIRES
- [ ] 428. LAMARR HOYT
- [ ] 461. RICH DOTSON
- [ ] 493. CHET LEMON
- [ ] 521. BILLY ALMON
- [ ] 563. ROSS BAUMGARTEN
- [ ] 597. WAYNE NORDHAGEN
- [ ] 599. JAY LOVIGLIO(FS)
- [ ] 599. REGGIE PATTERSON(FS)
- [ ] 599. LEO SUTHERLAND(FS)
- [ ] 622. DENNIS LAMP
- [ ] 654. JIM MORRISON
- [ ] 684. HAROLD BAINES
- [ ] 714. JERRY KOOSMAN
- [ ] 720. GREG LUZINSKI
- [ ] 736. JERRY TURNER
- [ ] 748. MARC HILL
- [ ] 778. KEVIN HICKEY

CINCINNATI REDS

- [ ] 30. TOM SEAVER
- [ ] 63. MARIO SOTO
- [ ] 97. PAUL MOSKAU
- [ ] 128. FRANK PASTORE
- [ ] 159. LARRY BIITTNER
- [ ] 169. CHARLIE LEIBRANDT
- [ ] 194. MIKE VAIL
- [ ] 228. SAM MEJIAS
- [ ] 294. MIKE LACOSS
- [ ] 327. JOE NOLAN
- [ ] 351. SCOTT BROWN(FS)
- [ ] 351. GEOFF COMBE(FS)
- [ ] 351. PAUL HOUSEHOLDER(FS)
- [ ] 361. RAFAEL LANDESTOY
- [ ] 400. JOHNNY BENCH
- [ ] 427. RON OESTER
- [ ] 459. BRUCE BERENYI
- [ ] 492. JOE PRICE
- [ ] 525. RAY KNIGHT
- [ ] 562. MIKE O'BERRY
- [ ] 595. DAVE COLLINS
- [ ] 620. KEN GRIFFEY
- [ ] 660. DAVE CONCEPCION
- [ ] 700. GEORGE FOSTER
- [ ] 723. JUNIOR KENNEDY
- [ ] 756. TEAM LEADER CARD
- [ ] 763. TOME HUME
- [ ] 785. DAN DRIESSEN

CLEVELAND INDIANS

- [ ] 26. JORGE ORTA
- [ ] 54. RON HASSEY
- [ ] 77. MIGUEL DILONE
- [ ] 141. CHRIS BANDO(FS)
- [ ] 141. TOM BRENNAN(FS)
- [ ] 141. VON HAYES(FS)
- [ ] 202. RICK MANNING
- [ ] 233. DUANE KUIPER
- [ ] 258. BO DIAZ
- [ ] 287. ALAN BANNISTER
- [ ] 310. MIKE HARGROVE
- [ ] 356. DENNY LEWALLYN
- [ ] 360. LEN BARKER
- [ ] 387. TOM VERYZER

☐ 417. H. PAT KELLY
☐ 446. WAYNE GARLAND
☐ 473. MIKE STANTON
☐ 512. JERRY DYBZINSKI
☐ 532. TOBY HARRAH
☐ 559. TEAM LEADER CARD
☐ 573. RICK WAITS
☐ 601. SID MONGE
☐ 630. JOE CHARBONEAU
☐ 664. DAN SPILLNER
☐ 685. BERT BLYLEVEN
☐ 724. DAVE ROSELLO
☐ 746. ANDRE THORNTON
☐ 773. JOHN DENNY

DETROIT TIGERS

☐ 39. LOU WHITAKER
☐ 64. LYNN JONES
☐ 105. KIRK GIBSON
☐ 133. PAT UNDERWOOD
☐ 137. GEORGE CAPPUZZELLO
☐ 184. MICK KELLEHER
☐ 211. DAN PETRY
☐ 238. KEVIN SAUCIER
☐ 261. HOWARD BAILEY(FS)
☐ 261. MARTY CASTILLO(FS)
☐ 261. DAVE RUCKER(FS)
☐ 266. RICK LEACH
☐ 286. BILL FAHEY
☐ 319. DAVE ROZEMA
☐ 369. CHAMP SUMMERS
☐ 391. DAVE TOBIK
☐ 423. STAN PAPI
☐ 450. JACK MORRIS
☐ 475. ALAN TRAMMELL
☐ 488. RON JACKSON
☐ 504. RICK PETERS
☐ 535. LANCE PARRISH
☐ 575. AL COWENS
☐ 603. RICH HEBNER
☐ 629. JOHNNY WOCKENFUSS
☐ 666. TEAM LEADER CARD
☐ 670. STEVE KEMP
☐ 691. DAN SCHATZEDER
☐ 728. AURELIO LOPEZ
☐ 753. TOM BROOKENS
☐ 784. MILT WILCOX

TIGERS
CATCHER LANCE PARRISH

HOUSTON ASTROS

☐ 34. JOE SAMBITO
☐ 57. CRAIG REYNOLDS
☐ 66. TEAM LEADER CARD
☐ 90. NOLAN RYAN
☐ 119. JOE PITTMAN
☐ 147. DANNY WALLING
☐ 190. J. R. RICHARD
☐ 218. DAVE W. ROBERTS
☐ 248. FRANK LACORTE
☐ 277. TERRY PUHL
☐ 305. DON SUTTON
☐ 325. JOSE CRUZ
☐ 377. KIKO GARCIA
☐ 404. DICKIE THON
☐ 433. ALAN ASHBY
☐ 441. DANNY HEEP(FS)
☐ 441. BILLY L. SMITH(FS)
☐ 441. BOBBY SPROWL(FS)
☐ 453. ART HOWE

☐ 483. GARY WOODS
☐ 509. HARRY SPILMAN
☐ 539. VERN RUHLE
☐ 582. LUIS PUJOLS
☐ 611. JOE NIEKRO
☐ 640. CESAR CEDENO
☐ 672. BOB KNEPPER
☐ 683. PHIL GARNER
☐ 698. TONY SCOTT
☐ 734. MIKE IVIE
☐ 761. DAVE SMITH

KANSAS CITY ROYALS

☐ 35. WILLIE AIKENS
☐ 67. RICH GALE
☐ 96. TEAM LEADER CARD
☐ 104. RANCE MULLINIKS
☐ 132. LEE MAY
☐ 173. JAMIE QUIRK
☐ 200. GEORGE BRETT
☐ 230. WILLIE WILSON
☐ 264. DAN QUISENBERRY
☐ 297. CLINT HURDLE
☐ 329. U.L. WASHINGTON
☐ 362. JIM L. WRIGHT
☐ 397. KEN BRETT
☐ 429. JOHN WATHAN
☐ 462. DAVE CHALK
☐ 471. ATLEE HAMMAKER(FS)
☐ 471. MIKE JONES(FS)
☐ 471. DARRYL MOTLEY(FS)
☐ 495. DENNIS LEONARD
☐ 594. RENIE MARTIN
☐ 625. HAL MCRAE
☐ 645. FRANK WHITE
☐ 693. CESAR GERONIMO
☐ 725. AMOS OTIS
☐ 759. PAUL SPLITTORFF
☐ 790. LARRY GURA

LOS ANGELES DODGERS

☐ 14. STEVE HOWE
☐ 48. BOBBY CASTILLO
☐ 82. BOB WELCH
☐ 114. KEN LANDREAUX
☐ 179. STEVE GARVEY
☐ 213. DAVE STEWART
☐ 247. PEDRO GUERRERO
☐ 279. BILL RUSSELL
☐ 311. TEAM LEADER CARD
☐ 315. BURT HOOTON
☐ 348. DERREL THOMAS
☐ 375. DUSTY BAKER
☐ 410. RON CEY
☐ 444. TERRY FORSTER
☐ 477. STEVE YEAGER
☐ 510. FERNANDO VALENZUELA
☐ 545. REGGIE SMITH
☐ 577. RICK MONDAY
☐ 609. RICK SUTCLIFFE
☐ 642. MIKE SCIOSCIA
☐ 674. DAVE GOLTZ
☐ 681. MIKE A. MARSHALL(FS)
☐ 681. RON ROENICKE(FS)
☐ 681. STEVE SAX(FS)
☐ 710. JERRY REUSS
☐ 740. DAVE LOPES
☐ 774. JAY JOHNSTONE

MILWAUKEE BREWERS

☐ 12. MOOSE HAAS
☐ 46. JERRY AUGUSTINE
☐ 68. ROY HOWELL
☐ 93. LARRY HISLE
☐ 122. JAMIE EASTERLY
☐ 150. TED SIMMONS
☐ 195. PAUL MOLITOR
☐ 221. JIM SLATON
☐ 268. RICKEY KEETON
☐ 280. BEN OGLIVIE
☐ 308. CHARLIE MOORE
☐ 333. FRANK DIPINO(FS)
☐ 333. MARSHALL EDWARDS(FS)
☐ 333. CHUCK PORTER(FS)
☐ 350. THAD BOSLEY
☐ 378. MIKE CALDWELL
☐ 408. ED ROMERO

☐ 435. ROBIN YOUNT
☐ 466. RANDY LERCH
☐ 487. BOB MCCLURE
☐ 517. MARK BROUHARD
☐ 542. NED YOST
☐ 585. ROLLIE FINGERS
☐ 613. JIM GANTNER
☐ 643. PETE VUCKOVICH
☐ 675. CECIL COOPER
☐ 703. TEAM LEADER CARD
☐ 709. DON MONEY
☐ 737. REGGIE CLEVELAND
☐ 765. GORMAN THOMAS

MINNESOTA TWINS

☐ 18. FERNANDO ARROYO
☐ 42. RICK SOFIELD
☐ 69. AL WILLIAMS
☐ 92. BRAD HAVENS
☐ 123. DANNY GOODWIN
☐ 153. ROGER ERICKSON
☐ 193. DARRELL JACKSON
☐ 222. BUTCH WYNEGAR
☐ 253. CHUCK BAKER
☐ 281. JOHN VERHOEVEN
☐ 309. PETE REDFERN
☐ 353. JACK O'CONNOR
☐ 379. ROB WILFONG
☐ 396. TEAM LEADER CARD
☐ 409. DON COOPER
☐ 438. PETE MACKANIN
☐ 467. MICKEY HATCHER
☐ 519. GLENN ADAMS
☐ 560. DOUG CORBETT
☐ 584. HOSKEN POWELL
☐ 612. GARY WARD
☐ 644. JOHN CASTINO
☐ 676. SAL BUTERA
☐ 738. DAVE ENGLE
☐ 766. LENNY FAEDO(FS)
☐ 766. KENT HRBEK(FS)
☐ 766. TIM LAUDNER(FS)
☐ 767. ROY SMALLEY

EXPOS
PITCHER BILL LEE

MONTREAL EXPOS

☐ 7. SCOTT SANDERSON
☐ 38. CHARLIE LEA
☐ 70. TIM RAINES
☐ 102. DAN BRIGGS
☐ 118. TERRY FRANCONA(FS)
☐ 118. BRAD MILLS(FS)
☐ 118. BRYN SMITH(FS)
☐ 131. STAN BAHNSEN
☐ 172. BILL GULLICKSON
☐ 191. TIM WALLACH
☐ 198. CHRIS SPEIER
☐ 227. RAY BURRIS
☐ 259. RODNEY SCOTT
☐ 292. DAVE PALMER
☐ 323. BILL LEE
☐ 354. ROBERTO RAMOS
☐ 386. JERRY WHITE
☐ 414. ELIAS SOSA
☐ 445. LARRY PARRISH
☐ 479. ROWLAND OFFICE
☐ 526. TEAM LEADER CARD
☐ 540. ANDRE DAWSON
☐ 605. STEVE ROGERS
☐ 638. JOHN MILNER

- ☐ 667. JEFF REARDON
- ☐ 695. WARREN CROMARTIE
- ☐ 730. GARY CARTER
- ☐ 762. MIKE PHILLIPS
- ☐ 779. GRANT JACKSON
- ☐ 788. WOODIE FRYMAN

NEW YORK METS

- ☐ 15. ELLIS VALENTINE
- ☐ 43. MIKE CUBBAGE
- ☐ 79. BOB BAILOR
- ☐ 121. ED LYNCH
- ☐ 143. MOOKIE WILSON
- ☐ 178. DYAR MILLER
- ☐ 205. NEIL ALLEN
- ☐ 234. RON HODGES
- ☐ 246. TEAM LEADER CARD
- ☐ 270. RUSTY STAUB
- ☐ 302. DOUG FLYNN
- ☐ 326. PETE FALCONE
- ☐ 368. ALEX TREVINO
- ☐ 399. PAT ZACHRY
- ☐ 432. MIKE SCOTT
- ☐ 465. LEE MAZZILLI
- ☐ 478. RAY SEARAGE
- ☐ 494. HUBIE BROOKS
- ☐ 524. TOM HAUSMAN
- ☐ 566. MIKE JORGENSEN
- ☐ 592. CRAIG SWAN
- ☐ 623. RON GARDENHIRE(FS)
- ☐ 623. TERRY LEACH(FS)
- ☐ 623. TIM LEARY(FS)
- ☐ 626. RANDY JONES
- ☐ 655. JOEL YOUNGBLOOD
- ☐ 690. DAVE KINGMAN
- ☐ 743. JOHN STEARNS
- ☐ 782. FRANK TAVERAS
- ☐ 783. GREG HARRIS

NEW YORK YANKEES

- ☐ 9. RON GUIDRY
- ☐ 45. RICK CERONE
- ☐ 75. TOMMY JOHN
- ☐ 83. STEVE BALBONI(FS)
- ☐ 83. ANDY MCGAFFIGAN(FS)
- ☐ 83. ANDRE ROBERTSON(FS)
- ☐ 109. DAVE REVERING
- ☐ 142. DAVE LAROCHE
- ☐ 154. DENNIS WERTH
- ☐ 175. JERRY MUMPHREY
- ☐ 208. BOBBY MURCER
- ☐ 240. BUCKY DENT
- ☐ 275. BOB WATSON
- ☐ 300. REGGIE JACKSON
- ☐ 334. AURELIO RODRIGUEZ
- ☐ 349. GEORGE FRAZIER
- ☐ 373. GENE NELSON
- ☐ 405. RICK REUSCHEL
- ☐ 439. DAVE RIGHETTI
- ☐ 472. OSCAR GAMBLE
- ☐ 486. TEAM LEADER CARD
- ☐ 505. GRAIG NETTLES
- ☐ 538. LOU PINIELLA
- ☐ 569. WILLIE RANDOLPH
- ☐ 600. DAVE WINFIELD
- ☐ 635. RON DAVIS
- ☐ 669. LARRY MILBOURNE
- ☐ 694. DAVE WEHRMEISTER
- ☐ 706. BARRY FOOTE
- ☐ 735. RUDY MAY
- ☐ 770. RICH GOSSAGE
- ☐ 791. BOBBY BROWN

OAKLAND A'S

- ☐ 29. DWAYNE MURPHY
- ☐ 60. TONY ARMAS
- ☐ 87. MATT KEOUGH
- ☐ 113. STEVE MCCATTY
- ☐ 139. JEFF JONES
- ☐ 148. MICKEY KLUTTS
- ☐ 156. TEAM LEADER CARD
- ☐ 187. JEFF NEWMAN
- ☐ 217. BO MCLAUGHLIN
- ☐ 243. BOB OWCHINKO
- ☐ 293. ROB PICCIOLO
- ☐ 318. MIKE HEATH
- ☐ 370. MIKE NORRIS
- ☐ 392. RICK BOSETTI
- ☐ 422. CLIFF JOHNSON

- ☐ 454. RICK LANGFORD
- ☐ 476. BRIAN KINGMAN
- ☐ 531. RICH BORDI(FS)
- ☐ 531. MARK BUDASKA(FS)
- ☐ 531. KELVIN MOORE(FS)
- ☐ 534. DAVE MCKAY
- ☐ 578. SHOOTY BABITT
- ☐ 610. RICKEY HENDERSON
- ☐ 633. MITCHELL PAGE
- ☐ 671. MIKE DAVIS
- ☐ 673. KEITH DRUMRIGHT
- ☐ 692. WAYNE GROSS
- ☐ 729. JIM SPENCER
- ☐ 757. TOM UNDERWOOD
- ☐ 787. FRED STANLEY

PHILADELPHIA PHILLIES

- ☐ 20. GARRY MADDOX
- ☐ 53. GREG GROSS
- ☐ 100. MIKE SCHMIDT
- ☐ 127. LONNIE SMITH
- ☐ 152. RAMON AVILES
- ☐ 183. MIKE PROLY
- ☐ 220. MANNY TRILLO
- ☐ 231. MARK DAVIS(FS)
- ☐ 231. BOB DERNIER(FS)
- ☐ 231. OZZIE VIRGIL(FS)
- ☐ 250. TUG MCGRAW
- ☐ 285. SPARKY LYLE
- ☐ 317. DICK RUTHVEN
- ☐ 352. DICK DAVIS
- ☐ 384. KEITH MORELAND
- ☐ 389. GEORGE VUKOVICH
- ☐ 416. MARTY BYSTROM
- ☐ 449. LUIS AGUAYO
- ☐ 480. STEVE CARLTON
- ☐ 515. LARRY BOWA
- ☐ 530. DICKIE NOLES
- ☐ 544. LARRY CHRISTENSON
- ☐ 581. RON REED
- ☐ 615. BOB BOONE
- ☐ 636. TEAM LEADER CARD
- ☐ 647. WARREN BRUSSTAR
- ☐ 680. GARY MATTHEWS
- ☐ 713. DEL UNSER
- ☐ 745. BAKE MCBRIDE
- ☐ 780. PETE ROSE

PITTSBURGH PIRATES

- ☐ 11. GARY ALEXANDER
- ☐ 40. DAVE PARKER
- ☐ 73. BUDDY SOLOMON
- ☐ 106. ENRIQUE ROMO
- ☐ 138. TONY PENA
- ☐ 160. LUIS TIANT
- ☐ 170. JIM BIBBY
- ☐ 207. ROD SCURRY
- ☐ 235. MIKE EASLER
- ☐ 263. VICTOR CRUZ
- ☐ 267. KURT BEVACQUA
- ☐ 291. VANCE LAW(FS)
- ☐ 291. BOB LONG(FS)
- ☐ 291. JOHNNY RAY(FS)
- ☐ 295. JASON THOMPSON
- ☐ 332. DON ROBINSON
- ☐ 365. BILL MADLOCK
- ☐ 383. PASCUAL PEREZ
- ☐ 395. OMAR MORENO
- ☐ 425. JOHN CANDELARIA
- ☐ 458. WILLIE MONTANEZ
- ☐ 485. KENT TEKULVE
- ☐ 513. RICK RHODEN
- ☐ 528. MATT ALEXANDER
- ☐ 543. BILL ROBINSON
- ☐ 588. DALE BERRA
- ☐ 618. TIM FOLI
- ☐ 652. STEVE NICOSIA
- ☐ 696. TEAM LEADER CARD
- ☐ 715. WILLIE STARGELL
- ☐ 752. LEE LACY

ST. LOUIS CARDINALS

- ☐ 27. TOM HERR
- ☐ 56. MARK LITTELL
- ☐ 86. DANE IORG
- ☐ 108. BOB SYKES
- ☐ 135. ANDY RINCON
- ☐ 181. SILVIO MARTINEZ

- ☐ 186. TEAM LEADER CARD
- ☐ 210. KEITH HERNANDEZ
- ☐ 236. JOHN MARTIN
- ☐ 260. BRUCE SUTTER
- ☐ 262. DOUG BAIR
- ☐ 288. GARRY TEMPLETON
- ☐ 316. STEVE BRAUN
- ☐ 367. JIM KAAT
- ☐ 420. GEORGE HENDRICK
- ☐ 447. DARRELL PORTER
- ☐ 474. KEN OBERKFELL
- ☐ 503. JULIO GONZALEZ
- ☐ 533. JOAQUIN ANDUJAR
- ☐ 561. GLENN BRUMMER(FS)
- ☐ 561. LUIS DELEON(FS)
- ☐ 561. GENE ROOF(FS)
- ☐ 574. MIKE RAMSEY
- ☐ 604. ORLANDO SANCHEZ
- ☐ 631. GENE TENACE
- ☐ 658. TITO LANDRUM
- ☐ 689. LARY SORENSEN
- ☐ 727. SIXTO LEZCANO
- ☐ 749. BOB SHIRLEY
- ☐ 775. BOB FORSCH

SAN DIEGO PADRES

- ☐ 28. JOHN URREA
- ☐ 65. TERRY KENNEDY
- ☐ 95. OZZIE SMITH
- ☐ 120. GARY LUCAS
- ☐ 151. DAVE EDWARDS
- ☐ 192. BRODERICK PERKINS
- ☐ 219. JOHN CURTIS
- ☐ 249. TIM FLANNERY
- ☐ 278. JOHN LITTLEFIELD
- ☐ 307. RANDY BASS
- ☐ 330. RICK WISE
- ☐ 366. TEAM LEADER CARD
- ☐ 376. CHRIS WELSH
- ☐ 407. DANNY BOONE
- ☐ 434. JOE LEFEBVRE
- ☐ 464. JUAN BONILLA
- ☐ 511. RUPPERT JONES
- ☐ 541. BARRY EVANS
- ☐ 587. TIM LOLLAR
- ☐ 614. JUAN EICHELBERGER
- ☐ 641. STEVE MURA
- ☐ 662. LUIS SALAZAR
- ☐ 708. GENE RICHARDS
- ☐ 731. MIKE ARMSTRONG(FS)
- ☐ 731. DOUG GWOSDZ(FS)
- ☐ 731. FRED KUHAULUA(FS)
- ☐ 764. STEVE SWISHER

SAN FRANCISCO GIANTS

- ☐ 17. DARRELL EVANS
- ☐ 47. JEFF LEONARD
- ☐ 84. RENNIE STENNETT
- ☐ 116. JIM WOHLFORD
- ☐ 144. FRED BREINING
- ☐ 171. BOB BRENLY(FS)
- ☐ 171. CHILI DAVIS(FS)
- ☐ 171. BOB TUFTS(FS)
- ☐ 182. LARRY HERNDON
- ☐ 209. GARY LAVELLE
- ☐ 242. MILT MAY
- ☐ 304. JOHNNIE LEMASTER
- ☐ 364. DOYLE ALEXANDER
- ☐ 406. AL HOLLAND
- ☐ 430. VIDA BLUE
- ☐ 460. JACK CLARK
- ☐ 498. DAVE BERGMAN
- ☐ 529. ALLEN RIPLEY
- ☐ 568. JOE PETTINI
- ☐ 576. TEAM LEADER CARD
- ☐ 593. BILLY E. SMITH
- ☐ 627. ENOS CABELL
- ☐ 656. EDDIE WHITSON
- ☐ 687. GREG MINTON
- ☐ 722. JERRY MARTIN
- ☐ 754. JOE MORGAN
- ☐ 777. TOM GRIFFIN

SEATTLE MARINERS

- ☐ 22. JIM BEATTIE
- ☐ 52. LARRY ANDERSON
- ☐ 72. RICK AUERBACH
- ☐ 98. TERRY BULLING

- ☐ 130. JULIO CRUZ
- ☐ 197. SHANE RAWLEY
- ☐ 224. BRUCE BOCHTE
- ☐ 283. BRIAN ALLARD
- ☐ 312. LENNY RANDLE
- ☐ 336. TEAM LEADER CARD
- ☐ 358. MIKE PARROTT
- ☐ 371. JERRY DON GLEATON
- ☐ 382. JOE SIMPSON
- ☐ 413. DAN MEYER
- ☐ 440. JEFF BURROUGHS
- ☐ 468. FLOYD BANNISTER
- ☐ 497. JIM ANDERSON
- ☐ 523. GARY GRAY
- ☐ 571. GLENN ABBOTT
- ☐ 598. BOB GALASSO
- ☐ 632. BRYAN CLARK
- ☐ 649. KEN CLAY
- ☐ 678. TOM PACIOREK
- ☐ 711. DAVE EDLER(FS)
- ☐ 711. DAVE HENDERSON(FS)
- ☐ 711. REGGIE WALTON(FS)
- ☐ 719. JERRY NARRON
- ☐ 742. DICK DRAGO
- ☐ 769. RICHIE ZISK

TEXAS RANGERS

- ☐ 16. STEVE COMER
- ☐ 36. TEAM LEADER CARD
- ☐ 50. BUDDY BELL
- ☐ 78. GEORGE MEDICH
- ☐ 103. BOB LACEY
- ☐ 112. BILLY SAMPLE
- ☐ 149. PAT PUTNAM
- ☐ 177. JOHN ELLIS
- ☐ 212. MARIO MENDOZA
- ☐ 239. JON MATLACK
- ☐ 272. BUMP WILLS
- ☐ 298. DANNY DARWIN
- ☐ 335. JIM SUNDBERG
- ☐ 402. BILL STEIN
- ☐ 418. JOHN BUTCHER(FS)
- ☐ 418. BOBBY JOHNSON(FS)
- ☐ 418. DAVE J. SCHMIDT(FS)
- ☐ 443. MARK WAGNER
- ☐ 463. JIM KERN
- ☐ 496. JOHNNY GRUBB
- ☐ 527. JOHN HERNY JOHNSON
- ☐ 567. BOB BABCOCK
- ☐ 590. AL OLIVER
- ☐ 624. FERGIE JENKINS
- ☐ 657. TOM POQUETTE
- ☐ 688. LEON ROBERTS
- ☐ 704. MICKEY RIVERS
- ☐ 718. CHARLIE HOUGH
- ☐ 751. RICK HONEYCUTT

TORONTO BLUE JAYS

- ☐ 19. ERNIE WHITT
- ☐ 49. ALVIS WOODS
- ☐ 71. ROY LEE JACKSON
- ☐ 99. BARRY BONNELL
- ☐ 125. DANNY AINGE
- ☐ 155. OTTO VELEZ
- ☐ 196. WILLIE UPSHAW
- ☐ 203. JESSE BARFIELD(FS)
- ☐ 203. BRIAN MILNER(FS)
- ☐ 203. BOOMER WELLS(FS)
- ☐ 223. LLOYD MOSEBY
- ☐ 254. JORGE BELL
- ☐ 282. KEN MACHA
- ☐ 314. BUCK MARTINEZ
- ☐ 380. DAVE STIEB
- ☐ 412. LUIS LEAL
- ☐ 437. JUAN BERENGUER
- ☐ 470. JOHN MAYBERRY
- ☐ 499. PAUL MIRABELLA
- ☐ 518. GARTH IORG
- ☐ 565. JACKSON TODD
- ☐ 596. DAMASO GARCIA
- ☐ 606. TEAM LEADER CARD
- ☐ 665. JIM CLANCY
- ☐ 677. ALFREDO GRIFFIN
- ☐ 707. MARK BOMBACK
- ☐ 739. JOEY MCLAUGHLIN
- ☐ 768. JERRY GARVIN

1982 TOPPS
TRADED (132)
2 1/2" X 3 1/2"

ORIOLES
CAL RIPKEN

ATLANTA BRAVES

- ☐ 4T. STEVE BEDROSIAN
- ☐ 125T. BOB WATSON

BALTIMORE ORIOLES

- ☐ 35T. DAN FORD
- ☐ 81T. JOE NOLAN
- ☐ 98T. CAL RIPKEN

BOSTON RED SOX

NO CARDS ISSUED

CALIFORNIA ANGELS

- ☐ 9T. BOB BOONE
- ☐ 21T. DOUG CORBETT
- ☐ 26T. DOUG DECINCES
- ☐ 34T. TIM FOLI
- ☐ 47T. REGGIE JACKSON
- ☐ 48T. RON JACKSON
- ☐ 53T. MICK KELLEHER
- ☐ 128T. ROB WILFONG

CHICAGO CUBS

- ☐ 10T. LARRY BOWA
- ☐ 11T. DAN BRIGGS
- ☐ 16T. BILL CAMPBELL
- ☐ 49T. FERGIE JENKINS
- ☐ 52T. JAY JOHNSTONE
- ☐ 55T. JUNIOR KENNEDY
- ☐ 76T. KEITH MORELAND
- ☐ 82T. DICKIE NOLES
- ☐ 92T. MIKE PROLY
- ☐ 99T. ALLEN RIPLEY
- ☐ 129T. BUMP WILLS
- ☐ 130T. GARY WOODS

CHICAGO WHITE SOX

- ☐ 54T. STEVE KEMP
- ☐ 85T. TOM PACIOREK
- ☐ 101T. AURELIO RODRIGUEZ

CINCINNATI REDS

- ☐ 19T. CESAR CEDENO
- ☐ 41T. GREG HARRIS
- ☐ 56T. JIM KERN
- ☐ 58T. WAYNE KRENCHICKI
- ☐ 72T. EDDIE MILNER
- ☐ 105T. BOB SHIRLEY
- ☐ 120T. ALEX TREVINO

CLEVELAND INDIANS

- ☐ 42T. VON HAYES
- ☐ 69T. BAKE MCBRIDE
- ☐ 71T. LARRY MILBOURNE
- ☐ 87T. JACK PERCONTE
- ☐ 111T. LARY SORENSEN
- ☐ 116T. RICK SUTCLIFFE
- ☐ 127T. EDDIE WHITSON

DETROIT TIGERS

- .☐ 15T. ENOS CABELL
- ☐ 43T. LARRY HERNDON
- ☐ 45T. MIKE IVIE
- ☐ 62T. CHET LEMON
- ☐ 112T. ELIAS SOSA
- ☐ 121T. JERRY TURNER

HOUSTON ASTROS

- ☐ 57T. RAY KNIGHT
- ☐ 61T. MIKE LACOSS

KANSAS CITY ROYALS

- ☐ 8T. VIDA BLUE
- ☐ 37T. DAVE FROST
- ☐ 46T. GRANT JACKSON
- ☐ 65T. JERRY MARTIN
- ☐ 93T. GREG PRYOR
- ☐ 126T. DENNIS WERTH

LOS ANGELES DODGERS

- ☐ 5T. MARK BELANGER
- ☐ 75T. JOSE MORALES
- ☐ 84T. JORGE ORTA
- ☐ 103T. STEVE SAX

MILWAUKEE BREWERS

- ☐ 89T. ROB PICIOLO

1ST BASE
TWINS
KENT HRBEK

MINNESOTA TWINS

- ☐ 13T. TOM BRUNANSKY
- ☐ 17T. BOBBY CASTILLO
- ☐ 25T. RON DAVIS
- ☐ 44T. KENT HRBEK
- ☐ 51T. RANDY JOHNSON
- ☐ 124T. RON WASHINGTON

MONTREAL EXPOS

- ☐ 7T. TIM BLACKWELL
- ☐ 83T. AL OLIVER
- ☐ 104T. DAN SCHATZEDER
- ☐ 118T. FRANK TAVERAS

NEW YORK METS

- ☐ 36T. GEORGE FOSTER
- ☐ 39T. RON GARDENHIRE
- ☐ 94T. CHARLIE PULEO
- ☐ 123T. TOM VERYZER

NEW YORK YANKEES

- ☐ 1T. DOYLE ALEXANDER
- ☐ 20T. DAVE COLLINS
- ☐ 30T. ROGER ERICKSON
- ☐ 40T. KEN GRIFFEY
- ☐ 67T. JOHN MAYBERRY
- ☐ 95T. SHANE RAWLEY
- ☐ 107T. ROY SMALLEY
- ☐ 131T. BUTCH WYNEGAR

OAKLAND A'S

- 14T. JEFF BURROUGHS
- 64T. DAVE LOPES
- 70T. DAN MEYER
- 102T. JOE RUDI

PHILADELPHIA PHILLIES

- 27T. IVAN DEJESUS
- 28T. BOB DERNIER
- 29T. BO DIAZ
- 32T. ED FARMER
- 59T. MIKE KRUKOW
- 73T. SID MONGE
- 100T. BILL ROBINSON

PITTSBURGH PIRATES

- 3T. ROSS BAUGARTEN
- 24T. DICK DAVIS
- 77T. JIM MORRISON
- 96T. JOHNNY RAY

ST. LOUIS CARDINALS

- 79T. STEVE MURA
- 108T. LONNIE SMITH
- 109T. OZZIE SMITH

SAN DIEGO PADRES

- 6T. KURT BEVACQUA
- 63T. SIXTO LEZCANO
- 74T. JOHN MONTEFUSCO
- 90T. JOE PITTMAN
- 106T. ERIC SHOW
- 119T. GARRY TEMPLETON

SAN FRANCISCO GIANTS

- 23T. CHILI DAVIS
- 38T. RICH GALE
- 60T. DUANE KUIPER
- 66T. RENIE MARTIN
- 110T. REGGIE SMITH
- 115T. CHAMP SUMMERS

SEATTLE MARINERS

- 12T. BOBBY BROWN
- 18T. BILL CAUDILL
- 22T. AL COWENS
- 31T. JIM ESSIAN
- 80T. GENE NELSON
- 88T. GAYLORD PERRY
- 113T. MIKE STANTON
- 114T. STEVE STROUGHTER
- 122T. ED VANDEBERG

TEXAS RANGERS

- 33T. DOUG FLYNN
- 50T. LAMAR JOHNSON
- 68T. LEE MAZZILLI
- 86T. LARRY PARRISH
- 117T. FRANK TANANA

TORONTO BLUE JAYS

- 2T. JESSE BARFIELD
- 78T. RANCE MULLINIKS
- 91T. HOSKEN POWELL
- 97T. DAVE REVERING

1983 TOPPS (792)
2 1/2" X 3 1/2"

ATLANTA BRAVES

- 26. JERRY ROYSTER
- 50. BOB HORNER
- 76. RICK MAHLER
- 104. BOB WALK
- 126. JOE TORRE(M)
- 157. STEVE BEDROSIAN
- 207. RICK CAMP
- 235. CLAUDELL WASHINGTON
- 255. GENE GARBER
- 288. JOE COWLEY
- 314. KEN DAYLEY
- 339. TERRY HARPER
- 364. BREET BUTLER
- 410. PHIL NIEKRO
- 417. TOM HAUSMAN
- 439. RAFAEL RAMIREZ
- 467. RUFINO LINARES
- 502. TEAM LEADER CARD
- 521. BRUCE BENEDICT
- 544. LARRY WHISENTON
- 572. BOB WATSON
- 596. RANDY JOHNSON
- 624. GLENN HUBBARD
- 649. TOMMY BOGGS
- 676. BIFF POCOROBA
- 760. DALE MURPHY
- 792. CHRIS CHAMBLISS

BALTIMORE ORIOLES

- 21. TEAM LEADER CARD
- 59. BENNY AYALA
- 85. KEN SINGLETON
- 138. RICK DEMPSEY
- 163. CAL RIPKEN
- 192. FLOYD RAYFORD
- 217. TIM STODDARD
- 242. JOE NOLAN
- 268. STORM DAVIS
- 293. GLENN GULLIVER
- 319. LENN SAKATA
- 347. SAMMY STEWART
- 372. TERRY CROWLEY
- 426. EARL WEAVER(M)
- 445. MIKE FLANAGAN
- 473. JOHN LOWENSTEIN
- 490. JIM PALMER
- 530. EDDIE MURRAY
- 553. DENNY MARTINEZ
- 579. RICH DAUER
- 605. GARY ROENICKE
- 631. TIPPY MARTINEZ
- 655. AL BUMBRY
- 683. DAN FORD
- 718. JIM DWYER
- 745. SCOTT MCGREGOR

BOSTON RED SOX

- 30. JIM RICE
- 56. CHUCK RAINEY
- 82. BRUCE HURST
- 108. GLENN HOFFMAN
- 135. DWIGHT EVANS
- 162. MARK CLEAR
- 188. RICK MILLER
- 213. TOM BURGMEIER
- 239. DAVE STAPLETON
- 270. DENNIS ECKERSLEY
- 295. JERRY REMY
- 318. JOHN TUDOR
- 344. ROGER LAFRANCOIS
- 381. TEAM LEADER CARD
- 419. STEVE CRAWFORD
- 446. REID NICHOLS
- 472. GARY ALLENSON
- 498. WADE BOGGS
- 523. CARNEY LANSFORD
- 550. CARL YASTRZEMSKI
- 577. LUIS APONTE
- 602. RICH GEDMAN
- 628. JULIO VALDEZ
- 654. BOB OJEDA
- 682. BOB STANLEY
- 715. TONY PEREZ
- 743. MIKE TORREZ
- 786. RALPH HOUK(M)

CALIFORNIA ANGELS

- 27. DOUG CORBETT
- 53. MIKE WITT
- 79. MICK KELLEHER
- 105. DON BAYLOR
- 131. ED OTT
- 158. ROB WILFONG
- 178. LUIS TIANT
- 184. BOB CLARK
- 200. ROD CAREW
- 236. STEVE RENKO
- 262. RON JACKSON
- 276. GENE MAUCH(M)
- 315. RICK BURLESON
- 341. DOUG DECINCES
- 416. JOE FERGUSON
- 442. BRIAN DOWNING
- 468. DAVE GOLTZ
- 500. REGGIE JACKSON
- 520. FRED LYNN
- 547. GEOFF ZAHN
- 573. ANDY HASSLER
- 599. DON AASE
- 623. LUIS SANCHEZ
- 625. KEN FORSCH
- 651. TEAM LEADER CARD
- 678. JUAN BENIQUEZ
- 712. BRUCE KISON
- 735. TOMMY JOHN
- 738. TIM FOLI
- 765. BOB BOONE
- 777. JOHN CURTIS
- 790. BOB GRICH

CHICAGO CUBS

- 22. RANDY MARTZ
- 51. TEAM LEADER CARD
- 73. ALLEN RIPLEY
- 83. RYNE SANDBERG
- 99. DICKIE NOLES
- 125. LEON DURHAM
- 152. JAY JOHNSTONE
- 204. JUNIOR KENNEDY
- 230. FERGIE JENKINS
- 250. BILL BUCKNER
- 305. LARRY BOWA
- 335. STEVE HENDERSON
- 356. GARY WOODS
- 436. BILL CAMPBELL
- 456. LEE ELIA(M)
- 481. SCOT THOMPSON
- 508. TOM FILER
- 542. JODY DAVIS
- 568. WILLIE HERNANDEZ
- 597. MIKE PROLY
- 619. KEITH MORELAND
- 643. BUMP WILLS
- 699. LEE SMITH
- 729. JERRY MORALES
- 759. DOUG BIRD
- 787. DICK TIDROW

CHICAGO WHITE SOX

- 20. CARLTON FISK
- 46. RICHARD DOTSON
- 72. TOM PACIOREK

☐ 98. VANCE LAW
☐ 124. MARC HILL
☐ 153. JERRY KOOSMAN
☐ 177. HAROLD BAINES
☐ 216. TONY LARUSSA(M)
☐ 260. STEVE KEMP
☐ 278. KEVIN HICKEY
☐ 310. GREG LUZINSKI
☐ 362. BILL ALMON
☐ 409. MARVIS FOLEY
☐ 434. DENNIS LAMP
☐ 461. STEVE TROUT
☐ 487. JERRY HAIRSTON
☐ 514. RUDY LAW
☐ 541. BRITT BURNS
☐ 560. RON LEFLORE
☐ 591. TEAM LEADER CARD
☐ 618. LAMARR LOYT
☐ 669. MIKE SQUIRES
☐ 693. SPARKY LYLE
☐ 698. TONY BERNAZARD
☐ 758. AURELIO RODRIGUEZ
☐ 772. JIM KERN

CINCINNATI REDS

☐ 34. PAUL HOUSEHOLDER
☐ 60. JOHNNY BENCH
☐ 86. TOM HUME
☐ 112. BOB SHIRLEY
☐ 139. BRUCE BERENYI
☐ 165. DAN DRIESSEN
☐ 191. JOE PRICE
☐ 215. MARIO SOTO
☐ 243. DUANE WALKER
☐ 269. RON OESTER
☐ 296. GREG HARRIS
☐ 322. DAVE VAN GORDER
☐ 351. TEAM LEADER CARD
☐ 374. WAYNE KRENCHICKI
☐ 423. TOM LAWLESS
☐ 449. EDDIE MILNER
☐ 475. CESAR CEDENO
☐ 527. LARRY BIITTNER
☐ 554. MIKE VAIL
☐ 580. TOM SEAVER
☐ 607. CHARLIE LEIBRANDT
☐ 632. ALEX TREVINO
☐ 658. FRANK PASTORE
☐ 684. RAFAEL LANDESTOY
☐ 720. DAVE CONCEPION
☐ 756. RUSS NIXON(M)

CLEVELAND INDIANS

☐ 48. LARY SORENSEN
☐ 91. LARRY MILBOURNE
☐ 120. LEN BARKER
☐ 141. TEAM LEADER CARD
☐ 182. MIKE FISCHLIN
☐ 227. CHRIS BANDO
☐ 248. BAKE MCBRIDE
☐ 280. BERT BLYLEVEN
☐ 289. JERRY DYBZINSKI
☐ 303. MIGUEL DILONE
☐ 325. VON HAYES
☐ 348. ALAN BANNISTER
☐ 367. BUD ANDERSON
☐ 429. EDDIE WHITSON
☐ 480. TOBY HARRAH
☐ 497. RICK SUTCLIFFE
☐ 524. TOM BRENNAN
☐ 546. DAVE GARCIA(M)
☐ 569. JACK PERCONTE
☐ 614. ED GLYNN
☐ 616. BILL NAHORODNY
☐ 640. ANDRE THORNTON
☐ 660. MIKE HARGROVE
☐ 689. RON HASSEY
☐ 725. DAN SPILLNER
☐ 757. RICK MANNING
☐ 779. RICK WAITS

DETROIT TIGERS

☐ 13. LARRY HERNDON
☐ 41. JERRY TURNER
☐ 65. JACK MORRIS
☐ 95. ALAN TRAMMELL
☐ 119. TOM BROOKENS

☐ 147. RICK LEACH
☐ 174. JERRY UJDUR
☐ 196. BILL FAHEY
☐ 225. ENOS CABELL
☐ 261. TEAM LEADER CARD
☐ 285. LANCE PARRISH
☐ 304. DAVE RUCKER
☐ 332. GLENN WILSON
☐ 373. KEVIN SAUCIER
☐ 430. KIRK GIBSON
☐ 457. MILT WILCOX
☐ 483. LYNN JONES
☐ 509. LOU WHITAKER
☐ 536. JOHNNY WOCKENFUSS
☐ 562. DAVE ROZEMA
☐ 588. PAT UNDERWOOD
☐ 613. MIKE IVIE
☐ 638. DAN PETRY
☐ 666. SPARKY ANDERSON(M)
☐ 691. DAVE TOBIK
☐ 727. CHET LEMON
☐ 753. ELIAS SOSA

HOUSTON ASTROS

☐ 14. FRANK LACORTE
☐ 39. TERRY PUHL
☐ 66. BOB LILLIS(M)
☐ 92. MIKE LACOSS
☐ 117. ALAN KNICELY
☐ 172. VERN RUHLE
☐ 193. HARRY SPILMAN
☐ 198. KIKO GARCIA
☐ 221. JOE NIEKRO
☐ 247. DAVE SMITH
☐ 275. RAY KNIGHT
☐ 328. CRAIG REYNOLDS
☐ 360. NOLAN RYAN
☐ 382. BOB KNEPPER
☐ 422. GEORGE CAPPUZZELLO
☐ 441. TEAM LEADER CARD
☐ 478. PHIL GARNER
☐ 507. TONY SCOTT
☐ 538. DANNY HEEP
☐ 558. DICKIE THON
☐ 585. JOSE CRUZ
☐ 611. BERT ROBERGE
☐ 639. ART HOWE
☐ 662. JOE SAMBITO
☐ 692. DENNY WALLING
☐ 723. RANDY MOFFITT
☐ 774. ALAN ASHBY
☐ 752. LUIS PUJOLS

KANSAS CITY ROYALS

☐ 25. HAL MCRAE
☐ 52. ONIX CONCEPCION
☐ 75. AMOS OTIS
☐ 96. DICK HOWSER (M)
☐ 136. WILLIE AIKENS
☐ 155. DAN QUISENBERRY
☐ 194. CESAR GERONIMO
☐ 219. MIKE ARMSTRONG
☐ 238. BUD BLACK
☐ 264. JAMIE QUIRK
☐ 316. PAUL SPLITTORFF
☐ 340. LARRY GURA
☐ 377. LEE MAY
☐ 418. GREG PRYOR
☐ 443. DON HOOD
☐ 471. TEAM LEADER CARD
☐ 525. FRANK WHITE
☐ 570. VIDA BLUE
☐ 600. GEORGE BRETT
☐ 626. JERRY MARTIN
☐ 656. DAVE FROST
☐ 687. U. L. WASHINGTON
☐ 710. WILLIE WILSON
☐ 746. JOHN WATHAN
☐ 785. DENNIS LEONARD

LOS ANGELES DODGERS

☐ 15. RON CEY
☐ 40. FERNANDO VALENZUELA
☐ 63. RICK MONDAY
☐ 90. JERRY REUSS
☐ 113. RON ROENICKE
☐ 170. STEVE HOWE
☐ 220. DUSTY BAKER

☐ 245. STEVE SAX
☐ 273. MARK BELANGER
☐ 306. TOM LASORDA(M)
☐ 324. MIKE MARSHALL
☐ 352. MIKE SCIOSCIA
☐ 376. KEN LANDREAUX
☐ 425. PEDRO GUERRERO
☐ 454. BOB WELCH
☐ 477. TOM NIEDENFUER
☐ 532. DAVE STEWART
☐ 555. STEVE YEAGER
☐ 583. TERRY FORSTER
☐ 610. STEVE GARVEY
☐ 633. VICENTE ROMO
☐ 661. BILL RUSSELL
☐ 681. TEAM LEADER CARD
☐ 722. JORGE ORTA
☐ 748. DERREL THOMAS
☐ 775. BURT HOOTON

MILWAUKEE BREWERS

☐ 10. GORMAN THOMAS
☐ 35. ROLLIE FINGERS
☐ 62. BOB MCCLURE
☐ 88. JIM GANTNER
☐ 114. JIM SLATON
☐ 142. MIKE CALDWELL
☐ 145. DON SUTTON
☐ 167. MARK BROUHARD
☐ 190. CECIL COOPER
☐ 218. ROY HOWELL
☐ 244. DWIGHT BERNARD
☐ 271. ED ROMERO
☐ 297. NED YOST
☐ 321. TEAM LEADER CARD
☐ 350. ROBIN YOUNT
☐ 375. PETE VUCKOVICH
☐ 424. JERRY AUGUSTINE
☐ 450. TED SIMMONS
☐ 476. ROB PICCIOLO
☐ 503. MOOSE HAAS
☐ 528. JAMIE EASTERLY
☐ 582. MARSHALL EDWARDS
☐ 608. DON MONEY
☐ 630. PAUL MOLITOR
☐ 659. CHARLIE MOORE
☐ 726. HARVEY KUENN(M)
☐ 750. BEN OGLIVIE
☐ 773. LARRY HISLE

MINNESOTA TWINS

☐ 11. BILLY GARDNER(M)
☐ 33. JACK O'CONNOR
☐ 67. SAL BUTERA
☐ 93. JOHN CASTINO
☐ 121. MICKEY HATCHER
☐ 166. JOHN PACELLA
☐ 181. TERRY FELTON
☐ 197. JIM EISENREICH
☐ 232. TOM BRUNANSKY
☐ 266. PAUL BORIS
☐ 294. DAVE ENGLE
☐ 308. JESUS VEGA
☐ 327. BOBBY CASTILLO
☐ 354. RANDY JOHNSON
☐ 380. RON DAVIS
☐ 431. GARY GAETTI
☐ 458. RON WASHINGTON
☐ 499. JEFF LITTLE
☐ 517. GARY WARD
☐ 529. TIM LAUDNER
☐ 559. PETE REDFERN
☐ 586. FRANK VIOLA
☐ 647. BOBBY MITCHELL
☐ 671. LENNY FAEDO
☐ 690. KENT HRBEK
☐ 731. AL WILLIAMS
☐ 751. BRAD HAVENS
☐ 771. TEAM LEADER CARD

MONTREAL EXPOS

☐ 31. BILL GULLICKSON
☐ 57. TIM BLACKWELL
☐ 111. TEAM LEADER CARD
☐ 137. WOODIE FRYMAN
☐ 164. DAVE PALMER
☐ 169. DOUG FLYNN

1983 Topps

☐ 189. DAN SCHATZEDER
☐ 214. JERRY WHITE
☐ 237. DAN NORMAN
☐ 265. JOEL YOUNGBLOOD
☐ 267. TERRY FRANCONA
☐ 290. JEFF REARDON
☐ 320. STEVE ROGERS
☐ 370. GARY CARTER
☐ 420. AL OLIVER
☐ 447. BRYN SMITH
☐ 474. RAY BURRIS
☐ 495. WARREN CROMARTIE
☐ 516. BILL VIRDON(M)
☐ 552. TIM WALLACH
☐ 595. TIM RAINES
☐ 629. CHARLIE LEA
☐ 657. MIKE GATES
☐ 680. ANDRE DAWSON
☐ 686. RANDY LERCH
☐ 717. SCOTT SANDERSON
☐ 744. BRAD MILLS
☐ 768. CHRIS SPEIER

NEW YORK METS

☐ 29. RANDY JONES
☐ 55. MOOKIE WILSON
☐ 80. GEROGE FOSTER
☐ 107. MIKE JORGENSEN
☐ 134. HUBIE BROOKS
☐ 160. DAVE KINGMAN
☐ 187. TERRY LEACH
☐ 212. JOHN STEARNS
☐ 246. GEORGE BAMBERGER(M)
☐ 292. CRAIG SWAN
☐ 317. GARY RAJSICH
☐ 343. BOB BAILOR
☐ 369. JESSE OROSCO
☐ 444. WALLY BACKMAN
☐ 469. RON GARDENHIRE
☐ 496. TOM VERYZER
☐ 522. PAT ZACHRY
☐ 548. BRIAN GILES
☐ 549. CHARLIE PULEO
☐ 575. NEIL ALLEN
☐ 601. ED LYNCH
☐ 621. TEAM LEADER CARD
☐ 653. ELLIS VALENTINE
☐ 679. MIKE SCOTT
☐ 713. RON HODGES
☐ 739. RICK OWNBEY
☐ 740. RUSTY STAUB
☐ 764. PETE FALCONE

NEW YORK YANKEES

☐ 8. STEVE BALBONI
☐ 19. OSCAR GAMBLE
☐ 45. JOHN MAYBERRY
☐ 81. TEAM LEADER CARD
☐ 110. KEN GRIFFEY
☐ 123. GEORGE FRAZIER
☐ 140. WILLIE RANDOLPH
☐ 176. DAVE RIGHETTI
☐ 203. MIKE MORGAN
☐ 240. RICH GOSSAGE
☐ 254. RICK CERONE
☐ 281. ANDRE ROBERTSON
☐ 307. LOU PINIELLA
☐ 333. DAVE LAROCHE

☐ 359. DAVE COLLINS
☐ 408. RUDY MAY
☐ 440. RON GUIDRY
☐ 460. ROY SMALLEY
☐ 486. CLYDE KING(M)
☐ 512. DOYLE ALEXANDER
☐ 539. ROGER ERICKSON
☐ 592. SHANE RAWLEY
☐ 617. BUTCH WYNEGAR
☐ 635. GRAIG NETTLES
☐ 652. BUTCH HOBSON
☐ 670. JERRY MUMPHREY
☐ 685. LEE MAZZILLI
☐ 697. BARRY FOOTE
☐ 770. DAVE WINFIELD
☐ 782. BOBBY MURCER

OAKLAND A'S

☐ 23. MIKE HEATH
☐ 47. DAVE MCKAY
☐ 87. JOE RUDI
☐ 102. DAVE BEARD
☐ 127. PRESTON HANNA
☐ 156. BILLY MARTIN(M)
☐ 180. RICKEY HENDERSON
☐ 208. DAN MEYER
☐ 233. WAYNE GROSS
☐ 259. JEFF JONES
☐ 286. RICK LANDFORD
☐ 312. BRIAN KINGMAN
☐ 338. BOB OWCHINKO
☐ 365. DAVE LOPES
☐ 413. MATT KEOUGH
☐ 435. TONY ARMAS
☐ 466. TOM UNDERWOOD
☐ 493. STEVE MCCATTY
☐ 513. FRED STANLEY
☐ 531. TEAM LEADER CARD
☐ 571. MICKEY KLUTTS
☐ 598. DWAYNE MURPHY
☐ 620. MIKE NORRIS
☐ 648. JEFF BURROUGHS
☐ 709. JIMMY SEXTON
☐ 737. MITCHELL PAGE
☐ 762. CLIFF JOHNSON
☐ 784. JEFF NEWMAN

PHILADELPHIA PHILLIES

☐ 16. GEORGE VUKOVICH
☐ 43. BOB DERNIER
☐ 70. STEVE CARLTON
☐ 100. PETE ROSE
☐ 148. DAVE W. ROBERTS
☐ 175. BO DIAZ
☐ 199. MARTY BYSTROM
☐ 211. JOHN DENNY
☐ 229. TEAM LEADER CARD
☐ 252. LUIS AGUAYO
☐ 279. GREG GROSS
☐ 300. MIKE SCHMIDT
☐ 331. MIKE KRUKOW
☐ 357. LEN MATUSZEK
☐ 383. OZZIE VIRGIL
☐ 432. PORFIRIO ALTAMIRANO
☐ 459. ED FARMER
☐ 484. DICK RUTHVEN
☐ 510. TUG MCGRAW
☐ 535. MANNY TRILLO
☐ 564. SID MONGE
☐ 587. IVAN DEJESUS
☐ 615. GARRY MADDOX
☐ 637. PAT CORRALES(M)
☐ 664. BOB MOLINARO
☐ 668. LARRY CHRISTENSON
☐ 728. RON REED
☐ 754. BILL ROBINSON
☐ 780. GARY MATTHEWS

PITTSBURGH PIRATES

☐ 17. KENT TEKULVE
☐ 44. DON ROBINSON
☐ 69. LEE LACY
☐ 97. ROSS BAUMGARTEN
☐ 122. JIMMY SMITH
☐ 149. JOHNNY RAY
☐ 173. JIM MORRISON
☐ 205. DAVE PARKER

☐ 226. ENRIQUE ROMO
☐ 253. LARRY MCWILLIAMS
☐ 291. TEAM LEADER CARD
☐ 329. RANDY NIEMANN
☐ 355. JIM BIBBY
☐ 385. MIKE EASLER
☐ 433. DALE BERRA
☐ 462. STEVE NICOSIA
☐ 485. OMAR MORENO
☐ 537. ROD SCURRY
☐ 566. MANNY SARMIENTO
☐ 590. TONY PENA
☐ 645. BILL MADLOCK
☐ 667. DICK DAVIS
☐ 696. CHUCK TANNER(M)
☐ 730. JASON THOMPSON
☐ 755. JOHN CANDELARIA
☐ 778. RICH HEBNER
☐ 781. RICK RHODEN

ST. LOUIS CARDINALS

☐ 24. STEVE MURA
☐ 49. WILLIE MCGEE
☐ 74. JULIO GONZALEZ
☐ 103. DARRELL PORTER
☐ 128. MIKE RAMSEY
☐ 150. BRUCE SUTTER
☐ 186. WHITEY HERZOG(M)
☐ 206. KEN OBERKFELL
☐ 228. JOAQUIN ANDUJAR
☐ 284. JEFF LAHTI
☐ 311. GLENN BRUMMER
☐ 337. TITO LANDRUM
☐ 363. JOHN STUPER
☐ 415. BOB FORSCH
☐ 438. DAVE LAPOINT
☐ 465. LONNIE SMITH
☐ 489. TOM HERR
☐ 515. GENE TENACE
☐ 540. OZZIE SMITH
☐ 561. TEAM LEADER CARD
☐ 578. DAVID GREEN
☐ 594. ERIC RASMUSSEN
☐ 627. DOUG BAIR
☐ 650. GEORGE HENDRICK
☐ 672. JIM KAAT
☐ 700. KEITH HERNANDEZ
☐ 721. JOHN MARTIN
☐ 734. STEVE BRAUN
☐ 788. DANE IORG

SAN DIEGO PADRES

☐ 7. GENE RICHARDS
☐ 38. TIM FLANNERY
☐ 68. ERIC SHOW
☐ 94. DAVE EDWARDS
☐ 118. CHRIS WELSH
☐ 168. JUAN EICHELBERGER
☐ 185. TIM LOLLAR
☐ 223. JOHN MONTEFUSCO
☐ 251. ALAN WIGGINS
☐ 274. TERRY KENNEDY
☐ 298. FLOYD CHIFFER
☐ 323. LUIS DELEON
☐ 346. JOE PITTMAN
☐ 366. DICK WILLIAMS(M)
☐ 384. DAVE DRAVECKY
☐ 455. SIXTO LEZCANO
☐ 482. TONY GWYNN
☐ 505. GARRY TEMPLETON
☐ 533. LUIS SALAZAR
☐ 563. JUAN BONILLA
☐ 593. BRODERICK PERKINS
☐ 612. STEVE SWISHER
☐ 644. JOE LEFEBVRE
☐ 674. KURT BEVACQUA
☐ 695. RUPPERT JONES
☐ 742. TEAM LEADER CARD
☐ 761. GARY LUCAS

SAN FRANCISCO GIANTS

☐ 32. DAVE BERGMAN
☐ 58. AL HOLLAND
☐ 84. MILT MAY
☐ 115. CHILI DAVIS
☐ 133. JIM BARR
☐ 143. JOE PETTINI

☐ 154. JOHNNIE LEMASTER
☐ 171. TEAM LEADER CARD
☐ 210. JACK CLARK
☐ 263. RENIE MARTIN
☐ 282. REGGIE SMITH
☐ 309. JEFF LEONARD
☐ 342. ATLEE HAMMAKER
☐ 379. GUY SULARZ
☐ 428. CHAMP SUMMERS
☐ 448. DARRELL EVANS
☐ 470. GREG MINTON
☐ 494. BOB BRENLY
☐ 518. BILL LASKEY
☐ 543. ALAN FOWLKES
☐ 576. FRANK ROBINSON(M)
☐ 603. JOE MORGAN
☐ 634. MAX VENABLE
☐ 663. TOM O'MALLEY
☐ 688. JIM WOHLFORD
☐ 719. RICH GALE
☐ 747. FRED BREINING
☐ 767. DUANE KUIPER
☐ 791. GARY LAVELLE

SEATTLE MARINERS

☐ 28. BRUCE BOCHTE
☐ 54. JIM MALER
☐ 78. BILL CAUDILL
☐ 106. GENE NELSON
☐ 132. TODD CRUZ
☐ 159. MIKE STANTON
☐ 183. ED VANDE BERG
☐ 195. BOB STODDARD
☐ 209. MIKE MOORE
☐ 234. LARRY ANDERSEN
☐ 258. MANNY CASTILLO
☐ 287. BOBBY BROWN
☐ 313. GARY GRAY
☐ 336. RENE LACHEMANN(M)
☐ 368. RICHIE ZISK
☐ 414. JULIO CRUZ
☐ 437. RICK SWEET
☐ 463. GAYLORD PERRY
☐ 492. PAUL SERNA
☐ 519. TERRY BULLING
☐ 545. FLOYD BANNISTER
☐ 567. JOE SIMPSON
☐ 622. DAVE EDLER
☐ 646. JIM ESSIAN
☐ 675. JIM BEATTIE
☐ 677. DAVE REVERING
☐ 711. TEAM LEADER CARD
☐ 732. DAVE HENDERSON
☐ 763. AL COWENS
☐ 789. BRYAN CLARK

TEXAS RANGERS

☐ 12. PAUL MIRABELLA
☐ 37. DARRELL JOHNSON(M)
☐ 64. BILL STEIN
☐ 116. DAVE J. SCHMIDT
☐ 144. MARK WAGNER
☐ 224. MICKEY RIVERS
☐ 272. FRANK TANANA
☐ 299. GEORGE WRIGHT
☐ 330. BUDDY BELL
☐ 353. STEVE COMER
☐ 371. MIKE RICHARDT

☐ 412. TEAM LEADER CARD
☐ 453. LAMAR JOHNSON
☐ 479. CHARLIE HOUGH
☐ 504. DON WERNER
☐ 534. JOHN BUTCHER
☐ 557. RICK HONEYCUTT
☐ 565. BUCKY DENT
☐ 584. DAVE HOSTETLER
☐ 609. DANNY DARWIN
☐ 641. BILLY SAMPLE
☐ 665. JIM SUNDBERG
☐ 724. JOHNNY GRUBB
☐ 749. JON MATLACK
☐ 776. LARRY PARRISH

TORONTO BLUE JAYS

☐   9. JOE MCLAUGHLIN
☐ 42. DALE MURRAY
☐ 77. HOSKEN POWELL
☐ 89. LEON ROBERTS
☐ 109. LUIS LEAL
☐ 130. DAVE STIEB
☐ 202. TEAM LEADER CARD
☐ 222. DAMASO GARCIA
☐ 257. JESSE BARFIELD
☐ 277. RANCE MULLINIKS
☐ 302. ERNIE WHITT
☐ 326. GARTH IORG
☐ 345. JIM CLANCY
☐ 358. JERRY GARVIN
☐ 427. ROY LEE JACKSON
☐ 452. LLOYD MOSEBY
☐ 488. ALFREDO GRIFFIN
☐ 506. JIM GOTT
☐ 556. WILLIE UPSHAW
☐ 574. GLENN ADAMS
☐ 589. ALVIS WOODS
☐ 606. BOBBY COX(M)
☐ 714. WAYNE NORDHAGEN
☐ 733. BUCK MARTINEZ
☐ 766. BARRY BONNELL

1983 TOPPS
TRADED (132)
2 1/2" X 3 1/2"

ATLANTA BRAVES

☐ 31T. PETE FALCONE
☐ 33T. TERRY FORSTER
☐ 51T. MIKE JORGENSEN
☐ 69T. CRAIG MCMURTRY
☐ 84T. PASCUAL PEREZ

BALTIMORE ORIOLES

☐   3T. JOE ALTOBELLI(M)
☐ 44T. LEO HERNANDEZ
☐ 97T. AURELIO RODRIGUEZ
☐ 102T. JOHN SHELBY

BOSTON RED SOX

☐   4T. TONY ARMAS
☐ 12T. DOUB BIRD
☐ 15T. MIKE BROWN
☐ 80T. JEFF NEWMAN

CALIFORNIA ANGELS

☐ 70T. JOHN MCNAMARA(M)
☐ 99T. DARYL SCONIERS
☐ 120T. ELLIS VALENTINE

CHICAGO CUBS

☐ 19T. RON CEY
☐ 39T. MEL HALL
☐ 92T. CHUCK RAINEY
☐ 98T. DICK RUTHVEN
☐ 117T. STEVE TROUT
☐ 121T. TOM VERYZER

CHICAGO WHITE SOX

☐   7T. FLOYD BANNISTER
☐ 23T. JULIO CRUZ
☐ 27T. JERRY DYBZINSKI
☐ 55T. RON KITTLE
☐ 112T. DICK TIDROW
☐ 124T. GREG WALKER

CINCINNATI REDS

☐ 11T. DANN BILARDELLO
☐ 35T. RICH GALE
☐ 57T. ALAN KNICELY
☐ 88T. CHARLIE PULEO
☐ 84T. GARY REDUS

CLEVELAND INDIANS

☐ 28T. JAMIE EASTERLY
☐ 29T. JUAN EICHELBERGER
☐ 30T. JIM ESSIAN
☐ 32T. MIKE FERRARO(M)
☐ 34T. JULIO FRANCO
☐ 86T. BRODERICK PERKINS
☐ 111T. GORMAN THOMAS
☐ 116T. MANNY TRILLO
☐ 122T. GEORGE VUKOVICH

DETRIOT TIGERS

☐   5T. DOUG BAIR
☐ 38T. JOHNNY GRUBB
☐ 63T. AURELIO LOPEZ

HOUSTON ASTROS

☐ 25T. FRANK DIPINO
☐ 26T. BILL DORAN
☐ 64T. MIKE MADDEN
☐ 76T. OMAR MORENO
☐ 100T. MIKE SCOTT

KANSAS CITY ROYALS

☐ 95T. STEVE RENKO
☐ 96T. LEON ROBERTS
☐ 104T. JOE SIMPSON

LOS ANGELES DODGERS

☐ 14T. GREG BROCK
☐ 59T. RAFAEL LANDESTOY
☐ 75T. JOSE MORALES
☐ 83T. ALEJANDRO PENA
☐ 131T. PAT ZACHRY

MILWAUKEE BREWERS

- ☐ 65T. RICK MANNING
- ☐ 109T. TOM TELLMANN
- ☐ 123T. RICK WAITS

MINNESOTA TWINS

- ☐ 17T. RANDY BUSH
- ☐ 126T. LEN WHITEHOUSE

MONTREAL EXPOS

- ☐ 22T. TERRY CROWLEY
- ☐ 62T. BRYAN LITTLE
- ☐ 93T. BOBBY RAMOS
- ☐ 119T. MIKE VAIL
- ☐ 125T. CHRIS WELSH
- ☐ 128T. JIM WOHLFORD

NEW YORK METS

- ☐ 41T. DANNY HEEP
- ☐ 43T. KEITH HERNANDEZ
- ☐ 47T. FRANK HOWARD(M)
- ☐ 101T. TOM SEAVER
- ☐ 105T. DOUG SISK
- ☐ 108T. DARRYL STRAWBERRY
- ☐ 115T. MIKE TORREZ

TOM SEAVER
PITCHER
METS

NEW YORK YANKEES

- ☐ 8T. DON BAYLOR
- ☐ 18T. BERT CAMPANERIS
- ☐ 53T. STEVE KEMP
- ☐ 54T. MATT KEOUGH
- ☐ 66T. BILLY MARTIN(M)
- ☐ 79T. DALE MURRAY
- ☐ 103T. BOB SHIRLEY

OAKLAND A'S

- ☐ 2T. BILL ALMON
- ☐ 6T. STEVE BAKER
- ☐ 13T. STEVE BOROS(M)
- ☐ 16T. TOM BURGMEIER
- ☐ 20T. CHRIS CODIROLI
- ☐ 24T. MIKE DAVIS
- ☐ 52T. BOB KEARNEY
- ☐ 60T. CARNEY LANSFORD
- ☐ 87T. TONY PHILLIPS

PHILADELPHIA PHILLIES

- ☐ 36T. KIKO GARCIA
- ☐ 40T. VON HAYES
- ☐ 45T. WILLIE HERNANDEZ
- ☐ 46T. AL HOLLAND
- ☐ 61T. JOE LEFEBVRE
- ☐ 72T. LARRY MILBOURNE
- ☐ 77T. JOE MORGAN
- ☐ 85T. TONY PEREZ

PITTSBURGH PIRATES

- ☐ 67T. LEE MAZZILLI
- ☐ 110T. GENE TENACE
- ☐ 118T. LEE TUNNELL

ST. LOUIS CARDINALS

- ☐ 1T. NEIL ALLEN
- ☐ 90T. JAMIE QUIRK

SAN DIEGO PADRES

- ☐ 37T. STEVE GARVEY
- ☐ 74T. SID MONGE
- ☐ 107T. ELIAS SOSA
- ☐ 127T. ED WHITSON

SAN FRANCISCO GIANTS

- ☐ 58T. MIKE KRUKOW
- ☐ 68T. ANDY McGAFFIGAN
- ☐ 130T. JOEL YOUNGBLOOD

SEATTLE MARINERS

- ☐ 9T. TONY BERNAZARD
- ☐ 42T. STEVE HENDERSON
- ☐ 71T. ORLANDO MERCADO
- ☐ 89T. PAT PUTNAM
- ☐ 129T. MATT YOUNG

TEXAS RANGERS

- ☐ 10T. LARRY BITTNER
- ☐ 48T. BOBBY JOHNSON
- ☐ 50T. ODELL JONES
- ☐ 81T. PETE O'BRIEN
- ☐ 91T. DOUG RADER(M)
- ☐ 106T. MIKE SMITHSON
- ☐ 113T. DAVE TOBIK
- ☐ 114T. WAYNE TOLLESON

TORONTO BLUE JAYS

- ☐ 21T. DAVE COLLINS
- ☐ 49T. CLIFF JOHNSON
- ☐ 56T. MICKEY KLUTTS
- ☐ 73T. RANDY MOFFITT
- ☐ 78T. MIKE MORGAN
- ☐ 82T. JORGE ORTA

1984 TOPPS (792)
2 1/2" X 3 1/2"

JIM DWYER OF

ATLANTA BRAVES

- ☐ 25. GLENN HUBBARD
- ☐ 50. CHRIS CHAMBLISS
- ☐ 77. BRETT BUTLER
- ☐ 104. KEN DAYLEY
- ☐ 126. TEAM LEADER CARD
- ☐ 150. DALE MURPHY
- ☐ 207. DONNIE MOORE
- ☐ 234. RAFAEL RAMIREZ
- ☐ 255. BRUCE BENEDICT
- ☐ 289. RANDY JOHNSON
- ☐ 313. MIKE JORGENSEN
- ☐ 365. STEVE BEDROSIAN
- ☐ 410. CLAUDELL WASHINGTON
- ☐ 438. BIFF POCORBA
- ☐ 466. GENE GARBER
- ☐ 502. JOE TORRE(M)
- ☐ 521. PETE FALCONE

- ☐ 543. CRAIG McMURTRY
- ☐ 572. JERRY ROYSTER
- ☐ 597. RICK CAMP
- ☐ 614. LEN BARKER
- ☐ 624. TERRY HARPER
- ☐ 650. PHIL NIEKRO
- ☐ 675. PASCUAL PEREZ
- ☐ 739. BOB WATSON
- ☐ 760. BOB HORNER
- ☐ 791. TERRY FORSTER

BALTIMORE ORIOLES

- ☐ 21. JOE ALTOBELLI(M)
- ☐ 59. SAMMY STEWART
- ☐ 71. LEO HERNANDEZ
- ☐ 86. JOHN SHELBY
- ☐ 106. TIM STODDARD
- ☐ 140. STORM DAVIS
- ☐ 165. KEN SINGLETON
- ☐ 191. MIKE BODDICKER
- ☐ 215. TIPPY MARTINEZ
- ☐ 240. EDDIE MURRAY
- ☐ 260. SCOTT McGREGOR
- ☐ 272. RICK DEMPSEY
- ☐ 295. MIKE FLANAGAN
- ☐ 319. AL BUMBRY
- ☐ 347. ALLAN RAMIREZ
- ☐ 372. GARY ROENICKE
- ☐ 426. TEAM CARD LEADER
- ☐ 443. BENNY AYALA
- ☐ 473. JIM DWYER
- ☐ 490. CAL RIPKEN
- ☐ 530. DAN FORD
- ☐ 553. JOE NOLAN
- ☐ 578. LENN SAKATA
- ☐ 604. JOHN LOWENSTEIN
- ☐ 631. DENNY MARTINEZ
- ☐ 682. DAN MOROGIELLO
- ☐ 723. RICH DAUER
- ☐ 750. JIM PALMER
- ☐ 773. TODD CRUZ

BOSTON RED SOX

- ☐ 30. WADE BOGGS
- ☐ 56. GARY ALLENSON
- ☐ 82. DOUG BIRD
- ☐ 105. TONY ARMAS
- ☐ 162. BOB OJEDA
- ☐ 187. LUIS APONTE
- ☐ 213. BRUCE HURST
- ☐ 238. REID NICHOLS
- ☐ 296. JEFF NEWMAN
- ☐ 320. BOB STANLEY
- ☐ 344. RICK MILLER
- ☐ 381. RALPH HOUK(M)
- ☐ 419. JOHN HENRY JOHNSON
- ☐ 445. JERRY REMY
- ☐ 472. MIKE BROWN
- ☐ 498. RICH GEDMAN
- ☐ 523. GLENN HOFFMAN
- ☐ 550. JIM RICE
- ☐ 577. MARK CLEAR
- ☐ 601. JOHN TUDOR
- ☐ 628. ED JURAK
- ☐ 653. DAVE STAPLETON
- ☐ 683. MARTY BARRETT
- ☐ 720. DWIGHT EVANS
- ☐ 745. DENNIS ECKERSLEY
- ☐ 786. TEAM LEADER CARD

CALIFORNIA ANGELS

- ☐ 27. DARYL SCONIERS
- ☐ 53. JUAN BENIQUEZ
- ☐ 79. ROB WILFONG
- ☐ 100. REGGIE JACKSON
- ☐ 158. JOHN CURTIS
- ☐ 184. MIKE O'BERRY
- ☐ 201. BRUCE KISON
- ☐ 236. ELLIS VALENTINE
- ☐ 258. LUIS SANCHEZ
- ☐ 266. STEVE LUBRATICH
- ☐ 276. TEAM LEADER CARD
- ☐ 315. BOB GRICH
- ☐ 342. TIM FOLI
- ☐ 414. TOMMY JOHN
- ☐ 442. BYRON McLAUGHLIN
- ☐ 468. GEOFF ZAHN

☐ 487. RICKY ADAMS
☐ 499. MIKE WITT
☐ 520. BOB BOONE
☐ 548. RON JACKSON
☐ 574. BRIAN DOWNING
☐ 600. ROD CAREW
☐ 626. BOB CLARK
☐ 643. MIKE BROWN
☐ 651. JOHN MCNAMARA(M)
☐ 680. FRED LYNN
☐ 719. ANDY HASSLER
☐ 735. RICK BURLESON
☐ 765. KEN FORSCH
☐ 790. DOUG DECINCES

CHICAGO CUBS

☐ 23. KEITH MORELAND
☐ 51. JIM FREY(M)
☐ 73. JODY DAVIS
☐ 99. CRAIG LEFFERTS
☐ 117. TOM VERYZER
☐ 151. STEVE TROUT
☐ 176. LEE SMITH
☐ 231. GARY WOODS
☐ 249. JAY JOHNSTONE
☐ 267. CARMELO MARTINEZ
☐ 304. WARREN BRUSSTAR
☐ 334. CHUCK RAINEY
☐ 357. RON CEY
☐ 437. MIKE PROLY
☐ 456. TEAM LEADER CARD
☐ 483. FERGIE JENKINS
☐ 508. MEL HALL
☐ 545. BILL BUCKNER
☐ 565. LEON DURHAM
☐ 596. RYNE SANDBERG
☐ 618. DICKIE NOLES
☐ 657. THAD BOSLEY
☐ 691. STEVE LAKE
☐ 736. DICK RUTHVEN
☐ 757. LARRY BOWA
☐ 787. BILL CAMPBELL

CHICAGO WHITE SOX

☐ 20. GREG LUZINSKI
☐ 47. RUDY LAW
☐ 72. MIKE SQUIRES
☐ 97. LAMARR HOYT
☐ 125. BRITT BURNS
☐ 153. DICK TIDROW
☐ 163. LORENZO GRAY
☐ 177. JERRY HAIRSTON
☐ 216. TEAM LEADER CARD
☐ 257. JULIO CRUZ
☐ 269. AURELIO RODRIGUEZ
☐ 280. FLOYD BANNISTER
☐ 311. JERRY KOOSMAN
☐ 364. SCOTT FLETCHER
☐ 382. CHRIS NYMAN
☐ 409. JUAN AGOSTO
☐ 434. HAROLD BAINES
☐ 459. KEVIN HICKEY
☐ 480. RON KITTLE
☐ 518. GREG WALKER
☐ 541. DENNIS LAMP
☐ 560. CARLTON FISK
☐ 591. TONY LARUSSA(M)
☐ 619. JERRY DYBZINSKI
☐ 664. DAVE STEGMAN
☐ 667. VANCE LAW
☐ 698. MARC HILL
☐ 759. RICHARD DOTSON
☐ 777. TOM PACIOREK

CINCINNATI REDS

☐ 34. EDDIE MILNER
☐ 55. DAVE CONCEPCION
☐ 87. FRANK PASTORE
☐ 113. KELLY PARIS
☐ 142. RICH GALE
☐ 160. MARIO SOTO
☐ 192. NICK ESASKY
☐ 214. PAUL HOUSEHOLDER
☐ 242. ALEX TREVINO
☐ 270. JEFF RUSSELL
☐ 273. CHARLIE PULEO
☐ 297. BRUCE BERENYI
☐ 323. ALAN KNICELY

☐ 351. RUSS NIXON(M)
☐ 373. BILL SCHERRER
☐ 424. DANN BILARDELLO
☐ 448. BEN HAYES
☐ 475. GARY REDUS
☐ 526. RON OESTER
☐ 554. TED POWER
☐ 585. DAN DRIESSEN
☐ 607. TOM HUME
☐ 632. TOM FOLEY
☐ 659. DUANE WALKER
☐ 686. JOE PRICE
☐ 725. CESAR CEDENO
☐ 756. TEAM LEADER CARD

CLEVELAND INDIANS

☐ 48. JULIO FRANCO
☐ 91. DAN SPILLNER
☐ 115. ANDRE THORNTON
☐ 141. PAT CORRALES(M)
☐ 212. BRODERICK PERKINS
☐ 226. JUAN EICHELBERGER
☐ 245. RICK SUTCLIFFE
☐ 286. LARY SORENSEN
☐ 308. RON HASSEY
☐ 329. PAT TABLER
☐ 348. TOBY HARRAH
☐ 367. JAMIE EASTERLY
☐ 431. CHRIS BANDO
☐ 478. ALAN BANNISTER
☐ 497. BUD ANDERSON
☐ 515. GORMAN THOMAS
☐ 546. TEAM LEADER CARD
☐ 569. BAKE MCBRIDE
☐ 638. GEORGE VUKOVICH
☐ 662. TOM BRENNAN
☐ 689. MIKE FISCHLIN
☐ 737. JIM ESSIAN
☐ 764. MIKE HARGROVE
☐ 789. BERT BLYLEVEN

DETROIT TIGERS

☐ 14. TOM BROOKENS
☐ 24. JOHN MARTIN
☐ 42. JOHNNY GRUBB
☐ 65. KIRK GIBSON
☐ 95. AURELIO LOPEZ
☐ 119. JOHNNY WOCKENFUSS
☐ 147. DAN PETRY
☐ 174. JUAN BERENGUER
☐ 195. JACK MORRIS
☐ 223. WAYNE KRENCHICKI
☐ 259. SPARKY ANDERSON(M)
☐ 284. HOWARD BAILEY
☐ 303. MARTY CASTILLO
☐ 333. LARRY HERNDON
☐ 356. GLENN ABBOTT
☐ 371. DAVE GUMPERT
☐ 427. RICK LEACH
☐ 457. DAVE ROZEMA
☐ 482. ENOS CABELL
☐ 510. ALAN TRAMMELL
☐ 536. DOUG BAIR
☐ 563. GLENN WILSON
☐ 588. MILT WILCOX
☐ 611. CHET LEMON
☐ 640. LANCE PARRISH
☐ 666. TEAM LEADER CARD
☐ 695. LOU WHITKER
☐ 731. LYNN JONES

HOUSTON ASTROS

☐ 36. DENNY WALLING
☐ 45. JERRY MUMPHREY
☐ 66. TEAM LEADER CARD
☐ 93. BOB KNEPPER
☐ 116. GEORGE BJORKMAN
☐ 127. MIKE MADDEN
☐ 172. FRANK DIPINO
☐ 198. BILL DORAN
☐ 217. ALAN ASHBY
☐ 248. BILL DAWLEY
☐ 292. TONY SCOTT
☐ 301. FRANK LACORTE
☐ 328. VERN RUHLE
☐ 361. DAVE SMITH
☐ 383. TERRY PUHL

☐ 422. JOSE CRUZ
☐ 441. BOB LILLIS(M)
☐ 446. LUIS PUJOLS
☐ 470. NOLAN RYAN
☐ 507. MIKE LACOSS
☐ 438. KEVIN BASS
☐ 559. MIKE SCOTT
☐ 586. JOE NIEKRO
☐ 612. HARRY SPILMAN
☐ 660. RAY KNIGHT
☐ 679. ART HOWE
☐ 692. DICKIE THON
☐ 752. PHIL GARNER
☐ 776. CRAIG REYNOLDS

MIKE SCOTT P

KANSAS CITY ROYALS

☐ 26. BUD BLACK
☐ 52. PAUL SPLITTORFF
☐ 74. JERRY MARTIN
☐ 96. TEAM LEADER CARD
☐ 121. PAT SHERIDAN
☐ 155. FRANK WHITE
☐ 196. DON SLAUGHT
☐ 219. JOE SIMPSON
☐ 247. ONIX CONCEPCION
☐ 294. U.L. WASHINGTON
☐ 317. GREG PRYOR
☐ 340. HAL MCRAE
☐ 375. DENNIS LEONARD
☐ 417. MIKE ARMSTRONG
☐ 444. STEVE RENKO
☐ 471. DICK HOWSER(M)
☐ 500. GEORGE BRETT
☐ 525. WILLIE WILSON
☐ 544. CESAR GERONIMO
☐ 570. DAN QUISENBERRY
☐ 602. JOHN WATHAN
☐ 625. LARRY GURA
☐ 655. AMOS OTIS
☐ 685. WILLIE AIKENS
☐ 724. ERIC RASMUSSEN
☐ 743. DON HOOD
☐ 784. LEON ROBERTS

LOS ANGELES DODGERS

☐ 15. BURT HOOTON
☐ 40. DUSTY BAKER
☐ 64. MIKE SCIOSCIA
☐ 90. PEDRO GUERRERO
☐ 112. TOM NIEDENFUER
☐ 142. JOSE MORALES
☐ 170. JERRY REUSS
☐ 220. FERANDO VALENZUELA
☐ 222. RICK HONEYCUTT
☐ 244. CANDY MALDONADO
☐ 263. JACK FIMPLE
☐ 274. RICK MONDAY
☐ 306. TEAM LEADER CARD
☐ 324. ALEJANDRO PENA
☐ 376. DAVE ANDERSON
☐ 425. STEVE HOWE
☐ 454. JOE BECKWITH
☐ 477. RAFAEL LANDESTOY
☐ 533. KEN LANDREAUX
☐ 555. GREG BROCK
☐ 583. DERREL THOMAS
☐ 610. STEVE SAX

1984 Topps

- [ ] 634. MIKE MARSHALL
- [ ] 661. STEVE YEAGER
- [ ] 681. TOM LASORDA(M)
- [ ] 722. BOB WELCH
- [ ] 747. PAT ZACHRY
- [ ] 792. BILL RUSSELL

MILWAUKEE BREWERS

- [ ] 10. ROBIN YOUNT
- [ ] 35. DON SUTTON
- [ ] 60. PAUL MOLITOR
- [ ] 88. ROB PICCIOLO
- [ ] 107. NED YOST
- [ ] 128. RICK MANNING
- [ ] 146. ED ROMERO
- [ ] 167. MARSHALL EDWARDS
- [ ] 190. BEN OGLIVIE
- [ ] 218. RICK WAITS
- [ ] 243. PETE LADD
- [ ] 262. TOM CANDIOTTI
- [ ] 271. MOOSE HAAS
- [ ] 298. JIM GANTNER
- [ ] 321. HARVEY KUENN(M)
- [ ] 349. BOB GIBSON
- [ ] 374. DON MONEY
- [ ] 420. CECIL COOPER
- [ ] 452. CHUCK PORTER
- [ ] 476. TOM TELLMANN
- [ ] 495. ROLLIE FINGERS
- [ ] 505. PETE VUCKOVICH
- [ ] 528. MARK BROUHARD
- [ ] 582. BOB McCLURE
- [ ] 605. MIKE CALDWELL
- [ ] 630. TED SIMMONS
- [ ] 658. JERRY AUGUSTINE
- [ ] 687. ROY HOWELL
- [ ] 726. TEAM LEADER CARD
- [ ] 738. BILL SCHROEDER
- [ ] 751. CHARLIE MOORE
- [ ] 772. JIM SLATON

MINNESOTA TWINS

- [ ] 11. TEAM CARD LEADER CARD
- [ ] 28. FRANK VIOLA
- [ ] 46. RAY SMITH
- [ ] 67. GARY WARD
- [ ] 84. LENNY FAEDO
- [ ] 157. GARY GAETTI
- [ ] 183. AL WILLIAMS
- [ ] 193. DARRELL BROWN
- [ ] 237. JOHN CASTINO
- [ ] 268. JACK O'CONNOR
- [ ] 307. BOBBY MITCHELL
- [ ] 322. KEN SCHROM
- [ ] 345. KENT HRBEK
- [ ] 363. TIM LAUDNER
- [ ] 411. HOUSTON JIMENEZ
- [ ] 429. RANDY BUSH
- [ ] 447. TOM BRUNANSKY
- [ ] 463. DAVE ENGLE
- [ ] 491. BOBBY CASTILLO
- [ ] 509. BRAD HAVENS
- [ ] 519. RON DAVIS
- [ ] 551. SCOTT ULLGER
- [ ] 568. PETE FILSON
- [ ] 598. RUSTY KUNTZ
- [ ] 623. RON WASHINGTON
- [ ] 639. RICK LYSANDER
- [ ] 648. LEN WHITEHOUSE
- [ ] 673. MIKE WALTERS
- [ ] 746. MICKEY HATCHER
- [ ] 771. BILLY GARDNER(M)

MONTREAL EXPOS

- [ ] 32. BOBBY RAMOS
- [ ] 57. DAN SCHATZEDER
- [ ] 80. STEVE ROGERS
- [ ] 111. BILL VIRDON(M)
- [ ] 164. SCOTT SANDERSON
- [ ] 180. MANNY TRILLO
- [ ] 188. BRYAN LITTLE
- [ ] 200. ANDRE DAWSON
- [ ] 232. TIM WALLACH
- [ ] 253. JIM WOHLFORD
- [ ] 287. WARREN CROMARTIE
- [ ] 318. BILL GULLICKSON
- [ ] 370. TIM RAINES
- [ ] 421. CHARLIE LEA

- [ ] 450. GARY CARTER
- [ ] 474. GREG BARGAR
- [ ] 496. TERRY FRANCONA
- [ ] 516. TEAM LEADER CARD
- [ ] 552. RAY BURRIS
- [ ] 579. BOB JAMES
- [ ] 595. JEFF REARDON
- [ ] 620. AL OLIVER
- [ ] 656. BRYN SMITH
- [ ] 678. CHRIS SPEIER
- [ ] 732. TERRY CROWLEY
- [ ] 749. DOUG FLYNN
- [ ] 766. MIKE VAIL

NEW YORK METS

- [ ] 13. SCOTT HOLMAN
- [ ] 29. DANNY HEEP
- [ ] 54. JESSE OROSCO
- [ ] 78. MIKE TORREZ
- [ ] 120. KEITH HERNANDEZ
- [ ] 161. JUNIOR ORTIZ
- [ ] 182. DARRYL STRAWBERRY
- [ ] 208. JOSE OQUENDO
- [ ] 246. TEAM LEADER CARD
- [ ] 293. ED LYNCH
- [ ] 316. MARK BARDLEY
- [ ] 350. GEORGE FOSTER
- [ ] 368. HUBIE BROOKS
- [ ] 418. RON HODGES
- [ ] 430. RUSTY STAUB
- [ ] 465. MOOKIE WILSON
- [ ] 492. TUCKER ASHFORD
- [ ] 524. CARLOS DIAZ
- [ ] 549. WALT TERRELL
- [ ] 573. DAVE KINGMAN
- [ ] 599. DOUG SISK
- [ ] 621. FRANK HOWARD(M)
- [ ] 654. BOB BAILOR
- [ ] 676. BRIAN GILES
- [ ] 740. TOM SEAVER
- [ ] 763. CRAIG SWAN
- [ ] 774. TOM GORMAN

NEW YORK YANKEES

- [ ] 8. DON MATTINGLY
- [ ] 16. OMAR MORENO
- [ ] 19. RAY FONTENOT
- [ ] 81. BILLY MARTIN(M)
- [ ] 110. RON GUIDRY
- [ ] 123. BUTCH WYNEGAR
- [ ] 139. BERT CAMPANERIS
- [ ] 175. GRAIG NETTLES
- [ ] 203. MATT KEOUGH
- [ ] 204. BOBBY MEACHAM
- [ ] 239. JAY HOWELL
- [ ] 254. SHANE RAWLEY
- [ ] 281. LARRY MILBOURNE
- [ ] 305. ROY SMALLEY
- [ ] 335. DON BAYLOR
- [ ] 360. WILLIE RANDOLPH
- [ ] 408. LOU PINIELLA
- [ ] 440. STEVE KEMP
- [ ] 460. DAVE WINFIELD
- [ ] 486. TEAM LEADER CARD
- [ ] 512. OSCAR GAMBLE
- [ ] 539. GEORGE FRAZIER
- [ ] 592. ANDRE ROBERTSON
- [ ] 617. RICK CERONE
- [ ] 635. DAVE RIGHETTI
- [ ] 652. RUDY MAY
- [ ] 670. RICH GOSSAGE
- [ ] 684. BOB SHIRLEY
- [ ] 697. DALE MURRAY
- [ ] 761. JOHN MONTEFUSCO
- [ ] 770. KEN GRIFFEY
- [ ] 782. STEVE BALBONI

OAKLAND A'S

- [ ] 33. TOM BURGMEIER
- [ ] 61. CHRIS CODIROLI
- [ ] 103. DWAYNE MURPHY
- [ ] 156. TEAM LEADER CARD
- [ ] 159. DARRYL CIAS
- [ ] 178. BILL KRUEGER
- [ ] 189. TIM CONROY
- [ ] 197. GARRY HANCOCK
- [ ] 230. RICKEY HENDERSON

- [ ] 241. BILL ALMON
- [ ] 265. DONNIE HILL
- [ ] 309. TONY PHILLIPS
- [ ] 326. BOB KEARNEY
- [ ] 338. MIKE WARREN
- [ ] 354. JEFF BURROUGHS
- [ ] 369. STEVE McCATTY
- [ ] 414. MITCHELL PAGE
- [ ] 436. RICK PETERS
- [ ] 464. JEFF JONES
- [ ] 493. MIKE NORRIS
- [ ] 513. DAVE BEARD
- [ ] 529. KEITH ATHERTON
- [ ] 521. STEVE BOROS(M)
- [ ] 558. MIKE DAVIS
- [ ] 567. MIKE HEATH
- [ ] 609. DAN MEYER
- [ ] 629. RICK LANGFORD
- [ ] 642. TOM UNDERWOOD
- [ ] 669. DAVE LOPES
- [ ] 741. WAYNE GROSS
- [ ] 767. CARNEY LANSFORD

PHILADELPHIA PHILLIES

- [ ] 17. JOHN DENNY
- [ ] 43. RON REED
- [ ] 70. GARY MATTHEWS
- [ ] 101. PORFIRIO ALTAMIRANO
- [ ] 158. JOE LEFEBVRE
- [ ] 185. SIXTO LEZCANO
- [ ] 199. WILLIE HERNANDEZ
- [ ] 210. JOE MORGAN
- [ ] 229. PAUL OWENS(M)
- [ ] 252. LARRY CHRISTENSON
- [ ] 275. LEN MATUSZEK
- [ ] 279. IVAN DEJESUS
- [ ] 300. PETE ROSE
- [ ] 332. KEVIN GROSS
- [ ] 358. BOB DERNIER
- [ ] 385. TONY PEREZ
- [ ] 432. CHARLIE HUDSON
- [ ] 458. KIKO GARCIA
- [ ] 484. OZZIE VIRGIL
- [ ] 511. MARTY BYSTROM
- [ ] 535. BO DIAZ
- [ ] 564. AL HOLLAND
- [ ] 587. VON HAYES
- [ ] 613. GREG GROSS
- [ ] 637. TEAM LEADER CARD
- [ ] 700. MIKE SCHMIDT
- [ ] 728. TUG McGRAY
- [ ] 755. GARRY MADDOX
- [ ] 780. STEVE CARLTON

PITTSBURGH PIRATES

- [ ] 18. DALE BERRA
- [ ] 44. JIM MORRISON
- [ ] 69. ROD SCURRY
- [ ] 122. CECILIO GUANTE
- [ ] 144. BRIAN HARPER
- [ ] 173. MARVELL WYNNE
- [ ] 209. MANNY SARMIENTO
- [ ] 225. LEE MAZZILLI
- [ ] 250. BILL MADLOCK
- [ ] 264. DOUG FROBEL
- [ ] 291. CHUCK TANNER(M)
- [ ] 330. JOHN CANDELARIA
- [ ] 355. JASON THOMPSON
- [ ] 384. LEE TUNNELL
- [ ] 433. RICH HEBNER
- [ ] 462. LEE LACY
- [ ] 485. RICK RHODEN
- [ ] 537. JOHNNY RAY
- [ ] 566. JIM BIBBY
- [ ] 581. JOSE DELEON
- [ ] 589. MIKE EASLER
- [ ] 616. DON ROBINSON
- [ ] 645. TONY PENA
- [ ] 668. LARRY McWILLIAMS
- [ ] 696. TEAM LEADER CARD
- [ ] 729. GENE TENACE
- [ ] 754. KENT TEKULVE
- [ ] 775. DAVE PARKER
- [ ] 788. MILT MAY

ST. LOUIS CARDINALS

- [ ] 49. JOHN STUPER
- [ ] 75. BOB FORSCH
- [ ] 102. KEN OBERKFELL
- [ ] 130. OZZIE SMITH
- [ ] 152. GLENN BRUMMER
- [ ] 186. TEAM LEADER CARD
- [ ] 206. ANDY VAN SLYKE
- [ ] 227. STEVE BRAUN
- [ ] 285. DARRELL PORTER
- [ ] 310. WILLIE MCGEE
- [ ] 337. KEVIN HAGEN
- [ ] 362. DAVID GREEN
- [ ] 416. DANE IORG
- [ ] 435. NEIL ALLEN
- [ ] 467. MIKE RAMSEY
- [ ] 489. GEORGE VON OHLEN
- [ ] 514. FLOYD RAYFORD
- [ ] 540. GEORGE HENDRICK
- [ ] 561. WHITEY HERZOG(M)
- [ ] 580. LONNIE SMITH
- [ ] 593. JEFF LAHTI
- [ ] 627. DAVE LAPOINT
- [ ] 649. TOM HERR
- [ ] 671. JAMIE QUIRK
- [ ] 699. DAVE RUCKER
- [ ] 730. BRUCE SUTTER
- [ ] 785. JOAQUIN ANDUJAR

SAN DIEGO PADRES

- [ ] 7. GARY LUCAS
- [ ] 38. LUIS DELEON
- [ ] 68. LUIS SALAZAR
- [ ] 94. MARIO RAMIREZ
- [ ] 168. JUAN BONILLA
- [ ] 224. SID MONGE
- [ ] 251. TONY GWYNN
- [ ] 261. BOBBY BROWN
- [ ] 277. EDDIE WHITSON
- [ ] 290. DAVE DRAVECKY
- [ ] 327. RUPPERT JONES
- [ ] 346. KURT BEVACQUA
- [ ] 366. TEAM LEADER CARD
- [ ] 380. STEVE GARVEY
- [ ] 455. TERRY KENNEDY
- [ ] 481. MARK THURMOND
- [ ] 503. ELIAS SOSA
- [ ] 532. ERIC SHOW
- [ ] 571. BRUCE BOCHY
- [ ] 594. GENE RICHARDS
- [ ] 615. GARRY TEMPLETON
- [ ] 644. TIM LOLLAR
- [ ] 674. TIM FLANNERY
- [ ] 693. ALAN WIGGINS
- [ ] 742. DICK WILLIAMS(M)
- [ ] 753. DOUG GWOSDZ
- [ ] 778. ANDY HAWKINS

SAN FRANCISCO GIANTS

- [ ] 31. ANDY MCGAFFIGAN
- [ ] 58. MAX VENABLE
- [ ] 85. ATLEE HAMMAKER
- [ ] 98. STEVE NICOSIA
- [ ] 109. BRAD WELLMAN
- [ ] 129. BILL LASKEY
- [ ] 145. GARY LAVELLE
- [ ] 171. FRANK ROBINSON(M)
- [ ] 205. GREG MINTON
- [ ] 228. JOHN RABB
- [ ] 282. JIM BARR
- [ ] 325. DARRELL EVANS
- [ ] 343. MARK DAVIS
- [ ] 378. BOB BRENLY
- [ ] 428. FRED BREINING
- [ ] 449. JOE PETTINI
- [ ] 469. TOM O'MALLEY
- [ ] 494. CHILI DAVIS
- [ ] 522. DAVE BERGMAN
- [ ] 542. DUANE KUIPER
- [ ] 576. TEAM LEADER CARD
- [ ] 603. RENIE MARTIN
- [ ] 633. MIKE KRUKOW
- [ ] 663. JOHNNIE LEMASTER
- [ ] 690. JACK CLARK
- [ ] 727. JOEL YOUNGBLOOD
- [ ] 748. JEFF LEONARD
- [ ] 768. CHAMP SUMMERS

SEATTLE MARINERS

- [ ] 22. BRYAN CLARK
- [ ] 41. TONY BERNAZARD
- [ ] 63. ED VANDE BERG
- [ ] 83. RICHIE ZISK
- [ ] 154. DAVE HENDERSON
- [ ] 166. JAMIE NELSON
- [ ] 181. ROY THOMAS
- [ ] 194. DOMINGO RAMOS
- [ ] 211. RICK SWEET
- [ ] 235. MATT YOUNG
- [ ] 288. JIM BEATTIE
- [ ] 314. ORLANDO MERCADO
- [ ] 336. TEAM LEADER CARD
- [ ] 413. SPIKE OWEN
- [ ] 439. BOB STODDARD
- [ ] 461. JIM MALER
- [ ] 501. STEVE HENDERSON
- [ ] 517. JOHN MOSES
- [ ] 547. MIKE MOORE
- [ ] 562. MANNY CASTILLO
- [ ] 622. AL COWENS
- [ ] 636. PAT PUTNAM
- [ ] 647. RON ROENICKE
- [ ] 672. RICKY NELSON
- [ ] 694. MIKE STANTON
- [ ] 721. DEL CRANDALL(M)
- [ ] 744. JAMIE ALLEN
- [ ] 769. BILL CAUDILL

TEXAS RANGERS

- [ ] 12. BILLY SAMPLE
- [ ] 37. TEAM LEADER CARD
- [ ] 62. DAVE HOSTETLER
- [ ] 89. MIKE SMITHSON
- [ ] 118. CHARLIE HOUGH
- [ ] 149. JON MATLACK
- [ ] 169. LARRY PARRISH
- [ ] 283. LARRY BITTNER
- [ ] 299. JOHN BUTCHER
- [ ] 331. BUCKY DENT
- [ ] 341. DAVE TOBIK
- [ ] 352. DAVE STEWART
- [ ] 353. JIM ANDERSON
- [ ] 377. DANNY DARWIN
- [ ] 412. DOUG RADER(M)
- [ ] 451. BOB JONES
- [ ] 479. FRANK TANANA
- [ ] 504. MICKEY RIVERS
- [ ] 534. PETE O'BRIEN
- [ ] 557. WAYNE TOLLESON
- [ ] 584. DAVE SCHMIDT
- [ ] 608. BOBBY JOHNSON
- [ ] 641. MIKE RICHARDT
- [ ] 665. BUDDY BELL
- [ ] 688. GEORGE WRIGHT
- [ ] 734. ODELL JONES
- [ ] 758. BILL STEIN
- [ ] 779. JIM SUNDBERG

TORONTO BLUE JAYS

- [ ] 9. JIM GOTT
- [ ] 39. GARTH IORG
- [ ] 76. ALFREDO GRIFFIN
- [ ] 92. LLOYD MOSEBY
- [ ] 108. RANDY MOFFITT
- [ ] 124. DAMASO GARCIA
- [ ] 179. BUCK MARTINEZ
- [ ] 202. BOBBY COX(M)
- [ ] 221. CLIFF JOHNSON
- [ ] 256. DAVE GEISEL
- [ ] 278. JORGE BELL
- [ ] 302. BARRY BONNELL
- [ ] 312. JORGE ORTA
- [ ] 339. ROY LEE JACKSON
- [ ] 359. JIM ACKER
- [ ] 423. MIKE MORGAN
- [ ] 453. WILLIE UPSHAW
- [ ] 488. JESSE BARFIELD
- [ ] 506. ERNIE WHITT
- [ ] 556. JOEY MCLAUGHLIN
- [ ] 575. JIM CLANCY
- [ ] 590. DAVE STIEB
- [ ] 606. TEAM LEADER CARD
- [ ] 677. DOYLE ALEXANDER
- [ ] 733. DAVE COLLINS
- [ ] 762. RANCE MULLINKS
- [ ] 783. LUIS LEAL

1984 TOPPS
TRADED (132)
2 1/2" X 3 1/2"

ATLANTA BRAVES

- [ ] 30T. JEFF DEDMON
- [ ] 85T. KEN OBERKFELL
- [ ] 92T. GERALD PERRY
- [ ] 120T. ALEX TREVINO

BALTIMORE ORIOLES

- [ ] 44T. WAYNE GROSS
- [ ] 96T. FLOYD RAYFORD
- [ ] 123T. TOM UNDERWOOD

BOSTON RED SOX

- [ ] 17T. BILL BUCKNER
- [ ] 33T. MIKE EASLER
- [ ] 40T. RICH GALE
- [ ] 46T. JACKIE GUTIERREZ

CALIFORNIA ANGELS

- [ ] 68T. FRANK LACORTE
- [ ] 93T. GARY PETTIS
- [ ] 94T. ROB PICCIOLO
- [ ] 102T. RON ROMANICK
- [ ] 107T. DICK SCHOFIELD
- [ ] 109T. JIM SLATON
- [ ] 116T. CRAIG SWAN

CHICAGO CUBS

- [ ] 31T. BOB DERNIER
- [ ] 34T. DENNIS ECKERSLEY
- [ ] 39T. GEORGE FRAZIER
- [ ] 49T. RON HASSEY
- [ ] 50T. RICH HEBNER
- [ ] 77T. GARY MATTHEWS
- [ ] 106T. SCOTT SANDERSON
- [ ] 112T. TIM STODDARD
- [ ] 115T. RICK SUTCLIFFE

CHICAGO WHITE SOX

- [ ] 98T. RON REED
- [ ] 108T. TOM SEAVER

CINCINNATI REDS

- [ ] 65T. WAYNE KRENCHICKI
- [ ] 90T. DAVE PARKER
- [ ] 91T. TONY PEREZ
- [ ] 95T. VERN RAPP(M)

CLEVELAND INDIANS

- [ ] 2T. LUIS APONTE
- [ ] 12T. TONY BERNAZARD
- [ ] 20T. BRETT BUTLER
- [ ] 47T. MEL HALL
- [ ] 55T. BROOK JACOBY
- [ ] 56T. MIKE JEFFCOAT
- [ ] 125T. TOM WADDELL

DETROIT TIGERS

- [ ] 11T. DAVE BERGMAN
- [ ] 36T. DARRELL EVANS
- [ ] 41T. BARBARO GARBEY
- [ ] 51T. WILLIE HERNANDEZ
- [ ] 59T. RUPPERT JONES
- [ ] 66T. RUSTY KUNTZ
- [ ] 80T. SID MONGE

HOUSTON ASTROS

- [ ] 21T. ENOS CABELL

KANSAS CITY ROYALS

- [ ] 6T. STEVE BALBONI
- [ ] 9T. JOE BECKWITH
- [ ] 45T. MARK GUBICZA
- [ ] 54T. DANE IORG
- [ ] 57T. LYNN JONES
- [ ] 88T. JORGE ORTA
- [ ] 104T. BRET SABERHAGEN

LOS ANGELES DODGERS

- [ ] 4T. BOB BAILOR
- [ ] 32T. CARLOS DIAZ
- [ ] 124T. MIKE VAIL

MILWAUKEE BREWERS

- [ ] 24T. BOB CLARK
- [ ] 26T. JAIME COCANOWER
- [ ] 67T. RENE LACHEMANN(M)
- [ ] 97T. RANDY READY
- [ ] 114T. JIM SUNDBERG

MINNESOTA TWINS

- [ ] 19T. JOHN BUTCHER
- [ ] 110T. MIKE SMITHSON
- [ ] 117T. TIM TEUFEL

MONTREAL EXPOS

- [ ] 16T. FRED BREINING
- [ ] 73T. GARY LUCAS
- [ ] 78T. ANDY MCGAFFIGAN
- [ ] 103T. PETE ROSE
- [ ] 118T. DERREL THOMAS

NEW YORK METS

- [ ] 10T. BRUCE BERENYI
- [ ] 27T. RON DARLING
- [ ] 37T. MIKE FITZGERALD
- [ ] 42T. DWIGHT GOODEN
- [ ] 57T. DAVE JOHNSON(M)
- [ ] 74T. JERRY MARTIN

NEW YORK YANKEES

- [ ] 3T. MIKE ARMSTRONG
- [ ] 13T. YOGI BERRA(M)
- [ ] 38T. TIM FOLI
- [ ] 48T. TOBY HARRAH
- [ ] 84T. PHIL NIEKRO
- [ ] 86T. MIKE O'BERRY
- [ ] 100T. JOSE RIJO

OAKLAND A'S

- [ ] 18T. RAY BURRIS
- [ ] 23T. BILL CAUDILL
- [ ] 35T. JIM ESSIAN
- [ ] 63T. DAVE KINGMAN
- [ ] 81T. JACKIE MOORE(M)
- [ ] 82T. JOE MORGAN
- [ ] 111T. LARY SORENSEN

PHIADELPHIA PHILLIES

- [ ] 22T. BILL CAMPBELL
- [ ] 64T. JERRY KOOSMAN
- [ ] 105T. JUAN SAMUEL
- [ ] 129T. GLENN WILSON
- [ ] 130T. JOHNNY WOCKENFUSS

PITTSBURGH PIRATES

- [ ] 89T. AMOS OTIS
- [ ] 122T. JOHN TUDOR

ST. LOUIS CARDINALS

- [ ] 29T. KEN DAYLEY
- [ ] 52T. RICKY HORTON
- [ ] 53T. ART HOWE
- [ ] 60T. MIKE JORGENSEN

SAN DIEGO PADRES

- [ ] 43T. RICH GOSSAGE
- [ ] 72T. CRAIG LEFFERTS
- [ ] 75T. CARMELO MARTINEZ
- [ ] 83T. GRAIG NETTLES
- [ ] 113T. CHAMP SUMMERS

RICH GOSSAGE P

SAN FRANCISCO GIANTS

- [ ] 5T. DUSTY BAKER
- [ ] 87T. AL OLIVER
- [ ] 99T. GENE RICHARDS
- [ ] 101T. JEFF ROBINSON
- [ ] 121T. MANNY TRILLO
- [ ] 128T. FRANK WILLIAMS

SEATTLE MARINERS

- [ ] 8T. DAVE BEARD
- [ ] 14T. BARRY BONNELL
- [ ] 15T. PHIL BRADLEY
- [ ] 28T. ALVIN DAVIS
- [ ] 61T. BOB KEARNEY
- [ ] 70T. MARK LANGSTON
- [ ] 79T. LARRY MILBOURNE
- [ ] 119T. GORMAN THOMAS

TEXAS RANGERS

- [ ] 7T. ALAN BANNISTER
- [ ] 76T. MIKE MASON
- [ ] 126T. GARY WARD
- [ ] 127T. CURT WILDERSON
- [ ] 131. NED YOST

TORONTO BLUE JAYS

- [ ] 1T. WILLIE AIKENS
- [ ] 25T. BRYAN CLARK
- [ ] 62T. JIMMY KEY
- [ ] 69T. DENNIS LAMP
- [ ] 71T. RICK LEACH

1985 TOPPS (792)
2 1/2" X 3 1/2"

RICKEY HENDERSON

ATLANTA BRAVES

- [ ] 25. STEVE BEDROSIAN
- [ ] 51. BOB WATSON
- [ ] 79. RICK MAHLER
- [ ] 106. PASCUAL PEREZ
- [ ] 129. GENE GARBER
- [ ] 167. RUFINO LINARES
- [ ] 195. GLENN HUBBARD
- [ ] 219. GERALD PERRY
- [ ] 248. TERRY FORSTER
- [ ] 292. BRAD KOMMINSK
- [ ] 320. DALE MURPHY
- [ ] 335. BRUCE BENEDICT
- [ ] 362. CRAIG MCMURTRY
- [ ] 410. BOB HORNER
- [ ] 438. JOE TORRE(M)
- [ ] 458. RANDY JOHNSON
- [ ] 491. RICK CAMP
- [ ] 518. CHRIS CHAMBLISS
- [ ] 540. CLAUDELL WASHINGTON
- [ ] 557. LEN BARKER
- [ ] 569. KEN OBERKFELL
- [ ] 602. JEFF DEDMON
- [ ] 618. PETE FALCONE
- [ ] 647. RAFAEL RAMIREZ
- [ ] 676. ALBERT HALL
- [ ] 699. DONNIE MOORE
- [ ] 747. ALEX TREVINO
- [ ] 776. JERRY ROYSTER

BALTIMORE ORIOLES

- ☐ 30. CAL RIPKEN
- ☐ 56. JIM DWYER
- ☐ 81. LENN SAKATA
- ☐ 109. GARY ROENICKE
- ☐ 147. BILL SWAGGERTY
- ☐ 173. MIKE YOUNG
- ☐ 199. DENNY MARTINEZ
- ☐ 225. MIKE BODDICKER
- ☐ 252. DAN FORD
- ☐ 289. TOM UNDERWOOD
- ☐ 316. JOHN LOWENSTEIN
- ☐ 341. FLOYD RAYFORD
- ☐ 366. TODD CRUZ
- ☐ 416. WAYNE GROSS
- ☐ 445. TIPPY MARTINEZ
- ☐ 469. SAMMY STEWART
- ☐ 494. RICH DAUER
- ☐ 508. JOHN SHELBY
- ☐ 521. RICK DEMPSEY
- ☐ 550. SCOTT MCGREGOR
- ☐ 574. JOE ALTOBELLI(M)
- ☐ 599. STORM DAVIS
- ☐ 624. BENNY AYALA
- ☐ 652. JOE NOLAN
- ☐ 700. EDDIE MURRAY
- ☐ 726. AL BUMBRY
- ☐ 755. KEN SINGLETON
- ☐ 780. MIKE FLANAGAN

BOSTON RED SOX

- ☐ 11. RALPH HOUK(M)
- ☐ 37. REID NICHOLS
- ☐ 65. BILL BUCKNER
- ☐ 89. JACKIE GUTIERREZ
- ☐ 116. DENNIS BOYD
- ☐ 150. JIM RICE
- ☐ 181. ROGER CLEMENS
- ☐ 207. MARK CLEAR
- ☐ 233. ED JURAK
- ☐ 259. GARY ALLENSON
- ☐ 298. MARTY BARRETT
- ☐ 322. DAVE STAPLETON
- ☐ 350. WADE BOGGS
- ☐ 376. JEFF NEWMAN
- ☐ 424. AL NIPPER
- ☐ 451. BRUCE HURST
- ☐ 477. BOB OJEDA
- ☐ 502. RICK MILLER
- ☐ 529. RICH GEDMAN
- ☐ 555. BOB STANLEY
- ☐ 580. DWIGHT EVANS
- ☐ 606. RICH GALE
- ☐ 633. GLENN HOFFMAN
- ☐ 661. STEVE CRAWFORD
- ☐ 686. MIKE EASLER
- ☐ 734. JOHN HENRY JOHNSON
- ☐ 761. JERRY REMY
- ☐ 785. TONY ARMAS

CALIFORNIA ANGELS

- ☐ 42. LUIS SANCHEZ
- ☐ 61. CURT KAUFMAN
- ☐ 86. DON AASE
- ☐ 111. DOUG DECINCES
- ☐ 153. FRANK LACORTE
- ☐ 179. TOMMY JOHN
- ☐ 200. REGGIE JACKSON
- ☐ 220. FRED LYNN
- ☐ 226. JUAN BENIQUEZ
- ☐ 234. JERRY NARRON
- ☐ 258. MIKE BROWN
- ☐ 300. ROD CAREW
- ☐ 309. MIKE WITT
- ☐ 348. BOB BOONE
- ☐ 374. BRIAN DOWNING
- ☐ 442. KEN FORSCH
- ☐ 465. BOB GRICH
- ☐ 497. GARY PETTIS
- ☐ 524. ROB WILFONG
- ☐ 544. BRUCE KISON
- ☐ 579. RON ROMANICK
- ☐ 604. DARYL SCONIERS
- ☐ 629. DICK SCHOFIELD
- ☐ 657. JIM SLATON
- ☐ 682. DOUG CORBETT

- ☐ 732. JOHN MCNAMARA(M)
- ☐ 756. ROB PICCIOLO
- ☐ 771. GEOFF ZAHN

CHICAGO CUBS

- ☐ 19. GEORGE FRAZIER
- ☐ 46. GARY WOODS
- ☐ 72. RICK SUTCLIFFE
- ☐ 98. STEVE LAKE
- ☐ 124. RICH HEBNER
- ☐ 163. DENNIS ECKERSLEY
- ☐ 189. WARREN BRUSSTAR
- ☐ 210. GARY MATTHEWS
- ☐ 241. JIM FREY(M)
- ☐ 267. HENRY COTTO
- ☐ 306. RICK REUSCHEL
- ☐ 330. LEON DURHAM
- ☐ 357. RICH BORDI
- ☐ 384. JODY DAVIS
- ☐ 405. TOM VERYZER
- ☐ 432. THAD BOSLEY
- ☐ 460. RYNE SANDBERG
- ☐ 484. LARRY BOWA
- ☐ 511. LEE SMITH
- ☐ 538. KEITH MORELAND
- ☐ 563. DICK RUTHVEN
- ☐ 589. BOB DERNIER
- ☐ 616. SCOTT SANDERSON
- ☐ 642. DAVE OWEN
- ☐ 668. STEVE TROUT
- ☐ 693. TIM STODDARD
- ☐ 742. RON HASSEY
- ☐ 768. RON CEY

CHICAGO WHITE SOX

- ☐ 26. ROY SMALLEY
- ☐ 52. JERRY DYBZINSKI
- ☐ 78. SCOTT FLETCHER
- ☐ 105. RON KITTLE
- ☐ 169. DAN SPILLNER
- ☐ 194. DAVE STEGMAN
- ☐ 216. JERRY DON GLEATON
- ☐ 221. RON REED
- ☐ 249. HAROLD BAINES
- ☐ 286. RUDY LAW
- ☐ 312. MARC HILL
- ☐ 338. BRITT BURNS
- ☐ 351. JUAN AGOSTO
- ☐ 364. RICHARD DOTSON
- ☐ 388. BERT ROBERGE
- ☐ 413. VANCE LAW
- ☐ 437. AL JONES
- ☐ 466. TONY LARUSSA(M)
- ☐ 488. JOEL SKINNER
- ☐ 520. LAMARR HOYT
- ☐ 543. MIKE SQUIRES
- ☐ 572. TOM PACIOREK
- ☐ 596. JERRY HAIRSTON
- ☐ 623. GREG WALKER
- ☐ 650. GREG LUZINSKI
- ☐ 670. TOM SEAVER
- ☐ 725. FLOYD BANNISTER
- ☐ 749. JULIO CRUZ
- ☐ 770. CARLTON FISK

CINCINNATI REDS

- ☐ 28. DANN BILARDELLO
- ☐ 54. CESAR CEDEON

- ☐ 82. JOE PRICE
- ☐ 107. TOM FOLEY
- ☐ 146. GARY REDUS
- ☐ 175. DAVE PARKER
- ☐ 198. EDDIE MILNER
- ☐ 223. TOM HUME
- ☐ 251. BRAD GULDEN
- ☐ 314. RON OESTER
- ☐ 323. ANDY MCGAFFIGAN
- ☐ 342. TED POWER
- ☐ 367. KEEFE CATO
- ☐ 417. JOHN FRANCO
- ☐ 441. DUANE WALKER
- ☐ 468. WAYNE KRENCHICKI
- ☐ 495. MARIO SOTO
- ☐ 515. DAVE CONCEPCION
- ☐ 547. PETE ROSE(M)
- ☐ 573. JAY TIBBS
- ☐ 597. BRAD LESLEY
- ☐ 600. PETE ROSE
- ☐ 627. ERIC DAVIS
- ☐ 651. JEFF RUSSELL
- ☐ 675. TONY PEREZ
- ☐ 727. FRANK PASTORE
- ☐ 752. BOB OWCHINKO
- ☐ 779. NICK ESASKY

CLEVELAND INDIANS

- ☐ 14. CHRIS BANDO
- ☐ 41. MIKE FISCHLIN
- ☐ 93. DON SCHULZE
- ☐ 119. PAT CORRALES(M)
- ☐ 158. PAT TABLER
- ☐ 184. CARMEN CASTILLO
- ☐ 212. GEORGE VUKOVICH
- ☐ 237. JULIO FRANCO
- ☐ 263. MEL HALL
- ☐ 303. MIKE JEFFCOAT
- ☐ 327. BROOK JACOBY
- ☐ 355. BERT BLYLEVEN
- ☐ 381. ROY SMITH
- ☐ 425. MIKE HARGROVE
- ☐ 453. TOM WADDELL
- ☐ 475. ANDRE THORNTON
- ☐ 504. JERRY WILLARD
- ☐ 533. TONY BERNAZARD
- ☐ 609. BRODERICK PERKINS
- ☐ 637. BRETT BUTLER
- ☐ 664. STEVE FARR
- ☐ 694. JOE CARTER
- ☐ 739. ERNIE CAMACHO
- ☐ 764. JAMIE EASTERLY
- ☐ 788. STEVE COMER

DETROIT TIGERS

- ☐ 20. CHET LEMON
- ☐ 47. DAVE ROZEMA
- ☐ 73. RUSTY KUNTZ
- ☐ 99. MILT WILCOX
- ☐ 126. RUPPERT JONES
- ☐ 160. LANCE PARRISH
- ☐ 192. HOWARD JOHNSON
- ☐ 243. BARBARO GARBEY
- ☐ 269. DOUG BAKER
- ☐ 307. SPARKY ANDERSON(M)
- ☐ 333. WILLIE HERNANDEZ
- ☐ 368. DAVE BERGMAN
- ☐ 408. SID MONGE
- ☐ 435. DAN PETRY
- ☐ 461. MARTY CASTILLO
- ☐ 480. LOU WHITAKER
- ☐ 512. TOM BROOKENS
- ☐ 539. AURELIO LOPEZ
- ☐ 565. KIRK GIBSON
- ☐ 586. BILL SCHERRER
- ☐ 591. LARRY HERNDON
- ☐ 610. JACK MORRIS
- ☐ 643. JOHNNY GRUBB
- ☐ 672. JUAN BERENGUER
- ☐ 690. ALAN TRAMMELL
- ☐ 744. DOUG BAIR
- ☐ 792. DARRELL EVANS

HOUSTON ASTROS

- ☐ 17. MIKE SCOTT
- ☐ 44. DICKIE THON
- ☐ 64. MARK BAILEY
- ☐ 95. JOSE CRUZ

- ☐ 123. DAVE SMITH
- ☐ 156. CRAIG REYNOLDS
- ☐ 186. BOB LILLIS(M)
- ☐ 206. PHIL GARNER
- ☐ 264. JOE SAMBITO
- ☐ 295. JOE NIEKRO
- ☐ 326. KEVIN BASS
- ☐ 353. JULIO SOLANO
- ☐ 382. DENNY WALLING
- ☐ 426. VERN RUHLE
- ☐ 455. BOB KNEPPER
- ☐ 479. MIKE MADDEN
- ☐ 482. HARRY SPILMAN
- ☐ 532. FRANK DIPINO
- ☐ 564. ALAN ASHBY
- ☐ 613. TERRY PUHL
- ☐ 634. BILL DAWLEY
- ☐ 666. MIKE LACOSS
- ☐ 684. BILL DORAN
- ☐ 736. JERRY MUMPHREY
- ☐ 760. NOLAN RYAN
- ☐ 786. ENOS CABELL

NOLAN RYAN

KANSAS CITY ROYALS

- ☐ 23. BRET SABERHAGEN
- ☐ 49. BUTCH DAVIS
- ☐ 77. JOE BECKWITH
- ☐ 100. GEORGE BRETT
- ☐ 127. MARK GUBICZA
- ☐ 164. JORGE ORTA
- ☐ 188. GREG PRYOR
- ☐ 217. LEON ROBERTS
- ☐ 244. MIKE JONES
- ☐ 270. DAN QUISENBERRY
- ☐ 308. JOHN WATHAN
- ☐ 334. DICK HOWSER(M)
- ☐ 359. PAT SHERIDAN
- ☐ 387. BUDDY BIANCALANA
- ☐ 412. BUD BLACK
- ☐ 431. U.L. WASHINGTON
- ☐ 459. CHARLIE LEIBRANDT
- ☐ 486. STEVE BALBONI
- ☐ 513. LYNN JONES
- ☐ 542. DON SLAUGHT
- ☐ 561. DARRYL MOTLEY
- ☐ 595. LARRY GURA
- ☐ 617. WILLIE WILSON
- ☐ 644. MARK HUISMANN
- ☐ 671. DANE IORG
- ☐ 697. ONIX CONCEPCION
- ☐ 743. FRANK WHITE
- ☐ 773. HAL MCRAE

LOS ANGELES DODGERS

- ☐ 31. TERRY WHITFIELD
- ☐ 57. PAT ZACHRY
- ☐ 85. MIKE MARSHALL
- ☐ 110. ALEJANDRO PENA
- ☐ 148. STEVE YEAGER
- ☐ 159. CARLOS DIAZ
- ☐ 174. RICK HONEYCUTT
- ☐ 201. BURT HOOTON
- ☐ 253. SID BREAM
- ☐ 291. BOB WELCH
- ☐ 343. BILL RUSSELL
- ☐ 369. R.J. REYNOLDS
- ☐ 418. KEN LANDREAUX
- ☐ 440. FERNANDO VALENZUELA

- ☐ 470. STEVE SAX
- ☐ 493. OREL HERSHISER
- ☐ 506. FRANKLIN STUBBS
- ☐ 523. CANDY MALDONADO
- ☐ 549. MIKE SCIOSCIA
- ☐ 575. PEDRO GUERRERO
- ☐ 601. TOM LASORDA(M)
- ☐ 626. GERMAN RIVERA
- ☐ 654. DAVE ANDERSON
- ☐ 680. JERRY REUSS
- ☐ 728. BOB BAILOR
- ☐ 753. GREG BROCK
- ☐ 782. TOM NIEDENFUER

MILWAUKEE BREWERS

- ☐ 32. CHUCK PORTER
- ☐ 59. RICK WAITS
- ☐ 83. CHARLIE MOORE
- ☐ 112. TOM TELLMANN
- ☐ 151. MOOSE HAAS
- ☐ 176. BILL SCHROEDER
- ☐ 203. BOB MCCLURE
- ☐ 228. DION JAMES
- ☐ 254. PETE VUCKOVICH
- ☐ 290. CECIL COOPER
- ☐ 317. JACK LAZORKO
- ☐ 318. TED SIMMONS
- ☐ 340. ROBIN YOUNT
- ☐ 372. ROY HOWELL
- ☐ 419. MIKE CALDWELL
- ☐ 446. JIM SUNDBERG
- ☐ 471. PETE LADD
- ☐ 498. ED ROMERO
- ☐ 522. PAUL MOLITOR
- ☐ 553. BOB CLARK
- ☐ 576. JAIME COCANOWER
- ☐ 603. RICK MANNING
- ☐ 628. RENE LACHEMANN(M)
- ☐ 653. MARK BROUHARD
- ☐ 681. BEN OGLIVIE
- ☐ 729. DON SUTTON
- ☐ 750. ROLLIE FINGERS
- ☐ 781. JIM GANTNER

MINNESOTA TWINS

- ☐ 18. MICKEY HATCHER
- ☐ 43. ANDRE DAVID
- ☐ 71. TIM LAUDNER
- ☐ 97. PETE FILSON
- ☐ 122. TOM BRUNANSKY
- ☐ 161. KEN SCHROM
- ☐ 187. MIKE WALTERS
- ☐ 213. BILLY GARDNER(M)
- ☐ 239. TIM TEUFEL
- ☐ 266. FRANK VIOLA
- ☐ 304. GARY GAETTI
- ☐ 329. RON WASHINGTON
- ☐ 356. DAVE MEIER
- ☐ 383. RICK LYSANDER
- ☐ 406. LEN WHITEHOUSE
- ☐ 430. RON DAVIS
- ☐ 452. JOHN CASTINO
- ☐ 483. MIKE SMITHSON
- ☐ 510. KENT HRBEK
- ☐ 535. PAT PUTNAM
- ☐ 536. KIRBY PUCKETT
- ☐ 562. HOUSTON JIMENEZ
- ☐ 577. CHRIS SPEIER
- ☐ 588. BOBBY CASTILLO
- ☐ 614. AL WILLIAMS
- ☐ 639. ED HODGE
- ☐ 667. DAVE ENGLE
- ☐ 692. RANDY BUSH
- ☐ 741. JOHN BUTCHER
- ☐ 767. DARRELL BROWN

MONTREAL EXPOS

- ☐ 36. FRED BREINING
- ☐ 62. MIKE RAMSEY
- ☐ 88. BRYN SMITH
- ☐ 114. BOB JAMES
- ☐ 154. ARGENIS SALAZAR
- ☐ 178. MIGUEL DILONE
- ☐ 205. STEVE ROGERS
- ☐ 230. GARY CARTER
- ☐ 257. BRYAN LITTLE
- ☐ 285. DAN DRIESSEN

- ☐ 297. GARY LUCAS
- ☐ 345. CHARLIE LEA
- ☐ 375. JEFF REARDON
- ☐ 407. BOBBY RAMOS
- ☐ 420. ANDRE DAWSON
- ☐ 448. DERREL THOMAS
- ☐ 473. TIM WALLACH
- ☐ 501. DAN SCHATZEDER
- ☐ 526. DAVE PALMER
- ☐ 554. DOUG FLYNN
- ☐ 578. TERRY FRANCONA
- ☐ 630. TIM RAINES
- ☐ 658. MIKE STENHOUSE
- ☐ 687. BILL GULLICKSON
- ☐ 733. TONY SCOTT
- ☐ 759. JIM FANNING(M)
- ☐ 787. JIM WOHLFORD

NEW YORK METS

- ☐ 27. BRUCE BERENYI
- ☐ 53. TOM GORMAN
- ☐ 67. RAFAEL SANTANA
- ☐ 80. KEITH HERNANDEZ
- ☐ 104. MIKE FITZGERALD
- ☐ 144. RON GARDENHIRE
- ☐ 170. GEORGE FOSTER
- ☐ 190. RUSTY STAUB
- ☐ 222. HUBIE BROOKS
- ☐ 250. JESSE OROSCO
- ☐ 287. WALT TERRELL
- ☐ 315. DOUG SISK
- ☐ 339. DANNY HEEP
- ☐ 363. RON HODGES
- ☐ 415. RON DARLING
- ☐ 439. JUNIOR ORTIZ
- ☐ 467. ED LYNCH
- ☐ 492. DAVE JOHNSON(M)
- ☐ 517. JERRY MARTIN
- ☐ 546. BRENT GAFF
- ☐ 570. DARRYL STRAWBERRY
- ☐ 590. RAY KNIGHT
- ☐ 598. JOSE EQUENDO
- ☐ 620. DWIGHT GOODEN
- ☐ 649. SID FERNANDEZ
- ☐ 677. WALLY BACKMAN
- ☐ 751. KELVIN CHAPMAN
- ☐ 775. MOOKIE WILSON

NEW YORK YANKEES

- ☐ 16. BOBBY MEACHAM
- ☐ 40. PHIL NIEKRO
- ☐ 70. DON BAYLOR
- ☐ 94. TOBY HARRAH
- ☐ 120. STEVE KEMP
- ☐ 155. YOGI BERRA(M)
- ☐ 180. DAVE WINFIELD
- ☐ 211. CLAY CHRISTIANSEN
- ☐ 238. JOSE RIJO
- ☐ 260. DAVE RIGHETTI
- ☐ 284. MARTY BYSTROM
- ☐ 301. JOHN MONTEFUSCO
- ☐ 328. BOB SHIRLEY
- ☐ 354. ANDRE ROBERTSON
- ☐ 380. KEN GRIFFEY
- ☐ 429. RICK CERONE
- ☐ 456. TIM FOLI
- ☐ 481. DALE MURRAY
- ☐ 507. RAY FONTENOT
- ☐ 534. BRIAN DAYETT
- ☐ 559. JAY HOWELL
- ☐ 585. BUTCH WYNEGAR
- ☐ 612. MIKE ARMSTRONG
- ☐ 638. MIKE PAGLIARULO
- ☐ 665. DON MITTINGLY
- ☐ 691. DENNIS RASMUSSEN
- ☐ 724. OSCAR GAMBLE
- ☐ 738. OMAR MORENO
- ☐ 765. WILLIE RANDOLPH
- ☐ 769. JOE COWLEY
- ☐ 790. RON GUIDRY

OAKLAND A'S

- ☐ 12. DAVE LOPES
- ☐ 38. JACKIE MOORE(M)
- ☐ 63. STEVE MCCATTY
- ☐ 91. JEFF BURROUGHS
- ☐ 115. RICKEY HENDERSON

- ☐ 166. KEITH ATHERON
- ☐ 197. MIKE WARREN
- ☐ 231. DWAYNE MURPHY
- ☐ 246. MIKE NORRIS
- ☐ 293. CURT YOUNG
- ☐ 319. JEFF JONES
- ☐ 347. RICK LANGFORD
- ☐ 352. JOE MORGAN
- ☐ 422. CARNEY LANSFORD
- ☐ 444. TONY PHILLIPS
- ☐ 472. JIM ESSIAN
- ☐ 503. TIM CONROY
- ☐ 528. BILL KRUEGER
- ☐ 552. CHRIS CODIROLI
- ☐ 581. MARK WAGNER
- ☐ 607. BILL ALMON
- ☐ 632. BRUCE BOCHTE
- ☐ 662. MIKE HEATH
- ☐ 685. BILL CAUDILL
- ☐ 730. DAVE KINGMAN
- ☐ 758. RAY BURRIS
- ☐ 778. MIKE DAVIS

PHILADELPHIA PHILLIES

- ☐ 15. JERRY KOOSMAN
- ☐ 39. JOHNNY WOCKENFUSS
- ☐ 68. VON HAYES
- ☐ 92. PAUL OWENS(M)
- ☐ 117. GREG GROSS
- ☐ 130. AL OLIVER
- ☐ 157. TUG MCGRAW
- ☐ 185. AL HOLLAND
- ☐ 209. BILL CAMPBELL
- ☐ 235. GARRY MADDOX
- ☐ 265. JUAN SAMUEL
- ☐ 302. TIM CORCORAN
- ☐ 325. JOHN DENNY
- ☐ 360. STEVE CARLTON
- ☐ 379. CHARLES HUDSON
- ☐ 428. LARRY ANDERSEN
- ☐ 454. GLENN WILSON
- ☐ 476. JEFF STONE
- ☐ 500. MIKE SCHMIDT
- ☐ 531. JOE LEFEBVRE
- ☐ 556. SIXTON LEZCANO
- ☐ 584. KEVIN GROSS
- ☐ 611. OZZIE VIRGIL
- ☐ 636. SHANE RAWLEY
- ☐ 663. LUIS AGUAYO
- ☐ 688. LEN MATUSZEK
- ☐ 737. BO DIAZ
- ☐ 763. KIKO GARCIA
- ☐ 791. IVAN DEJESUS

PITTSBURGH PIRATES

- ☐ 21. LEE TUNNELL
- ☐ 50. JOHN CANDELARIA
- ☐ 69. JIM WINN
- ☐ 96. JOHNNY RAY
- ☐ 125. KENT TEKULVE
- ☐ 162. BENNY DISTEFANO
- ☐ 183. LARRY MCWILLIAMS
- ☐ 214. JOHN TUDOR
- ☐ 268. CHUCK TANNER(M)
- ☐ 305. DALE BERRA
- ☐ 332. BRIAN HARPER
- ☐ 358. TONY PENA
- ☐ 385. JOSE DELEON
- ☐ 433. JIM MORRISON
- ☐ 457. CECILIO GUANTE
- ☐ 490. JASON THOMPSON
- ☐ 509. MILT MAY
- ☐ 537. DON ROBINSON
- ☐ 560. BILL MADLOCK
- ☐ 587. DOUG FROBEL
- ☐ 615. MARVELL WYNNE
- ☐ 641. ROD SCURRY
- ☐ 669. LEE LACY
- ☐ 695. RICK RHODEN
- ☐ 748. LEE MAZZILLI

ST. LOUIS CARDINALS

- ☐ 33. TITO LANDRUM
- ☐ 60. GEORGE HENDRICK
- ☐ 87. DAVID GREEN
- ☐ 113. TOM HERR
- ☐ 152. STEVE BRAUN
- ☐ 177. DAVE VON OHLEN
- ☐ 204. ART HOWE

- ☐ 229. DAVE LAPOINT
- ☐ 255. LONNIE SMITH
- ☐ 294. TOM JIETO
- ☐ 321. RICKY HORTON
- ☐ 346. TERRY PENDLETON
- ☐ 370. BRUCE SUTTER
- ☐ 421. DAVE RUCKER
- ☐ 447. JEFF LAHTI
- ☐ 474. KURT KEPSHIRE
- ☐ 499. DANNY COX
- ☐ 525. DARRELL PORTER
- ☐ 551. ANDY VAN SLYKE
- ☐ 605. OZZIE SMITH
- ☐ 631. BOB FORSCH
- ☐ 655. JOAQUIN ANDUJAR
- ☐ 683. WHITE HERZOG(M)
- ☐ 731. NEIL ALLEN
- ☐ 757. WILLIE MCGEE
- ☐ 783. MIKE JORGENSEN

SAN DIEGO PADRES

- ☐ 13. TIM LOLLAR
- ☐ 35. GRAIG NETTLES
- ☐ 66. DICK WILLIAMS(M)
- ☐ 90. RICH GOSSAGE
- ☐ 118. ERIC SHOW
- ☐ 182. TIM FLANNERY
- ☐ 208. CHAMP SUMMERS
- ☐ 236. MARK THURMOND
- ☐ 242. GREG HARRIS
- ☐ 262. GREG BOOKER
- ☐ 299. ANDY HAWKINS
- ☐ 324. BRUCE BOCHY
- ☐ 378. ALAN WIGGINS
- ☐ 427. MARIO RAMIREZ
- ☐ 450. STEVE GARVEY
- ☐ 478. KURT BEVACQUA
- ☐ 530. DAVE DRAVECKY
- ☐ 558. CARMELO MARTINEZ
- ☐ 583. BOBBY BROWN
- ☐ 608. CRAIG LEFFERTS
- ☐ 635. TERRY KENNEDY
- ☐ 660. TONY GWYNN
- ☐ 689. LUIS DELEON
- ☐ 735. GARRY TEMPLETON
- ☐ 762. EDDIE WHITSON
- ☐ 789. LUIS SALAZAR

SAN FRANCISCO GIANTS

- ☐ 22. DUANE KUIPER
- ☐ 45. GREG MINTON
- ☐ 74. MIKE KRUKOW
- ☐ 103. RANDY LERCH
- ☐ 165. DUSTY BAKER
- ☐ 191. STEVE NICOSIA
- ☐ 215. BOB BRENLY
- ☐ 245. CHILI DAVIS
- ☐ 283. FRAN MULLINS
- ☐ 310. MANNY TRILLO
- ☐ 331. BILL LASKEY
- ☐ 365. DANNY OZARK(M)
- ☐ 386. DAN GLADDEN
- ☐ 409. BRAD WELLMAN
- ☐ 434. GENE RICHARDS
- ☐ 462. GARY LAVELLE
- ☐ 487. FRANK WILLIAMS
- ☐ 514. JEFF CORNELL
- ☐ 541. MARK DAVIS
- ☐ 567. JOEL YOUNGBLOOD
- ☐ 592. JEFF ROBINSON
- ☐ 619. JEFF LEONARD
- ☐ 646. SCOT THOMPSON
- ☐ 674. ATLEE HAMMAKER
- ☐ 696. JOHN RABB
- ☐ 740. JACK CLARK
- ☐ 772. JOHNNIE LEMASTER

SEATTLE MARINERS

- ☐ 34. ED NUNEZ
- ☐ 58. ORLANDO MERCADO
- ☐ 84. SPIKE OWEN
- ☐ 108. DARNELL COLES
- ☐ 145. ALVIN DAVIS
- ☐ 172. JACK PERCONTE
- ☐ 202. GORMAN THOMAS
- ☐ 224. AL COWENS
- ☐ 232. DAVE BEARD
- ☐ 256. MIKE STANTON
- ☐ 296. RICKY NELSON
- ☐ 344. DAVE HENDERSON
- ☐ 349. DOMINGO RAMOS

- ☐ 373. MIKE MOORE
- ☐ 423. BARRY BONNELL
- ☐ 449. PHIL BRADLEY
- ☐ 485. MATT YOUNG
- ☐ 505. JIM BEATTIE
- ☐ 566. ED VAND BERG
- ☐ 582. KEN PHELPS
- ☐ 625. MARK LANGSTON
- ☐ 640. STEVE HENDERSON
- ☐ 656. CHUCK COTTIER(M)
- ☐ 679. BOB KEARNEY
- ☐ 754. LARRY MILBOURNE
- ☐ 766. PAUL MIRABRELLA

TEXAS RANGERS

- ☐ 29. ODELL JONES
- ☐ 55. FRANK TANANA
- ☐ 76. ALAN BANNISTER
- ☐ 102. TOMMY DUNBAR
- ☐ 149. DICKIE NOLES
- ☐ 171. BILL STEIN
- ☐ 196. PETE O'BRIEN
- ☐ 227. DANNY DARWIN
- ☐ 247. WAYNE TOLLESON
- ☐ 288. JEFF KUNKEL
- ☐ 313. DAVE SCHMIDT
- ☐ 337. BILLY SAMPLE
- ☐ 371. MICKEY RIVERS
- ☐ 414. GARY WARD
- ☐ 443. GEORGE WRIGHT
- ☐ 464. MIKE MASON
- ☐ 496. DONNIE SCOTT
- ☐ 519. DOUG RADER(M)
- ☐ 548. LARRY PARRISH
- ☐ 571. CHARLIE HOUGH
- ☐ 594. CURT WILKERSON
- ☐ 621. MARVIS FOLEY
- ☐ 648. BOB JONES
- ☐ 678. JOEY MCLAUGHLIN
- ☐ 723. DAVE STEWART
- ☐ 745. BUDDY BELL
- ☐ 777. NED YOST

TORONTO BLUE JAYS

- ☐ 24. JESSE BARFIELD
- ☐ 48. TONY FERNANDEZ
- ☐ 75. WILLIE UPSHAW
- ☐ 101. JIM ACKER
- ☐ 128. ERNIE WHITT
- ☐ 168. GARTH IORG
- ☐ 193. JIMMY KEY
- ☐ 218. DOYLE ALEXANDER
- ☐ 240. DAVE STIEB
- ☐ 311. JIM GOTT
- ☐ 336. RANCE MULLINIKS
- ☐ 361. ALFREDO GRIFFIN
- ☐ 411. BOBBY COX(M)
- ☐ 436. WILLIE AIKENS
- ☐ 463. DAVE COLLINS
- ☐ 489. BRYAN CLARK
- ☐ 516. ROY LEE JACKSON
- ☐ 545. LLOYD MOSEBY
- ☐ 568. CLIFF JOHNSON
- ☐ 593. RICK LEACH
- ☐ 622. LUIS LEAD
- ☐ 645. DAMASCO GARCIA
- ☐ 673. BUCK MARTINEZ
- ☐ 698. JORGE BELL
- ☐ 746. JIM CLANCY
- ☐ 774. DENNIS LAMP

U. S. OLYMPIC TEAM

- ☐ 389. ROD DEDEAUX (HC)
- ☐ 390. SID AKINS
- ☐ 391. FLAVIO ALFARO
- ☐ 392. DON AUGUST
- ☐ 393. SCOTT BANKHEAD
- ☐ 394. BOB CAFFREY
- ☐ 395. MIKE DUNNE
- ☐ 396. GARY GREEN
- ☐ 397. JOHN HOOVER
- ☐ 398. SHANE MACK
- ☐ 399. JOHN MARZANO
- ☐ 400. ODDIBE MCDOWELL
- ☐ 401. MARK MCGWIRE
- ☐ 402. PAT PACILLO
- ☐ 403. CORY SNYDER
- ☐ 404. BILLY SWIFT

1985 TOPPS TRADED (132) 2 1/2 X 3 1/2

ATLANTA BRAVES

- [ ] 20T. RICK CERONE
- [ ] 44T. EDDIE HAAS(M)
- [ ] 45T. TERRY HARPER
- [ ] 100T. PAUL RUNGE
- [ ] 115T. BRUCE SUTTER

BALTIMORE ORIOLES

- [ ] 1T. DON AASE
- [ ] 31T. KEN DIXON
- [ ] 70T. LEE LACY
- [ ] 77T. FRED LYNN
- [ ] 106T. LARRY SHEETS
- [ ] 110T. NATE SNELL
- [ ] 129T. EARL WEAVER(M)

BOSTON RED SOX

- [ ] 67T. BRUCE KISON
- [ ] 84T. JOHN MCNAMARA(M)

CALIFORNIA ANGELS

- [ ] 23T. PAT CLEMENTS
- [ ] 65T. RUPPERT JONES
- [ ] 81T. GENE MAUCH(M)
- [ ] 85T. DONNIE MOORE

CHICAGO CUBS

- [ ] 29T. BRIAN DAYETT
- [ ] 35T. RAY FONTENOT
- [ ] 111T. CHRIS SPEIER

CHICAGO WHITE SOX

- [ ] 8T. DARYL BOSTON
- [ ] 37T. OSCAR GAMBLE
- [ ] 43T. OZZIE GUILLEN
- [ ] 60T. TIM HULETT
- [ ] 61T. BOB JAMES
- [ ] 76T. TIM LOLLAR
- [ ] 86T. GENE NELSON
- [ ] 102T. LUIS SALAZAR

CINCINNATI REDS

- [ ] 11T. TOM BROWNING
- [ ] 68T. ALAN KNICELY

CLEVELAND INDIANS

- [ ] 3T. BENNY AYALA
- [ ] 21T. BRYAN CLARK
- [ ] 99T. VERN RUHLE
- [ ] 122T. RICH THOMPSON
- [ ] 127T. DAVE VON OHLEN

DETROIT TIGERS

- [ ] 91T. CHRIS PITTARO
- [ ] 119T. WALT TERRELL

HOUSTON ASTROS

- [ ] 79T. RON MATHIS

KANSAS CITY ROYALS

- [ ] 69T. MIKE LACOSS
- [ ] 109T. LONNIE SMITH
- [ ] 114T. JIM SUNDBERG

LOS ANGELES DODGERS

- [ ] 18T. BOBBY CASTILLO
- [ ] 32T. MARIANO DUNCAN
- [ ] 58T. KEN HOWELL
- [ ] 88T. AL OLIVER

MILWAUKEE BREWERS

- [ ] 5T. GEORGE BAMBERGER(M)
- [ ] 13T. RAY BURRIS
- [ ] 26T. DANNY DARWIN
- [ ] 39T. BOB GIBSON
- [ ] 53T. TEDDY HIGUERA

MINNESOTA TWINS

- [ ] 36T. GREG GAGNE
- [ ] 101T. MARK SALAS
- [ ] 108T. ROY SMALLEY
- [ ] 112T. MIKE STENHOUSE

MONTREAL EXPOS

- [ ] 9T. HUBIE BROOKS
- [ ] 34T. MIKE FITZGERALD
- [ ] 52T. JOE HESKETH
- [ ] 73T. VANCE LAW
- [ ] 87T. STEVE NICOSIA
- [ ] 94T. BERT ROBERGE
- [ ] 95T. BOB RODGERS(M)
- [ ] 128T. U.L. WASHINGTON
- [ ] 131T. HERM WINNINGHAM

NEW YORK METS

- [ ] 17T. GARY CARTER
- [ ] 64T. HOWARD JOHNSON
- [ ] 83T. ROGER MCDOWELL
- [ ] 103T. JOE SAMBITO

NEW YORK YANKEES

- [ ] 6T. DALE BERRA
- [ ] 7T. RICH BORDI
- [ ] 48T. RON HASSEY
- [ ] 49T. RICKEY HENDERSON
- [ ] 78T. BILLY MARTIN(M)
- [ ] 130T. EDDIE WHITSON

OAKLAND A'S

- [ ] 4T. DUSTY BAKER
- [ ] 25T. DAVE COLLINS
- [ ] 42T. ALFREDO GRIFFIN
- [ ] 50T. STEVE HENDERSON
- [ ] 54T. DONNIE HILL
- [ ] 57T. JAY HOWELL
- [ ] 90T. ROB PICCIOLO
- [ ] 116T. DON SUTTON
- [ ] 118T. TOM TELLMANN
- [ ] 120T. MICKEY TETTLETON

PHILADELPHIA PHILLIES

- [ ] 16T. DON CARMAN
- [ ] 33T. JOHN FELSKE(M)
- [ ] 62T. STEVE JELTZ
- [ ] 98T. DAVE RUCKER
- [ ] 104T. RICK SCHU
- [ ] 117T. KENT TEKULVE
- [ ] 121T. DERREL THOMAS

PITTSBURGH PIRATES

- [ ] 2T. BILL ALMON
- [ ] 51T. GEORGE HENDRICK
- [ ] 55T. AL HOLLAND
- [ ] 66T. STEVE KEMP
- [ ] 74T. JOHNNIE LEMASTER
- [ ] 75T. SIXTO LEZCANO
- [ ] 89T. JOE ORSULAK
- [ ] 93T. RICK REUSCHEL

ST. LOUIS CARDINALS

- [ ] 15T. BILL CAMPBELL
- [ ] 22T. JACK CLARK
- [ ] 24T. VINCE COLEMAN
- [ ] 30T. IVAN DEJESUS
- [ ] 124T. JOHN TUDOR

SAN DIEGO PADRES

- [ ] 12T. AL BUMBRY
- [ ] 28T. JERRY DAVIS
- [ ] 59T. LAMARR HOYT
- [ ] 96T. JERRY ROYSTER
- [ ] 113T. TIM STODDARD

SAN FRANCISCO GIANTS

- [ ] 10T. CHRIS BROWN
- [ ] 27T. JIM DAVENPORT(M)
- [ ] 38T. SCOTT GARRELTS
- [ ] 40T. JIM GOTT
- [ ] 41T. DAVID GREEN
- [ ] 71T. DAVE LAPOINT
- [ ] 123T. ALEX TREVINO
- [ ] 125T. JOSE URIBE

SEATTLE MARINERS

- [ ] 92T. JIM PRESLEY
- [ ] 105T. DONNIE SCOTT

TEXAS RANGERS

- [ ] 46T. TOBY HARRAH
- [ ] 47T. GREG HARRIS
- [ ] 56T. BURT HOOTON
- [ ] 63T. CLIFF JOHNSON
- [ ] 82T. ODDIBE MCDOWELL
- [ ] 97T. DAVE ROZEMA
- [ ] 107T. DON SLAUGHT
- [ ] 126T. BOBBY VALENTINE(M)

TORONTO BLUE JAYS

- [ ] 14T. JEFF BURROUGHS
- [ ] 19T. BILL CAUDILL
- [ ] 72T. GARY LAVELLE
- [ ] 80T. LEN MATUSZEK

1986 TOPPS (792)
2 1/2 X 3 1/2

EDDIE MURRAY

ATLANTA BRAVES

- ☐ 24. LEN BARKER
- ☐ 57. BOBBY WINE(M)
- ☐ 78. BRUCE BENEDICT
- ☐ 107. RAFAEL RAMIREZ
- ☐ 129. JEFF DEDMON
- ☐ 167. ZANE SMITH
- ☐ 194. CRAIG MCMURTRY
- ☐ 220. BOB HORNER
- ☐ 247. TERRY HARPER
- ☐ 293. CHRIS CHAMBLISS
- ☐ 319. RICK CAMP
- ☐ 334. KEN OBERKFELL
- ☐ 363. TERRY FORSTER
- ☐ 409. PAUL RUNGE
- ☐ 437. RICK MAHLER
- ☐ 456. TEAM LEADER CARD
- ☐ 491. PASCUAL PEREZ
- ☐ 517. MILT THOMPSON
- ☐ 539. GLENN HUBBARD
- ☐ 557. GERALD PERRY
- ☐ 572. PAUL ZUVELLA
- ☐ 600. DALE MURPHY
- ☐ 620. BRUCE SUTTER
- ☐ 648. STEVE BEDROSIAN
- ☐ 675. CLAUDELL WASHINGTON
- ☐ 698. BRAD KOMMINSK
- ☐ 747. RICK CERONE
- ☐ 776. GENE GARBER

BALTIMORE ORIOLES

- ☐ 30. EDDIE MURRARY
- ☐ 55. FRED LYNN
- ☐ 82. TIPPY MARTINEZ
- ☐ 110. SCOTT MCGREGOR
- ☐ 147. LARRY SHEETS
- ☐ 173. WAYNE GROSS
- ☐ 198. KEN DIXON
- ☐ 226. LEE LACY
- ☐ 251. RICH DAUER
- ☐ 279. AL PARDO
- ☐ 288. DON AASE
- ☐ 309. JOHN SHELBY
- ☐ 321. EARL WEAVER(M)
- ☐ 340. CAL RIPKEN
- ☐ 358. RICK DEMPSEY
- ☐ 365. MIKE FLANAGAN
- ☐ 416. DENNY MARTINEZ
- ☐ 446. LENN SAKATA
- ☐ 469. STORM DAVIS
- ☐ 494. GARY ROENICKE
- ☐ 508. ALAN WIGGINS
- ☐ 521. NATE SNELL
- ☐ 548. MIKE YOUNG
- ☐ 575. MIKE BODDICKER
- ☐ 597. SAMMY STEWART
- ☐ 623. FLOYD RAYFORD
- ☐ 653. JIM DWYER
- ☐ 726. TEAM LEADER CARD
- ☐ 753. DAN FORD
- ☐ 781. JOE NOLAN

BOSTON RED SOX

- ☐ 11. BOB OJEDA
- ☐ 38. GLENN HOFFMAN
- ☐ 60. DWIGHT EVANS
- ☐ 91. STEVE CRAWFORD
- ☐ 117. BRUCE KISON
- ☐ 151. DAVE STAPLETON
- ☐ 181. AL NIPPER
- ☐ 233. STEVE LYONS
- ☐ 255. TONY ARMAS
- ☐ 297. TIM LOLLAR
- ☐ 307. DAVE SAX
- ☐ 320. JIM RICE
- ☐ 349. MARK CLEAR
- ☐ 375. RICH GEDMAN
- ☐ 396. TEAM LEADER CARD
- ☐ 424. RICK MILLER
- ☐ 443. BILL BUCKNER
- ☐ 477. MIKE EASLER
- ☐ 510. WADE BOGGS
- ☐ 529. MARC SULLIVAN
- ☐ 581. BRUCE HURST
- ☐ 605. DENNIS BOYD
- ☐ 633. JACKIE GUTIERREZ
- ☐ 661. ROGER CLEMENS
- ☐ 687. MIKE TRUJILLO
- ☐ 734. MARTY BARRETT
- ☐ 749. ED JURAK
- ☐ 771. JOHN MCNAMARA(M)
- ☐ 785. BOB STANLEY

CALIFORNIA ANGELS

- ☐ 42. GEOFF ZAHN
- ☐ 62. BOB BOONE
- ☐ 81. GENE MAUCH(M)
- ☐ 124. LUIS SANCHEZ
- ☐ 127. JACK HOWELL
- ☐ 140. JOHN CANDELARIA
- ☐ 155. BOB GRICH
- ☐ 179. STU CLIBURN
- ☐ 190. GEORGE HENDRICK
- ☐ 193. DARYL SCONIERS
- ☐ 222. CRAIG GERBER
- ☐ 234. DOUG CORBETT
- ☐ 257. DOUG DECINCES
- ☐ 311. DICK SCHOFIELD
- ☐ 325. JUAN BENIQUEZ
- ☐ 335. DON SUTTON
- ☐ 345. DONNIE MOORE
- ☐ 369. AL HOLLAND
- ☐ 373. URBANO LUGO
- ☐ 400. ROD CAREW
- ☐ 464. RUPPERT JONES
- ☐ 486. TEAM LEADER CARD
- ☐ 524. DARRELL MILLER
- ☐ 543. JERRY NARRON
- ☐ 579. JIM SLATON
- ☐ 604. GARY PETTIS
- ☐ 628. KIRK MCCASKILL
- ☐ 658. ROB WILFONG
- ☐ 700. REGGIE JACKSON
- ☐ 733. RON ROMANICK
- ☐ 772. BRIAN DOWNING

CHICAGO CUBS

- ☐ 19. RICH HEBNER
- ☐ 46. BILLY HATCHER
- ☐ 72. SHAWON DUNSTON
- ☐ 98. DICK RUTHVEN
- ☐ 125. DAVE LOPES
- ☐ 188. BOB DERNIER
- ☐ 212. CHRIS SPEIER
- ☐ 231. JIM FREY(M)
- ☐ 266. KEITH MORELAND
- ☐ 284. BRIAN DAYETT
- ☐ 308. RAY FONTENOT
- ☐ 330. RICK SUTCLIFFE
- ☐ 355. LEE SMITH
- ☐ 384. STEVE TROUT
- ☐ 406. SCOTT SANDERSON
- ☐ 431. GOERGE FRAZIER
- ☐ 460. LEON DURHAM
- ☐ 485. GARY MATTHEWS
- ☐ 512. THAD BOSLEY
- ☐ 538. DENNIS ECKERSLEY
- ☐ 564. WARREN BRUSSTAR
- ☐ 588. STEVE LAKE
- ☐ 611. GARY WOODS

- ☐ 636. TEAM LEADER CARD
- ☐ 669. RON CEY
- ☐ 690. RYNE SANDBERG
- ☐ 744. LARY SORENSEN
- ☐ 767. JODY DAVIS

CHICAGO WHITE SOX

- ☐ 14. JULIO CRUZ
- ☐ 64. FLOYD BANNISTER
- ☐ 103. LUIS SALAZAR
- ☐ 123. GREG WALKER
- ☐ 139. DARYL BOSTON
- ☐ 156. TEAM LEADER CARD
- ☐ 187. SCOTT FLETCHER
- ☐ 227. AL JONES
- ☐ 239. JOEL SKINNER
- ☐ 254. OZZIE GUILLEN
- ☐ 290. CARLTON FISK
- ☐ 313. JOE DESA
- ☐ 346. BRYAN LITTLE
- ☐ 364. REID NICHOLS
- ☐ 390. TOM SEAVER
- ☐ 423. DAN SPILLNER
- ☐ 447. JERRY DON GLEATON
- ☐ 467. BOB JAMES
- ☐ 493. GENE NELSON
- ☐ 531. TONY LARUSSA(M)
- ☐ 552. MARC HILL
- ☐ 574. RON KITTLE
- ☐ 612. RICHARD DOTSON
- ☐ 637. RUDY LAW
- ☐ 657. JUAN AGOSTO
- ☐ 679. BRITT BURNS
- ☐ 724. TIM HULETT
- ☐ 755. HAROLD BAINES
- ☐ 778. JERRY HAIRSTON

CINCINNATI REDS

- ☐ 1. PETE ROSE
- ☐ 28. ERIC DAVIS
- ☐ 54. JOHN FRANCO
- ☐ 85. TONY PEREZ
- ☐ 108. TED POWER
- ☐ 133. ANDY MCGAFFIGAN
- ☐ 143. DAVE VAN GORDER
- ☐ 176. JAY TIBBS
- ☐ 195. DAVE CONCEPCION
- ☐ 253. DANN BILARDELLO
- ☐ 285. BUDDY BELL
- ☐ 314. FRANK PASTORE
- ☐ 342. GARY REDUS
- ☐ 366. TEAM LEADER CARD
- ☐ 428. MAX VENABLE
- ☐ 442. RON ROBINSON
- ☐ 497. JOHN STUPER
- ☐ 523. JOE PRICE
- ☐ 544. EDDIE MILNER
- ☐ 573. TOM HUME
- ☐ 595. DAVE PARKER
- ☐ 627. RON OESTER
- ☐ 639. BO DIAZ
- ☐ 652. TOM BROWNING
- ☐ 677. NICK ESASKY
- ☐ 725. MARIO SOTO
- ☐ 741. PETE ROSE(M)
- ☐ 777. WAYNE KRENCHICKI

CLEVELAND INDIANS

- ☐ 9. ROY SMITH
- ☐ 31. JAMIE EASTERLY
- ☐ 59. ANDRE THORNTON
- ☐ 86. TOM WADDELL
- ☐ 116. BROOK JACOBY
- ☐ 136. MIKE HARGROVE
- ☐ 149. BRETT BUTLER
- ☐ 172. JERRY REED
- ☐ 208. RAMON ROMERO
- ☐ 242. RICH THOMPSON
- ☐ 273. JERRY WILLARD
- ☐ 283. MIKE FISCHLIN
- ☐ 303. CURT WARDLE
- ☐ 336. TEAM LEADER CARD
- ☐ 354. TONY BERNAZARD
- ☐ 377. JOE CARTER
- ☐ 391. JULIO FRANCO
- ☐ 483. GEORGE VUKOVICH
- ☐ 509. ERNIE CAMACHO
- ☐ 542. DON SCHULZE

☐ 567. JEFF BARKLEY
☐ 594. CHRIS BANDO
☐ 632. DAVE VON OHLEN
☐ 647. MEL HALL
☐ 674. PAT TABLER
☐ 699. PAT CORRALES(M)
☐ 768. VERN RUHLE

DETROIT TIGERS

☐ 20. LOU WHITAKER
☐ 36. TEAM LEADER CARD
☐ 47. JUAN BERENGUER
☐ 73. RANDY O'NEAL
☐ 101. DAVE BERGMAN
☐ 121. NELSON SIMMONS
☐ 130. ALAN TRAMMELL
☐ 160. CHET LEMON
☐ 192. MILT WILCOX
☐ 217. BILL SCHERRER
☐ 243. JOHNNY GRUBB
☐ 270. JACK MORRIS
☐ 295. KIRK GIVSON
☐ 367. AURELIO LOPEZ
☐ 393. CHRIS PITTARO
☐ 411. SPARKY ANDERSON(M)
☐ 436. DOUG FLYNN
☐ 461. WALT TERRELL
☐ 479. BOB MELVIN
☐ 515. DARRELL EVANS
☐ 540. DAN PETRY
☐ 563. ALEJANDRO SANCHEZ
☐ 592. FRANK TANANA
☐ 609. BARBARO GARBEY
☐ 643. TOM BROOKENS
☐ 670. WILLIE HERNANDEZ
☐ 688. LARRY HERNDON
☐ 740. LANCE PARRISH
☐ 788. MARTY CASTILLO

HOUSTON ASTROS

☐ 26. FRANK DIPINO
☐ 57. BILL DORAN
☐ 83. PHIL GARNER
☐ 100. NOLAN RYAN
☐ 166. DICKIE THON
☐ 186. TEAM LEADER CARD
☐ 268. MIKE SCOTT
☐ 272. TIM TOLMAN
☐ 282. JERRY MUMPHREY
☐ 298. CRAIG REYNOLDS
☐ 331. ALAN ASHBY
☐ 352. HARRY SPILMAN
☐ 376. BILL DAWLEY
☐ 389. GLENN DAVIS
☐ 408. DAVE SMITH
☐ 432. MARK BAILEY
☐ 458. KEVIN BASS
☐ 476. RON MATHIS
☐ 504. DENNY WALLING
☐ 534. JEFF CALHOUN
☐ 561. BOB LILLIS(M)
☐ 590. BOB KNEPPER
☐ 618. JIM PANKOVITS
☐ 640. JOSE CRUZ
☐ 691. MIKE MADDEN
☐ 763. TERRY PUHL

KANSAS CITY ROYALS

☐ 25. WILLIE WILSON
☐ 50. DAN QUISENBERRY
☐ 77. CHARLIE LEIBRANDT
☐ 99. BUDDY BIANCALANA
☐ 128. JOHN WATHAN
☐ 164. STEVE BALBONI
☐ 199. DICK HOWSER(M)
☐ 215. FRANK WHITE
☐ 245. JIM SUNDBERG
☐ 269. DANE IORG
☐ 300. GEORGE BRETT
☐ 332. DARRYL MOTLEY
☐ 359. MIKE LACOSS
☐ 415. HAL MCRAE
☐ 487. BRET SABERHAGEN
☐ 514. MIKE JONES
☐ 541. JORGE ORTA
☐ 562. JOE BECKWITH
☐ 596. ONIX CONCEPCION
☐ 606. TEAM LEADER CARD

☐ 617. LONNIE SMITH
☐ 644. MARK GUBICZA
☐ 671. LYNN JONES
☐ 697. BUD BLACK
☐ 743. PAT SHERIDAN
☐ 773. GREG PRYOR

LOS ANGELES DODGERS

☐ 32. STEVE YEAGER
☐ 56. TOM NIEDENFUER
☐ 87. CANDY MALDONADO
☐ 109. LEN MATUSZEK
☐ 145. PEDRO GUERRERO
☐ 159. OREL HERSHISER
☐ 175. STEVE SAX
☐ 197. ENOS CABELL
☐ 252. BOBBY CASTILLO
☐ 291. TOM LASORDA(M)
☐ 318. TERRY WHITFIELD
☐ 343. CARLOS DIAZ
☐ 368. GREG BROCK
☐ 439. RICK HONEYCUTT
☐ 468. MIKE SCIOSCIA
☐ 470. BILL MADLOCK
☐ 496. JAY JOHNSTONE
☐ 506. BILL RUSSELL
☐ 522. BOB BAILOR
☐ 549. BOB WELCH
☐ 577. JERRY REUSS
☐ 602. MARIANO DUNCAN
☐ 630. FERNANDO VALENZUELA
☐ 654. KEN HOWELL
☐ 665. ALEJANDRO PENA
☐ 696. TEAM LEADER CARD
☐ 728. MIKE MARSHALL
☐ 758. DAVE ANDERSON
☐ 782. KEN LANDREAUX

MILWAUKEE BREWERS

☐ 21. GEORGE BAMBERGER(M)
☐ 49. RICK MANNING
☐ 76. DION JAMES
☐ 106. RAY BURRIS
☐ 137. CHARLIE MOORE
☐ 163. PETE LADD
☐ 185. ROLLIE FINGERS
☐ 209. RANDY READY
☐ 237. TED SIMMONS
☐ 267. PAUL MOLITOR
☐ 277. JAIME COCANOWER
☐ 292. CHUCK PORTER
☐ 317. ED ROMERO
☐ 347. TEDDY HIGUERA
☐ 372. BEN OGLIVIE
☐ 385. CECIL COOPER
☐ 398. EARNIE RILES
☐ 426. TEAM LEADER CARD
☐ 452. BOB CLARK
☐ 473. MARK BROUHARD
☐ 499. BOB GIBSON
☐ 519. DANNY DARWIN
☐ 554. PAUL HOUSEHOLDER
☐ 582. JIM GANTNER
☐ 614. RICK WAITS
☐ 642. RAY SEARAGE
☐ 662. BILL SCHROEDER
☐ 684. BOB MCCLURE
☐ 737. PETE VUCKOVICH
☐ 759. MOOSE HAAS
☐ 780. ROBIN YOUNT

MINNESOTA TWINS

☐ 17. MIKE STENHOUSE
☐ 43. DAVE ENGLE
☐ 71. KEN SCHROM
☐ 97. GARY GAETTI
☐ 122. PETE FILSON
☐ 162. GREG GAGNE
☐ 184. TIM LAUDNER
☐ 214. RANDY BUSH
☐ 236. FRANK EUFEMIA
☐ 265. RON DAVIS
☐ 329. KIRBY PUCKETT
☐ 356. MICKEY HATCHER
☐ 381. RAY MILLER(M)
☐ 430. KENT HRBEK
☐ 445. BERT BLYLEVEN

☐ 451. MARK BROWN
☐ 482. RICK LYSANDER
☐ 513. RON WASHINGTON
☐ 537. MARK SALAS
☐ 565. TOM BRUNANSKY
☐ 613. ROY SMALLEY
☐ 638. JOHN BUTCHER
☐ 667. TIM TEUFEL
☐ 695. MIKE SMITHSON
☐ 742. FRANK VIOLA
☐ 786. TEAM LEADER CARD

MONTREAL EXPOS

☐ 35. JEFF REARDON
☐ 89. RANDY ST. CLAIRE
☐ 93. SCOT THOMPSON
☐ 113. U.L. WASHINGTON
☐ 132. RAZOR SHINES
☐ 154. BERT ROBERGE
☐ 141. BOB RODGERS(M)
☐ 229. BILL GULLICKSON
☐ 258. TIM BURKE
☐ 280. TIM RAINES
☐ 299. BRYN SMITH
☐ 324. DAN SCHATZEDER
☐ 344. JIM WOHLFORD
☐ 374. TERRY FRANCONA
☐ 407. SAL BUTERA
☐ 421. DAVE PALMER
☐ 448. HERM WINNINGHAM
☐ 472. JOE HESKETH
☐ 503. MIKE FITZGERALD
☐ 526. CHARLIE LEA
☐ 555. HUBIE BROOKS
☐ 576. TEAM LEADER CARD
☐ 601. GARY LUCAS
☐ 603. BILL LASKEY
☐ 629. MITCH WEBSTER
☐ 685. TIM WALLACH
☐ 732. FLOYD YOUMANS
☐ 760. ANDRE DAWSON
☐ 787. VANCE LAW

LEN DYKSTRA

NEW YORK METS

☐ 18. BRENT GAFF
☐ 27. RAY KNIGHT
☐ 53. LEN DYKSTRA
☐ 68. ED LYNCH
☐ 80. DARRYL STRAWBERRY
☐ 104. SID FERNANDEZ
☐ 126. TEAM LEADER CARD
☐ 144. DOUG SISK
☐ 170. GARY CARTER
☐ 191. WALLY BACKMAN
☐ 210. CALVIN SCHIRALDI
☐ 225. RON DARLING
☐ 250. DWIGHT GOODEN
☐ 274. RON GARDENHIRE
☐ 287. JOHN CHRISTENSEN
☐ 315. MOOKIE WILSON
☐ 339. BRUCE BERENYI
☐ 362. TOM PACIOREK
☐ 414. TOM GORMAN
☐ 438. CLINT HURDLE
☐ 465. JESSE OROSCO
☐ 492. KELVIN CHAPMAN
☐ 501. DAVE JOHNSON(M)
☐ 520. KEITH HERNANDEZ
☐ 547. ROGER MCDOWELL

☐ 570. RUSTY STAUB
☐ 587. RAFAEL SANTANA
☐ 599. RICK AGUILERA
☐ 619. DANNY HEEP
☐ 649. RONN REYNOLDS
☐ 680. GEORGE FOSTER
☐ 751. HOWARD JOHNSON
☐ 774. TERRY LEACH

NEW YORK YANKEES

☐ 15. EDDIE WHITSON
☐ 40. KEN GRIFFEY
☐ 70. DAVE WINFIELD
☐ 94. RICH BORDI
☐ 135. JOE NIEKRO
☐ 157. RON HASSEY
☐ 180. DON MATTINGLY
☐ 213. BOB SHIRLEY
☐ 235. BUTCH WYNEGAR
☐ 259. DAN PASQUA
☐ 276. TEAM LEADER CARD
☐ 301. DENNIS RASMUSSEN
☐ 327. MIKE PAGLIARULO
☐ 379. BOBBY MEACHAM
☐ 427. JOE COWLEY
☐ 449. ROD SCURRY
☐ 455. WILLIE RANDOLPH
☐ 481. SCOTT BRADLEY
☐ 500. RICKEY HENDERSON
☐ 533. BILLY SAMPLE
☐ 560. DAVE RIGHETTI
☐ 584. BRIAN FISHER
☐ 610. RON GUIDRY
☐ 651. BILLY MARTIN(M)
☐ 663. NEIL ALLEN
☐ 692. DALE BERRA
☐ 723. MARTY BYSTROM
☐ 738. ANDRE ROBERTSON
☐ 765. DON BAYLOR
☐ 790. PHIL NIEKRO

OAKLAND A'S

☐ 8. DWAYNE MURPHY
☐ 29. TONY PHILLIPS
☐ 58. BILL KRUEGER
☐ 84. CURT YOUNG
☐ 115. JAY HOWELL
☐ 134. CARNEY LANSFORD
☐ 148. MIKE HEATH
☐ 165. MIKE DAVIS
☐ 216. TEAM LEADER CARD
☐ 240. TOMMY JOHN
☐ 271. DAVE COLLINS
☐ 281. STEVE MURA
☐ 304. MIKE GALLEGO
☐ 353. KEITH ATHERTON
☐ 378. BRUCE BOCHTE
☐ 410. DAVE KINGMAN
☐ 433. CHRIS CODIROLI
☐ 457. MICKEY TETTLETON
☐ 484. DONNIE HILL
☐ 507. STEVE ONTIVEROS
☐ 536. JOE RIJO
☐ 566. ALFREDO GRIFFIN
☐ 591. JACKIE MOORE
☐ 624. STEVE MCCATTY
☐ 645. DUSTY BAKER
☐ 672. ROB PICCIOLO
☐ 693. TOM TELLMAN
☐ 748. STEVE HENDERSON
☐ 766. RICK LANGFORD

PHILADELPHIA PHILLIES

☐ 16. RICK SCHU
☐ 39. DAVE RUCKER
☐ 69. LUIS AGUAYO
☐ 95. OZZIE VIRGIL
☐ 120. STEVE CARLTON
☐ 158. DERREL THOMAS
☐ 183. LARRY ANDERSEN
☐ 200. MIKE SCHMIDT
☐ 246. TEAM LEADER CARD
☐ 264. DARREN DAULTON
☐ 302. GREG GROSS
☐ 326. KENT TEKULVE
☐ 361. SHANE RAWLEY
☐ 392. JOHN RUSSELL
☐ 418. ALAN KNICELY

☐ 420. VON HAYES
☐ 453. STEVE JELTZ
☐ 466. TOM FOLEY
☐ 475. JUAN SAMUEL
☐ 505. JERRY KOOSMAN
☐ 532. DON CARMAN
☐ 556. JOHN DENNY
☐ 585. GARRY MADDOX
☐ 621. JOHN FELSKE(M)
☐ 664. TIM CORCORAN
☐ 686. JEFF STONE
☐ 689. DAVE STEWART
☐ 736. GLENN WILSON
☐ 764. KEVIN GROSS
☐ 792. CHARLES HUDSON

PITTSBURGH PIRATES

☐ 48. BILL ALMON
☐ 75. JOSE DELEON
☐ 102. JOE ORSULAK
☐ 114. MIKE BROWN
☐ 161. LEE TUNNELL
☐ 232. RICK RHODEN
☐ 260. TONY PENA
☐ 278. SIXTO LEZCANO
☐ 289. JOHNNIE LEMASTER
☐ 316. SAMMY KHALIFA
☐ 351. CHUCK TANNER(M)
☐ 387. STEVE KEMP
☐ 417. R.J. REYNOLDS
☐ 425. LARRY MCWILLIAMS
☐ 489. JIM WINN
☐ 525. MARVELL WYNNE
☐ 553. JIM MORRISON
☐ 578. LEE MAZZILLI
☐ 589. SID BREAM
☐ 615. JOHNNY RAY
☐ 635. JASON THOMPSON
☐ 668. CECILIO GUANTE
☐ 682. JUNIOR ORTIZ
☐ 731. DON ROBINSON
☐ 746. DENNY GONZALEZ
☐ 754. PAT CLEMENTS
☐ 756. TEAM LEADER CARD
☐ 779. RICK REUSCHEL

ST. LOUIS CARDINALS

☐ 33. JEFF LAHTI
☐ 66. TEAM LEADER CARD
☐ 88. TOM NIETO
☐ 112. BILL CAMPBELL
☐ 150. JOAQUIN ANDUJAR
☐ 178. IVAN DEJESUS
☐ 218. RANDY HUNT
☐ 224. CESAR CEDENO
☐ 228. TOM LAWLESS
☐ 256. KURT KEPSHIRE
☐ 294. DANNY COX
☐ 322. BOB FORSCH
☐ 350. JACK CLARK
☐ 370. VINCE COLEMAN
☐ 422. MIKE JORGENSEN
☐ 441. WHITEY HERZOG(M)
☐ 474. JOHN TUDOR
☐ 498. TITO LANDRUM
☐ 528. TERRY PENDLETON
☐ 550. TOM HERR
☐ 580. WILLIE MCGEE
☐ 607. KEN DAYLEY
☐ 631. STEVE BRAUN
☐ 656. BRIAN HARPER
☐ 683. ANDY VAN SLYKE
☐ 730. OZZIE SMITH
☐ 757. DARRELL PORTER
☐ 783. RICKY HORTON

SAN DIEGO PADRES

☐ 10. TONY GWYNN
☐ 37. MARK THURMOND
☐ 44. LANCE MCCULLERS
☐ 67. CARMELO MARTINEZ
☐ 90. GARRY TEMPLETON
☐ 118. JERRY ROYSTER
☐ 182. BOBBY BROWN
☐ 211. ED WOJNA
☐ 230. TERRY KENNEDY
☐ 244. CRAIG LEFFERTS
☐ 262. MARIO RAMIREZ

☐ 286. LUIS DELEON
☐ 306. TEAM LEADER CARD
☐ 323. JERRY DAVIS
☐ 380. LAMARR HOYT
☐ 413. TIM FLANNERY
☐ 429. GREG BOOKER
☐ 450. GRAIG NETTLES
☐ 478. ANDY HAWKINS
☐ 530. RICH GOSSAGE
☐ 558. TIM STODDARD
☐ 583. AL BUMBRY
☐ 608. BRUCE BOCHY
☐ 634. ROY LEE JACKSON
☐ 660. STEVE GARVEY
☐ 681. DICK WILLIAMS(M)
☐ 735. DAVE DRAVECKY
☐ 762. ERIC SHOW
☐ 789. KURT BEVACQUA

SAN FRANCISCO GIANTS

☐ 12. JOSE URIBE
☐ 41. BRAD WELLMAN
☐ 63. RON ROENICKE
☐ 65. DAN DRIESSEN
☐ 111. ROGER CRAIG(M)
☐ 138. MARK DAVIS
☐ 153. RICKY ADAMS
☐ 177. JOEL YOUNGBLOOD
☐ 223. ATLEE HAMMAKER
☐ 249. ROB DEER
☐ 310. GREG MINTON
☐ 341. FRANK WILLIAMS
☐ 383. CHRIS BROWN
☐ 395. SCOTT GARRELTS
☐ 444. ALEX TREVINO
☐ 463. JIM GOTT
☐ 490. JEFF LEONARD
☐ 516. TEAM LEADER CARD
☐ 551. DAVE LAPOINT
☐ 571. MIKE JEFFCOAT
☐ 625. BOB BRENLY
☐ 655. MANNY TRILLO
☐ 678. DAN GLADDEN
☐ 727. DAVID GREEN
☐ 752. MIKE KRUKOW
☐ 770. VIDA BLUE

SEATTLE MARINERS

☐ 13. BOB KEARNEY
☐ 34. KEN PHELPS
☐ 61. KARL BEST
☐ 92. AL COWENS
☐ 119. BARRY BONNELL
☐ 141. CHUCK COTTIER(M)
☐ 146. JACK PERCONTE
☐ 152. MIKE MORGAN
☐ 174. BRIAN SNYDER
☐ 221. DAVE HENDERSON
☐ 248. SPIKE OWEN
☐ 305. PHIL BRADLEY
☐ 337. DARNELL COLES
☐ 357. ED VANDEBERG
☐ 382. IVAN CALDERON
☐ 399. BILL SWIFT
☐ 419. FRANK WILLS
☐ 440. ALVIN DAVIS
☐ 462. DOMINGO RAMOS
☐ 495. MARK LANGSTON

☐ 511. ED NUNEZ
☐ 546. TEAM LEADER CARD
☐ 568. DONNIE SCOTT
☐ 598. JIM PRESLEY
☐ 626. ROY THOMAS
☐ 646. MIKE MOORE
☐ 676. MATT YOUNG
☐ 729. JIM BEATTIE
☐ 750. GORMAN THOMAS
☐ 769. HAROLD REYNOLDS

TEXAS RANGERS

☐ 22. DUANE WALKER
☐ 52. CHRIS WELSH
☐ 79. DAVE SCHMIDT
☐ 105. GARY WARD
☐ 142. BOB JONES
☐ 169. GEORGE WRIGHT
☐ 189. MIKE MASON
☐ 238. LARRY PARRISH
☐ 261. BOBBY VALENTINE(M)
☐ 275. CHARLIE HOUGH
☐ 296. GENO PETRALLI
☐ 328. PETE O'BRIAN
☐ 371. BILL STEIN
☐ 388. DICKIE NOLES
☐ 397. STEVE BUECHELE
☐ 434. CURT WILKERSON
☐ 454. BURT HOOTON
☐ 480. ODDIBE MCDOWELL
☐ 502. GLEN COOK
☐ 535. TOBY HARRAH
☐ 559. TOMMY DUNBAR
☐ 586. GREG HARRIS
☐ 616. GLENN BRUMMER
☐ 641. WAYNE TOLLESON
☐ 666. TEAM LEADER CARD
☐ 739. DAVE ROZEMA
☐ 761. DON SLAUGHT
☐ 784. ALAN BANNISTER

TORONTO BLUE JAYS

☐ 23. MANNY LEE
☐ 45. DAMASO GARCIA
☐ 74. RANCE MULLINIKS
☐ 96. TEAM LEADER CARD
☐ 168. JEFF BURROUGHS
☐ 196. DOYLE ALEXANDER
☐ 219. DENNIS LAMP
☐ 241. TONY FERNANDEZ
☐ 312. TOM FILER
☐ 333. TOM HENKE
☐ 338. JORGE BELL
☐ 348. CLIFF JOHNSON
☐ 360. LLOYD MOSEBY
☐ 386. CECIL FIELDER
☐ 412. JIM CLANCY
☐ 435. BILL CAUDILL
☐ 459. LUIS LEAL
☐ 471. BOBBY COX(M)
☐ 488. LOU THORNTON
☐ 518. BUCK MARTINEZ
☐ 545. JIMMY KEY
☐ 569. JIM ACKER
☐ 593. JESSE BARFIELD
☐ 622. GARY LAVELLE
☐ 650. DAVE STIEB
☐ 673. ERNIE WHITT
☐ 694. GARTH IORG
☐ 745. WILLIE UPSHAW
☐ 775. AL OLIVER

1986 TOPPS
TRADED (132)
2 1/2 X 3 1/2

PETE INCAVIGLIA

ATLANTA BRAVES

☐ 4T. PAUL ASSENMACHER
☐ 41T. KEN GRIFFEY
☐ 75T. OMAR MORENO
☐ 84T. DAVE PALMER
☐ 98T. BILLY SAMPLE
☐ 102T. TED SIMMONS
☐ 107T. CHUCK TANNER(M)
☐ 111T. ANDRES THOMAS
☐ 119T. OZZIE VIRGIL

BALTIMORE ORIOLES

☐ 8T. JUAN BENIQUEZ
☐ 13T. JUAN BONILLA
☐ 14T. RICH BORDI

BOSTON RED SOX

☐ 6T. DON BAYLOR
☐ 89T. REY QUINONES
☐ 95T. ED ROMERO
☐ 97T. JOE SAMBITO
☐ 101T. TOM SEAVER
☐ 103T. SAMMY STEWART

CALIFORNIA ANGELS

☐ 16T. RICK BURLESON
☐ 37T. TERRY FORSTER
☐ 51T. WALLY JOYNER

CHICAGO CUBS

☐ 38T. TERRY FRANCONA
☐ 73T. GENE MICHAEL(M)
☐ 76T. JERRY MUMPHREY
☐ 117T. MANNY TRILLO

CHICAGO WHITE SOX

☐ 2T. NEIL ALLEN
☐ 12T. BOBBY BONILLA
☐ 19T. JOHN CANGELOSI
☐ 29T. JOE COWLEY
☐ 30T. JOEL DAVIS
☐ 39T. JIM FREGOSI(M)
☐ 67T. STEVE LYONS
☐ 99T. DAVE SCHMIDT
☐ 115T. WAYNE TOLLESON

CINCINNATI REDS

☐ 32T. JOHN DENNY
☐ 42T. BILL GULLICKSON
☐ 104T. KURT STILLWELL

CLEVELAND INDIANS

☐ 1T. ANDY ALLANSON
☐ 5T. SCOTT BAILES
☐ 18T. TOM CANDIOTTI
☐ 21T. CARMEN CASTILLO

☐ 77T. PHIL NIEKRO
☐ 80T. OTIS NIXON
☐ 100T. KEN SCHROM

DETROIT TIGERS

☐ 17T. BILL CAMBELL
☐ 26T. DARNELL COLES
☐ 27T. DAVE COLLINS
☐ 53T. ERIC KING
☐ 59T. MIKE LAGA
☐ 61T. DAVE LAPOINT

HOUSTON ASTROS

☐ 45T. BILLY HATCHER
☐ 52T. CHARLIE KERFELD
☐ 60T. HAL LANIER(M)

KANSAS CITY ROYALS

☐ 35T. STEVE FARR
☐ 50T. BO JACKSON
☐ 62T. RUDY LAW
☐ 65T. DENNIS LEONARD
☐ 96T. ARGENIS SALAZAR

LOS ANGELES DODGERS

☐ 105T. FRANKLIN STUBBS
☐ 116T. ALEX TREVINO
☐ 118T. ED VANDEBERG

MILWAUKEE BREWERS

☐ 22T. RICK CERONE
☐ 25T. MARK CLEAR
☐ 31T. ROB DEER
☐ 64T. TIM LEARY
☐ 79T. JUAN NIEVES
☐ 87T. DAN PLESAC
☐ 92T. BILL JO ROBIDOUX
☐ 106T. DALE SVEUM
☐ 123T. BILL WEGMAN

MINNESOTA TWINS

☐ 85T. FRANK PASTORE

MONTREAL EXPOS

☐ 40T. ANDRES GALARRAGA
☐ 55T. WAYNE KRENCHICKI
☐ 71T. BOB MCCLURE
☐ 72T. ANDY MCGAFFIGAN
☐ 114T. JAY TIBBS
☐ 128T. GEORGE WRIGHT

NEW YORK METS

☐ 74T. KEVIN MITCHELL
☐ 78T. RANDY NIEMANN
☐ 81T. BOB OJEDA
☐ 109T. TIM TEUFEL

NEW YORK YANKEES

☐ 33T. MIKE EASLER
☐ 86T. LOU PINIELLA
☐ 94T. GARY ROENICKE
☐ 110T. BOB TEWKSBURY
☐ 131T. PAUL ZUVELLA
☐ 122T. CLAUDELL WASHINGTON

JOSE CANSECO

1986 Topps Traded

OAKLAND A'S

- ☐ 3T. JOAQUIN ANDUJAR
- ☐ 20T. JOSE CANSECO
- ☐ 44T. MOOSE HAAS

PHILADELPHIA PHILLIES

- ☐ 7T. STEVE BEDROSIAN
- ☐ 47T. TOM HUME
- ☐ 90T. GARY REDUS
- ☐ 112T. MILT THOMPSON

PITTSBURGH PIRATES

- ☐ 10T. MIKE BIELECKI
- ☐ 11T. BARRY BONDS
- ☐ 54T. BOB KNIPPER
- ☐ 66T. JIM LEYLAND(M)
- ☐ 120T. BOB WALK

ST. LOUIS CARDINALS

- ☐ 28T. TIM CONROY
- ☐ 46T. MIKE HEATH
- ☐ 82T. JOSE OQUENDO
- ☐ 127T. TODD WORRELL

SAN DIEGO PADRES

- ☐ 15T. STEVE BOROS(M)
- ☐ 49T. DANE IORG
- ☐ 56T. JOHN KRUK
- ☐ 91T. BIP ROBERTS
- ☐ 121T. GENE WALTERS

WILL CLARK

SAN FRANCISCO GIANTS

- ☐ 9T. JUAN BERENGUER
- ☐ 24T. WILL CLARK
- ☐ 57T. MIKE LACOSS
- ☐ 69T. CANDY MALDONADO
- ☐ 70T. ROGER MASON
- ☐ 93T. JEFF ROBINSON
- ☐ 113T. ROBBY THOMPSON

SEATTLE MARINERS

- ☐ 58T. PETE LADD
- ☐ 108T. DANNY TARTABULL
- ☐ 124T. DICK WILLIAMS(M)
- ☐ 130T. STEVE YEAGER

TEXAS RANGERS

- ☐ 36T. SCOTT FLETCHER
- ☐ 43T. JOSE GUZMAN
- ☐ 48T. PETE INCAVIGLIA
- ☐ 68T. MICKEY MAHLER
- ☐ 83T. TOM PACIOREK
- ☐ 88T. DARRELL PORTER
- ☐ 125T. MITCH WILLIAMS
- ☐ 126T. BOBBY WITT
- ☐ 129T. RICKY WRIGHT

TORONTO BLUE JAYS

- ☐ 23T. JOHN CERUTTI
- ☐ 34T. MARK EICHHORN
- ☐ 63T. RICK LEACH

1987 TOPPS (792)
2 1/2 X 3 1/2

LEE SMITH

ATLANTA BRAVES

- ☐ 31. TEAM LEADER CARD
- ☐ 49. TERRY HARPER
- ☐ 76. RAFAEL RAMIREZ
- ☐ 104. BILLY SAMPLE
- ☐ 132. PAUL ASSENMACHER
- ☐ 159. ED OLWINE
- ☐ 186. BRUCE BENEDICT
- ☐ 214. OMAR MORENO
- ☐ 242. RICH MAHLER
- ☐ 269. CLIFF SPECK
- ☐ 296. ANDRES THOMAS
- ☐ 324. DAVE PALMER
- ☐ 351. GENE GARBER
- ☐ 373. JEFF DEDMON
- ☐ 407. JIM ACKER
- ☐ 435. BRUCE SUTTER
- ☐ 461. CRAIG MCMURTRY
- ☐ 490. DALE MURPHY
- ☐ 516. TED SIMMONS
- ☐ 544. ZANE SMITH
- ☐ 571. OZZIE VIRGIL
- ☐ 593. CHUCK TANNER(M)
- ☐ 627. KEN OBERKFELL
- ☐ 639. GERALD PERRY
- ☐ 660. BOB HORNER
- ☐ 686. DOYLE ALEXANDER
- ☐ 711. KEN GRIFFEY
- ☐ 745. GLENN HUBBARD
- ☐ 777. CHRIS CHAMBLISS

BALTIMORE ORIOLES

- ☐ 28. RICK DEMPSEY
- ☐ 86. NATE SNELL
- ☐ 120. EDDIE MURRAY
- ☐ 154. TOM O'MALLEY
- ☐ 182. LEE LACY
- ☐ 208. JOHN SHELBY
- ☐ 246. JIM DWYER
- ☐ 276. JACKIE GUTIERREZ
- ☐ 309. MIKE YOUNG
- ☐ 349. STORM DAVIS
- ☐ 370. FRED LYNN
- ☐ 398. BRAD HAVENS
- ☐ 426. FLOYD RAYFORD
- ☐ 455. MIKE BODDICKER
- ☐ 484. JIM TRABER
- ☐ 506. TEAM LEADER CARD
- ☐ 528. KEN DIXON
- ☐ 552. LARRY SHEETS
- ☐ 563. JOHN STEFERO
- ☐ 568. EARL WEAVER(M)
- ☐ 638. RICH BORDI
- ☐ 668. JUAN BONILLA
- ☐ 688. JUAN BENIQUEZ
- ☐ 708. SCOTT MCGREGOR
- ☐ 728. TIPPY MARTINEZ
- ☐ 748. MIKE FLANAGAN
- ☐ 766. DON AASE
- ☐ 784. CAL RIPKEN

BOSTON RED SOX

- ☐ 12. JEFF SELLERS
- ☐ 39. MARTY BARRETT
- ☐ 66. MARC SULLIVAN
- ☐ 94. CALVIN SCHIRALDI
- ☐ 121. KEVIN ROMINE
- ☐ 150. WADE BOGGS
- ☐ 175. BOB STANLEY
- ☐ 204. SAMMY STEWART
- ☐ 230. DON BAYLOR
- ☐ 259. MIKE GREENWELL
- ☐ 285. DENNIS BOYD
- ☐ 306. TEAM LEADER CARD
- ☐ 340. ROGER CLEMENS
- ☐ 368. JOHN MCNAMARA(M)
- ☐ 374. GLENN HOFFMAN
- ☐ 396. TIM LOLLAR
- ☐ 425. TOM SEAVER
- ☐ 449. PAT DODSON
- ☐ 451. JOE SAMBITO
- ☐ 452. DAVE HENDERSON
- ☐ 480. JIM RICE
- ☐ 507. DAVE STAPLETON
- ☐ 535. TONY ARMAS
- ☐ 589. STEVE CRAWFORD
- ☐ 591. SPIKE OWEN
- ☐ 617. AL NIPPER
- ☐ 632. ROB WOODWARD
- ☐ 645. DWIGHT EVANS
- ☐ 675. ED ROMERO
- ☐ 705. BRUCE HURST
- ☐ 740. RICH GEDMAN
- ☐ 764. BILL BUCKNER

BRUCE HURST

CALIFORNIA ANGELS

- ☐ 22. DOUG DECINCES
- ☐ 53. RUPPERT JONES
- ☐ 80. WALLY JOYNER
- ☐ 92. URBANO LUGO
- ☐ 115. DONNIE MOORE
- ☐ 136. RON ROMANICK
- ☐ 139. DEVON WHITE
- ☐ 166. BOB BOONE
- ☐ 194. KIRK MCCASKILL
- ☐ 221. VERN RUHLE
- ☐ 251. ROB WILFONG
- ☐ 278. GARY PETTIS
- ☐ 300. REGGIE JACKSON
- ☐ 337. DARRELL MILLER
- ☐ 359. DOUG CORBETT
- ☐ 387. T.R. BRYDEN
- ☐ 422. JACK HOWELL
- ☐ 446. CHUCK FINLEY
- ☐ 474. JERRY NARRON
- ☐ 502. DICK SCHOFIELD
- ☐ 518. GENE MAUCH(M)
- ☐ 556. TEAM LEADER CARD
- ☐ 579. RICK BURLESON
- ☐ 630. JOHN CANDELARIA
- ☐ 652. TERRY FORSTER
- ☐ 673. DON SUTTON
- ☐ 677. BOB GRICH
- ☐ 696. GARY LUCAS
- ☐ 725. GEORGE HENDRICK
- ☐ 760. MIKE WITT
- ☐ 782. BRIAN DOWNING

CHICAGO CUBS

- ☐ 23. LEE SMITH
- ☐ 43. GENE MICHAEL(M)
- ☐ 58. THAD BOSLEY
- ☐ 142. RICK SUTCLIFFE
- ☐ 177. KEITH MORELAND
- ☐ 227. JAMIE MOYER
- ☐ 270. JODY DAVIS
- ☐ 290. LEON DURHAM
- ☐ 346. SHAWON DUNSTON
- ☐ 369. BRIAN DAYETT
- ☐ 372. JERRY MUMPHREY
- ☐ 383. RON DAVIS
- ☐ 390. GARY MATTHEWS
- ☐ 424. CHRIS SPEIER
- ☐ 459. DENNIS ECKERSLEY
- ☐ 487. DAVE GUMPERT
- ☐ 534. SCOTT SANDERSON
- ☐ 581. TEAM LEADER CARD
- ☐ 634. RAFAEL PALMEIRO
- ☐ 662. FRANK DIPINO
- ☐ 680. RYNE SANDBERG
- ☐ 695. CHICO WALKER
- ☐ 697. ED LYNCH
- ☐ 715. BOB DERNIER
- ☐ 732. MANNY TRILLO
- ☐ 750. STEVE TROUT
- ☐ 767. RON CEY
- ☐ 785. TERRY FRANCONA

CHICAGO WHITE SOX

- ☐ 27. JOE COWLEY
- ☐ 54. BILL DAWLEY
- ☐ 61. BOBBY THIGPEN
- ☐ 89. OZZIE GUILLEN
- ☐ 113. NEIL ALLEN
- ☐ 149. RAY SEARAGE
- ☐ 201. JOHN CANGELOSI
- ☐ 233. RUSS MORMAN
- ☐ 273. GENE NELSON
- ☐ 299. JOEL DAVIS
- ☐ 318. JIM FREGOSI(M)
- ☐ 342. BOB JAMES
- ☐ 356. TEAM LEADER CARD
- ☐ 397. GREG WALKER
- ☐ 421. JOSE DELEON
- ☐ 454. LUIS SALAZAR
- ☐ 482. DARYL BOSTON
- ☐ 491. RON KARKOVICE
- ☐ 511. STEVE LYONS
- ☐ 539. REID NICHOLS
- ☐ 566. TIM HULETT
- ☐ 667. RON HASSEY
- ☐ 685. JERRY HAIRSTON
- ☐ 703. DAVE SCHMIDT
- ☐ 718. STEVE CARLTON
- ☐ 720. RICHARD DOTSON
- ☐ 737. FLOYD BANNISTER
- ☐ 756. CARLTON FISK
- ☐ 772. HAROLD BAINES
- ☐ 790. JULIO CRUZ

CINCINNATI REDS

- ☐ 13. NICK ESASKY
- ☐ 41. BO DIAZ
- ☐ 65. TOM BROWNING
- ☐ 82. ROB MURPHY
- ☐ 101. CARL WILLIS
- ☐ 119. RON ROBINSON
- ☐ 146. TRACY JONES
- ☐ 172. RON OESTER
- ☐ 200. PETE ROSE
- ☐ 226. MAX VENABLE
- ☐ 253. EDDIE MILNER
- ☐ 281. TEAM LEADER CARD
- ☐ 305. JOHN FRANCO
- ☐ 332. JOE PRICE
- ☐ 358. SAL BUTERA
- ☐ 393. PETE ROSE(M)
- ☐ 412. ERIC DAVIS
- ☐ 437. TED POWER
- ☐ 453. SCOTT TERRY
- ☐ 466. KAL DANIELS
- ☐ 489. BILL GULLICKSON
- ☐ 517. MARIO SOTO
- ☐ 545. BUDDY BELL
- ☐ 569. WADE ROWDON
- ☐ 592. CHRIS WELSH

- ☐ 623. KURT STILLWELL
- ☐ 644. JOHN DENNY
- ☐ 648. BARRY LARKIN
- ☐ 691. DAVE PARKER
- ☐ 731. DAVE CONCEPCION

CLEVELAND INDIANS

- ☐ 11. TEAM LEADER CARD
- ☐ 51. MEL HALL
- ☐ 77. BRYAN OELKERS
- ☐ 107. JOHN BUTCHER
- ☐ 134. RICH YETT
- ☐ 160. JULIO FRANCO
- ☐ 192. CORY SNYDER
- ☐ 220. JOE CARTER
- ☐ 244. DICKIE NOLES
- ☐ 268. PAT CORRALES(M)
- ☐ 297. DON SCHULZE
- ☐ 319. GREG SWINDELL
- ☐ 322. CHRIS BANDO
- ☐ 353. ERNIE CAMACHO
- ☐ 405. BROOK JACOBY
- ☐ 436. ANDY ALLANSON
- ☐ 463. TOM CANDIOTTI
- ☐ 486. OTIS NIXON
- ☐ 513. CARMEN CASTILLO
- ☐ 551. FRANK WILLS
- ☐ 575. PAT TABLER
- ☐ 585. SCOTT BAILES
- ☐ 635. KEN SCHROM
- ☐ 657. TOM WADDELL
- ☐ 694. PHIL NIEKRO
- ☐ 723. BRETT BUTLER
- ☐ 758. TONY BERNAZARD
- ☐ 780. ANDRE THORNTON

DETROIT TIGERS

- ☐ 36. ERIC KING
- ☐ 72. WALT TERRELL
- ☐ 98. BILL SCHERRER
- ☐ 148. DAVE COLLINS
- ☐ 171. CHUCK CARY
- ☐ 196. RANDY O'NEAL
- ☐ 218. SPARKY ANDERSON(M)
- ☐ 234. PAT SHERIDAN
- ☐ 265. DARRELL EVANS
- ☐ 298. LARRY HERNDON
- ☐ 361. MARK THURMOND
- ☐ 384. JOHNNY GRUBB
- ☐ 411. DARNELL COLES
- ☐ 432. JIM SLATON
- ☐ 483. DWIGHT LOWRY
- ☐ 492. MIKE HEATH
- ☐ 515. WILLIE HERNANDEZ
- ☐ 631. TEAM LEADER CARD
- ☐ 661. LOU WHITAKER
- ☐ 674. BILL CAMPBELL
- ☐ 687. ALAN TRAMMELL
- ☐ 700. DAVE BERGMAN
- ☐ 713. TOM BROOKENS
- ☐ 726. FRANK TANANA
- ☐ 739. CHET LEMON
- ☐ 752. DAN PETRY
- ☐ 765. KIRK GIBSON
- ☐ 778. JACK MORRIS
- ☐ 791. LANCE PARRISH

HOUSTON ASTROS

- ☐ 24. TONY WALKER
- ☐ 50. DAVE SMITH
- ☐ 85. KEVIN BASS
- ☐ 112. ALAN ASHBY
- ☐ 145. CHARLIE KERFELD
- ☐ 157. DANNY DARWIN
- ☐ 167. JIM DESHAIES
- ☐ 197. MARK BAILEY
- ☐ 222. DENNY WALLING
- ☐ 249. JIM PANKOVITS
- ☐ 282. JEFF CALHOUN
- ☐ 304. PHIL GARNER
- ☐ 330. MIKE SCOTT
- ☐ 343. HAL LANIER(M)
- ☐ 386. DICKIE THON
- ☐ 408. JOHN MIZEROCK
- ☐ 445. DAVE LOPES
- ☐ 472. BILL DORAN
- ☐ 503. LARRY ANDERSON
- ☐ 531. TEAM LEADER CARD
- ☐ 560. GLENN DAVIS
- ☐ 578. BILLY HATCHER
- ☐ 659. AURELIO LOPEZ
- ☐ 670. JOSE CRUZ
- ☐ 693. TERRY PUHL
- ☐ 722. BOB KNEPPER
- ☐ 757. NOLAN RYAN
- ☐ 779. CRAIG REYNOLDS

KANSAS CITY ROYALS

- ☐ 18. DICK HOWSER(M)
- ☐ 38. DENNIS LEONARD
- ☐ 69. LONNIE SMITH
- ☐ 99. DARRYL MOTLEY
- ☐ 140. BRET SABERHAGEN
- ☐ 170. BO JACKSON
- ☐ 190. JIM SUNDBERG
- ☐ 203. MIKE KINGERY
- ☐ 223. CHARLIE LEIBRANDT
- ☐ 240. STEVE BALBONI
- ☐ 256. TEAM LEADER CARD
- ☐ 326. MARK GUBICZA
- ☐ 354. JAMIE QUIRK
- ☐ 382. RUDY LAW
- ☐ 400. GEORGE BRETT
- ☐ 473. STEVE FARR
- ☐ 508. SCOTT BANKHEAD
- ☐ 533. ARGENIS SALAZAR
- ☐ 554. BUDDY BIANCALANA
- ☐ 573. HAL MCRAE
- ☐ 669. BUD BLACK
- ☐ 692. FRANK WHITE
- ☐ 714. DAN QUISENBERRY
- ☐ 738. JORGE ORTA
- ☐ 761. GREG PRYOR
- ☐ 783. WILLIE WILSON

LOS ANGELES DODGERS

- ☐ 26. GREG BROCK
- ☐ 47. DENNIS POWELL
- ☐ 73. DAVE ANDERSON
- ☐ 116. BIL RUSSELL
- ☐ 144. MIKE SCIOSCIA
- ☐ 173. ALEX TREVINO
- ☐ 199. MARIANO DUNCAN
- ☐ 232. REGGIE WILLIAMS
- ☐ 266. JEFF HAMILTON
- ☐ 292. FRANKLIN STUBBS
- ☐ 328. BOB WELCH
- ☐ 360. PEDRO GUERRERO
- ☐ 385. OREL HERSHISER
- ☐ 410. FERNANDO VALENZUELA
- ☐ 431. TEAM LEADER CARD
- ☐ 457. LEN MATUSZEK
- ☐ 477. KEN HOWELL
- ☐ 493. TOM LASORDA(M)
- ☐ 509. ENOS CABELL
- ☐ 538. TOM NIEDENFUER
- ☐ 664. MIKE MARSHALL
- ☐ 682. JERRY REUSS
- ☐ 699. KEN LANDREAUX
- ☐ 717. ED VANDEBERG
- ☐ 734. BILL MADLOCK
- ☐ 753. RICK HONEYCUTT
- ☐ 769. STEVE SAX
- ☐ 787. ALEJANDRO PENA

MILWAUKEE BREWERS

- ☐ 10. CECIL COOPER
- ☐ 32. TIM LEARY
- ☐ 56. TEAM LEADER CARD
- ☐ 79. JUAN NIEVES
- ☐ 108. JIM GANTNER
- ☐ 129. RICK CERONE
- ☐ 179. BILL WEGMAN
- ☐ 216. B.J. SURHOFF
- ☐ 229. MIKE BIRKBECK
- ☐ 250. TEDDY HIGUERA
- ☐ 279. DAN PLESAC
- ☐ 302. BILL SCHROEDER
- ☐ 327. DALE SVEUM
- ☐ 352. MIKE FELDER
- ☐ 377. JOHN HENRY JOHNSON
- ☐ 401. BILL JO ROBIDOUX
- ☐ 423. JAIME COCANOWER
- ☐ 448. CHRIS BOSIO
- ☐ 468. GEORGE BAMBERGER(M)
- ☐ 495. GORMAN THOMAS
- ☐ 523. EARNIE RILES
- ☐ 547. ROB DEER
- ☐ 562. BRYAN CLUTTERBUCK
- ☐ 586. BEN OGLIVIE
- ☐ 622. GLENN BRAGGS
- ☐ 640. MARK CLEAR
- ☐ 676. CHARLIE MOORE
- ☐ 706. RICK MANNING
- ☐ 741. PAUL MOLITOR
- ☐ 773. ROBIN YOUNT

MINNESOTA TWINS

- ☐ 25. BERT BLYLEVEN
- ☐ 52. KEITH ATHERTON
- ☐ 87. MARK SALAS
- ☐ 114. BILLY BEANE
- ☐ 124. RAY FONTENOT
- ☐ 138. ROY LEE JACKSON
- ☐ 169. RON WASHINGTON
- ☐ 206. TEAM LEADER CARD
- ☐ 207. GEORGE FRAZIER
- ☐ 225. MIKE SMITHSON
- ☐ 247. JEFF REED
- ☐ 277. JUAN AGOSTO
- ☐ 310. FRANK VIOLA
- ☐ 336. ALLAN ANDERSON
- ☐ 364. RANDY BUSH
- ☐ 419. MARK PORTUGAL
- ☐ 450. KIRBY PUCKETT
- ☐ 478. TIM LAUDNER
- ☐ 504. MICKEY HATCHER
- ☐ 529. ALVARO ESPINOZA
- ☐ 558. GREG GAGNE
- ☐ 576. FRANK PASTORE
- ☐ 618. TOM KELLY(M)
- ☐ 679. KENT HRBEK
- ☐ 710. GARY GAETTI
- ☐ 744. ROY SMALLEY
- ☐ 776. TOM BRUNANSKY

MONTREAL EXPOS

- ☐ 9. JAY TIBBS
- ☐ 30. TIM RAINES
- ☐ 55. TIM WALLACH
- ☐ 78. TIM FOLEY
- ☐ 105. FLOYD YOUMANS
- ☐ 127. VANCE LAW
- ☐ 141. HERM WINNINGHAM
- ☐ 165. JEFF REARDON
- ☐ 189. JOE HESKETH
- ☐ 212. MIKE FITZGERALD
- ☐ 252. DENNY MARTINEZ
- ☐ 272. ANDRES GALARRAGA
- ☐ 293. BOB RODGERS(M)
- ☐ 323. AL NEWMAN
- ☐ 345. ANDRE DAWSON
- ☐ 381. TEAM LEADER CARD
- ☐ 416. TOM NIETO
- ☐ 442. MITCH WEBSTER
- ☐ 467. RANDY ST. CLAIRE
- ☐ 479. BOB SEBRA
- ☐ 505. BRYN SMITH
- ☐ 527. JIM WOHLFORD
- ☐ 577. DANN BILARDELLO
- ☐ 588. WALLACE JOHNSON
- ☐ 624. TIM BURKE
- ☐ 650. HUBIE BROOKS

- ☐ 707. BOB MCCLURE
- ☐ 742. ANDY MCGAFFIGAN
- ☐ 774. WAYNE KRENCHICKI

NEW YORK METS

- ☐ 20. GARY CARTER
- ☐ 48. WALLY BACKMAN
- ☐ 75. RON DARLING
- ☐ 103. RICK AGUILERA
- ☐ 130. DWIGHT GOODEN
- ☐ 147. RANDY NIEMANN
- ☐ 158. TIM TEUFEL
- ☐ 185. ROGER MCDOWELL
- ☐ 198. LEE MAZZILLI
- ☐ 213. RANDY MYERS
- ☐ 241. DANNY HEEP
- ☐ 267. HOWARD JOHNSON
- ☐ 295. LEN DYKSTRA
- ☐ 331. TEAM LEADER CARD
- ☐ 350. KEITH HERNANDEZ
- ☐ 378. RAFAEL SANTANA
- ☐ 404. DOUG SISK
- ☐ 433. ED HEARN
- ☐ 460. DARRYL STRAWBERRY
- ☐ 488. RAY KNIGHT
- ☐ 512. DAVE MAGADAN
- ☐ 543. DAVE JOHNSON(M)
- ☐ 570. SID FERNANDEZ
- ☐ 582. BRUCE BERENYI
- ☐ 594. RICK ANDERSON
- ☐ 625. MOOKIE WILSON
- ☐ 653. KEVIN MITCHELL
- ☐ 704. JESSE OROSCO
- ☐ 746. BOB OJEDA

NEW YORK YANKEES

- ☐ 15. CLAUDELL WASHINGTON
- ☐ 40. DAVE RIGHETTI
- ☐ 57. SCOTT NIELSEN
- ☐ 62. BOBBY MEACHAM
- ☐ 74. DAN PASQUA
- ☐ 102. PAUL ZUVELLA
- ☐ 135. MIKE EASLER
- ☐ 168. LOU PINIELLA(M)
- ☐ 174. HENRY COTTO
- ☐ 195. MIKE PAGLIARULO
- ☐ 224. WAYNE TOLLESON
- ☐ 236. TOMMY JOHN
- ☐ 239. JUAN ESPINO
- ☐ 254. BOB TEWKSBURY
- ☐ 283. DOUG DRABEK
- ☐ 316. BRIAN FISHER
- ☐ 344. JOE NIEKRO
- ☐ 375. RON GUIDRY
- ☐ 406. TEAM LEADER CARD
- ☐ 434. MIKE FISCHLIN
- ☐ 464. BUTCH WYNEGAR
- ☐ 500. DON MATTINGLY
- ☐ 524. BOB SHIRLEY
- ☐ 555. DENNIS RASMUSSEN
- ☐ 584. RON KITTLE
- ☐ 626. JOEL SKINNER
- ☐ 642. AL PULIDO
- ☐ 665. ROD SCURRY
- ☐ 683. GARY ROENICKE
- ☐ 701. WILLIE RANDOLPH
- ☐ 735. RICKEY HENDERSON
- ☐ 770. DAVE WINFIELD
- ☐ 788. TIM STODDARD

OAKLAND A'S

- ☐ 14. DAVE STEWART
- ☐ 34. JOSE RIJO
- ☐ 68. TONY LARUSSA(M)
- ☐ 83. MIKE DAVIS
- ☐ 111. ALFREDO GRIFFIN
- ☐ 137. JERRY WILLARD
- ☐ 161. STEVE ONTIVEROS
- ☐ 188. TONY PHILLIPS
- ☐ 217. CHRIS CODIROLI
- ☐ 238. BILL KRUEGER
- ☐ 263. STAN JAVIER
- ☐ 287. DAVE VON OHLEN
- ☐ 339. DONNIE HILL
- ☐ 366. MARK MCGWIRE
- ☐ 391. JAY HOWELL
- ☐ 413. MOOSE HAAS
- ☐ 441. DAVE LEIPER

- ☐ 456. TEAM LEADER CARD
- ☐ 496. BRUCE BOCHTE
- ☐ 519. CURT YOUNG
- ☐ 548. BILL MOONEYHAM
- ☐ 565. DUSTY BAKER
- ☐ 587. ERIC PLUNK
- ☐ 620. JOSE CANSECO
- ☐ 649. MICKEY TETTLETON
- ☐ 678. CARNEY LANSFORD
- ☐ 709. DAVE KINGMAN
- ☐ 743. DWAYNE MURPHY
- ☐ 775. JOAQUIN ANDUJAR

PHILADELPHIA PHILLIES

- ☐ 42. GARY REDUS
- ☐ 63. FRED TOLIVER
- ☐ 97. GLENN WILSON
- ☐ 163. KEVIN GROSS
- ☐ 191. CHARLES HUDSON
- ☐ 209. RICK SCHU
- ☐ 255. JUAN SAMUEL
- ☐ 294. STEVE JELTZ
- ☐ 329. RON ROENICKE
- ☐ 355. DON CARMAN
- ☐ 379. JOHN RUSSELL
- ☐ 409. MILT THOMPSON
- ☐ 430. MIKE SCHMIDT
- ☐ 443. JOHN FELSKE(M)
- ☐ 471. RONN REYNOLDS
- ☐ 481. TEAM LEADER CARD
- ☐ 499. BRUCE RUFFIN
- ☐ 532. JEFF STONE
- ☐ 553. MIKE MADDUX
- ☐ 636. DARREN DAULTON
- ☐ 666. VON HAYES
- ☐ 684. KENT TEKULVE
- ☐ 702. GREG GROSS
- ☐ 719. TOM HUME
- ☐ 736. STEVE BEDROSIAN
- ☐ 755. LUIS AGUAYO
- ☐ 771. SHANE RAWLEY
- ☐ 789. DAN SCHATZEDER

PITTSBURGH PIRATES

- ☐ 16. PAT CLEMENTS
- ☐ 35. SID BREAM
- ☐ 60. TONY PENA
- ☐ 93. JIM LEYLAND(M)
- ☐ 109. R.J. REYNOLDS
- ☐ 131. TEAM LEADER CARD
- ☐ 164. SAMMY KHALIFA
- ☐ 184. BOBBY BONILLA
- ☐ 219. CECILIO GUANTE
- ☐ 237. JIM MORRISON
- ☐ 262. JIM WINN
- ☐ 289. BOB KIPPER
- ☐ 320. BARRY BONDS
- ☐ 341. MIKE BROWN
- ☐ 365. RICK RHODEN
- ☐ 394. MIKE BIELECKI
- ☐ 414. JOE ORSULAK
- ☐ 447. BILL ALMON
- ☐ 469. MIKE DIAZ
- ☐ 494. BARY JONES
- ☐ 521. RICK REUSCHEL
- ☐ 541. RAFAEL BELLIARD
- ☐ 564. LARRY MCWILLIAMS
- ☐ 583. JUNIOR ORTIZ
- ☐ 628. BOB WALK
- ☐ 651. BENNY DISTEFANO
- ☐ 712. DON ROBINSON
- ☐ 747. JOHNNY RAY

ST. LOUIS CARDINALS

- ☐ 8. TERRY PENDLETON
- ☐ 33. ANDY VAN SLYKE
- ☐ 59. KEN DAYLEY
- ☐ 84. STEVE LAKE
- ☐ 110. JOHN TUDOR
- ☐ 133. JOSE OQUENDO
- ☐ 162. MIKE LAVALLIERE
- ☐ 181. TEAM LEADER CARD
- ☐ 211. JOHN MORRIS
- ☐ 243. WHITEY HERZOG(M)
- ☐ 257. BOB FORSCH
- ☐ 288. TITO LANDRUM
- ☐ 317. CLINT HURDLE

□ 321. MIKE LAGA
□ 338. TIM CONROY
□ 367. JEFF LAHTI
□ 399. CURT FORD
□ 417. PAT PERRY
□ 440. WILLIE MCGEE
□ 465. TODD WORRELL
□ 520. JACK CLARK
□ 542. RICKY HORTON
□ 567. GREG MATHEWS
□ 590. VINCE COLEMAN
□ 621. DANNY COX
□ 647. TOM LAWLESS
□ 671. RAY SOFF
□ 721. TOM HERR
□ 749. OZZIE SMITH

SAN DIEGO PADRES

□ 37. MARVELL WYNNE
□ 81. TEAM LEADER CARD
□ 88. ED WOJNA
□ 100. STEVE GARVEY
□ 123. JOHN KRUK
□ 143. STEVE BOROS(M)
□ 155. EDDIE WHITSON
□ 183. ANDY HAWKINS
□ 205. GRAIG NETTLES
□ 248. GENE WALTER
□ 275. LAMARR HOYT
□ 325. GARRY TEMPLETON
□ 348. CARMELO MARTINEZ
□ 380. RICH GOSSAGE
□ 403. JERRY ROYSTER
□ 428. BRUCE BOCHY
□ 429. TIM PYZNARSKI
□ 470. DAVE DRAVECKY
□ 501. CRAIG LEFFERTS
□ 530. TONY GWYNN
□ 540. TERRY KENNEDY
□ 559. LANCE MCCULLERS
□ 637. BIP ROBERTS
□ 690. DANE IORG
□ 730. ERIC SHOW
□ 754. DAVE LAPOINT
□ 763. TIM FLANNERY

SAN FRANCISCO GIANTS

□ 21. MARK DAVIS
□ 46. DANNY GLADDEN
□ 64. HARRY SPILMAN
□ 71. MIKE ALDRETE
□ 96. FRANK WILLIAMS
□ 125. BOB BRENLY
□ 151. MIKE LACOSS
□ 180. CHRIS BROWN
□ 193. ROGER CRAIG(M)
□ 231. TEAM LEADER CARD
□ 260. VIDA BLUE
□ 280. JEFFREY LEONARD
□ 286. MIKE WOODARD
□ 303. JUAN BERENGUER
□ 335. CANDY MALDONADO
□ 362. LUIS QUINONES
□ 389. JEFF ROBINSON
□ 420. WILL CLARK
□ 438. KELLY DOWNS
□ 475. SCOTT GARRELTS
□ 526 ROGER MASON
□ 536. TERRY MULHOLLAND
□ 549. BOB MELVIN
□ 580. MIKE KRUKOW
□ 633. JOSE URIBE
□ 658. ROBBY THOMPSON
□ 672. CHILI DAVIS
□ 724. GREG MINTON
□ 759. JOEL YOUNGBLOOD
□ 781. ATLEE HAMMAKER

SEATTLE MARINERS

□ 19. MATT YOUNG
□ 45. JIM PRESLEY
□ 67. BILL SWIFT
□ 91. HAROLD REYNOLDS
□ 117. JIM BEATTIE
□ 156. TEAM LEADER CARD
□ 187. MARK HUISMANN
□ 215. MARK LANGSTON

□ 235. ALVIN DAVIS
□ 258. STEVE YEAGER
□ 271. MIKE BROWN
□ 284. JOHN MOSES
□ 307. LEE GUETTERMAN
□ 333. KEN PHELPS
□ 347. MICKEY BRANTLEY
□ 357. STEVE FIREOVID
□ 376. SCOTT BRADLEY
□ 402. MIKE TRUJILLO
□ 418. DICK WILLIAMS(M)
□ 427. ED NUNEZ
□ 439. KARL BEST
□ 476. DANNY TARTABULL
□ 498. BOB KEARNEY
□ 525. PHIL BRADLEY
□ 546. MIKE MORGAN
□ 561. REY QUINONES
□ 572. PETE LADD
□ 619. JERRY REED
□ 641. DOMINGO RAMOS
□ 727. MIKE MOORE

TEXAS RANGERS

□ 17. PETE O'BRIEN
□ 44. GREG HARRIS
□ 70. CHARLIE HOUGH
□ 95. ODDIBE MCDOWELL
□ 118. BOBBY VALENTINE(M)
□ 126. MIKE LOYND
□ 152. TOBY HARRAH
□ 176. STEVE BUECHELE
□ 202. RICKY WRIGHT
□ 228. CURT WILKERSON
□ 261. RUBEN SIERRA
□ 291. MITCH WILLIAMS
□ 308. DON SLAUGHT
□ 334. ED CORREA
□ 363. JOSE GUZMAN
□ 388. GENO PETRALLI
□ 415. BOBBY WITT
□ 444. JEFF RUSSELL
□ 462. SCOTT FLETCHER
□ 497. DALE MOHORCIC
□ 514. ORLANDO MERCADO
□ 550. PETE INCAVIGLIA
□ 629. LARRY PARRISH
□ 646. MIKE MASON
□ 656. TEAM LEADER CARD
□ 689. DARRELL PORTER
□ 729. TOM PACIOREK
□ 762. GARY WARD

TORONTO BLUE JAYS

□ 29. JIMMY KEY
□ 90. DAVE STIEB
□ 106. TEAM LEADER CARD
□ 122. JIM CLANCY
□ 153. DUANE WARD
□ 178. CECIL FIELDER
□ 210. LLOYD MOSEBY
□ 245. WILLIE UPSHAW
□ 274. JEFF HEARRON
□ 301. LUIS AQUINO
□ 371. MARK EICHHORN
□ 395. DAMASO GARCIA
□ 458. KELLY GRUBER
□ 485. TONY FERNANDEZ
□ 510. TOM HENKE
□ 537. RANCE MULLINIKS
□ 557. JOHN CERUTTI
□ 574. MANNY LEE
□ 643. RON SHEPHERD
□ 655. JESSE BARFIELD
□ 663. CLIFF JOHNSON
□ 681. GEORGE BELL
□ 698. ERNIE WHITT
□ 716. RICK LEACH
□ 733. BILL CAUDILL
□ 751. GARTH IORG
□ 768. DENNIS LAMP
□ 786. JIMY WILLIAMS(M)

1987 TOPPS TRADED (132)
2 1/2 X 3 1/2

TERRY STEINBACH

ATLANTA BRAVES

□ 41T. ALBERT HALL
□ 54T. DION JAMES
□ 85T. GRAIG NETTLES
□ 105T. GARY ROENICKE

BALTIMORE ORIOLES

□ 3T. ERIC BELL
□ 37T. KEN GERHART
□ 57T. TERRY KENNEDY
□ 59T. RAY KNIGHT
□ 88T. TOM NIEDENFUER
□ 102T. CAL RIPKEN (M)
□ 110T. DAVE SCHMIDT
□ 126T. ALAN WIGGINS

BOSTON RED SOX

□ 14T. ELLIS BURKS

CALIFORNIA ANGELS

□ 13T. DEWAYNE BUICE
□ 35T. WILLIE FRASER
□ 62T. JACK LAZORKO
□ 75T. MARK MCLEMORE
□ 79T. GREG MINTON

CHICAGO CUBS

□ 27T. ANDRE DAWSON
□ 70T. GREG MADDUX
□ 73T. DAVE MARTINEZ
□ 92T. DICKIE NOLES
□ 119T. JIM SUNDBERG

CHICAGO WHITE SOX

□ 15T. IVAN CALDERON
□ 47T. DONNIE HILL
□ 67T. BILL LONG
□ 99T. GARY REDUS
□ 106T. JERRY RYOSTER
□ 130T. JIM WINN

CINCINNATI REDS

□ 34T. TERRY FRANCONA
□ 48T. GUY HOFFMAN
□ 93T. PAT PACILLO
□ 128T. FRANK WILLIAMS

CLEVELAND INDIANS

□ 19T. STEVE CARLTON
□ 28T. RICK DEMPSEY
□ 128T. ED VANDEBERG

DETROIT TIGERS

□ 46T. MIKE HENNEMAN
□ 71T. BILL MADLOCK
□ 91T. MATT NOKES
□ 104T. JEFF ROBINSON

1987 Topps Traded

HOUSTON ASTROS

- ☐ 77T. DAVE MEADS

KANSAS CITY ROYALS

- ☐ 4T. JUAN BENIQUEZ
- ☐ 7T. THAD BOSLEY
- ☐ 36T. BILLY GARDNER (M)
- ☐ 51T. DANNY JACKSON
- ☐ 111T. KEVIN SEITZER
- ☐ 120T. DANNY TARTABULL

LOS ANGLES DODGERS

- ☐ 12T. RALPH BRYANT
- ☐ 43T. MICKEY HATCHER
- ☐ 44T. BRAD HAVENS
- ☐ 49T. BRIAN HOLTON
- ☐ 64T. TIM LEARY
- ☐ 112T. JOHN SHELBY
- ☐ 131T. MATT YOUNG

MILWAUKEE BREWERS

- ☐ 9T. GREG BROCK
- ☐ 20T. JUAN CASTILLO
- ☐ 25T. CHUCK CRIM
- ☐ 121T. TOM TREBELHORN (M)

MINNESOTA TWINS

- ☐ 5T. JUAN BERENGUER
- ☐ 38T. DANNY GLADDEN
- ☐ 60T. GENE LARKIN
- ☐ 66T. STEVE LOMBARDOZZI
- ☐ 86T. AL NEWMAN
- ☐ 89T. JOE NIEKRO
- ☐ 90T. TOM NIETO
- ☐ 98T. JEFF REARDON
- ☐ 118T. LES STRAKER

MONTREAL EXPOS

- ☐ 17T. CASEY CANDAELE
- ☐ 45T. NEAL HEATON
- ☐ 87T. REID NICHOLS
- ☐ 100T. JEFF REED

NEW YORK METS

- ☐ 1T. BILL ALMON
- ☐ 24T. DAVE CONE
- ☐ 63T. TERRY LEACH
- ☐ 68T. BARRY LYONS
- ☐ 76T. KEVIN MCREYNOLDS
- ☐ 80T. JOHN MITCHELL

NEW YORK YANKEES

- ☐ 21T. RICK CERONE
- ☐ 40T. CECILIO GUANTE
- ☐ 50T. CHARLES HUDSON
- ☐ 101T. RICK RHODEN
- ☐ 107T. MARK SALAS
- ☐ 125T. GARY WARD

OAKLAND A'S

- ☐ 22T. RON CEY
- ☐ 31T. DENNIS ECKERSLEY
- ☐ 52T. REGGIE JACKSON
- ☐ 84T. GENE NELSON
- ☐ 96T. LUIS POLONIA
- ☐ 117T. TERRY STIENBACH

PHILADELPHIA PHILLIES

- ☐ 16T. JEFF CALHOUN
- ☐ 32T. LEE ELIA (M)
- ☐ 53T. CHRIS JAMES
- ☐ 94T. LANCE PARRISH
- ☐ 103T. WALLY RITCHIE

PITTSBURGH PIRATES

- ☐ 18T. JOHN CANGELOSI
- ☐ 29T. DOUG DRABEK
- ☐ 30T. MIKE DUNNE
- ☐ 33T. BRIAN FISHER
- ☐ 42T TERRY HARPER

- ☐ 61T. MIKE LAVALLIERE
- ☐ 114T. JOHN SMILEY
- ☐ 124T. ANDY VAN SLYKE

TONY PENA

ST. LOUIS CARDINALS

- ☐ 65T. JIM LINDEMAN
- ☐ 72T. JOE MAGRANE
- ☐ 95T. TONY PENA

SAN DIEGO PADRES

- ☐ 6T. GREG BOOKER
- ☐ 8T. LARRY BOWA (M)
- ☐ 26T. STORM DAVIS
- ☐ 55T. STAN JEFFERSON
- ☐ 69T. SHANE MACK
- ☐ 97T. RANDY READY
- ☐ 108T. LUIS SALAZAR
- ☐ 109T. BENNY SANTIAGO

SAN FRANCISCO GIANTS

- ☐ 39T. JIM GOTT
- ☐ 78T. EDDIE MILNER
- ☐ 81T. KEVIN MITCHELL
- ☐ 115T. CHRIS SPEIER
- ☐ 129T. MATT WILLIAMS

SEATTLE MARINERS

- ☐ 2T. SCOTT BANKHEAD
- ☐ 23T. JOHN CHRISTENSEN
- ☐ 58T. MIKE KINGERY
- ☐ 113T. STEVE SHIELDS
- ☐ 122T. DAVE VALLE
- ☐ 127T. BILL WILKINSON

TEXAS RANGERS

- ☐ 10T. BOB BROWER
- ☐ 11T. JERRY BROWNE
- ☐ 116T. MIKE STANLEY

TORONTO BLUE JAYS

- ☐ 56T. JOE JOHNSON
- ☐ 74T. FRED MCGRIFF
- ☐ 82T. CHARLIE MOORE
- ☐ 83T. JEFF MUSSELMAN

JEFF MUSSELMAN

1988 TOPPS (792)
2 1/2 X 3 1/2

ATLANTA BRAVES

- ☐ 13. ANDRES THOMAS
- ☐ 39. GERALD PERRY
- ☐ 67. KEN OBERKFELL
- ☐ 90. DALE MURPHY
- ☐ 134. CHUCK TANNER (M)
- ☐ 155. BRUCE SUTTER
- ☐ 179. CHARLIE PULEO
- ☐ 213. ALBERT HALL
- ☐ 241. DAMASO GARCIA
- ☐ 266. PAUL ASSENMACHER
- ☐ 297. ZANE SMITH
- ☐ 325. GLENN HUBBARD
- ☐ 353. ED OLWINE
- ☐ 379. RAFAEL RAMIREZ
- ☐ 408. DION JAMES
- ☐ 443. KEN GRIFFEY
- ☐ 469. JEFF DEDMON
- ☐ 523. GARY ROENICKE
- ☐ 549. TEAM LEADER CARD
- ☐ 574. GRAIG NETTLES
- ☐ 627. JOE BOEVER
- ☐ 652. BRUCE BENEDICT
- ☐ 678. JIM ACKER
- ☐ 706. RICK MAHLER
- ☐ 732. DAVE PALMER
- ☐ 755. OZZIE VIRGIL
- ☐ 779. TOM GLAVINE
- ☐ 791. TED SIMMONS

BALTIMORE ORIOLES

- ☐ 11. MIKE YOUNG
- ☐ 51. TEAM LEADER CARD
- ☐ 69. MIKE HART
- ☐ 98. RENE GONZALES
- ☐ 124. RAY KNIGHT
- ☐ 153. JOHN HABYAN
- ☐ 180. TERRY KENNEDY
- ☐ 214. DAVE SCHMIDT
- ☐ 242. TOM NIEDENFUER
- ☐ 271. KEN GERHART
- ☐ 296. FLOYD RAYFORD
- ☐ 327. LARRY SHEETS
- ☐ 352. BILLY RIPKEN
- ☐ 383. ERIC BELL
- ☐ 419. SCOTT MCGREGOR
- ☐ 444. CAL RIPKEN (M)
- ☐ 467. DON AASE
- ☐ 495. EDDIE MURRAY
- ☐ 521. JIM DWYER
- ☐ 544. JIM TRABER
- ☐ 571. MARK WILLIAMSON
- ☐ 598. LEE LACY
- ☐ 650. CAL RIPKEN
- ☐ 676. KEN DIXON
- ☐ 707. FRED LYNN
- ☐ 725. MIKE BODDICKER
- ☐ 782. JEFF BALLARD

BOSTON RED SOX

- ☐ 21. TEAM LEADER CARD
- ☐ 37. ED ROMERO
- ☐ 70. ROGER CLEMENS
- ☐ 96. TODD BENZINGER

□ 125. BRUCE HURST
□ 152. JODY REED
□ 189. WES GARDNER
□ 200. WADE BOGGS
□ 245. RICH GEDMAN
□ 269. ELLIS BURKS
□ 299. STEVE CRAWFORD
□ 326. AL NIPPER
□ 354. MARC SULLIVAN
□ 377. SAM HORN
□ 414. JOHN MCNAMARA (M)
□ 442. TOM BOLTON
□ 470. DWIGHT EVANS
□ 493. MIKE GREENWELL
□ 525. MARTY BARRETT
□ 573. BOB STANLEY
□ 599. CALVIN SCHIRALDI
□ 653. JEFF SELLERS
□ 675. JIM RICE
□ 704. DENNIS BOYD
□ 733. SPIKE OWEN
□ 757. JOHN MARZANO
□ 784. JOE SAMBITO

CALIFORNIA ANGELS

□ 16. KIRK MCCASKILL
□ 43. DICK SCHOEFIELD
□ 71. GARY PETTIS
□ 99. CHUCK FINLEY
□ 115. JOHNNY RAY
□ 129. GREG MINTON
□ 147. BILL BUCKNER
□ 162. MARK LCLEMORE
□ 192. DEVON WHITE
□ 216. JERRY REUSS
□ 243. MARK RYAL
□ 270. MIKE WITT
□ 304. GEORGE HENDRICK
□ 331. BRIAN DOWNING
□ 363. WILLIE FRASER
□ 381. TEAM LEADER CARD
□ 420. WALLY JOYNER
□ 446. DOUG DECINCES
□ 471. DONNIE MOORE
□ 498. BOB BOONE
□ 524. GARY LUCAS
□ 575. DON SUTTON
□ 601. JACK LAZORKO
□ 631. JACK HOWELL
□ 649. DEWAYNE BUICE
□ 679. DARRELL MILLER
□ 708. GUS POLIDOR
□ 737. BUTCH WYNEGAR
□ 761. TONY ARMAS
□ 774. GENE MAUCH (M)

CHICAGO CUBS

□ 10. RYNE SANDBERG
□ 36. JAMIE MOYER
□ 65. LEON DURHAM
□ 87. MIKE MASON
□ 112. LES LANCASTER
□ 136. BRIAN DAYETT
□ 171. TEAM LEADER CARD
□ 186. RAFAEL PALMEIRO
□ 211. FRANK DIPINO
□ 240. LEE SMITH
□ 262. DREW HALL
□ 287. MANNY TRILLO
□ 311. SCOTT SANDERSON

□ 336. ED LYNCH
□ 361. GREG MADDUX
□ 416. KEITH MORELAND
□ 439. DAVE MARTINEZ
□ 466. JERRY MUMPHREY
□ 500. ANDRE DAWSON
□ 516. JIM SUNDBERG
□ 542. PAUL NOCE
□ 564. FRANK LUCCHESI (M)
□ 593. BOB TEWKSBURY
□ 615. JODY DAVIS
□ 642. BOB DERNIER
□ 667. LUIS QUINONES
□ 695. SHAWON DUNSTON
□ 717. JAY BALLER
□ 740. RICK SUTCLIFFE
□ 768. DICKIE NOLES

CHICAGO WHITE SOX

□ 35. HAROLD BAINES
□ 86. RON KARKOVICE
□ 108. STEVE LYONS
□ 132. DONNIE HILL
□ 158. TIM HULETT
□ 184. IVAN CALDERON
□ 209. RICHARD DOTSON
□ 232. BOB JAMES
□ 281. JERRY HAIRSTON
□ 309. BILL LONG
□ 321. TEAM LEADER CARD
□ 334. DAVE LAPOINT
□ 357. FLOYD BANNISTER
□ 385. CARLTON FISK
□ 409. JOEL MCKEON
□ 437. FRED MANRIQUE
□ 458. RON HASSEY
□ 486. PAT KEEDY
□ 511. JOEL DAVIS
□ 559. KEN WILLIAMS
□ 585. OZZIE GUILLEN
□ 613. BOBBY THIGPEN
□ 634. JOSE DELEON
□ 657. JIM WINN
□ 714. JIM FREGOSI (M)
□ 739. DARYL BOSTON
□ 764. GREG WALKER
□ 788. RAY SEARAGE

CINCINNATI REDS

□ 17. RON OESTER
□ 42. BILL LANDRUM
□ 81. TEAM LEADER CARD
□ 102. BARRY LARKIN
□ 130. BUDDY BELL
□ 135. DENNIS RASMUSSEN
□ 150. ERIC DAVIS
□ 172. LLOYD MCCLENDON
□ 204. PAUL O'NEILL
□ 236. TED POWER
□ 265. BO DIAZ
□ 282. PAT PERRY
□ 288. PAT PACILLO
□ 315. DAVE PARKER
□ 339. KURT STILLWELL
□ 364. NICK ESASKY
□ 422. DAVE CONCEPCION
□ 477. JEFF MONTGOMERY
□ 475. PETE ROSE (M)
□ 496. GUY HOFFMAN
□ 517. RON ROBINSON
□ 553. TRACY JONES
□ 577. TOM BROWNING
□ 603. ROB MURPHY
□ 622. KAL DANIELS
□ 644. TERRY MCGRIFF
□ 666. MARIO SOTO
□ 686. TERRY FRANCONA
□ 730. JOHN FRANCO
□ 773. FRANK WILLIAMS

CLEVELAND INDIANS

□ 22. GREG SWINDELL
□ 49. DAVE CLARK
□ 75. JOE CARTER
□ 82. DARREL AKERFELDS
□ 107. SCOTT BAILES
□ 123. TOM CANDIOTTI
□ 144. DON GORDON
□ 230. PAT TABLER

□ 256. KEN SCHROM
□ 293. DOUG JONES
□ 318. MEL HALL
□ 341. CARMEN CASTILLO
□ 374. DOC EDWARDS (M)
□ 421. ED VANDEBERG
□ 479. BRETT BUTLER
□ 503. JUNIOR NOBOA
□ 531. RICH YETT
□ 533. JOHN FARRELL
□ 555. BROOK JACOBY
□ 576. TOMMY HINZO
□ 604. CHRIS BANDO
□ 620. CORY SNYDER
□ 637. JAY BELL
□ 683. JULIO FRANCO
□ 701. SAMMY STEWART
□ 728. ANDY ALLANSON
□ 758. EDDIE WILLIAMS
□ 789. TEAM LEADER CARD

DETROIT TIGERS

□ 14. SPARKY ANDERSON (M)
□ 78. DAN PETRY
□ 106. JIM WALEWANDER
□ 128. JOHNNY GRUBB
□ 145. BILL MADLOCK
□ 177. FRANK TANANA
□ 237. MIKE HEATH
□ 267. BILLY BEAN
□ 289. DAVE BERGMAN
□ 320. ALAN TRAMMELL
□ 340. JACK MORRIS
□ 366. CHET LEMON
□ 429. TEAM LEADER CARD
□ 449. JEFF ROBINSON
□ 474. TOM BROOKENS
□ 492. DOYLE ALEXANDER
□ 499. ERIC KING
□ 514. PAT SHERIDAN
□ 552. MARK THURMOND
□ 582. MIKE HENNEMAN
□ 605. KIRK GIBSON
□ 630. DARRELL EVANS
□ 645. MATT NOKES
□ 668. WALT TERRELL
□ 713. WILLIE HERNANDEZ
□ 743. LARRY HERNDON
□ 751. JIM MORRISON
□ 770. LOU WHITAKER

HOUSTON ASTROS

□ 24. JIM DESHAIES
□ 48. ALAN ASHBY
□ 64. KEN CAMINITI
□ 94. CHUCK JACKSON
□ 119. ROBBIE WINE
□ 151. BOB KNEPPER
□ 175. KEVIN BASS
□ 199. DAVE MEADS
□ 226. DAVE LOPES
□ 250. NOLAN RYAN
□ 278. JOSE CRUZ
□ 291. TEAM LEADER CARD
□ 306. BILLY HATCHER
□ 342. LARRY ANDERSON
□ 368. GERALD YOUNG
□ 430. GLENN DAVIS
□ 461. DANNY DARWIN
□ 487. JIM PANKOVITS
□ 520. DAVE SMITH
□ 557. CRAIG REYNOLDS
□ 587. TERRY PUHL
□ 608. CHARLIE KERFELD
□ 643. ROCKY CHILDRESS
□ 684. HAL LANIER (M)
□ 719. DENNY WALLING
□ 745. BILL DORAN
□ 760. MIKE SCOTT

KANSAS CITY ROYALS

□ 29. ARGENIS SALAZAR
□ 56. ED HEARN
□ 89. GARY THURMAN
□ 116. JERRY DON GLEATON
□ 141. TEAM LEADER CARD
□ 169. ROSS JONES
□ 195. DAN QUISENBERRY

□ 222. STEVE FARR
□ 247. THAD BOSLEY
□ 275. KEVIN SEITZER
□ 301. BUD BLACK
□ 324. DANNY JACKSON
□ 348. JIM EISENREICH
□ 433. BILL PECOTA
□ 452. WILLIE WILSON
□ 477. JAMIE QUIRK
□ 507. MARK GUBICZA
□ 534. JOHN WATHAN (M)
□ 540. BRET SABERHAGEN
□ 569. CHARLIE LEIBRANDT
□ 595. FRANK WHITE
□ 597. GENE GARBER
□ 638. STEVE BALBONI
□ 672. JIM DAVIS
□ 700. GEORGE BRETT
□ 724. DANNY TARTABULL
□ 750. BO JACKSON
□ 777. LONNIE SMITH

LOS ANGELES DODGERS

□ 23. KEN LANDREAUX
□ 40. OREL HERSHISER
□ 57. TIM CREWS
□ 62. JEFF HAMILTON
□ 74. TOM LASORDA (M)
□ 92. LEN MATUSZEK
□ 118. BOB WELCH
□ 149. KEN HOWELL
□ 174. PHIL GARNER
□ 198. FRANKLIN STUBBS
□ 202. GLENN HOFFMAN
□ 225. MIKE SCIOSCIA
□ 249. MIKE MARSHALL
□ 277. ALEJANDRO PENA
□ 305. STEVE SAX
□ 338. BRIAN HOLTON
□ 367. TIM LEARY
□ 428. JOHN SHELBY
□ 455. SHAWN HILLEGAS
□ 456. DAVE ANERSON
□ 481. MARIANO DUNCAN
□ 489. TEAM LEADER CARD
□ 512. ALEX TREVINO
□ 550. PEDRO GUERRERO
□ 581. TITO LANDRUM
□ 607. MICKEY HATCHER
□ 698. BARD HAVENS
□ 736. MATT YOUNG
□ 753. DANNY HEEP
□ 780. FERNANDO VALENZUELA

MILWAUKEE BREWERS

□ 12. BILL SCHROEDER
□ 33. ROB DEER
□ 61. MARK KNUDSON
□ 88. EARNIE RILES
□ 110. TEDDY HIGUERA
□ 137. CHRIS BOSIO
□ 165. ROBIN YOUNT
□ 187. STEVE KIEFER
□ 212. GREG BROCK
□ 224. TOM TREBELHORN (M)
□ 263. GLENN BRAGGS
□ 286. CHUCK CRIM
□ 312. JOEY MEYER
□ 337. JIM GANTNER
□ 362. JUAN CASTILLO
□ 417. MARK CIARDI
□ 441. RICK MANNING
□ 465. PAUL MOLITOR
□ 491. B.J. SURHOFF
□ 515. JUAN NIEVES
□ 538. BILL WEGMAN
□ 566. CHARLIE O'BRIEN
□ 592. DALE SVEUM
□ 616. JAY ALDRICH
□ 639. TEAM LEADER CARD
□ 670. DAN PLESAC
□ 692. MIKE BIRKBECK
□ 718. MIKE FELDER
□ 742. MARK CLEAR
□ 769. CECIL COOPER

MINNESOTA TWINS

□ 19. MARK DAVIDSON
□ 45. KENT HRBEK
□ 73. RANDY BUSH
□ 101. ALLAN ANDERSON
□ 120. KIRBY PUCKETT
□ 194. TOM KELLY (M)
□ 218. DAN SCHATZEDER
□ 239. ROY SMALLEY
□ 264. LES STRAKER
□ 295. BERT BLYLEVEN
□ 317. TOM NIETO
□ 343. GREG GAGNE
□ 375. TOM BRUNANSKY
□ 425. JEFF REARDON
□ 451. KEITH ATHERTON
□ 473. JOE NIEKRO
□ 502. DANNY GLADDEN
□ 526. JUAN BERENGUER
□ 545. DON BAYLOR
□ 554. MIKE SMITHSON
□ 578. GARY GAETTI
□ 609. TEAM LADER CARD
□ 625. FRANK VIOLA
□ 648. AL NEWMAN
□ 671. TIM LAUDNER
□ 697. STEVE LOMBARDOZZI
□ 709. GEORGE FRAZIER
□ 772. SAL BUTERA

MONTREAL EXPOS

□ 25. ANDRES GALARRAGA
□ 50. HUBIE BROOKS
□ 76. DENNY MARTINEZ
□ 93. BOB SEBRA
□ 111. TEAM LEADER CARD
□ 138. MITCH WEBSTER
□ 161. BRYN SMITH
□ 176. JEFF REED
□ 196. DAVE ENGLE
□ 228. WALLACE JOHNSON
□ 251. TOM FOLEY
□ 279. RANDY ST. CLAIRE
□ 313. BOB MCCLURE
□ 346. VANCE LAW
□ 365. FLOYD YOUMANS
□ 371. JOE HESKETH
□ 431. CASEY CANDAELE
□ 464. JAY TIBBS
□ 488. ANDY MCGAFFIGAN
□ 504. BOB RODGERS (M)
□ 529. TIM BURKE
□ 560. TIM WALLACH
□ 588. JEFF PARRETT
□ 614. HERM WINNINGHAM
□ 647. PASCUAL PEREZ
□ 674. MIKE FITZGERALD
□ 720. TIM RAINES
□ 748. REID NICHOLS
□ 765. NEAL HEATON

NEW YORK METS

□ 8. KEVIN ELSTER
□ 30. SID FERNANDEZ
□ 58. DAVE MAGADEN
□ 85. HOWARD JOHNSON
□ 105. JESSE OROSCO
□ 131. DON SCHULZE
□ 164. DAVE JOHNSON (M)
□ 181. DAVE CONE
□ 207. JOHN MITCHELL
□ 233. RAFAEL SANTANA
□ 255. MOOKIE WILSON
□ 308. LEE MAZZILLI
□ 333. WALLY BACKMAN
□ 355. ROGER MCDOWELL
□ 382. KEITH MILLER
□ 412. RANDY MYERS
□ 434. RICK AGUILERA
□ 457. TERRY LEACH
□ 480. DWIGHT GOODEN
□ 508. TIM TEUFEL
□ 530. GARY CARTER
□ 546. JOHN CANDELARIA
□ 558. BOB OJEDA
□ 579. TEAM LEADER CARD
□ 610. KEITH HERNANDEZ
□ 633. BARRY LYONS
□ 655. LEN DYKSTRA

□ 685. RON DARLING
□ 710. DARRYL STRAWBERRY
□ 735. KEVIN MCREYNOLDS
□ 746. BOB OJEDA
□ 763. DOUG SISK
□ 787. BILL ALMON

NEW YORK YANKEES

□ 18. AL LEITER
□ 44. LOU PINIELLA (M)
□ 60. RICKEY HENDERSON
□ 84. CECILIO GUANTE
□ 109. JOEL SKINNER
□ 159. BRAD ARNSBERG
□ 185. RICK RHODEN
□ 210. WILLIE RANDOLPH
□ 235. GARY WARD
□ 257. JERRY ROYSTER
□ 259. RON KITTLE
□ 283. PHIL LOMBARDI
□ 300. DON MATTINGLY
□ 335. CLAUDELL WASHINGTON
□ 359. TIM STODDARD
□ 384. NEIL ALLEN
□ 411. WAYNE TOLLESON
□ 435. MIKE PAGLIARULO
□ 459. TEAM LEADER CARD
□ 484. PAT CLEMENTS
□ 510. DAVE WINFIELD
□ 535. RON GUIDRY
□ 561. RICK CERONE
□ 584. STEVE TROUT
□ 611. TOMMY JOHN
□ 636. CHARLES HUDSON
□ 659. BOBBY MEACHAM
□ 691. DAN PASQUA
□ 711. BILL GULLICKSON
□ 716. LENN SAKATA
□ 741. MIKE EASLER
□ 766. HENRY COTTO
□ 790. DAVE RIGHETTI

OAKLAND A'S

□ 47. JOAQUIN ANDUJAR
□ 72. DENNIS ECKERSLEY
□ 103. CURT YOUNG
□ 122. TONY BERNAZARD
□ 143. MICKEY TETTLETON
□ 166. RICK RODRIGUEZ
□ 173. ERIC PLUNK
□ 238. LUIS POLONIA
□ 248. STORM DAVIS
□ 272. STEVE ONTIVEROS
□ 292. CARNEY LANSFORD
□ 316. JOSE RIJO
□ 328. GREG CADARET
□ 344. TONY LARUSSA (M)
□ 370. JOSE CANSECO
□ 424. DWAYNE MURPHY
□ 448. MIKE DAVIS
□ 476. DAVE STEWART
□ 501. TIM BIRTSAS
□ 527. STEVE HENDERSON
□ 551. TERRY STEINBACH
□ 580. MARK MCGWIRE
□ 606. MOOSE HAAS
□ 621. GENE NELSON
□ 641. RICK HONEYCUTT
□ 673. TONY PHILLIPS
□ 690. JAY HOWELL
□ 702. MIKE GALLEGO
□ 726. ALFREDO GRIFFIN
□ 759. TEAM LEADER CARD

PHILADELPHIA PHILLIES

□ 20. KEVIN GROSS
□ 38. JEFF CALHOUN
□ 66. SHANE RAWLEY
□ 95. LANCE PARRISH
□ 126. STEVE JELTZ
□ 154. JEFF STONE
□ 188. JOHN RUSSELL
□ 203. FRED TOLIVER
□ 215. VON HAYES
□ 254. LEE ELIA (M)
□ 268. BRUCE RUFFIN
□ 298. MILT THOMPSON

- ☐ 356. LUIS AGUAYO
- ☐ 378. TODD FROHWIRTH
- ☐ 415. DON CARMAN
- ☐ 440. STEVE BEDROSIAN
- ☐ 468. DARREN DAULTON
- ☐ 494. WALLY RITCHIE
- ☐ 518. GREG GROSS
- ☐ 543. KENT TEKULVE
- ☐ 572. CHRIS JAMES
- ☐ 600. MIKE SCHMIDT
- ☐ 626. GLENN WILSON
- ☐ 651. MIKE JACKSON
- ☐ 669. TEAM LEADER CARD
- ☐ 705. JUAN SAMUEL
- ☐ 731. RICK SCHU
- ☐ 756. MIKE MADDUX
- ☐ 781. KEITH HUGHES
- ☐ 783. RON ROENICKE

PITTSBURGH PIRATES

- ☐ 27. R.J. REYNOLDS
- ☐ 46. DARNELL COLES
- ☐ 127. JIM GOTT
- ☐ 142. ANDY VAN SLYKE
- ☐ 168. BARRY JONES
- ☐ 193. BRIAN FISHER
- ☐ 221. RAFAEL BELLIARD
- ☐ 231. TEAM LEADER CARD
- ☐ 244. JEFF ROBINSON
- ☐ 274. JUNIOR ORTIZ
- ☐ 294. AL PEDRIQUE
- ☐ 322. VICENTE PALACIOS
- ☐ 349. BOB WALK
- ☐ 423. JOHN SMILEY
- ☐ 436. MIKE BIELECKI
- ☐ 450. BARRY BONDS
- ☐ 478. SID BREAM
- ☐ 506. JOHN CANGELOSI
- ☐ 522. BOB PATTERSON
- ☐ 539. MIKE LAVALLIERE
- ☐ 547. FELIX FERMIN
- ☐ 567. MIKE DIAZ
- ☐ 591. DOUG DRABEK
- ☐ 619. MIKE DUNNE
- ☐ 624. JIM LEYLAND (M)
- ☐ 681. BOBBY BONILLA
- ☐ 723. BOB KIPPER
- ☐ 767. JOSE LIND

ST. LOUIS CARDINALS

- ☐ 34. RICKY HORTON
- ☐ 59. DANNY COX
- ☐ 83. JOSE OQUENDO
- ☐ 100. JACK CLARK
- ☐ 133. GREG MATHEWS
- ☐ 160. WILLIE MCGEE
- ☐ 183. TOM LAWLESS
- ☐ 208. STEVE LAKE
- ☐ 234. KEN DAYLEY
- ☐ 260. VINCE COLEMAN
- ☐ 310. TOM HERR
- ☐ 351. TEAM LEADER CARD
- ☐ 380. JOE MAGRANE
- ☐ 410. TONY PENA
- ☐ 460. OZZIE SMITH
- ☐ 483. ROD BOOKER
- ☐ 509. BILL DAWLEY
- ☐ 536. JOHN MORRIS
- ☐ 562. JIM LINDEMAN

- ☐ 586. BOB FORSCH
- ☐ 612. CURT FORD
- ☐ 635. TERRY PENDLETON
- ☐ 658. TIM CONROY
- ☐ 689. TOM PAGNOZZI
- ☐ 715. TODD WORRELL
- ☐ 744. WHITEY HERZOG (M)
- ☐ 792. JOHN TUDOR

SAN DIEGO PADRES

- ☐ 9. ANDY HAWKINS
- ☐ 31. BRUCE BOCHY
- ☐ 63. JIMMY JONES
- ☐ 91. JOEY CORA
- ☐ 117. JAMES STEELS
- ☐ 148. CARMELO MARTINEZ
- ☐ 170. RICH GOSSAGE
- ☐ 197. LANCE MCCULLERS
- ☐ 223. STAN JEFFERSON
- ☐ 276. LUIS SALAZAR
- ☐ 284. LARRY BOWA (M)
- ☐ 303. ERIC SHOW
- ☐ 330. EDDIE WHITSON
- ☐ 360. TONY GWYNN
- ☐ 426. RANDY READY
- ☐ 454. MARVELL WYNNE
- ☐ 482. MARK DAVIS
- ☐ 513. TIM FLANNERY
- ☐ 548. SHANE MACK
- ☐ 568. CHRIS BROWN
- ☐ 596. JOHN KRUK
- ☐ 640. GARY TEMPLETON
- ☐ 693. BENNY SANTIAGO
- ☐ 694. ERIC NOLTE
- ☐ 699. TEAM LEADER CARD
- ☐ 727. GREG BOOKER
- ☐ 752. MARK GRANT
- ☐ 778. KEITH COMSTOCK

SAN FRANCISCO GIANTS

- ☐ 15. CHILI DAVIS
- ☐ 41. BOB MELVIN
- ☐ 52. DON ROBINSON
- ☐ 68. DAVE DRAVECKY
- ☐ 97. SCOTT GARRELTS
- ☐ 157. ATLEE HAMMAKER
- ☐ 190. CANDY MALDONADO
- ☐ 217. HARRY SPILMAN
- ☐ 261. TEAM LEADER CARD
- ☐ 302. JOSE URIBE
- ☐ 329. CHRIS SPEIER
- ☐ 350. WILL CLARK
- ☐ 372. MATT WILLIAMS
- ☐ 418. JOEL YOUNGBLOOD
- ☐ 445. MIKE KRUKOW
- ☐ 472. ROBBY THOMPSON
- ☐ 497. KEVIN MITCHELL
- ☐ 570. JEFFREY LEONARD
- ☐ 602. MIKE ALDRETE
- ☐ 628. DAVE HENDERSON
- ☐ 629. KELLY DOWNS
- ☐ 654. ROGER CRAIG (M)
- ☐ 660. RICK REUSCHEL
- ☐ 677. EDDIE MILNER
- ☐ 703. BOB BRENLY
- ☐ 734. CRAIG LEFFERTS
- ☐ 754. MIKE LACOSS
- ☐ 786. JOE PRICE

SEATTLE MARINERS

- ☐ 32. MIKE MORGAN
- ☐ 55. PHIL BRADLEY
- ☐ 80. MARK LANGSTON
- ☐ 104. DICK WILLIAMS (M)
- ☐ 146. DONELL NIXON
- ☐ 156. GARY MATTHEWS
- ☐ 182. KEN PHELPS
- ☐ 206. DOMINGO RAMOS
- ☐ 246. MIKE CAMPBELL
- ☐ 258. ED NUNEZ
- ☐ 285. JIM PRESLEY
- ☐ 307. MIKE TRUJILLO
- ☐ 332. JERRY REED
- ☐ 358. REY QUINONES
- ☐ 376. BIL WILKINSON
- ☐ 413. JOHN CHRISTENSEN
- ☐ 432. MIKE MOORE
- ☐ 453. DENNIS POWELL
- ☐ 485. HAROLD REYNOLDS

- ☐ 519. TEAM LEADER CARD
- ☐ 532. MIKE KINGERY
- ☐ 556. STAN CLARKE
- ☐ 583. DAVE VALLE
- ☐ 632. STEVE SHIELDS
- ☐ 656. LEE GUETTERMAN
- ☐ 687. MIKEY BRANTLEY
- ☐ 712. JOHN MOSES
- ☐ 738. SCOTT BANKHEAD
- ☐ 762. SCOTT BRADLEY
- ☐ 785. ALVIN DAVIS

TEXAS RANGERS

- ☐ 26. MITCH WILLIAMS
- ☐ 53. CURT WILKERSON
- ☐ 77. TOM O'MALLEY
- ☐ 114. JEFF RUSSELL
- ☐ 139. JERRY BROWNE
- ☐ 163. DALE MOHORCIC
- ☐ 178. DWAYNE HENRY
- ☐ 201. TEAM LEADER CARD
- ☐ 219. MIKE STANLEY
- ☐ 227. ED CORREA
- ☐ 252. BOB BROWER
- ☐ 280. PETE INCAVIGLIA
- ☐ 319. MIKE LOYND
- ☐ 345. SCOTT FLETCHER
- ☐ 369. GREG HARRIS
- ☐ 427. PAUL KILGUS
- ☐ 462. DON SLAUGHT
- ☐ 490. LARRY PARRISH
- ☐ 537. STEVE BUECHELE
- ☐ 563. JOSE GUZMAN
- ☐ 589. GENO PETRALLI
- ☐ 594. BOBBY VALENTINE (M)
- ☐ 617. ODDIBE MCDOWELL
- ☐ 680. CHARLIE HOUGH
- ☐ 721. PETE O'BRIEN
- ☐ 747. BOBBY WITT
- ☐ 771. RUBEN SIERRA

TORONTO BLUE JAYS

- ☐ 28. JOSE NUNEZ
- ☐ 54. JIM CLANCY
- ☐ 79. ERNIE WHITT
- ☐ 113. KELLY GRUBER
- ☐ 140. JESSE BARFIELD
- ☐ 167. RANCE MULLINIKS
- ☐ 191. JOHN CERUTTI
- ☐ 205. NELSON LIRIANO
- ☐ 220. TOM HENKE
- ☐ 229. JEFF MUSSELMAN
- ☐ 273. GARTH IORG
- ☐ 290. TONY FERNANDEZ
- ☐ 314. JIMY WILLIAMS (M)
- ☐ 323. RICK LEACH
- ☐ 347. JOE JOHNSON
- ☐ 438. ROB DUCEY
- ☐ 463. FRED MCGRIFF
- ☐ 505. WILLIE UPSHAW
- ☐ 541. JUAN BENIQUEZ
- ☐ 565. LLOYD MOSEBY
- ☐ 590. GEORGE BELL
- ☐ 618. CECIL FIELDER
- ☐ 623. MIKE FLANAGAN
- ☐ 682. JIMMY KEY
- ☐ 696. DUANE WARD
- ☐ 722. MANNY LEE
- ☐ 729. TEAM LEADER CARD
- ☐ 749. MARK EICHHORN
- ☐ 775. DAVE STIEB

1988 TOPPS
TRADED (132)
2 1/2 X 3 1/2

ATLANTA BRAVES

- ☐ 29T. KEVIN COFFMAN
- ☐ 39T. RON GANT
- ☐ 76T. RUSS NIXON (M)
- ☐ 111T. PETE SMITH

BALTIMORE ORIOLES

- ☐ 10T. JOSE BAUTISTA
- ☐ 73T. MIKE MORGAN
- ☐ 78T. JOE ORSULAK
- ☐ 96T. FRANK ROBINSON (M)
- ☐ 114T. PETE STANICEK
- ☐ 120T. MICKEY TETTLETON

BOSTON RED SOX

- ☐ 5T. BRADY ANDERSON
- ☐ 27T. RICK CERONE
- ☐ 110T. LEE SMITH

CALIFORNIA ANGELS

- ☐ 32T. CHILI DAVIS
- ☐ 45T. BRYAN HARVEY
- ☐ 85T. DAN PETRY
- ☐ 97T. COOKIE ROJAS (M)

CHICAGO CUBS

- ☐ 15T. DAMON BERRYHILL
- ☐ 41T. RICH GOSSAGE
- ☐ 42T. MARK GRACE
- ☐ 56T. DARRIN JACKSON
- ☐ 60T. VANCE LAW
- ☐ 75T. AL NIPPER
- ☐ 87T. JEFF PICO
- ☐ 104T. CALVIN SCHIRALDI
- ☐ 131T. DON ZIMMER (M)

CHICAGO WHITE SOX

- ☐ 51T. RICKY HORTON
- ☐ 68T. JACK MCDOWELL
- ☐ 82T. DAN PASQUA
- ☐ 83T. MELIDO PEREZ
- ☐ 99T. MARK SALAS

CINCINNATI REDS

- ☐ 6T. JACK ARMSTRONG
- ☐ 55T. DANNY JACKSON
- ☐ 92T. JOSE RIJO
- ☐ 98T. CHRIS SABO
- ☐ 122T. JEFF TREADWAY

CLEVELAND INDIANS

- ☐ 16T. BUD BLACK
- ☐ 58T. RON KITTLE
- ☐ 123T. WILLIE UPSHAW
- ☐ 125T. RON WASHINGTON

DETROIT TIGERS

- ☐ 59T. RAY KNIGHT
- ☐ 86T. GARY PETTIS
- ☐ 100T. LUIS SALAZAR

HOUSTON ASTROS

- ☐ 2T. JUAN AGOSTO
- ☐ 13T. BUDDY BELL
- ☐ 90T. RAFAEL RAMIREZ

KANSAS CITY ROYALS

- ☐ 8T. FLOYD BANNISTER
- ☐ 62T. MIKE MACFARLANE
- ☐ 63T. SCOTTI MADISON
- ☐ 89T. TED POWER
- ☐ 115T. KURT STILLWELL
- ☐ 118T. PAT TABLER

LOS ANGELES DODGERS

- ☐ 12T. TIM BELCHER
- ☐ 33T. MIKE DAVIS
- ☐ 40T. KIRK GIBSON
- ☐ 43T. ALFREDO GIRFFIN
- ☐ 52T. JAY HOWELL
- ☐ 77T. JESSE OROSCO

MILWAUKEE BREWERS

- ☐ 7T. DON AUGUST
- ☐ 37T. TOM FILER
- ☐ 61T. JEFFREY LEONARD

MINNESOTA TWINS

- ☐ 49T. TOM HERR

MONTREAL EXPOS

- ☐ 94T. LUIS RIVERA
- ☐ 102T. NELSON SANTOVENIA

NEW YORK METS

- ☐ 54T. JEFF INNIS
- ☐ 103T. MACKEY SASSER

NEW YORK YANKEES

- ☐ 21T. JAY BUHNER
- ☐ 25T. JOHN CANDELARIA
- ☐ 28T. JACK CLARK
- ☐ 35T. RICHARD DOTSON
- ☐ 57T. ROBERTO KELLY
- ☐ 101T. RAFAEL SANTANA
- ☐ 108T. DON SLAUGHT

OAKLAND A'S

- ☐ 11T. DON BAYLOR
- ☐ 46T. RON HASSEY
- ☐ 48T. DAVE HENDERSON
- ☐ 53T. GLENN HUBBARD
- ☐ 81T. DAVE PARKER
- ☐ 126T. WALT WEISS
- ☐ 127T. BOB WELCH

PHILADELPHIA PHILLIES

- ☐ 18T. PHIL BRADLEY
- ☐ 79T. DAVE PALMER

PITTSBURGH PIRATES

NO CARDS ISSUED

ST. LOUIS CARDINALS

- ☐ 3T. LUIS ALICEA
- ☐ 20T. TOM BRUNANSKY
- ☐ 34T. JOSE DELEON
- ☐ 50T. BOB HORNER
- ☐ 70T. LARRY MCWILLIAMS
- ☐ 84T. STEVE PETERS
- ☐ 119T. SCOTT TERRY

SAN DIEGO PADRES

- ☐ 4T. ROBERTO ALOMAR
- ☐ 69T. JACK MCKEON (M)
- ☐ 72T. KEITH MORELAND
- ☐ 80T. MARK PARENT
- ☐ 91T. DENNIS RASMUSSEN
- ☐ 121T. DICKIE THON

SAN FRANCISCO GIANTS

- ☐ 22T. BRETT BUTLER
- ☐ 64T. KIRT MANWARING
- ☐ 93T. EARNIE RILES

SEATTLE MARINERS

- ☐ 31T. HENRY COTTO
- ☐ 105T. MIKE SCHOOLER
- ☐ 112T. JIM SNYDER (M)
- ☐ 117T. BILL SWIFT
- ☐ 129T. GLENN WILSON

TEXAS RANGERS

- ☐ 26T. JOSE CECENA
- ☐ 36T. CECIL ESPY
- ☐ 47T. RAY HAYWARD

TORONTO BLUE JAYS

- ☐ 17T. PAT BORDERS
- ☐ 24T. SIL CAMPUSANO
- ☐ 116T. TODD STOTTLEMYRE
- ☐ 128T. DAVID WELLS

U. S. OLYMPIC TEAM

- ☐ 1T. JIM ABBOTT
- ☐ 9T. BRET BARBERIE
- ☐ 14T. ANDY BENES
- ☐ 19T. JEFF BARNSON
- ☐ 23T. JIM CAMPANIS
- ☐ 30T. PAT COMBS
- ☐ 38T. MIKE FIORE
- ☐ 44T. TY GRIFFIN
- ☐ 65T. MARK MARQUESS (HC)
- ☐ 66T. TINO MARTINEZ
- ☐ 67T. BILLY MASSE
- ☐ 71T. MICKEY MORANDINI
- ☐ 74T. CHARLES NAGY

- ☐ 88T. JIM POOLE
- ☐ 95T. DOUG ROBBINS
- ☐ 106T. SCOTT SERVAIS
- ☐ 107T. DAVE SILVESTRI
- ☐ 109T. JOE SLUSARSKI
- ☐ 113T. ED SPRAGUE
- ☐ 124T. ROBIN VENTURA
- ☐ 130T. TED WOOD

1989 TOPPS (792)
2 1/2 X 3 1/2

ATLANTA BRAVES

- ☐ 11. BRUCE SUTTER
- ☐ 38. PAUL RUNGE
- ☐ 76. TERRY BLOCKER
- ☐ 83. JEFF BLAUSER
- ☐ 130. GERALD PERRY
- ☐ 157. TOM GLAVINE
- ☐ 171. TEAM LEADER CARD
- ☐ 179. OZZIE VIRGIL
- ☐ 210. DALE MURPHY
- ☐ 244. JIM ACKER
- ☐ 253. JOSE ALVAREZ
- ☐ 296. RON GANT
- ☐ 327. MARK LEMKE
- ☐ 382. JOHN SMOLTZ
- ☐ 433. ALBERT HALL
- ☐ 454. PAUL ASSENMACHER
- ☐ 488. KEVIN COFFMAN
- ☐ 523. ANDRES THOMAS
- ☐ 537. PETE SMITH
- ☐ 564. RUSS NIXON (M)
- ☐ 569. GERMAN JIMENEZ
- ☐ 586. JOE BOEVER
- ☐ 621. RICK MAHLER
- ☐ 678. DION JAMES
- ☐ 688. ZANE SMITH
- ☐ 728. CHARLIE PULEO
- ☐ 778. BRUCE BENEDICT
- ☐ 784. STEVE AVERY

BALTIMORE ORIOLES

- ☐ 13. DOUG SISK
- ☐ 69. JEFF BALLARD
- ☐ 98. LARRY SHEETS
- ☐ 124. JIM TRABER
- ☐ 152. MARK THURMOND
- ☐ 161. GREGG OLSON
- ☐ 181. CRAIG WORTHINGTON
- ☐ 213. RENE GONZALES
- ☐ 250. CAL RIPKEN
- ☐ 271. JAY TIBBS
- ☐ 297. OSWALD PERAZA
- ☐ 324. BOB MILACKI
- ☐ 352. RICK SCHU
- ☐ 381. TEAM LEADER CARD
- ☐ 469. JOSE BAUTISTA
- ☐ 497. PETE STANICEK
- ☐ 521. MICKEY TETTLETON
- ☐ 546. MARK WILLIAMSON
- ☐ 571. BILLY RIPKEN
- ☐ 598. KEN GERHART
- ☐ 625. EDDIE MURRAY
- ☐ 651. TOM NIEDENFUER
- ☐ 677. DAVE SCHMIDT
- ☐ 705. TERRY KENNEDY
- ☐ 727. JOE ORSULAK
- ☐ 757. BRADY ANDERSON

- ☐ 774. FRANK ROBINSON (M)
- ☐ 788. MIKE MORGAN

BOSTON RED SOX

- ☐ 37. BOB STANLEY
- ☐ 71. MIKE BODDICKER
- ☐ 96. RICK CERONE
- ☐ 123. SPIKE OWEN
- ☐ 155. MARTY BARRETT
- ☐ 188. DENNIS LAMP
- ☐ 205. DWIGHT EVANS
- ☐ 245. JIM RICE
- ☐ 269. TOM BOLTON
- ☐ 299. STEVE ELLSWORTH
- ☐ 321. TEAM LEADER CARD
- ☐ 326. DENNIS BOYD
- ☐ 354. LARRY PARRISH
- ☐ 377. MIKE SMITHSON
- ☐ 450. ROGER CLEMENS
- ☐ 471. STEVE CURRY
- ☐ 493. TODD BENZINGER
- ☐ 526. WES GARDNER
- ☐ 544. JEFF SELLERS
- ☐ 600. WADE BOGGS
- ☐ 630. MIKE GREENWELL
- ☐ 652. RICH GEDMAN
- ☐ 675. BRUCE HURST
- ☐ 704. CARLOS QUINTANA
- ☐ 714. JOE MORGAN (M)
- ☐ 734. JODY REED
- ☐ 760. LEE SMITH
- ☐ 785. ELLIS BURKS

CALIFORNIA ANGELS

- ☐ 17. BRIAN DOWNING
- ☐ 42. JIM EPPARD
- ☐ 51. TEAM LEADER CARD
- ☐ 68. DARRELL MILLER
- ☐ 99. SHERMAN CORBETT
- ☐ 129. TERRY CLARK
- ☐ 147. DEWAYNE BUICE
- ☐ 190. MIKE WITT
- ☐ 216. JACK HOWELL
- ☐ 243. BOB BOONE
- ☐ 270. WALLY JOYNER
- ☐ 332. TONY ARMAS
- ☐ 362. JACK LAZORKO
- ☐ 421. KIRK MCCASKILL
- ☐ 444. MOOSE STUBING (M)
- ☐ 455. JOHNNY RAY
- ☐ 477. DICK SCHOFIELD
- ☐ 525. CHILI DAVIS
- ☐ 547. MARK MCLEMORE
- ☐ 573. JIM ABBOTT
- ☐ 576. GREG MINTON
- ☐ 602. DEVON WHITE
- ☐ 632. BRYAN HARVEY
- ☐ 649. STEWART CLIBURN
- ☐ 679. WILLIE FRASER
- ☐ 708. CHUCK FINLEY
- ☐ 761. DANTE BICHETTE

CHICAGO CUBS

- ☐ 10. ANDRE DAWSON
- ☐ 36. MITCH WEBSTER
- ☐ 66. MANNY TRILLO
- ☐ 86. AL NIPPER
- ☐ 115. JODY DAVIS
- ☐ 134. DON ZIMMER (M)
- ☐ 140. SHAWON DUNSTON
- ☐ 149. DOUG DASCENZO
- ☐ 186. PAT PERRY
- ☐ 212. SCOTT SANDERSON
- ☐ 240. GREG MADDUX
- ☐ 262. JEFF PICO
- ☐ 286. DARRIN JACKSON
- ☐ 310. RAFAEL PALMEIRO
- ☐ 337. CALVIN SCHIRALDI
- ☐ 360. RYNE SANDBERG
- ☐ 415. RICH GOSSAGE
- ☐ 439. FRANK DIPINO
- ☐ 465. MARK GRACE
- ☐ 501. VANCE LAW
- ☐ 520. RICK SUTCLIFFE
- ☐ 543. DAMON BERRYHILL
- ☐ 549. TEAM LEADER CARD
- ☐ 593. DREW HALL
- ☐ 613. GARY VARSHO
- ☐ 642. ARGENIS SALAZAR

- ☐ 668. MIKE BIELECKI
- ☐ 694. LES LANCASTER
- ☐ 713. TY GRIFFIN
- ☐ 717. JAMIE MOYER
- ☐ 742. MIKE HARKEY
- ☐ 767. MIKE CAPEL

CHICAGO WHITE SOX

- ☐ 21. TEAM LEADER CARD
- ☐ 34. KEN WILLIAMS
- ☐ 108. FRED MANRIQUE
- ☐ 122. LANCE JOHNSON
- ☐ 133. BILL LONG
- ☐ 142. MIKE DIAZ
- ☐ 156. DAVE GALLAGHER
- ☐ 162. JOHN DAVIS
- ☐ 195. OZZIE GUILLEN
- ☐ 209. JEFF BITTIGER
- ☐ 247. SHAWN HILLEGAS
- ☐ 308. RON KARKOVICE
- ☐ 334. STEVE LYONS
- ☐ 357. JERRY REUSS
- ☐ 384. MARK SALAS
- ☐ 408. GREG WALKER
- ☐ 414. JIM FREGOSI (M)
- ☐ 434. KEN PATTERSON
- ☐ 458. DONN PALL
- ☐ 486. JACK MCDOWELL
- ☐ 512. DONNIE HILL
- ☐ 539. BARRY JONES
- ☐ 558. DAN PASQUA
- ☐ 585. HAROLD BAINES
- ☐ 616. STEVE ROSENBERG
- ☐ 633. DARYL BOSTON
- ☐ 656. IVAN CALDERON
- ☐ 695. CARLTON FISK
- ☐ 762. BOBBY THIGPEN
- ☐ 764. ROBIN VENTURA
- ☐ 786. MELIDO PEREZ

CINCINNATTI REDS

- ☐ 16. RON ROBINSON
- ☐ 45. KAL DANIELS
- ☐ 103. TIM BIRTSAS
- ☐ 111. TEAM LEADER CARD
- ☐ 135. JOSE RIJO
- ☐ 151. TERRY MCGRIFF
- ☐ 172. FRANK WILLIAMS
- ☐ 234. TOM BROWNING
- ☐ 264. ROB DIBBLE
- ☐ 290. JOHN FRANCO
- ☐ 317. JACK ARMSTRONG
- ☐ 330. ERIC DAVIS
- ☐ 366. HERM WINNINGHAM
- ☐ 422. BO DIAZ
- ☐ 446. ROB MURPHY
- ☐ 490. CHRIS SABO
- ☐ 505. PETE ROSE (M)
- ☐ 515. BARRY LARKIN
- ☐ 554. NICK ESASKY
- ☐ 604. PAUL O'NEILL
- ☐ 626. JEFF REED
- ☐ 644. LLOYD MCCLENDON
- ☐ 666. RANDY ST. CLAIRE
- ☐ 685. JEFF TREADWAY
- ☐ 711. CANDY SIERRA
- ☐ 730. DANNY JACKSON
- ☐ 737. NORM CHARLTON
- ☐ 772. RON OESTER

CLEVELAND INDIANS

- ☐ 31. TERRY FRANCONA
- ☐ 55. JULIO FRANCO
- ☐ 80. CORY SNYDER
- ☐ 106. WILLIE UPSHAW
- ☐ 141. TEAM LEADER CARD
- ☐ 144. JAY BELL
- ☐ 173. MEL HALL
- ☐ 204. BRAD HAVENS
- ☐ 222. MARK LEWIS
- ☐ 227. JOHN FARRELL
- ☐ 283. ANDY ALLANSON
- ☐ 315. GREG SWINDELL
- ☐ 339. SCOTT BAILES
- ☐ 363. RICH YETT
- ☐ 420. JOE CARTER
- ☐ 443. ROD NICHOLS
- ☐ 476. JON PERLMAN
- ☐ 509. BUD BLACK

☐ 528. LUIS MEDINA
☐ 534. DOC EDWARDS (M)
☐ 574. DAVE CLARK
☐ 599. TOM CANDIOTTI
☐ 637. CARMEN CASTILLO
☐ 690. DOUG JONES
☐ 721. RON TINGLEY
☐ 739. BROOK JACOBY
☐ 771. RON KITTLE

DETROIT TIGERS

☐ 43. WILLIE HERNANDEZ
☐ 77. DOYLE ALEXANDER
☐ 127. WALT TERRELL
☐ 146. GARY PETTIS
☐ 167. STEVE SEARCY
☐ 193. SPARKY ANDERSON (M)
☐ 238. ERIC KING
☐ 267. JEFF ROBINSON
☐ 288. PAT SHERIDAN
☐ 320. LOU WHITAKER
☐ 342. TOM BOOKENS
☐ 365. MIKE HENNEMAN
☐ 416. FRED LYNN
☐ 445. MATT NOKES
☐ 467. JIM WALEWANDER
☐ 487. SCOTT LUSADER
☐ 499. DON HEINKEL
☐ 514. CHET LEMON
☐ 553. LUIS SALAZAR
☐ 583. PAUL GIBSON
☐ 603. FRANK TANANA
☐ 609. TEAM LEADER CARD
☐ 631. DAVE BERGMAN
☐ 645. JACK MORRIS
☐ 667. DWAYNE MURPHY
☐ 743. MIKE HEATH
☐ 770. ALAN TRAMMELL
☐ 777. TED POWER

HOUSTON ASTROS

☐ 24. LARRY ANDERSEN
☐ 49. CRAIG BIGGIO
☐ 64. ALEX TREVINE
☐ 95. GERALD YOUNG
☐ 119. TERRY PUHL
☐ 153. JIM PANKOVITS
☐ 163. BOB FORSCH
☐ 164. HAL LANIER (M)
☐ 180. MIKE SCOTT
☐ 226. BILL DORAN
☐ 252. BILLY HATCHER
☐ 280. BOB KNEPPER
☐ 305. DAVE SMITH
☐ 341. JIM DESHAIES
☐ 369. KEN CAMINITI
☐ 428. CRAIG REYNOLDS
☐ 461. BUDDY BELL
☐ 492. ALAN ASHBY
☐ 530. NOLAN RYAN
☐ 559. JUAN AGOSTO
☐ 579. TEAM LEADER CARD
☐ 589. DAVE MEADS
☐ 607. WILLIE ANSLEY
☐ 643. LOUIE MEADOWS
☐ 646. KEVIN BASS
☐ 719. DANNY DARWIN
☐ 749. RAFAEL RAMIREZ
☐ 765. GLENN DAVIS

KANSAS CITY ROYALS

☐ 25. FRANK WHITE
☐ 56. PAT TABLER
☐ 87. LARRY OWEN
☐ 116. JEFF MONTGOMERY
☐ 148. BILL PECOTA
☐ 168. WILLIE WILSON
☐ 200. GEORGE BRETT
☐ 266. LUIS AQUINO
☐ 275. DANNY TARTABULL
☐ 301. CHARLIE LEIBRANDT
☐ 323. GARY THURMAN
☐ 348. ED HEARN
☐ 374. JOHN WATHAN (M)
☐ 430. MARK GUBICZA
☐ 452. ISRAEL SANCHEZ
☐ 479. MIKE MACFARLANE
☐ 507. STEVE FARR
☐ 540. BO JACKSON

☐ 596. KURT STILLWELL
☐ 638. FLOYD BANNISTER
☐ 670. KEVIN SEITZER
☐ 702. JAMIE QUIRK
☐ 724. JERRY DON GLEATON
☐ 750. BRET SABERHAGER
☐ 789. TEAM LEADER CARD

LOS ANGELES DODGERS

☐ 22. TIM CREWS
☐ 35. JOHN TUDOR
☐ 40. STEVE SAX
☐ 57. ALEJANDRO PENA
☐ 62. ALFREDO GRIFFIN
☐ 84. BILL BENE
☐ 93. KEN HOWELL
☐ 117. DAVE ANDERSON
☐ 150. FERNANDO VALENZUELA
☐ 175. JOHN SHELBY
☐ 198. DANNY HEEP
☐ 225. RAMON MARTINEZ
☐ 232. RICKY HORTON
☐ 249. TIM LEARY
☐ 254. TOM LASORDA (M)
☐ 277. MIKE DAVIS
☐ 306. TRACY WOODSON
☐ 340. KIRK GIBSON
☐ 368. BRIAN HOLTON
☐ 425. JAY HOWELL
☐ 456. TIM BELCHER
☐ 483. MICKEY HATCHER
☐ 513. JESSE OROSCO
☐ 550. OREL HERSHISER
☐ 582. MIKE MARSHALL
☐ 606. RICK DEMPSEY
☐ 669. TEAM LEADER CARD
☐ 697. FRANKLIN STUBBS
☐ 736. JEFF HAMILTON
☐ 755. MIKE SCIOSCIA

MILWAUKEE BREWERS

☐ 12. DALE SVEUM
☐ 33. B. J. SURHOFF
☐ 63. MARK CLEAR
☐ 88. DARRYL HAMILTON
☐ 110. PAUL MOLITOR
☐ 136. JOEY MEYER
☐ 160. JEFFREY LEONARD
☐ 192. PAUL MIRABELLA
☐ 214. CHARLIE O'BRIEN
☐ 263. MIKE FELDER
☐ 287. JUAN NIEVES
☐ 311. CHRIS BOSIO
☐ 338. JIM ADDUCI
☐ 343. GARY SHEFFIELD
☐ 344. TOM TREBELHORN (M)
☐ 364. ROB DEER
☐ 419. TOM FILER
☐ 466. CHUCK CRIM
☐ 491. MIKE BIRKBECK
☐ 517. GREG BROCK
☐ 538. JUAN CASTILLO
☐ 563. BILL SCHROEDER
☐ 595. TEDDY HIGUERA
☐ 615. ROBIN YOUNT
☐ 671. JIM GANTNER
☐ 696. DON AUGUST
☐ 718. GLENN BRAGGS
☐ 731. MIKE YOUNG
☐ 740. DAN PLESAC
☐ 759. TEAM LEADER CARD
☐ 768. BILL WEGMAN

MINNESOTA TWINS

☐ 14. TOM KELLY (M)
☐ 19. GREG GAGNE
☐ 46. MARK PORTUGAL
☐ 72. JOHN MOSES
☐ 101. LES STRAKER
☐ 120. FRANK VIOLA
☐ 220. GARY GAETTI
☐ 239. TIM LAUDNER
☐ 265. KENT HRBEK
☐ 294. JUAN BERENGUER
☐ 318. GENE LARKIN
☐ 376. STEVE LOMBARDOZZI
☐ 426. DANNY GLADDEN
☐ 429. TEAM LEADER CARD
☐ 451. MARK DAVIDSON

☐ 472. BRIAN HARPER
☐ 503. AL NEWMAN
☐ 555. BERT BLYLEVEN
☐ 577. RANDY BUSH
☐ 623. FRED TOLIVER
☐ 650. KIRBY PUCKETT
☐ 672. ALLAN ANDERSON
☐ 698. KEITH ATHERTON
☐ 709. TOM HERR
☐ 746. GERMAN GONZALEZ
☐ 775. JEFF REARDON

MONTREAL EXPOS

☐ 23. MIKE FITZGERALD
☐ 48. TIM BURKE
☐ 73. PASCUAL PEREZ
☐ 81. TEAM LEADER CARD
☐ 91. FLOYD YOUMANS
☐ 138. WALLACE JOHNSON
☐ 176. JEFF PARRETT
☐ 197. NEAL HEATON
☐ 228. NELSON SANTOVENIA
☐ 251. JOHN DOPSON
☐ 278. ANDY McGAFFIGAN
☐ 313. DENNY MARTINEZ
☐ 346. REX HUDLER
☐ 367. JOHNNY PAREDES
☐ 373. TRACY JONES
☐ 431. LUIS RIVERA
☐ 464. BRYN SMITH
☐ 474. BOB RODGERS (M)
☐ 485. HUBIE BROOKS
☐ 529. TOM FOLEY
☐ 560. TIM RAINES
☐ 590. ANDRES GALARRAGA
☐ 614. JOE HESKETH
☐ 647. RANDY JOHNSON
☐ 674. OTIS NIXON
☐ 720. TIM WALLACH
☐ 747. WIL TEJADA
☐ 763. DAVE MARTINEZ

NEW YORK METS

☐ 9. TIM TEUFEL
☐ 30. DWIGHT GOODEN
☐ 58. LEE MAZZILLI
☐ 85. KEVIN McREYNOLDS
☐ 105. RON DARLING
☐ 182. BOB McCLURE
☐ 207. TERRY LEACH
☐ 233. GREGG JEFFERIES
☐ 257. RICK AGUILERA
☐ 291. TEAM LEADER CARD
☐ 300. DARRYL STRAWBERRY
☐ 333. BOB OJEDA
☐ 356. KEVIN ELSTER
☐ 383. HOWARD JOHNSON
☐ 412. BARRY LYONS
☐ 435. LEN DYKSTRA
☐ 457. MACKEY SASSER
☐ 480. KEITH HERNANDEZ
☐ 508. WALLY BACKMAN
☐ 545. MOOKIE WILSON
☐ 557. KEITH MILLER
☐ 610. RANDY MYERS
☐ 655. DAVE MAGADAN
☐ 680. GARY CARTER
☐ 684. DAVE JOHNSON (M)
☐ 710. DAVE CONE
☐ 735. ROGER McDOWELL
☐ 787. DAVE WEST
☐ 790. SID FERNANDEZ

NEW YORK YANKEES

- ☐ 8. DAVE EILAND
- ☐ 18. RICK RHODEN
- ☐ 26. DALE MOHORCIC
- ☐ 61. NEIL ALLEN
- ☐ 104. DALLAS GREEN (M)
- ☐ 109. HIPOLITO PENA
- ☐ 159. PAT CLEMENTS
- ☐ 185. CLAUDELL WASHINGTON
- ☐ 211. MIKE PAGLIARULO
- ☐ 236. CHARLES HUDSON
- ☐ 255. RON GUIDRY
- ☐ 260. DAVE WINFIELD
- ☐ 285. JOHN CANDELARIA
- ☐ 302. GARY WARD
- ☐ 335. DAVE RIGHETTI
- ☐ 359. TOMMY JOHN
- ☐ 380. RICKEY HENDERSON
- ☐ 410. JACK CLARK
- ☐ 436. BOBBY MEACHAM
- ☐ 484. STEVE SHIELDS
- ☐ 511. RICHARD DOTSON
- ☐ 519. TEAM LEADER CARD
- ☐ 536. JOEL SKINNER
- ☐ 561. LUIS AGUAYO
- ☐ 584. RANDY VELARDE
- ☐ 611. DON SLAUGHT
- ☐ 635. WILLIE RANDOLPH
- ☐ 659. AL LEITER
- ☐ 691. ROBERTO KELLY
- ☐ 700. DON MATTINGLY
- ☐ 716. WAYNE TOLLESON
- ☐ 741. KEN PHELPS
- ☐ 792. RAFAEL SANTANA

OAKLAND A'S

- ☐ 47. CARNEY LANSFORD
- ☐ 70. MARK MCGWIRE
- ☐ 102. MIKE GALLEGO
- ☐ 131. DAVE OTTO
- ☐ 145. DAVE STEWART
- ☐ 166. DOUG JENNINGS
- ☐ 174. TODD BURNS
- ☐ 224. TONY LARUSSA (M)
- ☐ 237. GLENN HUBBARD
- ☐ 248. TONY PHILLIPS
- ☐ 272. RON HASSEY
- ☐ 292. JIM CORSI
- ☐ 316. WALT WEISS
- ☐ 328. RICK HONEYCUTT
- ☐ 370. DENNIS ECKERSLEY
- ☐ 424. LUIS POLONIA
- ☐ 448. ERIC PLUNK
- ☐ 475. DAVE PARKER
- ☐ 500. JOSE CANSECO
- ☐ 527. DAVE HENDERSON
- ☐ 552. GREG CADARET
- ☐ 581. GENE NELSON
- ☐ 605. BOB WELCH
- ☐ 622. STAN JAVIER
- ☐ 639. TEAM LEADER CARD
- ☐ 641. CURT YOUNG
- ☐ 673. DON BAYLOR
- ☐ 692. STEVE ONTIVEROS
- ☐ 701. STORM DAVIS
- ☐ 725. TERRY STEINBACH

PHILADELPHIA PHILLIES

- ☐ 20. STEVE BEDROSIAN
- ☐ 39. MIKE MADDUX
- ☐ 67. DAVE PALMER
- ☐ 74. NICK LEYVA (M)
- ☐ 100. MIKE SCHMIDT
- ☐ 128. MILT THOMPSON
- ☐ 154. DON CARMAN
- ☐ 187. DARREN DAULTON
- ☐ 202. BRAD MOORE
- ☐ 215. KEVIN GROSS
- ☐ 268. KEITH MILLER
- ☐ 298. CHRIS JAMES
- ☐ 349. RON JONES
- ☐ 358. RICKY JORDAN
- ☐ 385. VON HAYES
- ☐ 418. BOB DERNIER
- ☐ 438. GREG GROSS
- ☐ 470. LANCE PARRISH
- ☐ 489. TEAM LEADER CARD
- ☐ 494. SHANE RAWLEY
- ☐ 518. BRUCE RUFFIN

- ☐ 542. TODD FROHWIRTH
- ☐ 575. JUAN SAMUEL
- ☐ 608. PHIL BRADLEY
- ☐ 627. GREG HARRIS
- ☐ 634. MARVIN FREEMAN
- ☐ 653. TOMMY BARRETT
- ☐ 707. STEVE JELTZ

PITTSBURGH PIRATES

- ☐ 27. ORESTES DESTRADE
- ☐ 89. DAVE LAPOINT
- ☐ 114. BOB KIPPER
- ☐ 126. SID BREAM
- ☐ 165. MIKE DUNNE
- ☐ 218. MIKE LAVALLIER
- ☐ 273. JOSE LIND
- ☐ 281. GARY REDUS
- ☐ 284. JIM LEYLAND (M)
- ☐ 293. GLENN WILSON
- ☐ 303. FELIX FERMIN
- ☐ 322. JOHN SMILEY
- ☐ 350. ANDY VAN SLYKE
- ☐ 423. BRIAN FISHER
- ☐ 440. BOBBY BONILLA
- ☐ 453. TOM PRINCE
- ☐ 478. DOUG DRABEK
- ☐ 504. BOB WALK
- ☐ 522. RANDY KRAMER
- ☐ 566. AL PEDRIQUE
- ☐ 592. JOHN CANGELOSI
- ☐ 620. BARRY BONDS
- ☐ 658. R. J. REYNOLDS
- ☐ 681. JEFF ROBINSON
- ☐ 699. TEAM LEADER CARD
- ☐ 723. RAFAEL BELLIARD
- ☐ 751. KEN OBERKFELL
- ☐ 752. JIM GOTT
- ☐ 756. SCOTT MEDVIN
- ☐ 769. JUNIOR ORTIZ

ST. LOUIS CARDINALS

- ☐ 60. TOM BRUNANSKY
- ☐ 90. VINCE COLEMAN
- ☐ 97. GREG MATHEWS
- ☐ 107. JOSE DELEON
- ☐ 132. CURT FORD
- ☐ 184. JOHN COSTELLO
- ☐ 196. DENNY WALLING
- ☐ 208. TOM PAGNOZZI
- ☐ 230. OZZIE SMITH
- ☐ 259. LARRY MCWILLIAMS
- ☐ 261. TEAM LEADER CARD
- ☐ 282. CHRIS CARPENTER
- ☐ 312. TOM LAWLESS
- ☐ 375. TERRY PENDLETON
- ☐ 409. KEN DAYLEY
- ☐ 442. JOSE OQUENDO
- ☐ 463. STEVE LAKE
- ☐ 482. STEVE PETERS
- ☐ 510. BOB HORNER
- ☐ 535. TODD WORRELL
- ☐ 562. DANNY COX
- ☐ 578. JOHN MORRIS
- ☐ 588. LUIS ALICEA
- ☐ 612. DAN QUISENBERRY
- ☐ 640. WILLIE MCGEE
- ☐ 654. WHITEY HERZOG (M)
- ☐ 657. JOE MAGRANE
- ☐ 686. SCOTT TERRY
- ☐ 715. TONY PENA
- ☐ 780. PEDRO GUERRERO
- ☐ 791. JIM LINDEMAN

SAN DIEGO PADRES

- ☐ 32. DENNIS RASMUSSEN
- ☐ 59. MARK DAVIS
- ☐ 82. DAVE LEIPER
- ☐ 121. GARRY TEMPLETON
- ☐ 178. MARK GRANT
- ☐ 194. GREG HARRIS
- ☐ 206. ROBERTO ALOMAR
- ☐ 231. TEAM LEADER CARD
- ☐ 235. JOHN KRUK
- ☐ 256. BENNY SANTIAGO
- ☐ 307. LANCE MCCULLERS
- ☐ 319. GREG BOOKER
- ☐ 353. MARVELL WYNNE
- ☐ 379. TIM FLANNERY
- ☐ 427. ERIC SHOW

- ☐ 437. ANDY BENES
- ☐ 449. CARMELO MARTINEZ
- ☐ 481. CHRIS BROWN
- ☐ 516. EDDIE WHITSON
- ☐ 533. ANDY HAWKINS
- ☐ 551. RANDY READY
- ☐ 570. TONY GWYNN
- ☐ 617. MARK PARENT
- ☐ 624. JACK MCKEON (M)
- ☐ 648. SANDY ALOMAR
- ☐ 689. STAN JEFFERSON
- ☐ 726. DICKIE THON
- ☐ 748. JIMMY JONES
- ☐ 773. KEITH MORELAND

SAN FRANCISCO GIANTS

- ☐ 15. ROBBY THOMPSON
- ☐ 41. TERRY MULHOLLAND
- ☐ 52. BOB BRENLY
- ☐ 65. RICK REUSCHEL
- ☐ 94. CHRIS SPEIER
- ☐ 125. MIKE KRUKOW
- ☐ 158. MIKE ALDRETE
- ☐ 189. KEVIN MITCHELL
- ☐ 217. JOE PRICE
- ☐ 241. BRETT BUTLER
- ☐ 304. JOEL YOUNGBLOOD
- ☐ 329. BOB MELVIN
- ☐ 351. TEAM LEADER CARD
- ☐ 361. KELLY DOWNS
- ☐ 372. CRAIG LEFFERTS
- ☐ 417. MIKE LACROSS
- ☐ 447. DONELL NIXON
- ☐ 473. DON ROBINSON
- ☐ 495. CANDY MALDONADO
- ☐ 506. KIRT MANWARING
- ☐ 572. ATLEE HAMMAKER
- ☐ 601. DAVE DRAVECKY
- ☐ 628. MATT WILLIAMS
- ☐ 660. WILL CLARK
- ☐ 676. ERNIE RILES
- ☐ 703. SCOTT GARRELTS
- ☐ 733. RANDY BOCKUS
- ☐ 744. ROGER CRAIG (M)
- ☐ 753. JOSE URIBE
- ☐ 783. TREVOR WILSON

SEATTLE MARINERS

- ☐ 28. MIKE MOORE
- ☐ 44. JIM SNYDER (M)
- ☐ 54. STEVE TROUT
- ☐ 79. SCOTT BANKHEAD
- ☐ 112. JIM PRESLEY
- ☐ 143. MIKE CAMPBELL
- ☐ 169. MIKE JACKSON
- ☐ 199. MIKE SCHOOLER
- ☐ 223. JAY BUHNER
- ☐ 246. REY QUINONES
- ☐ 279. SCOTT BRADLEY
- ☐ 309. MARIO DIAZ
- ☐ 336. STEVE BALBONI
- ☐ 355. MARK LANGSTON
- ☐ 413. MIKE KINGERY
- ☐ 441. JERRY REED
- ☐ 459. TEAM LEADER CARD
- ☐ 468. HENRY COTTO
- ☐ 498. DAVE VALLE
- ☐ 531. DAVE HENGEL
- ☐ 556. BRUCE FIELDS
- ☐ 568. MICKEY BRANTLEY

1989 Topps

- ☐ 580. HAROLD REYNOLDS
- ☐ 597. TERRY TAYLOR
- ☐ 636. BILL WILKINSON
- ☐ 687. ALVIN DAVIS
- ☐ 712. BILL SWIFT
- ☐ 738. DARNELL COLES
- ☐ 758. GENE WALTER
- ☐ 781. GREG BRILEY

TEXAS RANGERS

- ☐ 53. RUBEN SIERRA
- ☐ 78. JIM SUNDBERG
- ☐ 92. JEFF KUNKEL
- ☐ 137. GENO.PETRALLI
- ☐ 177. MONTY FARISS
- ☐ 183. ODDIBE MCDOWELL
- ☐ 221. CECIL ESPY
- ☐ 242. ED VANDEBERG
- ☐ 276. PAUL KILGUS
- ☐ 295. SCOTT FLETCHER
- ☐ 314. BOBBY VALENTINE (M)
- ☐ 331. CURT WILKERSON
- ☐ 345. CHARLIE HOUGH
- ☐ 411. MITCH WILLIAMS
- ☐ 432. CHAD KREUTER
- ☐ 462. JOSE GUZMAN
- ☐ 496. DWAYANE HENRY
- ☐ 532. JERRY BROWNE
- ☐ 548. BOBBY WITT
- ☐ 565. JEFF RUSSELL
- ☐ 587. MIKE STANLEY
- ☐ 629. PETE O'BRIEN
- ☐ 683. JOSE CECENA
- ☐ 706. PETE INCAVIGLIA
- ☐ 729. TEAM LEADER CARD
- ☐ 732. STEVE BUECHELE
- ☐ 754. BOB BROWER
- ☐ 766. CECILIO GUANTE
- ☐ 779. CRAIG MCMURTRY

TORONTO BLUE JAYS

- ☐ 29. KELLY GRUBER
- ☐ 50. GEORGE BELL
- ☐ 75. TOM HENKE
- ☐ 113. LLOYD MOSEBY
- ☐ 139. MIKE FLANAGAN
- ☐ 170. TONY FERNANDEZ
- ☐ 191. SIL CAMPUSANO
- ☐ 201. TEAM LEADER CARD
- ☐ 203. ROB DUCEY
- ☐ 219. JIM CLANCY
- ☐ 229. JIMMY KEY
- ☐ 274. MARK EICHHORN
- ☐ 289. ERNIE WHITT
- ☐ 325. JESSE BARFIELD
- ☐ 347. JOHN CERUTTI
- ☐ 371. MANNY LEE
- ☐ 460. DAVE STIEB
- ☐ 502. DUANE WARD
- ☐ 541. CECIL FIELDER
- ☐ 567. DAVID WELLS
- ☐ 591. JEFF MUSSELMAN
- ☐ 594. JIMY WILLIAMS (M)
- ☐ 618. RANCE MULLINIKS
- ☐ 682. RICK LEACH
- ☐ 693. PAT BORDERS
- ☐ 722. TODD STOTTLEMYRE
- ☐ 745. FRED MCGRIFF
- ☐ 776. NELSON LIRIANO

1989 TOPPS TRADED (132) 2 1/2" X 3 1/2"

ATLANTA BRAVES

- ☐ 10T. GERONIMO BERROA
- ☐ 22T. JODY DAVIS
- ☐ 31T. DARRELL EVANS
- ☐ 39T. TOMMY GREGG
- ☐ 73T. DEREK LILLIQUIST
- ☐ 78T. ODDIBE MCDOWELL
- ☐ 114T. LONNIE SMITH
- ☐ 121T. JEFF TREADWAY

BALTIMORE ORIOLES

- ☐ 13T. PHIL BRADLEY
- ☐ 23T. MIKE DEVEREAUX
- ☐ 52T. BRIAN HOLTON
- ☐ 81T. RANDY MILLIGAN
- ☐ 89T. GREGG OLSON

BOSTON RED SOX

- ☐ 26T. JOHN DOPSON
- ☐ 29T. NICK ESASKY
- ☐ 64T. RANDY KUTCHER
- ☐ 86T. ROB MURPHY
- ☐ 105T. ED ROMERO

CALIFORNIA ANGELS

- ☐ 2T. JIM ABBOTT
- ☐ 3T. KENT ANDERSON
- ☐ 11T. BERT BLYLEVEN
- ☐ 96T. LANCE PARRISH
- ☐ 99T. DOUG RADER (M)
- ☐ 125T. CLAUDELL WASHINGTON

CHICAGO CUBS

- ☐ 60T. PAUL KILGUS
- ☐ 76T. LLOYD MCCLENDON
- ☐ 113T. DWIGHT SMITH
- ☐ 123T. JEROME WALTON
- ☐ 126T. CURT WILKERSON
- ☐ 130T. MITCH WILLIAMS
- ☐ 131T. STEVE WILSON

CHICAGO WHITE SOX

- ☐ 61T. ERIC KING
- ☐ 62T. RON KITTLE
- ☐ 75T. TOM MCCARTHY
- ☐ 120T. JEFF TORBORG (M)
- ☐ 127T. EDDIE WILLIAMS

CINCINNATI REDS

- ☐ 9T. TODD BENZINGER
- ☐ 40T. KEN GRIFFEY
- ☐ 74T. RICK MAHLER
- ☐ 116T. KENT TEKULVE

CLEVELAND INDIANS

- ☐ 4T. KEITH ATHERTON
- ☐ 16T. JERRY BROWNE
- ☐ 33T. FELIX FERMIN
- ☐ 88T. PETE O'BRIEN
- ☐ 91T. JESSE OROSCO

DETROIT TIGERS

- ☐ 83T. KEITH MORELAND
- ☐ 112T. RICK SCHU
- ☐ 124T. GARY WARD
- ☐ 128T. FRANK WILLIAMS
- ☐ 129T. KEN WILLIAMS

HOUSTON ASTROS

- ☐ 19T. JIM CLANCY
- ☐ 53T. ART HOWE (M)

KANSAS CITY ROYALS

- ☐ 12T. BOB BOONE
- ☐ 28T. JIM EISENREICH
- ☐ 38T. TOM GORDON
- ☐ 69T. TERRY LEACH

LOS ANGELES DODGERS

- ☐ 84T. MIKE MORGAN
- ☐ 87T. EDDIE MURRAY
- ☐ 100T. WILLIE RANDOLPH

MILWAUKEE BREWERS

- ☐ 21T. BRYAN CLUTTERBUCK
- ☐ 35T. TERRY FRANCONA
- ☐ 115T. BILLY SPIERS

MINNESOTA TWINS

- ☐ 5T. WALLY BACKMAN
- ☐ 18T. CARMEN CASTILLO
- ☐ 101T. SHANE RAWLEY

MONTREAL EXPOS

- ☐ 42T. KEVIN GROSS
- ☐ 66T. MARK LANGSTON
- ☐ 92T. SPIKE OWEN

NEW YORK METS

- ☐ 1T. DON AASE
- ☐ 108T. JUAN SAMUEL

NEW YORK YANKEES

- ☐ 6T. STEVE BALBONI
- ☐ 7T. JESSE BARFIELD
- ☐ 17T. CHUCK CARY
- ☐ 30T. ALVARO ESPINOZA
- ☐ 37T. BOB GEREN
- ☐ 43T. LEE GUETTERMAN
- ☐ 44T. MEL HALL
- ☐ 47T. ANDY HAWKINS
- ☐ 58T. JIMMY JONES
- ☐ 67T. DAVE LAPOINT
- ☐ 77T. LANCE MCCULLERS
- ☐ 94T. CLAY PARKER
- ☐ 110T. DEION SANDERS
- ☐ 111T. STEVE SAX

OAKLAND A'S

- ☐ 48T. RICKEY HENDERSON
- ☐ 82T. MIKE MOORE

PHILADELPHIA PHILLIES

- ☐ 27T. LEN DYKSTRA
- ☐ 49T. TOM HERR
- ☐ 54T. KEN HOWELL
- ☐ 63T. JOHN KRUK
- ☐ 65T. STEVE LAKE
- ☐ 79T. ROGER MCDOWELL
- ☐ 80T. LARRY MCWILLIAMS
- ☐ 90T. STEVE ONTIVEROS
- ☐ 95T. JEFF PARRETT
- ☐ 102T. RANDY READY
- ☐ 119T. DICKIE THON

PITTSBURGH PIRATES

- ☐ 25T. BENNY DISTEFANO
- ☐ 98T. REY QUINONES

ST. LOUIS CARDINALS

- ☐ 24T. FRANK DIPINO
- ☐ 50T. KEN HILL
- ☐ 118T. MILT THOMPSON

SAN DIEGO PADRES

- ☐ 20T. JACK CLARK
- ☐ 55T. BRUCE HURST
- ☐ 56T. CHRIS JAMES
- ☐ 103T. BIP ROBERTS
- ☐ 107T. LUIS SALAZAR
- ☐ 117T. WALT TERRELL

SAN FRANCISCO GIANTS

- ☐ 8T. STEVE BEDROSIAN
- ☐ 14T. JEFF BRANTLEY
- ☐ 59T. TERRY KENNEDY

SEATTLE MARINERS

- ☐ 41T. KEN GRIFFEY, JR.
- ☐ 45T. ERIK HANSON
- ☐ 46T. GENE HARRIS
- ☐ 51T. BRIAN HOLMAN
- ☐ 57T. RANDY JOHNSON
- ☐ 70T. JIM LEFEBVRE (M)
- ☐ 72T. JEFFREY LEONARD
- ☐ 97T. DENNIS POWELL
- ☐ 122T. OMAR VIZQUEL

TEXAS RANGERS

- ☐ 15T. KEVIN BROWN
- ☐ 34T. JULIO FRANCO
- ☐ 68T. RICK LEACH
- ☐ 85T. JAMIE MOYER
- ☐ 93T. RAFAEL PALMEIRO
- ☐ 104T. KENNY ROGERS
- ☐ 106T. NOLAN RYAN

TORONTO BLUE JAYS

- ☐ 32T. JUNIOR FELIX
- ☐ 36T. CITO GASTON (M)
- ☐ 71T. AL LEITER
- ☐ 109T. ALEX SANCHEZ

1990 TOPPS (792)
2 1/2" X 3 1/2"

ATLANTA BRAVES

- ☐ 55. DARRELL EVANS
- ☐ 111. ED WHITED
- ☐ 142. JEFF WETHERBY
- ☐ 152. LONNIE SMITH
- ☐ 171. RUSS NIXON (M)
- ☐ 199. SERGIO VALDEZ
- ☐ 223. TOMMY GREGG
- ☐ 251. JEFF BLAUSER
- ☐ 254. FRANCISCO CABRERA
- ☐ 282. DEREK LILLIQUIST
- ☐ 304. MARTY CLARY
- ☐ 329. ODDIBE MCDOWELL
- ☐ 358. ANDRES THOMAS
- ☐ 410. JOE BOEVER
- ☐ 451. MARK LEMKE
- ☐ 453. JODY DAVIS
- ☐ 486. JEFF TREADWAY
- ☐ 506. TOM GLAVINE
- ☐ 513. MARK EICHHORN
- ☐ 535. JOHN SMOLT
- ☐ 564. TYLER HOUSTON
- ☐ 567. RON GANT
- ☐ 583. BRUCE BENEDICT
- ☐ 617. GERONIMO BERROA
- ☐ 620. TONY CASTILLO
- ☐ 694. MIKE STANTON
- ☐ 744. KELLY MANN
- ☐ 750. DALE MURPHY
- ☐ 771. PETE SMITH
- ☐ 782. JOSE ALVAREZ
- ☐ 792. GERALD PERRY

BALTIMORE ORIOLES

- ☐ 13. MARK WILLIAMSON
- ☐ 73. BOB MILACKI
- ☐ 97. CURT SCHILLING
- ☐ 127. MIKE DEVEREAUX
- ☐ 153. RANDY MILLIGAN
- ☐ 163. PHIL BRADLEY
- ☐ 179. BRIAN HOLTON
- ☐ 212. JOE ORSULAK
- ☐ 249. MIKE SMITH
- ☐ 275. MICKEY TETTLETON
- ☐ 296. JEFF BALLARD
- ☐ 324. PETE HARNISCH
- ☐ 349. STEVE FINLEY
- ☐ 377. MICKEY WESTON
- ☐ 381. FRANK ROBINSON (M)
- ☐ 416. DAVE JOHNSON
- ☐ 468. BILLY RIPKEN
- ☐ 497. DAVE SCHMIDT
- ☐ 521. CRAIG WORTHINGTON
- ☐ 546. KEVIN HICKEY
- ☐ 570. CAL RIPKEN
- ☐ 598. BRADY ANDERSON
- ☐ 626. BOB MELVIN
- ☐ 655. GREGG OLSON
- ☐ 677. JAY TIBBS
- ☐ 708. LARRY SHEETS
- ☐ 724. JUAN BELL
- ☐ 758. MARK THURMOND
- ☐ 774. BEN MCDONALD
- ☐ 787. RENE GONZALES

BOSTON RED SOX

- ☐ 18. CARLOS QUINTANA
- ☐ 38. WES GARDNER
- ☐ 70. MIKE GREENWELL
- ☐ 96. JODY REED
- ☐ 123. RICH GEDMAN
- ☐ 155. ELLIS BURKS
- ☐ 188. MIKE SMITHSON
- ☐ 206. NICK ESASKY
- ☐ 245. ROGER CLEMENS
- ☐ 268. ROB MURPHY
- ☐ 303. RICK CERONE
- ☐ 321. JOE MORGAN (M)
- ☐ 338. DENNIS LAMP
- ☐ 355. MARTY BARRETT
- ☐ 375. DWIGHT EVANS
- ☐ 473. JOE PRICE
- ☐ 495. LEE SMITH
- ☐ 529. GREG HARRIS
- ☐ 544. DENNIS BOYD
- ☐ 573. DANNY HEEP
- ☐ 601. LUIS RIVERA
- ☐ 629. ERIC HETZEL
- ☐ 652. MIKE BODDICKER
- ☐ 676. RANDY KUTCHER
- ☐ 733. JOHN DOPSON
- ☐ 760. WADE BOGGS
- ☐ 785. JIM RICE

CALIFORNIA ANGELS

- ☐ 14. MIKE FETTERS
- ☐ 16. KENT ANDERSON
- ☐ 43. DANTE BICHETTE
- ☐ 51. DOUG RADER (M)
- ☐ 65. DEVON WHITE
- ☐ 99. RICH MONTELEONE
- ☐ 130. BERT BLYLEVEN
- ☐ 147. CHUCK FINLEY
- ☐ 189. DICK SCHOFIELD
- ☐ 215. KIRK MCCASKILL
- ☐ 244. BILL SCHROEDER
- ☐ 272. BRYAN HARVEY
- ☐ 334. JOHNNY RAY
- ☐ 363. DAN PETRY
- ☐ 421. GREG MINTON
- ☐ 444. KYLE ABBOTT
- ☐ 458. BOB MCCLURE
- ☐ 477. WILLIE FRASER
- ☐ 525. WALLY JOYNER
- ☐ 547. JACK HOWELL
- ☐ 575. LANCE PARRISH
- ☐ 603. TONY ARMAS
- ☐ 635. BRIAN DOWNING
- ☐ 650. MIKE WITT
- ☐ 675. JIM ABBOTT
- ☐ 705. CLAUDELL WASHINGTON
- ☐ 765. CHILI DAVIS

CHICAGO CUBS

- ☐ 12. JOE GIRARDI
- ☐ 37. DOMINGO RAMOS
- ☐ 67. SCOTT SANDERSON
- ☐ 86. PAUL KILGUS
- ☐ 114. MIKE BIELECKI
- ☐ 134. EARL CUNNINGHAM
- ☐ 140. ANDRE DAWSON
- ☐ 187. RICK WRONA
- ☐ 210. RYNE SANDBERG
- ☐ 240. MARK GRACE
- ☐ 256. MARVELL WYNNE
- ☐ 287. VANCE LAW
- ☐ 311. DWIGHT SMITH
- ☐ 337. LLOYD MCCLENDON
- ☐ 362. DAMON BERRYHILL
- ☐ 378. LUIS SALAZAR
- ☐ 415. SHAWON DUNSTON
- ☐ 437. LES LANCASTER
- ☐ 464. JEROME WALTON
- ☐ 502. MITCH WEBSTER
- ☐ 520. MITCH WILLIAMS
- ☐ 541. PAT PERRY
- ☐ 549. DON ZIMMER (M)
- ☐ 613. JEFF PICO
- ☐ 640. RICK SUTCLIFFE
- ☐ 644. PAUL ASSENMACHER
- ☐ 667. CURT WILKERSON
- ☐ 715. GREG MADDUX
- ☐ 741. STEVE WILSON
- ☐ 762. DOUG DASCENZO

CHICAGO WHITE SOX

- [ ] 21. JEFF TORBORG (M)
- [ ] 33. GREG WALKER
- [ ] 79. RON KITTLE
- [ ] 93. SHAWN HILLEGAS
- [ ] 121. ROBIN VENTURA
- [ ] 156. KEN PATTERSON
- [ ] 169. RICHARD DOTSON
- [ ] 219. DONN PALL
- [ ] 243. BARRY JONES
- [ ] 255. BOBBY THIGPEN
- [ ] 299. ADAM PETERSON
- [ ] 326. TOM MCCARTHY
- [ ] 365. OZZIE GUILLEN
- [ ] 379. STEVE ROSENBERG
- [ ] 414. FRANK THOMAS
- [ ] 420. CARLTON FISK
- [ ] 446. DAN PASQUA
- [ ] 461. CARLOS MARTINEZ
- [ ] 499. BILL LONG
- [ ] 524. DARYL BOSTON
- [ ] 565. SCOTT FLETCHER
- [ ] 569. IVAN CALDERON
- [ ] 587. LANCE JOHNSON
- [ ] 612. DAVE GALLAGHER
- [ ] 621. MELIDO PEREZ
- [ ] 692. SAMMY SOSA
- [ ] 717. RON KARKOVICE
- [ ] 751. STEVE LYONS
- [ ] 769. GREG HIBBARD
- [ ] 786. ERIC KING

CINCINNATI REDS

- [ ] 10. BARRY LARKIN
- [ ] 46. ROB DIBBLE
- [ ] 94. HERM WINNINGHAM
- [ ] 110. TOMMY HELMS (M)
- [ ] 120. JOHN FRANCO
- [ ] 151. RICK MAHLER
- [ ] 176. LUIS QUINONES
- [ ] 203. MIKE ROESLER
- [ ] 234. MARIANO DUNCAN
- [ ] 260. ERIC DAVIS
- [ ] 289. NORM CHARLTON
- [ ] 332. PAUL O'NEILL
- [ ] 364. ROLANDO ROOMES
- [ ] 418. TOM BROWNING
- [ ] 445. DANNY JACKSON
- [ ] 492. RON OESTER
- [ ] 516. TIM LEARY
- [ ] 553. SCOTT SCUDDER
- [ ] 581. KEN GRIFFEY
- [ ] 604. RON ROBINSON
- [ ] 627. JOSE RIJO
- [ ] 642. JACK ARMSTRONG
- [ ] 668. JOE OLIVER
- [ ] 687. TIM BIRTSAS
- [ ] 712. TODD BENZINGER
- [ ] 737. CHRIS SABO
- [ ] 772. JEFF REED

CLEVELAND INDIANS

- [ ] 32. JOHN FARRELL
- [ ] 54. JOEL SKINNER
- [ ] 75. DOUG JONES
- [ ] 108. ROD NICHOLS
- [ ] 141. JOHN HART (M)
- [ ] 144. BUD BLACK
- [ ] 172. TOM LAMPKIN
- [ ] 208. BROOK JACOBY
- [ ] 265. PETE O'BRIEN
- [ ] 283. JOEY BELLE
- [ ] 319. DION JAMES
- [ ] 339. DAVE CLARK
- [ ] 419. BEAU ALLRED
- [ ] 428. STEVE DAVIS
- [ ] 433. STEVE OLIN
- [ ] 442. JERRY BROWNE
- [ ] 476. BRAD KOMMINSK
- [ ] 514. ANDY ALLANSON
- [ ] 528. KEVIN WICKANDER
- [ ] 580. JOE CARTER
- [ ] 595. GREG SWINDELL
- [ ] 636. JESSE OROSCO
- [ ] 689. RICH YETT
- [ ] 722. FELIX FERMIN
- [ ] 743. TOM CANDIOTTI
- [ ] 770. CORY SNYDER
- [ ] 784. SCOTT BAILES

DETROIT TIGERS

- [ ] 11. PAUL GIBSON
- [ ] 42. JEFF ROBINSON
- [ ] 77. DAVE BERGMAN
- [ ] 107. FRED LYNN
- [ ] 131. MATT NOKES
- [ ] 146. ROB RICHIE
- [ ] 177. MIKE HENNEMAN
- [ ] 237. KEVIN RITZ
- [ ] 271. CHET LEMON
- [ ] 280. LOU WHITAKER
- [ ] 327. KEN WILLIAMS
- [ ] 343. FRANK TANANA
- [ ] 366. MIKE HEATH
- [ ] 413. BRIAN DUBOIS
- [ ] 440. ALAN TRAMMELL
- [ ] 471. MIKE BRUMLEY
- [ ] 487. STEVE SEARCY
- [ ] 498. RICK SCHU
- [ ] 512. GARY PETTIS
- [ ] 555. JACK MORRIS
- [ ] 586. ED NUNEZ
- [ ] 599. FRANK WILLIAMS
- [ ] 609. SPARKY ANDERSON (M)
- [ ] 632. SCOTT LUSADER
- [ ] 641. DOUG STRANGE
- [ ] 679. GARY WARD
- [ ] 748. DOYLE ALEXANDER
- [ ] 767. TRACY JONES

HOUSTON ASTROS

- [ ] 50. GLENN DAVIS
- [ ] 64. DANNY DARWIN
- [ ] 112. GLENN WILSON
- [ ] 157. CRAIG BIGGIO
- [ ] 164. JEFF JUDEN
- [ ] 181. JUAN AGOSTO
- [ ] 196. GERALD YOUNG
- [ ] 225. JIM DESHAIES
- [ ] 253. MARK PORTUGAL
- [ ] 267. MARK DAVIDSON
- [ ] 281. KEVIN BASS
- [ ] 309. ERIC YELDING
- [ ] 342. ALEX TREVINO
- [ ] 368. BILL DORAN
- [ ] 460. MIKE SCOTT
- [ ] 494. TERRY PUHL
- [ ] 531. KEN CAMINITI
- [ ] 534. LOUIE MEADOWS
- [ ] 558. RAFAEL RAMIREZ
- [ ] 579. ART HOWE (M)
- [ ] 588. RICK RHODEN
- [ ] 608. ERIC ANTHONY
- [ ] 637. CRAIG REYNOLDS
- [ ] 648. JIM CLANCY
- [ ] 746. DAVE SMITH
- [ ] 766. BRIAN MEYER

KANSAS CITY ROYALS

- [ ] 20. MARK GUBICZA
- [ ] 60. GEORGE BRETT
- [ ] 87. RICK LUECKEN
- [ ] 116. FLOYD BANNISTER
- [ ] 149. STEVE FARR
- [ ] 167. KEVIN APPIER
- [ ] 202. MIKE MACFARLANE
- [ ] 222. KURT STILLWELL
- [ ] 246. JIM EISENREICH
- [ ] 263. MEL STOTTLEMYRE, JR.
- [ ] 276. GARY THURMAN
- [ ] 300. BO JACKSON
- [ ] 323. WILLIE WILSON
- [ ] 350. BRET SABERHAGEN
- [ ] 435. KEVIN SEITZER
- [ ] 452. LUIS DE LOS SANTOS
- [ ] 479. FRANK WHITE
- [ ] 508. TERRY LEACH
- [ ] 540. DANNY TARTABULL
- [ ] 596. JOSE DEJESUS
- [ ] 638. JEFF MONTGOMERY
- [ ] 671. BOB BOONE
- [ ] 707. LUIS AQUINO
- [ ] 727. PAT TABLER
- [ ] 752. TOM GORDON
- [ ] 776. CHARLIE LEIBRANDT
- [ ] 789. JOHN WATHAN (M)

LOS ANGELES DODGERS

- [ ] 25. WILLIE RANDOLPH
- [ ] 40. JAY HOWELL
- [ ] 56. FRANKLIN STUBBS
- [ ] 62. RAMON MARTINEZ
- [ ] 84. RAY SEARAGE
- [ ] 98. JOSE GONZALEZ
- [ ] 117. MIKE SHARPERSON
- [ ] 150. KIRK GIBSON
- [ ] 173. TIM BELCHER
- [ ] 198. MIKE MARSHALL
- [ ] 226. MICKEY HATCHER
- [ ] 248. DAVE ANDERSON
- [ ] 277. LENNY HARRIS
- [ ] 305. EDDIE MURRAY
- [ ] 340. FERNANDO VALENZUELA
- [ ] 367. MIKE MORGAN
- [ ] 426. JEFF HAMILTON
- [ ] 456. CHRIS GWYNN
- [ ] 483. ALEJANDRO PENA
- [ ] 551. TIM CREWS
- [ ] 585. KAL DANIELS
- [ ] 605. MIKE SCIOSCIA
- [ ] 631. JOHN WETTELAND
- [ ] 643. ALFREDO GRIFFIN
- [ ] 669. TOM LASORDA (M)
- [ ] 697. MIKE DAVIS
- [ ] 736. RICK DEMPSEY
- [ ] 780. OREL HERSHISER

MILWAUKEE BREWERS

- [ ] 15. TEDDY HIGUERA
- [ ] 34. TONY FOSSAS
- [ ] 57. GREG VAUGHN
- [ ] 88. GLENN BRAGGS
- [ ] 106. CHARLIE O'BRIEN
- [ ] 139. GREG BROCK
- [ ] 159. MIKE FELDER
- [ ] 192. DON AUGUST
- [ ] 214. TERRY FRANCONA
- [ ] 264. BRYAN CLUTTERBUCK
- [ ] 290. ROBIN YOUNT
- [ ] 313. GUS POLIDOR
- [ ] 333. BILL WEGMAN
- [ ] 344. GEORGE CANALE
- [ ] 360. PAUL MOLITOR
- [ ] 417. JIM GANTNER
- [ ] 424. JERRY REUSS
- [ ] 467. JUAN NIEVES
- [ ] 490. DAN PLESAC
- [ ] 518. BILL KRUEGER
- [ ] 538. BILLY SPIERS
- [ ] 566. MARK KNUDSON
- [ ] 597. CHRIS BOSIO
- [ ] 615. ROB DEER
- [ ] 673. JOEY MEYER
- [ ] 696. B. J. SURHOFF
- [ ] 718. GARY SHEFFIELD
- [ ] 739. DALE SVEUM
- [ ] 759. TOM TREBELHORN (M)
- [ ] 768. CHUCK CRIM

MINNESOTA TWINS

- [ ] 19. AL NEWMAN
- [ ] 47. BRIAN HARPER
- [ ] 71. ALLAN ANDERSON
- [ ] 101. SHANE RAWLEY

☐ 125. KENT HRBEK
☐ 218. WALLY BACKMAN
☐ 227. KEVIN TAPANI
☐ 235. JEFF REARDON
☐ 266. GERMAN GONZALEZ
☐ 298. DANNY GLADDEN
☐ 317. MARK GUTHRIE
☐ 348. GARY WAYNE
☐ 357. DAVE WEST
☐ 427. CARMELO CASTILLO
☐ 429. TOM KELLY (M)
☐ 448. GREG GAGNE
☐ 503. RANDY ST. CLAIRE
☐ 556. GENE LARKIN
☐ 576. MIKE DYER
☐ 630. GARY GAETTI
☐ 653. JOHN MOSES
☐ 672. ROY SMITH
☐ 700. KIRBY PUCKETT
☐ 704. CHIP HALE
☐ 709. JUAN BERENGUER
☐ 711. RICK AGUILERA
☐ 713. TIM DRUMMOND
☐ 747. RANDY BUSH
☐ 777. TIM LAUDNER

MONTREAL EXPOS

☐ 24. JOE HESKETH
☐ 48. ZANE SMITH
☐ 72. JEFF HUSON
☐ 81. BOB RODGERS (M)
☐ 91. STEVE FREY
☐ 137. MARTY PEVEY
☐ 180. TIM RAINES
☐ 195. TIM BURKE
☐ 224. DELINO DESHIELDS
☐ 228. DAVE MARTINEZ
☐ 252. OTIS NIXON
☐ 278. PASCUAL PEREZ
☐ 284. MARK GARDNER
☐ 318. WALLACE JOHNSON
☐ 341. TOM FOLEY
☐ 352. BRYN SMITH
☐ 370. TIM WALLACH
☐ 432. DAMASO GARCIA
☐ 465. KEVIN GROSS
☐ 474. RICH THOMPSON
☐ 484. MIKE FITZGERALD
☐ 485. JOHN CANDELARIA
☐ 530. MARK LANGSTON
☐ 559. ANDY MCGAFFIGAN
☐ 589. MIKE ALDRETE
☐ 614. NELSON SANTOVENIA
☐ 647. REX HUDLER
☐ 674. SPIKE OWEN
☐ 714. MARQUIS GRISSOM
☐ 720. ANDRES GALARRAGA
☐ 745. HUBIE BROOKS
☐ 757. LARRY WALKER
☐ 763. DENNY MARTINEZ

NEW YORK METS

☐ 30. DAVID CONE
☐ 58. KEITH MILLER
☐ 85. JUAN SAMUEL
☐ 105. RANDY MYERS
☐ 135. DAVE MAGADAN
☐ 207. BOB OJEDA
☐ 230. KEITH HERNANDEZ
☐ 258. BARRY LYONS
☐ 291. DAVE JOHNSON (M)
☐ 301. DON AASE
☐ 330. RON DARLING
☐ 382. JEFF MUSSELMAN
☐ 434. MARK CARREON
☐ 457. GREGG JEFFERIES
☐ 470. FRANK VIOLA
☐ 480. SID FERNANDEZ
☐ 504. TOM O'MALLEY
☐ 510. DWIGHT GOODEN
☐ 545. KEVIN MCREYNOLDS
☐ 557. JEFF INNIS
☐ 600. DARRYL STRAWBERRY
☐ 656. MACKEY SASSER
☐ 680. HOWARD JOHNSON
☐ 684. JULIO MACHADO
☐ 719. WALLY WHITEHURST
☐ 734. KEVIN ELSTER
☐ 764. TIM TEUFEL
☐ 790. GARY CARTER

NEW YORK YANKEES

☐ 9. ERIC PLUNK
☐ 23. RANDY VELARDE
☐ 26. DON SLAUGHT
☐ 61. DEION SANDERS
☐ 83. HENSLEY MEULENS
☐ 109. ROBERTO KELLY
☐ 160. DAVE RIGHETTI
☐ 186. DAVE LAPOINT
☐ 200. DON MATTINGLY
☐ 236. HAL MORRIS
☐ 259. LANCE MCCULLERS
☐ 286. LEE GUETTERMAN
☐ 302. MARCUS LAWTON
☐ 335. ANDY HAWKINS
☐ 359. JIMMY JONES
☐ 380. DAVE WINFIELD
☐ 436. MEL HALL
☐ 511. CLAY PARKER
☐ 519. BUCKY DENT (M)
☐ 536. BOB GEREN
☐ 560. STEVE SAX
☐ 611. WALT TERRELL
☐ 634. LUIS POLONIA
☐ 651. RAFAEL SANTANA
☐ 659. GREG CADARET
☐ 691. CHUCK CARY
☐ 701. BERNIE WILLIAMS
☐ 716. STEVE BALBONI
☐ 740. JESSE BARFIELD
☐ 791. ALVARO ESPINOZA

OAKLAND A'S

☐ 45. DAVE PARKER
☐ 68. DAVE HENDERSON
☐ 102. STAN JAVIER
☐ 132. LANCE BLANKENSHIP
☐ 145. TERRY STEINBACH
☐ 165. WALT WEISS
☐ 175. MIKE MOORE
☐ 238. FELIX JOSE
☐ 250. JOSE CANSECO
☐ 270. DAVE STEWART
☐ 293. MIKE GALLEGO
☐ 316. CARNEY LANSFORD
☐ 328. CURT YOUNG
☐ 369. TODD BURNS
☐ 411. KEN PHELPS
☐ 450. RICKEY HENDERSON
☐ 475. BOB WELCH
☐ 501. MATT YOUNG
☐ 527. RON HASSEY
☐ 582. RICK HONEYCUTT
☐ 606. STORM DAVIS
☐ 623. JIM CORSI
☐ 639. TONY LARUSSA (M)
☐ 670. DENNIS ECKERSLEY
☐ 690. MARK MCGWIRE
☐ 702. TONY PHILLIPS
☐ 726. GENE NELSON

PHILADELPHIA PHILLIES

☐ 22. BRUCE RUFFIN
☐ 39. CURT FORD
☐ 69. TODD FROHWIRTH
☐ 74. JEFF JACKSON
☐ 103. MARVIN FREEMAN
☐ 129. RON JONES
☐ 154. MIKE MADDUX
☐ 183. STEVE LAKE
☐ 204. BOB DERNIER
☐ 216. RICKY JORDAN
☐ 269. DICKIE THON
☐ 297. TOM HERR
☐ 356. RANDY READY
☐ 384. PAT COMBS
☐ 439. JEFF PARRETT
☐ 469. JOHN KRUK
☐ 489. NICK LEYVA (M)
☐ 493. JASON GRIMSLEY
☐ 515. LEN DYKSTRA
☐ 542. DARREN DAULTON
☐ 577. CHARLIE HAYES
☐ 607. STEVE JELTZ
☐ 625. ROGER MCDOWELL
☐ 633. DENNIS COOK
☐ 657. TERRY MULHOLLAND
☐ 710. VAN HAYES

☐ 731. DON CARMAN
☐ 756. KEN HOWELL

PITTSBURGH PIRATES

☐ 29. JOHN CANGELOSI
☐ 119. BILLY HATCHER
☐ 126. RANDY KRAMER
☐ 143. RAFAEL BELLIARD
☐ 168. JOSE LIND
☐ 197. DOUG DRABEK
☐ 220. BARRY BONDS
☐ 273. BOBBY BONILLA
☐ 292. JIM GOTT
☐ 322. JUNIOR ORTIZ
☐ 354. STAN BELINDA
☐ 425. BILL LANDRUM
☐ 441. BOB KIPPER
☐ 454. JEFF KING
☐ 478. MIKE LAVALLIERE
☐ 482. STEVE CARTER
☐ 507. GARY REDUS
☐ 523. JAY BELL
☐ 539. NEAL HEATON
☐ 552. MIKE SMITH
☐ 568. JOHN SMILEY
☐ 592. R. J. REYNOLDS
☐ 622. SID BREAM
☐ 666. BRIAN FISHER
☐ 682. DANN BILARDELLO
☐ 699. JIM LEYLAND (M)
☐ 723. JEFF ROBINSON
☐ 754. BOB WALK
☐ 775. ANDY VAN SLYKE

ST. LOUIS CARDINALS

☐ 36. JOHN COSTELLO
☐ 59. TED POWER
☐ 82. SCOTT TERRY
☐ 95. TODD WORRELL
☐ 115. TONY PENA
☐ 133. RICKY HORTON
☐ 162. TODD ZEILE
☐ 184. DANNY COX
☐ 209. GREG MATHEWS
☐ 233. KEN HILL
☐ 257. JOSE DELEON
☐ 261. WHITEY HERZOG (M)
☐ 285. WILLIE MCGEE
☐ 312. DAN QUISENBERRY
☐ 383. JOHN MORRIS
☐ 409. TOM BRUNANSKY
☐ 443. CRIS CARPENTER
☐ 462. DENNY WALLING
☐ 509. TOM PAGNOZZI
☐ 533. TIM JONES
☐ 561. KEN DAYLEY
☐ 578. JOE MAGRANE
☐ 590. OZZIE SMITH
☐ 610. PEDRO GUERRERO
☐ 645. JOSE OQUENDO
☐ 654. PAUL COLEMAN
☐ 660. VINCE COLEMAN
☐ 688. MILT THOMPSON
☐ 725. TERRY PENDLETON
☐ 788. FRANK DIPINO

1990 Topps

SAN DIEGO PADRES

- ☐ 35. BENNY SANTIAGO
- ☐ 63. MIKE PAGLIARULO
- ☐ 90. JACK CLARK
- ☐ 122. SHAWN ABNER
- ☐ 178. CHRIS JAMES
- ☐ 193. ANDY BENES
- ☐ 205. MARK DAVIS
- ☐ 231. JACK MCKEON (M)
- ☐ 239. ERIC SHOW
- ☐ 307. BIP ROBERTS
- ☐ 315. BRUCE HURST
- ☐ 353. SANDY ALOMAR
- ☐ 423. FRED TOLIVER
- ☐ 449. DENNIS RASMUSSEN
- ☐ 481. GARRY TEMPLETON
- ☐ 517. ROBERTO ALOMAR
- ☐ 537. MARK GRANT
- ☐ 548. PAT CLEMENTS
- ☐ 572. GREG HARRIS
- ☐ 584. PHIL STEPHENSON
- ☐ 618. EDDIE WHITSON
- ☐ 624. DARRIN JACKSON
- ☐ 649. DAN MURPHY
- ☐ 686. CARMELO MARTINEZ
- ☐ 693. CALVIN SCHIRALDI
- ☐ 730. TONY GWYNN
- ☐ 749. MARK PARENT
- ☐ 773. DAVE LEIPER

SAN FRANCISCO GIANTS

- ☐ 17. KELLY DOWNS
- ☐ 41. MATT WILLIAMS
- ☐ 53. MIKE LACOSS
- ☐ 66. GREG LITTON
- ☐ 100. WILL CLARK
- ☐ 104. BOB KNEPPER
- ☐ 124. DAVE DRAVECKY
- ☐ 158. CRAIG LEFFERTS
- ☐ 190. RICK REUSCHEL
- ☐ 217. DON ROBINSON
- ☐ 241. MIKE KRUKOW
- ☐ 310. STEVE BEDROSIAN
- ☐ 325. ROBBY THOMPSON
- ☐ 351. ROGER CRAIG (M)
- ☐ 361. RANDY MCCAMENT
- ☐ 372. TERRY KENNEDY
- ☐ 408. TREVOR WILSON
- ☐ 422. PAT SHERIDAN
- ☐ 447. ATLEE HAMMAKER
- ☐ 472. JOSE URIBE
- ☐ 488. KEN OBERKFELL
- ☐ 500. KEVIN MITCHELL
- ☐ 571. BRETT BUTLER
- ☐ 602. SCOTT GARRELTS
- ☐ 628. CANDY MALDONADO
- ☐ 658. DONELL NIXON
- ☐ 678. KIRT MANWARING
- ☐ 703. JEFF BRANTLEY
- ☐ 732. ERNIE RILES
- ☐ 753. CHRIS SPEIER

SEATTLE MARINERS

- ☐ 31. HENRY COTTO
- ☐ 44. ROGER SALKELD
- ☐ 76. DAVE VALLE
- ☐ 89. CLINT ZAVARAS
- ☐ 118. ERIK HANSON
- ☐ 148. EDGAR MARTINEZ
- ☐ 161. HAROLD REYNOLDS
- ☐ 213. SCOTT BANKHEAD
- ☐ 232. DARNELL COLES
- ☐ 247. JERRY REED
- ☐ 288. GREG BRILEY
- ☐ 306. TOM NIEDENFUER
- ☐ 336. KEN GRIFFEY, JR.
- ☐ 346. JIM PRESLEY
- ☐ 373. ALVIN DAVIS
- ☐ 431. RANDY JOHNSON
- ☐ 455. JEFFREY LEONARD
- ☐ 459. JIM LEFEBVRE (M)
- ☐ 491. DAVE COCHRANE
- ☐ 522. MIKE DUNNE
- ☐ 554. JAY BUHNER
- ☐ 574. BILL SWIFT
- ☐ 593. SCOTT BRADLEY
- ☐ 616. BRIAN HOLMAN
- ☐ 681. MIKE SCHOOLER
- ☐ 698. OMAR VIZQUEL

- ☐ 738. GENE HARRIS
- ☐ 761. MIKE JACKSON
- ☐ 781. MARIO DIAZ

TEXAS RANGERS

- ☐ 1. NOLAN RYAN
- ☐ 27. RICK LEACH
- ☐ 52. JACK DAUGHERTY
- ☐ 80. JEFF RUSSELL
- ☐ 92. MIKE STANLEY
- ☐ 136. KEVIN BROWN
- ☐ 166. BOBBY WITT
- ☐ 174. JEFF JUNKEL
- ☐ 185. RUBEN SIERRA
- ☐ 221. GARY MIELKE
- ☐ 242. FRED MANRIQUE
- ☐ 279. STEVE BUECHELE
- ☐ 294. CRAIG MCMURTRY
- ☐ 308. JOSE GUZMAN
- ☐ 314. DONALD HARRIS
- ☐ 331. JUAN GONZALEZ
- ☐ 345. HAROLD BAINES
- ☐ 412. JAMIE MOYER
- ☐ 430. PETE INCAVIGLIA
- ☐ 463. DREW HALL
- ☐ 496. CECIL ESPY
- ☐ 532. CECILIO GUANTE
- ☐ 550. JULIO FRANCO
- ☐ 562. CHAD KREUTER
- ☐ 683. KENNY ROGERS
- ☐ 706. GENO PETRALLI
- ☐ 729. BOBBY VALENTINE (M)
- ☐ 735. CHARLIE HOUGH
- ☐ 755. RAFAEL PALMEIRO
- ☐ 778. MIKE JEFFCOAT

TORONTO BLUE JAYS

- ☐ 28. DUANE WARD
- ☐ 49. TOM LAWLESS
- ☐ 78. MIKE FLANAGAN
- ☐ 113. MANNY LEE
- ☐ 138. AL LEITER
- ☐ 170. GEORGE BELL
- ☐ 182. MOOKIE WILSON
- ☐ 191. PAT BORDERS
- ☐ 194. GLENALLEN HILL
- ☐ 201. CITO GASTON (M)
- ☐ 211. JOHN CERUTTI
- ☐ 229. DAVID WELLS
- ☐ 274. GOOSE GOZZO
- ☐ 295. FRED MCGRIFF
- ☐ 320. DAVE STIEB
- ☐ 347. JUNIOR FELIX
- ☐ 371. JIMMY KEY
- ☐ 374. STEVE CUMMINGS
- ☐ 438. GREG MYERS
- ☐ 466. RANCE MULLINIKS
- ☐ 505. KELLY GRUBER
- ☐ 543. NELSON LIRIANO
- ☐ 563. ALEX SANCHEZ
- ☐ 591. TODD STOTTLEMYRE
- ☐ 594. LUIS SOJO
- ☐ 619. ROB DUCEY
- ☐ 685. TONY FERNANDEZ
- ☐ 695. TOM HENKE
- ☐ 721. LEE MAZZILLI
- ☐ 728. JIM ACKER
- ☐ 742. ERNIE WHITT
- ☐ 779. LLOYD MOSEBY

T205 (208)
1 1/2" X 2 5/8"

BOSTON RED SOX

- WILLIAM CARRIGAN
- EDWARD V. CICOTTE
- CLYDE ENGLE
- EDWARD KARGER
- JOHN KLEINOW
- TRIS SPEAKER
- JACOB G. STAHL
- CHARLES WAGNER

BOSTON RUSTLERS

- EDW'D J. ABBATICCHIO
- FREDERICK T. BECK
- G.C. FERGUSON
- WILBUR GOOD
- GEORGE F. GRAHAM
- CHARLES L. HERZOG
- A.A. MATTERN
- BAYARD H. SHARPE
- DAVID SHEAN (BOSTON)

BROOKLYN SUPERBAS

- EDWARD B. BARGER
  (FULL B)
- EDWARD B. BARGER
  (PART B)
- GEORGE G. BELL
- WILLIAM BERGEN
- WILLIAM DAHLEN
- JACOB DAUBERT
- JOHN E. HUMMEL
- EDGAR LENNOX
- PRYOR MCELVEEN
- G.N. RUCKER
- W.D. SCANLAN
- TONY SMITH
- ZACH D. WHEAT
- IRVIN K. WILHELM

CHICAGO CUBS

- JAMES P. ARCHER
- MORDECAI BROWN
- FRANK L. CHANCE
- JOHN J. EVERS
- WILLIAM A. FOXEN
- GEORGE F. GRAHAM
- JOHN KLING
- FLOYD M. KROH
- HARRY MCINTIRE
- THOMAS J. NEEDHAM
- ORVAL OVERALL
- JOHN A. PFIESTER
- EDWARD M. REULBACH
- LEWIS RICHIE
- FRANK M. SCHULTE
- DAVID SHEAN (CUBS)
- JAMES T. SHECKARD
- HARRY STEINFELDT
- JOSEPH B. TINKER

CHICAGO WHITE SOX

- RUSSEL BLACKBURNE
- J. DONOHUE
- PAT'K H. DOUGHERTY
  (WHITE STOCKING)

- PAT'K H. DOUGHERTY
  (RED STOCKING)
- HUGH DUFFY
- FRANK LANG
- HARRY D. LORD
- AMBROSE MCCONNELL
- MATTHEW MCINTYRE
- FREDERICK OLMSTEAD
- F. PARENT
- FRED PAYNE
- JAMES SCOTT
- LEE FORD TANNEHILL
- EDWARD WALSH
- G.H. WHITE

CINCINNATI REDS

- ROBERT H. BESCHER
- THOMAS W. DOWNEY
- RICHARD J. EGAN
- ARTHUR FROMME
- HARRY L. GASPAR
- EDWARD L. GRANT
- CLARK GRIFFITH
- RICHARD HOBLITZELL
- JOHN B. MCLEAN
- MICHAEL MITCHELL
- GEORGE SUGGS

CLEVELAND NAPS

- NEAL BALL
- JOSEPH BIRMINGHAM
- A. JOSS
- GEORGE T. STOVALL
- TERENCE TURNER
- DENTON T. YOUNG

DETROIT TIGERS

- TYRUS RAYMOND COBB
- JAMES DELAHANTY
- HUGH JENNINGS
- DAVID JONES
- THOMAS JONES
- EDWARD KILLIAN
- GEORGE MORIARITY
- GEORGE J. MULLIN
- CHARLES O'LEARY
- CHARLES SCHMIDT
- GEORGE SIMMONS
- OSCAR STANAGE
- EDGAR SUMMERS
- EDGAR WILLETT

NEW YORK GIANTS

- LEON AMES
- BEALS BECKER
- ALBERT BRIDWELL
- OTIS CRANDALL
- ARTHUR DEVLIN
- JOSHUA DEVORE
- W.R. DICKSON
- LAWRENCE DOYLE
- ARTHUR FLETCHER
- W.A. LATHAM
- RICHARD MARQUARD
- CHRISTY MATHEWSON
- JOHN J. MCGRAW
- FRED MERKLE
- JOHN T. MEYERS
- JOHN J. MURRAY
- ARTHUR L. RAYMOND
- GEOREG H. SCHLEI

- FRED C. SNODGRASS
- GEORGE WILTSE
  (BOTH EARS)
- GEORGE WILTSE
  (RIGHT EAR ONLY)

NEW YORK YANKEES

- JAMES AUSTIN
- HAROLD W. CHASE
  (CHASE ONLY)
- HAROLD W. CHASE
  (HAL CHASE)
- LOUIS CRIGER
- RAY FISHER
- RUSSELL FORD
  (DARK CAP)
- RUSSELL FORD
  (LIGHT CAP)
- EARL GARDNER
- CHARLES HEMPHILL
- JACK KNIGHT
- JOHN QUINN
- EDWARD SWEENEY
- JAMES VAUGHN
- HARRY WOLTER

PHILADELPHIA ATHLETICS

- FRANK BAKER
- JOHN J. BARRY
- CHARLES A. BENDER
- EDWARD T. COLLINS
  (MOUTH CLOSED)
- EDWARD T. COLLINS
  (MOUTH OPEN)
- JAMES H. DYGERT
- FREDERICK T. HARTSEL
- HARRY KRAUSE
- PAT'K J. LIVINGSTON
- BRISCOE LORD
- DANIEL MURPHY
- RUEBEN N. OLDRING
- IRA THOMAS

PHILADELPHIA PHILLIES

- JOHN W. BATES
- WM. E. BRANSFIELD
- CHARLES S. DOOIN
- MICHAEL DOOLAN
- ROBERT EWING
- FRED JACKLITSCH
- JOHN LOBERT
- SHERWOOD R. MAGEE
- PATRICK J. MORAN
- GEORGE PASKERT
- JOHN A. ROWAN
- JOHN TITUS

PITTSBURGH PIRATES

- ROBERT BYRNE
- HOWARD CAMNITZ
- FRED CLARKE
- JOHN FLYNN
- GEORGE GIBSON
- THOMAS W. LEACH
- SAM LEEVER
- ALBERT P. LEIFIELD
- NICHOLAS MADDOX
- JOHN D. MILLER
- CHARLES PHILLIPPE
- KIRB WHITE
- J. OWEN WILSON

ST. LOUIS BROWNS

- WILLIAM BAILEY
- DANIEL J. HOFFMAN
- FRANK LAPORTE
- B. PELTY
- GEORGE STONE
- RODERICK J. WALLACE
  (WITH CAP)
- RODERICK J. WALLACE
  (WITHOUT CAP)

ST. LOUIS CARDINALS

- ☐ ROGER BRESNAHAN (MOUTH CLOSED)
- ☐ ROGER BRESNAHAN (MOUTH OPEN)
- ☐ FRANK J. CORRIDON
- ☐ LOUIS EVANS
- ☐ ROBERT HARMON (BOTH EARS)
- ☐ ROBERT HARMON (LEFT EAR ONLY)
- ☐ ARNOLD J. HAUSER
- ☐ MILLER HUGGINS
- ☐ EDWARD KONETCHY
- ☐ JOHN LUSH
- ☐ "REBEL" OAKES
- ☐ EDWARD PHELPS

WASHINGTON SENATORS

- ☐ NORMAN ELBERFELD
- ☐ GRAY
- ☐ ROBERT GROOM
- ☐ WALTER JOHNSON
- ☐ GEORGE F. MCBRIDE
- ☐ J. CLYDE MILAN
- ☐ HERMAN SCHAEFER
- ☐ CHARLES E. STREET

BALTIMORE

- ☐ DR. MERLE T. ADKINS
- ☐ JOHN DUNN

BUFFALO

- ☐ GEORGE MERRITT

JERSEY CITY

- ☐ CHARLES HANFORD

NEWARK

- ☐ FORREST D. CADY
- ☐ JAMES FRICK
- ☐ WYATT LEE
- ☐ LEWIS MCALLISTER
- ☐ JOHN NEE

PROVIDENCE

- ☐ JAMES COLLINS
- ☐ JAMES PHELAN

ROCHESTER

- ☐ HENRY BATCH

T206 (523)
1 1/2" X 2 5/8"

BOSTON RED SOX

- ☐ ARRELANES
- ☐ CARRIGAN
- ☐ CICOTTE
- ☐ KLEINOW
- ☐ LORD
- ☐ NILES
- ☐ SPEAKER
- ☐ SPENCER
- ☐ STAHL (PORTRAIT)
- ☐ STAHL (FIELDING)
- ☐ WAGNER (BATTING/WAIST)
- ☐ WAGNER (BATTING/HIPS)

BOSTON RUSTLERS

- ☐ BATES
- ☐ BEAUMONT
- ☐ BECK
- ☐ BECKER
- ☐ BOWERMAN
- ☐ DAHLEN
- ☐ FERGUSON
- ☐ GRAHAM
- ☐ HERZOG
- ☐ LINDAMAN
- ☐ MATTERN
- ☐ RITCHEY
- ☐ STARR
- ☐ SWEENEY

BROOKLYN SUPERBAS

- ☐ ALPERMAN
- ☐ BELL (PITCHING/HIPS)
- ☐ BELL (PITCHING/WAIST)
- ☐ BERGEN (BATTING)
- ☐ BERGEN (CATCHING)
- ☐ BURCH (BATTING)
- ☐ BURCH (FIELDING)
- ☐ DAHLEN
- ☐ DUNN
- ☐ HUMMEL
- ☐ HUNTER
- ☐ JORDAN (PORTRAIT)
- ☐ JORDAN (BATTING)
- ☐ LENNOX
- ☐ LUMLEY
- ☐ MARSHALL
- ☐ MCELVEEN
- ☐ MCINTYRE
- ☐ MCINTRYE (BROOKLYN & CHICAGO)
- ☐ PASTORIUS
- ☐ PATTEE
- ☐ RUCKER (PORTRAIT)
- ☐ RUCKER (PITCHING)
- ☐ H. SMITH
- ☐ WHEAT
- ☐ WILHELM (BATTING)
- ☐ WILHELM (PORTRAIT)

CHICAGO CUBS

- ☐ G. BROWN
- ☐ M. BROWN (PORTRAIT)
- ☐ M. BROWN (BLACK COLLAR)
- ☐ M. BROWN (BLUE COLLAR)
- ☐ CHANCE (BATTING)

- ☐ CHANCE (PORTRAIT/RED)
- ☐ CHANCE (PORTRAIT/YELLOW)
- ☐ EVERS (PORTRAIT)
- ☐ EVERS (BATTING/BLUE BACKGROUND)
- ☐ EVERS (BATTING/YELLOW BACKGROUND)
- ☐ HOFMAN
- ☐ HOWARD
- ☐ KLING
- ☐ KROH
- ☐ LUNDGREN
- ☐ MORAN
- ☐ NEEDHAM
- ☐ OVERALL (PORTRAIT)
- ☐ OVERALL (PITCHING/ARMS SIDE)
- ☐ OVERALL (PITCHING/ARMS UP)
- ☐ PFEFFER
- ☐ PFEISTER (PORTRAIT)
- ☐ PFEISTER (PITCHING)
- ☐ REULBACH (PORTRAIT)
- ☐ REULBACH (PITCHING)
- ☐ SCHULTE (BATTING/FRONT)
- ☐ SCHULTE (BATTING/BACK)
- ☐ SHECKARD (THROWING)
- ☐ SHECKARD (PORTRAIT)
- ☐ STEINFELDT (PORTRAIT)
- ☐ STEINFELDT (BATTING)
- ☐ TINKER (PORTRAIT)
- ☐ TINKER (HANDS ON KNEES)
- ☐ TINKER (BAT ON SHOULDER)
- ☐ TINKER (BAT OFF SHOULDER)
- ☐ ZIMMERMAN

CHICAGO WHITE SOX

- ☐ ATZ
- ☐ BURNS
- ☐ G. DAVIS
- ☐ DONOHUE
- ☐ DOUGHERTY (PORTRAIT)
- ☐ DOUGHERTY (FIELDING)
- ☐ DUFFY
- ☐ FIENE (PORTRAIT)
- ☐ FIENE (FIELDING)
- ☐ GANDIL
- ☐ HAHN
- ☐ ISBELL
- ☐ F. JONES (PORTRAIT/HIPS)
- ☐ F. JONES (PORTRAIT)
- ☐ OWEN
- ☐ PARENT
- ☐ PAYNE
- ☐ PURTELL
- ☐ SCOTT
- ☐ F. SMITH
- ☐ SMITH
- ☐ SMITH (CHICAGO & BOSTON)
- ☐ SULLIVAN
- ☐ L. TANNEHILL
- ☐ TANNEHILL
- ☐ WALSH
- ☐ WHITE (PORTRAIT)
- ☐ WHITE (PITCHING/WAIST)

CINCINNATI REDS

- ☐ BESCHER (PORTRAIT)
- ☐ BESCHER (FIELDING)
- ☐ CAMPBELL
- ☐ DOWNEY (BATTING)
- ☐ DOWNEY (FIELDING)
- ☐ DUBUC
- ☐ EGAN
- ☐ EWING
- ☐ FROMME
- ☐ GASPAR
- ☐ GRIFFITH (PORTRAIT)
- ☐ GRIFFITH (BATTING)
- ☐ HOBLITZELL
- ☐ HUGGINS (PORTRAIT)
- ☐ HUGGINS (PORTRAIT/HITTING)
- ☐ KARGER
- ☐ LOBERT
- ☐ MCLEAN
- ☐ MITCHELL
- ☐ MOWREY
- ☐ OAKES
- ☐ PASKERT
- ☐ SPADE

CLEVELAND NAPS

- ☐ BALL
- ☐ BERGER
- ☐ BIRMINGHAM
- ☐ BRADLEY (PORTRAIT)
- ☐ BRADLEY (BATTING)
- ☐ J. J. CLARKE
- ☐ EASTERLY
- ☐ FLICK
- ☐ GOODE
- ☐ HINCHMAN
- ☐ JOSS (PORTRAIT)
- ☐ JOSS (PITCHING)
- ☐ LAJOIE (PORTRAIT)
- ☐ LAJOIE (BATTING)
- ☐ LAJOIE (THROWING)
- ☐ LIEBHARDT
- ☐ PERRING
- ☐ RHOADES (PITCHING/WAIST)
- ☐ RHOADES (PITCHING/HIPS)
- ☐ STOVALL (PORTRAIT)
- ☐ STOVALL (BATTING)
- ☐ TURNER
- ☐ YOUNG (PORTRAIT)
- ☐ YOUNG (PITCHING/SIDE)
- ☐ YOUNG (PITCHING/FRONT)

DETROIT TIGERS

- ☐ BUSH
- ☐ COBB (PORTRAIT/RED)
- ☐ COBB (PORTRAIT/GREEN)
- ☐ COBB (BATTING/BLACK CAP)
- ☐ COBB (BATTING/GRAY CAP)
- ☐ CRAWFORD (BATTING)
- ☐ CRAWFORD (THROWING)
- ☐ DONOVAN (PORTRAIT)
- ☐ DONOVAN (PITCHING)
- ☐ JENNINGS (PORTRAIT)
- ☐ JENNINGS (PORTRAIT/WAIST)
- ☐ JENNINGS (PORTRAIT/HIPS)
- ☐ JONES
- ☐ KILLIAN (PORTRAIT)
- ☐ KILLIAN (PITCHING)
- ☐ MCINTYRE
- ☐ MORIARTY
- ☐ MULLEN
- ☐ MULLIN (BATTING)
- ☐ MULLIN (FIELDING/ HORIZONTAL)
- ☐ O'LEARY (PORTRAIT)
- ☐ O'LEARY (HANDS ON KNEES)
- ☐ ROSSMAN
- ☐ SCHAEFER
- ☐ SCHMIDT (PORTRAIT)
- ☐ SCHMIDT (THROWING)
- ☐ STANAGE
- ☐ SUMMERS
- ☐ WILLETT
- ☐ WILLETTS

NEW YORK GIANTS

- ☐ AMES (PORTRAIT)
- ☐ AMES (PITCHING/WAIST)
- ☐ AMES (PITCHING/HIPS)
- ☐ BRIDWELL (PORTRAIT)
- ☐ BRIDWELL (PORTRAIT/ SWEATER)
- ☐ CRANDALL(PORTRAIT)
- ☐ CRANDALL (PORTRAIT/ SWEATER)
- ☐ DEVLIN
- ☐ DEVORE
- ☐ DONLIN (PORTRAIT/KNEES)
- ☐ DONLIN (PORTRAIT/HANDS ON KNEES)
- ☐ DONLIN (BATTING)
- ☐ DOYLE (PORTRAIT/SWEATER)
- ☐ DOYLE (BATTING)
- ☐ DOYLE (THROWING)
- ☐ DURHAM
- ☐ FLETCHER
- ☐ HERZOG
- ☐ LATHAM
- ☐ MARQUARD (PORTRAIT)
- ☐ MARQUARD (PORTRAIT/HIPS)
- ☐ MARQUARD (PITCHING)
- ☐ MATHEWSON (PORTRAIT)

- ☐ MATHEWSON (PITCHING/WHITE CAP)
- ☐ MATHEWSON (PITCHING/BLACK CAP)
- ☐ MCCORMICK
- ☐ MCGRAW (PORTRAIT)
- ☐ MCGRAW (PORTRAIT/SWEATER)
- ☐ MCGRAW (PORTRAIT/HIPS)
- ☐ MCGRAW (PORTRAIT/KNEES)
- ☐ MERKLE (PORTRAIT)
- ☐ MERKLE (THROWING)
- ☐ MEYERS
- ☐ MURRAY (PORTRAIT)
- ☐ MURRAY (BATTING)
- ☐ MYERS (CATCHING)
- ☐ MYERS (BATTING)
- ☐ O'HARA
- ☐ RAYMOND
- ☐ SCHLEI (PORTRAIT/SWEATER)
- ☐ SCHLEI (BATTING)
- ☐ SCHLEI (CATCHING)
- ☐ SEYMOUR (PORTRAIT)
- ☐ SEYMOUR (BATTING)
- ☐ SEYMOUR (THROWING)
- ☐ SNODGRASS (BATTING)
- ☐ SNODGRASS (CATCHING)
- ☐ TENNEY
- ☐ WEIMER
- ☐ WILTSE (PORTRAIT)
- ☐ WILTSE (PORTRAIT/SWEATER)
- ☐ WILTSE (PITCHING)

NEW YORK YANKEES

- ☐ BALL
- ☐ CHASE (WITH CUP)
- ☐ CHASE (PORTRAIT/PINK)
- ☐ CHASE (PORTRAIT/BLUE)
- ☐ CHASE (THROWING/BLACK CAP)
- ☐ CHASE (THROWING/WHITE CAP)
- ☐ CHESBRO
- ☐ CREE
- ☐ DEMMITT
- ☐ DOYLE
- ☐ ELBERFELD
- ☐ ENGLE
- ☐ FORD
- ☐ FRILL
- ☐ HEMPHILL
- ☐ KEELER (PORTRAIT)
- ☐ KEELER (BATTING)
- ☐ KLEINOW (CATCHING)
- ☐ KLEINOW (BATTING)
- ☐ KNIGHT (PORTRAIT)
- ☐ KNIGHT (BATTING)
- ☐ LAKE
- ☐ LAPORTE
- ☐ MANNING (BATTING)
- ☐ MANNING (PITCHING)
- ☐ QUINN
- ☐ SWEENEY
- ☐ WARHOP

PHILADELPHIA ATHLETICS

- ☐ BAKER
- ☐ BARRY
- ☐ BENDER (PORTRAIT)
- ☐ BENDER (PITCHING/WITH TREES)
- ☐ BENDER (PITCHING/NO TREES)
- ☐ COLLINS
- ☐ DAVIS
- ☐ H. DAVIS
- ☐ DYGERT
- ☐ HARTSELL
- ☐ KRAUSE (PORTRAIT)
- ☐ KRAUSE (PITCHING)
- ☐ LIVINGSTONE
- ☐ MURPHY (BATTING)
- ☐ MURPHY (THROWING)
- ☐ NICHOLLS
- ☐ NICHOLS
- ☐ OLDRING (BATTING)
- ☐ OLDRING (FIELDING)
- ☐ PLANK
- ☐ POWERS
- ☐ THOMAS

PHILADELPHIA PHILLIES

- ☐ BRANSFIELD
- ☐ COVALESKI
- ☐ DOOIN
- ☐ DOOLAN (BATTING)
- ☐ DOOLAN (FIELDING)
- ☐ DOOLIN
- ☐ JACKLITSCH
- ☐ KNABE
- ☐ MAGEE (PORTRAIT)
- ☐ MAGIE (NAME MISSPELLED)
- ☐ MAGEE (BATTING)
- ☐ MCQUILLAN (BATTING)
- ☐ MCQUILLAN (PITCHING)
- ☐ TITUS

PITTSBURGH PIRATES

- ☐ ABBATICCHIO (BATTING/HIPS)
- ☐ ABBATICCHIO (BATTING/KNEES)
- ☐ ABSTEIN
- ☐ CAMNITZ (PORTRAIT)
- ☐ CAMNITZ (PITCHING/FRONT)
- ☐ CAMNITZ (PITCHING/SIDE)
- ☐ CLARKE
- ☐ F. CLARKE
- ☐ GIBSON
- ☐ LEACH (PORTRAIT)
- ☐ LEACH (FIELDING)
- ☐ LEIFIELD (PITCHING)
- ☐ LEIFIELD (BATTING)
- ☐ MADDOX
- ☐ MILLER
- ☐ PHILLIPPE
- ☐ WAGNER
- ☐ WILLIS
- ☐ WILSON

ST. LOUIS BROWNS

- ☐ CRIGER
- ☐ CRISS
- ☐ DEMMITT
- ☐ DINEEN
- ☐ FERRIS
- ☐ GRAHAM
- ☐ HOFFMAN
- ☐ HOWELL (PORTRAIT)
- ☐ HOWELL (PORTRAIT/HIPS)
- ☐ JONES
- ☐ LAKE (PITCHING)
- ☐ LAKE (HANDS ABOVE HEAD)
- ☐ MCALEESE
- ☐ PELTY (PITCHING)
- ☐ PELTY (HORIZONTAL)
- ☐ POWELL
- ☐ STEPHENS
- ☐ STONE
- ☐ WADDELL (PORTRAIT)
- ☐ WADDELL (PITCHING)
- ☐ WALLACE
- ☐ WILLIAMS

ST. LOUIS CARDINALS

- ☐ BARBEAU
- ☐ BLISS
- ☐ BRESNAHAN (PORTRAIT)
- ☐ BRESNAHAN (BATTING)
- ☐ BYRNE
- ☐ CHARLES
- ☐ EVANS
- ☐ GEYER
- ☐ GILBERT

T206

□ HULSWITT
□ KONETCHY (FIELDING/HIGH BALL)
□ KONETCHY (FIELDING/LOW BALL)
□ O'HARA
□ PHELPS
□ RHODES
□ SHAW
□ WILLIS (BATTING)
□ WILLIS (FIELDING)

WASHINGTON SENATORS

□ G. BROWN
□ CONROY (BATTING)
□ CONROY (FIELDING)
□ DELEHANTY
□ ELBERFELD (PORTRAIT)
□ ELBERFELD (FIELDING)
□ GANLEY
□ GRAY
□ GROOM
□ JOHNSON (PORTRAIT)
□ JOHNSON (PITCHING)
□ MCBRIDE
□ MILAN
□ SCHAEFER
□ SHIPKE
□ STREET (PORTRAIT)
□ STREET (CATCHING)
□ TANNEHILL
□ UNGLAUB

AMERICAN ASSOCIATION

COLUMBUS

□ CLARK
□ CLYMER
□ CONGALTON
□ KRUGER
□ SCHRECK

INDIANAPOLIS

□ BURKE
□ CARR
□ CROSS
□ DAVIDSON
□ HAYDEN

KANSAS CITY

□ BECKLEY
□ BRASHEAR
□ DORNER
□ HALLMAN
□ LUNGREN
□ RITTER
□ SHANNON

LOUISVILLE

□ DELAHANTY
□ PUTTMAN
□ THIELMAN

MILWAUKEE

□ BARRY
□ MCGANN
□ MCGLYNN
□ RANDALL

MINNEAPOLIS

□ COLLINS
□ CRAVATH
□ DOWNS
□ OBERLIN
□ O'NEIL
□ PICKERING
□ QUILLEN
□ YOUNG

ST. PAUL

□ ARMBRUSTER
□ O'BRIEN

TOLEDO

□ ABBOTT
□ FREEMAN
□ HINCHMAN
□ LATTIMORE
□ WRIGHT

EASTERN LEAGUE

BALTIMORE

□ ADKINS
□ CASSIDY
□ DESSAU
□ DUNN
□ HALL
□ JACKSON
□ POLAND
□ SLAGLE
□ STRANG

BUFFALO

□ BRAIN
□ BURCHELL
□ CLANCY
□ FLANAGAN
□ KISINGER
□ MALARKEY
□ NATTRESS
□ SCHIRM
□ SMITH
□ TAYLOR
□ WHITE

JERSEY CITY

□ HANNIFAN
□ MERRITT
□ MILLIGAN
□ MOELLER

MONTREAL

□ CASEY

NEWARK

□ MCGINNITY
□ SCHLAFLY
□ SHARPE

PROVIDENCE

□ ANDERSON
□ ARNDT
□ BLACKBURNE
□ HOFFMAN
□ LAVENDER
□ MORAN
□ PHELAN
□ SHAW

ROCHESTER

□ BARGER
□ BATCH
□ BUTLER
□ CHAPPELLE
□ GANZEL
□ MALONEY

TORONTO

□ GRINSHAW
□ KELLEY
□ MCGINLEY
□ MITCHELL
□ RUDOLPH

SOUTH ATLANTIC LEAGUE

AUGUSTA

□ COLES

CHARLESTON

□ FOSTER
□ PAIGE

COLUMBIA

□ KIERNAN
□ MANION

COLUMBUS

□ HELM

JACKSONVILLE

□ MULLANEY
□ VIOLAT

MACON

□ LAFITTE

SAVANNAH

□ HOWARD

SOUTHERN LEAGUE

ATLANTA

□ JORDAN
□ SMITH

BIRMINGHAM

□ MOLESWORTH

LITTLE ROCK

□ HART
□ LENTZ

MEMPHIS

□ CAREY
□ CRANSTON

MOBILE

□ HICKMAN
□ THORNTON

MONTGOMERY

□ GREMINGER
□ HART
□ PERSONS
□ ROCKENFELD

NASHVILLE

□ BAY
□ BERNHARD
□ ELLAM
□ PERDUE

NEW ORLEANS

□ BREITENSTEIN
□ FRITZ
□ REGAN

T206

TEXAS LEAGUE

DALLAS

☐ MILLER

HOUSTON

☐ WHITE

SAN ANTONIO

☐ BASTIAN
☐ STARK

SHREVEPORT

☐ SMITH
☐ THEBO

VIRGINIA LEAGUE

DANVILLE

☐ KING
☐ WESTLAKE

LYNCHBURG

☐ HOOKER
☐ ORTH

NORFOLK

☐ OTEY
☐ SEITZ

PORTSMOUTH

☐ GUIHEEN
☐ MCCAULEY

RICHMOND

☐ LIPE
☐ REVELLE

ROANOKE

☐ RYAN
☐ SHAUGHNESSY

T207 (207)
BROWN BACKGROUND
1 1/2" X 2 5/8"

BOSTON RED SOX

☐ BRADLEY
☐ BUSHELMAN
☐ CARRIGAN/CORRECT BACK
☐ CARRIGAN/ WAGNER BACK
☐ CICOTTTE
☐ ENGLE
☐ GARDNER
☐ HAGEMAN
☐ HALL
☐ HENRIKSEN
☐ HOOPER
☐ LEWIS
☐ NUNAMAKER
☐ O'BRIEN

☐ SPEAKER
☐ THOMAS
☐ WAGNER/CORRECT BACK
☐ WAGNER/CARRIGAN BACK
☐ WOOD
☐ YERKES

BOSTON RUSTLERS

☐ DEVLIN
☐ DONNELLY
☐ GOWDY
☐ HOUSER
☐ KIRKE
☐ KLING
☐ LEWIS
☐ MCDONALD
☐ MILLER
☐ PERDUE
☐ SPRATT
☐ SWEENEY
☐ TYLER

BROOKLYN SUPERBAS

☐ BARGER
☐ COULSON
☐ DAUBERT
☐ ERWIN
☐ KNETZER
☐ MILLER
☐ NORTHEN
☐ RAGAN
☐ RUCKER
☐ SCHARDT
☐ STACK
☐ TOOLEY
☐ WHEAT

CHICAGO CUBS

☐ CHANCE
☐ COLE
☐ LENNOX
☐ MCINTIRE
☐ MILLER
☐ NEEDHAM
☐ REULBACH
☐ SAIER
☐ SCHULTE
☐ TINKER

CHICAGO WHITE SOX

☐ BENZ
☐ BLACKBURNE
☐ BLOCK
☐ BODIE
☐ CALLAHAN
☐ COLLINS
☐ FOURNIER
☐ KUHN
☐ LANGE
☐ LORD
☐ MCINTYRE
☐ MOGRIDGE
☐ PETERS
☐ RATH
☐ SCOTT
☐ SULLIVAN
☐ TANNEHILL
☐ WEAVER
☐ WHITE
☐ ZEIDER

CINCINNATI REDS

☐ ALMEIDA
☐ BESCHER
☐ CLARKE
☐ FROMME
☐ MARSANS
☐ MCLEAN
☐ MITCHELL
☐ PHELAN
☐ SEVEROLD
☐ SMITH

CLEVELAND NAPS

☐ ADAMS
☐ BALL
☐ BIRMINGHAM
☐ BLANDING
☐ BUTCHER
☐ DAVIS
☐ EASTERLY
☐ GEORGE
☐ GRANEY
☐ GREGG
☐ KALER
☐ LIVINGSTON/"A" SHIRT
☐ LIVINGSTON/"C" SHIRT
☐ LIVINGSTON/SMALL "C" SHIRT
☐ MITCHELL
☐ OLSON
☐ RYAN
☐ TURNER

DETROIT TIGERS

☐ BAUMAN
☐ COVINGTON
☐ DELAHANTY
☐ DRAKE
☐ GAINOR
☐ LIVELY
☐ MORIARITY
☐ MULLINS
   WITH "D" ON CAP
☐ MULLINS
   WITHOUT "D" ON CAP
☐ STANAGE
☐ WORKS

NEW YORK GIANTS

☐ BECKER
☐ CRANDALL
☐ DEVORE
☐ DOYLE
☐ FLETCHER
☐ HARTLEY
☐ HERZOG
☐ HIGGINS
☐ LATHAM
☐ MARQUARD
☐ MCGRAW
☐ SNODGRASS
☐ WILSON
☐ WILTSE

NEW YORK YANKEES

☐ DANIELS
☐ FISHER
   WITH WHITE LETTERS ON CAP
☐ FISHER
   WITH BLUE LETTERS ON CAP
☐ HOFF
☐ QUINN
☐ STREET
☐ VAUGHN
☐ WARHOP
☐ WILLIAMS
☐ WOLVERTON

PHILADELPHIA ATHLETICS

☐ BARRY
☐ BENDER
☐ DANFORTH
☐ DERRICK
☐ KRAUSE
☐ LAPP

□ LORD
□ MORGAN
□ OLDRING
□ STRUNK

PHILADELPHIA PHILLIES

□ CHALMERS
□ DOOIN
□ DOWNEY
□ GRAHAM
□ KNABE
□ MOORE
□ MORAN
□ PASKART
□ RASMUSSEN
□ SCANLON

BYRNE-PITTSBURG-NAT.

PITTSBURGH PIRATES

□ BYRNE
□ CAMNITZ
□ CAREY
□ DONLIN
□ FERRY
□ HYATT
□ KELLY
□ LEACH
□ LEIFIELD
□ MCCARTHY
□ MCKECHNIE
□ MILLER
□ O'TOOLE
□ SIMON
□ WILSON

ST. LOUIS BROWNS

□ AUSTIN
 WITH STL ON SHIRT
□ AUSTIN
 WITHOUT STL ON SHIRT
□ HALLINAN
□ E. HAMILTON
□ HOGAN
□ KUTINA
□ NELSON
□ PELTY
□ STOVALL
□ WALLACE

ST. LOUIS CARDINALS

□ BRESNAHAN
□ ELLIS
□ EVANS
□ GOLDEN
□ HARMON
□ KONETCHY
□ LOUDERMILK
□ OAKES
□ SMITH
□ STEELE
□ STEINFELDT
□ WILIE
□ WINGO
□ WOODBURN

WASHINGTON SENATORS

□ AINSMITH
□ CUNNINGHAM
□ HENRY
□ JOHNSON
□ MCBRIDE
□ MILAN
□ MORGAN
□ SCHAEFER
□ WALKER

1989 UPPER DECK (800)
2 1/2" X 3 1/2"

Goose Gossage

ATLANTA BRAVES

□ 17. JOHN SMOLTZ
□ 19. MARK LEMKE
□ 52. JIM ACKER
□ 55. PAUL RUNGE
□ 71. ZANE SMITH
□ 74. RICK MAHLER
□ 93. ALBERT HALL
□ 104. OZZIE VIRGIL
□ 113. GERMAN JIMENEZ
□ 121. BRUCE BENEDICT
□ 132. JEFF BLAUSER
□ 144. ANDRES THOMAS
□ 357. DALE MURPHY
□ 360. TOM GLAVINE
□ 378. RON GANT
□ 396. CHUCK CARY
□ 399. TERRY BLOCKER
□ 412. PETE SMITH
□ 414. BRUCE SUTTER
□ 431. GERALD PERRY
□ 433. JERRY ROYSTER
□ 435. ED OLWINE
□ 566. PAUL ASSENMACHER
□ 568. JIM MORRISON
□ 570. TED SIMMONS
□ 587. DION JAMES
□ 589. CHARLIE PULEO
□ 672. TEAM CHECKLIST
□ 731. LONNIE SMITH
□ 734. JOSE ALVAREZ
□ 751. TOMMY GREGG
□ 753. DEREK LILLIQUIST
□ 795. JODY DAVIS

BALTIMORE ORIOLES

□ 254. LARRY SHEETS
□ 261. DOUG SISK
□ 275. EDDIE MURRAY
□ 283. BILLY RIPKEN
□ 294. JIM TRABER
□ 408. BRADY ANDERSON
□ 426. KEN GERHART
□ 429. JOE ORSULAK
□ 447. DAVE SCHMIDT
□ 450. DON AASE
□ 467. CAL RIPKEN
□ 469. TERRY KENNEDY
□ 486. JEFF STONE
□ 488. TOM NIEDENFUER
□ 490. RICK SCHU
□ 553. MICKEY TETTLETON
□ 571. MARK THURMOND
□ 574. JOSE BAUTISTA
□ 592. PETE STANICEK
□ 595. JEFF BALLARD
□ 651. OSWALD PERAZA
□ 653. MIKE MORGAN
□ 655. JAY TIBBS
□ 682. TEAM CHECKLIST
□ 723. GREGG OLSON
□ 725. CRAIG WORTHINGTON
□ 735. BOB MILACKI
□ 740. RANDY MILLIGAN
□ 742. STEVE FINLEY

□ 744. PETE HARNISCH
□ 747. JUAN BELL
□ 749. PHIL BRADLEY

BOSTON RED SOX

□ 26. CARLOS QUINTANA
□ 36. LARRY PARRISH
□ 38. MIKE SMITHSON
□ 40. ED ROMERO
□ 152. RICK CERONE
□ 161. SPIKE OWEN
□ 173. MARTY BARRETT
□ 184. TODD BENZINGER
□ 195. ROGER CLEMENS
□ 366. DWIGHT EVANS
□ 368. RICH GEDMAN
□ 370. JODY REED
□ 387. BRUCE HURST
□ 389. WADE BOGGS
□ 411. BOB STANLEY
□ 413. JIM RICE
□ 415. OIL CAN BOYD
□ 432. MIKE GREENWELL
□ 434. ELLIS BURKS
□ 503. DENNIS LAMP
□ 521. LEE SMITH
□ 524. KEVIN ROMINE
□ 542. MIKE BODDICKER
□ 545. TOM BOLTON
□ 687. TEAM CHECKLIST
□ 757. NICK ESASKY
□ 759. ROB MURPHY

CALIFORNIA ANGELS

□ 24. DANTE BICHETTE
□ 110. DEVON WHITE
□ 119. BOB BOONE
□ 126. CHILI DAVIS
□ 138. JACK HOWELL
□ 147. DEWAYNE BUICE
□ 201. DICK SCHOFIELD
□ 212. TONY ARMAS
□ 223. KIRK MCCASKILL
□ 234. TERRY CLARK
□ 245. MARK MCLEMORE
□ 462. DARRELL MILLER
□ 464. SHERMAN CORBETT
□ 481. JOHNNY RAY
□ 483. STU CLIBURN
□ 485. BRIAN DOWNING
□ 552. DAN PETRY
□ 555. MIKE WITT
□ 573. WALLY JOYNER
□ 591. THAD BOSLEY
□ 594. BRYAN HARVEY
□ 613. WILLIE FRASER
□ 614. JIM EPPARD
□ 632. CHUCK FINLEY
□ 635. GREG MINTON
□ 668. TEAM CHECKLIST
□ 712. BERT BLYLEVEN
□ 755. JIM ABBOTT
□ 775. LANCE PARRISH
□ 794. CLAUDELL WASHINGTON

CHICAGO CUBS

□ 6. ROLANDO ROOMES
□ 10. DOUG DASCENZO
□ 14. MIKE HARKEY
□ 61. FRANK DIPINO
□ 63. JAMIE MOYER
□ 65. MITCH WELSTER
□ 82. CALVIN SCHIRALDI
□ 84. LES LANCASTER
□ 107. SHAWON DUNSTON
□ 120. RYNE SANDBERG
□ 127. MANNY TRILLO
□ 140. MARK GRACE
□ 148. JODY DAVIS
□ 205. ANDRE DAWSON
□ 214. DARRIN JACKSON
□ 222. ANGEL SALAZAR
□ 235. RAFAEL PALMEIRO
□ 241. GREG MADDUX
□ 303. RICK SUTCLIFFE
□ 321. GARY VARSHO
□ 324. DREW HALL
□ 342. SCOTT SANDERSON
□ 345. PAT PERRY

- ☐ 452. GOOSE GOSSAGE
- ☐ 455. DAMON BERRYHILL
- ☐ 473. VANCE LAW
- ☐ 491. JEFF PICO
- ☐ 494. AL NIPPER
- ☐ 675. TEAM CHECKLIST
- ☐ 762. KEVIN BLANKENSHIP
- ☐ 765. JEROME WALTON
- ☐ 776. JOE GIRARDI
- ☐ 778. MITCH WILLIAMS
- ☐ 780. DWIGHT SMITH
- ☐ 797. PAUL KILGUS
- ☐ 799. STEVE WILSON

CHICAGO WHITE SOX

- ☐ 151. JERRY REUSS
- ☐ 164. DAVE GALLAGHER
- ☐ 175. OZZIE GUILLEN
- ☐ 183. RON KARKOVICE
- ☐ 192. KELLY PARIS
- ☐ 204. DAN PASQUA
- ☐ 211. HAROLD BAINES
- ☐ 224. STEVE LYONS
- ☐ 231. GREG WALKER
- ☐ 243. MELIDO PEREZ
- ☐ 457. BARRY JONES
- ☐ 460. MARK SALAS
- ☐ 478. SHAWN HILLEGAS
- ☐ 496. DARYL BOSTON
- ☐ 499. BILL LONG
- ☐ 506. KEN WILLIAMS
- ☐ 509. JEFF BITTIGER
- ☐ 527. DONNIE HILL
- ☐ 530. JACK MCDOWELL
- ☐ 548. JOHN DAVIS
- ☐ 606. MIKE DIAZ
- ☐ 609. CARLTON FISK
- ☐ 628. FRED MANRIQUE
- ☐ 647. BOBBY THIGPEN
- ☐ 650. IVAN CALDERON
- ☐ 692. TEAM CHECKLIST
- ☐ 711. RON KITTLE
- ☐ 715. STEVE ROSENBERG
- ☐ 790. EDDIE WILLIAMS

CINCINNATI REDS

- ☐ 23. VAN SNIDER
- ☐ 29. RANDY ST. CLAIRE
- ☐ 160. KAL DANIELS
- ☐ 169. BO DIAZ
- ☐ 180. CHRIS SABO
- ☐ 187. RON ROBINSON
- ☐ 196. DAVE CONCEPCION
- ☐ 257. JACK ARMSTRONG
- ☐ 270. BARRY LARKIN
- ☐ 276. JEFF REED
- ☐ 287. RON OESTER
- ☐ 299. NICK ESASKY
- ☐ 351. DAVE COLLINS
- ☐ 354. LEON DURHAM
- ☐ 372. ROB MURPHY
- ☐ 375. ROB DIBBLE
- ☐ 393. JEFF TREADWAY
- ☐ 407. JOHN FRANCO
- ☐ 410. ERIC DAVIS
- ☐ 428. PAUL O'NEILL
- ☐ 446. LLOYD MCCLENDON
- ☐ 449. FRANK WILLIAMS
- ☐ 617. TOM BROWNING
- ☐ 619. JOSE RIJO
- ☐ 636. HERM WINNINGHAM
- ☐ 638. TIM BIRTSAS
- ☐ 640. DANNY JACKSON
- ☐ 688. TEAM CHECKLIST
- ☐ 760. RICK MAHLER
- ☐ 781. LENNY HARRIS
- ☐ 783. NORM CHARLTON
- ☐ 785. TODD BENZINGER

CLEVELAND INDIANS

- ☐   2. LUIS MEDINA
- ☐ 32. DAN FIROVA
- ☐ 34. TOMMY HINZO
- ☐ 157. WILLIE UPSHAW
- ☐ 170. CORY SNYDER
- ☐ 186. JULIO FRANCO
- ☐ 190. JOE CARTER
- ☐ 198. BROOK JACOBY

- ☐ 209. SCOTT BAILES
- ☐ 217. ANDY ALLANSON
- ☐ 228. RON KITTLE
- ☐ 236. PAUL ZUVELLA
- ☐ 250. GREG SWINDELL
- ☐ 466. BUD BLACK
- ☐ 468. JOHN FARRELL
- ☐ 470. TOM CANDIOTTI
- ☐ 487. CARMEN CASTILLO
- ☐ 489. JAY BELL
- ☐ 517. DAVE CLARK
- ☐ 519. RON WASHINGTON
- ☐ 536. TERRY FRANCONA
- ☐ 538. MEL HALL
- ☐ 540. DOUG JONES
- ☐ 679. TEAM CHECKLIST
- ☐ 716. JOE SKALSKI
- ☐ 728. RICK YETT
- ☐ 796. ODDIBE MCDOWELL
- ☐ 800. PETE O'BRIEN

DETROIT TIGERS

- ☐ 47. PAUL GIBSON
- ☐ 49. LARRY HERNDON
- ☐ 106. TOM BROOKENS
- ☐ 117. GARY PETTIS
- ☐ 128. CHET LEMON
- ☐ 136. LUIS SALAZAR
- ☐ 150. MATT NOKES
- ☐ 259. RAY KNIGHT
- ☐ 266. DAVE BERGMAN
- ☐ 279. GUILLERMO HERNANDEZ
- ☐ 290. ALAN TRAMMELL
- ☐ 298. DOYLE ALEXANDER
- ☐ 352. JACK MORRIS
- ☐ 355. IVAN DEJESUS
- ☐ 373. MIKE HENNEMAN
- ☐ 391. FRANK TANANA
- ☐ 394. DARRELL EVANS
- ☐ 451. LOU WHITAKER
- ☐ 454. JIM WALEWANDER
- ☐ 472. JEFF ROBINSON
- ☐ 475. WALT TERRELL
- ☐ 493. ERIC KING
- ☐ 652. PAT SHERIDAN
- ☐ 654. MIKE HEATH
- ☐ 690. TEAM CHECKLIST
- ☐ 714. KEN WILLIAMS
- ☐ 761. FRED LYNN
- ☐ 764. STEVE SEARCY
- ☐ 782. TORY LOVULLO
- ☐ 784. CHRIS BROWN

HOUSTON ASTROS

- ☐ 58. CASEY CANDAELE
- ☐ 76. JIM DESHAIES
- ☐ 79. JOAQUIN ANDUJAR
- ☐ 97. DANNY DARWIN
- ☐ 100. JIM PANKOVITS
- ☐ 101. BILL DORAN
- ☐ 112. BUDDY BELL
- ☐ 135. GERALD YOUNG
- ☐ 141. KEN CAMINITI
- ☐ 145. NOLAN RYAN
- ☐ 251. JUAN AGOSTO
- ☐ 262. ALEX TREVINO
- ☐ 273. CRAIG BIGGIO
- ☐ 284. CRAIG REYNOLDS
- ☐ 295. MIKE SCOTT
- ☐ 302. DAVE SMITH
- ☐ 305. ALAN ASHBY
- ☐ 323. CHUCK JACKSON
- ☐ 341. RAFAEL RAMIREZ
- ☐ 344. BILLY HATCHER
- ☐ 401. LOUIE MEADOWNS
- ☐ 404. LARRY ANDERSEN
- ☐ 422. BOB KNEPPER
- ☐ 425. KEVIN BASS
- ☐ 443. GLENN DAVIS
- ☐ 669. TEAM CHECKLIST

KANSAS CITY ROYALS

- ☐ 12. LUIS DE LOS SANTOS
- ☐ 21. REY PALACIOS
- ☐ 37. BRET SABERHAGEN
- ☐ 42. ED HEARN
- ☐ 44. JIM EISENREICH
- ☐ 202. MARK GUBICZA

- ☐ 215. GEORGE BRETT
- ☐ 221. BO JACKSON
- ☐ 233. PAT TABLER
- ☐ 244. WILLIE WILSON
- ☐ 308. STEVE FARR
- ☐ 326. ISRAEL SANCHEZ
- ☐ 329. DANNY TARTABULL
- ☐ 347. GARY THURMAN
- ☐ 350. FRANK WHITE
- ☐ 507. BILL PECOTA
- ☐ 510. KEVIN SEITZER
- ☐ 528. LARRY OWEN
- ☐ 546. MIKE MACFARLANE
- ☐ 549. FLOYD BANNISTER
- ☐ 616. KURT STILLWELL
- ☐ 618. JEFF MONTGOMERY
- ☐ 620. JAMIE QUIRK
- ☐ 637. CHARLIE LEIBRANDT
- ☐ 639. BILL BUCKNER
- ☐ 689. TEAM CHECKLIST
- ☐ 736. TOM GORDON
- ☐ 767. BOB BOONE
- ☐ 769. JOSE DEJESUS

LOS ANGELES DODGERS

- ☐ 16. WILLIAM BRENNAN
- ☐ 18. RAMON MARTINEZ
- ☐ 20. JUAN BELL
- ☐ 53. STEVE SAX
- ☐ 66. JOHN TUDOR
- ☐ 68. MIKE DEVEREAUX
- ☐ 70. MIKE MARSHALL
- ☐ 72. BRIAN HOLTON
- ☐ 75. JOHN SHELBY
- ☐ 87. JESSE OROSCO
- ☐ 89. DAVE ANDERSON
- ☐ 91. FRANKLIN STUBBS
- ☐ 94. TIM LEARY
- ☐ 108. TRACY WOODSON
- ☐ 116. MIKE SCIOSCIA
- ☐ 130. OREL HERSHISER
- ☐ 137. ALEJANDRO PENA
- ☐ 146. MIKE DAVIS
- ☐ 607. CHRIS GWYNN
- ☐ 610. JAY HOWELL
- ☐ 611. TIM CREWS
- ☐ 615. JEFF HAMILTON
- ☐ 626. JOSE GONZALEZ
- ☐ 629. RICKY HORTON
- ☐ 631. ALFREDO GRIFFIN
- ☐ 633. KIRK GIBSON
- ☐ 648. TIM BELCHER
- ☐ 656. FERNANDO VALENZUELA
- ☐ 676. TEAM CHECKLIST
- ☐ 709. MICKEY HATCHER
- ☐ 713. RICK DEMPSEY
- ☐ 763. EDDIE MURRAY
- ☐ 777. WILLIE RANDOLPH

MILWAUKEE BREWERS

- ☐ 13. GARY SHEFFIELD
- ☐ 252. MIKE FELDER
- ☐ 263. JEFFREY LEONARD
- ☐ 274. JIM GANTNER
- ☐ 285. ROBIN YOUNT
- ☐ 292. CHRIS BOSIO
- ☐ 301. DARRYL HAMILTON
- ☐ 304. DAVE STAPLETON
- ☐ 322. PAUL MIRABELLA
- ☐ 325. DON AUGUST
- ☐ 343. B. J. SURHOFF
- ☐ 403. JOEY MEYER
- ☐ 421. DALE SVEUM
- ☐ 424. TED HIGUERA
- ☐ 442. ROB DEER
- ☐ 445. BILL WEGMAN
- ☐ 501. CHUCK CRIM
- ☐ 504. GLENN BRAGGS
- ☐ 522. JUAN CASTILLO
- ☐ 525. PAUL MOLITOR
- ☐ 543. GREG BROCK
- ☐ 608. ODELL JONES
- ☐ 627. BILL SCHROEDER
- ☐ 630. DAN PLESAC
- ☐ 646. JUAN NIEVES
- ☐ 649. MIKE YOUNG
- ☐ 673. TEAM CHECKLIST
- ☐ 745. BILL SPIERS
- ☐ 788. LAVEL FREEMAN

Ted Higuera

MINNESOTA TWINS

- ☐ 62. TIM LAUDNER
- ☐ 64. FRED TOLIVER
- ☐ 81. CHARLIE LEA
- ☐ 83. LES STRAKER
- ☐ 85. ALLAN ANDERSON
- ☐ 158. RANDY BUSH
- ☐ 166. GREG GAGNE
- ☐ 177. KELVIN TORVE
- ☐ 179. STEVE LOMBARDOZZI
- ☐ 197. AL NEWMAN
- ☐ 203. GARY GAETTI
- ☐ 213. KENT HRBECK
- ☐ 225. BERY BLYLEVEN
- ☐ 232. JUAN BERENGUER
- ☐ 242. JOHN MOSES
- ☐ 358. MARK PORTUGAL
- ☐ 376. KIRBY PUCKETT
- ☐ 379. BRIAN HARPER
- ☐ 397. FRANK VIOLA
- ☐ 400. DAN GLADDEN
- ☐ 558. TOMMY HERR
- ☐ 577. MARK DAVIDSON
- ☐ 580. GENE LARKIN
- ☐ 596. JEFF REARDON
- ☐ 599. KEITH ATHERTON
- ☐ 691. TEAM CHECKLIST
- ☐ 732. WALLY BACKMAN
- ☐ 786. SHANE RAWLEY

MONTREAL EXPOS

- ☐ 25. RANDY JOHNSON
- ☐ 57. JOHN DOPSON
- ☐ 60. JOE HESKETH
- ☐ 78. BRYN SMITH
- ☐ 96. TRACY JONES
- ☐ 99. NEAL HEATON
- ☐ 102. TIM WALLACH
- ☐ 115. ANDRES GALARRAGA
- ☐ 122. HUBIE BROOKS
- ☐ 124. WALLACE JOHNSON
- ☐ 133. MIKE FRITZGERALD
- ☐ 356. BRIAN HOLMAN
- ☐ 359. ANDY MCGAFFIGAN
- ☐ 377. DENNIS MARTINEZ
- ☐ 380. NELSON SANTOVENIA
- ☐ 398. JEFF PARRETT
- ☐ 402. TIM RAINES
- ☐ 405. REX HUDLER
- ☐ 423. LUIS RIVERA
- ☐ 441. TOM FOLEY
- ☐ 444. DAVE MARTINEZ
- ☐ 456. TIM BURKE
- ☐ 459. FLOYD YOUMANS
- ☐ 477. JOHNNY PAREDES
- ☐ 480. OTIS NIXON
- ☐ 498. PASCUAL PEREZ
- ☐ 677. TEAM CHECKLIST
- ☐ 717. SPIKE OWEN
- ☐ 719. KEVIN GROSS
- ☐ 738. MIKE ALDRETE

NEW YORK METS

- ☐ 7. DAVID WEST
- ☐ 9. GREGG JEFFERIES
- ☐ 159. RON DARLING
- ☐ 168. SID FERNANDEZ

- ☐ 176. BARRY LYONS
- ☐ 188. WALLY BACKMAN
- ☐ 199. MOOKIE WILSON
- ☐ 260. DARRYL STRAWBERRY
- ☐ 269. KEVIN ELSTER
- ☐ 277. TIM TEUFEL
- ☐ 288. TERRY LEACH
- ☐ 296. ROGER MCDOWELL
- ☐ 367. KEVIN MCREYNOLDS
- ☐ 369. LEN DYKSTRA
- ☐ 386. BOB OJEDA
- ☐ 388. DAVE MAGADAN
- ☐ 390. GARY CARTER
- ☐ 561. MACKEY SASSER
- ☐ 563. RICK AGUILERA
- ☐ 565. DWIGHT GOODEN
- ☐ 582. HOWARD JOHNSON
- ☐ 584. DAVID CONE
- ☐ 612. KEITH HERNANDEZ
- ☐ 634. RANDY MYERS
- ☐ 657. LEE MAZZILLI
- ☐ 681. TEAM CHECKLIST
- ☐ 737. WALLY WHITEHURST
- ☐ 739. KEITH MILLER

NEW YORK YANKEES

- ☐ 56. RICK RHODEN
- ☐ 59. DAVE RIGHETTI
- ☐ 77. BOBBY MEACHAM
- ☐ 80. RICHARD DOTSON
- ☐ 98. GARY WARD
- ☐ 156. LUIS AGUAYO
- ☐ 167. KEN PHELPS
- ☐ 178. DON SLAUGHT
- ☐ 189. RANDY VELARDE
- ☐ 200. DON MATTINGLY
- ☐ 210. RICKEY HENDERSON
- ☐ 216. RAFAEL SANTANA
- ☐ 230. TOMMY JOHN
- ☐ 237. WILLIE RANDOLPH
- ☐ 248. JOHN CANDELARIA
- ☐ 307. RON GUIDRY
- ☐ 310. CLAUDELL WASHINGTON
- ☐ 328. JOEL SKINNER
- ☐ 346. JACK CLARK
- ☐ 349. DAVE WINFIELD
- ☐ 567. NEIL ALLEN
- ☐ 569. MIKE PAGLIARULO
- ☐ 586. CHARLES HUDSON
- ☐ 588. AL LEITER
- ☐ 590. ROBERTO KELLY
- ☐ 693. TEAM CHECKLIST
- ☐ 702. JESSE BARFIELD
- ☐ 706. DAVE LAPOINT
- ☐ 708. ANDY HAWKINS
- ☐ 710. LANCE MCCULLERS
- ☐ 727. DALE MOHORCIC
- ☐ 729. MEL HALL
- ☐ 746. HENSLEY MEULENS
- ☐ 748. STEVE SAX

OAKLAND A'S

- ☐ 4. DAVID OTTO
- ☐ 15. LANCE BLANKENSHIP
- ☐ 22. FELIX JOSE
- ☐ 153. STORM DAVIS
- ☐ 162. LUIS POLONIA
- ☐ 174. DAVE HENDERSON
- ☐ 185. DAVE STEWART
- ☐ 191. BOB WELCH
- ☐ 256. TERRY STEINBACH
- ☐ 267. TONY PHILLIPS
- ☐ 278. RICK HONEYCUTT
- ☐ 289. DENNIS ECKERSLEY
- ☐ 300. MARK MCGWIRE
- ☐ 353. ERIC PLUNK
- ☐ 371. JOSE CANSECO
- ☐ 374. WALT WEISS
- ☐ 392. CURT YOUNG
- ☐ 395. GLENN HUBBARD
- ☐ 562. CARNEY LANSFORD
- ☐ 564. RON HASSEY
- ☐ 581. STAN JAVIER
- ☐ 583. MIKE GALLEGO
- ☐ 585. DOUG JENNINGS
- ☐ 601. DON BAYLOR
- ☐ 605. DAVE PARKER
- ☐ 624. ORLANDO MERCADO
- ☐ 643. GENE NELSON

- ☐ 670. TEAM CHECKLIST
- ☐ 718. TODD BURNS
- ☐ 756. OZZIE CANSECO
- ☐ 758. MIKE MOORE

PHILADELPHIA PHILLIES

- ☐ 11. RON JONES
- ☐ 31. KEVIN GROSS
- ☐ 33. JEFF CALHOUN
- ☐ 35. RICKY JORDAN
- ☐ 207. KENT TEKULVE
- ☐ 219. STEVE JELTZ
- ☐ 229. PHIL BRADLEY
- ☐ 240. LANCE PARRISH
- ☐ 246. VON HAYES
- ☐ 317. MILT THOMPSON
- ☐ 319. BRUCE RUFFIN
- ☐ 336. JUAN SAMUEL
- ☐ 338. MIKE MADDUX
- ☐ 340. BOB DERNIER
- ☐ 406. MIKE SCHMIDT
- ☐ 409. DON CARMAN
- ☐ 427. SHANE RAWLEY
- ☐ 430. JACKIE GUTIERREZ
- ☐ 448. DARREN DAULTON
- ☐ 511. STEVE BEDROSIAN
- ☐ 513. CHRIS JAMES
- ☐ 515. DAVID PALMER
- ☐ 532. JOHN RUSSELL
- ☐ 534. GREG GROSS
- ☐ 684. TEAM CHECKLIST
- ☐ 704. DICKIE THON
- ☐ 720. TOMMY HERR
- ☐ 730. FLOYD YOUMANS
- ☐ 741. JEFF PARRETT

PITTSBURGH PIRATES

- ☐ 3. TONY CHANCE
- ☐ 67. JOHN CANGELOSI
- ☐ 69. BRIAN FISHER
- ☐ 86. JUNIOR ORTIZ
- ☐ 88. FLEX FERMIN
- ☐ 90. RAFAEL BELLIARD
- ☐ 311. TOM PRINCE
- ☐ 313. KEN OBERKFELL
- ☐ 315. R. J. REYNOLDS
- ☐ 332. JEFF ROBINSON
- ☐ 334. JOSE LIND
- ☐ 417. MIKE LAVALLIERE
- ☐ 419. GARY REDUS
- ☐ 436. DAVE RUCKER
- ☐ 438. BOB WALK
- ☐ 440. BARRY BONDS
- ☐ 516. JOHN SMILEY
- ☐ 518. MIKE DUNNE
- ☐ 520. BOB KIPPER
- ☐ 537. ANDY VAN SLYKE
- ☐ 539. JIM GOTT
- ☐ 556. SID BREAM
- ☐ 559. RANDY MILLIGAN
- ☐ 578. BOBBY BONILLA
- ☐ 597. DOUG DRABECK
- ☐ 600. DAVE LAPOINT
- ☐ 685. TEAM CHECKLIST
- ☐ 750. REY QUINONES

ST. LOUIS CARDINALS

- ☐ 8. CRIS CARPENTER
- ☐ 103. JOE MAGRANE
- ☐ 114. KEN DAYLEY
- ☐ 125. BOB HORNER
- ☐ 131. TERRY PENDLETON
- ☐ 143. LARRY MCWILLIAMS
- ☐ 253. VINCE COLEMAN
- ☐ 265. OZZIE SMITH
- ☐ 272. TOM BRUNANSKY
- ☐ 281. LUIS ALICEA
- ☐ 293. JOSE DELEON
- ☐ 306. PEDRO GUERRERO
- ☐ 309. CURT FORD
- ☐ 327. DENNY WALLING
- ☐ 330. TONY PENA
- ☐ 348. TIMMY JONES
- ☐ 512. TODD WORRELL
- ☐ 514. JOSE OQUENDO
- ☐ 531. GREG MATHEWS
- ☐ 533. DAN QUISENBERRY
- ☐ 535. DANNY COX

☐ 602. TOM PAGNOZZI
☐ 621. WILLIE MCGEE
☐ 625. JOHN COSTELLO
☐ 644. ROD BOOKER
☐ 674. TEAM CHECKLIST
☐ 754. TODD ZEILE
☐ 771. STEVE PETERS

SAN DIEGO PADRES

☐   5. SANDY ALOMAR, JR.
☐ 30. JERALD CLARK
☐ 154. MARVELL WYNNE
☐ 165. BENITO SANTIAGO
☐ 171. ERIC SHOW
☐ 182. SHANE MACK
☐ 193. CHRIS BROWN
☐ 258. DICKIE THON
☐ 268. MARK DAVIS
☐ 280. JOHN KRUK
☐ 286. JIMMY JONES
☐ 297. GARRY TEMPLETON
☐ 361. KEITH MORELAND
☐ 363. DAVE LEIPER
☐ 365. CARMELO MARTINEZ
☐ 382. LANCE MCCULLERS
☐ 384. TONY GWYNN
☐ 453. ED WHITSON
☐ 471. ROBERTO ALOMAR
☐ 474. RANDY READY
☐ 492. MARK PARENT
☐ 495. ANDY HAWKINS
☐ 603. TIM FLANNERY
☐ 622. MARK GRANT
☐ 641. GREG BOOKER
☐ 645. DENNIS RASMUSSEN
☐ 683. TEAM CHECKLIST
☐ 703. WALT TERRELL
☐ 722. GARY GREEN
☐ 724. GREG HARRIS
☐ 726. TOM HOWARD
☐ 773. JACK CLARK
☐ 792. BRUCE HURST

SAN FRANCISCO GIANTS

☐ 39. DAVE DRAVECKY
☐ 46. MIKE KRUKOW
☐ 48. MIKE LACOSS
☐ 50. SCOTT GARRELTS
☐ 155. WILL CLARK
☐ 163. KEVIN MITCHELL
☐ 172. ROB THOMPSON
☐ 181. JOSE URIBE
☐ 194. RICK REUSCHEL
☐ 206. CHRIS SPEIER
☐ 218. BRETT BUTLER
☐ 227. BOB MELVIN
☐ 239. MIKE ALDRETE
☐ 247. MATT WILLIAMS
☐ 458. JOEL YOUNGBLOOD
☐ 476. KELLY DOWNS
☐ 479. BOB BRENLY
☐ 497. ERNIE RILES
☐ 500. KIRT MANWARING
☐ 502. CANDY MALDONADO
☐ 505. JOE PRICE
☐ 523. DON ROBINSON
☐ 541. CRAIG LEFFERTS
☐ 544. ATLEE HAMMAKER
☐ 678. TEAM CHECKLIST
☐ 707. CHARLIE HAYES
☐ 733. TREVOR WILSON
☐ 779. DENNIS COOK
☐ 798. TRACY JONES

SEATTLE MARINERS

☐   1. KEN GRIFFEY, JR.
☐ 28. MIKE SCHOOLER
☐ 105. ALVIN DAVIS
☐ 111. STEVE BALBONI
☐ 123. MIKE MOORE
☐ 134. HENRY COTTO
☐ 142. MIKE JACKSON
☐ 208. ROD SCURRY
☐ 220. JAY BUHNER
☐ 226. SCOTT BRADLEY
☐ 238. BRUCE FIELDS
☐ 249. HAROLD REYNOLDS
☐ 316. SCOTT BANKHEAD

☐ 318. MARIO DIAZ
☐ 320. DAVE VALLE
☐ 337. MIKE CAMPBELL
☐ 339. DARNELL COLES
☐ 508. REY QUINONES
☐ 526. MARK LANGSTON
☐ 529. JERRY REED
☐ 547. RICH RENTERIA
☐ 550. MICKEY BRANTLEY
☐ 604. GENE WALTER
☐ 623. BILL SWIFT
☐ 642. JIM PRESLEY
☐ 680. TEAM CHECKLIST
☐ 766. ERIK HANSON
☐ 768. EDGAR MARTINEZ
☐ 770. GREG BRILEY
☐ 787. OMAR VIZQUEL
☐ 789. JEFFREY LEONARD

TEXAS RANGERS

☐ 51. DWAYNE HENRY
☐ 54. PETE O'BRIEN
☐ 73. JOSE GUZMAN
☐ 92. CECIL ESPY
☐ 95. MITCH WILLIAMS
☐ 312. CHAD KREUTER
☐ 314. JERRY BROWNE
☐ 331. JIM SUNDBERG
☐ 333. ODDIBE MCDOWELL
☐ 335. PAUL KILGUS
☐ 416. RUBEN SIERRA
☐ 418. STEVE BUECHELE
☐ 420. SCOTT FLETCHER
☐ 437. CHARLIE HOUGH
☐ 439. BOB BROWER
☐ 461. JEFF RUSSELL
☐ 463. JEFF KUNKEL
☐ 465. CURTIS WILKERSON
☐ 482. GENO PETRALLI
☐ 484. PETE INCAVIGLIA
☐ 557. BOBBY WITT
☐ 560. JOSE CECENA
☐ 576. CECILIO GUANTE
☐ 579. MIKE STANLEY
☐ 598. EDWIN CORREA
☐ 686. TEAM CHECKLIST
☐ 752. KEVIN BROWN
☐ 772. RAFAEL PALMEIRO
☐ 774. NOLAN RYAN
☐ 791. JAMIE MOYER
☐ 793. JULIO FRANCO

Ruben Sierra

TORONTO BLUE JAYS

☐ 41. JEFF MUSSELMAN
☐ 43. RANCE MULLINIKS
☐ 45. SIL CAMPUSANO
☐ 109. NELSON LIRIANO
☐ 118. ERNIE WHITT
☐ 129. JOHN CERUTTI
☐ 139. TONY FERNANDEZ
☐ 149. JESSE BARFIELD
☐ 255. GEORGE BELL
☐ 264. TOM HENKE
☐ 271. MANNY LEE
☐ 282. JIM CLANCY
☐ 291. JIMMY KEY
☐ 362. TODD STOTTLEMYRE
☐ 364. CECIL FIELDER
☐ 381. LLOYD MOSEBY

☐ 383. DAVE STIEB
☐ 385. MIKE FLANAGAN
☐ 551. DUANE WARD
☐ 554. RICK LEACH
☐ 572. FRED MCGRIFF
☐ 575. KELLY GRUBER
☐ 593. PAT BORDERS
☐ 671. TEAM CHECKLIST
☐ 705. AL LEITER
☐ 721. ROB DUCEY
☐ 743. JUNIOR FELIX

1990 UPPER DECK (700+)
2 1/2" X 3 1/2"

Gregg Olson

ATLANTA BRAVES

☐ 33. KELLY MANN
☐ 49. TOMMY GREENE
☐ 61. MIKE STANTON
☐ 63. KENT MERCKER
☐ 64. FRANCISCO CABRERA
☐ 65. STEVE AVERY
☐ 84. TEAM CHECKLIST
☐ 101. GERALD PERRY
☐ 121. TOMMY GREGG
☐ 141. JEFF TREADWAY
☐ 143. DARRELL EVANS
☐ 145. ODDIBE MCDOWELL
☐ 212. ANDRES THOMAS
☐ 215. LONNIE SMITH
☐ 232. RON GANT
☐ 234. DEREK LILLIQUIST
☐ 406. JEFF BLAUSER
☐ 408. JOE BOEVER
☐ 429. JODY DAVIS
☐ 447. ED WHITED
☐ 531. GERONIMO BERROA
☐ 533. DALE MURPHY
☐ 535. JOHN SMOLTZ
☐ 551. TONY CASTILLO
☐ 571. TOM GLAVINE
☐ 611. JEFF WETHERBY
☐ 613. PETE SMITH
☐ 634. JOSE ALVAREZ
☐ 665. MARK LEMKE

BALTIMORE ORIOLES

☐   8. JOSE BAUTISTA
☐ 54. BEN MCDONALD
☐ 60. TEAM CHECKLIST
☐ 173. MARK WILLIAMSON
☐ 175. BRIAN HOLTON
☐ 184. BILLY RIPKEN
☐ 194. PHIL BRADLEY
☐ 259. JEFF BALLARD
☐ 266. CAL RIPKEN
☐ 268. JIM TRABER
☐ 270. JOE ORSULAK
☐ 287. LARRY SHEETS
☐ 290. BRADY ANDERSON
☐ 297. MICKEY TETTLETON
☐ 299. KEVIN HICKEY
☐ 401. KEITH MORELAND
☐ 425. DAVE JOHNSON
☐ 444. CRAIG WORTHINGTON
☐ 602. STEVE FINLEY
☐ 604. GREGG OLSON
☐ 623. PETE HARNISCH

□ 635. BOB MILACKI
□ 641. DAVE SCHMIDT
□ 644. BOB MELVIN
□ 663. RANDY MILLIGAN
□ 681. MIKE DEVEREAUX
□ 683. JAMIE WESTON

BOSTON RED SOX

□ 57. TEAM CHECKLIST
□ 112. DWIGHT EVANS
□ 133. MARTY BARRETT
□ 321. JODY REED
□ 323. ROGER CLEMENS
□ 343. ELLIS BURKS
□ 351. TOM BOLTON
□ 354. MIKE GREENWELL
□ 373. JIM RICE
□ 393. LEE SMITH
□ 402. RICH GEDMAN
□ 405. RICK CERONE
□ 441. KEVIN ROMINE
□ 461. ROB MURPHY
□ 463. NICK ESASKY
□ 465. CARLOS QUINTANA
□ 482. LUIS RIVERA
□ 484. OIL CAN BOYD
□ 555. WADE BOGGS
□ 610. MIKE SMITHSON
□ 652. MIKE BODDICKER
□ 654. BOB STANLEY
□ 671. JOHN DOPSON
□ 673. ERIC HETZEL
□ 694. MIKE ROCHFORD

CALIFORNIA ANGELS

□   5. TEAM CHECKLIST
□ 19. JACK HOWELL
□ 38. CHILI DAVIS
□ 58. TONY ARMAS
□ 77. BOBBY ROSE
□ 81. BOB MCCLURE
□ 83. GREG MINTON
□ 85. WILLIE FRASER
□ 129. DEVON WHITE
□ 146. BRIAN DOWNING
□ 149. BILL SCHROEDER
□ 395. CLAUDELL WASHINGTON
□ 506. KIRK MCCASKILL
□ 509. JOHNNY RAY
□ 527. BERT BLYLEVEN
□ 548. MIKE WITT
□ 645. JIM ABBOTT
□ 667. CHUCK FINLEY
□ 669. DICK SCHOFIELD
□ 672. JOHN ORTON
□ 674. LANCE PARRISH
□ 686. BRYAN HARVEY
□ 688. DANTE BICHETTE
□ 690. DAN PETRY
□ 691. KENT ANDERSON
□ 693. WALLY JOYNER

CHICAGO CUBS

□   6. LUIS SALAZAR
□ 14. MARVELL WYNNE
□ 39. SCOTT SANDERSON
□ 47. KEVIN BLANKENSHIP
□ 73. TEAM CHECKLIST
□ 107. MIKE HARKEY
□ 109. RICK SUTCLIFFE
□ 128. MARK GRACE
□ 147. CURTIS WILKERSON
□ 150. DOMINGO RAMOS
□ 153. MITCH WEBSTER
□ 155. PAUL KILGUS
□ 174. MITCH WILLIAMS
□ 211. DOUG DASCENZO
□ 213. GREG MADDUX
□ 231. SHAWON DUNSTON
□ 304. JOE GIRARDI
□ 322. DAMON BERRYHILL
□ 324. RYNE SANDBERG
□ 341. STEVE WILSON
□ 345. JEROME WALTON
□ 357. ANDRE DAWSON
□ 359. MIKE BIELECKI
□ 376. DWIGHT SMITH
□ 380. VANCE LAW
□ 398. LLOYD MCCLENDON

□ 582. RICK WRONA
□ 584. LES LANCASTER
□ 660. PAUL ASSENMACHER

Jerome Walton

CHICAGO WHITE SOX

□   3. TOM DRESS
□ 17. SAMMY SOSA
□ 21. ROBIN VENTURA
□ 67. MATT MERULLO
□ 69. RON KARKOVICE
□ 79. TEAM CHECKLIST
□ 90. LANCE JOHNSON
□ 267. OZZIE GUILLEN
□ 269. BOBBY THIGPEN
□ 286. DAN PASQUA
□ 289. EDDIE WILLIAMS
□ 310. SCOTT FLETCHER
□ 328. DAVE GALLAGHER
□ 347. CARLOS MARTINEZ
□ 350. GREG WALKER
□ 367. CARLTON FISK
□ 386. DONN PALL
□ 390. STEVE LYONS
□ 503. IVAN CALDERON
□ 522. STEVE ROSENBERG
□ 525. MELIDO PEREZ
□ 529. DARYL BOSTON
□ 541. SHAWN HILLEGAS
□ 543. GREG HIBBARD
□ 625. JACK MCDOWELL
□ 651. ERIC KING

CINCINNATI REDS

□ 52. CHRIS HAMMOND
□ 99. TEAM CHECKLIST
□ 116. ERIC DAVIS
□ 118. RON OESTER
□ 120. DANNY JACKSON
□ 137. TIM BIRTSAS
□ 139. JOHN FRANCO
□ 161. PAUL O'NEILL
□ 164. SCOTT SCUDDER
□ 165. JEFF REED
□ 167. BARRY LARKIN
□ 170. ROLANDO ROOMES
□ 181. CHRIS SABO
□ 186. TODD BENZINGER
□ 189. TOM BROWNING
□ 216. JOSE RIJO
□ 220. RICK MAHLER
□ 430. MARIANO DUNCAN
□ 566. NORM CHARLTON
□ 568. JOE OLIVER
□ 586. ROB DIBBLE
□ 589. HERM WINNINGHAM
□ 593. LUIS QUINONES
□ 662. TIM LEARY
□ 664. BO DIAZ
□ 682. KEN GRIFFEY
□ 684. JACK ARMSTRONG

CLEVELAND INDIANS

□ 53. TEAM CHECKLIST
□ 110. PETE O'BRIEN
□ 126. CORY SNYDER
□ 369. JOEL SKINNER
□ 375. JOE CARTER
□ 388. TOM CANDIOTTI

□ 409. FELIX FERMIN
□ 426. JERRY BROWNE
□ 428. BRAD KOMMINSK
□ 446. JOEY BELLE
□ 449. DAVE CLARK
□ 459. BROOK JACOBY
□ 498. BUD BLACK
□ 553. STEVE OLIN
□ 570. JOHN FARRELL
□ 572. ROD NICHOLS
□ 574. GREG SWINDELL
□ 588. JESSE OROSCO
□ 590. ANDY ALLANSON
□ 591. DION JAMES
□ 595. RICH YETT
□ 632. DOUG JONES

DETROIT TIGERS

□   2. RANDY NOSEK
□ 41. TEAM CHECKLIST
□ 76. ROB RICHIE
□ 78. BRIAN DUBOIS
□ 98. KEVIN RITZ
□ 226. MATT NOKES
□ 247. FRED LYNN
□ 249. KENNY WILLIAMS
□ 306. MIKE HEATH
□ 309. TRACY JONES
□ 312. MIKE BRUMLEY
□ 327. LOU WHITAKER
□ 330. DOYLE ALEXANDER
□ 332. TOREY LOVULLO
□ 348. CHET LEMON
□ 381. DAVE BERGMAN
□ 385. GARY PETTIS
□ 496. PAUL GIBSON
□ 516. FRANK TANANA
□ 518. GUILLERMO HERNANDEZ
□ 520. CHARLES HUDSON
□ 537. MIKE HENNEMAN
□ 539. FRANK WILLIAMS
□ 552. JEFF ROBINSON
□ 554. ALAN TRAMMELL
□ 573. JACK MORRIS
□ 575. STEVE SEARCY

HOUSTON ASTROS

□ 22. BRIAN MEYER
□ 28. ERIC ANTHONY
□ 43. JOSE CANO
□ 88. TEAM CHECKLIST
□ 104. CRAIG BIGGIO
□ 122. KEN CAMINITI
□ 125. MIKE SCOTT
□ 144. RAFAEL RAMIREZ
□ 160. LOUIE MEADOWS
□ 196. GERALD YOUNG
□ 198. BILL DORAN
□ 201. TERRY PUHL
□ 203. JIM CLANCY
□ 205. ALEX TREVINO
□ 221. JIM DESHAIES
□ 245. GLENN DAVIS
□ 302. KEVIN BASS
□ 305. DANNY DARWIN
□ 407. LARRY ANDERSEN
□ 410. GLENN WILSON
□ 427. ERIC YELDING
□ 448. DAVE SMITH
□ 450. JUAN AGOSTO
□ 502. MARK PORTUGAL
□ 504. RICK RHODEN

KANSAS CITY ROYALS

□ 32. TEAM CHECKLIST
□ 45. BOB HAMELIN
□ 102. KEVIN APPIER
□ 105. BO JACKSON
□ 124. GEORGE BRETT
□ 142. PAT TABLER
□ 252. BILL BUCKNER
□ 255. JOSE DEJESUS
□ 271. BOB BOONE
□ 274. LUIS AQUINO
□ 294. JIM EISENREICH
□ 307. MIKE MACFARLANE
□ 326. BRET SABERHAGEN
□ 349. WILLIE WILSON

□ 361. KURT STILLWELL
□ 363. KEVIN SEITZER
□ 365. TOM GORDON
□ 382. FRANK WHITE
□ 384. ISRAEL SANCHEZ
□ 524. MATT WINTERS
□ 621. RICK LUECKEN
□ 642. TERRY LEACH
□ 656. DANNY TARTABULL
□ 658. CHARLIE LEIBRANDT
□ 676. MARK GUBICZA
□ 680. STEVE FARR
□ 695. FLOYD BANNISTER
□ 698. JEFF MONTGOMERY

LOS ANGELES DODGERS

□ 10. TEAM CHECKLIST
□ 44. JOSE VIZCAINO
□ 46. JOSE OFFERMAN
□ 183. WILLIE RANDOLPH
□ 256. OREL HERSHISER
□ 258. MIKE DAVIS
□ 262. MIKE MARSHALL
□ 264. KIRK GIBSON
□ 277. EDDIE MURRAY
□ 279. ALEJANDRO PENA
□ 283. MICKEY HATCHER
□ 296. JEFF HAMILTON
□ 298. MIKE SCIOSCIA
□ 317. MIKE MORGAN
□ 338. ALFREDO GRIFFIN
□ 377. JOHN WETTELAND
□ 396. JOHN TUDOR
□ 423. LENNY HARRIS
□ 445. FERNANDO VALENZUELA
□ 508. JAY HOWELL
□ 510. DAVE ANDERSON
□ 526. CHRIS GWYNN
□ 547. TIM BELCHER
□ 550. FRANKLIN STUBBS
□ 603. KAL DANIELS
□ 666. JOSE GONZALEZ
□ 670. TIM CREWS
□ 675. RAMON MARTINEZ

MILWAUKEE BREWERS

□ 25. GREG VAUGHN
□ 59. GEORGE CANALE
□ 91. TEAM CHECKLIST
□ 96. JERRY REUSS
□ 157. GARY SHEFFIELD
□ 159. B. J. SURHOFF
□ 176. MIKE FELDER
□ 178. ROB DEER
□ 180. TERRY FRANCONA
□ 218. JIM GANTNER
□ 237. BILL SPIERS
□ 239. BRYAN CLUTTERBUCK
□ 254. PAUL MOLITOR
□ 293. CHRIS BOSIO
□ 295. DON AUGUST
□ 456. GLENN BRAGGS
□ 477. DAN PLESAC
□ 480. GUS POLIDOR
□ 499. DALE SVEUM
□ 511. CHUCK CRIM
□ 514. GREG BROCK
□ 567. ROBIN YOUNT
□ 627. TEDDY HIGUERA
□ 629. BILL WEGMAN
□ 646. JAIME NAVARRO
□ 648. JUAN NIEVES
□ 650. CHARLIE O'BRIEN

MINNESOTA TWINS

□ 11. RICK AGUILERA
□ 15. DAVID WEST
□ 48. TEAM CHECKLIST
□ 87. KEVIN TAPANI
□ 158. WALLY BACKMAN
□ 199. AL NEWMAN
□ 217. GREG GAGNE
□ 219. ALLAN ANDERSON
□ 236. KIRBY PUCKETT
□ 238. DAN GLADDEN
□ 240. JOHN MOSES
□ 281. CARMEN CASTILLO
□ 284. ROY SMITH

□ 352. GERMAN GONZALEZ
□ 372. GARY WAYNE
□ 374. MIKE DYER
□ 391. BRIAN HARPER
□ 417. JEFF REARDON
□ 419. TIM LAUDNER
□ 436. MARK GUTHRIE
□ 438. SHANE RAWLEY
□ 440. JUAN BERENGUER
□ 452. KENT HRBEK
□ 454. GARY GAETTI
□ 471. GENE LARKIN
□ 475. CHIP HALE
□ 493. RANDY BUSH

MONTREAL EXPOS

□   9. MARQUIS GRISSOM
□ 29. TEAM CHECKLIST
□ 177. TIM RAINES
□ 197. HUBIE BROOKS
□ 273. TIM WALLACH
□ 291. SPIKE OWEN
□ 356. ANDRES GALARRAGA
□ 379. OTIS NIXON
□ 411. REX HUDLER
□ 413. DENNIS MARTINEZ
□ 415. MIKE ALDRETE
□ 432. NELSON SANTOVENIA
□ 434. JEFF HUSON
□ 466. LARRY WALKER
□ 468. KEVIN GROSS
□ 470. DAVE MARTINEZ
□ 487. PASCUAL PEREZ
□ 489. TOM FOLEY
□ 512. JOE HESKETH
□ 515. TIM BURKE
□ 558. MIKE FITZGERALD
□ 579. BRYN SMITH
□ 597. ANDY MCGAFFIGAN
□ 607. ZANE SMITH
□ 628. MARTY PEVEY
□ 647. MARK LANGSTON
□ 649. DAMASO GARCIA

NEW YORK METS

□ 23. BLAINE BEATTY
□ 62. TEAM CHECKLIST
□ 93. JULIO MACHADO
□ 114. DWIGHT GOODEN
□ 131. DON AASE
□ 135. MARK CARREON
□ 162. JEFF MCKNIGHT
□ 166. GREGG JEFFERIES
□ 168. GARY CARTER
□ 182. DARRYL STRAWBERRY
□ 185. MACKEY SASSER
□ 187. KEVIN ELSTER
□ 190. KEITH MILLER
□ 204. BOB OJEDA
□ 222. KEITH HERNANDEZ
□ 224. DAVID CONE
□ 241. RON DARLING
□ 243. DAVE MAGADAN
□ 261. SID FERNANDEZ
□ 263. HOWARD JOHNSON
□ 265. KEVIN MCREYNOLDS
□ 473. BARRY LYONS
□ 492. TIM TEUFEL
□ 562. JEFF INNIS
□ 564. WALLY WHITEHURST
□ 581. RANDY MYERS
□ 583. JUAN SAMUEL
□ 585. JEFF MUSSELMAN
□ 626. FRANK VIOLA

NEW YORK YANKEES

□ 13. DEION SANDERS
□ 18. TEAM CHECKLIST
□ 31. HAL MORRIS
□ 70. KEVIN MAAS
□ 138. TOM BROOKENS
□ 152. DON SLAUGHT
□ 163. ALVARO ESPINOZA
□ 172. STEVE SAX
□ 191. DON MATTINGLY
□ 193. ROBERTO KELLY
□ 316. LUIS POLONIA
□ 318. LEE GUETTERMAN
□ 320. WAYNE TOLLESON

□ 337. DAVE WINFIELD
□ 339. ANDY HAWKINS
□ 458. MEL HALL
□ 476. JESSE BARFIELD
□ 479. DAVE RIGHETTI
□ 497. STEVE BALBONI
□ 507. DAVE LAPOINT
□ 528. CHUCK CARY
□ 530. DALE MOHORCIC
□ 546. HENSLEY MEULENS
□ 549. GREG CADARET
□ 608. BOB GEREN
□ 615. LANCE MCCULLERS
□ 630. ERIC PLUNK
□ 661. WALT TERRELL

OAKLAND A'S

□   4. CURT YOUNG
□ 36. TEAM CHECKLIST
□ 66. JOSE CANSECO
□ 80. GENE NELSON
□ 151. RICK HONEYCUTT
□ 154. TONY PHILLIPS
□ 171. MARK MCGWIRE
□ 192. DAVE PARKER
□ 195. RON HASSEY
□ 206. DAVE HENDERSON
□ 209. STAN JAVIER
□ 228. FELIX JOSE
□ 230. MIKE GALLEGO
□ 246. TERRY STEINBACH
□ 251. BOB WELCH
□ 253. CARNEY LANSFORD
□ 272. DAVE STEWART
□ 275. MIKE MOORE
□ 292. STORM DAVIS
□ 334. RICKEY HENDERSON
□ 513. DENNIS ECKERSLEY
□ 521. JIM CORSI
□ 542. WALT WEISS
□ 687. LANCE BLANKENSHIP
□ 689. TODD BURNS

PHILADELPHIA PHILLIES

□   7. TEAM CHECKLIST
□ 27. JASON GRIMSLEY
□ 35. SCOTT SERVICE
□ 71. DENNIS COOK
□ 92. JEFF PARRETT
□ 94. RON JONES
□ 404. RANDY READY
□ 416. ROGER MCDOWELL
□ 418. DARREN DAULTON
□ 420. DON CARMAN
□ 437. CHARLIE HAYES
□ 439. DICKIE THON
□ 443. TODD FROHWIRTH
□ 453. VON HAYES
□ 472. LEN DYKSTRA
□ 474. TERRY MULHOLLAND
□ 488. TOMMY HERR
□ 490. CURT FORD
□ 491. STEVE LAKE
□ 495. STEVE JELTZ
□ 559. KEN HOWELL
□ 576. RICKY JORDAN
□ 580. BRUCE RUFFIN
□ 668. JOHN KRUK

PITTSBURGH PIRATES

□ 16. TEAM CHECKLIST
□ 86. NEAL HEATON
□ 89. JIM GOTT
□ 97. BRIAN FISHER
□ 208. RAFAEL BELLIARD
□ 227. BARRY BONDS
□ 248. GARY REDUS
□ 250. SID BREAM
□ 366. BOBBY BONILLA
□ 368. STEVE CARTER
□ 370. JOHN CANGELOSI
□ 387. JOHN SMILEY
□ 389. JUNIOR ORTIZ
□ 403. JEFF ROBINSON
□ 422. DOUG DRABEK
□ 424. JOSE LIND
□ 442. BILL LANDRUM
□ 517. JAY BELL
□ 519. RANDY KRAMER

☐ 536. ANDY VAN SLYKE
☐ 538. MIGUEL GARCIA
☐ 540. R. J. REYNOLDS
☐ 557. JEFF KING
☐ 560. BOB KIPPER
☐ 578. MIKE LAVALLIERE
☐ 596. BOB WALK
☐ 598. BILLY HATCHER

ST. LOUIS CARDINALS

☐ 68. TEAM CHECKLIST
☐ 202. FRANK DIPINO
☐ 223. VINCE COLEMAN
☐ 225. OZZIE SMITH
☐ 242. JOE MAGRANE
☐ 244. PEDRO GUERRERO
☐ 257. TOM BRUNANSKY
☐ 260. SCOTT TERRY
☐ 276. TONY PENA
☐ 278. MILT THOMPSON
☐ 280. KEN DAYLEY
☐ 319. JOSE OQUENDO
☐ 336. KEN HILL
☐ 340. TED POWER
☐ 467. TODD WORRELL
☐ 469. TERRY PENDLETON
☐ 486. JOHN COSTELLO
☐ 501. TIMMY JONES
☐ 505. WILLIE MCGEE
☐ 523. CRIS CARPENTER
☐ 545. TODD ZEILE
☐ 659. DAN QUISENBERRY
☐ 678. GREG MATHEWS
☐ 697. JOSE DELEON

SAN DIEGO PADRES

☐ 12. TEAM CHECKLIST
☐ 51. ROB NELSON
☐ 55. ANDY BENES
☐ 288. GARRY TEMPLETON
☐ 301. SHAWN ABNER
☐ 303. BIP ROBERTS
☐ 308. ED WHITSON
☐ 325. BENITO SANTIAGO
☐ 329. MIKE PAGLIARULO
☐ 342. JACK CLARK
☐ 344. TONY GWYNN
☐ 346. ROBERT ALOMAR
☐ 412. MARK GRANT
☐ 414. DARRIN JACKSON
☐ 431. MARK DAVIS
☐ 433. BRUCE HURST
☐ 435. CHRIS JAMES
☐ 569. MARK PARENT
☐ 587. ERIC SHOW
☐ 592. CARMELO MARTINEZ
☐ 594. DENNIS RASMUSSEN
☐ 601. JOEY CORA
☐ 622. GREG HARRIS
☐ 624. JERALD CLARK
☐ 643. CALVIN SCHIRALDI
☐ 655. SANDY ALOMAR, JR.

SAN FRANCISCO GIANTS

☐ 40. TEAM CHECKLIST
☐ 117. KEVIN MITCHELL
☐ 119. BRETT BUTLER
☐ 136. CANDY MALDONADO
☐ 140. MIKE LACOSS
☐ 169. ROBBY THOMPSON
☐ 188. JOSE URIBE
☐ 358. JEFF BRANTLEY
☐ 360. KEN OBERKFELL
☐ 378. ERNIE RILES
☐ 397. TERRY KENNEDY
☐ 399. CRAIG LEFFERTS
☐ 457. KIRK MANWARING
☐ 460. PAT SHERIDAN
☐ 478. SCOTT GARRELTS
☐ 556. WILL CLARK
☐ 577. MATT WILLIAMS
☐ 599. BOB KNEPPER
☐ 616. DON ROBINSON
☐ 618. STEVE BEDROSIAN
☐ 620. ATLEE HAMMAKER
☐ 637. TREVOR WILSON
☐ 639. MIKE KRUKOW

☐ 657. RANDY MCCAMENT
☐ 677. GREG LITTON
☐ 679. DAVE DRAVECKY
☐ 696. RICK REUSCHEL
☐ 699. KELLY DOWNS

Will Clark

SEATTLE MARINERS

☐ 24. TEAM CHECKLIST
☐ 37. TINO MARTINEZ
☐ 156. KEN GRIFFEY, JR.
☐ 179. HAROLD REYNOLDS
☐ 207. HENRY COTTO
☐ 210. JERRY REED
☐ 214. MIKE SCHOOLER
☐ 229. DENNIS POWELL
☐ 233. OMAR VIZQUEL
☐ 235. ERIK HANSON
☐ 311. DARNELL COLES
☐ 313. BILL SWIFT
☐ 315. JIM PRESLEY
☐ 331. JEFFREY LEONARD
☐ 362. BRIAN HOLMAN
☐ 364. ALVIN DAVIS
☐ 383. SCOTT BRADLEY
☐ 451. DAVE VALLE
☐ 455. GREG BRILEY
☐ 494. MIKE JACKSON
☐ 532. EDGAR MARTINEZ
☐ 534. JAY BUHNER
☐ 561. SCOTT BANKHEAD
☐ 563. RANDY JOHNSON
☐ 565. GENE HARRIS

TEXAS RANGERS

☐ 42. SCOTT COOLBAUGH
☐ 72. JUAN GONZALEZ
☐ 74. DEAN PALMER
☐ 82. TEAM CHECKLIST
☐ 103. JULIO FRANCO
☐ 123. KEVIN BROWN
☐ 314. CHARLIE HOUGH
☐ 333. PETE INCAVIGLIA
☐ 335. RAFAEL PALMEIRO
☐ 353. HAROLD BAINES
☐ 355. RUBEN SIERRA
☐ 371. CECIL ESPY
☐ 392. FRED MANRIQUE
☐ 394. JEFF KUNKEL
☐ 544. NOLAN RYAN
☐ 606. KENNY ROGERS
☐ 609. CHAD KREUTER
☐ 612. GARY MIELKE
☐ 614. JACK DAUGHERTY
☐ 617. JOSE GUZMAN
☐ 619. JAMIE MOYER
☐ 631. DREW HALL
☐ 633. GENO PETRALLI
☐ 636. BOBBY WITT
☐ 638. JEFF RUSSELL
☐ 640. RICK LEACH
☐ 685. STEVE BUECHELE

TORONTO BLUE JAYS

☐ 26. XAVIER HERNANDEZ
☐ 30. DAVID WELLS
☐ 56. JOHN OLERUD
☐ 95. TEAM CHECKLIST
☐ 106. JUNIOR FELIX
☐ 108. FRED MCGRIFF
☐ 111. KELLY GRUBER
☐ 113. PAT BORDERS
☐ 115. KEVIN BATISTE
☐ 127. GEORGE BELL
☐ 130. TONY FERNANDEZ
☐ 132. RANCE MULLINIKS
☐ 134. NELSON LIRIANO
☐ 148. ERNIE WHITT
☐ 282. TOM HENKE
☐ 285. MANNY LEE
☐ 421. LLOYD MOSEBY
☐ 462. JIMMY KEY
☐ 464. ROB DUCEY
☐ 481. MOOKIE WILSON
☐ 483. MIKE FLANAGAN
☐ 485. JOHN CERUTTI
☐ 605. DAVE STIEB
☐ 653. DUANE WARD
☐ 692. TODD STOTTLEMYRE

SINGLE TEAM AND REGIONAL CARD SETS

The primary text of this book lists, by team, baseball cards from nationally issued card sets. This section lists, by team, non-nationally-issued card sets in which players from one team comprise all or a significant portion of the cards in the set. While not exhaustive, this list includes all of this type of card sets that have appeared in any of the first 12 editions of the Sport Americana Baseball Card Price Guide and the first two issues of the Sport Americana Baseball Collectibles Price Guide. The number in parentheses( ) indicates the number of cards of players of that team in the set. The asterisk* indicates that there are players of more that one team in the set. Major League teams only are included.

ATLANTA BRAVES

☐ 1966 KAHN'S WIENERS (9)*
☐ 1967 KAHN'S WIENERS (8)*
☐ 1968 KAHN'S WIENERS (5)*
☐ 1969 KAHN'S WIENERS (1)*
☐ 1981 POLICE (27)
☐ 1982 BURGER KING (27)
☐ 1982 POLICE (30)
☐ 1983 POLICE (30)
☐ 1984 POLICE (30)
☐ 1985 HOSTESS (22)
☐ 1985 POLICE (30)
☐ 1986 POLICE (30)

BALTIMORE ORIOLES

☐ 1954 ESSKAY (36)
☐ 1955 ESSKAY (27)
☐ 1987 FRENCH BRAY (30)
☐ 1988 FRENCH BRAY (30)
☐ 1989 FRENCH BRAY (32)

BOSTON BRAVES

☐ 1947 TIP TOP BREAD (15)

BOSTON RED SOX

☐ 1910 E91 AMERICAN
   CARAMELS (11)*
☐ 1947 TIP TOP BREAD (15)
☐ 1967 TOPPS STICKERS (33)
☐ 1981 COCA-COLA (12)
☐ 1981 TOPPS 5X7 (12)
☐ 1982 COCA-COLA (23)

BROOKLYN DODGERS

☐ 1947 TIP TOP BREAD (14)
☐ 1953-54 BRIGGS (4)*
☐ 1953 STAHL-MEYER (3)*
☐ 1954 N.Y. JOURNAL-
   AMERICAN (19)*
☐ 1954 STAHL-MEYER (4)*
☐ 1955 GOLDEN STAMPS (32)
☐ 1955 STAHL-MEYER (4)*

CALIFORNIA ANGELS

☐ 1981 TOPPS 5X7 (6)
☐ 1983 7-11 COINS (6)*
☐ 1984 SMOKEY THE BEAR (30)
☐ 1985 SMOKEY THE BEAR (24)
☐ 1986 SMOKEY THE BEAR (24)
☐ 1987 SMOKEY THE BEAR (24)
☐ 1988 SMOKEY THE BEAR (25)
☐ 1989 SMOKEY THE BEAR (20)

CHICAGO CUBS

☐ 1908 E91 AMERICAN
   CARAMELS (11)*
☐ 1910 E90-3 AMERICAN
   CARAMELS (11)*
☐ 1910 E91 AMERICAN
   CARAMELS (11)*
☐ 1947 TIP TOP BREAD (15)
☐ 1960 KAHN'S WIENERS (1)*
☐ 1968 KAHN'S WIENERS (3)*
☐ 1969 KAHN'S WIENERS (2)*

☐ 1969 SUNOCO PINS (9)*
☐ 1970 DUNKIN DONUTS (6)
☐ 1981 COCA-COLA (12)
☐ 1981 TOPPS 5X7 (9)
☐ 1982 RED LOBSTER (28)
☐ 1983 THORN APPLE VALLEY (28)
☐ 1985 SEVEN UP (28)
☐ 1986 GATORADE (28)
☐ 1987 DAVID BERG (28)
☐ 1988 DAVID BERG (27)
☐ 1989 MARATHON (25)

CHICAGO WHITE SOX

☐ 1910 E90-3 AMERICAN
   CARAMELS (9)*
☐ 1947 TIP TOP BREAD (15)
☐ 1960 KAHN'S WIENERS (1)*
☐ 1968 KAHN'S WIENERS (2)*
☐ 1969 KAHN'S WIENERS (2)*
☐ 1981 COCA-COLA (12)
☐ 1981 TOPPS 5X 7 (9)
☐ 1983 TRUE VALUE (23)
☐ 1984 TRUE VALUE (30)
☐ 1985 COCA-COLA (30)
☐ 1986 COCA-COLA (30)
☐ 1987 COCA-COLA (30)
☐ 1988 COCA-COLA (30)
☐ 1989 COCA-COLA (30)

CINCINNATI REDS

☐ 1938-39 W711-1 (32)
☐ 1941 W711-2 (32)
☐ 1955 KAHN'S WIENERS (6)
☐ 1956 KAHN'S WIENERS (15)
☐ 1957 KAHN'S WIENERS (19)*
☐ 1958 KAHN'S WIENERS (15)*
☐ 1959 KAHN'S WIENERS (10)*
☐ 1960 KAHN'S WIENERS (17)*
☐ 1961 KAHN'S WIENERS (15)*
☐ 1962 KAHN'S WIENERS (17)*
☐ 1963 FRENCH BAUER CAPS (25)
☐ 1963 KAHN'S WIENERS (14)*
☐ 1964 KAHN'S WIENERS (11)*
☐ 1965 KAHN'S WIENERS (15)*
☐ 1966 KAHN'S WIENERS (11)*
☐ 1967 KAHN'S WIENERS (14)*
☐ 1968 KAHN'S WIENERS (11)*
☐ 1969 KAHN'S WIENERS (8)*
☐ 1976 ICEE LIDS (12)
☐ 1981 COCA-COLA (12)
☐ 1981 TOPPS 5X7 (12)
☐ 1982 COCA-COAL (23)
☐ 1984 BORDEN'S STICKERS (8)
☐ 1986 TEXAS GOLD (28)
☐ 1987 KAHN'S (30)
☐ 1988 KAHN'S (26)
☐ 1989 PARTRIDGE (28)
☐ 1989 KAHN'S (26)

CLEVELAND INDIANS

☐ 1952 NUM-NUM POTATO
   CHIPS (20)
☐ 1955 GOLDEN STAMPS (32)
☐ 1959 KAHN'S WIENERS (14)*
☐ 1960 KAHN'S WIENERS (10)*
☐ 1961 KAHN'S WIENERS (12)*
☐ 1962 KAHN'S WIENERS (13)*
☐ 1962 SUGARDALE MEATS (22)
☐ 1963 SUGARDALE MEATS (31)

☐ 1964 KAHN'S WIENERS (10)*
☐ 1965 KAHN'S WIENERS (11)*
☐ 1966 KAHN'S WIENERS (6)*
☐ 1967 KAHN'S WIENERS (6)*
☐ 1968 KAHN'S WIENERS (7)*
☐ 1969 KAHN'S WIENERS (4)*
☐ 1982 BURGER KING (12)
☐ 1982 WHEATIES (30)
☐ 1983 WHEATIES (32)
☐ 1984 WHEATIES (29)
☐ 1985 POLAROID (32)
☐ 1986 OH HENRY (30)
☐ 1987 GATORADE (30)
☐ 1988 GATORADE (30)
☐ 1989 BB CARD DAY (28)

DETROIT TIGERS

☐ 1947 TIP TOP BREAD (15)
☐ 1954 GLENDALE MEATS (28)
☐ 1964 LIDS (14)
☐ 1968 KAHN'S WIENERS (4)*
☐ 1978 BURGER KING (23)
☐ 1981 COCA-COLA (12)
☐ 1985 CAIN'S DISCS (20)
☐ 1985 WENDY'S (22)
☐ 1987 CAIN'S DISCS (20)
☐ 1987 COCA-COLA (18)
☐ 1988 PEPSI/KROGER (25)
☐ 1988 POLICE (14)
☐ 1989 MARATHON (28)
☐ 1989 POLICE (14)

HOUSTON ASTROS

☐ 1978 BURGER KING (23)
☐ 1981 COCA-COLA (12)
☐ 1981 TOPPS 5X7 (6)
☐ 1984 MOTHER'S COOKIES (28)
☐ 1985 MOTHER'S COOKIES (28)
☐ 1986 MOTHER'S COOKIES (28)
☐ 1986 POLICE (26)
☐ 1987 MOTHER'S COOKIES (28)
☐ 1987 POLICE (26)
☐ 1988 MOTHER'S COOKIES (28)
☐ 1988 POLICE (26)
☐ 1989 LENNOX/HSE (26)
☐ 1989 MOTHER'S COOKIES (28)

HOUSTON COLT .45'S

☐ 1963 PEPSI-COLA (16)
☐ 1989 SMOKEY THE BEAR (29)

KANSAS CITY ATHLETICS

☐ 1955 RODEO MEATS (47)
☐ 1956 RODEO MEATS (13)

KANSAS CITY ROYALS

☐ 1981 COCA-COLA (12)
☐ 1981 POLICE (10)
☐ 1983 POLICE (10)
☐ 1986 KITTY CLOVER DICS (20)
☐ 1986 NATIONAL PHOTO (24)
☐ 1988 SMOKEY THE BEAR (28)

SINGLE TEAM & REGIONAL SETS

LOS ANGELES DODGERS

☐ 1958 BELL BRAND (10)
☐ 1959 MORRELL MEATS (12)
☐ 1960 BELL BRAND (20)
☐ 1960 MORRELL MEATS (12)
☐ 1961 BELL BRAND (20)
☐ 1961 MORRELL MEATS (6)
☐ 1962 BELL BRAND (20)
☐ 1980 POLICE (30)
☐ 1981 POLICE (32)
☐ 1981 TOPPS 5X7 (12)
☐ 1982 POLICE (30)
☐ 1983 POLICE (30)
☐ 1983 7-11 COINS (6)*
☐ 1984 POLICE (30)
☐ 1984 SMOKEY THE BEAR (4)
☐ 1986 POLICE (30)
☐ 1987 MOTHER'S COOKIES (28)
☐ 1987 POLICE (30)
☐ 1988 MOTHER'S COOKIES (28)
☐ 1988 POLICE (30)
☐ 1988 SMOKEY THE BEAR (32)
☐ 1989 MOTHER'S COOKIES (28)
☐ 1989 POLICE (30)
☐ 1989 SMOKEY THE BEAR (100)

MILWAUKEE BRAVES

☐ 1953 JOHNSTON COOKIES (25)
☐ 1954 JOHNSTON COOKIES (35)
☐ 1955 GOLDEN STAMPS (32)
☐ 1955 JOHNSTON COOKIES (35)
☐ 1960 LAKE TO LAKE DAIRY (28)
☐ 1965 KAHN'S WIENERS (9)*

MILWAUKEE BREWERS

☐ 1969 SUNOCO PINS (9)*
☐ 1982 POLICE (30)
☐ 1983 GARDNER'S BREAD (22)
☐ 1983 POLICE (30)
☐ 1984 GARDNER'S BREAD (22)
☐ 1984 POLICE (30)
☐ 1985 GARDNER'S BREAD (22)
☐ 1985 POLICE (30)
☐ 1986 POLICE (32)
☐ 1987 POLICE (30)
☐ 1988 POLICE (31)
☐ 1989 GARDNER'S (15)
☐ 1989 POLICE (30)

MINNESOTA TWINS

☐ 1961 PETER'S MEATS (26)
☐ 1961-62 CLOVERLEAF DAIRY (31)
☐ 1962 KAHN'S WIENERS (1)*
☐ 1985 7-11 (13)
☐ 1988 MASTER BREAD (12)
☐ 1988 SMOKEY THE BEAR (12)

MONTREAL EXPOS

☐ 1969 FUD'S PHOTOGRAPHY (14)
☐ 1971 LA PIZZA ROYALE (14)
☐ 1974 WESTON (10)
☐ 1982 HYGRADE MEATS (24)
☐ 1982 ZELLER DEPARTMENT
    STORE (20)
☐ 1982 O-PEE-CHEE POSTERS (12)*
☐ 1983 STUART (30)
☐ 1984 STUART (40)
☐ 1985 O-PEE-CHEE POSTERS (12)*
☐ 1986 PROVIGO (28)
☐ 1988 HOSTESS DISCS (12)*

NEW YORK GIANTS

☐ 1908 E91 AMERICAN
    CARAMELS (11)*
☐ 1910 E91 AMERICAN
    CARAMELS (11)*
☐ 1947 TIP TOP BREAD (15)
☐ 1953-54 BRIGGS (4)*
☐ 1953 STAHL-MEYER (3)*
☐ 1954 N.Y. JOURNAL-
    AMERICAN (20)
☐ 1954 STAHL-MEYER (4)*
☐ 1955 GOLDEN STAMP (32)
☐ 1955 STAHL-MEYER (4)*

NEW YORK METS

☐ 1967 KAHN'S WIENERS (6)*
☐ 1968 KAHN'S WIENERS (2)*
☐ 1970 TRANSOGRAM (15)
☐ 1981 COCA-COLA (12)
☐ 1981 TOPPS 5X7 (6)
☐ 1984 FAN CLUB (8)
☐ 1985 FAN CLUB (8)
☐ 1986 FAN CLUB (8)
☐ 1987 FAN CLUB (8)
☐ 1988 FAN CLUB (9)
☐ 1988 KAHN'S (31)
☐ 1989 FAN CLUB (9)
☐ 1989 KAHN'S (32)

NEW YORK YANKEES

☐ 1947 TIP TOP BREAD (15)
☐ 1953-54 BRIGGS (4)*
☐ 1953 STAHL-MEYER (3)*
☐ 1954 N.Y. JOURNAL-
    AMERICAN (20)*
☐ 1954 SYAHL-MEYER (4)*
☐ 1955 STAHL-MEYER (4)*
☐ 1963 KAHN'S WIENERS (6)*
☐ 1977 BURGER KING (24)
☐ 1978 BURGER KING (23)
☐ 1979 BURGER KING (23)
☐ 1981 TOPPS 5X7 (12)
☐ 1983 ROY ROGERS DISCS (12)
☐ 1989 SCORE NATIONAL
    WESTMINSTER BANK (33)

OAKLAND A'S

☐ 1981 GRANNY GOOSE (15)
☐ 1982 GRANNY GOOSE (15)
☐ 1983 GRANNY GOOSE (15)
☐ 1984 MOTHER'S COOKIES (28)
☐ 1985 MOTHER'S COOKIES (28)
☐ 1986 MOTHER'S COOKIES (28)
☐ 1987 MOTHER'S COOKIES (28)
☐ 1988 MOTHER'S COOKIES (28)
☐ 1989 MOTHER'S COOKIES (28)

PHILADELPHIA ATHLETICS

☐ 1908 E91 AMERICAN
    CARAMELS (11)*
☐ 1910 E91 AMERICAN
    CARAMELS (11)*

PHILADELPHIA PHILLIES

☐ 1949 LUMMIS PEANUT
    BUTTER (12)
☐ 1949 SEALTEST DAIRY (12)
☐ 1958 KAHN'S WIENERS (1)*
☐ 1979 BURGER KING (23)
☐ 1980 BURGER KING (23)
☐ 1981 COCA-COLA (12)
☐ 1981 TOPPS 5X7 (12)
☐ 1985 CIGNA (16)
☐ 1986 CIGNA (16)
☐ 1986 KELLER'S (6)
☐ 1986 TASTYCAKE (49)
☐ 1987 TASTYCAKE (46)
☐ 1988 TASTYCAKE (30)

PITTSBURGH PIRATES

☐ 1910 E90-2 AMERICAN
    CARAMELS (11)
☐ 1910 E91 AMERICAN
    CARAMELS (11)*
☐ 1947 TIP TOP BREAD (14)
☐ 1957 KAHN'S WIENERS (10)*
☐ 1958 KAHN'S WIENERS (13)*
☐ 1959 KAHN'S WIENERS (14)*
☐ 1960 KAHN'S WIENERS (12)*
☐ 1961 KAHN'S WIENERS (16)*
☐ 1962 KAHN'S WIENERS (10)*
☐ 1963 KAHN'S WIENERS (9)*
☐ 1964 KAHN'S WIENERS (10)*
☐ 1965 KAHN'S WIENERS (10)*
☐ 1966 EAST HILLS SHOPPING
    CENTER (25)
☐ 1966 KAHN'S WIENERS (6)*
☐ 1967 KAHN'S WIENERS (7)*
☐ 1967 TOPPS STICKERS (33)
☐ 1968 KAHN'S WIENERS (4)*
☐ 1969 KAHN'S WIENERS (4)*
☐ 1981 COCA-COLA (12)
☐ 1989 VERY FINE (30)

ST. LOUIS BROWNS

☐ 1941 W753 (29)
☐ 1947 TIP TOP BREAD (15)

ST. LOUIS CARDINALS

☐ 1941 W754 (29)
☐ 1947 TIP TOP BREAD (15)
☐ 1953 HUNTER'S WIENERS (26)
☐ 1954 HUNTER'S WIENERS (30)
☐ 1955 HUNTER'S WIENERS (30)
☐ 1960 KAHN'S WIENERS (1)*
☐ 1963 KAHN'S WIENERS (1)*
☐ 1969 KAHN'S WIENERS (1)*
☐ 1981 COCA-COLA (12)
☐ 1986 KAS DISCS (20)
☐ 1986 SCHNUCKS MILK (26)
☐ 1987 SMOKEY THE BEAR (25)
☐ 1988 SMOKEY THE BEAR (25)
☐ 1989 SMOKEY THE BEAR (25)

SAN DIEGO PADRES

☐ 1984 MOTHER'S COOKIES (28)
☐ 1984 SMOKEY THE BEAR (29)
☐ 1985 MOTHER'S COOKIES (28)
☐ 1987 BOHEMIAN BREAD (22)
☐ 1988 COCA-COLA (20)
☐ 1988 SMOKEY THE BEAR (31)
☐ 1989 COCA-COLA (21)
☐ 1989 SMOKEY THE BEAR

SAN FRANCISCO GIANTS

☐ 1958 SAN FRANCISCO CALL-
    BULLETIN (25)
☐ 1979 POLICE (30)
☐ 1980 POLICE (31)
☐ 1983 MOTHER'S COOKIES (20)
☐ 1984 MOTHER'S COOKIES (28)
☐ 1985 MOTHER'S COOKIES (28)
☐ 1986 MOTHER'S COOKIES (28)
☐ 1987 MOTHER'S COOKIES (28)
☐ 1988 MOTHER'S COOKIES (28)
☐ 1989 MOTHER'S COOKIES (28)

SEATTLE MARINERS

☐ 1981 POLICE (16)
☐ 1983 NALLEY'S POTATO
    CHIPS (6)
☐ 1984 MOTHER'S COOKIES (28)
☐ 1985 MOTHER'S COOKIES (28)
☐ 1986 MOTHER'S COOKIES (28)
☐ 1987 MOTHER'S COOKIES (28)
☐ 1988 MOTHER'S COOKIES (28)
☐ 1988 NORTHWEST BELL (29)
☐ 1989 MOTHER'S COOKIES (28)

TEXAS RANGERS

☐ 1978 BURGER KING (23)
☐ 1981 TOPPS 5X7 (6)
☐ 1983 AFFILIATED FOOD
    STORES (28)
☐ 1984 JARVIS PRESS (30)
☐ 1985 PERFORMANCE
    PRINTING (28)
☐ 1986 PERFORMANCE
    PRINTING (28)
☐ 1987 MOTHER'S COOKIES (28)
☐ 1988 MOTHER'S COOKIES (28)
☐ 1988 SMOKEY THE BEAR (21)
☐ 1989 MOTHER'S COOKIES (28)
☐ 1989 SMOKEY THE BEAR (34)

TORONTO BLUE JAYS

☐ 1982 O-PEE-CHEE POSTERS (12)*
☐ 1984 FIRE SAFETY (36)
☐ 1985 O-PEE-CHEE POSTERS (12)*
☐ 1985 FIRE SAFETY (36)
☐ 1986 AULT FOODS (24)
☐ 1986 FIRE SAFETY (36)
☐ 1987 FIRE SAFETY (36)
☐ 1988 FIRE SAFETY (36)
☐ 1988 HOSTESS DISCS (12)*
☐ 1989 FIRE SAFETY (36)

WASHINGTON SENATORS

☐ 1910 E91 AMERICAN
    CARAMELS (11)*
☐ 1953-54 BRIGGS (25)*

'TWO' GOOD TO BE TRUE

Two great new magazines in the tradition of
Beckett Baseball Card Monthly.
Up-to-date, accurate, and reliable prices • interesting articles
full-color superstar cover photos • hobby tips • answers to your questions

🏈 Beckett Football Card Magazine Subscriptions

Name _____ Age _____
(Please Print)

Address _____

City _____ State _____ Zip _____

Type of Subscription: ☐ New Subscription ☐ Renewal

Payment enclosed via: ☐ Check or Money Order ☐ VISA/MasterCard

Signature _____

Acct. # _____ Exp. _____

Check one please:

	Your Price
8 issues (a savings of $8.65)	**$14.95**
16 issues (a savings of $21.25)	**$25.95**
24 issues (a savings of $33.85)	**$36.95**
32 issues (a savings of $46.45)	**$47.95**

All foreign addresses add $12 per 8 issues for postage. All payments payable in U.S. funds.
Beckett Football Card Magazine is published 8 times a year.

Mail to: Beckett Publications, Football Subscriptions, 4887 Alpha Rd., Suite 200,
Dallas, Texas 75244

🏀 Beckett Basketball Card Magazine Subscriptions

Name _____ Age _____
(Please Print)

Address _____

City _____ State _____ Zip _____

Type of Subscription: ☐ New Subscription ☐ Renewal

Payment enclosed via: ☐ Check or Money Order ☐ VISA/MasterCard

Signature _____

Acct. # _____ Exp. _____

Check one please:

	Your Price
6 issues (a savings of $4.75)	**$12.95**
12 issues (a savings of $13.45)	**$21.95**
18 issues (a savings of $23.15)	**$29.95**
24 issues (a savings of $33.85)	**$36.95**

All foreign addresses add $9 per 6 issues for postage. All payments payable in U.S. funds.
Beckett Basketball Card Magazine is published 6 times a year.

Mail to: Beckett Publications, Basketball Subscriptions, 4887 Alpha Rd., Suite 200,
Dallas, Texas 75244

EVEN MORE FOR LESS!

More color
superstar covers

More collectable
superstar photos

More answers to
your hobby questions

More accurate prices
to all the new sets

**The best-selling magazine in the hobby just got better.
More color, more photos, more enjoyment for less
money. More than just a price guide, *Beckett Monthly*
is a quality baseball entertainment magazine.
Subscribe today!**